D1365875

ORGANIZATIONAL BEHAVIOR

SECOND
EDITION

ORGANIZATIONAL BEHAVIOR

The Management of Individual and Organizational Performance

David J. Cherrington

Brigham Young University

Allyn and Bacon

Boston • London • Toronto • Sydney • Tokyo • Singapore

Vice President, Publisher: Susan Badger
Editor-in-Chief, Business and Economics: Rich Wohl
Senior Series Editor: Suzy Spivey
Series Editorial Assistant: Karen Joseph
Series Development Editor: Judith S. Fifer
Composition Buyer: Linda Cox
Manufacturing Buyer: Megan Cochran
Cover Administrator: Linda Dickinson
Editorial-Production Service: The Book Company
Text Designer: Wendy Calmenson/The Book Company
Photo Researcher: Susan Duane

Copyright © 1994, 1989 by Allyn and Bacon
A Division of Paramount Publishing
160 Gould Street
Needham Heights, Massachusetts 02194

All rights reserved. No part of the material protected by this copyright notice may be reproduced or utilized in any form or by any means, electronic or mechanical, including photocopying, recording, or by any information storage and retrieval system, without written permission from the copyright owner.

Library of Congress Cataloging-in-Publication Data

Cherrington, David J.
    Organizational behavior : the management of individual and
organizational performance / David J. Cherrington. — 2nd ed.
        p.   cm.
    Includes bibliographical references and index.
    ISBN 0-205-15550-2
    1. Organizational behavior.   I. Title.
HD58.7.C4845   1994
658—dc20   93-33568
                                                                      CIP
                                                                      Rev

Printed in the United States of America
10 9 8 7 6 5 4 3 2 1   98 97 96 95 94 93

Photo Credits: Section I: Jon Riley/Tony Stone Worldwide; Section II: Courtesy of IBM; Section III: Bruce Ayres/Tony Stone Worldwide; Section IV: Joseph Pobereskin/Tony Stone Worldwide; Section V: Chuck Keeler/Tony Stone Worldwide; Exhibit 4.5: David Dempster; page 175: Gale Zucker/Stock Boston.

CONTENTS

Preface xx
A Word to the Student xxiv

SECTION III   GROUP AND INTERGROUP BEHAVIOR

SECTION IV   ORGANIZATIONS

SECTION V   ORGANIZATIONAL PROCESSES

PREFACE

To the Instructor

I have used several organizational behavior texts in my teaching and most have been excellent. My students, however, have often had trouble understanding certain topics. Although these ideas seemed clear to me, they were not clear for the students. When I looked at the topics from the students' perspective, I could see that the assumptions made about the students' prior knowledge were wrong. The explanations were simply insufficient. I decided to create a text that gave a fundamentally solid explanation of organizational behavior, but written so that students could clearly understand these topics and see how to apply them.

This text builds on the successful foundation of the first edition and follows the same primary objectives of helping students understand and implement important insights about human behavior. This edition has benefited from the valuable suggestions of the students and instructors who used the first edition. As you examine this book, you will notice that the important concepts are carefully explained and illustrated.

New Features

Three new boxed features have been added to this edition:

- "Applying Organizational Behavior in the News" gives students the opportunity to read about an organizational behavior topic and then consider a real management situation, by viewing an accompanying CNN video that has been specially edited for this text. Topics include how companies employ self-managing teams of workers to increase productivity, and why sexual harassment is an abuse of power.

- "Applying Organizational Behavior Research" reinforces the research conclusions in the chapter and helps students understand how knowledge of organizational behavior is acquired.

- "Applying Organizational Behavior Across Cultures" illustrates the importance of understanding diversity in our global environment and shows how principles of organizational behavior differ among various cultures.

New Content

Several important new topics have emerged in the past five years. The introductory section has been condensed from two chapters into one, to provide a more streamlined background for this new material.

In Section II, the popular Myers-Briggs Type Indicator has been added to Chapter 2, along with some of the recent research showing how different personality types are related to specific occupations and behaviors. Chapter 2 also describes self-efficacy—another personality dimension that has attracted considerable research attention. Control theory is a new motivation theory that helps integrate the other theories in Chapters 3 and 4. Although control theory is not widely known, it holds great promise because it explains a broad range of behaviors. Another important addition to Section II is a discussion of the interactions between work and family and how people are responding to the conflicts that seem to be inevitable.

The section on group norms in Section III has been supplemented with a more complete discussion of equity and equality norms. Also, the section on intergroup conflict in Chapter 10 has been strengthened with a discussion of recent research on organizational citizenship behaviors (OCB). *OCB* is the new term used to describe altruism in organizations.

Strategy has become such an important topic in management that many business schools now offer strategy courses. Chapter 11 of Section IV explains the relationship between strategy and organizational theory by explaining how the value chain used in strategic management relates to the subsystems of an organization.

Some of the most significant changes involve the organizational processes described in Section V. The electronic transmission of information is discussed in both Chapters 13 and 14; this new communication technology has subtly but significantly influenced both communication and decision making in organizations. Organizations are only beginning to comprehend and use the power of electronic information processing. The contrast between transactional and transformational leadership, discussed in Chapter 15, has likewise created a new paradigm for thinking about leadership. This paradigm requires people to re-evaluate the implications and prescriptions of all the traditional leadership theories. Sexual harassment is a new topic discussed within Chapter 16, Power and Politics in Organizations. Finally, Chapter 17 provides a new discussion of the processes recommended for revitalizing a mature organization, including recent developments in sociotech redesign, self-directed work teams, and Total Quality Management. These processes help students comprehend the complexity and difficulty in making major changes in a large, bureaucratic company.

Special Features Designed to Enhance Student Learning

Several features of this text were purposely designed to enhance student learning. The following list identifies these features and explains the benefits of each.

Chapter Outline. Each chapter begins with a chapter outline that previews the text material and helps students keep the information in perspective while they are reading.

Learning Objectives. At the beginning of each chapter, learning objectives serve as guidelines on how to study the chapter.

Introductory Cases. In the opening pages of each chapter, a case study introduces readers to organizational behavior problems related to the chapter content. Each case concludes with discussion questions designed to help instructors lead a class discussion.

Exhibits. Each chapter contains several figures, line drawings, or charts that are used to explain or clarify the theoretical concepts and to present visual models to help students remember the insights.

Chapter Summaries. At the end of each chapter, a summary helps to organize the content of the chapter and to identify the most important information.

Discussion Questions. In the concluding pages of each chapter, a set of discussion questions test the students' understanding of the chapter material and can serve as vehicles for class discussion.

Chapter Glossaries. Each chapter contains a glossary of key terms and ideas. The glossaries summarize the major ideas of each chapter and define vocabulary that may be new to the student.

Concluding Cases. At the end of each chapter, a case further applies the chapter material to a real organizational behavior situation. Some of these cases refer to real-life organizational situations, while others are composite situations taken from multiple organizations. These cases have been condensed and simplified to make them more useful for class discussion.

Experiential Exercises. Each chapter concludes with an experiential exercise to help students apply insights from the chapters in a learning environment. The experiential exercises help students learn from their own experiences. Most of these exercises involve group activities that are appropriate for small classes or laboratory sessions in large classes.

Supplements

Valuable supplements have been provided, to help instructors increase their teaching effectiveness. The needs of instructors and the kinds of activities that improve classroom instruction were paramount in the creation of these supplements.

Instructor's Manual. The *Instructor's Manual* has been revised and expanded to provide useful teaching suggestions. These suggestions include lecture ideas, discussion questions for leading a class discussion, experiential exercises to help students learn from their own experience, case discussions to apply the concepts in the chapters, and a guide for using the CNN videos for maximum effectiveness in the classroom.

Transparency Masters. A separate package of Transparency Masters is available to provide an extra dimension for lectures.

Test Bank. A large test bank has been created with true–false, multiple-choice, and essay questions. The bank of questions for each chapter is adequate to generate multiple forms of a test, for instructors who allow retesting.

Computerized Test Bank. The Test Bank is available in a computerized format for the IBM-PC or IBM-compatible computers. The Allyn & Bacon Test Manager lets you choose specific test questions, edit the questions, or create your own tests.

CNN Video. Through an exclusive agreement between the Cable News Network (CNN) and Allyn and Bacon, a CNN video has been developed to accompany this text. Available to qualified adopters, it contains CNN business news programming to accompany each of the "Applying Organizational Behavior in the News" boxes. The video segments have been specially edited to run 8–12 minutes, allowing you to use them at any point in your class to stimulate discussion or to provide a real-life example of the topic. Information about how to use the CNN video to maximum advantage in your classroom is included in the *Instructor's Manual.*

The Mosaic Workplace Video Series. This series of six video programs was developed for U.S. businesses by Films for the Humanities and Sciences, to provide companies with practical assistance in adapting to an increasingly diverse workforce. Each video provides insight into the realities of the changing U.S. workforce, and suggestions for how to deal with an increasingly diverse workplace. The programs cover a range of issues that includes the benefits of having a diverse workforce, definitions of sexual harassment, how to avoid discrimination in hiring, how to avoid biases in interviewing, and how to make new employees feel comfortable at work.

Acknowledgments

As with the development of all texts, this one combines the efforts of several people. I would like to express appreciation and give credit where credit is due. The person who deserves to be thanked first is my research assistant, Laura Zaugg, who is also an outstanding scholar and NCAA heptathlete. Laura has contributed importantly to the quality of this edition by helping me identify and explain the new topics.

Valuable assistance in writing this text came from a number of highly respected colleagues who devoted time and energy to conscientiously reviewing the manuscript at various stages of completion. The collective wisdom of the following people helped improve this text:

Royce L. Abrahamson, Southwest Texas State University

Peggy A. Anderson, University of Wisconsin—Whitewater

Debra A. Arvanites, Villanova University

D. Neil Ashworth, University of Richmond

Joanna Banthin, New Jersey Institute of Technology

David A. Bednar, Texas Tech University

W. Randy Box, University of Mississippi

John F. S. Bunch, Lehigh University

Charles J. Capps III, Sam Houston State University

William E. Cayley, University of Wisconsin—Eau Claire

Roy A. Cook, Fort Lewis College

Steven E. Field, University of West Florida

David H. Holt, James Madison University

Conrad N. Jackson, The University of Tulsa

Mary C. Kernan, University of Delaware

Jeffrey Lewis, Pitzer College

Michael McCuddy, Valparaiso University

Paul Preston, The University of Texas, San Antonio

Walter W. Smock, Rutgers University

Leigh Stelzer, Seton Hall University

Jerald T. Storey, Weber State University

M. Susan Taylor, University of Maryland

The people at Allyn and Bacon deserve special thanks. I am impressed with the professional expertise and cheerful cooperation of many employees I have never met, but whose skill and contributions I have admired from afar. I am especially grateful for the assistance of my editor, Suzy Spivey, and my developmental editor, Judy Fifer, who both gave valuable suggestions and encouragement.

Typing a lengthy manuscript, and especially cutting and pasting a revised edition, even in the age of word processors, is always a difficult chore. I appreciate the cheerful service provided by all the secretaries in the Word Processing Center, who not only accomplished the task but said they enjoyed doing it. I'm especially grateful for the dedicated efforts of two supervisors, Linda Veteto and Catherine Shumway, and to four typists, Laura Collins, Cathleen Cornaby, Nancy Elkington, and Amberly Knight, who were as pleasant in revising the manuscript the third and fourth times as the first time.

Finally, the personal support of my family enabled me to complete this project within the context of a team effort. Very special thanks go to the members of my team: Marilyn, David, Kristy, Nathan, Jana, Jennifer, and Jill. And thanks also to some special people: my parents, Jack A. and Virginia F. Cherrington, and my parents-in-law, Dr. Robert Ho and Anna M. Daines, whose standards of excellence and constant encouragement will be an inspiration throughout my life.

The purpose of this book is to increase your knowledge of organizational behavior and make you a better leader and manager, regardless of whether you are leading a large organization or simply managing your own career. The people who have the greatest impact on designing and changing organizations are leaders and managers. They can create order out of chaos and can direct the coordinated efforts of people and organizations. After studying this text, you should be better at diagnosing what happens in organizations and more capable of influencing the situation to improve organizational functioning.

Society is filled with organizations, and you spend your life interacting with them. In fact, on a daily basis people spend the majority of their time interacting in organizations either as members, customers, clients, or patients. These interactions may be good, bad, or mixed. An important reason for studying organizations is because people who are organized and working together can accomplish important goals that they cannot accomplish alone. So organizations are an essential part of society, and they need to function effectively.

Whether your interactions with organizations are good or bad is largely determined by whether they are operating efficiently and producing the kinds of goods and services they are expected to provide. The quality of your life and many of your physical comforts are produced by a multitude of organizations in diverse industries, such as manufacturing, mining, transportation, finance, medical care, education, religion, and government services. When these organizations are operating effectively and responding to human needs, they increase the quality of life and improve your standard of living. However, inefficient organizations can be extremely frustrating and irritating. Because people spend the bulk of their lives in organizations, they need to create healthy ones that contribute to the quality of life, rather than inefficient organizations that harass and destroy individuals.

How This Text Will Help You

The insights in this text are designed to increase your personal effectiveness. After studying this text, you will not only *know* about organizational behavior, you should also *be* more effective—as an individual, as a member of a group, and as a leader in an organization. It is not enough, for example, to simply know the principles of supportive communication; these principles are written and illustrated in a way to help you *apply* them. Likewise, all the other topics, such as motivation, leadership, and power, are designed to teach you how to motivate, lead, and influence others.

Several teaching devices are used to help you learn the material in this book. This text contains many examples, comprehensive coverage of current research, and boxed inserts illustrating the ideas. These boxed inserts include research summaries of

A WORD TO THE STUDENT

empirical studies, cross-cultural comparisons explaining how organizational behavior differs among cultures, and applications of organizational behavior from news broadcasts. A boxed insert in each chapter describes how the associated video segment from an actual CNN business news program applies to the material in that chapter. Each chapter contains two cases and an experiential exercise to help you apply what you learned in the chapter. If this is your first course in management, you will find the first chapter helpful as a review of the basic principles of management and a foundation for the material that follows.

■ People and Organization

INTRODUCTION TO ORGANIZATIONAL BEHAVIOR

O rganizational behavior is the study of individuals, organizations, and the way people behave in organizations. And we study organizations because we spend our lives interacting with them. If all the world is a stage, it is a stage filled with organizations. Regardless of the part we play—student, manager, customer, or employee—we act our parts on an organizational stage. The quality of our lives is influenced by our interactions with organizations and by whether these interactions are satisfying and fulfilling. Many of our emotional gratifications and physical comforts depend on the products and services of organizations. Whether we participate as members, managers, or customers, we need to understand organizational behavior; we need to know how organizations influence us and how we influence organizations.

An understanding of organizational behavior requires a careful analysis of the interactions that occur at three different levels: the individual, the group, and the organization. Organizational behavior is defined in Chapter 1, and the reasons why we should study organizational behavior are explained. This introductory chapter focuses especially on the basic characteristics of managerial work, because managers play such an important role in creating organizations and helping them operate effectively.

Chapter 1 also explains how behavioral science research contributes to our knowledge of organizational behavior through a variety of research methods, including the personal experiences of managers, field surveys, and laboratory experiments. Through history and research, we have accumulated a wealth of knowledge to help us explain, predict, and control organizational behavior.

People and Organization

LEARNING OBJECTIVES

After studying this chapter, you should be able to

1. Define organizational behavior, and explain why the study of organizational behavior is important.

2. Identify and describe the three different levels used in analyzing organizational behavior.

3. Define an organization, and describe the variables used to study organizations.

4. Describe the inducements–contributions balance, explaining the interactions of people and organizations.

5. Describe the characteristics of managerial work, and describe the roles managers perform.

6. Explain how theories help us understand organizational behavior.

7. Describe the major characteristics of the scientific method, and explain how science differs from experiential learning.

8. Identify four research methods for conducting behavioral science research, and describe the strengths and limitations of each method.

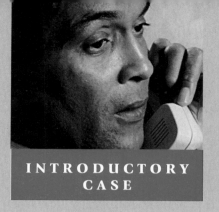

HOW MUCH DO YOU KNOW ABOUT
ORGANIZATIONAL BEHAVIOR?

Before you begin reading the text, see how well you can answer these simple true–false statements. Read each statement and decide whether it is always true, mostly true, mostly false, or always false.

1. Satisfied workers are more productive than dissatisfied workers.

2. Bureaucracies are inefficient and represent a bad form of organizational structure.

3. Workers should participate in making decisions that concern them.

4. Workers want challenging jobs.

5. Cohesive work groups are more productive than noncohesive work groups.

6. Effective leaders are more concerned about people than about the task.

7. Where there is a conflict, cohesive work groups make better group decisions than groups.

8. Telling employees they will receive a $25 bonus will make them happy.

9. The communication in a company is more accurate if employees are free to talk with anyone they want.

10. Organizations are generally more effective when they eliminate rules and give employees more freedom.

How confident are you in your answers? Could you write a brief paragraph explaining your answer?

None of these statements is always true or false, and more information is needed to decide whether any one is mostly true or mostly false. For example, the first statement reiterates the popular proverb "A happy worker is a productive worker," and for many years managers assumed that a positive relationship existed between job satisfaction and productivity. The human relations movement encouraged managers to treat their employees well and to give them personalized attention. If they were more satisfied, employees were supposed to be more productive, although it was not clear why. Perhaps contented employees were supposed to be more productive for the same reason that contented cows produce more milk. Or perhaps happy employees were supposed to feel such loyalty to the company that they would feel guilty if they didn't produce well. Apparently, neither of these explanations is accurate, since research studies fail to show that job satisfaction is correlated with productivity.[1] Sometimes it is, sometimes not. Managers have learned that happy workers are not necessarily more productive workers. Indeed, some workers are satisfied because they are playing rather than working. The relationship between satisfaction and productivity is explained more fully in Chapter 7; the other nine statements are discussed in other chapters.

DEFINING THE STUDY OF ORGANIZATIONAL BEHAVIOR

Organizational behavior encompasses the interactions of people and organizations, and the field of organizational behavior involves the systematic study of the behaviors, the processes, and the structures found in organizations. An organization is difficult to study because it is not a visible physical object. However, the study is exciting because it is real and relevant: You will be studying your own behavior and your own attitudes and how people respond in organizations. Although organizations have existed for thousands of years, the study of organizational behavior is relatively recent.

Why Study Organizational Behavior?

Being an effective manager of organizational behavior requires a combination of knowledge and experience; neither one alone is sufficient. Knowing the principles of organizational behavior does not guarantee that you will be able to apply them; you will also need practice and experience. The term **"experiential learning"** refers to learning from our own experiences. As we observe the consequences of our behavior and discover how others respond to what we do, we gain new insights into human behavior and we learn how to be more effective when working in groups and organizations. Being able to learn from our own experience is a valuable skill. However, experience alone is also not enough. We do not adequately learn from our own experiences because life is so complex and our experiences are so limited. We are not exposed to enough information to make broad generalizations about any more than a few topics. Consequently, we must use the insights of others to broaden our knowledge.

As you study this text, apply what you learn and practice using your new skills. This text contains knowledge and insights that can help you develop a mental picture or "road map" for understanding organizational behavior. Your reading will probably be combined with class activities that include case discussions, personal assessments, and group activities. These learning opportunities allow you to practice different interpersonal skills, receive feedback from others, and learn from observing them. Learning new skills usually feels uncomfortable because it involves uncertainty and mistakes; but the benefits are worthwhile. Don't be afraid to try something new or to learn from your mistakes. Experiential learning is a skill that improves with practice.

The study of organizational behavior is rather abstract and often very frustrating. Rather than producing a series of simple principles, it often produces complex conditional statements where the explanations depend on the situation. Introductory students sometimes feel the study of organizational behavior is "common sense made difficult" or "the painful elaboration of the obvious."

If organizational behavior were indeed just simple common sense, it would not be worth spending much time studying. However, organizational behavior is not just simple common sense. Many concepts are not immediately obvious; they are obscure and often difficult to understand. Furthermore, some ideas many people accept as simple common sense are wrong. Although these ideas may seem right at first, research shows they are counterintuitive; that is, disproves them. The world isn't always as it appears, nor as we think it should appear. Behavioral science research relies on the scientific method to identify myths.

Many simple statements that sound good are only correct under a limited number of conditions. The ten statements in the introductory case illustrate the **contingency approach to organizational behavior.** This approach rejects the idea that universal principles can be applied to all situations. Managing would be much easier if managers could follow a simple set of general principles. As a general rule, however, there are no simple principles to guide managerial actions. The contingency approach explains why there is no "one best way" to design organizations, motivate workers, lead subordinates, or conduct group discussions. Instead, a variety of managerial behaviors may be appropriate to a particular situation, and the most appropriate behavior depends on the circumstances at the time. The contingency approach teaches managers to diagnose a problem within the context of the situation. Learning to diagnose situations and adapt to the demands of each situation is like the idea expressed in an old Chinese proverb: "Give a person a fish and you feed that person for a day; teach a person to fish and you feed that person for life." The study of organizational behavior can sharpen your thinking about organizational phenomena and help you diagnose and interpret what is happening around you.

The Creation of Organizational Behavior

The field of organizational behavior emerged as a unique field of study during the early 1960s as an interdisciplinary combination of three disciplines: psychology, sociology, and anthropology, as illustrated in Exhibit 1.1.

Psychology. The discipline that has had the greatest influence on the field of organizational behavior is psychology, because it focuses directly on understanding and predicting individual behavior. During the 1800s, sufficient research and writing about individual behavior had accumulated so that by 1900 the field of psychology emerged as a well-respected discipline. As this field became larger and more complex, it divided into a number of subdisciplines, such as experimental psychology, clinical psychology, social psychology, educational psychology, and organizational psychology. Some topics, such as motivation and learning, are common to all of these areas as well as to organizational behavior, and they are described in Chapters 3 and 4, which explore the determinants of individual behavior and how behavior can be changed.

Some of the earliest attempts to apply psychology to organizational problems occurred in the early 1900s. In 1913, for example, Hugo Munsterberg's book, *Psychology and Industrial Efficiency*, outlined the contributions that psychology could make to the areas of employment testing, training, and industrial efficiency.[2] Munsterberg suggested that individual differences in personality and abilities should be considered when selecting electric railway engineers and telephone operators. Today, psychological studies are still highly relevant to organizational behavior because they increase our understanding of how people behave in organizations. Individual differences are described in Chapter 2.

Sociology. The discipline of sociology also has a lengthy history that reaches back to the nineteenth century. Auguste Comte, a French philosopher of the nineteenth century, is generally credited with coining the term *sociology* as part of his attempt

8

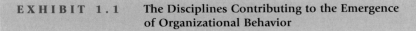

EXHIBIT 1.1   The Disciplines Contributing to the Emergence
of Organizational Behavior

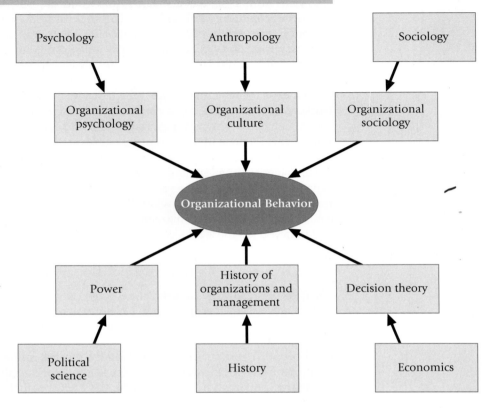

to reclassify and rearrange the field of science.[3] Sociology is the study of social systems and the interactions of people within a social setting. Comte believed that the scientific method could be used to investigate the effects of society, and that these social phenomena were subject to general laws that could be identified and meaningfully described. The fields of sociology and social psychology have made valuable contributions to our understanding of group dynamics within organizations. The concepts of group dynamics presented in Chapters 9 and 10 have largely been derived from the study of groups and social interactions within the field of sociology or social psychology.

Anthropology. Anthropologists study the relationships among individuals and their environments. Groups of individuals living together create a body of shared ideas called *culture*. Culture is embodied in the system of symbols shared by people in a group and is reflected in the group's language and beliefs. The culture of a civilization and the subculture of a defined group are transmitted by the stories and myths told by members of the group. These stories and myths help the group members understand who they are and what things are important. Likewise, organizations create a unique culture that influences the way organizational members think about the organization and how they should behave. Some important insights about organizational culture, derived from the field of anthropology, are described in Chapter 12. Today we are using important insights about culture to understand serious organizational problems such as why some U.S. manufacturers are struggling to compete effectively with foreign competitors.

Other Social Sciences. Three other disciplines have also contributed to our understanding of organizational behavior: economics, political science, and history. Several economic models describe the behavior of individuals when they are confronted with a choice, and these economic models have made valuable contributions to our understanding of both individual and organizational decision-making processes. Power, authority, and politics are popular topics that come from the field of political science; they are seeing increased use in organizational behavior to explain specific influence processes. In addition, history has contributed valuable insights to our understanding of organizational behavior by describing the lives of great leaders and the successes and failures of the organizations they managed.

Some of the most significant historical events and the people who contributed to the development of management and organizational behavior include the following:

1. *Egyptian pyramid building.* The planning and organizing involved in building the pyramids, with construction technology that must have been very primitive by modern standards, simply staggers the imagination. Although most details are lacking, several writings have been preserved from the period 2700 to 1500 B.C. and, most remarkably, many pyramids are still standing.[4]

2. *Decentralized leadership in Israel and Rome.* The principles of delegation and decentralized authority are first attributed to the advice **Moses** received from Jethro, his father-in-law, as he was leading the Israelites out of Egypt. Later, this principle was used extensively by the Roman military and government as they managed a massive empire that ruled an estimated fifty million people, including Europe and all of North Africa from Great Britain in the west to Syria in the east.[5]

3. *Venetian shipbuilding.* The greatest showplace of organizational efficiency during the medieval period was the **Arsenal of Venice,** where galleys were assembled in assembly-line fashion along canals. The arsenal operated for almost six hundred years and for much of this time it was perhaps the largest and most efficient industrial plant of the world.[6]

4. *Management philosophy.* During the medieval period, several books were written describing management and organizational practices, such as Daniel Defoe's (1661–1731) *The Compleat English Tradesman,* Sir Thomas More's (1478–1535) *Utopia,* and Niccolò Machiavelli's (1469–1527) *The Prince* and *The Discourses.* Many of these ideas, especially Machiavelli's discussions about power, are still highly relevant and studied by today's managers.[7]

5. *Scientific management.* From about 1880 to 1930, the **scientific management** movement significantly improved manufacturing productivity both in the United States and other industrialized countries. This movement, which is discussed further in Chapter 6, focused on the use of time-and-motion studies, piece-rate incentives, and job redesign to make work more efficient.[8]

6. *The human relations movement.* The human relations movement began with a series of studies from 1924 to 1933 at the Hawthorne works of the Western Electric Company on factors influencing morale and productivity. These studies concluded that friendly supervision and the influence of the work group had a greater impact on satisfaction and productivity than did financial incentives or task design. Although their findings have since been discredited, the **Hawthorne Studies** had a major impact on redirecting the thinking of managers.[9]

Goals of Organizational Behavior

The goals of organizational behavior are description, explanation, and control of behavior in organizations. For example, Chapter 8 describes the physiological responses of stress and how they are associated with a stressful situation. If we regularly observe people showing signs of stress, we can identify patterns of consistent behavior. The regularity of our observations allows us to seek an explanation. By understanding the determinants of stress and learning how to manage them, we gain greater control over stressful situations and reduce their harmful effects.

Description. The first goal in studying organizational behavior is to recognize and describe the things that happen regularly in organizations. If all we observed were random events, our efforts to study organizational behavior would be thwarted. We need to develop a way of thinking and talking about the events in our environment, because it makes the environment more secure and comfortable. When we see something occur with regularity and predictability, we want to recognize it, identify it, and develop a way to discuss it. **Description** requires us to label and define organizational events. If the comments of women in a mixed-sex committee are consistently ignored, the first goal is to describe what is happening and then to identify the problem of sexism. An accurate description of the problem is needed before we try to understand or explain it. If we find that study groups tend to achieve greater academic performance when they compete against each other, our observations will encourage us to study the effects of competition versus cooperation.

Explanation and Prediction. The second goal of organizational behavior is **explanation**—to explain and predict the events that occur. When we see recurring events, we want to identify the forces contributing to them. This allows us to predict what will happen in the future when these same conditions are present, thereby making our world more stable and secure. For example, if a professor places an article in the reserve library for students to read, we can predict how many students will read it by knowing whether the professor says the exam will include questions about the article. We can also predict when most students will read it if we know when the exam will be given. But we want to do more than just predict the study habits of students; we also want to explain student behavior. Why aren't students adequately motivated by the excitement of learning something new, and why do they wait until just before the exam to read the article when it has been available for several weeks?

We develop our own theories to explain what we observe. These theories represent our own efforts to explain the relationships between variables and the motives that cause people to behave the way they do. Even though we may not think of ourselves as behavioral scientists, we generate our own theories to explain the world around us. For example, we have our own working theories to explain why some people refuse to accept welfare, why supervisors get angry, why people play lotteries, why students are so concerned about grades, and why people quit their jobs. The characteristics of good theories and the process of testing them are explained later in this chapter.

Control. The third goal of organizational behavior is to **control** the behavior that occurs in organizations. If behavior has been carefully explained, and we know what causes it, we can create situations that elicit desirable behaviors and eliminate undesirable behaviors. Organizational behavior contains a variety of techniques and interventions to change the behaviors of individuals, groups, and organizations.

Controlling behavior, however, creates a difficult ethical problem: some people are firmly opposed to the idea of using organizational behavior knowledge to control the behavior of people at work. Organizational control is criticized as a form of bribery, coercion, or manipulation. Those who object to the idea of controlling behavior have a legitimate concern, because organizations can have a destructive influence on individuals and society. However, organizations can also provide excellent opportunities for personal growth and self-fulfillment. This issue points to the continuing need for students to study the ethics of organizational behavior.

Some organizations do much more than others to control the behavior of their members. The military is well known for its structured environment, which controls to a great extent both thoughts and behaviors. The control process in the military is apparent from the very first minute new recruits begin basic training. Other organizations, especially fraternities and sororities, also use social pressures and rigorous initiation rituals to influence the attitudes and behaviors of new members, and some of these practices have led to public censure when they have become extreme. Smoking is a behavior that is becoming increasingly controlled by organizations. Some companies, such as U.S. Gypsum, use a variety of rewards, punishments, and counseling to induce their employees to completely stop smoking both on and off the job.

Attempts to control behavior are not necessarily unethical. Essentially all managerial actions are designed to influence individual behavior and control what occurs in organizations. Organizations control behavior whether we like it or not, and it only seems reasonable that we should try to design them to enhance the quality of life. As an ethical concern, managers should seek to control behavior in a way that contributes to both individual growth and organizational goal achievement.

Levels for Analyzing Organizational Behavior

Organizational behavior can be examined from three distinct levels of analysis: the individual, the group, and the organization. Each event can be analyzed from these three levels, and the kinds of behavior we observe and the types of problems we diagnose will depend on the level of analysis. For example, a dispute between the purchasing supervisor and the warehouse superintendent could be analyzed quite differently depending on whether it was viewed as a conflict between personalities at the individual level, a problem between members of a task force at a group level, or a conflict between two division heads at the organizational level. Analyzing a given problem from all three levels is necessary to develop a proper diagnosis of the problem, as shown in Exhibit 1.2.

EXHIBIT 1.2   **Three Levels for Analyzing Organizational Events**

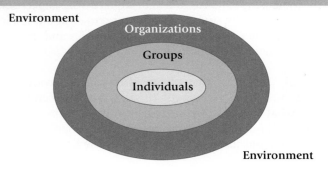

Individual Level. At the individual level, events are diagnosed in terms of the behaviors and personalities of the people interacting in the situation. Each individual brings to the organization a unique history of attitudes, values, and past experiences. Individuals have unique personalities that predispose them each to behave in characteristic ways. If an organization announced that it was sponsoring a competitive incentive program, this program would be greeted enthusiastically by employees with a high need for achievement, while employees with a low need for achievement might feel threatened. When the warehouse superintendent and the purchasing supervisor debate the merits of a proposed change, their comments reflect their own personal attitudes and values. How forcefully they express their attitudes will be influenced by their own personal self-esteem and assertiveness. The fate of the proposed change may rest on which individual uses greater personal power and aggressiveness.

Group Level. Although groups are made of individuals, the events that occur within a group are not simply the sum of individual behaviors. Groups develop their own norms of acceptable behavior, and these general expectations may be shared by members of the group even though none of them would be willing to accept the same norms outside the group. The behavior of group members is influenced by group dynamics, group roles, and status. For example, in a task force meeting, the warehouse superintendent could suggest a superior solution to a crucial problem. But, because of group dynamics, the task force may compel a premature majority decision that protects the interests of the purchasing supervisor, who is chairing the task force.

Organizational Level. Organizations are more than just the sum of individuals. Events occur within the context of an organizational structure. This structure and the location of people within it has an impact on virtually every social interaction, including casual conversations. Secretaries and production workers do not speak to the president of the company with the same degree of candor and ease as they use when they speak with each other. An organizational structure with hierarchical reporting relationships gives certain individuals the power and the authority to influence others. This structure affects the way information is communicated and the way decisions are made. A decentralized organizational structure, for example, allows lower-level managers to participate in making decisions, thereby raising their status and providing greater variety in their jobs. Returning to the previous example, let's say the purchasing supervisor is opposed to the warehouse superintendent's recommendation to adopt a computerized inventory system because the people in the warehouse would then have immediate access to all inventory information. In the past this information was controlled by purchasing supervisors, who used it as a weapon and source of power to influence other areas of the organization, particularly accounting.

Environment. In an analysis of behavior at the individual, group, or organizational level, it is important to consider the effects of the external environment. Individuals do not interact in a vacuum, and events do not occur in isolation. External forces may exert a powerful influence on what is observed at each of these three levels. For example, low productivity, careless work, excessive absenteeism, and frequent tardiness are serious problems that need to be analyzed at more than just the individual, group, and organizational levels. The seriousness of these problems becomes evident only when we realize that the environment includes both consumers who demand high-quality products, and competing firms in Korea, Japan, or Singapore that have workers who are willing to dependably produce high-quality items for considerably lower wages. Returning to our earlier example: the purchasing supervisor's desire to maintain control of the inventory data may be inconsistent with the organization's need to install a computerized inventory system. The survival of the organization may be threatened by other organizations who use "just-in-time" manufacturing and have a competitive advantage because they require less working capital for raw materials and finished goods. Organizations face a variety of significant environmental forces that influence their effectiveness, including changes in the labor force, evolving social customs, fluctuating economic conditions, and the enactment of laws by federal or state legislatures.

What Are Organizations?

Since organizational behavior is the study of organizations, it is useful at the beginning to dispel some of the popular myths about organizations and help students develop a better way of thinking about them. Knowing how to think about organizations and how to understand the behavior that occurs in them is very difficult for many students because organizations do not exist as physical objects in the same way that people, machines, and chemical compounds exist.

When students are asked to define an organization, they usually say an organization is a group of people who are working together to achieve a common goal. In spite of its popularity, this definition is not very useful for studying organizations. The two basic elements of this definition are "a group of people" and "a common purpose," and neither of these elements can be clearly defined.

Rather than thinking about an organization as a group of people with common goals, students need a better model that defines the common characteristics of organizations. Four of the most basic statements defining organizations include the following: (1) organizations consist of the patterned activities of people, (2) organizations are social inventions, (3) organizations involve goal-oriented activities, and (4) organizations are open systems.[10]

Patterned Activities. An organization consists of the **patterned activities** of people. These patterned activities relate to the recurring events that happen over and over in organizational life. For a university, the most obvious illustrations of patterned activities are the classes that are held at specified times. For example, every Monday, Wednesday, and Friday at 10 A.M. a group of students and a professor meet for one hour to discuss organizational behavior. Other patterned activities include seminars, faculty meetings, admitting students, processing loan applications, and typing correspondence. Activities that occur only once or at unpredictable times, such as a mob or a student demonstration, are not characteristic of an organization. Thinking of an organization as a system of patterned activities is probably the most important and yet the most difficult concept for students who are starting to learn about organizational behavior.

Social Inventions. Organizations are **social inventions** created by people; therefore, an organization is a social reality rather than a physical reality. As long as individuals are willing to continue participating in the patterned activities defining the organization, it will continue to exist. The physical facilities do not define the organization, although they may be necessary for the organization to continue its activities. When an organization dies, it does not leave behind a physical object for conducting a postmortem examination, such as the cadaver of a dead person or the remains of a wrecked vehicle. Some organizations may have virtually no physical assets. A trucking company, for example, may consist of only a few pieces of paper, including a corporate charter or permit, contracts with drivers who own their own trucks, and a schedule showing the materials to be picked up and delivered. This organization may operate indefinitely and even outlast the individuals who created it. When the activities defining this situation cease to occur, the trucking company will die and the only thing left behind will be a file cabinet of contracts and schedules. Although organizations face the possibility of falling apart and disintegrating overnight, they also have the capacity to continue indefinitely and survive many generations after the individuals who created them.

Goal Orientation. To understand organizations, we must make a distinction between individual goals and organizational goals. Organizational members have their own individual goals that justify their participation in the organization. As long as individuals are reasonably satisfied that their personal goals are being met, they are willing to continue participating in the organization. However, the goals of individual members are not identical, and each has his or her own reasons for participating.

We often assume that organizations are **goal oriented** in the same way that people have goals. However, this is not exactly true. On the one hand, it can be argued that organizations do not speak or think; therefore, they cannot be said to have their own goals. On the other hand, it is meaningful to talk about organizational goals because in most organizations a general consensus emerges about the goals of that organization. Organizational members have their own individual goals, but they also share a general consensus about the purpose of the organization. This consensual validation of the organization's goals is even supported by individuals outside the organization who have expectations about what the organization should be doing. For example, colleges and universities are expected to educate people; hospitals are supposed to treat the sick; churches are expected to teach moral values; and manufacturing companies are expected to produce consumer products.

Open System. An organization is an open system in the sense that it interacts with the environment and depends on the environment for people, resources, and acceptance of its products. People are constantly entering and leaving organizations as members, customers, and stakeholders. The term **stakeholders** refers to the people who have a genuine interest in an organization. The stakeholders of a community hospital, for example, include administrators and medical staff who are paid by the hospital and also the patients who are treated there, the doctors who refer them, the bondholders who invested their money to build it, the neighbors in the area, and members of the community who may need its services.

Although an organization requires the presence of people, it is not defined by identifying who those people are. In fact, in many organizations it is impossible to construct a list of names where everyone on this list is a member of the organization and those not on the list are nonmembers. Which of the following would you include as members of a university, for example: faculty, students, administration, high school counselors, placement officials, campus recruiters, alumni, contributors, parents, taxpayers? Those who want a restricted list of members would exclude alumni, part-time faculty, and part-time students, while those who want a more expansive list would include all these plus the board of education, the state legislature who approves the budget, and all employers who hire the graduates. This illustration explains why an organization cannot be defined by the people associated with it. Although an organization requires the presence of people, knowing who those people are is neither helpful nor necessary.

Rather than thinking of an organization as a specified group of people working together to achieve a goal, it is better to think of an organization as a loose structure where individuals are continually coming and going. The organizational members who are "in" the organization today may not be the same members who are "in" tomorrow. Organizations are constantly interacting with the environment. The participation of individuals is voluntary; therefore, in this sense organizations are open to the environment and depend on the environment for a constant input of people and materials. This concept is explained further in Chapter 11.

In many ways, modern organizations are very different from organizations fifty or even five years ago. Today's organizations are characterized by much greater diversity and technological advancement than in earlier years, and the amount of change in organizations seems to increase each year. Many factors have contributed to the growing diversity of the labor force, including an increase in the percentage of female and minority employees and a larger number of ethnic groups represented in the labor force. Scientific discoveries have made dramatic changes in technology, especially in the transmission of information. New products emerge almost instantaneously, making old products obsolete. The world has increasingly become one global economy requiring organizations to interact across national and cultural boundaries as competitors and/or partners. To survive, organizations have had to change their orientation from being product-producing organizations to service-producing organizations. The forces of change and how organizations can adapt to them are discussed further in Chapter 17 at the end of the text. In spite of these changes, however, organizations share certain common characteristics that help us understand what they are and what has to happen so they can survive.

What Characteristics Do We Study?

The study of organizational behavior focuses on three characteristics of organizations: behavior, structure, and processes.

Behavior. At times the study of organizational behavior focuses on the behavior of individuals. For example, the study of perception, job satisfaction, motivation, and learning are all concerned with the behavior of individuals. The study of behavior includes how individuals respond to a new incentive program, an autocratic supervisor, group pressures, or job redesign. To understand organizational behavior, we must be able to understand the behavior of individuals.

Structure. Another characteristic of organizational behavior is the structure of organizations and groups. The term *structure* refers to the fixed relationships of the organization, such as how jobs are assigned to departments, who reports to whom, and how the jobs and the departments are arranged in an organizational chart. The structure of an organization has a large influence on the behavior of individuals and the effectiveness of the organization.

Processes. The third characteristic of organizational behavior is organizational processes: the interactions among members of the organization. Some of the major organizational processes include communication, decision making, leadership, and power. These topics are covered in Chapters 13 through 16. A major consideration in designing an effective organizational structure is providing for these processes to be accomplished efficiently. For example, effective methods for collecting and communicating useful information need to be integrated within the organizational structure.

ORGANIZATIONS AND PEOPLE AT WORK

The relationship between people and organizations is a central issue in the study of organizational behavior. Organizations are created by people to benefit people. Social institutions are designed for specific purposes, and they continue to exist only if at least part of our society agrees that the organization is producing worthwhile products or services. Organizations do not have an inherent right to exist; instead, they exist only because people have created them as a means of achieving worthwhile objectives. Too often we forget that organizations exist to serve people rather than the reverse.

At the same time, however, individuals need organizations. The organized efforts of a group of people provide a variety of goods and services that individuals could not produce for themselves alone. Many economic and technological contributions are beyond the capacity of individuals to create for themselves, such as roads, utilities, medical services, education, and personal protection. Therefore, individuals and organizations share a symbiotic relationship. Organizations need people or they cannot exist, and people need organizations to achieve something greater than primitive life.

When individuals decide to work for an organization, they enter into a voluntary agreement regarding the conditions of employment. This agreement is called an "employment exchange": the individuals agree to work in exchange for wages, benefits, and other rewards. The voluntary nature of this employment exchange and the expectations of each party represent an important foundation for understanding organizational behavior and other management actions.

Since the abolition of slavery following the Civil War, a basic principle in America is that people cannot be held in servitude. Consequently organizations must compete for members. The survival of any organization is influenced by its ability to attract individuals to join and stay with it. An organization that loses its ability to attract new members will eventually disintegrate and disappear. Business organizations usually rely on monetary incentives to attract an adequate supply of labor. Political parties, religious organizations, and voluntary associations, however, rely mostly on nonmonetary incentives to attract new members.

The Inducements–Contributions Balance

An **employment exchange** occurs when individuals are willing to exchange labor for rewards and when an organization is willing to exchange rewards for labor. This employment exchange has been referred to as an "inducements–contributions balance."[11] The inducements people receive for working must be balanced with the contributions they make to the organization. A state of equilibrium or balance is achieved if the inducements are essentially equal to the contributions.

Inducements. Inducements are all the rewards that accrue to individuals from working. One of the most important inducements is money in the form of wages, salaries, and benefits. Other inducements include satisfying work that creates feelings of fulfillment and involvement, friendly co-workers and supervisors who make life pleasant and meaningful, the opportunity to provide service to others and to society, and the opportunity for self-expression and economic security. The inducements provided by various occupations vary greatly. Some jobs, such as senator, judge, lifeguard, and movie star, provide desirable inducements in the form of social status, power, prestige, or service. Individuals also vary in how they evaluate the value of inducements offered by the job. For example, a job with high status and extensive responsibility is not universally desired. Some employees simply do not want additional responsibilities or opportunities for promotion.

Contributions. Contributions are the things people offer to the organization, such as effort, skill, knowledge, and creative ideas. The essential contributions that enable an organization to survive include (1) dependable attendance, (2) dependable performance, and (3) spontaneous and innovative behaviors.[12] Dependable attendance means joining an organization and staying with it. Employees must be at work when they are expected to be there, and they must also be on time. Dependable performance concerns the quantity and quality of employees' performances. Employees must perform their jobs well enough to satisfy the needs of the organization. Spontaneous and innovative behaviors are those contributions to organizational effectiveness that are above and beyond the formal job description. Examples of such behaviors include cooperative acts that help the organization operate smoothly, creative suggestions, self-training for additional responsibility, acts that are protective of the organization, and conduct that creates a positive climate and pleasant environment.

Employees usually participate in the employment exchange only as long as the inducements offered to them are as great as or greater than the contributions they are asked to make. Likewise, the organization will support the employment exchange only as long as the employees' contributions are equal to or greater than the rewards offered by the organization. This inducements–contributions balance is illustrated in Exhibit 1.3. If either party believes the situation is out of balance, the employment contract may be terminated.

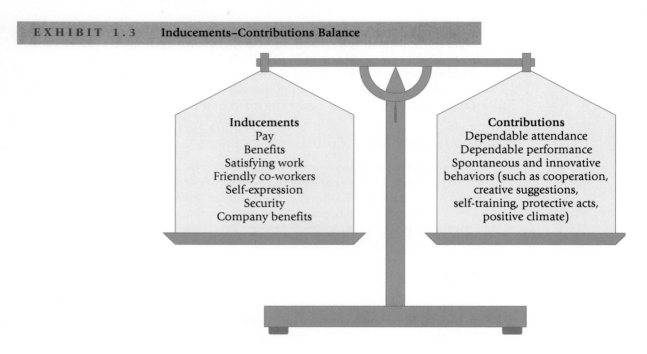

EXHIBIT 1.3   Inducements–Contributions Balance

Inducements
Pay
Benefits
Satisfying work
Friendly co-workers
Self-expression
Security
Company benefits

Contributions
Dependable attendance
Dependable performance
Spontaneous and innovative
behaviors (such as cooperation,
creative suggestions,
self-training, protective acts,
positive climate)

The inducements–contributions balance is based on the subjective perceptions of individuals. The relative value of money, satisfying work, and other inducements are subjectively assessed. Employees working in identical situations do not necessarily evaluate the inducements they receive equally. Moreover, two employees may not feel the same about the contributions they are making even though they are performing identical jobs. How employees evaluate their contributions is largely determined by their personal values and by how they assess alternative activities. Working for an organization may be very costly to someone who places a higher value on leisure and other activities. For example, an employee who is typically satisfied with the inducements received from working may be very dissatisfied with the same inducements on the day his or her softball team plays for the city championship. Generally, the inducements match the contributions, but now the costs of contributing have increased dramatically because of a highly valued alternative activity. To entice the individual to work rather than play softball, the organization needs to provide sufficient inducements in the form of added rewards for staying or sufficient penalties for leaving to offset the change in the cost of contributing.

The Effects of Organizations on People

An unbalanced employment exchange is not always terminated. Sometimes a serious inequity may persist for a long time and results in individuals abusing the organization or in the organization abusing individuals. This abuse may occur as an intentional strategy by either party, but it can also occur through careless innocence. An individual's personal life or self-esteem can be seriously damaged by events occurring at work even though no one meant harm to occur. Consequently, you need to know how to protect yourself; you need to recognize abusive treatment when it happens and know what you can do about it.

Abuse of Organizations. Abusive actions toward an organization may take the form of employee theft or fraud, for example. In retail stores, theft by the store's own employees is a serious problem. Employee theft is measured in terms of inventory shrinkage—the reduction in merchandise that stores ought to have, versus what they actually have. Only 10 percent of this loss is attributed to clerical errors and 30 percent to shoplifting. The remaining 60 percent is attributed to theft by the store's own employees. The statistics for bank fraud are equally serious: for every $1 banks lose to robberies, burglaries, and larceny, they lose $20 to internal fraud and embezzlement.[13] Employee theft occurs at all levels in an organization, with some of the major fraud being committed by top-level managers.

A more subtle form of abuse occurs when employees are paid for work that is not performed. This type of abuse includes loafing on the job, coming late to work, taking extra personal time or lengthy coffee breaks, abusing sick leave, and performing careless and sloppy work. Employees often get away with these types of careless performance because they are protected by work rules in a labor agreement or because the organization has not developed adequate appraisal procedures for evaluating and correcting problems.

Abuse of Individuals. Organizations also have the power to abuse individuals. The balance of power is clearly in the hands of the organization in power struggles over wages, benefits, and working conditions. Although disgruntled employees are free to quit, the consequences of quitting are clearly more costly to the individuals than to the organization. The loss of a job to an employee is more catastrophic than the loss of an employee to an organization.

Employers are generally free to dismiss their employees for good reasons, for bad reasons, or even for reasons that are normally wrong without breaking the law. This idea is called the "employment-at-will" doctrine because employers have the discretion to create jobs and hire whom they want for as long as they want. The employment exchange can be terminated at the will of either the employer or the employee for almost any reason. Employees who belong to labor unions sometimes enjoy a measure of protection against arbitrary management decisions, but over four-fifths of the employees in America are not union members.

Although the Bill of Rights guarantees certain freedoms to citizens in society, employees in organizations do not enjoy many of the same rights. For example, freedom of speech is sometimes constrained by company regulations, such as this one established by a private bus company on the West Coast: "The company requires its employees to be loyal. It will not tolerate words or acts of hostility to the company, its officers, agents, or employees, its services, equipment or its condition, or . . . criticisms of the company to others than . . . superior officers."[14] Employees who violate this company regulation can be fired even though their criticisms may be legitimate and in the best interests of society.

The rights of privacy and security guaranteed to citizens by the Bill of Rights are often not extended to employees at work. Although employees' homes are protected from arbitrary search and seizure, their lockers, desks, and files at work can be inspected.

In some situations, employees are faced with moral dilemmas because they are asked to perform unethical or illegal acts. Sometimes employees are told to falsify reports, to dump toxic wastes in streams, to use substandard materials in construction, or to fire employees because of their age or race. These orders are immoral and illegal, and employees should never be expected to obey them. Even minor instructions, such as telling a secretary to say that a manager is out when the manager is really in can create an uncomfortable situation in which the secretary is forced to compromise personal standards of integrity.

Unintentional Abuse. When organizations condone illegal or immoral activities, the potential for abuse is obvious. However, organizations also abuse employees in subtle ways that may be entirely unintended. Every organization has the potential to abuse individuals—even benign organizations that sincerely try to help and support their employees. An organization does not have a heart and a mind or a soul, and employees who have contributed years of faithful service may be forced to find a new job or a new career because of forces beyond the control of the organization, such as a technological advance or an economic collapse. A new management team often has little knowledge about the devoted service of some long-term employees who deserve to be protected.

Organizations cannot control the expectations of employees, and there are natural tendencies for employees to develop false expectations. Employees are often seduced into thinking that someone in top management is looking after them and that they should just quietly serve the organization. When their jobs are eliminated because of a merger or new technology, these people feel abused and mistreated. The real irony here is that organizations with active career development programs have the greatest potential for abuse because they create the greatest expectations.

Job opportunities—even those that are typically valued by employees, such as promotions, transfers, and sales contests—can result in unintended abuse. Marriages can be damaged by long separations or pressure to relocate. Families may suffer because parents miss important events, such as graduations and Little League games, or are not available to provide guidance and support at crucial times. Excessive job stress may impair health and leave employees too emotionally exhausted to cope with other demands. It is natural for employees in large and powerful organizations to succumb to the belief that the organization's goals are inherently right and that the interests of the organization are more important than their personal welfare.

The hierarchical authority structure in organizations creates a natural opportunity for adversely influencing employees because they tend to develop a distorted concept of authority. When a person is promoted to a high-level position, the promotion somehow seems to imply moral superiority, innate goodness, or some other virtuous quality. As a result, employees do not question the decisions of upper-level managers, and they give too much import to managers' opinions. The blind obedience that results often does a disservice to the employee, the manager, and the organization.

A partial solution to organizational abuse is to change organizations in order to eliminate improper and unfair treatment. But more importantly, individuals must learn how to protect themselves from organizational influences. Organizations can be improved to make them safer for people, but people must also learn to protect themselves from both intentional and unintentional organizational abuse.

Managers and Leaders

This book takes a managerial perspective and is designed to teach you how to think about people and organizations, how to diagnose problems, how to formulate new policies, and how to implement them. At one time or another, we all serve as lead-

APPLYING ORGANIZATIONAL BEHAVIOR
IN THE NEWS

Becoming an Entrepreneur

CNN Philippe Kahn, founder and CEO of Borland International, is an entrepreneur. He didn't want to be an entrepreneur; he didn't even want to manage his own company. But he didn't have any choice at the time.

Kahn never studied management or marketing. He was born in France to Jewish parents who fled persecution, first in Russia, then in Germany. Although his mother survived the concentration camps, she died of cancer when Kahn was 13 years old. His parents had divorced, and he did not live with his father; but his father's engineering background inspired in him a fascination for technology.

During the 1970s, Kahn became involved by accident with the computer industry. In 1974, at the age of 21, he left his wife and two daughters in France and migrated to Silicon Valley because that is where he thought his ideas for new software could be developed. He had no intentions of starting a company. But without a legal work permit, he didn't have much luck finding a job. He had even less luck trying to interest investors in the software program he had developed.

Kahn decided the only way to sell his first products—Turbo Pascal and SideKick—was by mail order, a method shunned by other software producers. But since he couldn't afford to pay for an ad, he devised a clever scheme to secure advertising which has become a Borland legend. He invited a salesman from *Byte* magazine, filled the office with temporary workers to make the company look vibrant, and let the salesman "accidentally" catch sight of a list of magazines with his title crossed off. Kahn professed that his media plan was complete and he couldn't afford more ads. But he willingly agreed to buy space in the magazine when the salesman offered credit. When the ad reaped over $100,000 sales in its first month, Kahn easily repaid the salesman's loan.

Kahn tries to avoid bureaucratic procedures in Borland and encourage people to make decisions for themselves. The employees can expect Kahn to drop by unexpectedly to learn what they are thinking about. Furthermore, any employee can contact him directly by e-mail, thereby bypassing traditional chains of command.

Source: CNN *Pinnacle* news programming.

ers in some kind of organization, whether it is a business, family, church, neighborhood, or political organization.

Managers and leaders have a large influence on the success of organizations. Studies on the reasons why organizations succeed or fail typically point to the significant role of managers. Key managerial decisions in formulating strategic plans and organizational policies primarily account for the survival or the demise of organizations. Effective managers make things happen. They are largely responsible for establishing organizations that create new jobs and produce useful products and services. Dynamic leaders who have the vision and foresight to create an enterprise and who can excite the minds of followers to coalesce around their vision can be valuable national treasures.

Some writers like to make a distinction between managers and leaders to emphasize the importance of vision and foresight in directing a dynamic organization. According to this distinction, managers manage things while leaders lead people; managers do things right, while leaders do the right things; managers rely on control, while leaders rely on trust; managers maintain employees in the organization, while leaders develop the people in the organization.[15] Although this distinction helps emphasize the need for inspired direction in a rapidly changing environment, it is also true that effective managers must also be good leaders and that effective leaders are also good managers. Effective leadership is described further in Chapter 15.

Characteristics of Managerial Work

When asked, "What do managers do?" most people say managers plan, organize, direct, and control. These four management functions were first proposed at the beginning of this century, and for many years they dominated the vocabulary and literature of management. The central elements comprising these four management functions are illustrated in Exhibit 1.4. However, these four functions do not adequately describe what managers actually do.

A significant contribution toward understanding managerial work was made by Henry Mintzberg, who observed a group of managers and recorded their behavior.[16] Through structured observations, Mintzberg observed five chief executives of medium to large organizations for one-week periods. Other researchers have replicated Mintzberg's study and identified similar characteristics of managerial work by actually observing managers to learn what they do.[17] These observations have identified six characteristics of managerial work.

1. *Managers perform a great quantity of work at an unrelenting pace.* Mintzberg's study found that there was virtually no break in the frantic pace of activity for managers either at work or after work. In performing their work, they responded to an average of thirty-six pieces of mail per day, five telephone calls, and eight meetings, which accounted for almost every minute from the moment they entered their offices in the morning until they departed in the evenings. Coffee was taken during meetings, and lunchtimes were typically devoted to formal or informal meetings. When pressing problems were resolved, subordinates seemed to be ever present to usurp free time. The work of managing an organization may be described as a very taxing responsibility.

2. *Managerial activity is characterized by variety, fragmentation, and brevity.* Managerial activities are not structured or scheduled. Instead, they are fragmented as successive activities force managers to deal with one issue after another. Managers must be prepared to shift moods quickly and frequently. Most managerial actions are brief and take less than nine minutes. Telephone calls are quick and to the point, and average about six minutes. Unscheduled meetings are about twelve minutes long, and routine desk work, such as dictating letters and reading the *Wall Street Journal*, takes about fifteen minutes. Few managers have time to do more than merely skim long reports or memos. Recent college graduates who submit lengthy reports for managers to read soon learn that they are expected to begin their report with an executive summary, which is typically all that is read.

3. *Managers prefer issues that are current, specific, and ad hoc.* Managers tend to have a greater interest in and are more influenced by spontaneous reports, gossip, and speculation rather than routine operating reports. Managers seem to have a strong desire for current information, and they are more inclined to act on instant communication rather than routine reports. Since routine reports do not contain the latest information, managers tend to pay little if any serious attention to them. Although most managers are required to write reports as part of their job, few managers take the time to read reports written by others. Top managers are espe-

EXHIBIT 1.4   The Cycle of Management Functions

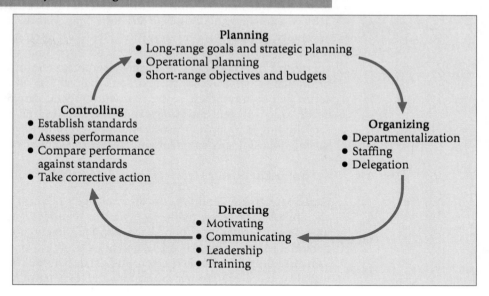

cially concerned with today and tomorrow, and prefer to deal with specific issues rather than general trends.

4. *Managers demonstrate a strong preference for spoken media.* They typically use five methods of communication: mail, telephone calls, unscheduled meetings, scheduled meetings, and tours. Processing mail is usually viewed as an unpleasant chore. Because mail does not deal with live action, managers tend to avoid using it and ignore most of what they get. Telephone calls and unscheduled meetings account for about two-thirds of their contacts with others. Although these contacts are brief, they generally provide pressing information about specific problems that attract the manager's attention. Scheduled meetings are generally lengthy, and the most important part of scheduled meetings consists of the incidental information at the beginning and end of such meetings. A walking tour around the organization is generally a powerful tool for gaining information in an informal way, but Mintzberg discovered that these tours were not used very frequently. Only 3 percent of the manager's time was spent touring the organization to collect information.

5. *The manager stands between the organization and a network of other contacts.* Managers generally spend a surprisingly large amount of time in horizontal communication with a variety of other contacts, such as clients, associates, suppliers, outside staff experts, trade organizations, government officials, and other directors. The job of a manager was described as "the neck of an hourglass," in which managers are responsible for sifting information into their organization from the environment. Much of this information is filtered by subordinates who condense it to prevent information overload on the chief executive.

6. *Managers appear to control their own affairs despite the preponderance of obligations and interruptions.* The endless barrage of unscheduled meetings, telephone calls, uninvited visitors, and sporadic problems create the impression that managers have little control over their time and activities. Managers are often viewed as slaves to

pressures beyond their control, such as appointments, requests for authorizations, meetings, and mail. In spite of these external pressures, however, managers still achieve a considerable degree of freedom. Managers exert their own will by taking advantage of opportunities to further their own interests. For example, an obligation to speak provides a manager with an opportunity to lobby for a cause, and committee meetings allow managers a forum to reinforce their views of the organizational mission. Although managers may appear on the surface to be puppets controlled by an endless string of environmental demands, successful managers decide who will pull the strings and how, and they take advantage of each move they are forced to make. Unsuccessful managers, however, generally fail to exploit this high-tension environment and are destroyed by their demanding jobs.

Managerial Roles

Henry Mintzberg identified ten roles managers perform in doing their jobs. A role encompasses the task activities or behaviors required of an individual performing a job. These ten roles are grouped according to three major classifications: (1) **interpersonal roles** as a figurehead, leader, or liaison; (2) **informational roles** as a monitor, disseminator, or spokesperson, and (3) **decisional roles** as an entrepreneur, disturbance handler, resource allocator, and negotiator. Although these roles are described separately, as shown in Exhibit 1.5, in practice they are highly integrated. The importance of each role varies according to the managerial level. Some roles are more important for top-level managers, while other roles have greater importance to first-level supervisors.

EXHIBIT 1.5	Mintzberg's Categories of Managerial Roles

Interpersonal Relationship Roles

1. Symbolic figurehead: represents the organization to the outside world.
2. Liaison: maintains contact with people and groups outside the organization.
3. Leader: hires, trains, motivates, evaluates, and supervises subordinates.

Informational Roles

4. Monitor: collects and analyzes data from outside and inside the unit.
5. Disseminator: circulates vital information to members of the unit.
6. Spokesperson: circulates relevant information to outside parties.

Decision Roles

7. Entrepreneur: innovates, initiates change, designs new products.
8. Disturbance handler: resolves nonroutine problems.
9. Resource allocator: distributes money, materials, time, and other resources.
10. Negotiator: secures resources and arranges favorable conditions from others.

APPLYING ORGANIZATIONAL BEHAVIOR
ACROSS CULTURES

Managers and Organizations: National Resources

 Samuel R. Daines is a colorful entrepreneur, a humanitarian who believes that significant social and economic improvements must be profitable if they hope to survive. After graduating from Harvard, where he studied law and economics, Sam worked five years each for the Agency for International Development (AID) and the Ford Foundation, advising the leaders of underdeveloped countries. His advice, however, went unheeded because the people he advised lacked the managerial and organizational skills to use it. In frustration, Sam decided to act on his own advice and purchased his first farm in 1969 near Lago Ranco, Chile, with money from family and friends.

Before Sam arrived, southern Chile had plenty of peasants, fertile highlands, and ample sunshine, but they were not organized or managed. Sam created an organization that included technological advances in harvesting and preserving raspberries, strawberries, and blueberries; training and supervising an unskilled labor force; and managing a massive worldwide network of distribution and marketing centers.

The key to the operation was effective field management control. Ripe raspberries spoil within two to three hours if they are picked from the vine and kept in the sun. To extend their "shelf life," they must be harvested before they are fully ripe, when they are "salmon pink," and cooled to 31°F within fifteen minutes of leaving the vine. Field workers are required to sort the berries by color to prevent ripe ones from spoiling during transportation.

During the two-month harvesting season, the farm near Llanquihue employs more than seven hundred workers, who come from as far away as Chiloe Island 200 miles away, for employment. The wages and benefits obtained from this seasonal employment have significantly enhanced the quality of these workers' lives.

By 1981, Sam Daines had major marketing and distribution centers in New York City, Chicago, Los Angeles, Paris, Amsterdam, and London. In the middle of winter, consumers in Europe and North America were able to enjoy fresh raspberries that had been picked the day before in Southern Chile, where it was summer, and air-lifted to northern markets.

In the past decade, Sam has extended his economic assistance to other underdeveloped countries, including India, Jordan, Pakistan, and Sri Lanka. In 1988, for example, Sam turned his attention to strife-torn Sri Lanka in an effort to help that country develop a viable export product and improve its struggling economy. After examining the availability of labor, the growing conditions, and possible agricultural exports, Sam decided that Sri Lanka had the potential to be a major exporter of ambul bananas. The ambul variety is resistant to sigaturka disease, a contagious leaf disease that can quickly destroy entire plantations; it grows well in many parts of the island with minimum care; and it grows evenly and does not fall off the comb when ripe. When properly handled and stored, the ambul banana produces an attractive bright yellow color with a blemish-free peel and a delicious flavor that competes effectively in European markets.

Sam recommends an unorthodox but effective growing method that consists of covering the young stems with a polyurethane bag containing durzban, an insecticide. The bags are secured to the stalk with color-coded ribbons to indicate when the fruit should be picked. Ambul bananas are harvested green after thirteen weeks and ripen in market areas. These bags have to be imported and they add to the expense and labor, but they protect the fruit from leaf scarring and insects and make the fruit exportable by looking attractive on produce shelves.

Sam's managerial talent, combined with his knowledge of global markets, is an extremely valuable international resource. His efforts have significantly improved the economic conditions of several countries.

Source: Mahan Besnarsalinghe, "Big Market Awaiting Export of 'Ambul' Bananas," *Daily News* (in Sri Lanka) (September 10, 1991), p. 1; "Chilean Blueberry Output Set to Double," *Eurofruit Magazine* (December 1992–January 1993), p. 30.

BEHAVIORAL SCIENCE RESEARCH

Behavioral science research contributes to our knowledge of organizational behavior by allowing us to make observations, formulate theories to explain our observations, and then test the accuracy of the theories. Good managers need to understand behavioral science research. Students who are studying organizational behavior also need to understand the scientific method and know how research is used in organizational behavior. Behavioral science research is as important for managers as biological research is for medical students.

The Usefulness of Theory in Understanding Behavior

Behavioral science research involves developing and testing theories. A theory consists of a statement of functional relationships among variables; we are stating a theory when we attempt to explain a recurring type of event.

How Theories Help. To some extent, we all act like behavioral scientists as we observe events around us and try to make sense out of them. We develop our own working **theories** to help us interpret what is happening, and what the consequences of our behavior will be. We rely on our theories to guide our actions. If our theories are wrong, we can make serious mistakes without realizing that the problem stemmed from a bad theory. The skills of a good behavioral scientist—observing, interpreting, generalizing, and explaining—are essential for managers because they are required to collect data, analyze them logically, and act on them.

Some theories are very simple, involving only two variables, while other theories are extremely complex. Theories are useful because they direct our observations and tell us what to look for, they help us interpret and explain our observations, and they help us predict future behavior.

Many valuable insights have been gained from the formal theories that have emerged in the behavioral science literature. However, we also develop our own informal theories to help us organize and interpret our observations. These are some examples of theories:

1. Dissatisfied employees are more likely to steal from their employers.
2. How people dress has a significant influence on their career success.
3. Students do not learn very effectively when they study organizational behavior while the television is on.
4. People who have the most power are able to manipulate situations so they get more power.

In our day-to-day activities, we develop a large repertoire of theories similar to these, and use them to guide our thinking. By making careful observations to test our theories, we can refine them and improve the accuracy of our predictions and the likelihood of behaving effectively.

Characteristics of Good Theories. There are no perfect theories in organizational behavior; each theory has advantages and limitations. Good theories generally contain the following characteristics.

1. A good theory is stated in simple terms. A theory that can explain an event in only a few terms is superior to a theory requiring a more complex set of variables and relationships to explain the event. Simple theories are called *parsimonious* theories.

2. Good theories are testable. Although we cannot prove a theory is true, a testable theory allows us to estimate the probability of its truth. If a theory cannot be confirmed or disproved through research, the accuracy of the theory cannot be assessed.

3. A good theory should be logically consistent with itself and with other known facts. A good theory should build on what has already been learned.

4. The conditions that indicate when a theory is relevant need to be clearly defined, so that the theory will not be erroneously applied in situations to which it does not apply. Some attempts should be made to indicate when a theory would be expected to hold and when the conditions do not apply.

Most theories presented in this book do not satisfy all these criteria. None of the theories have been so extensively researched that they can be pronounced conclusively true. Rather, the theories that have been the most extensively studied are usually the most qualified. Extensive research helps to identify the conditions when the theory applies and the conditions when it does not. Although students usually want to know only if a theory is true or false, this is not the best question to ask. It is better to ask when the theory is *useful*.

Paradigm Shifts. Occasionally the development of new knowledge produces a dramatic shift in the way a problem is analyzed and in the way the situation is perceived. This change, which is called a **paradigm shift,** results in a total restructuring in the way we think about a situation and the kinds of assumptions we make about former observations. A paradigm is a method of approaching a problem or situation and the kinds of assumptions, values, and attitudes associated with thinking about the situation.[18]

A very dramatic illustration of a paradigm shift was the shift from the Ptolemaic theory, seeing the earth as the center of the universe, to the Copernican theory, seeing the sun as the center of the universe. A more modest illustration of a paradigm shift was the shift from scientific management to the human relations movement during the 1930s. The focus of scientific management was on task efficiency; consequently, the development of time and motion studies, piece-rate incentives, and division of labor were analyzed and evaluated according to the criteria of how they influenced task efficiency. In contrast, the human relations movement focused on the dignity and individuality of people. Therefore, all corporate policies and management practices were evaluated with respect to their impact on the dignity and worth of the employee.

The Scientific Method

The **scientific method** is a systematic, controlled, and objective process of discovering and verifying new knowledge. The greatest advantage of the scientific method that distinguishes it from other methods of obtaining knowledge is its capacity for self-correction. The scientific method contains built-in checks to control extraneous explanations and verify the conclusions. This method tries to minimize the effects of the scientist's own biases and preconceptions.

The scientific method provides a way of obtaining information that is quite different from the way we learn about life from personal experiences and casual observations. It involves a systematic approach to developing and testing new ideas. At its most basic level, it consists of stating a proposition or theory and testing whether the proposition is true. Some of the major characteristics of the scientific method that distinguish it from the methods of analysis used in experiential learning, such as literature, art, and daily events, concern the use of hypotheses, constructs, and observations.[19]

1. *Hypothesis.* A **hypothesis** is a provisional statement describing the potential relationship between two or more variables. In the scientific method, the hypotheses used to explain and predict behavior are stated in ways that are rigorous and precise. In literature, art, and daily events, however, the hypotheses are very intuitive and general, and therefore not testable. An example of a testable hypothesis is "If meatcutters are offered a financial incentive to work safely then their accident rates will decrease." Because the hypotheses in science are testable, the procedures are therefore open to the public. Both the methods and the results are clearly described, and other researchers have the opportunity to replicate the results.

Hypotheses:
Testability

Experiential learning |———————————————————————————| Science

Intuitive and general   Rigorous and precise

2. *Constructs.* A **construct** is a word or concept that refers to relationships between objects or events. Intelligence, company loyalty, job satisfaction, and commitment are examples of constructs. In literature, art, and daily events, the constructs purposefully contain considerable surplus meaning and evoke a variety of feelings. In science, however, constructs must be operationally defined to make them very specific and empirical. An operational definition consists of defining a construct by specifying the operation or activity involved in measuring it. An IQ test, for example, is an operational definition of intelligence. "Bright" students could be operationally defined as those with grade-point averages in the top 10 percent. Job satisfaction has been operationally defined in a variety of ways, including responses on an attitude questionnaire, number of grievances submitted, turnover rates, and percent of negative comments expressed during staff meetings.

Constructs:
Operational specificity

Experiential learning |———————————————————————————| Science

Rich with surplus meaning   Specific and empirical

3. *Observations.* Observations vary in the degree of control and whether extraneous factors can influence them. In experiential learning, for example, the observations are loosely controlled and ambiguous; no attempt is made to control the environment in which they are made. In science, however, observations are carefully controlled through a variety of experimental methods.

Observations:

Control

Experiential learning |————————————————————————————————| Science

Loosely controlled   Experimental
and ambiguous

The theory that corporate mergers destroy company loyalty can be used to illustrate the difference between the scientific method and intuition. A newspaper article describing the angry feelings of a worker whose job was terminated after a corporate merger supports the theory that mergers destroy corporate loyalty. However, this newspaper article would be classified as literature or daily events, because the hypothesis is not operationally defined, and the observation comes from one randomly selected person rather than from a representative sample of the affected population. The scientific method requires that a testable hypothesis using operationally defined constructs be stated and examined in a controlled setting. Here is an example of a testable hypothesis: "If one company is acquired by another company through a leveraged buyout, the average organizational commitment scores of the employees in the acquired company will be lower after the acquisition than before." Here loyalty is operationally defined by responses to the organizational commitment questionnaire.

Research Methods

Behavioral scientists use a variety of research methods to obtain knowledge about organizational behavior. These methods are usually referred to as *research designs.* Four basic research designs include observational studies, field surveys, field experiments, and laboratory experiments, as shown in Exhibit 1.6.

Observational Studies. Observational research techniques are the most direct method of learning about organizational behavior. This method explains how we develop most of our common-sense views about organizations and people. In observational studies, researchers examine the natural activities of real people in an organizational setting by listening to what they say and watching what they do. Behavioral scientists are trained to describe the behavior they see, using specific terms that could be confirmed by others. They try to avoid drawing unwarranted conclusions about things they cannot observe, such as motives and attitudes. By limiting their observations to what they can see, their observations can be confirmed by others and are therefore more objective. Their observations are also more systematic, because they have been trained to look for certain crucial events, and they record them as they happen rather than trusting their memories to reconstruct them.

EXHIBIT 1.6	The Continuum of Scientific Research Methods

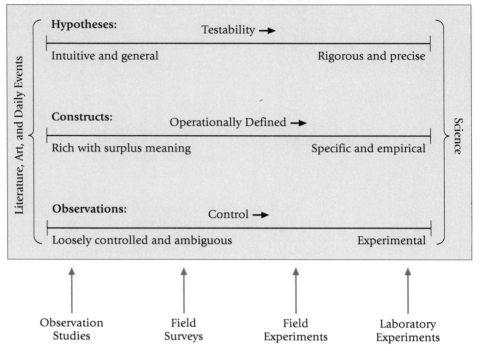

Observation   Field   Field   Laboratory
Studies   Surveys   Experiments   Experiments

Source: Adapted from *Theories in Contemporary Psychology,* by Melvin H. Marx. Macmillan Publishing Company. Used with permission of the author.

The most common form of observational studies is called a *case study.* The case study seeks to examine many characteristics of one or more people, usually over an extended period of time. Occasionally the experimenter joins the group and actively participates in group activities. Here the researcher becomes a functioning member of the group in what is called *participant observation.* This method has often been used by anthropologists who study the customs and norms of various cultures by actually living among them. The advantage of participant observation is that the researcher can obtain more spontaneous and unbiased information about the group, because the group is not as conscious about being watched. The disadvantage is that participating observers lose some of their objectivity and occasionally influence the group by their involvement.

Case studies are often used to help students learn how to diagnose organizational problems and formulate possible solutions. Although useful for educational purposes, the case study method is not good for research. The insights and conclusions from a case study depend entirely on the skill of the observer. Although a trained researcher may be able to make some valuable observations, the results are based on a sample of 1 ($N = 1$), so they cannot be generalized to other situations, and rarely can case studies be repeated or their findings verified. Even if the researcher accurately describes what occurred, a lack of experimental control prevents the researcher from explaining why it occurred or eliminating other explanations.

Field Surveys. A **field survey,** sometimes called a *correlational study,* involves measuring a few characteristics about a large number of people at one point in time. One major advantage of a field survey is that it examines people who are involved in real-life situations in actual organizations. Its major disadvantage is that it does not allow researchers to explain what caused the event.

Most field surveys involve *correlational studies* in which researchers measure two or more variables and then test whether they are related. For example, a correlation study could be used to test whether there is a relationship between office size and job satisfaction. A questionnaire could be used to measure job satisfaction and a correlation coefficient could be computed between this variable and office space measured in square feet.

A correlation coefficient is a number that shows the relationship between two variables. The statistical formula for computing a correlation coefficient always produces a number between −1.0 and +1.0. A positive correlation coefficient close to +1.0 indicates that people who have high scores on one variable tend to have high scores on the other variable, while those who have low scores on one variable tend to be low on both. A negative correlation coefficient suggests that people with high scores on one variable tend to have low scores on the other variable. An illustration of a negative correlation coefficient is shown in Exhibit 1.7, which shows the relationship between absenteeism and job satisfaction for a group of twenty employees.

A correlation coefficient indicates the degree of association or relationship between two variables, but does not imply causality. Although the analysis may produce a positive correlation between office space and job satisfaction, nothing of a causal nature can be concluded. A positive correlation cannot be interpreted to mean that larger offices make people more satisfied with their jobs. Instead, both variables may be caused by a third variable, such as status within the organization or nearness to the company cafeteria.

Field Experiments. In a **field experiment,** a researcher attempts to manipulate and control variables in the natural setting of the organization. The subjects being observed continue to work as employees in an ongoing organization, and certain

EXHIBIT 1.7 **Relationship Between Absenteeism and Job Satisfaction for Twenty Employees (Correlation Coefficient = −.65)**

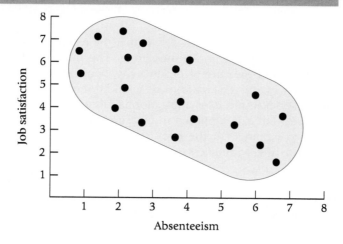

important organizational variables are manipulated or changed to examine their effects on behavior. An example of a field experiment is offering a select group of employees a financial incentive for every day they work without a recordable accident and then measuring the reduction in their accidents.

The advantage of a field experiment is that the individuals continue to interact in a real situation under relatively normal circumstances. The effects of different variables can be assessed by varying them one at a time. The results of the experiment allow the researchers to draw causal inferences in which they say a change in variable A caused a change in variable B. The disadvantages of a field experiment are (1) the results cannot always be generalized to other organizations and (2) some experiments can disrupt the organization.

Laboratory Experiments. In a laboratory experiment, the environment is created by the researcher and extraneous influences can be controlled. The carefully controlled environment of a laboratory study is both an advantage and disadvantage. It is an advantage because it eliminates competing explanations for the observed changes, and it is a disadvantage because it creates an artificial environment that does not necessarily represent reality.

In laboratory and field experiments, the variable controlled by the researcher is the **independent variable.** It is called the *independent variable* because the researcher has control over it and can decide such things as when it will be presented, in what form, or how much. The **dependent variables** are the variables that are measured to see if the independent variable had an influence. For example, in a study that tests whether financial incentives influence productivity, the independent variable is the change in financial incentives, while the dependent variable is the level of productivity.

Data Collection Methods

All data collection methods need to satisfy two requirements: the data must be both reliable and valid. The term **reliability** refers to the consistency of the measure. A research instrument is said to be reliable if it produces consistent and repeatable measures each time it is used. Counting the number of bricks a mason has laid should be a very reliable measure of productivity, because the results should be the same each time they are counted. Questionnaires are usually reliable if the questions are clear; if they are ambiguous, the responses will be random and the instrument will be unreliable.

The term **validity** refers to whether the research instrument actually measures what it is supposed to be measuring. The number of bricks a mason has laid is a very valid measure of productivity, because laying bricks is what a mason is supposed to do. The validity of a questionnaire, however, is more difficult to assess. For example, does a questionnaire measuring company commitment really measure what it is supposed to measure? Are people with high scores more loyal to the company? Do the people who leave have lower scores? Are the scores related to the willingness of employees to defend the company against public criticism?

Three of the most frequently used methods in collecting research data include observations, interviews, and questionnaires. Each of these methods has advantages and disadvantages and is appropriate for a particular type of research.

APPLYING ORGANIZATIONAL BEHAVIOR RESEARCH

Using a Quasi-experiment to Evaluate Office Decisions

A practical architectural design question for managers is whether several workstations should be located in a large open area, or should employees have their own individual offices? Walls are costly; they reduce interaction between employees; and they reduce the number of employees who can work in a given area. Yet walls provide privacy and reduce noise and distractions.

A large insurance company used a quasi-experimental research method to evaluate the reactions of employees to three office designs. A quasi-experiment is a field experiment that examines intact work groups rather than experimental groups to which subjects have been randomly assigned. "True experiments" that can randomly assign subjects to an experimental condition provide better control. Unfortunately, organizations cannot randomly assign members to groups, so a quasi-experiment randomly assigns groups to the experimental conditions.

In this study, conducted by Greg Oldham, three offices of a large insurance company were assigned to different experimental conditions and evaluated at two time periods, July and December. In office C, the control group, no changes were made in the open office plan where employees had approximately 140 square feet per office. In office D, the density of the employees was changed in October when they moved from an open office plan with 125 square feet per employee to another open office plan with 260 square feet per employee. In office P, the employees moved in October from an open office plan with 150 square feet per employee to a new office that had about the same social density, but the workstations were separated on three sides by 4- to 6-foot partitions.

The evaluations in July and December measured the employees' reactions to crowding, task privacy, communication privacy, office satisfaction, job satisfaction, perceived performance, and need for privacy. The results of this study indicated that moving from an open office plan to either an open office with relatively low levels of social density or to an office with three partitions surrounding the employees' workstation had generally positive effects on employees' perceptions on crowding, task and communication privacy, and office satisfaction. Self-rated performance was not affected by the new office designs, and job satisfaction was only improved in office D, where the density was reduced. Finally, the effects of the new designs were more important to employees with high needs for privacy; these employees reported the greatest decreases in perceived crowding after the office changes.

Source: Greg R. Oldham, "Effects of Changes in Workspace Partitions and Spatial Density on Employee Reactions: A Quasi-Experiment," *Journal of Applied Psychology,* vol. 73 (1988), pp. 253–58.

Observations. Direct **observation** allows researchers to record specific behaviors. As long as the observations are measuring specific observable behaviors, these measures tend to be both reliable and valid.

A problem with direct observation is that the observation process itself sometimes influences behavior. This problem was recognized in the Hawthorne experiments (1927–1935) and has come to be known as the *Hawthorne effect:* when people know they are being observed, they tend to behave differently.[20]

Having an observer stand next to an employee with a clipboard and record the employee's behavior is a very obtrusive method of data collection. To prevent the observation process from influencing behavior, experimenters often use a variety of unobtrusive measures.[21] These methods typically involve indirect measures that may be more accurate than direct measures in some situations. For example, adults

EXHIBIT 1.8 **Questionnaire Measuring Attitudes Toward an Incentive Commission Program**

Here are some statements about how some people feel about the commission incentive program. You may agree with certain items and disagree with others. Please circle the number that comes closest to indicating your true feelings.

	No Opinion	Strongly Disagree	Neutral		Strongly Agree
1. My pay is too low, considering the work I do.	X	1	2	3	4	5
2. I have always been treated fairly by the company.	X	1	2	3	4	5
3. The incentive commission program is unfair because some get higher commissions than others.	X	1	2	3	4	5
4. The customers get much better service because of the incentive commission program.	X	1	2	3	4	5
5. The incentive commission program should be eliminated and replaced with straight hourly wages.	X	1	2	3	4	5
6. Because of the incentive commission program, my income fluctuates wildly, and I'd like it to be a little more stable.	X	1	2	3	4	5
7. The incentive commission program is an excellent program for motivating and rewarding employees.	X	1	2	3	4	5
8. There is a crucial need to change the incentive commission program so that it is more fair.	X	1	2	3	4	5

9. What changes are needed to make conditions in this organization more fair and equitable?

_____

_____

may not be willing to admit their interest in the hatching chick display at the National Museum of Science and Industry in Chicago. Therefore, a better measure of the public interest in this display is a record of how frequently the linoleum has to be replaced in front of this display. Likewise, to assess the interest of students in different library books, alternatives to asking the students about their interest are measuring the dust on the top of each book and counting how many times each book has been checked out.

Interviews. Interviews are useful when a researcher wants to assess the personal feelings and attitudes of employees. A nondirective interview, where employees talk about issues important to them, provides a rich and meaningful description for a researcher. This type of interview is particularly helpful when a researcher does not know what to look for and is searching for an explanation. The major disadvantage of nondirective interviews is that they are not reliable. What people say in an interview tends to vary from time to time and may be highly influenced by the unique circumstances of the interview. To increase the reliability of interviews, researchers can develop a patterned interview schedule in which they ask specific written questions and the interviewee may even be given a list of alternatives for making a multiple-choice answer. A highly patterned interview, however, fails to generate the richness, diversity, and creative insight that makes interviewing so valuable, and it becomes more like an oral questionnaire.

Questionnaires. One major advantage of a questionnaire is that it can be used to collect extensive information from a large sample of people at the same time. Furthermore, questionnaire data can be conveniently analyzed using a variety of statistical procedures. Most well-developed questionnaires have also been found to be reliable and valid measures of specific variables. An example of a questionnaire measuring attitudes toward an incentive commission program is illustrated in Exhibit 1.8.

SUMMARY

1. An important reason why we study organizational behavior is because it helps us understand and improve the interactions of people and organizations. Although many ideas in organizational behavior appear to be simple common sense, a careful analysis reveals that many of the basic principles of management cannot be applied universally to all situations. Instead, they depend on the situation. This is referred to as the "contingency approach to organizational behavior."

2. The field of organizational behavior developed primarily from the contributions of psychology, sociology, and anthropology. Each of these three disciplines contributed ideas relevant to organizational events that were combined into a separate field, the study of organizational behavior. Three other disciplines that had a minor influence on the development of organizational behavior include economics, political science, and history.

3. The goals of studying organizational behavior are, first, to recognize and describe events that occur with regularity in organizations; second, to explain the causes of these events; and third, to control the situations in a way that elicits desirable behavior and eliminates undesirable behavior.

4. A careful analysis of organizational events requires that they be analyzed from three different levels—the individual level, the group level, and the organizational level. The effects of the environment must also be considered, because it influences and constrains the events we observe.

5. An organization is a difficult object to describe, because it is not a physical object. Four of the most important common characteristics defining organizations are (a) they consist of patterned activities of recurring events, (b) they are social inventions created by people and only exist as long as they serve the needs of people, (c) they are goal oriented and designed to achieve both individual and organizational goals, and (d) they are open systems in the sense that they are influenced by external forces from the environment and internal forces such as revolving memberships.

6. Three of the most important characteristics we study in organizational behavior include the behaviors of individuals, the structure of fixed relationships and authority patterns within the organization, and organizational processes such as communication, leadership, and decision making.

7. People depend on the goods and services they receive from organizations, and organizations depend on people to survive. An organization that loses its capacity to attract sufficient numbers of people cannot continue to survive.

8. If organizations are willing to hire people and people are willing to work, this reciprocal relationship is called an "inducements–contributions balance." The inducements are all of the rewards individuals receive from working, including both monetary and nonmonetary rewards. The contributions are the performance and dedication of the workers.

9. The effects of organizations on people can be either positive or negative. A healthy organizational environment can significantly enhance the quality of life for workers. However, organizations also have the capacity to abuse members through a variety of intentional or unintentional processes.

10. The four traditional management functions include planning, organizing, directing, and controlling. Although these functions help identify the knowledge managers need to acquire, they are not good descriptions of how managers spend their time. The people who have the greatest influence on the creation and effective functioning of organizations are managers. Managers serve a crucial role in helping to create organizations and operate them effectively.

11. Studies of managerial work indicate that managers perform an enormous quantity of work at an unrelenting pace, and they are constantly involved in activities that are characterized by variety, fragmentation, and brevity. Managers are required to make effective decisions with limited information. Therefore, they are constantly seeking immediate and specific information and usually prefer verbal communication. Although many demands are made on their time from a variety of sources, effective managers develop a method of advancing their own issues and accomplishing their own agendas as they respond to the pressures of others.

12. An analysis of the activities managers perform has produced a list of ten managerial roles that are grouped according to three major classifications: (a) interpersonal roles as a figurehead, leader, or liaison; (b) informational roles as a monitor, disseminator, or spokesperson; and (c) decisional roles as an entrepreneur, disturbance handler, resource allocator, and negotiator.

13. Our knowledge of organizational behavior has been extended through behavioral science research. Through research, we are able to develop theories explaining the world around us and test their accuracy.

14. The development of a theory is a creative endeavor in which we attempt to explain recurring events or phenomena. Good theories help to direct our observations, interpret our observations, predict future behavior, and direct our research efforts.

15. The scientific method consists of a process of testing and refining propositions. Three characteristics—hypotheses, constructs, and observations—help to define the scientific method. In science, hypotheses need to be testable and precise, constructs need to be operationally defined, and observations need to be experimentally controlled.

16. Four basic research designs are observational studies, field surveys, field experiments, and laboratory experiments. These four methods can be placed along a continuum of experimental rigor. Observational studies are the easiest but least rigorous research method to use.

Laboratory experiments are the most rigorous and controlled research method. However, laboratory experiments are often performed in a rather artificial environment.

17. Three of the most frequently used methods for collecting research data include observations, interviews, and questionnaires. Two requirements of data collected through any of these methods are reliability and validity. The term *reliability* refers to consistency of measurement, while *validity* refers to the degree to which the data measure what they are actually supposed to measure.

DISCUSSION QUESTIONS

1. A philosophy called "reductionism" suggests that a complex phenomenon such as sociology can best be studied by reducing it to lower levels of analysis. For example, societies consist of organizations, organizations consist of groups, and groups consist of people. Therefore, societies, organizations, and groups can best be studied by carefully analyzing individual personalities. How would you argue against the idea that the organizational behavior field should focus exclusively on the study of individual personalities?

2. Because of the contingency approach to organizational behavior, some students believe that the correct answer to any question about organizational behavior is "It depends." What are the implications of the contingency approach for the study of organizational behavior?

3. One goal of organizational behavior is to control behavior. How do you feel about the morality of one person influencing or controlling the behavior of another? Why (and when) is such control moral or not?

4. What is meant when we say an organization is a social invention that consists of patterned activities? Identify an organization, and use some specific activities from its repertoire to illustrate these two characteristics.

5. How would you respond to someone who made the statement "An organization doesn't have goals, only people have goals"? Provide some illustrations of goals.

6. The idea of an inducements–contributions balance suggests that individuals will continue to work for the organization only as long as they find it rewarding. If this is true, why do so many people continue to work for organizations they despise and in jobs they dislike?

7. How would you respond to someone who made the statement "All organizations are immoral because of the way they mistreat and abuse individuals"?

8. Do managers receive too much credit and attention? Everyone has a job to do, and the success of the organization depends on everyone doing a good job—so how is it fair for someone to claim that managerial jobs are more important?

9. What is a theory? Describe two informal theories you have created to explain things you have observed.

10. What is the relationship between a theory and a hypothesis? Identify two or three testable hypotheses derived from the informal theory that

sitting in the front of the classroom helps students improve their academic performance.

11. What are the strengths and weaknesses of the four basic research designs: observational studies, field surveys, field experiments, and laboratory experiments?

12. The professional journals in organizational behavior contain a wide variety of articles including thought pieces, empirical reports, case studies, and editorial opinions. What criteria should you use in evaluating the significance and accuracy of an article published in a management journal?

GLOSSARY

construct A word or concept that refers to or describes the relationships between objects or events. In empirical research, constructs need to be operationally defined.

contingency approach to organizational behavior An approach to the study of organizational behavior that recognizes the effects of the situation on determining the most appropriate behavior or decision.

control the third goal in studying organizational behavior, structuring situations to elicit acceptable behaviors from organizational members.

decisional roles Four crucial managerial roles that involve making important decisions as an entrepreneur, disturbance handler, resource allocator, or negotiator.

dependent variables The variables that are measured in an experimental study to determine whether an experimental change had an effect.

description The first goal in studying organizational behavior, recognizing events that occur with regularity and predictability.

employment exchange The reciprocal interaction between people and organizations that exists when an individual is willing to exchange work for rewards and the organization is willing to pay the individual for his or her contribution.

experiential learning Learning from personal experiences by observing the consequences of one's behavior and diagnosing the behaviors of others.

explanation The second goal of organizational behavior; identifying the forces or causes for the events that are observed.

field experiment A research study that occurs in a natural setting of an organization and where an independent variable is manipulated to determine its effects on dependent variables.

field survey A research study in which variables in an actual organization are measured and correlated; sometimes called a *correlational study.*

goal-oriented A common characteristic defining an organization and suggesting that the activities within an organization focus on achieving individual and organizational goals.

Hawthorne Studies A series of experiments conducted at the Hawthorne Works of the Western Electric Company from 1924 to 1934. These studies were the foundation of the human relations movement.

hypothesis A proposition, usually stated in the form of a conjecture or provisional explanation, that states a testable relationship between variables that can be measured.

independent variables The variables in a research study that can be controlled by the experimenter in terms of when and how much of it will be administered.

inducements–contributions balance A central concept of the employment exchange in which the inducements of monetary and nonmonetary rewards for the employees are roughly equivalent to the contributions they make in the form of productivity and dedication.

informational roles Three important managerial roles associated with dispensing information as a monitor, disseminator, or spokesperson.

interpersonal roles Three crucial managerial roles associated with interacting with others as a figurehead, leader, or liaison.

laboratory experiment A research study that is conducted in a controlled environment where outside influences can be eliminated or controlled.

Machiavelli, Niccolò An Italian philosopher who lived in the latter part of the fifteenth century and wrote about power and the dependence of leaders on the mass consent of the public.

Moses An Old Testament prophet whose leadership demonstrated the importance of decentralized authority and the exception principle as he led the Israelite nation out of Egypt.

observation A research method that consists of observing events as they occur and then trying to interpret and describe what occurred and why.

open systems One of the common characteristics defining an organization, suggesting that it is influenced by both internal forces within the organization and external forces from the environment.

paradigm shift A dramatic change in the way we think about a problem or situation involving significantly different assumptions, values, and attitudes about it. A dramatic paradigm shift was changing from the Ptolemaic theory of the earth as the center of the universe to the Copernican theory of the sun as the center of the universe.

patterned activities One of the common characteristics defining an organization, suggesting that the organization consists of recurring activities and events that occur at regular and predictable times.

reliability Repeatability or consistency of measurement.

scientific management A theory of management, particularly popular during the early 1900s, that emphasized performing tasks in the one best way, using task analysis, time and motion studies, and piece-rate incentives to motivate workers.

scientific method An approach to studying problems and testing propositions. It is a systematic, controlled, and objective process of discovering and verifying new knowledge whereby results can be replicated, errors can be corrected, and observations can be examined by the public.

social inventions A common description of an organization, suggesting that organizations are created by people for specified purposes.

stakeholders Individuals who have a genuine interest in the performance of an organization, including employees, managers, stockholders, suppliers, customers, and members of the surrounding community.

theory A formal statement explaining the relationship between variables; any generalized explanatory principle.

validity The quality of a measurement, referring to its ability to measure or predict what it actually intends to measure or predict.

Venice, Arsenal of A famous Italian shipyard of the fifteenth and sixteenth centuries that was probably the largest and most efficient manufacturing organization of its time.

NOTES

1. A. H. Brayfield and W. H. Crockett, "Employee Attitudes and Employee Performance," *Psychological Bulletin*, vol. 52 (1955), pp. 396–424.

2. Hugo Munsterberg, *Psychology and Industrial Efficiency* (Boston: Houghton Mifflin, 1913).

3. Auguste Comte, *The Positive Philosophy*, trans. and ed. Harriet Martineau (London: Ball, 1915).

4. Claude S. George, Jr., *The History of Management Thought*, 2nd ed. (Englewood Cliffs, N.J.: Prentice-Hall, 1972), p. 5.

5. Op. cit., pp. 23–25.

6. Frederick C. Lane, *Venetian Ships and Shipbuilders of the Renaissance* (Baltimore: Johns Hopkins Press, 1934).

7. Daniel Defoe, *The Compleat English Tradesman*, vols. 1 and 2 (Oxford: D. A. Talboys for Thomas Tegg, 1726–1727); Sir Thomas More, *Utopia*, trans. Ralph Robinson (London: Dent, [1516 in Latin] 1898); Niccolò Machiavelli, *The Prince* (New York: Modern Library, 1940).

8. Frederick W. Taylor, *Principles of Scientific Management* (New York: Harper, 1911).

9. Fritz J. Roethlisberger and William J. Dickson, *Management and the Worker* (Cambridge, Mass.: Harvard University Press, [1939] 1967); Alex Carey, "The Hawthorne Studies: A Radical Criticism," *American Sociological Review*, vol. 32 (June 1967), pp. 403–16; H. M. Parsons, "What Happened at Hawthorne?" *Science*, vol. 183 (March 1974), pp. 922–932.

10. Daniel Katz and Robert Kahn, *The Social Psychology of Organizations*, 2nd ed. (New York: Wiley, 1978), chap. 2.

11. James G. March and Herbert A. Simon, *Organizations* (New York: Wiley, 1966), chap. 4.

12. Katz and Kahn, op. cit., chap. 13.

13. Federal Bureau of Investigation, "Bank Crime Statistics" (Washington, D.C.: U.S. Government Printing Office, 1985); Errol M. Cook, Stephanie M. Shern, and Richard I. Hersh, (eds.), *Ounce of Prevention* (New York: National Mass Retailing Institute, 1985).

14. David W. Ewing, *Freedom Inside the Organization* (New York: McGraw-Hill, 1977), p. 7.

15. Warren Bennis and Burt Nanus, *Leaders: The Strategies for Taking Charge* (New York: Harper & Row, 1985).

16. Henry Mintzberg, *The Nature of Managerial Work* (New York: Harper & Row, 1973).

17. Lance B. Kurke and Howard E. Aldrich, "Mintzberg was Right!: A Replication and Extension of the Nature of Managerial Work," *Management Science*, vol. 29 (August 1983), pp. 975–84.

18. Thomas S. Kuhn, *The Structure of Scientific Revolutions* (Chicago: University of Chicago Press, 1952).

19. Melvin H. Marx, "The General Nature of Theory Construction," in Melvin H. Marx, (ed.), *Theories of Contemporary Psychology* (New York: MacMillan, 1963), pp. 4–46.

20. Roethlisberger and Dickson, op. cit.

21. Eugene J. Webb, Donald T. Campbell, Richard D. Schwartz, and Lee Sechrist, *Unobtrusive Measures: Nonreactive Research in the Social Sciences* (Chicago: Rand-McNally, 1966).

THOMPSON DORMITORY COUNCIL

PART I

The first week of university life was a shocking and aggravating experience for Lance and Tadd. After traveling 1200 miles, they were prepared for the intellectual and social challenges of college life, but they weren't prepared for the irritating challenges of dormitory living.

Rather than being a meaningful academic experience, the first week of dormitory life was more like a summer camp with practical jokes, loud stereos, and noise. Lance and Tadd's room was directly across the hall from the bathroom, the noisiest location on the floor. Most of the students had their own stereos which they played constantly, even in the bathrooms. The ultimate aggravation occurred at the end of the week while Lance was writing a paper. Using pieces of plywood and plastic garbage bags, some students created a hot tub in the showers and held a noisy party that started shortly after midnight and ended just before dawn.

Lance and Tadd decided dormitory living was intolerable and tried to withdraw their deposit to move off campus. The housing authority, however, refused to cancel their contract and refund their money. Instead, they suggested that Lance and Tadd organize a student group to correct the problem of noise in the dorms. Lance and Tadd were assured that the majority of students disapproved of the excessive noise since many students had complained about the problem.

The Thompson dormitories consisted of four dormitory buildings, and each building contained three floors with 24 rooms. Three outdoor basketball courts were located between the buildings, and two tennis courts were located behind the buildings. The grass areas on the sides of the buildings provided excellent areas for playing soccer, football, and other lawn games.

Questions

1. Is it realistic to think that Lance and Tadd can actually do something to solve this problem? What would you do?

2. Who should feel responsible for this problem: someone in the university administration, the housing authority, or the students?

3. What power or authority do Lance and Tadd have to solve the problem?

PART II

Lance and Tadd decided to accept the challenge of organizing a dormitory council to govern the behavior of students living in the Thompson dormitory complex. To organize a dormitory council, Lance and Tadd decided to have each floor elect a representative, thus forming a council with twelve representatives. These twelve representatives would be responsible for listening to the suggestions of dormitory members, formulating policies to eliminate problems, and submitting the council's recommendations for ratification by the membership.

Lance and Tadd described their ideas for the council on a one-page flyer and distributed it at informal meetings with each of the twelve floors. The flyer described the formation and the purpose of the council and called for each floor to hold elections at the end of the third week of school. Dormitory members were also invited to prepare written statements of problems or issues they would like the council to address.

The proposal to form a dormitory council was well received. By the end of the third week, twelve representatives had been elected, representing each of the twelve floors in the Thompson dormitories. As Lance and Tadd had anticipated, the most pressing issue for the council to consider was noise in the dormitories. Other issues included the scheduling of the tennis courts, the creation of an interdorm football and soccer program, plus a suggestion that everyone contribute to the purchase of some weight-training equipment to be installed in one of the laundry rooms.

After considerable discussion, the dormitory council developed a noise control act that the representatives were expected to discuss with the students on their floors and ratify by a majority vote. This proposal largely focused on reducing noise by encouraging students to show greater common courtesy. The proposal specifically prohibited students taking stereos into the bathrooms; also, no conversations were to be held in the hallways between the hours of 11:00 P.M. and 7:00 A.M. If stereos were played in the individual rooms, the volume was to be low enough that, outside the room with the door closed, the sound would be no more than "barely audible."

The noise control act was passed by an overwhelming majority on ten of the twelve floors and by a narrow margin on the other two. Lance and Tadd were pleased with the results of the election and even more pleased with the reduction in noise on their floor. No more stereos could be heard in the bathroom, and the laughter and conversations were at an acceptable level. Students were pleased with the council's success in reducing noise levels. The dormitory council met on a regular basis every Monday evening at 9:00 P.M. under the direction of an elected president who was responsible for developing an agenda and leading the discussions. Also elected was a recorder who was responsible for keeping minutes and publishing a weekly bulletin announcing the council's decisions. Three athletic committees were formed to develop basketball, football, and soccer programs.

Questions

1. Is the dormitory council an organization? Who are its members?

2. What are its goals?

3. What is necessary for the dormitory council to survive as an ongoing organization?

PART III

Because of his involvement in creating the council, Lance was elected as the first president, a position that generated both status and criticism. The council's success and the visibility of its athletic programs created much public recognition for Lance. He found that he was well known by all the students living in the Thompson dorms, plus other student leaders and members of the university administration who were aware of his activities and who often praised him for his accomplishments.

The most painful part of being the president was the criticism Lance received for playing tennis. As an enthusiastic tennis player, Lance agreed to schedule the use of the tennis courts. Since he knew when the courts were available and when someone needed a partner, Lance spent a considerable amount of time playing tennis. Other students, seeing Lance on the courts so frequently, criticized him for using his position to serve his own interests. Before long Lance found that he was criticized for playing tennis regardless of how frequently he played. Finally Lance discovered that his position on the council had placed him in an impossible situation. Because of his love of tennis he did not want to quit playing, but he also didn't want to appear to be abusing his position as president of the dormitory council. Even though he thought it was unfair, Lance felt very hurt by the criticism he received for playing tennis.

Questions

1. Is Lance a manager? Is he a leader? What is the difference between a manager and a leader?

2. How should Lance respond to those who criticize him for playing tennis?

3. Should managers and leaders receive special privileges or considerations because of their position? If so, what and why?

OFFICE BUILDING CONSTRUCTION EXERCISE

Purpose. As you begin your study of organizational behavior, it is useful for you to experience the problems of organizing, planning, decision making, leadership, implementation, communication, and other aspects of group dynamics. It is easier to appreciate organizational problems after you have experienced an actual task and discussed the problems with others. This exercise is also designed to acquaint you with other class members.

Objective. The objective of your group is to build an attractive and structurally sound two-story office building using cards and tape. The building should have floors and a roof.

Activity. The class should be divided into groups of four to seven members. Each group should have a stack of cards (5- by 7-inch cards or computer cards, if you can still find them), tape, and scissors. Your group will have 40 minutes to plan and then 6 minutes to construct your office building. During the planning period, no trial assembly of any sort is allowed. The instructor will start and stop the planning and construction periods, but the instructor will not give advice or tell the amount of time remaining.

Evaluation. Your group will be awarded one point per cubic inch of office space in your building subject to the following costs: each card costs ten points and tape costs ten points per inch. After your building has been constructed, it will be judged by an impartial committee according to two criteria: aesthetic beauty and structural stability. For aesthetic beauty, you can receive up to plus or minus 50 percent of your initial points. For structural stability, you may also receive up to plus or minus 50 percent of your initial points. There are two tests of structural stability. First, it must be dropped from an elevation of 6 feet to the floor without being deformed. Second, this textbook will be dropped on it from a height of 3 feet, and again, your building must not be deformed or fall apart. (Before you think this is impossible, you should know that one group built a structure using computer cards that supported the weight of a 95-pound student.)

Discussion. (1) How well did the group work together? Did everyone cooperate, and if so, how did a group of strangers succeed in obtaining the immediate cooperation of all members? (2) How were decisions made—by consensus, by majority rule, by a powerful leader, or by default? Did anyone make a suggestion that was ignored? (3) Which members exerted the greatest influence and served as leaders? Was there a power struggle? Did coalitions emerge? Does everyone agree which member exerted the greatest influence? (4) How were people treated? Did everyone participate equally, or were some more quiet? Was there a difference in the participation of men and women? Were the ideas of women received with as much consideration as the ideas of men? (5) What was the climate of the group; were the members serious and task-oriented, happy and friendly, sarcastic and critical, competitive, or apathetic? Did the group members enjoy their interactions?

INDIVIDUAL BEHAVIOR

T wo people facing the same situation will not necessarily behave the same. Their perceptions of the situation will almost never be identical; therefore, we shouldn't be surprised if their attitudes and responses are also quite different.

Several good reasons explain why we need to understand individual behavior. First, this knowledge is particularly useful when we seek to diagnose organizational problems or improve organizational efficiency. Some organizational problems are caused by unique individual differences. Second, when people are assigned to jobs, their abilities and skills should be matched with the demands of the job. An understanding of the major individual differences can help managers avoid the serious mistakes that occur when people are assigned to jobs for which they are not well suited. Third, this information contributes to greater self-awareness. Knowing more about perception, personality, and motivation provides us with useful insights for analyzing our own behavior.

This section describes the topics that help us understand individual behavior. These topics include perception, personality, motivation, punishment, reinforcement, job design, job satisfaction, attitudes, careers, and stress.

Organizational behavior research plays an important part in helping us understand individual behavior and individual differences. Therefore, each chapter contains an "Applying Organizational Behavior Research" box describing a recent research study. Information about cultural differences also helps us understand individual differences; therefore, an "Applying Organizational Behavior Across Cultures" box is also included in each chapter. Finally, the "Organizational Behavior in the News" features help you understand that the study of individual behavior can be used every day, as you watch and read about different companies and individuals in business.

CHAPTER 2

Individual Characteristics: Perception and Personality

LEARNING OBJECTIVES

After studying this chapter, you should be able to

1. Describe the perceptual process, and explain why two individuals observing the same event may describe it quite differently.

2. Identify some of the characteristics of the stimulus, the situation, and the perceiver that influence perception.

3. Describe some of the most common perceptual errors, and explain what can be done to minimize or reduce them.

4. Describe the differences between theory X and theory Y, and explain their impact on managerial behavior.

5. Describe the perceptual tendencies that contribute to prejudice and discrimination.

6. Describe the self-fulfilling prophecy phenomenon, and explain why it occurs.

7. Explain how attribution theory contributes to our understanding of the causes of behavior.

8. Define *personality,* and explain how personalities are developed and measured.

9. List some of the major personality dimensions, and describe the kinds of behaviors associated with them.

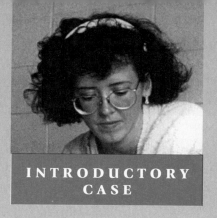

BANK RUNS: THE CLASSIC SFP

Friday morning, January 4, 1991, the Bank of New England announced a $450 million fourth-quarter loss. Through the remainder of Friday and into Saturday morning, anxious depositors jammed bank offices withdrawing their accounts and straining the bank's liquidity. Many customers demanded cash rather than accept cashiers' checks even though they did not know where they would keep their money. The situation was so delicate that the bank's chairman, Lawrence K. Fish, drove from branch to branch personally assuring crowds of anxious depositors that their money was safe. On Sunday, the FDIC took control of the bank in an effort to halt the erosion of confidence in the banking system.[1]

A bank run is a classic self-fulfilling prophecy. A healthy bank experiences unusually brisk activity one morning, generating a rumor that the bank will fail. Before the day ends, the bank is forced to close early because of the rush of depositors withdrawing their accounts. Although the rumor is false at the time, it becomes true as nervous depositors act on it, forcing the bank into insolvency. Because of bank runs during the Great Depression, the U.S. Congress created the Federal Deposit Insurance Corporation and guaranteed people's deposits to maintain investor confidence. In spite of these assurances, January 1991 saw a return to bank runs in the Northeast.

Before the month ended, runs occurred at other banks, even though they were healthy. The run on Old Stone Corporation's banks in Rhode Island occurred without warning Thursday, January 24. By Friday, crowds of anxious depositors filled Old Stone's branch offices, demanding cash. Bank executives were forced to request an emergency truckload of cash from the Federal Reserve and tried to assure customers. Even the new governor, Bruce G. Sundlun, who had closed forty-five small banks on New Year's Day, made a visit to the Providence branch to remind investors that their money was federally insured. Although many depositors were assured, others insisted on withdrawing their money in cash. The bank's liquidity and assets decreased significantly, threatening the survival of the bank, but the bank stayed open. Events like these illustrate how fragile public confidence is and how false expectations can become a reality when people believe them.[2]

Questions

1. Why do bank runs occur? Why don't federal guarantees that deposits are secure prevent bank runs?
2. What conditions contribute to a bank run? How can they be prevented?

PERCEPTION

Although the study of perception belongs primarily to the field of psychology, a brief survey of perception is important because it has such an enormous impact on organizational behavior. No two people share the same reality; for each of us, the world is unique. We cannot understand organizational behavior unless we understand perception and why two individuals observing the same event can honestly see something entirely different. Furthermore, we need to understand that through our perceptions we are not simply passive observers of the drama of life, but active participants helping to write the script and play the roles. The behavior of others is influenced by how you perceive them.

The Perceptual Process

Perception is the process of receiving and interpreting environmental stimuli. In a world filled with complex environmental stimuli, our perceptions help us categorize and organize the sensations we receive. We behave according to our interpretation of the reality we see. What we fail to appreciate is that the reality we see is almost never the same as the reality perceived by others.

If your supervisor rates your performance as good and says you will receive a 2 percent pay increase, you may feel criticized because you expected more. Because your raise was less than before, however, does not necessarily mean that your efforts have gone unrecognized. You may not realize that the company's profits were down and your raise was the largest for managers at your level. Or you may be aware of the fact that you received the largest raise, but still be dissatisfied because you expected more.

The perceptual process consists of three major components as shown in Exhibit 2.1: sensation, attention, and perception. These three components are important in the perception of both physical objects and social events.

Sensations. At any given moment, we are surrounded by countless environmental stimuli. We are not aware of most of these stimuli, either because we have learned to ignore them, or because our sense organs are not capable of receiving them. The five major sense mechanisms include sight, smell, taste, touch, and hearing. Those who have studied perception in a psychology course are well aware of the limitations of these senses. For example, our sense of hearing is only capable of sensing a very narrow range of frequencies. Certain high-frequency sounds are not audible to human beings, but can be sensed by other animals such as dogs. Some individuals have developed their senses much more than others have. People who are blind, for example, typically achieve a highly developed sense of hearing and touch. Although most people have no idea what the level of their blood sugar is, some people with diabetes and hypoglycemia can estimate their blood glucose levels with remarkable accuracy.

Environmental stimuli only produce **sensations** on the human body if the body has developed the sensing mechanism to receive them. Whether you are consciously aware of these sensations, however, depends on the next step in the perception process—attention.

EXHIBIT 2.1 **Perceptual Process**

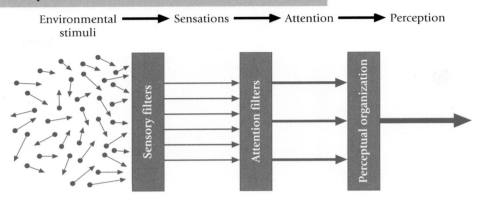

Attention. Although we are capable of sensing many environmental stimuli, we attend to only a very small portion of them and ignore the rest. Many factors influence the attention process.

1. *Size.* The larger the size of a physical object, the more likely it is to be perceived.
2. *Intensity.* The greater the intensity of a stimulus, the more likely it is to be noticed. A loud noise, such as shouting, is more likely to get attention than a quiet voice.
3. *Frequency.* The greater the frequency with which a stimulus is presented, the greater are the chances you will attend to it. This principle of repetition is used extensively in advertising to attract the attention of buyers.
4. *Contrast.* Stimuli that contrast with the surrounding environment are more likely to be selected for attention than stimuli that blend with the environment. The contrast can be created by color, size, or any other factor that distinguishes one stimulus from others, as shown in Exhibit 2.2.
5. *Motion.* Because movement tends to attract attention, a moving stimulus is more likely to be perceived than a stationary object. An animated sign, for example, attracts more attention than a fixed billboard.
6. *Change.* Objects are more likely to be noticed if they display some form of change. An object with lights blinking on and off, such as a Christmas tree or sign, attracts more attention than one without blinking lights.
7. *Novelty.* A stimulus that is new and unique will often be perceived more readily than stimuli that have been observed on a regular basis. Advertisers use the impact of novelty by creating original packaging or advertising messages.

Perception. The process of perception involves organizing and interpreting the sensations we attend to. Visual images, sounds, odors, and other sensations do not simply enter our consciousness as pure, unpolluted sensations. As we attend to them, we consciously try to organize or categorize the information into a meaningful perception that will somehow make sense to us.

| EXHIBIT 2.2 | The Effects of Size, Intensity, and Contrast on Attention |

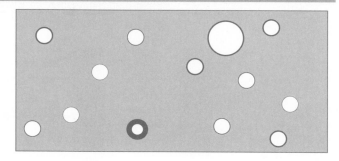

Although we would like to think of ourselves as open-minded, unbiased, and non-judgmental in our perceptions, the demands of the situation make it impossible; we are forced to draw quick inferences based on very sparse information. If you were working as a counselor in a college advisement center and a student came for assistance, you would be required to make rapid inferences based on only limited information. Your recommendations on course loads and elective classes would depend on your perception of the student's situation.

We tend to categorize people using limited pieces of information and then act on this information, even though most of our inferences have not been confirmed. This process is called "making **perceptual inferences**" because we are required to diagnose our situation and make rapid inferences about it from scanty clues.

We cannot wait until we have complete information about each individual before we respond to the person. If we waited until we were fully informed about each person's unique personality and problems, we would never respond. Instead, we develop a system of categories based on only a few pieces of information and use this system to organize our perceptions. For example, college students tend to categorize other college students according to gender, marital status, year in school, and major. If you started a casual conversation with another student, your conversation would likely be quite different depending on whether you thought that student was a married graduate student majoring in engineering or an unmarried first-year student majoring in sociology.

The process of grouping environmental stimuli into recognizable patterns is called **perceptual organization**. Rather than just seeing the stimuli as random observations, we seek to organize them into meaningful, recognizable patterns. Some of the principles we use to organize these sensations include the following:

1. *Figure–ground contrast.* People tend to perceive objects standing against a background. The figure–ground principle is illustrated by the picture in Exhibit 2.3. This picture is an illustration of a reversible figure–ground pattern. Do you see a white vase against a gray background, or do you see two facing silhouettes on a white background? The figure–ground contrast is particularly relevant in observing social events. In a committee meeting, for example, most people see the verbal conversation as figure, and fail to attend to the background of nonverbal messages that may be far more meaningful in understanding the group processes. Likewise, on a study date, if you viewed the discussion of academic subjects as figure and the flirtatious

EXHIBIT 2.3	Principles Influencing Perceptual Organization

Figure–Ground Contrast

Do you see a vase or two silhouettes facing each other?

Similarity

Because of similarity, we tend to see four rows on the left
and four columns on the right.

Proximity

Because of proximity, we see three columns of six dots, not six rows of three dots.

Closure

Although the triangle on the left isn't complete, we see it anyway.
If the Pacmen on the right are arranged correctly, we see a star.

hand-holding and touching as background, you would overlook the beginning of a library romance.

2. *Similarity.* Stimuli that have common physical similarities are more likely to be grouped together, as illustrated in Exhibit 2.3. Athletic teams wear uniforms to help players recognize their teammates. Some organizations color-code memos to

identify messages about the same topic. Some companies that have open floor plans color-code the partitions and other furniture to visually define separate functions and responsibilities. Because of the principle of similarity, the management style of top managers sets the stage for how the feedback and instructions of middle managers will be perceived by their subordinates.

3. *Proximity.* Stimuli that occur in the same proximity, either in space or in time, are often associated. For example, if you see two people together frequently, you will tend to attribute the characteristics you learn about one individual to the other until your perceptions become more accurate. An illustration of proximity in time occurs, for example, when some boxes in the hall are removed the same day you complain about them. You may assume your complaints led to their removal, without realizing it would have occurred anyway.

4. *Closure.* Because most of the stimuli we perceive are incomplete, we naturally tend to extrapolate information and project additional information to form a complete picture. For example, a pole placed in front of a stop sign may prevent you from seeing the entire eight-sided sign. But since you have seen many stop signs before, the principle of closure causes you to "see" the complete sign. This principle is illustrated in Exhibit 2.3 by the lines we "see" as a triangle. If we watch an employee work for fifteen minutes and complete the first half of a task, and return twenty minutes later to find the task completed, we attribute the entire task to the employee because of the principle of closure. Actually, however, we only saw this person perform half the task, and our inference about the last half may be incorrect.

Characteristics of the Object Perceived

Perceiving social events and people is more difficult and challenging than perceiving physical objects. If two people disagree about the length of an object, they can use a yardstick to measure it. But if they disagree about whether a supervisor was pleased with their work, they may have difficulty verifying which one was right, even if the supervisor's response was filmed. The major characteristics influencing social perception include characteristics of the person perceived, characteristics of the situation, and characteristics of the perceiver, as shown in Exhibit 2.4.

Although the inferences we make about someone's personality should be based on the behavior we observe, our perceptions are actually influenced by a variety of physical characteristics and attributes. Three characteristics that influence our perceptions are appearance, communication, and status.

Appearance. Although two people behave identically, we might describe their behavior quite differently if their physical appearances are different. For example, if a child were tearing the pages of a magazine in a doctor's waiting room, and another person took the magazine from the child, our description of the event would probably depend on the person's appearance. A well-dressed, middle-aged man would probably be described as kind and considerate—he was helping the mother tend the child. A poorly dressed man would more likely be described as cruel and impatient—he had no consideration for the child's feelings as he impatiently took the magazine from the child.

Our visual images of what we think people should look like influence how we interpret what they do. One study found that most people agree on the physical attributes of leaders; however, there was no relationship between the attributes peo-

EXHIBIT 2.4   Characteristics Influencing Social Perception

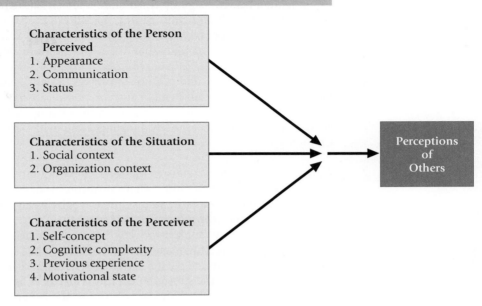

ple expected to find in leaders and the attributes of actual leaders. Nevertheless, when we see individuals who appear to be confident, articulate, assertive, and goal-oriented, we infer that these people are natural leaders.[3]

The appearance of others not only influences how we perceive their behavior, but influences how we respond to them. The dress-for-success literature has amply demonstrated the effects of appearance on how people are perceived and treated. Although many people, especially college students, feel somewhat repulsed by the implications of the research, the data nevertheless show that people who dress in conservative business attire are more likely to be hired, be promoted, make a sale, obtain service, and be treated as important.[4] We generally assume that people who are dressed in business suits and uniforms are professional or technical employees performing their assigned functions. Therefore, we tend to respond to them with respect and deference, and willingly comply with their requests. However, we assume that people dressed in work clothes are lower-level employees, who possess little, if any, authority to tell us what to do. We are more likely to treat them in a discourteous manner. Whether we respond to others in a polite or inconsiderate manner will be influenced by their physical appearance, especially when it is some-one we have never seen before.

Communication. As we listen to people talk, we make rapid inferences about their personalities, backgrounds, and motives. We notice the tone of voice to detect whether individuals are happy, sad, angry, or impatient. We notice the precision and clarity in the messages communicated to us, and generally assume that a message spoken in a very emphatic and distinct manner is supposed to be carefully attended to. When people speak in a particular dialect or accent, we make inferences about their geographic and cultural background. The topics people choose to discuss not only reveal their educational training, but also their personal interests and ways of thinking. In a leaderless group discussion, a female student with a soft, unassertive voice frequently has difficulty getting the other group members to listen to her ideas. In contrast, people who speak with a distinct, authoritative tone of voice often receive greater credibility than their contributions deserve.

We also draw many inferences from nonverbal communications such as eye contact, hand motions, and posture. Sitting up straight, looking the other person in the eye, and nodding your head in agreement indicate to other people that you are interested in them, and they will perceive you as being friendly and concerned. Such actions are referred to as body language, and will be examined more fully in Chapter 13.

Status. The term *status* refers to the level of esteem attributed to individuals, and is based primarily on the individual's position in an organization. Although two people may behave similarly, status differences between them cause us to perceive or assign different motivations for their behavior.

In an experiment, subjects observed two people behave exactly the same, but one was described as a high-status person and the other a low-status person. In this experiment, a high-status person and a low-status person were introduced to the subject and asked by the subject to comply with his or her requests. Although both people agreed to comply at the same point in the experiment, the subject did not perceive them as equally cooperative. The high-status person was perceived as wanting to cooperate, while the low-status person was perceived as having to cooperate. The subject expressed more liking and attraction to the high-status person.[5] This experiment suggests that the friendly actions of high-status people are perceived as more friendly, spontaneous, and genuine than the same responses of lower-status people. Having your supervisor say "Good morning" to you will be perceived as a more friendly and thoughtful expression than if the same comment were made by a subordinate.

Our perceptions are also influenced by the occupations and group memberships of the people we see. Our assessment of a speech about the long-term investment advantages of life insurance will be greatly influenced by whether the speech is delivered by a life insurance salesperson, an economist, or a retired banker. Comments about the threats of foreign competition will be perceived quite differently if they are stated by a labor union leader or a business executive.

Several studies have shown that a variety of personal characteristics influence our perceptions of other people. For example, in one study a speaker was introduced to a group by written descriptions. The descriptions were identical except that one form described him as being, among other things, very warm, and the other form called him rather cold. Although everyone saw the same speaker, he was described as more sociable, more popular, more humorous, more humane, and more considerate by those who were told he was warm.[6] In another experiment, subjects were led to believe that certain employees were more trustworthy than others even though both groups of employees produced equal amounts of work. One group was perceived as less trustworthy simply because a supervisor was located in a position where the group's performance could be frequently observed. Therefore, the subjects inferred that the supervisor's presence was necessary for these employees to perform, while the other group could be trusted to work reliably on their own. Therefore, differences in the degree of trust were created by the supervisor, and not by the workers.[7]

Characteristics of the Situation

Occasionally the situation can play a major role in determining how an object or event is perceived. The situational context can provide added information about the stimulus (person or event), or it can serve as a filter through which only biased observations are passed. Two contexts that influence our perceptions are the organizational culture and the organizational structure.

Organizational Culture. Our perceptions are influenced by a variety of factors in the social setting that are referred to generally as *organizational culture*. Organizational culture consists of the shared beliefs about how things are done and what is important. The process by which culture is created and transmitted to new members through stories, legends, and myths is described in Chapter 11.

One important cultural variable is whether there is a competitive or a cooperative climate. In a competitive group situation, communication is guarded, people tend to behave defensively, and they tend to perceive the comments and actions of others as threatening and challenging. However, in a cooperative situation group members display greater openness and trust, and the comments and behaviors of others are perceived as friendly and helpful.

Another important variable in the social context is whether there is a commitment to integrity or an acceptance of dishonesty. If everyone is expected to be completely honest and forthright, people can be more open in their interpersonal relationships and have greater trust in what they see and hear. However, if dishonesty and misrepresentation are common, people learn to guard what they say and to interpret a wink or a shrug as an indication that they shouldn't ask questions.

The pursuit of excellence is also a crucial cultural variable. The members will perceive things differently depending on whether they know they are expected to strive for excellence in performing their jobs, or if they think the organization accepts mediocre performance. For example, if superior quality and outstanding service have been emphasized in the past, a simple suggestion to hide a defective part in the middle of a box to be shipped would be perceived as a joke, while in a context where mediocrity was accepted it would be perceived as a realistic suggestion.

Organizational Structure. What we are prepared to see is influenced by the organizational level and the department where the event occurs. This process was illustrated by a study of managers in a training program. In this study, executives from various departments (production, accounting, sales) studied a detailed and factual case about a steel company and tried to identify the major problem a new president would need to solve. The results showed that the executives' perceptions of the most significant problems were influenced by the departments in which they worked. For example, sales executives perceived sales problems as the most significant, while production executives said the most significant problems were production issues.[8]

Characteristics of the Perceiver

The way we organize and interpret environmental stimuli is also influenced by our own personal characteristics. Four of the most important personal characteristics influencing perception include self-concept, cognitive complexity, previous experience, and motivational state.

Self-concept. Several studies have identified a common tendency of people to use themselves as a norm or standard to judge others. Consequently, how we feel about ourselves has an enormous influence on how we perceive others. Research on this relationship has identified these conclusions:[9]

1. When we understand ourselves and when we can accurately describe our own personal characteristics, we can more accurately perceive others.

2. Our own personal characteristics influence the characteristics we see in others. For example, secure people tend to see others as warm rather than cold, and our own sociability influences the importance we attach to the sociability of others. People with authoritarian personalities are more likely to view others in terms of status and power, and they are more insensitive to others' personality traits.

3. When we accept ourselves and have a positive self-image, we tend to see favorable characteristics in others. We are not as negative or critical about others if we accept ourselves as we are.

4. As we observe people we like, we tend to perceive more accurately the ways in which they are similar to us and overlook the ways they are different.

These conclusions emphasize the importance of being able to understand ourselves. They also explain the self-defeating spiral found in people who do not feel good about themselves. Because of their low self-esteem, they make serious errors in their perceptions of others and tend to see everything as negative and threatening. Consequently, their poor self-esteem is reinforced by their misperceptions.

Cognitive Complexity. The term **cognitive complexity** refers to the way people structure their thinking and reasoning. People with high cognitive complexity have a complex system of categories for storing information; they are more sensitive to a greater breadth of information, which they use in their thinking and analysis. Cognitively simple individuals, however, use only a few categories for storing information and overlook subtle differences. For example, an American with little cognitive complexity would fail to recognize cultural differences between tourists from China and Japan, or Japan and Korea, while an American with high cognitive complexity would perceive significant differences in the tourists' cultures, customs, and habits.

Cognitive complexity allows us to use multiple criteria to differentiate between people, and thereby increases the accuracy of our perceptions. Evidence indicates that individuals tend to make more positive appraisals of others if they use greater cognitive complexity in their assignments. This research suggests that cognitive complexity may be an important characteristic for effective executives.[10]

Previous Experience. Past experience has taught us to perceive objects and events in characteristic ways. Although no two events may be exactly the same, having seen an event before conditions us to see the same thing again. From our past experiences, we develop expectations and these expectations influence our current perceptions. This process is referred to as *perceptual set:* we are "set" to perceive an event in a particular way. Unless the sensations are significantly different from what we expected, we will see what we expected to see.

Motivational State. Perceptions are influenced by temporary motives and emotions. Research has shown, for example, that people who have been deprived of food tend to see more edible objects in ambiguous pictures than do people who have been recently fed.[11] When they are driving, many people have found that as they get hungrier they tend to notice more billboards advertising restaurants and food. Similar studies that asked children to describe the size of various coins found that low-income children perceived the coins as being significantly larger than did high-income children.[12] When we are angry or emotionally upset, our perceptual processes can be distorted and we can seriously misinterpret simple comments by others. Fear is another emotional state that tends to influence the perceptions of a perceiver. Small problems and challenges can be entirely blown out of proportion when we are afraid.

Personal Values. Some objects or ideas are more important to us because of our personal values. Consequently, we are more prepared to perceive certain objects or events, and we have ready-made mental processes for evaluating or reinterpreting new information. Our values influence our perceptual organization and guide decision making. Those who value altruism and cooperation are more inclined to perceive opportunities to be helpful. Those who value pride in craftsmanship are more likely to notice quality defects and errors that need repair. Those who hold strong feelings for or against power are more prone to recognize attempts by themselves or others to dominate or control behavior.

A study of 103 students demonstrated the effects of personal values on perception and decision making. On a perceptual task where students were shown words for a fraction of a second and on a decision task where they evaluated the performance of twenty employees, the students' responses were related to their personal values. Students were more likely to "see" things that were consistent with their values.[13]

McGregor's Theory X Versus Theory Y. An excellent illustration of how a perceptual set influences the behavior of managers is provided by Douglas McGregor's **theory X versus theory Y.**[14] McGregor developed his theory at a time when television commercials were contrasting brand X, the ineffective product, with brand Y, the effective one. According to McGregor, theory X represents an outdated, repressive view of human nature that assumes people are lazy, they don't want to work, and management's job is to force or coerce them.

Theory X contains three assumptions:

1. The average human being inherently dislikes work and will avoid it if possible.
2. Because they dislike work, most people must be coerced, controlled, directed, and threatened with punishment to get them to achieve organizational objectives.
3. The average human being prefers to be directed, wishes to avoid responsibility, has relatively little ambition, and wants security above all.

McGregor said employees would behave much differently if managers adopted a different set of assumptions. In contrast to his pessimistic theory X view of human nature, McGregor presented a set of six assumptions that he called theory Y:

1. The expenditure of physical and mental effort in work is as natural as play or risk. The average human being does not inherently dislike work.

2. External control and the threat of punishment are not the only means of motivating people to achieve organizational objectives. People will exercise self-direction and self-control in the pursuit of objectives to which they are committed.

3. Commitment to objectives is a function of the rewards associated with their achievement. The most significant rewards, the satisfaction of ego and self-actualization needs, can be obtained from effort directed toward organizational objectives.

4. The average human being learns, under proper conditions, not only to accept but to seek responsibility. Avoidance of responsibility, lack of ambition, and an emphasis on security are generally consequences of experience, not inherent human characteristics.

5. The capacity to exercise a relatively high degree of imagination, ingenuity, and creativity in solving organizational problems is widely, not narrowly, distributed in the population.

6. Under the conditions of modern industrial life, the intellectual potentialities of the average human being are only partially realized.

According to theory X, poor performance can be blamed on the employees' failure to demonstrate initiative and motivation. In contrast, theory Y represented an enlightened view of human nature suggesting that organizational inefficiencies must be blamed on management. If employees are lazy, indifferent, unwilling to take responsibility, uncooperative, or uncreative, these problems indicate that management has failed to tap the potential of its employees.

These two views of human nature represent significantly different perceptual sets that managers use in perceiving the behavior of their subordinates. McGregor explained how these two views cause managers to behave quite differently in response to organizational problems. Most of the techniques involved in organizational change and development described later in Chapter 17 are based on McGregor's theory Y assumptions. In his own writing, McGregor used theory Y to redesign such management practices as performance appraisal, wage and salary administration, profit sharing, promotions, and participative management.

Perceptual Errors

As we observe people and events, we make countless perceptual errors day to day. This section analyzes seven of the most frequent perceptual errors.

The Halo Effect. The **halo effect** is the tendency to allow one personality trait to influence our perceptions of other traits. For example, if we see a person smiling and looking pleasant, we may conclude, as one study found, that the person is more honest than someone who frowns. However, there is no necessary connection between smiling and honesty. Another study of army officers found that those who were well liked were also judged to be more intelligent than those who were disliked, even though both groups had equivalent IQ test scores.[15] The halo effect also appears in the perception of organizations. When one company went into receivership, insecurity about the company's financial problems created a generalized negative attitude toward the company and specific complaints about low pay. Even though the company was in receivership, however, it continued to pay relatively high salaries and provided excellent working conditions and supervision. The actual conditions were clearly more favorable than suggested by the negative perceptions caused by the halo effect.

One potentially serious application of the halo effect is when it occurs in a performance evaluation. If one particular attribute, positive or negative, colors a supervisor's perception of other unrelated attributes, the performance evaluation process can be extremely unfair and misleading.[16] However, a study that measured the amount of halo effect in performance evaluations and statistically controlled for it found that its influence on the overall performance evaluation is usually trivial.[17]

Perceptual Defense. Occasionally we face stimuli that are so threatening or embarrassing that we refuse to perceive them. This process is called **perceptual defense** or *denial*. Information that is personally threatening or culturally unacceptable tends to be ignored unless it is more intense than normal. The process of perceptual defense lets us ignore events we are incapable of handling and helps us dissipate our emotions by directing our attention to other objects. When we confront threatening stimuli, we typically respond in one of four ways:[18]

1. We deny the existence of the perception and totally ignore it.
2. We modify or distort the perception to make it acceptable or consistent with our other beliefs.
3. We accept the perception and make corresponding changes in our other beliefs.
4. We acknowledge the threatening stimuli but refuse to change.

Selective Perception. The process of systematically screening out information we don't wish to hear is referred to as **selective perception.** This process is a learned response; we learn from past experience to ignore or overlook information that is uncomfortable and unpleasant. For example, most teachers illustrate the process of selective perception in listening to the comments of students evaluating their courses. From past experience, they have learned to overlook criticism, and as a consequence they honestly think their courses are wonderful.

Implicit Personality Theories. We all tend to create our own system of personality profiles, based on our experiences with a variety of people. For example, many people have a mental profile of accountants as somewhat shy, nonassertive, soft spoken, honest, and obedient, while insurance salespeople are seen as outgoing, friendly, insincere, sociable, talkative, and persistent. To the extent that such personality profiles are accurate, they facilitate our ability to perceive more rapidly and accurately. Because everyone is unique, however, **implicit personality theories** can serve at best as only a rough approximation for categorizing people. If we continue to observe carefully, we may find that many expectations are not correct. Hardworking people may not be honest. Happy employees are not necessarily highly productive. Intelligent people are not the most creative. And workers who have a high need for achievement may not be loyal to the organization.

Projection. The tendency to attribute our own feelings and characteristics to others is called **projection.** As with other perceptual errors, occasionally projection is an efficient and reasonable perceptual strategy. If we don't like to be criticized, harassed, or threatened, it is reasonable to assume that others would not like it any better. However, *projection* usually refers to more than just attributing our thoughts and feelings to others. Instead, it is used to describe the dysfunctional process of attributing to others the undesirable thoughts and traits we ourselves possess but are not willing to admit. In essence, we attribute or project onto others the characteristics or feelings we have about ourselves. Projection serves thereby as a defense mechanism to protect our self-concept and makes us more capable of facing others whom we see as imperfect. As a defense mechanism, however, projection involves erroneous perceptions. It has been demonstrated, for example, that people high in such traits as obstinacy, disorderliness, and stinginess tend to rate others as being much higher in these traits and themselves as being low in these traits.[19]

First Impressions. When we meet people for the first time, we form an impression, based on limited information, that should be open for correction on subsequent encounters. Research evidence indicates, however, that first impressions are remarkably stable. In recruiting interviews, for example, it has been found that recruiters form a fairly stable impression of the applicant within the first three or four minutes. Negative first impressions seem to require abundant favorable information to change them, and some recruiters are so opinionated they refuse to perceive contradictory information.[20]

Allowing first impressions to have a disproportionate and lasting influence on later evaluations is known as the **primacy effect.** The primacy effect explains why the first few days on the job may have a large impact on the attitudes and performance of new employees. Likewise, the opening comments in a committee meeting may have a lasting impact on the remainder of the group discussion because of the primacy effect.

Stereotyping. The process of **stereotyping** involves categorizing individuals based on one or two traits and attributing characteristics to them based on their membership. Stereotypes are frequently based on sex, race, age, religion, nationality, and occupation. Although stereotypes help us interpret information more rapidly, they also cause serious perceptual errors. When we create fixed categories based on variables such as gender, race, and age, and resist looking more carefully to confirm our expectations, we make serious perceptual errors that damage ourselves and others. Perceptual errors due to stereotyping based on age, race, or gender can be extremely troublesome and have generated extensive research.

The effects of stereotypes in organizational settings have been demonstrated in a variety of studies. One study examined the stereotypes of industrial relations managers and union leaders toward themselves and each other. The photographs of two men, along with a brief biographical sketch, were shown to these subjects, who were then asked to describe the people in both pictures, using a list of adjectives. Half the members of each group were told that the first man was a plant manager and that the second man was a labor official. The other half were shown the same photographs, but the descriptions were reversed. Several differences were observed in the stereotypes of these two men. For example, over 70 percent of the managerial group described the manager as honest, while only 50 percent described the union representative as honest.[21] Another study asked samples of male and female managers to describe the characteristics, attitudes, and temperaments more commonly associated with successful managers. The results indicated that both the male and female managers had strong male-oriented stereotypes of successful managers. Both groups described successful managers as exhibiting primarily masculine traits.[22]

The Equal Employment Opportunity Act (1972) prohibits discrimination on the basis of race, religion, sex, or national origin. Within the past twenty years, significant progress has been made in reducing the use of stereotypes, particularly in hiring new employees. However, we continue to use stereotypes because they serve a useful purpose and facilitate rapid perceptions of others. Occasionally these stereotypes are very useful, especially age and sex stereotypes. For example, it is reasonable to guess that older workers are not as interested in opportunities for promotion and new training programs as younger workers, because such differences have indeed been documented. Likewise, it may seem reasonable to think that female employees would be less interested in working overtime, since many women, especially those with small children in the home, find working overtime a particular burden. But just because these attributes are true in general, does not mean they are true for a particular person. Some older workers may be very excited about a new training program, and some mothers may be very anxious to work overtime. Although it is impossible to confirm all our stereotypes, we should constantly question the accuracy of our perceptions, and maintain a flexible system of categories.

Discrimination and Prejudice

Discrimination and prejudice are two serious organizational problems that originate naturally from basic perceptual processes, but often lead to vicious manifestations of racism and sexism. Behaviors that are demeaning and disrespectful to someone because of the person's race or sex are referred to as *racist* or *sexist* behaviors. Serious attempts have been made for many years to eliminate these kinds of behavior both at work and within society, and it is important to understand how perceptual processes contribute to them.

Discrimination is defined as recognizing the differences between or differentiating between items or people. According to this definition, discrimination is not necessarily good or bad. When consumers discriminate between two items on the basis of quality, or when employers discriminate between two job applicants on the basis of job qualifications, discrimination is positive. However, when individuals are discriminated against on the basis of race, religion, or sex and mistreated because of these characteristics, discrimination is both morally and legally wrong.

Discrimination on the basis of race, religion, or sex typically occurs because of prejudice. Prejudice is defined as an incorrect judgment or opinion that is held in disregard of contradictory facts—an unreasonable bias—and it is associated with suspicion, intolerance, or an irrational dislike for people of a particular race, religion, or sex.

In understanding the nature of prejudice, it is important to appreciate the psychological impact of individuality and uniqueness. The simple fact that one or two individuals differ significantly from other members of the group will cause them to be perceived and treated differently regardless of whether the differences are on the basis of race, religion, sex, or any other visible characteristic. This can best be illustrated by looking at these letters:

X X x x x X x O x X

If you studied this configuration briefly and then attempted to describe it, you would probably say that it consisted of some big and little X's with an O. Unless you studied it carefully, you would probably not remember how many big X's and little *x's* there were or how they were arranged in the configuration, but you would probably remember the *O* and where it was located.

The same process occurs among a group of individuals when one or more individuals differ significantly from the others by sex or race. They are perceived differently, and they attract more attention regardless of which race or sex constitutes the majority. This perceptual process occurs simply because the minority stands out from the majority. Four types of groups can be formed depending on the percentages of minorities and majorities, as shown in Exhibit 2.5. A *uniform group* exists when all group members are of the same category, such as all females or all males. A *balanced group* consists of approximately equal numbers of both categories. A *skewed group* consists of a large proportion of one type of people, called the *dominants,* and a very small ratio of members from the other category, called the *tokens.* A *tilted group* falls between a skewed group and a balanced group and contains both minority and majority populations.[23]

Three perceptual tendencies explain why tokens and minorities experience prejudice within the group. These three tendencies are visibility, contrast, and assimilation.[24]

Visibility. As a smaller percent of the group belongs to a particular category, regardless of whether the situation is one or two females in a predominantly male group or the reverse, these individuals tend to become more visible. Therefore, if a committee consisted of one female and several males, it is likely that everyone will remember where the woman sat in the committee meeting, what she wore, what she said, and how she voted. The minority tends to capture a larger share of the awareness within that group.

Contrast. When one or more individuals who are different are added to a group, their presence creates a self-consciousness of the dominant group about what makes the dominants a separate class. Each group defines itself partly by knowing what it isn't. Consequently, a polarization and exaggeration of differences occurs, highlighting the differences between the minorities and majorities. Both groups

EXHIBIT 2.5   Minorities and Majorities

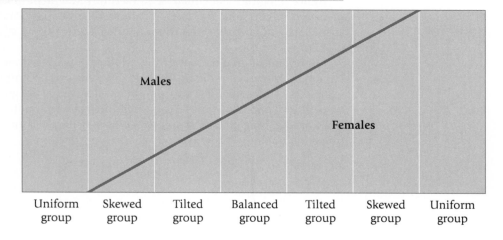

| Uniform group | Skewed group | Tilted group | Balanced group | Tilted group | Skewed group | Uniform group |

APPLYING ORGANIZATIONAL BEHAVIOR
ACROSS CULTURES

The Fear of a Japanese Takeover

 Perceptions can be very damaging, especially when they involve unfounded fears. Some observers have become very concerned about "culture bashing" between the United States and Asian countries, especially Japan. To many frightened Americans, Japan is an "evil empire" whose corporations have a hostile conspiracy bent on capturing U.S. companies.

Concerned about the spread of misinformation, some Asian scholars have attempted to separate perception from reality by describing Japanese corporations in the United States. A study by Yoshi Tsurumi, professor of international business at Baruch College in New York City, examined the effects of Japanese ownership of U.S. companies.

He reported there were over 7,000 "workplace units" in the United States that are owned and operated by Japanese corporations, with over 2,000 in manufacturing. Fear that the Japanese are targeting big business is not correct: 40 percent of these companies each employs less than a hundred employees.

The fear that Japanese ownership means massive unemployment is also unfounded. The total number of Americans employed by these Japanese companies was approximately 850,000 in 1992, which was up from 50,000 in 1982. In many instances, Japanese corporations bought failing U.S. companies and made them profitable, thereby preserving thousands of jobs. Although Japanese investments have increased significantly in the past decade, total Japanese investments are still a distant third behind those of Great Britain and the Netherlands.

Rather than fearing Japanese ownership, there is much to be grateful for. Over three-quarters of Japanese businesses in the United States practice a "no layoff" policy. During the recent recession, very few Japanese companies experienced layoffs, whereas most U.S. companies had massive layoffs.

In addition to providing better job security, Japanese firms in the United States pay their U.S. employees on the average 20 percent higher wages and salaries than their U.S. counterparts. Contrary to the general perceptions created by news reports of selected incidents, there is no evidence of a systemic "glass ceiling" preventing the promotion of U.S. employees into top executive positions. Furthermore, Japanese-owned firms in the United States employ just as many minority and female employees as U.S. firms.

Finally, the success of Japanese firms in America has not been achieved by imposing Japanese cultural values on U.S. workers. Rather, it is argued that this success has come from adopting Japanese management principles that involve hands-on management, teamwork, and a cooperative corporate culture.

Source: Yoshi Tsurumi, "Japanese Corporations in America: Managing Cultural Differences," *Pacific Basin Quarterly* 19 (Fall 1992): 3–7.

become more aware of their commonalities and their differences, and group processes tend to accentuate the differences by creating stereotypes to separate the two groups.

Assimilation. The third perceptual tendency, assimilation, involves the application of stereotypes and familiar generalizations about a person's social category. Minority group members and tokens are not perceived as unique individuals but as representatives of a particular category. In essence, their behavior is assimilated into a stereotype of how members of their particular group are expected to behave. An illustration of assimilation is when a Japanese business executive who is meeting with a group of U.S. executives is asked how other Japanese executives would react to a particular proposal. The question assumes that all Japanese executives respond alike and that one person can represent them all.

Assimilation and contrast appear to be a function of how much effort people are willing to make to form accurate impressions. Some people challenge their assumptions and seek additional information; others label behavior and ignore uniqueness.[25]

Prejudice and discrimination occur in a variety of settings and range in intensity from very innocent and unintended to very nasty and invidious. Some of the most obvious forms of racism and sexism include name calling and slurs directed toward a specific individual. Such cruel behavior is considered entirely unacceptable in today's organizations; it is both immoral and illegal. Other forms of prejudice and discrimination, however, are much more subtle because the acts are not directed toward a specific individual and are often said in humor or jest. Such behavior, however, is still considered inappropriate. Jokes and other comments that reflect negatively on another person's race or sex are both insulting and demeaning to everyone.

Self-fulfilling Prophecies

An interesting application of the perceptual process to organizational behavior is the **self-fulfilling prophecy.** This phenomenon was first described by Robert Merton in 1948 to explain why healthy banks failed during the Depression because of a false public belief that became true when all the investors tried to withdraw their savings. Later this phenomenon was called the "Pygmalion effect," after a character in Greek mythology, by Robert Rosenthal when he observed the results of an experiment. The results were created not by the independent variable but by the expectations that the researcher unwittingly communicated to the subjects. Knowing that they were supposed to behave in a certain way caused them to behave as expected.[26]

Expectations. We are not passive observers of our own social worlds, but active forces in shaping those worlds. To an important extent, we create our own social reality by influencing the behavior we observe in others. The self-fulfilling prophecy explains how the expectations in the mind of one person about how others should behave are apparently communicated in a variety of ways until these individuals actually behave in the way expected. However, the self-fulfilling prophecy involves more than just one person having strong expectancies that influence the behavior of others. It requires (1) that the expectancies have a particular effect on the behavior of the person holding them, (2) that this behavior in turn affect the behavior of the other person, (3) that the other person's behavior confirm the first person's expectancies, and (4) that the first person view this behavior as unsolicited evidence that the expectancy was right all along. This relationship between the perceiver and the target person is illustrated in Exhibit 2.6.

The self-fulfilling prophecy has been demonstrated in several experiments. In one setting, second-grade children were administered a test of mental ability. The teacher was told that certain students had been identified as "early bloomers" and that she should expect significant academic progress from these students over the next few months. Actually, however, the children had been selected at random. Nevertheless, the teacher's expectations that these students should show the most progress became a self-fulfilling prophecy. By the end of the term the achievement scores of these randomly selected students were significantly greater than the other class members.[27]

Similar results have been achieved with adult students. In an adult training class, the welding instructor of fifteen adults was told that some of the trainees were high-aptitude students who should acquire skills more rapidly than others.

EXHIBIT 2.6 A Social Interaction Sequence in Which Both Perceptual and Behavioral Confirmation Create the Self-fulfilling Prophecy

Self-Fulfilling Prophecy

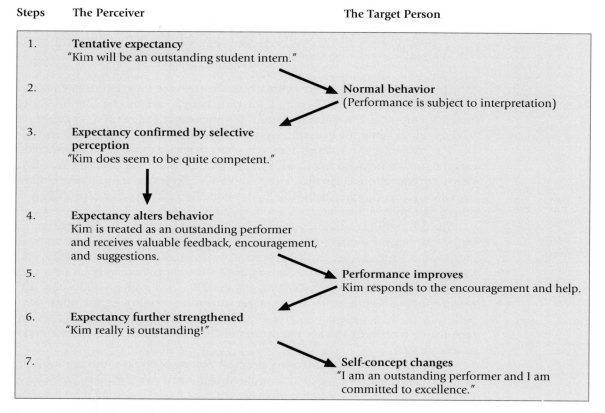

Steps	The Perceiver	The Target Person
1.	**Tentative expectancy** "Kim will be an outstanding student intern."	
2.		**Normal behavior** (Performance is subject to interpretation)
3.	**Expectancy confirmed by selective perception** "Kim does seem to be quite competent."	
4.	**Expectancy alters behavior** Kim is treated as an outstanding performer and receives valuable feedback, encouragement, and suggestions.	
5.		**Performance improves** Kim responds to the encouragement and help.
6.	**Expectancy further strengthened** "Kim really is outstanding!"	
7.		**Self-concept changes** "I am an outstanding performer and I am committed to excellence."

Source: E. E. Jones, "Interpreting Interpersonal Behavior: The Effects of Expectancies," *Science,* vol. 234 (October 3, 1986): pp. 41–46. Copyright 1986 by the AAAS.

Although these individuals had been selected at random, and the only person to whom they were identified was the instructor, this group achieved higher proficiency ratings in welding at the end of the training, and during the training they were identified as the informal leaders who assisted other trainees.[28]

Four elements have been proposed to explain why the self-fulfilling prophecy occurs.[29]

1. *Input.* Individuals who are expected to do well receive better ideas and suggestions than people who are expected to do poorly. As the quantity and quality of information increases, it helps them perform better and communicates a sense of urgency and importance about the task.

2. *Output expected.* Specific comments about how much individuals are expected to achieve help them establish realistic levels of aspiration and higher performance goals.

3. *Reinforcement*. Individuals from whom high performance is expected tend to be rewarded more frequently when they achieve their performance goals. Individuals from whom low performance was expected usually perform poorly and are not reinforced. But they may not be rewarded even if they perform well, because their supervisors feel threatened or irritated that their expectations are disconfirmed.

4. *Feedback*. Managers who communicate high performance expectations typically provide greater feedback. This feedback occurs more frequently and usually contains specific suggestions for improvement.

The self-fulfilling prophecy normally starts when the expectations are planted in the minds of the leader. However, the expectations can also be communicated directly to the actor. Positive expectations of competence and mastery are called the "Galatea effect" after the beautiful ivory statue who came to life in Greek mythology. The "Golem effect," named after a character in Jewish folklore, occurs when the expectations are negative and filled with doubt and failure. The Galatea and Golem effects are part of the Pygmalion effect, and both effects can be cyclically reinforcing when actors produce behaviors that eventually influence the expectations of others. The process then becomes a self-sustaining prophecy.[30]

The self-fulfilling prophecy has been recommended as a valuable strategy for improving organizational performance. The key is to start the sequence by creating positive expectations in managers and workers about the organization and themselves. These expectations can originate with upper management or a consultant and must be both challenging and realistic. This strategy works best with new beginnings before either the manager or workers develop expectations about performance. If a Golem effect is already established, a fresh start is recommended by transferring either the leaders or the members or by making a major restructuring.[31]

When new employees are introduced into an organization, the self-fulfilling prophecy phenomenon contributes importantly to their career success. Some theorists argue that the expectations of managers may be more important than the skills and training of the new trainees in determining their success.[32] An analysis of management training programs suggests that the self-fulfilling prophecy is particularly crucial to the success of new managers.

Hawthorne Effect. Another example of behavior being influenced by the expectations of others is called the Hawthorne effect. This process occurs when people know their behavior is being observed and they behave differently as a result of being evaluated. The label *Hawthorne effect* comes from a series of experiments conducted at the Hawthorne Works of Western Electric from 1927 to 1933. These experiments, known as the Hawthorne Studies, are probably the most famous experiments in organizational behavior.[33] The first experiments examined the effects of light intensity on worker productivity. In these experiments, the intensity of lighting was increased or decreased while productivity levels were measured. The results were puzzling, since productivity was not related to the levels of illumination. Productivity often increased when the light intensity was changed regardless of whether the lighting was brighter or darker. When a parallel control group was used for comparison, the productivity of the control group often increased about the same as that of the test group.

Thinking that the workers were responding to something other than their physical environment, the investigators conducted another experiment. This time they asked the women how they felt about changes in illumination and were told that they preferred working under bright lights. When the researchers *actually* increased the light, the women said they liked it and thought they worked better. Then the investigators *pretended* to increase the light, and the women said they liked it even better. When they decreased the light and announced what they had done, the women complained. Later they only *pretended* to decrease the light, and again the women complained and claimed that the work was not as pleasant. Throughout this experiment, however, production did not materially change.

As a result of the illumination studies, the researchers concluded that light was only a minor and largely insignificant factor affecting employee output. They finally concluded that productivity was influenced more by the measuring process than by the illumination. Knowing that their performance was being measured caused the employees to increase their productivity, a phenomenon that has come to be known as the *Hawthorne effect*.

The Hawthorne effect is an important consideration in behavioral science research because when they are being studied participants behave differently from when they are not. The Hawthorne effect is recognized as one of the major biases that can threaten the internal validity of a research study. In organizations, however, some managers attempt to use the Hawthorne effect to improve productivity by measuring employee performance. How well this intervention works depends on goal setting and how performance is evaluated and rewarded. These topics are discussed in Chapters 3 and 5.

Attribution Theory

When we perceive social events, part of the perceptual process includes assigning responsibility for behavior. Are people responsible for their own behavior because of their personal characteristics, or were they forced to behave as they did because of the situation? The assignment of responsibility and the cognitive processes by which people interpret the reasons for their own behavior and the behavior of others is known as **attribution theory.**

Attribution theory is based largely on the work of Fritz Heider, who claimed that behavior is determined by a combination of external forces (for example, luck, chance, the environment) and internal forces (for example, ability, effort, or knowledge).[34] Heider noted that the actual determinants of behavior are not as important as the perceived determinants. Therefore, when we observe behavior, do we perceive that it is caused by internal personality factors or external situational factors?

According to attribution theory, the assignment of responsibility stems from our observations of people over time. For example, if we observe a group of people trying to use a word processor and find that many of them have trouble getting the printer to function properly, we perceive the problem as being caused by the situation. But if only one person has difficulty with the printer, we attribute the cause of the problem to that individual's personal skills or abilities. Studies on attribution theory have generated the following conclusions:

1. When we observe someone else's behavior, we tend to overestimate the influence of personality traits and underestimate situational influences.

APPLYING ORGANIZATIONAL BEHAVIOR
IN THE NEWS

Rising Above Prejudice Through Personal Fortitude

CNN James Bruce Llewellyn, chairman of Philadelphia Coca-Cola Bottling Company, is a strong believer in the values of hard work and education to overcome the problems of poverty and discrimination. Philadelphia Coca-Cola is the third largest black-owned business in the United States, and Llewellyn is also involved with two other companies that are among the top fifty black-owned businesses.

Bruce Llewellyn's parents came from Jamaica, and they taught him early to make his own luck and work hard. They instilled in him the value of education and offered to do all they could to help him obtain as much education as he wanted. He completed a graduate degree in business and also graduated from law school before he became the regional director of the Small Business Administration in 1960.

A significant opportunity that helped launch Llewellyn's success was a $3 million loan by Prudential Life Insurance Company. A friend at Prudential was willing to risk money on Llewellyn if he were willing to risk all that he owned. With this loan, he bought a supermarket chain in the riot-torn south Bronx and through hard work he made it a success.

Llewellyn was greatly disappointed by the theft and destruction that followed the 1977 blackout of New York City. His warehouse and computer operations center were looted and burned, and eighteen of his stores were broken into and looted. The damage amounted to $1.25 million; but his disappointment with the people who he thought he was serving was more heartbreaking than the monetary loss.

Although Llewellyn thinks prejudice is a natural human response, he opposes it and works to eliminate it. Rather than being known as an Afro-American or an African American, he prefers to be known and treated as just an American. Although he says he may have to work harder for less, he believes that success depends on him and his determination.

Source: CNN *Pinnacle* 26, news programming.

2. When we are explaining our own behavior, we tend to overestimate the importance of the situation and underestimate our own personality characteristics.

The explanation for these two conclusions is that as actors we are more aware of the differing situations we face and, therefore, we attribute our behavior to these differing situations. But since we are not as knowledgeable about the variety of situations others face, we overlook the situation and attribute their behavior to their personality. This explanation has been confirmed by a study showing that when observers had empathy for another person they were more likely to take the actor's perspective and were better able to notice situational causes for the actor's behavior. Conversely, distant observers only tended to notice personality characteristics.[35]

3. In casual situations, as we observe the successes and failures of others, we tend to attribute their successes to personality traits such as effort and ability, and their failures to external factors such as the difficulty of the task.

It is not clear in casual situations why we attribute success to the person and failure to the situation, but apparently this tendency does not extend to an organizational setting. In fact, studies of the attribution process within organizations suggest that the results are the opposite.

4. In evaluating the performance of employees, poor performance is generally attributed to internal personal factors, especially when the consequences are serious.

A study of nursing supervisors found that they were more likely to hold their employees accountable for poor performance as performance problems became more serious.[36] The behavior of subordinates reflects on their managers; therefore, when subordinates do well, managers are quick to accept partial credit for success; but when problems occur, they are quick to blame subordinates, in order to exonerate themselves.

5. Employees tend to attribute their successes to internal factors and their failures to external causes.

Because of our need to maintain a positive self-image, we attribute our own successes to our personal skills and abilities. When we fail, however, we look for external causes to blame.

PERSONALITY

Personality is defined as the stable set of characteristics and tendencies that determines the commonalities and differences among people. These commonalities and differences have continuity in time, resulting in consistent ways of behaving in a variety of situations, in spite of momentary social or biological pressures.

For many years, the basic formula of Kurt Lewin has been used to explain behavior. According to Lewin, behavior is a function of the personality and the environment: $B = fn\ (P,\ E)$. This formula suggests that our behavior at any given time is a complex combination of our unique personality traits, and the demands of the environment. The relative contribution of these two variables was examined in the previous section on attribution theory.

The study of personality seeks to answer two basic questions: How are we alike, and how are we different? Many personality theories have tried to identify the basic personality dimensions we all share. This list of common characteristics is referred to as the **"core of personality."** The way in which we differ because of unique traits or personality dimensions is referred to as the **"periphery of personality."**

Personality Theories

There are many personality theories, and no single theory is widely accepted as right or best. In some situations, one personality theory may be superior in explaining behavior or predicting how people will respond. In other situations, a different theory may be more useful. Salvatore Maddi has made a comparative analysis of the major personality theories and condensed them into three categories: conflict theories, fulfillment theories, and consistency theories.[37] For each of these categories, Maddi identifies the core characteristics common to all individuals plus the peripheral characteristics explaining individual differences.

Conflict Theories. According to **conflict theories,** people are continually and inevitably caught between two opposing forces. Our day-to-day life is a compromise between opposing forces as we struggle to maintain a dynamic state of balance. The most famous conflict theory is the **psychoanalytic theory** of Sigmund Freud (1856–1939).[38]

According to Freud, the personality consists of three distinct parts or systems: the id, the ego, and the superego. The most basic personality system and the first to develop in childhood is the id, which contains the basic impulses to achieve gratification and to pursue pleasure. The ego personality system develops as people mature and learn to channel the impulses from the id into socially acceptable behaviors. The final personality system to be developed, according to Freud, is the superego, which represents the values and traditions of society, especially as taught by parents. The superego has been described as the conscience and is the moral segment of personality.

According to Freud, the most significant form of instinctual gratification came from the libido, which is the desire for sexual gratification. Although the term *id* referred to the composite of all human instincts craving gratification, the desire for sexual gratification was clearly the most prominent in Freud's writings. Freud believed there was a constant battle between the libidinal impulses of the id and the constraining forces of both the ego and the superego to channel these impulses into socially acceptable behaviors. From Freud's writings, a list of defense mechanisms has been created to explain how individuals control their instinctual impulses and make them socially acceptable. Some of the most frequently used defense mechanisms are described in Exhibit 2.7.

Although Sigmund Freud's psychoanalytic theory is clearly the most popular conflict theory, other personality theories also contain the basic premise that life consists of resolving inevitable conflicts between opposing forces. In some theories, the conflict is between individual instincts and the demands of society for acceptable living, while in other theories both opposing forces come from within the individual. Several of these theories agree with Freud that the unconscious domain of the mind contains repressed thoughts and feelings. These hidden urges and passions may be unknown to the individual and still direct and explain much of human behavior. The psychoanalytic technique of Freud and other conflict theorists focuses on helping people become aware of their unconscious mental thoughts and desires so they can better understand and deal with their problems. Helping people acquire greater self-awareness and insight is a central focus of sensitivity training, encounter groups, and other organizational development interventions described in Chapter 17.

Fulfillment Theories. Rather than postulating two opposing forces, the **fulfillment theories** are based on the premise that individuals possess only one basic force that is constantly pushing them toward self-actualization and fulfillment. The most popular fulfillment theories came from the work of Carl Rogers (1902–1987) and Abraham Maslow (1908–1970). As clinical psychologists, both these men were greatly concerned about the growth and human potential of people. They each pos-

EXHIBIT 2.7   Defense Mechanisms

Rationalization: Developing logical justifications or excuses for what we do impulsively. Compulsive or irrational behavior becomes socially acceptable if an explanation can be provided for it.

Projection: Falsely attributing to others the undesirable traits we possess. We protect ourselves from recognizing our own undesirable qualities by assigning them in exaggerated amount to other people.

Repression: Conveniently forgetting what might otherwise be troublesome or embarrassing. Unpleasant memories are simply erased.

Identification: To mentally associate yourself with others and take their desirable qualities as your own. By identifying with someone you admire, you automatically acquire all of that person's positive attributes.

Reaction Formation: To conceal a motive from yourself by giving strong expression to its opposite, such as working on a student honor council to eliminate cheating because of guilty feelings about your own earlier cheating.

Sublimation: The process whereby socially unacceptable motives find expression in socially acceptable forms, such as channeling the desire for sexual gratification into writing love letters and poems or other creative expressions.

Compensation: Exerting a strenuous effort to make up for failure or weakness in one activity through excelling in either a different or an allied activity.

sessed a very optimistic assessment of human nature and believed that everyone was capable of becoming a healthy, well-adjusted person. Both men believed in the concept of **self-actualization,** where people constantly strive toward fulfillment and growth.[39] Rogers particularly emphasized the unlimited potential for continuous improvement in life, and emphasized the freedom and capacity for growth of human beings. Rogers and Maslow believed that each individual has a genetic blueprint identifying the unique characteristics and potentialities he or she can achieve.

According to fulfillment theories, the true nature of the human personality with its striving for maintenance and enhancement is consistent with the demands of society. Only when inherent opportunities for growth and development become thwarted and frustrated do people become maladjusted and exhibit behavior destructive to themselves and others. When people feel hopeless and unworthy, they tend to disregard others and treat them poorly, but when they accept themselves they appreciate and accept others. According to fulfillment theories, life is an unfolding of our inherent human nature.

Consistency Theories. The fulfillment theories all share a belief that individuals have an innate tendency toward actualization; other personality theories make no assumption about the innate nature of humans. These theories suggest instead that personality is learned from experience and represents the history of feedback and interaction with the world. These theories are referred to as **consistency theories,** because individuals seek to perceive the world about them and then to develop attitudes and behaviors consistent with the demands of their world.

One of the most popular consistency theories is called "**cognitive dissonance theory.**"[40] Cognitions are thoughts, expectations, attitudes, opinions, and perceptions. According to cognitive dissonance theory, we have a desire to maintain consistency in our attitudes, expectations, and behaviors. When a discrepancy exists, we are motivated to reduce the discrepancy by either changing our attitudes, changing our behaviors, or some other form of mental restructuring, such as redefining the situation.

Another popular consistency theory is the cognitive theory of George Kelly (1905–1966) who believed that people function much like scientists in trying to understand their world.[41] They anticipate events and purposefully strive to predict and control their environment by creating personal constructs or interpretations of reality. According to Kelly, the personal constructs are like the lens through which we look as we attempt to understand the world. How we see events largely determines our behavior. As we observe social events, we mentally synthesize, refine, and discard constructs about reality in much the same way as scientists develop and test hypotheses. Therefore, according to Kelly, our expectations of the future are generally more important than our past experiences. Our unique patterns of viewing life and the personal constructs we have created for interpreting reality create our unique personalities.

Personality Dimensions

Many personality traits have been identified to account for differences in individual behavior. Some traits have only been proposed as theoretical constructs and await empirical support. Other traits have been clearly identified, measured, and associated with overt behavior. This section describes some of the major personality dimensions that influence how people behave in organizations.

Locus of Control. The **locus of control** is one of the most extensively studied personality dimensions. This belief system refers to the degree to which people believe that their actions influence the rewards they receive in life. People with an internal locus of control believe that the rewards they receive are internally controlled by their own actions, whereas individuals with an external locus of control believe external forces such as luck, chance, or fate control their lives and determine their rewards and punishments.[42] If an unexpected opportunity for advancement were presented to two people, the externally controlled person would probably attribute it to luck or being in the right place at the right time. The internally controlled individual would be more inclined to attribute the opportunity to hard work, effort, and knowledge. As with other personality factors, however, people vary along a continuum and cannot be neatly placed into one category or the other.

People behave differently depending on whether they believe their rewards are internally or externally controlled. In contrast to externals, internals believe how hard they work will determine how well they perform and how well they will be rewarded. Consequently, internals generally perceive more order and predictability in their job-related outcomes and usually report higher levels of job satisfaction.[43] Because managers are required to initiate goal-directed activity, it is not surprising that they tend to be very internally controlled.

In times of upheaval and disruption, externals generally experience more frustration and anxiety than internals and are less able to cope with the situation. A study of how people responded to a flood following a hurricane found that externals were more concerned than internals about coping with their own tension and frustration. They tended to withdraw from the task of rebuilding and to express bit-

APPLYING ORGANIZATIONAL BEHAVIOR
RESEARCH

The Locus of Control as a Moderator of Incentives and Participation

 A laboratory study examined the relationship between the locus of control, incentives, and participation using forty-four undergraduate business students. It was predicted that the locus of control would help to explain when financial incentives and participation lead to greater productivity.

People who have an internal locus of control believe success results from hard work and individual responsibility. Therefore, internals are expected to respond more favorably to situations that offer performance incentives and allow them to participate in setting their own goals because in these situations they are in control and they are rewarded for their efforts.

Intuition suggests that because people like to participate in setting goals and making decisions, this participation will make them more productive. Empirical evidence, however, is mixed. Some evidence indicates that participation increases goal acceptance, thereby leading to improved performance, while other studies have found no relationship.

In this study, students were required to solve a business problem through an interactive computer simulation. Some students were paid a fixed rate of pay for participating in the study, while others could earn a financial incentive depending on the quality of their decisions. Some students participated in deciding budget projections, while others had less participation, because their budget projections were presented to them. The locus of control was measured with a fifteen-item questionnaire and the students were divided into two equal groups of internals and externals.

The results indicated that internals were more productive with incentives than without, while externals were equally productive with or without incentives. Internals also responded more to participation. When participation was absent, internals and externals performed about evenly. But when participation was present, internals outperformed externals.

Although this study used a unique and difficult task, and the sample size was small, the results indicate that the locus of control is an important moderating variable that influences how people respond to various organizational situations. Internals tend to adopt a more proactive orientation to the environment than externals. Therefore, some management controls work better with internals, such as contingent incentives, while other management controls work better with externals, such as direct supervision.

Source: Leslie Kren, "The Moderating Effects of Locus of Control on Performance Incentives and Participation," *Human Relations*, vol. 45 (1992), pp. 991–1012.

terness and aggression about the "rotten hand" they had been dealt. Internals, in contrast, went immediately to the task of acquiring new loans, gathering new resources, and rebuilding their homes and businesses. Obviously, no one could have prevented the storm from happening, but the internals had faith that an active problem-solving response could determine whether the flood would be a conclusive tragedy or only a temporary setback.[44]

The locus of control is determined largely by an individual's past experiences. Internals are the product of an environment where their behaviors largely decided their outcomes, while externals experienced futility in trying to set their own rewards. Child-rearing practices are thought to have an important influence on the development of locus of control: an internal locus of control is created by predictable and consistent discipline, by parental support and involvement, and by parental encouragement of autonomy and self-control. Some evidence also suggests that the locus of control can be influenced over a long period of time by the way employees are reinforced at work. At least one study has shown that the locus of control becomes more internal as a result of exposure to a work environment where important rewards are consistently associated with individual behavior.[45]

Jungian Personality Types. Carl Gustav Jung (1921–1971) developed a personality theory that is widely used in psychology, education, and organizational behavior.[46] Jung's theory claims that the major differences between individuals stem from basic differences in the processes of perception and judgment. Perception involves all the ways people become aware of other people, ideas, and events. Judgment involves all the ways people form conclusions about what they have perceived. According to Jung, differences in the way people perceive information and make judgments about it explain why they differ in their attitudes, values, interests, motivations, and skills.

Several typologies for classifying individuals are derived from Jung's theory of personality types.[47] The most popular instrument is the Myers-Briggs Type Indicator (MBTI), developed by Isabel Briggs Myers and Katherine C. Briggs. The MBTI measures four personality dimensions and places people in 16 categories based on their preference for each of the four dimensions. The four preferences are extraversion–introversion, sensing–intuition, thinking–feeling, and judgment–perception.[48]

1. *Extraversion-introversion (EI)*. Individuals differ in their sociability: some are outgoing and friendly, while others prefer to remain alone. **Extraverts** tend to direct their attention toward people and events in the outside world and to derive satisfaction from external sensory stimulation. **Introverts** tend to spend most of their time looking toward their inner or personal worlds and to derive pleasure from their own thoughts and feelings.

2. *Sensing–intuition (SN)*. The SN index measures a person's preferred perceptual style. Those who focus their perceptions on observable facts or events they perceive through one of the five senses are characterized as sensing (S) individuals. Those who tend to look beyond the known facts for relationships and possibilities that extend beyond the reach of the conscious mind are characterized as intuitive (N) individuals.

3. *Thinking–feeling (TF)*. The TF index measures a person's preferred style of decision making. Those who prefer logical and rational decision making based on impersonal criteria are characterized as thinking (T) individuals. A contrasting style exhibited by those who prefer to make emotional decisions on the basis of personal or social values is feeling (F).

4. *Judgment–perception (JP)*. The JP index measures how individuals like to interact with the outside world. Those who prefer a planned, orderly, structured way of life that focuses on achieving and doing are said to use a judgment (J) process. Those who prefer a flexible, spontaneous way of life that focuses more on experiencing and observing are said to use a perception (P) process.

The sixteen personality types created by these dimensions are shown in Exhibit 2.8. Some personality styles appear to be more prevalent than others. About three-fourths of the United States' population are extraverts (E), and about the same percentage prefer sensing (S) over intuition (N). About 60 percent prefer judgment (J)

EXHIBIT 2.8 Sixteen Personality Types of the Myers-Briggs Type Indicator

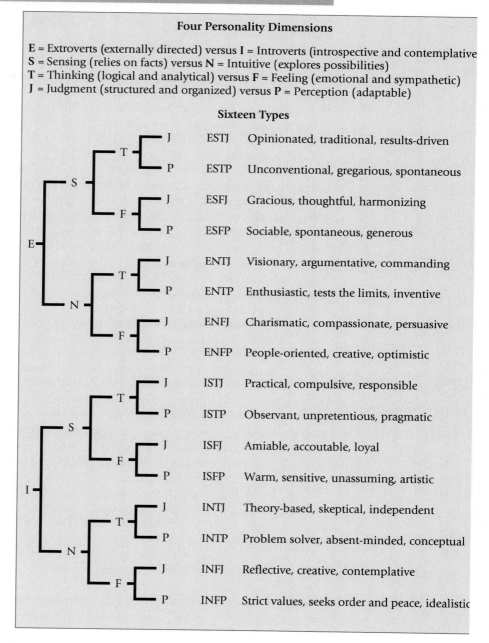

Four Personality Dimensions

E = Extroverts (externally directed) versus **I** = Introverts (introspective and contemplative
S = Sensing (relies on facts) versus **N** = Intuitive (explores possibilities)
T = Thinking (logical and analytical) versus **F** = Feeling (emotional and sympathetic)
J = Judgment (structured and organized) versus **P** = Perception (adaptable)

Sixteen Types

ESTJ	Opinionated, traditional, results-driven
ESTP	Unconventional, gregarious, spontaneous
ESFJ	Gracious, thoughtful, harmonizing
ESFP	Sociable, spontaneous, generous
ENTJ	Visionary, argumentative, commanding
ENTP	Enthusiastic, tests the limits, inventive
ENFJ	Charismatic, compassionate, persuasive
ENFP	People-oriented, creative, optimistic
ISTJ	Practical, compulsive, responsible
ISTP	Observant, unpretentious, pragmatic
ISFJ	Amiable, accoutable, loyal
ISFP	Warm, sensitive, unassuming, artistic
INTJ	Theory-based, skeptical, independent
INTP	Problem solver, absent-minded, conceptual
INFJ	Reflective, creative, contemplative
INFP	Strict values, seeks order and peace, idealistic

Source: Adapted from Isabel Briggs Myers, *Introduction to Type: A Description of the Theory and Applications of the Myers-Briggs Type Indicator* (Palo Alto, Calif.: Consulting Psychologists Press, 1987).

to perception (P). Thinking–feeling appears to be gender related: the majority of males (60 percent) prefer thinking (T) while the majority of females (65 percent) prefer feeling (F).[49] This gender difference in preferred decision-making style appears to be an important explanation for the differences in the working styles of male and female managers.[50]

Only one of the four preferences, SN, appears to be related to intelligence or mental ability. On most mental ability and aptitude tests, individuals who prefer intuition (N) have significantly higher average scores than those who prefer sensing (S). On the Scholastic Aptitude Test, for instance, the average verbal score was 45 points higher for N than for S.[51] Intuition also seems to play an important role in entrepreneurial success. A stronger preference for intuition was observed among the founders of growth-oriented *Inc.* magazine 500 firms than among the founders of slow-growth firms.[52]

Research using the MBTI suggests that certain personality types are best suited for particular occupations and this information can be used for career counseling and job placement.[53] On the SN index, for example, over 80 percent of steelworkers, police detectives, and factory supervisors prefer S (sensing) over N, while over 80 percent of research assistants, social scientists, writers, artists, and entertainers prefer N (intuition) over S. On the TF index, over 75 percent of auditors, operations analysts, and sales managers prefer T (thinking) over F, while over 75 percent of clergy, receptionists, and preschool teachers prefer F (feeling) over T.[54] An experiment on learning effectiveness using self-paced computer-assisted instruction found that people who prefer T performed 10–15 percent better than those who prefer F.[55] These conclusions would probably be reversed, however, if the training involved case discussions or counseling for those in the helping professions, because they prefer F.

The introversion–extraversion dimension involves more than just the individual's preference for social interaction. According to Jung, these two traits are tied to the development of a person's nervous system and serve to regulate the optimal levels of external sensory stimulation. Extraverts need more generalized stimulation than introverts to achieve an optimal state of sensory balance.[56]

Extraverts have a great need for stimulation in the form of social activity, crowds, adventure, frequent changes in the environment, and intense colors or noises. They prefer job environments that provide opportunity, variety, unpredictability, and sporadic bursts of intensity. Even an occasional crisis may appeal to extraverts. If the job environment is not sufficiently stimulating, extraverts may play practical jokes and games or display other kinds of distracting behavior to produce additional stimulation. Introverts do not require as much excitement from external stimulation, and consequently they tend to perform better than extraverts on repetitive tasks or tasks occurring in environments that offer very little sensory stimulation.

Whether an individual is an introvert or an extravert ought to be considered in selecting personnel and designing jobs. Introverts may not respond well to an enriched job that provides frequent contact with customers and/or other employees. Significant differences also would be expected in the ways introverts and extraverts respond to training and development activities. Introverts are more inclined to study on their own and to avoid the group involvements that are such a large part of management development.

Authoritarianism. The events of World War II stimulated a series of behavioral science studies of the relationship between personality and the way individuals respond to power and authority in organizations. Shocked by some of the inhumane events of World War II, behavioral scientists first tried to explain the events by identifying an authoritarian personality dimension that caused individuals to be susceptible to autocratic leadership. Since then investigations of how people respond to organizational authority have examined a variety of similar personality traits, such as **authoritarianism,** dogmatism, Machiavellianism, and the bureaucratic orientation. All four of these personality dimensions are associated with how people respond to power and authority relationships within an organization.

People with strong authoritarian personalities believe there should be clearly defined status and power positions in organizations, strict adherence to conventional values, and unquestioned obedience to a recognized authority. If they are leading, they expect respect for their authority; and if they are following, they willingly submit to the authority of the leader. Because of their concern for power and influence, they believe decisions should be based on the desires of higher-level leaders rather than on subjective feelings, emotions, or logic. Whether authoritarians are effective as either leaders or subordinates depends on the demands of the situation and on whether their associates share their expectations about strict obedience to authority.[57]

Dogmatism is closely associated with the authoritarian personality, but the term particularly describes the rigidity of one's belief systems. Highly dogmatic individuals believe that organizational authority should be absolute, and they tend to accept or reject other people on the basis of their agreement or disagreement with accepted authority or doctrine. Because they believe right and wrong are determined by higher-level authority or rigid doctrine, dogmatic individuals tend to keep closed minds and be unwilling to listen to reason or logic.[58]

The **Machiavellian personality** was named after Niccolò Machiavelli, a fifteenth-century public employee in Florence, Italy, who wrote a blunt and forthright analysis of power and political manipulation. Machiavelli discarded the theological and sanctimonious quality of other traditional writings of his time, and frankly described the manipulations of power and influence within political circles. In his writing, he attempted to expose the abuses of power. Many of Machiavelli's principles of leadership and power are as relevant now as they were then, and many modern writers still make reference to Machiavelli's writings regarding leadership, cohesiveness, and the reliance of those in power on the mass consent of the public. Machiavelli taught that although princes may usurp power or inherit it, to win firm control of the state they must win the approval of the people. Princes must remember that authority flows from the bottom up within an organization, and not from the top down.

Two of Machiavelli's books, *The Discourses* and *The Prince,* were written over 450 years ago but have been resurrected in recent years to describe opportunistic, self-serving leaders.[59] Although modern references tend to seriously distort Machiavelli's writings, they are used nevertheless to describe people who are willing to behave in any manner that will further their own needs, regardless of the impact on others. People with strongly Machiavellian personalities are not team players. Rather than responding to the needs of the other group members, they attempt to manipulate others through conniving, lying, the use of false praise, and other subversive methods to achieve their own objectives. In contrast, individuals who are low in Machiavellian personality attributes believe there is no excuse for manipulating or lying to others. They are sensitive to the effects of their decisions on others and believe they should take action only when they are sure it is morally right.[60]

Bureaucratic orientation is a personality trait derived from Max Weber's description of bureaucracy. According to Weber, an ideal bureaucratic organization is a highly structured, impersonal organization that relies on rules, standard operating procedures, and conformity. Some individuals seem to thrive in a highly structured bureaucratic environment. People who have a bureaucratic orientation believe in self-subordination—they willingly accept higher authority and comply with the directives of their superiors, prefer the impersonal, formal relationships found in a bureaucratic organization rather than informal friendships, believe in strict rule conformity, and feel a sense of security from following organizational rules and regulations. And they feel a sense of traditionalism and believe in loyalty to the organization and conformity to the attitudes expressed by experienced leaders.[61]

Individuals who have a strong bureaucratic orientation also tend to believe that people at higher levels in the organization are in the best position to make important decisions for the people below them. To them, relationships within the organization should be based on position or level, rather than on personal considerations, and individuals should think of themselves as members of the organization first and as individuals second. Research has shown that people who have a strong bureaucratic orientation tend to choose jobs in more structured organizations, such as the military, and they display lower turnover rates and higher job satisfaction in a structured environment.

Self-esteem.   Our self-concept is presumed to be a particularly human manifestation and refers to our own conscious awareness of who we are. We see ourselves relative to others and form evaluative impressions about our skills, abilities, and behaviors.

Many personality theories discuss self-concept, especially the humanistic personality theory of Carl Rogers. According to Rogers, our self-concept is a collection of the attitudes, values, and beliefs we have acquired about ourselves from our own unique experiences. We form opinions of our behavior, ability, appearance, and overall worth as people from our own personal observations and the feedback we receive from others.[62]

Over time, our accumulated experiences establish our self-concept. This self-concept determines how we feel about ourselves and influences how we respond to others. Individuals with high self-esteem are generally more creative, independent, and spontaneous in their interactions with others. Because of their positive feelings about themselves, they can concentrate on the issues at hand and focus on new and original ideas without being as concerned about how people feel about them. People with low self-esteem tend to feel overly concerned about the evaluations of others, which dilutes their ability to concentrate on problems and to think creatively. Their low self-esteem often causes them to withdraw from tasks or social situations.

Extensive research has shown that the behaviors of individuals are consistent with their self-concepts. Students, for example, who see themselves as competent academic achievers quite consistently perform better in school. Individuals with high self-esteem are generally more accurate in their perceptions of social situations.[63]

Problems of low self-esteem are often attributed to inadequate positive reinforcement from others. Although people whose self-esteem is low have usually experienced less praise than others, the solution is not to simply give them more praise and recognition. Self-esteem is greatly influenced by how well we have actually performed. Although the comments of others help us interpret our performance, how well we have actually done has a greater impact on our self-esteem. Therefore, to raise an individual's self-esteem, praise and compliments may not be as effective as actually helping the individual perform better.

Self-efficacy. Self-efficacy is one's belief in one's capability to perform a specific task. In many respects, the concept of self-efficacy is similar to the concepts of self-esteem and locus of control. However, self-efficacy is task specific rather than a generalized perception of overall competence.

Self-efficacy emerged from the research on social cognitive theory (discussed in Chapter 3) and represents an important personality variable that explains variations in individual performance. Several studies suggest that self-efficacy is a better predictor of subsequent performance than past behavior.[64] Although knowing how well people have performed in the past helps to predict their future performance, an even better predictor is knowing how capable they feel regarding a specific task.[65]

Self-efficacy has three dimensions: magnitude, strength, and generality. Magnitude concerns the level of task difficulty that a person believes he or she can attain, and is related to the concept of goal setting. Some people think they can achieve very difficult goals. Strength concerns the amount of confidence one has in one's ability to perform, and it can be strong or weak. Some people have strong convictions that they will succeed even when they face difficult challenges. Generality indicates the degree to which one's expectations are generalized across many situations or restricted to an isolated instance. Some people believe they can succeed in a variety of situations.

Self-efficacy is a learned characteristic that is acquired by four kinds of information cues:

1. *Enactive mastery.* The most influential stimulus contributing to the development of self-efficacy is enactive mastery, which concerns the repeated performance or practicing of the task. For example, a nurse who has inserted many IV needles should feel a sense of high self-efficacy in being able to do it again.

2. *Vicarious experience.* Observing the behavior of others (modeling) can almost be as effective as enactive mastery, especially when the person and the model are similar in terms of age, capability, and other characteristics and when the model's behavior is clearly visible.

3. *Verbal persuasion.* In developing self-efficacy, verbal persuasion is less effective than practicing or modeling; nevertheless, it can be an important source of efficacy information, especially if the source has high credibility and expertise and if there are multiple sources who all agree.

4. *Perceptions of one's physiological state.* Efficacy perceptions are influenced by momentary levels of arousal, as illustrated by these statements by athletes: "We were ready for them," "They were really up for this game," "I was mentally prepared," and "He was really psyched for this match."

Efficacy perceptions appear to be self-reinforcing. Self-efficacy influences the kinds of activities and settings people choose to participate in, the skills they are willing to practice and learn, the amount of energy they are willing to exert, and the persistence of their coping efforts in the face of obstacles. People with high self-efficacy tend to engage more frequently in task-related activities and persist longer in coping efforts; this leads to more mastery experiences, which enhance their self-efficacy. People with low self-efficacy tend to engage in fewer coping efforts; they give up more easily under adversity and demonstrate less mastery, which in turn reinforces their low self-efficacy.[66]

Self-efficacy can predict performance in a variety of settings as long as the efficacy measure is tailored to the specific tasks being performed. Consequently, efficacy perceptions are relevant in many organizational settings, such as employee selection, training and development, and vocational counseling. Employees with high self-efficacy would be expected to respond more favorably to most personnel programs, such as performance evaluation, financial incentive, and promotion programs.[67]

Need for Achievement. Extensive research by David McClelland and others on the achievement motive has identified this factor as a basic personality dimension. McClelland found that individuals differ in their **need for achievement,** and this difference serves as a basic personality trait leading to consistent behavior patterns in a variety of situations. From his research, McClelland identified three characteristics of high-need achievers.[68]

1. They want to be personally responsible for the successful completion of the task.
2. They prefer moderate levels of risk where achieving success is a realistic challenge rather than an extremely difficult or easy challenge.
3. They want immediate feedback on their performance.

Because McClelland's research on the need for achievement is also a motivation theory, the characteristics of high-need achievers and the research supporting them are described in Chapter 4.

Management Style. If this chapter failed to discuss management style, most employees would think it overlooked the most important personality characteristic. Most employees believe management style is a personality dimension, and they talk about the good and bad management styles of their supervisors. Although many personality dimensions contribute to a supervisor's management style, the most important dimension to employees is whether the supervisor is abrasive and punitive or friendly and considerate. Supervisors who have abrasive personalities tend to make arbitrary decisions, issue authoritarian demands, hold unrealistic expectations, seldom smile, criticize employees frequently and publicly, and seldom recognize good performance. Employees dislike working for supervisors who have abrasive personalities. Consequently, the work groups of abrasive supervisors are typically plagued by higher absenteeism, higher turnover, more grievances, and lower satisfaction.

The central theme of the human relations movement focused on the importance of friendly supervision, respect for employees, and personal consideration. The way managers treat their subordinates is the core of Rensis Likert's "principle of supportive relationships."[69] This principle says that all employees perform better and prefer to work in an environment where their supervisors are supportive, trusting, encouraging, respectful, and considerate. Likert argued that this principle was universally relevant in every superior–subordinate relationship, and his research data from organizational surveys seemed to support his claims.

SUMMARY

1. The perceptual process consists of three major components: sensation, attention, and perception. Human beings only perceive a small fraction of the sensations that are present in the external environment. Stimuli must pass through the filters of sensation and attention and be interpreted before they are perceived.

2. The major characteristics that determine whether we will attend to stimuli are size, intensity, frequency, contrast, motion, change, and novelty.

3. Perception is the process of organizing and interpreting the sensations we attend to. Some of the processes that facilitate our perceptual organization include figure–ground separation, similarity, proximity, and closure.

4. Our ability to perceive social events is influenced by characteristics of the person perceived, characteristics of the situation, and characteristics of the perceiver. Appearance, communication, and status are three of the most important characteristics influencing our perceptions of other people. Characteristics of the situation include both the social context and the organizational context of the event. Four important characteristics of the perceiver include the person's self-concept, cognitive complexity, previous experience, motivational state, and personal values.

5. Two contrasting perceptions of managers that significantly impact how they interact with employees are called theory X and theory Y. Theory X assumes people are lazy and dislike work, while theory Y assumes people are ambitious, responsible, and creative and they want to contribute to the company.

6. Our perceptions may be wrong for a variety of reasons. Some of the most frequent causes of perceptual errors include stereotyping, the halo effect, perceptual defenses, selective perception, implicit personality theories, projection, and excessive reliance on first impressions.

7. Prejudice is an unreasonable bias that leads to intolerance or an irrational dislike for people of a particular race, religion, or gender. Prejudice on the basis of race, religion or gender is both immoral and illegal and ought to be eliminated. However, the psychological processes that contribute to prejudice are very natural and stem from perceptual differences of minorities and majorities of any sort. Three perceptual tendencies that explain why minorities experience prejudice are visibility because of their smaller numbers, contrast because they are different, and assimilation into projective stereotypes.

8. An impressive illustration of how perceptions influence behavior in organizations is the self-fulfilling prophecy. Here the expectations in the mind of one person about how others should behave are communicated through subtle ways and actually influence the behaviors of others. The factors that appear to create the self-fulfilling prophecy include the amount of input given to others, the amount of output expected, the reinforcement they receive, and the kind of feedback given to them.

9. The Hawthorne effect occurs when people know their performance is being evaluated and they behave differently as a result. This effect was discovered in the famous Hawthorne Studies (1924–1933).

10. Attribution theory attempts to explain how we interpret the behavior of others—whether their behavior is caused by personality characteristics or environmental circumstances. In general we attribute the behavior of others to their personality and explain our own behavior by environmental circumstances.

11. Personality theories address two basic issues: how we are the same, called the "core of personality," and how we are different, called the "periphery of personality."

12. Personality theories can be categorized according to their basic premises into conflict theories, fulfillment theories, and consistency theories. Conflict theories postulate two opposing forces within the person. How individuals

resolve this conflict determines their basic personality. According to fulfillment theories, there is one basic force constantly pushing toward self-actualization and fulfillment. The premise of consistency theories is that personality represents an integrated composite of everything individuals have experienced and learned. Personality is determined by the way individuals organize these elements into a consistent cognitive system.

13. Several personality traits have been identified to explain differences in individual behavior. Some of the traits most relevant to the field of organizational behavior include locus of control, which refers to whether people believe the rewards they receive are based on their own effort or external factors, introversion versus extraversion, authoritarianism, self-esteem, self-efficacy, need for achievement, and management style.

DISCUSSION QUESTIONS

1. If two people disagree in their perceptions of a social event, but each has a sincere desire to know whose perceptions are most correct, how could they decide?

2. Explain how implicit personality theories influence perceptions. Describe your implicit personality theories for the following people: a welfare recipient, an FBI agent, a leader of the PLO, a city judge, and a university president.

3. Since first impressions play such a major role in our perceptions, what recommendations would you make to an interviewer and to an interviewee to improve the accuracy of an interview?

4. What are the causes of prejudice, and how much of a problem is it today? If someone recognized that he or she had feelings of prejudice and knew that it was wrong, how should he or she go about changing them?

5. How does the self-fulfilling prophecy occur and how large a factor do you think it is in determining the success of new employees?

6. According to attribution theory, what are the factors that influence how we assign responsi-

bility? How would friendship influence our attributions?

7. How are perceptual inferences both good and bad? How does stereotyping both help and hinder us? How is projection both useful and dysfunctional?

8. What are the basic differences between conflict, fulfillment, and consistency theories of personality? Which of these theories appeals most to you and why?

9. How would you expect the locus of control to be different for minority individuals? How would you expect internals to respond differently than externals to such organizational events as a job enrichment program, a profit-sharing plan, a management development program, a bonus system, and a union election?

10. Describe the differences you would expect between the behavior of someone highly authoritarian and someone who was not. Which person would be most effective as the leader of an organization and when?

GLOSSARY

attention Part of the perceptual process in which we acknowledge the reception of sensations from the environment. The major characteristics of physical stimuli that affect attention include size, intensity, frequency, contrast, motion, change, and novelty.

attribution theory A theory that explains how we assign responsibility for behavior either to personality characteristics or to environmental circumstances.

authoritarianism A personality trait of people who believe in strict adherence to conventional values, clearly defined status and power positions, and unquestioned obedience to recognized authority.

bureaucratic orientation A personality trait of people who thrive in a bureaucratic organization characterized by formal relationships, reliance on rules and standards, highly structured activities, and conformity to higher-level authority.

cognitive complexity The degree to which people have developed complex categories for organizing information.

cognitive dissonance theory A theory claiming that people try to maintain a state of balance between their cognitions and behaviors and explaining how people adjust their attitudes or behaviors when these are dissonant or inconsistent.

conflict theories A category of personality theories that focuses on the idea that people are affected by two opposing forces. Personality traits are determined by the way these conflicts are resolved.

consistency theories A classification of personality theories that claim that the core of personality consists of the composite experiences and learning events people have experienced. The process of achieving consistency among these constructs determines our personality traits.

core of personality The central elements of a personality theory that identify the common dimensions all people share.

dogmatism A personality trait of someone who has rigid belief systems and believes right and wrong are determined by higher-level authority.

extravert People who direct their attention toward other people and events and who desire a variety of external sensory stimulation.

fulfillment theories A classification of personality theories in which the core personality dimension consists of a force pushing people in the direction of self-actualization and fulfillment.

halo effect One of the perceptual errors in which people allow one characteristic to influence their evaluations of other personality characteristics.

implicit personality theories The process of allowing our personal stereotypes and expectations regarding certain kinds of people to create a perceptual set that influences how we respond to other people.

introverts People who prefer to spend their time focusing on their inner thoughts and feelings and who prefer a minimum of external sensory stimulation.

locus of control A personality trait that is determined by whether people think the rewards they obtain are based on internal factors such as knowledge, effort, and skill, or external factors such as luck, chance, and fate.

Machiavellian personality A personality trait of someone who attempts to exert power over others through manipulation, conniving, lying, and other subversive methods designed to help them achieve their own objectives.

need for achievement A personality trait that reflects the importance of achievement and upward striving within a person's life. High need achievers are characterized by a desire for personal responsibility, moderate levels of risk, and immediate feedback on their performance.

perception The process of interpreting and organizing the sensations we attend to.

perceptual defense A defense mechanism in which we protect our personalities by overlooking or ignoring threatening stimuli; denial.

perceptual inferences The process of extrapolating from a small amount of information to form a complete perception about an object or event. Often we are required to act on only limited pieces of information from which we infer what more information might tell us.

perceptual organization The process of organizing our perceptions into recognizable patterns. Four of the principles we use to assist in this effort include figure–ground separation, similarity, proximity, and closure.

periphery of personality The dimensions of personality theories that differ from individual to individual.

primacy effect The tendency for first impressions and early information to exert a particularly profound influence on our evaluations and judgment.

projection A form of perceptual bias in which we project our own personal feelings and attitudes onto others as a means of helping us interpret their attitudes and feelings.

psychoanalytic theory A theory developed by Sigmund Freud that analyzes three personality systems, the id, the ego, and the superego, and how they interact.

selective perception A source of perceptual errors that occurs when people choose to perceive only that information which they find acceptable.

self-actualization The tendency for people to become fulfilled and achieve all that they have the potential to achieve according to their genetic blueprint.

self-fulfilling prophecy A process that explains how the expectations in the mind of one person, such as a teacher or researcher, come to influence the behaviors of others, such as students, or subjects, in such a way that the latter achieves the former's expectations.

sensations Environmental stimuli that we are capable of receiving through one or more of the five sense mechanisms—sight, smell, taste, touch, and hearing.

stereotyping The process of using a few attributes about an object to classify it and then responding to it

as a member of a category rather than as a unique object.

theory X versus theory Y A theory proposed by Douglas McGregor that explains two opposite perceptual styles of managers. Managers who espouse theory X see employees as lazy and refusing to work while managers who espouse theory Y believe employees are dedicated and willing to work.

NOTES

1. Ron Suskind and Kenneth H. Bacon, "Financial Casualty: U.S. Recession Claims Bank of New England as First Big Victim," *Wall Street Journal* (January 7, 1991), p. A1.

2. John R. Wilke, "Fear Strikes Old Stone Depositors in Rhode Island, Prompting Many to Demand Cash Immediately," *Wall Street Journal* (January 28, 1991), p. A2.

3. D. J. Mason, "Judgments of Leadership Based on Physiognomic Cues," *Journal of Abnormal and Social Psychology*, vol. 54 (1957), pp. 273–274.

4. J. T. Malloy, *Dress for Success* (New York: Warner Books, 1975); M. Snyder, E. D. Tanke, and E. Berscheid, "Social Perception and Interpersonal Behavior: On the Self-fulfilling Nature of Social Stereotypes," *Journal of Personality and Social Psychology*, vol. 35 (1977), pp. 656–666; D. Gilbert and Edward E. Jones, "Perceiver-Induced Constraint: Interpretations of Self-generated reality," *Journal of Personality and Social Psychology*, vol. 50 (1986), pp. 269–280.

5. John W. Thibaut and H. W. Riecker, "Authoritarianism, Status and the Communication of Aggression," *Human Relations*, vol. 8 (1955), pp. 95–120.

6. J. L. Hilton and J. M. Darley, "Constructing Other Persons: A Limit on the Effect," *Journal of Experimental Social Psychology*, vol. 21 (1985), pp. 1–18.

7. L. H. Strickland, "Surveillance and Trust," *Journal of Personality*, vol. 26 (1958), pp. 200–215.

8. D. C. Dearborn and H. A. Simon, "Selective Perception: A Note on Departmental Identification of Executives," *Sociometry*, vol. 21 (1958), p. 142.

9. R. D. Norman, "The Interelationships Among Acceptance–Rejection, Self–Other, Insights into Self, and Realistic Perception of Others," *Journal of Social Psychology*, vol. 37 (1953), pp. 205–235; P. A. McCarty, "Effects of Feedback on the Self-confidence of Women," *Academy of Management Journal*, vol. 29 (1986), pp. 840–847.

10. K. J. Fraunenfelder, "A Cognitive Determinant of Favorability of Impression," *Journal of Social Psychology*, vol. 94 (1974), pp. 71–81.

11. R. Levine, I. Chein, and G. Murphy, "The Relation of the Intensity of a Need to the Amount of Perceptual Distortion, a Preliminary Report," *Journal of Psychology*, vol. 13 (1942), pp. 283–293.

12. H. G. McCurdy, "Coin Perception Studies and the Context of Schemata," *Psychological Review*, vol. 63 (1956), pp. 160–168.

13. Elizabeth C. Ravlin and Bruce M. Meglino, "Effect of Values on Perception and Decision Making: A Study of Work Values Measures," *Journal of Applied Psychology*, vol. 72 (November 1987), pp. 666–673.

14. Douglas McGregor, *The Human Side of Enterprise* (New York: McGraw-Hill, 1960).

15. Sheldon S. Zalkind and Timothy W. Costello, "Perception: Some Recent Research and Implications for Administration," *Administrative Science Quarterly*, vol. 9 (1962), pp. 218–235.

16. K. R. Murphy and W. K. Balzar, "Systematic Distortions in Memory-based Behavior Ratings and Performance Evaluations: Consequences for Rating Accuracy," *Journal of Applied Psychology*, vol. 17 (February 1986), pp. 39–43.

17. Brian E. Becker and Robert L. Cardy, "Influence of Halo Error on Appraisal Effectiveness: A Conceptual and Empirical Reconsideration," *Journal of Applied Psychology*, vol. 71 (1986), pp. 662–671.

18. Mason Haire and W. F. Grunes, "Perceptual Defenses: Processes Protecting an Organized Perception of Another Personality," *Human Relations*, vol. 3 (1950), pp. 403–412.

19. R. R. Sears, "Experimental Studies of Perception: Attribution of Traits," *Journal of Social Psychology*, vol. 7 (1936), pp. 151–163.

20. Eugene Mayfield, "The Selection Interview—A Reevaluation of Published Research," *Personnel Psychology*, vol. 17 (Autumn 1964), pp. 239–260; S. W. Constantin, "An Investigation of Information Favorability in the Employment Interview," *Journal of Applied Psychology*, vol. 61 (1976), pp. 743–749; O. R. Wright, "Summary of Research on the Employment Interview Since 1964," *Personnel Psychology*, vol. 22 (1969),

pp. 391–413; B. Brophy, "First Impressions Can Last Forever," *U.S. News and World Report,* vol. 101 (July 14, 1986), p. 48; Angelo J. Kinicki, Peter W. Hom, Chris A. Lockwood, and Roger W. Griffeth, "Interviewer Predictions of Applicant Qualifications and Interviewer Validity: Aggregate and Individual Analyses," *Journal of Applied Psychology,* vol. 75 (October 1990), pp. 477–486.

21. Mason Haire, "Role Perception in Labor–Management Relations: An Experimental Approach," *Industrial and Labor Relations Review,* vol. 8 (1955), pp. 204–216.

22. V. E. Schein, "The Relationship Between Sex-Role Stereotypes and Requisite Management Characteristics," *Journal of Applied Psychology,* vol. 57 (1973), pp. 95–100; V. E. Schein, "Relationships Between Sex-Role Stereotypes and Requisite Management Characteristics Among Female Managers," *Journal of Applied Psychology,* vol. 60 (1975), pp. 340–344.

23. Rosabeth Moss Kanter, *Men and Women of the Corporation* (New York: Basic Books, 1977), Chap. 8.

24. Ibid.

25. Leonard L. Martin, John J. Seta, and Rick A. Crelia, "Assimilation and Contrast as a Function of People's Willingness and Ability to Expend Effort in Forming an Impression," *Journal of Personality and Social Psychology,* vol. 59 (July 1990), pp. 27–37.

26. Robert Rosenthal and L. Jacobson, *Pygmalion in the Classroom* (New York: Holt, Rinehart, and Winston, 1968).

27. Rosenthal and Jacobson, op. cit.; see also Jack Horn, "Pygmalion vs. Golem in a High School Gym," *Psychology Today,* vol. 18 (July 1984), pp. 9–10.

28. Rosenthal and Jacobson, op. cit.; Horn, op. cit.; see also "Productivity and the Self-Fulfilling Prophecy: The Pygmalion Effect," CRM Management Films Series, 1975.

29. "Productivity and the Self-Fulfilling Prophecy."

30. Dov Eden, *Pygmalion in Management: Productivity as a Self-Fulfilling Prophecy* (Lexington, Mass.: Lexington Books, 1990).

31. R. H. G. Field, "The Self-Fulfilling Prophecy: Achieving the Metharme Effect," *Journal of Management Studies,* vol. 26 (March 1989), pp. 151–175; J. Sterling Livingston, "Pygmalion in Management," *Harvard Business Review,* vol. 66 (September–October 1980), pp. 121–130; Barbara Whitaker Shimko, "Using Positive Pygmalion to Build Your Workforce," *Cornell Hotel and Restaurant Administration Quarterly,* vol. 30 (November 1989), pp. 90–94.

32. J. Sterling Livingston, "Pygmalion in Management," *Harvard Business Review,* vol. 55 (July–August 1969), pp. 81–89; L. Sandler, "Self-fulfilling Prophecy: Better Training by Magic," *Training: The Magazine of Human Resource Development,* vol. 23 (February 1986), pp. 60–64.

33. Fritz J. Rothlisberger and William J. Dickson, *Management and the Worker* (Cambridge, Mass.: Harvard Uni-

versity Press, [1939] 1967); "The Hawthorne Studies: A Synopsis." pamphlet (Cicero, Ill.: Western Electric, 1974), p. 2.

34. F. Heider, *The Psychology of Interpersonal Behavior* (New York: Wiley, 1958); Steven E. Kaplan, "Improving Performance Evaluation," *CMA—The Management Accounting Magazine,* vol. 61 (May–June 1987), pp. 56–59.

35. Jean M. Bartunek, "Why Did You Do That? Attribution Theory in Organizations," *Business Horizons,* vol. 24, No. 5 (1981), pp. 66–71; Edward E. Jones and Richard E. Naisbett, *The Actor and the Observer, Divergent Perceptions of the Causes of Behavior* (Morristown, N.J.: General Learning Press, 1971); J. C. McElroy and C. B. Shrader, "Attribution Theories of Leadership and Network Analysis," *Journal of Management,* vol. 12 (Fall 1986), p. 35.

36. Harold H. Kelley and John L. Michela, "Attribution Theory and Research," *Annual Review of Psychology,* vol. 31 (1980), pp. 457–501; Terence R. Mitchell and Robert E. Wood, "Supervisors' Responses to Subordinates' Poor Performance: A Test of an Attributional Model," *Organizational Behavior and Human Performance,* vol. 22 (1980), pp. 123–128.

37. Salvatore R. Maddi, *Personality Theories: A Comparative Analysis* (Homewood, Ill.: Dorsey Press, 1972).

38. Sigmund Freud, "The Ego and the Id," trans. Joan Riviere, in Jonathan Cape and Harrison Smith (eds.), *Collected Essays* (London: Hogarth Press, 1930).

39. Carl R. Rogers, "Some Basic Propositions of a Growth and Self-Actualization Psychology," in *Perceiving, Behaving, Becoming: A New Focus for Education* (Washington, D.C.: Yearbook of the Association for Supervision and Curriculum Development, 1962); Carl R. Rogers, *On Becoming a Person* (Boston: Houghton Mifflin, 1961); Carl R. Rogers, "Actualizing Tendency in Relation to 'Motives' and to Consciousness," in M. R. Jones (ed.), *Nebraska Symposium on Motivation* (Lincoln: University of Nebraska Press, 1963).

40. Leon Festinger, *A Theory of Cognitive Dissonance* (Stanford, Calif.: Stanford University Press, 1957).

41. George A. Kelly, *The Psychology of Personal Constructs,* vol. 1 (New York: Norton, 1955).

42. Julian B. Rotter, "Generalized Expectancies for Internal Versus External Control of Reinforcement," *Psychological Monographs,* vol. 80 (1966), pp. 1–28.

43. Virginia T. Geurin and Gary F. Kohut, "The Relationship of Locus of Control and Participative Decision Making Among Managers and Business Students," *Mid-Atlantic Journal of Business,* vol. 25 (February 1989), pp. 57–66; John R. Hollenbeck, Arthur P. Brief, Ellen M. Whitener, and Karen E. Pauli, "An Empirical Note on the Interaction of Personality and Aptitude in Personnel Selection," *Journal of Management,* vol. 14 (September 1988), pp. 441–451; Lokman Mia, "Participation in Budgetary Decision Making, Task Difficulty, Locus of Control, and Employee Behavior: An Empirical Study," *Decision Sciences,* vol. 18 (Fall 1987),

pp. 547–561; Paul E. Spector, "Development of the Work Locus of Control Scale," *Journal of Occupational Psychology,* vol. 61 (December 1988), pp. 335–340.

44. C. Anderson, Donald Hellriegel, and John Slocum, "Managerial Response to Environmentally Induced Stress," *Academy of Management Journal,* vol. 20 (1977), pp. 260–272; see also Phillip L. Storms and Paul E. Spector, "Relationships of Organizational Frustration with Reported Behavioral Reactions: The Moderating Effect of Locus of Control," *Journal of Occupational Psychology,* vol. 60 (December 1987), pp. 227–234.

45. S. Eitzen, "Impact of Behavior Modification Techniques on Locus of Control of Delinquent Boys," *Psychological Reports,* vol. 35 (1974), pp. 1317–1318; Charles J. Cox and Gary L. Cooper, "The Making of the British CEO: Childhood, Work Experience, Personality, and Management Style," *Academy of Management Executive,* vol. 3 (August 1989), pp. 241–245.

46. Carl G. Jung, *The Undiscovered Self* (Boston: Little, Brown, 1958); Rowan Bayne, "A New Direction for the Myers-Briggs Type Indicator," *Personnel Management,* vol. 22 (March 1990), pp. 48–51.

47. Roger T. O'Brien, "Using Jung More (And Etching Him in Stone Less)," *Training,* vol. 22 (May 1985), pp. 53–66.

48. Isabel Briggs Myers and Mary H. McCaulley, *A Guide to the Development and Use of the Myers-Briggs Type Indicator* (Palo Alto, Calif.: Consulting Psychologists Press, 1985).

49. Ibid., p. 45.

50. Susan Vinnicombe, "What Exactly Are the Differences in Male and Female Working Styles?" *Women in Management Review,* vol. 3, no. 1 (1987), pp. 13–21.

51. Myers and McCaulley, op. cit., p. 102.

52. Charles W. Ginn and Donald L. Sexton, "A Comparison of the Personality Type Dimensions of the 1987 *Inc.* 500 Company Founders/CEOs with Those of Slower-Growth Firms," *Journal of Business Venturing,* vol. 5 (September 1990), pp. 313–326.

53. Christine F. Lindgard and Noel W. Bates, "Do Police Departments Recruit Different Types of Officers?" *Journal of Managerial Psychology* 4, no. 2 (1989), pp. 3–12; George H. Rice and David P. Lindecamp, "Personality Types and Business Success of Small Retailers," *Journal of Occupational Psychology,* vol. 62 (June 1989), pp. 177–182.

54. Myers and McCaulley, op. cit., pp. 246–250.

55. Gary M. Kern and Khalil F. Matta, "Learning Style as an Influence on the Effectiveness of Self-Paced Computer-Assisted Instruction: Preliminary Results," *Computers and Industrial Engineering,* vol. 13 (1987), pp. 203–207.

56. Hans J. Eysenck, *The Biological Basis of Personality* (Springfield, Ill.: Thomas, 1967); Hans J. Eysenck (ed.), *Eysenck on Extraversion* (New York: Wiley, 1973).

57. T. W. Adorno, E. Frenkel-Brunswik, D. J. Levinson, and R. N. Sanford, *The Authoritarian Personality* (New York: Harper & Row, 1950). See also a series of conference presentations on authoritarianism and dogmatism reported in *The High School Journal,* vol. 68 (February–March 1985).

58. Milton Rokeach, *The Open and Closed Mind* (New York: Basic Books, 1960); J. Garvey, "Deeper than emotions: The guiding role of dogma," *Commonweal,* vol. 112 (June 21, 1985), pp. 357–358.

59. Niccolò Machiavelli, *The Prince* (New York: Modern Library, 1940).

60. R. Christie and F. Geis, *Studies in Machiavellianism* (New York: Academic Press, 1970); F. L. Geis and T. H. Moon, "Machiavellianism and Deception," *Journal of Personality and Social Psychology,* vol. 41 (1981), pp. 766–775; Carroll N. Mohen, "Machiavellian Marketing Research," *European Research,* vol. 16 (August 1988), pp. 145–148; Gerald C. Parkhouse, "An Interview with Niccolò Machiavelli," *Business Horizons,* vol. 33 (May–June 1990), pp. 3–6.

61. L. V. Gordon, "Measurement of Bureaucratic Orientation," *Personnel Psychology,* vol. 23 (1970), pp. 1–11.

62. Rogers, *On Becoming a Person.*

63. R. H. Combs and V. Davies, "Self-conception and the Relationship Between High School and College Scholastic Achievement," *Sociology and Social Research,* vol. 50 (1966), pp. 460–471; B. Borislow, "Self-evaluation and Academic Achievement," *Journal of Counseling Psychology,* vol. 9 (1962), pp. 246–254; D. E. Hamachek (ed.), *The Self in Growth, Teaching, and Learning* (Englewood Cliffs, NJ: Prentice-Hall, 1965).

64. Albert Bandura, "Self-Efficacy: Toward a Unifying Theory of Behavioral Change," *Psychological Review,* vol. 84 (1977), pp. 191–215; Albert Bandura, "Self-Efficacy Mechanism in Human Agency," *American Psychologist,* vol. 37 (1982), pp. 122–147; Albert Bandura, N. E. Adams, A. B. Hardy, and G. N. Howells, "Tests of the Generality of Self-Efficacy Theory," *Cognitive Therapy and Research,* vol. 4 (1980), pp. 39–66.

65. John Lane and Peter Herriot, "Self-Ratings, Supervisor Ratings, Positions and Performance," *Journal of Occupational Psychology,* vol. 63 (March 1990), pp. 77–88; Robert Wood, Albert Bandura, and Trevor Bailey, "Mechanisms Governing Organizational Performance in Complex Decision-Making Environments," *Organizational Behavior and Human Decision Processes,* vol. 46 (August 1990), pp. 181–201.

66. Albert Bandura and D. H. Shunk, "Cultivating Confidence, Self-Efficacy, and Intrinsic Interest Through Proximal Self Motivation," *Journal of Personality and Social Psychology,* vol. 41 (1981), pp. 586–598.

67. Marilyn E. Gist, "Self-Efficacy: Implications for Organizational Behavior and Human Resource Management," *Academy of Management Review,* vol. 12 (July 1987), pp. 472–485.

68. David McClelland, *The Achieving Society* (Princeton, N.J.: Van Nostrand, 1961).

69. Rensis Likert, *The Human Organization* (New York: McGraw-Hill, 1967).

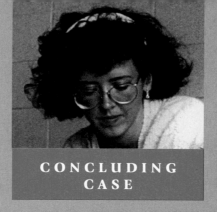

USING POSITIVE PYGMALION IN THE FAST FOOD INDUSTRY

The fast food industry is plagued by high turnover and labor shortages. Many entry-level employees leave because they lack the basic interpersonal skills managers expect of all employees. Several Philadelphia fast food restaurants have found a solution to their turnover and labor shortage problems by using the Pygmalion effect—the influence that one person's expectations can have on another person's behavior.

Project Transition started when a fast food chain in Philadelphia hired a consultant to reduce turnover. He suggested that welfare recipients would be good employees for entry-level positions if they could acquire basic interpersonal skills. Project Transition screens and trains welfare recipients, and places them in full-time jobs with participating restaurants. Experience has shown that the managers of the fast food restaurants adequately explain the technical requirements of the job, but they fail to convey important behavioral expectations.

Therefore, each new employee is paired with a volunteer coach who helps the person make the transition from welfare to employment. The coaches, who are graduate students from business schools, explain to the employees what they are expected to do and how to create favorable expectations in the managers so the managers are willing to give them the help they need to succeed. The training is very simple; they tell the employees to smile instead of frown, how to dress and groom themselves, and to use good posture and positive body language.

These simple interventions improve the managers' perceptions of employees and thus increase their expectations. Because the managers expect them to succeed, they stay and succeed. During the first year of Project Transition, all fifty-seven participants stayed off welfare and remained gainfully employed.

Project Transition aids former welfare recipients by helping them understand how they are perceived by their managers and how they can enhance that perception. As the managers' perceptions improve, their expectations also increase, and consequently the performance of the employees improves to meet those higher expectations.

Questions

1. What is the Pygmalion effect? How does it function?
2. What are some specific daily events that must occur for it to happen?
3. How can managers use the Pygmalion effect as a conscious strategy to increase productivity?
4. To what extent can any of your successes and failures be explained as self-fulfilled prophecies?

Source: Barbara Whitaker Shimko, "Using Positive Pygmalion to Build Your Work Force," *Cornell HRA Quarterly*, vol. 30, no. 3 (November 1989), pp. 91–94; Barbara Whitaker Shimko, "The McPygmalion Effect," *Training and Development Journal*, vol. 44 (June 1990), pp. 64–70.

MEASURING PERSONALITY

PART I: LOCUS OF CONTROL

This is an exercise designed to reveal how certain important events in our society affect different people. Each item consists of a pair of alternatives, lettered *a* and *b*. Please circle the statement that you more strongly believe to be true. Be sure to mark the one you actually believe to be true, rather than the one you think you should choose or the one you would like to be true. This is a measure of personal belief. Obviously there are no right or wrong answers.

Please answer these items carefully, but do not spend too much time on one item. In some instances you may discover that you believe both statements or neither. In such cases, select the one you more strongly believe to be the case. Try to respond to each item independently; do not be influenced by your previous choices.

1. a. Promotions are earned through hard work and persistence.
   b. Getting promoted is really a matter of being a little luckier than the next guy.
2. a. Succeeding in your chosen occupation is mainly a matter of social contacts—knowing the right people.
   b. Succeeding in your chosen profession is mainly a matter of personal competence—how much you know.
3. a. Achieving a successful marriage depends on the devotion and commitment of both partners to each other.
   b. The most important element in a happy marriage is being lucky enough to marry the right person.
4. a. It is silly to think that you can really change another person's basic attitudes.
   b. When I am right, I can convince others.
5. a. In our society, your future earning power depends on your ability.
   b. Making a lot of money is largely a matter of getting the right breaks.

6. a. I have little influence over the way other people behave.
   b. If you know how to deal with people, you can lead them and get them to do what you want.
7. a. In my case, the grades I make are the results of my own efforts; luck has little or nothing to do with them.
   b. Sometimes I feel that I have little control over the grades I get.
8. a. Marriage is largely a gamble that can end in divorce no matter how hard the partners try.
   b. Most divorces could be avoided if both partners were determined to make their marriage work.
9. a. Success in an occupation is mainly a matter of how much effort you put into it.
   b. Success in an occupation is mainly a matter of luck—being in the right place at the right time.
10. a. Often, the way teachers assign grades seems haphazard to me.
    b. In my experience, I have noticed that there is usually a direct connection between how hard I study and the grades I get.
11. a. People like me can change the course of world affairs if we make ourselves heard.
    b. It is only wishful thinking to believe that you can really influence what happens in society at large.
12. a. A great deal that happens to me is probably a matter of chance.
    b. I am the master of my fate.
13. a. Getting along with people is a skill that must be practiced.
    b. It is almost impossible to figure out how to please some people.

Scoring For each of the thirteen items, one statement reflects an internal response and the other statement reflects an external response. For the odd items, the internal response is the first statement (a). For the even items, the internal response is the second statement (b). After completing the exercise, count how many internal choices you have circled. Your score is the total number of internal choices.

This questionnaire is adapted from Julian B. Rotter's internal–external control scale, which measures the extent to which individuals believe that the rewards that come to them are controlled by internal forces, such as their own ability and effort, as opposed to external forces, such as luck, chance, fate, or "the system." In this exercise, extreme externals would score between 0 and 3, while extreme internals would score between 10 and 13.

Question How would you expect extreme internals to respond differently from extreme externals to the following kinds of personnel activities: job search, performance evaluation, a piece-rate incentive system, training and development activities, safety programs, physical fitness centers?

Source: Adapted from Julian B. Rotter, "Internal Control–External Control: A Sampler." *Psychology Today,* vol. 5 (June 1971), p. 42. *See also* Julian B. Rotter, "Generalized Expectancies for Internal vs. External Control of Reinforcement," *Psychological Monographs* (vol. 80, no. 1, Whole no. 609, 1966). Reprinted with permission from Psychology Today Magazine Copyright © 1971 (PT Partners, L.P.)

PART II: MACHIAVELLIAN PERSONALITY

The following statements are part of a Machiavellianism questionnaire measuring attitudes toward power and the ethics of influencing others. There are no right or wrong answers. Answer each question the way you believe, rather than the way you think you should believe.

Each statement is followed by a five-point scale that ranges from strongly disagree to strongly agree (SD = strongly disagree; D = disagree; N = neutral; A = agree; SA = strongly agree). Read each statement and decide the extent to which you agree or disagree with it. Circle the letter that comes closest to indicating your true feelings.

1. Never tell anyone the real reason you did something unless it is useful to do so.   SD D N A SA
2. Most people are basically good and kind.   SD D N A SA
3. The best way to handle people is to tell them what they want to hear.   SD D N A SA
4. Most people who get ahead in the world lead clean, moral lives.   SD D N A SA
5. It is wise to flatter important people.   SD D N A SA
6. All in all, it is better to be humble and honest than to be important and dishonest.   SD D N A SA
7. Generally speaking, people won't work hard unless they are forced to do so.   SD D N A SA
8. Most people are brave.   SD D N A SA
9. It is hard to get ahead without cutting corners here and there.   SD D N A SA
10. It is possible to be good in all respects.   SD D N A SA
11. Anyone who completely trusts anyone else is asking for trouble.   SD D N A SA
12. Honesty is the best policy in all cases.   SD D N A SA

Scoring In these twelve statements, the odd items endorse a Machiavellian personality orientation, while the even items are just the opposite. Therefore, to calculate your score, you need to reverse the scoring of the odd and even items. For the odd items; SD = 1, D = 2, N = 3, A = 4, SA = 5. For the even items; SD = 5, D = 4, N = 3, A = 2, SA = 1. Calculate your score by adding the number of points for the twelve items. The scores will range from a low of 12 to a high of 60.

Questions Compare your score with your classmates' scores, and answer the following questions:

1. Is your score higher or lower than others' scores, and does your score seem "right" to you?

2. How would individuals with high scores and low scores differ in these management activities: promotions, job assignments, salary increases, intergroup conflict, committee assignments, and leadership opportunities?

Source: Items selected from Richard Christie and Florence L. Geis, *Studies in Machiavellianism* (New York: Academic Press, 1970).

Motivation: Learning and Reinforcement

LEARNING OBJECTIVES

After studying this chapter, you should be able to

1. Describe the principles of classical conditioning, operant conditioning, and social learning theory, and explain the differences among them.

2. Explain the differences between primary and secondary rewards and between intrinsic versus extrinsic rewards, and list several examples of each.

3. Identify five reinforcement contingencies for changing behavior, and present an illustration of each.

4. Explain continuous, intermittent, and interval reward schedules, and describe their effects on behavior.

5. Describe the principles of behavior modification, and apply them to the problem of changing behavior within organizations.

6. Describe the effects of feedback and goal setting on motivation, and explain why they influence behavior.

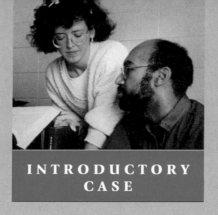

INCREASING PRODUCTIVITY WITH EMPLOYEE CONTESTS

The Maid Bess Corporation, an apparel manufacturer in Salem, Virginia, decided to sponsor a contest among its 370 employees to increase productivity.[1] The contest rewarded outstanding producers with travel or cash awards. Three separate contests were conducted within a two-year period, and each contest lasted three months. The employees, who were already paid on a piece-rate basis, were grouped into six groups based on their average hourly earnings over the previous thirteen weeks' performance. For example, those whose earnings fell between $6 and $6.50 per hour competed in the same contest group. The person in each of the six groups who had the highest productivity level during the three-month contest period won the prize—a trip to the World's Fair or a cash prize.

During the three contest periods, the average productivity rate increased from 83.5 percent to 87.3 percent of standard, which produced an increase of $103,800 in profit. Because the costs of the program were only $1,800, the company realized a sizable return on its investment.

The company also benefited from reduced absenteeism. During periods when the contests were in effect, absenteeism averaged about 5.4 percent, which was noticeably better than the 7.1 percent rate when the contests were not in effect. Even the employees who didn't win benefited from increased productivity, because they received more earnings.

Questions

1. If these contests are so effective and everyone benefits from them, should the company use them more often?

2. Could they be used continuously?

3. Could other companies also benefit from employee contests?

4. What theories of human behavior can be used to answer these questions, and do all these theories produce similar answers?

Motivation is probably the most popular topic in organizational behavior because it involves such crucial questions as "Why do people behave the way they do?" and "How do we motivate employees to perform their jobs?" Many motivation theories address these basic questions. These theories can generally be placed into one of three categories: (1) reinforcement or learning theories, (2) need or content theories, and (3) process or decision-making models. Because so much has been written about motivation, this information has been divided into two chapters. Reinforcement theories are described in this chapter, while content and process theories are described in the following chapter.

The word "motivation" is derived from the Latin word *movere*, which means "to move." In the context of organizational behavior, motivation is what "energizes, directs, and sustains human behavior."[2] Thus, motivation has three basic characteristics. The first characteristic is the amount of energy or effort individuals are willing to exert; those who exert more effort are more highly motivated. The second characteristic is that their effort must be goal directed. The activity should focus on achieving some objective, because motivation is more than just being busy. The third characteristic is that people persist in sustained activity. Highly motivated people will continue in goal-directed efforts for an extended period of time.

THEORIES OF LEARNING AND REINFORCEMENT

Learning is defined as "a relatively permanent change in potential behavior as a result of practice or experience." People are said to have learned something when they consistently exhibit a new behavior over time. Learning is an inferred process, and cannot be observed directly. Instead, we must infer the existence of learning from observing changes in behavior. A change in behavior is an *observable* change in behavior, not just a change in the way people think or feel. Although we typically talk as though learning involves acquiring new insights and knowledge, no learning has occurred unless these new insights and knowledge result in an overt change in behavior.

Because learning is a relatively permanent change in behavior, temporary changes or adaptations to unique situations are not considered learning. The words *practice* and *experience* suggest that behavioral changes are not caused by factors such as biological maturity or chemical changes. Thirteen-year-old boys begin to sing in a deeper tone of voice because of maturity, not because of practice and experience. Likewise, changes in behavior after taking stimulants or depressants are not an indication that learning has occurred.

Learning normally involves some form of practice or experience; however, practice may consist of mentally rehearsing a response so that when it is finally performed it is performed correctly. Defining learning as a relatively permanent change in behavior is intended to exclude the effects of warmup or fatigue. Just because you make lots of errors when you first begin to type or after you have typed for several hours doesn't mean you haven't learned to type. Saying that it is a change in potential behavior acknowledges the fact that an individual may have acquired a new response but does not consistently demonstrate it because of the situation. For example, a receptionist may have learned how to greet customers politely but may choose to be nasty to irate customers.

Theories of learning help to explain why people behave the way they do and how new behaviors are acquired. Consequently, learning theories are also motivation theories, because they explain the forces that energize, direct, and sustain human behavior. The three major learning theories include classical conditioning, operant conditioning, and social cognitive theory. These three theories are also known as *reinforcement theories,* because they explain behavior in terms of the reinforcing consequences of behavior—they explain how people acquire new behaviors and why their present behavior is sustained.

Classical Conditioning

Classical conditioning consists of connecting or pairing a neutral stimulus with a reflexive response. Reflexive responses, also called *respondent behaviors,* consist of responses controlled by the autonomic nervous system, such as blood pressure changes, salivation, and the secretion of adrenalin. These responses are normally caused by specific unconditioned (unlearned) stimuli. For example, the taste of food causes salivation, peeling onions causes eyes to water, and a state of stress causes blood pressure to rise. However, these same responses can be conditioned to otherwise neutral stimuli by repeated pairings or associations of the unconditioned stimuli with the conditioned stimuli.[3]

Establishing Conditioned Responses. The process of establishing a **conditioned response** (CR) is illustrated by the early work of Ivan Pavlov, the noted Russian physiologist who pioneered the early research in classical conditioning. While studying the automatic reflexes associated with digestion in dogs, Pavlov noted that the secretion of saliva and gastric juices were innate unlearned responses caused by the chemical reactions of food. However, salivating at the sight of food was a learned response, and Pavlov succeeded in training the dogs to salivate not only to the sight of food but also to various other signals, such as rotating disks, a metronome, or the sound of a bell. The training process consisted of presenting a dog with meat powder and the sound of a bell at the same time. After repeated pairings of the food with the bell, the dog became conditioned to salivate to the sound of the bell.[4] Exhibit 3.1 illustrates how a **conditioned stimulus** (bell) can become paired with an **unconditioned stimulus** (food) to evoke a conditioned response (salivation).

Classical conditioning is also called **respondent conditioning** or **reflexive conditioning** because the conditioned responses are innate reflexive responses. Some conditioned responses can be acquired quite rapidly with very few pairings of the conditioned and unconditioned stimuli. Conditioned responses also tend to extinguish rather rapidly. After the dog was conditioned to salivate to the sound of the bell, salivation would occur to the sound of the bell alone without the meat powder. However, if the meat powder was not occasionally presented with the sound of the bell, the conditioned response of salivating was soon extinguished. A dog will not continue to salivate endlessly to the sound of the bell if the bell is not periodically accompanied by the presentation of meat powder. However, some reflexive responses, especially those associated with pain, are much more resistant to extinction than others.

EXHIBIT 3.1   Classical Conditioning Process: Pairing a Conditioned
                   Stimulus with a Conditioned Response

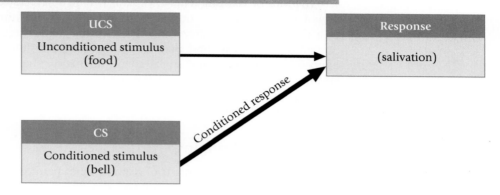

When a reflexive response is conditioned to one stimulus, other similar stimuli will also elicit the response. If a dog is conditioned to salivate to the sound of a bell producing a tone of middle C, it will also salivate to slightly higher or lower tones without further conditioning. This principle is called **stimulus generalization** and explains how we are able to respond to novel situations because of their similarities to familiar ones.

Extinction does not actually destroy a conditioned response. After a period of time, a conditioned stimulus may elicit the conditioned response again even if it has not recently been paired with the unconditioned stimulus. This return of the conditioned response is called *spontaneous recovery*, and it suggests that extinction is some sort of active inhibition or suppression of the conditioned response, not a permanent forgetting or disappearance of the response.

Applications of Classical Conditioning. Classical conditioning has not been discussed as much as operant conditioning, because the study of motivation is primarily concerned with voluntary behaviors. However, several interesting applications of classical conditioning have emerged in recent years, especially in marketing, stress management, and emotional control.

Although the term *classical conditioning* is seldom heard in the field of marketing, its techniques are frequently used. Many advertising campaigns seek to associate a particular product or brand name with a conditioned response. Showing pictures of popcorn, candy, and drinks in theaters is intended to sell more products. Commercials are designed to associate a neutral stimulus such as a new product or a brand name, with another stimulus such as the sound of pleasant music or the sight of an exciting activity to evoke a favorable emotional feeling as a conditioned response. A soft drink should not only taste good but also make you feel the exhilaration of surfing, skiing, or boating through white-water rapids.[5]

Stress, anxiety, and fear are largely responses of the autonomic nervous system that have been classically conditioned to other stimuli. If telephone calls consist of one harassing problem after another, the sound of a ringing telephone can become a conditioned stimulus eliciting high blood pressure. If the telephone continues to ring throughout the day, and most of the calls are unpleasant hassles, the consequence could be chronically high blood pressure. Many stress management programs seek to reduce excessive stress, anxiety, and fear by eliminating the association between the stimulus and the conditioned response.

Emotions are largely influenced by autonomic nervous system responses, which can be classically conditioned to otherwise neutral stimuli. The classical conditioning process is the same for positive emotions such as love and satisfaction, as for negative emotions such as hatred and anger. Job satisfaction research has demonstrated that a pay increase not only evokes a positive emotion toward pay, but also greater satisfaction with the supervisor who administered the pay increase.[6] Negative emotions such as hatred and anger often create difficulty in solving intergroup conflicts. These classically conditioned negative responses sometimes need to be eliminated before the work groups can function amicably together.

Operant Conditioning

Operant conditioning focuses on the learning of voluntary behaviors—behaviors controlled by the muscle system of the body. Consequently, operant conditioning involves a much wider range of potential behavior than does classical conditioning. The term **operant conditioning** is derived from the idea that people learn to operate on their environment to achieve desired consequences. People learn to repeat certain behaviors because they are rewarded by the environment, and these voluntary behaviors are called *operant responses.*

Stimulus–response Bonds. Operant conditioning is the process of reinforcing a response that is made in the presence of a stimulus. This process is diagramed this way:

Stimulus–response bonds are created by the consequences of the response. In operant conditioning, an environmental stimulus (S) is followed by a response (R), which is followed by an environmental consequence that can be either a positive or negative reinforcer. The response is said to be "instrumental" in the receipt of the consequence, which explains why operant conditioning is also called *instrumental conditioning.*[7]

According to operant conditioning theory, if a response occurs in the presence of a stimulus, and this response is reinforced, this increases the probability that on future occasions the same response will be made in the presence of similar stimuli. An important aspect of this definition is the word *probability.* The stimulus does not cause the response, and it is not certain that an operant response will be made after the stimulus is presented. Operant conditioning is a probabilistic model, which simply means that the probability of a response in a given situation is more likely if it has been positively reinforced in the past.

The principles of operant conditioning are similar to the law of effect proposed in 1911 by Edward L. Thorndike (1874–1949). The **law of effect** states that "of several responses made to the same situation, those which are accompanied or closely followed by satisfaction (reinforcement) . . . will be more likely to occur, those which are accompanied or closely followed by discomfort (punishment) . . . would be less likely to occur."[8] In essence, the law of effect claims that behaviors leading

to positive, or pleasurable, outcomes will tend to be repeated, while behaviors leading to negative outcomes, or punishment, tend to be avoided.

The principles of operant conditioning have been amply demonstrated in thousands of experimental studies using many different organisms including humans
and animals, especially rats and pigeons. So much of the work on operant conditioning was pioneered by B. F. Skinner that the experimental chamber where rats
and pigeons are tested has come to be known as a Skinner box. A Skinner box typically consists of three glass walls to observe the animal, a fourth wall containing a
food box, a device for making a response (such as a lever for rats to press or a key
for pigeons to peck), and a wire grid floor to stand on. This experimental chamber
allowed the researchers to eliminate extraneous environmental stimuli and carefully reinforce a specific operant response. The basic principles of operant conditioning so amply demonstrated in animal studies have been extensively replicated
with human subjects.[9]

Stimulus Generalization and Discrimination.   In a typical organization, employees are simultaneously bombarded with dozens of stimuli. Even a relatively calm
office environment contains countless stimuli such as lighting, color of walls,
sound of typewriters, conversation at the next desk, humming of the air-condi-
tioner, odor of perfume, and the feel of clothes that fit too tightly.

Within this massive stimulus environment, the telephone rings and the
employee is expected to respond to this unique stimulus by making a unique
response. In this situation, the ringing of the telephone is considered a **discriminative stimulus** because the person is required to discriminate the sound of the
phone from all the other environmental stimuli and make a differential response.
Helping people identify the discriminative stimulus is an important part of operant conditioning and a crucial part of many training and development programs.
For example, basketball players must be trained to recognize a teammate breaking toward the basket as the discriminative stimulus for the response of passing
the ball, without being distracted by thousands of screaming fans and other distracting stimuli.

Someone who has learned to discriminate the sound of a ringing telephone
should be able to recognize a slightly different ringing sound and still make the correct response because of the principle of *stimulus generalization*. If the new stimulus
is radically different, however, then a response will probably not be emitted until
the individual learned to associate it with the new response. For example, most people would have difficulty learning to respond to a telephone that ticked like a clock
when someone phoned.

Operant Responses.   Individuals have the capacity to produce a wide variety of
potential responses, called a "response repertoire." Different organisms have different response repertoires. For example, rats cannot be trained to fly, and pigeons cannot be trained to dribble a basketball and shoot free throws like humans.
Nevertheless, animals have been trained to make remarkable responses that are
both astonishing and entertaining. For example, chickens have been trained to play
poker, ducks have been trained to play the piano, and porpoises have been trained
to sing. People have been entertained by a variety of animal shows starring farm
animals such as pigs, dogs, and horses, and aquatic animals such as whales, wal-
ruses, and porpoises.[10]

Chaining. Most of the responses we make are not simple responses to a discriminative stimulus. Many of the things we do are far more complex behaviors. We usually make a series of responses, each one altering the environment and setting the stage for the next response. For example, in shooting a lay-up the player dribbles the basketball several times while running toward the basket, jumps, and then shoots. Each response of running, dribbling, jumping, and shooting changes the stimulus environment and calls for the next response. Frequently only the last response of seeing the ball go through the basket is reinforced. This process of stringing together stimulus–response bonds is called *chaining* and is diagramed like this:

$$S \longrightarrow R \longrightarrow S \longrightarrow R \longrightarrow S \longrightarrow R$$

The concept of chaining is particularly important in the design of training programs. Rather than an activity in which learners are expected to perform a complex series of responses, the task is divided into smaller steps and each stimulus–response association is presented to the learners separately. As the learners practice each response, they are reinforced and receive feedback on their performance. Gradually the responses are combined until the learners can perform the entire complex response, and reinforcement is provided only for the final response.

Shaping. Shaping is the process of acquiring a unique response by reinforcing closer and closer approximations of it. This process is also called the **"method of successive approximations."** During the early stages of learning, any response that remotely resembles the correct response is reinforced. However, as learning continues, only the responses that most closely approximate the correct response are reinforced. The process of shaping is used extensively in animal training such as in teaching porpoises to sing and ducks to play the piano. At first the porpoise is reinforced for making any sound, but gradually the sounds must become closer and closer approximations to the desired sound before reinforcement is given. The process of shaping also occurs in human learning, especially in the development of skills such as in learning to ice skate, dance, shoot a jump shot, or operate a machine.

Feedback. Performance feedback is a necessary prerequisite to learning. One of the early studies on the importance of feedback was conducted by Thorndike in which blindfolded students were asked to draw a 3-inch line.[11] Students who received no feedback regarding the lengths of their lines did not improve in their ability to draw 3-inch lines even after several thousand trials. Although less variability in the lengths of the lines existed after many trials, the students were no closer to the goal after thousands of trials than at the start. However, significant improvements were noted in the lengths of the lines of the blindfolded students who were told whether their lines were too long or too short.

Feedback improves performance not only by helping employees correct their mistakes but also by providing reinforcement for learning. Knowledge of results is a positive form of reinforcement by itself. Learning activities have more intrinsic interest when performance feedback is available. Performance feedback should do more than tell employees whether they were right or wrong; it should also tell them how they can avoid making mistakes in the future.[12] Merely informing individuals of their incorrect responses can be very frustrating for those who want to know why they were wrong. Studies on feedback have concluded that it is a valuable resource for individuals and it is perceived as especially important to employees who are new, who face ambiguous situations, who have ambiguous roles, and who are highly involved in their work.[13]

In general, knowledge of results is essential for learning, and the sooner this knowledge comes after the learner's response the better. Studies in animal learning suggest that the ideal timing of the feedback is almost immediately after the response has been made.[14] Some training programs are able to provide this kind of ideal feedback, but not all. Management development programs typically fail to provide any form of feedback, mainly because the managers are not given opportunities to respond until they are back on the job.

Social Cognitive Theory

Social cognitive theory developed during the 1960s and 1970s, primarily as a result of the research of Albert Bandura and others who recognized the need to consider cognitive thought processes in understanding human behavior.[15] Social cognitive theory, which was first called "social learning theory," also developed in part as a reaction against operant conditioning's refusal to consider thinking processes or any other psychological functions that could not be openly observed.

A basic proposition central to both operant conditioning and social cognitive theory is that behavior is influenced by its consequences. Responses that are rewarded are more likely to occur in the future, while responses that are punished probably will be terminated.

Reciprocal Determinism. One important difference between operant conditioning and social cognitive theory concerns the degree to which individuals are controlled by the environment. According to operant conditioning, behavior is environmentally determined: the environment contains the cues for responding as well as the reinforcement; and if the environment changes, the behavior of individuals will also change. Although this position, called *environmental determinism*, is a bit oversimplified, it illustrates why so much concern exists about the possibility of cultural engineering to control the behavior of people and the loss of freedom and dignity that might accompany it.

According to social cognitive theory, behavior is determined by more than just the environment; the environment, behavior, and personal factors such as skills, values, and physical limitations interact to influence each other. This interaction, called *reciprocal determinism*, is illustrated in Exhibit 3.2. According to reciprocal determinism, behavior, personality, and the environment operate as interlocking determinants of one another. Behavior is influenced by the environment, but the environment is also influenced by behavior. Individuals have the capacity to change their environment if they don't like the effect it is having on their personality and behavior. The strength of these three influences (behavior, personality, and environment) vary over time and in various settings. At times environmental factors may exercise powerful constraints on behavior while at other times personal factors may override or alter environmental conditions.[16]

Vicarious Learning. Another important difference between operant conditioning and social cognitive theory concerns the analysis of thought processes. Social cognitive theory emphasizes the importance of **vicarious learning,** symbolic thinking,

EXHIBIT 3.2 **Reciprocal Determinism**

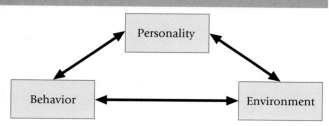

and self-regulatory processes in understanding human behavior. Vicarious learning, also called **imitative learning,** is the process of learning by observing others—watching how they behave, and seeing the consequences that they experience from their behavior. An enormous amount of human learning occurs through observational learning. By observing other people perform complex behaviors, we learn quickly, and sometimes with very few errors, how to competently perform the same behaviors. Imitative learning is especially superior to trial-and-error learning when mistakes can produce costly or even fatal consequences. When teaching children to swim, adolescents to drive a car, or novice medical students to perform surgery, a trainer cannot rely on trial-and-error learning or simply wait to reinforce correct responses.

Behavior modeling is an extremely useful training technique for helping trainees acquire a variety of responses. Training that contains a clear demonstration usually leads to faster learning with fewer errors.[17] Cognitive modeling is also an effective training method for improving innovative problem-solving skills and idea generation. A study of 60 managers compared their problem-solving skills after two types of training: one method involved lecture and practice alone, while the other method included cognitive modeling with vicarious reinforcement of the model's performance. Participants in the modeling training significantly outperformed those in the lecture condition in both the quantity and divergence of ideas generated.[18]

Another distinguishing feature of social cognitive theory is the idea that people can regulate their own behavior. People can effectively control their own behavior by arranging environmental rewards, by generating cognitive supports, and by producing consequences for their own actions. For example, students who think their poor academic performances are caused by a lack of study can decide to do something about it. The student can find a quiet place to study, remove all distracting materials such as magazines and newspapers, record the hours spent each day in studying, set daily study goals, and give a friend $6 to be returned at the rate of $1 per day only if the goals for that day are met. Although individual behavior is influenced by the reinforcers that exist in the environment, people have the ability to change their environment both physically and psychologically so that they are reinforced for doing what they want to do.

Symbolic Learning. The use of symbols either as words, pictures, or mental images greatly facilitates learning. Humans use symbols to represent events, to analyze conscious experiences, to communicate with others at any distance in time and space, to imagine, to create, to plan, and to engage in purposeful action. The use of symbols also contributes to the effectiveness of imitative learning. When a model is present, the trainee can observe the model and immediately try to reproduce the same behavior. But when a model is absent, the trainee must rely on symbols such as mental images, verbal statements, or written descriptions to reproduce the behavior. Without symbols, humans would be unable to engage in reflective thought or foresightful planning. Even conducting a careful analysis of the present environment requires being able to use symbols to represent objects, events, and relationships. According to social cognitive theory, symbolic activities cannot be ignored in understanding human behavior.

Our ability to use symbols presents an important implication for assessing the effects of practice on learning: according to social cognitive theory, practice is not as important as thinking in some learning situations. Operant conditioning claims that practice and repetition are necessary to help trainees learn the correct responses; learned behavior must be overlearned to ensure smooth performance and a minimum of forgetting at a later date. Social cognitive theory, however, claims that practice is not especially necessary for learning certain behaviors. Although practice may be necessary for developing motor skills, it is not important for behavior that is learned symbolically through "central processing" of the response information. Learning how to produce an income statement, for example, does not require practicing each component activity. Instead, it involves central processing, using symbols to know how to handle cash, accounts receivable, debts, and other items. Many human behaviors are performed with little or no practice. Studies of imitative behavior have shown that after watching models perform a novel behavior, observers can later describe it with considerable accuracy and, given appropriate incentives, they can often reproduce it exactly on the first trial.

REINFORCEMENT CONTINGENCIES

Reinforcement theories (both operant conditioning and social cognitive theory) claim that behavior is a function of the consequences associated with the behavior. Very simply, people tend to do things that lead to positive consequences and avoid doing things that lead to unpleasant consequences. The relationship between behavior and its consequences is called a *reinforcement contingency*. Knowing the reinforcement contingencies associated with a person's behavior allows you to diagnose and predict that person's behavior. To change behavior requires a change in the reinforcement contingencies.

Reinforcers

Five of the major reinforcement contingencies are described here, along with a description of reinforcers.

Positive and Negative Reinforcers. The consequences associated with a response may be either positive, negative, or a combination of both. Positive reinforcers are desirable consequences that people normally report as pleasant and enjoyable. Negative reinforcers are negative consequences and are described as undesirable and disliked. Negative reinforcers are also referred to as **aversive stimuli.**

These definitions of positive and negative reinforcers are not acceptable to a strict behaviorist, because they rely on subjective judgments to decide whether a consequence is pleasant or aversive. Strict behaviorists define positive and negative reinforcers according to their influence on behavior. Anything that increases the probability of a response is a positive reinforcer, and anything that decreases the probability of a response is a negative reinforcer or punisher. These operational definitions are especially useful for conducting research on animal behavior, because they do not require behavioral scientists to decide what is pleasant or aversive.

Primary and Secondary Reinforcers. Reinforcers can also be categorized as primary and secondary rewards. **Primary rewards** are those associated with physiological needs such as food, water, sex, sleep, and removal of pain. These rewards are satisfying because of their association with physical comforts and survival. They do not have to be learned. Food is innately satisfying to a hungry person, and sex is innately pleasurable. However, various cultural forces and personal experiences influence the strength and attraction of these primary rewards. For example, food may be more reinforcing and the threat of going without food more punishing to someone who has experienced periods of starvation.

Secondary rewards are learned or acquired reinforcers. Examples of secondary reinforcers include social approval, money, recognition, and pride in craftsmanship. These reinforcers are not innate; an individual is not born with a need for recognition or a desire for money. Furthermore, these reinforcers may not contribute to physical comfort. In fact, the hard work and effort required to obtain secondary rewards might be physically painful.

Calling them *secondary* and saying that they are acquired rather than innate does not mean that their influence on behavior is less than that of primary rewards. Indeed, just the opposite seems to be true; secondary rewards usually have a much greater influence on day-to-day behavior than primary reinforcers. Social approval, for example, has been shown to be an extremely powerful secondary reward, especially during adolescence, that has a major impact on behavior and often overrides the effects of other reinforcers.[19] Because of their desire to be approved and accepted by their peers, most teenagers allow peer pressures to guide their behavior even if it is physically uncomfortable, and sometimes socially illegal. Clothing and jewelry are determined by what is socially approved, not by what is comfortable. Diet fads and the unhealthy conditions of anorexia and bulimia can occur when the desire for social approval is more rewarding than other primary rewards.

Primary rewards are ineffective motivators after people become satiated. For example, after people have eaten they are no longer motivated to do something for food. However, secondary rewards do not cause satiation; instead, they tend to become increasingly reinforcing the more they are used. People do not get tired of being praised and complimented. In fact, as people receive increasing amounts of praise and recognition, they tend to place a higher value on praise and recognition and they are more influenced by them in the future.

Money is a generalized secondary reinforcer—its affects can be generalized to numerous behaviors.[20] Praise and recognition are generalized secondary reinforcers that have been used extensively to influence job performance. By carefully constructing the presentations of these rewards, their strength can be increased and their effects can be generalized to other related behaviors. For example, a twenty-five-year service pin can be a very powerful secondary reinforcer, not because of its economic value, but because of the symbolic meaning attached to it.[21]

Another significant form of secondary reinforcement comes from the intrinsic satisfaction people receive from their work. Intrinsic feelings of pride and craftsmanship are very important to most people, especially those with a strong work ethic. Managers should learn what rewards mean the most to which employees. A meaningless reward may have the same effect as no reward at all. Effective reward systems should be flexible, visible, and reviewed regularly, and employees need to know exactly what they must do to earn a specific reward.[22]

Extrinsic and Intrinsic Reinforcers. When analyzing reinforcers, it is also useful to distinguish between extrinsic and intrinsic rewards. This distinction is useful because managers only have direct control over extrinsic rewards in terms of the level of rewards and how they are distributed.

Extrinsic rewards are the rewards people receive from others; they are administered by external sources such as co-workers, supervisors, or the organization. Financial compensation is clearly the most popular form of extrinsic rewards, including wages, salaries, bonuses, profit sharing, and incentive plans. Promotions to higher jobs and recognition from peers are also extrinsic rewards, because they too are administered by external sources. Even though these rewards are not physical and tangible, they are classified as extrinsic rewards because they are administered by others. Compliments from friends and supervisors are likewise extrinsic rewards.

Intrinsic reinforcers are associated with the job itself and are the positive feelings people derive from the work they do. Intrinsic rewards are self-administered and are based on the personal values of each individual. For example, people who have a strong work ethic will derive satisfaction from successfully performing an outstanding job. People who value being considerate and helpful will derive intrinsic satisfaction from helping someone in need. People who have a high need for achievement feel rewarded when they achieve challenging goals.

The relationship between extrinsic and intrinsic rewards has been closely examined because in some situations it appears that extrinsic rewards destroy the effects of intrinsic rewards. For example, in a laboratory study when students were asked to perform an intrinsically satisfying task of solving puzzles, they tended to persist in working on the puzzles after the experiment was over longer if they were not paid for their participation. It was suggested that extrinsic rewards in the form of money tended to divert the students' interest from the intrinsically rewarding nature of the tasks themselves. The implications of this study were that people should not receive pay incentives for performing a job since pay incentives destroy the intrinsic satisfaction inherent in a job.[23]

Subsequent research, however, has failed to show that extrinsic rewards necessarily inhibit intrinsic rewards, especially on actual jobs where people expect to be paid for their employment. If the extrinsic rewards are exorbitant sums that make people feel bribed or paid off, the extrinsic rewards may contribute to destroying the intrinsic satisfaction. However, if extrinsic rewards appear to be fair and equitable and based on a careful assessment of performance, the extrinsic rewards do not destroy intrinsic rewards. Instead, the extrinsic rewards combine with intrinsic rewards to create higher levels of motivation and task satisfaction.[24]

People obviously derive many rewards from work, most of which are learned rewards. To predict how an individual will behave in a given situation, we must

APPLYING ORGANIZATIONAL BEHAVIOR
ACROSS CULTURES

Reinforcing Employee Suggestions

Why do the employees of Japanese companies submit so many more suggestions than U.S. employees? They don't submit 20 to 30 *percent* more—they submit twenty to thirty *times* more.

In a typical U.S. company, the average employee submits about two suggestions per year. In a Japanese company, it is not uncommon for employees to submit and implement between forty and a hundred new suggestions per person each year. Consider some of the data provided by the Japan Human Relations Association on the number of suggestions per employee per year:

Company	Number of Suggestions	Number of Employees	Number per Employee
Nissan	1,393,745	48,849	38.5
Toyota	2,648,710	55,578	47.6
Matsushita	6,446,935	81,000	79.6
Mazda	3,025,853	23,929	126.5
Tohoku Oki	734,044	881	833.2

An important principle in designing any motivation program is "What you reward is what you get." A corollary to this principle is "If you don't reward it, you don't get it." These principles help to explain the enormous differences in the number of creative suggestions submitted by employees.

An examination of a large Japanese consumer electronics firm explains how submitting suggestions is rewarded both individually and as a group with powerful intrinsic incentives. Monetary incentives are awarded for most ideas, but the awards are small. The most important incentives are intrinsic satisfactions from creating and implementing new ideas and the praise and recognition of team members. Employees are members of quality circle teams that meet regularly to explore ways to improve the company. Individuals are also encouraged to submit their own ideas to the employee suggestion system. The team gets credit every time one of its members submits a suggestion. Major celebrations are held by top management each year honoring teams and their members who have accomplished significant innovations. All new employees are trained the first day on the job about the importance of the suggestion system and how it works. Managers and supervisors are trained to work closely with employees to help them find and solve problems.

Sources: Min Basadur, "Managing Creativity: A Japanese Model," *Academy of Management Executive*, vol. 6 (1992), pp. 29–41.

know all the significant rewards and the attractiveness of each reward. In most instances, however, people are confronted with conflicting rewards, which makes it difficult to predict how they will behave.

Positive Reinforcement Contingencies

A **positive reinforcement contingency** consists of providing a positive reinforcement after the correct response has been emitted. When the pigeons made the correct response by pecking at the disk, they were reinforced with a kernel of grain. The effect of a positive reinforcement contingency is to increase the probability of the response. Consequently, the pigeon was more likely to continue pecking at the disk.

Most things we do in life are the result of positive reinforcement contingencies; the majority of our behaviors occur because positive consequences are associated with them. We go to movies, attend sports events, and watch TV because it is entertaining; we attend parties and visit with friends because it is fun; we eat, sleep, and rest because it makes us feel better; we study to get good grades; and we work to earn money. When you pass a friend in the hall, you smile and nod, because you have learned that this friendly gesture increases the probability that your friend will also smile and say hello—a pleasant experience. When we carefully examine our behavior, we usually find that most of it can be explained by some form of positive reinforcement.[25]

It is easy to underestimate the effects of positive reinforcement contingencies because so many of the situations where we think they exist do not produce high levels of motivation. A careful examination of these situations usually indicates that the relationship between behavior and the reward is very weak. Compensation programs illustrate this problem. Although being paid for work is a positive contingency, most employees do not think their pay is closely associated with their performance. Except for a few jobs that use direct incentives, such as commission sales or piece-rate incentives, pay is not directly tied to performance. Consequently, we tend to underestimate the potential effect of compensation on employee performance. Supervisor compliments and the recognition of others are recognized as powerful reinforcers, probably because they are more closely tied to performance.

Punishment Contingencies

A **punishment contingency** consists of administering a punisher or an aversive stimulus after the response has been made. In animal studies, punishment contingencies were usually created by administering an electrical shock after the animal made a response. The effect of a punishment contingency is to decrease the probability that the response will be emitted on future occasions.

Punishment contingencies also occur frequently in everyday life, because we are surrounded by many forms of physical or psychological pain. When children touch things they are not supposed to, their parents slap their hands. When employees make mistakes, their supervisors reprimand them. When drivers change lanes without signaling and looking, they may either cause an accident or provoke a blaring horn from another driver. When people run on an icy sidewalk, they may fall down.

Learning theorists claim that punishment is not the most effective method of changing behavior. Several reasons have been proposed to explain why punishment might not be effective.[26]

1. Punishment is only effective when the threat of punishment is present. If the only reason employees do not engage in horseplay is because the supervisor is there to discipline them, the horseplay is likely to begin as soon as the supervisor leaves.

2. Punishment indicates what is wrong but not what is right. One wrong response might be replaced with another wrong response. When students are criticized for coming late to class, they might choose to avoid class altogether the next time they are behind schedule. When individuals are criticized for attempting to resolve interpersonal conflicts, they may decide to quit talking, and the interpersonal conflict continues to smolder.

3. Punishment may eliminate both good and bad behavior if both behaviors are tied together. For example, trying to help a co-worker might be seen as

"getting in the way" and result in punishment. Employees may feel their helpfulness was being punished.

4. Punishment may cause fixated behavior because the individual's thinking becomes fixed on past errors rather than on searching for a correct solution. For example, a new employee maybe so humiliated in a public meeting after incorrectly giving the name of his new department that he makes the same mistake again because the humiliation prevents him from thinking of anything else.

5. Punishment creates a negative feeling toward the punishing agent, such as a supervisor, and interferes with relationships regarding other issues. When supervisors are highly critical and constantly harass subordinates or when parents constantly criticize children, they tend to create such a negative emotional feeling that even friendly comments and legitimate requests are ignored.

6. Punishment is sometimes a reward, because any form of attention is better than being ignored. Grade school teachers are often surprised to find that rowdy students seem to enjoy being disciplined, because it tends to raise their status in the eyes of their peers.

Escape Contingencies

An **escape contingency** is a situation where an aversive stimulus is present, and the individual makes a response to terminate or eliminate it. In animal studies, for example, a loud buzzer or electric shock was presented to the animal, and the animal was required to make a response to eliminate it. The effect of an escape contingency is to increase the probability of a response; the individual does not like the aversive stimulus and acts to remove it.

Escape contingencies are illustrated by many of the little annoying things in life. For example, when the wind is blowing unpleasantly through the window, we close it; we fasten our safety belts to eliminate the sound of a buzzer; we go to the kitchen to get a bottle of milk to feed a crying baby; we stumble out of bed to turn off an obnoxious, irritating alarm clock; we take antacid to ease stomach discomfort; and we complete a weekly report to silence a nagging supervisor. Advertising that emphasizes the removal of aversive stimuli capitalizes on escape contingencies.[27]

An escape contingency tends to increase the probability of responding, but the response normally is only a minimal act to terminate the aversive condition. When employees are demoted or placed on probation for poor performance, for example, they improve their performance just enough to be promoted or removed from probation. Unless other reinforcers are present, they are not motivated to achieve outstanding performance; instead, they are content with minimally acceptable performance.

Avoidance Contingencies

An **avoidance contingency** consists of making a response to avoid an aversive consequence. If the response is not made, the aversive consequence is experienced. In animal studies, for example, a light may indicate that within a matter of seconds the animal will receive an unpleasant electrical shock unless it responds by pressing a lever.

Some illustrations of avoidance contingencies are taking an umbrella to avoid getting drenched, studying late at night to avoid failing an exam, completing a report to avoid being humiliated by a supervisor, and paying your phone bill to avoid having your phone service cut off. Like an escape contingency, avoidance contingencies are based on a motive of avoiding failure or pain, rather than seeking success and rewards. Therefore, even though avoidance contingencies tend to increase the probability of a response, the response tends to be the least possible effort needed to avoid the unpleasant consequence.

Extinction Contingencies

An **extinction contingency** consists of not reinforcing a response. When the response is made, the individual receives no reinforcement, either positive or negative. This contingency is based on the premise that people do what they are reinforced for doing. Behaviors that are not reinforced are extinguished; in other words, not displayed any more. In animal studies, extinction contingencies are created by discontinuing any form of reinforcement and observing how long the animal continues to perform without any form of reinforcement. Some responses are much more persistent than others, depending on the schedules of reinforcement. In time, nonreinforced responses are terminated.

Examples of extinction contingencies include ignoring students who talk without raising their hands, failing to notice good performance from employees who have attempted to do a good job, and not responding to written reports. An extinction contingency tends to decrease the probability of responding. If written reports are continually ignored, before long they will no longer be prepared.

These five reinforcement contingencies, summarized in Exhibit 3.3, describe the major approaches to changing behavior. They indicate the kinds of consequences that should follow behavior in order to increase or decrease the probability of a response in the future.

EXHIBIT 3.3	Summary of Reinforcement Contingencies

Label	Effect on Behavior	Nature of the Contingency
1. Positive	increases	Correct response is followed by a positive reinforcing stimulus.
2. Punishment	decreases	Behavior is followed by an aversive stimulus.
3. Escape	increases	An aversive stimulus is present and the correct response terminates it.
4. Avoidance	increases	An aversive event will occur unless the correct response is made.
5. Extinction	decreases	The behavior is ignored. No reinforcement is associated with the response.

REWARD SCHEDULES

The timing of the reinforcement also influences behavior. Reinforcers are most effective when they occur immediately after a response, but not necessarily after each response. Delayed reinforcement tends to lose its reinforcing effect. If reinforcement is delayed too long, it might be associated with some other response and lose its effect altogether. Immediate reinforcement is especially important for learning new behaviors. New behavior can be learned faster if the learner receives immediate performance feedback and reinforcement. After the response has been learned, however, every response does not have to be reinforced. In fact, intermittent schedules of reinforcement are often more effective in maintaining high levels of responding.[28]

A reinforcement schedule shows how often the correct response is reinforced. There are three major reinforcement schedules: continuous, intermittent, and interval.

Continuous Reward Schedules

A **continuous reward schedule** reinforces each correct response. Each time the person makes the correct response, it is reinforced. Most of our day-to-day behavior is maintained on a continuous reinforcement schedule. Every time we push the knob on the drinking fountain, we get a drink; when we push the horn, it honks; if we twist the knob, the door opens; when we turn the key, the car starts; when we pick up the phone, we get a dial tone.

Continuous reinforcement schedules tend to produce a steady rate of performance as long as reinforcement continues to follow every response. However, a high frequency of reinforcement may lead to early satiation. In animal studies, for example, pigeons would develop a fairly consistent rate of response when each response was reinforced on a continuous reinforcement schedule. However, after many reinforcements the response declined, because the pigeon was apparently no longer hungry.

When reinforcement is terminated, behaviors that have been maintained on a continuous reinforcement schedule tend to extinguish rapidly. If you twist the knob on the drinking fountain and nothing comes out, you will probably conclude that the water has been turned off temporarily. Rather than continuing to turn the knob, you will probably turn the knob another time or two to make certain that it doesn't work, and then leave until you think the water has been turned on again.

In training programs, continuous reinforcement schedules are ideal during the early training periods when learners are attempting to acquire a new response. Continuous reward schedules provide immediate feedback on performance to help the learners evaluate their performance and correct their mistakes.

Intermittent Reinforcement Schedules

An **intermittent reinforcement schedule** occurs when only a portion of the correct responses are reinforced. Only every nth response is reinforced, which explains why they are also called "partial reward schedules." However, n can be either a fixed or a variable number.

Fixed Ratio Reinforcement Schedules. If *n is* a fixed number, the reinforcement schedule is called a **"fixed ratio schedule."** Here a fixed number of responses must be made before a reinforcement occurs. Fixed ratio schedules are easy to construct in animal studies by requiring the pigeon to peck at a disk five times before being reinforced. In organizational life, however, fixed ratio schedules are rarely observed. Some piece-rate incentive plans and commission sales programs are fixed ratio schedules where a dozen units must be produced and submitted, or three subscriptions must be sold before the order forms can be submitted.

Fixed ratio schedules tend to produce a vigorous and steady rate of response that is typically a little higher than continuous reward schedules. Since the number of responses being reinforced is less, the individuals tend to perform at a higher rate to obtain higher levels of reinforcement. Like a continuous reinforcement schedule, behaviors maintained on fixed ratio schedules tend to extinguish quite rapidly when reinforcement is terminated.

Variable Ratio Reinforcement Schedules. If *n* is a variable number, the reinforcement schedule is called a **"variable ratio schedule."** Here a varying or random number of responses must be made before reinforcement occurs.

Most social reinforcers are administered on a variable ratio schedule. Employees never know for certain whether their outstanding performance will be recognized, but they have learned from past experience that occasionally it will be. Sales also tend to occur on a random basis, so that sales representatives are reinforced on a variable ratio schedule in making sales. One plan for applying a variable ratio schedule to salespeople involves the use of a token reward system. They receive tokens for each sale equivalent to the dollar value of the sales. The tokens are deposited into a computerized video machine that uses a random number-generating program to select a winner after a given number of tokens are deposited. A wide range of rewards can be used with this reward system.[29]

Variable ratio schedules tend to produce a very high rate of response that is vigorous, steady, and resistant to extinction. Variable ratio schedules are especially effective in maintaining behavior long after the reinforcement has been terminated. Games of chance such as bingo and slot machines are excellent illustrations of variable ratio reinforcement schedules. For example, people play slot machines for long periods of time even though they are infrequently reinforced. In fact, most people who play slot machines know they will go broke if they play long enough. To comprehend the power of variable ratio schedules, remember that playing slot machines is a very repetitive (that is, boring) activity according to industrial engineering standards. Nevertheless, many people pay to play them in an atmosphere where the noise and air pollution might not meet acceptable industrial requirements.

Interval Schedules

In some situations, the timing of a reinforcer is based on an interval of time that can be of either fixed or variable length.

Fixed Interval Schedules. With a **fixed interval schedule,** the first response after a fixed period of time is reinforced. In animal studies, for example, a pigeon may be required to wait for a period of time, such as one minute, before any responses are reinforced. Responses made before the one minute ends are ignored. The most popular example of a fixed interval schedule is a weekly or monthly paycheck. How-

APPLYING ORGANIZATIONAL BEHAVIOR
IN THE NEWS

The Excitement of Variable Ratio Reinforcement

CNN Television game shows use variable ratio reinforcement schedules to create the excitement and glamour that attracts regular viewers. In animal studies, variable ratio reinforcement schedules consistently lead to high levels of responding, and the behavior persists long after the reinforcement is terminated. The effects of variable ratio reinforcement schedules help explain the popularity of TV game shows.

The king of TV game shows is Mark Goodson. In the 1940s, Goodson moderated a successful radio game show called "Pop the Question." In 1946, he met Bill Todd and together they produced such winning favorites as "What's My Line," "Password," and "Match Game," plus TV's longest-running game show—"The Price Is Right." Although Bill Todd died in 1979, Mark Goodson Productions continues to produce successful game shows and some of them, such as "Family Feud," are even syndicated in foreign countries.

Some game shows are not successful. Goodson estimates that only one in five of his shows actually succeeds. Success is measured by television ratings, and game shows must attract regular viewers week after week to survive. Successful game shows use a combination of knowledge, skill, and luck. The shows are spontaneous and do not follow a script, the participants are real people who are usually selected at random, and the reinforcements are usually substantial but uncertain rewards. The television audience vicariously participates in the tension and excitement of both the players and the studio audience. The variable ratio reinforcements are a central source of the tension and excitement.

Source: CNN *Pinnacle* news programming.

ever, this illustration has to be treated somewhat cautiously because even though the pay comes only after a specified interval of time, employees are expected to perform during that period. A failure to perform might result in being fired. Therefore, a weekly salary only partially illustrates a fixed interval schedule.

Fixed interval schedules tend to produce an uneven response pattern that varies from a very slow, lethargic response rate immediately after being reinforced to a very fast, vigorous response rate immediately preceding reinforcement. This pattern of responding can be illustrated by a monthly board-of-directors meeting. The reinforcements to managers occur on a fixed interval schedule once each month. Prior to each board meeting, managers are frantically gathering data, preparing reports, and supervising their staffs as they work ten and twelve hours per day. After the board meeting, however, their rate of activity declines precipitously and they work only two or three hours each day to answer their mail. The same response pattern is observed in the study habits of students. Much more reading occurs just before each exam.

Variable Interval Schedules. When the interval is of a varying or random length of time, the reinforcement schedule is called a **"variable interval schedule."** Again, responses made during the interval of time are ignored, only the first correct response after the end of the variable interval is reinforced. Conceptually, variable interval schedules are different from variable ratio schedules since one depends on an interval of varying time, while the other depends on a varying number of responses. To the person being reinforced, however, these schedules are essentially

**EXHIBIT 3.4   Schedules of Reinforcement and
                        Their Effects on Behavior**

1. *Continuous reinforcement schedule.* Reinforcement follows every correct response.
   - Produces a steady rate of performance as long as reinforcement continues to follow every response.
   - High frequency of reinforcement may lead to early satiation.
   - Behavior extinguishes rapidly when reinforcement is terminated.
   - Best schedule for teaching new behavior.

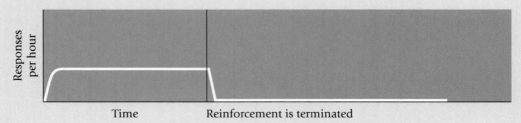

2. *Fixed ratio (FR)* A fixed number of responses must be made before a reinforcement occurs.
   - Tends to produce a vigorous and steady rate of response that is higher than continuous reinforcement.
   - Tends to extinguish rapidly when reinforcement is terminated.
3. *Variable ratio (VR)* A varying or random number of responses must be made before reinforcement occurs.
   - Capable of producing a very high rate of response that is vigorous, steady, and resistant to extinction.
4. *Variable interval (VI)* The first correct response after a varying or random interval of time is reinforced.
   - Capable of producing a very high rate of response that is vigorous, steady, and resistant to extinction.

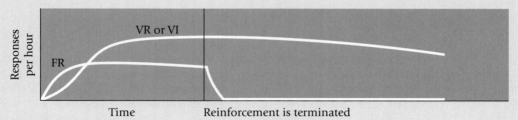

5. *Fixed interval (FI)* The first response after a fixed period of time is reinforced.
   - Produces an uneven response pattern that varies from a very slow, lethargic response rate immediately following reinforcement to a very fast, vigorous response rate immediately preceding reinforcement.

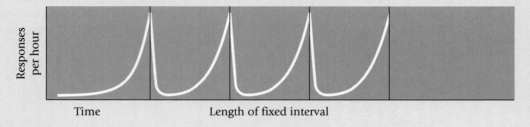

Source: David J. Cherrington, *Personnel Management* (Dubuque, Iowa: Wm. C. Brown Company Publishers, 1983), p. 260.

the same. Reinforcements are delivered on an irregular and unpredictable schedule. Promotions often occur on a variable interval schedule. New college graduates are often told that after a year or two they will probably be promoted. However, the promotion may occur earlier or later depending on other employment factors in the organization.

Like a variable ratio schedule, variable interval schedules are capable of producing a very high rate of response that is vigorous, steady, and resistant to extinction. Individuals who have been on a variable interval schedule tend to persist in their performance long after the reinforcement has been terminated. Gamblers will tend to continue playing slot machines long after the machines have quit paying off. Sales representatives continue to make sales calls long after the product has stopped selling. Managers continue to operate outdated companies and produce obsolete products even though they are consistently losing money. The effects of these reinforcement schedules on behavior are illustrated in Exhibit 3.4.

BEHAVIOR MODIFICATION

One of the earliest applications of reinforcement theories to individual behavior was called *behavior modification.* The principles of operant conditioning had been examined in thousands of animal studies, and the results were ultimately applied to changing individual behavior by using appropriate rewards and reinforcement contingencies. Through behavior modification, the behavior of individuals is modified by analyzing the antecedents (environmental cues) and consequences of behavior and changing them as necessary. Individuals are assisted in acquiring desirable behaviors by creating positive rewards for good behavior and by designing appropriate reward contingencies. For example, a high school student was so shy and self-conscious that she had difficulty developing friends. She requested help from a school counselor who developed a behavior modification program that taught the girl three simple responses: smiling and nodding her head, introducing herself by telling her name, and asking the question "What do you like most about school?" The girl wore a simple counter on her wrist that looked like a watch, which she used to record how many times she made a response each day. The reinforcement came first from the counselor's praise, then from the counter recording her new behavior, and eventually from the acceptance of her new friends. Simple behavior modification programs such as this have proven to be very effective at helping people change their behavior and make the kinds of responses they want to make.

The extension of behavior modification into organizations is called "organizational behavior management" (OBM) or "organizational behavior modification" (OB Mod). Principles of reinforcement theory are applied to human resource management problems to change and direct organizational behavior toward the attainment of organizational and societal objectives. OB Mod is not a theory of work motivation; instead, it is a technique for motivating employees using principles of reinforcement theory. OB Mod focuses on observable and measurable behaviors instead of needs, attitudes, or internal states.[30]

Behavioral Events

Performance problems can be analyzed from three different levels of analysis: (1) behavioral events, (2) performance, and (3) organizational consequences. The basic units of analysis in OB Mod are **behavioral events,** that is, the specific acts people perform in the course of working. As individuals perform their jobs, their specific task activities are the behavioral events used in OB Mod. Performance includes behaviors that are measured in terms of their contribution to the goals of an organization. Organizational consequences are measures of organizational effectiveness associated with the long-range survival and success of an organization. These three levels vary along a continuum from specific acts to general outcomes:

Very specific actions	Intermediate outcomes	Very general outcomes
Behavioral events	Performance	Organizational consequences

An illustration of a behavioral event is cleaning up an oil spill on the shop floor. At the performance level, cleaning up oil spills improves safety, and the organizational consequence is a reduction in accidents. Other behavioral events include coming to work, punching in on time, or being at the workstation by 8 A.M. These events are dependable attendance at the performance level, and the organizational consequence is reduced absenteeism and tardiness.

The identification of behavioral events is important in OB Mod because these are the specific acts that are measured and reinforced. Desirable organizational consequences are pursued through a strategy of obtaining the desired behavioral events that create them.

Behavioral Contingency Management (BCM)

The process of implementing OB Mod is called **"behavioral contingency management"** or **BCM.** This model provides a general methodology for identifying and managing the critical behaviors of employees in all types of organizations.[31] The BCM methodology consists of a five-step process for solving performance problems as illustrated in Exhibit 3.5.

1. *Identify performance-related events.* The first step consists of identifying the specific behaviors that contribute to effective performance. These behaviors must be observable and countable. For example, if the performance problem is late reports, the behavioral events could refer to the number of reports submitted by a specified date.

2. *Measure the frequency of response.* Before trying to change a behavior, a baseline measure of its frequency must be established. Sometimes a behavior believed to be problematic turns out to have a low frequency, and the manager realizes that the behavior is not really a problem after all. In measuring the frequency of a response, all responses can be counted if they are infrequent, such as absenteeism and tardiness. If the responses are frequent, however, only samples of behavior need to be counted, such as the number of correct strokes of a data entry operator during a 5-minute sample every two hours.

EXHIBIT 3.5   **Behavioral Contingency Management**

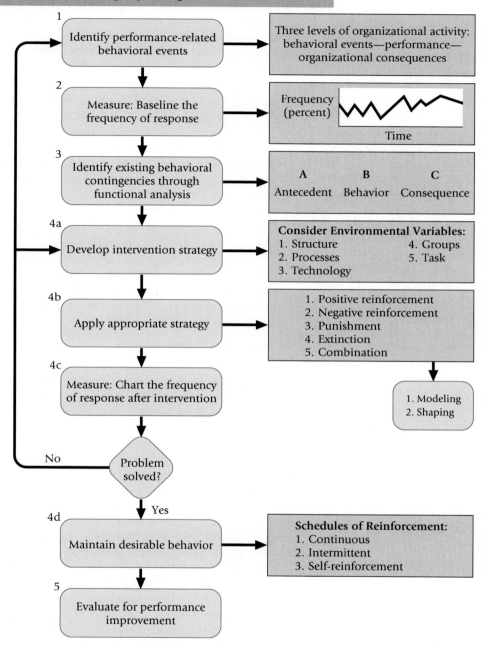

1. Identify performance-related behavioral events → Three levels of organizational activity: behavioral events—performance—organizational consequences

2. Measure: Baseline the frequency of response → Frequency (percent) / Time

3. Identify existing behavioral contingencies through functional analysis → A Antecedent B Behavior C Consequence

4a. Develop intervention strategy → Consider Environmental Variables: 1. Structure 4. Groups 2. Processes 5. Task 3. Technology

4b. Apply appropriate strategy → 1. Positive reinforcement 2. Negative reinforcement 3. Punishment 4. Extinction 5. Combination → 1. Modeling 2. Shaping

4c. Measure: Chart the frequency of response after intervention

Problem solved? — No / Yes

4d. Maintain desirable behavior → Schedules of Reinforcement: 1. Continuous 2. Intermittent 3. Self-reinforcement

5. Evaluate for performance improvement

Source: Reprinted by permission of the publisher, from "Behavioral Contingencies Management" by F. Luthans and R. Kreitner, *Personnel:* July–August, 1974, © 1974 American Management Association, New York. All rights reserved.

3. *Identify existing contingencies through a functional analysis.* A functional analysis is an examination of the antecedents and consequences of behavior. The antecedents consist of environmental conditions surrounding the behavior and any actions that occurred immediately prior to the behavior. The consequences consist of all the outcomes associated with the behavior, both positive and negative. Since human behavior is so complex, identifying all the antecedents and consequences is extremely difficult.

4. *Develop intervention strategies.* The first three steps provide a foundation for altering behaviors by changing the reinforcement contingencies. The success of OB Mod depends on selecting and implementing an appropriate intervention strategy. The basic strategies were described earlier: positive reinforcement, punishment, escape, avoidance, and extinction contingencies, or a combination of these. The goal of the intervention is to change the frequency of the identified behavior. Once the strategy is applied, the results are monitored and charted.

5. *Evaluate.* The final step of behavioral contingency management is to evaluate whether the changes in behavior resulted in performance improvement and contributed to desirable organizational consequences. BCM is supposed to be directed toward performance improvement and bottom-line results. Several successful applications of OB Mod have been reported in various organizations, including industry, government, and the military.

Applications of OB Mod

One of the earliest and best known applications of OB Mod occurred at Emery Air Freight. The behavior modification program was designed to reduce the persistent problems of inefficiency and low productivity. Success in the air freight industry requires processing parcels rapidly and efficiently. The containers in which the parcels are transported need to be filled. Before the program was implemented, workers estimated that 90 percent of the containers were filled. However, a performance audit indicated that they were filled only about 45 percent of the time.[32]

The OB Mod program implemented at Emery Air Freight used feedback in the form of self-report checklists and positive reinforcement in the form of praise and recognition from the supervisors. Almost overnight the percentage of full containers rose from 45 to 90 percent. The cost savings for the first year exceeded $500,000 and totaled $2 billion during the first three years. To maintain a high rate of efficiency in later years, Emery Air Freight adopted a variety of other positive reinforcers, including invitations to business lunches, formal letters of public commendation, and job enrichment.

Applications of OB Mod in other organizations have been equally effective. The city of Detroit implemented an OB Mod program among garbage collectors to increase the efficiency of garbage collection, reduce overtime, and reduce the number of citizen complaints. Feedback to the garbage collectors was provided daily and quarterly based on a formula negotiated by the city and the sanitation union. The reinforcers consisted of a combination of praise and a profit-sharing bonus based on the efficiency of garbage collection. The increase in efficiency was so great that the city was able to provide a $350 annual profit-sharing bonus for each employee, and the city saved $1.6 million in the first year after the bonus was paid. The number of citizen complaints also declined significantly.[33]

An OB Mod program implemented among the manufacturing employees at B. F. Goodrich Chemical Company was equally successful. Production increased over 300 percent in a program that provided weekly feedback to employees who received praise and recognition for increasing their productivity and greater freedom to choose how they would perform their work. A survey of ten companies using OB Mod found that the results of all ten programs were consistently described as successful. The reinforcers most frequently used in these programs were praise, recognition, and positive feedback. Only two of the ten programs included monetary reinforcers as part of the program.[34]

Criticisms of OB Mod

Although studies show that OB Mod has the capacity to significantly improve productivity and help organizations function more effectively, it is not without its criticisms. Three of the major criticisms against OB Mod include its tendency to ignore individual differences and preferences regarding rewards, the potential threat that it poses to individual freedom, and its failure to accommodate group norms.[35]

OB Mod Ignores Individual Reward Preferences. Each person has a unique history of reinforcement conditioning. Consequently, people vary in the type of secondary reinforcers they prefer. For example, hanging an employee's picture on a wall below a sign saying "Outstanding Employee of the Month" could be perceived by one employee as a meaningful form of recognition, while another employee could view it as a degrading experience. OB Mod programs are frequently designed to provide the same type of praise and recognition for all employees without recognizing that some forms of praise and recognition are more valued by some employees than others.

Employees also differ in their personal circumstances. For employees who have little need for additional income, time off from work is a positive reward and working overtime is a punishment. However, employees who are heavily in debt feel just the opposite.

The recommended solution for this problem is to involve employees in the design of an OB Mod program. Employees should have an opportunity to express their preferences regarding rewards and the frequency of feedback.

OB Mod Is a Threat to Individual Freedom. Because behavior modification programs have been so successful in changing behavior, their success causes us to question the morality of changing another person's behavior. Does OB Mod cause people to lose their individuality and force them to behave differently? OB Mod programs are not necessarily unethical simply because they change individual behavior. Like other social influence processes the determination of whether they are unethical depends on a variety of circumstances, particularly on how they are developed and implemented. An OB Mod program is not considered unethical in these situations: (1) when it helps people pursue their own personal and social ideals, (2) when it uses positive rather than negative techniques, (3) when the participants are fully aware of the methods and goals used in the program, (4) when there is a clearly established need for it and widespread agreement that change is necessary, or (5) when those who design the program have ample opportunity to discuss the consequences of the program and its potential side effects.

There is a dramatic difference in the ethical implications of an OB Mod program designed to force employees to behave in ways they consider immoral or illegal versus an OB Mod program designed to help employees succeed in an organization or pursue their own personal goals. One program is viewed as an invidious form of manipulation, while the other is viewed as constructive assistance.

OB Mod Disregards Group Norms. OB Mod programs are designed by establishing reinforcement contingencies that are usually applied universally regardless of group norms and expectations. The problem with overlooking group norms is that while the organization may reinforce employees for good performance, this behavior may be punished by peer group pressures. For example, a group norm that restricts productivity is usually maintained by a variety of punishments for group members who violate the norm. This problem has occurred frequently when employees are paid a piece-rate incentive.

GOAL SETTING

Many managers have discovered the influence of goal setting on performance. People perform significantly better when they are trying to achieve a specific goal such as completing a project before noon, increasing productivity by 5 percent, working for the next hour without making a mistake, maintaining 100 percent attendance, and getting a research paper submitted on time.

Goal-setting Theory

Goal-setting theory is an important motivation theory that can be discussed as an application of reinforcement theory in this chapter or as a cognitive theory of motivation in the next chapter. The major concepts are presented here.

In 1968 Edwin A. Locke first presented a theory of goal setting and a series of studies showing the effects of goal setting on performance. Continuing research in both laboratory and field studies supports Locke's theory.[36] Reinforcement theory explains why goal setting has such a powerful influence on behavior.[37]

A goal is simply a standard of performance an individual is trying to achieve. For example, "completing a project before noon" or "increasing productivity by 5 percent" describe specific actions individuals must perform in a specified period of time. Some of the earliest work on goal setting was performed by Frederick W. Taylor in his work on scientific management. Taylor attempted to identify appropriate goals for workers using time-and-motion studies and a careful task analysis. The methods and procedures by which employees were to perform their assigned tasks, such as tools, pacing, and physical movement were specified in great detail. Rather than referring to them as goals derived from a goal-setting process, however, Taylor referred to them as standards derived from a time-and-motion study.

The basic elements of goal setting theory are illustrated in Exhibit 3.6. Given our own personal values, we have a concept of what we desire. After examining our present circumstances, we compare our actual conditions with our desired conditions. If we are achieving what we want to achieve, we experience a sense of satis-

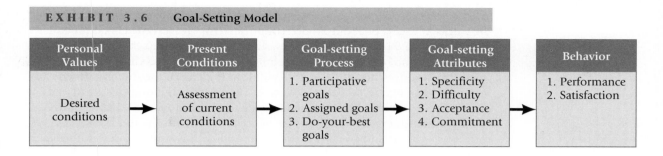

EXHIBIT 3.6   Goal-Setting Model

Personal Values	Present Conditions	Goal-setting Process	Goal-setting Attributes	Behavior
Desired conditions	Assessment of current conditions	1. Participative goals 2. Assigned goals 3. Do-your-best goals	1. Specificity 2. Difficulty 3. Acceptance 4. Commitment	1. Performance 2. Satisfaction

faction and fulfillment and follow the same course. However, if there is a discrepancy, we will go through a goal-setting process.

Students go through the goal-setting model frequently during their educational program. Given their personal values, students have an idea of what they want, such as graduating from college, going on to graduate school, or securing an attractive job. As they assess their present conditions, however, they often discover that their test scores are low, their class attendance is down, and their term papers are behind schedule. These discrepancies between their desired and actual conditions frequently cause students to initiate a goal-setting process. They establish such goals as raising the next test score from a C+ to an A–, attending every lecture, and having the first draft of a term paper written within the next two weeks.

The process of establishing goals frequently occurs in three different ways. *Participative goals* allow employees to participate in the process of setting goals by providing information and contributing to the goal selection. If they believe the goals are too high or too low, they can express their opinions and try to influence the goal statements. *Assigned goals* are determined by management and simply assigned to the employees. In scientific management, the standards of performance are determined by industrial engineers with almost no input from the employees. *Do-your-best goals* allow employees to control their own goals; management simply asks the employees to do their best without getting involved in approving or vetoing their goals. A do-your-best goal is usually not a specific quantifiable standard of performance but only a general principle that usually means "We'll keep going the way we are."

Goal-setting Attributes

The effects of goal setting on behavior are influenced by four major goal-setting attributes: goal specificity, goal difficulty, goal acceptance, and goal commitment. There is also some indication that individual differences seem to influence the effects of goal setting on behavior.

Goal Specificity. Numerous studies have shown a very direct relationship between **goal specificity** and increased performance. When employees are working toward specific goals, they consistently perform at higher levels than when they are simply told to do their best or are allowed to work at their own rate with no instructions at all. An excellent illustration of the effects of specific goals was a study of truck drivers in a logging company. The drivers were responsible for loading their own trucks, but the only instruction drivers received in loading their trucks was the general goal to "do your best." An analysis revealed that the drivers seldom loaded the trucks in excess of about 60 percent of capacity. The researchers decided that a specific goal of 94 percent of capacity should be assigned to the drivers with the provision that no one would be disciplined for failing to reach the goal, nor would financial incentives be available if they did. At the end of the first month the performance increased to 80 percent of the trucks' capacity but dropped to 70 percent during the second month. At the end of the third month and thereafter, however, the performance exceeded 90 percent of capacity. The drivers did not receive any form of specific training or instructions other than the expectation that their performance should be increased to 94 percent. Consequently, this study illustrates the effects of specific goals in increasing performance.[38]

Since do-your-best goals are only loose guidelines rather than specific goals, they have approximately the same effect on performance as no goals at all. Studies indicate that when workers are simply told to do their best, this instruction is considered equivalent to not having goals. A review by Locke and his associates of field experiments using a wide variety of different jobs found that 99 out of the 110 studies they reviewed found that specific goals led to better performance than did vague goals.[39]

Goal Difficulty. Studies on the effects of **goal difficulty** have found a direct linear relationship between an increase in goal difficulty and an increase in task performance. In other words, higher goals lead to higher performance. These results have been observed for brief one-time tasks lasting as little as one minute, and for ongoing tasks lasting as long as seven years.[40] Again, these studies investigated a wide variety of different jobs with participants ranging in age from 4 years to adulthood.[41]

The relationship between goal difficulty and task performance, however, does not hold for unreasonably difficult goals. When the goals are so high that they become unreasonably difficult or impossible, individuals tend to ignore the goals, and performance may be only slightly better than with no goals at all. When a goal is perceived as so difficult that it is virtually impossible to attain, the result is often frustration rather than achievement. Dreaming the impossible dream does not improve performance as much as a difficult but realistic goal. Research on the effects of various probabilities of success suggest that the optimum levels of motivation occur when the probability of success is .5. Here the probability of success is equal to the probability of failure and, according to a formula by Atkinson, the highest levels of motivation occur when the probability of success is equal to the probability of failure.[42] Therefore, to obtain high performance levels goals should be difficult and challenging, but the difficulty should not be so great that people believe their chances of succeeding through a dedicated effort are less than 50–50.

Goal Acceptance. **Goal acceptance** concerns the degree to which individuals accept a specific goal as their own. People need to feel that the goal belongs to them: "This is my goal." Goals are typically resisted or ignored when they are too difficult and out of reach. However, goals can also be rejected for a variety of other reasons, such as that the employees distrust management, they feel they are being exploited by the organization, the goals are not fair and consistent, or the activity is meaningless and irrelevant.[43]

Unrealistically high goals are not always entirely rejected. There is some indication that unreachable goals are reinterpreted by employees rather than rejected altogether.[44] For example, if a music student has been practicing only fifteen minutes a day and then is told that he should be practicing four hours daily, rather than totally disregard the four-hour goal, he may adopt a compromise position and practice two hours per day.

Goal Commitment. **Goal commitment** concerns the degree to which people are dedicated to reach the goals they have adopted and it is determined by both situational (goal origin and public announcement) and personal (need for achievement and locus of control) variables. The evidence suggests that participatively set goals contribute to higher levels of goal commitment. When people participate in setting their goals, they generally display a sense of ownership of the goals and are highly committed to achieving them.[45] There is also some indication that goal commitment is greater when people have declared their intentions publicly. Failing to meet publicly declared goals can be embarrassing. Goal-setting research shows that commitment to difficult goals is higher when (1) goals are self-set rather than assigned, (2) goals are made public rather than private, (3) the locus of control is internal, and (4) subjects are high in need for achievement.[46] High levels of goal commitment can also be expected regarding goals associated with one's self-esteem. To the extent that people become ego invested in achieving a goal, their level of goal commitment can be expected to be very high.[47]

Individual Differences. There is some indication that the goal-setting process is influenced by individual differences. Everyone does not respond similarly to a suggestion to increase productivity. In fact, some people are defiant and belligerent when told that they are expected to achieve a minimum level of performance. When given the opportunity to set their own goals, some individuals set very high, rigorous goals, while others set goals below their current performance with the expectation of reducing their effort.

Research on personality variables that moderate the effects of goal setting has been rather limited. One study found that high-need achievers perform better when they are given very specific goals and high levels of feedback, while low-need achievers perform better when allowed to participate in goal setting.[48] Another study found that education levels seem to moderate the effects of goal setting—the relationship between goal specificity and performance seems to be much stronger for employees with less education. Apparently, highly educated people are able to take general goals and make them more specific for themselves while less educated people require specific goals because they tend not to make general goals more specific on their own.

Criticisms of Goal Setting

Although many studies have shown that goal setting increases performance, it is not without critics. The criticisms include both practical and ethical concerns:

1. Goal setting works better for simple jobs than for complex jobs. Goal setting is particularly difficult for jobs that do not produce a physical product or where the time required to produce a definable product requires several months or years.

2. Goal setting encourages employees to be manipulative and deceitful. Goal-setting activities often encourage employees to get involved in playing games where they set low goals to look good later rather than setting high goals to encourage

APPLYING ORGANIZATIONAL BEHAVIOR
RESEARCH

Feedback, Goal Setting, and Incentives: A Field Experiment

 Extensive research has shown that feedback, goal setting, and incentives can increase individual productivity. The United States Air Force wanted to know if similar performance increases would occur among the five sections of an Air Force base in the Southwest. With the assistance of a research team from the University of Houston led by Robert D. Pritchard, the Air Force conducted a field experiment using a time series design. A time series design involves measuring performance for several time periods and allows researchers to use baseline measures as a control for assessing before-and-after effects of experimental changes.

The first step of the project was to develop a productivity measuring system so that the performance of each unit could be accurately measured and meaningfully compared. Once the measures were developed, performance was assessed monthly for an eight-month baseline period. Next, performance feedback was provided for each unit for a five-month period. Goal setting was then added to feedback for each unit and continued for another five months. Finally, incentives were added to feedback and goal setting for five months.

Feedback consisted of formal computer-generated reports that were distributed monthly showing basic productivity data plus information comparing the productivity of different units. The goal-setting program encouraged each unit to set difficult but attainable goals that would not be reported to senior management. The incentive was time off from work: a half day off if the unit's performance exceeded the average performance of the previous five months and a whole day off if it exceeded the previous five months by 5 percent.

The results indicated that the average monthly productivity during the five months when feedback was provided was 50 percent over baseline performance, goal setting and feedback increased productivity to 75 percent above baseline, and when incentives were added productivity was 76 percent above baseline. The effects of these changes were also assessed on job attitudes and it was found that job satisfaction and the intent to stay were just as good or better than before. Furthermore, performance did not decline after the research team left.

Source: Based on Robert D. Pritchard, Steven D. Jones, Philip L. Roth, Karla K. Stuebing, and Steven E. Ekeberg, "Effects of Group Feedback, Goal Setting, and Incentives on Organizational Productivity," *Journal of Applied Psychology Monograph*, vol. 73 (1988), pp. 337–358.

greater performance. Managers play the same game if they set unrealistically high performance goals when all they expect is a small increase in performance.

3. Goal setting can lead to a narrow-minded focus on measurable goals while other important aspects of performance are ignored because they are not measurable. This criticism does not stem from the failure of goal setting but from its success. Goal-setting activities are designed to focus the attention of employees on achieving the measurable goals. To the extent that important dimensions of a job are not included in the goal statements, employees will have a tendency to overlook these crucial activities.

4. Goal-setting activities are often difficult to sustain when they are not combined with other forms of reinforcement. When employees achieve higher levels of performance, they think it is only fair that their increased performance be recognized and rewarded. Financial reinforcement is not the only acceptable reward for good

performance, but many employees feel that praise alone is not entirely fair if their extra efforts have significantly increased the company's profitability.

5. Goal setting is another device to control and monitor employee behavior. The same criticisms made of OB Mod are relevant to goal setting because both programs attempt to reduce the variability of human behavior and encourage employees to behave in predictable ways. Goal-setting programs are not necessarily unethical simply because they are attempting to control behavior, and the same questions about goal-setting programs need to be asked: Do employees understand the goal-setting program? Is it necessary? Do they accept it? Does it help them achieve both their personal and organizational objectives?

In spite of these criticisms, however, the powerful effects of goal setting on motivation should not be overlooked or minimized. Goal setting appears to be one of the most consistent and powerful processes influencing motivation. An extensive review of the goal-setting studies reported that over 90 percent of both laboratory and field experiments found that specific, challenging goals lead to higher performance than do-your-best or no goals.[49] The consistency of these results extends across hard (measurable) and soft (subjective) performance criteria, quantity and quality of performance, and individual and group goals. Clearly, goal setting is one of the most "robust" findings in the psychological literature.

SUMMARY

1. Learning occurs when practice or experience leads to a relatively permanent change in potential behavior. No learning is said to have occurred unless there is a change in overt behavior.

2. Classical conditioning is a theory of learning that explains how reflexive responses governed by the autonomic nervous system become paired with a conditioned stimulus. This pairing occurs by simultaneously presenting the conditioned and unconditioned stimulus. Emotions and stress reactions are illustrations of classically conditioned responses.

3. Operant conditioning is a theory of learning that explains how reinforcing consequences influence behavior. When a response that is made in the presence of a stimulus is reinforced, this will increase the probability that on future occasions the same response will be made in the presence of a similar stimulus.

4. The process of chaining explains how a series of stimulus–response associations are combined to form complex behaviors.

5. The process of shaping is the process of acquiring a unique response by a selective reinforcement process, called the method of successive approximations.

6. Social cognitive theory emphasizes the role of thinking as a central processing activity in learning new behaviors. Three central elements of social cognitive theory include reciprocal determinism, vicarious learning, and symbolic learning.

7. Any stimulus that has the effect of increasing the probability of a response is defined as a positive reinforcer. A stimulus that has the effect of decreasing the probability of a response is a negative reinforcer or punisher. Primary rewards are reinforcers associated with the physiological needs of the body, while secondary rewards are learned or acquired reinforcers. Intrinsic rewards concern reinforcers associated with activities that are self-administered, while extrinsic rewards are reinforcers that are administered by others.

8. Behavior is a function of its consequences, and five reinforcement contingencies explain the

relationship between behavior and consequences. These five reinforcement contingencies are positive reinforcements, punishment, escape, avoidance, and extinction.

9. Reward schedules concern the timing of the reinforcement—how often the correct response is reinforced. The three major reinforcement schedules include continuous, intermittent, and interval schedules. Both intermittent and interval schedules can be either fixed or variable. Variable ratio and variable interval schedules tend to produce a very high rate of response that is vigorous, steady, and resistant to extinction.

10. Behavior modification programs in organizations, called OB Mod, are an application of operant conditioning principles to organizational problems. OB Mod is implemented through behavioral contingency management (BCM), which identifies behavioral events and modifies them by altering the reinforcement contingencies.

11. OB Mod has been criticized for ignoring individual reward preferences, for disregarding group norms, and for threatening individual freedom and dignity.

12. Goal-setting theory claims that the performance of employees can be significantly increased by setting realistic but challenging goals. Considerable evidence has shown that realistic but challenging goals significantly improve performance, especially when the goal-setting program is accompanied by other reinforcers. Four important attributes of the goal-setting process include goal specificity, goal difficulty, goal acceptance, and goal commitment.

DISCUSSION QUESTIONS

1. Since emotions are classically conditioned responses to thoughts or situations, how would you propose to change someone's emotions such as the irritation people feel about waiting in line?

2. What are the differences between operant and classical conditioning? What are some examples of each that might be found in either an industrial or an educational setting?

3. What are the major differences between operant conditioning and social cognitive theory in describing the learning process? How are these theories similar?

4. What are the most useful reinforcement contingencies for changing employee behavior at work? How should they be used?

5. Behavioral scientists have strongly discouraged the use of punishment as a means of influencing behavior. However, punishment is frequently used in disciplining children, students, and employees. What are your recommendations about the use of punishment and how effective or destructive do you think it is?

6. If variable ratio schedules are so effective in maintaining a high and steady rate of responding, why are they not used more frequently in organizations? How could variable ratio schedules be used more frequently to reward employee performance?

7. How are secondary rewards learned? Identify a secondary reward that is important to you, and describe how it became an important reward.

8. OB Mod focuses on specific behavioral events rather than on more general performance or organizational responses. What are some examples of behavioral events, and why are they so important in OB Mod?

9. It has been said that goals that have not been written are only wishes. Do you agree that the process of recording goals makes a significant difference in goal accomplishment? What are your goals, how many of them are written, and what progress have you made in achieving them?

10. Performance feedback is generally considered a form of reinforcement, but is this always true? If people have performed poorly, do you think they want to know about it? How important is feedback to you and are there ever times when you really don't want to know how well you've done?

11. If variable ratio and variable interval schedules are so effective in increasing the rate of responding and preventing extinction, is there any way they can be used to pay employees?

GLOSSARY

aversive stimulus An unpleasant or punishing stimulus.

avoidance contingency A reinforcement contingency in which the person is required to make a response to avoid an aversive stimulus.

behavioral contingency management (BCM) The process of implementing an OB Mod program in which behavioral events are specified and the conditions to achieve them are created.

behavioral event The basic unit of OB Mod, which consists of a specific act or response.

chaining The process of combining several stimulus–response associations to form a complex behavior.

classical conditioning A form of learning involving responses of the autonomic nervous system where a conditioned stimulus is associated with a conditioned response.

conditioned response (CR) A response that has been paired with a conditioned stimulus.

conditioned stimulus (CS) A neutral stimulus that has become paired with a conditioned response through the process of classical conditioning.

continuous reward schedule A reward schedule that reinforces every correct response.

discriminative stimulus A specific environmental stimulus that a person has learned to distinguish from other environmental stimuli and to respond to.

escape contingency A reinforcement contingency that requires a person to make a correct response in order to terminate a negative condition that is already present in the environment.

extinction contingency A reinforcement contingency in which no reinforcement, either positive or negative, is associated with a response. In time the person stops making the response.

extrinsic reward Rewards that are administered by others or are under the control of an external source.

fixed interval schedule A reward schedule in which no reinforcement is given during a predetermined period of time, but after the end of that time interval, the first correct response is reinforced.

fixed ratio schedule A reward schedule that rewards every nth response, where n is a fixed number.

goal acceptance An attribute of the goal-setting process that concerns the degree to which people accept a specific goal as their own.

goal commitment An attribute of the goal-setting process that concerns the degree to which people are dedicated to reach the goals they have adopted.

goal difficulty An attribute of the goal-setting process that concerns the amount of effort required to achieve the goal.

goal specificity An attribute of the goal-setting process that concerns how clearly defined and measurable the goals are.

imitative learning The process of learning new behaviors by observing others and by modeling their behavior.

intermittent reward schedule A reward schedule that does not reward every correct response. Only a certain percentage, one nth, of the correct responses are reinforced on either a fixed or variable schedule.

intrinsic reinforcer Self-administered rewards; the positive feelings people receive from performing an activity.

law of effect An early description of operant conditioning by Thorndike that states that rewarded behaviors will be repeated while punished behaviors will not.

method of successive approximations The process of reinforcing closer and closer approximations of the correct behavior, sometimes referred to as the *shaping process.*

OB Mod Organizational behavior modification; the application of reinforcement theories to organizational behavior.

operant conditioning A form of learning involving the association of a stimulus and a response that the person makes to obtain reinforcement.

positive reinforcement contingency A reinforcement contingency in which positive reinforcement is presented when the correct response is made.

primary rewards Rewards or outcomes that are desirable because of their association with physiological requirements or comforts, especially food, water, sex, rest, and the removal of pain.

punishment contingency A reinforcement contingency in which negative reinforcement or punishment is associated with a specific response.

reciprocal determinism A basic philosophy of social cognitive theory suggesting that the environment influences individual behavior but that individuals also influence their environment and can change it.

reflexive conditioning Another name for classical conditioning, where reflexive behavior governed by the autonomic nervous system is associated with a conditioned stimulus.

reinforcement contingency The relationship between behavior and the reinforcing consequences of that behavior. The five major reinforcement contingencies are positive reinforcement, punishment, avoidance, escape, and extinction.

respondent conditioning Another name for classical conditioning, where autonomic nervous system responses are associated with a neutral stimulus.

secondary rewards Learned rewards or outcomes that have a powerful influence on behavior because they are self-administered. They can become increasingly important or valued, and they do not become satiated or filled.

shaping The process of refining a response by selectively reinforcing closer and closer approximations of the desired response.

social cognitive theory A major theory of learning based on observational and symbolic learning. Learning is influenced by what is reinforced, either extrinsically or through self-administered reinforcement, especially the anticipations of future events. The environment influences individual behavior, but people can influence their environment through a process called *reciprocal determinism.*

spontaneous recovery The reappearance of a conditioned response that had been created earlier and then extinguished.

stimulus generalization The process of using a slightly different stimulus to elicit a response.

symbolic learning A process of learning that uses symbols such as words, mental images, and other cognitive associations.

unconditioned stimulus A stimulus that naturally elicits a reflexive response. By associating an unconditioned stimulus with another neutral stimulus, the neutral stimulus can become a conditioned stimulus that produces the same response, which is then called a *conditioned response.*

variable interval schedule A reinforcement schedule based on an interval of time. However, the length of the time interval is not constant; it varies on a random basis.

variable ratio schedule An intermittent reinforcement schedule in which rewards are administered on the basis of a variable number of correct responses. Variable ratio schedules lead to high rates of responding and are very resistant to extinction.

vicarious learning The process of learning by observing the actions and behaviors of a model.

NOTES

1. K. D. Scott, S. E. Markham, and R. W. Robers, "Boost Productivity with Employee Contests," *Personnel Journal,* vol. 65 (September 1986), pp. 114–116.

2. Richard M. Steers and Lyman W. Porter, *Motivation and Work Behavior* (New York: McGraw-Hill, 1975), p. 406.

3. Fred S. Keller, *Learning: Reinforcement Theory* (New York: Random House, 1967).

4. Ivan P. Pavlov, *Conditioned Reflexes* (New York: Oxford University Press, 1927).

5. C. T. Allen and T. J. Madden, "A Closer Look at Classical Conditioning," *Journal of Consumer Research,* vol. 12 (December 1985), pp. 301–315; Chris T. Allen and Chris A. Janiezewski, "Assessing the Role of Contingency Awareness in Attitudinal Conditioning with Implications for Advertising Research," *Journal of Marketing Research,* vol. 25 (February 1989), pp. 30–43; O. Lee Reed and Douglas Whitman, "A Constitutional and Policy-Related Evaluation of Prohibiting the Use of Certain Nonverbal Techniques in Legal Advertising," *BYU Law Review,* vol. 1988, no. 2 (1988), pp. 265–341; Elnora W. Stuart, Terrence A. Shimp, and Randall W. Engle, "Classical Conditioning of Consumer Attitudes: Four Experiments in an Advertising Context," *Journal of Consumer Research,* vol. 14 (December 1987), pp. 334–349.

6. David J. Cherrington, "The Effects of a Central Incentive Motivational State on Measures of Job Satisfaction," *Organizational Behavior and Human Performance,* vol. 10 (1973), pp. 271–289.

7. George S. Reynolds, *A Primer of Operant Conditioning,* Revised Edition (Glenview, Ill.: Scott Foresman, 1975).

8. E. C. Tolman, "Principles of Purposive Behavior," in S. Koch (ed.), *Psychology: A Study of a Science,* Vol. 2 (New York: McGraw-Hill, 1959).

9. B. F. Skinner, *Contingencies of Reinforcement: A Theoretical Analysis* (Englewood Cliffs, N.J.: Prentice-Hall, 1969); B. F. Skinner, *Science and Human Behavior* (New York: Macmillan, 1953).

10. Beth Nissen, "Can a Chicken Play Poker? Maybe If It's Been to Hot Springs," *Wall Street Journal* (February 1, 1979).

11. Edward L. Thorndike, *The Fundamentals of Learning* (New York: Teachers College, Columbia University, 1932).

12. S. Nelton, "Feedback to Employees Can Nourish Your Business," *Nation's Business*, vol. 73 (July 1985), pp. 62–63; P. C. Earley, "Trust, Perceived Importance of Praise and Criticism, and Work Performance: An Examination of Feedback in the United States and England," *Journal of Management*, vol. 12 (Winter 1986), pp. 457ff.

13. S. J. Ashford and L. L. Cummings, "Proactive Feedback Seeking: The Instrumental Use of the Information Environment," *Journal of Occupational Psychology*, vol. 58 (1985), pp. 67–79.

14. George S. Reynolds, op. cit., chaps. 2–4.

15. Albert Bandura, *Social Learning Theory* (Englewood Cliffs, N.J.: Prentice-Hall, 1977). Albert Bandura, *Principles of Behavior Modification* (New York: Holt, Rinehart and Winston, 1969).

16. Robert Wood and Albert Bandura, "Social Cognitive Theory of Organizational Management," *Academy of Management Review*, vol. 14 (July 1989), pp. 361–384.

17. Marilyn E. Gist, Catherine Schwoerer, and Benson Rosen, "Effects of Alternative Training Methods on Self-Efficacy and Performance in Computer Software Training," *Journal of Applied Psychology*, vol. 74 (December 1989), pp. 884–891.

18. Marilyn E. Gist, "The Influence of Training Method on Self-Efficacy and Idea Generation Among Management," *Personnel Psychology*, vol. 42 (Winter 1989), pp. 787–805.

19. Richard W. Mallott, *Contingency Management in Education* (Kalamazoo, Mich.: Behaviordelia, 1972), chap. 9.

20. Robert L. Opsahl and Marvin B. Dunnette, "The Role of Financial Compensation in Industrial Motivation," *Psychological Bulletin*, vol. 66, no. 2 (1966), pp. 94–118.

21. D. J. Cherrington and B. J. Wixom, "Recognition Is Still a Top Motivator," *Personnel Administrator* (May 1983), pp. 87–91; David J. Cherrington, "Designing an Effective Recognition Award Program: Dispelling the Myths," *Clinical Laboratory Management Review*, vol. 7 (May–June 1993), pp. 106–111.

22. Pat Buhler, "Rewards in the Organization," *Supervision*, vol. 50 (January 1989), pp. 5–7.

23. Edward L. Deci, "Intrinsic Motivation, Extrinsic Reinforcement, An Inequity," *Journal of Personality and Social Psychology*, vol. 22 (1972), pp. 113–120.

24. H. J. Arnold, "Effects of Performance Feedback and Extrinsic Reward upon High Intrinsic Motivation," *Organizational Behavior and Human Performance*, vol. 17 (1976), pp. 275–288. Also, Barry M. Staw, *Intrinsic and Extrinsic Motivation* (Morristown, N.J.: General Learn-

ing Press, 1976); Thomas C. Mawhinney, Alyce M. Dickinson, and Lewis A. Taylor III, "The Use of Concurrent Schedules to Evaluate the Effects of Extrinsic Awards on 'Intrinsic Motivation,'" *Journal of Organizational Behavior Management*, vol. 10, no. 1 (1989), pp. 109–129; Thomas C. Mawhinney, "Decreasing Intrinsic 'Motivation' with Extrinsic Rewards: Easier Said Than Done," *Journal of Organizational Behavior Management*, vol. 11, no. 1 (1990), pp. 175–191.

25. Blase J. Bergiel and Christine Trosclair, "Instrumental Learning: Its Application to Consumer Satisfaction," *Journal of Consumer Marketing*, vol. 2 (Fall 1985), pp. 23–28.

26. W. K. Estes, "An Experimental Study of Punishment," *Psychological Monograph*, vol. 57, whole no. 263 (1944).

27. Stanley M. Widrick, "Concept of Negative Reinforcement Has Place in Marketing Classroom," *Marketing News*, vol. 20 (July 18, 1988), pp. 48–49.

28. George Reynolds, op. cit.; R. D. Tustin and P. Morgan, "Choice of Reinforcement Rates and Work Rates with Concurrent Schedules," *Journal of Economic Psychology*, vol. 6 (1985), pp. 109–141.

29. Stephen O. Bushardt, Aubrey R. Fowler, Jr., and Sukumar Debneth, "Sales Force Motivation: A Theoretical Analysis," *Human Relations*, vol. 41 (December 1988), pp. 901–913.

30. Fred Luthans and Robert Kreitner, *Organizational Behavior Modification* (Glenview, Ill.: Scott Foresman, 1975).

31. Ibid., Chap. 8.

32. W. C. Hamner and E. P. Hamner, "Behavior Modification on the Bottom Line," *Organizational Dynamics*, vol. 4, no. 4 (1976), pp. 8–21.

33. Ibid., pp. 12–14.

34. Ibid., pp. 12–14; See also Edward M. Kinselle, "Achieving First-Class Customer Service," *Small Business Reports*, vol. 15 (August 1990), pp. 28–32.

35. Edwin A. Locke, "The Myths of Behavior Mod in Organizations," *Academy of Management Review*, vol. 2 (1977), pp. 543–553.

36. Edwin A. Locke, "Toward a Theory of Task Performance and Incentives," *Organizational Behavior and Human Performance*, vol. 3 (1968), pp. 157–189; "The Motivational Effects of Knowledge of Results: Knowledge or Goal Setting?" *Journal of Applied Psychology*, vol. 51 (1967), pp. 324–329.

37. V. L. Huber, "The Interplay of Goals and Promises of Pay-for-Performance on Individual and Group Performance: An Operant Interpretation," *Journal of Organizational Behavior Management*, vol. 7 (Fall–Winter 1985), pp. 45–64.

38. Gary Latham and Jay James Balds, "The Practical Significance of Locke's Theory of Goal Setting," *Journal of Applied Psychology*, vol. 60 (February 1975), pp. 122–124.

39. Edwin A. Locke, Karyll N. Shaw, Lise M. Saari, and Gary P. Latham, "Goal Setting and Task Performance: 1969–1980," *Technical Report*, GS-1, Office of Naval Research, Washington, D.C., June 1980.

40. Edwin A. Locke and Gary P. Latham, *Goal Setting: A Motivational Technique That Works!* (Englewood Cliffs, N.J.: Prentice-Hall, 1984).

41. Christopher P. Earley, Cynthia Lee, and Alice L. Hanson, "Joint Moderating Effects of Job Experience and Task Component Complexities: Relations Among Goal Setting, Task Strategies, and Performance," *Journal of Organizational Behavior*, vol. 11 (January 1990), pp. 3–15; John P. Meyer and Ian R. Gellatly, "Perceived Performance Norm as a Mediator in the Effect of Assigned Goal on Personal Goal and Task Performance," *Journal of Applied Psychology*, vol. 73 (August 1988), pp. 410–420.

42. John W. Atkinson, *An Introduction to Motivation* (Princeton, N.J.: D. Van Nostrand, 1964, chap. 9); Sandra Hile Hart, William C. Moncrief, and A. Parasuraman, "An Empirical Investigation of Salespeople's Performance, Effort, and Selling Method During a Sales Contest," *Journal of the Academy of Marketing Science*, vol. 17 (Winter 1989), pp. 29–39; Zur Chapira, "Task Choice and Assigned Goals as Determinants of Task Motivation and Performance," *Organizational Behavior and Human Decision Processes*, vol. 44 (October 1989), pp. 141–165.

43. Philip M. Podsakoff and Jiing-Lih Farh, "Effects of Feedback Sign and Credibility on Goal Setting and Task Performance," *Organizational Behavior and Human Decision Processes*, vol. 44 (August 1989), pp. 45–67.

44. H. Garland, "Influence of Ability-Assigned Goals, and Normative Information of Personal Goals and Performance: A Challenge to the Goal Attainability Assumption," *Journal of Applied Psychology*, vol. 68 (1983), pp. 20–30.

45. William B. Werther, Jr., "Workshops Aid in Goal Setting," *Personnel Journal*, vol. 68 (November 1989), pp. 32–38.

46. John R. Hollenbeck, Charles R. Williams, and Howard J. Kline, "An Empirical Examination of the Antecedents of Commitment to Difficult Goals," *Journal of Applied Psychology*, vol. 74 (February 1989), pp. 18–23.

47. D. J. Cherrington and J. O. Cherrington, "Appropriate Reinforcement Contingencies in the Budgeting Process," *Empirical Research in Accounting: Selected Studies* (1973), pp. 225–253.

48. Richard M. Steers, "Task–Goal Attributes, *n* Achievement, and Supervisory Performance," *Organizational Behavior and Human Performance*, vol. 13 (1975), pp. 392–403.

49. Gary P. Latham and Thomas W. Lee, "Goal Setting," in Edwin A. Locke (ed.), *Generalizing from Laboratory to Field Settings* (Lexington, Mass.: D. C. Heath, 1988), pp. 101–118.

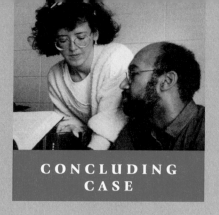

REWARDS OR PUNISHMENTS: WHICH WORKS BEST?

GTE Corporation in California tells employees to be customer oriented, but they pay them to be fast. They talk about the importance of good customer service, but they continue to press employees for productivity and efficiency gains. This inconsistency is confusing to employees.

GTE executives were surprised to learn from a company survey that most customer service representatives thought speed was more important than customer service. To change this impression, GTE invested $170,000 in weekend seminars for 850 employees, who were paid to attend. The events featured actors, singers, and a motivational speaker who preached the concept that when you pick up the phone to help a customer you own the problem. Asking the customer to call another department is not an acceptable solution. Instead, you should put the caller on hold and make the call yourself.

Although the training was entertaining, the message was still muddled. GTE says both speed and quality count, but only speed is measured. GTE continues to time how long workers talk on the phone. The only reward for customer service is the intrinsic satisfaction that comes from helping customers; but helping a customer with a problem takes time.

Scott DeGarmo, the manager of *Success* magazine, does not use incentives. Instead, he imposes monetary fines on his six senior editors for printing articles containing typographical errors and grammatical mistakes. Most typos and misplaced commas cost $25, while misspelling the name of the main person in a story costs $500. The fines are deducted from the next year's pay raises for the six editors.

Although the fines seem excessive to some, DeGarmo considers them rather lenient. On his first newspaper job, writers who made serious misspelling errors were automatically fired. DeGarmo instituted his system of fines when other strategies failed to reduce the frequency of errors. He says he tried all the positive things, such as praising perfect copy and gently citing mistakes, to no avail.

The system of fines immediately reduced the number of errors. During the first six weeks after the penalties started, fines amounting to $625 were assessed for one misspelled name, three misspelled words, and two grammatical errors. DeGarmo finds that when employees are motivated by the threat of punishment they quickly learn to do it right.

Questions

1. Why are fines working so well at *Success* magazine? List some situations in which you would expect fines to function effectively.

2. How could GTE use incentives to improve customer service? What fines could they use?

3. What has the greatest impact on behavior, incentives or fines, and when would you recommend each?

Source: Joan E. Rigdon, "More Firms Try to Reward Good Service, But Incentives May Backfire in Long Run," *Wall Street Journal* (December 5, 1990), pp. B1, B4; Gilbert Fuchsberg, "Now You Know What We Know About How Most Writers Write," *Wall Street Journal* (December 18, 1990), p. B1.

CONTINGENCY MANAGEMENT

If people do what they are given reinforcement to do, then why do people have so much trouble accomplishing some of their cherished goals? Why do some people have so much trouble trying to quit smoking? Why do students have so much trouble studying to get good grades? Why do overweight people have so much difficulty losing weight?

One of the useful insights of learning theory that helps to explain why large reinforcers such as losing weight, quitting smoking, and passing a course are ineffective is the following principle: "Our behavior is more easily influenced by small, immediate, and definite reinforcers than it is by large, distant, and uncertain reinforcers." The problem is not that getting a good grade, passing a course, or getting a college degree are unimportant—getting a degree is a large, significant reinforcer. But at a given moment in the life of a college student, receiving a degree is a distant and uncertain reinforcer. The student thinks, "I am not going to graduate today, and I do not think a few minutes of goofing off will hurt my chances of getting a degree." This principle is illustrated in this diagram:

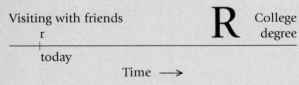

Since behavior is more easily influenced by small, immediate, and definite reinforcers than by large, distant, and uncertain reinforcers, how can individuals achieve long-term goals? The answer is to bring some of the large reinforcers from the future into the present in the form of small, immediate reinforcers. This process is called *contingency management*. New reinforcement contingencies are created to reinforce small, specific steps leading to the attainment of a large, distant objective. The following examples illustrate the principles of contingency management.

Four students who shared an apartment found that their academic performance was suffering because of inadequate study. To reinforce their studying, they used a small financial incentive. Each Sunday evening the roommates identified their daily reading assignments for the coming week and put five quarters into a jar. For each day they completed their assignments, they were allowed to remove one of their quarters from the jar. If someone didn't achieve her daily goal, her quarter remained in the jar that day. At the end of the week, any money that remained was used to buy snacks.

A graduate student who was an avid football fan made an agreement with his wife that he could watch Monday night football if he studied enough the week before. He put a chart above his desk at home, and each day he recorded the number of hours he spent either in class or studying. Unless he had sixty-four hours of study or class time the previous week, he could not watch Monday night football.

STEPS OF CONTINGENCY MANAGEMENT

Since behavior is a function of the reinforcement contingencies that maintain it, the best way to change behavior is to change the reinforcement contingencies. The following six steps describe the procedure.

1. *Identify the undesirable behavior that you want to eliminate or change.* It is important to identify the undesirable behavior, rather than a personality trait or characteristic. For example, laziness is a personality trait, and some people think that they would like to stop being so lazy. In contingency management, however, it is important to identify the specific behavior that needs to be changed, such as spending time at the snack bar or visiting with friends.

2. *Identify the consequences that maintain the undesirable behavior.* What rewards or punishments are associated with the present behavior? For example, going to the snack bar and discussing politics with friends is a form of social affiliation, which is a powerful reinforcement.

3. *Specify the desired behavior.* Identify the specific actions that you need to perform in order to achieve your long-range goal. For example, reading a chapter from a textbook may be one of the specific behaviors needed to pass a course and obtain a college degree.

4. *Design new contingencies to reinforce the desired behavior.* Sometimes, especially in the beginning, it is important to reward each step of the behavioral sequence. For example, instead of waiting until halfway through a semester to experience the positive or negative consequences of reading ten chapters, you should have specific consequences for each chapter. Although it is usually best to take advantage of natural consequences, in which the behavior itself provides the reinforcement, sometimes artificial consequences have to be created to reward the behavior. Performance records, gold stars, recognition awards, and other secondary reinforcers can be used effectively to reward good performance.

5. *Devise a method to observe and measure the new behavior.* In order for the new behavior to be reinforced, there must be some way of observing or measuring when it occurs. Although measuring the new behavior is very important, the measuring process should not be so inconvenient that it defeats its purpose.

6. *Arrange for the new reinforcement contingency to be administered.* Getting others involved in administering the rewards, such as roommates or friends, usually helps to keep the program running and keep it honest. After the new reinforcement contingencies have been designed and the behavior is evaluated, consequences must be administered consistently. To illustrate, a student who was leaving for college promised her parents that she would write to them each week. The parents also said they would write to her each week, and they agreed to include a check for $25 only if they received a letter from her the previous week. The letter did not have to be long, but it should at least contain a brief description of how she was doing in school and a specific request for $25. The parents wrote each Sunday afternoon, and if they had not heard from their daughter, they did not include the check. On one occasion, the daughter's letter did not arrive until Monday. The following Sunday, the parents thanked her for sending two letters that week, enclosed one check for $25, and expressed regret that she had missed receiving a check the week before.

Directions. Identify a behavior in your own life that you would like to change, and use the six steps of contingency management to develop an effective change program. Some illustrations of the kinds of behaviors that you may choose to develop include adopting better study habits, quitting smoking, exercising regularly, losing weight, writing to parents, and maintaining a personal journal. Use your creativity to design reinforcement contingencies to support your new behavior. As you try to arrange for the new reinforcement contingencies to be administered, try to involve others who can help to keep you honest and increase the probability of a successful change.

Motivation: Needs and Outcomes

LEARNING OBJECTIVES

After studying this chapter, you should be able to

1. Describe the needs in Maslow's needs hierarchy, and explain the concept of prepotency as it applies to them.

2. Identify the characteristics of high-need achievers, explain how the need for achievement is acquired, and explain the effects of achievement motivation on entrepreneurial activity and economic development.

3. Explain the differences between motivators and hygienes, and describe their effects on satisfaction and motivation.

4. Describe the components of expectancy theory, and explain how this theory helps managers solve motivation problems.

5. Explain the conditions that lead to feelings of inequity, and describe the effects of overpayment and underpayment on performance.

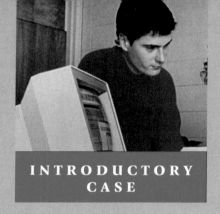

FREE TURKEY DINNERS

For the past several years, the employees at Wright's Furniture Manufacturing Company have received free turkey dinners on Wednesday before Thanksgiving.[1] The free dinners were intended as an expression of appreciation by the company to its employees. Management viewed the dinner as an important event to build company loyalty and improve job motivation.

Last year, however, there were several complaints about the dinner: the meal was not ready on time, service was too slow, the lines were too long, the food was not as good at the end because all the good pieces of turkey had been taken, and the food was cold. Douglas Wright, the president of the company, was very irritated by the employees' criticisms because he thought they showed a total lack of gratitude for the company and a self-centered disregard for the problems associated with feeding 200 people at the same time.

Wright decided that this year the company would distribute free turkeys the day before Thanksgiving and let the employees prepare their own meals. Giving each employee a full-size turkey was considerably more expensive for the company, but Wright thought it was a good solution to the problem of trying to feed a large crowd.

Unfortunately, some of the employees did not think getting a free turkey was all that great. Repre-sentatives of the union threatened to submit the issue as a grievance, complaining that it altered a condition of employment. The most negative reactions came from the six employees in the machine shop. Four of them, who were all single men, did not take their turkeys home and one left an anonymous note: "Give my bird to Mr. Wright and tell him to stuff it!" The most offensive reaction, however, was an obscene caricature drawn on a bathroom wall of Wright as a turkey.

Wright was so incensed by the picture that he ordered the personnel director to fire the entire department. "If they don't appreciate what we do for the employees, we'll get someone who does. How can anyone be so ungrateful?"

Questions

1. How should this episode be interpreted? Does it mean that employees dislike gifts or that they just dislike turkeys?

2. Should companies give rewards to all employees, or just some employees? What kinds of rewards should they give, or does it matter?

3. What theories of human behavior can be used to answer these questions, and do all these theories produce similar conclusions?

Motivation theories explain why people behave as they do. As noted at the beginning of the previous chapter, motivation theories seek to explain the intensity, the direction, and the persistence of behavior. Over the years, literally hundreds of theories have been proposed to explain human behavior, including macro theories describing the nature of humans, and micro theories explaining specific behaviors such as political involvement, sexual arousal, and aggression.

Virtually all motivation theories assume that behavior is caused; how we behave is not simply the result of random influences. The theories of motivation described in the previous chapter emphasized the consequences of behavior, especially the role of positive reinforcement. The theories in this chapter emphasize the role of cognitions; they assume that human behavior is purposive, or goal directed—that people can think, reason, and process information. These cognitive theories of motivation can be separated into **content theories** and **process theories.** Content theories explain *what* motivates behavior while process theories explain *how* or *why* we are motivated. Content theories are also called *needs theories,* because psychological needs comprise the core content that creates motivated behavior. Process theories, in contrast, explain how we use information to decide what to do. This chapter describes three needs theories: Maslow's needs hierarchy, McClelland's learned needs, and Herzberg's motivator-hygiene theory, plus three process theories: expectancy theory, equity theory, and control theory.

NEED THEORIES: THE CONTENT OF MOTIVATION

Content theories of motivation describe the psychological constructs within people that energize and sustain behavior. In other words, content theories examine the specific things inside people that motivate them.

Early Theories of Motivation

The most prominent historical views of human nature were based on the assumption that people are essentially rational beings with conscious desires and capacities to fulfill these desires. These ideas were central to the thinking of ancient philosophers such as Aristotle and Plato, medieval philosophers such as Thomas Aquinas, and more recent philosophers such as Descartes, Hobbes, and Spinoza.

For many years the idea of a person's "will" played a large role in explaining human behavior. Will was considered to be a faculty of the mind, similar to thoughts and feelings. The notions of being "strong willed" and having "will power" are current concepts derived from the early idea that people can consciously determine how they are going to behave. The implication of this idea is that to get people to change their behavior, you have to convince them to change their will, as expressed in the proverb "A man convinced against his will is of the same opinion still." Since people had the capacity to control their own will, they were responsible for their actions.[2]

In spite of all that was written about it, however, the concept of will was never very adequate for explaining human behavior. The failure of will to help predict and describe behavior finally gave way to other conceptualizations of motivation.

Hedonism. An important construct in many early philosophical writings was **hedonism,** or hedonistic calculus. The ancient Greek philosophers used this principle as the core concept to explain what motivated human behavior. In the West, it served as a philosophical foundation for several centuries and was especially popular in the eighteenth and nineteenth centuries among such philosophers as John Locke, Jeremy Bentham, and John Stuart Mill.[3]

Basically, the principle of hedonism states that individuals seek pleasure and avoid pain—they pursue things that bring comfort and satisfaction and avoid things that bring pain and discomfort. Hedonism was a very simple principle that focused specifically on physical gratification and pain.

The basic principle of hedonism is still found in many of our current theories of motivation; however, it is far too simplistic to adequately explain the complexity of human behavior. Hedonism fails to explain why people engage in activities that are physically unpleasant. For example, this simple principle cannot explain why the early Puritans rejected physical comforts and intentionally pursued an ascetic life of arduous physical toil.

Instinct Theory. Another early explanation for behavior was based on a theory of **instincts.** According to Charles Darwin's theory of evolution, certain intelligent actions were inherited. The simplest of these were reflexes such as the sucking reflex of newborn infants. More complex behaviors, which were also more variable and adapted by individuals to the circumstances, were called *instincts.* Darwin believed instincts arose through natural selection and were necessary for survival.

Around the turn of the century, several psychologists used instincts as part of their theories of motivation, especially William James, William McDougall, and Sigmund Freud. James defined an instinct as the ability to perform an action without having previously learned how to perform it. Instincts were natural, unlearned behaviors, and James believed that an important difference between humans and other mammals was that humans had a great many more instincts than did other mammals.[4] McDougall claimed that instincts were inherited, purposive, goal-seeking tendencies that explained how people perceived objects and were aroused to take action regarding them. In 1908, McDougall published a list of twelve instincts: flight, repulsion, curiosity, cognacity, self-abasement, self-assertion, parenting, reproduction, hunger, gregariousness, acquisitiveness, and constructiveness.[5] Freud's writings were largely centered around two instincts, aggression and sex, although toward the end of his career when he was suffering from cancer of the mouth, he also wrote extensively about the death instinct.[6]

During the first quarter of this century, instincts were used extensively to explain behavior. In the 1920s, however, instincts were discredited for two reasons. First, the lists of instincts become both unwieldy and unreasonable. The list of instincts totaled nearly 6,000, including an "instinct to avoid eating apples in one's own orchard." The most significant attack against instincts, however, came from a group of behaviorists and cultural anthropologists who began to show that these behaviors were learned rather than inherited. Today, the notion of instincts is no longer used to explain behavior except for some animal behaviors and a few innate responses of newborn infants, such as the knee-jerk response to tapping the patella tendon, blinking in response to tapping the eyebrow, and head turning in response to touching the cheek. However, these actions are generally called *reflex responses* rather than *instincts.*

Needs. After instincts were discredited, explanations for behavior shifted to the notion of needs. A **need** was defined as an internal state of disequilibrium or deficiency that has the capacity to energize or trigger a behavioral response. The cause of the deficiency can be physiological, such as hunger; psychological, such as a need for power; or sociological, such as a need for social interaction. The presence of a need motivates a person to action to restore a state of equilibrium, as shown in Exhibit 4.1. A basic assumption of all need theories is that when deficiencies exist, people are motivated to action to satisfy them.

One of the earliest theories of needs was the **manifest need theory** proposed by Henry A. Murray.[7] Murray believed that needs are mostly learned rather than inherited and are activated by cues from the external environment. For example, an employee who has a high need for affiliation will pursue that need by associating with others only when the environmental conditions are appropriate. Only then will the need be *manifest*. When the need is not cued, the need is said to be *latent* or not activated.

Murray identified a wide range of needs that people supposedly acquire to one degree or another through interaction with their environment. Murray first developed a list of fifteen needs that were classified as viscerogenic (primary) and psychogenic (secondary). The needs for food, water, sex, urination, defecation, and lactation, all associated with physiological functioning, are examples of Murray's viscerogenic needs. Murray's psychogenic needs include abasement, achievement, affiliation, aggression, autonomy, deference, dominance, and power.

Murray's need categories focused on specific, relatively narrow need-related issues, and a separate need was created for almost every human behavior. Murray's list of needs was not derived from empirical research but from his personal observations and clinical experience. Periodically he added additional needs to his list, and the length of the list increased with his career.

Maslow's Needs Hierarchy

Abraham Maslow was a clinical psychologist whose theory of motivation was part of a larger theory of human behavior. Maslow was a humanist who was deeply concerned about the dignity and worth of individuals. He frequently talked of the differences between healthy and unhealthy people, and believed that people had a positive capacity to improve the quality of their lives. His theories of behavior emerged from his clinical experiences as he attempted to sift and integrate the ideas of other leading psychologists.[8]

Hierarchy of Needs. Using his experience as a therapist and counselor, Maslow formulated a theory that explained human behavior in terms of a **needs hierarchy.** He believed everyone has a common set of five universal needs, ordered in a hierarchy of importance from the lowest-level basic needs through the highest-order needs.

1. *Physiological needs.* Physiological needs are the most basic needs in Maslow's hierarchy and include needs that must be satisfied for the person to survive, including food, water, oxygen, sleep, sex, and sensory satisfaction.
2. *Safety and security needs.* If the physiological needs are relatively satisfied, Maslow claimed, safety and security needs emerge. These needs include a

EXHIBIT 4.1   Relationship Between Needs and Motivated Behavior

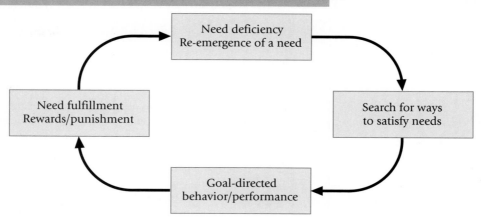

desire for security, stability, dependency, protection, freedom from fear and anxiety, and a need for structure, order, and law. Threats of physical harm, assault, tyranny, or wild animals prevent people from satisfying their safety needs and cause them to focus their energies almost exclusively on eliminating these threats.

3. *Social needs.* Originally Maslow referred to this need as the need for belongingness and love. Social needs include the need for emotional love, friendship, and affectionate relationships with people in general, but especially for a spouse, children, and friends. People who are unable to satisfy this need will feel pangs of loneliness, ostracism, and rejection.

4. *Ego and esteem.* The need for ego and esteem includes the desire for self-respect, self-esteem, and for the esteem of others, and may be focused either internally or externally. When focused internally, the esteem needs include a desire for strength, achievement, adequacy, mastery, confidence, independence, and freedom. When focused externally, this need consists of a desire for reputation or prestige, status, fame and glory, dominance, recognition, attention, importance, dignity, and appreciation.

5. *Self-actualization.* The highest need in Maslow's hierarchy was for **self-actualization,** which refers to the needs for self-realization, continuous self-development, and the process of becoming all that a person is capable of becoming.

According to Maslow, these five needs are arranged in a hierarchy of importance that he called **prepotency;** that is, higher-level needs are not important and are not manifest until lower-level needs are satisfied. Once lower-level needs are satisfied, needs at the next highest level emerge and influence behavior. The levels of the need hierarchy are not rigidly separated but overlap to some extent. Thus, it is possible for a higher-level need to emerge before a lower-level need is completely satisfied. In fact, Maslow estimated that average working adults have satisfied about 85 percent of their physiological needs, 70 percent of their safety needs, 50 percent of their social needs, 40 percent of their self-esteem needs, and 10 percent of their

EXHIBIT 4.2	Applying Maslow's Needs Hierarchy

Need Levels	General Rewards	Organizational Factors
1. Physiological	Food, water, sex, sleep	a. Pay b. Pleasant working conditions c. Cafeteria
2. Safety	Safety, security, stability, protection	a. Safe working conditions b. Company benefits c. Job security
3. Social	Love, affection, belongingness	a. Cohesive work group b. Friendly supervision c. Professional associations
4. Esteem	Self-esteem, self-respect, prestige, status	a. Social recognition b. Job title c. High-status job d. Feedback from the job itself
5. Self-actualization	Growth, advancement, creativity	a. Challenging job b. Opportunities for creativity c. Achievement in work d. Advancement in the organization

self-actualization needs. Although Maslow never collected data to support these estimates, many studies have found that lower-level needs are more satisfied than higher-level needs.[9]

Maslow's theory has been widely adopted by organizations and is frequently used as the foundation for organizational development programs such as participative management, job enrichment, and quality-of-work-life projects. According to his theory, an organization must use a variety of factors to motivate behavior, because people will be at different levels of the needs hierarchy. A list of the general rewards and organizational factors used to satisfy different needs is illustrated in Exhibit 4.2. Maslow encouraged managers to become more sensitive to the needs of employees, and he called the convergence of management and human relations "enlightened management."[10]

In Maslow's needs hierarchy, the effects of money are often misunderstood. The needs most directly related to money are physiological and security needs, because money contributes significantly to securing a comfortable and safe environment. Money is usually considered relatively unimportant for satisfying higher-level needs, and the general belief is that most American workers are mainly concerned about higher-level needs. Therefore, according to Maslow's needs hierarchy, money typically is not considered an effective motivator. However, this view overlooks the fact that money is usually essential to self-actualization because it buys the necessary time and resources that allow for self-actualizing activities.

Self-actualization. One of Maslow's unique contributions to motivation theory was his description of self-actualization. Self-actualization is the process of developing one's true potential as an individual to the fullest extent, and expressing skills, talents, and emotions in the most personally fulfilling manner. Self-actualization is a process, not an end state—people do not become self-actualized in the sense that they have finally reached an ultimate goal. Instead they are continually in the process of becoming more and more of what they are uniquely capable of becoming.

In his later writings, Maslow suggested that the need for self-actualization could not be gratified or satiated like the other needs. Instead, the need for self-actualization tends to increase in potency as people engage in self-actualizing behaviors. Thus, self-actualization is an ongoing process of becoming that is intensified and sustained as people achieve self-fulfillment.

How self-actualization is manifest varies greatly from person to person. Maslow believed that each person has a genetic potential, a blueprint, to describe what that person is uniquely capable of becoming. In one individual, the process of self-actualization might take the form of becoming an outstanding father or mother, while other people might express the same need athletically, musically, artistically, or administratively. Self-actualization does not demand that people excel as the best in the world, but only as the best they can possibly be. For example, people expressing their self-actualization through athletics do not have to be world-class athletes in order to develop and enjoy their athletic talents. Fulfillment can also be derived from achieving one's personal best performances. Although Maslow said self-actualization could not be defined precisely, he did describe some characteristics manifested by people he thought were advanced in self-actualization. These characteristics are shown in Exhibit 4.3.

Alderfer's ERG Theory. Maslow's research supporting his theory was largely limited to analyzing biographies of self-actualizing people and to his own clinical experiences. Maslow acknowledged that the research supporting his theory was weak and inadequate, and expressed the hope that more research would ultimately be directed toward confirming and refining his theory. He noted, however, that neither

---

EXHIBIT 4.3   Characteristics of Self-Actualizing People

1. Superior perception of reality
2. Increased acceptance of self, of others, and of nature
3. Increased spontaneity
4. Increase in problem centering
5. Increased detachment and desire for privacy
6. Increased autonomy and resistance to restrictive cultural norms
7. Greater freshness of appreciation and richness of emotional reaction
8. Greater frequency of peak experiences
9. Increased identification with the human species
10. Improved interpersonal relations
11. More democratic values and character structure
12. Greatly increased creativity
13. A carefully designed system of values

animal nor human laboratory studies could possibly examine the full range of human needs in an acceptable way.[11]

The most popular refinement of Maslow's theory is one proposed by Clayton Alderfer. Based on a series of studies, Alderfer condensed Maslow's needs hierarchy from five needs to just three, which he referred to as the **ERG theory**.[12]

1. *Existence needs.* The existence needs are all the material and physiological factors necessary to sustain human existence. This need encompassed Maslow's physiological and safety needs.
2. *Relatedness needs.* These needs include all socially oriented needs, which include Maslow's social needs and parts of the safety and esteem needs.
3. *Growth needs.* Growth needs are those related to the development of human potential, which includes Maslow's self-actualization plus the internally based portion of self-esteem needs.

Alderfer agreed with Maslow that people tended to move up the hierarchy as they satisfied lower-level needs. However, Alderfer did not believe that one level of needs had to be satisfied before the next-level need would emerge. All the needs could be simultaneously active for a given individual. Studies examining the ERG theory using bank employees, nurses, and life insurance personnel seem to suggest that Maslow's theory can be condensed from five needs to three, and that all three needs can be simultaneously active in motivating behavior.

Research on the Needs Hierarchy Theory. Maslow's theory has generated several research studies in organizational settings. One study, for example, found that managers in higher organizational levels place greater emphasis on self-actualization needs and are generally more able to satisfy their growth needs than lower-level managers.[13] These results were interpreted to support Maslow's theory, because higher-level managers tend to have more challenging, autonomous jobs where it is possible to pursue growth needs, while lower-level managers tend to have more routine jobs, making it more difficult to satisfy these needs.

Support for Maslow's theory has also come from the observations of those who have traveled in foreign countries and studied the effects of economic conditions on cultural development. Cultural arts and creative expression are found much more frequently in countries where the basic survival needs are largely satisfied. Higher-level expressions of self-esteem and self-actualization are not found as frequently in poorer countries where the majority of people are struggling for survival. However, the differences in the desire for actualization and creative expression between developed and underdeveloped countries seem to be vanishing with global communication and the spread of materialistic values.[14]

Although some evidence seems to support Maslow's theory, an extensive review of the research findings on the needs hierarchy concept concluded with an interesting paradox: the theory is widely accepted, but there is little research evidence to support it.[15] This extensive review examined three propositions of Maslow's model: (1) the existence of the hierarchy itself, (2) the proposition that an unfulfilled need leads people to focus exclusively on that need, and (3) the proposition that gratification of one need activates the next higher need.

Seventeen studies were reviewed to examine the first issue, and the results indicated that there was no clear evidence showing that human needs are classified into five distinct categories, or that these categories are structured in any special hierarchy. Most of these studies instead condensed the needs to just two categories—deficiency and growth needs. The deficiency needs, also called *lower-order needs*, refer to physiological, safety, and social needs. The growth needs, also called *higher-order needs*, are comprised of the needs for self-esteem and self-actualization. Occasionally needs are also categorized into extrinsic, interactive, and intrinsic needs. Extrinsic needs are associated with biological comforts and physical rewards; interactive needs are associated with the desire for social approval, affiliation, and companionship; and intrinsic needs concern yearnings for self-development, confidence, mastery, and challenge. These needs categories help to explain the nature of rewards and how they influence behavior. A comparison of these need theories is presented in Exhibit 4.4.

The second proposition, that unfulfilled needs lead people to focus exclusively on them, produced mixed results. Some studies supported this proposition while others failed to support it. The third proposition, that lower-level needs must be filled before higher-level needs are activated, was also not supported. Apparently higher-level needs can influence behavior even when lower-level needs are largely unfulfilled. Indeed, a review of some of the greatest artistic and cultural contributions in society showed that they were produced by people whose lower-level needs were seriously unfulfilled.[16]

Although it lacks empirical support, Maslow's need hierarchy continues to be a very popular theory of motivation. His description of self-actualizing people and his enduring belief in the developmental potential of people provide a useful model of personal development that is consistent with what Maslow hoped to achieve by his theory. Maslow's theory was not intended as a model for predicting individual behavior, but as a model describing the potential of a fully functioning human being.

McClelland's Learned Needs Theory

Another well-known need theory is the **learned needs** theory, developed by David McClelland and his associates. McClelland's theory is closely associated with learning theory, because he believed that needs were learned or acquired by the kinds of events people experienced in their culture. These learned needs represented behavioral predispositions that influence the way people perceive situations and motivate them to pursue a particular goal. People who acquire a particular need behave differently from those who do not have it. McClelland and his associates, particularly John Atkinson, investigated three of Murray's needs: achievement, affiliation, and power. In the literature, these three needs are abbreviated "nAch," "nAff," and "nPow."[17]

The Need for Achievement—nAch. The most thorough series of studies conducted by McClelland and his associates concerned the need for achievement. They defined the need for achievement as behavior directed toward competition with a standard of excellence.

McClelland's first step in studying the need for achievement was to develop a method for measuring achievement. Rather than simply infer achievement from a person's behavior or a self-report questionnaire, McClelland and his associates developed a projective test called the Thematic Apperception Test (TAT). The test consists of showing people a series of pictures, such as the one shown in Exhibit 4.5,

EXHIBIT 4.4	Comparison of Need Theories

Murray	Maslow	Alderfer	A Popular Classification Today
Psychogenic: Abasement Achievement Affiliation Aggression Autonomy Deference Dominance etc.	Self-actualization	Growth	Intrinsic
	Esteem		
	Social	Relatedness	Social interaction
Viscerogenic: Food Water Sex Urination Defecation Lactation	Safety	Existence	Extrinsic
	Physiological		
Divided into two categories but not arranged according to level or importance	Arranged in a hierarchical level of prepotency	Arranged in a hierarchy, but all can be simultaneously active	No order of importance implied

Source: David J. Cherrington, *Personnel Management* (Dubuque, Iowa: Wm. C. Brown Company Publishers, 1983), p. 255.

and asking them to write a story about each picture. Their scores are calculated by counting how many times they referred to achievement-oriented ideas in their stories. McClelland believed that analyzing these fantasies is the best way to measure the strength of their needs. People with high needs for achievement write stories about people who are striving to accomplish a particular goal and think about how to do it. In contrast, individuals who write stories that center on social interactions and being with others have a high need for affiliation, while stories about dominating, controlling, and influencing others indicate a high need for power.

Through his research, McClelland identified three characteristics of high-need achievers:

1. *High-need achievers have a strong desire to assume personal responsibility for performing a task or finding a solution to a problem.* Consequently, they tend to work alone rather than with others. If the task requires the presence of others, they tend to choose co-workers depending on their competence rather than their friendship.

EXHIBIT 4.5   Sample Picture for Measuring Achievement Motivation
(subjects are asked to write a story about this picture).

2. *High-need achievers tend to set moderately difficult goals and take calculated risks.*
   Consequently, in a ring toss game where children tossed rings at a peg at
   any distance they chose, high-need achievers chose an intermediate distance
   where the probability of success was moderate, while low-need achievers
   chose either high or low probabilities of success by standing extremely close
   or very far away from the peg.

3. *High-need achievers have a strong desire for performance feedback.* These people
   want to know how well they have done, and they are anxious to receive feedback regardless of whether they have succeeded or failed.

   In his research on the need for achievement, McClelland found that money did
not have a very strong motivating effect on high-need achievers; they were already
highly motivated. In a laboratory study, for example, high-need achievers performed very well with or without financial incentives.[18] Low-need achievers did not
perform well without financial incentives, but when they were offered money for
their work they performed noticeably better. This study does not mean that money

APPLYING ORGANIZATIONAL BEHAVIOR
IN THE NEWS

Developing a Need for Achievement

CNN Josie Natori spent nine years on Wall Street as one of Merrill Lynch's first female vice presidents before she left the finance world to become the founder and president of the Natori Company, a $25 million high-fashion women's lingerie company. Her status as an Asian woman has not inhibited her success; indeed, she claims that status as her biggest asset. She also says that her success does not come from being a great designer, because she sees herself as a business woman first. Her success can be attributed to her entrepreneurial spirit and her intense need for achievement, characteristics she acquired in her youth.

Josie Natori, the oldest of six children, was reared in the Philippines and attended a Catholic girls' school. Her father was a self-made man, the first member of his family to graduate from col-

lege. Her mother was a talented musician. Natori describes her upbringing as very strict, but says her family was very close and loving. At age 4 she was playing the classics on the piano, and at age 9 she gave her first solo performance with the Manila Philharmonic Orchestra.

Much of her entrepreneurial spirit came from her grandmother, who was nicknamed "Supreme Commander in Chief." Her grandmother was a matriarch who had her own business and served as an excellent role model for Josie.

Consistent with high need achievers, Josie Natori has a vision of what she wants to achieve, even though her long-range goals are not written, and she enjoys taking reasonable risks. She likes the challenge of business and is confident of her ability to excel.

Source: CNN *Pinnacle* news programming.

is unimportant to high-need achievers. Instead, to them, money is a form of feedback and recognition. When high-need achievers succeed, they look to monetary rewards as evidence of their success.

High-need achievers are characterized by their single-minded preoccupation with task accomplishment. Consequently, the need for achievement is an important motive in organizations because many managerial and entrepreneurial positions require such a single-minded preoccupation in order for the person to be successful. McClelland believed that a high need for achievement was essential to entrepreneurial success. In a series of rather unique and interesting studies, McClelland examined the need for achievement among managers in a number of current societies, to show that a high need for achievement was correlated with managerial success and economic activity. By examining the literature of earlier civilizations, McClelland was also able to show that the rise and fall of economic activity within the civilization was correlated with the rise and fall of the achievement motive.

This line of research is perhaps best illustrated by a study of the need for achievement in England between A.D. 1500 and 1850. To measure the achievement orientation of the English culture, the literature written at various points during this period was analyzed. The need for achievement was measured by counting the number of achievement themes per 100 lines of literature. The measure of economic activity came from historical records showing the tons of coal exported from England. The results, summarized in Exhibit 4.6, show that the rise and fall of economic activity followed the rise and fall of the need for achievement by about fifty years.[19]

EXHIBIT 4.6 **The Relationship Between the Need for Achievement and Economic Activity in England: A.D. 1500 to 1850**

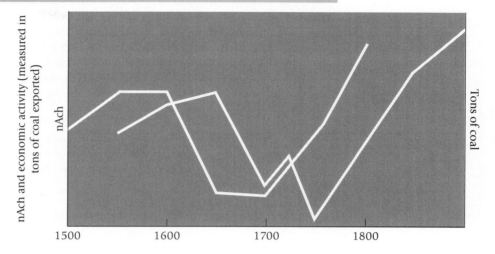

Source: David C. McClelland, *The Achieving Society,* New York: Free Press © 1967, p. 139. Reprinted with permission.

McClelland concluded from his research that the need for achievement, like other personality characteristics, is apparently learned at an early age and largely influenced by child-rearing practices and other influences of parents. Children tend to have a fairly high need for achievement if they have been raised by parents who have fairly strict expectations about right and wrong behavior, who provide clear feedback on the effectiveness of their performance, and who help their children accept personal responsibility for their actions.[20]

The need for achievement appears to be an important personal characteristic for entrepreneurs. A willingness to take reasonable risks, personal accountability, and a constant striving for goal accomplishment seem to be essential traits for successful entrepreneurs. A review of twenty-three studies that sought to link achievement motivation and entrepreneurship found a positive relationship in twenty of the studies.[21]

McClelland argued that economic development and national prosperity were closely related to the need for achievement and recommended that U.S. foreign aid programs to poorer countries focus on raising the need for achievement rather than on providing financial aid. He argued that the achievement motive could be taught, and described the kinds of training needed to raise the need for achievement. The training focused on four objectives. First, managers were encouraged to set personal goals and keep a record of their performance. Second, they were taught the language of achievement—to think, talk, and act like people with a high achievement motive. Third, managers were given cognitive or intellectual support—they were taught why the achievement motive was important to success. Fourth, they were provided with group support—a group of budding entrepreneurs met periodically to share success stories. In short, the managers were taught how to think and behave as entrepreneurs with a high achievement motive. Their new success-oriented behavior was reinforced verbally, intellectually, and through peer group influences.

Following this model, McClelland conducted a training program for fifty-two business executives in Hyderabad, India. Six to ten months after the course, many executives had doubled their natural rate of entrepreneurial activity. These findings have important implications for efforts to help underdeveloped nations because they suggest that beyond giving economic aid lies a greater need to instill the achievement motive in the population.[22]

The Need for Affiliation—nAff. The need for affiliation is defined as a desire to establish and maintain friendly and warm relations with other people. In many ways the need for affiliation is similar to Maslow's social needs. People with a high need for affiliation have these characteristics:

1. They have a strong desire for approval and reassurance from others.
2. They have a tendency to conform to the wishes and norms of others when they are pressured by people whose friendship they value.
3. They have a sincere interest in the feelings of others.

People with a high need for affiliation seek opportunities at work to satisfy this need. Therefore, people with a high nAff prefer to work with others rather than to work alone, and they tend to have good attendance records. Evidence also indicates that people with a high nAff tend to perform better in situations where personal support and approval are tied to performance.[23]

The implications for organizations of the need for affiliation are fairly straightforward. To the extent that managers can create a cooperative, supportive work environment where positive feedback is tied to task performance, employees with a high nAff tend to be more productive. The explanation for this is rather simple. By working hard in such an environment, people with high nAff can satisfy their affiliation needs. In contrast, people who have a low need for affiliation should be placed in positions allowing them to work fairly independently, since they prefer to work alone.

The Need for Power—nPow. The need for power has been studied extensively by McClelland and others.[24] This need is defined as the need to control others, to influence their behavior, and to be responsible for them. Some psychologists have argued that the need for power is the major goal of all human activity. These people view human development as the process by which people learn to exert control over the forces that exert power over them. According to this view, the ultimate satisfaction comes from being able to control environmental forces, including other people.

People who have a high need for power are characterized by

1. A desire to influence and direct somebody else
2. A desire to exercise control over others
3. A concern for maintaining leader–follower relations

People who have a high need for power tend to make more suggestions, offer their opinions and evaluations more frequently, and try to bring others around to their way of thinking. They also tend to seek positions of leadership in group activities, and their behavior within a group, either as leader or member, is described as verbally fluent, talkative, and sometimes argumentative.

In his research on the need for power, McClelland describes "two faces of power." The need for power can take the form of **personal power,** in which people strive for dominance almost for the sake of dominance, or **social power,** in which people are more concerned with the problems of the organization and what can be done to facilitate goal attainment. People with a high need for personal power tend to behave like conquistadors or tribal chiefs who inspire their subordinates to heroic performance, but they want their subordinates to be accountable to the leader, not to the organization. People with a high need for social power, however, satisfy their power needs by working with the group to formulate and achieve group goals. This method of satisfying power needs is oriented toward achieving organizational effectiveness rather than satisfying a self-serving egotism.[25]

Power needs are especially salient when the time comes for an entrepreneur to step aside and place the direction of a company under the control of a successor. Entrepreneurs high in personal power have more difficulty relinquishing control than those who are high in social power. A study of succession planning among entrepreneurs found that social power entrepreneurs are likely to have less trouble turning over their positions of power to someone else than will entrepreneurs who need personal power.[26]

McClelland argues that the need for social power is the most important determinant of managerial success. Although a high need for achievement may be necessary for entrepreneurial activity, most managerial positions in today's corporate world require managers who have a strong need for social power. Successful managers also need to have a relatively high need for achievement, but achievement is not as important for corporate managers in large corporations as it is for entrepreneurs.

Although people with a high need for social power tend to be more effective managers, McClelland provides some evidence suggesting that they pay a fairly high price for their success in terms of their own personal health. McClelland measured the need for power among a group of Harvard graduates and followed their careers over a twenty-year period. He found that 58 percent of those rated high in nPow either had high blood pressure or had died of heart failure.[27]

Herzberg's Motivator-Hygiene Theory

The **motivator-hygiene theory** was developed by Frederick Herzberg, a behavioral scientist whose initial training was in the field of public health. The theory was based on an extensive literature review on job attitudes and a series of interviews with engineers and accountants. From this survey, Herzberg separated the factors influencing satisfaction and motivation into two lists: hygiene factors and motivator factors.

Hygienes and Motivators. In his study, Herzberg and two colleagues asked 203 accountants and engineers to discuss times when they felt exceptionally good and times when they felt exceptionally bad about their jobs.[28] When these descriptions were analyzed, Herzberg found the employees tended to use different factors to describe their good and bad feelings. When describing what made them feel bad about their jobs, they usually mentioned factors in the context surrounding the job, such as company policy and administration, supervision, salary, interpersonal relations, and working conditions. These factors were referred to as maintenance factors or dissatisfiers, because they had the potential to make employees unhappy with their jobs, but lacked the potential to make them satisfied. Herzberg also labeled them hygienes to emphasize their preventive nature. When these context factors were present, they prevented dissatisfaction. Thus, context factors = dissatisfiers = hygienes.

When employees described the times they felt especially good about their jobs, they tended to identify factors directly associated with the content of the job: achievement, recognition, the work itself, responsibility, and advancement. These content factors were directly associated with the task itself and were called *satisfiers* or *motivators.* Herzberg claimed they were effective in motivating the individual to superior performance and effort. Thus, content factors = satisfiers = motivators.

Perhaps the most significant (and most controversial) concept in Herzberg's motivator-hygiene theory is his suggestion that the hygienes and motivators represent two different factors associated with satisfaction and motivation. Most conventional views say that job satisfaction is a bipolar concept ranging from extreme satisfaction to extreme dissatisfaction.

Dissatisfaction ←————————————————————————→ Satisfaction

However, Herzberg claimed that one simple continuum overlooks the unique difference between the motivators and the hygienes and the ways in which they influence satisfaction and motivation. He proposed a two-factor theory in which the opposite of dissatisfaction was simply no dissatisfaction, while the opposite of satisfaction was no satisfaction.[29]

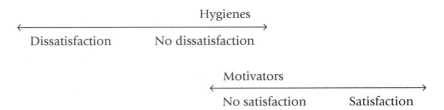

Hygienes
Dissatisfaction ←————————→ No dissatisfaction

Motivators
No satisfaction ←————————→ Satisfaction

According to Herzberg, therefore, the factors that create satisfaction and dissatisfaction are qualitatively distinct. Herzberg suggests that these two factors are as separate in influencing job attitudes as vision and hearing are in perceiving the environment. Just as increasing or decreasing light will have no effect on a person's hearing, neither will increasing or decreasing the hygienes have any impact on motivation. If the hygiene factors are not present, however, there will be no dissatisfaction, but increasing them further will not lead to satisfaction. Likewise, if the motivators are present, employees will feel satisfied and motivated, but their absence will not create dissatisfaction.

The organizational implications of Herzberg's theory are significant and controversial. The theory suggests that hygiene factors, especially pay and working conditions, will not effectively motivate workers. The only potential organizational benefit of providing hygienes is to avoid dissatisfaction. Therefore, Herzberg recommends that hygiene factors should be given adequate attention in order to maintain a healthy environment, but they should not attract excessive attention. Herzberg encourages managers to provide an equitable wage for employees and then avoid talking about it or drawing attention to compensation. Because Herzberg's motivators are related to the content of the job, his two-factor theory has been extensively used in job enrichment and job redesign projects. Applications of the motivator-hygiene theory to job redesign are described in Chapter 6.

Controversy and Criticism. Although Herzberg's theory has been widely accepted by managers, it has produced widespread controversy and criticism among behavioral scientists.[30] The results of the initial study have been replicated by Herzberg and his associates, using the same methodology on a variety of different employee groups and in many countries. Other researchers using the same methodology have also found what appears to be supporting evidence. However, studies using a different methodology fail to support Herzberg's theory.[31]

A major criticism of the motivator-hygiene theory is that it is "method bound"; in other words, it only produces supportive results when one method is used. Other methods produce different results. One explanation why Herzberg's methodology is the only method that supports his theory is based on attribution theory (explained in Chapter 2). People want to defend their self-esteem and to look good in the eyes of others. Therefore, when they describe the times they feel particularly good, they attribute these successful experiences to their own efforts and skills and thus to the intrinsic motivator factors. However, when they are asked to describe negative experiences they tend to blame context factors over which they have no control.

Two highly criticized implications of Herzberg's theory are first, the idea that the motivators and hygienes are separate factors representing distinctly different continua, and second, the idea that the hygiene factors, especially pay, cannot be used to motivate performance. One of the most extensive reviews of Herzberg's theory claims that it oversimplifies the complex sources of satisfaction and dissatisfaction and the relationship between satisfaction and motivation. This study re-examined the data from seventeen samples and concluded that (1) a given factor can cause both satisfaction and dissatisfaction in the same group of workers, (2) intrinsic motivator factors (such as achievement, which is directly tied to self-esteem) actually produce a greater influence on both satisfying and dissatisfying events than do extrinsic hygiene factors, and (3) while a particular event may cause job satisfaction for one person, the same event may be dissatisfying for another.[32]

Although the motivator-hygiene theory appears to be partially incorrect as it was originally stated by Herzberg, it has contributed to our understanding of motivation by identifying a wide range of organizational factors capable of influencing worker reactions. Furthermore, it has focused our attention on the intrinsic content factors of the job and provided a valuable framework for analyzing the relevant factors to be considered in a job redesign program. Herzberg's ideas have been applied extensively in job redesign projects in a wide range of organizations, including AT&T and Texas Instruments. Herzberg's theory is also an excellent illustration of how a theory need not be perfect to provide a valuable contribution. As is the case with most theories, we need to be more concerned with when it is helpful rather than whether it is right or wrong.

COGNITIVE THEORIES: THE PROCESS OF MOTIVATION

Although the need theories of motivation concentrate on what motivates people, the process theories focus on how motivation occurs. The process theories discussed in this section include expectancy theory, equity theory, and control theory. Both these theories are also cognitive theories of motivation, because they assume that people think and process information as rational decision makers.

Expectancy Theory

Expectancy theory is a cognitive model of motivation based on people's conscious thought processes as they evaluate a situation. It is also a decision-making theory that explains how people decide what to do by evaluating the outcomes and the probabilities associated with them.

Expectancy theory was derived from the research and thinking of many people, including philosophers, economists, psychologists, and managers. The earliest roots of expectancy theory stemmed from the English utilitarians of the eighteenth and nineteenth centuries, most notably Jeremy Bentham and John Stuart Mill, and the principle of hedonism described earlier. The utilitarians claimed that people compute a "hedonistic calculus" that lets them choose among possible alternatives on the basis of their assumptions about the relative amounts of pleasure and pain each had to offer.

During the 1930s and 1940s, significant contributions toward the development of expectancy theory were made by Kurt Lewin and Edward Tolman. These psychologists sought to move beyond the theory of motivation then being used to explain animal behavior, called "drive theory," to describe how people respond in a given situation. Basic to the theories of both men was the idea that people have behavioral expectations or anticipations about future events. These expectations are in the form of beliefs concerning the likelihood that a particular act will be followed by a particular outcome. These expectations were viewed as probabilities that could take values between zero (no chance of a rewarding outcome) and 1 (completely sure the reward would follow). Both Tolman and Lewin emphasized the subjective nature of these probabilities and noted that behavior was determined by the subjective rather than the objective probability.[33]

Similar concepts about subjective probabilities and the subjective value attached to the outcomes were concurrently being developed by economists, especially Ward Edwards. It was suggested that people would make choices based on the combination of the perceived value of the outcomes and the subjective probabilities that a particular event would occur. The subjective expected utility (SEU) of a particular alternative was calculated by multiplying the subjective probability of an outcome by the utility or value of that outcome, and summing the products across all possible outcomes. This process is explained further in Chapter 14 on decision making.

The first systematic and comprehensive formulation of expectancy theory was presented by Victor Vroom in his classic book, *Work and Motivation*.[34] Many theorists have sought to extend and refine expectancy theory; consequently, many different models of expectancy theory have been presented in the literature. Although each model may be slightly different, the basic components are essentially similar in each model. Expectancy theory has also been called "expectancy–valence theory," "instrumentality theory," and "valence–instrumentality–expectancy (VIE) theory."

The Determinants of Effort. The basic idea of expectancy theory is that motivation is determined by the outcomes people expect to occur as a result of their actions. The basic elements of this theory are shown in Exhibit 4.7 and outlined in the following diagram: the amount of effort a person is willing to exert depends on (1) the perceived relationship between effort and performance (expectancy), (2) the perceived relationship between performance and the outcomes (instrumentality), and (3) the value of the outcomes (valence).

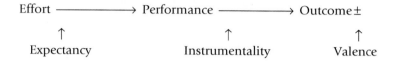

Expectancy is the probability that effort will lead to performance, as expressed in the questions "If I really try hard, can I do this job?" "If I exert enough effort, can I perform well?" This relationship is viewed as a probability, and in research on expectancy theory, people are asked to estimate the perceived probability that if they put out a certain level of effort, they will achieve a particular level of performance. Workers who are highly skilled and have direct control over their work normally report a high expectancy, because they know they can perform well if they try. Expectancies are much lower on jobs where employees see little relationship between their effort and performance, such as sales jobs where sales depend more on the customer's needs than the efforts of the sales representatives. Students complain about low expectancies when there is no relationship between how diligently they study and how well they perform in class. These low expectancies can be caused by a variety of reasons, such as the test questions are too ambiguous, the textbook is too difficult to understand, or students lack the prerequisites.

Instrumentality is the relationship between performance and outcomes. "If I perform well, will I be rewarded?" "What are the consequences for performing well?" Most situations produce a variety of consequences, and some outcomes are more likely than others. Because several outcomes are possible, individuals subjectively calculate several instrumentalities to decide what to do—one for each outcome. Instrumentalities are typically viewed as a correlation coefficient showing the relationship between two variables. An instrumentality of +1.0 implies a direct relationship between performance and outcomes, such as piece-rate incentives. People who are paid a fixed salary regardless of their performance, however, would report an instrumentality close to zero, indicating no relationship between pay and performance. Instrumentalities can also be negative. For example, leisure time would probably be negatively associated with performance, because employees are forced to relinquish some of their leisure and free time to increase their performance.

Valence is the value of the outcomes and the extent to which they are attractive or unattractive to the individual. Some rewards are almost universally valued, such as praise, recognition, and compliments by others, while other outcomes may only

EXHIBIT 4.7   The Determinants of Effort: Expectancy Theory

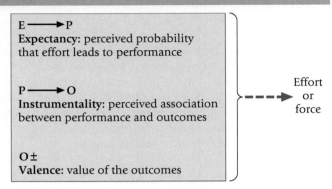

appeal to certain employees, such as promotions and opportunities to work over-time. Research studies measuring expectancy theory typically use an arbitrary scale, such as one that ranges from +10 to –10, to measure the valence of various out-comes. Pay increases, feelings of pride in craftsmanship, and feelings of being of ser-vice to others typically have positive valences, while being fired, being criticized by the supervisor, and feeling fatigue typically have negative valences.

Effort or force is the combination of expectancy, instrumentality, and valence. People who expect to receive highly valued outcomes if they perform well, and who expect to perform well if they exert sufficient effort, should be highly motivated employees. The components of expectancy theory—expectancy, instrumentality, and valence—can be multiplied together to measure individual effort. Because the components are multiplied together, expectancy theory is sometimes described as a *multiplicative* model.[35] The formula for combining expectancy, instrumentality, and valence, is

$$\text{Effort} = \exp \Sigma \, (\text{I} \cdot \text{V})$$

A recent refinement of expectancy theory suggests that measuring the incre-mental benefits of greater effort will provide more accurate predictions of behavior. This approach, called the *return-on-effort* (ROE) method, entails asking people to estimate the likelihood of an outcome as a result of working hard and then sub-tracting the likelihood that the same outcome will occur as a result of little effort. This refinement is more sensitive to the perceived relationship between effort and outcomes. Research indicates that the ROE method produces more accurate pre-dictions of behavior among both student subjects and employees.[36]

Although expectancy theory appears rather complex, the central ideas underly-ing it can be simply stated in a way that is easily understood. People are motivated to exert effort if by doing so they can perform well and attain desired outcomes. It is important to remember that expectancy theory is based on personal perceptions. Two workers placed in an identical situation may not exert equal effort, because they perceive different expectancies, instrumentalities, or valences. These percep-tions are influenced by past experiences, observations of the rewards others receive, and future anticipations.

Some descriptions of expectancy theory discuss two levels of outcomes: first-level outcomes and second-level outcomes. First-level outcomes usually concern performance variables, such as quantity and quality of productivity and attendance, while second-level outcomes usually concern all the consequences of performance, such as pay, promotion, fatigue, and a sense of accomplishment.[37]

Appendix 4-A at the end of this chapter shows how expectancy theory can be applied to a decision. This example illustrates how the components of expectancy theory can be combined to predict behavior; it also illustrates how the computations can be unreasonably complex. Does this model really describe the way people behave? Do we actually make all these calculations before deciding what to do? The answer to these questions is clearly no. But even though we do not make all these explicit calculations, it is still reasonable to assume that we implicitly estimate both the probability of being able to perform well if we put forth sufficient effort and the likelihood that the performance will be followed by desirable outcomes.

Research on Expectancy Theory. Extensive research has examined expectancy theory, and most studies have produced positive results in spite of some difficult methodological problems. Perhaps the greatest difficulty in testing expectancy theory stems from the fact that the theory is so comprehensive that it is virtually impossible to concurrently test all aspects of the theory. Consequently, most studies have only examined a limited part of the theory in any given study. Another problem in testing the theory stems from having many versions of the theory. Although they are generally similar, there are enough differences to create some confusion regarding the right way to measure the components and combine the numbers.

Although various modifications and extensions have been proposed, the basic concepts of expectancy theory have remained unchanged: effort is determined by the combination of expectancy, instrumentality, and valence. The correlations between the levels of effort predicted by expectancy theory and actual job performance have generally been low, ranging between .20 and .70. However, correlations of this size are quite encouraging, because performance is determined by other variables than just individual effort. Reviews of research studies investigating expectancy theory have generally concluded that sufficient empirical support has been generated to safely conclude that expectancy theory accurately describes human motivation. Although expectancy theory may not be able to explain fully all motivated behavior, the results are sufficiently impressive to support the basic components of the model.[38]

The Expanded Expectancy Model. In addition to describing the determinants of effort, expectancy theory has been expanded to explain job performance and satisfaction.[39] This expanded model is illustrated in Exhibit 4.8. According to this model, job performance is a multiplicative combination of abilities and skills, effort, and role perceptions. If people have clear role perceptions, if they have the necessary skills and abilities, and if they are motivated to exert enough effort, the model suggests that they will perform well. Abilities and skills include both physical and psychological characteristics, such as finger dexterity, mental ability, and the proficiency people have developed from experience or training.

Role perceptions concern the clarity of the job description and whether individuals know how to direct their efforts toward effectively completing the task.

EXHIBIT 4.8   **Expectancy Theory Model**

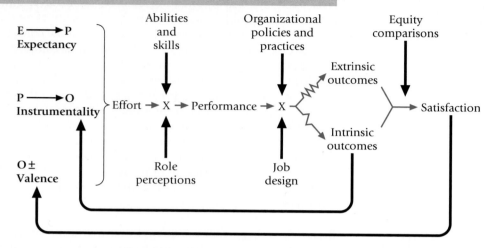

Source: Adapted from L. W. Porter and E. E. Lawler, *Managerial Attitudes and Performance* (Homewood, Ill.: Richard D. Irwin, 1968), p. 165.

Those who have clear perceptions of their role responsibilities apply their efforts where they will count and perform the correct behaviors. Those who have incorrect role perceptions tend to spend a large part of their time in unproductive efforts that do not contribute to effective job performance.

According to the model, performance produces extrinsic and intrinsic outcomes. The wavy lines are intended to indicate that the relationship between performance and rewards is not direct, but that the relationship for intrinsic rewards tends to be more direct than for extrinsic rewards. Whether job performance will produce intrinsic outcomes is primarily determined by the design of the job and the values of the worker, while the relationship between performance and extrinsic outcomes is determined by the organizational policies regarding such things as pay and promotions.

The model predicts that satisfaction levels are determined by the levels of intrinsic and extrinsic outcomes. These outcomes, however, are influenced by equity comparisons, suggesting that satisfaction is determined not only by the actual outcomes people receive, but also by the level of outcomes they expect to receive and how these outcomes compare with the rewards of others.

The feedback loops in the model explain how the expectancy components are created and can be changed. Because expectancy is the perceived relationship between effort and performance, it is reasonable to assume that future expectancies will be influenced by previous experience. People who have performed well in the past expect to perform well again. Instrumentalities are influenced even more by past experiences. Those who in the past have experienced contingent rewards—rewards tied to performance—expect the same in the future. The valences of outcomes are also derived in part from the types of satisfactions people have experienced in the past. Outcomes that have been associated with pleasant experiences in the past tend to have higher valences in the future.

Applying Expectancy Theory

According to Expectancy Theory, How Do Supervisors Motivate Employees? Expectancy theory provides a convenient model for diagnosing performance problems and motivating employees. When supervisors describe poor performance, they often use such phrases as "lacks initiative," "insufficient dedication," "no commitment," or "bad attitude." Unfortunately, these explanations do not help supervisors know what to do differently to obtain greater motivation.

Rather than attributing motivation problems to a lack of initiative or other personality traits, expectancy theory provides specific recommendations for improving motivation. Motivation problems are solved by altering the components of expectancy theory: expectancy, instrumentality, and valence.

1. *Examine the effort–performance relationships.* Employees are not willing to put forth much effort if they think their efforts are unproductive. They need to see a strong relationship between their efforts and how well they perform. Low expectancies are usually an indication that supervisors need to provide job training to help employees make their efforts more productive.

2. *Examine the performance–reward relationships.* Since people do what they are reinforced for doing, the performance–reward relationship should provide rewards that are tied to performance.

3. Use highly valued rewards to reinforce good performance. The consequences of good performance should possess a high positive valence. Money is a positive reward for most employees, but it is not the only valuable reward. Intrinsic rewards, such as achievement and feelings of pride in craftsmanship, also can reinforce outstanding performance.

Equity Theory

Equity theory is another cognitive theory of human behavior that has been used to explain motivation problems and levels of job satisfaction. Equity theory comes from the field of social psychology and is based on a series of studies examining social comparison processes. Social comparison theories focus on the feelings and perceptions of individuals and on whether they think they are treated fairly compared to others.

According to social comparison theory, people evaluate their social relationships in much the same way economists describe the economic exchanges in the marketplace. Social relationships are viewed as an exchange process in which people expect certain outcomes in return for the contributions or investments they make. The inducements–contributions theory of James March and Herbert Simon described earlier in Chapter 1 is an illustration of social comparison theory.[40] Equity theory represents an extension of social comparison theories and specifically examines the expectations individuals have about the outcomes they receive as a result of their contributions of time and effort.

Comparison Processes. According to equity theory, people evaluate their inputs to the job relative to the outputs they receive.[41] However, this evaluation is based on a relative comparison rather than a comparison against a fixed standard. Employees compare what they receive for their inputs relative to what they believe others received for theirs. "Did I get as much from my inputs as my co-workers received for theirs?" According to equity theory, therefore, attitudes toward pay are influenced by how much pay people receive, what they had to do to earn it, and whether they feel their ratio of pay to work was fair compared to the pay-to-work ratios of others. Those who think their ratios are unfair experience dissatisfaction that motivates them to change the situation in the direction of greater equity.

Inputs are all the relevant factors people bring to the exchange. The typical inputs include effort, performance, education, skills, time, and opportunity costs. It is important to note that the value attached to an input is based on the person's *perception* of its value, rather than its objective worth. Outcomes include all the rewards people receive from the exchange. Although pay is the most obvious organizational outcome, many other positive and negative outcomes may also be viewed as relevant and valuable, such as working conditions, social interactions, stress, and fatigue. Again, the value is determined by the person's perceptions rather than by any objective value.

The basic comparisons of equity theory can be illustrated by the following formula comparing the input–outcome ratios of a person relative to the input–outcome ratios of others.

$$\frac{O_p}{I_p} \overset{?}{=} \frac{O_o}{I_o}$$

where O = outcomes
I = inputs
o = others
p = person

In this formula, O_p divided by I_p refers to the ratio of a person's outcomes to inputs while the O_o divided by I_o refers to the outcomes–inputs ratio of others. A state of equity exists when the two ratios are essentially equal. But this state of equity can be destroyed by changing any of the four values. For example, you could feel underpaid because your outcomes were decreased ("My shift differential was eliminated"), because your inputs were increased ("I have to travel further to get to the workplace"), because the outcomes of the others were increased ("Sam got a production bonus"), or because the inputs of others were decreased ("Sam's new machine is easier to operate than mine").

A state of inequity exists whenever the two ratios are unequal, and it can be caused by either ratio being greater than the other. In other words, inequity can exist because people are either overpaid or underpaid. Not surprisingly, the available research suggests that people are more easily upset by underpayment than by overpayment. Therefore, people are more willing to accept overpayment in a social exchange than underpayment. Nevertheless, according to equity theory, both conditions of inequity motivate individuals to establish a more equitable exchange.

Equity theory explains why employee performance is often less than expected. Employees typically have inflated perceptions of a "fair wage" because high wages are mentioned more frequently in the popular literature. Because the actual wages employees receive are generally less than what they perceive as fair wages, workers supply a corresponding fraction of their normal effort.[42]

Equity theory is a general theory, believed to apply to most people in most situations. The importance of equity, however, is not universally accepted by everyone.

Research has shown that the norm of equity is an individual characteristic, somewhat linked to gender, wherein some people, especially men, are more prone than women to distribute outcomes to other people in direct proportion to their inputs. This is not to say that men are more concerned than women with being fair in allocating rewards. Rather, men are more apt to use a norm of equity, whereas women are more apt to adopt an equality norm in which outcomes are distributed equally regardless of inputs.[43]

Consequences of Inequity. When a perceived state of equity exists, people tend to feel satisfied and report that the conditions are fair. When a perceived condition of overreward exists, however, people tend to feel guilty and dissatisfied and they are motivated to correct the imbalance. Likewise, when a perceived state of underreward exists, people tend to feel dissatisfied and angry, and again they are motivated to do something about it. According to equity theory, a perceived state of inequity creates tension within individuals and the tension is proportionate to the magnitude of the inequity.

Six methods have been proposed to explain how people try to reduce inequity.[44]

1. People may alter their inputs. Underpaid workers could reduce their level of effort while overpaid workers could increase theirs.

2. People may alter their outcomes. People who feel overrewarded can share their rewards with others (although they usually don't), while underrewarded people will try to obtain greater rewards by increasing prices, requesting a raise, or joining a union.

3. People may cognitively distort their inputs and outcomes. People who are underrewarded may cognitively distort both their inputs ("I don't really work that hard, after all") or their outcomes ("Besides, I get a lot of satisfaction living in this community"). Cognitive distortion is especially likely for overrewarded people who may distort either their inputs ("I bring with me a lot of experience and leadership from my earlier jobs") or their outcomes ("Even though I get more money, I pay more taxes").

4. People may distort the inputs or outcomes of others. It is just as easy for people to distort their perceptions of others' outcomes and inputs as it is to distort their own.

5. People may change objects of comparison. Sometimes the easiest adjustment is to adopt a different comparison group. For example, if a group of executive secretaries received a substantial pay increase, an easy way to rationalize it is to think of themselves more as executives and less as secretaries.

6. People may leave the field. If they can't change the actual inputs or outcomes, and cognitive distortion becomes too difficult or painful, people may choose to leave the situation by transferring to another job or quitting.

The object of these methods is to re-establish a condition of equity and reduce the tension created by the former inequitable state. Because equity theory is a cognitive theory of motivation, it is frequently rather difficult to predict which method of tension reduction someone may adopt. Over time, it is likely that a given person will use them all.

Research on Equity Theory. Equity theory has generated a substantial body of research to assess the validity of the theory. Most of this research has focused on equity theory's predictions of how employees react to pay. These studies focused on two types of pay inequity, overpayment and underpayment, and two methods of compensation—hourly pay and piece-rate pay. The results of several studies generally support these conclusions:[45]

1. When people are underpaid on a piece-rate system, they tend to increase the quantity of their work while letting the quality decline. Because they get paid only for what they produce, they try to correct for the underpayment by producing more units while allowing the quality to decline.

2. People who are underpaid on an hourly rate tend to respond by reducing their effort and allowing both the quantity and quality of their work to decline. Because they can't change their hourly rate of pay, their outcomes are fixed. Therefore, they try to correct the underpayment by reducing their inputs of effort.

3. People who are overpaid on a piece-rate system tend to reduce the quantity of their work and increase their quality. Because overpayment is created by more outputs than inputs, they tend to reduce their pay by producing fewer units, but invest significantly greater effort, thereby raising the quality.

4. People who are overpaid on an hourly rate tend to increase both the quantity and quality of their performance. Because their outcomes are set at a fixed hourly rate, they can correct the imbalance only by increasing their inputs. Consequently, by exerting greater effort they increase both the quantity and quality of their work.

Studies on the effects of overpayment have sometimes been clouded by weak results and competing explanations. Part of this difficulty comes from how perceptions of overpayment were created: the subjects' qualifications for their jobs were challenged in order to make them feel overpaid relative to their qualifications. Making people feel unqualified, however, influences more than their perceptions of pay equity: it also threatens their self-esteem. An illustration of equity theory and the way overpayment perceptions were created is described in Appendix 4-B. Research studies examining the effects of underpayment, however, are much more consistent. Equity theory appears to be a useful tool in predicting whether employees will believe their pay is fair or unfair, and how they might respond when they feel underpaid.

Applying Equity Theory. The most significant implication of equity theory for managers is that perceived underpayment will have a variety of negative consequences for the organization such as low productivity, turnover, grievances, absenteeism, and dissatisfaction. When evaluating and rewarding employees, managers need to remember that the objective reality of how much people are paid is not as important as the subjective perceptions of equity. Rewarding one individual is not an isolated event. A sizable bonus awarded to one employee may cause that individual to feel rewarded, but it may create intense dissatisfaction among many others because of their perceived state of inequity.

According to equity theory, individuals should increase the quantity and quality of their performance when they feel overpaid. Overpayment can be created by actually paying employees more than they are worth, or by manipulating them to

APPLYING ORGANIZATIONAL BEHAVIOR
ACROSS CULTURES

Equity and Outrageous Executive Pay

In the United States, some of the highest-paid CEOs receive more than a thousand times as much money as the lowest-paid full-time employees. Such large pay multiples are simply outrageous, and they have also been called immoral. Such inequities in executive compensation have become sensationalized. In the U.S. auto industry, for example, the ratio is 192 to 1, while in the Japanese auto industry the ratio is only 20 to 1. Pay ratios vary greatly across cultures, but the differences are not always this sensational.

According to equity theory, people compare their input–outcome ratios with the input–outcome ratios of others to decide if they are being treated fairly. But how do workers make meaningful comparisons between their wages and the exorbitant salaries of corporate executives? And who should international executives use for their comparison person?

In the fifth century B.C., Plato wrote that no man in the community should earn more than five times what the lowest-paid worker makes. Many years later, financier J. P. Morgan suggested that the ratio should never exceed a 20–1 ratio. Morgan observed that many of his less successful clients paid exorbitant salaries to top executives and concluded that their disproportionately high executive salaries created internal dissension and conflict. Management expert Peter Drucker also claims that ratios greater than 20 to 1 have an adverse impact by provoking

inflationary wage demands and creating divisive class conflict.

A recent study shows that in the United States the average compensation of CEOs is twenty-six times greater than the compensation of an average manufacturing employee. Here, compensation includes cash pay, stock options, benefits, and perquisites (perks), and the data include both large and small companies. The pay ratios in other industrial countries are not as great.

United States	26–1	Canada	12–1
Britain	17–1	Japan	11–1
France	16–1	Germany	11–1
Italy	15–1		

Compensation specialists suggest that large pay multiples create feelings of inequity and a lack of trust among members of a management team. Reducing the gap between executives' salaries and the wages of workers is seen as an important step in creating better equity and trust. Contributing to this perception is the observation that Japan and Germany, two economically strong countries, have low pay multiples.

Sources: Amanda Bennett, "Executive Pay: An International Survey; Managers' Incomes Aren't Worlds Apart," *Wall Street Journal* (October 12, 1992), p. B1; Bob Daily, "Compensation: Multiple Pay, Multiple Problems," *Business Month* (June 1990), pp. 76–77; D. Keith Denton, "Equity, the Unifying Factor," *HR Magazine*, vol. 37 (February 1992), pp. 111–112.

believe they receive more than they are worth, such as by downgrading the quality of their inputs. Overpayment is not really an effective long-term strategy to increase productivity, however, because feelings of overpayment appear to be extremely temporary. People can cognitively change their perceptions very rapidly. Rather than continuing to feel overpaid and working harder, they very quickly come to believe their efforts are worth what they receive.

Control Theory

Several attempts have been made to combine the diverse theories of motivation into one integrated model. One of the most complete integrated models that manages to incorporate many of the major theories of human behavior is called **control theory.**[46] This theory is reasonably parsimonious, and the model explaining it is dynamic and focuses on self-regulation and the underlying cognitive mechanisms of motivation. A basic outline of the model is shown in Exhibit 4.9.

Control theory in the behavioral sciences is an elaboration of control theory in the physical sciences with simple feedback loops. The classic illustration is a thermostat that controls room temperature by activating a furnace or air conditioner when room temperature deviates from the designated standard. When this model is applied to human behavior, goals or performance standards incite people to action and lead to motivated behavior. Motivated behavior is like the furnace in the physical example and is referred to as the **effector** because it makes things happen and gets things done.

The result of motivated behavior (effort) is organizational performance, which is measured either objectively or subjectively and provides feedback to the individual. Feedback is called the **sensor** and is similar to the device in a thermostat that measures room temperature. And just as a thermostat acts as a **comparator,** comparing current room temperature against the thermostat setting, so also people evaluate their performance against their goals. If their performance is on target, they continue; if they are off target, their response will depend on whether they know what to do to take corrective responses. If they know what went wrong, their response will be almost automatic, like an unconscious scripted response. But if they don't know, they might begin a lengthy investigation that could result in trying new behaviors, revising their goals, reassessing the value of the rewards, or possibly leaving the field.

Control theory contains both cognitive (knowledge) and affective (feeling) elements. The cognitive component consists of internal goals, performance information, and the comparison between them. The affective component occurs when behavior is initiated because of the perceived discrepancy between the goals and performance.

Control theory accommodates all the research conclusions regarding goal setting and feedback. It explains very nicely, for example, why specific measurable goals lead to higher performance than vague do-your-best goals. It also incorporates the ideas of programed versus nonprogramed decision making (discussed in Chapter 14) and the individual versus situational sources of variance discussed in attribution theory. The principles of social cognitive theory are consistent with control theory, as shown most clearly by the inclusion of unconscious scripted responses. Scripts are overlearned performance programs or routines that provide sequences of events for common problems. Many routine work behaviors are executed via scripts. When performance is inadequate and people know how to improve, they automatically adopt a scripted response that has been reinforced in the past. Control theory similarly accommodates expectancy and equity theories, largely through the evaluation process, as people consider both their first- and second-level outcomes and decide whether the rewards they receive are adequate and fair.

Research using control theory has sought to explain three kinds of reactions: task performance, affective reactions to various organizational conditions, and behavioral withdrawal from unpleasant situations. The predictions of control theory tend to be more accurate for people who are high in private self-consciousness because they seem to be more aware of what they are trying to accomplish and how

EXHIBIT 4.9   Control Theory of Work Motivation

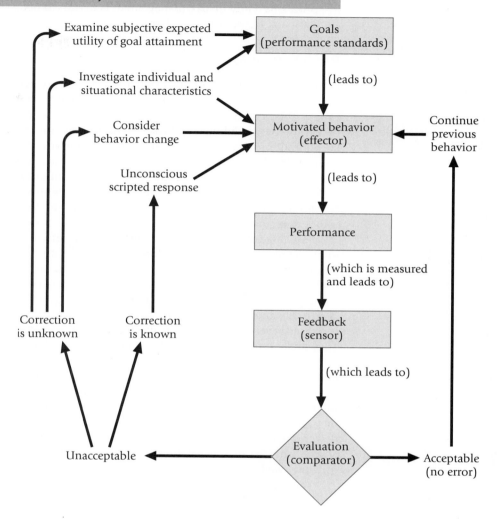

well they are succeeding. One study using control theory found that people who show high levels of private self-consciousness tend to suffer most from the effects of chronic work stressors.[47]

INTEGRATING AND APPLYING MOTIVATIONAL THEORIES

The theories described in this chapter have spawned a wide variety of management programs to motivate employees. Some of the most popular programs include participative management, job enrichment, quality-of-work-life programs, alternative patterns of work, employee recognition programs, and a variety of financial incentive programs. Participative management is discussed here, and the other programs are discussed in the next two chapters.

Participative Management

Participative management, also called "employee involvement" and "participative decision making," or PDM, invites employee involvement in managing the organization. This is accomplished by allowing subordinates to share in making material decisions, by including employees in the budgeting and goal-setting processes, keeping subordinates informed about the economic condition of the organization, inviting employees to recommend innovative ideas and suggestions, treating subordinates with consideration and respect, supporting employees even when they make mistakes, and providing training and development opportunities to help employees advance. Employee ownership, the ultimate in employee participation, is described in the next chapter.

Participative management has generated an emotional debate among behavioral scientists. Some argue that there are moral reasons why employees should be permitted to participate in management decisions. Denying employees the opportunity to participate in making decisions is interpreted as evidence that managers are exploitative, autocratic, and even suppressive. These advocates assume that everyone wants to participate in managing the organization, and they point to the increased level of education in the population as evidence for their assumption. They argue that today's workforce is better educated and more highly skilled than ever before and that educated people generally seek autonomy, self-actualization, and the right to make decisions. Some advocates have even called for government legislation that would force organizations to be more participative by requiring them to allow employee participation on boards of directors and employee involvement in making significant managerial decisions about such things as new product development and plant closings. Some European countries, such as Germany, have already enacted such legislation, called *codetermination,* and it seems to be operating quite well.

The arguments against participative management are that sometimes it doesn't work and sometimes people don't want it. Participation does not always lead to better performance. Some experiments found that participative management reduced productivity and it was considered a failure. For many employees, participation is not appropriate for their jobs. Even unions have occasionally refused to accept management's invitation to participate in making managerial decisions. The attitude of many union leaders is that it is management's responsibility to manage the company in a profitable way; the union members are only concerned about receiving a fair wage. Participative management also takes more time. The more people involved in making a decision, the longer it takes and the more difficult it is to reach a consensus decision. Furthermore, if they are involved, employees expect to be rewarded financially for their contribution. Occasionally, however, there are no rewards for them to share.[48]

A review of the research on participative decision making found that participation tends to increase subordinates' satisfaction, but it is no more likely to increase productivity than authoritative decision making. The results from both laboratory and field studies agree that performance is unchanged. Although we want to believe participation enhances productivity because it is "good," the results fail to support

APPLYING ORGANIZATIONAL BEHAVIOR
RESEARCH

Motivation in a Russian Factory

 Three motivation techniques that have been widely used in U.S. companies were examined in a Russian factory: extrinsic rewards, behavioral management, and participation. Although all three of these techniques have been successfully implemented in U.S. firms, participation was not expected to improve the productivity of Russian workers because it violates some of their cultural values.

The participants were ninety-nine workers in the Tver Cotton Mill, located 90 miles northwest of Moscow. Groups of workers were randomly assigned to one of three conditions. Those in the extrinsic reward condition received valued American products if they increased their performance, such as soap, clothes, canned goods, and music tapes. Those in the behavioral management intervention received praise and feedback for such functional behaviors as checking the looms, making repairs, and changing the rolls of cloth. For dysfunctional behaviors, such as absenteeism or dirty hands, they were given reminders and encouragement. Those in the participative intervention attended open-ended discussions asking workers for their input on how to improve performance in their area of responsibility.

The experiment lasted six weeks. Baseline measures were obtained for the first two weeks, followed by two weeks of the intervention, plus another two weeks of postintervention measures. The dependent variable was the average meters of top-grade fabric produced per worker.

The extrinsic rewards groups significantly increased their production from a baseline of 18,954, to 22,248 while the rewards were available, and to 21,401 in the final period. Likewise, the behavioral management groups increased their production from a baseline of 18,864, to 20,587 while they received feedback and recognition, and to 19,207 in the final period. The participative groups, however, showed a decline from a baseline of 20,130, to 18,144 during the discussions, and 18,384 after the intervention ended.

Historically, Lenin suggested the use of team meetings to get workers to provide input for improving performance. However, the Russian culture has not supported it. Russian workers are loyal to each other, and their work groups have established a culture that values cohesion, solidarity, and camaraderie. Participative efforts that require a company-wide perspective threaten to disrupt the Russian cultural value of communal work.

Source: Dianne H. B. Welsh, Fred Luthans, and Steven M. Sommer, "Managing Russian Factory Workers: The Impact of U.S.-Based Behavioral and Participative Techniques," *Academy of Management Journal,* vol. 36 (1993), pp. 58–79.

it. There were as many studies showing participation leading to inferior performance as leading to superior performance, but the large majority of studies found no difference.[49]

People Do What They Expect to Be Rewarded for Doing

Perhaps the best summary principle explaining human behavior is that people do what they expect to be rewarded for doing. This principle, which sounds much like the earlier principle of hedonism, serves as a useful foundation for analyzing motivation problems. The difference between this principle and hedonism, however, is that this principle recognizes the complexity of determining what is rewarding to the individual and it is based on more than physical gratification.

This general principle is largely consistent with each of the theories of motivation, and each of these theories helps to identify what will be rewarding and when.

Studies in operant conditioning found that animal behaviors were greatly influenced by food because the animals were hungry and because they were rewarded with food when they made the correct response. In a typical experiment with pigeons, the birds were reduced to 80 percent of their free-feeding weight to make sure that food would be a valued reward.

Social cognitive theory recognizes more clearly the complexity of rewards and how they can be derived vicariously and symbolically. Secondary rewards, for example, are learned and can be derived from past experience. Whether a particular event will be rewarding is often based on a person's value system.

Maslow's theory emphasizes the importance of self-esteem and self-actualization as secondary rewards for those who have acquired them. His theory is particularly useful in understanding the indomitable human spirit and the heights of creativity and greatness people can aspire to attain. Likewise, McClelland's research on the need for achievement helps us understand how the achievement need is acquired as a secondary reinforcer and how it influences both individual accomplishments and economic success. Apparently, other secondary rewards, such as the need for power, the need for affiliation, and the work ethic are acquired through a similar process. Organizational behavior modification programs rely on a functional analysis of the reinforcement contingencies and the kinds of reinforcers available to people to understand and alter their behavior. Expectancy theory and equity theory explain how perceptions of rewards and the ways in which they are obtained may be more important than the actual rewards in determining behaviors.

In summary, each theory of motivation contributes to our understanding of the kinds of rewards that may be considered important to people and of the conditions under which they will be rewarded. Although people do what they are rewarded for doing, sometimes it is difficult to know for certain that a specific outcome will in fact be perceived as a reward or that it will be the most important reward. The best motivation theory for analyzing a motivation problem may depend on the situation; different theories may be more helpful at different times.

SUMMARY

1. Some of the earliest explanations for motivation were based on the concept of a person's will or inherited instincts. The most popular idea, however, was the principle of hedonism, which states that people seek pleasure and avoid pain.

2. The concept of needs developed as psychologists began to realize that instincts were learned rather than inherited behaviors. A need was defined as an internal state of disequilibrium or deficiency that had the capacity to energize behavior to satisfy the need.

3. One of the earliest theories of needs was the manifest need theory proposed by Henry A. Murray. Although at first he proposed only a limited number of viscerogenic and psychogenic needs, his list ultimately became rather lengthy and unwieldy.

4. The most popular need theory is the hierarchy of needs proposed by Abraham Maslow. The five needs proposed by Maslow include physiological needs, safety and security needs, social needs, ego and esteem needs, and self-actualization needs. These needs are arranged in a hierarchy of importance that he called *prepotency*. Lower-level needs must be largely satisfied before needs at the next level appear.

5. Self-actualization is the process of personal fulfillment in which people become more of what they are uniquely capable of becoming. Self-actualization is a process rather than an end

state. It is not a need that becomes satiated but one that grows in importance with each exposure.

6. Maslow's needs hierarchy was refined by Clayton Alderfer, who proposed the ERG Theory of three needs rather than five: existence, relatedness, and growth needs.

7. David McClelland's learned needs theory examined the needs for achievement, affiliation, and power and described how they were acquired, their behavioral characteristics, and their effects on society. The need that received the greatest research attention was the need for achievement. High need achievers are characterized by personal responsibility, moderate risk, and a strong desire for feedback. McClelland found that the need for achievement was important for economic activity and entrepreneurial success.

8. Frederick Herzberg proposed a motivator-hygiene theory suggesting that the motivator variables contributing to satisfaction and productivity were completely separate from the hygiene factors that determined levels of dissatisfaction. Although research has failed to support Herzberg's claim of two separate factors, his theory has been successfully applied to job redesign programs where significant job enrichment has occurred by focusing on the motivator factors.

9. Expectancy theory is a cognitive motivation model in which people decide what to do by evaluating the probable outcomes of their behavior. The basic components of expectancy theory include expectancy (relationship between effort and performance), instrumentality (relationship between performance and outcomes), and valence (the importance of the outcomes). These three components can be measured, and the numbers can be combined quantitatively to derive a measure of effort.

10. Expectancy theory has been expanded in a model that suggests that effort is combined multiplicatively with ability and role perceptions to determine job performance. Job performance in turn determines the levels of both intrinsic and extrinsic rewards, and these rewards determine job satisfaction.

11. Expectancy theory is a useful model for diagnosing performance problems. Three components should be analyzed and possibly changed: the effort–performance relationships, the performance–reward relationships, and the value or importance of the rewards.

12. Equity theory is derived from social comparison theory and suggests that people compare their output–input ratios with the output–input ratios of others. A state of inequity exists when people think their ratios are not equal to the ratios of others. A state of imbalance caused either by being overrewarded or underrewarded motivates people to change the situation and re-establish a state of balance.

13. Control theory is a theory of motivation modeled after control theory in the physical sciences. Goals, or performance standards, incite people to action and lead to motivated behavior, called the *effector*. The results of motivated behavior are measured and compared, through a process called the *comparator*, against the goals. If performance is on target, performance continues; if it is off target, corrective actions are made.

14. Many companies have tried to achieve higher levels of motivation by installing some form of participative management program. These programs allow employees to be involved in making managerial decisions and provide other forms of involvement that are designed to satisfy their needs for self-esteem and self-actualization. The results of participative management programs are mixed. Although most employees like greater participation, some do not. Some programs have increased productivity while others have caused production to decline. Participation usually takes more time and often creates the expectation that employees should be rewarded financially for their participation.

15. A basic principle of motivation that is generally consistent with each motivation theory is that people do what they expect to be rewarded for doing. Knowing what will be rewarding to a specific individual, however, may be difficult to determine. Different motivation theories may be relatively more useful in certain situations to predict what will be rewarding and when.

DISCUSSION QUESTIONS

1. What does it mean to say that self-actualization needs cannot be satiated like other needs?

2. Do you agree that we all have an innate blueprint that tells us what we need to do to pursue self-actualization? What do you think you have the unique capacity to do or become?

3. How is the need for achievement learned? What experiences in your life helped you acquire your need for achievement? What moral implications regarding personal responsibility are associated with low need achievers who prefer to receive unemployment or welfare?

4. Using Herzberg's methodology, describe a time in your life when you felt particularly good and a time when you felt particularly bad. Do the factors con-

tributing to these times correspond to Herzberg's motivator and hygiene lists?

5. What are the most important outcomes associated with taking a class in organizational behavior? Using a scale from +10 to –10, how would you assess the valences of these outcomes?

6. According to expectancy theory, what should a supervisor do to motivate an employee?

7. Apply equity theory to your organizational behavior class. What are the inputs and outputs?

8. How does the general principle that people do what they expect to be rewarded for doing, differ from the principle of hedonism? Are there times when you think this general principle does not hold? Explain.

GLOSSARY

comparator The evaluation process in control theory that compares performance with goals to decide whether performance is acceptable or unacceptable.

content theories Motivation theories that describe the specific constructs within the individual that energize and sustain behavior. Content theories explain what motivates behavior.

control theory A motivation theory that explains behavior in terms of goals and feedback loops indicating whether performance is on target or if a change is needed.

effector The mechanism in control theory that creates motivated behavior aimed at achieving the goals.

equity theory A motivation theory derived from social comparison theory in which people compare their output–input ratios with the output–input ratios of others.

ERG theory A refinement of Maslow's needs hierarchy by Clayton Alderfer, which reduced the number of needs to three needs: existence, relatedness, and growth needs.

expectancy (E→P) The component of expectancy theory that consists of the subjective probability that performance levels are based on the amount of effort exerted.

expectancy theory A process theory of motivation in which people decide what to do by subjectively esti-

mating the probability of being able to perform an activity and whether that activity will be rewarding. The three components of expectancy theory include expectancy, instrumentality, and valence.

hedonism A principle, described in early philosophical writings, claiming that people behave in a way that increases their pleasure and avoids pain.

Herzberg's motivator-hygiene theory A motivation theory that claims the factors in a work setting can be separated into two lists of motivator factors and hygiene factors. Motivators create satisfaction and motivation but do not create dissatisfaction, while hygienes can create dissatisfaction but do not create motivation or satisfaction.

hygienes Job factors associated with the job context, such as pay, working conditions, interpersonal relationships, and company policies.

instinct An unlearned behavior that is inherited, purposive, and goal seeking.

instrumentality (P→R) The component of expectancy theory that consists of the correlation between performance levels and possible rewards. The association can be positive or negative.

learned needs Needs that have been acquired by the events people have experienced within their culture. David McClelland studied three learned needs—for achievement, affiliation, and power—and described how these needs were acquired and how they influenced behavior.

Maslow's needs hierarchy A theory of motivation proposed by Abraham Maslow that focused on five needs arranged in ascending order of importance: physiological needs, safety needs, social needs, esteem needs, and self-actualization needs.

motivators Job factors associated with the content of a job such as achievement, recognition, the work itself, responsibility, advancement and the possibility of growth.

Murray's manifest needs theory A need theory proposed by Henry A. Murray that contained a lengthy list of potential needs. However, the needs were only expected to influence behavior when they were triggered by the appropriate environmental conditions. Only then would the need be manifest. Otherwise it remained latent or not activated.

need An internal state of disequilibrium or deficiency that causes people to interact with their environment to satisfy the needs.

personal power A manifestation of the need for power in which people strive for dominance and control over others.

prepotency The idea that a list of needs can be arranged in a hierarchy of importance in which basic needs take precedence and prevent higher-level needs from emerging until lower-level needs have been largely satisfied.

process theories Motivation theories that explain how or why people are motivated: expectancy theory, equity theory, and control theory describe how information is processed to motivate people.

self-actualization The highest-order need in Maslow's needs hierarchy, the need for self-realization, continuous self-development, and ever-increasing personal fulfillment.

sensor The mechanism in control theory that obtains feedback information for the comparator.

social power A form of the need for power in which people attempt to satisfy their power needs by working with a group to achieve group and organizational goals.

valence A component of expectancy theory that refers to the subjective value, positive or negative, of the various work outcomes.

NOTES

1. This case is adapted from the experience of Quill Corporation, which ordered 10,000 pounds of turkey for its 700 employees, as described in the "Labor Letter," *Wall Street Journal* (November 5, 1985), p. 1.

2. William James, *Principles of Psychology,* 2 vols. (1890). Republished in *The Great Books* collection, Vol. 53 (Chicago: Encyclopaedia Britannica, 1952), chap. 26.

3. John Locke, *An Essay Concerning Human Understanding,* Book II (1689), chaps. 7, 10, and 11. In *Great Books,* vol. 35 (Chicago: Encyclopaedia Britannica, 1952). John Stewart Mill, *On Liberty* (1859), *Utilitarianism* (1863). In *Great Books,* vol. 43 (Chicago: Encyclopaedia Britannica, 1952).

4. William James, op. cit., chap. 24.

5. William McDougall, *An Introduction to Social Psychology* (London: Methuen, 1908).

6. Sigmund Freud, *Beyond the Pleasure Principle* (Vienna: 1920) translated by C. J. M. Hubback (London: Hogarth Press, 1930); *Civilization and Its Discontents* (Vienna, 1929), English translation by Joan Riviere (London: Hogarth Press, 1930).

7. Henry A. Murray, *Explorations in Personality* (New York: Harper, 1954, 1970).

8. Abraham H. Maslow, *Motivation and Personality* (New York: Harper, 1954).

9. Abraham H. Maslow, "A Theory of Human Motivation," *Psychological Review,* vol. 1 (1943), pp. 370–396.

10. Edward Hoffman, "Abraham Maslow: Father of Enlightened Management," *Training,* vol. 25 (September 1988), pp. 79–82.

11. Abraham H. Maslow, *Toward a Theory of Being* (New York: Van Nostrand Reinhold, 1968).

12. Clayton P. Alderfer, "An Empirical Test of a New Theory of Human Needs," *Organizational Behavior and Human Performance,* vol. 4 (1969), pp. 142–175.

13. Lyman W. Porter, "A Study of Perceived Need Satisfactions in Bottom and Middle Management Jobs," *Journal of Applied Psychology,* vol. 45 (1961), pp. 1–10; Lyman W. Porter, "Job Attitudes in Management: I. Perceived Deficiencies in Need Fulfillment as a Function of Job Level," *Journal of Applied Psychology,* vol. 46 (1962), pp. 375–384.

14. Chunoh Park, Nicholas P. Lovrich, Brent S. Steel, "Post-Materialistic Values in the Post-Industrial Workplace: A Test of Inglehart's Theory of Value Change in the Context of U.S./Korean Comparisons," *Public*

Administration Quarterly, vol. 13 (Summer 1989), pp. 273–292.

15. M. A. Wahba and L. G. Bridwell, "Maslow Reconsidered: A Review of Research on the Need Hierarchy Theory," *Organizational Behavior and Human Performance,* vol. 15 (1976), pp. 212–240.

16. Salvatore Maddi, *Theories of Personality, A Comparative Analysis,* rev. ed. (Homewood, Ill.: Dorsey Press, 1972).

17. David C. McClelland, "Toward a Theory of Motive Acquisition," *American Psychologist,* vol. 20 (1965), pp. 321–333.

18. J. W. Atkinson and W. R. Reitman, "Performance as a Function of Motive Strength and Expectancy of Goal-Attainment," *Journal of Abnormal Social Psychology,* vol. 53 (1956), pp. 361–366.

19. David C. McClelland, *The Achieving Society* (New York: Free Press, 1961). However, McClelland's research findings were not confirmed in a follow-up study thirty years later by Christopher J. Gilleard, "The Achieving Society Revisited: A Further Analysis of the Relation Between National Economic Growth and Need Achievement," *Journal of Economic Psychology,* vol. 10 (March 1989), pp. 21–34.

20. David C. McClelland, "Achievement Motivation Can Be Developed," *Harvard Business Review,* vol. 43 (November–December 1965), pp. 6–24.

21. Bradley R. Johnson, "Toward a Multi-Dimensional Model of Entrepreneurship: A Case of Achievement Motivation and the Entrepreneur," *Entrepreneurship: Theory and Practice,* vol. 14 (Spring 1990), pp. 39–54; See also Ari Ginsberg and Ann Buchholtz, "Are Entrepreneurs a Breed Apart? A Look at the Evidence," *Journal of General Management,* vol. 15 (Winter 1989), pp. 32–40.

22. David C. McClelland, "Business Drive and National Achievement," *Harvard Business Review,* vol. 40 (July 1962), pp. 99–112.

23. Reviewed by Kae H. Chung, *Motivational Theories and Practices* (Columbus, Ohio: Grid, 1977), pp. 47–48.

24. David C. McClelland, "The Two Faces of Power," *Journal of International Affairs,* vol. 24 (1970), pp. 29–47; Jeffrey Pfeffer, *Power in Organizations* (Marshfield, Mass.: Pitman, 1981).

25. David C. McClelland, "The Two Faces of Power," *Journal of International Affairs,* vol. 24 (1970), pp. 29–47.

26. Roger T. Peay and W. Gibb Dyer, Jr., "Power Orientations of Entrepreneurs and Succession Planning," *Journal of Small Business Management,* vol. 27 (January 1989), pp. 47–52.

27. David C. McClelland, "Power Is the Great Motivation," *Harvard Business Review,* vol. 54, no. 2 (1976), pp. 100–110.

28. Frederick Herzberg, B. Mausner, and B. Snyderman, *The Motivation to Work* (New York: Wiley, 1959).

29. Frederick Herzberg, *Work and the Nature of Man* (New York: Crowell, 1966).

30. Robert J. House and L. A. Wigdor, "Herzberg's Dual Factor Theory of Job Satisfaction and Motivation: A Review of the Evidence and a Criticism," *Personnel Psychology,* vol. 20 (1967), pp. 369–389; N. King, "Clarification and Evaluation of the Two Factor Theory of Job Satisfaction," *Psychological Bulletin,* vol. 74 (1970), pp. 18–31; L. K. Waters and C. W. Waters, "An Empirical Test of Five Versions of the Two Factor Theory of Job Satisfaction," *Organizational Behavior and Human Performance,* vol. 7 (1972), pp. 18–24.

31. Frederick Herzberg, "Workers' Needs," *Industry Week,* vol. 234 (September 21, 1987), pp. 29–32; J. Daniel Cougar, "Motivators Versus De-motivators in the IS Environment," *Journal of Systems Management,* vol. 39 (June 1988), pp. 36–41; Chunoh Park, Nicholas P. Lovrich, and Dennis L. Soden, "Testing Herzberg's Motivation Theory in a Comparative Study of U.S. and Korean Public Employees," *Review of Public Personnel Administration,* vol. 8 (Summer 1988), pp. 40–60; David Shipley and Julia Kiely, "Motivation and Dissatisfaction of Industrial Salespeople—How Relative Is Herzberg's Theory?" *European Journal of Marketing,* vol. 22, no. 1 (1988), pp. 17–30.

32. House and Wigdor, op. cit.

33. Kurt Lewin, *Field Theory in Social Science* (New York: Harper, 1951); E. C. Tolman, "The Determiners of Behavior at a Choice Point," *Psychological Review,* vol. 43 (1938), pp. 1–41.

34. Victor Vroom, *Work and Motivation* (New York: Wiley, 1964).

35. Lyman W. Porter and Edward E. Lawler, *Managerial Attitudes and Performance* (New York: Irwin Dorsey, 1968).

36. Richard E. Kopelman, "Across-Individual, Within-Individual and Return-on-Effort Version of Expectancy Theory," *Decision Sciences,* vol. 8 (1977), pp. 651–662; Gerald Biberman, Galen L. Baril, and Richard E. Kopelman, "Comparison of Return-on-Effort and Conventional Expectancy Theory Predictions of Work Effort and Job Performance: Results from Three Field Studies," *Journal of Psychology,* vol. 120 (1986), pp. 229–237.

37. George B. Graen, "Instrumentality Theory of Work Motivation: Some Experimental Results and Suggested Modifications," *Journal of Applied Psychology,* Monograph 53 (1969), pp. 1–25.

38. Richard E. Kopelman and Paul H. Thompson, "Boundary Conditions for Expectancy Theory Predictions of Work Motivation and Job Performance," *Academy of Management Journal,* vol. 19 (1976), pp. 237–258; Terrence R. Mitchell, "Expectancy Models of Job Satisfaction, Occupational Preference, and Effort: A Theoretical, Methodological, and Empirical Appraisal," *Psychological Bulletin,* vol. 81 (1974), pp. 1053–1077.

39. Lyman W. Porter and Edward E. Lawler, *Managerial Attitudes and Performance* (New York: Irwin Dorsey, 1968).

40. Paul S. Goodman, "Social Comparison Processes in Organizations," in Barry M. Staw and Gerald R. Salancik (eds.), *New Directions in Organizational Behavior* (Chicago: St. Clair Press, 1977), pp. 97–131.

41. J. S. Adams, "Injustice in Social Exchange," in Leonard Berkowitz (ed.), *Advances in Experimental Social Psychology*, vol. 2 (New York: Academic Press, 1965); Karl E. Weick, "The Concept of Equity in the Perception of Pay," *Administrative Science Quarterly*, vol. 11 (1966), pp. 414–439.

42. George A. Akerlof and Janet L. Yellen, "The Fair Wage–Effort Hypothesis and Unemployment," *Quarterly Journal of Economics*, vol. 105 (May 1990), pp. 255–283. However, the predictions of equity theory did not hold in a study of retail salespeople by Alan J. Dubinsky and Michael Levy, "Influence of Organizational Fairness on Work Outcomes of Retail Salespeople," *Journal of Retailing*, vol. 65 (Summer 1989), pp. 221–252.

43. Joel Brockner and Laury Adsit, "The Moderating Impact of Sex on the Equity–Satisfaction Relationship," *Journal of Applied Psychology*, vol. 71 (1986), pp. 585–590.

44. Adams, op. cit.

45. R. T. Mowday, "Equity Theory Predictions of Behavior in Organizations," in Richard M. Steers and Lyman W. Porter (eds.), *Motivation and Work Behavior*, 2nd ed. (New York: McGraw-Hill, 1979).

46. C. S. Carver and M. F. Scheier, *Attention and Self-Regulation: A Control Theory Approach to Human Behavior* (New York: Springer-Verlag, 1981); Howard J. Klein, "An Integrated Control Theory Model of Work Motivation," *Academy of Management Review*, vol. 14 (April 1989), pp. 150–172; R. G. Lord and P. J. Hanges, "A Control Systems Model of Organizational Motivation: Theoretical Development and Applied Implications," *Behavioral Science*, vol. 32 (1987), pp. 161–178.

47. Michael R. Frone and Dean B. McFarlin, "Chronic Occupational Stressors, Self-Focused Attention, and Well-Being: Testing a Cybernetic Model of Stress," *Journal of Applied Psychology*, vol. 74 (December 1989), pp. 876–883; John R. Hollenbeck, "Control Theory and the Perception of Work Environments: The Effects of Focus of Attention on Affective and Behavioral Reactions to Work," *Organizational Behavior and Human Decision Processes*, vol. 43 (1989), pp. 406–430.

48. Adrienne E. Eaton, "The Extent and Determinants of Local Union Control of Participative Programs," *Industrial and Labor Relations Review*, vol. 43 (July 1990), pp. 604–620; Gerald T. Gabris, Kenneth Mitchell, and William A. Giles, "Motivating the Uninvolved Worker: Some Conceptual and Empirical Observations," *International Journal of Public Administration*, vol. 11 (January 1988), pp. 27–63; Lokman Mia, "Managerial Attitude, Motivation, and the Effectiveness of Budget Participation," *Accounting Organizations and Society*, vol. 13, no. 5 (1988), pp. 465–475; Lokman Mia, "The Impact of Participation in Budgeting and Job Difficulty on Managerial Performance and Work Motivation: A Research Note," *Accounting Organizations and Society*, vol. 14, no. 4 (1989), pp. 347–357.

49. David M. Schweiger and Carrie R. Leana, "Participation in Decision Making," in Edwin A. Locke (ed.), *Generalizing from Laboratory to Field Setting* (Lexington, MA: Heath, 1986), pp. 147–166.

AN ILLUSTRATION OF EXPECTANCY CALCULATIONS

An illustration explains how the components of expectancy theory can be combined to predict behavior. Suppose your research paper must be submitted Wednesday afternoon before 5 P.M., and you have allocated Tuesday and Wednesday to write it. However, Tuesday morning you are surprised to learn that your best friend is in town and wants to take you golfing. You have to decide whether to go golfing or use the time to write your paper. As you evaluate the situation, you identify the three most relevant outcomes associated with each option. If you go golfing, the three outcomes are (1) the friendship and satisfaction of being with your friend again, (2) the entertainment of playing a round of golf, and (3) the effect it will have on your grades. Using a scale from +10 to –10, you assign a high valence of +9 to friendship, because you haven't been together recently; a valence of only +3 to playing golf, because it isn't your favorite sport; and a valence of +8 to grades, because you're interested in graduate school. If you forgo the golf and write a paper, the three outcomes are (1) disappointing your best friend, (2) enduring the stress and pain of actually researching the literature and writing the paper, and (3) getting a better grade. The valences of these outcomes are –7 for disappointing your friend, –3 for the stress because it isn't all that bad, and +8 for grades thanks to graduate school. These valences are shown in Exhibit 4.10.

Next you evaluate your expectancies. If you decide to go golfing, what is the probability you will actually be able to do it? Because you know where

to go, you've done it before, and the weather looks good, you assign a high probability of .9. Your expectancy of writing a research paper is also high, .8, but slightly lower since you're a little concerned about finding the literature you need in the library.

The instrumentalities are the most difficult numbers for you to assess. Instrumentality, the correlation coefficient between performance and each outcome, is a number between +1.00 and –1.00. The correlation between playing golf and enjoying friendship is very high, at least .9. Since you are not a good golfer, the relationship between playing it and enjoying it is slightly lower, .6. The real disadvantage of golfing is its effect on your grades, and you assign a negative correlation of –.7 because the longer you golf the lower your grade will be. However, the correlation between working on the paper and getting a good grade is a positive correlation of +.8. The reason it isn't higher is because you are not sure how carefully your paper will be graded. You decide the relationship between writing papers and feeling stress is only .5 because some aspects of research aren't too bad, and the instrumentality for disappointing your friend is only .2, because you hope he will understand your situation.

The total effort you might be expected to exert for either of these options can be calculated by multiplying the expectancies, instrumentalities, and valences, using the formula shown at the top of Exhibit 4.10. When the products are summed for option A, the total effort is 3.87 while the total effort for option B is 2.80. These two numbers indi-

EXHIBIT 4.10   Illustration of Expectancy Calculations

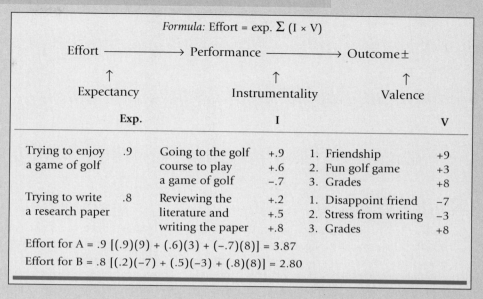

Formula: Effort = exp. Σ (I × V)

Effort   ⟶   Performance   ⟶   Outcome±

↑ Expectancy   ↑ Instrumentality   ↑ Valence

	Exp.		I		V
Trying to enjoy a game of golf	.9	Going to the golf course to play a game of golf	+.9 +.6 −.7	1. Friendship 2. Fun golf game 3. Grades	+9 +3 +8
Trying to write a research paper	.8	Reviewing the literature and writing the paper	+.2 +.5 +.8	1. Disappoint friend 2. Stress from writing 3. Grades	−7 −3 +8

Effort for A = .9 [(.9)(9) + (.6)(3) + (−.7)(8)] = 3.87

Effort for B = .8 [(.2)(−7) + (.5)(−3) + (.8)(8)] = 2.80

---

cate that you are more likely to go golfing. Getting a good grade is important to you, but not as important as the satisfaction of enjoying a game of golf with a friend. These two numbers, 3.87 and 2.80, are only meaningful when comparing them with each other, because they cannot be compared against an absolute scale. The size of these numbers depends on the subjective estimates assigned by each person, the number of outcomes included in the computations and how the valences are scaled.

According to the calculations shown in Exhibit 4.10, you would choose to go golfing. Several small changes, however, could produce a different outcome. For example, if a cloudy sky dropped the expectancy of golfing from .9 to .6, the total effort for golf would drop to 2.58 and you would work on your paper instead. You would also reject golfing if you thought golf was a poor way to visit with your friend and reduced the instrumentality from .9 to .7 or lower.

AN ILLUSTRATION OF EQUITY THEORY

The following illustration helps to clarify the motivational implications of equity theory. Suppose you saw an ad in the student newspaper inviting students who wanted to work part time as a research assistant to apply for employment at a research institute. After completing the necessary application forms at the student employment office, you report to work the first day to be trained with a small group of other students who are also starting work. Your job consists of conducting interviews, something you think you can do, but you are surprised to learn that only students with a master's degree and six months of interviewing experience were to have been hired. All the others claim to be graduate students possessing the necessary qualifications. In spite of the grumbling by the director, you are hired, trained, and sent out to conduct interviews. Since you will receive $8 per hour, the same hourly rate as the other interviewers, you will probably have a perception of inequity. While your pay is the same, your inputs are less than others.

$$\frac{O = \$8/\text{per hour}}{I = \text{undergraduate student, no experience}} > \frac{O = \$8/\text{per hour}}{I = \text{Graduate student, previous experience}}$$

You   Other Interviewers

In this situation, you should feel overpaid and will likely feel some tension, particularly if you are required to interact with the other interviewers. People who find themselves in this situation tend to produce more interviews to reduce the perception of inequity.

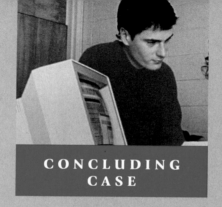

CONCLUDING CASE

FALSIFYING SAFETY REPORTS

PART I

During the past two years, Wardley Home Products has witnessed a serious deterioration in its safety record. During this time its worker compensation payments have increased from $200,000 to $500,000 per year.

The safety director recommended that the company develop a recognition and reward program to reduce the number of accidents. This suggestion was made after reviewing the success other companies had achieved in using incentives to reduce the number of accidents. Based on the safety director's advice, three incentive programs were developed: (1) at the end of each month, group photographs would be taken of departments that did not have any lost-time accidents (time lost because of work injuries), and these photographs would be prominently displayed in the front office; (2) at the end of the year, workers in the department with the best safety record would be invited with their spouses to attend a recognition banquet with the company administration; (3) any department that went through the entire year without a lost-time accident would be rewarded with a $500 savings bond for each member of the department.

Questions

1. Are these incentive programs well designed? How effective do you expect them to be?
2. Do you think safety incentives will reduce the number of accidents? How would you respond to some-

one who says, "No one wants to have accidents, they just happen. Therefore, you can't reward people for something that is out of their control"?
3. What other incentive programs would you recommend for this company?

PART II

Nine months after the new safety incentives were announced, Bill Barber, the president of Wardley Home Products, was the speaker at the Chamber of Commerce monthly meeting. His talk focused on the benefits of strong leadership, and he referred to the new safety program as an illustration of dynamic leadership.

"Everyone knows how we feel about the importance of providing a safe working environment. We take safety very seriously, and these efforts have really paid off. All three of our production departments have worked for more than 140 days without a lost-time accident, whereas we used to have at least one or two accidents per week. We think this is a marvelous improvement, and it will reduce our worker compensation payments to less than $200,000."

After the luncheon, a member of the audience approached Bill Barber and asked him if he was sure about the safety records of his production departments. "My neighbor, Sue Arnold, works in your liquid cleaner department, and last month she suffered a serious accident that prevented her from using her left hand for at least two weeks."

Mr. Barber said he didn't know anything about it, but later decided it was important enough to investigate. He reviewed the accident reports from the liquid cleaner department and found no recorded accidents. When he phoned the medical clinic that provides medical services for his company, the records of the liquid cleaner department were again clean. However, the accident coverup was discovered the next day when he phoned the emergency center at the hospital in an adjacent city and learned that Sue Arnold had indeed been treated for a severe laceration of the left hand. Although the hospital record said the accident was not employment related, the records indicated that the accident had occurred during working hours. When Mr. Barber checked with the accounting department, he learned that a check for the exact amount of Sue's accident had been sent to the hospital, but the explanation for the check was listed as medical supplies.

When Mr. Barber talked with Sue Arnold, he was told, "Oh, it was just a little cut, something that happened at home, but it didn't interfere with my work." When he asked the accounting department to explain the medical supplies expense, no one seemed to remember anything about it. Finally Mr. Barber confronted Karen Hill, the supervisor of the liquid cleaner department, and she admitted that she and several others had falsified the reports to maintain a clean record. She said that several months ago the entire department decided they wanted to win the safety contest, and the decision to falsify the report was a group decision. Even Sue refused to go to the medical clinic to be treated, and the group offered to pay for the hospital emergency bill if the accounting department refused to cooperate. While Sue was unable to work, other members of the department worked faster to carry her load and maintain the same rate of production.

Questions

1. Should Mr. Barber ignore the incident, or take some type of corrective action? What action?

2. Are the safety incentives responsible for this problem, and if so, should they be revised or discontinued?

3. Since failing to report an accident violates the federal Occupational Safety and Health Act, should someone be terminated or disciplined?

MEASURING MOTIVATION

PART I: EXPECTANCY CALCULATIONS

Expectancy theory predicts that the amount of effort an individual will exert ultimately depends on three perceptual relationships: expectancy, instrumentality, and valence. Here is one formula for illustrating how these three variables are combined to measure effort.

$$\text{Effort} = \text{Exp.} \sum (I \times V)$$

According to this formula, effort is equal to expectancy times the sum of the instrumentalities times the valences. This formula can be used to estimate the amount of effort students would be expected to exert in an organizational behavior course.

Valence. When using expectancy theory, all the important outcomes associated with performance must be identified. The following list shows seven outcomes associated with taking an organizational behavior course. If other outcomes are important to you, add them to this list. If you plan to compare your scores with other class members, however, everyone should have the same list of outcomes. After making sure that the list contains the most important outcomes, evaluate the valence of each outcome using a scale that ranges from –5 to +5. This is an arbitrary scale. Unpleasant outcomes have a negative valence number, while desirable outcomes have a positive valence number.

–5	–4	–3	–2	–1	0	+1	+2	+3	+4	+5

Extremely undesirable	Slightly undesirable	Neutral	Slightly desirable	Extremely desirable

Instrumentality. Instrumentality is the relationship between performance and rewards: P→R. This is your subjective belief about the reinforcement contingencies in this class. Is performance instrumental in obtaining rewards and avoiding punishments? In this exercise, instrumentality is measured by a correlation coefficient between performance and each outcome. Correlation coefficients range from –1.0 to +1.0 depending on whether there is a negative or positive association between performance and the outcome. A correlation of zero means there is no relationship between performance and the outcome. If you think there is a fairly strong relationship between performance and rewards, the instrumentality will probably be between +.8 and +1.0. However, if you think that performing well will result in receiving less of an outcome, the instrumentality coefficient will be a negative number. Use a correlation coefficient to estimate the instrumentality of the seven following outcomes. In estimating the instrumentality, ask yourself, "What is the relationship between performing well in this class and receiving this outcome?" You will probably have a negative correlation coefficient between performing well and having free time or visiting with friends, since leisure time and friendships usually must be sacrificed in order to have time to perform well in class.

Expectancy. Expectancy concerns the relationship between effort and performance: E→P. "If I put forth adequate effort, what is the probability that I will be able to perform well?" "If I try, will I succeed?" In this exercise you should estimate your expectancy by asking yourself the question, "What is the probability that I will be able to perform well if I put forth adequate effort?" The expectancy term should be a probability that ranges from zero to 1.0.

Outcomes	Instrumentality	×	Valence	=	I × V
Receiving good grades in this class	_____		_____		_____
Learning new ideas about OB	_____		_____		_____
Obtaining credit toward graduation	_____		_____		_____
Having free time to spend the way I want	_____		_____		_____
Being able to earn a lot of money in the future	_____		_____		_____
Visiting with my friends and goofing off with them	_____		_____		_____
Feeling good about myself as a dedicated student	_____		_____		_____

$$\Sigma(I \times V) = \underline{\hspace{2cm}}$$
$$\times \text{ Expectancy} = \underline{\hspace{2cm}}$$
$$\text{Effort} = \underline{\hspace{2cm}}$$

After you have assigned numbers to each value, you can calculate your level of effort by multiplying the instrumentality and valence numbers, and summing them across all products. This sum should then be multiplied by the expectancy term. After you have calculated the level of effort from this formula, compare your number with the numbers of other classmates. If you used seven outcomes, the maximum score anyone could have is 35. But since two of the outcomes probably have negative instrumentalities, it is very doubtful that any one will have a score greater than 15, and most will probably have scores between 0 and 10. When you compare your effort score with your classmates' scores, do the numbers seem reasonable? Would you expect the effort scores to be positively correlated with grades at the end of the semester?

PART II: MEASURING ACHIEVEMENT MOTIVATIONS

Study the following photograph for about twenty seconds, and then write an imaginative story that is suggested to you by the picture. Do not spend more than about five minutes writing your story. As you write, do not worry about whether there are right or wrong kinds of stories to write. The most important goal is to write a vivid or imaginative story about the picture. The picture is designed to give you an idea, but do not be concerned about describing it perfectly. To help you think about possible story elements, consider the following four questions: (1) What is happening? Who are the people? (2) What has led to this situation? What has happened in the past? (3) What is being thought? What is wanted by whom? (4) What will happen in the future?

Scoring. After you have written your story, you can analyze it to measure your achievement motivation. First analyze it to see if it meets the prime test for the achievement motive. If it passes the prime test, your story can then be analyzed further to measure the amount of achievement imagery. If it does not pass the prime test, the story is scored a zero on the need for achievement. The maximum number of points your story can obtain is eleven points.

1. *Prime test for achievement motive.* Determine whether any of the characters in the story have an achievement goal. Do they want to perform better or do they care about performing better? Performing better is indicated by one or more of the following things: (a) outperforming someone else, such as making more sales or getting better grades; (b) meeting or surpassing some self-imposed standard of excellence, such as doing something faster or cheaper; (c) doing something unique, such as inventing or designing something; (d) being involved over a long period of time in doing something well when there is an indication of great involvement in the achievement goal, such as being a success in life, or achieving a career goal.

   If any of the four characteristics is present in the story, you can score the story further by determining how much achievement imagery it contains. Each story receives one point if it meets the prime test and one point for each category of achievement imagery it contains. The rule to follow in scoring each story is that you must be able to point to the sentence or clause that you have scored for that category.

2. *Stated need for achievement.* Someone in the story explicitly states the desire to meet an achievement goal.

3. *Activity.* Action is taken in the story toward the attainment of the achievement goal.

4. *Anticipating success.* Someone in the story thinks about or anticipates reaching the achievement goal.

5. *Anticipating failure.* Someone in the story thinks about failing to reach the achievement goal or doubts that it will be reached.

6. *Personal block.* Some characteristic of a person in the story will be a block to his or her achievement.

7. *Environmental block.* Something in the environment is mentioned in the story as a block to achievement.

8. *Help.* The person with an achievement goal receives aid or encouragement from someone else in the story.

9. *Positive feelings.* The person is pleased when an achievement goal is reached.

10. *Negative feelings.* The person is discouraged when an achievement goal is not reached.

11. *Theme.* The central plot of the imaginative story contains achievement thoughts and activities.

CHAPTER 5

Job Motivation: Evaluating and Rewarding Performance

LEARNING OBJECTIVES

After studying this chapter, you should be able to

1. Describe the types of motivational patterns used to motivate employees.

2. Discuss the role of performance evaluation in organizations.

3. Identify and describe the major criticisms of performance evaluation.

4. Identify and contrast different methods for evaluating performance.

5. Explain the philosophy and practice of management by objectives.

6. Describe the potential problems caused by punishment, and explain the conditions necessary for effective punishment.

7. Explain the differences between system rewards and individual rewards, and describe the effects of each.

8. List the major system rewards, and explain their effects on satisfaction and productivity.

9. Identify the most effective recognition rewards, and explain why they are so effective.

10. Identify different types of financial incentives, and explain their effects on behavior.

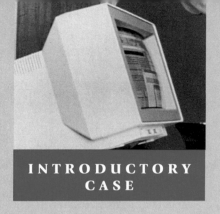

SUPERVISING AN OBNOXIOUS EMPLOYEE

Michelle Boyd is the supervisor of the customer support department and she wants to fire one of her six staff members, Donald Harrison. She thinks Don's behavior is rude and obnoxious, and she wants to terminate him. Michelle is required to evaluate the performance of her staff, and she thinks this is a good time to get rid of him.

Don has more seniority than Michelle: he has been with the company for three years, while she was hired two years ago. She has been a supervisor for nine months. Don is probably the most technically competent member of the staff, and he is usually the one who solves the most difficult customer problems. But he is also very arrogant and self-centered, and he brags about the difficult problems he solves.

Between customer calls, Don dominates the group conversation with discussions of politics, current events, or personal feelings. Other staff members enjoy listening to him, but Michelle finds him argumentative and abrasive. What she objects to most is his teasing and questions about personal topics. Some staff members don't seem to mind discussing intimate feelings and personal opinions, but Michelle finds it very threatening and does not like being questioned. Don is a master of practical jokes that are harmless but usually embarrassing.

When she announced her decision to terminate Don, the human resource manager did not support her decision. The human resource manager says Don has a record of excellent performance reviews—including the one Michelle submitted six months ago as a new supervisor. According to the company's personnel policies, Don should not be terminated without a warning and a hearing. Michelle's supervisor also disagrees with firing Don for a different reason: he thinks Don should only be fired if he is incompetent. Since Don is highly competent, her supervisor thinks Michelle should either tolerate Don's personality and teasing or get him to change.

Questions

1. Should Michelle be allowed to fire Don? Since she also recommends semiannual pay increases, should she withhold Don's pay increase to punish him?

2. Is being obnoxious a legitimate reason to fire an employee? What process should a company follow to terminate employees who deserve to be fired?

3. Can supervisors change the personality of subordinates? If so, how?

BEHAVIORAL REQUIREMENTS OF ORGANIZATIONS

What are the behavioral requirements of organizations? What kinds of behaviors do organizations desire from their members? If an organization is to survive and operate effectively, it must require not one but several different types of behavior from most of its members. The first section examines the variety of behaviors organizations require of their members, and the types of motivational patterns available for eliciting them.

Multidimensionality of Performance

Before we design a program to motivate people, we need to know what we want to motivate them to do. In most attempts to describe essential behaviors, we make the mistake of either overdescribing or underdescribing what is necessary. We underdescribe when we assume that employee performance consists of only one thing: productivity. This approach assumes that every employee's performance can be placed along one dimension of overall performance that ranges from high to low, although separate dimensions are sometimes used to measure quantity and quality performance. This overly simplistic approach is frequently observed in research reports where we read that variable X increases productivity or variable Y decreases productivity.

We make the mistake of overdescribing behavior when we expect employees to perform behaviors that are not really necessary for the effectiveness of the organization. Sometimes we expect employees to display acts of loyalty and commitment to the organization that have little to do with how well the organization operates. The dress codes of some organizations have been challenged as an unnecessary extension of organizational requirements.

A useful framework that identifies the essential behaviors necessary for organizational effectiveness includes three basic types of behavior: (1) people must be induced to enter and remain within the organization; (2) they must perform their role assignments in a dependable fashion; (3) there must be spontaneous and innovative behaviors beyond the formal job descriptions that contribute to achieving organizational objectives.[1]

Attracting and Holding People in the System. The first requirement of every organization is to attract enough people into the organization and to persuade them to stay for at least a reasonable period of time. Organizations other than the military (when the draft is in effect) depend on their ability to attract members, and the failure to attract enough new members could keep the organization from functioning effectively and even cause it to die. High turnover and absenteeism are very costly to an organization, and as a general rule organizations that are more successful in attracting and holding people are more effective.

Dependable Role Performance. Members of an organization are assigned to perform their individual roles, and it is essential to the organization that these people achieve minimal levels of quantity and quality performance. The members of an organization are expected to know their major responsibilities, and these duties are often described in a formal job description. In general, organizations are more effective if their members are motivated to do their assigned jobs and to do them well—if the members show **dependable role performance.**

Spontaneous and Innovative Behaviors. In addition to the formal task requirements, numerous other behaviors profoundly influence the effectiveness of an organization. These are called **spontaneous and innovative behaviors,** because they are not stated in the formal task requirements. Because an organization cannot foresee all contingencies within its operations, its effectiveness is influenced by the willingness of its employees to perform spontaneous and innovative behaviors as the need arises. Some of the most important spontaneous and innovative behaviors include these:

1. *Cooperation:* coming to the aid of co-workers and helping them achieve the organization's goals
2. *Protective acts:* going out of one's way to remove hazards or eliminate threats to the organization
3. *Constructive ideas:* contributing constructive and creative ideas to improve the organization
4. *Self-training:* engaging in self-training programs to help the organization fill its ever-present need for better-trained personnel
5. *Favorable attitudes:* where employees strive to develop favorable attitudes about the organization among themselves, the customers, and the public, thus facilitating recruitment, retention, and sales

Types of Motivational Patterns

In addition to realizing that human behavior consists of multiple dimensions, it is important to understand that these behaviors are elicited by a variety of motives. The conditions that motivate someone to join and stay with an organization may not motivate dependable role performance. Different motivational patterns are effective in eliciting different behaviors. At least six different motivational patterns are available within organizations to achieve the necessary behaviors.[2]

Rule Enforcement. People in our culture have acquired a generalized expectation that they should conform to rules and social norms. If we want to remain in the game, we are expected to play by the recognized rules of the game. The rules of an organization are described in its policies and procedures, and employees know that their continued membership in the organization is contingent on adhering to these rules. Most of the time, employees willingly follow the rules.

Occasionally, however, an employee's behavior is unacceptable. Every organization needs an effective **rule enforcement** procedure to redirect people who are willing to change and expel those who are not. Although the threat of punishment or expulsion cannot be ignored, most organizational members adhere to the rules simply because they have been socialized to comply with generally accepted norms. Nevertheless, every organization needs to establish punishment and discipline procedures for the times when they are needed.

System Rewards. Rewards that come to individuals by virtue of their membership in the organization are called **system rewards.** These rewards are distributed equally to all members of a given classification in the organization. Some examples of system rewards include benefits, recreational facilities, and working conditions. A later section describes additional examples of system rewards and explains why they are effective in enticing people to enter and remain with the organization.

Individual Rewards. Although system rewards are allocated equally to all members of a subsystem, **individual rewards** are granted only to those who deserve them because of their individual performance. Individual rewards include both financial incentives, such as piece rates and merit pay, and nonfinancial rewards, such as recognition and status. Additional examples of individual rewards are described in a later section, with an assessment of their effectiveness.

Intrinsic Satisfaction from Work Itself. Some activities are intrinsically satisfying because they are a form of self-expression. Those who find work intrinsically satisfying may be willing to continue working even when extrinsic rewards are insufficient or absent altogether. Whether an activity will be perceived as intrinsically satisfying depends both on the nature of the activity and on how the person evaluates it. Chapter 6 explains how an individual's self-concept and personal values help to determine whether an activity will be perceived as intrinsically rewarding.

Internalized Values. Some individuals are motivated to perform an activity because they embrace the goals of the organization and believe their activity will facilitate the organization's goal accomplishment. Here the activity itself may not be an expression of the person's skill; instead, the individual is driven by a sense of commitment or loyalty to the mission of the organization. Organizational commitment and loyalty are two of the topics discussed in Chapter 7.

Group Relationships. Social satisfactions derived from interpersonal relationships represent an important source of gratification for group members. Interactions with other group members provide an important source of friendship, social support, and emotional understanding. Chapter 9 explains how group relationships become a powerful motivation force, and why friendships can either facilitate organizational success or resist organizational objectives.

EVALUATING PERFORMANCE

Performance evaluation programs represent a significant application of motivation theory. The process of evaluating an individual's performance contains elements of both positive and negative reinforcement. How well people perform is largely determined by whether their performance is evaluated and rewarded.

Role of Performance Evaluation

Performance evaluation programs are often challenged, and one of the first philosophical questions that needs to be answered is "Why do we evaluate performance?" Performance evaluation programs serve at least five important organizational functions.[3]

1. *To reward and recognize performance.* Merit pay programs, for example, base the size of pay increases on performance. Without performance data, everyone must be rewarded equally or rewards must be distributed subjectively—

conditions that are perceived as inequitable by the recipients. Performance appraisals also provide intrinsic rewards, because outstanding performers receive positive recognition for their efforts.

2. *To guide personnel actions such as hiring, firing, and promoting.* Performance information is necessary for making rational decisions about whom to promote and terminate. When this information is not available, personnel actions are made by subjective impressions. It is more desirable to make careful, defensible decisions based on good performance data. Organizations that fail to have a formal evaluation program are vulnerable to costly legal challenges. Without accurate performance data, organizations cannot show that their personnel decisions are free from illegal discrimination on the basis of race, religion, sex, national origin, age, or disability.

3. *To provide people with information for their own personal development.* People need performance feedback to help them improve; accurate and timely feedback facilitates the learning of new behavior. Furthermore, most people want to know how well they are doing and where they need to improve.

4. *To identify training needs for the organization.* A well-designed performance evaluation system helps to identify which individuals or departments could benefit from training, and what abilities and skills are needed for each job.

5. *To integrate human resource planning and coordinate other personnel functions.* The information obtained from a performance evaluation is essential for individual career planning and for organizational staffing. Performance information is used to identify high-potential people, who are known as "fast-track" employees.

Criticisms of Performance Evaluation

In spite of its importance, the performance evaluation process has been severely criticized, and the criticisms have prompted many managers to abandon performance evaluation as a useless and perhaps harmful practice. Many people, especially low performers and people who dislike work, simply dislike being evaluated. These individuals are basically opposed to having anyone conduct any sort of evaluation of their performance. They view any efforts to evaluate their performance, either formally or informally, as a threat.

The process of evaluating performance can also be threatening to supervisors. Evaluating the performance of subordinates is a basic supervisory responsibility, and a supervisor who lacks the skills to evaluate performance and to provide performance feedback simply cannot be a good supervisor. Nevertheless, some supervisors do not like to evaluate their subordinates, and they feel threatened by having to explain their evaluation. These supervisors argue that having to evaluate subordinates creates role conflict by forcing them to be a judge, coach, and friend at the same time. And many supervisors do not have the interpersonal skills needed to handle evaluation interviews.

On some jobs, especially jobs that do not produce a physical product, performance is difficult to define. Managers provide leadership, engineers create new ideas, and trainers present information, but these products cannot be meaningfully counted. So how do we know what to measure? Some argue that intangible products such as new ideas, leadership, and training cannot be reliably measured; others argue that everyone can be measured even if it is only by a subjective rating scale.

These people argue that if an evaluator has an attitude about an employee's performance, this attitude can be evaluated like any other attitude, regardless of how subjective it is. Organizations need to be careful, however, that these subjective judgments are job related. Because subjective evaluations can give rise to discrimination against certain groups, the federal courts have not been willing to accept evaluation procedures that allow "unfettered subjective judgments." In some instances, organizations have been required by the courts to establish objective formal guidelines for evaluation, promotion, and transfer.[4]

Evaluating performance and assigning a number to represent it often creates feelings of anxiety in both the evaluator and the person being evaluated. Eight of the most frequent criticisms of performance evaluation are described in Exhibit 5.1. Although these criticisms represent legitimate problems, they should be treated as problems needing to be resolved rather than as insurmountable obstacles.

Performance Evaluation Methods

Performance evaluations occur whether or not a formal evaluation program exists. The demands to hire, fire, promote, and compensate all necessitate some form of evaluation. Supervisors have always evaluated their subordinates and formed impressions about each employee's work, and these informal, subjective evaluations have influenced personnel decisions just as much as formal written evaluations. The advantage of an informal system is that it is easier to design and administer; the advantage of a formal program is that it is more unbiased, defensible, and open to inspection.

The popular proverb—what you evaluate is what you get—emphasizes the importance of evaluating behaviors that are essential to organizational effectiveness. The importance of evaluating relevant behaviors was illustrated by the experience of a military officer who included "orderliness" as one of the criteria for evaluating a unit of clerk-typists.[5] The officers who conducted the evaluation defined orderliness in terms of how clear and uncluttered the clerk-typists kept their desks. The clerk-typists responded by removing everything from the tops of their desks and keeping it in their desk drawers. Although the procedure was inefficient, and the volume of work dramatically declined, the clerk-typists obtained high performance evaluations.

Deciding what to evaluate is in part a value judgment. The personal values of those who design the evaluation system will be reflected in it. In deciding what to evaluate, an important issue is whether the evaluation should focus on outcomes (results) or behaviors (activities).[6] For example, the performance evaluation of a salesclerk could focus on the number of products sold per hour or it could focus on the behaviors required to produce the sale such as describing the product, arranging for financing, and making repeat calls. When asked, most people say outcomes are more important to measure than behaviors; they are primarily interested in measuring results. However, most performance evaluations focus more on behaviors than on results, especially when evaluating managers and supervisors.

The major advantage of focusing on outcomes is that attention is directed toward producing specific results. The primary objective of all employees should be to produce results, not behaviors. Unfortunately, some employees perform many of the right behaviors and still fail to produce results. This situation can be illustrated by examining the behaviors of a student writing a research paper. The right behaviors include finding references, reading articles, making notes, and studying the

EXHIBIT 5.1 **Criticisms of Performance Appraisals**

1. *Halo effect.* Sometimes one characteristic about a person, positive or negative, strongly influences all other attitudes about that person.
2. *Leniency-strictness effect.* Some evaluators give mostly favorable ratings, while other evaluators evaluate the same performance more unfavorably.
3. *Central tendency effect.* Some evaluators give average ratings to everyone to avoid sticking their necks out to identify marginal or outstanding performance.
4. *Interrater reliability.* Two evaluators, seeing the same behavior, may disagree and give different ratings.
5. *Contrast effect.* The evaluation of one employee's performance may be influenced by the relative performance of the preceding individual.
6. *Zero-sum problem.* Some appraisal systems require supervisors to balance high ratings given to some employees with low ratings given to others.
7. *Numbers fetish.* An excessive focus is sometimes placed on numbers, which may be treated as though they possessed unquestioned accuracy.
8. *Recency effect.* Recent events are unduly reflected in the appraisal to the exclusion of events earlier in the year.

materials. A student can perform all these activities very well and still fail to get the paper written.

A potential problem with exclusively evaluating outcomes is that the results can sometimes be achieved by unethical or undesirable means. By exerting excessive pressure on subordinates, supervisors usually can increase performance. But over time, excessive pressure can lead to turnover, dissatisfaction, and unethical conduct. In managing people, the way it is done (behaviors) is just as important as the results (outcomes).

An increasing number of companies include self-evaluation and peer evaluations in their formal appraisal program. Self-evaluations tend to increase the employees' feelings of involvement and commitment to the evaluation process and generally enhance goal setting when there is a cooperative organizational setting. Peer evaluations also operate best in a cooperative setting where co-workers are motivated to evaluate each other accurately rather than maliciously. In some situations, peer evaluations are more accurate and valid and provide more useful feedback than ratings by supervisors. Although self and peer evaluations may provide unique and valuable information, the hierarchical structure of organizations confirms the general expectation that supervisors have the major responsibility for collecting, integrating, and reporting performance information.[7]

Good performance evaluation programs depend more on the competence of the evaluator than on the specific evaluation technique. Nevertheless, some appraisal techniques are considerably better than others, depending on the purpose of the evaluation and the nature of the work being done.

Literally thousands of performance evaluation forms have been developed in various companies. These forms include ranking procedures, classification procedures, graphic rating scales, behaviorally anchored rating scales, forced-choice procedures, and descriptive essays.

APPLYING ORGANIZATIONAL BEHAVIOR
RESEARCH

How the Social Context Influences Performance Evaluations

 When your performance is being evaluated, should you only be concerned about your performance, or should you also care whether your supervisor likes you, works with you, has frequent opportunities to observe you, and is similar to you in age and experience?

A study of eighty-one registered nurses and their supervisors examined how these social context variables influence the way performance evaluation decisions are made. The researchers developed a model showing how these seven social context variables were predicted to influence evaluation decisions:

1. *Opportunity to observe a subordinate's job performance.* The ease of observation was expected to result in more favorable evaluations because supervisors tend to search for positive information. Increased liking comes from increased familiarity.

2. *Span of control.* A large span of control means supervisors have less opportunity to observe each subordinate's performance and thus means lower performance ratings.

3. *Supervisor's experience.* Less experienced supervisors were expected to rate more harshly to demonstrate their ability to handle tough decisions and handle the job of supervisor.

4. *Supervisor–subordinate demographic similarity.* People feel more favorable to others who are like them. Interpersonal similarity leads to attraction and complexity. Demographic similarity also helps people develop a prototype that they can

use to organize their perceptions and simplify the processing of information.

5. *Supervisor's affect toward subordinates.* A positive emotional feeling toward subordinates tends to cause supervisors to make more positive evaluations.

6. *Supervisor–subordinate work relationship.* Supervisors who work more closely with certain subordinates in terms of the frequency and quality of their daily interactions would be expected to like those subordinates more than others.

7. *Supervisor's perception of subordinates' self-rating.* When supervisors think subordinates believe they have performed well, the supervisors feel pressured to conform to the subordinate's wishes.

This model was tested using a path analysis, and all but two of the hypothesized relationships were confirmed. A supervisor's experience and span of control were not significantly related to the supervisor's ratings; however, the other five variables were.

This study demonstrates that the social context surrounding the evaluation process influences how an employee's performance will be judged. Some employees may be rated higher simply because their work requires them to work closely with their supervisor or because their supervisor happens to be like them. Employees may have little they can do to control or influence some of these factors.

Source: Timothy A. Judge and Gerald R. Ferris, "Social Context of Performance Evaluation Decisions," *Academy of Management Journal,* vol. 36 (1993), pp. 80–105.

Ranking Procedures. The objective of a **ranking procedure** is to order a group of employees from highest to lowest along some performance dimension, usually overall performance. Ranking is frequently used when making promotion decisions and occasionally used when making compensation decisions to decide which employees should get the largest financial bonuses. However, ranking is not helpful for providing personal feedback.

Classification Procedures. Classification procedures simply categorize individuals into one of several categories, such as outstanding, excellent, good, fair, and poor. This procedure is typically used to evaluate an individual's overall performance, as shown in Exhibit 5.2, although people can also be classified on specific performance dimensions, such as quantity of work, quality of work, and cooperativeness.

Graphic Rating Scales. **Graphic rating scales** are the most frequently used method of evaluating performance for nonmanagerial workers.[8] Some of the most popular characteristics measured by graphic rating scales include quantity of work, quality of work, cooperativeness, job knowledge, dependability, initiative, creativity, and overall performance. The scales used to measure these characteristics are typically seven- or ten-point scales that are described to at least some extent by such words as "high" versus "low," or "exceeds job requirements" versus "needs improvement," as shown in Exhibit 5.3. The accuracy of graphic rating scales and their freedom from bias and subjectivity improve as the points along the scale are more accurately described in behavioral terms. Ideally, each point along the scale should be defined by a specific behavioral description.

Behavior-based Rating Scales. When the points along a graphic rating scale are clearly defined by specific behavioral descriptions, as shown in Exhibit 5.4, these scales are then called **"behavior-anchored rating scales" (BARS).** Another behavior-based rating system, called "behavioral observation scales" (BOS), consists of a list of the key behaviors employees are expected to perform and the evaluator simply reports how frequently they are observed. Research indicates that behaviorally-anchored rating scales and behavioral observation scales are superior to regular

EXHIBIT 5.2   Illustration of a Classification Procedure

Name _____   Position _____
Date of appraisal _____   Months in position _____

Evaluate the overall performance of this person, considering accuracy of performance, attendance, helpfulness, safety consciousness, economical use of company resources, attitude toward the job, and proficiency in task performance.

Overall Job Performance

[ ] *Outstanding*—exceptionally high performance (among the top 2–5% of company)
[ ] *Excellent*—significantly exceeds job requirements (among the top 10–15% of the company)
[ ] *Good*—exceeds requirements (less than 50% should be rated good or better)
[ ] *Satisfactory*—meets job requirements
[ ] *Fair*—improvement needed
[ ] *Poor*—unsatisfactory, significant improvement needed

| EXHIBIT 5.3 | Illustration of a Graphic Rating Scale |

Name of employee _____   Job title _____

Department _____   Rated by _____

Date _____

Instructions: Rate this employee on the basis of the actual work he or she is now doing. Read the definitions very carefully. Compare this employee with others in the same occupation in this company or elsewhere. In the space before each number, rate the employee according to the following scale.

1	2	3	4	5	6	7	8	9
Fair				Average				Excellent

[ ] 1. *Quantity of work.* How does the quantity of this employee's work compare with what you expect? Is this employee energetic and industrious, or does he or she waste time?

[ ] 2. *Quality of work.* How does the quality of this employee's work compare with what you expect? Consider the degree of completeness and the number of errors and mistakes.

[ ] 3. *Dependability and responsibility.* Habits of punctuality and attendance. Can this employee be trusted to complete work with a minimum of supervision?

[ ] 4. *Initiative, resourcefulness, and leadership.* Consider the employee's ability to proceed without supervision and achieve results without being told. How does this employee affect the output of co-workers? Does he or she have the ability to direct and train others and use company resources and properties effectively?

[ ] 5. *Intelligence, mental alertness, and flexibility.* Does this employee understand instructions and comprehend the equipment and processes associated with his or her job? Is follow-up necessary for desired results? Is a lack of understanding due to inability to comprehend? Is the employee adaptable and capable of thinking through a problem?

[ ] 6. *Judgment.* Does the employee strike you as a person whose judgment would be dependable even under stress? Is the employee likely to be excitable or hasty when making decisions in an emergency? Are decisions objective and rational, or swayed by feelings and the opinions of others?

[ ] 7. *Personality, attitudes, and stability.* How well does this employee interact with subordinates and superiors, command the respect of associates, avoid complaints, maintain a good safety record, accept criticism from others, and avoid bringing personal problems to work? Is the employee loyal to the company and self-confident, or easily upset?

[ ] 8. *Ability, training, skill, and experience.* Does the employee have sufficient job knowledge to perform the job satisfactorily? Does the employee need additional training on the job?

[ ] 9. *Personal appearance and speech.* Does the employee make a good first impression? Is the employee well groomed, or slovenly? Does the employee have a pleasant speaking voice? Does he or she express thoughts and ideas clearly?

EXHIBIT 5.4	Illustration of a Behaviorally-Anchored Rating Scale

The phrase "cooperation and dependability" refers to spontaneous and innovative behaviors beyond the formal job description that contribute significantly to the effectiveness of the company, such as dependability, willingness to accept assignments, cooperation in working with others, initiative in seeing what needs to be done and doing it willingly.

Excellent attitude	7	Always acts enthusiastic and demonstrates a positive commitment to the company.
Good attitude	6	Excellent and enthusiastic worker, willing to do more than expected. Always pleasant and cooperative unless criticized or mistreated.
Slightly good attitude	5	Performs assigned work but conveys the attitude that they would rather not be asked to do anything special.
Average attitude	4	Adequate worker, but occasionally allows personal problems to influence work much of the day.
Slightly poor attitude	3	Sometimes resistive; may even resist performing tasks that are part of the normal job.
Poor attitude	2	Frequently resistive; often resists performing tasks that are part of the normal job. Argumentative and sometimes nasty to co-workers.
Very poor attitude	1	Occasionally acts belligerently and in a hostile manner to supervisors.

graphic rating scales because they are more reliable, less ambiguous, and less biased; furthermore, they are more accurate measures of performance and provide better feedback to employees.[9] The disadvantage of using behavior-based rating scales is that more time and effort are required to develop these scales.

Forced-Choice Evaluations. Some companies have developed **forced-choice rating scales** to minimize the potential bias of the evaluators. Forced-choice procedures consist of statements arranged in pairs, and the evaluator is asked to check which statement is most descriptive of the employee's performance. The pairs of statements are designed so that both statements appear equally favorable or unfavorable, but one statement is actually more descriptive of an outstanding or poor performer. Experiments comparing the forced-choice technique with other rating procedures have shown that less bias is evident in the forced-choice method than in other methods.[10] Six pairs of statements are illustrated in Exhibit 5.5. The forced-choice method seems to allow greater objectivity than other methods. However, the disadvantage again is the time required to develop this method.

Descriptive Essays. Some performance evaluation forms simply provide a blank space for the evaluator to write a **descriptive essay** summarizing the employee's performance. New and inexperienced evaluators find this procedure extremely challenging and unpleasant. However, experienced evaluators are able to use this

EXHIBIT 5.5   Illustration of Six Forced-Choice Rating Scales

Evaluate the performance of this manager using a 9-point scale where 1 = not at all descriptive and 9 = very descriptive of the manager's behavior. Do not use the same number twice with a pair of statements. You must decide which statement in each pair is most descriptive.

1. A follower rather than a leader ____
   Tends to resolve problems with routine approaches ____

2. Fails to consider consequences of decisions ____
   Narrow in outlook ____

3. Not really involved with work ____
   Works with uneven application of effort ____

4. Inquisitive ____
   Gets the best out of people ____

5. Generates enthusiasm ____
   Skillful in dealing with people ____

6. Persuasive ____
   Gives adequate balance to long- and short-range considerations ____

method quite effectively. The essay description typically identifies the employee's job responsibilities on one side of the page, and the other side of the page contains a description of how well these duties have been performed. If they want to, evaluators are free to construct and use their own scales to facilitate their essay descriptions, as shown in Exhibit 5.6. A major benefit of a descriptive essay procedure is that it provides valuable feedback to help employees improve their performance. The major disadvantage is that the information cannot be used effectively to make comparisons among employees.

Management by Objectives

Many organizations emphasize individual accountability through a results-oriented approach to performance evaluation. Less emphasis is placed on the activities employees perform and more emphasis is placed on the results employees are expected to produce. Many labels have been attached to these results-oriented evaluations. The most popular label is **"management by objectives" (MBO)**.[11]

Peter Drucker is credited with first publicizing MBO in his 1954 book, *The Practice of Management*.[12] Drucker noted the advantages of managing managers by "objectives" rather than by "drives." The advantages are that each manager from the highest level to the lowest has clear objectives that reflect and support the objectives of the organization. All managers participate in the goal-setting process and then exercise "self-control" over their own performance; that is, they monitor their own performance and take corrective actions as necessary. To do this, their performance is measured and compared with their objectives. The measurements do not need to be rigidly quantitative or exact, but they must be clear and rational.

A Philosophy of Management. MBO is applied not only as a performance evaluation procedure, but also as a general management philosophy. It is not a prescribed procedure for managers to follow or a cookbook approach to managing.

EXHIBIT 5.6   Illustration of a Descriptive Essay

Name: Cindy Lowe		Date: February 12, 19xx
Position: Departmental Secretary and Receptionist		Tenure: 8 mo.

Duties and Responsibilities	Description of Performance
Responsible for greeting students when they come to the departmental office for information and advice. Percent of job equals 40%.	I would rate Cindy about a 6 on a 1 to 10 scale where 10 is high. She is generally pleasant when meeting students, but she responds very defensively and uncooperatively when students are disrespectful or demanding. Cindy is generally well informed and able to answer the majority of students questions accurately.

Moreover, there is no one best way to manage by objectives. Each program must be adapted to the needs and circumstances of the organization.

MBO is primarily a philosophy of management that reflects a positive, proactive way of managing rather than a reactive way. The focus is on (1) predicting and shaping the future of the organization by developing long-range organizational objectives and strategic plans, (2) accomplishing results rather than performing activities, (3) improving both individual competence and organizational effectiveness, and (4) increasing the participation and involvement of employees in the affairs of the organization.

MBO is also a process consisting of a series of integrated management functions: (1) the development of clear, precise organizational objectives; (2) the formulation of coordinated individual objectives designed to achieve the overall organizational objectives; (3) the systematic measurement and review of performance; and (4) the use of corrective action as needed to achieve the planned objectives.

The Three Phases of MBO. Implementing an effective management-by-objectives program in an organization requires considerable coordination and planning. The implementation typically occurs in three phases.[13] Phase 1 focuses primarily on evaluating the performance of managers. The emphasis is on developing measurable objectives for each manager and evaluating how well they have achieved these objectives at the end of a period.

In phase 2, MBO programs are integrated into an organization's planning and control processes. Greater support is obtained from both top management and line managers, and the MBO program becomes tied to the organization's planning and budgeting cycle. Emphasis also is placed on training and developing subordinates.

Phase 3 is a fully implemented MBO system. In this phase, all the major organizational functions are integrated in a logical manner. These functions include performance evaluations, budgeting and financial planning, the development of strategic plans and overall goals, staffing, compensation, human resource development, and management training and development. This integration is achieved by emphasizing teamwork and flexibility during the goal-setting process, and by emphasizing individual growth and development during the performance review process.

The effectiveness of management by objectives has been examined in dozens of case studies and surveys of managerial opinions. A limited number of studies have even measured changes in objective performance measures before and after the implementation of an MBO program.[14] Like most field experiments, these studies could not control all extraneous influences and the results are therefore somewhat tenuous. Nevertheless, most of the evidence has found that MBO increases organizational efficiency, reduces costs, and improves managerial practices. Perhaps the best evidence supporting the value of MBO comes from research concerning goal setting, performance feedback, participation, delegation, budgeting, and reinforcement, which are the major processes included in an MBO program. Extensive research has been conducted on these processes, and from this research it appears safe to conclude that MBO is an effective process for managing an organization and evaluating performance.

Performance Feedback

The importance of performance feedback is introduced in Chapter 3. Operant conditioning explains how feedback is essential for acquiring new responses and why learning cannot occur without timely feedback. Performance feedback is also a central element in goal-setting theory, because the goals are meaningless and have no impact on behavior when feedback is absent. There is no uncertainty about the importance of feedback, but there are questions about the most helpful forms of feedback and how it should be given.

Some popular recommendations for giving feedback are inconsistent with empirical research. For example, learning theory recommends that for optimal learning feedback should occur immediately after the response. However, supervisors are also cautioned to postpone telling employees what they did wrong until they can do so privately, to avoid public humiliation. Another popular recommendation is that supervisors should limit their feedback to positive comments and avoid criticism. Studies on discipline have shown, however, that criticism is useful and even necessary to improve performance.[15] The interesting paradox regarding criticism is that those who need it most are usually the most threatened by it and the least capable of benefiting from it.

Research on the effects of performance feedback on behavior in organizations has produced these conclusions:

1. Supervisors give subordinates feedback more often after instances of good performance than about instances of poor performance. People dislike being criticized, and giving negative feedback creates an uncomfortable discussion. Consequently, many supervisors avoid giving negative feedback.[16]

2. When they are compelled to give negative feedback, supervisors tend to distort the feedback to make it less negative or convey the feedback in very specific terms in order to convince the subordinate that the evaluation was not

APPLYING ORGANIZATIONAL BEHAVIOR
ACROSS CULTURES

The Effects of Culture on Performance Appraisals

 An American manager assigned to supervise an international division in Japan made the mistake of publicly recognizing an employee for her outstanding work. The compliments seriously embarrassed her, and she declined to accept the small gift recognizing her performance. Two weeks later she asked to be transferred to a new work group.

Evaluating the performance of subordinates and conducting feedback interviews is a difficult challenge for most supervisors. Cross-cultural situations make the process even more difficult. People raised in different cultures give and receive feedback in ways that may differ significantly from one culture to another. It is not uncommon for people raised in an Asian culture to display little or no emotion when they are paid a compliment, and they tend to deny that they have done anything worthy of special recognition.

The Asian cultures, especially the Japanese, emphasize loyalty to the company and a commitment to the group. Employees perceive themselves as members of a team, and they succeed as the team succeeds. This group approach to work is quite unlike the individualism found in the United States, and it means that individual feedback, even positive recognition, may create problems, especially if it occurs in public.

Business in Hispanic cultures, especially in Mexico, tends to be more relaxed and easygoing than in the United States. Consequently, a Mexican employee being evaluated with direct, businesslike efficiency by a U.S. manager could feel threatened by the manager's manner and may respond defensively. Hispanic cultures place a high priority on personal relationships; business will get done when the time is right. Before the review focuses on performance, a Hispanic employee expects the evaluator to engage in a personal conversation and to be well acquainted with the person and the person's family.

Even the European cultures seem to differ from the United States and from each other in their attitudes toward performance feedback. Although the differences may be small, at least two studies have concluded that the performance of U.S. workers is influenced more by feedback than the performance of English workers is. U.S. workers expect and accept feedback. Therefore, they exhibited a stronger relationship between the amount of feedback they received and their performance improvement than did English workers, who were more indifferent to feedback.

Sources: Louis A. Allen, "Working Better with Japanese Managers," *Management Review,* vol. 77 (November 1988), pp. 55–56; James B. Stull, "Giving Feedback to Foreign-Born Employees," *Management Solutions,* vol. 33 (July 1988), pp. 42–45; P. Christopher Earley, "Trust, Perceived Importance of Praise and Criticism, and Work Performance: An Examination of Feedback in the United States and England," *Journal of Management,* vol. 12 (Winter 1986), pp. 457–473. See also Clive Morton, "Bringing Manager and Managed Together," *Industrial Society,* vol. 70 (September 1988), pp. 26–27.

biased.[17] Distorting the feedback is dysfunctional, while giving specific comments is generally beneficial and helps the person know how to improve.

3. Supervisors have traditionally been told that discussions about performance levels and pay increases should be separated. Research evidence does not support this, however. Discussions about pay increases represent a significant form of feedback that clarifies and reinforces other comments about performance. Therefore, performance reviews should include information about the recommended pay increase that accompanies this performance level.[18]

4. Feedback tends to improve performance to the extent it indicates that prior performance levels are inadequate for reaching the goal. Therefore, negative feedback that implicitly calls for greater effort tends to improve performance more than positive feedback that endorses current performance levels.[19]

5. People who are high in self-efficacy and self-esteem can respond more adaptively to criticism than people who are low. People with high self-efficacy and high self-esteem are more likely to use the feedback to diagnose their performance and make adaptive changes while people who are low are more inclined to coast or quit.[20]

Performance interviews are usually uncomfortable experiences for both supervisors and subordinates. But they are also significant events that have an enormous impact on employee motivation, personal development, and job satisfaction. Good performance reviews require good interpersonal skills, accurate performance information, and careful preparation. The feedback is most helpful when supervisors describe behavior in a way that is direct, specific, and nonpunishing.

RULE ENFORCEMENT AND DISCIPLINE

As noted earlier, rule enforcement and the threat of punishment are one of the major motivational patterns. Although most applications of motivation theories focus on rewards or need fulfillment to elicit desired behaviors, we should not overlook the effects of punishment and rule enforcement to eliminate undesirable behavior. In fact, some have argued that rule enforcement and punishment are used far more frequently than rewards in influencing everyday behavior.[21]

Compliance with Rules

Much of the behavior of organizational members can be explained by examining the rules of the organization. The rules tell people how they should behave and most members willingly comply with them. To change behavior simply requires a change in the rules. In his discussion of bureaucratic functioning, Max Weber argued that the acceptance of legal rules served as the foundation of much of organizational behavior. He noted, however, that the rules had to be rational and legitimately tied to the functioning of the organization. Weber referred to this as rational-legal authority and it served as a central concept in explaining why officeholders within a bureaucracy faithfully followed the guidelines and procedures required of their office.[22]

To some extent, adherence to organizational rules is enforced by discipline or the threat of punishment. To a much larger extent, however, compliance is a function of generalized habits and attitudes toward symbols of authority. In other words, most people in our society believe in following the rules; observing legitimate rules has become an accepted social value. Once we know the legitimate norms and appropriate symbols of authority for a given situation, we can accurately predict how well people will behave.

Rule enforcement explains much of our behavior, even though this motivational pattern is very limited in the intensity of its influence on behavior. Although it will not create a commitment to excellence, legal compliance can effectively motivate behaviors that are governed by established rules, such as absenteeism, tardiness, and minimum standards of quantity and quality performance. Several field experiments have demonstrated that rule enforcement can effectively improve the quality of performance. In one experiment, reprimands and warnings were combined with feedback to reduce the number of errors by operators in a manufacturing plant. The number of errors was reduced to zero and remained there for the next six weeks, while performance was observed and the rules were enforced.[23]

Legal compliance is especially effective in creating acceptable levels of performance when the tasks are routine and paced by some type of mechanical control, such as an assembly line. However, legal compliance and rule enforcement are notoriously deficient in motivating performance beyond the minimum standards. Emphasis on rule compliance tends in practice to mean that the minimum acceptable standard becomes the maximum standard. A minimum standard of sixty units per hour, for example, soon becomes interpreted by employees as the maximum required and the speed of work is gauged to achieve that standard but never higher.

Another problem with relying excessively on rule compliance as a motivational pattern is that it is largely ineffective at motivating spontaneous and innovative acts that go beyond the call of duty. Because these acts are not part of the formal job description, they are not included in the rules. Organizations cannot stimulate innovative acts by decreeing them. In general, when there is greater emphasis on rule compliance, there is less motivation for people to do more than is specified by their job descriptions.

Punishment

As described in Chapter 3, the effect of punishment is to reduce the probability of a response. Some managers are opposed to the use of punishment for moral reasons, although some forms of punishment are unavoidable.

Types of Punishment. Punishment occurs when an aversive stimulus follows a response. An aversive stimulus is something unpleasant and whose removal is reinforcing. Physical pain, criticisms, and being fired are examples of aversive stimuli, and we try to avoid doing things that elicit these consequences. Punishment plays a major role in shaping the behavior of people in organizations. Some managers argue that there is no justification for the use of punishment in organizational settings. Others believe that sometimes punishment is the most effective and timely way to change behavior.

Three significantly different kinds of punishment occur in organizations: natural consequences, logical consequences, and contrived consequences.[24] **Natural consequences** occur when behavior violates the laws of nature or society, such as being injured because you followed unsafe work procedures, or being excluded from a lunchroom clique because you have body odor. Virtually every form of misbehavior creates some form of undesirable natural consequence, although some consequences are difficult to recognize immediately.

Logical consequences are punishment that contains a logical relationship to the violated rule. An example of a logical consequence is requiring employees to wait for an assigned secretary to make copies for them because they misuse the copy machine or fail to record the number of copies when they use it themselves.

Contrived consequences involve punishment for wrongdoing where the punishment is unrelated to the misbehavior. Fining a football player $100 for missing practice and revoking an employee's use of a company privilege for a late report are examples of contrived punishments. Because no one has to initiate action to create natural consequences, nor can anyone really prevent them from occurring, the following discussion focuses largely on logical and contrived punishment. In organizational leadership, as in parenting, the use of logical consequences is probably much more effective in changing behavior than contrived consequences.

A highly recommended procedure for administering punishment is called the **"hot stove rule."** A hot stove with its radiating heat provides a warning that it should not be touched. Those who ignore the warning and touch it, like employees who violate a rule, are assured of being burned. The punishment, in this case the burn, is immediate and directly associated with violating the rule. Like the hot stove, which immediately burns anyone who touches it, an established rule for employees to follow should be consistently enforced and should apply to all employees. The pain of a hot stove is administered in a rigid and impersonal way to everyone who touches it.[25]

Punishment does not need to be experienced personally in order to change behavior. Just as we learn vicariously from observing others what will be rewarding, we also learn through vicarious punishment what we should avoid. We are less likely to imitate those behaviors for which we see others punished. Studies of punishment have shown that people who have observed others being punished change their behavior almost as much as those who were actually punished.[26]

Conditions for the Effective Use of Punishment. Some of the major criticisms of punishment were described in Chapter 3. The most severe criticisms are that punishment is only effective when the punishing agent is present, it creates a negative attitude toward the punishing agent, it only tells people what they did wrong and not what they should do right, and it creates a negative emotional feeling. In spite of these criticisms, however, there are appropriate times when punishment should be used, and there is considerable evidence that punishment can be an effective tool if the conditions are right. Seven conditions have been proposed for the effective use of punishment.[27]

1. Punishment is more effective when it is administered immediately after an undesirable response. The longer the delay in administering punishment, the more likely the punishment will be perceived as arbitrary, unfair, and unrelated to the undesired behavior.

2. Punishment should be unpleasant but not severe. If it is too mild, the punishment will be ignored; but if it is too severe, the people who are punished will think too much about the pain and discomfort and not enough about how they need to change their behavior to avoid it in the future.

3. Punishment should focus on a specific act, not on the person or on general behavior patterns. Punishment should not be a means of revenge or a way of venting frustrations. Instead, it should be tied to a specific act that can be described.

4. Punishment should be consistent across persons and across time. Whether or not punishment is administered should not depend on who misbehaved, how they get along with the manager, or whether things are running smoothly or otherwise.

5. Punishment should be administered in a way that informs people what they did wrong and also how they must change to do it right. Simply knowing that what they did was wrong, without knowing how to change, can be very frustrating.

6. Punishment is most effective when it occurs in the context of a loving and nurturing relationship. Because punishment naturally creates a negative emotional feeling toward the punishing agent, it is essential that on other occasions a warm and supportive relationship be developed to withstand the strain of punishment. When the relationship between a person and the punishing agent is strained or distant, the punishment tends to be perceived as a personal attack that creates a feeling of hatred rather than an indication of wrongdoing that needs to be changed.

7. Punishment should not be followed by undeserved rewards. Although greater efforts should be made after punishment to re-establish an interpersonal relationship, these efforts should not include showering the person with undeserved rewards, thereby encouraging him or her to misbehave again.

There are numerous reasons why punishment cannot be administered as quickly or as intensely in organizations as the theory would recommend. Many undesirable behaviors such as leaving the workstation, sleeping on the job, fighting, theft, and damaging equipment cannot be punished as immediately or as severely as the hot stove rule recommends. Furthermore, most managers prefer to delay punishment until an appropriate time in order to avoid socially humiliating an employee. Because punishment is often delayed, it is important for the person administering punishment to explain the importance of the rules and provide what is called *cognitive structuring*. Evidence has shown that clear and reasonable explanations for punishment significantly increase the effectiveness of punishment and produce desirable behavior.[28] Reasonable explanations help people understand why their behavior was wrong and how their behavior needs to change in the future.

Progressive Discipline

Discipline is the use of some form of punishment or sanction when employees deviate from the rules. The overall objective of a disciplinary action is to remedy a problem and to help employees behave acceptably in their work. Although some organizations have lists of rules and unacceptable behavior, the disciplinary processes in most organizations are simply based on two concepts of administrative justice. These two basic concepts are "due process" and "just cause."[29]

The concept of **due process** means that disciplinary actions must follow an accepted procedure that protects employees from arbitrary, capricious, and unfair treatment. Due process normally involves providing people with written statements of the charges against them as well as the reasons for the penalties. The charged employees must have full opportunity to defend themselves and to use the formal grievance procedure if one exists, or an impartial hearing if a formal procedure does not exist. The employer is normally expected to bear the burden of proof; that is, the employer must show both the evidence of wrongdoing and the need for discipline.

The concept of **just cause** means that disciplinary actions will be taken only for good and sufficient reasons. Discipline should not be administered for trivial matters or for obscure and irrelevant rules. However, every employee is expected to know that certain behaviors are never tolerated, such as insubordination, employee theft, alcoholism, drug use, sexual harassment, and violence.

The disciplinary procedures in most organizations follow a process called **progressive discipline** in which the disciplinary actions become increasingly severe. Most progressive discipline procedures include these five steps:[30]

1. *Verbal warning.* A simple comment, usually by a supervisor, warning employees that certain acts are not acceptable.

2. *Verbal reprimand.* A verbal discussion, usually by a supervisor, informing employees that the situation is not acceptable and that improvement is required. This reprimand is more than a casual comment, and both the misbehavior and the desired change need to be carefully described.

3. *Written reprimand.* A written record summarizing the history of the problem and identifying the kinds of changes that are required and the consequences of failing to make them. This step is more formal than the first two steps. The company may need to use this written record to defend itself in court on a case of wrongful discharge.

4. *Suspension.* Employees who fail to improve may be suspended for a few days to think about whether they are willing to change their behavior to keep their job.

5. *Discharge.* Those who persist in wrongdoing and who fail to respond to previous disciplinary action are terminated.

Demotions and transfers are sometimes used as disciplinary actions, although they are not highly recommended. Personal problems such as drug abuse, embezzlement, and habitual tardiness are problems that demotion and transfer are not likely to correct. Consequently, demotions and transfers are usually recommended only for problems of unsatisfactory performance when employees have been promoted to a job that is too demanding for them to handle. Even then, demotion may not be a viable form of discipline because of the stigma attached to it.

SYSTEM REWARDS

System rewards are rewards granted to people because of their membership in the organization. Normally, all members enjoy equal participation in system rewards. This category of rewards includes benefits, recreational facilities, cost-of-living pay increases, job security, and pleasant working conditions. A unique system reward for the employees of Apple Computer, Inc., is a personal computer. Each new employee receives a computer for use at home, and the employee takes ownership of the PC after one year of service.[31]

The purpose of system rewards is to attract employees and to encourage them to stay. If system rewards are distributed on the basis of how long individuals have been in the system, people will want to stay because the rewards become increasingly attractive over time. Since system rewards are given across the board to all members, however, they do not motivate people to do more than meet the minimum standards necessary to remain in the organization. Sometimes it is assumed that system rewards will make the organization more attractive and will generalize into greater productivity and satisfaction. Managers have learned, however, that the gratitude of workers for a new benefit or recreation facility does not become translated into higher productivity or general satisfaction. A new benefit might make employees want to stay with the organization, but it will not motivate them to work harder. Three of the major kinds of system rewards include benefits, employee ownership, and stock options.

Benefits

Employee benefits represent a very significant and costly system reward. Before 1970, benefits were usually called "fringe benefits," suggesting that these nonwage benefits represented a small addition to the regular pay to make the compensation package more attractive. In recent years, the word "fringe" has been dropped because benefits no longer represent a small addition to compensation. Expressed as a percentage of total payroll costs, benefits have increased significantly. In 1929 the average benefits cost to the employer equaled only 3 percent of total wages and salaries. In recent years, the cost of benefits equals almost 40 percent of payroll.[32]

Surveys on the effectiveness of employee benefit plans suggest that employees generally are not very knowledgeable about the benefits offered by their employers.[33] Most employees are aware only of the benefits they regularly use. For example, the parents of children who wear braces know about the dental benefits, and older workers understand the pension plan. These surveys also indicate that benefits do not increase job satisfaction, nor do they encourage employees to produce more. Whether benefits help in recruiting and retaining new employees is unclear. Some recruiters think an attractive benefits package helps in recruiting some employees, but most new employees are more concerned about the starting salary than the benefits.

Kinds of Benefits. Employers are legally required to provide three benefits: unemployment compensation, workers' compensation, social security, and family leave. Other benefits are optional, and benefit packages vary dramatically from company to company. The various kinds of benefits can be classified into these five categories:

1. *Health and accident insurance.* This benefit might include hospitalization, doctor's fees, dental care, psychiatric care, and vision care.
2. *Life insurance and income continuation.* This benefit might provide term life insurance, accidental death and dismemberment insurance, and long-term disability insurance, severance pay, and sick leave.

3. *Pay for time not worked.* This benefit might provide for paid vacations, paid holidays, and personal time off with pay for family emergencies or other important events.

4. *Employee services.* This benefit may include a broad range of services such as a credit union, emergency loans, tuition reimbursement, child care facilities, legal assistance, and recreational facilities.

5. *Pensions.* This benefit, when it is provided, provides retiring employees with a continuing income that is based on either how many years they worked for the company or how much was contributed to their retirement fund during their working years.

Flexible Benefits. Since the benefit needs of employees vary dramatically, some companies allow their employees to choose the kinds of benefits in their program. These plans are called **flexible benefit plans** because employees are permitted to choose the type of coverage they prefer, subject to certain constraints. Some plans even allow employees to choose fewer benefits and put the remaining cash in a deferred savings plan. Flexible benefit programs, sometimes called *cafeteria benefits,* have become increasingly popular, although they are more difficult to administer.

Stock Options

Stock option plans provide employees with the opportunity to buy shares of the company's stock at a lower price than if they bought them on the open market. When a stock option plan is available, the employees enjoy certain financial benefits if they purchase stock through the plan. Although many kinds of stock option plans exist, the basic premise of most is that employees are given the option of buying a specified number of shares at a fixed price. The option can be exercised over a period of time, which allows employees to wait and see if the value of the stock appreciates before buying it. During periods of rising stock prices, the income from stock options can be very sizable.

Stock options are designed to motivate managers to perform well, since the value of the stock depends largely on how well managed the company is and whether it grows and produces a sizable profit. Therefore, managers can obtain a sizable financial reward by purchasing large shares of stock and making them appreciate in value through good management. For key managers who have a significant impact on the value of the company's stock, stock options represent an important individual reward, motivating them to do better. However, the market value of the stock can be materially influenced by only a few top executives, and even these executives frequently believe that the relationship between their performance and the stock price is very weak at best.

As a general rule, therefore, stock options for most employees are a system reward, and then only a reward if they have the financial resources to invest in the stock. The history of stock options indicates that their popularity has been determined primarily by tax considerations. Stock options were more attractive during the years when the income from them was taxed at a lower capital gains tax rate than during the years when it was taxed at a higher rate as ordinary income. Stock options provided a way for companies to pay large sums to executives in a way that minimized how much they would lose to taxes.

APPLYING ORGANIZATIONAL BEHAVIOR
IN THE NEWS

The Rewards of Work

CNN Larry Phillips, chairman of shirt manufacturer Phillips-Van Heusen, was asked in an interview how he felt about his job and whether the people working in his company liked their work. Although he likes his work now, he says, and wants his employees to feel the same, it hasn't always been fun.

Phillips-Van Heusen was founded more than 100 years ago, in 1881, when Larry's great, great grandfather Moses Phillips immigrated from Russia and began peddling shirts from a push-cart in Pottsville, Pennsylvania. Leadership of the company, as a family business, has passed from father to son, and Larry Phillips knew he would one day run the company. But he didn't always want to. During his youth, he would have preferred a different career. Even after he was the president, he did not feel competent to shoulder the responsibility for the first fifteen years.

As his competence increased, however, Larry Phillips eventually found his work invigorating and he wants his employees to feel the same fulfillment. The company avoids "frills," such as company cars for managers. But all employees, whom he calls "associates," are well paid, and 72 percent of them own stock in the company. He is proud of the fact that the employees have never had to ask for a raise. He attributes the company's nonunion status to its generous reward systems.

Intrinsic rewards are just as important as pay raises and stock ownership. Phillips wants his associates to feel intrinsically rewarded from their work and to think that their work is meaningful. The company has a very well-developed policy regarding the environment and ethics. All 13,000 associates are encouraged to extend their enthusiasm at work to improving the environment, even if it is only cleaning a stretch of highway.

Source: CNN *Pinnacle* (December 5, 1992).

Employee Ownership

Employee stock ownership plans (ESOPs) are a type of system reward that has become increasingly common in America. In 1976 there were fewer than 1,000 ESOP companies in the United States. However, favorable tax laws over the next decade led to the existence of more than 10,000 by the end of 1989.[34] Employee stock ownership plans are a deferred employee benefit through which employees acquire company stock. Occasionally employees buy the stock themselves either directly or through wage concessions. Generally, however, the company gives the employees stock as a benefit in addition to salary and other benefits.

The most popular method for creating employee ownership is through an ESOP trust, in which the company makes annual donations into a trust of stock or cash to buy stock. Company contributions to the ESOP trust are tax deductible for the company. Stock in the trust is allocated to the employees' individual accounts either on an equal basis or relative to the employees' salaries. Typically, all full-time employees over the age of 21 are automatically included in the plan after one year of service with the company.

Over time the shares of stock assigned to each employee become "vested." Vesting refers to rights to ownership which means that over a period of time, usually five years, employees earn the right to keep a gradually increasing amount of their allocations even if they leave the company. Employees receive the vested portion of their ESOP accounts when they leave the company or when they reach retirement age. Employees in privately held companies may sell their ESOP shares back to the company at the current market value of the stock. Employees in publicly held companies can sell their ESOP shares on the stock market.

One of the most popular reasons for creating an ESOP is to rescue a failing firm by having the employees purchase the stock through an employee buyout. In spite of the publicity about them, however, employee buyouts represent less than 2 percent of all ESOPs. The most popular motives for establishing an ESOP program include these: (1) to provide greater democratic participation of employees in the management of the firm, (2) to provide a means of sharing the wealth in society and creating a broader base of capitalism, (3) to provide a source of money to finance capital acquisitions, (4) to motivate employees by providing a financial incentive, and (5) to finance the employee purchase of the company during a threatened corporate takeover.

Employee ownership is not a new idea. During the mid 1800s, employee ownership was a popular idea in the form of worker cooperatives. Many union leaders and social reformers thought that worker cooperatives were the answer to the industrial problems of the time. Several cooperatives were started, but very few survived for long. At that time, the major problem in starting a cooperative involved collecting enough money from the workers to provide sufficient plant, equipment, and working capital. After the cooperative had been started, the major problem again concerned finances. The goal was for all workers to share in the ownership of the cooperative, preferably on an equal basis, but troubles were created when new members were added and old members left. New workers did not have enough capital to buy into the cooperative, and old members could not get their money out.

The advocates of ESOPs enthusiastically claim that employee ownership improves company performance, productivity, worker participation, and employee morale. In spite of this enthusiasm, however, empirical research has not consistently shown that owner-controlled ESOP companies are more productive than the traditional manager-controlled firms.[35] Employee ownership does not necessarily elicit higher levels of motivation to ensure the success of the company, as conventional wisdom would suggest. Instead, the results of employee ownership are extremely mixed.

Some experiments in employee ownership have been success stories, such as the ESOP at Okonite Company, a cable manufacturer in New Jersey.[36] All the company's stock was placed in an ESOP trust and used as collateral for loans of $44 million, which included $13 million in federally subsidized credit. The 1,600 workers were not required to pay anything into the trust or make any wage concessions. Over a period of about eight years, the company paid off the debts through contributions to the ESOP, which built the workers' equity from zero to $45.3 million. Okonite's success was attributed to good management plus a favorable economic climate that saw its major competitors go out of business.

The employee ownership at Okonite did not solve all its labor relations problems, however. During the first few years of employee ownership, there were four strikes by the employee owners against the company they owned. Although the workers were grateful for the stock in their individual stock accounts, this fringe benefit did not automatically make them satisfied with their pay or working conditions.

One review of employee ownership found that the satisfaction of employee owners with the firm and their jobs depended largely on their perceptions of the firm's financial performance and the effectiveness of their co-workers.[37] To the extent that the employee owners were dissatisfied with the financial performance of the organization, they became increasingly interested in influencing the decision making.

Studies on the effects of ownership on job satisfaction suggest that owning a part of the company does not make employees happier either with their specific job or the company in general. One study found that among nonmanagerial employees of an employee-owned trucking firm, the satisfaction of those who owned shares of the company did not differ from that of nonowners.[38] Similar results have been found in other industries, confirming the idea that owning part of the company does not make work more interesting.

Research studies have also discredited the idea that ownership increases a person's desire to participate in management and decision making. A study of employee attitudes in an employee-owned furniture-manufacturing company suggested that, if anything, share ownership decreased the desire of workers to perform managerial functions.[39] Likewise, ownership in an employee-owned electronics firm was associated with a decline in the desire of the new owners to participate in managerial decisions.[40]

Employee buyouts of troubled companies generally come as a pragmatic response to a financial crisis when alternative forms of restructuring are not feasible. These buyouts are typically accompanied with wage concessions, cuts in employment, and a plea for greater labor–management cooperation. Although the initial results of employee buyouts look promising, the long-term financial security of employee-owned companies is not assured. A troubled company before the employee buyout is still a troubled company after the buyout unless significant changes are made in the way the firm is managed. The existing evidence suggests that the key variable determining success is not ownership but management. Regardless of who owns the company, a firm will be successful only if it is well managed. Employee ownership appears to do little or nothing to increase levels of motivation or guarantee labor peace or profitability.

PERFORMANCE REWARDS

Performance rewards are any type of incentive that is based on the actual performance of employees. Unlike system rewards that are granted to employees because of their membership in the organization, performance rewards are administered differentially to those who merit them because of their performance. The purpose of performance rewards is to motivate employees to perform better.

Formulating an effective reward system that motivates employees is a difficult design problem. The reason why the design is so complicated is because there is such a wide variety of both financial and nonfinancial rewards and because so many different reinforcement contingencies can be used to administer them. Nonfinancial rewards can be broadly classified as recognition programs.

Recognition Programs

Nonmonetary reward systems have been used effectively to improve employee motivation. Every motivation theory agrees that praise and recognition are effective rewards. Companies have created a variety of nonmonetary reward programs to recognize employees, and some of them have been more effective than monetary incentives.[41]

Types of Recognition Programs. The following illustrations demonstrate the diversity of recognition rewards:

- A storage company paneled one of the walls inside its warehouse and used it to display the photographs of the employee with the best safety record each month. The number of accidents in the warehouse was greatly reduced, and the forklift operators were pleased with the recognition they received, even though the public could not see their photographs.

- Sewing machine operators receive silver stars on their nameplates if they exceed 120 percent of their production quotas every day for a week. After they get ten silver stars, they receive a purple seal. Ribbons are awarded for high-quality production, and the operators display them with pride.

- A hospital gives five-, ten-, fifteen-, twenty-, and twenty-five-year service pins to recognize employees for their years of service. The pins are top-quality jewelry, made with diamonds and gold, that show the hospital's logo. When the price of gold increased, the hospital decided to give savings bonds rather than pins, but the administrators abandoned the idea when they discovered that the pins were far more important to and valued by the employees than the savings bonds.

- To reduce absenteeism and tardiness, a small apparel manufacturer decided to give gifts of $10 to $15 to randomly selected employees who had perfect attendance. At the end of each week, the names of those who had perfect attendance records were placed in a drawing. For every twenty names in the drawing, one name was selected to receive a gift. After three months, tardiness was only a third of what it had been, and absenteeism was cut in half.

Learned Rewards. Recognition awards, such as silver stars, purple seals, and photographs hung on a wall, are not inherently rewarding. Primary rewards such as food, water, rest, and the removal of pain are reinforcing because of their relationship to the innate physiology of the body. However, secondary rewards such as recognition awards do not directly satisfy physiological needs. Instead, they become powerful reinforcers as people come to place value on them. Consequently, social approval, recognition, status, and feelings of pride and craftsmanship are secondary or learned rewards because their reinforcing properties are acquired through experience with them. Although a person may not immediately see the secondary reinforcer as a highly motivating award, over time it can become a powerful form of reinforcement. Recognition awards are often inconsequential to new employees, but as new workers observe their co-workers participate in meaningful recognition experiences, the reward comes to be a highly valued reinforcer. For example, a twenty-five-year service pin can be an extremely motivating reward, not because of its financial worth but because of the symbolic meaning associated with it. In some organizations, the service pins are distributed at an annual awards banquet where the recipients are recognized individually. Employees who observe this ritual year after year come to appreciate the ceremony and see the pin as a highly valued reward.[42]

To assess the popularity of recognition programs, the *Personnel Journal* asked its subscribers to describe the kinds of programs they sponsor and the rewards they offer.[43] Length-of-service programs were the most popular; 90 percent said they recognized employees for the number of years spent with the organization, and two-thirds recognized employees at retirement. Attendance programs that recognize employees for not being tardy or absent were reported by one-fourth of the respondents. A quarter of the respondents also said they have safety programs to reduce accidents, and about the same percentage have some form of productivity improvement programs to save money or streamline procedures. Six percent have a suggestion program to reward employees for creative ideas. To recognize employees who make that extra service step, 13 percent of the companies have a customer service program. Approximately one-third of the companies have a sales incentive program that provides recognition beyond the regular sales commissions.

The most popular type of recognition award was a certificate or plaque sometimes accompanied by a gift certificate or cash award. Two-thirds of the companies reported using plaques and certificates in their award programs. Other rewards included accessory jewelry, watches, travel, rings, trophies, and ribbons. Travel and paid vacations have become increasingly popular in recent years, especially for sales incentives.

Financial Incentives

The effects of money on motivation depend primarily on whether pay is based on performance. In spite of this relationship, however, it is surprising to discover how seldom pay is based on performance. For example, when employees are asked what would happen if they doubled their efforts and produced twice as much, very few report that they would receive additional income. Some say their supervisors would recognize their efforts and commend them, and a few think they might eventually receive a pay increase. However, most report that the consequences of doubling their effort would be negative: it would disrupt the flow of work, their co-workers would hassle them, and they would eventually be expected to work at that rate all the time without additional compensation.

Incentive compensation can be granted on the basis of individual performance, group performance, or company-wide performance.

Individual Incentives. The most popular forms of individual incentive pay include merit pay, piece-rate incentives, and commission sales. **Merit pay** plans are based on a subjective assessment of each employee's performance, and the merit pay is typically awarded in the form of an increase to base pay for the coming year.

The most direct relationship between pay and performance generally appears in the form of **piece-rate incentives,** where workers receive a specified amount for each unit of work. The effectiveness of piece-rate incentives has been studied for many years. Frederick W. Taylor, the father of scientific management, defended his recommendations of piece-rate incentives on the basis of research showing that workers paid on a piece-rate basis produced more work and earned more money. Taylor argued that piece-rate incentive programs would increase productivity by at least 25 percent.

Most surveys of piece-rate plans over the past seventy years have suggested that Taylor underestimated the actual results. Most surveys have found that productivity under piece work has increased between 30 to 40 percent and in some cases greater than 60 percent.[44]

Although piece-work incentive systems predictably increase productivity, there is some question whether the increase is due to financial incentives alone or to other changes that accompany piece-work plans. Two variables that accompany piece-work programs are (1) changes in the design of the work and (2) higher performance goals. When a piece-work plan is installed, a careful analysis of the job is usually conducted to ensure that it is being performed efficiently. A careful job analysis often identifies more efficient methods of performing the task. Moreover, when the task is being timed to establish pay rates, a goal-setting process occurs, followed by performance feedback. The question, then, is whether goal-setting, measurement, and job redesign are more responsible than pay incentives for increasing productivity. Studies generally show that each factor alone has a positive influence on productivity, but that the impact is far greater when all three factors are present. Thus, incentive systems contribute to productivity increases due to improved work methods, higher performance goals with specific performance feedback, and monetary incentives that induce greater effort.[45]

An alternative to paying people for what they do is to pay them for what they are capable of doing. This alternative pays employees for the skills and knowledge they possess rather than for the work they produce or for a particular job category. Skill-based pay systems reward employees for acquiring additional knowledge and skill within the same job category. These skill-based compensation plans reinforce employees for their growth and development and hopefully result in more creative ideas and quality performance.[46]

Group Incentives and Bonuses. Although piece-work plans are typically based on individual performance, they can also be based on group production, with all members of the group sharing the money earned by the group. Group incentive plans have some important advantages over individual incentive plans, because they create greater cooperation among co-workers. This climate of cooperation usually reduces the need for direct supervision and control, since workers are supervised more by their co-workers than by their supervisors. In such a climate, slow workers are pressured by their co-workers to increase their productivity. Moreover, the flow of work and flexibility in job assignments are greatly facilitated by group incentives. When the normal work routine is disrupted because of unique problems such as illness or broken machines, individuals paid on a group incentive plan are more willing to adapt to the problem and solve it themselves.

Group incentives have certain limitations, however. When their jobs are independent, group members feel responsible only for their own jobs and think they should be paid individually. In this situation, group incentives provide little incentive to produce because extra efforts by one worker will only result in a small increase in that worker's weekly pay. As the group gets larger, this problem becomes more severe. Thus, group incentives are most useful when jobs are interdependent, when the output of the group can be counted, and when the group is small.

The powerful influence of group pressure explains why piece-rate incentives are sometimes not effective. Although many studies have shown that incentive pay systems increase productivity, other studies have found examples where groups restrict output to arbitrarily low levels. Group norms restricting productivity are very troublesome to managers, and they are particularly perplexing because they seem to be so irrational. Why should a group of workers collectively decide to restrict their productivity when they are paid only for what they produce? This behavior is not so irrational when it is examined from the workers' perspective. The problem centers on how the performance standards are established. Workers know that performance standards are somewhat arbitrary. They believe that if they consistently produce more than the standard, the industrial engineer will return and retime the job. Then they will be expected to produce more work for the same amount of pay.

Management has been guilty of retiming jobs often enough in some organizations to justify the workers' fears. Several interesting case studies have described the games played by workers and industrial engineers in setting performance standards. Since industrial engineers know the workers intentionally work slowly, they arbitrarily tighten the standards above the measured times. But the workers know the industrial engineer suspects them of working slowly so they add unnecessary and inefficient movements to look busy, which the industrial engineers expect and try to disregard.

Company-wide Incentives. In some organizations, financial incentives are based on the performance of the entire organization. These programs are called *gain-sharing plans* because they share the financial gains of productivity improvements with the employees who helped produce them. Two of the most popular forms of company-wide incentives include profit-sharing plans and Scanlon plans. Profit sharing is the most popular company-wide incentive, and in some companies the employees have been highly motivated to perform as a result of a generous profit-sharing plan. A typical profit-sharing plan distributes 25 percent of the pretax profit to the employees according to an allocation formula combining years of service and base wages. The major types of profit-sharing plans are *cash plans* and *deferred plans.* Cash plans are most directly tied to performance because payments are made to employees at the end of each period such as quarterly or annually. However, deferred plans are more popular because of tax considerations. Under a deferred plan, an employee's share of the profit is held in an individual account where it grows without being taxed until it is received at a later period, usually retirement. Some deferred plans provide very sizable sums of money to their participants.

Profit-sharing plans have generally succeeded in reducing conflict between managers and production workers. Many companies claim that their plans have created a sense of partnership between employees and management and have increased employee interest in the company. In turn, many profit-sharing plans have contributed to the financial security of employees. Profit-sharing plans typically increase productivity through higher levels of motivation. However, the motivating impact of profit sharing is typically less than for piece-rate plans, because the individual worker's share of the profit is not directly tied to individual productivity. Immediate rewards that are directly tied to specific individual behaviors are more effective than profit-sharing plans, especially for motivating employees who have short attention spans and who cannot delay gratification. Deferred compensation plans, for example, are more effective for older workers than younger workers because retirement is not so far away.

Scanlon plans were named after their founder, Joseph Scanlon, an accountant and union steward in a steel mill. While negotiating a new labor agreement, Scanlon proposed that the percent of revenue allocated to labor costs be maintained at a fixed ratio of what it had been over the past few years. Scanlon believed that the employees would be highly motivated to increase their productivity if they knew that a fixed percent of the revenue would be paid in wages. Scanlon believed that significantly higher revenues could be obtained without an increase in the number of employee hours by motivating the employees to submit productivity improvement suggestions and to work harder. Since 1941, when Scanlon first proposed his idea, Scanlon plans have grown in popularity, and the results have shown that they tend to increase both company profits and employee wages.[47]

Executive Bonuses. Executives and managers often participate in an additional bonus program designed specifically for them. The basic philosophy behind executive bonuses is to reward managers for good performance. When bonuses are tied to the overall performance of a company, the bonuses are expected to create greater creativity and better cooperation between managers.

The size of executive bonuses is typically larger for upper-level managers than for middle-level managers even when expressed as a percentage of salary. At upper levels of a company, a typical bonus might be 50 to 80 percent of salary. At lower levels of the company, supervisors typically receive bonuses that are only 15 to 40 percent of their salaries, if they receive a bonus at all.

The bonus plans of many companies are not carefully designed and administered. Although bonuses are intended to improve the performance of individual managers and the organization as a whole, the research evidence evaluating bonuses does not entirely support their effectiveness.[48] Because management performance is difficult to evaluate, most bonus plans distribute money based on the manager's position rather than on the manager's performance. Consequently, these plans typically do little to motivate greater performance. Even though they are very expensive and the research evidence regarding their effectiveness is mostly negative, they are still widely used.

Fine-Tuning the Compensation Plan. In designing an effective compensation program, organizations need to find the proper balance between base pay and incentive pay, including individual incentives, group incentives, and company-wide incentives. This process of balancing the various incentives is called **"fine-tuning" the compensation system.** Compensation managers must fine-tune the compensation system just as a mechanic fine-tunes an engine. The engine needs to be adjusted for the load it must pull, the quality of fuel it will use, and even the altitude at which it will operate. Similarly, a compensation system needs to be fine-tuned to balance the employees' needs for security, equity, and motivation.

Employees who have a sizable base pay feel very secure, but they are not motivated. However, if the total compensation consists only of incentive pay, several potential problems could develop, such as increased turnover because of inadequate security, dissatisfaction over inaccurate performance evaluations, and dysfunctional competition between coworkers.

The fine-tuning process consists of adjusting the base pay, individual incentives, group incentives, and profit sharing to create feelings of security and motivation. Security is provided by a stable base pay that provides a dependable weekly or monthly income. Equity and motivation, however, are provided through incentive plans. Some organizations choose to pay large base salaries and give small bonuses. General Motors and Ford, for example, pay their managers a small base pay with large bonuses, while General Electric does just the opposite.

In fine-tuning a compensation system, managers need to carefully evaluate the performance of employees and diagnose the jobs they are performing. These variables need to be considered:

1. To what extent can individual performance be measured accurately, objectively, and conveniently? As a larger portion of the total compensation is determined by individual incentives, the measurement of individual performance must be more precise. Occupations that are difficult to measure precisely, such as engineer, lawyer, and college professor, should not have as large an individual incentive component determining their compensation as occupations that are easier to measure, such as sewing machine operator or salesperson.

2. How much control do workers have over their rate of production? Individual incentives are not very useful when workers have no control over the quantity or quality of their performance. Most assembly-line workers, for example, can control the quality of their work, but not the quantity. Likewise, security guards at a front gate do not control how many people they allow to pass through or direct elsewhere.

3. How much interdependence and cooperation is required by the work itself? When individuals work together to produce a group product, their pay should be based on the level of group performance rather than on individual performance.

4. What is the size of the work group and the organization? As work groups and organizations become larger, the measurable influence of a single worker shrinks. In large work groups and large organizations, group incentives and profit-sharing plans lose some of their motivating influence.

5. Does the organization produce a profit, and can it obtain accurate and timely measures of performance? A profit-sharing plan not only requires profits to share, which largely excludes most nonprofit organizations, but also an acceptable procedure for measuring the profits and a formula for dividing them.

SUMMARY

1. Effective organizations are required to elicit multiple behaviors from their members. Three essential behaviors necessary for organizational effectiveness are (a) people must be induced to enter and remain in the organization, (b) they must perform their role assignments in a dependable fashion, and (c) they must be motivated to voluntarily contribute spontaneous and innovative behaviors.

2. Organizations use six different motivational patterns to achieve the necessary behaviors: rule en-

forcement, instrumental system rewards, instrumental individual rewards, intrinsic satisfaction for the work itself, internalized values, and group relationships.

3. Performance evaluation is an important element in the employment exchange, and serves at least five important organizational functions: (a) to guide personnel actions such as hiring, firing, and promoting; (b) to reinforce behavior through pay increases and other rewards; (c) to aid personal development; (d) to identify

training needs; and (e) to integrate the personnel functions and facilitate career planning.

4. Because the performance appraisal process has been extensively criticized, many different procedures have been developed for evaluating performance, including ranking procedures, classification procedures, graphic rating scales, behaviorally-anchored rating scales, forced-choice evaluations, and descriptive essays.

5. Management by objectives is a results-oriented form of evaluating performance. It is also a philosophy of management that focuses on developing long-range organizational goals, translating these goals into specific objectives for every employee, delegating to each employee the responsibility and authority to act, evaluating the accomplishment of the objectives, and allowing all members of the organization to participate in the decision-making process and control of the organization. MBO is usually implemented in an organization as a performance evaluation procedure built on setting goals and objectives. Gradually, the MBO program encompasses other management functions, such as strategic planning, compensation, training, and human resource planning.

6. Much of the behavior in organizations can be explained by understanding the organization's rules. People comply with the rules because they have been socialized to accept them, and because of the threat of punishment. Three major types of punishment include natural consequences, logical consequences, and contrived consequences.

7. Although punishment is not highly recommended as a means of controlling behavior, it can be an effective tool when these conditions exist: (a) when it is administered immediately after an undesirable behavior; (b) when it is unpleasant but not severe; (c) when it focuses on a specific act, not on the person or general behavior patterns; (d) when it is consistent across persons and across time; (e) when it is administered in a way that informs people of what they did wrong; (f) when it occurs in the context of a loving and nurturing relationship; and (g) when it is not followed by undeserved rewards.

8. Employees should be disciplined for just cause only after a fair procedure providing for due process has been followed. The customary steps in a progressive discipline procedure include verbal warning, verbal reprimand, written reprimand, suspension, and discharge.

9. System rewards are granted to people because of their membership in the organization. They include such things as employee benefits, recreational facilities, and working conditions. System rewards motivate employees to join an organization and remain in it.

10. Employee benefits are an expensive system reward that typically costs about 40 percent as much as wages and salaries. The typical benefits include (a) health and accident insurance; (b) life insurance and income continuation; (c) pay for time not worked, such as holidays; (d) employee services such as tuition reimbursement; and (e) pensions.

11. Stock options have typically been used to reward managers with large sums of money in a way that minimizes the amount they will lose because of taxes. Since stock options are largely unrelated to individual performance, they do almost nothing to increase motivation.

12. Employee stock ownership plans (ESOPs) have been created as a way to help employees own the company. Company contributions are paid to an ESOP trust that buys the company's stock and holds it for the individual employees. Because of favorable tax incentives, ESOPs have grown considerably over the past decade. Like stock option plans, however, they do very little, if anything, to motivate employee performance.

13. Performance rewards include both recognition programs and financial incentives. Recognition programs are especially effective because they are learned rewards that possess symbolic meaning. Awards such as service pins, certificates, and plaques have been used effectively to improve attendance, increase productivity, and reduce accidents.

14. Financial incentives can be based on individual performance, group performance, or company-wide profitability. The two major individual rewards include merit pay and piece-rate incentives. Two of the most popular company-wide incentives include Scanlon plans and profit-sharing plans. Because these incentive plans are closely tied to productivity, they tend to significantly increase motivation. Piece-rate incentives, for example, often increase productivity by 40 to 60 percent.

15. Fine-tuning a compensation plan involves creating a balance between the employees' needs for security, equity, and motivation. Security is provided by a stable base pay, while motivation is created through incentive plans that pay people only when they perform.

DISCUSSION QUESTIONS

1. Many employees dislike performance evaluations. Many students dislike grades. What would happen if teachers quit giving grades? What if everyone received the same grade? What if everyone received an A?

2. How would you respond to an executive who said, "I do not want any personality factors on the company's performance evaluation. I only want to measure quantity and quality. It is results we are after!"

3. What difference does it make to you in terms of effort and learning to take a course on a pass–fail basis rather than on a grade basis?

4. What changes would you recommend for solving the problem of grade inflation at colleges and universities? How would you apply these recommendations in an actual work group where the norm is to rate everyone as outstanding?

5. Identify the natural consequences, logical consequences, and contrived consequences associated with these acts: missing class, coming to class late, writing a careless term paper, submitting a term paper late, and missing an exam.

6. Describe the type of discipline system you would propose for reducing noise in the library. How effective do you think your discipline procedure would be?

7. What conditions make a group incentive system superior to an individual incentive system?

8. In designing an incentive compensation system, what problems would occur if excessive weight were placed on individual incentives? on group incentives? on profit sharing? on base salary?

GLOSSARY

behaviorally-anchored rating scales (BARS) A form of graphic rating scales in which the scales are accompanied by specific behavioral descriptions.

contrived consequences Consequences created by the person administering punishment that bear no relationship to the wrongdoing.

dependable role performance One of the essential behaviors organizations require of their employees. The phrase refers to adequate quantity and quality production.

descriptive essays A method of performance evaluation that consists of a free-form essay describing the employee's performance.

due process A major concept of administrative justice that requires disciplinary actions to follow a process that provides for fair and unbiased treatment. Such a process requires that specific charges of wrongdoing must be stated, that evidence of wrongs must be presented, that employees must be allowed to defend themselves, and that cases must be decided by an impartial judge.

ESOP (employee stock ownership plan) A method for helping employees to participate in the ownership of the company, by which the company places stock in an ESOP trust that is gradually purchased and given to employees through company contributions.

fine-tuning compensation Adjusting a compensation package to achieve a balance between security and motivation. Security is provided by a stable base pay, and motivation is provided by incentives that associate pay with performance.

flexible benefit plans A plan that allows employees to choose which benefits they desire, subject to certain limitations and total cost constraints.

forced-choice rating scales An evaluation procedure that contains pairs of items that sound equally desirable, even though only one item in each pair is actually descriptive of an outstanding performer.

graphic rating scales An evaluation procedure consisting of specified dimensions of performance and a scale for each dimension to evaluate the employee's behavior.

hot stove rule A recommended procedure for administering discipline that involves advance warning as well as immediate and impartial punishment for wrongdoing.

individual rewards Rewards that are distributed to individuals according to their individual performance.

just cause A major concept of administrative justice in which disciplinary actions are taken for good and sufficient reasons. For good and sufficient reasons to be established, company rules must be related to safe and efficient operations and must be clearly communicated to employees. Moreover, employees must have been warned about the consequences of rule violations, and objective evidence must show that rules have actually been violated.

logical consequences A form of discipline in which the nature of the punishment is logically related to the nature of the wrongdoing. Although the punishment is determined by the person administering it, the punishment is not arbitrary or unrelated to the misbehavior.

management by objectives (MBO) A results-oriented type of performance evaluation in which every employee identifies specific measurable objectives against which the employee is evaluated at the end of each period.

merit pay A form of individual incentive in which pay increases are tied to the individual's performance evaluation.

natural consequences A form of punishment that occurs naturally because of the nature of the misbehavior. No one is required to administer natural consequences, because they occur naturally. Because they are automatic, natural consequences are the most effective form of punishment.

piece-rate incentives A form of individual incentive wherein employees are paid a specific amount of money for each unit they produce.

progressive discipline A sequence of disciplinary actions that specify increasingly severe penalties for repeated violations, such as verbal warning, verbal reprimand, written reprimand, suspension, and discharge.

ranking procedures An evaluation procedure that involves ranking a group of employees from best performer to worst performer.

rule enforcement A motivational pattern that has a large impact on individual behavior because people have internalized the rules and are willing to live by them.

Scanlon plans A company-wide incentive plan that combines profit sharing with a suggestion system. The amount of money distributed to employees is based on a fixed ratio of labor costs to total revenues.

spontaneous and innovative behaviors Behaviors that are important for organizational effectiveness but that are not typically considered part of an employee's formal job description. They include such things as cooperative actions, creative suggestions, and protective acts.

system rewards Rewards that are given to people because they are members of the organization or one of its subsystems. These rewards are not based on individual performance.

NOTES

1. Daniel Katz and Robert L. Kahn, *The Social Psychology of Organizations*, 2nd ed. (New York: Wiley, 1978), pp. 402–405.

2. Daniel Katz, "The Motivational Basis of Organizational Behavior," *Behavioral Science*, vol. 9 (April 1964), pp. 131–146.

3. David J. Cherrington, *The Management of Human Resources* (Needham Heights, Mass.: Allyn & Bacon, 1990), chap. 7.

4. *Baxter v. Savannah Sugar Refining Corp.*, 495 F2d 437 (1974); *Brito v. Zia Co.*, 478, F2d, 1200 (1973); *Albemarle Paper Company v. Moody*, 95 SCt 2362 (1974);

Rowe v. General Motors Corp., 457 F2d 348, 1972; *Wade v. Mississippi Cooperative Extension Service*, 528 F2d 508 (1976).

5. Personal communication from the commanding officer.

6. Kathleen M. Eisenhardt, "Control: Organizational and Economic Approaches," *Management Science*, vol. 31 (February 1985), pp. 134–149.

7. Donald J. Campbell and Cynthia Lee, "Self-appraisal in Performance Evaluation: Development vs. Evaluation," *Academy of Management Review*, vol. 13 (April 1988), pp. 302–314; Mark R. Edwards, "Implementation Strategies for Multiple Rater Systems," *Personnel Journal*, vol. 69 (September 1990), pp. 130–141; Barron Wells and Nelda Spinks, "How Companies Are Using Employee Self-Evaluation Forms," *Journal of Compensation and Benefits*, vol. 6 (November–December 1990), pp. 42–47.

8. "Performance Appraisal Programs," *Personnel Policies Forum*, Survey no. 135, February 1983, p. 6.

9. John P. Campbell, R. Darvey, Marvin D. Dunnette, and L. V. Hellervik, "The Development and Evaluation of Behaviorally Based Rating Scales," *Journal of Applied Psychology*, vol. 57, no. 1 (1973), pp. 15–22; Donald P. Schwab, Herbert G. Heneman, and T. A. DeCotis, "Behaviorally-Anchored Rating Scales: A Review of the Literature," *Personnel Psychology*, vol. 28, no. 4 (Winter 1975), pp. 549–562; Aharon Tziner and Richard Kopelman, "Effects of Rating Format on Goal-Setting Dimensions: A Field Experiment," *Journal of Applied Psychology*, vol. 73 (May 1988), pp. 323–326; Aharon Tziner and Gary P. Latham, "The Effects of Appraisal Instrument, Feedback and Goal-Setting on Worker Satisfaction and Commitment, *Journal of Organizational Behavior*, vol. 10 (April 1989), pp. 145–153.

10. Lee W. Cozan, "Forced-choice: Better Than Other Rating Methods?" *Personnel*, vol. 36, no. 3 (May–June 1955), pp. 80–83; Donald E. Sisson, "Forced-Choice: The New Army Rating," *Personnel Psychology*, vol. 1, no. 3 (Autumn 1948), pp. 365–381; Mary L. Tenopyr, "Artifactual Reliability of Forced-Choice Scales," *Journal of Applied Psychology*, vol. 73 (November 1988), pp. 749–751.

11. See Stephen J. Carroll and Henry L. Tosi, *Management by Objectives: Applications and Research* (New York: Macmillan, 1973).

12. Peter F. Drucker, *The Practice of Management* (New York: Harper & Row, 1954).

13. Anthony P. Raia, *Managing by Objectives* (Glenview, Ill.: Scott Foresman, 1974).

14. Anthony P. Raia, "Goal Setting and Self-control," *Journal of Management Studies*, vol. 2 (February 1965), pp. 34–53; Anthony P. Raia, "A Second Look at Management Goals and Controls," *California Management Review*, vol. 8 (Summer 1966), pp. 49–58; Dennis Daley, "Performance Appraisal and Organizational Success: Public Employee Perceptions in an MBO-based Appraisal System, *Review of Public Personnel Administration*, vol. 9 (Fall 1988), pp. 17–27; Albert W. Schrader and G. Taylor Seward, "MBO Makes Dollar Sense," *Personnel Journal*, vol. 68 (July 1989), pp. 32–37.

15. Stephen G. Green, Gail T. Fairhurst, and B. Kay Snavely, "Chains of Poor Performance and Supervisory Control," *Organizational Behavior and Human Decision Processes*, vol. 38 (1986), pp. 7–27.

16. James R. Larson, Jr., "Supervisors' Performance Feedback to Subordinates: The Impact of Subordinate Performance Valence and Outcome Dependence," *Organizational Behavior and Human Decision Processes*, vol. 37 (1986), pp. 391–408.

17. C. D. Fisher, "Transmission of Positive and Negative Feedback to Subordinates: A Laboratory Investigation," *Journal of Applied Psychology*, vol. 64 (1979), pp. 533–540; Daniel R. Ilgen and W. A. Knowlton, "Performance Attributional Effects on Feedback from Superiors," *Organizational Behavior and Human Performance*, vol. 25 (1980), pp. 441–456.

18. J. Bruce Prince and Edward E. Lawler, III, "Does Salary Discussion Hurt the Developmental Performance Appraisal?" *Organizational Behavior and Human Decision Processes*, vol. 37 (1986), pp. 357–375.

19. Tamao Matsui, Akinori Okada, and Osamu Inoshita, "Mechanism of Feedback Affecting Task Performance," *Organizational Behavior and Human Performance*, vol. 31 (1983), pp. 114–122.

20. Albert Bandura, "Self-efficacy Mechanism in Human Agency," *American Psychologist*, vol. 37 (February 1982), pp. 122–147.

21. Dennis W. Organ and Thomas Bateman, *Organizational Behavior: An Applied Psychological Approach*, 3rd ed. (Plano, Texas: Business Publications, 1986), p. 320.

22. Max Weber, *The Theory of Social and Economic Organization*, translated by A. M. Henderson and Talcott Parsons (New York: Free Press, 1947).

23. A classic study reported by L. Miller, "The Use of Knowledge of Results in Improving the Performance of Hourly Operators" (Crotonville, NY: General Electric Company Behavioral Research Service). Cited by Katz and Kahn, op. cit., p. 409.

24. Rudolf Dreikurs and Loren Grey, *Logical Consequences: A New Approach to Discipline* (New York: Hawthorn Books, 1968).

25. This principle is attributed to Douglas McGregor. See George Strauss and Leonard Sayles, *Personnel: The Human Problems of Management* (Englewood Cliffs, N.J.: Prentice-Hall, 1967); Walter Kiechel, III, "How to Discipline in the Modern Age," *Fortune*, vol. 121 (May 7, 1990), pp. 179–180.

26. R. Di Giuseppe, "Vicarious Punishment: An Investigation of Timing," *Psychological Reports*, vol. 36 (1975), pp. 819–824; Charles A. O'Reilly, III, and Sheila M. Puffer, "The Impact of Rewards and Punishments in a

Social Context: A Laboratory and Field Experiment," *Journal of Occupational Psychology,* vol. 62 (March 1989), pp. 41–53.

27. Organ and Bateman, op. cit., chap. 11; Robert A. Baron, "Negative Effects of Destructive Criticism: Impact on Conflict, Self-efficacy, and Task Performance," *Journal of Applied Psychology,* vol. 73 (May 1988), pp. 199–207; Appa Rao Korukonda and James G. Hunt, "Pat on the Back vs. Kick in the Pants: An Application of Cognitive Inference to the Study of Leader Reward and Punishment Behaviors," *Group and Organizations Studies,* vol. 14 (September 1989), pp. 299–324.

28. Martin L. Hoffman, "Moral Internalization, Parental Power, and the Nature of Parent–Child Interaction," *Developmental Psychology,* vol. 11, no. 2 (1975), pp. 228–239.

29. Darryel Roberds, "Supervisors Must Occasionally Fire Someone," *Supervision,* vol. 51 (December 1990), pp. 14–18.

30. Elaine Hobbs Fry, Blaise J. Bergiel, and Nicholas E. Fry, "Organizational Discipline: Does the Punishment Fit the Crime?" *Mid-Atlantic Journal of Business,* vol. 26 (Fall 1989), pp. 41–52; Richard C. Kearney and Frank Whitaker, "Behaviorally Anchored Disciplinary Scales (BADS): A New Approach to Discipline," *Public Personnel Management,* vol. 17 (Fall 1988), pp. 341–350.

31. Jim Braham, "A Rewarding Place to Work," *Industry Week,* vol. 238 (September 18, 1989), pp. 15–19.

32. "Employee Benefits, 1990," Chamber of Commerce of the United States, 1615 H Street, Washington, D.C. 20062, 1990.

33. Survey by the author of 3,300 employees in a major corporation.

34. Corey Rosen, Kathryn J. Klein, and Karen M. Young, *Employee Ownership in the United States: The Equity Solution* (Lexington, Mass.: Lexington Books, 1986). Jon L. Pierce, Stephen A. Rubenfield, and Susan Morgan, "Employee Ownership: A Conceptual Model of Process and Effects," *Academy of Management Review,* vol. 16 (1991), pp. 121–144.

35. J. Lawrence French, "Employee Perspectives on Stock Ownership: Financial Investment or Mechanism of Control?" *Academy of Management Review,* vol. 12 (1987), pp. 427–435; Kathyrn J. Klein, "Employee Stock Ownership and Employee Attitudes: A Test of

Three Models," *Journal of Applied Psychology Monograph,* vol. 72, no. 2 (1987), pp. 319–332.

36. William Baldwin, "The Myths of Employee Ownership," *Forbes,* vol. 133 (April 23, 1984), pp. 108–111.

37. French, op. cit.

38. R. Long, "Desire for and Patterns of Worker Participation in Decision Making After Conversion to Employee Ownership," *Academy of Management Journal,* vol. 22 (1979), pp. 611–616.

39. T. Hammer and R. Stern, "Employee Ownership: Implications for the Organizational Distribution of Power," *Academy of Management Journal,* vol. 23 (1980), pp. 78–100.

40. R. Long, "The Effects of Formal Employee Participation in Ownership and Decision-Making on Perceived and Desired Patterns of Organizational Influence: A Longitudinal Study," *Human Relations,* vol. 34 (1981), pp. 847–876.

41. Skip Derra, "Honoring the Stars of Research," *Research and Development,* vol. 31 (August 1989), pp. 48–52; Jennifer J. Koch, "Recognition: Ross Employees Are in the Company of Excellence," *Personnel Journal,* vol. 69 (June 1990), pp. 108–110; Marilyn Kay Zelinsky, "A Spotless Program: A Building Services Firm Cleans Up Its Turnover Rate," *Incentive,* vol. 164 (July 1990), pp. 51–52.

42. David J. Cherrington and B. Jackson Wixom, Jr., "Recognition Is Still a Top Motivator," *Personnel Administrator,* vol. 28 (May 1983), pp. 87–91.

43. M. Magnus, "Surveying the Diversity of Rewards," *Personnel Journal,* vol. 65 (December 1986), pp. 69–74.

44. Surveyed by Allan N. Nash and Stephen J. Carroll, Jr., *The Management of Compensation* (Monterey, Calif.: Brooks-Cole, 1975), p. 199.

45. James S. Devlin, "Wage Incentives: The Aetna Plan," presented at the LOMA work measurement seminar (April 1975).

46. Fred Luthans and Marilyn L. Fox, "Update on Skill-based Pay," *Personnel,* vol. 66 (March 1989), pp. 26–31.

47. Brian E. Moore and T. L. Ross, *The Scanlon Way to Improve Productivity* (New York: John Wiley and Sons, 1978).

48. J. Perham, "What's Wrong with Bonuses?" *Dun's Review of Modern Industry,* vol. 98 (1981), pp. 40–44.

CONSTRUCTIVE DISCIPLINE

Daniel Salazar, age 23, is the son of an immigrant family of seven children. Despite the family's poverty, Dan stayed in school and graduated from technical school in drafting. His father has been dead for seven years and his mother receives welfare. It is well known at the company that part of Dan's earnings help to support the family.

During his schooling, Dan denied himself ordinary social activities because he was required to work part time to help his family. Within the past year, however, he has made several remarks, suggesting that he has felt a little resentful at having to spend so many hours working and would now like to have more social contacts.

Dan's performance at work has been outstanding. Both his supervisors and his co-workers were impressed with how rapidly he learned his job. Recently, however, his supervisor has become concerned about an attendance problem. On one occasion, Dan called his supervisor and requested a substitute because of illness. A substitute was not available, and the other members of his department decided to complete Dan's work. That evening the supervisor called to see how Dan was feeling and found that he was on a date. The supervisor noted the incident on Dan's record and warned him that a similar occurrence would lead to disciplinary action. In the past Dan has maintained a good relationship with the other members of the department, yet some of them felt irritated when they learned that Dan was not actually ill.

Two months later it was again learned that in a period of claimed illness, Dan was not at home. He was reprimanded by the supervisor, but he claimed he was helping an older sister take care of a family emergency. In the past week it has come to the attention of the supervisor that a similar breach of conduct has occurred. The supervisor consulted with the area supervisor, who contacted the plant manager. The plant manager decided that the other area supervisors should be involved in the development of a general policy. The plant manager has accordingly called a meeting involving all the area supervisors plus Dan's supervisor. The purpose of the meeting is to determine what course of action should be taken regarding Dan's problem.

Alternatives

What are the arguments for and against each of the following alternatives?

1. Be supportive of Dan and try for the time being to overlook his misbehavior.

2. Counsel Dan regarding both his personal and family problems and help him manage them more effectively so that they do not interfere with his work.

3. Make it very clear to Dan that he has violated the standards of the plant, and help him see the difficulty his absence creates for others. Make arrangements for him to make up the time.

4. Tell Dan that he is now on probation and that another incident of this nature will lead to his dismissal.

5. Tell Dan that since he has been warned about missing work, he is now terminated, but give him a favorable recommendation to help him find another job.

6. Since Dan has ignored two previous warnings and continued in the same pattern, he should be terminated from the plant, and this termination should appear on any recommendation for future employment.

DECIDING PAY INCREASES

In the College of Business, all salary changes, including merit increases and cost-of-living adjustments, are decided by the department heads. This year, the dean's office has allocated $16,000 for salary increases to the six members of one depart-ment. The six faculty members and some information about them are shown in Exhibit 5.7.

In the past, pay increases have largely been tied to the rate of inflation, and everyone has received about the same percentage increase. The rate of

EXHIBIT 5.7   Faculty Profiles

Professor	Present Salary	Years of Teaching	Performance Information
Brooks	$44,800	15	Students say he is a horrible teacher. Never keeps his office hours, spends most of his time doing outside consulting, and hasn't written anything but consulting project reports for nine years.
Falk	$32,100	3	Excellent researcher; good teacher of graduate classes; receives mixed evaluations from undergraduate students because most class activities are used to collect research data. Published six articles last year in leading journals.
Hunter	$45,100	12	Students say she is a very good teacher and is very helpful to students; a member of the College Advisory Council; published three articles last year in practitioner journals and one article in an academic journal.
Moore	$30,200	2	New to the job; students say she is entertaining in class, but her lectures are weak because she lacks experience; spent first year finishing dissertation and has been working on other research projects since then, but nothing is finished.
Stephens	$55,600	28	Former associate dean and department head, influential in college politics but is not on any committees; author of three books, including a textbook he revised eight years ago. Has written nothing in the last four years. Students complain that his lectures are boring and obsolete. He spends much of his time at his hobby, training dogs.
Walker	$52,200	26	Considered an outstanding teacher at both graduate and undergraduate levels. Served on several thesis committees last year; involved in two major research projects; has solo-authored two and coauthored six research articles; wrote about 40 percent of a textbook last year; serves on the review board for a research journal.

inflation this year has been about 6 percent, and everyone would normally receive a cost-of-living adjustment of at least that amount. However, during its fall retreat, the college executive committee decided that pay increases should be based primarily on performance rather than on cost-of-living increases. The committee concluded that greater efforts should be made to reward outstanding faculty members for teaching, research, and professional service to the university or to society. When this decision was announced, some of the faculty members objected, and the dean said publicly that everyone would probably receive some increase, but that weak faculty members might not keep up with inflation.

Directions. Decide how you would allocate the $16,000 salary increases, using Exhibit 5.8. After you have made your own decisions, discuss your recommendations with four or five other students and try to reach a group consensus based on similar arguments. Pretend that you are the department head who must justify these decisions to the faculty members.

EXHIBIT 5.8   **Recommended Salary Increases**

Professor	Salary Increase		Explanation
	amount	*% increase*	
Brooks			
Falk			
Hunter			
Moore			
Stephens			
Walker			

CHAPTER 6

Job Design: Intrinsic Motivation

CHAPTER OUTLINE

LEARNING OBJECTIVES

After studying this chapter, you should be able to

1. Explain the advantages of job specialization and the role it has played in industrial development.

2. Describe the problems created by highly specialized jobs, and describe how job enrichment and job enlargement programs are designed to correct these problems.

3. Describe the job characteristics model of job enrichment, and explain how this model can be used for analyzing jobs to determine whether they should be redesigned and how.

4. Summarize the research conclusions concerning the effects of job enrichment on employee attitudes and performance.

5. Describe five alternative patterns of work schedules—flextime, permanent part time, job sharing, compressed workweeks and telecommuting—and list the advantages and disadvantages of each.

6. Identify the goals of quality-of-work-life (QWL) programs, and describe some of the major QWL programs.

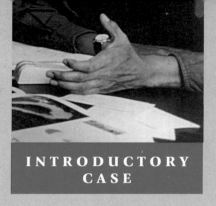

JOB SPECIALIZATION AT UPS

Although some companies use job enrichment to increase motivation, United Parcel Services uses job specialization to improve efficiency. The delivery routes of its 62,000 drivers have been calibrated down to the minute to eliminate wasted motions and unnecessary delays. The drivers are trained to perform with mechanical efficiency, always conscious of their schedule.[1]

Activities that do not require total concentration are performed simultaneously with other activities, such as completing paperwork while walking back to the truck. Routine actions are performed in a studied sequence of flowing hand motions, such as unhooking the safety belt, tooting the horn, cutting the engine, yanking on the emergency brake, and shoving the gear shift into first gear ready to take off again. Equipment has been engineered to minimize time and effort; for example, the seat is placed at an optimal height with a beveled edge that makes it easier to get onto and off.

Although the daily UPS routines have been described as mind-numbing efficiency, there is a very good reason to use a time-and-motion study. For a driver who makes an average of 145 stops to deliver 246 packages and to pick up a similar number, adding just a few seconds to each transaction extends the average day by an hour or more. And when multiplied by 62,000 drivers, these few seconds make a dramatic difference in labor costs.

Questions

1. Is this kind of "hurry-up" really necessary? Are there long-term hidden costs?

2. How will this focus on task efficiency influence the drivers?

3. Customer service takes time. How should UPS balance the needs for task efficiency and customer service?

JOB SPECIALIZATION, JOB ENLARGEMENT, AND JOB ENRICHMENT

While financial incentives provide extrinsic motivation, job design programs try to provide intrinsic rewards from the job itself. Job design involves structuring the tasks and social relationships of a job to create optimal levels of variety, responsibility, autonomy, and interaction. Carefully designed jobs that minimize wasted effort and maximize employee motivation can significantly improve productivity, attendance, and organizational effectiveness. Job satisfaction and satisfaction with life in general are greatly influenced by the demands of the job and by the extent to which these demands are consistent with the individual's abilities and interests. Sometimes very simple job changes can make a big difference to employees.

The history of organizational behavior contains a continuous stream of job redesign programs, each with its own distinctive focus.

As mentioned earlier, the greatest showplace of organizational efficiency during the medieval period was the Arsenal of Venice. Most people are surprised to learn that assembly lines and specialized jobs were effectively used so many years ago. The arsenal was created by the Venetian Senate in 1104 and eventually covered sixty acres of the lagoon. It normally employed about two thousand employees to build or repair ships; but at times as many as 16,000 people were involved in the entire process of procuring, assembling, warehousing, and outfitting the ships. The arsenal was called "the heart of the state of Venice" and the crafts workers, called *arsenalotti*, were privileged citizens who served at coronations and were the only ones permitted to work in the mint.[2]

Over the centuries, significant improvements were made in the arsenal's management and work design. Specialized tasks, production quotas, and financial incentives were refined to improve productivity. Much of the arsenal was located along canals that served as assembly lines in the construction and outfitting of ships. Rather than carry equipment to the ships, the galleys were outfitted by towing them along the canals past warehouses that efficiently equipped the galleys for service. An elaborate inventory system was used to record materials available in the warehouses, and elaborate accounting reports provided an excellent system of controls and costs. Employees who produced a specific product that could be counted (such as oars) were paid on a piece-rate basis, while others received day wages and participated in a merit-rating plan administered by a committee that met in March and September to review the merits of each employee and raise his pay if he deserved it. The efficiency of the arsenal was widely recognized. In 1570, when the Turks planned to attack Cyprus, the arsenal succeeded in assembling a total of 100 ships that were totally equipped with arms and supplies in a period of two months. In 1574 Henry III of France visited the arsenal and observed a galley as it was assembled, launched, and completely armed within one hour.

The cottage industry of the fifteenth and sixteenth centuries allowed workers to produce at home as independent contractors, occasionally with the assistance of family members. During the eighteenth and nineteenth centuries, self-directed work teams of skilled craftsmen worked together as autonomous groups in craft guilds such as the barrel makers, the hat makers, and the cordwainers (boot makers).[3] Elements of these early job design programs are visible in recent programs such as "flexible manufacturing systems" that require workers with broad skills to work on alternating product lines, flexible work scheduling that allows workers to select their own working hours, and sociotechnical redesign where workers participate in redesigning both their social interactions and the work they do.[4]

Other recent job design programs also use strategies of earlier periods, such as job rotation (moving employees from one job to another), job enlargement (combining previously fragmented tasks into one job), job enrichment (increasing job responsibility and the variety of tasks performed), self-directed work teams (giving a group a task and discretion regarding how it will be accomplished), job sharing (two people share one job), and telecommuting (workers work at home with a computer and telephone). Job design strategies continue to reappear because jobs and workers are not stable—the ideal job design is a moving target. Competitive pressures often drive companies to implement job design programs as they try to create high-performance work teams.[5] The advantages and limitations of these and other job design programs are described in this chapter.

The two major strategies of job redesign are **job specialization** (sometimes called *job simplification*), and **job enlargement.** These two strategies are almost exact opposites. Job specialization involves simplifying a job by reducing the number of elements performed by the worker. Job enlargement involves making a job more complex by combining elements to increase the number of activities performed by each worker.

Job Specialization

The job specialization versus job enlargement controversy has a long history. One of the major themes of the industrial revolution was task specialization: complex jobs were divided into separate tasks and assigned to separate individuals. Indeed, the history of the industrial revolution was the history of task specialization. When the production of a product was separated into many highly specialized tasks, manufacturing was taken out of the craft shops and brought into the factories. One of the earliest descriptions of the advantages of task specialization was Adam Smith's book, *The Wealth of Nations,* published in 1776. Smith described how one person could make 20 ordinary pins per day, whereas ten specialized workers could make 48,000 per day.[6]

Task Analysis. Although the modern factory system existed throughout most of the nineteenth century, the development of highly specialized jobs became much more widespread at the end of that century, thanks to the scientific management movement. Under the leadership of Frederick Winslow Taylor, scientific management significantly changed the practices of management from traditional "handed-down" methods to carefully analyzed tasks, methods, and piece-rate incentives.

Scientific management involves a detailed analysis of each task to identify the one best way of performing it. The goal is to find the ideal method for reducing fatigue, eliminating wasted motions, and maximizing productive efficiency. The ideal timing of rest periods is studied to reduce fatigue, and changes are made in the equipment, such as using large shovels for loading light materials and small shovels for loading heavy materials. The workers are "scientifically" selected to match job requirements with the workers' abilities. Piece-rate incentives are established to motivate employees to perform the highly specialized repetitive tasks.

One of the most popular illustrations of Taylor's work was the study of handling pig iron at Bethlehem Steel Company in the 1890s. For years Bethlehem Steel had been dumping pig iron in an open field as a by-product of its smelting process.

During the Spanish-American War, however, the price of pig iron increased enough to create a market for it, and the mountains of pig iron needed to be loaded onto railroad cars. When Taylor first analyzed the task he found a group of seventy-five men working at the rate of 12 1/2 tons per man per day. By calculating the ideal walking speed and the percent of time a worker needed to be free of a load to avoid excessive fatigue, Taylor designed a method of increasing productivity almost four-fold. By following Taylor's instructions of when to lift, when to carry, and when to rest, the workers succeeded in loading 47 1/4 tons per day, and found that the new method was no more exhausting than the old method.[7]

Although Taylor is frequently criticized for ignoring the feelings of workers, this criticism is unjust and overlooks a major component of Taylor's work in scientific management. Taylor clearly recognized the need for a cooperative relationship between managers and workers and the powerful influence of cohesive group norms. Scientific management's concern for the dignity of workers is illustrated by the list of thirteen aims of scientific management published by the Taylor Society and shown in Exhibit 6.1. Taylor assumed that the most effective way to gain the cooperation of the workers was through a system of piece-rate incentives that rewarded workers for their productivity. Taylor outlined his incentive plan in one of his early articles, "A Piece-Rate System," in which he proposed a differential piece-rate incentive system, consisting of a low piece rate for substandard workers and a higher piece rate for those who exceeded the standard performance.

Taylor strongly disagreed with those who criticized his principles of scientific management. Following his procedures and observing the prescribed rest pauses, Taylor claimed, the workers reported less fatigue, even though they were perform-ing three or four times the volume of work. Taylor argued that scientific manage-ment was in the best interests of the company, because it reduced labor costs; it was in the best interests of the workers, because it increased their wages; and it was in the best interests of society, because it increased the production of consumer goods and improved the overall economy.[8]

The popularity of scientific management increased significantly in 1911 when Taylor participated in a special hearing conducted by the Interstate Commerce Commission on the efficiency of railroads. Later he was asked to testify before a spe-cial House of Representatives committee on the effects of a scientific management program implemented at the Watertown Arsenal. Knowledge of scientific manage-ment quickly spread to other countries, especially France, Italy, Germany, Holland, Russia, and Japan.

Perhaps the most colorful contributors to scientific management were Frank B. and Lillian M. Gilbreth, who were the parents of twelve children, and the topic of a popular movie and book, *Cheaper by the Dozen*.[9] After studying the methods of several bricklayers, Frank Gilbreth developed an improved method that reduced the number of motions required to lay interior brick from 18 motions to 4 1/2 motions per brick. By reducing the number of motions, Gilbreth increased the rate of brick laying from 120 to 350 bricks per hour.[10]

Although the Gilbreths are remembered for many of their applications of sci-entific management, their most significant contributions were in the development of motion films to analyze and improve motion sequences. By analyzing films, they were able to simplify and improve the sequence of motions required to perform a task and determine how long each motion required. Since the early cameras did not run at a constant speed but were hand cranked, the Gilbreths invented a microchronometer, a clock with a large, sweeping hand capable of recording time

EXHIBIT 6.1   Thirteen Aims of Scientific Management Published by the Taylor Society

1. To gauge industrial tendencies and the market in order to thereby regularize operations in a manner which will serve the investment, sustain the enterprise as an employing agency, and assure continuous operation and employment.

2. To assure the employee not only continuous operation and employment by correct gauging of the market, but also to assure by planned and balanced operations a continuous earning opportunity while on the payroll.

3. To earn, through a waste-saving management and processing technique, a larger income from a given expenditure of human and material energies, which shall be shared through increased wages and profits by workers and management.

4. To make possible a higher standard of living as a result of increased income to workers.

5. To assure a happier home and social life to workers through removal, by increase of income, of many of the disagreeable and worrying factors in the total situation.

6. To assure healthful as well as individually and socially agreeable conditions of work.

7. To assure the highest opportunity for individual capacity through scientific methods of work analysis and of selection, training, assignment, transfer, and promotion of workers.

8. To assure by training and instructional foremanship the opportunity for workers to develop new and higher capacities, and eligibility for promotion to higher positions.

9. To develop self-confidence and self-respect among workers through opportunity afforded for understanding of one's own works specifically, and of plans and methods of work generally.

10. To develop self-expression and self-realization among workers through the stimulative influence of an atmosphere of research and valuation, through understanding of plans and methods, and through the freedom of horizontal as well as vertical contacts afforded by functional organization.

11. To build character through the proper conduct of work.

12. To promote justice through the elimination of discrimination in wage rates and elsewhere.

13. To eliminate factors of the environment which are irritating and the causes of friction, and to promote common understandings, tolerances, and the spirit of teamwork.

Source: Excerpt from *Scientific Management in American Industry* by H. S. Person, pp. 16–17. Reprinted by permission of Harper & Row, Publishers, Inc.

to one two-thousandth of a minute. By placing this clock in the field of work being photographed, the length of time for each required motion could be determined. The Gilbreths' microchronometer is still used today in photographing and studying motion patterns.

In their study of hand motions, the Gilbreths found that the common descriptions of hand motions were not sufficiently precise for their purposes.

Consequently, the Gilbreths developed a refined list of seventeen basic or funda-mental motions that were more precise, such as "grasp," "load," and "position." These basic motions were called "therbligs," which is *Gilbreth* spelled backward.

The principles of scientific management significantly increased manufacturing productivity in the early 1900s. Many of these same principles are still used in job redesign, such as time-and-motion studies, work simplification, piece-rate incen-tives for individuals or groups, and error analysis to improve quality.

Ergonomics. The professional disciplines that study job design include industrial psychology, human factors engineering, and **ergonomics,** sometimes called *biotech-nology.* Ergonomics is that aspect of technology concerned with the application of biological and engineering factors to problems relating to the mutual adjustment of people and machines. Professionals in ergonomics are concerned with adapting technology to improve productive efficiency and human life.

An illustration of ergonomics is research on the health problems associated with working at a computer terminal. People who work long continuous hours at a computer terminal often experience a variety of problems such as carpal tunnel syndrome, arm and shoulder muscle cramps, back strain, and eye fatigue. Concern has also been expressed about the possibility that radiation from the video display terminal (VDT) causes birth defects, cancer, or eye cataracts. Although research indi-cates that the radiation from the VDT is no more harmful than emissions from an ordinary electrical appliance, the physical problems caused by repetitive motions can be quite serious, especially back and wrist problems.[11] Through ergonomic research, wrist braces have been developed to reduce the incidence of carpal tunnel syndrome, and special chairs have been designed to reduce back strain by provid-ing lumbar support, adjustable arm rests, and an adjustable front edge.[12]

Advantages of Specialization. The advantage of job specialization is increased efficiency; highly specialized jobs can be performed more efficiently in terms of greater quantity and quality of output than nonspecialized jobs. This efficiency has been well recognized since the early writings of Adam Smith and Charles Babbage. In 1776, Adam Smith attributed the increase in productivity to greater individual dexterity, decreased time spent in changing from one task to another, and the inven-tion of specialized machines.[13] In 1832, Charles Babbage advocated specialization because of decreased learning time, decreased waste, fewer tool changes, and increased skill due to repetition.[14] These ideas are summarized in Exhibit 6.2.

The advantages of job specialization can be readily observed by visiting com-panies that use an assembly-line procedure. In the sewing industry, for example, one company has 425 employees; only 120 of these employees are sewing machine operators, and the remainder work in other departments such as shipping, receiv-ing, and cutting. All jobs in this company are highly specialized, and each worker performs the same repetitive activity hundreds of times each day. Rather than using scissors to cut cloth, several dozen layers of material are rolled onto a large table and are cut simultaneously by a cutter who uses a specialized cutting tool. The materials then go from operator to operator along an assembly line. For example, one operator sews two button holes on the back of each dress and is paid $.38 per dozen dresses. Each bundle of one dozen dresses is then passed to the next opera-tor, who sews two buttons adjacent to the holes and receives $.37 per dozen. Two operators tend a row of specialized machines that are guided by a computer pro-gram, as they make ruffles and special design markings.

| EXHIBIT 6.2 | Advantages of Job Specialization |

1. *Learning time.* Training time is dramatically reduced, since the worker only masters a small segment of the job. Complex and highly sophisticated products can be produced by relatively unskilled workers who are required to master only the skills needed for their particular job rather than the entire production process.

2. *Time spent changing jobs.* Workers performing highly specialized jobs are able to perform the same repetitive motions without losing time changing from one activity to another. Workers who are required to perform a variety of tasks are less efficient because of the time required to change their physical position, move from one station to another, or pick up different tools.

3. *Increased proficiency.* By performing the same repetitive activity, workers are able to develop greater proficiency and speed in their work. Practicing the same motions time after time helps workers develop habits and work more rapidly.

4. *Development of technology.* Highly specialized jobs are more conducive to the development of new machines and unique tools to help workers eliminate wasted motions, perform several activities simultaneously, or perform each activity more rapidly.

5. *Greater precision and control.* When each worker performs a small definable task, it is easier for management to observe the quantity and quality of performance, detect errors, and pay each worker for the exact amount produced. Supervisors have better control over workers, since deviations from standards can be easily recognized and corrected.

Using highly specialized jobs, this sewing company produces an average of 7,000 dresses per day. If job specialization were eliminated and each worker had to design, cut, and sew an entire dress, even experienced workers could not make two dresses per day. These data illustrate the advantages of job specialization. With job specialization, the employees produce over seven thousand dresses per day; without it, they could produce less than seven hundred dresses, and these dresses would lack the ruffles, special design markings, and periodic design changes. The enormous advantages of job specialization have led some to conclude that the real revolutionaries who have significantly improved life in our society are not the leaders of revolts who overthrow oppressive governments, but the leaders of industry who mass-produce abundant and inexpensive consumer goods that raise the standard of living.[15]

Disadvantages of Specialization. The major disadvantage of task specialization is that highly specialized jobs are extremely repetitive, causing workers to feel bored and alienated. Workers are expected to perform like machines, they do not see the final product, and they never have the satisfaction of pointing to a finished product and saying, "I made that myself."

The disadvantages of specialization—boredom and worker dissatisfaction—were apparent from the beginning. These problems were ignored, however, as the productive efficiency and increased profitability of task specialization led to the widespread adoption of assembly-line manufacturing. During the 1950s, a large-scale study of assembly-line work, particularly in the auto industry, identified a list of criticisms, as shown in Exhibit 6.3.

EXHIBIT 6.3   Disadvantages of Job Specialization on Assembly Lines

1. *Mechanical pacing.* The production rate is determined by the speed of the conveyor line rather than by the workers' natural rhythm or inclination.

2. *Repetitiveness.* Workers are required to perform the same short work cycle over and over each day. Most work cycles are less than one minute, and workers may be required to perform the same activity over five hundred times a day.

3. *Low skill requirements.* Highly specialized jobs prevent workers from developing and displaying a variety of skills and talents.

4. *Concentration on only a fraction of the product.* Each job represents only a small fraction of the total product, and workers cannot see the final product.

5. *Limited social interaction.* Even though they work as a team, the workers feel socially isolated because they are physically separated along an assembly line. The speed of the line and the noise levels prevent workers from interacting or developing meaningful relationships.

6. *Elimination of the need to think.* The production techniques, equipment design, and selection of tools are determined by staff specialists to maximize the efficiency of operations.

Source: Adapted from C. R. Walker and R. Guest, *The Man on the Assembly Line* (Cambridge, Mass.: Harvard University Press, 1952), pp. 71–83.

The effects of depersonalization and loss of control in auto assembly lines was dramatically highlighted in 1972 by a wildcat strike at the General Motors assembly plant in Lordstown, Ohio. This new plant was an engineering showplace in which jobs had been carefully designed using the latest information in engineering technology, and even using computers. This unauthorized strike lasted twenty-two days and attracted public attention to the workers' dissatisfaction with assembly-line work. The issues were not pay, benefits, or any of the traditional grievances; the workers went on strike over what they called dehumanizing work. Chevrolet Vegas were coming off the assembly line at the rate of 101.6 per hour—a pace that required each worker to perform the same specialized task every thirty-six seconds. The assembly line had been recently designed to represent the best in engineering knowledge, and the workers were mostly young employees who had the health and stamina to make Lordstown the most productive assembly line in the world. But for twenty-two days they produced nothing. The initial complaint was that the line was moving faster than it should. Further examination, however, concluded that the problem was the very existence of a line. All assembly-line work was condemned as monotonous, boring, and dehumanizing.[16]

Job Enlargement and Job Enrichment

During the 1940s the trend toward highly specialized jobs was countered by a trend toward job enlargement. The proponents of job enlargement argued that it created greater satisfaction and productivity. Even though enlarged jobs were less efficient than specialized jobs, the proponents argued that increased motivation more than compensated for the loss in efficiency. Job enlargement gradually came to be seen as the solution to many organizational problems. By the 1970s, job enlargement was being proposed as the primary cure for such diverse forms of worker discontent as job dissatisfaction, labor grievances, careless work, and drug abuse.[17]

Job Enlargement. Job enlargement consists of making a job larger in scope by combining additional task activities into each job through what is called "**horizontal loading**," or expansion. An example of job enlargement would be to allow a sewing machine operator to sew both sleeves on a piece of clothing, rather than just one. Job enlargement tries to increase task variety by extending the length of the work cycle, which refers to the length of time required to complete a task from start to finish before the worker begins the same activity again. In addition to lengthening the work cycle, some job enlargement programs allow workers to determine their own pace of work (within limits), to serve as their own inspectors by giving them responsibility for quality control, to repair their own mistakes, to be responsible for their own machine setup and repair, and to select their own work procedures.

Some of the earliest reported uses of job enlargement occurred at IBM, Detroit Edison Company, AT&T, the civil service, and Maytag. The general conclusion from these early experiences was that job enlargement improved worker satisfaction, decreased production costs, and increased quality. However, no empirical evidence was provided to support these claims. Interviews with workers produced mixed conclusions, because the majority of them liked, rather than disliked, the job specialization aspects of assembly lines and conveyor belts.

Job Enrichment. The greatest criticism of job enlargement is that it does not really change the essential nature of the task; sewing two sleeves is not materially different from just sewing one. To make a noticeable change in the job requires **vertical loading** rather than horizontal loading; the job must be redesigned to include components previously held by the employee's supervisor.

Many **job enrichment** programs extensively rely on Frederick Herzberg's motivator-hygiene theory. Herzberg argues that meaningful job changes can occur only if the job is redesigned to include more of these seven motivator factors.[18]

1. *Accountability.* Workers should be held responsible for their own performance.
2. *Achievement.* Workers should feel that they are accomplishing something worthwhile.
3. *Control over resources.* If possible, workers should have control of their resources and costs. Cost and profit centers should be delegated to lower levels in the organization.
4. *Feedback.* Workers should receive direct and timely information from the job itself regarding their performance.
5. *Personal growth and development.* Workers should have the opportunity to learn new skills.
6. *Work pace.* Within constraints, workers should be able to set their own work pace and have the flexibility to schedule rest pauses and work breaks.
7. *Client relationships.* When possible, workers should develop a relationship with the customers who use the products they produce to know if they are satisfied.

Herzberg's theory guided the job enrichment and job redesign programs in many companies, such as AT&T, which conducted a series of nineteen generally successful experiments in job enrichment.[19] Job enrichment can make a significant change in a job. Unlike simple job enlargement, job enrichment seeks to improve both task efficiency and personal satisfaction by building into a job a greater scope for personal achievement and its recognition, more challenging and responsible work, and more opportunity for individual growth and advancement.

Job Characteristics

In job redesign projects, managers need to analyze the characteristics of each job, called the "job scope," and decide which characteristics to change. This analysis involves reviewing the range of activities performed by the worker and the types of decisions a job holder must make.

Job Scope. **Job scope** is defined by the breadth and depth of the job. The dimension **job breadth** concerns the number of different activities included as part of the job, while **job depth** concerns the degree of discretion or control the worker has over how these tasks are to be performed. Jobs are said to have a greater breadth if the person is required to perform a wide range of different activities. In general, the greater the number of tasks performed and the longer it takes to complete the job, the greater is the job breadth.

Job depth concerns the degree of discretion or control the worker has over how these tasks are to be performed. Workers who have control over when they do the job, how it is to be done, and the order in which the activities are to be performed, are said to have jobs with greater depth.

Assembly-line work is the classic example of jobs with low depth and low breadth. Assembly-line workers perform the same repetitive activities with little variation and no control over when or how they perform them. Other jobs may vary from organization to organization in the depth and breadth of the job. For example, in some hospitals nursing jobs are highly specialized, creating very limited job breadth. At other hospitals, the nurses perform a wide variety of tasks, making for a very wide range of activities and greater job breadth. The nurses in intensive care units typically have greater job depth than the nurses in other units, because they have greater discretion in making decisions about the care of patients. These combinations of job depth and job breadth are illustrated in Exhibit 6.4.

Task Attributes. An important step in studying job design is identifying the crucial dimensions or attributes of a task that make a difference in how workers feel about the job. An almost endless list of job characteristics could be compiled, such as whether it is an indoor or outdoor job; whether it is a day shift or night shift job; and whether it involves reading, writing, computing, standing, or sitting. Most of these, however, are not relevant characteristics.

One of the first significant attempts to measure the degree of job enrichment was a study by Arthur Turner and Paul Lawrence of forty-seven different jobs.[20] Turner and Lawrence attempted to develop an index that measured the most important attributes of each task. They identified six attributes they claimed were the most important factors determining the desirability of a job:

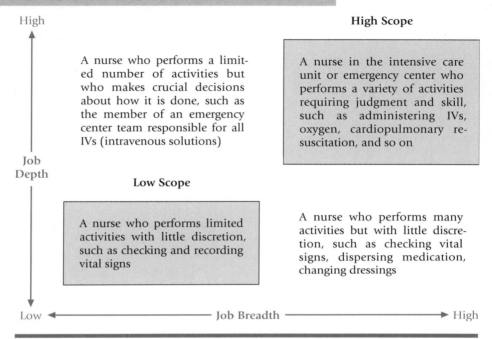

EXHIBIT 6.4   Job Scope of a Nursing Job

High   **High Scope**

A nurse who performs a limited number of activities but
who makes crucial decisions
about how it is done, such as
the member of an emergency
center team responsible for all
IVs (intravenous solutions)

A nurse in the intensive care
unit or emergency center who
performs a variety of activities
requiring judgment and skill,
such as administering IVs,
oxygen, cardiopulmonary re-
suscitation, and so on

Job
Depth

Low Scope

A nurse who performs limited
activities with little discretion,
such as checking and recording
vital signs

A nurse who performs many
activities but with little discretion, such as checking vital
signs, dispersing medication,
changing dressings

Low ◄——————————— Job Breadth ———————————► High

1. *Variety:* the number of different activities that had to be completed in performing each job
2. *Autonomy:* the amount of discretion the worker was expected to exercise in
   completing the assigned activities
3. *Required interaction:* the amount of interdependence between workers, particularly direct face-to-face communication required to perform the task
   properly
4. *Optional interaction:* the amount of voluntary communication permitted by
   the noise and layout of the work
5. *Knowledge and skill required:* the degree of mental preparation or learning
   involved in performing the job adequately
6. *Responsibility:* the level of accountability required for task performance

These six attributes were measured independently by the researchers and combined mathematically into one scale called the "requisite task attributes" (RTA)
index. According to Turner and Lawrence, the most highly enriched and desirable
jobs were those which had a high RTA index score.

Job Characteristics Model of Job Enrichment

The best conceptual framework for examining the effects of job enrichment on work
attitudes and behavior is the **job characteristics model.**[21] This model explains the
psychological impact of various job characteristics and predicts what effects the

resultant psychological states will have on work attitudes and performance. The usefulness of a job enrichment program can be predicted from this model by analyzing how the program changes the core dimensions of the job and thereby influences the behavior of the worker. Questionnaires measuring each concept in the model have been developed and tested in numerous companies. The results indicate that the interactions specified in the model, as shown in Exhibit 6.5, are generally correct.[22]

Work Outcomes. The model is explained best by starting at the outcome end and working backward. Organizations desire four important outcomes from each worker.[23]

1. *Dependable performance:* high quantity and quality work
2. *Good attendance:* low absenteeism and low tardiness
3. *High satisfaction with work:* positive feelings about the job, the company, and the treatment received at work
4. *Spontaneous and innovative behaviors:* doing more than is called for in the formal job description, such as showing initiative, making creative suggestions, cooperating with fellow workers, and pursuing self-development and training

These four outcomes are clearly in the organization's best interests. An organization that can elicit such behavior from its members will be more effective than an organization that cannot. Generally, these outcomes are also in the individual's best interest, because pay and other rewards are usually associated with good performance.

Psychological States. The desired work outcomes result from three psychological states, as shown in Exhibit 6.5. These three states represent the **motivators** behind all activity (including nonwork activity, such as practicing a golf swing at a driving range).

1. *Meaningful.* The activity must have a purpose and be perceived as important and worthwhile.
2. *Responsibility.* Employees must believe that they are personally accountable for results and that their efforts will influence the outcome.
3. *Knowledge of results.* Employees need systematic and timely information about how well they are performing so they can make corrective adjustments if necessary.

When these three conditions are present, workers are expected to feel good about their activities and perform well because of their own internal motivation. They are willing to continue performing the activity because of the positive internal feelings created by the activity itself. If any one of the three psychological states is missing, motivation will decline significantly. When all three are present, however, employees demonstrate dependable performance, good attendance, high satisfaction, and spontaneous and innovative behaviors.

EXHIBIT 6.5   **Job Characteristics Model**

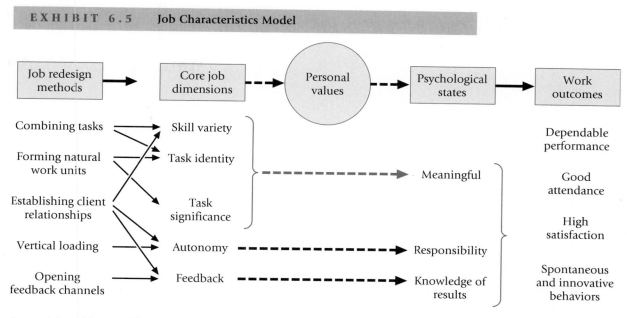

Source: Adapted from J. Richard Hackman, Greg Oldham, Robert Janson, and Kenneth Purdy, "A New Strategy for Job Enrichment," *California Management Review,* vol. 17, no. 4 (1975), p. 62. By permission of the Regents.

Core Job Dimensions. The three psychological states are created by five core job dimensions, as shown in Exhibit 6.5. However, the relationships between the core dimensions and the psychological states are influenced by the personal values of the worker, as indicated by the dashed arrows. The five core dimensions include the following:

1. *Skill variety:* the degree to which a job allows workers to develop and use their skills and to avoid the monotony of performing the same task repeatedly

2. *Task identity:* the degree to which a task consists of a whole or complete unit of work as opposed to a small, specialized, repetitive act

3. *Task significance:* the degree to which a task has a significant impact on the organization, the community, or the lives of other people

4. *Autonomy:* the degree to which workers are free of the direct influence of a supervisor and can exercise discretion in scheduling their work and in deciding how it will be done

5. *Feedback:* the degree to which workers obtain evaluative information about their performance in the normal course of doing their jobs

A questionnaire for measuring these five job dimensions is shown in Exhibit 6.6. According to the model, skill variety, task identity, and task significance contribute to the meaningfulness of a job, as indicated by the arrows in Exhibit 6.5. Responsibility and personal accountability are created by autonomy, the ability of

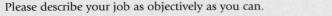

EXHIBIT 6.6   Selected Questions from the Job Diagnostic Survey

Please describe your job as objectively as you can.

1. How much *variety* is there in your job? That is, to what extent does the job require you to do many different things at work, using a variety of your skills and talents?

1———2———3———4———5———6———7

Very little; the job requires me to do the same routine things over and over again.

Moderate variety.

Very much; the job requires me to do many different things, using a number of different skills and talents.

2. To what extent does your job involve doing a *"whole" and identifiable piece of work?* That is, is the job a complete piece of work that has an obvious beginning and end? Or is it only a part of the overall piece of work, which is finished by other people or by automatic machines?

1———2———3———4———5———6———7

My job is only a tiny part of the overall piece of work; the results of my activities cannot be seen in the final product or service.

My job is a moderate-sized "chunk" of the overall piece of work; my own contribution can be seen in the final outcome.

My job involves doing the whole piece of work, from start to finish; the results of my activities are easily seen in the final product or service.

3. In general, how *significant or important* is your job? That is, are the results of your work likely to significantly affect the lives or well-being of other people?

1———2———3———4———5———6———7

Not very significant; the outcomes of my work are *not* likely to have important effects on other people.

Moderately significant.

Highly significant; the outcomes of my work can affect other people in very important ways.

4. How much *autonomy* is there in your job? That is, to what extent does your job permit you to decide *on your own* how to go about doing the work?

1———2———3———4———5———6———7

Very little; the job gives me almost no personal "say" about how and when the work is done.

Moderate autonomy; many things are standardized and not under my control, but I can make some decisions about the work.

Very much; the job gives me almost complete responsibility for deciding how and when the work is done.

5. To what extent does *doing the job itself* provide you with information about your work performance? That is, does the actual *work itself* provide clues about how well you are doing—aside from any "feedback" co-workers or supervisors may provide?

1———2———3———4———5———6———7

Very little; the job itself is set up so I could work forever without finding out how well I am doing.

Moderately; sometimes doing the job provides "feedback" to me; sometimes it does not.

Very much; the job is set up so that I get almost constant "feedback" as I work about how well I am doing.

Source: J. Richard Hackman and Greg R. Oldham, "The Job Diagnostic Survey: An Instrument for the Diagnosis of Jobs and the Evaluation of Job Redesign Projects," Technical Report No. 4, Department of Administrative Sciences, Yale University, May 1974, pp. 2–3.

workers to schedule their own work and decide how it will be done. Performance feedback provides employees with knowledge about the results of their efforts.

To measure the motivating potential of a given job, the five core characteristics can be combined algebraically into a "motivating potential score" (MPS). The MPS provides a single summary index of the degree to which the objective characteristics of a job will provide high internal work motivation. The formula for the MPS score is

$$MPS = \frac{(variety + identity + significance)}{3} \times autonomy \times feedback$$

According to the job characteristics model, a job high in motivating potential will create a higher state of internal work motivation than a job with a low motivating potential score.[24]

Job Redesign Methods. Numerous job enrichment programs have been proposed to establish optimal levels of each core job dimension. Five methods are recommended as guides to managers in redesigning jobs:

1. Combine tasks to eliminate highly specialized jobs and to make larger work modules; this approach is called *horizontal loading*.
2. Form natural work units—teams of workers—in which each person feels part of the team, and where jobs can be rotated among team members. Job rotation increases the variety of skills workers can use and it contributes to greater task identity. Rotation can occur informally, such as when workers trade assignments, or it can be a formal program, such as when workers are assigned to a new department.
3. Establish client relationships to help workers know who uses the products or services they produce and how the clients feel about their work.
4. Give workers greater authority and discretion by allowing them to perform functions previously reserved for higher levels of management, called *vertical loading*.
5. Open feedback channels so that information about the quality of performance goes directly to the employee performing the job.

This model provides a useful framework for diagnosing jobs and for deciding whether they ought to be enriched. The core dimensions represent the important areas of each job that need to be examined. If the decision is made to redesign a job, the model suggests some of the most appropriate changes that ought to be considered. In recent years, a broad assortment of changes have been tried and are frequently referred to as "quality-of-work-life" (QWL) programs.

Which of these job redesign methods is best, and should they be used in combination? A review of thirty job enrichment studies where productivity was measured suggested that the most effective redesign method was opening feedback channels so that workers could learn how well they were doing from the job itself rather than from someone's description of how well they were doing. A comparison of the studies that opened feedback channels with those that didn't found that more feedback led to increased productivity, higher quality of work, and a decrease in absenteeism. Although opening feedback channels appeared to have the greatest impact, other redesign methods were also effective, especially if they were used in combination. This review also revealed that the productivity increases were related to the number of redesign methods that were used. All five redesign methods were used in eight studies, three or four methods were used in another eight studies, and only one or two methods were used in the remaining fourteen studies. The median increases in productivity were 10.2 percent, 7.7 percent, and 2.5 percent, respectively.[25]

Personal Values. The job characteristics model recognizes that not everyone will respond equally to the core job dimensions. According to the model, skill variety, task identity, and task significance should contribute to the meaningfulness of a job. But whether an activity is actually perceived as meaningful or meaningless depends on an employee's personal values. Some people (such as social workers and school-teachers who complain of burnout) think their jobs are meaningless even though they contain extensive variety, identity, and significance. The same principle applies to assembly-line work. Sewing pockets inside the waistbands of tennis shorts is a meaningful activity if you perceive it as a necessary step in producing a useful product. But if you think tennis shorts are worthless products consumed by a self-indulgent group of idlers in society, the same activity could be perceived as meaningless.

The job characteristics model, as originally proposed, claims that the effects of the core dimensions on the psychological states is moderated (or influenced) by an individual's growth need strength. This moderator, derived from Maslow's needs hierarchy, concerns whether the individual is primarily interested in satisfying lower-level survival needs or higher-level growth needs. People who are striving to satisfy their growth needs should respond more favorably to an enriched job. It is reasonable to expect, however, that many other personal values will also serve as moderator variables. Whether workers perceive a task as meaningful and whether they feel a sense of accountability or responsibility for it, depends not only on the core job dimensions, but also on their own personal values.

EFFECTS OF JOB ENRICHMENT

Many studies have examined the effects of job enrichment programs on both organizational effectiveness and individual responses. The results have been both positive and negative, and part of this inconsistency seems to be explained by individual differences.[26]

Organizational Effectiveness

Most early reports about job enrichment programs indicated that the results were positive. Although these reports were usually case studies that relied extensively on subjective impressions, more recent studies using better experimental designs have been almost as supportive. Higher levels of satisfaction and productivity were often achieved by adding variety, responsibility, and other enriching characteristics to specialized jobs.

APPLYING ORGANIZATIONAL BEHAVIOR
ACROSS CULTURES

Job Redesign in Sweden, Japan, and the Israeli Kibbutz

 An analysis of the factors that have motivated other countries to adopt job redesign programs helps to explain why job redesign programs in the United States have been so slow to develop. The adoption of intrinsically satisfying jobs is essentially a function of the demand and supply for less alienating work.

- *Demand factors.* Important factors that lead workers to demand more enriched jobs include higher education levels, increased income, and more attractive job opportunities.
- *Supply factors.* The most important factors influencing the decision to supply enriched jobs are how much it will cost to create them and what will be the loss in productivity.

Sweden. Sweden is internationally recognized for its job redesign efforts. New factories have been designed around the concept of autonomous work teams that have replaced the traditional assembly line. Small groups of workers work together at separate workstations and enjoy considerable autonomy in how they organize themselves. Every member is trained to perform all the functions, which facilitates job rotation. The need for first-line supervisors is reduced because their duties are limited mainly to coordinating the groups and training new workers.

Sweden leads the world in per capita use of industrial robots, which means that most repetitive jobs have been mechanized. Contributing to the demand for enriched jobs is Sweden's high labor union participation rate (83 percent, compared with 33 percent in Japan and 16 percent in the United States). Unions have pressed for the enactment of laws restricting foreign workers and giving unions the right to negotiate nonwage workplace issues.

Japan. Japanese workers are also recognized for the extensive mechanization, skill utilization, and job complexity, but these characteristics are a product of Japan's social structure rather than unions or legislation. Japanese unions are mostly company unions oriented to cooperation with management.

After World War II, Japanese companies emphasized a classless corporate community where employees are treated equally. Japan's norms of equality and collectivism promote sentiments of loyalty, togetherness, and commitment. Most Japanese employees work in small groups with supervisors who have small spans of control. This allows supervisors to develop strong personal ties with their subordinates and function more as facilitators than bosses.

Employees are typically trained to perform the entire range of group tasks. In Japan's auto industry, for example, there is only one large job category with a single wage rate for assemblers, while U.S. auto assembly plants have up to two hundred designated jobs with different wage rates.

Over three-fourths of Japanese companies have employees participate in formal and informal meetings to offer suggestions for improving product quality or other aspects of the production process. These groups play a significant role even though they have no legally binding decision-making power, as in Sweden.

The Israeli Kibbutz. The major demand for enriched jobs in the Israeli kibbutz comes from the members' refusal to perform alienating jobs. Membership in the kibbutz is voluntary, and members play an active role in deciding what they want to do. If no one wants to perform a boring job, the job is either eliminated or redesigned.

Almost all the 260 kibbutz communities in Israel have been established since the late 1960s. The typical kibbutz contains 30 to 120 workers, with very few nonmembers employed as wage laborers. To attract members and motivate them to work well, both industrial and agricultural jobs have to maximize the opportunities for members to use their skills, structure their work, and obtain intrinsic satisfaction.

The Kibbutz Industrial Association has worked with Scandinavian experts in a sociotechnical intervention to replace dirty, dangerous, or boring jobs with robots and computerized technology. Consequently, the kibbutz factories, which represent only 4 percent of Israel's industrial jobs and 6.5 percent of its output, has 60 percent of the nation's robots.

Source: Menachem Rosner and Louis Putterman, "Factors Behind the Supply and Demand for Less Alienating Work, and Some International Illustrations," *Journal of Economic Studies,* vol. 18 (1991), pp. 18–41.

In a British chemical company, for example, five job enrichment experiments were conducted. The job enrichment changes consisted of creating greater autonomy and responsibility for the technical control, financial accountability, and managerial authority of each job. For each experiment, there was an experimental and a control group. In all, 100 employees were in the five experimental groups, and the estimated annual savings were $200,000, or $2,000 per person. Job satisfaction also increased in the experimental groups, but the improvement in satisfaction was not as dramatic as the cost improvement.[27]

Another case study showing the benefits of job enrichment involved a group of women assembling radar equipment. The procedures used for assembling the radar had been developed by the engineering department, and the time required to assemble each unit averaged 138 hours. As part of a job enrichment program, the women were given the responsibility for devising their own manufacturing processes and goals. After the group implemented its own methods and goals, the assembly time per unit dropped from 138 hours to 86 hours. During a subsequent group discussion, the women suggested that they did not need a supervisor; they said they could exercise self-direction and supervise themselves. The women were allowed to supervise themselves, although they kept their supervisor informed. Eventually the assembly time per unit was reduced to 36 hours.[28]

A review of thirty-two job enrichment studies found that job redesign programs typically contribute to organizational effectiveness. The studies included in this review all assessed the impact of job redesign in terms of either measurable productivity, production quality, or absenteeism.[29] In thirty studies where productivity was measured, the median result was an increase in production of 6.4 percent. In eleven of these thirty experiments, however, the results were zero or negative. The effects on quality were more encouraging; twenty-one studies measured quality and only one experiment reported a decline. The median result was a 28 percent increase in production quality. Absenteeism was measured in only nine experiments, and the median result was a decrease of 14.5 percent in absenteeism. All in all, the evidence suggests that job redesign frequently improves production quality, modestly reduces absenteeism, and occasionally increases productivity.

The effects of job redesign, however, are not permanent. At least one study found that the desirable results that were so encouraging after the first five months had essentially disappeared at the end of fourteen months.[30] Escalating levels of challenge may be required to prevent boredom and frustration. The temporary nature of these results underscores the disturbing question asked by those who have tried job enrichment: "What can we do next to keep our employees challenged and interested in their work?"

Individual Differences

The early reports about job enrichment generally implied that every job should be redesigned, since every worker wants an enriched job. During the 1960s, however, research evidence indicated that job enrichment was not good for everyone. Some workers did not want job enrichment and did not respond favorably to it. A review of job enrichment research suggests that the ambiguous effects of job enrichment are partially due to individual differences; only those workers who accept middle-class work values will respond favorably to job enrichment.[31]

Several variables have been proposed to predict the effects of job enrichment on employee responses. Most of this research has focused on three types of variables: urban versus rural cultures, the Protestant work ethic, and the strength of growth needs.

Urban Versus Rural Culture. One of the earliest studies to show that workers respond differently to job enrichment was the study by Turner and Lawrence of forty-seven jobs.[32] Turner and Lawrence measured the amount of enrichment of each job and assumed that highly enriched jobs would create greater satisfaction and motivation. When they first analyzed their data, however, they were surprised to find that none of their expectations were confirmed. Instead, they found that enriched jobs created greater satisfaction and motivation only for workers from factories located in small towns, but not in large urban cities. In urban areas, workers reported less satisfaction with enriched jobs. Turner and Lawrence concluded that the urban versus rural location of the company was a "moderator" variable that influenced the relationship between job enrichment and job satisfaction. They reasoned that workers in large cities were likely to be "normless" because of the absence of cohesive cultural norms in heavily populated areas. Consequently, urban workers do not possess middle-class work values and do not respond well to challenging, skilled, autonomous jobs. Subsequent research, however, has not consistently supported their conclusions.[33]

Protestant Work Ethic. A second explanation for why some people respond more positively to enriched jobs than others was based on whether they accept the ideals of the Protestant work ethic. It was suggested that people who are raised in rural areas, particularly in farming communities, have a stronger belief in the Protestant work ethic because they have observed the effects of diligent work on their success. Those who accept the Protestant work ethic believe they ought to work diligently and demonstrate a devotion to their labors, a belief that should lead them to respond more favorably to an enriched job. In contrast, people who reject the Protestant work ethic view work as an unpleasant necessity, and dislike work that requires greater responsibility, initiative, and variety.[34] Although some research evidence shows that individuals who accept the Protestant work ethic respond more favorably to enriched jobs, again the evidence is weak and inconsistent.[35]

Higher-Order Needs. Another potential moderator of the enrichment–satisfaction relationship is the individual's desire for a job that provides greater opportunities to satisfy higher-level needs. This variable, called "growth needs strength," was based largely on Maslow's hierarchy and refers to needs for self-esteem, self-actualization, and the enhancement of one's creative potential. People who have strong needs for growth and advancement ought to respond more favorably to an enriched job.

The strength of higher-order needs is measured by asking people what type of job they prefer. A desire for higher-order needs is indicated when people choose jobs characterized by variety, independence, challenge, expression of creativity, and opportunity for learning over jobs stressing high pay, fringe benefits, job security, friendly co-workers, and considerate supervisors. In essence, people with high growth need report that they want more enrichment in the jobs they perform.

Studies on the effects of higher-order needs generally found that people who had high growth needs were more satisfied with enriched jobs. Again, however, the relationships were not particularly strong.[36]

In summary, all three moderators produce similar but weak conclusions. People raised in rural cultures, those who espouse the Protestant work ethic, and those who have higher-order needs are more inclined to display high satisfaction and high productivity if they have an enriched job. But the results are not strong enough to make useful predictions. It is not safe to assume, for example, that urban workers do not want an enriched job or that everyone who espouses the Protestant work ethic is more productive in an enriched job.

There is some evidence to suggest that the best way to predict which employees will respond favorably to enriched jobs is simply to ask them what types of jobs they prefer. Rather than using a host of indirect variables such as urbanization, Protestant work ethic, and growth needs strength to predict a worker's response to job enrichment, it is much simpler and far more direct to just ask the individual for a preference.[37]

An individual's desire for an enriched job is apparently influenced by a complex set of variables, including personality variables, cultural variables, career stages, social expectations, and specific company conditions. This point is illustrated by the following comment: "They tried to get us to do all the jobs but no one liked it. We couldn't get near as much done that way. This way is lots faster. My job is coating, and I can do it twice as fast as anyone else. I don't think I could ever learn to do their jobs as fast as them. We like it the way it is now." This comment was made by the informal leader of a group of eight women in a group interview. They worked in a small electronics manufacturing plant performing a series of extremely repetitive tasks. The routine tasks, the rural location of the company, and the generally strong work-oriented attitudes of these women would lead some to conclude that here was an ideal opportunity to see the benefits of job enrichment. Such a program had been tried earlier and failed—a combination of both horizontal and vertical enrichment had been introduced but gradually discontinued. Job specialization was more efficient. The satisfaction of the women seemed to be helped more by the positive feelings of task accomplishment than it was harmed by the routine nature of their tasks.[38]

Criticisms of Job Enrichment

Some reviews of job enrichment are not favorable. One review is very critical of job enrichment as an attempt by behavioral scientists to impose their values on others. To illustrate the point, a statement is quoted from a union newspaper denouncing General Electric's job enrichment program: "Makes no difference how you slice it, it's still monotony and more speedup."[39]

Some of the strongest criticisms of job enrichment come from labor unions. One union leader makes the following statement, "If you want to enrich the job, enrich the paycheck. . . . If you want to enrich the job, do something about the nerve-shattering noise, the heat, the fumes. . . . Worker dissatisfaction diminishes with age and that's because older workers have accrued more of the kinds of job enrichment that unions have fought for—better wages, shorter hours, vested pensions, a right to have a say in their working conditions, the right to be promoted on the basis of seniority, and all the rest. That's the kind of job enrichment that unions believe in."[40]

Another criticism of job enrichment programs is that some jobs are already too enriched. "When I read this stuff on job enrichment, it makes me shake my head. My job is already too enriched for me or anyone else. Everyday I'm being called on to make decisions I'm not prepared to make. I don't have enough time and I've got too many things to do. It's frustrating to be spread so thin."[41]

Many of these criticisms about job enrichment are well deserved. The success of a job enrichment program depends not only on its design, but also on how well it is implemented. Even if appropriate job changes are made, the change may be resisted if it is not implemented properly. Six major implementation problems are described in Exhibit 6.7. Many job enrichment failures could have been avoided if the conditions had been more carefully diagnosed and the job enrichment program more carefully implemented. However, some problems cannot be eliminated, no matter how well implemented they are.

There are also limits to how much some jobs can be improved; work is still work even in an enriched job. Ford Motor Company produced a film called *It Ain't Disney* to help its workers recognize the limits of their job redesign programs. The central message of the film was that the company had made many serious attempts to enrich the jobs and improve the working conditions, but the jobs were still hard work with much repetition.

EXHIBIT 6.7 **Problems in Implementing a Job Enrichment Program**

1. *Inadequate diagnosis before jobs are redesigned.* Some job enrichment projects have tried to enrich jobs that did not need to be changed because they were adequately enriched or already too complex. Because of a faulty diagnosis, some jobs have been changed improperly.

2. *The work itself remains unchanged.* Some job redesign efforts involve such trivial and minor changes that the work itself is not actually changed.

3. *Failure to consider unexpected effects.* Changes in one part of an organization almost always entail consequences for other parts of the organization. The benefits of a job enrichment program may be offset by the dysfunctional consequences to the nonenriched jobs.

4. *Inadequate evaluation.* Most job evaluation programs are not adequately evaluated, and managers have inadequate information to refine or make continued improvements in the job design program.

5. *Lack of training in job enrichment.* Managers may receive inadequate training in job redesign and feel overwhelmed by its demands. They may also lack the knowledge required to deal with the technology and complexity of the redesign.

6. *Creeping bureaucracy.* Many job enrichment efforts are casually inserted into the existing management processes without being carefully integrated into the organization. As a consequence, the organization tends to revert to its old, established methods when the job enrichment program fails to achieve its expected results.

ALTERNATIVE WORK SCHEDULING

Since the Great Depression, the typical workweek for most employees has been a five-day, 40-hour week. Five 8-hour days from Monday through Friday have generally represented the standard workweek in the minds of most people. However, many exceptions to the standard workweek have always existed, particularly in the farming and transportation industries. In recent years, many employees enjoy considerable flexibility in scheduling the hours they work.

Five of the most popular alternatives to the standard workweek include flextime, permanent part time, job sharing, the compressed workweek, and telecommuting. These five alternative patterns of work have both advantages and disadvantages. They are not universally desirable to all workers, and they are not feasible for some jobs. But the fact that they are being implemented in so many companies indicates the concern of top managers for improving the quality of life at work. The major reason for trying these alternatives is that they contribute to the quality of life by being more consistent with the unique circumstance of workers and the nonwork demands of their lives.

Flextime

An attractive alternative to the standard workweek is the concept of flexible working hours, or **flextime.** For many years, professionals, managers, salespeople, and the self-employed have had considerable freedom in setting their own hours of work. Flextime allows organizations to extend this same privilege to clerical, production, and other service workers. Flextime as a formal innovation was started in Germany in 1967 and spread rapidly to America. By 1990, one survey indicated that about 45 percent of the 521 responding companies offered some form of flexible scheduling.[42]

Under flexible work hours, employees choose when to arrive at work and sometimes when to depart, subject to limits set by management. Usually the organization establishes a **core period** when all employees are expected to be at work and allows flexible hours at both ends of the workday. Three typical flextime schedules are illustrated in Exhibit 6.8.

Flextime cannot be extended to all employees because of the demands of certain jobs. Jobs that require continuous coverage, such as receptionist, switchboard operator, and bus driver, make flextime inappropriate unless employees cover these jobs during their core hours and perform other discretionary activities during their flexible hours. Assembly-line jobs and other activities that require interdependence with other employees also are not appropriate for flextime. Some of the major advantages and disadvantages of flextime are presented in Exhibit 6.9.

Studies on the effects of flextime indicate that it creates more favorable job attitudes. Employees say that flextime makes them feel more trusted, and they report higher levels of satisfaction. The effects of flextime on productivity are not as clear. Most studies have indicated that flextime either increases productivity or has no effect. However, these studies generally relied on the perceptions of employees regarding their performance rather than on objective measures of productivity. Nevertheless, very few companies that have tried flextime have reported undesirable results.[43]

EXHIBIT 6.8   Three Flextime Schedules

1. Flexible starting time

Flexible period	Core time	Flexible period

6 A.M.   10 A.M.   3 P.M.   7 P.M.

Employees can choose to start their workday anytime between 6 A.M. and 10 A.M. Quitting time is nine hours later. Everyone stops for lunch between 12 P.M. and 1 P.M.

2. Flexible starting time and lunch period

Flexible period	Core time	Flexible period	Core time	Flexible

6 A.M.   9 A.M.   11 A.M.   2 P.M.   4 P.M.   7 P.M.

Employees must work a full eight-hour day, and they must be present during the core periods. However, they can start their workday anytime between 6 A.M. and 9 A.M. and take their lunch break anytime between 11 A.M. and 2 P.M. This schedule makes it possible for employees to run errands and shop in the middle of the day.

3. Flexible workday

Flexible period	Core time	Flexible period

Employees are required to work during the core hours each day, but they do not have to work exactly eight hours every day. Employees are allowed to work more or less than eight hours per day provided that they work the required number of hours each week. This arrangement provides employees with a debit–credit option in which extra hours can be banked or borrowed. For those who like shorter workdays on Friday, this is an attractive alternative. Some companies even allow hours to be carried over from week to week as long as employees do not have to be paid overtime and they work the required hours per month.

Because most executives enjoy the luxury of setting their own hours of work, they usually feel inclined to allow their employees to have the same privileges when possible. Many companies have found that most employees do not make extensive use of flextime when the option is offered to them. Even on jobs where flextime is appropriate and employees are free to set their own work hours, companies find that employees tend to follow the standard workday and generally vary their starting times by fewer than plus or minus thirty minutes. The typical response of most employees is to start work a few minutes earlier. But even if employees do not use flextime much, they like having the option of flexible hours.

Permanent Part Time

Part-time employment is defined as a job consisting of less than thirty-five hours per week and is usually considered temporary work. However, many part-time employees do not consider themselves temporary. Working less than thirty-five hours per week is a permanent position for them. In recent years, the part-time work force has increased significantly; more workers are choosing to work less than full time.[44]

One reason for the growth of **permanent part-time** employment is that it fits the needs of people who prefer working shorter hours. Mothers who have children at home and older employees who have less stamina are two groups who especially prefer part-time employment. For many people, having a job that allows

EXHIBIT 6.9   Advantages and Disadvantages of Flextime

Advantages	Disadvantages
1. Tardiness is virtually eliminated since employees are not tardy unless they miss the core hours.	1. Communication problems increase since employees frequently need to communicate during the flexible hours.
2. Absenteeism is reduced, especially the one-day absences caused by employees deciding to miss work rather than come to work late.	2. Keeping attendance records can become a problem. Employees do not like time clocks, but some tend to misrepresent their hours when they are on their own.
3. It is easier to schedule personal appointments and personal time.	3. If administrative decisions need to be made throughout the day, providing supervision for twelve to fifteen hours a day can become a problem.
4. Employees can schedule their work to match their biorhythm or internal clock. Some people work best early in the day, and others work better late in the day.	4. Legislation presents some obstacles to the use of flextime since overtime pay is required for certain jobs that exceed the standard workweek.
5. It reduces traffic congestion and creates less stress on getting to work on time.	5. Utility costs may be higher with flextime because of longer operating hours.
6. It provides greater flexibility in handling uneven workloads.	
7. It provides increased customer service because the company is open longer.	

them to work shorter hours makes the difference between having a job and having no job at all.

Additional part-time positions would likely increase the size of the workforce. Many people who are unable to work full time could probably be attracted to part-time work if more part-time jobs were available. Other advantages of part-time employment include (1) greater job satisfaction for those who need to work but do not want to work full time, and (2) greater flexibility in hiring employees to meet erratic work requirements.[45]

One major disadvantage of part-time employment is that it creates additional administrative and scheduling difficulties. All part-time workers need to be supervised, and half-time employees require almost as much supervision as full-time employees. Another problem is the cost of providing full-time benefits. However, this problem is not always relevant, because some part-time employees participate in their spouses' full-time benefit programs and do not need additional benefits.

Job Sharing

One of the most popular variations of permanent part-time employment is **job sharing.** Here a full-time position is divided into two part-time positions, and the duties and responsibilities of the job are assigned to two separate employees.

In some cases, the job functions of the two people may be distinctly different, because each may be responsible for separate activities. Accountability for the total job may be divided between the two sharers, or both may assume equal and full accountability. Job sharing usually involves a splitting of the responsibilities and the accountability between the sharers. When both part-time employees are held responsible for the whole job, it is sometimes called "job pairing."

The initial interest in job sharing was expressed by female professionals who were interested in maintaining a better balance between their career and family responsibilities. Two successful job-sharing experiments in the mid 1960s—one with social workers and the other with teachers—stimulated a considerable interest in this work arrangement. Approximately 80 percent of the job sharers are women.[46]

An example of job sharing is the case of a husband and wife who share one teaching position in the history department of a university. He teaches American history classes, his specialty, and she teaches Asian history classes, her specialty. Together their combined teaching loads, committee assignments, and salary are equivalent to one position.

Job sharing has been tried successfully among many different employees, including clerical and office workers, elementary school teachers, district attorneys, librarians, and various production-level workers. In most instances, job sharing has been initiated by two people who submitted a proposal to split a job in response to a job opening. Two mothers, for example, prepared a proposal to split the job of an elementary school teacher. They convinced the school district that their combined efforts and unique contributions were superior to what was offered by any of the alternative full-time applicants for the job.

Some major advantages of job sharing include these:[47]

1. Productivity is usually higher because two people sharing one job have higher levels of energy and enthusiasm than one full-time person. In an early study of job sharing among social workers, it was found that half-time social workers handled 89 percent as many cases as full-time workers.[48] Other studies have also reported greater productivity for job sharers. However, most of the evidence relies on subjective perceptions.

2. Increased flexibility in scheduling work assignments allows for better coverage during peak periods.

3. Reduced absenteeism and turnover have resulted from job sharing. One of the major causes of absenteeism is the need for more personal time than a forty-hour workweek allows. Job sharing not only provides more personal time but also provides the option of trading hours between partners during times of crisis or illness. Reduced turnover rates are probably an indication that part-time work is more consistent with the personal needs of employees as they try to balance competing responsibilities and interests.

4. Job training is improved by job sharing. When one member of a team quits, the remaining partner can provide on-the-job training and coaching for the new employee. The remaining partner also provides continuity during the transition period.

5. Better employment options are provided through job sharing for people who cannot perform a full-time job. Job sharing provides greater employment opportunities not only for parents but also for people who are older, handicapped, or disabled. Part-time employment in the form of job sharing may provide meaningful employment to people who might otherwise be unable to work.

Job sharing also has certain disadvantages. The most serious problem concerns the allocation of benefits. Generally benefits are prorated to each partner according to the percentage of the job that each performs. If they want full benefits, job sharers are sometimes allowed to pay the additional costs themselves; however, job sharers are usually surprised at the cost of benefits and sometimes prefer to take fewer benefits. A growing number of companies have decided to provide full benefits to job sharers. A 1987 survey indicated that 50 percent provide full health insurance, 60 percent provide full pension retirement benefits, 90 percent provide vacation pay, and 90 percent provide holiday pay.[49]

Other disadvantages of job sharing stem from the fact that employing twice as many people requires greater supervision, additional paperwork, and added communication problems. These problems are usually not very serious, however, if the partners work well together. Most job sharers say that a cooperative working relationship between the job sharers is a prerequisite for a successful team. Another problem that has to be resolved in a job-sharing situation is how a team should be promoted, fired, or evaluated. If one member is fired or promoted, what happens to the partner? Can two people sharing the job of a university professor submit combined résumés and expect to be promoted?

Compressed Workweek

The **compressed workweek** consists of scheduling a full-time job in fewer than five workdays per week. The most typical compressed workweek consists of four workdays of ten hours per day. This alternative is usually referred to as the 4/40 alternative. A workweek that is further compressed consists of three twelve-hour days; however, this 3/36 alternative has not been very popular except in some hospitals.

The idea of a compressed workweek was quite exciting when it was first tried in a few companies. Working a couple of extra hours each day did not seem like much of an added burden, because many employees frequently worked overtime anyway. The tradeoff was a free day with no work. The compressed workweek was typically scheduled to free either a Friday or a Monday to provide an extended weekend.

The advantages of a compressed workweek include these:

1. It reduces the time and costs of commuting to work.
2. It increases the leisure time of employees.
3. It creates greater job satisfaction and morale for employees who like it.
4. It reduces the setup and cleanup costs on certain jobs.

In a field experiment, it was found that the initial enthusiasm for a 4/40 workweek led to increased employee satisfaction and performance. After two years, however, the novelty and enthusiasm for change disappeared and performance had returned to original levels.[50]

The disadvantages of a compressed workweek usually outweigh the advantages. The early proponents of the compressed workweek expected it to increase productivity and lead to higher-quality work. The results have suggested just the opposite. Working more than eight hours per day generally increases fatigue. An extended schedule of ten-hour days (beyond two or three weeks) often results in less total productivity during a ten-hour day than during a regular eight-hour day. Heavy physical work or taxing mental work is generally not suited to a compressed workweek schedule. Accidents and safety violations are likely to increase with a compressed workweek schedule because of fatigue and carelessness.[51]

The compressed workweek is not popular with some employees.[52] Even though the initial response to a compressed schedule is usually favorable, many dislike it after a short time. This schedule is not convenient for working parents who want a steady daily routine that enables them to handle family responsibilities, for older employees who are prone to fatigue, or for young employees who do not want long work schedules to interfere with their social lives. A compressed workweek appears to be most suitable for middle-aged men, especially those who want to hold a second job. Compressed workweeks usually lead to increased moonlighting.

Compressed workweeks are best suited for jobs where the responsibility to initiate action comes from the job itself rather than from the worker. Security guards, hospital nurses, and refinery workers who monitor dials are examples of jobs where actions are made in response to a job demand. These jobs are better suited for compressed workweeks than physically tiring jobs that require the worker to initiate action, such as most construction jobs.[53]

Telecommuting

For some people, the epitome of flexible work and job enhancement is working at home. Technological advances in computer networks, phone-mail systems, and facsimile machines have made it possible for many jobs to be performed at home more effectively and efficiently than at the office. Working at home eliminates the disadvantages of lengthy commutes to work and reduces the number of unnecessary interruptions.

Working at home or at a satellite office and communicating with the home office by phone, usually with a computer terminal, is called **telecommuting** or *teleworking*. Some companies have found that telecommuting is advantageous to both the employees and the company. Some managers of employees who work at home report that these workers actually work more hours, significantly improve their productivity, and are easier to manage. For example, DuPont Company's Wilmington, Delaware, office has over 1,000 sales representatives and managers telecommuting. The company reports that the administrative workload of each sales representative has been reduced and morale, communications, and information turnaround have been improved.[54] Aetna Life and Casualty Company allows some of its office employees to work at home three days a week, using a computer and a modem. For Aetna, the benefit is staffing jobs in a tight labor market.[55]

The disadvantage of telecommuting is the lack of person-to-person communication and the loss of benefits that come from such encounters. Face-to-face conversations satisfy affiliation needs and help employees feel part of a group. Creative ideas and improved work procedures occasionally come from such casual conversations.

QUALITY-OF-WORK-LIFE PROGRAMS

Quality-of-work-life (QWL) programs generally encompass a variety of changes in the traditional methods of working. Job enrichment programs and alternative work schedules are examples of QWL programs. Some QWL programs, such as autonomous work teams, represent a dramatic departure from the traditional methods of doing business, while other QWL programs, such as labor–management committees, have a 200-year history. The major component that all QWL programs have in common is that they seek to improve the quality of life by creating better jobs. Almost all QWL programs share four common goals that comprise what is sometimes referred to as "industrial democracy":

1. They seek to create a more democratic organization where all members have more voice in deciding issues that influence their lives.

2. They try to share the financial rewards of the organization so that everyone benefits from greater cooperation, high productivity, and increased profitability.

3. They seek to create greater job security by increasing organizational vitality and furthering employee rights.

4. They try to enhance individual development by establishing conditions that contribute to personal growth and adjustment.

The major QWL programs discussed in this section include (1) self-directed work teams, (2) quality circles, (3) representation on the board of directors, (4) labor–management committees, and (5) humor in the workplace.

Self-directed Work Teams

A self-directed work team consists of a small group of workers, usually less than fifteen or twenty workers, who are responsible for performing a series of jobs. This group is also called an **"autonomous work team"** because it is directed by its own informal leadership rather than through a layer of supervisors. Members of the team are free to rotate jobs as they choose. Someone may perform the same repetitive job day after day while another team member may shift from one job to another or even build a complete unit alone. Some groups handle their own personnel functions, such as hiring new people, evaluating each other's performance, and determining each member's pay increase.[56]

Several companies have eliminated the traditional assembly line and changed to a production system based on self-directed work teams. The two most widely known experiments in self-directed work teams are the Swedish car companies Volvo and SAAB. Each company tried to outdo the other in its attempts to introduce a radical departure from the traditional assembly line. Volvo, for example, built an entirely new assembly plant in Kalmar, Sweden, where assembly lines were replaced with workstations for each autonomous group. Partially completed cars are moved from station to station on small electric carts.[57]

In America, the most widely publicized attempt to use autonomous work teams occurred at the General Foods plant in Topeka, Kansas, which produces pet food.

APPLYING ORGANIZATIONAL BEHAVIOR
IN THE NEWS

Quality-of-Work-Life Programs

CNN Organizations have experimented with a variety of job redesign programs to increase productivity and improve the quality of life at work. These programs have included self-directed work teams and intrepreneurship initiatives. But, these programs have not been trouble free.

Federal Express experimented with self-directed work teams almost by accident. When a group of managers was promoted out of one facility and not immediately replaced, workers asked that they be allowed to manage themselves. Upper management agreed. For a while, everyone was satisfied with the workers' progress, but eventually the workers asked for the managers to return. Without the managers, they lacked essential connections to the rest of the corporation and they had difficulty obtaining essential resources. They discovered that someone in the group needed to perform the managerial role.

Managers were assigned, but the employees were invited to participate in quality action teams to preserve their involvement in generating new ideas.

Intrepreneurship programs encourage small dynamic groups of workers within a larger corporation to create and produce innovative products. Minnesota Mining and Manufacturing Company encourages intrepreneurship by inviting technical workers to spend 15 percent of their time on their own projects. 3M's Post-It Notes and Gillette's Sensor Razor are two of the most successful consumer products to result from intrepreneurship. A potential problem with intrepreneurship is having employees with new ideas leave and become part of the competition. Experience suggests, however, that employees with new ideas are generally motivated to remain and develop them.

Source: CNN *Inside Business* news programming.

When this new plant was constructed, it was designed especially for autonomous work groups. Seventy workers were carefully selected and organized into six teams. Each team was comprised of from seven to fourteen operators plus a team leader. Although each operator had primary responsibility for a set of tasks, the tasks could be shared or rotated.

Early reports about the General Foods-Topeka experiment were extremely favorable. After eighteen months, the fixed overhead was reduced 33 percent, quality rejects were down 92 percent, and the annual savings were estimated at $600,000.[58] Later results, however, were not so favorable, and the program finally had to revert to a more traditional work setting. In some teams serious inequities were observed, such as discriminatory hiring practices, unfair work assignments, and arbitrary restrictions on opportunities for training. Apparently the leaders in some teams abused the freedom they were given.[59]

Other companies in both Europe and America have expanded the use of autonomous work teams. General Mills allowed its work groups to become self-directed as part of its focus on high-performance work teams. Productivity at General Mills' cereal plant in Lodi, California, increased 40 percent above comparable plants after it installed self-directed work teams.[60] Some companies (such as Signetics and Procter & Gamble) prefer to use the label "semiautonomous work teams" to emphasize the fact that the teams are still subject to the direction of management and must comply with company personnel policies. Although the results

APPLYING ORGANIZATIONAL BEHAVIOR
RESEARCH

A Longitudinal Study of Autonomous Work Groups

 A carefully designed longitudinal study of autonomous work groups concluded that these groups improve productivity, increase satisfaction, and produce other desirable results. A critical review of this experiment, however, illustrates the difficulties of field research and questions the conclusions.

The participants in this study were 900 blue-collar and 100 white-collar workers who repaired locomotives and railway wagons in the largest heavy engineering workshop in Western Australia. The data in this longitudinal study were collected six times at two-month intervals measuring productivity, job satisfaction, job motivation, role perceptions, task characteristics, participation in decision making, accidents, and attendance.

The study employed the use of a Solomon four-group design which is considered one of the most powerful research techniques. This design randomly assigns groups to experimental and control conditions and only half the groups in each condition are pretested to control for the effects of testing.

The fifteen experimental groups in this study held 30-minute weekly meetings to discuss work-related problems. They were encouraged to set goals and determine the strategies for attaining them. They had ready access to needed information, plus the authority to make decisions and implement changes in their work processes. They were called "autonomous groups" even though they continued to have an assigned supervisor. The thirteen control groups continued to use traditional bureaucratic management practices that had evolved since 1904.

The results found significant differences between the autonomous groups and the control groups, but the differences were caused by declines within the control groups rather than by improvements in the autonomous groups. The control groups experienced significant declines in job motivation and job satisfaction, and significant increases in role ambiguity and role conflict. The autonomous groups did not show significant improvement in any of the measures except for a slight improvement in job satisfaction.

At the beginning of the study, productivity did not differ significantly between the control and autonomous groups, but by the end of the study slight differences appeared. Again, this difference was due to a decline in the productivity of the control groups rather than to an increase in the autonomous groups. Likewise, there were differences in accidents—not because the autonomous groups were safer, but because the control groups experienced an increase in their accident rate. The control groups also had an increase in absenteeism.

These results do little to endorse the value of autonomous work groups. However, the author explains that the mysterious deterioration in the control groups and lack of improvement in the autonomous groups may have been caused by troublesome economic conditions. The state railway lost its protected status and was required to reduce its budget deficits. Consequently, it was undergoing restructuring. Consumer confidence was very low because of adverse economic and employment conditions.

Even if the autonomous groups had shown significant improvements, these gains should not be attributed directly to the value of self-directed work teams. The goal-setting process used by the experimental groups probably had a greater impact on improving performance than the benefits of self-determination.

Source: C. A. L. Pearson, "Autonomous Workgroups: An Evaluation at an Industrial Site," *Human Relations*, vol. 45 (1992), pp. 905–935.

of using work teams are not spectacular, and some employees transfer out of them, most companies report favorable results.

The effects of autonomous work teams were carefully investigated in a quasi-experimental field study of a British confectionery company. In the experimental condition, production employees working in groups of eight to twelve people were responsible for allocating jobs among themselves, meeting quality and hygiene standards, solving local production problems, organizing breaks, ordering and collecting raw materials, delivering finished goods to stores, and selecting and training new employees. Supervisory positions were eliminated, and the groups worked under the general guidance of a support manager. Evaluations of the autonomous and nonautonomous work groups after six, eighteen, and thirty months indicated that those who participated in the autonomous groups liked it and consistently reported higher levels of intrinsic job satisfaction; they appreciated their autonomy. However, none of the other benefits typically attributed to autonomous work groups were found; there were no improvements in job motivation, work performance, organizational commitment, mental health, or extrinsic job satisfaction. And contrary to what might be expected, labor turnover increased. The only other benefit, in addition to the fact that those who stayed liked it, was a decrease in indirect labor costs since the supervisory positions were eliminated. But even though managers and employees liked it, there were definite costs in terms of personal stress arising from the difficulties involved in managing and maintaining the system.[61]

Quality Circles and Total Quality Management

The term "**quality circle**" comes primarily from Japan and describes the process used by many Japanese firms to involve employees in work redesign experiments. A quality circle consists of a group of workers who meet periodically to discuss methods of increasing productivity. Participation in the group discussion is voluntary. The group meets regularly, such as one hour each week, usually on company time. The discussions are led by a supervisor or a group facilitator. The purposes of the meeting are to identify and diagnose problems, to explore alternative solutions, and to recommend the best solution. The members of the group are encouraged to discuss only problems they can do something about; problems out of their control are referred elsewhere. In union companies, quality circle members are generally instructed to avoid discussing the labor contract because of anxiety that the quality circle will reduce the union's power or threaten management's prerogatives.[62]

During the 1980s, quality circle programs rapidly proliferated throughout the United States and Europe. Their popularity stemmed from the glowing reports of companies who used them plus the reasonable belief that the people who do the work are in the best position to know how it can be improved. The use of quality circles was also the most prominent explanation given for the superiority of Japanese management and the declining competitiveness of U.S. manufacturing. Three benefits are attributed to quality circles. First, the creative suggestions of team members reduce costs and produce greater productivity and efficiency. Second, quality circles improve communication within the group, between groups, and with upper levels of management. Third, quality circles enhance the level of morale and increase the employees' commitment to their work and satisfaction with the company.

Quality performance has become so important to the economic survival of some companies that they have implemented a company-wide program called "total quality management" (TQM). The purpose of TQM is to reduce errors to essentially zero and improve the quality of service. Four influential contributions to the development of total quality management include W. Edwards Deming's fourteen-point philosophy that quality begins with a commitment by top management and cascades throughout the company, Philip Cosby's zero-defects approach to prevention through statistical process control, Armand V. Feigenbaum's discussion regarding the competitive advantages of total quality management, and Joseph M. Juran's encouragement to make quality the focus of interdepartmental problem-solving groups. A central concept common to all four theorists is that quality must start at the design stage: quality must be built in, not inspected in.[63]

The focus of total quality management is on giving customers what they have a right to expect. Total quality is achieved with a system designed to keep the customer's interests continuously in the product cycle. Statistical methods are used to evaluate both management and production processes at each point of functional accountability. Variance analyses and joint problem solving at each control point eventually leads to continuous improvement. Every employee is expected to be involved in identifying obstacles and implementing solutions.[64]

Like other job redesign projects, the research on quality circles and TQM has not been universally positive. By a wide margin, most of the published reports about quality circles and TQM have been anecdotal appraisals and estimates of anticipated savings due to productivity improvements or labor efficiencies. The bottom-line benefits described in these reports have fueled the aspirations of managers who want to duplicate these programs in their companies and achieve identical benefits.[65]

Good empirical studies that actually measured the results of quality circles, especially those with experimental designs that included control groups, found that quality circles were successful less than half the time. One study found that only eight out of twenty-nine companies using quality circles reported that they were successful as measured by the cost of the program relative to the gains in productivity.[66] Another review of fourteen empirical studies found that seven of them failed to find any positive benefits for quality circles, and the benefits in some of the other seven studies were mixed and meager.[67]

An analysis of the quality control failures suggests that the major causes of failure stem from poor communication with employees before the program is started and inadequate training and leadership once it begins. Some companies have not done a good job selling quality circles and TQM and explaining why they are necessary. Consequently, some employees see them as a management ploy to reduce overtime, to increase productivity, to reduce the work force, or to eliminate the union. The supervisors or facilitators selected to lead the groups sometimes receive inadequate training in human relations and group dynamics. Consequently, group members may feel that the meetings fail to accomplish anything and they are a waste of time. Team members also feel frustrated if worthwhile suggestions are not implemented in a timely way, due to delay and indecision.[68]

Representation on the Board of Directors

Many companies, especially in Europe, have placed employees on their boards of directors. These members are elected by the workforce to represent the workers' interests and participate on the board of directors as voting members. In many European companies, this practice has been mandated by national law. In Sweden, for example, a law passed in 1973 requires all corporations with more than 100 people on the payroll to have worker representatives on their boards. German companies adopted this practice many years ago to minimize labor disputes, and it seems to be effective, since the number of lost days due to strikes has been reduced. Several major American corporations, especially in the automobile, steel, and airline industries, have included worker representatives on their boards of directors.

The reason for placing production workers on the board is to assure that the interests of workers will be considered. During a board's deliberations, when decisions of tremendous economic importance to the employees are being made, the board members can be reminded about the employees' interests. Employee participation on a board represents to some extent a significant value reorientation away from the single-minded focus of a traditional board on profits. The presence of employee representatives is a recognition that preserving jobs is a goal at least as important as producing profits; decisions that lead to maximum profitability might be bad decisions if they eliminate jobs.

The benefits of workers participating on a board have been mixed. Announcing that the employees will be invited to send representatives to the board as voting members is largely a symbolic act signaling a desire for a more harmonious working relationship between management and workers. However, the employee representatives do not have enough influence or votes to materially alter the board's decisions. Therefore, including employee representatives does not guarantee the cooperation of the employees or the success of the company.

Several companies, such as Hyatt Clark Industries, Rath Packing, and LTV Steel, have found that employee representation on the board does not guarantee labor cooperation, profitability, or job protection; such participation does not prevent competitive pressures nor compensate for bad management decisions. Placing employee representatives on the boards at Eastern Airlines and Continental Airlines, likewise, failed to solve their financial problems.[69] Nevertheless, many other corporations in the United States and Europe report positive benefits from including employee representatives on their boards of directors.

Labor–Management Committees

To reduce conflict and create a more cooperative climate, some unions and companies have formed committees with representatives from both sides. This committee does not perform the traditional collective bargaining functions; in fact, the committee must be careful not to interfere in the collective bargaining process. The purpose of the committee is to resolve conflicts between management and union and help both survive. Many labor–management committees have originated in response to severe economic threats, such as an economic depression, a plant closing, declining markets, or intense foreign competition. Effective programs have evolved in many different industries, most having been created in response to specific economic needs.

Labor–management committees have survived a long history, especially in the United States and Europe.[70] Between 1820 and 1840, when manufacturing was still in its infancy, groups of crafts workers and employers held committee meetings to discuss quality improvements, production standards, and pricing. These committees were destroyed by the depression of 1837, but similar committees were active again after the Civil War under the title of "worker councils" or "shop councils." During the 1920s, labor–management committees were jointly recommended as a means of improving production efficiency by a surprising coalition of the American Federation of Labor (AFL) and the disciples of Frederick Taylor's scientific method of management.

The greatest popularity of labor–management committees occurred during World War I and World War II when government pressure led to the formation of hundreds of committees in almost every industry to discuss a wide range of topics such as labor productivity and turnover, living and working conditions, terms of employment, and social and recreational needs of employees. Most of these committees were terminated after the war, however, because they threatened the power positions of both management and union. Even though people on both sides generally recognized the contributions of the committees, these contributions were ignored in favor of skepticism regarding future benefits.

Managers have had low expectations of the workers' willingness or ability to make contributions. They also have feared that such participation would reduce their prestige and authority and add to the strength of the union. Meanwhile, unions have been concerned about the effect of productivity gains on job opportunities and fearful that cooperation would weaken their bargaining power.

Labor–management committees have been remarkably successful in several industrial countries, most notably in Japan, Switzerland, and Singapore.[71] In the United States, joint committees are often viewed as essential to organizational improvement, and their success is crucial for the organization to succeed in foreign competition.

One of the best illustrations of labor–management cooperation is the joint venture between the United Auto Workers, General Motors, and Toyota. The GM assembly plant in Fremont, California, was forced to close because of ineffective management, a militant union, and foreign competition. Two years later, GM and Toyota reached an agreement with the union and reopened the plant with new management, a new labor relations system, and new technology. This plant, called NUMMI (New United Motor Manufacturing Incorporated), is one of the most efficient auto assembly plants in the world, and absenteeism has been reduced from 20 percent to 2 percent.[72]

Like other QWL programs, however, labor–management committees are not a guarantee of cooperation or financial success. A climate of selfishness, distrust, or suspicion can destroy a joint effort. In the steel industry, for example, Jones and Laughlin Steel Corporation and LTV Steel created several labor–management participation teams, or "LMPTs" as they were called, in cooperation with their labor unions. In 1984 LTV Steel announced that its LMPTs cost the company $600,000 a year, but their ideas would save the company over $4 million per year. In spite of the company's efforts to preserve the joint committees, the union employees voted two years later not to participate in the LMPTs, complaining that they were being used by the company to increase productivity, eliminate jobs, ignore grievances, and generate more profits that wouldn't be shared with the employees.[73] Such complaints explain why labor–management committees have such a long history of mixed success.

Humor in the Workplace

Some efforts have been directed toward making work more fun. Laughter can enhance the work environment because it creates positive physiological and psychological effects on the human body and mind. Humor appears to be a useful tool for motivating employees, stimulating creativity, and improving job performance. One survey found that employees who have fun at work tend to have better attendance records and report higher levels of motivation and productivity.[74]

Three strategies are recommended for making work more fun:

1. *Talk mostly about subjects that are interesting and pleasant.* Do not discuss problems and criticisms any more than necessary. Identify topics related to shared goals, goal success, common interests, and enjoyable experiences, and let these topics become the center of conversation.

2. *Interpret situations and events in humorous ways.* One way to diminish a problem and, at the same time, open avenues of solution is to imagine how a situation could be worse. Clever analogies or labels can insert an element of humor without trivializing the seriousness of a problem.

3. *Keep humorous objects in the surrounding environment.* Objects that are silly or unusual make offices seem less formal and serve as fun conversation pieces. Favorite cartoons and caricatures of oneself hanging on the wall communicate that laughter is encouraged, especially if you can laugh at yourself.

Humor in the workplace does more than make work fun. It also improves the rapport between employees, diminishes feelings of unequal status among individuals, helps groups achieve a consensus, reduces conflicts and tension, and diminishes boredom and fatigue.[75]

SUMMARY

1. Job specialization and job enrichment are essentially opposite strategies of redesigning jobs. While job specialization involves simplifying the job to make it more repetitive, job enrichment makes jobs more complex and variable.

2. Job specialization was a major contributor to the industrial revolution and was epitomized by the scientific management movement with its emphasis on task analysis and time-and-motion studies.

3. The major advantage of job specialization is greater efficiency through reduced learning time, increased proficiency, and the development of technology. The disadvantage of job specialization is that it creates extremely repetitive jobs that contribute to boredom and alienation.

4. The opposite of job specialization is job enlargement. The arguments in favor of job enlargement are that it creates greater satisfaction and motivation. Although enlarged jobs are less efficient than specialized jobs, the increase in motivation and satisfaction are expected to more than compensate for the loss in efficiency.

5. Job enlargement is not the same as job enrichment. Job enlargement consists of adding similar elements to enlarge a task; job enrichment consists of giving the job holder greater achievement, recognition, responsibility, advancement, and growth in competence. Increases in satisfaction and productivity are more likely to result from job enrichment than from job enlargement.

6. Job scope concerns the characteristics of the job and is defined by job breadth and job depth. Breadth concerns the number of different activities involved in the job, while depth concerns the degree of decision making and control exercised by the worker.

7. A useful model for diagnosing a job and deciding how it should be enriched is the job characteristics model. This model shows how job changes influence the core dimensions of the job, which in turn influence the psychological reactions to the job, which in turn influence the work outcomes.

8. Studies on the effects of job enrichment programs have produced generally mixed results. Numerous case studies describing the effects of specific job enrichment programs report significant cost savings and increases in organizational effectiveness. Many of these case studies also suggest that employees respond favorably to job enrichment programs with less absenteeism, less tardiness, lower turnover, greater satisfaction, and higher productivity.

9. Numerous experimental studies of job enrichment have failed to find the positive results described in case studies. Job enrichment has been criticized as an imposition of management's values on workers and a method of coercing workers to work harder for the same pay.

10. Some people do not respond favorably to job enrichment programs, and three variables have been proposed to predict these individual differences: (a) urban versus rural culture, (b) the Protestant work ethic, and (c) higher-order needs. Rather than using these indirect variables, however, a better way to predict how people will respond to job enrichment is simply to ask them how they would like their jobs to be changed.

11. There are five major alternatives to the standard five-day, 40-hour week: flextime, permanent part-time work, job sharing, the compressed workweek, and telecommuting. Flextime is a schedule where workers set their own starting time, subject to certain constraints. Permanent part-time work is treating a part-time job of less than thirty-five hours per week as a permanent job. Job sharing consists of allowing two employees to perform one full-time position. The compressed workweek alternative involves working longer hours per day but fewer days per week, such as the 4/40 plan of working four 10-hour days each week. Telecommuting lets employees work at home with the aid of telephones, computers, and facsimile (fax) machines. Each of these alternatives has advantages and disadvantages, but the advantages generally far outweigh the disadvantages for all but the compressed workweek.

12. Quality-of-work-life programs involve changing the traditional methods of work to improve the quality of life. QWL programs have four common goals: (a) more democratic participation of all employees, (b) sharing the financial rewards of the organization, (c) greater job security, and (d) greater personal development. Some major QWL programs include autonomous work teams, quality circles, representation on boards of directors, and labor–management committees.

DISCUSSION QUESTIONS

1. How do job enrichment and job specialization contribute to increased productivity? Is job enrichment the opposite of job specialization?

2. What changes would you recommend for enriching the job of a teaching assistant who grades exams and papers?

3. What is the best way to decide which jobs should be enriched and what changes need to be made?

4. How do you evaluate the contributions of scientific management today? Did scientific management make a significant positive contribution to management theory during its day, and does it have anything to offer today?

5. Are repetitive jobs necessarily boring? Why are some activities with a short work cycle not perceived as boring, such as playing slot machines and bingo?

6. Is it possible to enrich a job without necessarily enlarging it?

7. Provide different illustrations of the job scope for the job of a university professor, including high and low depth and high and low breadth.

8. What major task attributes can be changed in a job enrichment program?

9. In the job characteristics model, personal values moderate the effects of the core job dimensions on the psychological states. What are some examples of personal values that influence how individuals respond to different job characteristics?

10. Which jobs are particularly well suited for flextime, permanent part-time work, job sharing, the compressed workweek, and telecommuting? What are some jobs that are poorly suited for these alternative patterns of work?

11. What are the advantages of self-directed work teams? Can a work group really be free of the influence and control of management? What constraints are necessary?

12. How are quality circles different from a regular employee suggestion system?

13. Should labor–management committees get involved in discussions about the labor agreement that is normally negotiated at the bargaining table? Why or why not?

GLOSSARY

autonomous work teams A group of workers who are largely self-managed and only loosely directed by management. The group collectively decides who will perform which job, and members typically rotate from job to job.

compressed workweek An alternative work schedule in which employees work fewer days per week by working more hours on the days they work. The most typical compressed workweek schedule is four 10-hour days, called the 4/40 plan.

core period The period of time during the workday when employees on flexible working hours must be at work.

ergonomics The application of technology and engineering to human abilities, interests, and feelings. Sometimes called *biotechnology*, it considers the mutual adjustment of people and machines in improving organizational effectiveness.

flextime An alternative work schedule that allows employees to set their own work hours, subject to specific constraints, such as requiring them to work a specific number of hours per day or per week and to be at work during the core period.

horizontal loading A form of job enrichment where the job is enlarged by combining additional tasks or elements into a job. On an assembly line, horizontal loading involves combining elements from the preceding or following jobs to enlarge a particular job.

job breadth As one dimension of job scope, job breadth is defined by the number of different activities performed by a job holder.

job characteristics model A model explaining how job enrichment programs change the core dimensions of the job, which in turn influence the psychological states of workers, which in turn influence the work outcomes.

job depth As one dimension of job scope, job depth is defined by the degree of decision making or control the worker exercises over how the job is to be performed.

job enlargement Making a job larger by adding more of the same kinds of elements.

job enrichment Changing a job to make it significantly different in terms of the amount of variety, autonomy, and responsibility for the job. Job enrichment involves a significant change in the content of the job, rather than just making it more of the same.

job scope Job scope concerns the characteristics or attributes of a job and is defined by the breadth and depth of a job.

job sharing A work arrangement whereby two workers split one job, each worker being responsible for his or her share of the job. The workers split the salary, the benefits, and the responsibilities.

job specialization Simplifying a job by reducing the number of elements or activities performed by a job holder. Job specialization normally involves more repetitive activities with short work cycles.

motivators Characteristics associated with the content of a job, such as achievement, accountability, feedback, and personal growth. Significant job enrichment involves enhancing these characteristics.

permanent part time　A work arrangement permitting employees to work less than thirty-five hours per week. This arrangement is considered a permanent rather than a temporary part-time job.

quality circles　An organizational improvement strategy that involves work groups meeting periodically, usually one hour per week, to discuss ways to improve productivity.

telecommuting　A work arrangement permitting employees to work at home and use telephones, computers, and facsimile (fax) machines to communicate with the office.

vertical loading　A form of job enrichment in which higher-level administrative and supervisory responsibilities are included in the job to create greater levels of responsibility.

NOTES

1. Todd Vogel, "Hello, I Must Be Going: On the Road with UPS," *Business Week*, vol. 4 (June 1990), p. 82.

2. Frederic C. Lane, *Venetian Ships and Shipbuilders of the Renaissance* (Baltimore: Johns Hopkins University Press, 1934); John J. Norwich, *Venice: The Rise to Empire* (New York: Penguin Books, 1977); Alvise Zorzi, *Venice: The Golden Age, 697–1797* (New York: Abbeville Press, 1980).

3. Herbert G. Gutman, *Work, Culture, and Society in Industrializing America* (New York: Vintage Books, 1977); Daniel T. Rodgers, *The Work Ethic in Industrial America: 1850–1920* (Chicago: University of Chicago Press, 1978).

4. Yash P. Gupta and M. D. Yakimchuk, "Impact of Advanced Manufacturing Technology on Industrial Relations: A Comparative Study," *Engineering Management International*, vol. 5 (May 1989), pp. 291–298.

5. David Buchanan, "Job Enrichment Is Dead: Long Live High Performance Work Design," *Personnel Management*, vol. 19 (May 1987), pp. 40–43.

6. Adam Smith, *An Inquiry into the Nature and Causes of the Wealth of Nations*, 3 vols. Reprinted in (London: W. Lewis, 1811, volumes). See Vol. 1, chap. 1. First published in five books, 1776.

7. Frederick W. Taylor, *The Principles of Scientific Management* (New York: Harper, 1911).

8. Frederick W. Taylor, *Shop Management* (New York: Harper, 1911).

9. Frank B. Gilbreth, Jr., and Ernestine Gilbreth Carey, *Cheaper by the Dozen* (New York: Crowell, 1949).

10. Claude S. George, Jr., *The History of Management Thought*, 2nd ed. (Englewood Cliffs, N.J.: Prentice-Hall, 1972), pp. 99–101.

11. Jan Stafford, "Is Your Office Making You Sick?" *Today's Office*, vol. 25 (October 1990), pp. 28–33.

12. Patricia M. Fernberg, "Sitting in Judgment on Chairs," *Modern Office Technology*, vol. 35 (November 1990), pp. 62–66.

13. Smith, op.cit.

14. Charles Babbage, *On the Economy of Machinery and Manufactures* (London: Charles Knight, 1932).

15. Samuel Hayakawa, "The Musings of Senator Sam," speech reported in the *San Francisco Chronicle* about 1978.

16. See Paul Dickson, *The Future of the Work Place* (New York: Weybright and Talley, 1975), p. 14.

17. See *Work in America: A Report of a Special Task Force to the Secretary of Health, Education, and Welfare* (Cambridge, Mass.: MIT Press, 1973), especially chap. 4; Stephen M. Pittell, "Addicts in Wonderland: Sketches for a Map of a Vocational Frontier," *Journal of Psychedelic Drugs*, vol. 6 (April–June, 1974), pp. 231–241; Arthur S. Grecham and Yoash Wiener, "Job Involvement and Satisfaction as Related to Mental Health and Personal Time Devoted to Work," *Journal of Applied Psychology*, vol. 60 (1975), pp. 521–523.

18. Frederick Herzberg, *Work and the Nature of Man* (Cleveland, Ohio: World Publishing, 1966); Frederick Herzberg, "The Wise Old Turk," *Harvard Business Review*, vol. 52 (September–October 1974), pp. 70–80.

19. Robert N. Ford, "Job Enrichment Lessons from AT&T," *Harvard Business Review*, vol. 51 (January–February 1973), pp. 96–106.

20. Arthur N. Turner and Paul R. Lawrence, *Industrial Jobs and the Worker* (Boston: Harvard University, Graduate School of Business Administration, 1965).

21. This section is a summary and adaptation of the job characteristics model presented in these publications: J. Richard Hackman and Greg R. Oldham, "The Job Diagnostic Survey: An Instrument for the Diagnosis of Jobs and the Evaluation of Job Redesign Projects" (Technical Report 4, Yale University, School of Organization and Management, 1974); J. Richard Hackman and Greg R. Oldham, "Motivation Through the Design of Work: Test of a Theory," *Organizational Behavior and Human Performance*, vol. 7 (1976), pp. 250–279; J. Richard Hackman, Greg R. Oldham, Robert Janson, and Kenneth Purdy, "A New Strategy for Job Enrichment," *California Management Review*, vol. 17 (Summer 1975), pp. 57–71; and Greg R. Oldham, "Job Charac-

teristics and Internal Motivation: The Moderating Effect of Interpersonal and Individual Variables," *Human Relations*, vol. 29, no. 6 (1976), pp. 559–569.

22. Brian T. Loher, Raymond A. Noe, Nancy L. Moeller, and Michael P. Fitzgerald, "A Meta-analysis of the Relation of Job Characteristics to Job Satisfaction," *Journal of Applied Psychology*, vol. 70 (1985), pp. 280–289; Thomas C. Head and Peter F. Sorenson, "A Multiple Site Comparison of Job Redesign Projects: Implications for Consultants," *Organizational Development Journal*, vol. 3 (Fall 1985), pp. 37–44.

23. According to the job characteristics model, the fourth outcome is "internal work motivation." Since this is really a personal value, it has been replaced with a more general outcome that has been carefully described in the literature. See Daniel Katz and Robert Kahn, *The Social Psychology of Organizations* (New York: Wiley, 1965), chap. 12. For further explanation, see David J. Cherrington, *The Work Ethic: Working Values and Values that Work* (New York: AMACOM Publishing, 1980), chap. 11.

24. Daniel J. Cougar, "Effect of Cultural Differences on Motivation of Analysts and Programmers: Singapore vs. the United States," *MIS Quarterly*, vol. 10 (June 1986), pp. 189–196.

25. Richard E. Kopelman, "Job Redesign and Productivity: A Review of the Evidence," *National Productivity Review*, vol. 4 (Summer 1985), pp. 237–255.

26. Preston C. Bottger and Irene K-H Chew, "The Job Characteristics Model and Growth Satisfaction: Main Effects of Assimilation of Work Experience and Context Satisfaction," *Human Relations*, vol. 39 (1986), pp. 575–594; Yitzhak Fried and Gerald R. Ferris, "The Validity of the Job Characteristics Model: A Review and Meta-Analysis," *Personnel Psychology*, vol. 40 (Summer 1987), pp. 287–322; Shaul Fox and Gerald Feldman, "Attention State and Critical Psychological States as Mediators Between Job Dimensions and Job Outcomes," *Human Relations*, vol. 41 (March 1988), pp. 229–245; George B. Graen, Terri A. Scandura, and Michael R. Graen, "A Field Experimental Test of the Moderating Effects of Growth Need Strength on Productivity," *Journal of Applied Psychology*, vol. 71 (August 1986), pp. 484–491; Eileen A. Hogan and Daniel A. Martell, "A Confirmatory Structural Equations Analysis of the Job Characteristics Model," *Organizational Behavior and Human Decision Processes*, vol. 39 (April 1987), pp. 242–263.

27. William J. Paul Jr., Keith B. Robertson, and Frederick Herzberg, "Job Enrichment Pays Off," *Harvard Business Review*, vol. 47 (March–April, 1969), pp. 61–78.

28. Charles L. Hughes, "Applying Behavioral Science in Manufacturing Supervision: Case Report," *Proceedings of the 9th Annual Midwest Management Conference* (Carbondale: Southern Illinois University, 1966), pp. 85–89.

29. Kopelman, op. cit.

30. Charles N. Greene, "Some Effects of a Job Enrichment Program: A Field Experiment," *Proceedings*, 41st Annual Academy of Management Meetings, Academy of Management, 1981, pp. 281–282.

31. Charles L. Hulin and Milton R. Blood, "Job Enlargement, Individual Differences, and Worker Responses," *Psychological Bulletin*, vol. 69 (1968), pp. 41–55.

32. Arthur N. Turner and Paul R. Lawrence, *Industrial Jobs and the Worker* (Boston: Harvard University, Graduate School of Business Administration, 1965).

33. John P. Wanous, "Individual Differences and Reactions to Job Characteristics," *Journal of Applied Psychology*, vol. 59 (1974), pp. 67–622; J. Kenneth White, "Individual Differences and the Job Quality—Worker Response Relationship: Review, Integration, and Comments," *Academy of Management Review*, vol. 3 (April 1978), pp. 267–279.

34. E. F. Stone, "Job Scope, Job Satisfaction, and the Protestant Ethic: A Study of Enlisted Men in the U.S. Navy," *Journal of Vocational Behavior*, vol. 7 (1975), pp. 215–224; E. F. Stone, "The Moderating Effect of Work-Related Values on the Job Scope—Job Satisfaction Relationship," *Organizational Behavior and Human Performance*, vol. 15 (1976), pp. 147–177.

35. Wanous, op. cit.; White, op. cit.; David J. Cherrington and J. Lynn England, "The Desire for an Enriched Job as a Moderator of the Enrichment—Satisfaction Relationship," *Organizational Behavior and Human Performance*, vol. 25 (1980), pp. 139–159.

36. Wanous, op. cit.; Greg R. Oldham, "Job Characteristics and Internal Motivation: The Moderating Effect of Interpersonal and Individual Variables," *Human Relations*, vol. 29 (1976), pp. 559–569; Henry P. Sims and Andrew D. Szilagyi, "Job Characteristics Relationships: Individual and Structural Moderators," *Organizational Behavior and Human Performance*, vol. 17 (1976), pp. 211–230; P. E. Spector, "Higher-order Need Strength as a Moderator of the Job Scope—Employee Outcome Relationship: A Meta-analysis," *Journal of Occupational Psychology*, vol. 58 (1985), pp. 119–127.

37. Cherrington and England, op. cit.; Rintaro Muramatsu, Haruo Miyazaki, and Kazuyoshi Ishii, "A Successful Application of Job Enlargement/Enrichment at Toyota," *IIE Transactions*, vol. 19 (December 1987), pp. 451–459.

38. Ibid., p. 156.

39. Mitchell Fein, "Job Enrichment: A Re-evaluation," *Sloan Management Review*, vol. 15, no. 2 (Winter 1974), p. 75.

40. W. Winpisinger, "Job Satisfaction: A Union Response," *AFL-CIO American Federationist*, vol. 80 (February 1973), pp. 8–10.

41. Cherrington and England, op. cit., p. 156.

42. Kathleen Christensen, "Here We Go into the 'High-Flex' Era," *Across the Board*, vol. 27 (July–August 1990), pp. 22–23; John A. Hollingsworth and Frank A. Wiebe,

"Flex Time: An International Innovation with Limited U.S. Acceptance," *Industrial Management*, vol. 31 (March–April 1989), pp. 22–26.

43. Ellen Ernst Kossek, "The Acceptance of Human Resource Innovation by Multiple Constituencies," *Personnel Psychology*, vol. 42 (Summer 1989), pp. 263–281; Robert N. Lussier, "Should Your Organization Use Flex-Time?" *Supervision*, vol. 51 (September 1990), pp. 14–16; David A. Ralston, "The Benefits of Flex-Time: Real or Imagined?" *Journal of Organizational Behavior*, vol. 10 (October 1989), pp. 369–373; Pam Silverstein and Jozetta H. Srb, *Flex-Time: Where, When, and How* (Ithaca, N.Y.: Cornell University Press, 1979).

44. Roberta Graham, "In Permanent Part-Time Work, You Can't Beat the Hours," *Nations Business*, vol. 67 (January 1979), pp. 65–68.

45. Carol S. Greenwald and Judith Liss, "Part-Time Workers Can Bring Higher Productivity," *Harvard Business Review*, vol. 51 (September–October 1973), pp. 20–22; Frank W. Schiff, "Short-time Compensation: Assessing the Issues," *Monthly Labor Review*, vol. 109 (May 1986), pp. 28–30; Robert N. Lussier, "Should Your Organization Use Job-Sharing?" *Supervision*, vol. 51 (April 1990), pp. 9–11.

46. Nancy Connors, "Job Sharing: Beyond Maternity Leave," *CFO: The Magazine for Chief Financial Officers*, vol. 6 (March 1990), pp. 47–49.

47. David Clutterbuck, "Why a Job Shared Is Not a Job Halved," *International Management*, vol. 35 (October 1979), pp. 45–47; Gretel S. Meier, *Job Sharing: A New Pattern for Quality of Work Life* (Kalamazoo, Mich.: W. E. Upjohn Institute for Employment Research, 1978); Barney Olmstead, "Job Sharing: A New Way to Work," *Personnel Journal*, vol. 56 (February 1977), pp. 78–81; Robert I. Lazer, "Job Sharing as a Pattern for Permanent Part-Time Work," *Conference Board Record*, Volume 12, no. 10 (October 1975), pp. 57–61; Felice N. Schwartz, "New Work Patterns for Better Use of Woman Power," *Management Review*, vol. 63 (May 1974), pp. 5–12; Christina Scordato and Julie Harris, "Workplace Flexibility," *HR Magazine*, vol. 35 (January 1990), pp. 75–78.

48. Greenwald and Liss, op. cit.

49. Edward G. Thomas, "Flextime Doubles in a Decade," *Management World*, vol. 16 (May 1987), pp. 18–19.

50. John M. Ivancevich and H. C. Lyon, "The Shortened Workweek: A Field Experiment," *Journal of Applied Psychology*, vol. 62 (1977), pp. 41–55.

51. "Effect of Scheduled Overtime," in *Coming to Grips with Some Major Problems in the Construction Industry* (New York: Business Round Table Report, 1974), pp. 1–14.

52. Stu Newman, "Working Alternatives," *Supervision*, vol. 50 (July 1989), pp. 11–13.

53. Sandy Gould, "12-hour-shift Plant Schedule Improves Operator Productivity," *Power Engineering*, vol. 92 (November 1988), pp. 38–39.

54. Lad Kuzela, "Sandy's Working at Home Today," *Industry Week*, vol. 233 (June 1, 1988), pp. 34–35.

55. Janet Ruhl, "Part-time Jobs Are Catching On," *Computer World*, vol. 24 (May 21, 1990), p. 111.

56. Anna Versteeg, "Self-Directed Work Teams Yield Long-Term Benefits," *Journal of Business Strategy*, vol. 11 (November–December 1990), pp. 9–12.

57. The experiments at Volvo and SAAB and many other QWL experiments are described in Paul Dickson, *The Future of the Work Place* (New York: Weybright and Talley, 1975); Ira P. Krepchin, "Report from Sweden: The Human Touch in Automobile Assembly," *Modern Materials Handling*, vol. 45 (November 1990), pp. 52–55.

58. Richard E. Walton, "How to Counter Alienation in the Plant," *Harvard Business Review*, vol. 50 (November–December 1972), pp. 70–81.

59. Personal communication with the consultant of the aggrieved employees.

60. "Self-Directed Work Teams: Are They Effective?" *HR Update*, vol. 11 (July–August 1991), pp. 1–2.

61. Toby D'Wall, Nigel J. Kemp, Paul R. Jackson, and Chris W. Clegg, "Outcomes of Autonomous Workgroups: A Long-term Field Experiment," *Academy of Management Journal*, vol. 29 (1986), pp. 280–304.

62. H. N. Seelye and J. A. Sween, "Quality Circles in U.S. Industry: Survey Results," *Quality Circles Journal*, vol. 5, no. 4 (1982), pp. 26–29.

63. Yunis Kathawala, "A Comparative Analysis of Selected Approaches to Quality," *International Journal of Quality and Reliability Management*, vol. 6, no. 5 (1989), pp. 7–17.

64. William B. Scott, "TQM Expected to Boost Productivity, Insure Survival of U.S. Industry," *Aviation Week and Space Technology*, vol. 131 (December 4, 1989), pp. 64–69; Lawrence M. Tobin, "The New Quality Landscape: Total Quality Management," *Journal of Systems Management*, vol. 41 (November 1990), pp. 10–14.

65. Shoukry D. Saleh, Zengying Guo, and Treat Hull, "The Use of Quality Circles in the Automobile Parts Industry," *IEEE Transactions on Engineering Management*, vol. 37 (August 1990), pp. 198–202.

66. Matthew Goodfellow, "Why Quality Circles Failed at 21 Firms," *Management Review*, vol. 71, no. 9 (September 1982), pp. 56–57.

67. Robert P. Steel and Guy S. Shane, "Evaluation Research on Quality Circles: Technical and Analytical Implications," *Human Relations*, vol. 39 (1986), pp. 449–468.

68. Berkley Rice, "Square Holes for Quality Circles," *Psychology Today*, vol. 18 (February 1984), p. 17.

69. Ernest Blum, "Gap Continues to Grow Between Eastern's Unions and Management," *Travel Weekly*, vol. 45 (December 8, 1986), p. 2; Paul G. Engel, "Union Board Power," *Industry Week*, vol. 220 (February 6, 1984), pp. 52–53.

70. This review is based largely on Henry P. Guzda, "Industrial Democracy: Made in U.S.A.," *Monthly Labor Review*, vol. 107 (May 1984), pp. 26–33; Ron Mitchell, "Rediscovering Our Roots: Quality Circles in the U.S., 1918–1948," *Journal for Quality and Participation*, vol. 10 (December 1987), pp. 56–66.

71. David J. Cherrington, "Lessons from Singapore," *Exchange* (Spring 1983), pp. 12–15; Elaine Gale Wrong, "Labor–Management Conflict Resolution in Switzerland," *Akron Business and Economic Review*, vol. 15 (Spring, 1984), pp. 27–33.

72. William Brock III, "The Importance of Labor–Management Cooperation," *Journal of Labor Research*, vol. 11 (Summer 1990), pp. 225–230.

73. Loretta Ashyk, "A Better Way for LTV Steel?" *Crain's Cleveland Business*, December 10, 1984, pp. 1, 31, 32, 38; M. B. Gary, "Why Our Local Dumped LMPT," *Labor Today*, vol. 25 (March 1986), p. 6; James Lyons and Jim Lang, "QWL to the Max—A Saturn Agreement," *Labor Today*, vol. 25 (March 1986), p. 6; Bryan H. Berry, "Teamwork Boosts LTV's Efficiency," *Iron Age*, vol. 5 (August 1989), pp. 41–45; Brad Stratton, "Steel U.S.A.: The Struggle to Be Profitable," *Quality Progress*, vol. 22 (July 1989), pp. 18–24.

74. Sheila Feigelson, "Mixing Mirth and Management," *Supervision*, vol. 50 (November 1989), pp. 6–8; Barbara Smith Lee, "'Humor Relations' for Nurse Managers," *Nursing Management*, vol. 21 (May 1990), pp. 86–92.

75. Barbara Mandell, "Does a Better Worklife Boost Productivity?" *Personnel*, vol. 66 (October 1989), pp. 48–52.

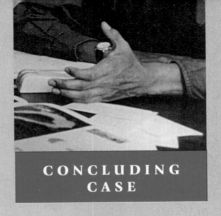

LABOR–MANAGEMENT PARTICIPATION TEAMS

During the 1980s, many employers adopted one variant or another of quality-of-work-life programs. In many instances, unions and their members enthusiastically jumped at the chance to finally have a say about production problems. Occasionally, however, these programs created skepticism or outright resistance.

In 1983, LTV Steel Company negotiated a basic steel agreement with members of the United Steel Workers of America union (USWA) that created a program called labor–management participation teams (LMPTs). The union was willing to accept the company's invitation to participate in these committees because at that time the steel industry faced massive layoffs and the closure of several steel mills. For a time, it appeared that the entire hot end of the steel industry would entirely disappear from the United States.

The LMPTs were not entirely new. In the early 1970s, the steel companies and the USWA worked together in what was then called *productivity committees.* The benefits of these committees were somewhat mixed. Although they produced some valuable suggestions for increasing productivity, the union criticized the steel companies for attempting to weasel productivity ideas out of union members without paying for these ideas. Furthermore, the union claimed that the goal of these committees was to eventually combine or eliminate jobs and, ultimately, to eliminate the union.

After two years of participating in the LMPTs, the members of USWA Local 1033 at LTV Steel company's South Chicago plant voted to discontinue their participation. The desire to scrap the LMPTs was not universal, however, and some union members wanted to continue the cooperative effort. The company was reluctant to abandon the LMPTs and tried to continue meeting with union representatives in spite of the resistance.

An article written by two members of USWA Local 1033 explained why the union rejected LMPTs. The union criticized LTV for trying to manipulate the union by encouraging union members sympathetic to the LMPTs to disrupt union meetings. The union alleged that at a membership meeting the company planted about forty union members and had them demonstrate in favor of restoring the LMPTs.

The union also criticized LTV for using LMPTs to circumvent the labor agreement, especially the grievance process:

> Even before 1983, the company had begun to ignore grievances and the grievers and increased their violations of the contract. But with the advent of LMPTs, the company began to engage in a total stonewalling of the grievance procedure, circumventing the grievers whenever possible . . .
>
> Instead of making progress with the union through our bargained procedure, the company kept pushing the LMPTs, encouraging workers to 'talk to your team' about the water fountain, about the parking lot, about all the frills and none of the real issues.

Since the company failed to participate with us, the union could see no reason to continue in a one-sided labor–management team which was neither fair nor just, neither democratic nor reasonable.

We could only see how the company was trying to use the teams to stifle the militancy of our members and to undercut the union's fight. . . .

Historically speaking, any time the company has 'offered' workers the 'opportunity to participate on a management team', they have really had in mind how to get more from us for less and how to undermine our unity and strength. Today's LMPTs are no exception.

Questions

1. What are the potential benefits of an LMPT for the company? What are the potential benefits of an LMPT for the union?

2. What are the union's criticisms about the LMPTs, and are these criticisms reasonable?

3. Why did the LMPT fail at LTV Steel, and what should this company or any other company do differently to successfully implement a quality-of-work-life program?

Source: James Lyons and Jim Lang, "QWL to the Max—a 'Saturn' Agreement," *Labor Today,* vol. 25 (March 1986), p. 7.

MEASURING GROWTH NEED STRENGTH

Purpose. The job characteristics model of job enrichment shows that people respond differently to job enrichment programs depending on the strength of their individual growth needs. This exercise is designed to measure your growth need strength and help you understand more about it by comparing your score with the scores of your classmates.

A Measure of Growth Need Strength

Instructions

People differ in what they like and dislike in their jobs. Listed here are twelve pairs of jobs. For each pair, indicate which job you would prefer. Assume that everything else about the jobs is the same—pay attention only to the characteristics actually listed for each pair of jobs.

If you would prefer the job in the left-hand column (Job A), indicate how much you prefer it by putting a checkmark in a blank to the left of the "neutral" point. If you prefer the job in the right-hand column (Job B), check one of the blanks to the right of "neutral." Check the "neutral" blank only if you find the two jobs equally attractive or unattractive. Try to use the "neutral" blank rarely.

Job A		Job B
1. A job where the pay is very good.	Strongly prefer A — Neutral — Strongly prefer B	A job where there is considerable opportunity to be creative and innovative.
2. A job where you are often required to make important decisions.	Strongly prefer A — Neutral — Strongly prefer B	A job with many pleasant people to work with.
3. A job in which greater responsibility is given to those who do the best work.	Strongly prefer A — Neutral — Strongly prefer B	A job in which greater responsibility is given to loyal employees who have the most seniority.
4. A job in an organization that is in financial trouble—and might have to close down within the year.	Strongly prefer A — Neutral — Strongly prefer B	A job in which you are not allowed to have any say whatever in how your work is scheduled or in the procedures to be used in carrying it out.
5. A very routine job.	Strongly prefer A — Neutral — Strongly prefer B	A job where your co-workers are not very friendly.
6. A job with a supervisor who is often very critical of you and your work in front of other people.	Strongly prefer A — Neutral — Strongly prefer B	A job that prevents you from using a number of skills that you worked hard to develop.
7. A job with a supervisor who respects you and treats you fairly.	Strongly prefer A — Neutral — Strongly prefer B	A job that provides constant opportunities for you to learn new and interesting things.

8. A job where there is a real chance you could be laid off.

|L____|____|____|____|____|
Strongly prefer A   Neutral   Strongly prefer B

A job with very little chance to do challenging work.

9. A job in which there is a real chance for you to develop new skills and advance in the organization.

|L____|____|____|____|____|
Strongly prefer A   Neutral   Strongly prefer B

A job that provides lots of vacation time and an excellent fringe benefit package.

10. A job with little freedom and independence to do your work in the way you think best.

|L____|____|____|____|____|
Strongly prefer A   Neutral   Strongly prefer B

A job where the working conditions are poor.

11. A job with very satisfying teamwork.

|L____|____|____|____|____|
Strongly prefer A   Neutral   Strongly prefer B

A job that allows you to use your skills and abilities to the fullest extent.

12. A job that offers little or no challenge.

|L____|____|____|____|____|
Strongly prefer A   Neutral   Strongly prefer B

A job that requires you to be completely isolated from co-workers.

Source: J. R. Hackman and G. R. Oldman (1974), *The Job Diagnostic Survey: An Instrument for the Diagnosis of Jobs and the Evaluation of Job Redesign Projects,* Technical Report No. 4, New Haven, Conn.: Yale University Department of Administrative Sciences, pp. 1–2.

Scoring. Each of the 12 items uses a five-point scale. However, the direction of the scale is reversed for half the items. "Strongly prefer A" is scored 1, and "Strongly prefer B" is scored 5 for these items: 1, 5, 7, 10, 11, and 12. On the other six items (2, 3, 4, 6, 8, and 9), the scoring is reversed, so that "Strongly prefer A" is scored 5, and "Strongly prefer B" is scored 1. Compute your growth need strength score by averaging the numbers you indicated for all twelve items. To help you interpret your score, the authors of this instrument report that the mean growth need score is approximately 3.0. Therefore, individuals who have growth need scores greater than 3.0 tend to prefer jobs where they have greater opportunities for personal growth and self-actualization.

Questions

1. How does your score compare with the scores of your classmates? As you compare your scores, does it seem intuitively right to you?

2. What types of jobs have you performed, and how enriched have they been? Does your growth need score appear to be related to your job satisfaction and productivity on these jobs?

Job Attitudes and Behavior

LEARNING OBJECTIVES

After studying this chapter, you should be able to

1. Define *attitudes,* and explain the difference between attitudes and beliefs.

2. Explain how attitudes and beliefs are formed and changed.

3. Describe the concept of behavioral intentions and how it relates to both attitudes and behaviors.

4. Explain the relationship between attitudes and behaviors and why it is typically so weak.

5. Define the concept of values, and explain how values are developed.

6. Explain how job involvement, organizational commitment, and work values are created and how they are related to behavior.

7. Explain the concept of job satisfaction, and describe three theories that can be used to explain changes in job satisfaction.

8. Explain how to measure job satisfaction, and summarize the results of studies measuring the overall levels of satisfaction in society.

9. Describe the relationships between job satisfaction and employee behaviors such as performance, attendance, turnover, and physical and mental health.

HOW DO YOU FEEL ABOUT YOUR JOB?

These comments were made by people when asked how they feel about their job.

SEWING MACHINE OPERATOR—ABOUT 40 YEARS OLD, MOTHER OF THREE

I have the best job in the world. I come here every morning and check out what we're doing. Then I turn my hands on and my mind is free to go where it wants. I like to recite stuff and I do it all day long—mostly Shakespeare and the New Testament. I like [Shakespeare's] sonnets because I had a class on them. I used to memorize a lot more than I do now, but I still love finding something new to learn. It's too noisy to talk to anyone, so I just talk to myself. It makes time fly by, and I work faster; I usually get my work done in six hours and then sometimes I go home and take care of the family. I don't think I could ask for a better job.

CUSTOMER SUPPORT—ABOUT 25 YEARS OLD, HUSBAND, SOLVES CUSTOMER PROBLEMS BY TELEPHONE

I hate my job; it's terrible. Its definitely a high-stress job. We never get to see the customers we help; we have to answer one question after another; and some of the people are just plain stupid. We never see any productivity. . . . Actually, it isn't really stressful, but you have to concentrate. . . . I feel like an animal on a chain with my headset on. Sunday nights I feel really depressed just thinking that tomorrow I'm back on the phones. I can't even enjoy the weekend, 'cause I know it's going to end. . . . The only decent thing I like is the people I work with. We visit during breaks and between calls. I don't think anyone really likes this job—they're just waiting for something better. Karen is putting her husband through college; Kim is waiting to go to law school; and the rest are hoping to get advanced to something else, like programing. I'm going to quit in 325 days and there are exactly 1,203 more hours I have to spend on phones.

Questions

1. How can these differences in job attitudes be explained? Is job satisfaction a function of the job requirements, the interactions with others, the need to think, or something else?

2. How much do individual personalities contribute to differences in job attitudes?

ATTITUDES

Attitudes are involved in almost every aspect of organizational life. Employees have attitudes about hundreds of things, including their pay, their supervisors, top management, the work they do, and their co-workers. Outstanding employees are commended for their good attitudes, while uncooperative workers are reprimanded for having bad attitudes. Managers worry about the effects of their decisions on employee attitudes and about whether the employees will resist change. Events that occur away from work influence the attitudes of employees, who carry these attitudes into the work setting. Customers form attitudes about the quality of a company's products and services, and their buying behavior influences organizational survival and effectiveness. Consequently attitudes play an important role in the study of organizational behavior.

Knowing about attitudes is important for four reasons. First, in some situations attitudes influence behavior. For many years, managers assumed that happy workers were more productive, and they tried to increase productivity by increasing job satisfaction. Years of research have shown that the relationship between attitudes and behavior is not so simple. The relationship appears to be a reciprocal interaction in which attitudes and behavior influence each other, and managers need to understand this interaction.

The second reason for studying attitudes is because favorable job attitudes are desirable for humanitarian reasons. Creating positive job attitudes is a worthwhile goal regardless of whether it leads to higher productivity.

The third reason for studying attitudes is because so many organizational programs are designed to create positive attitudes. Programs such as leadership training, career counseling, and job enrichment are created in part to improve employee attitudes.

Finally, a fourth reason for studying attitudes is because they play an important role in many organizational behavior theories, especially theories of motivation. An understanding of attitudes is necessary to comprehend the intricacies of these theories.

What Are Attitudes?

An **attitude** is a "hypothetical construct"; it is not something real or something you can see, taste, or touch. Consequently, it is something that exists only because we can define it or infer it from the things people say or do.

An attitude is defined as the positive or negative feelings one holds toward an object. Therefore, when we speak of positive job attitudes we mean the pleasant feelings one has when one thinks about one's jobs. However, it is possible to have positive feelings about some aspects of the job and negative feelings about other aspects.

Attitude Objects. People have specific attitudes toward specific objects, including both physical objects (such as people, places, and things) and nonphysical objects (such as ideas and beliefs). Some of the most relevant attitude objects in the study of organizational behavior are those associated with the job, such as the job itself, pay, working conditions, supervision, and one's co-workers. These job attitudes are what comprise job satisfaction or dissatisfaction, and we will discuss them in a later section. Self-esteem consists of the attitudes we have about ourselves. The different aspects of personality, such as intelligence, integrity, and talents, may serve as the objects of self-esteem attitudes. Personal values can be viewed as attitudes, the object of which is an idea or an abstract concept such as pride in craftsmanship, loyalty, and organizational commitment. These values are also examined in later sections.

Components of Attitudes. The early research on attitudes identified three attitude components: cognitive, affective, and behavioral tendency.[1] The **cognitive component** is the information a person possesses about the attitude object. This information includes descriptive data such as facts, figures, and other specific knowledge. The **affective component** is the person's feelings and emotions toward the attitude object. This component involves evaluation and emotion and is often expressed as a liking or disliking for the attitude object. The behavioral tendency component is the way the person intends to behave toward the object, such as whether the person is inclined to follow, help, injure, abandon, or ignore the attitude object.

Attitudes are best viewed as a combination of the cognitive and affective components, as illustrated in Exhibit 7.1. For example, your attitude about working overtime consists of cognitive information, such as knowing you will get more money and knowing the job is important and needs to be completed, combined with affective feelings, such as the desire for more money or the dislike of feeling tired. The kind of information you have and how you feel about it determines your attitude. The behavioral tendency component is best viewed as a separate construct that may or may not be consistent with the cognitive and affective components. For example, just because you have a positive attitude about working overtime does not mean you will have a positive behavioral tendency to do it ("I'd like to stay and help you, but I have tickets to the ball game"). The relationship between attitudes and behavioral intentions are examined later.

Attitude Formation.[2] Personal attitudes are formed when affective feelings are attached to beliefs. These affective feelings can be either conditioned emotions or feelings associated with personal values. Emotions are classically conditioned responses associated with a conditioned stimulus, as explained in Chapter 3. The conditioned stimulus creating the emotion could be any stimulus in the environment, including another person. Criticism by a supervisor, for example, usually arouses an emotion of anger or defensiveness because these emotions have been conditioned to criticisms. Attitudes toward the supervisor are formed when these feelings are combined with data (beliefs) about the supervisor.[3]

EXHIBIT 7.1   The Components of Attitudes and Values

Attitudes and Values	
Affective component	Cognitive component
• Feelings	• Knowledge
• Emotions	• Beliefs

Affective feelings are also associated with personal values, since values indicate what is important and desirable and what we feel good about. These feelings can be generalized to other attitude objects. Values produce a more stable affective component than the temporary nature of emotions.

Three different types of **beliefs** have been identified, each formed by a different means: observational beliefs, inferential beliefs, and external information.[4] **Observational beliefs** are formed on the basis of our own observations. For example, the belief that our job is repetitive and dirty comes from performing the same tasks over and over in a filthy environment.

Inferential beliefs result from the logical connections we make between certain thoughts or events. For example, if you think salary is associated with status, you infer that your supervisor earns more than you do. Knowing that it is true in one or more instances makes you feel certain that your belief is correct. Although you may feel very secure about your inferences, they may be wrong. A person's beliefs need to be internally consistent. Inconsistent beliefs create a state of tension that motivates a person to correct this state of inconsistency.

A third source of beliefs comes from **external information,** such as other people, newspapers, or television. The beliefs acquired from external sources are similar to the beliefs formed from personal observations, except that they are not as stable. In general, the beliefs acquired through personal observations tend to be more resistant to change than those learned from logical inferences or external sources. However, beliefs acquired from inferences and external sources may also be very stable and resistant to change if they are part of a mutually reinforcing cluster of other beliefs and values.[5]

How Stable Are Attitudes? The stability of attitudes varies dramatically, depending on the individual, the attitude, and the situational context. Evidence shows that when people are placed in a different social context, their attitudes can change dramatically. For example, the attitudes of union employees in one manufacturing company were very antimanagement. However, when certain union members were promoted into managerial ranks, their attitudes became substantially more pro-management. A short time later, however, some of these supervisors returned to the ranks of the union because the workforce was reduced, and almost immediately their attitudes returned to being antimanagement.[6]

There is also evidence to suggest that some attitudes are remarkably stable over time and in different situations. A study evaluating how employees perceived certain job characteristics, such as autonomy, variety, and feedback, found that these attitudes were remarkably stable over a three-month period. However, the emotional reactions of job satisfaction and satisfaction with the supervisor were not especially stable and showed considerable variation among some employees.[7] As a general rule, emotions are very unstable and often change dramatically in a short time, while attitudes are much more stable.

An **information-processing theory** has been proposed to explain how additional information contributes to attitude formation.[8] According to this theory, an attitude is an integration of the evaluative meanings regarding a set of beliefs held in the memory of an individual. The memory function includes both long-term and short-term memory. Long-term memory provides the ongoing storage of information about an attitude, while short-term memory processes and interprets new incoming information. As we interact with our surroundings, we continually gather additional information about attitude objects. This information is interpreted and analyzed in short-term memory with the help of information that has been stored in long-term memory. Long-term memory provides a framework for evaluating new information that may bias, distort, or emphasize portions of it. In this way, the contents of long-term memory contribute to the stability of our attitudes and beliefs by influencing how we perceive and interpret new information. The most relevant portions of the information in short-term memory are retained and moved into long-term memory.

Attitude Change

Occasionally we want to change employee attitudes. Because some attitudes resist change, it is important to know how to change them and what the likelihood is of succeeding. Attitude change can involve the addition, removal, or modification of either the beliefs or the affective components. Four of the most popular methods of changing attitudes include providing new information, fear arousal and reduction, dissonance arousal and reduction, and participating in a group discussion.[9]

Providing New Information. The most popular method of changing attitudes is to provide new information that alters beliefs. Since attitudes are a composite of the feelings and beliefs, attitudes can be changed by creating new beliefs or changing the present ones. The effectiveness of new information depends on whether the individual perceives the source of the new information as being credible and believable. In general, the most credible sources are people who are considered expert, unbiased, and likable. For example, your attitude about the value of a new training program could be changed more easily by a close friend who recently completed it than by an external consultant who wants to sell it to you. Persuasive communication is discussed further in Chapter 13.

Fear Arousal and Reduction. The use of fear in changing attitudes has been examined in a variety of studies and is also discussed further in Chapter 13. The results of this research suggest that mild fear increases the likelihood of attitude change, because people are more attentive to the message and motivated to change. Beyond a certain point, however, intense fear in the form of severe threats and punishments tends to reduce the probability of attitude change. Apparently the presence of moderate fear causes individuals to be more attentive and willing to change their attitudes, while extreme fear causes them to completely ignore or reject the fear message.

Dissonance Arousal and Reduction. Extensive research has shown that people try to maintain consistency between their beliefs, attitudes, and behaviors. This theory, called *cognitive dissonance theory,* states that when people behave in a way that is inconsistent with their attitudes and beliefs, they experience tension and a need to reduce this tension.[10] For example, suppose you agreed to circulate a petition to request a union election, but your basic attitudes are antiunion because you believe unions have made exorbitantly high wage demands. In this situation, you would experience intense cognitive dissonance because your behavior in support of the union is inconsistent with your antiunion attitude. Because cognitive dissonance is uncomfortable, you would try to re-establish a condition of cognitive consistency by doing one of two things. Your first effort would probably be to recant your offer to circulate the petition. But if you can't get out of it gracefully and feel compelled to complete the assignment, you would probably change your attitude and think more positively about labor unions.

Participation in Group Discussion. The effects of a group discussion on changing attitudes is mentioned here and described more fully in later chapters. Studies in group decision making have shown that the opportunity to participate in a group discussion provides a powerful force for changing individual attitudes.[11] Several explanations have been proposed to explain why group discussions are so effective. When people are considering a change in their behavior or attitudes, they are reinforced when they see others in the same position make a similar change. Furthermore, when people participate in a group discussion, they are forced to come to a decision point and publicly commit themselves to change. This sort of active involvement is far more effective than passively listening to new information. Furthermore, if the decision is reached by a unanimous group consensus, responsibility for the change does not belong solely to one individual but is shared by everyone in the group. The effectiveness of group discussions in changing attitudes explains why they are used so frequently in the form of task forces, committees, and quality circles.

The Relationship Between Attitudes and Behavior

We often assume that attitudes cause behavior; therefore, if you want to get people to change their behavior, you must first get them to change their attitudes. Unfortunately, the relationship is much more complex. The relationship between attitudes and behavior appears to be a reciprocal interaction in which each factor influences the other, as shown in Exhibit 7.2. Attitudes influence behavior by first influencing the behavioral intentions, whereas behavior influences attitudes by requiring individuals to justify their behavior.

Behavioral Intentions. Most of our attitudes do not have a direct impact on our behavior. We have an enormous number of attitudes about countless objects, and only a small percentage of these attitudes ever get translated into behavior. An intervening process between attitudes and behavior is **behavioral intentions,** the extent to which we actually expect to perform a given act.

Intentions are similar to goals, but they are more than goals. An *intention* is defined as a cognitive representation of both the objective (or goal) you are striving for and the action plan you intend to use to reach your objective. Intentions can range along a continuum of abstraction. They can be very specific, such as to call a client or to take a patient's blood pressure, or they can also be very general, such as to increase sales or to provide quality patient care.[12]

According to the model shown in Exhibit 7.2, attitudes affect behavior only to the extent that they influence our intentions to act. To illustrate, suppose you have a dozen positive attitudes about safety and the importance of safe working procedures. You have heard countless safety lectures about accidents and how easily they could have been avoided, and you believed all you heard. You even agree that safety reports reduce accidents by emphasizing the need for safety. Nevertheless, you may not intend to submit your weekly accident report on time because of more pressing responsibilities. And even though you believe safety belts save lives, you may not intend to wear them all the time.

EXHIBIT 7.2   Reciprocal Interaction of Attitudes and Behavior

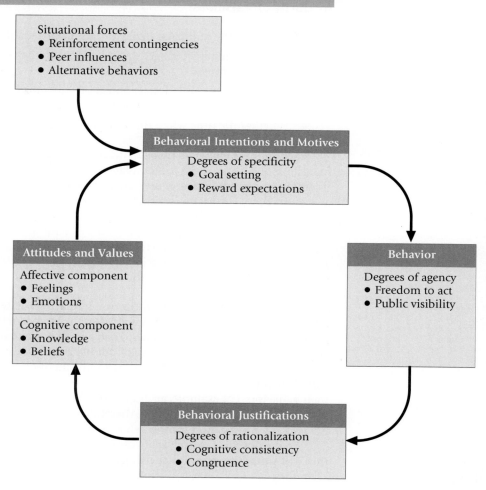

So the next question is "How are behavioral intentions formed?" The model indicates that behavioral intentions are influenced to some extent by attitudes, but they are also influenced by other situational forces that may be more important:

- Reinforcement contingencies providing specific rewards or punishments
- Normative pressures from peer expectations and group norms
- Random situational influences and alternative behaviors

The relationship between attitudes and behavioral intentions is not especially strong. However, the effects of behavioral intentions on behavior tend to be much stronger if our intentions are specific and not limited by environmental constraints. People usually strive to do what they intend to do.[13]

Specificity of Intentions. As explained in Chapter 3, goal setting and reward expectations have a sizable impact on our behavioral intentions and help us develop specific intentions to act. Specific intentions, once formed, are usually associated with specific behaviors. Four elements determine the degree of **specificity of intentions:**

1. How well the particular behavior has been visualized in clear detail
2. Whether the target object toward which the behavior will be directed has been determined
3. How clearly the situational context in which the behavior will be performed has been defined, including where and with whom
4. Whether the time when the behavior should occur has been established[14]

Each of these elements helps to determine whether the behavior is specifically identified or only loosely contemplated. The most specific situation involves an intention to perform a clearly defined act toward a specific target in a defined place at a given time. For example, the behavioral intention to "learn something about computers as soon as it's convenient" is a very loosely defined behavioral intention that would not have as much impact on behavior as the behavioral intention to "meet Larry in the computer lab tomorrow at 10 A.M. to learn how to format a disk." To the extent that distinct behaviors are specifically articulated, the intentions are more closely tied to actual behavior.

Behavioral Justifications.   The reciprocal interaction between attitudes and behaviors, as illustrated in Exhibit 7.2, emphasizes the impact of behavior on attitudes. An intervening process between behavior and attitudes is **behavioral justifications:** our efforts to interpret and make sense of our behavior. One explanation of this idea is called *self-perception theory.*[15] According to this theory, people form attitudes as a result of their behaviors—their attitudes are formed as a rationale or justification for their behaviors. For example, an employee who continues to perform a repetitive job may say, "I continue to do this job, therefore I must like it." Here, the attitude "I like my job" is a justification for the behavior of continuing to perform it.

We do not view ourselves or others as capricious, random actors. We like to think of ourselves as rational beings whose behavior is conscious and planned. Therefore, we feel a need to explain and justify our behavior both to others and especially to ourselves. According to consistency theory and cognitive dissonance theory, our attitudes and behaviors need to be in harmony. When they are dissonant, the easiest way to create harmony is by changing one's attitudes.

According to this model, the effects of behavior on attitudes are a function of the felt need to justify behavior. Therefore, the amount of attitude change increases as the need to justify behavior increases. This occurs when (1) people are asked to explain their behavior, (2) when the explanation is a public declaration, (3) when there are alternative ways to behave, and (4) when they are free to choose how to behave.

VALUES

Personal values play an important role in understanding individual behavior and how people respond in organizations. In fact, the importance of understanding values has already been observed in our study of perception and rewards. Our values influence our perceptions by causing us to selectively attend to attractive stimuli consistent with our values. Our values also determine whether a particular outcome will be rewarding. Sometimes a brief event, such as a handwritten thank-you note, is a highly valued reward because it is an intrinsic reward consistent with the person's values of pride in craftsmanship. This section explains how values are formed and describes three significant values: job involvement, organizational commitment, and the work ethic.

What Are Values?

A **value** is defined as a constellation of attitudes about a concept that contains a moral quality of like or dislike, desirable or undesirable, and should or should not. To say that a particular concept is a value, such as honesty, loyalty, or beauty, is to say that the concept is desirable, important, and personally meaningful. Our values define the things that we strive for, extol, embrace, and celebrate if it is a positive value. Concepts that we ignore, reject, avoid, escape from, or attack constitute negative values.

Once a value constellation has become internalized, it serves either consciously or subconsciously as a standard or criterion for guiding our actions. Values are the criteria we use in assessing our daily lives, arranging priorities, measuring pleasures and pains, and choosing between alternative courses of action. Values affect our perceptions of what we see and also our interpretation of the sensations we receive. Like attitudes, values do not exist as actual, physical objects. They are hypothetical constructs that help us understand the way people think and behave. An important difference, however, between attitudes and values is that values are more generalized than attitudes and possess a moral quality of "ought" or "should."

Many values come from interaction with culture. In fact, the entire social system is designed to teach and reinforce the values society deems appropriate. These values are taught and reinforced by parents, teachers, supervisors, and civic leaders in a variety of settings. Although the most significant value learning occurs in the home during early formative years, many values continue to be shaped and formed in other settings, especially school and work.

A **cultural value** is something that is widely believed throughout a society to be desirable or worthy of esteem for its own sake. Honesty, cooperation, and patriotism are examples of well-established cultural values. Even though many values are widely shared, not everyone holds the same values. The Rokeach Scale of Values, one of the most popular instruments for measuring values, identifies six values: intellectual, economic, aesthetic, social, political, and religious. Studies of values among people in different occupations suggest that managers usually score higher than average on economic values, while college professors score higher than average on intellectual values.[16]

Moral Development

Research on moral development helps to explain how values are acquired. Most of the research has focused on three moral behaviors: aggression, honesty, and prosocial behaviors, especially altruism. Theories of moral development help to explain why some people espouse certain important values while others do not.

Moral values do not always produce moral behaviors; studies have shown that the relationship between moral values and moral behaviors is not a direct relationship.[17] Moral behaviors are influenced by our moral values plus other situational forces. Occasionally these outside forces are strong enough to override the influence of our values and we may behave contrary to our own personal values. For example, even though employees may have high standards of integrity, they may still commit theft or fraud because of situational pressures, such as an intense need for money, and convenient opportunities. Two theories have been proposed to explain how moral values are acquired. These two theories are Lawrence Kohlberg's cognitive-developmental stage theory and social cognitive theory.

Cognitive-Developmental Stage Theory. Kohlberg's theory of moral development (**cognitive-developmental stage theory**) is based on the sequential development of increasingly complex cognitive or mental structures that allow people to think more abstractly and to acquire a greater understanding of the extended consequences of their behavior.[18] Kohlberg identified six stages of moral reasoning, which he separated into three levels as shown in Exhibit 7.3. The first two stages are in level I, which he called the *preconventional level*. This level is particularly characteristic of young children. Stage 1 is oriented toward obedience to avoid punishment, while stage 2 is a naively egotistic orientation seeking rewards and need satisfaction. Here the right way to behave is defined as what is fair and what creates an equal exchange or agreement.

The moral development of a person in stage 3 is oriented toward social approval and pleasing others. Stage 3 individuals feel a concern for others and are able to develop a perspective of seeing their own personal interests relative to someone else's. Stages 3 and 4 are called the *conventional level*, since they focus on following social conventions. As people advance to Stage 4, they extend their level of thinking from another individual to a collection of individuals in a social group or an organization. These people can adopt the point of view of the system or organization that defines the rules and standards. In this stage, right and wrong are defined in terms of fulfilling social responsibilities within organizations and thereby contributing to society or the organization.

Stages 5 and 6 comprise level III, the *postconventional* or principle level of moral reasoning. At this level, people define right and wrong according to their own carefully considered standards rather than the conventions of society. In stage 5, people are aware that people hold a variety of values and that most values and rules are relative to their group. Although they agree that these relative rules should usually be upheld, they recognize the potential inadequacy or incompleteness inherent within rules, and the need for supplementing the social contract beyond the specific rules. In stage 6, Kohlberg's highest level of moral reasoning, people follow their self-chosen ethical principles based on universal principles of justice, the equality of human rights, and respect for the dignity of human beings as individuals. Here moral reasoning is based on personal conscience as a directing agent and on mutual respect and trust.

Kohlberg's theory of moral development suggests that values are acquired through a process of thinking and reasoning. An important event that helps people advance to a higher stage is to experience conflict in explaining their opinions when interacting with people who are at higher levels. For example, when people in stage 3 debate with others whose reasoning is at stage 4, they experience conflict that forces them to consider more carefully about the basis of their thinking. According to Kohlberg, the majority of college students are at stages 3 and 4, the conventional level of moral development.[19]

EXHIBIT 7.3   Stages of Moral Development

Level and Stage	Defining What Is Right
Level I: Preconventional **Stage 1:** Heteronomous morality	To avoid breaking rules backed by punishment, and avoiding physical damage to persons and property; obedience is required for its own sake.
Stage 2: Individualism and instrumental exchange	Following rules only when it is in your immediate interest; acting to satisfy your own interests and needs and letting others do the same. Right is also what is fair, what is an equal exchange, a deal, an agreement.
Level II: Conventional **Stage 3:** Mutual interpersonal expectations and conformity	The need to be a good person in your own eyes and the eyes of others. Caring for others. Belief in the Golden Rule. Desire to maintain rules and authority that support stereotypical good behavior.
Stage 4: Social system and conscience	Contributing to society, the group, or institution and fulfilling the actual duties to which you have agreed as an imperative of conscience. To keep the institution going and avoid the breakdown in the system that would occur "if everyone did it."
Level III: Postconventional or principled **Stage 5:** Social contract and individual rights	A sense of obligation to make and abide by laws for the welfare of all and for the protection of all people's rights. Concern that laws and duties be based on a rational calculation of overall utility: "the greatest good for the greatest number."
Stage 6: Universal ethical principles	Following self-chosen ethical principles. The belief as a rational person in the validity of universal moral principles, and a sense of personal commitment to them. The principles are universal principles of justice: the equality of human rights and respect for the dignity of human beings as individual persons.

Source: Adapted from Lawrence Kohlberg, "Moral Stages and Moralization: The Cognitive-Developmental Approach," in *Moral Development and Behavior: Theory, Research, and Social Issues,* Thomas Lickona, ed. (New York: Holt, Rinehart and Winston, 1976), pp. 34–35. Used with permission.

Social Cognitive Theory. The **social cognitive theory** of moral development claims that moral values are learned responses acquired through experience.[20] This theory emphasizes the role of antecedent and consequent environmental events, especially the presence or absence of a model displaying moral behaviors, and seeing this behavior reinforced. According to social cognitive theory, the most effective method for learning moral behaviors is to observe someone else displaying that behavior and to see it reinforced. According to social cognitive theory, people do not acquire values in a fixed sequence; instead, values are acquired in whatever sequence they are modeled and reinforced.

Job Involvement

Job involvement is a work value that has been loosely defined as the strength of the relationship between an individual's work and his or her self-concept. People are said to be highly involved in their jobs if they (1) actively participate in them, (2) view their jobs as central life interests, and (3) see their jobs and how well they perform as a central part of their self-concepts.[21]

People who are highly involved in their jobs tend to be ego involved with their work. They spend long hours working at their jobs and think about them when they are away from work. If a project they have completed fails, they may feel intense feelings of personal frustration and despair. When they perform poorly, they feel embarrassed and disappointed. Because they identify with their work, they want others to know them for their work and to know that they do it well. For a highly job-involved person, work is the most important aspect of life.

Causes of Job Involvement. Job involvement seems to result from a combination of personal characteristics and organizational factors. People tend to display greater job involvement if they are more committed to the work ethic or if they define their self-concepts according to their job performance. Higher job involvement has also been associated with the length of time a person has performed the job and the extent to which the job is enriched and provides people with an opportunity to participate in making important job decisions. Consequently, job involvement results from a combination of the individual value orientations of the worker and desirable job characteristics that reward greater involvement.

Consequences of Job Involvement. What are the consequences of job involvement, and is it a good thing? Some evidence indicates that people who are highly involved in their jobs tend to be more satisfied than those who are not as involved. The evidence also indicates that employees who are highly involved in their jobs are likely to be happier with the organization, more committed to it, and absent less frequently.[22] This evidence suggests that job involvement is a desirable characteristic that managers ought to encourage. However, an important question is whether job involvement can be carried to an unhealthy or undesirable extreme.

Some individuals become so highly involved in their job that they become workaholics. A *workaholic* is someone who is literally addicted to work. By definition, the addiction is an unhealthy condition in which the individual feels an uncontrollable need to work incessantly.[23] The need to work can arise from many different sources. People may feel anxious or guilt ridden and turn to work as a means to salve their conscience; or they may suffer from feelings of insecurity and turn to work to obtain a sense of permanence, usefulness, and competence. Some people rely on their work to support their feelings of self-righteousness and self-worth.

A central element defining a workaholic is an irrational commitment to excessive work. Workaholics are unable to take time off from their job or to comfortably divert their interests.

Someone who works long hours and has an intense interest in work is not necessarily a workaholic. Defining the word that way would be like calling anyone who drinks alcohol an alcoholic. The characteristics that are missing are an addiction and an inability to function normally. Many outstanding workers have been called **workaholics** mistakenly. Some people consider work their real hobby;

APPLYING ORGANIZATIONAL BEHAVIOR
IN THE NEWS

A Successful Work Ethic

CNN The road to success for S. Truett Cathy, owner and operator of Chick-fil-A, followed the pathway of diligence and hard work. He believes that commitment, dedication, and desire are important personal attributes, not just because they lead to success, but because they are fundamental virtues of a good character.

As a boy, Truett Cathy didn't have much. His father's rural insurance route was shattered by the Depression and his mother supported the family by running their home as a boardinghouse. He learned at an early age that if he wanted a bicycle or a wagon, he had to earn it.

Cathy's first taste of business came at home, where all seven Cathy children were expected to help shop, cook, and clean to support the family. But to earn cash, Cathy had to look outside the home. When he was 8, he discovered that he could buy a six-pack of Coca-Colas for a quarter and sell them to his neighbors for a nickel apiece. Soon he was buying Cokes by the case and making forty cents profit on each case.

When Cathy left the army in 1946, he and his brother, Ben, bought a piece of land and opened the Dwarf Grill, a 24-hour, six-day-a-week coffee shop. Cathy rented a room next door so he could mind the shop and always be available. Two years later, Ben was killed in a plane accident and Truett was left to carry on alone. Three years after Ben's death, he opened a second Dwarf Grill and continued to experiment with different recipes to please his customers.

During the 1960s, Cathy developed a chicken-breast sandwich recipe that was extremely popular with his customers. Through diligence and hard work, he expanded his Chick-fil-A fast-food restaurants into malls and today he has over 460 outlets in thirty-one states. But success has not changed his basic religious beliefs or his work values. The company's mission statement, inscribed on a stone marker outside the headquarters, states, "That we may glorify God by being faithful stewards." In respect for the Sabbath day, Cathy insists on keeping all his outlets closed on Sunday.

Source: CNN *Pinnacle* news programming.

it satisfies their ambitions and is an exciting and exhilarating activity. Many hard workers think that their work is not really work; it is play to them. For example, Mark Twain was well known for the long hours he spent working. But at the age of 73 he wrote, "I have always been able to gain my living without doing any work. I enjoy the writing of books and magazine matter. It was merely billiards to me."[24] Consequently, a distinction needs to be made between job involvement and workaholism.

People can be extremely involved in their jobs without necessarily being workaholics. Not every hard worker is a workaholic. The hard worker may put in long hours and take an extra job in order to meet a mortgage payment or support a child in college. The workaholic, however, puts in long hours all the time not to earn extra money or to oblige a supervisor, but to satisfy an inner compulsion. Both may arrive early, leave late, take work home, and prefer short vacations. But a hard worker retains a sense of meaning and purpose in work, and can place it within the larger context of the meaning of life. For the workaholic, however, life revolves around work and lacks meaning away from work. Hard workers can stop working when they want to and turn to other activities without suffering acute withdrawal pains. Workaholics often try to create the impression that they are indispensable to the organization, and sometimes they are, because of their unwillingness to delegate effectively. Although workaholics may create the impression that they are highly productive workers, such is frequently not the case. Many workaholics lack creativity and are unable to work effectively with other co-workers. Other difficulties associated with workaholics are found away from the job. They tend to be isolated from their friends and strangers to their children. Their marriages frequently suffer greater strains, reducing the quality of family life. To prevent excessive job involvement, some organizations require people to take periodic vacations and insist that they divert their attention for at least brief periods.

Organizational Commitment

Organizational commitment is another personal value, sometimes referred to as *company loyalty* or *company commitment*. Organizational commitment is the relative strength of an individual's identification with and involvement in an organization. Three characteristics are associated with organizational commitment: (1) a strong belief in and acceptance of the organization's values and goals, (2) a willingness to exert considerable effort on behalf of the organization, and (3) a strong desire to maintain membership in the organization.[25] These three characteristics suggest that organizational commitment involves more than mere passive loyalty to the organization. It involves an active relationship with the organization in which employees are willing to give of themselves and make a personal contribution to help the organization succeed.

Causes of Commitment. What causes employees to commit to an organization? Studies on organizational commitment have identified many factors that have been summarized into four categories called "antecedents of organizational commitment."[26]

1. *Personal factors.* Organizational commitment is generally higher among older and more tenured employees. Those who have greater intrinsic work values are more committed.[27] As a group, female employees tend to be more committed to organizations than are males, and employees who have less education also tend to display more commitment than do highly educated employees.

2. *Role-related characteristics.* Organizational commitment tends to be stronger among employees in enriched jobs and jobs that involve low levels of role conflict and ambiguity.[28]

3. *Structural characteristics.* Organizational commitment is stronger among employees in worker-owned cooperatives and among employees in decentralized organizations, who are more involved in making crucial organizational decisions.

4. *Work experiences.* Organizational commitment tends to be stronger among employees who have had favorable experiences at work, such as positive group attitudes among one's peers, feelings that the organization has met the employees' expectations, feelings that the organization could be relied on to fulfill its commitments to its personnel, and feelings that the individual is important to the organization. Employees show more commitment when firms have well-developed recruitment and orientation procedures and well-defined organizational value systems.[29]

One theory suggests that organizational commitment is largely determined by the rewards offered by the organization, particularly financial rewards. Pensions and other benefit plans sometimes constitute so-called golden handcuffs that make it increasingly difficult for employees to consider leaving. However, studies of organizational commitment have identified two different types of commitment called *continuance* and *affective* commitment and these golden handcuffs only increase continuance commitment.[30] Also called **calculative commitment,** continuance commitment is the individual's willingness to remain with a particular organization because of the economic rewards associated with staying. For example, continuance commitment to an organization occurs when employees believe that their organization offers more pay, higher status, friendlier co-workers, and more interesting work than other organizations. Affective commitment, also called **moral commitment,** is the individual's personal acceptance of the organization's values and goals. Employees feel a moral commitment to the organization to the extent that their personal identity and self-esteem are consistent with the goals of the organization.

Consequences of Commitment. Studies on organizational commitment suggest that employees who have high levels of either affective or continuance commitment have better attendance records and are more likely to stay with the company. Consequently, most managers think that affective commitment and loyalty should be cultivated in the workforce as positive social values.[31] Other consequences, however, depend on the nature of the commitment. One study found that job performance correlated positively with affective commitment, but negatively with continuance commitment.[32] Other research has also found that people who have high levels of affective commitment tend to be more satisfied with their jobs, they feel better about their opportunities for career advancement, and they find greater fulfillment in life away from work. These benefits do not seem related to continuance commitment.[33]

There is some indication, however, that extremely high levels of organizational commitment can be undesirable for both the organization and the individual. Extreme levels of commitment tend to reduce the involvement of employees in other organizations and concerns. This loss of interest in other concerns may be particularly dysfunctional for professional and technical employees. One study found that research and development engineers who were more committed to their organization tended to be less creative and innovative than those who showed a greater commitment to their scientific discipline.[34]

Continuance commitment may also be dysfunctional for individual employees. Organizations are complex social systems that are designed primarily to survive. They do not have memories and they do not have hearts; therefore, the intense loyalty people feel for an organization may be very one-sided and leave them open to disappointment and abuse. Top executives may remember who deserves to be rewarded for their loyalty in the past, but senior executives come and go. Loyal service rendered during one era may lose all value and go unrewarded as a new management team evolves. When economic pressures threaten the survival or effectiveness of an organization, many employees who are terminated may justly feel abused because their loyal service for several years has gone unrecognized.

Corporate restructurings brought about by takeovers, leveraged buyouts, and downsizing have altered the meaning of corporate loyalty. Rather than feeling a total fealty to the company, employees are more prone to make short-term commitments with top management to perform their jobs in return for good pay and career advancement. There is a shared recognition that relationships will not be long term.[35]

The Work Ethic

The **work ethic** is the value of work and work-related activities to an individual. Although the work ethic is similar to job involvement and organizational commitment, the work ethic is a broader value that concerns the value of work in one's life. The study of the work ethic largely originated with Max Weber's famous treatise *The Protestant Ethic and the Spirit of Capitalism* (1904–1905).[36] Weber used the term "Protestant work ethic" because it encompassed a philosophy of life that he attributed to the Protestant Reformation. The Protestant work ethic taught that people have a moral and religious obligation to fill their lives with productive work. Dedicated work was seen as a form of worshiping God and serving humanity. Both men and women were expected to spend long hours at work and to lead a strictly regimented life of work and worship in which physical pleasures and enjoyments were limited. Although neither Weber nor the Protestant theologians he quoted said so, many people have come to believe that, in the extreme, the Protestant work ethic demanded heavy physical toil, drudgery, and an ascetic existence devoid of all comforts or pleasures.

For the most part, there are three motives behind a belief in the work ethic:[37]

1. *Terminal value.* Dedicated work is a desirable activity in and of itself. It is considered a mark of good character and equated with industry, perseverance, diligence, and initiative. Some people believe they have a moral obligation to be diligent and industrious.

2. *Instrumental value.* Work is good because of its contribution to society, the community, or an organization. Work itself is not considered a personal virtue; instead, it is instrumental in achieving other virtues such as greater national productivity, organizational effectiveness, personal happiness, self-discipline, or some form of service to society.

3. *Self-worth.* Work is valued for its role in building a person's self-esteem. A worker develops feelings of confidence and mastery by successfully accomplishing a task.

The traditional work ethic consists primarily of two values: the moral importance of work, and pride in craftsmanship. The moral importance of work is the moral obligation that an individual feels to have a job that provides a useful product or service for society. Pride in craftsmanship concerns the quality of performance and involves doing a job well. Surveys of both work values indicate that most Americans have rather strong attitudes about the importance of pride in craftsmanship. They value this attribute highly, and they generally believe in the importance of doing a good job. However, the moral importance of work is not as widely accepted. Some Americans believe they have a moral obligation to perform a useful job but others believe work is not important, and if they had a choice they would choose not to work.[38]

International comparisons suggest that the work ethic is stronger in some countries than others. One study evaluated the meaning of work by asking a representative sample of workers in seven countries if they would continue working even if they won a lottery or inherited a large sum of money. Japan had the highest percentage of employees who said they would continue to work (93 percent), followed by the United States (88), Israel (87), the Netherlands (86), Belgium (84), Germany (70), and Great Britain (68). These differences in work values are generally related to differences in manufacturing productivity of the respective countries.[39]

Causes of the Work Ethic. Studies on the development of the work ethic suggest that it is strongly influenced by childhood experiences and the expectations of significant others, especially parents, in early life. Those who have the strongest work ethic typically come from homes in which children are expected to participate in family chores and work activities. Children who are raised in homes by parents who emphasized discipline and obedience tend to have stronger work values and display greater social responsibility.[40]

Although research indicates that family expectations and early-life experiences play a major role in the development of work values, the work ethic can also be influenced by a variety of organizational experiences among adult employees. Eight principles for developing stronger work values among employees have been proposed. These eight principles, shown in Exhibit 7.4, emphasize the importance of good leadership and supervision.[41]

Consequences of the Work Ethic. Studies on the work ethic suggest that people who have strong work values tend to report greater job satisfaction. However, the relationship is not very strong. Studies have also shown that there is a relationship between the work ethic and job performance. But, this relationship is even weaker. People with strong work values tend to be slightly happier and more productive than those who reject the work ethic, but the work ethic is apparently only one of many variables influencing satisfaction and productivity.[42]

Concern has been expressed that the work ethic in society is declining. Unfortunately we do not have evidence from longitudinal studies to show whether the

---

EXHIBIT 7.4   Principles for Developing the Work Ethic

1. Establish a climate that fosters positive work values and a commitment to excellence.
2. Communicate clear expectations about productivity and high-quality craftsmanship.
3. Teach and explain the value of work, the dignity of labor, and the job of service.
4. Establish individual accountability through effective delegation.
5. Develop personal commitment and involvement through individual choice and participation.
6. Provide feedback on performance through effective performance appraisals.
7. Reward effective performance with pay and other social reinforcers.
8. Continually encourage employees in their personal growth and skill development.

Adapted by permission of the publisher from *The Work Ethic: Working Values and Values That Work* by David J. Cherrington, pp. 181–183 © 1980 by AMACOM, a division of American Management Association. All rights reserved.

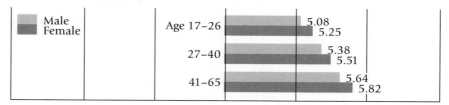

EXHIBIT 7.5   Age Differences in the Responses of Employees to Two Work Values (*N* = 3053)

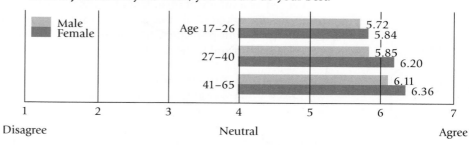

"Working hard makes you a better person."

| Male | | |
| Female | | |

Age 17–26 — 5.08 / 5.25
27–40 — 5.38 / 5.51
41–65 — 5.64 / 5.82

"Even if you dislike your work, you should do your best."

| Male | | |
| Female | | |

Age 17–26 — 5.72 / 5.84
27–40 — 5.85 / 6.20
41–65 — 6.11 / 6.36

1   2   3   4   5   6   7
Disagree   Neutral   Agree

Adapted by permission of the publisher from *The Work Ethic: Working Values and Values That Work* by David J. Cherrington, p. 51 © 1980 by AMACOM, a division of American Management Association. All rights reserved.

work ethic is increasing, decreasing, or remaining constant. However, good evidence suggests the work ethic is associated with age. Older workers generally report much stronger work-oriented values than do younger workers, as shown in Exhibit 7.5. Three explanations have been proposed to explain why older workers have consistently more favorable attitudes toward the work ethic:

1. *Maturity.* As workers become older, their values and perspectives change.
2. *Historical experiences.* Older workers have experienced unique events that taught the value of work, especially the Great Depression and World War II.
3. *Training and indoctrination.* During their youth, older workers were taught work values that differ from values taught to younger workers.[43]

JOB SATISFACTION

Some of the most important attitudes in an organizational setting are attitudes of job satisfaction. Managers have been concerned about the job satisfaction of their employees for many years. High job satisfaction contributes to organizational commitment, job involvement, improved physical and mental health, and improved quality of life both on and off the job. Job dissatisfaction contributes to absenteeism, turnover, labor problems, labor grievances, attempts to organize labor unions, and a negative organizational climate.

The Concept of Job Satisfaction

Although the terms *job satisfaction* and *employee morale* are often used interchangeably to refer to the same thing, occasionally a distinction is made between them. Job satisfaction concerns the attitudes of a single individual, while **morale** describes the overall feelings of a group of workers.[44]

Job satisfaction basically concerns how much employees like their jobs. Research on job satisfaction has produced two approaches to help us understand it: component satisfaction and overall satisfaction.[45]

Component Satisfaction. Component satisfaction is sometimes called the "facet" or the **"attitudes toward things" approach,** because it assumes that job satisfaction really consists of many different attitudes about various components of the job. Therefore, employees have specific attitudes about their pay, their supervisors, the reports they have to complete, the cafeteria, and dozens of other external objects called *referents.* Some attitudes can be positive, and others can be negative. Not all these attitudes are equally important. The attitudes that appear to be the most important are those concerning the work itself, whether it is challenging, stimulating, and attractive; the supervisors, whether they are considerate, fair, and competent; and the pay, whether it is adequate and equitable.[46] A cross-cultural study on the meaning of work found that when employees in six industrial nations were asked to rank the importance of eleven work goals, "interesting work" and "good pay" were the most pre-eminent work goals regardless of sex, age, and nationality.[47]

Overall Satisfaction. Another approach to studying job satisfaction treats it as a general internal state of satisfaction or dissatisfaction within the individual. This internal state approach assumes that employees have a central internal feeling of overall satisfaction or dissatisfaction. Positive experiences, as a result of friendly co-workers, good pay, helpful supervisors, and attractive jobs, create a positive internal state. Negative experiences that stem from low pay, boring jobs, and criticism create a negative internal state. The feeling of **overall satisfaction** or dissatisfaction is a global feeling determined by the intensity and frequency of positive and negative experiences.

The internal state approach assumes that job satisfaction can be measured by asking employees about the specific components of their jobs, and then averaging their attitudes to arrive at a global satisfaction measure. The attitudes-toward-things approach claims that combining attitudes in this way is like mixing apples and oranges. Attitudes about different things should not be mixed; they should be measured and analyzed separately. Research evidence provides support for both these approaches. Job satisfaction questionnaires have identified several specific attitudes about important components of the job. Feelings of satisfaction or dissatisfaction with each component have been found to vacillate with changes in the job. For example, a promotion to a new job might increase pay satisfaction and satisfaction with the work itself but decrease satisfaction with fellow workers or working conditions.

Evidence of an internal state has been provided by experimental studies.[48] Changes in pay, for example, influenced satisfaction with pay as well as other attitudes closely associated with pay, such as feelings toward the supervisor who recommended the pay increase. However, attitudes about other aspects unrelated to pay, such as working conditions, did not change. The internal state can be conditioned by positive and negative experiences. A positive internal state or emotion is created by a rewarding environment and probably explains why some employees have a positive orientation toward work, and why they perceive new situations favorably.

Determinants of Job Satisfaction

Four theories have been used to determine whether people will feel satisfied or dissatisfied in a particular situation. These four theories include fulfillment theory, reward theory, discrepancy theory, and equity theory. There is also evidence that job satisfaction is influenced by genetic factors.

Fulfillment Theory. According to **fulfillment theory,** job satisfaction is a function of need satisfaction. It is indicated by the degree of correspondence between an individual's needs and the extent to which the needs are satisfied. Insofar as an individual's needs are fulfilled, that person will experience job satisfaction. Dissatisfaction occurs when important needs are not met.

Although this explanation seems plausible, it is not a useful theory for predicting job satisfaction. The term *needs* refers to internal deficiencies of a physiological or psychological nature that cannot be observed directly. Needs are usually inferred after the fact as an explanation for behavior. Therefore, it is difficult to know beforehand whether an individual will respond to a situation favorably or unfavorably without knowing whether a need actually exists.

Reward Theory. Perhaps the most useful theory for understanding job satisfaction is **reward theory,** which suggests that job satisfaction is a function of the rewards people receive. Both the amount and the timing of the rewards influence satisfaction levels. As a general rule, people feel greater satisfaction to the extent that they are more highly rewarded.

Reward theory emphasizes the role of values in determining satisfaction, because a person's values determine whether a particular event or outcome is actually rewarding. To the extent that people receive highly valued rewards, they are highly satisfied. To the extent that people are punished, they will be dissatisfied.

One inadequacy of reward theory is not knowing in advance whether someone will perceive a particular event as rewarding or punishing. The other two theories, discrepancy theory and equity theory, help to determine how a person will perceive a specific situation.

Discrepancy Theory. Job satisfaction is influenced by the expectations of employees. Discrepancy theory claims that job satisfaction results from a comparison between what ought to be and what is. A favorable comparison, showing that the employees received more than they expected, creates high job satisfaction. However, an unfavorable comparison, showing that "what is" falls short of "what ought to be," leads to dissatisfaction.[49] For example, an announcement that every employee will receive a $50 bonus would not necessarily create satisfaction if the employees were expecting a considerably larger bonus. This theory emphasizes the importance of understanding employee expectations when examining job satisfaction.

Equity Theory. Another theory that helps to explain job satisfaction focuses on the relative comparison of an individual's inputs and outcomes to the inputs and outcomes of others. **Equity theory,** which was explained in Chapter 4, describes how people compare their inputs and outcomes to the inputs and outcomes of others. To the extent that their ratios compare favorably with the ratios of others, they are satisfied. But to the extent there is inequity, they will feel dissatisfied.[50] Therefore, a group of employees might feel extremely happy about receiving a $500 pay increase until they hear that one person received a $1000 increase for the same effort and performance.

Heredity. Job satisfaction is also influenced by hereditary factors that people bring with them to the job. A study of job attitudes among thirty-four monozygotic (identical) twins who were reared apart concluded that genetic factors influence how people react to their work environments. In this study, about 30 percent of the variance in general job satisfaction was attributed to genetic factors. These data suggest that people bring important predispositions to the job that cause satisfaction levels to be influenced by more than just the objective conditions.[51]

One predisposition associated with job dissatisfaction is called "negative affectivity." Negative affectivity is an individual difference variable characterized by a disposition to experience aversive emotional states. People high in negative affectivity tend to be distressed, agitated, pessimistic, and dissatisfied. In studies where job enrichment is systematically varied people with negative affectivity predictably report lower satisfaction than others.[52] Both genetic and learned factors may contribute to a predisposition toward negative affectivity.

Measuring Job Satisfaction

Measuring job satisfaction is important to both behavioral scientists and managers. The effects of many management decisions and organizational interventions have been examined with respect to their impact on job satisfaction. Developing a means of measuring job satisfaction has been essential to behavioral science research in assessing the effects of organizational change. Measuring job satisfaction is important to managers because satisfaction is viewed as an important indicator of organizational effectiveness. Morale surveys are administered periodically in some organizations and used to develop a change strategy.

Unlike physical factors such as height and weight, job satisfaction exists only inside a person's head and cannot be measured directly. Three of the most popular methods for indirectly measuring job satisfaction include observing workers, interviewing them, and asking them to complete a written survey. Because personal observations and interviews are so time consuming, questionnaires are the most popular method of assessing job satisfaction. Although some questionnaires have poor reliability and validity, others have been carefully developed and are reliable and valid measures of both component satisfaction and overall job satisfaction.

One of the most popular instruments for measuring job satisfaction is the Job Descriptive Index (JDI).[53] This instrument measures attitudes toward the work itself, pay, the supervisor, co-workers, and promotion opportunities. Sample items from the JDI measuring the work itself are presented in Exhibit 7.6. Employees are asked to indicate whether each statement does or does not describe their jobs. Positive statements are scored +1, negative statements −1, and undecided statements 0. The higher the score, the greater the job satisfaction.

EXHIBIT 7.6   Job Descriptive Index: Sample Items

Directions:

Think of your present work. What is it like most of the time?

Circle YES if it describes your work.
Circle NO if it does NOT describe it.
Circle ? if you cannot decide.

Fascinating	YES	NO	?
Routine	YES	NO	?
Satisfying	YES	NO	?
Boring	YES	NO	?
Good	YES	NO	?
Creative	YES	NO	?
Respected	YES	NO	?

From P. C. Smith, L. M. Kendall, and C. L. Hulin, *The Measurement of Satisfaction in Work and Retirement.* © Rand McNally, 1969.

Another popular scale for measuring job satisfaction is the Minnesota Satisfaction Questionnaire (MSQ).[54] This instrument uses a Likert response format to generate satisfaction scores from twenty-six scales. Examples of the MSQ questions are shown in Exhibit 7.7.

A unique method of measuring job satisfaction that does not require good reading skill is a faces scale.[55] A sample item from such a scale is shown in Exhibit 7.8. Employees are asked to circle the face that best describes their feelings about the overall job or specific aspects of it.

One of the most sensitive instruments for measuring job satisfaction is a semantic differential scale, which consists of bipolar adjective pairs set against concepts representing important components of the job.[56] An example of a semantic differential scale is shown in Exhibit 7.9. Semantic differential scales have also been proposed as a method of measuring specific job attitudes as well as the internal state.

Paper-and-pencil questionnaires have several advantages for evaluating job satisfaction. Most satisfaction questionnaires are relatively short, they are easy to understand, and they can be administered to large numbers of employees simultaneously. Because most of these surveys are worded in general terms, the instruments can be administered to a wide range of employees in various jobs, allowing for comparisons across jobs and across organizations. In some situations, however, managers or researchers may be interested in assessing attitudes toward a specific facet of job satisfaction. In this situation, unique scales would need to be developed and refined. Open-ended interviews with a few employees are often used to help develop such items. Items are constructed regarding the most frequently mentioned issues during the interviews.

EXHIBIT 7.7   **Minnesota Satisfaction Questionnaire: Sample Items**

On my present job, this is how I feel about . . .

	Not Satisfied	Slightly Satisfied	Satisfied	Very Satisfied	Extremely Satisfied
My job security	1	2	3	4	5
The amount of pay for the work I do	1	2	3	4	5
The working conditions (heating, lighting, ventilation, etc.) on this job	1	2	3	4	5
The opportunities for advancement on this job	1	2	3	4	5
The technical "know-how" of my supervisor	1	2	3	4	5

Source: D. J. Weiss, R. V. Dawis, G. W. England, and L. H. Lofquist (1967). *Manual for the Minnesota Satisfaction Questionnaire* (Minnesota Studies in Vocational Rehabilitation No. 22), Minneapolis: University of Minnesota Industrial Relations Center, Work Adjustment Project. Reproduced by permission. Copyright 1977 by Vocational Psychology Research, University of Minnesota.

Levels of Job Satisfaction

Job satisfaction is determined primarily by the kinds of rewards, the amount of rewards, and the reward expectations of employees. Several factors contribute to the rewarding or nonrewarding nature of a job. These factors include characteristics of the job itself, characteristics of the organization, and characteristics of the person.

Characteristics of Jobs Affecting Satisfaction. Many job characteristics influence satisfaction, especially role clarity, job scope, and intrinsic rewards. Role clarity concerns how well employees understand their assigned tasks and responsibilities. Employees seem to prefer jobs where they know what is expected of them and where they have clear task goals. Role ambiguity and role conflict contribute to stress and reduce job satisfaction among employees.[57]

Job scope concerns the amount of variety, autonomy, responsibility, and feedback provided by the job itself. Job scope is higher as more of these attributes are present in the job. Studies on the effects of job scope on employee attitudes have generally found that increased job scope is related to increased satisfaction.[58] However, for some people this relationship is not true, because they do not want enriched jobs.

Employees may not perceive their jobs accurately, and satisfaction is influenced more by the job characteristics they perceive than by the actual job characteristics. One study found only modest agreement between how employees evaluated their jobs and how the jobs were evaluated by job analysts. Desirable jobs, as perceived by the workers, tended to create greater job satisfaction, less work frustration, reduced anxiety on the job, and a strong desire to remain with the company.

EXHIBIT 7.8   Faces Scales: Sample Items

Adapted from T. Kunin, "The Construction of a New Type of Attitude Measure," in *Personnel Psychology* 8 (1955), 65–68; and R. B. Dunham and J. B. Herman, "Development of a Female Faces Scale for Measuring Job Satisfaction," in *Journal of Applied Psychology* 60 (1975): 630. © 1975 American Psychological Association, Washington, D.C. Reprinted by permission.

Objective measures of the job characteristics, however, tended to be unrelated to worker outcomes. How employees respond to their work is apparently based on their values and predispositions, and how they perceive their jobs has a greater impact on their satisfaction than how their jobs really are.[59]

Employees receive a variety of intrinsic and extrinsic rewards from their job. Some of the most important intrinsic rewards include achievement, recognition, and opportunity for personal growth. These rewards generally have a strong impact on raising job satisfaction. Important extrinsic rewards include salary, company benefits, and status. These rewards also tend to increase satisfaction, but not always. The most controversial relationship is the influence of money on satisfaction. The relative importance of pay and other job factors has been examined in a host of opinion surveys. A review of these studies indicates that pay is more important to workers than some theories of motivation suggest. For example, one review of these studies found that pay was ranked as the most important job characteristic in 20 percent of the studies. It should be noted, however, that whether pay is ranked first or somewhat lower often depends more on how the questions are asked and the employees' financial situations, because it is difficult to evaluate the importance of pay in an artificial setting.[60]

Characteristics of Organizations Affecting Satisfaction. Certain characteristics of organizations are perceived as rewarding events that affect job satisfaction. There is evidence that both administrative and technological improvements improve worker satisfaction. For example, the opportunity to participate in organizational decision making seems to be a rewarding experience. A field experiment among four clerical divisions of a large organization found that more autonomy and a greater voice in making decisions created greater job satisfaction. In the other divisions, however, the organizational structure was changed to a more hierarchically

EXHIBIT 7.9   Semantic Differential Scales

Me at Work—How I Feel Most of the Time

	Extremely	Quite	Slightly	Neutral	Slightly	Quite	Extremely	
Appreciated	1	2	3	4	5	6	7	Unappreciated
Efficient	1	2	3	4	5	6	7	Inefficient
Penalized	1	2	3	4	5	6	7	Rewarded
Satisfied	1	2	3	4	5	6	7	Dissatisfied
Unproductive	1	2	3	4	5	6	7	Productive
Encouraged	1	2	3	4	5	6	7	Discouraged
Ineffective	1	2	3	4	5	6	7	Effective
Valuable	1	2	3	4	5	6	7	Worthless

My Pay

	Extremely	Quite	Slightly	Neutral	Slightly	Quite	Extremely	
Annoying	1	2	3	4	5	6	7	Pleasing
Reasonable	1	2	3	4	5	6	7	Unreasonable
Satisfying	1	2	3	4	5	6	7	Dissatisfying
Penalizing	1	2	3	4	5	6	7	Rewarding

controlled setting that prevented the clerical workers from making as many decisions. The resulting loss of control reduced job satisfaction.[61]

Satisfaction surveys typically find a relationship between job satisfaction and job level. Higher levels of satisfaction are usually reported by people in higher-level positions in the organizational hierarchy—managers tend to be more satisfied than nonmanagers. This relationship is not very surprising, since higher-level jobs tend to have better pay, greater variety, more challenge, and better working conditions.

These two variables, decision-making authority and job level, appear to be the only organizational factors consistently related to satisfaction. Some studies have suggested that line managers are more satisfied than staff managers for reasons that are not clear. However, small correlations and inconsistent results suggest that line versus staff differences and other organizational variables such as size and span of control, do not have a large influence on satisfaction levels.[62]

Characteristics of the Person. Job satisfaction surveys have consistently shown that certain groups of workers are more satisfied than others. Age, education, and occupation are three personal characteristics that have been consistently related to job satisfaction.[63] Older workers consistently report greater satisfaction, probably because they receive higher pay, they have longer tenure with the company, they have more responsible jobs at higher levels in the organization, and their educational levels tend to be lower, which supposedly reduces their expectations. The relationship between satisfaction and education is negative, suggesting that the most highly educated employees are the least satisfied, probably because they expect more from their jobs.

Older workers may report greater job satisfaction for two other reasons: they have greater self-assurance and stronger work values. Because of their maturity, self-assurance, and decisiveness, older workers tend to have higher levels of self-esteem and studies have suggested that people with high self-esteem tend to be more satisfied with their work and to take more pleasure from a job well done. Also, people with stronger work values tend to report greater job satisfaction and studies have shown that older workers have stronger work values than do younger workers.[64] In summary, several personal characteristics seem to influence satisfaction: age, job tenure, job level, education, self-esteem, and the work ethic. It should be remembered, however, that none of them have as great an impact on job satisfaction as the work itself.

Changes in Satisfaction Over Time. How satisfied are employees? Many people think that most U.S. workers are extremely dissatisfied despite being among the most highly paid workers in the world. The common belief is that U.S. workers feel enormously frustrated and alienated because of the dehumanizing aspects of modern technology.[65]

This assessment of extreme dissatisfaction is not consistent with the available evidence. National surveys of worker attitudes conducted by the University of Michigan, the University of California, and the National Opinion Research Center (Gallup) find that workers generally report that they are largely satisfied with their jobs. Although the method of measurement has varied slightly over the years since these surveys first started in 1958, the percentage of workers reporting that they were satisfied with their work has fluctuated between approximately 80 and 90 percent.[66]

The results of these surveys suggest that organizational policies and management practices are generally successful in creating satisfied employees. However, the results have been questioned because they rely on the employees' self-assessments. Because absenteeism, turnover, and work stoppages are so prevalent in organizations, some have wondered if these surveys overstate how satisfied employees really are. The results are obtained by asking people, "How satisfied are you with your job?" It has been suggested that such a question threatens people's self-esteem and creates a response bias by pushing people to report that they are satisfied. If they report they are dissatisfied, they are admitting they made a poor job choice, they don't have control over their lives, or they let others push them around.[67]

A more conservative estimate of the percentage of satisfied employees is obtained by asking, "What type of work would you try to get into if you could start all over?" The results suggest that many workers would not choose the same occupation. Most surveys find that about three-fourths of professional and white-collar workers would choose the same occupation if they could start all over, while only one-fourth of blue-collar workers would make the same choice.[68]

Job Satisfaction and Life Satisfaction. People do not compartmentalize their lives into life at work and life away from work. What happens at home influences life at work, and vice versa. Life satisfaction is the overall quality of life and the degree of satisfaction people achieve in both the work and nonwork aspects of their lives.[69] Several studies have shown that overall life satisfaction is related to a variety of job characteristics. For example, overall life satisfaction is positively related to occupational prestige; higher-prestige jobs provide more responsibility and challenge. In fact, just being employed in work outside the home seems to increase overall life satisfaction. Indeed, one study even showed that suicide rates were lower among women who were employed outside the home.[70]

Studies examining the effects of work on life satisfaction have generally focused on three areas: political behavior, leisure behavior, and family activities. Political activities and conservative attitudes are consistently related to occupational level and job characteristics. Workers with jobs high in variety, autonomy, and responsibility tend to be more actively involved in political activities away from work and have more conservative political views. Workers who tend to feel alienated at work also tend to feel alienated in political activities, to the extent that they are less likely to vote and they tend to feel more politically ineffective.

Activities at work also spill over into leisure activities. Since people are free to choose their own leisure activities, we might expect workers to choose leisure activities that satisfy different needs and compensate for any job deficiencies. Such is not the case, however. People tend to choose leisure activities that are similar in nature to their occupation. Someone who is involved in frequent social interaction and extensive decision making on the job, tends to choose leisure activities with these same characteristics, such as being an officer in a private club. People who are isolated from social interaction at work tend to choose leisure activities that perpetuate their social isolation in spite of their needs for interaction.[71]

Characteristics of the work environment have also been shown to spill over into the family environment in a variety of ways. Time pressures and job responsibilities often limit a worker's involvement in family activities. Few people can psychologically leave their jobs each day as they return home from work. Instead, they carry with them a residue of feelings and emotions. Conflicts and frustrations at work are often translated into conflicts and frustrations at home. Conversely, feelings of happiness and satisfaction at work are also transported to the home environment. Some spillover even occurs with child-rearing practices, career expectations, and interaction patterns within the family. Characteristics of the parents' jobs are related to the values imparted to their children. The interaction patterns of families in the home tend to mirror those at work; even at home, parents expect their children to show qualities needed for success in their professional careers. One study found that husbands of employed women reported lower levels of job satisfaction, marital adjustment, and quality of life than husbands of housewives. These effects were mediated somewhat by flexible work schedules and satisfaction with child care.[72] Another study of educators found that job satisfaction was caused by stress and burnout, which was related to mental problems and a negative home environment.[73] In summary, life at work is not divorced from life away from work. The quality of life a person enjoys away from work is closely related to the quality of life on the job.

APPLYING ORGANIZATIONAL BEHAVIOR
ACROSS CULTURES

The Relative Importance of Work Goals

 What do people seek from working, and do their goals differ from one culture to another? Almost every employee wants good pay and pleasant working conditions, but are these the most important work goals?

International comparisons of work goals have reported cultural differences; however, these differences have not been especially consistent. For example, a study by Dowling and Nagel (1986) reported that Australians placed greater emphasis on extrinsic values, whereas Americans stressed self-fulfillment. But a study by Bass and Eldridge (1979) found that U.S. managers strongly valued the profit motive, while Danish managers emphasized societal concerns.

A study by Bigoness and Hofstede (1987) compared the work goals from 13 nations at two points in time, 14 years apart. The importance rankings of ten work goals remained highly similar for both time periods. Both samples listed job challenge, job freedom, good relations with one's superior, and advancement opportunities as the four most important work goals.

An extensive study of work goals in seven countries by the Meaning-of-Work International Research Team found both similarities and differences across cultures. Their survey included 8,192 respondents chosen by a random quota sampling from Belgium, Great Britain, Germany, Israel, Japan, the Netherlands, and the United States. The respondents were asked to rank eleven work goals.

There was remarkable intercultural consistency for the most important and least important goals. The goals ranked first and second in almost every country were interesting work and pay, while working conditions and opportunities for promotion were usually ranked last. These results suggest that both intrinsic and extrinsic rewards are important goals for workers everywhere.

Some cultural differences were also interesting. Most countries ranked "match between person and job" about sixth, but Japan ranked it first. "Autonomy" was ranked first by the Netherlands, but only tenth by Britain. The culture that seemed most unique, however, was Israel. While most countries ranked "job security" second or third, Israel ranked it tenth. Other countries ranked "interpersonal relations" from fourth to seventh, while Israel ranked it second. And while other countries ranked "variety" about sixth or seventh, Israel ranked it eleventh.

So, even though these results suggest many similarities, there are also important cultural differences in what employees seek. What employees rank as important work goals probably indicates what they do not have. For example, it is easy to understand why the Japanese rank "match between person and job" so highly, because they are highly trained but join one company for life, and their career path is largely controlled by that company.

Source: Itzhak Harpaz, "The Importance of Work Goals: An International Perspective," *Journal of International Business Studies,* vol. 21 (1990), pp. 75–93; P. J. Dowling and T. W. Nagel, "Nationality and Work Attitudes: A Study of Australian and American Business Majors," *Journal of Management,* vol. 12 (1986), pp. 121–128; B. Bass and L. Eldridge, "Accelerated Managers' Objectives in Twelve Countries," *Industrial Relations,* vol. 12 (1973), pp. 158–171; W. J. Bigoness and G. Hofstede, "A Cross National Study in Managerial Work Goals: A Quasi-longitudinal Investigation," paper presented at the Annual Academy of Management meeting, 1987.

JOB SATISFACTION AND BEHAVIOR

What are the consequences of job satisfaction or dissatisfaction? Many people respond by saying that a happy worker is a productive worker; therefore, increasing job satisfaction should raise productivity. In spite of how reasonable it seems, however, this answer is wrong. In this section, we examine the relationships between job satisfaction and some of the most important responses people make in organizations, including performance, attendance, turnover, physical and mental health, union activity, and frustration and aggression.

Performance

The idea that satisfaction causes performance has always been a popular belief, and the Hawthorne Studies reinforced the idea. However, extensive research failed to support the relationship. Although some correlations between job satisfaction and productivity were positive, others were negative, and almost all were close to zero. A major review during the 1950s concluded that the evidence did not support the belief that a happy worker would be a productive worker.[74] This conclusion suggested that increasing the levels of satisfaction would not necessarily increase productivity. Unproductive workers can be very satisfied. In fact, their high satisfaction might result from not having to work hard. Highly satisfied employees, for example, may become complacent, resting on their reputations and assuming that contributions made in the past have earned them the right to coast on the job.

During the 1960s it was argued that performance causes satisfaction, and an intervening process between performance and satisfaction was added to explain the relationship.[75] This notion was derived from the expanded model of expectancy theory, explained in Chapter 4, in which intrinsic and extrinsic rewards from performance determine satisfaction.

Studies have concluded that no necessary relationship exists between satisfaction and productivity.[76] Rather than causing each other, they are both caused by the rewards employees receive and by how the rewards are administered. Satisfaction is primarily a function of the amount and timing of the rewards, and the employee's personal expectations, as explained earlier. Productivity is primarily a function of the reward contingencies, as explained in Chapter 3. Organizations can establish a positive relationship between satisfaction and productivity by rewarding high performance. A negative relationship can be created by unfair compensation policies that reward low performers or everyone equally.

The effects of rewards were demonstrated in a laboratory study in which workers performed a task for two 1-hour periods.[77] At the end of each hour, their performance was evaluated, they were paid a financial bonus for their performance, and their satisfaction was measured. Although they were told the bonuses would be based on performance, the money was given randomly to half the best workers and half the poorest workers at the end of each hour.

In this study, there were four groups of workers, as shown in Exhibit 7.10. Those who received bonuses (groups 1 and 2) reported significantly greater satisfaction than did those who were not rewarded (groups 3 and 4). Clearly, satisfaction depended on rewards and not on performance. Likewise, the best performance improvement during the second hour came from those whose performance had been appropriately rewarded the first hour. Clearly, performance depended on reward contingencies and not on satisfaction. When satisfaction was correlated with performance for all four groups, the correlations were zero. However, the correlations were positive for those who were appropriately reinforced (groups 2 and 3), while they were negative for those who were inappropriately rewarded (groups 1 and 4). These results suggest that managers can create either a positive or negative relationship between satisfaction and performance depending on the extent to which rewards are based on performance.

EXHIBIT 7.10	Relationship Between Satisfaction and Performance

	Low performers	High performers
Rewarded	Group 1 Inappropriately rewarded	Group 2 Appropriately rewarded
Nonrewarded	Group 3 Appropriately rewarded	Group 4 Inappropriately rewarded

Attendance: Absenteeism and Tardiness

Absenteeism and tardiness are sometimes considered withdrawal or avoidance behaviors and they are consistently, though only moderately, related to job satisfaction. People who are unhappy or dissatisfied at work tend to miss work or come late more frequently than those who are satisfied.

The costs of absenteeism are extremely high. To diagnose attendance problems, a distinction should be made between voluntary and involuntary absenteeism. **Voluntary absenteeism** is when employees have a choice of working or not working, and they intentionally decide to miss work. **Involuntary absenteeism** is when employees miss work for reasons beyond their control. Some examples of involuntary absenteeism include health problems, the death or serious illness of a family member, transportation problems, and bad weather.

Although this distinction is helpful in diagnosing absenteeism, the definition is not entirely clear. When is a problem beyond a person's control? Major surgery and serious illnesses may force employees to be absent, but some return to work much sooner than others. Some football players have appendectomies and return only a few days later to play a game. When their cars are broken, some employees miss several days of work while others take public transportation, ride a bike, or walk several miles. For some employees, a heavy snowstorm means getting up an hour earlier to get to work on time; for others, it means sleeping in. Consequently, it is difficult to decide when an absence is truly involuntary or when the employee could have taken an aspirin and gone back to work. Most managers believe job satisfaction and motivation make a big difference in situations such as these.

Attendance is related to self-efficacy: people who are confident in their ability to perform their jobs and who have strong feelings of competence and self-mastery tend to have better attendance records. One study examined the effects of self-management training and found that better self-management through goal setting, feedback, and self-reinforcement increased self-efficacy and attendance.[78]

Attendance behavior is also influenced by job satisfaction and pressures to attend. Several studies have shown that job satisfaction is correlated with attendance at work, which means that managers should try to maintain a positive work environment.[79] People who are highly satisfied with their jobs are seldom absent from work and faithfully see that their job is performed in spite of personal illnesses, family emergencies, or bad weather.

Pressures to attend may appear in the form of incentives for attendance or punishments for failure to attend. Studies have shown that specific incentives for good attendance, including punishment for being absent, decrease absenteeism. An electrical manufacturing firm, for example, studied the effects of rewards and punishment on absenteeism in two divisions. They found that absenteeism declined by 40 percent when positive rewards were provided for good attendance. However, absenteeism declined by only 14 percent when negative sanctions were provided for poor attendance. In the control divisions, those who did not implement either rewards or sanctions, no changes in the absenteeism rate were reported during the same period of time.[80]

Turnover

The analysis of absenteeism and turnover statistics show that these factors are highly correlated. When absenteeism rates are high, turnover rates are likely to be quite high. Apparently absenteeism and turnover are not alternative ways of expressing dissatisfaction; they are both caused by many of the same factors. As working conditions become undesirable, employees may first start to miss a few days and then leave permanently.

Like absenteeism, the costs of turnover are surprisingly high, much higher than most people suspect. Because turnover can be so costly, organizations need to reduce it to an acceptable level. Maintaining a zero turnover rate, however, is unrealistic and even undesirable. A small amount of turnover is necessary and desirable as employees develop new skills and advance to higher levels of responsibility.

The two variables most significantly related to turnover are (1) job dissatisfaction and (2) economic conditions. The highest turnover levels are found in companies where employees report the greatest dissatisfaction. Consequently, most explanations of turnover maintain that employees leave their jobs when alternative jobs that better satisfy their needs become available. Therefore, turnover levels are generally high in companies with poor working conditions, undesirable jobs, wage inequities, poor communication, and limited opportunities for advancement. To reduce turnover, companies should improve the quality of the work environment. A field experiment, for example, involving 350 clerical employees found that improved pay and promotion policies reduced turnover from over 30 percent to 18 percent the first year and to 12 percent the next year.[81]

Turnover rates are strongly influenced by economic conditions. When unemployment levels are high because of a depressed economy, turnover in most companies is greatly reduced. An analysis of turnover levels and unemployment levels over a period of several years shows an inverse relationship between these two variables. Apparently high unemployment levels reduce the perceived and real opportunities of changing to another job. Employees are reluctant to leave one job unless they know another is available. Because managers cannot control economic conditions or unemployment levels, their turnover levels may fluctuate widely regardless of other actions they take.

Physical and Mental Health

Sometimes people complain, "My work is ruining my health" or "My job is driving me crazy." Although these people may be overstating the impact of their work, consistent evidence shows that job satisfaction is related to physical and mental health. One study has shown a fairly strong relationship between the incidence of death due to heart disease and job dissatisfaction caused by stress, conflict, and

APPLYING ORGANIZATIONAL BEHAVIOR
RESEARCH

The Effects of Employee Ownership on Attitudes and Turnover

 Do employees like employee stock ownership programs (ESOPs) because of (a) the intrinsic satisfaction of ownership, (b) the instrumental satisfaction of being able to influence company actions, or (c) the extrinsic monetary returns? Previous research suggests that ESOPs do not really create much intrinsic satisfaction; but they do contribute to instrumental and extrinsic satisfactions.

The popularity of employee ownership has increased dramatically in the past two decades. From 1974 to 1989, the number of companies with ESOPs increased from 1,000 to 10,000. It is estimated that over ten million workers participate in some type of employee ownership. Their popularity is due to favorable tax legislation and reports that employee-owned firms are more profitable and competitive than companies under traditional ownership. But how do employees feel about them?

A study examined the effects of employee ownership on worker attitudes and turnover during a thirty-two month period. This study was conducted at a medium-sized company in the Midwest that created an ESOP in 1983 so employees could participate in the ownership of the company. The company employed 376 people, and in 1987, 218 of them completed a questionnaire measuring their attitudes about the company, the ESOP plan, com-

pany commitment, their intention to leave, and involvement in the company. Turnover data were obtained thirty-two months later from company records and these data showed that 29 people had left the company.

The results indicated that employees who thought ownership increased their perceived influence in the company (instrumental satisfaction) were more satisfied with the ESOP, more committed to the organization, had lower intentions to leave, and were actually less likely to leave the company. Likewise, those who had a larger financial stake in the ESOP (extrinsic satisfaction) were more satisfied with the ESOP, were more committed to the organization, and said they did not intend to leave. However, actual turnover was unrelated to the participant's financial stake in the ESOP.

This study suggests that ESOPs contribute to several desirable consequences for both organizations and employees. Employees like to participate in ESOPs because they feel more involved in the management of the company and they are monetarily rewarded from their ownership. Both these motives (instrumental satisfaction and extrinsic rewards) help explain why employees like ESOPs.

Source: Aaron A. Buchko, "Employee Ownership, Attitudes, and Turnover: An Empirical Assessment," *Human Relations,* 45 (1992), pp. 711–733.

boredom.[82] An even more dramatic study was a longitudinal study of life expectancy. An analysis of numerous physical and attitudinal variables, including physical condition and tobacco use, revealed that the single best predictor of longevity was work satisfaction. Those who felt their work was meaningful and useful outlived their less satisfied co-workers.[83]

Job satisfaction also contributes to better overall mental health. A study of blue-collar workers revealed consistent relationships between job satisfaction and mental health. The most important job attributes for good mental health were challenging work and opportunities to use their abilities and skills.[84]

Intense dissatisfaction can arise from jobs that are extremely frustrating and filled with ambiguity and conflict. These jobs tend to make people feel more physically tired and more mentally fatigued than they otherwise would. The consequences of extreme dissatisfaction are generally rather widespread in the lives of workers. Frustration and despair caused by an unpleasant job permeate an individual's life and makes the worker feel depressed both on the job and at home. Leisure activities, vacations, and off-the-job social interactions become increasingly important for such individuals, and yet the spillover from the job prevents them from pursuing meaningful relaxations. As a consequence, job dissatisfaction is a major contributor to poor mental health and it contributes to a variety of dysfunctional behaviors.[85]

If people continually face a frustrating and unpleasant situation at work, there is a growing likelihood that they will eventually respond with aggression, fixation, or withdrawal either on the job or off the job. The symptoms will depend on the person and the situation. Some of the specific forms of extreme job dissatisfaction include bickering, theft, deliberate tardiness, insubordination, sabotage, and union activity. These responses reflect impulses of aggression and anger directed at the job or the organization. Occasionally, however, anger and frustration from work produce displaced aggression at home in the form of child abuse and spouse beating.

SUMMARY

1. An attitude consists of a combination of cognitive beliefs and the affective feelings or emotions attached to these beliefs.

2. A belief is information held about objects, people, or things. Beliefs are acquired from personal observations, from the inferences we make, or from external sources of information.

3. Some attitudes are easily changed, while others are remarkably stable. The information-processing theory of attitude change suggests that we process new information within short-term memory and interpret it in a manner consistent with information retained in long-term memory.

4. Four of the most popular methods of changing attitudes include (a) providing new information to change an individual's belief system; (b) creating a feeling of fear or anxiety; (c) creating a feeling of dissonance or inconsistency; and (d) having people participate in a group discussion.

5. Changing a person's attitudes will not necessarily create a change in behavior. The relationship between attitudes and behavior is mediated by behavioral intentions. Only attitudes associated with specific behavioral intentions are likely to lead to a change in behavior.

6. In many situations, attitudes are a function of behavior, so that a change in behavior creates a change in attitudes. This relationship is explained by the self-perception theory, which suggests that people form attitudes as a rationale for or justification of their behavior.

7. Personal values are a constellation of related attitudes containing a moral quality that characterizes something as "desirable" and important. Values are more generalized than attitudes and possess a moral quality of right and proper. Like attitudes, however, there is not a direct relationship between values and behavior.

8. Moral development is the process of acquiring moral values and behaviors. The two leading theories explaining the process of moral development include Lawrence Kohlberg's cognitive-developmental stage theory, in which values are acquired in six stages, and social cognitive theory, which suggests that values are acquired through a learning process facilitated by modeling and teaching.

9. Job involvement is a work value of people who participate actively in their work and view it as a central life interest. People tend to display greater job involvement if they are more committed to the work ethic, define their

self-concepts according to their job performance, and have an enriched job. Studies of
job involvement suggest that people who are
highly involved in their work tend to achieve
higher job satisfaction and greater intrinsic
motivation. However, people can become so
highly involved in their jobs that they become obsessed with their work and become
workaholics.

10. Organizational commitment is a work value
that is characterized by a feeling of loyalty to
the organization and desire to maintain membership in it. Organizational commitment
tends to be stronger among older employees,
higher-level officials, and employees who have
a stake in the ownership or success of the organization. The two types of organizational
commitment include calculative commitment,
where commitment is associated with the
rewards offered by the organization, and moral
commitment, which is based on the person's
acceptance of the organization's values and
goals.

11. Although the work ethic encompasses a variety
of work values, the traditional work ethic is
specifically concerned with the moral importance of work and pride in craftsmanship. The
moral importance of work concerns the moral
obligation a person feels to have a job, while
pride and craftsmanship concern the importance of doing a job well. Employees with a
strong work ethic tend to report higher levels
of job satisfaction and productivity. Older
workers consistently report stronger work values than younger workers, because of maturity,
historical experiences, and the kinds of training and indoctrination they received earlier in
life.

12. Job satisfaction includes the attitudes of satisfaction or dissatisfaction people hold toward
their jobs. The component satisfaction
approach suggests that people have job attitudes toward a variety of objects in their job
setting. The overall satisfaction approach suggests that all the attitudes a person has toward

various job components can be combined into
one overall measure.

13. The four theories that explain job satisfaction
include (a) fulfillment theory, in which satisfaction comes from fulfilling personal needs;
(b) reward theory, in which satisfaction comes
from the rewards people receive; (c) discrepancy theory, wherein satisfaction results from a
comparison of the rewards employees think
they should receive with the rewards they actually receive; and (d) equity theory, which suggests that people compare their own rewards
and effort to the rewards and effort of others.

14. Questionnaires provide a convenient method
of measuring job satisfaction. Some of the
most popular job satisfaction instruments
include the job descriptive index, the Minnesota Satisfaction Questionnaire, and the
semantic differential scale.

15. Higher levels of job satisfaction are typically
reported by people who have clear job descriptions, whose jobs are relatively free of conflict
and ambiguity, whose jobs are at higher levels
in the organizational hierarchy, and who are
older.

16. Surveys of job satisfaction over the past twenty
years suggest that the level of job satisfaction
has remained fairly constant, although the evidence is somewhat equivocal. The effect of job
satisfaction on life satisfaction, however, seems
to be very consistent. Greater job satisfaction
contributes to the quality of life both on and
off the job and to greater longevity.

17. There is no necessary relationship between job
satisfaction and productivity. Managers can
create either a positive or negative relationship
between satisfaction and performance depending on whether rewards are based on
performance.

18. Job satisfaction is inversely related to absenteeism and turnover. Dissatisfied employees
are more likely than satisfied employees to be
absent or leave the organization.

DISCUSSION QUESTIONS

1. Identify two or three of your attitudes, and describe the cognitive belief component and the affective emotional component accompanying each of them.

2. If you were a new supervisor and the members of your work group resented you because you were hired into that position directly out of college, while they have worked for the company for years, how would you try to change their attitudes?

3. What is the relationship between attitudes and behavior? When does a change in attitude cause a change in behavior, and when does a change in behavior cause a change in attitudes?

4. How does the cognitive-developmental stage theory of moral development differ from social cognitive theory? Identify one of your personal values that you consider extremely important, such as honesty, achievement, or chastity, and describe how you acquired it.

5. How can you tell when someone is so highly involved in a job that she or he is becoming a workaholic?

6. What are the consequences of excessive organizational commitment?

7. Describe a situation in which you expect to find a positive relationship between satisfaction and productivity. Where would you expect to find a negative relationship?

8. When job satisfaction is being measured, does it matter whether satisfaction is viewed as an internal state or as an attitude toward things? Why or why not?

9. When measuring absenteeism and turnover, why is it useful to distinguish between voluntary and involuntary causes?

GLOSSARY

affective component The emotional or feeling component that contributes to the formation of an attitude.

attitude The combination of cognitive beliefs and affective feelings toward an attitude object.

attitudes-toward-things approach An approach that views job satisfaction as a collection of unique attitudes toward different objects within the work environment.

behavioral intentions A potential outcome of a group of attitudes that refers to the individual's intentions to display a particular behavior.

behavioral justifications A part of self-perception theory that concerns the rationale or explanations people use to justify their behavior.

beliefs The knowledge, information, or data we store within our memory.

calculative commitment A type of organizational commitment that explains commitment in terms of the rewards or economic advantages that come from organizational membership.

cognitive component The belief component of attitudes that contains the knowledge and information.

cognitive-developmental stage theory A theory of moral development, proposed by Lawrence Kohlberg, suggesting that people acquire moral values in a sequential process advancing from stage 1 to stage 6.

component satisfaction An approach suggesting that job satisfaction consists of different attitudes toward a variety of components or objects within the work environment.

cultural value A value that is widely accepted within a society.

discrepancy theory A theory of job satisfaction suggesting that satisfaction levels are a function of the difference between what people expect and what they actually obtain.

equity theory A theory of job satisfaction suggesting that people compare their inputs and outputs with the inputs and outputs of others.

external information A source of data that contributes to the formation of a belief system.

fulfillment theory An explanation of job satisfaction that explains satisfaction in terms of the fulfillment of personal needs.

inferential beliefs A source of information contributing to the formation of a belief system in which the information comes from the inferences and probability estimates people make within their environment.

information-processing theory of attitude formation A theory of attitude formation suggesting that new information is processed in short-term memory according to the biases and frameworks created by the information stored in long-term memory.

involuntary absenteeism Absenteeism caused by reasons beyond the control of the employee.

job involvement A work value characteristic of people who participate actively in their work, view it as a central life interest, and define their self-concept in terms of their performance.

moral commitment A form of organizational commitment that refers to the extent to which people personally accept the organization's values and goals.

morale The general level of job satisfaction within a work group.

observational beliefs A source of information contributing to a person's belief system in which information comes from the individual's personal observations.

organizational commitment A work value that concerns the extent to which people have a strong belief and acceptance of the organization's values and goals, they are willing to exert effort on behalf of the organization, and they have a strong desire to maintain membership in it.

overall satisfaction An approach to understanding job satisfaction that assumes the various job attitudes can be combined to form an overall level of satisfaction.

reward theory A theory that explains job satisfaction in terms of the level of rewards or outcomes that people receive.

social cognitive theory A theory that explains moral development in terms of the kinds of values people learn because they are modeled and reinforced within their environment.

specificity of intentions The degree of specificity associated with behavioral intentions in terms of (a) how well the particular behavior has been visualized in detail; (b) whether the target object has been determined; (c) how clearly the situational context has been defined; and (d) whether a time schedule has been established.

values A constellation of generalized attitudes about a concept that possesses a moral quality of right and desirable.

voluntary absenteeism Absenteeism caused by reasons that are under the control of the individual employee.

workaholic A person who feels an irrational compulsion to work and experiences withdrawal symptoms when not at work. Workaholics typically suffer from a lack of meaning and fulfillment in their work and life in general.

work ethic The values that people hold toward the importance of work. The traditional work ethic emphasizes the importance of work as a moral and religious obligation of people and suggests that people should feel a moral obligation to have a job and a personal responsibility to do it dependably.

NOTES

1. D. Krech, R. S. Crutchfield, and E. L. Balachey, *Individual in Society* (New York: McGraw-Hill, 1962).

2. Many ideas in this section are taken from M. Fishbein and I. Ajzen, *Belief, Attitude, Intention, and Behavior* (Reading, Mass.: Addison-Wesley, 1975).

3. L. R. James and L. E. Tetrick, "Confirmatory Analytic Tests of Three Causal Models Relating Job Perceptions to Job Satisfaction," *Journal of Applied Psychology*, vol. 71 (1986), pp. 77–82.

4. Craig C. Pinder, *Work Motivation: Theory, Issues and Applications* (Glenview, Ill.: Scott Foresman, 1984), chap. 5.

5. Alison Hubbard Ashton and Robert H. Ashton, "Sequential Belief Revision in Auditing," *Accounting Review*, vol. 63 (October 1988), pp. 623–642.

6. S. Lieberman, "The Effects of Changes in Roles on the Attitudes of Role Occupants," *Human Relations*, vol. 9 (1956), pp. 385–402.

7. R. W. Griffin, "A Longitudinal Investigation of Task Characteristics Relationships," *Academy of Management Journal*, vol. 24 (1981), pp. 99–113.

8. Bobby J. Calder and P. H. Schurr, "Attitudinal Processes in Organizations," *Research in Organizational Behavior*, Vol. 3 (Greenwich, Conn.: JAI Press, 1981).

9. Harry C. Triandis, *Attitude and Attitude Change* (New York: Wiley, 1971); William J. McGuire, "Personality and Attitude Change: An Information Processing Theory," in A. G. Greenwald, T. C. Brock, and T. M. Ostrum (eds.), *Psychological Foundations of Attitudes* (New York: Academic Press, 1968), pp. 171–196.

10. Leon Festinger, *A Theory of Cognitive Dissonance* (Stanford, Calif.: Stanford University Press, 1957).

11. Victor H. Vroom, *Some Personality Determinants of the Effects of Participation* (Englewood Cliffs, N.J.: Prentice-Hall, 1960); D. R. Nelson and T. E. Obremski, "Promoting Moral Growth Through Intra-group Participation," *Journal of Business Ethics*, vol. 9 (September 1990), pp. 731–740.

12. Mark E. Tubbs and Steven E. Ekeberg, "The Role of Intentions in Work Motivation: Implications for Goal-Setting Theory and Research," *Academy of Management Review*, vol. 16 (1991), pp. 180–199.

13. Lucinda I. Doran, Arthur P. Brief, Veronica K. Stone, and Jennifer M. George, "Behavioral Intentions as Predictors of Job Attitudes: The Role of Economic Choice," *Journal of Applied Psychology*, vol. 76 (1991), pp. 40–45.

14. Fishbein and Ajzen, op. cit.

15. Daryl J. Bem, "Self-Perception Theory," in L. Berkowitz (ed.), *Advances in Experimental Social Psychology*, Vol. 6 (New York: Academic Press, 1972).

16. Milton Rokeach, *The Nature of Human Values* (New York: Free Press, 1973); Lawrence A. Crosby, Mary Jo Bitner, and James D. Gill, "Organizational Structure of Values," *Journal of Business Research*, vol. 20 (March 1990), pp. 123–134.

17. Reviewed by J. Philippe Rushton, "Socialization and the Altruistic Behavior of Children," *Psychological Bulletin*, vol. 83 (1976), pp. 898–913.

18. Lawrence Kohlberg, "Stage and Sequence: The Cognitive Developmental Approach to Socialization," in D. Goslin (ed.), *Handbook of Socialization: Theory and Research* (New York: Rand McNally, 1969).

19. James Weber, "Managers' Moral Reasoning: Assessing Their Responses to Three Moral Dilemmas," *Human Relations*, vol. 43 (1990), pp. 687–702.

20. Albert Bandura, *Social Learning Theory* (Englewood Cliffs, N.J.: Prentice-Hall, 1986).

21. S. D. Saleh and J. Hosek, "Job Involvement: Concepts and Measurements," *Academy of Management Journal*, vol. 19 (1976), pp. 213–224.

22. R. N. Kanungo, "Worker Alienation and Involvement: Problems and Prospects," *International Review of Applied Psychology*, vol. 31 (1981), pp. 1–15; S. Rabinowitz, "Towards a Developmental Model of Job Involvement," *International Review of Applied Psychology*, vol. 30 (1981), pp. 31–50.

23. David J. Cherrington, *The Work Ethic: Working Values and Values That Work* (New York: AMACOM Publishing, 1980), chap. 12.

24. Quoted by Warren Boroson, "The Workaholic," *Money*, vol. 5 (June 1976), pp. 32–35.

25. R. T. Mowday, L. W. Porter, and R. M. Steers, *The Employee–Organization Linkages: The Psychology of Commitment, Absenteeism and Turnover* (New York: Academic Press, 1982).

26. Richard M. Steers, "Antecedents and Outcomes of Organizational Commitment," *Administrative Science Quarterly*, vol. 22 (1977), pp. 46–56.

27. Joseph M. Putti, Samuel Aryee, and Tan Kim Liang, "Work Values and Organizational Commitment: A Study in the Asian Context," *Human Relations*, vol. 42 (1989), pp. 275–288.

28. Mark W. Johnston, A. Parasuraman, Charles M. Futrell, and William C. Black, "A Longitudinal Assessment of the Impact of Selected Organizational Influences on Sales People's Organizational Commitment During Early Employment," *Journal of Marketing Research*, vol. 27 (August 1990), pp. 333–344; Ronald E. Michaels, William L. Cron, Alan J. Dubinsky, and Erich A. Joachimsthaler, "Influence of Formalization on the Organizational Commitment and Work Alienation of Sales People and Industrial Buyers," *Journal of Marketing Research*, vol. 25 (November 1988), pp. 376–383.

29. David F. Caldwell, Jennifer A. Chatman, and Charles A. O'Reilly, "Building Organizational Commitment: A Multi-firm Study," *Journal of Occupational Psychology*, vol. 63 (September 1990), pp. 245–261.

30. Natalie J. Allen and John P. Meyer, "The Measurement and Antecedents of Affective, Continuance, and Normative Commitments to the Organization," *Journal of Occupational Psychology*, vol. 63 (1990), pp. 1–18; Aaron Cohen and Geula Lowenberg, "A Reexamination of the Side-bet Theory as Applied to Organizational Commitment: A Meta-analysis," *Human Relations*, vol. 43 (October 1990), pp. 1015–1050; John P. Meyer, Natalie J. Allen, and Ian R. Gellatly, "Affective and Continuance Commitment to the Organization: Evaluation of Measures and Analysis of Concurrent and Time Lagged Relations," *Journal of Applied Psychology*, vol. 75 (1990), pp. 710–720; H. S. Becker, "Notes on the Concept of Commitment," *American Journal of Sociology*, vol. 66 (1960), pp. 32–40; J. Meyer and N. Allen, "Testing the 'Side-bet Theory' of Organizational Commitment: Some Methodological Considerations," *Journal of Applied Psychology*, vol. 69 (1984), pp. 372–378.

31. H. Angle and J. Perry, "An Empirical Assessment of Organizational Commitment and Organizational

Effectiveness," *Administrative Science Quarterly,* vol. 26 (1981), pp. 1–14; H. Angle and J. Perry, "Organizational Commitment: Individual and Organizational Influences," *Work and Occupations,* vol. 10 (1983), pp. 123–146; R. T. Mowday, R. M. Steers, and L. W. Porter, "The Measurement of Organizational Commitment," *Journal of Vocational Behavior,* vol. 14 (1979), pp. 224–247; Barbara M. Romzek, "Personal Consequences of Employee Commitment," *Academy of Management Journal,* vol. 32 (1989), pp. 649–661.

32. John P. Meyer, Sampo V. Paunonen, Ian R. Gellatly, Richard D. Goffin, and Douglas N. Jackson, "Organizational Commitment and Job Performance: It's the Nature of the Commitment That Counts," *Journal of Applied Psychology,* vol. 74 (1989), pp. 152–156.

33. Donna M. Randall, "The Consequences of Organizational Commitment: Methodological Investigation," *Journal of Organizational Behavior,* vol. 11 (1990), pp. 361–378; Romzek, op. cit.

34. T. Rotondi, "Organizational Identification: Issues and Implications," *Organizational Behavior and Human Performance,* vol. 13 (1975), pp. 95–109.

35. Clive Fullager and Julian Barling, "Predictors and Outcomes of Different Patterns of Organizational and Union Loyalty," *Journal of Occupational Psychology,* vol. 64 (1991), pp. 129–143.

36. Max Weber, "Die Protestantische Ethik und der Geist des Kapitalismus," *Archiv für Sozialwissenschaft,* Vols. 20 and 21 (1904 and 1905), translated from the German by Talcott Parsons as *The Protestant Ethic and the Spirit of Capitalism* (New York: Scribners, 1958).

37. Cherrington, op. cit.

38. Ibid., chap. 4.

39. Itzhak Harpaz, "Nonfinancial Employment Commitment: Across-national Comparison," *Journal of Occupational Psychology,* vol. 62 (1989), pp. 147–150.

40. Cherrington, op. cit., chap. 5.

41. Ibid., chap. 8.

42. Ibid., chap. 6.

43. Ibid., chap. 5.

44. William E. Scott, Jr., "The Development of Semantic Differential Skills as Measures of 'Morale'," *Personnel Psychology,* vol. 20 (1967), pp. 179–198.

45. G. H. Ironson, P. C. Smith, M. T. Brannick, W. M. Gibson, and K. B. Hall, "Construction of a Job in General Scale: A Comparison of Global, Composite, and Specific Measures," *Journal of Applied Psychology,* vol. 74 (1989), pp. 193–200; Robert W. Rice, Douglas A. Gentile, and Dean B. McFarlin, "Facet Importance and Job Satisfaction," *Journal of Applied Psychology,* vol. 76 (1991), pp. 31–40.

46. Clifford J. Mottaz, "Work Satisfaction Among Hospital Nurses," *Hospital and Health Services Administration,* vol. 33 (Spring 1988), pp. 57–74.

47. Itzhak Harpaz, "The Importance of Work Goals: An International Perspective," *Journal of International Business Studies,* vol. 21 (Spring 1990), pp. 75–93.

48. David J. Cherrington, "The Effects of a Central Incentive-Motivational State on Measures of Job Satisfaction," *Organizational Behavior and Human Performance,* vol. 10 (1973), pp. 271–289.

49. Robert W. Rice, Debbie E. Bennett, and Dean B. McFarlin, "Standards of Comparison and Job Satisfaction," *Journal of Applied Psychology,* vol. 74 (1989), pp. 591–598; Robert W. Rice, Suzanne M. Phillips, and Dean B. McFarlin, "Multiple Discrepancies and Pay Satisfaction," *Journal of Applied Psychology,* vol. 75 (1990), pp. 386–393.

50. Paul D. Sweeney, Dean B. McFarlin, and Edward J. Inderrieden, "Using Relative Deprivation Theory to Explain Satisfaction with Income and Pay Level: A Multi-study Examination," *Academy of Management Journal,* vol. 33 (1990), pp. 423–436.

51. Richard D. Arvey, Lauren M. Abraham, Thomas J. Bouchard, Jr., and Nancy L. Segal, "Job Satisfaction: Environmental and Genetic Components," *Journal of Applied Psychology,* vol. 74 (April 1989), pp. 187–192; Russ Cropanzano and Keith James, "Some Methodological Considerations for the Behavioral Genetic Analysis of Work Attitudes," *Journal of Applied Psychology,* vol. 75 (August 1990), pp. 733–739.

52. Ira Levin and Joseph P. Stokes, "Dispositional Approach to Job Satisfaction: Role of Negative Affectivity," *Journal of Applied Psychology,* vol. 74 (October 1989), pp. 752–758.

53. P. C. Smith, L. M. Kendall, and C. L. Hulin, *The Measurement of Satisfaction in Work and Retirement* (Chicago: Rand McNally, 1975).

54. D. J. Weiss, R. V. Dawis, G. W. England, and L. H. Lofquist, *Manual for the Minnesota Satisfaction Questionnaire* (Minnesota Studies in Vocational Rehabilitation, no. 22 (Minneapolis: 1967).

55. T. Kunin, "The Construction of a New Type of Attitude Measure," *Personnel Psychology,* vol. 8 (1955), pp. 65–78; Randall B. Dunham and Jeanne V. Herman, "Development of a Female Faces Scale for Measuring Job Satisfaction," *Journal of Applied Psychology,* vol. 60 (1975), pp. 629–631.

56. William E. Scott, Jr., and Kendrith M. Rowland, "The Generality and Significance of Semantic Differential Scales as Measures of 'Morale', " *Organizational Behavior and Human Performance,* vol. 5 (1970), pp. 576–591.

57. John H. Howard, David A. Cunningham, and Peter A. Rechnitzer, "Role Ambiguity, Type A Behavior, and Job Satisfaction: Moderating Effects on Cardiovascular and Biochemical Responses Associated with Coronary Risk," *Journal of Applied Psychology,* vol. 71 (1986), pp. 95–102; Karin E. Klenke-Hamel and John E. Mathieu, "Role Strains, Tension, and Job Satisfaction Influ-

ences on Employees' Propensity to Leave: A Multi-Sample Replication and Extension," *Human Relations,* vol. 43 (August 1990), pp. 791–807.

58. J. Richard Hackman and Edward E. Lawler, "Employee Reactions to Job Characteristics," *Journal of Applied Psychology,* vol. 55 (1971), pp. 259–286.

59. Paul E. Spector and Steve M. Jex, "Relations of Job Characteristics from Multiple Data Sources with Employee Affect, Absence, Turnover Intentions, and Help," *Journal of Applied Psychology,* vol. 76 (February 1991), pp. 46–53.

60. Daniel C. Feldman and U. J. Arnold, "Position Choice: Comparing the Importance of Organizational and Job Factors," *Journal of Applied Psychology,* vol. 63 (1978), pp. 706–710; Abraham E. Haspel, "A Study in Occupational Choice: Managerial Positions," *Southern Economics Journal,* vol. 44 (April 1978), pp. 958–967; Moshe Krausz, "A New Approach to Studying Worker Job Preferences," *Industrial Relations,* vol. 17, no. 1 (February 1978), pp. 91–95.

61. N. Morse and E. Reimer, "The Experimental Change of a Major Organizational Variable," *Journal of Abnormal and Social Psychology,* vol. 52 (1956), pp. 120–129.

62. Larry L. Cummings and Chris J. Berger, "Organization Structure: How Does It Influence Attitudes and Performance?" *Organizational Dynamics,* vol. 5 (no. 2, 1976), pp. 34–49.

63. Frederick Herzberg, B. Mausner, R. O. Peterson, and D. F. Capwell, *Job Attitudes: Review of Research and Opinion* (Pittsburgh: Psychological Services of Pittsburgh, 1957); Patricia C. Smith, L. M. Kendall, and Charles L. Hulin, *The Measurement of Satisfaction in Work and Retirement* (Chicago: Rand McNally, 1969); Gerald Zeitz, "Age and Work Satisfaction in a Government Agency: A Situational Perspective," *Human Relations,* vol. 43 (1990), pp. 419–438.

64. David J. Cherrington, Spencer J. Condie, and J. Lynn England, "Age and Work Values," *Academy of Management Journal,* vol. 22 (1979), pp. 617–623; K. Michele Macmar and Gerald R. Ferris, "Theoretical and Methodological Considerations in the Age–Job Satisfaction Relationship," *Journal of Applied Psychology,* vol. 74 (1989), pp. 201–207; Scott J. Vitell and D. L. Davis, "The Relationship Between Ethics and Job Satisfaction: An Empirical Investigation," *Journal of Business Ethics,* vol. 9 (June 1990), pp. 489–494.

65. Studs Terkel, *Working: People Talk About What They Do all Day and How They Feel About What They Do* (New York: Avon Books, 1972), p. xiii.

66. Conference Board, "Job Satisfaction High in America," *Monthly Labor Review,* vol. 108 (February 1985, p. 52); Robert P. Quinn, Graham L. Staines, and Margaret R. McCullough, *Job Satisfaction: Is There a Trend?* Manpower Research Monograph, no. 30, (1974), Manpower Administration, U.S. Department of Labor.

67. Robert L. Kahn, "The Meaning of Work: Interpretations and Proposals for Measurement," In A. A. Campbell and P. E. Converse (eds), *The Human Meaning of Social Change* (New York: Basic Books, 1972).

68. Elizabeth Dougherty, "Career Satisfaction: Would You Do It Again?" *Research and Development,* vol. 32 (July 1990), pp. 40–47; Michael R. Kagay, "Most Job Holders Content, Poll Says; But Workers Born After 1945 Are Far Less Satisfied, the Gallup Survey Reports," *New York Times* (September 4, 1989), p. A-8; Donna Coco, "And the Survey Says . . ." *EDN Magazine,* vol. 36 (May 16, 1991), pp. S32–33.

69. Marianne Tait, Margaret Youtz Padgett, and Timothy T. Baldwin, "Job and Life Satisfaction: A Reevaluation of the Strength of the Relationship and Gender Effects as a Function of the Date of the Study," *Journal of Applied Psychology,* vol. 74 (June 1989), pp. 502–507; Kno-Tsai Liou, Ronald D. Silvia, and Gregory Brunk, "Non-work Factors and Job Satisfaction Revisited," *Human Relations,* vol. 43 (January 1990), pp. 77–86.

70. E. Cummings, C. Lazer, and L. Chisholm, "Suicide as an Index of Role Strain Among Employed and Not Employed Married Women in British Columbia," *Canadian Review of Sociology and Anthropology,* vol. 12 (1975), pp. 462–470.

71. Janet P. Near, Robert W. Rice, and Raymond G. Hunt, "The Relationship Between Work and Non-work Domains: A Review of Empirical Research," *Academy of Management Review,* vol. 5 (1980), pp. 415–429; Garnet S. Shaffer, "Patterns of Work and Non-work Satisfaction," *Journal of Applied Psychology,* vol. 72 (1987), pp. 115–124; Jeffrey S. Rain, Irving M. Lane, and Dirk D. Steiner, "A Current Look at the Job Satisfaction/Life Satisfaction Relationship: Review and Future Considerations," *Human Relations,* vol. 44 (March 1991), pp. 287–307.

72. Saroj Parasuraman, Jeffrey H. Greenhaus, Samuel Rabinowitz, Arthur G. Bedeian, and Kevin W. Mossholder, "Work and Family Variables as Mediators of the Relationship Between Wives' Employment and Husbands' Well-Being," *Academy of Management Journal,* vol. 32 (March 1989), pp. 185–201.

73. Jacob Wolpin, Ronald J. Burke, and Esther R. Greenglass, "Is Job Satisfaction an Antecedent or a Consequence of Psychological Burnout?" *Human Relations,* vol. 44 (February 1991), pp. 193–209.

74. A. H. Brayfield, and W. H. Crockett, "Employee Attitudes and Employee Performance," *Psychological Bulletin,* vol. 52 (1955), pp. 396–424; Dennis W. Organ, "A Restatement of the Satisfaction-Performance Hypothesis," *Journal of Management,* vol. 14 (December 1988), pp. 547–557.

75. Edward E. Lawler, III, and Lyman W. Porter, "The Effect of Performance on Job Satisfaction," *Industrial*

Relations, a Journal of Economy and Society, vol. 7, no. 1 (October 1967), pp. 20–28.

76. David J. Cherrington, H. Joseph Reitz, and William E. Scott, Jr., "Effects of Contingent and Non-Contingent Reward on the Relationship Between Satisfaction and Task Performance," *Journal of Applied Psychology,* vol. 55 (1971), pp. 531–537; Dennis W. Organ, "A Reappraisal and Reinterpretation of the Satisfaction-Causes-Performance Hypothesis," *Academy of Management Journal,* vol. 2, no. 1 (1977), pp. 46–53.

77. Cherrington, Reitz, and Scott, op. cit.

78. Gary P. Latham and Collette A. Frayne, "Self-Management Training for Increased Job Attendance: A Follow Up and A Replication," *Journal of Applied Psychology,* vol. 74 (June 1989), pp. 411–416.

79. Gary J. Blau, "Relationship of Extrinsic, Intrinsic, and Demographic Predictors to Various Types of Withdrawal Behaviors," *Journal of Applied Psychology,* vol. 70 (1985), pp. 442–450; P. Muchinsky, "Employee Absenteeism: A Review of the Literature," *Journal of Vocational Behavior,* vol. 10 (1977), pp. 316–340.

80. E. Pedalino and V. U. Gamboa, "Behavior Modification and Absenteeism: Intervention in One Industrial Setting," *Journal of Applied Psychology,* vol. 59 (1974), pp. 694–698.

81. Charles L. Hulin, "Job Satisfaction and Turnover in a Female Clerical Population," *Journal of Applied Psychology,* vol. 50 (1966), pp. 280–285.

82. M. J. Cavanagh, M. W. Hurst, and R. Rose, "The Relationship Between Job Satisfaction and Psychiatric Health Symptoms for Air Traffic Controllers," *Personnel Psychology,* vol. 34 (1981), pp. 691–707.

83. E. Palmore, "Predicting Longevity: A Follow-up Controlling for Age," *Gerontologist,* vol. 9 (1969), pp. 247–250.

84. M. Jamal and V. F. Mitchell, "Work, Non-Work, and Mental Health: A Model and a Test," *Industrial Relations,* vol. 19 (1980), pp. 88–93.

85. Chris Clegg and Toby Wall, "The Relationship Between Simplified Jobs and Mental Health: A Replication Study," *Journal of Occupational Psychology,* vol. 63 (December 1990), p. 289.

THE DECLINE OF CORPORATE LOYALTY

Decor Design was a small division of Arrowhead Plastics that was largely built by Helmut Schultz. Helmut was responsible for hiring, training, and supervising the twenty-five employees. Under Helmut's leadership, this group had developed numerous unique designs for the interiors of restaurants and fast food outlets. During the past fifteen years, many of the ideas had been copyrighted and the designs had been patented.

Because of financial difficulty, Arrowhead Plastics found it necessary to sell Decor Design to Freemont Industries. The division was sold as an entire unit, including the building, the patents, and the equipment. With Helmut's reassurance that work would continue as before, none of the employees quit. Although the acquisition was a little unsettling, the employees continued to work hard to achieve the division's goals. It was not uncommon for some employees to work overtime when deadlines were approaching, and some employees even worked over twenty hours per day during crucial periods.

After just ten months of ownership by Freemont Industries, Decor Design was again sold, this time to the Coronet Group, a financial holding company. The new management did not retain Helmut Schultz as the manager. Instead, they promoted Rosemary Olsen, who had served as Helmut's administrative assistant. When they saw that Helmut was not going to be offered a position with the new company, four other members of the division decided to find jobs elsewhere. Rosemary's request to replace those who left was denied by the management of the Coronet Group.

Although the leadership of the Coronet Group was friendly and respectful, the morale among the Decor Design employees deteriorated rapidly. All the employees were very suspicious that their company would soon be sold again. Consequently, none of them were willing to extend themselves to achieve the division's goals or meet the deadlines.

The employees' suspicions were correct. Four months after being bought by the Coronet Group, Decor Design was again sold to Bates United Incorporated. During the negotiations for the sale, the executives from Bates United asked Rosemary if she would continue to manage Decor Design, and which employees she would retain. Rosemary insisted that all eighteen were outstanding employees. The executives of Bates United, however, pointed to the poor performance of the past four months and suggested that, at the most, only three or four of them should be retained.

Questions

1. Is it fair to judge the performance of the employees by what they accomplished during the preceding four months?

2. Before their division was first sold, the employees demonstrated extreme organizational loyalty. Was this loyalty and commitment misguided?

3. What type of performance can the management of Bates United expect from the former employees if they agree to hire them? Would you be willing to hire them? Would you hire them on probationary terms?

4. How can organizational mergers and acquisitions be accomplished without destroying organizational commitment and loyalty?

JOB ATTITUDES

PART I: WORK VALUES

Directions. Read each of the following statements about work and decide the extent to which you agree or disagree with it. Circle the number that comes closest to indicating your true feelings.

	Strongly disagree			Neither			Strongly agree
1. Being a dedicated worker makes you a better person.	1	2	3	4	5	6	7
2. A good indication of your personal worth is how well you do your job.	1	2	3	4	5	6	7
3. Work should be one of the most important parts of a person's life.	1	2	3	4	5	6	7
4. Rich people should feel obligated to work even if they do not need to.	1	2	3	4	5	6	7
5. Unproductive workers are not loyal to their country.	1	2	3	4	5	6	7
6. If I inherited a lot of money I would keep working; I work for reasons other than just to earn wages.	1	2	3	4	5	6	7
7. A worker should do a decent job whether or not the supervisor is around.	1	2	3	4	5	6	7
8. A worker should feel a sense of pride in his or her work.	1	2	3	4	5	6	7
9. An individual should enjoy his or her work.	1	2	3	4	5	6	7
10. Even if you dislike your work, you should do your best.	1	2	3	4	5	6	7
11. Getting recognition for my own work is important to me.	1	2	3	4	5	6	7
12. It's wrong to do a poor job at work just because you think you can get away with it.	1	2	3	4	5	6	7

Scoring. Of the preceding twelve statements, the first six measure the moral importance of work and the last six measure pride in craftsmanship. To compute your moral-importance-of-work score, add your responses to the first six items and divide by 6. To compute your pride-in-craftsmanship score, add your responses to items 7 through 12 and divide by 6. The average scores for 3,000 American workers were moral importance of work = 4.95, and pride in craftsmanship = 6.23.

Questions

1. How would people with strong work values be expected to differ from people who do not believe in the importance of work or do not have pride in craftsmanship, in terms of their responses to career development, motivation, leadership, performance evaluation, compensation, and discipline?

2. What is the difference between a person with high work values and a workaholic?

Adapted, by permission of the publisher, from David J. Cherrington, *The Work Ethic: Working Values and Values That Work*, © 1980 by AMACOM, a division of American Management Association, New York. All rights reserved.

PART II: ATTITUDES AND BEHAVIORS

Purpose. The purpose of this exercise is to examine the relationships between attitudes and behaviors. Use the following questionnaire to measure your attitude toward movies, and then respond to the questions following it.

Read each of the following statements about movies, and decide the extent to which you agree or disagree with it. Circle the number that comes closest to indicating your true feelings.

SD = strongly disagree, D = disagree, N = neutral, A = agree, SA = strongly agree

	SD	D	N	A	SA
1. I really enjoy going to the movies.	1	2	3	4	5
2. Movies are an expensive waste of time.	1	2	3	4	5
3. Going to a movie is a great fantasy experience for me because I escape from reality and identify with the characters in the movie.	1	2	3	4	5
4. Excessive sex and violence in movies is damaging to our society.	1	2	3	4	5
5. Going to movies together is great family entertainment.	1	2	3	4	5
6. I get really irritated at the greasy armrests, sticky floors, and litter scattered in movie theaters.	1	2	3	4	5
7. The motion picture producers have made hundreds of outstanding movies over the years.	1	2	3	4	5
8. Most movie stars do not deserve the wealth and social status they have gained. It is basically unfair.	1	2	3	4	5

Calculate a score measuring your attitude toward movies by adding the numbers you circled for the odd items, and subtracting the numbers you circled for the even items. Your score will be somewhere between minus 16 and plus 16.

1. Within the past month, how many movies have you seen at a theater?

2. Within the past month, how many movies have you seen on a VCR?

3. Within the past month, how many movies have you seen on television?

Questions

1. Does there appear to be any relationship between your attitudes toward movies and the number of movies you have seen?

2. If you correlated movie attitudes and movie attendance for your entire class, what do you think the correlation coefficient would be?

3. If you actually computed the correlations for your class, you would probably find that movie attitudes are more highly correlated with movies seen on TV than in a theater. How do you explain this relationship?

Job Adaptation:
Careers and Stress

LEARNING OBJECTIVES

After studying this chapter, you should be able to

1. Describe the socialization process, and explain how people adapt to organizational requirements.

2. Define the concept of a career and the meaning of career success.

3. List the typical stages employees pass through during their careers.

4. Identify the major variables people consider in selecting an occupation, an organization, and a job.

5. Describe some of the most prominent career-planning programs for helping people develop their careers.

6. Explain the differences among anxiety, depression, burnout, and stress.

7. Describe stress, and explain the physiological responses associated with it.

8. List the most prominent causes and consequences of stress.

9. Identify and describe the major methods for managing stress.

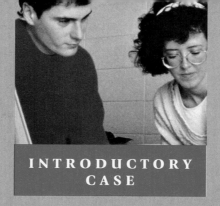

ON BEING AN EMERGENCY MEDICAL TECHNICIAN

"I always planned to be a doctor; I remember announcing in the first grade that some day I would be a doctor. I still felt that way when I started college, but I didn't get the kind of grades I needed to go to medical school. My first two years were horrible; I just didn't take my career very seriously. But back then it didn't seem like anyone else did either, with all the protests and demonstrations.

"A major turn in my career path was when I spent time in the Army and served as a medic in Vietnam. I got some good training in the military and I started to take my career seriously again. I really liked that work; there was something very exciting about patching people up and saving their lives. When I got home, I got a job as an emergency medical technician and finished my college degree. I still wanted to be a doctor. I was married and didn't have enough money for graduate school. Besides, my grades weren't good enough anyway. I've been doing the same thing ever since then.

"We moved out of the city ten years ago when this community decided to start an emergency ambulance service. I was hired to manage the service, and it sounded like a good opportunity. But now I'm not sure what I want. I don't like being an administrator; that just means headaches and ulcers. Besides, it keeps me from doing what I like to do. I still like putting accident victims together; that's still my first love. But I've started to think that ambulance running is for the young. Sure, it's exciting, but it's also emotionally draining and physically taxing. No doubt it's a high-stress job. Sometimes I think that if I don't change careers soon it's going to be me lying in that ambulance."

Questions

1. What is this person's career? How would you evaluate this person's career success? What constitutes a "successful career"?

2. What career advice would you give this person?

CAREERS

This chapter explains how people adapt to work and specifically addresses the concepts of careers and stress. When people decide to work for an organization, they make a significant career decision. Although individuals do influence the organization, the organization has a much larger influence on them. What they think, how they behave, and their choice of friends and associates are all influenced by the organization.

Because such a large portion of a person's life revolves around work, it is not surprising that people want jobs that fulfill their personal needs. Maslow found evidence of this connection between career demands and personal needs in a study that indicated that highly self-actualized people identified with their career work. When Maslow asked the people in his study what they would be if they were not in their respective jobs, many hesitated and had difficulty answering. Others responded with comments such as "I can't say. If I weren't a _____ , I just wouldn't be me, I would be someone else."[1]

Socialization

The process of molding the attitudes and behaviors of people to socially acceptable standards is called **socialization.** This process is particularly important during the formative years of childhood, but it continues during education and employment. Through the socialization process, people acquire the kinds of attitudes and behaviors that are considered necessary to participate as members of an organization. The purpose of socialization is to teach people how to behave in socially acceptable ways consistent with social customs and organizational demands.

Socialization Processes. Organizations have an important stake in the socialization process. To the extent that the goals of the organization are consistent with the members' goals, the organization is more effective and the people are more satisfied and successful.

The socialization process is a continuous activity throughout an individual's career. As the needs of the organization change, and as jobs are redefined, employees must adapt to these changes; that is, they must be socialized. Socialization is especially important when employees begin their first job or change jobs. Organizations use a variety of methods to help people conform to the ever-changing needs of the organization. Three of the most prominent socialization processes include new employee orientations, training and development programs, and performance appraisal.[2]

New employee orientation programs are designed to inform new employees about the mission of the organization and the basic rules and procedures they will be expected to follow. The most basic expectations include such topics as hours of employment, safe working procedures, relationships with co-workers, and job assignments. Most new-employee orientation programs make the mistake of overloading new employees with far too much detailed information to remember at one time. An employee handbook or a procedures manual often helps clarify what is expected of employees.

Training and development programs help to socialize employees by teaching specific job skills, plus the proper attitudes and values demanded by the organization. For example, an effective safety training program not only teaches employees how to perform their jobs safely, but also creates an appropriate attitude about the importance of safety and the need to follow safe procedures.

Performance appraisals are a powerful socializing influence when they are done properly. The appraisal process provides feedback to employees about the appropriateness of their behaviors and attitudes. It also serves as a form of reward or punishment for acceptable behavior, because important outcomes are associated with the appraisal.

In addition to these formal programs, organizations use a variety of informal socialization processes that are described in later chapters, such as the role episode (Chapter 9), communication processes (Chapter 13), decision making (Chapter 14), and organizational development interventions (Chapter 17).

Individuals are effectively integrated into an organization when their interests and goals are consistent with the mission of the organization. This consistency, referred to as **organizational integration,** is maximized when individuals' goals are congruent with the goals of the organization. Occasionally these goals are naturally consistent, such as with most voluntary associations. More frequently, however, people are required to go through a relearning process to acquire the necessary values and behaviors.[3] The most extreme form of this undoing and relearning process involves debasement techniques designed to eliminate individuality, such as those experienced by fraternity pledges, Marine Corps recruits, and military academy plebes. Rigorous initiation ceremonies typically increase the perceived value of membership to new recruits and help them acquire the appropriate attitudes and behaviors.

In socializing new employees, organizations must achieve a balance between oversocialization and undersocialization. This balance is illustrated by Exhibit 8.1. On the one hand, if new employees are undersocialized, their behavior will violate the social norms of the organization and they will rebel against organizational policies and procedures. On the other hand, if people are oversocialized, their behavior will be excessively rigid and conforming. At this end, people lose creativity, individuality, and spontaneity as their behavior adheres to fixed and unquestioned expectations. Between these two extremes, there should be a point where people can display their own creative individuality while still adhering to the social expectations of the organization. At this point they would adhere to those expectations that are required for organizational effectiveness, and they would still maintain a degree of flexibility and autonomy in their own behavior.[4]

Role Transition Process. A person's life history may be viewed as a series of passages from one role to another—from high school student to college student to company trainee to junior partner to senior partner, and so on. The process of advancing from one stage to another has been termed "rites of passage."[5] Three phases are associated with moving from one stage to another: **separation** of the person from the former role, **initiation** into the new role, and **incorporation** into the new environment. These three phases are illustrated in Exhibit 8.2. As people move from one role to another, they experience a form of identity change. The new role requires them to develop a different self-perception regarding their feelings of competency, responsibility, relationships with others, and status.[6]

EXHIBIT 8.1   Balance in Socialization

Undersocialization	Oversocialization
• Poor performance	• Mindless conformity
• Rule violation	• Lack of creativity
• Rebelliousness	• Loss of spontaneity
• Unacceptable conduct	• Dogmatic thinking

Two psychological processes occur between the stages of the **role transition process.** As people who are being advanced begin to separate themselves from their previous environment, they typically experience **anticipatory socialization** in which they begin to adopt the attitudes, attributes, and self-perceptions of the new role before entering it. For example, as MBA students approach graduation, they begin to anticipate what it will be like to be a manager, and they begin to prepare themselves to think and act like professionals in their new role.

The other psychological change occurs as people are incorporated into the new role. The discrepancy between an individual's work expectations before and after joining an organization is referred to as occupational **"reality shock."** Here, people realize that their new role involves more than just the glamour they perceived before. The new role also involves a lot of hard work and responsibility. One study has shown that during the anticipatory socialization, the identity perceptions and self-esteem of those expecting promotion tend to be more favorable than usual, while their self-perceptions and identity become less favorable after the advancement. Studies of Catholic priests and public school teachers, for example, have both shown that the positive self-perception they experienced before a role change were replaced by negative self-perceptions after they were advanced. In both studies, the people reported feeling disillusioned about their new positions.[7]

Before new employees join an organization, they have already experienced a variety of socialization processes. These anticipatory socialization experiences occur long before the person enters the organization, and they help employees anticipate and prepare for working in an organization. Anticipatory socialization comes from many sources, such as formal schooling, actual work experience, and company publications.

Organizations contribute to anticipatory socialization by their recruiting activities and the information they provide to job applicants. Unfortunately, the recruiting activities in many organizations overstate the benefits of working for the company and glorify the job descriptions. Thus organizations often create unrealistic expectations that produce a severe reality shock after the employees join the organization.

A strategy designed to reverse the problem of exaggerated recruiting is giving **"realistic job previews" (RJPs).** Here, recruits are given a balanced presentation that describes both the favorable and unfavorable aspects of the job and the company. For example, a realistic job preview for a school bus driver might include the negative aspects of promptness, rigid scheduling, low pay, and noisy students plus the positive aspects of serving the students and not being confined to an office. Studies have shown that the recruitment rate is about the same for those who

EXHIBIT 8.2	Role Transition Process: Rites of Passage

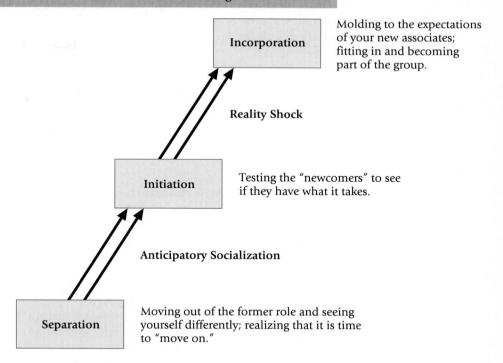

Incorporation

Molding to the expectations of your new associates; fitting in and becoming part of the group.

Reality Shock

Initiation

Testing the "newcomers" to see if they have what it takes.

Anticipatory Socialization

Separation

Moving out of the former role and seeing yourself differently; realizing that it is time to "move on."

receive realistic job previews as for those who do not. More importantly, however, those who receive realistic previews are more likely to remain on the job and to express greater job satisfaction than those who received one-sided presentations. Realistic information facilitates the socialization process by helping people adjust to their jobs and the work environment.[8] Because it contributes to lower turnover and helps employees accommodate better, several companies now use realistic job previews.[9]

Understanding Careers[10]

Discussions of career planning and career development are sometimes confusing because the concept of careers is unclear. For some, "having a career" means working for a large organization and steadily advancing to higher levels of leadership. This view of a career is what some people have in mind when they talk about a "military career": those who remained in the military for twenty years had a career in the military, while those who left after four years did not have a career. Another popular definition of a career is to equate it with a profession. Professional people such as doctors, lawyers, and dentists are thought to have careers, while workers in construction and manufacturing do not. In spite of their popularity, neither definition of careers is acceptable.

Definition of a Career. Every employee has a career. Although career patterns vary considerably, each of us experiences a variety of work-related events that comprise a career. Some people join an organization early in their careers and remain until retirement. Others make significant changes by either changing companies or changing their entire vocation. Nevertheless, everyone experiences a unique sequence of work activities. Two basic assumptions are central to this definition of a career:

1. A career is best viewed as a process of work-related experiences that may include both paid or unpaid work in either one organization or several organizations or as a self-employed person. In essence, everyone who works has a career.

2. The concept of a career does not imply success or failure. Career success or failure is best evaluated by the person whose career is being considered rather than by others.[11]

Career Success. Everyone wants to be successful in life and have a satisfying career. Deciding whether someone has achieved success is difficult, however, because career effectiveness can be measured in many ways. The most popular methods of measuring career effectiveness are career performance, satisfaction, adaptability, and identity.

1. *Career performance.* Career performance is largely measured in terms of the popular symbols of success: money and position. Financial indicators include salary, pay increases, bonuses, and executive perks. Evidences of position and status include the number of employees the individual supervises, the size of the budget for which the person is responsible, the revenue generated by the organizational unit the person manages, and the level of the person's position on the organizational chart.

2. *Satisfaction.* Because people make their own career decisions, success or failure should be judged by each individual. Your success should be determined by whether you are happy with your job and with the company. This criterion is an extremely individual judgment in which we each measure our own career success by deciding whether we like what we do.

3. *Adaptability.* People face a constant threat of obsolescence because new knowledge is created and old knowledge is forgotten. Therefore, another criterion is whether or not people are qualified to perform the new demands placed on them. According to this criterion, career success is measured by maintaining the technical competence needed to adapt to new changes. Adaptability comes from acquiring new skills and knowledge through such activities as self-training, continuing education seminars, job rotation, and independent study.

4. *Career identity.* Career identity is the integration of the individual's work activity and self-esteem. Each of us has a sense of identity that defines who we are. Therefore, an important measure of career success is whether our daily occupations are consistent with our self-identity. A woman who thinks of herself as an interior design decorator and is working in such a position would feel that she had a successful career. But someone would be considered to have an unsuccessful career if, when asked what he did, said, "I'm a clarinet player but I don't have time to join an orchestra because I have to work at the mill." The enormous influence of work on self-identity is reflected by the fact that most people, when asked who they are, describe themselves in terms of their occupation.

Stages of Career Development

Young children progress through a sequence of predictable developmental stages. These stages are characterized by both physical and psychological development, and they are remarkably stable across individuals. Thus, we can explain much of the behavior of young children by knowing their chronological age.

Adults, likewise, progress through a sequence of phases associated with their work experiences. However, the adult phases are not as easy to delineate. The stages of transition in childhood, such as entering grade school, graduating from high school, and becoming old enough to drive or to vote are common experiences to almost all youth, while most of the clear advancements of adults are specific to their occupations. Nevertheless, even during adulthood, a series of relatively discrete career stages common to most people can be identified. Numerous models of career stages have been proposed, including comprehensive models of general life stages and work-related models describing a specific profession.

Life Stages.   One of the most popular developmental stage theories was developed by Erik H. Erikson.[12] His theory begins with infancy and is not restricted to work-related experiences. According to Erikson, people must pass through eight developmental stages on their way to complete maturity. The first four stages—oral, anal, genital, and latency—describe childhood, and, therefore, are not relevant here. The last four stages, which are shown in Exhibit 8.3, describe the process of development from adolescence through maturity. Erikson believes that each stage is characterized by a particular developmental task or crisis that the person must resolve before advancing fully into the next stage.

During the **adolescent stage,** a person seeks to establish a personal identity that includes both sexual identity as a male or female and occupational identity as a person who is expected to eventually become a working, functioning adult. Adolescents begin to develop their occupational interests and to solidify their career preferences during this stage.

During the **young adulthood stage**, a person learns how to work and to love and how to pursue an intensity in both areas without destroying the balance that should exist between them. The developmental task at this stage is to develop involvements that include interpersonal intimacy along with learning how to let oneself become ego involved with another person, group, organization, or cause.

People who resolve crises during the first six stages exceptionally well become trustworthy, autonomous, industrious, highly competent at a variety of tasks, sure of their social and personal roles, and able to identify with and understand the intimate feelings of others. According to Erikson, however, very few people are fortunate enough to successfully pass through all six stages, and therefore most of us are a mixture of partial successes and failures.

During the **adulthood stage,** a person is concerned with **generativity,** the process of helping to socialize and establish the next generation. In a work setting, generativity may be achieved through endeavors such as developing creative theories, building organizations, coaching and sponsoring younger colleagues, and teaching and guiding students. The opposite of generativity is what Erikson calls **stagnation,** which means standing still, producing nothing, and becoming obsolete.

Erikson's eighth stage—**maturity**—occurs during the final years of life when an individual must face the termination of life and thoughts of death. People who are

EXHIBIT 8.3   **The Last Four Developmental Stages of Erik Erikson**

Stage 5   Adolescence

Identity. Being able to find oneself and establish an accurate self-concept in terms of sexual identity and occupational aspirations.

versus

Role confusion. Uncertainty regarding one's sexual identity and an inability to plan one's life in the direction of becoming a working functioning adult.

Stage 6   Young Adulthood

Intimacy. Learning how to become ego-involved with other people, groups, organizations, and causes; learning how to work and love and achieve a balance between them.

versus

Isolation. Becoming absorbed in oneself or afraid to become involved with others; unable to share oneself with others.

Stage 7   Adulthood

Generativity. A concern for establishing and guiding the next generation; having the power to produce things and generate new ideas or new inventions.

versus

Stagnation. Standing still, producing nothing, becoming obsolete.

Stage 8   Maturity

Ego integrity. Satisfaction with the life one has lived; an acceptance of the character one has acquired.

versus

Despair. Dissatisfaction with the life one has lived; a feeling of despair because time is too short to start another life or to try alternate roads to integrity.

---

satisfied with their lives and who can accept the qualities of character they have developed, can integrate the inevitability of death into their patterns of existence.

According to Erikson's theory, people behave differently depending on which developmental stage they are in and how well they have resolved the crises and tasks of earlier stages. Erikson's theory is particularly useful in understanding career development and career stages. Research shows that career stages influence how people perceive organizational events, such as the appointment of a new president or the introduction of a quality improvement program. Career stage provides a frame of reference through which organizational events are interpreted.[13]

Career Stages. Consistent with Erikson's theory of life stages, most career development models identify four career stages as shown in Exhibit 8.4. These four stages include exploration, establishment, maintenance, and decline.[14]

EXHIBIT 8.4   Career Stages

15	**Exploration Stage (ages 15–24)**
20	
25	Self-examination and occupational exploration occur in school, leisure activities, and part-time work.
30	**Establishment Stage (ages 25–44)**
35	
40	After finding an acceptable field, the person strives to make his or her place in it. There may be some trial and experimentation in this stage with consequent restarting.
45	
50	**Maintenance Stage (ages 45–64)**
55	Having made a place in the world of work, the concern is now to hold it. Little new ground is broken, but there is continuation along established lines.
60	
65	**Decline Stage (ages 65+)**
70	As physical and mental powers decline, work activities change and eventually cease. New roles must be developed; first as a limited participant and
75	then as an observer.

Source: Reprinted by permission of the publisher from Donald Super, J. Crites, R. Hummel, H. Moser, P. Overstreet,, and C. Warnath, *Vocational Development: A Framework for Research* (New York: Teachers College Press © 1957 by Teachers College, Columbia University, all rights reserved), pp. 40–41.

During the **exploration stage**, people are completing school, solidifying their career choices, and searching for their first employment. During the stage of exploration, people are primarily concerned about two issues: finding and securing an ideal job. High turnover among younger employees reflects their efforts to improve their employment. Young workers try to match their interests and abilities with the demands of a job. They anxiously pursue better opportunities whenever possible.

During the **establishment stage**, people strive to create a permanent position within their chosen occupation. There may be some trial and error early in this stage, with subsequent career changes, but eventually people seek to create a stable place within the organization to establish their worth and make their contribution. During this period, the organization is also assessing the long-term worth of the individual.

During the **maintenance stage**, people try to protect themselves and secure their positions within the organization. Leaving the organization to pursue a different career is much more difficult at this stage, and people who are laid off or terminated feel very threatened by such actions. The performance levels of people in this stage vary considerably. Some people continue to develop and grow and are highly productive; others begin to stagnate and deteriorate. Problems of obsolescence become particularly acute during this stage. Although some people continue to reach out and grasp new opportunities, others become overly concerned with security and survival.

The final stage is the **decline stage,** in which people approach the end of their employment years and enter retirement. Although the decline stage is typically accompanied by a reduction in the physical and mental abilities of older employees, many older people are capable of contributing far more to the organization than the organization or society allows.

The issues and concerns of people in the establishment stage are not the same as the issues of those in the maintenance stage. During their early career years, when they are becoming established, people are primarily concerned about opportunities for advancement, social status, prestige, doing something important, recognition by others, opportunities to use special aptitudes, opportunities to be creative, and high salary. Many people early in their careers have unrealistically high aspirations and frequently feel a sense of reality shock as they realize their expectations were overly ambitious and unrealistic.

Career success during the establishment stage is greatly influenced by the person's work assignment. The first year is a particularly crucial period, when new employees are susceptible to learning new attitudes and adjusting to the requirements of the job. Competent supervisors who patiently coach and encourage can have a profound influence on the career success of new employees.

During the middle of their careers, when employees are in the maintenance stage, their concerns involve a different set of issues than earlier. Physical aging contributes to an awareness of the inevitability of death. People begin to realize that many of their career goals may never be achieved, and some are forced to search for more realistic life goals.

During their early forties, many people experience a "mid-life crisis" that can be very traumatic and difficult. A variety of threatening circumstances often contribute to a feeling of anxiety and despair, such as rebellious teenagers at home, financial pressures, a growing sense of obsolescence on the job, and a threat of being replaced by a younger employee. While these problems are viewed as challenges by some employees to spur them to higher levels of performance and competence, others are thrown into a state of constant defensiveness in which they simply try to endure.

During the mid-life decade, which typically occurs between the ages of 35 and 45, people tend to appraise their life accomplishments and ask such questions as "What have I done with my life? What do I really get from and give to my spouse, children, friends, work, community, and self? What are my real values and how are they reflected in my life?" One study of men in mid-career found that 80 percent experienced significant struggles over career or family that frequently resulted in moderate or severe crises, forcing these men to question every facet of their lives. To resolve these crises, many people were required to make new choices about career and family and accept a more realistic view of themselves and their limitations of time and ability.[15]

Professional Career Stages. A model of career development that focuses specifically on professionals (engineers, lawyers, and accountants) has been developed by Gene Dalton and Paul Thompson.[16] Their research identified four career stages, as shown in Exhibit 8.5. Stage I professionals are typically new employees who have recently completed their professional training and must now learn to

EXHIBIT 8.5   Professional Career Stages

Central Activities, Relationships, and Psychological Issues in Four Career Stages

	Stage I	Stage II	Stage III	Stage IV
Central activity	Helping Learning Following directions	Independent contributor	Training Interfacing	Shaping the direction of the organization
Primary relationship	Apprentice	Colleagues	Mentor	Sponsor
Major psychological issues	Dependence	Independence	Assuming responsibility for others	Exercising power

Reprinted by permission of the publisher, from "The Four Stages of Professional Careers—A New Look at Performance by Professionals," by Gene W. Dalton, Paul H. Thompson, and Raymond L. Price, *Organizational Dynamics* (Summer 1977), p. 23. © 1977 AMACOM, a division of American Management Association, New York. All rights reserved.

work under the direction of someone who supervises their activities and evaluates their performance.

After the new professionals have demonstrated their abilities to follow directions and perform competently, they advance to Stage II, where they are independent contributors. Here, they work on their own in performing their professional activities. Professionals in Stage III are involved in training and directing the work of others, particularly those who are in Stage I. Professionals at this level are evaluated not only on their own performance but also on their ability to supervise others. Professionals in Stage IV are involved in making strategic decisions that guide the organization and shape its direction. Those who are most active in shaping the mission of the organization are the professionals in Stage IV.

Dalton and Thompson examined the relationship between career stages and performance. They found that the performance ratings of professionals depended in part on whether they were performing the "right" activities or, in other words, activities that were consistent with their career stage. For example, their data suggested that professionals older than 40 were generally not considered above-average performers unless they had moved into Stages III and IV. Only 18 percent of those over age 40 who were still in stage I or II were rated as above-average performers. Apparently, age and experience are associated with fairly well-accepted expectations about the kinds of activities people should be performing. Those who are performing activities inconsistent with their professional career stage generally suffer from a lack of social acceptance.

Career Choices

As their careers unfold, people make numerous career choices. Some of these decisions are irreversible, because decisions made early in one's career can eliminate options later in life. For example, deciding to drop out of high school and not go to college immediately eliminates many professional and technical jobs from the individual's later choices. However, most career decisions are not permanent, and there is little need for anyone to feel locked into a dead-end job. People who are not satisfied with the work they are doing are free to pursue something more suitable. Most people's careers involve working in a variety of jobs in multiple organizations. A study of college graduates indicated that five years after graduation, at least 50 percent had changed organizations and some had even changed occupations.[17]

It is not unusual for people to make a significant career change and pursue a totally different line of work. In fact, it has been estimated that the average person will pursue at least three different careers during his or her lifetime. Making a significant career change usually helps people acquire new skills, avoid obsolescence, and become more enthusiastic about life and work. A gardening metaphor is used to explain the rejuvenating effects of changing careers in mid-life. These people are called "repotters." The most common motivation for changing careers is to find more meaningful work.[18]

Career decisions involve many choices. Three of the most important choices include (1) occupational choice—selecting a vocation or profession; (2) organizational choice—deciding which company to work for; and (3) job choice—selecting a desirable job.

Occupational Choice. The selection of an occupation is not a decision that is made once and for all at one dramatic point in life. Instead, occupational choices are made and revised repeatedly throughout a person's life. Earlier choices influence later choices and generally restrict the range of future possibilities.

Many studies have examined the variables that influence occupational choice. This research indicates that the factors of socioeconomic status, race, gender, community, intelligence, and aptitudes and interests have a significant influence on the kinds of occupations people select.[19]

1. *Socioeconomic status.* The socioeconomic status of parents has a large influence on the occupations selected by children. Children from families at higher socioeconomic levels are more likely to choose careers in law, medicine, or business management than in nonsalaried professions.[20] The socioeconomic levels of parents appears to influence the kinds of career information and opportunities open to their children. Children raised in families from higher socioeconomic level receive more information about the educational opportunities and professional training required for higher professional occupations. Furthermore, their parents communicate higher expectations about the amount of discipline and study necessary for success.

2. *Race.* Although considerable progress has been made in providing more equal employment opportunities, a larger proportion of minorities than whites enter lower-status occupations. This discrepancy occurs even though the vocational preferences (the ideal jobs they would like to have) of minorities and whites are similar. Apparently, minorities are forced to compromise their eventual career choices more than whites.[21]

3. *Gender.* For many years, certain jobs were classified as either male or female jobs. For example, mining and construction jobs were considered male occupations while nursing and telephone operator jobs were considered female occupations.

Although significant efforts have been made in recent years to eliminate these stereotypes, cultural norms, child-rearing practices, and other social expectations continue to perpetuate the feeling among many people that certain jobs are primarily intended for a particular sex.

4. *Communities.* Occupational choice is influenced by the occupational structure found in a community. Significant differences have been found between rural and urban locations.[22] People who are reared in rural communities generally aspire to occupations with lower prestige than those from urban communities. These differences have been attributed to the limited educational opportunities found in rural areas and the lack of career information available to people.

5. *Intelligence.* A relationship has been observed between average intelligence levels and occupational choice.[23] For example, taken as a group, people in accounting, mechanical engineering, medicine, chemistry, and electrical engineering have intelligence levels that are slightly above average. However, teamsters, miners, farmworkers, and lumberjacks have below-average intelligence, when considered as a group. It should be noted, however, that even though a relationship exists between intelligence and occupation when considering large sample sizes, a broad range of intelligence is found in every occupation. A certain minimum intelligence is important in any occupation, and people who are more intelligent have more opportunities for promotion.

6. *Aptitudes and interests.* Probably the greatest determinants of occupational choice are aptitudes and interests. Often we allow our vocational interests to override considerations about our aptitudes and abilities. What we want to do becomes more important than what we are capable of doing best. Indeed, asking young adults what occupation they want to enter is generally the best predictor of their eventual occupation.[24]

People who have special aptitudes and abilities typically try to find occupations where they can use these skills to achieve success in their work. Because occupational success often depends on having the necessary skills, people should carefully assess their aptitudes and use this information to make wise occupational choices. The evidence shows, however, that many people do not assess their abilities very accurately. One study found mainly low correlations between the self-evaluations of a group of adolescents and how these people were measured on a battery of tests.[25]

These six factors have long been operating in the lives of people and have significantly influenced occupational preferences. Their implications should not be overlooked. Long-term career choices can limit an organization's ability to attract and retain new employees and can influence the effectiveness of recruiting activities. Before a recruiter tries to sell a job opening, the applicants may have already decided that they are not willing to consider it. Consequently, these background variables may represent formidable obstacles to organizations who are attempting to achieve affirmative action goals of hiring larger percentages of women and members of minorities. For example, a decision by AT&T to employ women in outdoor crafts jobs was found to be more difficult to implement than anticipated. To achieve its goals, the company had to launch an aggressive educational program in the public schools to convince girls that outdoor crafts jobs are a legitimate occupation for women.

**APPLYING ORGANIZATIONAL BEHAVIOR
IN THE NEWS**

The Stress of Termination

CNN Being fired from a job is a traumatic experience. Job loss ranks close to the death of a close family member in terms of stress and is one of the major causes of suicide.

Drake Beam Morin, the nation's largest outplacement firm, tries to help people when they are terminated, by providing professional social support. Drake is hired by companies planning cuts. These companies recognize that hiring an outplacement firm not only helps soften the blow of firing, but also decreases lawsuits and reduces stress among the remaining employees.

In recent years, with the economic upheaval of mergers, acquisitions, and downsizing, job security has eroded. Hundreds of thousands of workers have been terminated as a result of corporate restructurings. Top and middle managers, who almost always assumed their jobs were perfectly secure, were just as vulnerable as those at the bottom of the wage scale.

Outplacement services often mean the difference between hope and despair. An outplacement counselor can provide valuable social support plus insightful suggestions regarding such issues as how to explain your termination to your family, what to say to your friends, how to begin a new job search, and whether you want to remain in the same career. Drake Beam Morin boasts that about 97 percent of the ex-employees it helps find new jobs, with more than 70 percent finding jobs that pay as well as or better than their old jobs.

Source: CNN *Pinnacle* news programming.

Organizational Choice. In addition to choosing an occupation, people also choose the organization in which their occupation will be performed. Occasionally people choose an organization when they choose a job, because their job offers come from different organizations. Three characteristics seem to influence organizational choice: the organization's mission, its image, and its culture or personality.

1. *Organizational mission.* Organizations serve a wide variety of societal purposes, and people may be attracted to an organization because of its particular mission. Since people have their own career interests, they typically select an organization whose mission is consistent with their career interests. For example, people with social interests may prefer occupations in teaching and helping others, such as a mental hospital or a government welfare agency. And people who have intellectual interests may prefer scientific occupations and choose to work for a university or a research and development institute.

2. *Organizational image.* Some people are attracted to an organization because of the status and prestige associated with the organization or the industry to which it belongs. In recent years, chemical companies have had a reputation for polluting the environment, government agencies have had a reputation for bureaucratic inefficiencies, and railroads have had an image of financial decline. Although these reputations are not entirely accurate and some organizations are quite different from their industry's image, individuals' perceptions of an organization influence their employment decisions.

The image of the organization also influences the status and social life of employees outside the work setting. Employees tend to transfer the status and prestige of the organization to their own status and prestige in society. The image of their organization becomes part of their own self-concept. A study examining the reasons why employees decided to remain with or leave an organization found that the decision was greatly influenced by the prestige of the organization as viewed by an employee's spouse.[26] Consequently, the image of an organization and the status of the industry seem to be important in attracting and keeping employees.

3. *Organizational personality.* Some evidence demonstrates that people are attracted to organizations that show "personalities" or styles similar to their own. In one study, the personalities of a group of subjects were measured in a number of dimensions and the subjects were then asked to describe the personalities of the organizations in which they would most prefer and least prefer to work. The results of this study indicated that the same dimensions were used for describing both the personality of the individual and the personality of their preferred organization. The better the match of personalities, the more highly the organization was preferred.[27] These results are consistent with other studies suggesting that people choose vocations consistent with their self-esteem or self-concept.

Job Choice. Several factors associated with the job itself influence an individual's job choice. The job factors most frequently examined in studies of job choice include:

1. Pay and benefits
2. Geographical location
3. The level of responsibility and leadership
4. Flexible work hours and an opportunity to pursue a particular lifestyle
5. Autonomy and independence
6. Opportunity to use special skills and abilities
7. Providing essential services and products for society
8. Friendly co-workers
9. Friendly supervision

Several studies have tried to estimate the relative importance of these job factors. The results generally show that pay and benefits are the most important factors involved in choosing a job.[28] However, the results are not entirely consistent, and the evidence seems to suggest that the results are influenced greatly by the method used to collect the information. When people are asked to rank the job factors in order of importance, they usually rank responsibility, opportunities for growth, and the opportunity to provide essential services as the most important factors. However, when they are shown job descriptions and asked to select between several pairs of jobs, their preferences seem to be most strongly influenced by pay and benefits.[29]

A hierarchical decision framework has been proposed to explain the relative importance of these job choice factors.[30] This framework suggests that applicants first consider **objective factors** associated with alternative job offers, such as salary, benefits, location, and the job requirements. These factors can be objectively evaluated and, in some cases, a dollar figure can be assigned to them. Objective job factors that can be easily measured, such as a job having a $200-higher starting salary or being located two hundred miles closer to home, appear to be the most important factors involved in choosing a job.

If the objective factors are roughly comparable, applicants are likely to turn to **subjective factors** and base their decisions on such things as the organization's image and the opportunity to serve society. Subjective factors are concerned with how well alternative jobs will satisfy personal needs and career goals; they may include such things as organizational prestige, responsibility, freedom from supervision, and the opportunity to benefit society. These subjective factors tend to be emotional and intuitive rather than objective.

If both the objective and subjective factors are roughly comparable, new recruits tend to base their decision on **critical contacts** with the organization. Recruits are influenced by how they feel about their interview and the interviewer, how speedily the organization handled the correspondence, and how hospitable the company representatives were during visits to the company offices. Critical contacts with the company are usually influential only if the objective and subjective factors are comparable, or when the recruits do not know enough about the organization to rate one above the other.

Career Planning

People differ in terms of how well they plan their careers. Some people develop elaborate career plans with specific timetables and clearly defined goals, while others do essentially no planning at all. During the last three or four weeks of spring semester, college placement offices are typically flooded with students who have failed to plan what they want to do after graduation. Other students do an excellent job of managing their careers. They know which careers they want to pursue, and they arrange their educational training to prepare them for their careers. Long before graduation they conduct an aggressive job search to find which organizations offer them the best opportunities to fulfill their career aspirations.

Importance of Career Planning. The responsibility for career planning is an individual responsibility. Finding a job does not just happen; people have to make it happen. Every person should be responsible for managing his or her own career regardless of economic factors influencing the supply and demand of labor. A useful concept in career planning is for people to view themselves as one-person corporations. Corporations must be responsible for producing products and services, for research and development, and for marketing their products. Likewise, people must be concerned about being able to provide useful products and services, maintaining relevant skills and knowledge, and finding ways to sell their efforts and abilities.

A major ingredient of successful career planning is looking ahead. College placement directors report that because some college students fail to plan adequately, about 10 percent of each graduating class is unemployed and another 20 percent are grossly underemployed or working below their levels of education or expectations. Approximately three out of ten college students usually fail to find compatible, fulfilling jobs because they spent too little effort in matching their interests and abilities with job opportunities.[31]

Finding a good job does not simply depend on luck or chance. It involves a careful process of assessing one's own abilities and interests, becoming aware of job opportunities, preparing an effective resume, locating job opportunities, interviewing prospective employers, and then assessing the job offers. Each of these activities takes time. You should begin to look for a job before graduation or before terminating other employment.

Effective career planning benefits both the employee and the company. For the individual, the most immediate benefits of career development include a better job, more money, increased responsibility, greater mobility, better use of skills, and higher productivity. Career development also provides less tangible benefits for people, such as increased satisfaction. The development of a career orientation rather than a job orientation is another valuable by-product of career planning that leads to increased involvement in work, greater exposure and visibility to top management, a better understanding of what is expected, and a broader knowledge of additional areas of career interest.[32]

Career planning benefits organizations by identifying and developing future managers. Career-planning activities are designed to nurture employees and increase their capacity to achieve organizational goals. When competent replacements are available, an organization can adopt a policy of promotion from within which motivates aspiring managers. Employees who remain in the same position for an extended period typically become obsolete. Career planning helps to avoid the problems of obsolescence by training employees and stimulating their desires to maintain their job skills.

Career-Planning Programs. Many organizations provide a broad assortment of activities to help employees manage their careers. Some of the most frequently used career development programs include these:[33]

1. *Career counseling and performance evaluation*: career-oriented discussions between supervisors and subordinates regarding their current performance and future goals.[34]

2. *Career pathing*: identifying the sequence of jobs through which people are expected to progress and how long they can expect to be in each job.

3. *Human resource planning*: developing a succession plan and a replacement chart showing the most likely replacements for each position on the organization chart. Some organizations use special career information systems such as job posting and bidding systems or announcements on bulletin boards or in company newsletters to make people aware of promotion opportunities.

4. *Training and development programs:* programs providing specific developmental experiences such as job rotation, conferences, seminars, technical skills training, intern programs, tuition reimbursement, and in-house supervisory and management development training.

5. *Special-interest programs*: programs designed to fill special needs such as pre-retirement counseling for employees soon to retire and orientation programs for the handicapped or members of minorities.

6. *Mentoring:* assigning an experienced employee to work closely with a new employee to provide on-the-job coaching and encouragement.

Work and Family

Most people feel a constant tension between the demands of work and family responsibilities. Maintaining a comfortable balance between these two factors has become increasingly difficult because of changes in the traditional family structure, the increase in female employment, and the shortage of skilled workers in some industries. Everyone who works must resolve the conflict between work and family responsibilities. Dual-career families, where both husband and wife pursue full-time employment, present special challenges to both organizations and individuals, especially when employees are responsible for the care of young children or aging parents.

Dual-career Families. After World War II, the dominant labor market trend was to release women from the workforce, where they had supported the war effort, and allow them to remain at home raising the baby boom generation. This trend was reversed in the 1960s, however, as increasing numbers of women joined the labor force. The growth in **dual-career families** is reflected in the changes in the participation rates of women: from 1960 to 1990, the percent of eligible women in the 25-to-34 age category who joined the labor force increased from 36.0 percent to 78.1 percent.[35] This increase in female employment represents a profound social trend that requires families and organizations to develop new patterns of accommodation.

The most difficult problems accompanying this change concern the care of young children and balancing other family responsibilities when both parents work. While some couples have joint career aspirations and both want to pursue careers outside the home, many couples prefer having one partner remain at home or only hold part-time employment when there are young children in the home.

The percentage of children living in dual-career families and single-parent families continues to increase. From 1975 to 1990, the number of children under 18 years of age decreased from 63.5 million to 58.4 million. During this time, the percentage of children living in traditional families (with the father employed and mother not employed) decreased from 46 to 26 percent, while the percentage of children in dual-career families increased from 30 to 44 percent and in single-parent families increased from 16 to 24 percent.[36] Forecasts indicate that the percentages of dual-career and single-parent families will continue to increase because of two primary reasons: career fulfillment and money.

Money is usually an important consideration in the decision to have both partners work; having two incomes is an economic necessity for some couples. The average income of a dual-career family is about 25 percent higher than a traditional family.[37] But while the incomes of dual-career families are higher, so are the costs: spending patterns indicate that dual-career families spend more on services and nondurable goods.[38] Consequently, the average disposable incomes of a dual-career family may not be much different from those of traditional families if they must pay more for taxes, child care, elder care expenses, household services, clothing, and prepared foods.

Studies on the effects of dual-career families indicate that the lives of both parents and children are affected by the decision to have both parents work full time. Having a second source of income creates a greater sense of financial security for both partners, and the feelings of freedom and professional self-determination are especially pronounced in men.[39] However, other results are not so positive.

The growth in dual-career families has been accompanied by an increase for women in physical and social problems that were once dominated by men, such as heart disease, heart attacks, ulcers, hypertension, and white-collar crime. Dual-career partners typically experience greater stress as they try to balance housework and child care, and this burden falls unevenly on women in most families. Significant feelings of guilt are reported by both dual-career partners, with women usually reporting slightly higher levels.[40] In dual-career families, wives spend more hours doing housework than husbands, although dual-career husbands do more than traditional husbands. Daughters in dual-career families do 25 percent more housework than the daughters in traditional homes. The sons of dual-career families, however, only do about one-third as much housework as sons in traditional families, and they often develop very chauvinistic attitudes.[41] Men in dual-career families report lower job satisfaction than men in traditional families.[42]

There is little doubt that some dual-career families experience intense stress that reduces the quality of life for all family members, both at home and at work. There is also evidence, however, that these problems are not universal in all dual-career families and the stress can be reduced by satisfactory child care facilities and flexibility in work schedules. Employers are being asked to provide greater flexibility to accommodate family demands of workers.[43]

Balancing Work and Family. Adapting work demands to family responsibilities has been referred to as **accommodation.**[44] People who give the highest priority to family responsibilities, while work and other outside interests remain secondary, are said to be the most accommodative. The most nonaccommodative are those for whom work and career interests are always a higher priority than family responsibilities. In the past, the most accommodative people were the wives and mothers in traditional families, who assumed responsibility for the family needs; the most nonaccommodative were career-oriented male executives, who focused their interests and attention almost exclusively on work.

In recent years, new patterns of accommodation have emerged, largely because husbands are becoming more accommodative. Most women who are employed outside the home think their husbands should share household responsibilities. To achieve a successful marriage, dual-career couples need to decide who is responsible for such things as child care, meal preparation, housecleaning, shopping, yard work, and other family responsibilities. Unplanned events and emergencies often present special problems of accommodation, such as deciding which spouse remains home with a sick child or who should arrange for the repair of a household appliance.

The trend toward greater accommodation in our society on the part of husbands is indicated by the number of successful managers who, at mid-career, reject advancement opportunities because their new responsibilities would interfere with family commitments.

Organizations have been encouraged to develop alternative career tracks for mothers and fathers, letting them sacrifice career advancement for the chance to spend more time with their families. A separate "mommy" or "daddy" track lets parents hold flexible jobs with less travel and fewer time demands while they have responsibilities for young children at home.[45] When their parenting demands ease,

APPLYING ORGANIZATIONAL BEHAVIOR
RESEARCH

Work and Family Conflict in Dual-Career Families

Although we try to separate life and keep work problems at work and family problems at home, it doesn't seem to happen that way. Problems at work spill over into family life, and family problems create conflicts at work.

An empirical study examined conflicts at work and at home and how these conflicts influenced the quality of work life, the quality of family life, and overall life satisfaction. The participants were 220 professional employees, each with a working spouse and children in the home. Each person responded to a 135-item questionnaire.

The study found highly significant and positive relationships between work conflict and family conflict, indicating that work and family are not independent dimensions of life. Conflict on the job increases conflict in the home, and *vice versa.* Having both parents in the workforce has a profound impact on the family, especially if either one experiences a high degree of work conflict on the job.

When there is conflict at work or in the home, this conflict apparently causes conflict between work and home. Both work conflict and family conflict were significantly related to work–family conflict.

The results also indicated that we pay a heavy price for these conflicts. Conflicts either at home or at work diminish the quality of life and overall life satisfaction. Both the quality of work life (QWL) and the quality of family life (QFL) were negatively affected by work–family conflict. By lowering the QWL and the QFL, the clash between work roles and family roles also affects other factors such as absenteeism, turnover, marital discord, family breakdowns, and productivity. Furthermore, QWL and QFL are both shown to be strong predictors of overall life satisfaction.

Life can be very difficult for dual-career families, especially when both partners hold professional jobs and there are young children in the home. From 1981 to 1986, the proportion of women in the workforce who had children increased from 34 to 55 percent. These women face very difficult challenges as they try to balance family responsibilities with demanding work schedules. The lives of men are also affected, as they have to assume more family responsibilities and adjust their priorities toward the family and away from work. The consequence for both husbands and wives is greater work–family conflict.

Source: Christopher Alan Higgins, Linda Elizabeth Duxbury, and Richard Harold Irving, "Work–Family Conflict in the Dual-Career Family," *Organizational Behavior and Human Decision Processes*, vol. 51 (1992), pp. 51–75.

they once again pursue a fast track. Having a separate mommy track has been severely criticized, however, by those who fear it will be used as a pretext for discrimination against women, or as proof that women can't "have it all"—both motherhood and a career.[46]

A major problem for a dual-career couple is a job transfer involving relocation. This situation poses a problem not only for the couple but also for the organization. Some organizations offer to help an employee's spouse find a job when it wants to relocate an employee. Some dual-career couples find they must live in a metropolitan area to increase the career opportunities of both partners.[47]

Many couples have decided that the benefits of dual careers are not worth the costs, and a growing number of women have decided that the joys of mothering justify interrupting their careers. The process of leaving the workforce to raise a family and then returning is called **sequencing**, and an informal survey indicates that a growing number of career women are choosing sequencing as a means of balancing career and family interests.[48] Women who elect to sequence their career first complete their education and work a short time, usually two to eight years, in their chosen careers. Then they leave full-time work during the years they bear and care for their young children, and then—as their children grow—innovate new ways to incorporate professional activities into their lives so that mothering and profession do not conflict.

Employment gaps by women, especially for child rearing, are generally perceived as acceptable career decisions that do not seriously damage their career advancement. An investigation of employment gaps among MBA graduates revealed that discontinuous employment histories were negatively associated with future income and satisfaction for men, but not as much for women. Although an employment gap for women who return to work reduces their income 9 percent below what it would have been with continuous employment, a corresponding gap for men reduces their income by 21 percent.[49]

Some of the innovative ways women become reincorporated in the workforce, such as through job sharing and permanent part-time employment, were discussed in Chapter 6. Other programs designed to help dual-career families include flexible work hours, work-at-home programs, relocation help for the spouse of a transferred employee, child care and day care assistance, time management and stress management workshops, and employee assistance programs.

Another specific way organizations can help employees cope with the stress of dual-career families is to legitimize boundaries between work and home. For example, when professional employees are home in the evenings, are they still on call, or can they dedicate themselves to home and family? Some organizations help create boundaries by stating that evenings and weekends are viewed as family time, and employees and their supervisors should not allow work to encroach on family time. A consequence of this policy is that people who stay late are not seen as superachievers, but as poor time managers.[50]

STRESS

A major component of adapting to work is learning to manage **stress.** Everyone experiences stress and its effects can be either positive or negative. People who achieve an optimal level of stress tend to work at peak efficiency, report high levels of job satisfaction, and experience a sense of accomplishment and well-being. Unfortunately, many people experience levels of stress that are either too high or too low. When stress is too low, we tend to feel lethargic, lazy, and bored. However, excessive levels of stress can produce a loss of efficiency, excessive accidents, ill health, drug abuse, alcoholism, and other undesirable physical consequences.

Excessive stress caused by pressures both on and off the job represents a major problem in industry today. Everyone should understand what causes stress and appreciate the effects of stress on physical and mental well-being. Many of the physical and emotional problems college students experience are partially created by unhealthy levels of stress that they don't understand and don't know how to control. Too many people mistakenly associate stress with mental illness and are unwilling to recognize the causes or consequences of stress in their lives.

Mental Health

The mental health of employees is just as important as their physical health. A highly stressful work environment can be extremely destructive to the mental health of employees; it can also be a major cause of accidents and inefficiency. Mental illness is caused by many factors both on and off the job, including child abuse and other traumatic childhood experiences, marital conflicts and an unhappy family life, peer pressure and social ridicule, and a stressful work environment. Everyone occasionally feels frustrated, depressed, and a bit insecure, but most people are able to cope with temporary setbacks.

Maintaining good mental health requires a healthy environment just as the maintenance of good physical health requires good hygiene. Mental illness sometimes involves serious emotional problems that require professional psychiatric help. However, the emotional problems of most people are not that severe. Most employees can adjust to everyday problems and can live reasonably healthy, normal lives. A stressful, unpleasant work environment can cause severe trouble for some employees by destroying their self-esteem and making them feel inadequate. Creating a healthier work environment can make a big difference in improving their mental health.

Anxiety and Depression. Two of the most common mental disorders are anxiety and depression. **Anxiety** is a state of tension associated with worry, apprehension, guilt, and a constant need for reassurance. Anxiety is more than the ordinary fear and apprehension that is consistent with reality. For example, if a person is scheduled to speak to an executive board, some fear and apprehension are normal and even desirable. Moderate amounts of tension help to improve performance—without some degree of concerned anticipation, a person might be indifferent and apathetic. Anxiety, however, is a general state of fear and apprehension that is abnormally high and is not associated with a specific cause.

Depression is a mood that is characterized by dejection and gloom and that usually contains feelings of worthlessness, guilt, and futility. Depression is more than just being unhappy or sad: unhappiness is usually associated with a specific unpleasant event; depression is an intense sadness that has lost its relationship to a specific series of events. Moreover, depression may be mild or severe. When it is severe, someone may be unable to make even simple decisions or to respond to customary, everyday situations. In its extreme form, depression occasionally leads to suicide.

Both anxiety and depression are accompanied by a host of physiological effects. Anxiety usually leads to profuse perspiration, difficulty in breathing, gastric disturbances, rapid heartbeat, frequent urination, muscle tension, diarrhea, or high blood pressure. Depression is usually associated with a series of biochemical disturbances that may be linked to a genetic predisposition. Both anxiety and depression have been treated with drugs. However, recent reports discourage the use of drugs, especially as a long-term solution. Drug treatments often have undesirable side effects and usually do not solve emotional problems in the long run. Various forms of psychiatric counseling are recommended for severe cases. For mild forms, a good book, a vacation, or talks with close friends are highly recommended.[51]

Burnout and Boredom. An inability to handle continued stress on the job that results in demoralization, frustration, and reduced efficiency, has been called **burnout.** Some occupations are particularly prone to burnout, mainly those which require great personal commitment and involvement. Burnout was first observed as a general problem among people who work in the helping professions, especially psychiatrists, social workers, and counselors. Similar problems were observed among medical personnel who work with patients, especially nurses and physical therapists. The term has also been used to explain the frustration and apathy of schoolteachers who have taught for many years. Burnout has even been used to describe the apathy of dentists, office managers, personnel directors, and students. The concept of burnout is popular because it helps to explain why people who are constantly asked to give of themselves can come to feel emotionally drained. However, the concept also has been abused, because it has been used as a socially acceptable excuse for indolence among white-collar workers who are simply bored with their jobs.[52]

Boredom encompasses the psychological responses of workers to repetitive jobs. Not all repetitive activities, however, are boring. For example, playing a slot machine is a very repetitive activity that some people find very interesting. But jobs that have short work cycles and require the workers to do the same thing again and again are usually described as boring. Assembly-line jobs are frequently described as the most boring jobs.

Although boredom and burnout are different problems, they are both caused in part by a lack of meaning in work. Burnout occurs on jobs that usually provide a considerable amount of variety, significance, skill, and responsibility. At first, employees feel excited about their work and their opportunities to make a significant contribution. They invest themselves in their jobs and often work extra hours. After a while the excitement wears off, yet the job still demands much effort and commitment. However, the jobs are no longer meaningful to the employees, and they feel unwilling to exert the effort needed. Periodic vacations are usually recommended for professionals to take time to reassess the meaning and importance of their work. But like blue-collar workers who are bored with their work, some professionals feel they have to find a different job.[53]

Stress. **Stress** is the nonspecific response of the body to stressors within the environment. Stressors can appear in a variety of forms, and almost any physical or psychological demand can serve as a stressor. Some examples of stressors include a barking dog about to attack you, a speeding auto about to hit you, an executive committee you are planning to address, or a disciplinary hearing to suspend an employee. The variety of potential stressors is shown in Exhibit 8.6. All these stressors have one thing in common: they represent a potential demand that may exceed the person's ability or capacity to respond. Thus stress involves an interaction between the person and the environment. It should be remembered, however, that not all people perceive the environment similarly, and an extremely stressful situation for one person may not be stressful for another. Stressful events are not necessarily negative; a passionate kiss and receiving an award are positive experiences even though they create the same physiological responses as negative stressors.

Physiology of Stress

To understand stress properly requires an understanding of the physiological changes that occur during stress. Our bodies experience a predictable series of physiological changes during periods of extreme stress, regardless of whether the stressors are positive or negative.

EXHIBIT 8.6   **Typical Stressors**

Physical Environment Stressors
- Hazardous jobs and toxic substances
- Busy highways and bad driving conditions
- Stormy weather

Individual Stressors
- Type A personality
- Low tolerance for ambiguity

Job Stressors
- Time pressures and deadlines
- Pressure to perform and exposure to the public
- Limited control over important matters
- Responsibility for the well-being of others
- Too much or too little work to do

Organizational Stressors
- Inefficient work procedures
- Unfair policies and inequitable practices
- Office politics
- Role conflict

Life Stressors
- Death of a spouse or serious illness
- Divorce or family conflicts
- Financial problems
- Pregnancies and childbirth
- Marriage and falling in love

General Adaptation Syndrome. Occupational stress has received a considerable amount of attention in recent years largely because of the pioneering research of Hans Selye, a famous endocrinologist. In 1936 Selye described a **general adaptation syndrome (GAS),** which was a major discovery in understanding the stress response.[54] Selye made a clear distinction between stress and a stressor. Stress is the nonspecific response of the body to any demand placed on it. A stressor is the object or event that caused the stress.

When a stressor is present, a sequence of biological events occurs. The same sequence of biological events can be triggered by many different situations, both pleasant and unpleasant. Because the same syndrome of physiological responses is elicited by many different situations, Selye called it the *general adaptation syndrome (GAS).* The GAS consists of three stages: alarm, resistance, and exhaustion.

The **alarm reaction** occurs when a stressor is recognized. A biochemical message is sent from the brain to the pituitary gland, which is a small gland just below the brain. The pituitary gland, the master control of the endocrine system, secretes adrenocorticotrophic hormone (ACTH) which causes the adrenal gland to secrete corticosteroids such as adrenalin. Immediately the entire endocrine system is engaged in the secretion of complex hormones, and a general alarm is sent to all systems of the body.

During the **resistance stage,** the body tries to return to a state of equilibrium once the immediate threat has passed. The physiological changes in this stage are mostly the exact opposite of those that characterize the alarm reaction. The body tries to regain a state of balance even if the stressor is present.

If the stressor continues and the body exhausts its ability to adapt, the **exhaustion stage** sets in. The symptoms of the exhaustion stage are similar to the alarm reaction. If the stress persists, severe wear and tear will occur, resulting in damage to a local area or death to the organism as a whole.

The alarm reaction also has been called the "fight or flight" response. In this stage, the autonomic nervous system makes dozens of immediate responses to prepare the body for physical action. When pedestrians are crossing the street and suddenly see a car speeding toward them, the alarm reaction prepares their bodies to quickly get out of the way. Some of the major responses that the body makes during the alarm reaction are listed in Exhibit 8.7.

The alarm reactions are very useful when a physical threat demands an immediate physical response. If you attempted to flee from a dog that was about to bite you or a car about to hit you and your body failed to make the appropriate alarm reactions, you would very quickly become unconscious because of a lack of oxygen or blood glucose. However, the stressors most people face do not call for an immediate physical response. The most typical kinds of alarm reactions are such things as taking exams, being called on in class, speaking before an executive committee, or seeing another motorist cut in front of you. A strenuous physical response is not appropriate in such situations, even though the alarm reaction prepares your body to make such a response.

The alarm reaction is a major source of distress when it is constantly turned on without being used for its intended purpose. When the alarm reaction is fired too often or too long, the body may remain in a constant state of mobilization. The alarm reaction can become classically conditioned to inappropriate conditioned stimuli. The body may remain in a state of chronic tension, with high blood pressure, rapid heartbeat, and disrupted digestion. The consequences are usually very serious. Damage can occur to the nervous system itself or to many vital organs. The results may range from simple hypertension to fatal heart disease.

The consequences of excessive stress may lead to a wide variety of health problems. A useful analogy is to think of a chain that is subjected to increasing levels of tension until it breaks. The increasing tension will cause the chain to break at its weakest link. Likewise, excessive levels of stress will result in injury to the weakest system of the body. Some people will respond to excessive stress by experiencing coronary heart disease, others by digestive problems such as ulcers, while others experience nervous disorders and hypertension. During periods of intense pressure, such as the week of midterms and final exams, students may experience a variety of physiological problems, especially sore throats, indigestion, and headaches.

Stress Versus Distress. Not all stress is unpleasant. Selye described stress as the spice of life and said that the absence of stress is death. He differentiated between positive stress, which he called **eustress,** and negative, harmful stress, which he called **distress.**[55] Some examples of eustress are falling in love, winning a contest,

EXHIBIT 8.7   Physiological Responses to an Alarm Reaction

1. The breath rate increases to provide more oxygen.
2. Red blood cells flood the bloodstream to carry more oxygen to the muscles.
3. The heart beats faster, and blood pressure soars to provide blood to needed areas.
4. Stored sugar and fats are converted to blood glucose to provide fuel for quick energy.
5. Blood-clotting mechanisms are activated to protect against possible bleeding.
6. Digestion ceases so that blood may be diverted to muscles and brain.
7. Perspiration and saliva increase.
8. Bowel and bladder muscles loosen.
9. Muscles tense in preparation for strenuous activity.
10. The pupils dilate, allowing more light to enter the eye.
11. The endocrine system increases the production of hormones.

and receiving an award. Because stress is the nonspecific response of the body to any demand, the physiological responses of distress and eustress are virtually the same. However, eustress causes much less damage to the body because the person is more inclined to successfully adapt to the change. How the person chooses to respond to a stressor has a large influence on how much damage is likely to occur. If the person sees the stressor as an opportunity, the situation is much more likely to produce a growth-enhancing reaction.

A common assumption is that top executives experience the most stressors. Stress-related illnesses, however, do not increase at higher organizational levels. A study of 270,000 male employees in major corporations showed that the rate of coronary disease was lower at successively higher levels of the organization. Top-level executives probably experience less stress than might be expected because they have greater control and predictability over their own situations than do people at lower levels, and the results of their decisions are more predictable.[56] Rather than feeling stress themselves, they are more inclined to create stress for others. People who have more perceived control over their environments experience less stress and fewer somatic disorders.[57]

Individual Differences. Large individual differences have been observed in the way people respond to stressors. Speaking before a large audience is a frightening and stressful experience for most people. But some people enjoy speaking to large audiences and would gladly accept the opportunity even though they might feel a little nervous. Individual differences such as these are caused by many factors, including biochemistry, physical strength, psychological and emotional makeup, past experience, and personal values.[58]

Research suggests that the negative effects of stress have been more evident in the lives of men than women. Women have a longer life expectancy than men, and at certain ages men are four times more likely to die of coronary heart disease and five times more likely to die of alcohol-related disease than women. Although these differences may be partially attributed to biological sex differences, they are also caused by role differences. Men have historically held occupations involving higher levels of stress and limited opportunities for physical exercise to manage the stress. Today, however, the differences between male and female occupational roles are being reduced as more women move into the mainstream of organizational life. Consequently, an increasing number of women are now beginning to experience stress-related health problems. As the occupational differences between male and female roles have narrowed, so also have the differences in stress-related health problems. For example, peptic ulcers and coronary disease among women below age 45 are increasing.[59]

Self-esteem is a personality characteristic that appears to moderate the effects of stress. People with high self-esteem have greater confidence and can deal successfully with stressors. These people are more inclined to perceive a stressful situation as a challenge or opportunity than as a threat. People with high self-esteem have been found to experience fewer coronary heart disease risk factors. Even when the situation is beyond their control, people with high self-esteem are influenced less by stressful events. Research on survivors of war-time prison camps found that high levels of self-esteem helped the prisoners endure the stress of captivity.[60]

Type A Versus Type B Behavior. Perhaps the most extensively researched individual characteristic associated with stress is the **type A versus type B behavior pattern**. The type A behavior pattern was discovered by Meyer Friedman and Ray Rosenman, two medical practitioners and researchers who found that the traditional coronary heart risk factors such as diet, cholesterol, blood pressure, and heredity could not totally explain or predict coronary heart disease.[61] Through their interviews and observations, they found that certain personality characteristics predisposed some people to coronary heart disease. The person with type A behavior pattern has these characteristics:

Chronically struggles to get as many things done as possible in the shortest time period

Speaks explosively

Rushes others to finish what they're saying

Is always in a struggle with people, things, and events

Is preoccupied with deadlines and highly work oriented

Is impatient, hates to wait; considers waiting a waste of precious time

Is aggressive, ambitious, competitive, and forceful

The type B behavior pattern is characterized by a person who is contemplative and feels no need to hurry or race against the clock. Although type B people may have considerable drive and want to accomplish things, they tend to work at a steady pace and do not feel the intense pressures of time and deadlines. Type B people are not as easily angered or disappointed by their own work or the work of others. They tend to be more relaxed and noncompetitive. Because of their contemplative approach to problem solving, type B people tend to be more creative than type A.[62]

Some jobs are better suited for a particular type A or type B personality. For example, type A people are generally superior to type B in real estate sales jobs.[63]

However, studies have found that coronary heart disease is much more prevalent among type A people. In fact, recent investigations suggest that type A people have approximately twice the risk of developing coronary heart disease as type B people.

Almost all change in life can contribute to a feeling of stress. Most stress comes from major changes, such as divorce, marriage, the death of a family member, and so on. Even positive events such as vacations and Christmas can contribute to stress levels because of the excitement, time pressures, and self-imposed deadlines associated with them. A study of over 5,000 patients suffering from stress-related illnesses produced a list of major life changes and a numerical rating of their relative impact on an individual. This list of life events, called the Social Readjustment Rating Scale, is illustrated in Exhibit 8.8 along with the numbers showing the degree of adjustment required following the event. For example, with a mean value of 100 the death of a spouse requires twice as much readjustment as a marriage with a score of 50.[64] To evaluate the amount of stress in your life, identify how many of these changes have occurred within the last twelve months and add the points for these events. A score of 150 or less indicates a relatively manageable degree of readjustment and a low susceptibility to stress-related illness. A score in the range of 150 to 300 indicates a 50 percent probability of a stress-induced health problem during the next two years. The probability of stress-induced health problems rises to about 80 percent for scores greater than 300. The developers of this scale suggest that those who have scores exceeding 300 should seriously seek to reduce the number of changes in their lives and recommend that they become involved in some form of stress management exercise.

Stress Management

Because stress cannot be eliminated from daily life—nor should it be—the solution is to manage it effectively. Managed effectively, stress can enhance rather than diminish individual productivity, interpersonal relationships, and a general zest for living. Many books explain how to benefit from stress and how to use it to improve the quality of life.

The basic principle involved in managing stress is to reverse the stress response when it occurs inappropriately. The alarm reaction needs to be extinguished when it occurs at the wrong time. For pedestrians who see a car speeding toward them, the alarm reaction is appropriate, but it is not appropriate for motorists idled in heavy traffic. Several techniques have been proposed for controlling the stress response. The most popular techniques are (1) eliminating the stressor, (2) relaxation techniques, (3) social support systems, and (4) physical exercise.[65]

Eliminating the Stressor. In some cases, the easiest way to manage stress is to avoid it. Not all stress can or should be avoided, but much unnecessary stress can be avoided by changing the environment or by altering one's interpretation of the stressor. Some executives avoid the stress of traffic jams by being chauffeured. By writing a criticism in a memo, supervisors can avoid the stress of criticizing an employee face to face. Employees can avoid the stress of supervisory responsibilities by refusing promotions. Students avoid the stress of difficult exams by taking easy classes and not applying to graduate school. Some people avoid the stress of marital conflict by getting a divorce. Some parents avoid the stress of having children around during the summer by sending them to summer camp.

EXHIBIT 8.8   Social Readjustment Rating Scale

Rank	Life Event	Mean Value
1	Death of spouse	100
2	Divorce	73
3	Marital separation	65
4	Jail term	63
5	Death of close family member	63
6	Personal injury or illness	53
7	Marriage	50
8	Fired at work	47
9	Marital reconciliation	45
10	Retirement	45
11	Change in health of family member	44
12	Pregnancy	40
13	Sex difficulties	39
14	Gain of new family member	39
15	Business readjustment	39
16	Change in financial state	38
17	Death of close friend	37
18	Change to different line of work	36
19	Change in number of arguments with spouse	35
20	Mortgage over $10,000	31
21	Foreclosure of mortgage or loan	30
22	Change in reponsibilities at work	29
23	Son or daughter leaving home	29
24	Trouble with in-laws	29
25	Outstanding personal achievement	28
26	Wife beginning or stopping work	26
27	Beginning or ending school	26
28	Change in living conditions	25
29	Revision of personal habits	24
30	Trouble with boss	23
31	Change in work hours or conditions	20
32	Change in residence	20
33	Change in schools	20
34	Change in recreation	19
35	Change in church activities	19
36	Change in social activities	18
37	Mortgage or loan less than $10,000	17
38	Change in sleeping habits	16
39	Change in number of family get-togethers	15
40	Change in eating habits	15
41	Vacation	13
42	Christmas	12
43	Minor violations of the law	11

The amount of stress a person has experienced in a given period of time, say one year, is measured by the total number of life change units (LCUs) associated with the events that the person has experienced.

Source: Thomas H. Holmes and Richard H. Rahe, "The Social Readjustment Rating Scale," *Journal of Psychosomatic Research*, vol. 11 (1967), pp. 213–18.

APPLYING ORGANIZATIONAL BEHAVIOR
ACROSS CULTURES

Karoshi: Working Oneself to Death in Japan

The Japanese have become famous for their productivity, quality, and economic success in global markets. With only 2 percent of the world population, they produce 10 percent of the world's exports. Their work ethic has been applauded, and their work processes have been emulated. The Japanese work longer hours than workers in any other industrialized country. Japanese workers averaged 2,150 hours in 1989, compared with 1,924 hours for Americans and 1,643 for the French.

But Japan's dedication to work has not come without a price. The physiological stress of working excessive overtime has led to what the Japanese refer to as *karoshi:* death from chronic fatigue caused by overwork. No official statistics are available, but it has been estimated that 10,000 Japanese workers die every year from *karoshi.*

A recent survey found that more than 40 percent of Japanese employees fear they might die from overwork. But since Japanese employees think working overtime is a way to show dedication to their companies, few are likely to slow down. Furthermore, Japanese managers often demand overtime work and use it as a criterion for promotion.

A group of lawyers, doctors, and victims' spouses are trying to raise public awareness about *karoshi.* They published a book entitled *Karoshi: When the Corporate Warrior Dies,* which describes the lives of some of its victims. In 1988, a *karoshi* hotline was established in Japan and 135 people called for help on the first day.

Despite these efforts to increase public awareness and to pressure employers to change, little progress has been made in the battle against *karoshi.* Managers have grown accustomed to overtime work, and they rely on it to reach their production goals. The government is hesitant to tamper with the country's work ethic for fear that it would hamper productivity and tarnish Japan's image.

Sources: Jim Impoco, "Dying to Work," U.S. News and World Report (March 18, 1991), p. 24; Louise de Rosario, "Dropping in Harness: Salarymen Stalked by 'Unmentionable' Killer," *Far Eastern Economic Review,* vol. 15 (April 25, 1991), pp. 30–31; Ruth Haas, "Strategies to Cope with a Cultural Phenomenon—Workaholism," *Supervisory Management,* vol. 36 (November 1991), p. 4.

Sometimes the stressor can be eliminated psychologically, by changing the meaning of the situation. The objective here is to reassess the seriousness of the situation. Sometimes this is done by asking people to think about the worst consequences that could possibly occur and then decide how serious they really would be. "If I don't get this project finished by the deadline, will I die? No. Will my family leave me? No. Will I lose my job? Well, maybe. So how bad is that? It would be a real blow and I don't want that to happen, but I could get another job."[66]

Much of the stress students experience in preparing for final exams can be handled quite effectively by this form of reassessment. "If I'm not prepared, will I fail the exam? No, but I'll probably get a low score. So, how bad is that?" Generally, the worst possible consequence does not happen, yet seriously thinking about it helps people remove the stress psychologically. This method is particularly useful for those who suffer from vague premonitions of disaster. When two or three problems occur simultaneously, we often feel overwhelmed and think everything is crumbling around us. These vague premonitions of disaster can often be relieved by making a written list of our specific responsibilities or problems and ranking them by priority.

Relaxation Techniques. Several stress management techniques involve some form of physical or mental **relaxation.** Some of these techniques have been advocated with the zeal and enthusiasm of new fads. However, the research evaluating their effectiveness is quite impressive.

Two simple relaxation techniques are muscle massage and abdominal breathing. A muscle massage, which is something people can do while sitting on a chair or sofa, is recommended to relieve muscle tension. Because muscle tension is part of the classically conditioned physiological responses of stress, the idea behind a muscle massage is to extinguish the conditioned response producing the muscle tension. The recommended procedure is to start at the top of the head, massaging slowly, and moving down the neck to the arms, back, legs, and feet. However, some other sequence or even part of a sequence that allows the body enough time to relax and regain a state of equilibrium should be helpful. Abdominal breathing involves taking long, deep breaths that cause the body to relax and counteract the stress responses associated with an alarm reaction. This is an especially effective technique for most stress situations because it can be done without breaking a person's routine. A few deep breaths can effectively calm a person and yet go unnoticed in a committee meeting or during a phone call. Several organizations hire onsite massage therapists to help employees manage job stress more effectively. The onsite massage is generally done on a fully clothed employee who is in a seated position. Most employees find it provides immediate relief from stress without causing drowsiness or lethargy.[67]

Transcendental meditation (TM) is a relaxation technique derived from the ancient traditions of India. The practice of TM involves the use of an otherwise meaningless sound called a *mantra*. The mantra is assigned to the individual meditator by a trained instructor, and proper use of the mantra is said to automatically reduce the level of excitation and disorderly activity of the nervous system and to quiet the mind while maintaining its alertness. Evidence evaluating TM indicates that metabolic changes occur during meditation that move the body toward a deep state of rest. Advocates of TM maintain that the rejuvenating effects on the mind are even more profound. Although research is limited, a few studies have shown that employees who practice TM have high levels of satisfaction and productivity and good relationships with supervisors and co-workers. The mantra is classically conditioned to evoke a state of calm and quiet within the nervous system, which serves to replace the conditioned responses evoking stress.[68]

Another relaxation technique that is growing in popularity is **biofeedback.** This technique uses sophisticated equipment to observe some of the internal body processes and to report this information in observable ways. Biofeedback equipment can monitor events such as muscular tension, skin temperature, heartbeat, blood pressure, and brain waves. This information is reported to the person in the form of sounds, lights, or wavy lines on a graph. When people are able to observe recordings of their brain waves or blood pressure, they can begin to control them by observing the internal and external conditions that made them change. Once people are aware that their internal body responses are in a state of stress, they can begin to adjust, altering their environment or their frame of mind to reduce the stress.[69]

Social Support. Another method of managing stress is to develop a social support system. A social support system is an interlocking network of people with whom a person can interact to satisfy important human needs. A wide variety of people may be part of a social support system, including a spouse, family members, other relatives, friends, neighbors, a work supervisor, co-workers, members of self-help groups, and health and welfare professionals. Because people spend such a large part of their lives at work, the social support they obtain from work associates represents a major part of their total social support.[70]

An effective social support system may provide four major types of supportive behaviors.

1. *Emotional support:* Providing empathy, love, caring, and trust
2. *Instrumental support:* Providing direct help to people in need, such as doing their work, taking care of them, or helping them pay their bills
3. *Informational support:* Providing knowledge or information to help people cope with personal or environmental problems
4. *Appraisal support:* Providing specific evaluative information to help people with their self-evaluations

Each form of social support serves a different function, but the most important form is emotional support. When people think of others being supportive toward them, they usually think of emotional support—providing empathy, love, caring, and trust. Most research showing that social support reduces occupational stress and improves health has focused specifically on emotional support.[71]

The evidence indicates that the most important source of social support comes from the family unit, especially from one's spouse. The death of a spouse is usually a traumatic experience that influences both the physical and mental health of the surviving partner. The trauma is much less severe, however, if people have other social supports that can help them, such as an understanding supervisor, co-workers who are willing to listen and empathize, and a counselor who can provide supportive, nondirective counseling.

Physical Exercise. Exercise enthusiasts argue that the best technique for managing stress is a regular program of physical exercise. They claim that exercise prevents many physical and mental health problems and significantly reduces the seriousness of others. Although these claims may be a bit overstated, an enormous flood of studies has shown that a well-designed physical exercise program can significantly improve both physical and emotional health.[72] Some of the major benefits are listed in Exhibit 8.9.

Many different kinds of exercise programs exist. Some isometric routines are very brief and can be done sitting in a chair or standing in an office. An isometric routine involves tightening the different muscle groups and holding them tight for a short time, such as 10 seconds. These exercises are designed to maintain good muscle tone and to strengthen the ligaments and tendons.

Almost any form of physical activity can provide good exercise if it is done properly. Basketball, football, and tennis are good activities for staying in shape, but they are not recommended for getting into shape because of the potential harm from jarring and abrupt movements. A common mistake in exercising is overdoing it and tearing the body down rather than building it up. Exercise should be systematic and regular and never too much at one time. People who have been inactive for several years need to start slowly when they begin exercising again.

EXHIBIT 8.9   Benefits of Regular Exercise

General Benefits to Overall Health

1. Person gains increased strength and endurance.
2. Energy used more efficiently, even in mental tasks.
3. Proper circulation is maintained.
4. Grace, poise, and appearance improve.
5. Posture and muscle tone improve.
6. Chronic tiredness and tension are reduced.
7. Ideal weight is more effectively maintained.
8. Aches, pains, and stiffness are reduced.
9. Degenerative risk factors decline.

Specific Benefits to the Heart

1. Resting heart rate is lowered, meaning that the heart does not have to work as hard to circulate blood to the body.
2. Cardiac output is increased, meaning that under stress the heart is better able to distribute blood.
3. Number of red blood cells is increased, meaning that more oxygen can be carried per pint of blood.
4. Elasticity of the arteries is increased.
5. Blood cholesterol level and triglyceride levels are lowered.
6. Adrenal secretions in response to emotional stress are lowered.
7. Lactic acid causing fatigue is more effectively eliminated.
8. Heart muscle is strengthened, and additional blood vessels within it are formed.

Since 1970, aerobic exercises have gained in popularity because of their contribution to cardiovascular conditioning. **Aerobic exercises** raise the heart and breath rate to a training range and keep them within that range for a period of time. Some of the best aerobic exercises are jogging, cycling, swimming, brisk walking, and aerobic dancing, because they involve a constant level of activity. It is recommended that aerobic exercise be done a minimum of three times each week for at least 12 to 15 minutes each time. More exercise is better, but the gains are not very large for exercise beyond 45 minutes daily. A major argument for aerobic exercise is that it reduces stress and prevents heart disease. Although some debate exists over the conclusiveness of the evidence, it is generally believed that regular, vigorous exercise helps prevent heart disease and reduce stress, for the reasons listed in Exhibit 8.9.

Many executives recognize the value of physical exercise programs, and many large corporations have some form of in-house physical fitness facilities. The use of these facilities is sometimes limited to managers and executives, but increasingly the facilities are being made available to all members of the organization. A growing number of organizations encourage everyone to participate, and some organizations even offer financial incentives to participating employees. For example, the Hospital Corporation of America gives its employees 4¢ a mile for cycling, 16¢ per mile for walking or jogging, and 64¢ per mile for swimming. Some organizations spend considerable money providing physical fitness centers for their employees, and claim these centers more than pay for themselves by reducing health insurance costs and benefits claims.[73] Students reluctant to begin a physical exercise program, especially those who claim to be too busy with the pressures of exams and research papers, should memorize the following lament of a graduating doctoral student: "We labored all our days to stuff a million-dollar mind into a ten-cent body."

SUMMARY

1. Socialization is the process of acquiring the kinds of attitudes and behaviors that are considered necessary for people to become members of an organization.

2. Organizational integration is the process of integrating the goals and objectives of individuals with the goals and objectives of the organization. The degree of integration influences the commitment and satisfaction of members.

3. Three of the most prominent socialization processes include new employee orientations, training and development programs, and performance appraisal reviews. Employees who are undersocialized tend to be poor performers who violate rules, while oversocialized employees tend to be overly submissive and lack the creativity and spontaneity needed. The ideal degree of socialization tries to achieve an appropriate balance.

4. Role transition includes the changes that occur when people move from one stage in life to the next. The three phases associated with moving from one stage to another include separation, initiation, and incorporation.

5. A career is the work-related experiences of an individual and may include both paid or unpaid work in either one organization or several organizations. Everyone who works has a career.

6. Career success should be determined by each individual according to his or her personal criteria. Four of the most popular methods for measuring career effectiveness are career performance, satisfaction, adaptability, and identity.

7. One of the most popular theories of personal development is Erik Erikson's eight stages of development. The last four stages involving adult development include the adolescent stage, the young adulthood stage, the adulthood stage, and the maturity stage.

8. Four stages of career development have been identified to describe the typical stages of a career. These four stages include exploration, where people are concerned about finding and securing a job; establishment, where people strive to demonstrate competence and create a permanent position in a company; maintenance, where people try to perform dependably and protect their positions; and decline, where people reduce their involvement in work and prepare for retirement.

9. The decision to accept a job is determined largely by a person's occupational choice, the choice of an organization, and the choice of specific job characteristics. Occupational choice is heavily influenced by social background factors such as socioeconomic status, race, gender, aptitudes, and interests. Organizational choice is influenced by the kinds of rewards the organization offers, especially the mission and image of the organization. Job choice is influenced by many characteristics, especially pay, the level of responsibility, and the opportunity to perform a worthwhile job.

10. Career planning is important for people who desire meaningful employment. People should be responsible for their own career planning,

and they should not assume that organizations will direct their careers.

11. Career planning can benefit people by helping them find satisfying and profitable employment. It can benefit organizations by preparing employees for promotion, and by increasing their abilities to make meaningful contributions.

12. The most prominent kinds of career development activities include career counseling, career pathing, human resource planning, training and development programs, mentoring, and special programs such as minority training or preretirement counseling.

13. In career development, the term *accommodation* refers to balancing the requirements of family and work responsibilities. Accommodative people place family responsibilities ahead of work, while nonaccommodative people focus their attention and time on work and career advancement rather than on family. The increase in dual-career families has required new patterns of accommodation where husbands are beginning to share more responsibilities for household tasks. Employers need to provide greater flexibility for dual-career and single-parent families to accommodate work and family responsibilities, such as flexible work schedules, job sharing, part-time employment, and paid work at home.

14. Anxiety and depression are two of the major mental illnesses observed in the workplace. Anxiety is an excessive state of tension or fear that is general and not associated with a specific problem. Depression is a mood of gloom and dejection that creates a general state of unhappiness and may lead to suicide.

15. Burnout is the inability to handle continued stress on the job and is usually associated with people in the helping professions, such as nurses, counselors, psychiatrists, and social workers. Burnout is similar to the boredom of blue-collar workers who do not find their work meaningful.

16. Stress is a physiological reaction to stressors in the environment. Stress can result from both pleasant (eustress) and unpleasant (distress) experiences. The three stages of stress are the alarm stage, the resistance stage, and the exhaustion stage. During the alarm stage, the body's endocrine system prepares it for "fight or flight" reactions. If there is a physical danger, this reaction is desirable; however, most stress situations do not call for a vigorous physical effort, and the body therefore responds to a false alarm. If too many false alarms occur, the body stays in a chronic state of alarm, and the body's vital organs may be damaged.

17. The recommended methods for managing stress include eliminating the stressors, relaxation techniques, social support, and physical exercise.

18. Studies show that physical exercise not only helps to reduce stress, but also improves physical health and increases job satisfaction and productivity. Consequently, many companies have developed physical exercise programs for their employees. The evidence indicates that these exercise programs are cost–benefit effective.

DISCUSSION QUESTIONS

1. What is organizational integration? Is it really possible for the goals and objectives of the individual to be consistent with the organization's goals and objectives? Is it desirable?

2. What are the consequences of being oversocialized and undersocialized? What criteria should you use for deciding whether someone is over- or undersocialized?

3. What is anticipatory socialization? How do realistic job previews contribute to anticipatory socialization?

4. What is meant by the term *career success*? What criteria do you use for measuring your own personal career success?

5. What kinds of forces would cause someone in the adulthood stage to move toward generativity while others move toward stagnation?

6. What are the consequences of someone advancing too fast or too slowly through the various career stages?

7. If occupational choice is heavily influenced by social background factors, especially socioeconomic status, can organizations realistically expect to attract people into novel occupations? Why or why not?

8. Studies on why people choose one job over another are not consistent. Why do you suppose some studies show that pay is the most important factor, while other studies show that the nature of the job is the most important factor?

9. What are some consequences of inadequate career planning?

10. What are the typical situations in a student's life that can create alarm reactions?

11. What are the advantages and disadvantages of different stress management techniques?

12. Do you think it is legitimate for a company to become involved in employees' personal lives, even if the purpose is to help them solve their personal problems or to improve their mental health? Why or why not?

GLOSSARY

accommodation The process of achieving a balance between family demands and responsibilities at work. The most accommodative people are those who place the highest priority on family responsibilities.

adolescent stage The fifth stage of development, when individuals begin to develop their sexual and occupational identity.

adulthood stage The seventh stage of development, when people are concerned about generativity versus stagnation.

aerobic exercise A type of physical exercise that is regular and rhythmic and uses the large-muscle systems to raise the heart rate to a training range and maintain it for a period of time. Aerobic exercise contributes to cardiovascular conditioning.

alarm reaction The first stage of stress in which the body prepares for a "fight or flight" response by activating the endocrine system.

anticipatory socialization The process of acquiring the attitudes and behaviors associated with a new role as people anticipate changing from one role to another.

anxiety An intense feeling of fear and apprehension that is not associated with a specific threatening situation.

biofeedback The use of electronic monitoring equipment to measure internal body functions of which people are normally unaware, such as blood pressure and muscle tensions. Being able to observe measurements of these functions helps people control them.

burnout The inability to handle continued stress on the job, and the feeling of psychological exhaustion.

critical contacts An explanation of how people choose a job in which the decision to accept a job offer is based on the interpersonal contacts the applicant has with representatives of the company.

decline stage The fourth and last stage of career development, in which people begin to prepare themselves for retirement.

depression A feeling of intense gloom and despair that is not associated with a specific unpleasant event.

distress Unpleasant or disease-producing stress that is destructive to physical and mental well-being.

dual-career family A family where both father and mother are pursuing careers outside the home.

establishment stage The second stage of career development, in which people seek to create a secure position and contribute effectively to the organization.

eustress Pleasant or curative stress that contributes to interest, enthusiasm, and a zest for living.

exhaustion stage The third and final stage of the general adaptation syndrome where physical damage occurs because the person cannot adapt to the stress.

exploration stage The first stage of career development, in which people try to identify and obtain suitable jobs.

general adaptation syndrome (GAS) How people respond to stress; the syndrome contains three phases: alarm reaction, resistance, and exhaustion.

generativity A positive growth-oriented response of people in the adulthood stage of career development. Generativity involves a concern for establishing and guiding the next generation, having the power to produce things, and generating new ideas or new inventions.

incorporation The final stage of the role transition process in which people are integrated into the new role.

initiation The second stage in the role transition process wherein new members are tested and expected to prove themselves to be accepted in full fellowship.

maintenance stage The third stage of career development, in which people seek to secure their position within the organization and protect themselves from being replaced.

maturity The eighth and final stage of development when people face what they have made of their lives and either feel a sense of ego integrity or despair.

objective factors theory An explanation of job choice suggesting that people choose jobs based on objective considerations, such as pay, benefits, and working conditions.

organizational integration The process of integrating people into the organization by matching the individual's objectives and goals with the objectives and goals of the organization.

realistic job previews (RJPs) A recruiting strategy that involves telling applicants both the favorable and unfavorable aspects of the job.

reality shock Realizing that a new role is not as glamorous as it appeared at first.

relaxation techniques Methods of relaxation to reverse the alarm reaction and avoid stress, such as abdominal breathing, transcendental meditation, and biofeedback.

resistance stage The second stage of the general adaptation syndrome, in which people attempt to re-establish a state of balance after first responding to stress.

role transition process The process in which people advance from one role in life to another.

separation The first stage of the role transition process where people begin to disassociate themselves from their former role.

sequencing The process of structuring one's career in sequential phases to accommodate the demands and interests of different stages of life.

socialization The process of acquiring socially acceptable attitudes and behaviors according to the standards of society or of the organization.

stagnation A negative response by someone in the adulthood stage, characterized by standing still, producing nothing, and becoming obsolete.

stress The physiological response of the body to a stressor. The initial stage is the alarm reaction, which readies the body to make an immediate response. The resistance stage attempts to return the body to a state of balance. The third stage, exhaustion, occurs when the body experiences repeated alarm reactions.

subjective factors An explanation of job choice behavior suggesting that people base their job preferences on subjective considerations that concern how well an organization will satisfy personal needs and career goals.

type A versus type B behavior patterns A personality dimension related to the way people respond to stressors. Type A people are intense, high-strung, and impulsive, while type B people are contemplative and relaxed.

young adulthood stage The sixth stage of development when people learn how to work and to love, and how to develop a balance between work and love.

NOTES

1. Abraham H. Maslow, "A Theory of Metamotivation: The Biological Rooting of the Value-Life," *Psychology Today*, vol. 2 (July 1968), pp. 38, 39, 58–61.

2. Bruna Nota, "The Socialization Process at High-Commitment Organizations," *Personnel*, vol. 65 (August 1988), pp. 20–23.

3. Marie Day, "Organizational Integration," *Canadian Manager*, vol. 15 (June 1990), pp. 16–18.

4. Natalie J. Allen and John P. Meyer, "Organizational Socialization Tactics: A Longitudinal Analysis of Links to Newcomers' Commitment and Role Orientation," *Academy of Management Journal*, vol. 33 (December 1990), pp. 847–858.

5. Arnold van Gennep, *The Rights of Passage* (Chicago: University of Chicago Press, 1960).

6. Douglas T. Hall, *Careers in Organizations* (Pacific Palisades, Calif.: Goodyear Publishing Company, 1976), chap. 5.

7. Benjamin Schneider and Douglas T. Hall, "Toward Specifying the Concept of Work Climate: A Study of Roman Catholic Diocesan Priests," *Journal of Applied Psychology,* vol. 56 (1972), pp. 447–455; H. Walberg, "Professional Role Discontinuities in Education Careers," in J. R. Hackman (Chairman), *Longitudinal Approaches to Career Development,* American Psychological Association Annual Convention, San Francisco, 1968; Roger A. Dean, Kenneth R. Ferris, and Constantine Constans, "Occupational Reality Shock and Organizational Commitment: Evidence from the Accounting Profession," *Accounting, Organizations and Society,* vol. 13, no. 3 (1988), pp. 235–250.

8. Robert J. Vandenberg and Vida Scarpello, "The Matching Model: An Examination of the Processes Underlying Realistic Job Previews," *Journal of Applied Psychology,* vol. 75 (1990), pp. 60–67.

9. John P. Wanous, "Tell It Like It Is at Realistic Job Previews," *Personnel,* vol. 52, no. 4 (1975), pp. 50–60; John P. Wanous, "Organizational Entry: Newcomers Moving from Outside to Inside," *Psychological Bulletin,* vol. 84 (1977), pp. 601–618; John P. Wanous, "Installing the Realistic Job Preview: Ten Tough Choices," *Personnel Psychology,* vol. 42 (June 1989), pp. 117–134; Bruce M. Meglino, Angelo S. DeNisi, and Stewart A. Youngblood, "Effects of Realistic Job Previews: A Comparison Using an Enhancement and a Reduction Preview," *Journal of Applied Psychology,* vol. 73 (May 1988), pp. 259–266; Alan M. Saks and Steven F. Crownshaw, "A Process Investigation of Realistic Job Previews: Mediating Variables and Channels of Communication," *Journal of Organizational Behavior,* vol. 11 (May 1990), pp. 221–236.

10. The ideas in this section are largely taken from Hall, op. cit.

11. Urs E. Gattiker and Laurie Larwood, "Predictors for Career Achievement in the Corporate Hierarchy," *Human Relations,* vol. 43 (August 1990), pp. 703–726.

12. Erik H. Erikson, *Childhood and Society,* 2nd ed. (New York: Norton, 1963).

13. Lynn A. Isabella, "The Effect of Career Stage on the Meaning of Key Organizational Events," *Journal of Organizational Behavior,* vol. 9 (October 1988), pp. 345–358.

14. Donald Super, J. Crites, R. Hummel, H. Moser, P. Overstreet, and C. Warnath, *Vocational Development: A Framework for Research* (New York: Teachers College Press, 1957), pp. 40–41.

15. D. J. Levinson, "The Mid-life Transition: A Period in Adult Psychological Development," *Psychiatry,* vol. 40 (1977), pp. 99–112.

16. Gene W. Dalton, Paul H. Thompson, and Ray L. Price, "The Four Stages of Professional Careers: A New Look at Performance by Professionals," *Organiza-*

tional Dynamics, vol. 6 (1977), pp. 19–42; Gene W. Dalton and Paul H. Thompson, *Novations: Strategies for Career Management* (Glenview, Ill.: Scott, Foresman, 1986).

17. Lyman Porter, Edward E. Lawler, III, and J. Richard Hackman, *Behavior in Organizations* (New York: McGraw-Hill, 1975), pp. 200.

18. O. C. Brenner and Marc G. Singer, "Career Repotters: To Know Them Could Be to Keep Them," *Personnel,* vol. 65 (November 1988), pp. 554–558.

19. John Saltiel, "The Wisconsin Model of Status Attainment and the Occupational Choice Process," *Work and Occupations,* vol. 15 (August 1988), pp. 334–355; see Benjamin Schneider, *Staffing Organizations* (Pacific Palisades, California: Goodyear, 1976), chap. 4.

20. Donald Robertson and James Symons, "The Occupational Choice of British Children," *Economic Journal,* vol. 100 (September 1990), pp. 828–841; Robert F. Sherer, Janet S. Adams, Susan S. Carley, and Frank A. Wiebe, "Role Model Performance Effects on Development of Entrepreneurial Preference," *Entrepreneurship: Theory and Practice,* vol. 13 (Spring 1989), pp. 53–71; Milton Rosenberg, *Occupations and Values* (Glencoe, Ill.: Free Press, 1957).

21. J. J. Kirkpatrick, "Organizational Aspirations, Opportunities, and Barriers," in K. S. Miller and R. M. Dreger (eds.), *Comparative Studies of Blacks and Whites in the United States* (New York: Seminar Press, 1973); Jeffrey H. Greenhaus, Saroj Parasuraman, and Wayne M. Wormley, "Effects of Race on Organizational Experiences, Job Performance Evaluations, and Career Outcomes," *Academy of Management Journal,* vol. 33 (March 1990), pp. 64–86.

22. W. H. Sewell and A. M. Orenstein, "Community of Residence and Occupational Choice," *American Journal of Sociology,* vol. 70 (1965), pp. 551–563.

23. Naomi Stewart, "Sources of Army Personnel Grouped by Occupation," *Occupations, the Vocational Guidance Journal,* vol. 20, no. 1 (1947), pp. 5–41; George D. Dreher and Robert D. Bretz, "Cognitive Ability and Career Attainment: Moderating Effects of Early Career Success," *Journal of Applied Psychology,* vol. 76 (June 1991), pp. 392–397.

24. David Hammond and James Dingley, "Sex Differences in Career Preferences of Lower Sixth Formers in Belfast Grammar Schools," *Journal of Occupational Psychology,* vol. 62 (September 1989), pp. 263–264.

25. R. P. O'Hara and D. V. Tiedman, "Vocational Self-Concept in Adolescence," *Journal of Counseling Psychology,* vol. 6 (1959), pp. 292–301.

26. Benjamin Schneider and L. K. Olson, "Effort as a Correlate of Organizational Reward System and Individual Values," *Personnel Psychology,* vol. 23 (1972), pp. 313–326.

27. V. R. Tom, "The Role of Personality and Organizational Images in the Recruiting Process," *Organiza-*

tional Behavior and Human Performance, vol. 16 (1971), pp. 573–592.

28. Daniel C. Feldman and U. J. Arnold, "Position Choice: Comparing the Importance of Organizational and Job Factors," Journal of Applied Psychology, vol. 63 (1978), pp. 706–710; Abraham E. Haspel, "A Study in Occupational Choice: Managerial Positions," Southern Economics Journal, vol. 44 (April 1978), pp. 958–967; Sara L. Rynes, "Compensation Strategies for Recruiting," Topics in Total Compensation, vol. 2 (Winter 1987), pp. 185–196; A. G. Peppercorn and G. A. Skoulding, "How Do Managers Position Themselves?" Industrial Management and Data Systems (September–October 1987), pp. 12–16.

29. Moshe Krausz, "A New Approach to Studying Worker Job Preferences," Industrial Relations, vol. 17 (February 1978), pp. 91–95.

30. Thomas J. Hosnik, "Aiming for the Right Company: Choosing from Among Job Offers," SAM Advanced Management Journal, vol. 44 (Spring 1979), pp. 44–54.

31. John Shingleton and Robert Bao, College to Career (New York: McGraw-Hill, 1977), chap. 3.

32. Karen M. Gaertner and Stanley D. Nollen, "Career Experiences, Perception of Employment Practices, and Psychological Commitment to the Organization," Human Relations, vol. 42 (November 1989), pp. 975–991.

33. Stephen M. Colarelli and Ronald C. Bishop, "Career Commitment: Functions, Correlates, and Management," Group and Organization Studies, vol. 15 (June 1990), pp. 158–176; Idalene F. Kesner, "Succession Planning," Credit, vol. 15 (May–June 1989), pp. 29–33; Donald L. Kirkpatrick, "Supervisory and Management Development: Update from an Expert," Training and Development Journal, vol. 42 (August 1988), pp. 59–63; William Whitely, Thomas W. Dougherty, and George F. Dreher, "Relationship of Career Mentoring and Socioeconomic Origin to Managers' and Professionals' Early Career Progress," Academy of Management Journal, vol. 34 (June 1991), pp. 331–350.

34. Robert L. Laud, "Performance Appraisal and Its Link to Strategic Management Development," Management Decision, vol. 27 (June 1989), pp. 82–85.

35. From the Bureau of Labor Statistics published in the Monthly Labor Review.

36. Howard V. Hayghe, "Children in Two-Worker Families and Real Family Income," Monthly Labor Review, vol. 112 (December 1989), pp. 48–52.

37. Ibid.

38. Stephanie Shipp, Eva Jacobs, and Gregory Brown, "Families of Working Wives Spending More on Services and Nondurables," Monthly Labor Review, vol. 112 (February 1989), pp. 15–21; Paul N. Strassels, "It's Your Money; A Spouse's Income Costs as Well as Pays," Nation's Business, vol. 77 (March 1989), p. 66; Mary Rowland, "Can You Afford Not to Work?" Women's Day (March 28, 1989), pp. 54–56.

39. Hazel M. Rosin, "Consequences for Men of Dual Career Marriages: Implications for Organizations," Journal of Managerial Psychology, vol. 5, no. 1 (1990), pp. 3–8.

40. "Housework Gap," Executive Female, vol. 12 (September–October 1989), p. 8; Jack L. Simonetti, Nick Nykodym, and Janet M. Goralske, "Family Ties: A Guide for HR Managers," Personnel, vol. 65 (January 1988), pp. 37–41; Uma Sekaran, "Understanding the Dynamics of Self-Concept of Members in Dual-Career Families," Human Relations, vol. 42 (February 1989), pp. 97–116.

41. Thomas Exter, "Everybody Works Hard Except Junior," American Demographics, vol. 13 (May 1991), pp. 14.

42. Saroj Parasuraman, Jeffrey H. Greenhaus, Samuel Rabinowitz, Arthur G. Bedeian, and Kevin W. Mossholder, "Work and Family Variables as Mediators of the Relationship Between Wives' Employment and Husbands' Well-Being," Academy of Management Journal, vol. 32 (March 1989), pp. 185–201.

43. Hazel M. Rosin, "The Effects of Dual Career Participation on Men: Some Determinants of Variation in Career and Personal Satisfaction," Human Relations, vol. 43 (February 1990), pp. 169–182; Alan L. Otten, "How Work, Home Stress Affects Working Couples," The Wall Street Journal (February 22, 1991), p. B-1.

44. Lotte Bailyn, "Accommodation of Work to Family," in R. N. Rappoport and R. Rappoport (eds.), Working Couples (New York: Harper & Row, 1980).

45. Felice Schwartz, "Management Women and the New Facts of Life," Harvard Business Review, vol. 67 (January–February, 1989), pp. 65–76; Douglas T. Hall, "Promoting Work/Family Balance: An Organization-Change Approach," Organizational Dynamics, vol. 18 (Winter 1990), pp. 4–18.

46. Joani Nelson-Horchler, "Derailing the Mommy Track," Industry Week, vol. 239 (August 6, 1990), pp. 22–26.

47. Calvin Reynolds and Rita Bennett, "The Career Couple Challenge," Personnel Journal, vol. 70 (March 1991), pp. 46–49.

48. Daniel F. Jennings, "Special Problems of Married Women at Work," Baylor Business Review, vol. 8 (Summer 1990), pp. 9–11.

49. Joy A. Schneer and Frieda Reitman, "Effects of Employment Gaps on the Careers of MBA's: More Damaging for Men Than for Women?" Academy of Management Journal, vol. 33 (June 1990), pp. 391–406.

50. Hall, "Promoting Work/Family Balance."

51. Brent Q. Hafen, Alcohol: The Crutch That Cripples (St. Paul, Minn.: West, 1977); Brent Q. Hafen and Brenda Peterson, Medicines and Drugs: Problems and Risks, Use and Abuse, 2nd ed. (Philadelphia: Lea & Febiger, 1978).

52. A. V. Boy and G. J. Pine, "Avoiding Counselor Burnout Through Role Reversal," Education Digest, vol. 46 (January 1981), pp. 50–52; Michael R. Daley, "Burnout:

Smoldering Problem in Protective Services," *Social Work*, vol. 24, no. 5 (September 1979), pp. 375–379; John G. Nelson, "Burnout — Business' Most Costly Expense," *Personnel Administrator*, vol. 25 (August 1980), pp. 81–87.

53. Charles Polance, "Avoiding Burnout," *American Salesman*, vol. 33 (May 1988), pp. 9–11; Randolph L. Mase, "The Battle Against Burnout," *Training and Development Journal*, vol. 43 (June 1989), pp. 35–36.

54. Hans Selye, *The Stress of Life* (New York: McGraw-Hill, 1956, 1976).

55. Ibid, p. 74; Hans Selye, *Stress Without Distress* (New York: Lippincott, 1974).

56. Philip Goldberg, *Executive Health* (New York: McGraw-Hill, 1978), p. 29.

57. Cynthia Lee, Susan J. Ashford, and Philip Bobko, "Interactive Effects of 'Type A' Behavior and Perceived Control of Worker Performance, Job Satisfaction, and Somatic Complaints," *Academy of Management Journal*, vol. 33 (December 1990), pp. 870–881.

58. Freddie Choo, "Accountants' Personality Typology and Perceptions of Job-Related Stress: An Empirical Study," *Accounting and Finance*, vol. 27 (November 1987), pp. 13–23; Debra L. Nelson and Charlotte Sutton, "Chronic Work Stress and Coping: A Longitudinal Study and Suggested New Directions," *Academy of Management Journal*, vol. 33 (December 1990), pp. 859–869.

59. M. A. Chesney and R. H. Rosenman, "Type A Behavior in the Work Setting," in C. Cooper and R. Payne (eds.), *Current Concerns in Occupational Stress* (New York: Wiley, 1980), pp. 187–212.

60. Goodson, op. cit., p. 159.

61. Meyer Friedman and Ray H. Rosenman, *Type A Behavior and Your Heart* (New York: Knopf, 1974).

62. Muhammad Jamal, "Relationship of Job Stress and Type-A Behavior to Employees' Job Satisfaction, Organizational Commitment, Psychosomatic Health Problems, and Turnover Motivation," *Human Relations*, vol. 43 (August 1990), pp. 727–738.

63. Kenneth R. Bartkus, Mark F. Peterson, and Danny N. Bellenger, "Type A Behavior, Experience, and Sales Person Performance," *Journal of Personal Selling and Sales Management*, vol. 9 (Summer 1989), pp. 11–18.

64. Thomas H. Holmes and Richard H. Rahe, "The Social Readjustment Rating Scale," *Journal of Psychosomatic Research*, vol. 11 (1967), pp. 213–217.

65. Kenneth E. Hart, "Introducing Stress and Stress Management to Managers," *Journal of Managerial Psychology*, vol. 5, no. 2 (1990), pp. 9–16; Dorothy Schwimer, "Managing Stress to Boost Productivity," *Employment Relations Today*, vol. 18 (Spring 1991), pp. 23–26.

66. Teresa Foot, "Stress Management," *Management Services*, vol. 34 (September 1990), pp. 12–14; David Hingsburger, "Learning How to Face That Stressful Situation," *Management Solutions*, vol. 33 (February 1988), pp. 41–45.

67. Aric Sigman, "Hands On Management," *Personnel Management*, vol. 23 (March 1991), p. 17.

68. Reviewed in Goldberg, op. cit., pp. 211–213. See also Daniel Goleman, "Meditation Helps Break the Stress Spiral," *Psychology Today*, vol. 9 (February 1976), pp. 82–93.

69. Barbara B. Brown, *Stress and the Art of Biofeedback* (New York: Harper & Row, 1977).

70. Kathy E. Kram and Douglas T. Hall, "Mentoring as an Antidote to Stress During Corporate Trauma," *Human Resource Management*, vol. 28 (Winter 1989), pp. 493–510.

71. James S. House, *Work, Stress and Social Support* (Reading, Mass.: Addison-Wesley, 1981); Jeffrey R. Edwards and A. J. Baglioni, Jr., and Cary L. Cooper, "Stress, Type A, Coping and Psychological and Physical Symptoms: A Multi-Sample Test of Alternative Models," *Human Relations*, vol. 43 (October 1990), pp. 919–956.

72. Some of the best references summarizing the benefits of physical exercise programs are Goldberg, op. cit., chap. 6; Kenneth H. Cooper, *The Aerobics Way* (New York: Lippincott, 1977); Kenneth H. Cooper, *The New Aerobics* (New York: Lippincott, 1970); Valerie DeBenedette, "Getting Fit for Life: Can Exercise Reduce Stress?" *Physician and Sports Medicine*, vol. 16 (June 1988), pp. 185–191.

73. David Clutterbuck, "Executive Fitness Aids Corporate Health," *International Management*, vol. 35 (February 1980), pp. 18–22.

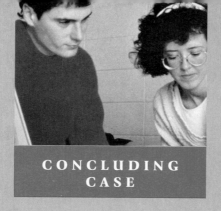

RITES OF PASSAGE OR SEX DISCRIMINATION?

Since engineering has been a male-dominated profession, Patricia Davis was very pleased when she landed an engineering job with the Streuling Scientific Company even though she was the only female engineer. Patricia did well in graduate school, and she anticipated acceptance as a competent professional within the company. As a graduate student, Pat often received differential treatment, and she struggled to be accepted as a legitimate student. Pat resolved that on her first job she would not allow anyone to treat her as a second-class citizen. Instead, she would insist on being treated as a professional equal to others in the engineering department.

During her first six weeks on the job, Pat was generally pleased with how well she had been accepted. She found her first job assignment challenging, and many of her colleagues had willingly offered to help her. At the end of six weeks, she had finished her first project and was looking forward to presenting it to the engineering group in a "project defense" meeting.

During lunch hour the day before Pat was to make her project defense, one of the engineers tried to warn Pat about what she would face the next day. In a hushed voice he said, "You'd better be ready for tomorrow because they're coming after you with all their guns loaded."

Because she was disturbed by this comment, Pat called Carl Mahoney in advertising. Carl was the husband of a former roommate in college, and she trusted him to give her a straight answer. Carl told her he didn't think the comment meant anything,

but after he hung up, he decided to check into it. Carl was very disturbed by what he learned.

When junior engineers completed a project, the practice in the company was to have them present their project to a group of senior engineers. Anyone interested was invited to attend these presentations. Normally, only a few people attended, but when it was the first presentation for a new engineer, the custom had developed for many people to attend and ask tough questions. The first project defense for new engineers was viewed as an initiation ceremony during which the work of a new engineer was severely challenged. Many of the engineers referred to their first project defense as "baptism by fire," and it was generally believed that no one was accepted fully as a member of the engineering department until he or she had survived his first project defense. Although the event was extremely threatening and unpleasant, the engineers viewed it as a valuable ritual that helped new engineers understand the importance of thorough and careful work.

Carl learned that the entire engineering department planned to attend Pat's project defense. Realizing how threatening this situation would be, several of the engineers were informally betting on how long Pat would last before she left the room in tears. Carl was told not to warn Pat because there was nothing she could do at this point, and she would probably perform better if she entered the room expecting a positive experience rather than feeling threatened.

Questions

1. Do you agree that the project defense is a useful rite of passage, and what are the consequences of changing or eliminating it for Patricia Davis?

2. How is this an illustration of sex discrimination?

3. Should Carl say anything to Pat, or should he try to intervene by talking to anyone else in the organization?

4. Do any of the engineers have a moral or social responsibility to protect Pat?

STRESS AND ADAPTATION: SELF-ASSESSMENT

This exercise provides an opportunity to examine the levels of stress in your life. Our knowledge about stress and the effects of stress on the body have been greatly enhanced by the pioneering work of Hans Selye, a Vienna-born endocrinologist associated with the University of Montreal. Selye defined stress as the nonspecific response of the body to any demand made upon it. Not all stress is unpleasant; according to Selye, "stress is the spice of life," and the absence of stress is death. Selye uses the labels "eustress" and "distress" to distinguish between the healthy and destructive forms of stress. "Eustress" refers to pleasant or curative stress that contributes to interest, enthusiasm, and a zest for living. "Distress" refers to unpleasant or disease-producing stress that is destructive to physical and mental well-being. Therefore, stress is not just nervous tension or the body's reaction to bad events. Nor is stress entirely bad, since we all need a certain amount of stimulation in life, and most people can thrive on some forms of stress. Stress can be caused by quite ordinary and even positive events, such as a game of tennis or a passionate kiss.

The amount of stress that people experience results from a complex interaction between their personalities and their circumstances. People who have experienced a large number of significant changes in their lives tend to be more susceptible to stressful situations. Part I identifies some of the major life changes people experience and examines the relationship of these experiences to mental health. Two contrasting personality types, type A and type B, are revealed by stress responses, and these have been used to describe the characteristic behavior patterns of different individuals. These two personality types are described in Part II, along with a self-assessment questionnaire for measuring them.

PART I: SUSCEPTIBILITY TO STRESS

Thomas Holmes and Richard Rahe of the University of Washington School of Medicine studied the clinical effects of major life changes over a twenty-year period. They asked people from diverse racial and ethnic backgrounds to rank specific life changes according to their degree of impact on health, and found virtually universal agreement. From their research, they were able to assign a numerical value to each life event. Then they compared the life change scores of some five thousand people with their respective medical histories. Those who had a high rating on the life change index were more likely to contract illness following the events.

Question Which of the following changes have occurred in your life during the past year?

After checking the items in Exhibit 8.8 on page 335, add the point values for all the items checked. If your total score for the year was under 150 points, your level of stress based upon life change is low. If your total was between 150 and 300, your stress levels are borderline, and you are advised to minimize other changes in your life at this time. If your total was more than 300, your life change levels of stress are high and it is recommended that you not only minimize any other changes in your life but also begin some form of stress reduction technique, such as an exercise program.

PART II: BEHAVIOR ACTIVITY PROFILE

The type A versus type B personality patterns were described by two San Francisco cardiologists, Meyer Friedman and Ray Rosenman, who were investigating the relationship between behavior and heart disease. (See M. Friedman and R. Rosenman, *Type A Behavior and Your Heart*, New York: Alfred A. Knopf, 1974.) Their observations led them to suspect that the effects of competition and job deadlines were more damaging than had been previously imagined. From their research, they concluded that people who had what they called type A personalities were more susceptible to coronary heart disease. Before studying more about type A versus type B personalities, complete the following behavior activity profile.

The behavior activity profile measures the characteristic style or approach you exhibit in a number of situations. There are no right or wrong answers. The best answer to each item is the response that most nearly describes the way you feel, behave, or think.

Directions. Each item in Exhibit 8.10 contains two alternatives. Indicate which of the two alternatives is more descriptive of you. In some items you may feel that the alternatives are equally descriptive; for other items you may feel that neither is descriptive. Nevertheless, try to determine which alternative is more descriptive of you. For each item you have five points that you may distribute between the two alternatives however you choose. For instance, if X is totally descriptive of you and Y is not at all descriptive, place a 5 by the X and a 0 by the Y. If Y is slightly more descriptive of you than X is, place a 3 by the Y and a 2 by the X. There are six possible combinations for responding to each pair of alternatives. Whatever combination you use, be sure that the points you allocate to each item add to 5. Remember, answer on the basis of what you honestly feel *is* descriptive—not how you feel you should be or how you would like to be.

Scoring. Calculate and interpret your score on the behavior activity profile using the following information. Add your responses to 1Y, 2X, 3Y, 4X, 5Y, 6Y, 7X, 8X, 9X, 1OX, 11Y, 12X, 13Y, 14Y, 15X, 16Y. The average score for a group of 364 male students ages 18 to 25 was 49, while the average score of a sample of 397 female students was 42.

71–80	Hard-core type A
56–70	Strong type A
47–55	Moderate type A
41–46	Low type A
40	A and B tendency
32–39	Low type B
24–31	Moderate type B
12–23	Strong type B
0–11	Hard-core type B

Although people cannot be easily categorized as having either type A or type B personalities, the research of Friedman and Rosenman indicates that the incidence of coronary heart disease is more prevalent among people whom they categorized as having type A personalities. The following is true of type A people:

- They chronically struggle to get as many things done as possible in the shortest amount of time.
- They are aggressive, ambitious, competitive, and forceful.
- They speak explosively, hurrying others to finish what they are saying.
- They are impatient, and they consider waiting a waste of precious time.
- They are preoccupied with deadlines and are highly work oriented.
- Their lives always seem to be a struggle with people, things, and events.

EXHIBIT 8.10   Behavior Activity Profile Questionnaire

	X	Y	

1. ___ ___ X. I guess I'm just interested in what other people have to say—I seldom find my attention wandering when someone is talking to me.
   Y. Often when someone is talking to me I find myself thinking about other things.

2. ___ ___ X. When I talk, I tend to accent words with increased volume, and my delivery is staccato, but rapid.
   Y. My speech usually flows slowly in a smooth amplitude, without changes in speed.

3. ___ ___ X. I like to enjoy whatever it is I'm doing; the more relaxed and noncompetitive I can be, the more I enjoy the activity.
   Y. In just about everything I do, I tend to be hard-driving and competitive.

4. ___ ___ X. I prefer being respected for the things that I accomplish.
   Y. I prefer being liked for who I am.

5. ___ ___ X. I let people finish what they are doing or saying before I respond in any way—no use in jumping the gun and making a mistake.
   Y. I usually anticipate what a person will do or say next; for example, I'll start answering a question before it has been completely asked.

6. ___ ___ X. My behavior is seldom or never governed by a desire for recognition and influence.
   Y. If I were really honest about it, I'd have to admit that a great deal of what I do is designed to bring me recognition and influence.

7. ___ ___ X. I often get upset or angry with people, even though I may not show it.
   Y. I rarely get upset with people; most things simply aren't worth getting angry about.

8. ___ ___ X. I frequently feel impatient with others, either for their slowness or for the poor quality of their work.
   Y. While I may be disappointed in the work of others, I don't let it frustrate me.

9. ___ ___ X. My job provides me with my primary source of satisfaction; I don't find other activities nearly as gratifying.
   Y. Although I like my job, I regularly find satisfaction in other things, such as spectator sports, hobbies, friends, and family.

10. ___ ___ X. If I had to identify one thing that really frustrates me, it would be standing in line.
    Y. I find it kind of amusing the way some people get upset about waiting in line.

11. ___ ___ X. I don't have to control my temper; it's just not a problem for me.
    Y. I frequently find it hard to control my temper, although I usually manage to do so.

12. ___ ___ X. I work hard at my job because I have a very strong desire to get ahead.
    Y. I work hard at my job because I owe it to my employer, who pays my salary.

13. ___ ___ X. It's very unusual for me to have difficulty getting to sleep because I'm excited, keyed up, or worried about something.
    Y. Many times I'm so keyed up that I have difficulty getting to sleep.

14. ___ ___ X. I may not be setting the world on fire, but I don't really want to, either.
    Y. I often feel uncomfortable or dissatisfied with how well I am doing in my job or career.

15. ___ ___ X. It really bothers me when, for some reason, plans I've made can't be executed.
    Y. Few plans I make are so important that I get upset if something happens and I can't carry them out.

16. ___ ___ X. Such things as achieving peace of mind or enjoyment of life are as worthy ambitions as a desire to get ahead.
    Y. People who do not want to get ahead professionally or career-wise simply don't have any ambition.

Source: This survey was developed by Michael T. Matteson and John M. Ivancevich, and is copyrighted by Fred Dorin, Associates, P.O. Box 31753, Houston, TX 77231.

■ Group Dynamics

■ Intergroup Behavior and Conflict

GROUP AND INTERGROUP BEHAVIOR

Behavior can be analyzed from three levels—the individual, the group, and the organization—and each level provides a unique perspective. This section explains how behavior is influenced by group processes. As members of a group, people behave differently from the way they behave when they are are acting alone, and their behavior may change dramatically as they go from one group to another. Consequently, when people are members of a group we cannot understand their individual behavior without also understanding the group.

People join groups for a variety of reasons, as explained in Chapter 9, and the dynamics of the group, especially group roles and group norms, have a powerful influence on individual behavior. Group members often experience intense pressures to conform to group norms, and the status they derive from their group membership usually represents a major component of their self-esteem.

Chapter 10 explains why the behavior of people in groups is influenced by the relationships between groups. Competition between two groups can motivate group members to perform better; but it can also create unhealthy conflict. Simply separating people into two separate groups is sometimes all that is needed to create hostility and intergroup conflict. Conflict tends to inhibit communication between groups, making the conflict even more intense, while within the group the growing conflict leads to greater cohesiveness among the group members. Although conflict is not always undesirable, it may become too intense. Chapter 10 explains how managers can either increase or decrease the level of intergroup conflict to improve performance.

Group Dynamics

LEARNING OBJECTIVES

After studying this chapter, you should be able to

1. Describe the different types of groups typically found in organizations.

2. Explain why people join groups.

3. List the stages of group development.

4. Explain the effects of group size on member satisfaction and group performance.

5. Explain the differences between work roles and maintenance roles.

6. Describe the causes and consequences of role ambiguity and role conflict.

7. Explain how norms are developed, and list some of the most prominent in our society.

8. Describe two kinds of pressures causing people to conform to group norms.

9. Explain how people acquire status through both formal and informal group processes and how status influences the interactions of group members.

10. Explain why the presence of other group members sometimes facilitates or hinders individual performance.

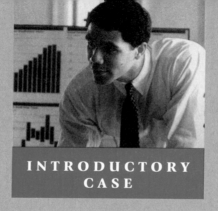

COVERING THE RECEPTION DESK

In their weekly productivity improvement meeting, the twelve committee members listened to a recommendation from Karen Nichols, one of the lead interviewers. The twelve committee members work for the placement division of the Job Service Agency. The purpose of the committee is to improve the performance of the agency by eliminating inefficiencies. Three weeks earlier, the committee identified the problem of inadequate staffing of the reception desk during the heavy midday demand. The busiest part of the day is from 12 to 2, and the receptionist's lunch break is scheduled at noon. Before the recent budget cuts, two receptionists worked at the desk and scheduled their lunch breaks so they were usually both there.

Karen proposed to have the five employer relations representatives assigned to work at the reception desk on a rotating schedule. "You can't expect us to do that," replied Janet Andrus, one of the employer relations representatives. "That's not part of our job. As ER reps we have our own responsibilities." "So who should do it?" Karen asked. "Do you have a better idea?"

"I think the interviewers should do it. We have fourteen interviewers, and one or two of them should be able to handle it," Janet responded.

"But if you take them away from interviewing," Karen persisted, "the whole process slows down. We've got to keep the interviewers talking to the applicants. I think the ER reps could fill in one day a week without hindering their work very much."

"If we have to do it, then I think everyone should have to take a turn, including Barry," said another ER rep. Barry Walker, the placement director, smiled at the suggestion and his smile was all the encour-

agement Paul and Ernest needed. Suddenly, the meeting degenerated into a comedy as Paul and Ernest began to mimic Barry's voice and facial expressions. "Could ah hep ya pleeze?" "Have ya filled out yer blue card, partner?"

Karen was disappointed that the committee had dismissed her proposal without really considering it. Janet thought the committee was wasting time with silly jokes, but she was glad no one was taking the proposal seriously.

Paul enjoyed making the group laugh at his antics and he tried to have them imagine how Barry would look in a wig, a skirt, false eyelashes, and long fingernails. Louise, the receptionist, was not amused at his humor. After listening to three or four of Paul's comments, Louise quietly left the room.

After she saw Louise leave, Janet decided the group had been clowning long enough. Turning to Paul and Ernest, she announced that it was time to quit fooling around. Stunned by Janet's reproof, they listened quietly as she redirected the group to the reception desk problem. Janet summarized Karen's proposal, explained her objection to it, and suggested they go around the room and each express his or her opinion.

Questions

1. Although Barry is the official leader of this group, who seems to be the real leader in this episode? Why do groups need leaders? What purposes do they serve?

2. What happens to the performance of a group when one or more members begin to act like comedians?

3. What are the other positions or roles that group members played in this episode?

An understanding of group dynamics is essential for understanding organizational behavior. Groups are a central part of our everyday lives, and at any given time we are members in many different groups, such as work groups, student clubs, church groups, professional associations, dormitory groups, political parties, and our family. At any one time the average individual belongs to five or six different groups.[1]

Why do we study groups? The study of group dynamics is important for three reasons. First, groups exert an enormous influence on individuals. Our attitudes, values, and behaviors are greatly influenced by our interactions with other group members. We rely on groups to teach us how to behave and to help us understand who we are.

The second reason to study group dynamics is because groups have such a powerful influence on other groups and on the organization. Much of the work that gets done in organizations is done by groups, and the success of an organization is limited by the effectiveness of its groups. The collective action of a group of individuals is much greater than the sum of individuals acting alone.

The third reason to study group dynamics is because it helps to explain behavior. Unique behavior occurs within groups that can only be explained by understanding group processes. Group members perform specialized functions that can be explained best by knowing the kinds of roles and norms found in groups. An understanding of group dynamics is essential for analyzing human interactions and diagnosing problems.

TYPES OF GROUPS

A group consists of two or more people interacting interdependently to achieve a common goal or objective. The principal characteristics of this definition are people, face-to-face interaction, and at least one common goal. A collection of people who use the same copy machine is not a group even though they have face-to-face contact, because they are not interacting interdependently. Members of a group must think they belong together; they must see themselves as forming a single unit. This feeling of self-awareness usually results because the group members share common beliefs and attitudes and accept certain group norms.

To understand why people join groups and why groups have such a great impact on behavior, it is necessary to distinguish between formal and informal groups. Different kinds of formal and informal groups are listed in Exhibit 9.1.

Formal Groups

Groups established by the organization to achieve organizational goals are referred to as *formal work groups,* and the most common formal groups are command groups and task groups. A **command group** consists of a supervisor and the subordinates who report to that supervisor. Membership in a command group is specified by the organizational chart. In a university, for example, a department chairman and the nine faculty members in that department would comprise a command group. A *task group* consists of the people who work together on a common task; they are united by the work they do. A task group would also be a command group if it included all members of the same department and the supervisor. But some task groups

EXHIBIT 9.1	Types of Group

Formal Groups	Informal Groups
Command group	Friendship group
Task group	Interest group
Project group	Reference group
Committees	

include members who report to different supervisors. Task groups and command groups are what people usually refer to when they talk about "my work group," "my co-workers," or "my friends at work."

Many organizations create additional work groups, such as task forces, project groups, and committees. A **task force** is a group that is organized on a temporary basis to achieve a particular goal or solve a specific problem. **Project groups,** likewise, are created to complete a specific project, and the life of the group normally coincides with the length of the project. *Committees* are usually created outside the usual command group structure to solve recurring problems, and the life of a committee may be relatively long or short. **Standing committees** are relatively permanent and survive by rotating members, such as a grievance committee created by a union contract. An **ad hoc committee** is a temporary group created "for this case only," such as a committee formed to resolve a specific complaint.

Informal Groups

Some of the most important group dynamics occur in informal groups that are not created or controlled by the organization. *Informal groups* are groups that emerge naturally in response to the common interests and shared values of individuals, such as friendship groups and interest groups.

Friendship groups are associations of people who like each other and who like to be together. They are formed because members have something in common, such as social activities, political beliefs, religious values, or other bonds of attraction. Friendship groups in organizations often extend their interactions to off-the-job activities, such as bowling leagues, softball teams, and bridge clubs.

Interest groups are composed of individuals who may not be members of the same organizational unit, but they are united by their interest in a common issue. Some examples of interest groups include a group of scientists who organize a study group to learn about new developments, a group of nurses who combine their efforts to create a daycare center at the hospital, or the group of employees from three different airlines who maintain a refrigerator stocked with refreshments in a break room. The objectives uniting interest groups are specific to each group rather than related to the goals of the organization.

A **reference group** is a special type of informal group that people use to evaluate themselves. Reference groups serve two important and related functions: social validation, which helps us justify and legitimate our attitudes and values; and social comparison, which helps us evaluate what we do by comparing ourselves to others.[2]

In serving these two functions, reference groups exert an enormous influence on the behavior of group members. Through social comparison processes, we assess whether our behavior is acceptable and whether our appearance conforms to group standards. Through social validation processes, we decide whether our attitudes and values are right or wrong. For example, our reference group helps us decide whether we should feel good about such things as accurately reporting our expense accounts, remaining calm when being yelled at by irate customers, and going out of our way to help a co-worker. We assume a particular standard of behavior is right if our reference group says it is right. A reference group may not be an actual group that meets together; it can be an imaginary group. The reference group for a new college professor, for example, may be other scholars in the same discipline at other universities. The reference group for a union steward could be the memory of "all the renowned union leaders" this person remembers, both living and dead.

An excellent illustration of reference groups and their enormous impact on individual behavior occurred in the prisoner of war camps during the Korean War. The Chinese Communists effectively disrupted most of the informal groups among the POWS, which made them very vulnerable to social influence attempts. Unlike the daring escape attempts among POWs in World War II, the Korean POWs made very few attempts to escape or harass their captors. The Chinese succeeded in systematically undermining the group solidarity by creating doubt and mistrust among the POWS. After the return of the POWs, rumors circulated regarding mysterious brainwashing and thought control techniques, but these mysterious forces consisted of nothing more than a sophisticated understanding of reference groups and a systematic method for destroying their influence. Without a reference group for social support and evaluation, many prisoners became doubtful, insecure, and susceptible to the influence of their captors. Prisoners were used to spy on other prisoners and create doubt and suspicion. Those who showed leadership capacities were systematically removed, and group memberships were frequently shuffled. Organized activities, such as sports, social events, and religious gatherings, were strictly forbidden. Contrived confessions by some prisoners were used to pressure other prisoners into confessing, and the anchors of social comparison and social validation were destroyed by creating the impression that everyone was collaborating with the enemy. The prisoners who most successfully avoided the influence of the Chinese Communists were those whose reference group identifications were beyond the boundaries of the camp (such as family, school, and religious reference groups). The POWs who used the enforced solitude as a time to think and reflect were able to strengthen their self-concepts and resist the attempts to induce collaboration.[3]

GROUP FORMATION

Formal groups are typically created to satisfy a particular organizational objective or to solve a specific problem. Informal groups, however, are created for a variety of reasons, and these reasons explain why people maintain their membership in them. This section examines the reasons individuals join groups and the stages of group development.

Why Groups Form

When individuals join a group, they voluntarily surrender part of their personal freedom, since they must be willing to accept the standards of the group and behave in prescribed ways that are sometimes very restrictive. Musical groups and athletic teams, for example, place heavy demands on members regarding attendance at practices and performances, dressing in the proper attire, and behaving in prescribed ways even outside the group. Although the loss of freedom varies from group to group, every individual voluntarily relinquishes at least some personal freedom as a member of a group. Why then do individuals want to join a group and sacrifice part of their personal freedom?

According to operant conditioning, individuals join groups because of the positive reinforcement that comes from group membership, such as friendly interaction and being able to achieve something they cannot obtain by acting alone. **Cooperant behavior** is the behavior that group members perform to obtain reinforcement.[4] Some of the specific reinforcement accompanying cooperant behavior is goal accomplishment, affiliation, emotional support, and social validation.

Social identity theory provides another explanation for why members join a group.[5] According to social identity theory, people tend to classify themselves and others according to salient social categories, such as gender, age, interests, religion, and organizational affiliations, and they define themselves partly in terms of these group memberships. This categorization process helps people define who they are; for example, "I am a second-year, married, female, MBA student at _____ University; and I am an alumni of _____ High School and a member of the _____ Church."

Social identification creates a perception of oneness with and belongingness to a group that allows members to experience either directly or vicariously the group's characteristics and its successes and failures. Identity with a group is more pronounced when the group's values and practices are more distinctive, when the group is a highly prestigious group, and when out-groups are highly salient, providing a contrast that defines who group members are not.

Metaphors and idiomatic expressions contribute to a group's development.[6] Social groups develop self-reinforcing and group reinforcing patterns of speech that help construct a collective social reality. Athletic teams are especially known for their mascots, nicknames, and peculiar jargon that have unique significance only to other team members. The use of a shared vernacular increases group contact among the group members, lets members express themselves both as individuals and group members, develops a group consciousness, facilitates group learning, and overcomes a social resistance of recalcitrant members. These idioms and metaphors are generative in the sense that they help people conceptualize the group as a viable living unit apart from the individual identities that comprise it.

Goal Accomplishment. People work together in groups because they need the help of others to achieve important goals. Physical goals, such as building a high-rise tower, extinguishing a forest fire, and playing a basketball game, require the cooperative efforts of other group members. Intellectual goals may also require help from others, such as developing a new consumer product, restructuring the production process, and evaluating applications for college scholarships. Here members of the group contribute to the group's success by suggesting new ideas and helping to evaluate them.

Many situations require people to work together for economic benefits. An organized work group performing specialized jobs can produce significantly more than it could if the members worked independently, as explained in Chapter 6. Another form of economic benefit comes from the power exerted by special-interest groups such as political action committees, investment clubs, and unions. For example, workers have succeeded in raising their wage levels by organizing a union and collectively pressuring management to make wage and benefit concessions.

Successful groups have a better chance than unsuccessful groups of attracting new members and maintaining their membership. Achieving a group goal is a reinforcing event that allows the successful groups to reward their members. A winning football team, for example, is in a better position than a losing team to recruit new players and make them feel proud to belong to the team.

Affiliation. Group members enjoy associating with other group members, particularly if they like them and have something in common with them. The mere presence of others provides friendship, social stimulation, and personal acceptance. College students and factory workers alike form informal peer groups simply to avoid the discomfort of being alone.

Membership in a group often results in **ego extension.** By being part of something beyond our physical self, we achieve a sense of belongingness and participate in accomplishments beyond our individual powers. The members of a winning basketball team participate equally in the glory of success—even the third team players who didn't play in any of the tournament games. Likewise, when a new product is developed everyone on the research and development team glories in the success.

When individuals form a group, do they select associates who have similar or different personalities? In short, do "opposites attract" or do "birds of a feather flock together"? As a general rule, people prefer to associate with co-workers who are like them. Research suggests that individuals tend to be attracted to others of similar age, sex, religion, and socioeconomic status.[7] However, this rule does not always hold for people who have a high achievement orientation. When choosing co-workers, people with a high achievement orientation tend to base their decisions on competence rather than friendship, which means that they usually select people different from themselves who have complementary skills. People with a low achievement orientation, however, tend to choose as co-workers the people they like and who are like them.[8]

Emotional Support. When situations are threatening or uncertain, people rely on others for emotional support. Research shows that people facing a stressful situation are comforted by the physical presence of another person facing the same stress.[9] Without doing or saying anything, just the physical presence of another person provides emotional support. During times of natural disasters, people join together to talk about their misfortune and express sympathy. The uncertainty of joining an organization and being accepted by new co-workers encourages new employees to form a group to create a sense of security. New employees typically search for other new employees and form a peer group in part as a defense against the potential power of the organization.[10]

Social Validation. Individuals join groups for purposes of self-identity. We want to know who we are and we learn about ourselves from the feedback we receive from others, as expressed in these lines: "Each to each a looking glass,/ Reflects the other that doth pass."[11] The comments we receive from others help us evaluate our personalities and behaviors.

The comments of peer group members generally have a great impact on our self-esteem because they come from people we respect. Because of our association with them, we have greater confidence in what they say; we can tell the difference between friendly sarcasm and serious criticism. Their comments are also more credible because we assume they know us better and are concerned about our well-being. Sometimes personal feedback is so threatening that it is useful only when it comes from close peers who can help us respond to the criticism.

Physical Factors. **Proximity,** or physical distance, is an important physical factor influencing the formation of groups. People who are physically close together for an extended period of time tend to develop mutual attraction for each other and form a group. Just being close together in face-to-face interaction usually creates feelings of friendship and affiliation. Architectural barriers that prevent face-to-face interaction, such as a movable partition or a row of file cabinets, can effectively disrupt or alter the formation of groups.

The effects of proximity on group formation have been supported in organizational studies. A study of clerical employees in a large organization found that the distance between their desks was the most important variable explaining the interaction between any two employees. Those who interacted frequently developed bonds of friendship that resulted in the formation of informal peer groups. Similar results showing that physical proximity contributes to interaction and attraction have been found in research and development laboratories and university faculty office buildings. Among bomber crews, the seat locations that allowed the most frequent interactions produced the greatest attraction between crew members.[12]

Group Development

The developmental processes for most groups are quite similar. Even though their functions and purposes may be very different, most groups experience similar conflicts and challenges that need to be resolved as they strive to become effective.

Characteristics of Effective Groups. Some groups are considerably more successful than others in accomplishing their goals and satisfying the needs of their members. Douglas McGregor identified eleven dimensions of group functioning and argued that these dimensions made the difference between highly effective groups and ineffective groups.[13] These eleven dimensions are listed in Exhibit 9.2, with brief descriptions showing the differences between effective and ineffective groups.

Effective groups have several characteristics: the atmosphere is close and friendly; all members participate in the group; all members are committed to the group's goals; members listen to each other and share information; decisions are made by consensus; conflict is dealt with openly and resolved; members receive frank and objective feedback and feel free to express their feelings openly; there is a division of labor with shared leadership; and the group is aware of its own operations and able to monitor itself.

Stages of Group Development. After a group is initially formed, it does not immediately function as a highly effective team until after it has gone through various stages of development and addressed the kinds of issues that

EXHIBIT 9.2   Characteristics of Effective Groups

Ineffective		Effective

1. *Atmosphere and relationships:* What kinds of relationships exist among group members?

   Formal and reserved ←————————————→ Close and friendly

2. *Member participation:* Does everyone participate in the group?

   Some participate more ←————————————→ There is equal
   than others.   participation.

3. *Goal understanding and acceptance:* How well do members accept the objectives of the group and commit themselves to them?

   No commitment ←————————————→ Total commitment

4. *Listening and sharing information:* Are people willing to listen to each other or are they afraid of looking foolish for suggesting creative ideas?

   There is no listening or sharing. ←————————→ People listen and share.

5. *Handling conflicts and disagreements:* Is conflict and disagreement tolerated and used to improve the group or is it avoided, brushed aside, or flamed into conflict?

   If it's not ignored, it ←————————————→ Conflict is dealt
   results in hostility.   with and resolved.

6. *Decision making:* How are decisions made? Does everyone have an opportunity to provide input?

   Autocratically ←————————————→ By consensus

7. *Evaluation of member performance:* What kind of feedback do members receive about their performance?

   Criticism and ←————————————→ Frank, frequent, and
   personal attacks   objective feedback

8. *Expressing feelings:* Do members feel free to express their feelings openly on more than just task issues?

   True feelings must ←————————————→ Open expression
   remain hidden.   is welcomed.

9. *Division of labor:* Are task assignments clearly made and willingly accepted?

   Poorly structured ←————————————→ Effective job
   job assignments   specialization

10. *Leadership:* How are the leaders selected, and are the leadership functions shared?

    Leadership is lacking or ←————————————→ Leadership is shared
    dominated by one person.   and effective.

11. *Attention to process:* Is the group conscious of its own operations and can it monitor and improve its own processes?

    Unaware of group ←————————————→ Aware of operations
    operations   and monitors them

Source: Adapted from Douglas McGregor, *The Human Side of Enterprise* (New York: McGraw-Hill, 1960), pp. 232–235.

separate effective from ineffective groups. Every work group, whether it is a surgical team, a quality control circle, or a production crew, has to resolve the same general issues, and the way these issues are resolved determines the group's effectiveness.

In spite of variability in how groups develop, there appears to be a basic model of development that applies to most groups.[14] Although the developmental process is not highly standardized, most effective groups go through four stages: orientation, confrontation, differentiation, and collaboration, as shown in Exhibit 9.3. A useful mnemonic for remembering these developmental stages is forming, storming, norming, and performing. Groups do not necessarily advance through each of these four stages; indeed, some groups never advance to the later stages, because of internal conflicts.

Orientation ("Forming"). The first stage for almost every group is an orientation stage when members learn about the purposes of the group and the roles of each member. This stage is marked by caution, confusion, courtesy, and commonality. Individual members have to decide how the group will be structured and how much they are willing to commit themselves to the group. The formal leader, or someone who assumes the leadership role, typically exerts a great influence in structuring the group and shaping member expectations. Members strive to discover the rules of the game and the biases and motives of other group members. During this stage, members need to get acquainted with each other and share their expectations about the group's goals and objectives. Efforts to rush this process by expecting members to be fully open and express their real feelings can be very destructive, both to the individuals and to the group. The trust and openness necessary for members to feel willing to share intimate details of themselves comes in later stages of development.

EXHIBIT 9.3   Stages of Group Development

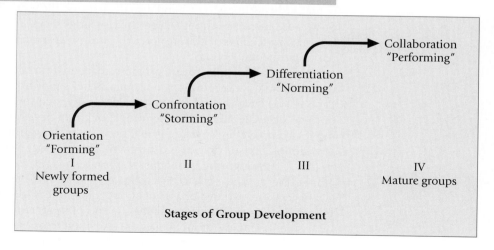

Stages of Group Development

Confrontation ("Storming").   Although conflict is not a necessary phase of group development, the purposes of the group and the expectations of group members are eventually challenged in most groups. This stage contains conflict, confrontation, concern, and criticism. Struggles for individual power and influence are common. Challenging the group's goals can be a healthy process if the conflict results in greater cohesiveness and acceptance. But if the conflict becomes extremely intense and dysfunctional, the group may dissolve or continue as an ineffective group that never advances to higher levels of group maturity.

Differentiation ("Norming").   The major issues at this stage of development are how the tasks and responsibilities will be divided among members and how members will evaluate each other's performance. Individual differences are recognized, and task assignments are based on skills and abilities. If a group can resolve its authority conflicts and create shared expectations regarding its goals and task assignments, it can become a cohesive group and achieve its goals. At this stage, the members often feel the group is successful as they pursue their group goals, and indeed their short-term effectiveness may look rather impressive. As unique situations arise that violate personal expectations, however, the long-term effectiveness of the group will require additional maturity in resolving conflicts and re-establishing shared expectations.

Collaboration ("Performing").   The highest level of group maturity is the stage of collaboration, where there is a feeling of cohesiveness and commitment to the group. Individual differences are accepted without being labeled as either good or bad. Conflict is neither eliminated nor squelched but is identified and resolved through group discussion. Conflict is real and concerns substantive issues relevant to the group task rather than emotional issues regarding group processes. Decisions are made through rational group discussion, and no attempts are made to force decisions or to present a false unanimity. The members of the group are aware of the group's processes and the extent of their own involvement in the group.

Separation ("Adjourning").   Some groups go through an "adjourning" stage by consciously deciding to disband, usually because the group has completed its tasks or because members choose to go their separate ways. This stage is typically characterized by feelings of closure and compromise as members prepare to leave, often with sentimental feelings.

The idea that all groups progress through four stages—forming, storming, norming, and performing—is a popular belief supported by common experience. People who have worked in groups can usually identify group events that fit each of these stages. However, another model of group development comes from studying the complete life spans of actual decision-making groups.[15] Each of these project groups had to diagnose a problem and produce a group product before a deadline. Although the problems, the products, and the deadlines varied greatly among the groups, each group followed the same developmental process. Each group goes through two phases of about equal time. Phase 1 is the initial period of movement whose direction is set by the end of the group's first meeting. When the time is half spent, the group makes the transition to phase 2 as it reviews its progress and revises its strategy. At the end of phase 2, there is a final meeting marked by accelerated activity to complete the project and prepare an acceptable group product. This study provides an alternative way to examine group development.

GROUP STRUCTURE

As a group develops, a structure emerges that influences what it does and how effectively it performs. Group structure is not an easy concept to explain because it does not refer to a specific observable object. Group structure is the stable pattern of relationships among group members that maintain the group and help it work toward its goal. The major variables defining group structure are the concepts of group roles, group norms, and status. *Group roles* are the task activities and responsibilities performed by the group members; *group norms* are general expectations about how members ought to behave; and *status* is the social position accorded to various group members by the awards and prestige ascribed to them. Situational factors also influence group structure by influencing the relationships among group members. This section will examine three of these situational factors: group size, social density, and nature of the task. Later sections examine group roles, group norms, and status in greater detail.

Group Size

Perhaps the most visible factor influencing group structure is the size of the group. Groups vary enormously in size from as small as a dyad (two-person group) or a triad (three-person group) to as large as 400 to 500 members (such as the House of Representatives).

Size and Participation. Small groups provide each member with an opportunity to be actively involved in the group. As the group gets larger, however, participation declines rather rapidly. A small graduate seminar with four students, for example, allows each student to participate freely in the discussion. In large classes, however, students have limited opportunities to participate. Large informal groups must develop a method for allowing members to participate in an orderly manner so that everyone doesn't speak at once. When an informal group gets to be larger than eight to twelve individuals, a significant part of the time, called *process time,* can be wasted simply trying to decide who should participate next.

Size and Satisfaction. As the size of a group increases, the satisfaction of the group members with the group and their involvement in it tend to increase up to a point—"the more the merrier." A five-person group provides twice as many opportunities for friendly interaction as a three-person group. Beyond a certain point, however, which is probably less than ten to fifteen members, increasing size results in reduced satisfaction. Members of an extremely large group cannot identify with the group's accomplishments nor experience the same degree of cohesiveness and participation as members of a smaller group.[16]

Size and Performance. The relationship between group size and performance depends on whether the task is an additive task, conjunctive task, or disjunctive task.

On **additive tasks** the final group product is the sum of the individual contributions. Additive tasks are sometimes referred to as *pooled interdependence,* since the

APPLYING ORGANIZATIONAL BEHAVIOR
RESEARCH

Using Electronic Brainstorming to Overcome Process Losses

Brainstorming has been recommended as an effective group method for generating creative ideas. The theory is that groups can generate more ideas if their members express whatever ideas occur to them, regardless of their feasibility, and the ideas of one group member will stimulate the thinking of others.

Although this theory sounds good, research evidence has shown that people usually create a higher quantity and quality of ideas while working alone than in a group. Apparently the presence of others creates process losses that inhibit the generation of new ideas.

The two major process losses are called *production blocking* and *evaluation apprehension.* Production blocking occurs when people cannot express their ideas spontaneously because someone else is talking. As groups become larger, each member has less opportunity to talk. Evaluation apprehension occurs when people withhold their ideas because of shyness or a concern that others will ridicule them. Again, as groups become larger, members feel increasingly reluctant to express their ideas.

A new technique that overcomes these process losses is electronic brainstorming. In electronic brainstorming, group members enter their ideas into a computer, which immediately distributes the ideas to the screens of other group members. Since each person has access to a keyboard, production blocking should not be a problem; nor should evaluation apprehension be a problem, because the ideas are anonymous.

Electronic brainstorming was examined in a study that involved two experiments at two college campuses. In one study, 120 students were assigned to groups of two, four, or six members and in the second study 144 students were assigned to groups of six or twelve members. In both experiments, the students were asked to brainstorm two problems for 15 minutes: "How can tourism be improved at _____?" and "How can campus security be improved at _____?" Each group used electronic brainstorming for one question, but for the other they met in a face-to-face group and dictated their ideas into a tape recorder.

The results indicated that the electronic brainstorming groups produced more nonredundant ideas and more high-quality ideas than the nonelectronic brainstorming groups. The electronic groups also reported less production blocking, less evaluation apprehension, and greater satisfaction than the nonelectronic groups.

Furthermore, the benefits of electronic brainstorming became even more pronounced as the group became larger. In the first experiment, with groups of two, four, or six people per group, the average number of ideas per person in the nonelectronic groups declined from 13.10 to 7.95, to 5.98. But for the electronic groups, the means were 12.40, 10.55, and 11.64. In the second experiment, the average number of ideas per person in the nonelectronic groups was 5.0 for six-person groups and 2.5 for twelve-person groups. But for the electronic groups, the means were essentially unchanged (6.0 and 7.2). Thus, the per-person productivity fell as nonelectronic brainstorming groups became larger, but remained steady for electronic brainstorming groups.

This experiment demonstrates how process losses can dramatically reduce the generation of ideas in a decision-making group and how the damages become more severe as the group becomes larger.

Source: R. Brent Gallupe, Alan R. Dennis, William H. Cooper, Joseph S. Valacich, Lana M. Bastianutti, and Jay F. Nunamaker, Jr., "Electronic Brainstorming and Group Size," *Academy of Management Journal,* vol. 35 (1992), pp. 350–369.

individual contribution of each member simply adds to the group product. Interviewing customers leaving a store as part of a consumer survey is an example of an additive task. In additive tasks, the group's performance will almost always be better than the performance of a single individual, even though the average individual in the group usually does not perform as well in the group as if the individual were performing alone.

Three interviewers working together will survey more customers than one interviewer working alone, but the three working together in one location will probably not conduct as many interviews as if they were working alone in separate locations.

Conjunctive tasks are those that can be divided into interdependent subtasks and then assigned to various group members. The overall performance depends on the successful completion of each subtask. The group's maximum performance is limited by the capacities of the least capable member. A chain, for example, is only as strong as its weakest link. An example of a conjunctive task is a TV news team filming an event. A mistake by any member means failure for the whole group, whether it is a bad interview, a bad picture, or bad sound.

Disjunctive tasks require the group to make an "either–or" decision. Most problem-solving and decision-making tasks are disjunctive tasks that require the group to select the best solution. An early study on the performance of individuals and groups in performing a disjunctive task, asked individuals working alone or groups working together to arrive at a solution to the following problem: "On one side of a river are three wives and three very jealous husbands. All of the men but none of the women can row. Get them all across the river in the smallest number of trips by means of a boat carrying no more than three people at one time. No man will allow his wife to be in the presence of another man unless he is also there."[17] Disjunctive tasks require at least one individual with sufficient insight to solve the problem. As a group gets larger, there is a greater probability that the group will contain at least one person with superior insight. In the study just mentioned, correct solutions to the problem of the three couples were produced by 60 percent of the groups, but only 14 percent of the individuals who worked alone.

On disjunctive tasks, therefore, the potential performance of the group depends on the performance of its best member. The term "potential performance" is used here instead of "actual performance" because the actual performance is usually something less than the potential performance. Although the potential performance of a group performing a disjunctive task increases with group size, the actual performance is typically less because the group suffers from process losses. **Process losses** are the inefficiencies that arise from having to organize and coordinate larger groups. Large groups tend to restrict communication, inhibit creative thought processes, and reduce the personal commitment of group members. Therefore, actual performance equals potential performance minus process losses.

Social Density

The interactions among group members are influenced by the physical or spatial locations of group members—whether they are physically separated or close together. Consequently, considerable interest has been expressed in the effects of modern architectural arrangements. Many modern offices use an open office plan with many desks in a large open room or small cubicles separated by partitions rather than separate rooms connected by long hallways. The concentration of people within an area is called **social density,** which is measured by square feet per person or the number of group members within a certain walking distance. Walking distance is used rather than straight-line distance since it is the distance someone must go to have face-to-face contact that is important.

Some organizational studies have found that greater social density improves performance because of greater accessibility. In a research-and-development organization, for example, reducing the distance between desks tended to improve performance by increasing the flow of technical information. In another technical organization, engineers reported less stress and tension where colleagues and other authority figures were located in close proximity. Likewise, the employees of a petroleum company reported greater feedback, friendship opportunities, and satisfaction with work when their social density was increased because of a relocation.[18]

Obviously, the performance of a group will not endlessly increase as the level of social density increases. At some point, the conditions become too crowded and people get in each other's way. The optimal social density depends on the nature of the task, the amount of feedback members need from each other, and their needs for privacy. Most studies of open office plans have found that employees generally dislike open office plans because of a lack of privacy. A large number of studies have shown that high levels of social density in organizations produce feelings of crowdedness, intentions to quit, high levels of stress, and low levels of satisfaction and performance. Although high social density normally has only a small effect on performance, the effects appear to be larger among employees who have a high need for privacy and for complex tasks that require intense concentration.[19]

Nature of the Task

Since the interactions among group members are influenced by the nature of the task, the group structure needs to adapt to the demands of the task. Three types of tasks have already been described: additive, conjunctive, and disjunctive tasks. The need for coordination among group members is much greater for conjunctive tasks than for additive or disjunctive tasks. For example, if five students decided to sell tickets by telephone soliciting, they could divide the student directory into five sections and each one could call the students in one section. Since this is an additive task, the need for coordination is minimal, and the performance of the group would simply be the sum of each individual's sales. Deciding how to divide the student directory would be a disjunctive task and it, too, requires minimal coordination. With a conjunctive task, however, the need for coordination increases as the task becomes more complex. Organizing and presenting a new product development conference is a conjunctive task that would require the coordinated efforts of many people from several departments, including research, sales, training, production, and finance. Playing basketball, another conjunctive task, is an even more complex activity that requires team members to constantly coordinate their efforts and even anticipate each other's moves.

The relationship between group structure, the nature of the task, and task difficulty is a topic we will discuss in Chapter 12. There we will see that the organizational structure needs to vary depending on the nature of the task and how much coordination is required to keep everyone working cooperatively together. Organizations that have highly specialized tasks require special efforts to coordinate the activities of employees, especially when the activities change frequently. The same general conclusion applies here in the study of groups, Groups that perform complex conjunctive tasks require greater coordination between group members than groups performing simple additive or disjunctive tasks. With the basketball team, for example, as the team develops more complex offensive and defensive plays and assigns team members to perform specialized activities, the need for constant coordination between team members during the game increases.

GROUP ROLES

The concept of role is very useful in understanding the behavior of individuals in both groups and organizations. A role encompasses the expected behaviors attached to a position or job. In an organization, an employee's role is briefly indicated by a position title and elaborately specified by a job description. Group roles are usually not explicitly stated in informal groups; and one group member may perform several roles or several members may alternate performing the same role. In formal groups, some roles are designated or assigned. These **assigned roles** are prescribed by the organization as a means of dividing the labor and assigning responsibility. **Emergent roles** develop naturally to meet the needs of group members or assist in achieving formal goals. The dynamics in many groups often results in emergent roles replacing assigned roles as people express their individuality and assertiveness.

Typical Group Roles

Group members may be expected to perform a variety of different behaviors. A complete listing of these group roles would be very lengthy. However, two popular classifications have identified the most relevant group roles and categorized them into meaningful schemes. Both classifications make a distinction between task-oriented roles and social-emotional roles.

Work Roles and Maintenance Roles. The classification of group roles illustrated in Exhibit 9.4 makes a distinction between three major kinds of group roles: work roles, maintenance roles, and blocking roles.[20] **Work roles** are task-oriented activities involved in accomplishing the work and achieving the group objective. Work roles include such activities as clarifying the purpose of the group, developing a strategy for accomplishing the work, delegating job assignments, and evaluating progress.

Maintenance roles are the social-emotional activities of group members that maintain their involvement and personal commitment to the group. These roles include encouraging other members to participate, praising and rewarding others for their contributions, reconciling arguments and disagreements, and other activities designed to maintain a friendly group atmosphere.

Blocking roles are activities that disrupt or destroy the group. These activities include such things as dominating the discussion, attacking other group members, disagreeing unreasonably with other group members, and distracting the group by irrelevant issues or unnecessary humor. Deciding that a group member is performing a blocking role is sometimes difficult because the behavior may not be intended to block the group. For example, a member may question a conclusion to force the group to think more carefully about an issue. Other group members may feel that this person is stubbornly resisting the emerging consensus and simply trying to

EXHIBIT 9.4   Group Roles

Work Roles	Maintenance Roles	Blocking Roles
1. *Initiator:* Proposing tasks or actions; defining group problems; suggesting a procedure.	1. *Harmonizer:* Attempting to reconcile disagreements; reducing tension; getting people to explore differences.	1. *Aggressor:* Deflating other's status; attacking the group or its values; joking in a barbed or semi-concealed way.
2. *Informer:* Offering facts; giving expression of feeling; giving an opinion.	2. *Gatekeeper:* Helping to keep communication channels open; facilitating the participation of others; suggesting procedures that permit sharing remarks.	2. *Blocker:* Disagreeing and opposing beyond reason; resisting stubbornly the group's wish for personally oriented reasons; using hidden agenda to thwart the movement of a group.
3. *Clarifier:* Interpreting ideas or suggestions; defining terms; clarifying issues for the group.	3. *Consensus tester:* Asking to see if a group is nearing a decision; sending up a trial balloon to test a possible conclusion.	3. *Dominator:* Asserting authority or superiority to manipulate the group or certain of its members; interrupting contributions of others; controlling by means of flattery or other forms of patronizing behavior.
4. *Summarizer:* Pulling together related ideas; restating suggestions; offering a decision or conclusion for the group to consider.	4. *Encourager:* Being friendly, warm and responsive to others; indicating by facial expression or remark the acceptance of others' contributions.	4. *Comedian:* Making a display in comical fashion by one's lack of involvement; abandoning the group while remaining physically with it; seeking recognition in ways not relevant to group task.
5. *Reality tester:* Making a critical analysis of the idea; testing an idea against some data trying to see if the idea would work.	5. *Compromiser:* When his own idea or status is involved in a conflict, offering a compromise which yields status; admitting error; modifying an interest of group cohesion or growth.	5. *Avoidance behavior:* Pursuing special interests not related to task; staying off the subject to avoid commitment; preventing the group from facing controversy.

Source: Kenneth D. Benne and Paul Sheats, "Functional Roles of Group Members," *Journal of Social Issues,* 2 (1948), pp. 42–47.

disrupt its progress. Likewise, a good joke may help to relieve tension and keep the group working cooperatively together, or it may disrupt the group discussion and prevent the group from returning to a crucial issue.

Interaction Process Analysis.   Another classification for analyzing group roles was developed by R. F. Bales. This classification system, which he called Interaction Process Analysis (IPA), was originally designed as an instrument for recording what happened in group research projects.[21] Bales developed twelve categories of interactions, as shown in Exhibit 9.5, that he considered a reasonably complete list of the unique interactions that might be observed within a group.

EXHIBIT 9.5 Bales' System of Categories Used to Observe Individuals in Groups

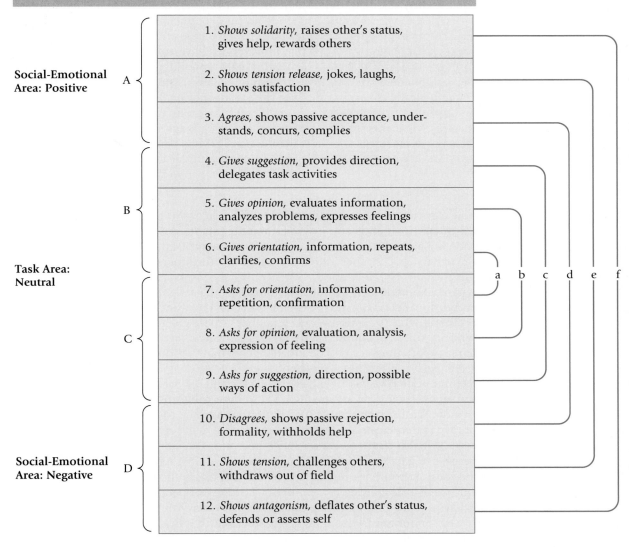

Social-Emotional Area: Positive — A

1. *Shows solidarity*, raises other's status, gives help, rewards others

2. *Shows tension release*, jokes, laughs, shows satisfaction

3. *Agrees*, shows passive acceptance, understands, concurs, complies

Task Area: Neutral — B

4. *Gives suggestion*, provides direction, delegates task activities

5. *Gives opinion*, evaluates information, analyzes problems, expresses feelings

6. *Gives orientation*, information, repeats, clarifies, confirms

C

7. *Asks for orientation*, information, repetition, confirmation

8. *Asks for opinion*, evaluation, analysis, expression of feeling

9. *Asks for suggestion*, direction, possible ways of action

Social-Emotional Area: Negative — D

10. *Disagrees*, shows passive rejection, formality, withholds help

11. *Shows tension*, challenges others, withdraws out of field

12. *Shows antagonism*, deflates other's status, defends or asserts self

a b c d e f

Key:
A Positive reactions
B Attempted answers
C Questions
D Negative reactions

a Problems of communication
b Problems of evaluation
c Problems of information and delegation
d Problems of agreement
e Problems of tension reduction
f Problems of reintegration

Source: From Robert Bales, "Bales' System of Categories," *Interaction Process Analysis* (University of Chicago Press, 1950), p. 9. Copyright 1950 by the University of Chicago. All rights reserved.

The twelve categories are divided into six social-emotional responses—three positive and three negative—and six task-oriented or problem-solving responses—three involve asking questions and the other three involve providing answers.

When the IPA was used to study group dynamics, an observer would classify each comment according to one of these twelve areas and record who said it. Given his research, Bales concluded that most groups have at least two leaders who perform the majority of these roles. The formally appointed leader typically performs the task-oriented roles to help the group achieve its objectives, but an informal leader typically emerges to perform the social-emotional roles. Both the work roles and maintenance roles are necessary for effective group functioning, and it appears, therefore, that they can be performed either as assigned roles by the designated leader or as emergent roles by someone else. These two group roles will be discussed again in Chapter 15, where they will be used to understand leader behaviors.

Role Episode

Role expectations are communicated to individuals during a **role episode,** which is the interaction between role senders and the person receiving the role.[22] A role episode is diagrammed in Exhibit 9.6. A *role sender* may be anyone attempting to change the behavior of another individual, called the **focal person.** In formal groups, the most legitimate role senders are generally supervisors, project directors, and other organizational leaders responsible for delegating assignments. In reality, however, every group member participates as a role sender to other group members. Even subordinates tend to communicate how they expect their superiors to behave. Role senders typically communicate only a small percentage of their role expectations. Some expectations seem to be so self-evident that they do not need to be communicated (such as answering your telephone when you hear it ring), while others are not communicated because of uncertainty on the part of the role sender (such as whether the supervisor should say anything to group members involved in horseplay).

The focal person may or may not respond to the role sender. Communication problems may create a discrepancy between the sent role and the received role. But even if the expectations are accurately received, the focal person may not respond because of a lack of motivation or inadequate ability. A feedback loop, going from the focal person back to the role sender, illustrates the ongoing nature of a role episode. A role episode is a continuous process of people evaluating each other's behavior and communicating expectations, both overtly and covertly.

An important factor influencing how well the focal person will respond to a sent role is the focal person's state of role readiness. **Role readiness** concerns the focal person's ability and willingness to accept the responsibility associated with a new role. For example, a new employee who has had a broad background of relevant experience and is prepared to immediately perform a new job would have a high degree of role readiness. An illustration of a lack of role readiness is union stewards who resist promotions into supervisory positions because they have difficulty changing their thinking from hourly wages, seniority, and job security to salary, merit pay, and raising productivity.

Role Ambiguity

Role ambiguity concerns the discrepancy between the sent role and the received role, as shown in Exhibit 9.6. Ambiguity frequently results from the confusion that surrounds the delegation of job responsibilities. Many jobs do not have a written

EXHIBIT 9.6   The Role Episode: Role Ambiguity and Role Conflict

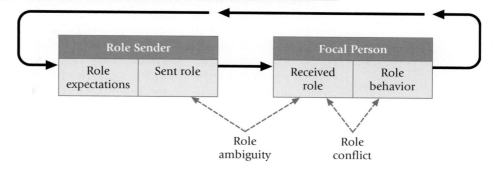

Source: Adapted from Daniel Katz and Robert Kahn, *The Social Psychology of Organizations,* 2nd ed. (New York: Wiley, 1978), p. 196.

job description and when employees are told what to do, their instructions are not clear. Supervisors may not understand how the job should be done, what the standards of acceptable performance are, how performance will be evaluated, or the limits of the employees' authority and responsibility. Even when the supervisors know this information, the orientation training usually overwhelms the new employees.

The consequences of role ambiguity are frustration, dissatisfaction, and evidences of stress. Moderate levels of ambiguity may be tolerable and even desirable, since some employees like to structure their own environment. However, extreme role ambiguity can create an unhealthy condition contributing to dissatisfaction and turnover.[23]

Role Conflict

Role conflict exists when someone faces inconsistency between the received role and role behavior, as shown in Exhibit 9.6. The conditions that create role conflict and role ambiguity are apparently highly variable and individual. Research efforts to develop standard measures of role conflict and role ambiguity have not been very successful because working conditions and other artifacts seem to influence the measurement of these constructs.[24] Role conflict is not the same as role ambiguity, because the received role may be very clear and specific. In fact, additional communication often serves to intensify the role conflict rather than reduce it. The inconsistency between the received role and role behavior can produce four types of role conflict.[25]

Intrasender Role Conflict. When a single role sender communicates incompatible role expectations to the focal person, the focal person experiences **intrasender role conflict.** For example, a manager could tell the staff members that they are each expected to perform the role of critical evaluator and challenge every decision, but they are also expected to work together cooperatively and be team players.

Intersender Role Conflict. If two or more role senders communicate incompatible expectations to the focal person, **intersender role conflict** results. The first-line supervisors in most organizations typically experience rather intense intersender role conflict. Upper management expects them to tighten the controls to increase productivity, reduce errors, and eliminate wasted time. In contrast, their subordinates send messages that the supervisors need to loosen the controls and be less interested in productivity, quality, and wasted time. Boundary role occupants, those who straddle the boundary between the organization and its clients and customers, are also prone to experience intersender role conflict. Salespeople, schoolteachers, and purchasing agents, for example, often receive incompatible instructions from people within the organization and external clients or customers.

Person–role conflict.   When people are asked to behave in ways that are inconsistent with their personal values, **person-role conflict** occurs. An administrative aide, for example, may be told that a report must be completed before going home, even if it means several hours of overtime. But working overtime would mean missing the school play, and the aide's daughter is the star of the play. Employees experience person–role conflict when they are asked to do something illegal or unethical, such as falsifying reports or lying to customers.

Role Overload.   The conflicting demands of too many roles causes role overload, sometimes called **interrole conflict.** People fill a variety of roles, both within the organization and in their personal lives. We cannot be in two places at one time, and conflicting time schedules often create severe role overload, forcing us to reassess which role should take precedence. A personnel director, for example, may experience role overload because of the inconsistent demands accompanying numerous roles such as affirmative action officer, safety director, facilitator of a quality control circle, career development counselor, and manager of the human resource planning system. In addition to the roles she fills in the organization are her roles outside the organization as a wife, mother, and fund raiser for the United Way campaign. These multiple roles contain conflicts of time, interests, and loyalty, because they cannot all be filled simultaneously.

GROUP NORMS

Group norms are the commonly held beliefs of group members about appropriate conduct. As such, they represent general expectations or codes of conduct that contain a quality of demand. Group norms identify the standards against which the behavior of group members will be evaluated and help group members know what they should or should not do. Group norms typically develop around the eleven issues presented earlier regarding group formation.

Every group creates its own norms and standards for evaluating the appropriateness of individual behavior. To illustrate, the members of a fraternity created a group norm that it wasn't "cool" to act like a dedicated student. A little studying was OK if it didn't interfere with social activities. To get good grades, several fraternity members had to lie about how they spent their time and not admit that their dates and weekend trips were actually to the library. The members of an engineering firm created the norm that no one should leave until after the supervisor had left. None of the engineers actually accomplished very much after the regular quitting hours; but even though they quit working, they did not leave.

On the one hand, norms limit individuality and restrict the creativity and autonomy of individuals. But on the other hand, norms create greater predictability within the group and help to structure the group's activities. In a typical classroom, for example, most students adhere to the norm of raising their hands when they want to contribute to the class discussion and waiting until they are called on. This hand-raising norm prevents some class members from making insightful comments, but it also creates a structure that helps the class. Although everyone may not be able to participate, the teacher is able to guide the discussion without the chaos that would result if everyone spoke at once.

Development of Norms

Over time, groups develop a variety of norms regarding many aspects of behavior. The most crucial group norms are those regarding issues of central concern to the group. In general, groups tolerate less deviation from norms regarding important group concerns. For the offensive unit of a football team, for example, a highly enforced norm is that no one talks in the huddle but the quarterback. Accuracy in listening to the quarterback's instructions is vital to the success of the team. Wearing wristbands and putting stickers on helmets, however, are not closely enforced norms because they are not as important to the team's success.

Group norms are typically created and enforced for four reasons: (1) they facilitate group survival, (2) they simplify the requirements and make the behavior of group members more predictable, (3) they help the group avoid embarrassing situations, and (4) they express the central values of the group and clarify what is distinctive about its identity.[26]

Two almost opposite theories are used to explain how group norms are developed.[27] In one explanation, norms are viewed as the product of the shared attitudes and beliefs of group members. These shared attitudes result from either a group consensus after the group discusses the issue or from a dominant group member who simply voices an opinion. If no one expresses a dissenting view, the group may adopt the dominant member's viewpoint. For example, a norm of no smoking during the weekly planning meetings was created when one of the division managers took the ashtray off the table, put it on the shelf behind her, and said, "There's no need to get lung cancer." Her action went uncontested and no one said anything; but thereafter, a no-smoking norm existed.

Another explanation for how group norms are created is that they are the product of the group's behavior. Individuals form a group and begin to behave in predictable ways. They didn't decide how to behave first; instead, they just began to interact and then felt a need to explain or justify their behavior. According to this explanation, norms are viewed as justifications or explanations for the group's behavior. Many performance norms are simply justifications for what has happened in the past, such as stopping the machines twenty minutes early to wash up and considering 38 pallets a full day's work. These standards were never part of a labor agreement; this was just how the employees behaved from the start.

Generally Accepted Norms

Our day-to-day behavior is influenced by so many general social norms that we often fail to recognize them. Most people are members of numerous groups, and these multiple memberships generate a lengthy list of norms providing regularity and predictability to our behavior.

Social Conduct. Social conduct norms are designed to create a pleasant social atmosphere, such as smiling when you pass a friend in a hallway, answering the phone when it rings by saying hello, and saying goodbye before you hang up. When we are introduced, we shake hands and say, "I'm pleased to meet you," whether it's true or not. If someone asks, "How are you?" the norm is to say, "Fine!" not to give a full medical report. Walking away while someone is talking to you is considered a norm violation and leaving in the middle of a lecture or public address is generally considered poor taste. "The customer is always right" is a social norm that reduces conflict with the public but occasionally contributes to abusive acts by customers.

Dress Codes. Some organizations specify formal dress standards for their members, such as the military, police, hospitals, restaurants, and hotels. The dress codes in other organizations may not be quite as official, and nothing may be written; nevertheless, the dress norms may be just as powerful. Many organizations, especially banks and insurance companies, expect employees to wear conservative dresses, shirts, ties, and suits. Heavy equipment operators and factory workers, however, would look quite out of place in a white shirt and three-piece suit.

Performance Norms. How fast group members are expected to work and how much they should produce are important issues to most groups. Therefore, performance norms are created to guide individual efforts. Performance norms can be very frustrating to managers because the norms may be inconsistent with the organization's goals. Sometimes they appear to be very irrational because they are not in the worker's best interests either. In the bank-wiring experiment of the Hawthorne Studies, for example, a group of men maintained an arbitrarily low production norm that restricted productivity even though the workers were paid according to how much work they did, and this study was conducted during the Depression when the workers needed additional income. In many work groups, productivity is determined more by the group's performance norms than by the ability and skill of the employees.

Reward Allocation Norms. Groups develop norms governing how rewards should be distributed to the group members. Three allocation norms have been investigated to determine which norm is the most widely accepted.[28]

The norm of equality suggests that everyone should be treated the same. Everyone shares equally in his or her status as a group member; therefore, the rewards that come to the group should be distributed equally to everyone.

The norm of equity suggests that the rewards should be allocated according to the contribution to the group product or on the basis of merit. According to the norm of equity, people who have contributed the greatest effort and made the

APPLYING ORGANIZATIONAL BEHAVIOR
IN THE NEWS

Group Norms: Customer Service

A company that has succeeded in making customer satisfaction a group norm among its sales associates is Hechinger's Hardware and Home Improvement. Every retail company would like to have customer service entrenched as a central group norm. Hechinger's success comes from selecting employees on the basis of their knowledge about hardware and their enthusiasm for teaching do-it-yourself skills to customers. Their project experts average over ten years' experience in their respective fields.

Hechinger's is one of the giants in the home improvement business, with more than 120 stores along the East Coast. Most of Hechinger's customers are typical homeowners trying to tackle a renovation project by themselves, often for the first time. They enter Hechinger's not knowing what products are available, how much they cost, or exactly how to install the product once they buy it. This uncertainty is not too serious if you're just looking for a shower curtain, but if you plan to remodel your entire bathroom, the project can be frightening. Hechinger's sales associates are prepared to help customers design an entirely new bathroom and teach them how to build it.

Customer service is a top priority for all of Hechinger's employees. Every facet of Hechinger's operations stresses the importance of customer service to employees and customers alike. When the company transformed some of its stores into Home Project Centers, it surveyed the opinions of 3,500 customers about the products they preferred, how they thought the stores should be laid out, and what the displays should be like. Hechinger's responded by changing its inventory, rotating its traditional horizontal aisles to face front and center as customers enter the store, and showing specialized displays of remodeled rooms, such as bathrooms and kitchens.

Even the president of the company, John Hechinger, Jr., encourages total customer service by occasionally helping customers in the store. He claims the greatest lesson he has learned is to listen to the customers and give them what they want the way they want. That lesson is imparted to Hechinger's employees every day, in word and in deed.

Source: CNN *Pinnacle* news programming.

largest contribution to the group product, either through effort, skill, or ability, should receive a larger share of the rewards.

The norm of social responsibility suggests that the rewards should be allocated on the basis of need. People who have special needs, especially those who are disadvantaged or handicapped, should receive special consideration and obtain a larger share of the rewards.

Norm of Reciprocity. The norm of reciprocity suggests that when people make an effort to help you, you should feel an obligation to help them at a later time. Among some people, this norm is a very firmly held expectation, and they keep track of favors and who owes whom. Although some people feel that service should be rendered specifically to those who have helped them, others have a much broader interpretation of whom they should help. For example, a mentor may be very happy to help a new employee, not because the mentor expects help from the new employee in the future, but because of the help that the mentor received as a new employee from someone else in the past.

Norm Violation

Although group norms are a group product, they may not match the private beliefs of all members. Norms are accepted in various degrees by the group members. Some norms may be completely accepted by all group members, while other norms are only partially accepted. Norms vary according to their inclusivity, or the number of people to whom they apply. Some norms are nearly universal in nature, such as the prohibition against murder, which applies to all members of society. Other norms, however, apply to only specific group members. Production norms, for example, may not apply to a lead worker who is expected to spend part of the time training other employees.

For a group norm to be created and maintained, a majority of the active members must agree that the norm specifies appropriate and required behavior. Furthermore, there must be a shared awareness that the group supports a given belief. Although some members may violate the norm, it will continue to survive as long as the majority uphold and accept it. If adherence to the norm continues to erode, it will eventually collapse and no longer serve as a standard for evaluating behavior. Most students have witnessed the disintegration of student conduct norms. Two or three students may violate the norm of raising their hands without the norm being destroyed, but when three or four more students begin to violate the norm, the class dissolves into a shouting match in which all the students are speaking at once rather than raising their hands and waiting to be acknowledged.

Conformity to the essential group norms is a requirement of sustained group membership. Group members who do not conform to important norms are punished by the group by being excluded, ignored, or ridiculed. The ultimate punishment is to be banished from membership in the group.

Because of their status, group leaders are in a better position to violate the norms than are other group members. Indeed, leaders sometimes deviate slightly from accepted group norms as a means of asserting their uniqueness or superiority over other group members. Group members must not come late to work, but managers think they can come when they want as a privilege of being a manager. Studies have shown that highly intelligent group members are also less likely to conform to group norms than less intelligent members. However, group members with a strong authoritarian personality are more likely to conform to group norms than nonauthoritarians.[29]

Group norms are difficult to change. Since they were created by the group, they need to be changed by the group. Organizational leaders are sometimes successful in helping groups change norms by communicating new expectations of behavior. They are successful to the extent that they can get the group to accept what they say as the new standard of behavior.

CONFORMITY

Group norms provide regularity and predictability to the behavior of group members, but only if they conform to the group norms. Norms do not exist without conformity. Unless the members create pressure to enforce the group norms, these norms will disappear and be replaced by other norms.

APPLYING ORGANIZATIONAL BEHAVIOR
ACROSS CULTURES

Group Norms: Equity Versus Equality

 When a supervisor is told to divide a financial bonus among the members of a group, what criteria does the supervisor use to divide the money? How people allocate rewards among group members is apparently influenced by culture, but the cultural differences are not very great. The three dominant allocation norms are equity, equality, and need.

- *Equity:* Rewards are allocated according to each member's contribution to the task. Those who contribute more receive more.

- *Equality:* Rewards are allocated equally to all members of the group.

- *Need (or social responsibility):* Rewards are allocated according to financial need.

In cultures that are highly individualistic, such as the United States, the dominant norm is equity. In cultures where individualism is less important, however, the norm of equity can create problems. In a group-oriented, tightly knit society, people may consider highly differentiated rewards inherently detrimental to group harmony, even when they are given to recognize a member's contributions to the groups.

Research has shown that people in the United States rate much higher on individualism than people from Hong Kong (91 versus 25 on a scale that ranges from a low of zero to a high of 100). A study compared the allocation norms of U.S. and Hong Kong college students. In this study, both groups exhibited a preference for using an equity norm,

but the preference was much stronger for U.S. students than for Hong Kong students.

Another study compared how college students from the United States, Japan, and South Korea allocated rewards in a student study group. The students were asked to evaluate a group member who was described as high, medium, or low in contributing to the group task and high, medium, or low in contributing to group harmony. U.S. students are much more individualistic than Japanese or Korean students (scores of 91, 46, and 18, respectively). Therefore, U.S. students were expected to allocate rewards according to how members contributed to the task accomplishment, while Korean students were expected to allocate rewards according to how members contributed to group harmony. The results indicated that there were some cultural differences as predicted, but that the students from all three cultures predominantly adopted an equity norm in allocating rewards.

Thus, the norm of equity appears to be a widely accepted norm in many cultures. The strength of the equity norm, however, is apparently greater in more individualistic cultures such as the United States than in group-oriented Asian cultures.

Source: Ken I. Kim, Hun-Joon Park, and Nori Suzuki, "Reward Allocations in the United States, Japan, and Korea: A Comparison of Individualistic and Collectivistic Cultures," *Academy of Management Journal,* vol. 33 (1990), pp. 188–198; M. H. Bond, K. Leung, and K. C. Wan, "How Does Cultural Collectivism Operate? The Impact of Task and Maintenance Contribution on Reward Distribution," *Journal of Cross-Cultural Psychology,* vol. 13 (1982), pp. 186–200.

Conformity is yielding to group influence by doing or saying something you might otherwise choose not to do. To say you have conformed means you have succumbed to social influence and behaved differently from how you would have behaved in the absence of the influence. Therefore, conformity is distinguished from uniformity, which indicates that several people are behaving similarly for reasons other than social pressure. Moving away from the doors of a crowded elevator to allow others to get off is probably an illustration of uniformity, since it is required by the situation. But facing the doors and looking at the floor numbers while riding in an elevator illustrates conformity because it is a social norm most people follow. Conformity involves yielding to group pressures and involves some form of conflict, because you would behave differently in the absence of group pressure. Adhering to simple social conventions, such as using the right hand to shake hands, would probably not be considered conformity; whereas saluting a senior officer probably would.[30]

Why do people conform? Social critics have referred to modern times as the age of conformity, and large organizations are criticized for needless pressures that force people to conform in their thinking, dress, and living habits. Although conformity does reduce variability in the ways people behave, it also increases individual freedom by providing greater predictability and regularity of behavior. Group norms help the group achieve its goals. The success of the group then depends on how effectively it can influence group members to conform to these norms. As conformity increases, the likelihood of success also increases. On the one hand, therefore, conformity reduces individuality and personal autonomy, but on the other hand, it contributes to greater success for both the group and its members.

Pressures to Conform

Two major social influence processes are used by groups to obtain conformity: reward dependence and information dependence.[31]

Reward Dependence (Effect Dependence). A group can influence its members because it has the capacity to create rewarding or punishing effects for their actions. This capacity to reward or punish member behavior is referred to as *reward* or **effect dependence.** In an organizational setting, supervisors have numerous rewards and punishments available for inducing conformity, such as promotions, pay increases, performance evaluations, and job assignments. The rewards and punishments in an informal group may be just as powerful in inducing conformity among group members. Praise, recognition, and social approval are very powerful social reinforcers, while criticism, ridicule, and harassment are very effective forms of punishment for deviant behavior.

The classic study by Solomon Asch illustrates reward dependence.[32] In this experiment, students were shown two cards and asked to indicate which of the three lines on the comparison card were equal in length to the standard line on the other card. The students who were asked to do this task alone were able to choose the correct comparison line virtually every time. However, Asch had students participate as members of a group with seven to nine other individuals who were confederates. The seating was arranged so the naive subject sat at the end of the row and gave his judgments last. On the first two trials, the confederates gave the correct answer, but starting on the third trial, the confederates gave unanimously incorrect answers. The naive subject was asked to respond after each of the other confederates had unanimously agreed on an incorrect answer, and Asch wanted to know whether the naive subject would go along with the group or resist the pressures to conform. In Asch's first experiments, 123 naive subjects were tested on twelve critical judgments and of the total judgments given, 37 percent were in error. Some individuals yielded to the unanimous majority on all twelve critical trials, while other individuals were completely independent. Most subjects, however, yielded at least some of the time.

After each session, the naive subjects were asked how they felt about the group pressures. None of the subjects entirely disregarded the majority, and most said they longed to agree with them. Evidence of reward dependence was illustrated by some of their comments: "Despite everything, there was a lurking fear that in some way I did not understand I might be wrong; fear of exposing myself as inferior in some way. It is more pleasant if one is really in agreement." "I felt awfully funny, everything was going against me." "I felt disturbed, puzzled, separated, like an outcast from the rest. Every time I disagreed I was beginning to wonder if I wasn't beginning to look funny."

Information Dependence. The other major source of social influence is called **information dependence.** Individuals conform to group pressure because they depend on others for information about the appropriateness of their thoughts, feelings, and behavior. An individual is particularly dependent on others when faced with a novel situation or an unfamiliar problem.

Our need for information is a central concept of *social comparison theory*, discussed in Chapter 4, which suggests that people want to compare their feelings, thoughts, and actions with those of others. Studies have shown that individuals rely heavily on others to interpret their feelings and help them define their emotions. In one study, for example, subjects agreed to participate in a study and then learned that the study involved potentially painful electrical shocks. The subjects were required to wait for the equipment to be prepared, and they could choose to wait either alone or with someone else. The subjects generally chose to wait with others, but not with just anyone. They wanted to wait with someone else who faced the same threatening situation. In essence, the subjects wanted to be with someone who could help them understand how they should be feeling and behaving in this threatening situation.[33]

Another study illustrated how people rely on others to help them define their emotions. In this study people were injected with a small amount of adrenalin, which raised their level of arousal. With their internal physiology slightly altered, they were ready to respond differently but not sure which emotion to display. The behavior of another individual in the same room served as a source of social information that helped them define how they should feel and respond.[34]

A classic study illustrating the influence of information dependence was reported by Muzafer Sherif.[35] In this study, the subjects were placed in a dark room where the only thing they could see was a very small point of light in the distance. The subjects were asked to estimate how much the light moved. Actually the light was absolutely stationary, but in this situation, the light appears to move because of a physiological process known as the *autokinetic* (self-movement) *effect.* The light appears to move because of muscle twitches in the muscles of the eye. The absence of other visual cues in the completely darkened room prevent the subject from having any idea how much actual movement there may have been. Sherif tested people individually to measure their estimates without any social influence. The subjects were then tested in groups over a series of trials. Sherif found that in this ambiguous situation, the estimates of movement reported by a subject were greatly influenced by the estimates of other group members. After a series of trials, the estimates began to converge, and those who reported large movements reduced their estimates while those who reported small movements increased theirs.

In one experiment, Sherif used confederates to create a group norm regarding the amount of movement. The confederates were then replaced one at a time over a series of trials with naive subjects. Sherif found that the group norm survived after all the confederates had been rotated out of the group and even persisted four and five generations later after several subjects had been rotated through the group membership. The reason why the experimental subjects continued to conform to the group norm in this situation is quite obvious: the subjects did not really know how much movement had actually occurred; therefore, they were greatly influenced by the estimates of others.

Levels of Conformity

People conform to social pressure at different levels of conformity, and the level depends on the motive for conforming. Writing your name and address on a check so you can cash it is a different level of conformity from refusing to accept a bribe from a client because it violates company policy. When driving an automobile, you are expected to obey speed limits, stop at stop signs, and yield the right of way to pedestrians. When you follow these accepted norms, what are your motives? Conforming to group norms occurs for three significantly different motives: compliance, identification, and internalization.[36]

Compliance. At the lowest level of conformity, people comply with social pressure either to obtain rewards or to avoid punishment. Peer pressure and the fear of harassment or criticism induce group members to comply. **Compliance,** however, is usually quite temporary and limited to the specific situation. If a police officer is parked at an intersection, the fear of being ticketed will probably induce compliance to stop for the stop sign. If the fines for overdue library books are exorbitantly high, students will probably return them on time. If supervisors receive a $50 bonus for a good safety rating, they will probably conduct periodic safety inspections simply to obtain the reward.

Identification. The second level of conformity is called **identification** because the motive is to be accepted by others who are perceived as important and respected individuals. Identification is the process of behaving like "significant others" and adopting their characteristics and personal attributes. Not only do we want to be like them and acquire their attributes, we also want them to think well of us and to approve of our attitudes and actions. Through imitative learning, we tend to model their behavior and accept what they say and how they behave. People who identify with a significant other will stop at stop signs, return library books, and work independently on a take-home exam if that is the way they think the significant other expects them to behave.

Internalization. At the highest level of conformity, the standards of behavior are internalized and become part of the person's basic character. At the **internalization** level of conformity norms are followed because the person accepts the beliefs, attitudes, and values supporting the norms. This level of conformity is characteristic of Kohlberg's highest level of moral development, as discussed in Chapter 7. Conformity does not occur because it achieves rewards, avoids punishments, or pleases others; it occurs because the behavior is perceived as morally right and proper. At this level you stop for stop signs, return library books, and avoid cheating on exams not to avoid punishment nor to receive the praise of others, but because you personally believe it is right and you are committed to abide by your own personal standards of right and wrong.

Factors Influencing Conformity

Whether group pressures influence behavior depends on many factors. Research has shown that conformity is influenced by the nature of the group influence, the individual being influenced, and the specific issue at hand.[37]

Group Size. In general, group pressure tends to increase as the size of the majority arrayed against the individual increases. Beyond a certain point, however, additional members do not add appreciably to the effectiveness of the pressure. The number of people needed to get maximum conformity depends on the nature of the influence attempt. In judging the length of lines Asch discovered that when the individual was opposed by a single other person, there was very little yielding. With two opposing him, there was some yielding; with three or four opposing him the amount of yielding approached the maximal level and was just about as great as with groups of fifteen or more. However, in Sherif's study measuring the movement of a point of light, a single individual produced almost as much influence as a large group because of the ambiguity of the situation.

Group Composition. The qualifications of other group members influence the likelihood of conformity. Group members who are perceived as experts or as highly qualified or experienced people exert greater pressures to conform. Minority group members tend to be highly influenced by group pressure. People belonging to ethnic and racial minorities are more likely to conform to group pressures, especially when the person is the only minority member in the group.

Unanimity of Group Consensus. A united group exerts much greater pressure to conform than a group divided by dissension. Asch discovered that the amount of conformity dropped precipitously when the group contained just one dissenter who might be perceived as a partner for the subject.

Ambiguity. The influence of the group, from both information dependence and effect dependence, becomes increasingly powerful as the situation becomes more ambiguous. Some ambiguity is inherent in almost every situation, but group members can create greater ambiguity as an intentional strategy for inducing conformity by raising irrelevant questions and suggesting immaterial facts to confuse the situation. When people do not know what is expected of them, they become increasingly dependent on available norms.

Goal Achievement. The pressure to adhere to a social norm increases as the necessity of going along with the group to accomplish a goal increases. As a group gets closer and closer to achieving its goal, the anticipation of success increases the pressure to conform and makes nonconformity less acceptable. During the playoff games at the end of a season, team members experience particularly strong pressures to abide by the group norms. As the probability of a strike increases, unions demand greater conformity among union members as a show of strength to management. Deviation from the group norm becomes absolutely unacceptable at crucial times.

Self-confidence. Individuals who are highly confident of their skills and abilities are less susceptible to the influence of group members. When individuals are faced with a discrepant judgment by a unanimous majority, their first step in seeking to reconcile the difference is to blame their own judgments and perceptions. Individuals who are high in self-confidence, however, generally resist blaming themselves and prefer instead to blame the group for the discrepant judgments.

STATUS

Status is the rank or social position ascribed to members of a group. A group member's status reflects how that individual is evaluated by other group members. If there is **status congruence**, everyone agrees on the status ascribed to each group member. Status incongruence occurs when individuals disagree about the social position of a group member, such as whether the spokesperson for the committee should be the committee chair or the recorder. Status incongruence also occurs when a member's behavior is inconsistent with his or her position in the group, such as when a new member tries to restructure the task or tell others what to do. Status is derived from a combination of formal status systems and informal status systems.

Formal Status Systems

Formal status systems are created within the organization and are usually accompanied by status symbols. A status symbol is a tangible indicator of a person's importance. Formal status within the organization and the status symbols accompanying it generally come from the following sources: titles, working relationships, pay and fringe benefits, work schedules, and work location.

Titles. Every employee likes to have a job that sounds important; sanitary engineer sounds more impressive than janitor or garbage collector. Organizations generally create titles to indicate the relative level of each position in the organizational hierarchy. Titles such as head supervisor, division chief, and managing director are used to denote the status of people in the organization.

Working Relationships. Whom you work with influences your status in the organization. A secretary to a division manager has higher status than the secretary to a supervisor, even though both jobs have similar responsibilities. Individuals have higher status if their work requires them to associate with higher-ranking officers or if they work on a crucial assignment or in an important group.

Pay and Fringe Benefits. Pay and fringe benefits are used to ascribe status; people who receive more money tend to have higher status than lower-paid individuals. Expense accounts, travel opportunities, a company car, and other fringe benefits are also important status symbols. A reserved parking space with a name on it can be a very visible symbol of status.

Work Schedule. Because managers have the freedom to come and go as they please, autonomy is usually perceived as a status symbol. Therefore, status is generally ascribed to people who do not have to punch a time clock, who have the freedom to start and stop work when they choose, or who work the day shift rather than the evening or swing shift.

Work Location. The status associated with the work location is illustrated by the conflict that arises when a company moves to a new location. Many irrelevant variables suddenly become important status symbols, such as the office size, the color scheme in the office, the size of the desk and whether it is made of metal or wood, whether the chair is a swivel rocker with a high back, whether the office has a window, the thickness of the carpeting, the number of pictures on the wall, and how far the office is from secretaries, restrooms, and drinking fountain.

Informal Status Systems

In addition to the status ascribed by the formal organization, status can also be ascribed by an informal status system. Informal status is largely derived from the personal qualities of group members or their past experience. People who are empathic and compassionate develop a reputation for kindness and are recognized as valuable group members who attract friends and influence group behavior. Other people are known for their ability to remain calm in tense situations and make effective decisions for the group. These individuals are known for their rationality, and other members trust their judgment and rely on them for leadership. Another valuable quality that contributes to ascribed status is a quick wit with a pleasant sense of humor. People who are humorous without being sarcastic or cynical usually attract the attention of the group and are recognized for their skill.

Informal status also comes from unique past experiences. Men and women who have been professional athletes find that many years later people still show deference and respect for their accomplishment. Similar deference and respect is often accorded people who have accomplished unique feats such as performing a dangerous stunt, surviving a serious disaster, or saving someone's life. Academic credentials also serve as a basis for ascribing informal status even when education is not relevant to the situation.

Status in Organizations

To diagnose an organizational situation accurately, you need to know how status can influence individual and group behavior. Status relationships influence such things as interpersonal communication, personal associations, and the formation of group norms.

Interpersonal Communication. The communication between people reflects their status differentials. Higher-status people are allowed to issue directives and speak in an authoritative tone of voice to lower-status individuals. While lower-status people may be told they are wrong in definite terms, higher-status people are usually informed of their errors in a very tactful or tentative manner. Higher-status people may address lower-status members by their first names, but lower-status individuals usually address higher-status people by title or by Mr. or Ms.

Associations. People generally prefer to associate with others who have essentially equal status. Division managers associate with other division managers, supervisors associate with other supervisors, and production workers associate with members of their own production crew. Lower-status individuals often enjoy briefly associating with higher-status people because of the temporary excitement of being in the presence of a high-status person. Likewise, high-status individuals sometimes enjoy brief association with lower-status members because they are treated with ego-inflating deference. As an ongoing association, however, individuals of significantly different status levels usually begin to feel uncomfortable and prefer the company of people at their own status level.

Influence on Group Norms. Because of the deference and respect accorded to higher-status people, they have a larger influence on defining acceptable standards of behavior. Higher-status individuals exert more influence on the decisions made by a group because their comments carry greater credibility, and lower-status members are less inclined to counter or disagree.

Deviation from Group Norms. When nonconformity occurs, it usually occurs among low-status members who have been actively rejected by the group or by high-status members who have achieved the right to deviate from the norms. Failing to adhere to group norms helps to explain why lower-status members are rejected. Because of their failure to conform to the group norms, they are socially isolated and may serve as scapegoats for the group. High-status members, however, are often allowed to deviate from group norms because they have acquired idiosyncrasy credits from the group.[38] Because they have conformed to group norms in the past or made significant contributions to the group's success, the group allows high-status individuals to deviate from some group norms without fear of censure. **Idiosyncrasy credits** are the reserve fund of positive sentiments accorded a group member who has contributed significantly in some other way to the group.

External Status. The status of people inside the organization influences their status outside the organization as well. The social status of individuals and their standing in the community is directly related to their status in organizations. Therefore, high-status members such as professionals and administrators are the people most frequently selected to serve on school boards and boards of directors for community organizations. In a PTA meeting, greater deference would most likely be shown to a doctor or a corporate executive than to a production worker. The production worker would also have more difficulty expressing an opinion and the opinion would not be considered as credible, nor would it have as much impact on the group's decisions.

THE EFFECT OF THE GROUP ON INDIVIDUAL BEHAVIOR

How does the presence of a group influence an individual's performance? Suppose you were laying bricks with four other bricklayers. Would more bricks get laid if the five of you worked together as a group along one side of a wall, or would it be better to assign each of you to different walls on the construction site? Two contrasting processes have been identified to explain the effects of the group on individual performance: social facilitation and social loafing. Another concept called *deindividuation* has also been proposed to explain the effects of a group on individual behavior.

Social Facilitation

Early studies in social psychology noted that people performed better as members of a group than when performing alone. It was observed, for example, that cyclists rode more rapidly when they raced in head-to-head competition than when they raced alone to beat the clock. Subsequent research showed that the presence of an audience or crowd or simply the presence of other co-workers facilitated the performance of well-learned responses such as crossing out letters and words, doing multiplication problems, and other simple tasks. This process, called the **social facilitation effect,** is caused by the mere presence of others rather than direct competition between individuals, since a number of studies found that subjects performed better even in front of a passive audience. The social facilitation effect has been observed not only on people, both adults and children, but also on an unusual assortment of other animals including ants, fish, chickens, rats, and cockroaches.[39]

One of the most popular explanations for the social facilitation effect is called **evaluation apprehension.** According to this explanation, the presence of others creates a higher level of arousal and motivation because we expect others to evaluate our performance and we are concerned about the outcomes of their evaluation. When others are watching we want to look good, if for no other reason than that we want others to think well of us.

Although the presence of others may improve performance, it can also inhibit performance on some tasks. This process, called **social inhibition effect,** has been observed on complex learning tasks such as learning a maze or a list of nonsense syllables. Since the social inhibition effect is the opposite of the social facilitation effect, it is important to know when the presence of others will inhibit and when it will facilitate an individual's performance.

Perhaps the best explanation of the contradictory results relies on an important distinction between learning a new task and performing a well-learned task. The presence of others increases the level of arousal and motivation, and this increase helps people perform their dominant response as shown in Exhibit 9.7.[40] This is the response that is the easiest to make because of previous habits and practice. Therefore, if the response is a well-learned response such as walking, running, bicycling, or playing the piano (for a highly skilled musical performer), then the presence of others tends to improve the individual's performance. However, if the response has not been well learned, which is the case with all new learning

EXHIBIT 9.7   The Interaction Between Response Skill and
the Presence of Others on Performance

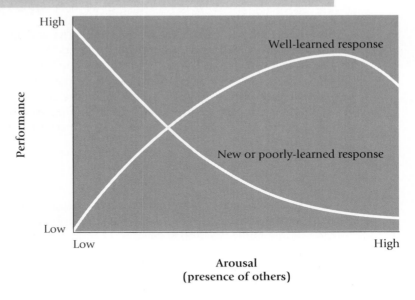

situations, then the presence of others will inhibit performance. In a learning situation, the new response, such as playing a new piano piece, has not yet become the dominant response. Many hours of practice are needed on a piano piece before a performer's dominant response will be the correct motions of the fingers on the keyboard. Therefore, according to social facilitation the learning of complex new tasks is best accomplished in isolation, but the performance of well-learned tasks will be facilitated by an audience.

Social Loafing

Social loafing occurs when the members of a group exert less effort while working as a group than when working as individuals. Social loafing is the opposite of social facilitation but it is different from social inhibition. The social inhibition effect is typically ascribed to a reduction in the individual's ability to perform because of the presence of others. Social loafing, in contrast, is not attributed to a decline in ability but a decline in motivation or the amount of effort. One of the earliest studies in social loafing examined how much effort individuals exerted in pulling on a rope, either individually or in a group. The average pressure exerted by each individual was 63 kilograms, which was more than double the average pressure exerted by a group of eight people pulling together (248 kilograms per group, or 31 kilograms per person).[41] Later studies have shown that social loafing also occurs in decision-making groups with cognitive tasks: people in groups exert less effort and less concentration, and they also use less complex judgment strategies than single judges or judges working in pairs.[42]

Subsequent research has concluded that social loafing occurs because being in a group reduces the individual's identifiability.[43] As members of a group, individuals know their efforts cannot be identified; therefore, they display only mediocre effort. The social loafing effect becomes increasingly apparent in larger groups because of reduced personal identifiability. When individuals cannot be identified, there is no relationship between their efforts and their outcomes; therefore, they cannot be rewarded for good effort or punished for poor performance.

Deindividuation

The issue of identifiability is related to another process of group dynamics: **deindividuation.** Individuals often become lost in crowds and perform acts they would not perform if they were alone. Unruly crowds at rock concerts have produced hysterical screaming and uncontrolled emotions, angry fans at athletic contests have thrown objects at athletes and assaulted referees, and groups of union picketers have destroyed property and committed acts of violence. Stories of lynch mobs illustrate how individuals in a group get carried away and do things they would not have done without the presence of the group. Crowds have the capacity to create a mental homogeneity, referred to as a *collective mind,* that is frequently irrational and often functions at an intellectual level below that of the isolated individual.

Three mechanisms have been proposed to explain the process of deindividuation in groups. First, the individual is anonymous because he or she loses a sense of individual responsibility. Second, the contagion of the group causes people to act differently by reducing their inhibitions and allowing them to behave as other group members. Third, people become more suggestible in groups where they feel greater pressures to conform.

The loss of individuality has often been associated with rather undesirable social consequences. In a study of the warfare patterns of many cultures, for example, it was found that in cultures where warriors deindividuated themselves by wearing masks and paint, there was a greater tendency to torture captives than in cultures whose warriors were not deindividuated. Another study of trick-or-treaters on Halloween found that they were more likely to steal when they wore masks and remained anonymous than when they were clearly identifiable.[44]

Perhaps the most shocking study of deindividuation was the Stanford Prison study, conducted by Phillip Zimbardo.[45] In this study, twenty-four male students who were described as mature, emotionally stable, normal, intelligent students were randomly assigned to play the roles of guards or prisoners. Both the prisoners and the guards were given appropriate uniforms, and the prisoners were placed in three-man cells for the duration of the experiment, which was to be two weeks. The guards were instructed to run the prison, and the experimenter served only as a warden. Silver reflector sunglasses were worn by the guards, which served to increase the level of deindividuation. The prisoners made only meager attempts to escape, and their behavior was described as that of servile, dehumanized robots. The behavior of the guards became tyrannical and brutal, and the situation became so ugly and repressive that the experiment had to be terminated after only 6 days instead of the two weeks originally planned.

Deindividuation does not necessarily create undesirable social behavior; it can also be positive. Although they don't attract as much attention, many groups have noble purposes and worthwhile social goals that sweep people along in productive activities. Schools, charitable foundations, religious groups, and even business organizations frequently create groups where individuals lose a sense of their own personal identity and are carried along as part of the group in activities that contribute to their own growth and development and to the betterment of society.[46] Therefore, although groups can be destructive and nasty, they don't necessarily need to be that way. Anyone who has enjoyed the exhilaration of wildly cheering in a large crowd for a favorite football team knows how much fun being "lost in the crowd" can be.

SUMMARY

1. People belong to a variety of formal and informal groups. Formal groups are established by the organization to achieve organizational goals. Informal groups are created by individuals who share common interests and values.

2. Individuals join groups because of the positive reinforcement they derive from group membership. The positive reinforcement includes being able to accomplish something as a group that cannot be accomplished individually, affiliating with friends, obtaining emotional support, and receiving social validation.

3. Effective groups are different from ineffective groups. They are open and friendly; all members participate in the group and are committed to it; members listen to one another and make decisions by consensus; they face conflicts and resolve them; they express opinions and give feedback openly and honestly; and they share the leadership responsibilities. Mature groups typically progress through four stages of development: orientation (forming), confrontation (storming), differentiation (norming), and collaboration (performing).

4. Group structure is the predictable relationships among group members that maintain the group and help it achieve its goals. The major variables defining group structure are group roles, group norms, and status.

5. The structure of a group is greatly influenced by the nature of the group task—whether it is an additive task, conjunctive task, or disjunctive task. Conjunctive tasks require much greater coordination than additive or disjunctive tasks.

6. A group role is the task activities or expected behaviors assigned to a position in the group. While there are many different roles group members can perform, two types of roles are essential for an effective group: work roles and maintenance roles. Work roles are the task-oriented activities involved in achieving the group's objectives, while maintenance roles are the social-emotional activities that maintain the involvement and commitment of group members.

7. Individuals learn about their responsibilities during a role episode, when role senders communicate their expectations to the focal person. Unclear communication creates role ambiguity. When the received role is inconsistent with the individual's role behavior, the individual experiences role conflict.

8. Group norms identify the general expectations about how group members are supposed to behave. Although group norms limit individuality, they create greater predictability of behavior and allow groups to operate more effectively.

9. Group norms may be created through a conscious decision-making process by the group, or they may emerge over time through customary practices. But regardless of whether they are created intentionally or unintentionally, social norms exert an enormous influence on a person's day-to-day behavior.

10. Group norms are enforced by social pressure that forces members to conform. The two major social influence processes used to

obtain conformity are reward dependence and information dependence. Reward dependence comes from the capacity of the group to reward or punish its members, while information dependence is created by the needs of group members for information, particularly in ambiguous situations.

11. Behavior within a group is influenced by the status of individuals. High-status members enjoy a higher level of rank or social position because of either the formal or the informal status systems. Formal status is acquired through titles, working relationships, pay and fringe benefits, work schedules, and location. Informal status is acquired through the individual's personal attributes. Status influences interpersonal communications and association as well as the development of group norms.

12. The presence of other group members tends to influence an individual's performance. On well-learned tasks, the presence of others tends to increase motivation and thereby improve performance. This is called the *social facilitation effect*. On a new task, or when the response has not been well learned, the presence of others tends to inhibit performance. This is called the *social inhibition effect*. When people work as part of a group and their individual contribution cannot be identified, they tend to exert less effort. This is called *social loafing*.

13. When people become members of a large group, they may experience a loss of individuality and personal responsibility, and they may be carried away in their behavior. This process, called *deindividuation*, may create either desirable or undesirable behavior, depending on the crowd.

DISCUSSION QUESTIONS

1. Why do you join groups? Identify one or two formal and informal groups you have joined, and list the specific reasons why you joined them and why you continue your membership.

2. What functions do reference groups perform for individuals? What are some of the reference groups in your life?

3. List some examples of additive, conjunctive, and disjunctive tasks. What type of tasks would the following groups most likely have: (a) a semi-autonomous work team in an electronics manufacturing firm, (b) a group of students working on a research project for an organizational behavior class, (c) an executive search committee trying to hire a new manager, (d) a swimming team, and (e) a fraternity.

4. Does every group require both work roles and maintenance roles to be effective? Which work roles and maintenance roles are necessary, and what would happen if they were not performed?

5. What are the different kinds of role conflict? List some specific instances of role conflict you have experienced recently.

6. What are some of the most important norms regulating your behavior at your residence? How did these norms develop? What forms of social pressure are used to enforce compliance with these norms?

7. Compare and contrast reward dependence with information dependence. What are the conditions that make both reward dependence and information dependence effective forms of pressure for creating conformity?

8. Identify at least two examples illustrating the three levels of conformity: compliance, identification, and internalization.

9. Suppose you were a new member of a group, such as a campus service club, and you wanted to increase your status through the informal status system. What would you do?

10. How does a study group influence individual learning? If you formed a study group with some of your classmates, would you expect the effects of studying together to produce social facilitation, social inhibition, or social loafing?

GLOSSARY

additive tasks An independent group task in which the contribution of each member is simply summed or pooled to form the group product.

ad hoc committee A formal group created for a specific purpose; a committee designed to resolve a specific issue.

assigned roles Group roles that are formally assigned to group members.

command group A formal group consisting of a supervisor and his or her direct subordinates as specified by an organization chart.

compliance The first level of conformity, in which the individual's motive is to obtain rewards or avoid punishment.

conjunctive tasks A group task that is divided into interdependent subunits, and the successful completion of each subpart is necessary to the overall task.

cooperant behavior The behavior of group members in a group setting designed to elicit positive reinforcement.

deindividuation The loss of individuality that occurs by being a member of a large crowd.

disjunctive tasks A group task involving some form of decision making or problem analysis that requires a yes or no decision.

effect dependence A social influence process created by the capacity of a group to reward or reinforce its members.

ego extension An inflated feeling of self-esteem that occurs when the success of the group is viewed by the group members as their own personal success.

emergent roles Group roles that are voluntarily performed by group members without being formally assigned.

evaluation apprehension A general concern about being evaluated by others, which creates a desire to perform well and look impressive.

focal person The person in a role episode to whom the role expectations are communicated.

friendship group An informal group created for the purpose of affiliating with friends.

identification The second level of conformity, in which the motive to conform is to please others.

idiosyncrasy credits A reservoir of positive sentiments allowing certain group members who have made significant contributions to the group to deviate from the group norms.

information dependence A social influence process created by an ambiguous situation in which individuals need to know how to behave.

interest group An informal group created by individuals who share common interests and values.

internalization The highest level of conformity, in which the motive to conform is based on the group member's acceptance of the prescribed behavior as a basic principle of right and wrong.

interrole conflict Conflict created by the multiple-role demands individuals experience.

intersender role conflict Role conflict created by incompatible demands and expectations of two or more role senders.

intrasender role conflict Role conflict created by incompatible demands of a single role sender.

maintenance roles A category of group roles designed to maintain the members' willingness to participate in the group.

person–role conflict Role conflict created by asking people to behave in ways that violate their personal values.

process losses The loss of time and efficiency created by the need to integrate and coordinate a large group.

project group A formal group created by the organization to accomplish a specific objective or work on an assigned project.

proximity The physical nearness of group members, which influences the likelihood of group formation.

reference group An informal group that exists largely in the mind of an individual and serves as a basis for personal evaluation and a source of acceptance.

role episode An encounter between a role sender and the focal person in which role expectations are sent, received, and evaluated.

role readiness An individual's preparation to perform a group role by possessing the appropriate motivation and/or ability.

social density The number of people physically located within a confined area.

social facilitation effect The tendency for the presence of other people to increase motivation and arousal, which tends to help the individual perform better.

social inhibition effect The tendency for the presence of other people to disrupt performance and cause them to perform poorly.

social loafing The tendency to exert less effort when working as a member of a group than when working alone.

standing committee A formal committee created to resolve recurring problems. The life of the committee is intended to be indefinite.

status congruence Consistency or agreement among the members of a group regarding the status assigned to each member.

task force A formal group assigned to accomplish a specific objective or resolve a unique problem.

work roles One of the major types of roles found in a group that help the group accomplish its task and pursue its goals; for example, structuring the tasks, delegating assignments, and initiating action.

NOTES

1. P. M. Mills, *The Social Psychology of Small Groups* (Englewood Cliffs, N.J.: Prentice-Hall, 1967).

2. Rodney W. Napier and Matti K. Gershenfeld, *Groups: Theory and Experience,* 3rd ed. (Boston: Houghton Mifflin Co., 1985), pp. 87–92.

3. Edgar H. Schein, "Interpersonal Communication, Group Solidarity, and the Social Influence," *Sociometry,* vol. 23 (1960), pp. 148–161; Edgar H. Schein, Imge Schneier, and Curtis Barber, *Coercive Persuasion* (New York: Norton, 1961).

4. William E. Scott, Jr., and Phillip M. Podsakoff, *Behavioral Principles in the Practice of Management* (New York: Wiley, 1985), chap. 7.

5. Blake E. Ashforth and Fred Mael, "Social Identity Theory and the Organization," *Academy of Management Review,* vol. 14 (January, 1989), pp. 20–39.

6. Suresh Srivastva and Frank J. Barrett, "The Transforming Nature of Metaphors in Group Development: A Study in Group Theory," *Human Relations,* vol. 41 (January 1988), pp. 31–63.

7. Edward E. Jones and Harold B. Gerard, *Foundations of Social Psychology* (New York: Wiley, 1967), chap. 8.

8. David C. McClelland, *The Achieving Society* (New York: Van Nostrand, 1961).

9. Stanley Schachter, *The Psychology of Affiliation: Experimental Studies of the Sources of Gregariousness* (Stanford, Calif.: Stanford University Press, 1959).

10. Edgar Schein, "Organizational Socialization and the Profession of Management," *Sloan Management Review,* vol. 30 (Fall 1988), pp. 53–65.

11. Source unknown. Quoted by James Sherman in a graduate social psychology course at Indiana University, (October–November 1968).

12. John T. Gullahorn, "Distance and Friendship as Factors in the Gross Interaction Matrix," *Sociometry,* vol. 15 (1952), pp. 123–134; D. M. Kipnis, "Interaction Between Members of Bombing Crews as a Determinant of Sociometric Choice," *Human Relations,* vol. 10 (1957), pp. 263–270.

13. Douglas McGregor, *The Human Side of Enterprise* (New York: McGraw-Hill, 1960), pp. 232–240.

14. B. W. Tuckman, "Developmental Sequences in Small Groups," *Psychological Bulletin,* vol. 63 (1965). pp. 384–399; M. F. Maples, "Group Development: Extending Tuckman's Theory," *Journal for Specialists in Group Work,* vol. 13 (1988), pp. 17–23.

15. Connie J. G. Gersick, "Time and Transition in Work Teams: Toward a New Model in Group Development," *Academy of Management Journal,* vol. 31 (March 1988), pp. 9–41.

16. B. Mullen, C. Symons, L. Hu, and E. Salas, "Group Size, Leadership Behavior, and Subordinate Satisfaction," *Journal of General Psychology,* vol. 116 (1989), pp. 155–170.

17. Marjorie Shaw, "A Comparison of Individuals and Small Groups in the Rational Solution of Complex Problems," *American Journal of Psychology,* vol. 44 (1932), pp. 491–504.

18. T. J. Allen and D. I. Cohen, "Information Flow in R&D Laboratories," *Administrative Science Quarterly,* vol. 14 (1969), pp. 12–25; Robert H. Miles, "Roles Set Configuration as a Predictor of Role Conflict and Ambiguity in Complex Organizations," *Sociometry,* vol. 40 (1977), pp. 21–34; Andrew D. Szilagyi and W. E. Holland, "Changes in Social Density: Relationships with Perceptions of Job Characteristics, Role Stress, and Work Satisfaction," *Journal of Applied Psychology,* vol. 65 (1980), pp. 28–33.

19. Greg R. Oldham, "Effects of Changes in Workspace Partitions and Spatial Density on Employee Reactions: A Quasi-Experiment," *Journal of Applied Psychology,* vol. 73 (1988), pp. 253–258; Eric Sundstrom, *Work Places* (Cambridge, England: Cambridge University

Press), 1986; Eric Sundstrom, Robert E. Burt, and Douglas Kamp, "Privacy at Work: Architectural Correlates of Job Satisfaction and Job Performance," *Academy of Management Journal*, vol. 23 (1980), pp. 101–107.

20. Kenneth D. Benne and P. Sheats, "Functional Roles of Group Members," *Journal of Social Issues*, vol. 2 (1948), pp. 42–47; Hal B. Gregersen, "Group Observer Instructions," in J. B. Ritchie and Paul Thompson, *Organization and People*, 3rd ed. (St. Paul, Minn.: West, 1984), pp. 231–234.

21. Robert F. Bales, *Interaction Process Analysis: A Method for the Study of Small Groups* (Cambridge, Mass.: Addison-Wesley, 1950).

22. Daniel Katz and Robert L. Kahn, *The Social Psychology of Organizations*, 2nd ed. (New York: Wiley, 1978), chap. 7.

23. Samuel Rabinowitz and Stephen A. Stumpf, "Facets of Role Conflict, Role-Specific Performance, and Organizational Level Within the Academic Career," *Journal of Vocational Behavior*, vol. 30 (1987), pp. 72–83; Shaker A. Zahra, "A Comparative Study of the Effect of Role Ambiguity and Conflict on Employee Attitudes and Performance," *Akron Business and Economic Review*, vol. 16 (Spring 1985), pp. 37–42.

24. Karin E. Klenke-Hamel and John E. Mathieu, "Role Strains, Tension, and Job Satisfaction Influences on Employees' Propensity to Leave: A Multi-Sample Replication and Extension," *Human Relations*, vol. 43 (August 1990), pp. 791–807; Gail W. McGee, Carl E. Ferguson, Jr., and Anson Sears, "Role Conflicts and Role Ambiguity: Do the Scales Measure These Two Constructs?" *Journal of Applied Psychology*, vol. 74 (October 1989), pp. 815–818; Richard G. Netemeyer, Mark W. Johnston, and Scot Burton, "Analysis of Role Conflict and Role Ambiguity in a Structural Equations Framework," *Journal of Applied Psychology*, vol. 75 (April 1990), pp. 148–157; Michael M. Harris, "Role Conflict and Role Ambiguity as Substance Vs. Artifact: A Confirmatory Factor Analysis of House, Schuler, & Levanoni's (1983) Scales," *Journal of Applied Psychology*, vol. 76 (February 1991), pp. 122–126.

25. Robert L. Kahn, D. M. Wolfe, R. P. Quinn, J. D. Snoek, and R. A. Rosenthal, *Organizational Stress: Studies in Role Conflict and Ambiguity* (New York: Wiley, 1964).

26. Daniel C. Feldman, "The Development and Enforcement of Group Norms," *Academy of Management Review*, vol. 9 (1984), pp. 47–53.

27. Kenneth L. Bettenhausen and Jay Keith Murnighan, "The Development of an Intragroup Norm and the Effects of Interpersonal and Structural Challenges," *Administrative Science Quarterly*, vol. 36 (March 1991), pp. 20–35.

28. Jerald Greenberg, "Equity, Equality, and the Protestant Ethic: Allocating Rewards Following Fair and Unfair Competition," *Journal of Experimental Social Psychology*,

vol. 14 (1978), pp. 217–226; Boris Cabanoff, "Equity, Equality, Power and Conflict," *Academy of Management Review*, vol. 16 (April 1991), pp. 416–431.

29. Bernard M. Bass, C. R. McGehee, W. C. Hawkins, P. C. Young, and A. S. Gebel, "Personality Variables Related to Leaderless Group Discussion," *Journal of Abnormal and Social Psychology*, vol. 62 (1953), pp. 120–128; E. B. Nalder, "Yielding, Authoritarianism, and Authoritarian Ideology Regarding Groups," *Journal of Abnormal and Social Psychology*, vol. 68 (1959), pp. 408–410.

30. Paul R. Nail, "Toward an Integration of Some Models and Theories of Social Responses," *Psychological Bulletin*, vol. 100 (1986), pp. 190–206.

31. Edward E. Jones and Harold B. Gerard, *Foundations of Social Psychology* (New York: Wiley, 1967), chaps. 3 and 4.

32. Solomon E. Asch, "Studies of Independence and Conformity: A Minority of One Against a Unanimous Majority," *Psychological Monographs*, vol. 70, no. 9 (1956, whole no. 416).

33. Stanley Schachter, *The Psychology of Affiliation: Experimental Studies in the Sources of Gregariousness* (Stanford, Calif.: Stanford University Press, 1959).

34. Stanley Schachter and J. E. Singer, "Cognitive, Social, and Physiological Determinants of Emotional State," *Psychological Review*, vol. 69 (1962), pp. 379–399.

35. Muzafer Sherif, "A Study of Some Social Factors in Perception," *Archives of Psychology*, vol. 27 no. 187 (1935), pp. 1–60.

36. H. C. Kelman, "Compliance, Identification, and Internalization: Three Processes of Opinion Change," *Journal of Conflict Resolution*, vol. 2 (1958), pp. 51–60; Nail, op. cit.

37. See the literature review by David Krech, Richard S. Krutchfield, and Egerton L. Ballachey, *Individual in Society* (New York: McGraw-Hill, 1962), pp. 512–529.

38. Gary M. Katz, "Previous Conformity, Status, and the Rejection of the Deviant," *Small Group Behavior*, vol. 13 (1982), pp. 402–414.

39. Reviewed by Stephen Worchel and Joel Cooper, *Understanding Social Psychology*, 3rd ed. (Homewood, Ill.: Dorsey Press, 1983), pp. 485–488.

40. Robert Zajonc, "Social Facilitation," *Science*, vol. 149 (1965), pp. 269–274.

41. This early study by Ringelmann is reported by J. F. Dashiel, "Experimental Studies of the Influence of Social Situations on the Behavior of Individual Human Adults," in Carl Murchison (ed.), *The Handbook of Social Psychology* (Worcester, Mass.: Clark University Press, 1935).

42. Kenneth H. Price, "Decisions Responsibility, Task Responsibility, Identifiability, and Social Loafing," *Organizational Behavior and Human Decisions Processes*, vol. 40 (December 1987), pp. 330–345; Elizabeth Wel-

don and Elisa L. Mustari, "Felt Defensibility in Groups of Coactors: The Effects of Shared Responsibility and Explicit Anonymity on Cognitive Effort," *Organizational Behavior and Human Processes,* vol. 41 (June 1988), pp. 330–351.

43. Norbert L. Kerr and Steven E. Brunn, "Dispensability of Member Effort and Group Motivation Losses: Free Rider Effects," *Journal of Personality and Social Psychology,* vol. 44 (1983), pp. 78–94; Norbert L. Kerr and Steven E. Brunn, "Ringelmann Revisited: Alternative Explanations for Social Loafing Effect," *Journal of Personality and Social Psychology,* vol. 7 (1981), pp. 224–231.

44. R. I. Watson, "Investigation into Deindividuation Using A Cross Cultural Survey Technique," *Journal of Personality and Social Psychology,* vol. 25 (1973), pp. 342–345; E. Diener, S. Fraser, A. Beaman, and Z. Kellem, "Effects of Deindividuation Variables on Stealing Among Halloween Trick-or-Treaters," *Journal of Personality and Social Psychology,* vol. 33 (1976), pp. 178–183.

45. Phillip Zimbardo, *The Psychological Power and Pathology of Imprisonment,* statement prepared for the U.S. House of Representatives Committee on the Judiciary, (Subcommittee No. 3, Robert Kastemeyer, Chairman, Hearings on Prison Reform). Unpublished paper, Stanford University, 1971.

46. Michael T. Farrell, "Artists' Circles and the Development of Artists," *Small Group Behavior,* vol. 13 (1982), pp. 451–474.

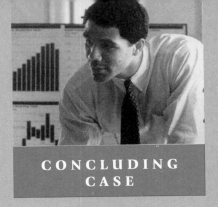

INCREASING WORK STANDARDS

Scott Condie is a union steward. It's not a job he really wanted, but after he was elected he decided to do his best. Scott has worked for the company for eight years, and as long as he can remember, a full day's work in the mixing building has been thirty-six pallets with fifty-six sacks on each pallet. He assumed the standard had been negotiated with management many years ago. Everyone knew, however, that it was a loose standard, and one night two college students on summer employment proved it convincingly.

The work in the mixing building is performed by seven men: five sackers, a control operator, and a chemical mixer. The five sackers alternate working on the sacking machine since only two can work at the same time. When the other three are not sacking, they prepare the next pallet and wait for their turn to sack.

One night the two college students boasted that with the cooperation of the operator and mixer, they could meet an eight-hour quota in the first two and a half hours all by themselves. Since they worked on the night shift with little supervision, the other three sackers called their challenge. Without any help from the other three, they made the full quota of 36 pallets in just two and one quarter hours. They used a slightly different procedure that required more effort. When one sack was filled, they pulled it off the machine with one hand and started the next sack with the other hand so that it was filling while they stacked the first one. Since each sack weighed 50 pounds, this pro-

cedure required more effort but was considerably faster.

The rest of the crew went on to create an additional 36 pallets that night. Thereafter, the new standard became 50 pallets. When the day shift heard about the night shift's new standard, some members stayed after work to get the night shift "straightened out." The meeting was very unsatisfactory, with a lot of name-calling and threats. After it was over, the night shift decided that they would raise the standard to 60 pallets just to make the day shift look bad.

The day shift supervisor was willing to accept 36 pallets as the quota for his shift. However, one day a broken chain idled them for six hours and they only produced 8 pallets. To make up for the loss, their supervisor wanted them to produce an extra 7 pallets each of the next four days and threatened to give them only seven hours' work on their time cards if they refused.

Since Scott was the union steward, the day shift crew warned him that they would pull a wildcat strike and shut the entire plant down if the supervisor didn't back off. To add to the problem, Scott has also received instructions from the night shift crew to warn the day shift about alleged acts of violence. Two night shift workers had their cars damaged in the company parking lot, and they are convinced that it was done by the day shift. Members of the day shift have threatened additional violence if the night shift doesn't adhere to the original standard. Because of these threats, Scott carefully checked the labor agreement and discussed the issue with management. He was surprised to find that nothing was written about 36 pallets being the standard. The contract only says that management would direct the employees in the performance of their work, and unfair treatment would be handled through the grievance procedure. The 36-pallet standard was simply an informal quota that was never questioned. Scott informed both the day and night crews about the right of management to determine the work standards.

Questions

1. What should Scott say to the day shift, to the night shift, and to management?

2. What will likely happen if the day shift supervisor only credits them with seven hours work if they fail to produce an extra 7 pallets daily? Should management try to mediate this dispute? What should be the company's policy, and whose side should management take?

THE COLLEGE SCHOLARSHIP COMMITTEE MEETING

In this exercise, participants are assigned as members of a college scholarship committee and asked to allocate $10,000 among six applicants.

Directions. Six people should be selected as participants and assigned to represent one of the scholarship applicants. Six or more others should be selected as observers and assigned to observe a specific participant. Each participant should read the description of the scholarship applicant he or she is assigned to represent. However, the participants should not read any information about any of the other applicants.

After the participants have had time to study their applicants and prepare what they want to say, the committee should decide how to allocate the $10,000 among the applicants.

Setting. *To each participant:* You are a member of the scholarship committee of a small private college. This year the school must cut back on the amount of money awarded; only those students with the most crucial needs can be recipients.

Essential costs for the school year include $2,000 for room and board, $4,000 for tuition, and $1,000 for fees and books. Your committee has already awarded several scholarships and has only $10,000 left. The final result of the committee's discussion should be the allocation of this money to one student or to several students.

You have examined the applications and other supporting data and have identified the student whom you think should receive a substantial amount of money. Each of the other committee members will also have a student to sponsor. You must try to convince the other members that your proposal suggests the best use of the money. You are aiming to get as much money as possible for this student while still helping the group to swiftly and fairly accomplish its task. The following material describes the needs of each student. Examine the information for the applicant you will sponsor and decide which points you wish to present.

Applicant A Kyle Anderson will be a junior next fall. He is a B student majoring in history and minoring in physical education. Kyle plays varsity football, hockey, and golf. Last year he was second in the conference in golf. He plans to coach college football. Kyle is also first vice-president of his fraternity and is a member of the Interfraternity Council.

Kyle's parents have an above-average income, but they have two other children in college and one son in medical school. They can't afford to continue to send Kyle here. His brothers and sister are at state universities, and Kyle says he will have to transfer to a state school if he doesn't receive financial help from the college. Kyle's application contains a letter from the athletic department describing his contributions to the university and recommending that he receive a scholarship. Kyle works during the summer as a lifeguard, but cannot work during the school year because of all his other activities. He has not received financial aid before.

Applicant B Larry Bellows will be a sophomore next fall. He is an A student majoring in biology and minoring in chemistry. He was the only first-year student ever taken into the Biology Society. He plans to become a doctor.

Larry's father is dead, and his mother is sending him to school. She has sold their house and has moved into an apartment to try to help with expenses. Larry says his mother is going to cash in her life insurance and sell everything she has of value to help raise money for his education if he doesn't get a scholarship. He doesn't want her to give up everything for him to continue going to school. Larry works during the summer and works in the college library for a few hours a week during the school year. He has received no other financial aid from the school.

Applicant C Ann Marie Carter will be a senior next fall. She is a C student majoring in English and minoring in speech. Ann Marie is a student senator and a varsity debater. Last year she was on the top national-level varsity team and won fifteen trophies in debate tournaments all over the country. She hopes to go to graduate school and debate.

Ann Marie's parents have very little money. Her father has quit three jobs in eighteen months, and the family is living on the money they have saved for her to go to college. She works during the summer and used to work during the school year, but it became too much for her to handle and she got very ill. She will have to drop debate and work to stay in school if she receives no scholarship. Last year Ann Marie received a scholarship of $1,200 for the second semester after she became ill and had to quit her job.

Applicant D Alan Dickson will be a first-year student in the fall. He was an A student in high school and made very high scores on his College Boards. He was vice president of his high school student body, and he won national recognition during high school for his chemistry projects. Alan wants to attend graduate school and eventually go into research.

Alan's parents are very poor. His father is a janitor, and his mother doesn't work. Alan worked this past summer and plans to borrow money, but it still won't be enough. He will be carrying a very difficult course load this year, and he is afraid that he won't be able to keep up with his studies if he finds a job. He plans to continue with this heavy course load and go to summer school while he works so that he can finish in three years. He has a sister three years younger than he who also wants to go to college.

She couldn't hope to go, he says, if he is still in school.

Applicant E Sally Ensley will be a junior next fall. She is a B student majoring in speech and minoring in drama. She is a member of the Drama Honorary, the Forensics Honorary, is Secretary of the Women's Service Sorority, and was treasurer of the sophomore class. On graduation, she wants to work with children's theater and speech correction.

Sally's parents are getting a divorce, and neither will pay for her to finish college. Sally has no other relatives who can finance her next two years here, so she will have to quit school if she receives no scholarship. Sally has not worked in the past because there had never been a need. She has received no previous financial aid.

Applicant F Diane Fautz will be a senior next fall. She was formerly a low C student, but now is making Bs and a few As. She is majoring in education and minoring in political science. Diane has been a student senator for three years and is a member of the Faculty-Student-Administration Relations Committee. She wants to finish school and join the Peace Corps. Currently, she works weekends and three nights a week as a volunteer for the YMCA's enrichment program for underprivileged children.

Diane's parents have cut her off financially because they violently disagree with her political and social beliefs. An aunt has agreed to pay her tuition, but can't afford anything else. Diane works summers as a YMCA camp counselor, but makes very little above living expenses. To earn more money, she would have to take another summer job that pays more. She wants to finish school but will quit before she stops working at the YMCA. She has received no previous aid.

Intergroup Behavior and Conflict

LEARNING OBJECTIVES

After studying this chapter, you should be able to

1. Explain the differences among altruism, cooperation, and conflict.

2. Describe the conditions that contribute to cooperation and competition.

3. Describe the conditions that create a cohesive group, and explain how cohesiveness influences group dynamics.

4. Explain why conflict can either help or hinder an organization.

5. Identify the major causes of intergroup conflict.

6. Describe the consequences of intergroup conflict both within and between the competing groups.

7. List the major methods of resolving conflict between groups, and discuss the usefulness of each method.

8. Explain why managers may want to create conflict within an organization and describe some methods for stimulating conflict.

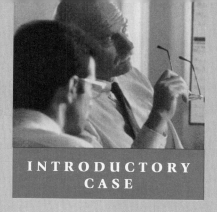

WHO SHOULD BE MOVED TO THE TRAILER?

Before the idea of moving to a mobile trailer was proposed, Carol and Marie were hostile co-workers. Carol was hired first and assigned the position of head nurse. Marie was hired two months later and continually challenged Carol's leadership because she had more education and experience. Both women were highly respected nurses who specialized in heart disease before joining Dr. Bachman's cardiology staff. The other four staff members tried to avoid taking sides, but conflicts erupted almost daily.

The conflict between Carol and Marie changed to cooperativism almost overnight when it was announced that the cardiology unit would be moved to a mobile trailer to relieve the over-crowded conditions in the clinic. After reaching an agreement between themselves, Carol and Marie prepared a memo explaining why they shouldn't be moved and convinced the other four staff members to sign it. They threatened to leave if they were forced to move, since they thought a mobile trailer was unprofessional.

Dr. Bachman joined the clinic 2 years ago with two other doctors: Dr. Adams, a urologist, and Dr. Turner, a dermatologist. The staff members reporting to these two doctors realized that they might be moved to the trailer if the memo from Carol and Marie was convincing. To discredit the cardiology staff memo, the urology and dermatology staffs issued a joint memo, arguing that the cardiology unit should be moved since the basement room was poorly ventilated and not the best place to conduct stress tests and other examinations.

During the next three weeks, the conflict and antagonism at the clinic became so intense that it reduced the quality of patient care for all nine doctors and their staffs at the clinic.

The problem was resolved when the oncology staff under Dr. Cohen volunteered to move to the trailer. The announcement that they were willing to move surprised the other staff groups because Dr. Cohen was one of the three founders of the clinic and everyone assumed that, with her seniority and influence, she and her staff would maintain their position near the front of the clinic. The decision, however, was a consensus decision by Dr. Cohen and her staff and once the trailer was in place, they moved quickly and efficiently. This voluntary move by the oncology staff restored a spirit of cooperation among the other staff groups.

Questions

1. What was the cause of the conflict between Carol and Marie? Why did they decide to unite to issue a joint memo? Has the conflict between them been eliminated?

2. Why did the urology and dermatology staffs form a coalition? Why do coalitions form?

3. What motivated the oncology staff to move voluntarily? What are the motives behind cooperative behavior, and what impact does it have on others?

COMPETITION AND COOPERATION

This chapter examines the interactions between groups and between individuals within a group. These interactions have an enormous influence on the effectiveness and survival of an organization. Individuals and groups depend on each other for information, assistance, and coordinated effort, and this interdependence may foster either a competitive or a cooperative relationship.

The relationship between two groups does not need to be viewed as a conflict situation, although it often is. The interaction can be viewed just as easily as a situation calling for a cooperative or helping response. Frequently, however, the situation becomes a competitive interaction as the two groups become locked in intergroup conflict. This chapter examines the interactions between individuals and groups and the circumstances that determine whether a cooperative or conflict relationship will exist between them. When will two groups choose to cooperate or compete? How can intergroup conflict be resolved and be replaced by a cooperative relationship?

Differences Between Competition and Cooperation

Interpersonal relationships vary along a continuum representing different degrees of concern for others versus self-interest, as shown in Exhibit 10.1. At one extreme individuals or groups have a high concern for others and are willing to go out of their way to help them. At the other extreme, individuals are concerned only for their own self-interest, even to the point of attempting to injure or destroy the other party. Four types of interactions can be defined along this continuum of concern for others versus self-interest: altruism, cooperation, competition, and conflict.

Altruism. Behavior that is motivated by a regard for others is called **altruism.** Altruism usually involves at least some cost to the helper, such as physical, mental, or emotional effort, for which the helper does not expect to be compensated. Altruism includes both small acts of courtesy, such as holding the door open for the next person, and heroic acts, such as risking your life to rescue someone facing an eminent hazard. The conditions that contribute to altruism are discussed later.

Cooperation. Altruism and cooperation are often confused. **Cooperation** means working together for a joint goal or mutual benefit. The major difference between altruism and cooperation lies in the outcomes to the helper. When you help someone without benefit to yourself or at some personal sacrifice, your behavior is altruistic. But if you help another and in so doing help yourself, you are being cooperative. An example of cooperation is that of two people moving supplies: one person holds the elevator door while the other moves both of their boxes into the elevator. A group of doctors and a team of medical technicians cooperate when one group refers patients for medical tests and the other group analyzes the tests. In a cooperative situation, both parties benefit from their combined efforts.

Competition. **Competition** occurs when two or more individuals or groups are striving for a goal that can be obtained by only one. Fixed or limited resources is one of the basic characteristics of a competitive situation: the person with the most

EXHIBIT 10.1 Continuum of Self-interest Versus Concern for Others

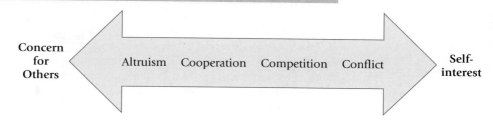

sales wins the sales contest; the group with the lowest bid is granted the contract; only one individual can be promoted to division manager. Three different types of competition can be created by altering the reward structures.

Intragroup competition exists when the members of a group compete against each other for a reward.

Intergroup competition exists when one group is competing against another group for the rewards.

Individual competition (sometimes called *noncompetition*) is when individuals work independently against an external standard.

To illustrate: if four members of a group ran a race to see who was the fastest, they would be participating in intragroup competition. If they formed a relay, however, and challenged another group to see which team was the fastest, they would be competing in intergroup competition. If they ran individually, however, and measured their times, they would be engaging in individual competition against their own previous record.

Conflict. **Conflict** occurs when one party perceives that another party has frustrated, or is about to frustrate, its efforts to achieve a desired outcome. Conflict is not limited to interacting groups, since it can also occur within groups, within and between individuals, and within and between organizations. Conflict occurs when two groups have mutually exclusive goals and their interactions are designed to defeat, suppress, or inflict damage on the other. For example, conflict usually occurs when labor–management negotiations reach a stalemate and the union decides to go on strike. Both sides attempt to strengthen their positions by winning public support and weaken their opponents by creating an economic hardship for them.

Interpersonal, intergroup, and interorganizational conflicts are conflicts between individuals, groups, and organizations respectively. Intragroup and intra-organizational conflict are conflict within groups or within an organization. Intrapersonal conflict is usually described in other terms, such as person–role conflict or personality disorders.

Effects of Competition and Cooperation

Competition has a pervasive influence in our Western civilization and can be clearly observed in family relationships, athletic activities, education, business, and community living. Many social observers have noted that Western cultures are far more competitive than Asian cultures, and competition has been condemned for creating hostility, suspicion, and destructive rivalry among family members, business associates, and friends.[1]

Some of the early research on the effects of competition and cooperation claimed that cooperation produced higher levels of satisfaction and productivity in experimental groups.[2] For example, a classic study reported that cooperative groups performed better and learned more than competing groups. This study involved 10 groups of five students each who met weekly to solve puzzles and discuss human relations problems. In the five competitive groups, the members in each group competed to see which one would receive the reward. In the five cooperative groups, the groups competed with other groups, and all the members of the winning group received a reward. The reward consisted of being excused from writing a term paper and of receiving an A on the assignment.

The groups were evaluated on how well they performed the task functions, how well they worked together as a unit, and how well each individual contributed to the group. The cooperative groups were judged to be superior in all three areas.

The harmful effects of competition are not as clear as this study suggests, however. In this study the cooperative groups had a cooperative relationship within the group, but they competed against the other groups. To understand the effects of competition and cooperation, therefore, the relationships both within the group and between groups must be carefully evaluated. The effects of competition have been examined on both productivity and satisfaction.

Competition and Productivity. Competition typically increases arousal and motivation, which leads to higher productivity. Workers who compete to finish their job first or to obtain the highest sales generally achieve higher levels of productivity. The enthusiasm and excitement accompanying a contest usually raises performance levels. As a general rule, competition increases productivity.

Although some of the earliest studies found that competition on simple tasks induced higher levels of motivation and facilitated performance, other studies found that competition was detrimental to the group processes and destroyed the cooperative working relationship necessary to perform well. The discrepancy in these studies has been explained by examining the degree of task interdependence in each study.[3] A review of twenty-four studies found that competition improved performance when the tasks were independent and did not require the subjects to work together. However, when the tasks were interdependent, requiring cooperative effort, competition resulted in lower levels of performance.

In conclusion, whether competition increases or decreases performance depends on the nature of the group's task as shown in Exhibit 10.2. Competition generally increases motivation and raises productivity when people work alone on independent tasks. But when the tasks are interdependent and require a cooperative effort among individuals, the reward system needs to reward cooperation. A system of differential rewards that creates a competitive relationship is not compatible with interdependent tasks because it produces behavior that interferes with the task performance. Committee meetings, for example, are interdependent activities where all members contribute ideas and express opinions. If the committee members compete to see who suggests the most ideas, everyone would talk at once and no one would be listening. Many sales jobs, however, are inde-

EXHIBIT 10.2   **Influence of the Task on the Effects
of Competition and Cooperation**

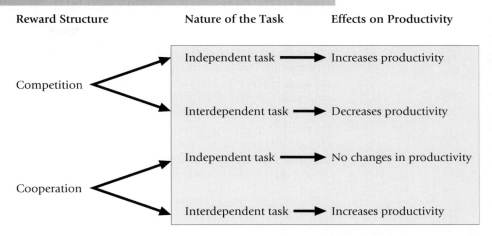

Reward Structure	Nature of the Task	Effects on Productivity
	Independent task ⟶	Increases productivity
Competition		
	Interdependent task ⟶	Decreases productivity
	Independent task ⟶	No changes in productivity
Cooperation		
	Interdependent task ⟶	Increases productivity

pendent tasks, with sales representatives calling on customers in separate areas. Therefore, competition between the sales representatives should increase their performance.

Competition and Satisfaction. The effects of competition on satisfaction depend largely on the outcome of the situation and whether the competition is so intense that it destroys friendships. Competition tends to destroy interpersonal relationships by creating a feeling of antagonism, distrust, and dislike for the other person. These results, however, do not occur with all competitive situations.

Some **mixed-motive conflicts** involve a combination of competition and cooperation. Most athletic activities, for example, involve competing and cooperating. In a tennis match, for example, both players are competing to see who wins, but unless they cooperate the match will never occur. The cooperation includes agreeing to play, deciding on a time and place, and following a set of consistent rules. If either player decides that the game is dissatisfying and not worth playing, the match will not occur.

Television sportscasting has popularized the phrase "the thrill of victory and the agony of defeat." Obviously, one of the major variables influencing satisfaction in competitive conditions is whether you win or lose. Winning is fun, and the extrinsic rewards are only part of the satisfaction. In addition to the money, prizes, or trophies, there are intrinsic rewards associated with the thrill and elation from excelling in competition.

An important by-product of competition is being able to compare and evaluate our abilities. In novel situations we don't know how well we should be able to perform, so we use the performance of others as a standard for assessing our own behavior. In some experimental situations, subjects have voluntarily changed a cooperative situation into a competitive situation just to have a basis for comparing their own abilities. An explanation for why people may choose a competitive situation is suggested by the theory of social comparison processes, which argues that the absence of information regarding the quality of our performance causes our self-esteem to be unstable. Therefore, we seek a competitive situation to obtain personal feedback. We measure our ability by comparisons with others and establish a level of aspiration from the feedback we obtain.

In summary, the effects of competition on satisfaction are determined primarily by the outcome of the competitive situation.[4] Since competitive situations present such a complex combination of rewards and punishments, it is very difficult to predict the final outcome. Although the winners are usually happy and the losers unhappy, many considerations influence the outcome. For example, if a work unit competes aggressively to determine which member will be promoted to a new position, both the winner and the losers may be very dissatisfied if the competition destroys the interpersonal relationships within the group. In contrast, Olympic athletes usually report that the competition was exciting and satisfying even though they lost. Just the thrill of being at the Olympic games and the privilege of representing their country was a satisfying experience in spite of the defeat.

ALTRUISM

Altruism is defined as behavior that is motivated by a regard for others with no immediate extrinsic reward for the helper. This definition still applies even if it can be argued that the helper always expects some reward, such as a simple thank you. Sometimes it is difficult to know what motivated a helping response; even the helper can't explain why. Furthermore, if someone received a sizable reward for helping, we would still call it altruism if it was motivated by a selfless desire to render assistance.[5] The motive or desire to render assistance is an important element in understanding altruism.

The study of altruism was stimulated by a tragic event that occurred on March 13, 1964, in the borough of Queens, New York. A young woman named Kitty Genovese, returning to her home at 3 A.M., was attacked by a man with a knife. Her screams of terror attracted the attention of at least thirty-eight neighbors along Austin Street, who looked from their apartment windows as the young woman was attacked and beaten on the street below. These thirty-eight people watched in horror as her assailant assaulted her in three separate attacks lasting over half an hour and listened to her calls for help, "He stabbed me! . . . Please help me! I am dying, I am dying!" Not one of her neighbors came to her aid, and the police were called only after Ms. Genovese lay dead on the street and her assailant had fled.

Failing to render help to people in distress has been referred to as "bystander apathy." People were shocked by the apathy of neighbors who watched and did nothing. We would like to think that as human beings we are compassionate and would render assistance to someone in need. Many experiments have examined bystander apathy and attempted to describe the conditions that lead people to either intervene in an emergency or ignore it. These studies indicate that altruism is not just a simple dichotomous process of deciding whether to help or not to help in a given situation. Several steps are involved in an altruistic response. First, the person must notice the situation and interpret it as an emergency. Next, the person must accept a personal responsibility for taking action and must know how to render assistance. Finally, the person must make the decision to render assistance and then implement the decision. Failing to render help can result from a break in any part of this complex process. The first step, recognizing the need for help, is probably the biggest cause of apathy since we tend to be preoccupied with our own problems.

Organizational Citizenship Behavior (OCB). When an employee voluntarily helps other employees with no promise of rewards, this behavior is called **organizational citizenship behavior (OCB).** It consists of going above and beyond the formal job description and doing more than the job normally requires. An understanding of OCB requires distinguishing between three different behaviors: role requirements, compliance, and altruism.[6]

1. *Role requirements* are activities associated with completing the assigned duties specified by the job description. These behaviors are not considered OCB; employees who do these behaviors well are deemed good employees, but citizenship behaviors involve doing more than just what is required.

2. *Compliance* is a form of organizational citizenship behavior directed toward benefiting the organization. An example of compliance is when two department secretaries return to the office late at night during the first week of the semester to organize class lists and assemble orientation materials. University policy prohibits working overtime, so they covertly return late at night and prepare for the next day to minimize the amount of time students will have to wait in long lines. Another example of compliance is when an electrician cancels a Thanksgiving trip and works through the weekend so other subcontractors on a construction period will not have to wait for the wiring to be installed.

3. *Altruism* is a form of organizational citizenship behavior directed toward helping others. An example of altruism is the help a group of high school English teachers voluntarily provided for another teacher who was absent for six weeks after surgery. While she was absent, her colleagues arranged to teach her classes during their preparation periods and they stayed after school to do their preparation. Although altruism is directed toward helping people, it indirectly benefits the organization.

Leader Fairness and Task Characteristics. Organizational citizenship behaviors are much more likely to occur when employees are in a good mood than when they are in a bad mood. Research has consistently shown a positive relationship between the amount of job satisfaction employees report and the number of citizenship behaviors they perform as reported by their supervisors.[7] There is some evidence to suggest, however, that OCB is determined by something more fundamental than the individual's mood state; both the mood state and OCB are created specifically by the fairness of the leader and the nature of the task.[8]

According to this explanation, employees appraise their working relationships and decide whether the conditions are fair enough to allow them to voluntarily help others and do more than required without having others take advantage of them by expecting them to do more all the time and never reciprocating. To the extent that fairness does not exist, people will choose to contribute less and work according to the rules by doing only what is required.

Similarly, the nature of the task can stimulate organizational citizenship behaviors depending on the degree of responsibility and meaningfulness of the job. Intrinsically motivating tasks create a sense of responsibility that causes people to feel personally accountable for completing the job and doing it well. Their determination to succeed induces them to go beyond the formal job requirements when needed to achieve excellence in their work. Work is meaningful to the extent that it is perceived as personally and socially valued, especially if it directly improves the quality of life and serves society. The internal satisfaction derived from performing a meaningful job rewards employees for doing more than just what is required.[9]

Personal Responsibility. Research studies on altruism have identified some of the environmental conditions and personal characteristics that contribute to a helping response. Certain situations are more likely to elicit altruistic responses than others, and certain people are more likely to be helped than others. People are more inclined to render assistance if they feel a personal sense of responsibility for taking action. When other people are present, a person does not feel the same degree of personal responsibility as when others are not present. In one experiment, for example, subjects thought a female experimenter fell to the floor and heard her scream in agony, crying out that her ankle had been hurt and she could not get the chair off her. Subjects who were alone responded to the call for help 70 percent of the time. By contrast, only 40 percent of the subjects who came in pairs offered help. Furthermore, if the other individual was actually an experimental confederate who acted as though nothing had happened, the number of subjects who rendered help dropped to only 7 percent.[10]

The presence of other people, however, does not necessarily eliminate the feeling of personal responsibility. A sense of personal responsibility can be created by asking people to be responsible. On a crowded beach, for example, an experimenter placed his blanket and portable radio next to a subject and a few minutes later asked the subject to watch his things while he went to the boardwalk for a few minutes. When another confederate attempted to steal the portable radio, 95 percent of the subjects attempted to intervene in the theft. If the subjects were not asked specifically to watch the experimenter's things, the number who responded directly dropped to only 20 percent.[11]

Personality Development. Since altruism involves some degree of self-sacrifice in helping others, it is reasonable to expect people who behave altruistically to be relatively unselfish and emotionally mature. People who are more psychologically healthy and whose character is more developed are more inclined to help others. The degree of personality development has been shown to influence the motives of men in caring for their families. Men who are at higher stages of personality development are more committed to serving their families and their organization, and they will sacrifice some of their egoistic concerns for the benefit of others.[12]

Research on why people willingly participate in voluntary activities has identified an altruistic motive that seems to apply to many types of voluntary activities: Some people are simply more predisposed than others to volunteer assistance.[13] This motive appears to be associated with the degree of personality development.

Models. Altruistic behavior appears to be particularly responsive to the example of others. Studies of both children and adults have found that charitable contributions and assistance to others increase when someone observes another person contributing or sharing. One reason why modeling is so effective in influencing behavior is because in uncertain situations, when we don't know what to do, we tend to follow the example of someone else. The behavior of others not only identifies an alternative way to behave, but signals that this way is appropriate.

People are more inclined to behave altruistically if they have observed someone else behave that way. One study recorded how many male motorists stopped on a highway to assist a woman who was trying to change a flat tire.[14] The study found that motorists were much more likely to stop if they had recently passed a similar scene in which a male driver had stopped to help a woman change a tire. Those who had observed an altruistic model were more inclined to behave altruistically themselves. Another study, which also demonstrated the effects of modeling on altruistic behavior, looked at the contributions that were made to a Salvation Army collection box.[15] A significantly larger percent of the people were willing to make a contribution if they observed a model making a contribution. In fact, the percentage of the people contributing was just about as high when the model considered the issue but decided not to contribute. If the subject saw the model seriously consider making a contribution, the percentage of subjects contributing increased even though in one condition the model decided not to contribute.

Perception of Need. People are more inclined to help another if they have a clear perception that the individual needs help. When the situation is ambiguous or uncertain, people tend not to help. Serious situations, in which a helpless victim is in dire need of assistance, may be ignored because people failed to appreciate the situation. However, as the need for assistance becomes increasingly apparent, the likelihood of obtaining assistance increases. The more serious the plight, the more likely the victim is to receive help. Studies have found that when people are in a hurry and have important business to perform, they are less likely to behave altruistically.[16] Part of the reason why they fail to help is that they think they are too busy and they assume someone else should lend assistance. But another part of the reason why they don't help is that they simply fail to notice the need for help or appreciate the seriousness of the situation.

Similar People. Since altruism is helping others when there is no anticipation of a reward other than our own good feelings, it should not be surprising to learn that people are more inclined to help those whom they like. Indeed, some research efforts have shown that greater help is given to those who are liked than those who are disliked. People seem to derive greater satisfaction from helping someone they admire and respect and for whom they have positive feelings. Since we tend to like people who are similar to us, we would expect people to be more inclined to help others who have similar personal characteristics. Indeed, studies have shown that people are more inclined to render assistance to those of similar race, dress, and appearance.[17]

Implications for Organizations. Studies on altruism and bystander apathy indicate that people are more inclined to behave altruistically when they feel a personal sense of responsibility for providing assistance, when they see others model helping behavior, when they have a clear perception of the need for rendering assistance, and when the person they are helping is someone they like. Managers who want to increase the frequency of altruistic responses should first set a proper example by modeling the behaviors they desire. Managers are usually very visible, high-status models who have a significant influence on the behavior of employees. A manager who makes a concerted effort to assist others communicates an important message that altruism is appropriate and desirable.

In addition to setting a proper example, managers should also communicate a sense of personal responsibility and the need for helping behavior. Employees can be told that they are specifically expected to go out of their way when necessary to help others in need. They can also be taught to look for specific cues that would indicate that their help is needed. In retail stores, for instance, employees can be encouraged to look for opportunities to help customers.[18]

The effectiveness of an organization is greatly influenced by its ability to obtain altruistic responses from its employees. When employees are willing to go out of their way to help each other, the work is performed more efficiently and a higher level of morale is maintained in the organization.

COALITION FORMATION

Some competitive situations require at least partial cooperation for anyone to achieve success. For example, the faculty members of a college faculty may have different opinions about which courses should be required for a degree program. The marketing professors think students should take additional marketing classes, and other faculty, likewise, argue that students should be required to take their classes. Unless a majority of the faculty can agree on the required curriculum, the proposed program will not be approved. In this situation, some of the units must cooperate by supporting a compromise program. Uniting together to endorse a compromise proposal is called "**coalition** formation." For a coalition to occur, at least three parties must be involved in a competitive situation that allows cooperation between any two of the parties.

In some competitive situations, coalitions are not possible because the relationships are independent and the behavior of one party does not affect the rest. For example, in a tennis tournament three tennis players cannot eliminate a fourth tennis player with superior ability simply by forming a coalition. However, the accounting and finance faculty could form a coalition to remove the marketing classes from the required curriculum.

Coalitions allow individuals or groups to exert greater influence than they could if they retained their independence. Coalitions are particularly prevalent in political campaigns. By forming a coalition, two minority parties may be able to pass legislation and elect officers over the opposition of a much more powerful third party. An organized coalition of minorities is typically much more powerful than a disorganized majority.

Although a long-term relationship may develop, coalitions are typically temporary alliances between individuals or groups whose long-term goals may be very different. The purpose of the coalition is to achieve short-run benefits by agreeing to cooperate. Within a group, certain individuals may form a coalition to control the group. Likewise, within an organization, groups may form a coalition for the purpose of structuring the organization's activities and allocating resources. Coalitions can also be formed between competing political parties within a nation as well as between competing nations. NATO represents a relatively long-term coalition of nations that united to provide greater security for each nation. Other alliances have been very short-term. The classic example occurred during World War II when Russia first formed an alliance with Germany against Poland and then entered an alliance with the United States and England against Germany.

Most of the research on coalition formation has tried to predict which coalitions will form and why. This research has focused on the resources each group brings to the coalition. The two leading theories are the minimum resource theory and the bargaining theory of coalitions.

Minimum-Resource Theory. Initially, it seems reasonable to assume that a small, weaker party would want to form an alliance with the strongest and most powerful party for protection or influence. Research on coalition formation, however, indicates this is not true. In a three-person group, for example, the two weakest members usually form a coalition if their combined power is adequate to form a majority.

One explanation why the two weakest parties form a coalition is called the **minimum-resource theory.**[19] This theory focuses on the potential resources each party contributes to the coalition and predicts that people enter into coalitions that maximize their gains. It assumes that when people form a winning coalition, the rewards of the coalition will be divided according to how many resources each party contributed. Suppose, for example, three subjects were offered six dollars provided they could reach a majority agreement about how the money should be allocated. Suppose further that person A has four votes, person B has three votes, and C has two votes. In this situation, studies have shown that a B–C coalition with five votes is clearly the most popular coalition.[20]

The reason for a B–C coalition, according to minimum-resource theory, is that this coalition maximizes the gains for persons B and C. If B forms a coalition with A, B could expect only three-sevenths of the rewards. By forming a coalition with C, however, B expects three-fifths of the rewards. Likewise, C expects a greater share of the rewards by forming a coalition with B than with A.

Bargaining Theory of Coalitions. Although several studies have supported the minimum-resource theory, recent research indicates this theory is overly simplistic. One overlooked point involves the reasoning of the low-resource person in the coalition. Although that individual may bring fewer resources to the coalition, without these resources the coalition could not win. In one sense, then, both B and C are equally important because without the resources of either person, the coalition could not succeed.

Although the lower-resource person has fewer resources to contribute to the coalition, the other parties may be powerless unless they can attract that person to form a coalition. In an A–B–C triad, for example (A = 4, B = 3, C = 2), C can refuse to form a coalition with either A or B unless the rewards are shared equally. However, if C sticks to its demands and refuses to accept anything less than equality, A and B may form a coalition and leave C with nothing.

Recognizing the negotiating process that occurs in coalitions has led to the **bargaining theory of coalitions.**[21] This theory also assumes that people form coalitions to obtain the highest expected rewards. However, the rewards are not necessarily distributed according to the proportion contributed by each party. Instead, they may be divided equally. Consequently, this theory suggests that coalitions will often be unstable because those who are excluded from a coalition will try to entice one of the other parties to join them by offering higher outcomes than they are getting from the present coalition. The bargaining theory of coalitions helps to explain why the allocation of rewards among coalitions is usually less than equality but greater than parity (according to the sources they contribute).

Characteristics of Individuals or Groups.   Coalition formation is also influenced by two additional characteristics: philosophical agreement and affiliation. People are more likely to form an alliance with another party if they believe its position is reasonable and they endorse a similar philosophy or ideology. Similarly, people choose to associate with those who have similar attitudes and goals and with whom they feel an interpersonal attraction.

Research indicates that when subjects have equal resources, they choose to form coalitions with others who have similar attitudes. When there are resource differences, however, the subjects tend to choose coalitions that offer the highest potential payoff. Therefore, although resource allocations may be the most important variable influencing the formation of coalitions, other factors are also important in understanding the behavior of coalitions.[22]

COHESIVENESS

Before we discuss conflict, it is necessary to discuss cohesiveness and explain the causes and consequences of cohesive groups. **Cohesiveness** is the attraction that group members have for each other and for the group as a whole. In some groups there is an atmosphere of solidarity with common attitudes and behavior, while in other groups members possess only minimal interest in one another. Obviously, group members must have some attraction for one another or the group would cease to exist. Highly cohesive groups provide satisfaction for their members, who may in turn feel an intense loyalty and commitment to the group. Group cohesiveness has important consequences for the degree of conflict or cooperation in an organization. This section identifies the causes and consequences of cohesive groups.

Factors Influencing Cohesiveness

Group cohesiveness is created by a combination of factors within the group as well as by factors in the external environment beyond the group's control.

Frequency of Interaction. Cohesiveness increases as group members have more opportunities to interact with one another. Frequent contact allows people to communicate more openly and develop greater interpersonal attraction for one another. The frequency of interaction can be increased by increasing the number of formal and informal meetings and physically moving people closer together.

The size of the group influences opportunities for interaction. As the group gets larger, it becomes increasingly difficult for the members to interact with or possibly even know other group members. As group size increases, therefore, cohesiveness tends to decrease. The optimal group size for maximum cohesiveness is probably from six to ten individuals.

Interpersonal Attraction. The most important variable influencing cohesiveness is the interpersonal attraction of members for each other.[23] People are attracted to others who are fun to be with and for whom they feel a mutual trust and respect. Individuals tend to be attracted to those of similar socioeconomic status, religion, sex, and age. Therefore, cohesiveness tends to increase as group members share common interests and attitudes toward religion, politics, and philosophical ideas. The key factor is that cohesiveness increases when people enjoy working with and being with each other.

Rigor of Initiation. Groups that are more elite in selecting new members and that require more rigorous and severe initiation rites tend to be more cohesive. Some organizations require members to perform acts that are humiliating, physically exhausting, or perhaps illegal before they are accepted as full members. Fraternities, lettermen clubs, and youth gangs have been particularly noted for their severe initiation rites. Although these practices are unwise when there is danger of physical or psychological harm, they do tend to unite the group members into a cohesive unit. Military organizations try to create cohesive groups by their rigorous training of new recruits in basic training. Academic institutions often try to foster a feeling of cohesiveness through a psychological initiation created by advertising very high academic standards and requiring very high test scores for admission. Other organizations attempt to create the same perception by advertising that they only accept the cream of the crop. This practice is designed to make students and new employees feel they are part of a select group and their elite membership provides higher status and prestige for them.

Agreement on Group Goals. Groups tend to be more cohesive when the members agree on the purpose and direction of the group's activities. When the group members have a common feeling about the purpose of the group and what it should be doing, there is a greater sense of unity and cohesiveness.

Group Success. Successful groups tend to be more cohesive than unsuccessful groups. Individuals are more attracted to a winning group than a losing group. If two sales units have been competing for a prize, and one sales unit is declared the winner and the other the loser, the winning team will develop greater cohesiveness while the losing team may become less cohesive, depending on how they interpret their defeat. If they can blame defeat on an outside force, they may remain a fairly cohesive group. But if they blame other members of the group, their level of cohesiveness will decline.

Outside Threats. Groups facing an outside threat will often close ranks and form a more cohesive unit. Intergroup competition usually provides an outside threat, causing the group to become more cohesive. Threat is an effective means of producing cohesiveness when the following conditions exist: (1) the threat comes from outside the group; (2) there is little chance for escape; and (3) cooperation is necessary to resist or overcome the threat. Sometimes leaders attempt to create a more cohesive group by convincing the members that they face a serious external threat. Coaches and military officers often talk about the power of the enemy as a way of creating greater cohesiveness within their unit. Political leaders and business executives talk about the dangers of foreign competition, high interest rates, and a bad economy for similar reasons. For years the Soviet Union relied on its ability to convince the Soviet citizens that the United States was intent on imperial aggression as a means of uniting the Soviet citizens and making them willing to make heavy economic and personal sacrifices. Likewise, labor union leaders try to develop cohesiveness by convincing union members that management is trying to destroy the union and their jobs.

Consequences of Cohesiveness

Cohesive groups generally achieve better results than noncohesive groups. However, the effects of cohesiveness are not universally positive and need to be examined with respect to four aspects of group functioning: participation, conformity, success, and productivity.

Participation. Cohesive groups elicit greater levels of participation from group members. Because of their attraction for the group, individuals are willing to devote more time and energy to group activities. A highly cohesive work group, for example, may interact more frequently on the job and even meet informally in recreational activities off the job. For example, some cohesive work groups form bowling teams, softball teams, and other interest groups, which sometimes dominate their lives away from work, particularly when a local tournament is held. Members of cohesive groups generally spend more time communicating with each other than noncohesive groups do. This increase in communication and participation serves to further strengthen the cohesiveness within the group. In other words, increased communication and participation increases the interpersonal attraction and cohesiveness the members feel for each other, and increased cohesiveness, in turn, leads to greater communication and participation.

Conformity. As discussed in Chapter 9, cohesive groups create intense pressures for conformity. Because of the attraction of the group, people value their group membership and are willing to conform to the group's norms and expectations. As groups become more highly cohesive, group norms become more clearly specified, and the behavior of group members conforms more closely to these norms. One of the ways cohesive groups enforce conformity is through greater communication. As they become more cohesive, they communicate more openly and create more explicit expectations regarding acceptable behavior. In groups that are not very cohesive, members can sometimes express deviant views without repercussions or challenges. In a highly cohesive group, however, deviant attitudes are not acceptable, and other group members try to reform the deviant members. Those who refuse to change are ostracized.

Success. Successful groups tend to be more cohesive, but cohesive groups also tend to be more successful.[24] On interdependent tasks requiring cooperation, cohesive teams are generally superior because they work well together. Winning athletic teams often attribute their success to teamwork. Although their success is probably due to more than just cohesive teamwork, their cohesiveness contributes importantly to their success.

Productivity. Because cohesive groups tend to elicit more conformity, more participation, and more communication, shouldn't they also be more productive? Studies on the relationship between cohesiveness and performance indicate that highly cohesive groups are not always the most productive. For example, a major review of thirty-four studies of cohesiveness and productivity found that the relationship was neither direct nor simple.[25] Eleven studies found that cohesiveness and productivity were unrelated; another eleven studies found that more cohesive groups were less productive; and only twelve studies found that cohesive groups were more productive. The studies involved a wide variety of groups, including radar crews, decision-making groups, basketball teams, combat units, bomber crews, factory workers, college students, nurses, and forest rangers.

There is a good reason why highly cohesive groups are not always the most productive. Cohesive groups would only be expected to be highly productive if the group norms support high productivity and are consistent with the organization's goals. If the group's goals are inconsistent with the organization's goals, a highly cohesive group may be counterproductive and may engage in such activities as sabotaging the organization or avoiding work.

The relationship between performance and cohesiveness is illustrated in Exhibit 10.3. The performance of noncohesive groups tends to be about average, but the performance of highly cohesive groups may be high or low depending on the performance norms of the groups. If a cohesive group has high performance norms, the members will accept the group norms and be highly productive. A cohesive group with low performance norms, however, will have low performance.

Another characteristic of cohesive groups is that there is usually less variation in the performance of individuals. Highly cohesive groups tend to have members who all perform at the same level, while noncohesive groups may have both high producers and low producers within the group.

Three additional reasons have been suggested to explain why cohesive groups are not necessarily more productive. One reason is that cohesive groups tend to spend more time socializing than working because they enjoy being with each other. If work interferes with visiting, a highly cohesive group may sacrifice some of their working time to spend more time visiting. Another reason why cohesive groups may perform more poorly is because they may be subject to "groupthink," a phenomenon described further in Chapter 14 that refers to rigid thinking controlled by the group. The desire to maintain a cohesive group may prevent members from challenging ideas and confronting issues and thereby cause cohesive groups to make bad decisions. Furthermore, as groups become more cohesive, they tend to become more conservative in their approach to solving problems and less willing to take chances. As a result, the group may produce less creative solutions to their problems.

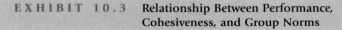

EXHIBIT 10.3   **Relationship Between Performance, Cohesiveness, and Group Norms**

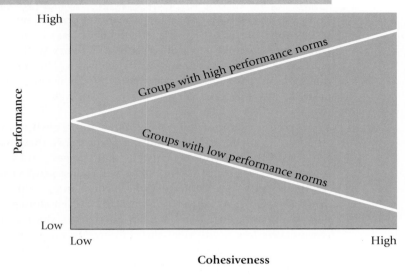

CONFLICT AND ORGANIZATIONAL PERFORMANCE

Like competition, conflict occurs when two or more parties engage in activities that are in some sense incompatible. Both parties cannot win, and the success of one prevents the other from achieving success. Although we often talk about competition and conflict as though they were the same, they differ in the degree of self-interest displayed by each side. This small difference has important consequences for the success of a group or an organization.

Competition does not involve direct action by one party to interfere with the activities of the other. With conflict, however, one party tries to prevent or inhibit the success of the other. This difference is clearly illustrated in sports. Track events are examples of competition rather than conflict since each runner attempts to run faster than the others but no one is allowed to trip or interfere with the others. In contrast, games of football, hockey, and rugby involve both competition and conflict because each team acts directly to interfere with the activities of the other. The degree of conflict is limited by the rules of the game, and penalties are assessed when players violate the rules.

Conflict designed to destroy the other party is not uncommon in organizations. Price wars involve conflict between organizations, with one company trying to drive its competitors out of business. Conflict between union and management sometimes becomes so intense that the union forces the company to go out of business by making unreasonable demands, and management tries to destroy the union by refusing to accept an agreement or hiring replacements. Conflict between nations that could result in nuclear war probably represents the epitome of conflict.

Social conflict, then, is a struggle in which the aims of the conflicting parties are not only to obtain the desired outcomes, but also to injure or eliminate their rivals. Intense conflict involves not only hindering one's opponents but also injuring and retaliating against them.

Functional and Dysfunctional Conflict

Many people believe that all conflict is dysfunctional and that efforts should be made to eliminate it. This common belief is wrong, however. Some conflict is inevitable in every organization because of the inherent struggle for organizational survival. Every organization exists within an environment that requires organizations to compete for limited resources. Even within friendly work groups there are limited resources that create some degree of conflict, regardless of how cooperatively the members try to allocate resources. Furthermore, all conflict is not bad because some conflict situations produce desirable results. Therefore, a distinction needs to be made between functional and dysfunctional conflict.

Functional Conflict. **Functional conflict** is a confrontation between two parties that improves or benefits the organization's performance. For example, two divisions of a public health agency may be in conflict over which should be allowed to serve a neighborhood. In their attempts to prove they are better prepared to provide the service, both divisions may create new services and improved methods of delivery that benefit not only the neighborhood in question but other areas as well.

Studies have suggested that some conflict not only helps but may be a necessary condition for creativity. Experimental studies have shown that heterogeneous groups whose members represent a diversity of opinion produce better solutions and more creative ideas.[26] These studies on group decision making have led theorists to conclude that conflict may produce many positive benefits for organizations if it is properly managed. It has been suggested, for example, that functional conflict can lead to the discovery of more effective ways to structure an organization, better recognition of the strategic changes necessary for survival, and a better accommodation and acceptance of the power relationships within and between organizations.[27]

At the individual level, functional conflict can create a number of desirable consequences. Individuals require a certain level of stimulation and excitement to feel enthusiastic about their work. Within certain limits, conflict produces an element of tension that motivates individuals to action.[28] Channeling this level of tension can produce high levels of productivity and satisfaction. It has been suggested that conflict contributes to personal interest, curiosity, and the full use of individual capacities. To produce the desired results, however, the conflict must somehow be limited or contained to appropriate levels of intensity. Otherwise, dysfunctional consequences occur.

Dysfunctional Conflict. **Dysfunctional conflict** is any interaction between two parties that hinders or destroys the achievement of organizational or group goals. Some organizations are prepared to handle higher levels of conflict than others, such as professional sports teams, crisis organizations, police and fire departments, and commodity traders. Most organizations, however, have more conflict than is desirable, and performance would improve if the level of conflict was reduced. When conflict becomes too great, the performance of every organization begins to deteriorate. In research and development companies and universities, for example, intense conflict destroys the working relationships between members and seriously reduces the level of organizational performance.

The relationship between conflict and organizational performance is illustrated in Exhibit 10.4. Organizational performance is low when the level of intergroup conflict is either extremely high or extremely low, while moderate levels of inter-group conflict contribute to high organizational performance. When the level of conflict is too low, such as at point A on the curve, performance suffers because of a lack of arousal and stimulation. Individuals find their environment too comfort-able and complacent, and they respond with apathy and stagnation. When they are not challenged and confronted, they fail to search for new ideas, and the organiza-tion is slow to adapt to environmental changes. Yet when the level of conflict is extremely high, performance suffers because of inadequate coordination and coop-eration. The organization is in a state of chaos because of disruption and interfer-ence to crucial activities. Individuals spend more time defending themselves or attacking others than accomplishing productive work.

Maximum organizational performance occurs somewhere between these two extremes, where there is an optimal level of intergroup conflict. In this situation, at point B on the curve, there is sufficient conflict to stimulate new ideas and a cre-ative search for solutions to problems. However, the conflict is not so great that it prevents the organization from moving effectively toward its goals. Individuals and groups need to assess the situation and adapt to environmental change. Such adap-tation may produce innovation and creativity.

Studies of Conflict

Conflict has been a very popular research topic because of its perceived value in reducing organizational conflicts and international tensions. Much of the research on conflict comes from two research methods: the prisoner's dilemma game and

EXHIBIT 10.4   **Relationship Between Conflict and Organizational Performance**

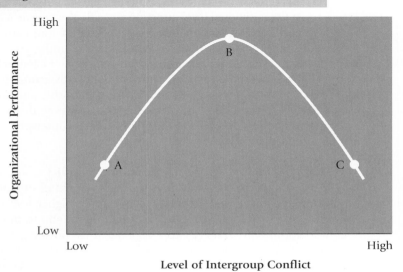

APPLYING ORGANIZATIONAL BEHAVIOR
RESEARCH

Using Diversity and Constructive Conflict to Improve Decisions

 Homogeneous groups communicate more effectively, and they are more harmonious than heterogeneous groups. When group members all come from the same ethnic membership, there is usually more participation and openness and greater interpersonal attraction than when there is diversity.

Diversity can be used to advantage, however, when it stimulates constructive conflict in a decision-making group. Constructive conflict enhances decision outcomes by exposing members to a broader variety of ideas, forcing them to consider alternative ideas, and encouraging them to carefully critique each idea.

The benefits of constructive conflict were examined in a study of 180 business students in a Canadian university, of which 47 were from mostly Asian minorities. The students were formed into forty-five multicultural groups with 4 members per group, 1 of whom was from an ethnic minority. Each group had an hour to analyze a business case and recommend a solution. After writing their report, the members rated the amount of constructive conflict in their group and evaluated each member's contribution to the decision. Judges evaluated the quality of the decisions.

The results indicated that the contributions made by members of minorities were considerably less than those of nonminority members. In 76 percent of the groups, the member who contributed the least was from an ethnic minority. However, the groups that reported greater minority involvement also reported greater constructive conflict and these groups made better decisions. Although minority members contributed less to the decision, they were just as committed to the decision and just as committed to the group as the nonminority members.

Because constructive conflict can improve group decision making, group leaders are encouraged to consider a variety of ways to stimulate constructive conflict, such as expressing their opinions and uncertainties, actively soliciting the viewpoints of others, demonstrating a willingness to change their own positions, critiquing the discussion, and rewarding members for independent thinking.

Source: Catherine Kirchmeyer and Aaron Cohen, "Multicultural Groups: Their Performance and Reactions with Constructive Conflict," *Group and Organization Management,* vol. 17 (June 1992), pp. 153–170.

the trucking game. These two research designs have been very popular because they allow experimenters to obtain extensive data in a short time from many subjects, and the experimental conditions can be easily varied in a controlled situation. A classic study by Muzafer Sherif called the Robber's Cave experiment has also contributed greatly to our understanding of conflict. The results of these studies will be discussed in later sections after the research methods have been described.

The Prisoner's Dilemma Game. A convenient method for studying conflict between two people is to present them with a two-by-two payoff matrix, similar to the one shown in Exhibit 10.5, and ask them to choose either response 1 or response 2. If person A and person B both choose response 1, B will receive four points while A loses four points. This payoff matrix is called a *zero-sum* or *pure conflict* situation because what one person gains the other loses. **Zero-sum conflicts** occur in organizations whenever the rewards to one group cause losses to another group, such as budget allocations, territorial assignments, and staffing decisions that reassign employees to different departments.

EXHIBIT 10.5   Payoff Matrix for a Zero-Sum or Pure Conflict Situation

Person A

	a_1	$a_2{}^*$
$b_1{}^*$	+4, −4	+1, −1
b_2	+7, −7	−6, +6

Person B

Many organizational situations, especially interpersonal interactions, are not zero-sum situations because both parties can win by cooperating but one can win more at the expense of the other person by not cooperating. The numbers in the payoff matrix can be changed to create a *mixed-motive* situation. In these situations people can either maximize their own personal gains or maximize the gains for both parties. One mixed-motive situation, called the **prisoner's dilemma game,** concerns two suspects who are taken into custody and placed in separate cells. The district attorney is certain they are guilty of a specific crime but does not have adequate evidence to convict them in a trial. The district attorney tells the prisoners, however, that they have two alternatives: they can confess or not confess. If neither confesses, the district attorney threatens to prosecute them on a minor charge and they will both receive minor punishments. If they both confess, they will be prosecuted but he (or she) will recommend a light sentence. But if one confesses and the other does not, then the confessor will receive lenient treatment for providing evidence whereas the latter will receive a severe sentence.[29]

The payoff matrix for the prisoner's dilemma is illustrated in Exhibit 10.6. If the prisoners trust each other and neither confesses, they will each receive only a one-year sentence. But if only one confesses and testifies against the other, that one will receive an even lighter sentence of only three months while his (or her) partner receives a ten-year sentence. The essential features of this and other mixed-motive situations is that one person's gain is not necessarily the other person's loss and motives of both cooperation (not confess) and conflict (confess) are involved.

The Trucking Game. In the trucking game, pairs of subjects are asked to imagine that they are managers of opposing trucking companies that transport merchandise over a road. One player's company is called Acme and the other's is called Bolt. Both players are told that each time their truck completes a delivery trip they will make sixty cents less their operating expenses, which are determined by the time required to complete the trip (one cent per second). Thus, a trip taking 20 seconds would earn the company forty cents.

The players are then shown a road map, illustrated in Exhibit 10.7, which indicates each player's starting point and destination. Each player has two routes; the main route is clearly the shortest but contains a section in the middle wide enough for only one truck at a time. If the two trucks meet in this section, the only way either

EXHIBIT 10.6   Matrix for the Prisoner's Dilemma Mixed-Motive Payoff

		Prisoner A	
		Not confess	Confess
Prisoner B	Not confess	One year each	3 months for A 10 years for B
	Confess	10 years for A 3 months for B	4 years for each

truck can continue is for the other truck to back up. The alternate route is much longer, and the subjects are told they will lose at least ten cents if they take this route. In playing this game, the two players experience conflict because each knows the only way to win money is to use the one-way pass, but only one person's truck can move down that section at a time. If either player waits to allow the other to pass first, the one who waits makes less money than the one who goes through first.

In some experiments, the trucking game was modified slightly to study the effects of threat. At each end of the one-lane section, a gate was installed. Each gate was controlled by one player and only that player's truck could pass through the gate. In conditions of unilateral threat, only one player had a gate while in conditions of bilateral threat, both players had access to a gate.[30]

The trucking game was typically played over twenty trials, which allowed the experimenters to observe the degree of cooperation or conflict of the subjects and the effects of threat on conflict resolution.

EXHIBIT 10.7   Diagram of the Trucking Game

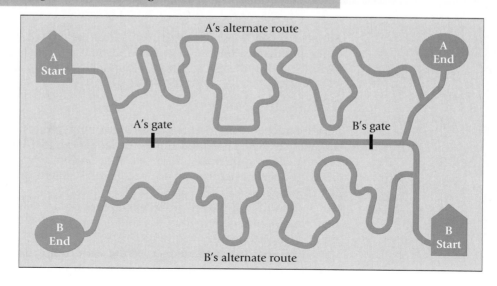

The Robber's Cave Experiment. The effects of conflict have been studied extensively by observing the interaction of groups in a natural setting. Some of the most well-known studies in conflict were conducted by Carolyn and Muzafer Sherif and their colleagues, who observed the interactions of boys in summer camps in Connecticut (1949), New York (1953), and Oklahoma (1954). The 1954 experiment in Oklahoma is sometimes called the Robber's Cave experiment, referring to the name of the campsite where the two groups of boys stayed.[31]

The boys in each camp were divided into two groups and given a week to develop intragroup cohesiveness. Each group participated in activities that stimulated cooperation. They lived together in bunk houses, cooked their own meals, cleaned their own campsites, and organized their own activities and games. During the first week, each group became a cohesive unit with its own leadership structure and group norms. The groups were originally assigned the name of a color to differentiate them, such as the Blue Group, but each group quickly coined its own name, such as Eagles, Rattlers, and Bulldogs. After the first week, the two groups were brought together to compete for prizes and participate in games of football, tug-of-war, and baseball. They competed to see which team could have the best skit, have the cleanest cabin, or pitch a tent faster.

The effects of bringing the groups together and introducing competition were striking. The peaceful camp environment was quickly turned into a miniature battleground as the two groups began to attack and insult each other. Derogatory terms, such as "pigs," "dirty bums," and "jerks," were used to describe the rival team. Posters were made insulting the other team, and the opposing team's flags were stolen and mutilated. Incidents of open warfare occurred as food fights erupted in the dining hall and artillery attacks were staged in the surrounding fields using apples as ammunition. A variety of competitive and cooperative activities were introduced in the boys' camps to examine their effects on stimulating or reducing the level of conflict.

CAUSES OF INTERGROUP CONFLICT

Studies on conflict suggest that conflict can be created by a variety of situations. Some of the most important causes of conflict include task interdependence, goal incompatibility, the use of threats, group identification, and win–lose attitudes.

Task Interdependence

Task interdependence occurs when two or more groups depend on each other to accomplish their tasks, and the potential for conflict increases as the degree of interdependence increases. Three types of task interdependence have been identified: pooled interdependence, sequential interdependence, and reciprocal interdependence.

A condition of **pooled interdependence** occurs with additive tasks when the performance of different groups is simply combined or added together to achieve the overall performance.

Sequential interdependence occurs with conjunctive tasks when one group cannot complete its task until the preceding group has finished. In assembly line manufacturing, for example, the products must first pass through department A before they can proceed to department B.

Reciprocal interdependence also occurs with conjunctive tasks when each group depends upon the performance of each of the other groups. A depends upon B and C, while B and C depend on each other as well as A. Reciprocal interdependence occurs in many organizations, such as the various departments in a hospital: the x-ray unit, the blood laboratory, the nursing unit, the emergency center, and the anesthesiology staff all depend on each other to provide skilled patient care.

Goal Incompatibility

Although managers try to avoid having incompatible goals for different organizational units, inherent incompatibility sometimes exists between groups because of their individual goals. The goal of a production department is to have low production costs with long production runs, which means fewer models, colors, and styles. These goals conflict with the aim of the marketing department, which attempts to increase sales by promising customers unique products in a unique style and color with a delivery this week. The marketing department also wants to allow customers to pay nothing down and have the first payment postponed for six months. The credit department, however, wants to have cash in hand before the product is shipped.

The likelihood of conflict increases in conditions of scarcity. When resources such as money, space, labor, or materials are limited, the groups are forced to compete for them in a win–lose competition that frequently results in dysfunctional conflict. The Robber's Cave experiment indicated that little conflicts typically lead to larger conflicts. After the competitive sports had concluded, for example, the boys escalated the conflict by food fights, scuffles, and taunting insults.

Use of Threats

The level of conflict appears to increase when one party has the capacity to threaten the other. The effects of threat were studied in the trucking game by giving one or both players access to a gate. The results indicated quite dramatically that the quickest resolution to the problem and the best payoff for the players occurred when neither player had access to a threat. In fact, the players were able to obtain a profit only in the no-threat condition.32 The slowest resolution occurred when both players could threaten. Therefore, the absence of threat seems to encourage players to cooperate more and develop a compatible, cooperative relationship. However, when they have access to threats, the evidence seems to show that the players not only communicate the threat, but actually use it.

Group Identification

When two groups are competing for scarce resources, it is easy to understand why conflict would occur. Both groups are striving for the same goal, and only one can obtain it. Research has shown, however, that a competitive situation is not necessary for conflict to exist. Simply assigning people to different groups and allowing them to develop a feeling of cohesiveness is all that is necessary for conflict to result. As the groups become more cohesive, the intergroup conflict increases. One of the major conclusions of the Robber's Cave experiment was that conflict between the groups was a natural outcome of group cohesiveness. The feelings of solidarity and in-group favoritism seem to contribute to unfavorable attitudes and negative stereotypes of the out-group. This suggests that a feeling of hostility and criticism could exist between two groups who work side by side in an organization, even though there is no interaction between the two groups and they do not compete for scarce resources. And as these two groups become more cohesive, the potential for conflict between them increases.

Win–lose Attitudes

When two groups interact in zero-sum competition, it is easy to understand why conflict occurs. Whatever one group wins, the other group loses. Unfortunately, many situations are perceived as win–lose situations when in reality they are not. Industrial conflict frequently pits union against management, with each side bargaining for a larger share of dwindling profits. Rather than fighting for a larger share of a smaller pie, management and union ought to be cooperating to increase the size of the profit pie.

Although win–lose situations do not have to occur, they appear frequently when any of these conditions exist:

When someone defines or interprets the situation as a win–lose conflict

When one group chooses to pursue its own goals

When one group understands its needs but publicly disguises them

When one group attempts to increase its power position

When one group uses threats to obtain submission

When one group overemphasizes its needs, goals, and position

When one group adopts an attitude of exploiting the other group whenever possible

When one group attempts to isolate the other group

Getting two groups to change from a win–lose attitude to a win–win attitude is a difficult task because the groups develop perceptual stereotypes that reinforce their win–lose attitudes. Furthermore, rather than communicating openly, their communication becomes guarded or discontinued, which further reinforces a win–lose attitude. Research using the prisoner's dilemma game found that if the parties were able to communicate before they made their decisions, the level of cooperation increased. Cooperation also increased when the numbers in the pay-off matrix were changed to reward players for cooperating.

A very interesting conclusion from the prisoner's dilemma game is that cooperation did not increase just because one player decided to cooperate. Several studies attempted to analyze how subjects would respond to a pacifistic partner who constantly made cooperative choices. The experiments found that subjects tended to exploit a pacifistic partner who continually made cooperative choices. This exploitation occurred even when the other player's consistent cooperation was explained in terms of religious convictions or personal morality.[33] At least in the laboratory, unconditional cooperation does not create reciprocal cooperation. Instead, it seems to lead to exploitation.

The most effective strategy for obtaining cooperation was the strategy of conditional cooperation. Here one partner first makes a cooperative move and continues to make cooperative responses as long as the other responds cooperatively. If the cooperative initiative is met with aggression, however, the aggression is reciprocated; on a later trial, the cooperative response is again taken on the same conditional basis.[34]

CONSEQUENCES OF INTERGROUP CONFLICT

The consequences of intergroup conflict can be summarized in one simple statement: conflict begets conflict. When conflict occurs, the consequences of this conflict frequently lead to further conflict and create a vicious cycle of spiraling conflict. The consequences of intergroup conflict can be analyzed in terms of the changes that occur both within the group and between groups.

Changes Within the Group

When two groups are involved in intergroup conflict, the following changes are likely to occur within each group.

Increased Cohesiveness. Conflict, competition, and external threats usually cause group members to set aside their personal differences and close ranks. Group members become more loyal to the group and committed to its goals. Group norms are followed more closely, and less deviation is tolerated.

Increased Loyalty. When one group is threatened by another group, both groups will demand greater loyalty from their members. Deviant behavior is not tolerated, and friendliness with members of the opposing group is viewed with suspicion if not hostility. Personal sacrifice for the group is highly rewarded and expected. Group goals take precedence over individual satisfaction as members are expected to demonstrate their loyalty.

Rise in Autocratic Leadership. In normal conditions, democratic leadership methods are popular because they allow group members to participate in making decisions and to satisfy their needs for involvement and affiliation. In extreme conflict situations, however, democratic leadership is generally perceived as time consuming and ineffective. Members demand strong leadership and not only tolerate but seem to prefer autocratic leaders.[35]

Activity Orientation. Groups in conflict tend to focus on achieving their goal. Groups are more concerned about identifying what it is they do well and then proceeding to do it. Group members are not allowed to visit or waste time if these activities reduce the group's effectiveness in defeating the enemy.

Inflated Evaluation. The perceptions of group members become distorted as they tend to overevaluate their own performance and underevaluate their opponent's performance. Everything within the group is considered good, and a general halo effect tends to bias and inflate the group's perceptions of its members.

APPLYING ORGANIZATIONAL BEHAVIOR
IN THE NEWS

The Escalation of Conflict

CNN The consequences of intergroup conflict can be seen when union and management teams are trying to negotiate a new labor agreement. Small disagreements often escalate into major conflicts. At a time when empathy and understanding are essential to resolving problems, the dynamics of conflict create negative stereotyping, distorted perceptions, and reduced communication between the groups.

In 1992, a simple dispute over pattern bargaining—where one contract is patterned after another one within the industry—led the members of the United Auto Workers Union to strike Caterpillar Company. Caterpillar refused to offer the same contract as its rival, John Deere. Tensions and bad feelings increased during the bitter five-month strike. Finally, Caterpillar issued an ultimatum: Return to work by Monday or lose your jobs. Enough strikers crossed the picket lines and returned to work to break the strike; the bitterness and conflict between union and management was not resolved.

Caterpillar's conflict took its toll on employee morale, but it was not as bitter or divisive as some earlier strikes have been. When the Professional Air Traffic Controllers Organization went on strike in 1981, the bargaining positions of each side became so inflexible that a negotiated settlement could not be reached. The striking union members were ultimately replaced. Although the new Republican administration was praised for having the courage to make a tough decision, it was never free from criticism for failing to resolve the dispute.

In Austin, Minnesota, the members of the United Food and Commercial Workers Union refused to accept the offers of George A. Hormel & Company even though their national leaders urged them to do so. During a bitter strike, the union even tried to use economic pressure to force local banks to cease dealing with the company. Five months after the workers walked off the job, and after the local union refused to accept a federal mediator's proposal for a settlement, the company reopened the plant with 700 nonunion workers. Harassment, vandalism, and threats of violence forced the governor to send the National Guard and armored trucks to restore order. The dispute divided a once-friendly town and left permanent emotional scars.

Sources: CNN *Moneyweek* news programming.

Changes Between Groups

Intergroup conflict creates three predictable changes between the groups.

Decreased Communication. At the time when the groups are most in need of open communication to enable them to discuss the problem and resolve the conflict, the communication processes become most strained. As the conflict increases, communication tends to decrease. Both groups tend to be more guarded in their communication. Rather than openly confronting the problems, each side becomes more cautious and formal. The frequency of communication between the two groups continues to decline until it finally breaks down entirely.

Distorted Perceptions. Conflict creates suspicion and prevents people from accurately perceiving the behaviors and motives of the other party. People think everything about their own group is good while everything about the opponent group is perceived as bad. These distorted perceptions are created, in part, by negative stereotypes. The distorted perceptions cause members in each group to misperceive the others' intentions and misinterpret their communications. The performance and success of the other group is underevaluated and minimized. Even simple estimates of factual information, such as time estimates, can be enormously distorted by conflict. In the Robber's Cave experiment, for example, a tug-of-war was declared a tie after 55 minutes. When the members of the group on the verge of victory were asked to estimate the actual time of the tug-of-war, the estimates ranged from 20 to 50 minutes. However, the group that was on the verge of losing estimated the time from 65 to 210 minutes. Many other factual observations were distorted, making the in-group look good and the out-group look bad.

Negative Stereotyping. Group members in one group tend to create negative stereotypes regarding the opposing group. Negative characteristics are used to describe the opposing group, such as greedy, dishonest, unethical, and unfriendly. In a labor–management conflict, for example, management typically views labor leaders as greedy agitators who are out to destroy the company. And union leaders tend to view management as greedy profit grabbers who are trying to exploit labor and keep all the rewards.

RESOLVING INTERGROUP CONFLICT

The dynamics of interacting groups is such that conflict begets conflict. Unless something is done to reverse the process, the two groups will be the victims of a spiraling escalation of conflict. Conflict causes each group to become more cohesive and task oriented, with a rigid structure and an autocratic leader. Individuality is replaced by loyalty as each group demands greater unity within the group. The cohesiveness, loyalty, and task orientation within each group only contributes to more biased perceptions, negative stereotypes, hostility, and aggression between the groups.

Because conflict is inherent in complex organizations, managers must be capable of resolving it before dysfunctional consequences destroy the organization's effectiveness. The ability to resolve conflict is a valuable managerial skill. The most popular strategies for reducing conflict can be classified into four categories: (1) avoidance strategies, (2) power intervention strategies, (3) diffusion strategies, and (4) resolution strategies. Although the most effective strategy depends in part on the situation and the time available for resolving the conflict, the following strategies are arranged in order from generally least effective to most effective.[36]

Avoidance Strategies

Avoidance strategies generally disregard the cause of conflict but allow it to continue only under controlled conditions. Two types of avoidance strategies include ignoring the conflict and physical separation.

Ignore the Conflict. If the conflict is not too severe and the consequences are not very costly, managers frequently prefer to ignore it and pretend that it doesn't exist. Some managers think conflict reflects badly on the organization, so they ignore the

APPLYING ORGANIZATIONAL BEHAVIOR
ACROSS CULTURES

The Fine Art of International Negotiation

 International negotiations are greatly influenced by two crucial cultural factors. One focuses on the outcome of the negotiation, and the other focuses on the style of communication.

The outcome of the negotiation can be based on either **position** or **interest.** *Position-based negotiation* is based on a win–lose paradigm that assumes resources are limited. If one party receives more, the other party receives less. Consequently, both parties seek to maximize their returns by arguing for their position, protecting the confidentiality of their position, and insisting on concessions in return for anything they yield.

Interest-based negotiations are based on a win–win paradigm that assumes a mutually advantageous agreement is possible and desirable. Both parties expect to benefit from their collaboration, and they strive to secure the long-term survival of each. Negotiations involve sharing information in a spirit of openness and trust, visiting each other's facilities, and designing systems to share the gains and risks.

The style of the communication can focus on either the *content* or the *context* of the communication. High-content communication focuses on the words and ideas being communicated and relies extensively on position papers, written agreements, legal contracts, and written correspondence.

High-context communication assumes that the most important meanings are communicated by contextual factors such as the interpersonal relationship, the location, the timing, and the feelings between the parties. Context communication is subtle and highly personal and considers both what is said and what is left unsaid.

	Content	Context
Position	A	B
Interest	C	D

The combination of position versus interest-based outcomes and content versus context communication creates four different negotiating styles that are characteristic of particular cultures. Managers in the United States, Germany, and Switzerland tend to use content–position-based (style A) negotiating, whereas executives in Mexico, Spain, Egypt, and the Philippines tend to use context–position-based (style B) negotiating. Executives from Sweden and Iceland tend to use content–interest-based (style C) negotiating, while a context–interest-based style (style D) is characteristic of executives from Japan.

Negotiations between executives from different cultures often produce predictable conflicts. D would be prone to perceive A as pushy, aggressive, impatient, naive, greedy, and narrow minded. In contrast, A would likely perceive D as vague, evasive, difficult to understand, and misleading. B would probably perceive C as formal, cold, overly serious, inflexible, and moralistic; while C would perceive B as manipulative, glib, and untrustworthy. An effective cross-cultural negotiator would need to anticipate these problems and avoid them through greater self-awareness and cultural insight.

Source: Gary M. Wederspahn, "The Fine Art of International Negotiation . . . It Can Really Make a World of Difference," *HRNews*, vol. 12 (January 1993), pp. C6–7.

conflict and hope it will eventually resolve itself. Because the sources of conflict are neither identified nor resolved, however, this strategy is seldom effective. Instead, the situation continues to worsen over time.

Physical Separation. If two combative groups are physically separated, the likelihood of open hostility and aggression are reduced. Unless the source of the conflict is eliminated, however, acts of sabotage and aggression may continue. Physical separation is generally an effective strategy only when the two groups do not need to interact and the separation eliminates the symptom of the conflict. If the two groups are required to interact, however, separating them only contributes to poorer performance.

Power Intervention Strategies

When two groups are unable to resolve the conflict on their own, some form of **power intervention strategies** may be used. The source of power may come from higher levels within the organization in the form of regulated interaction, or the power may come from political maneuvering by either of the groups.

Regulated Interaction. When the conflict becomes too great to ignore, higher-level managers may become irritated and impatient and try to resolve the conflict by authoritative command. "All right, you guys, that's the end of it, no more!" In addition to the unilateral decree that the conflict will go no further, the command may be accompanied by threats such as termination or transfer to a different group. Higher-level officers may also establish rules and procedures that limit the conflict to an acceptable level. This procedure, sometimes called *encapsulating* the conflict, occurs when managers establish specific rules and procedures regulating the interactions between the groups and defining their relationship.

Political Maneuvering. The two groups may decide to end the conflict by some form of political maneuvering in which one party attempts to accumulate sufficient power to force compliance on the other party. A democratic process is often used to settle the issue by bringing it to a vote. Both groups try to sway the outcome of the balloting by soliciting outside support and encouraging marginal opponents to defect to their side.

A difficulty with trying to encapsulate the conflict or vote on the issues is that these strategies typically tend to intensify win–lose situations. The source of the conflict has not been eliminated, and both parties feel a greater commitment to their position. Even after fair elections, the losers may feel resentment and continue to oppose the winners.

Diffusion Strategies

Diffusion strategies try to reduce the level of anger and emotion and buy time until the conflict between the two groups can be resolved. Diffusion strategies generally focus on surface issues rather than strike at the roots of the conflict. Three diffusion strategies have been used to reduce the level of emotion: smoothing, compromise, and identifying a common enemy.

Smoothing. The process of smoothing involves accentuating the similarities and common interests between the two groups and minimizing or rationalizing their differences. Stressing the similarities and common interests helps the groups see that their goals are not so far apart and there is something to be gained by working together. Although smoothing may help the groups realize they have common interests, it is only a short-term solution when it fails to resolve the basic underlying conflicts.

Compromise. Compromise strategies between two groups involve bargaining over the issues, and they require some degree of flexibility on the part of both sides. If the parties are so inflexible that they are not willing to concede, the negotiation will reach a stalemate and the conflict will continue. Once a compromise solution has been negotiated, the two groups should be able to work together harmoniously. Frequently, however, compromise decisions are inferior solutions, and neither side is happy with the settlement. With labor–management negotiations, for example, both sides may be unhappy with the current labor agreement, and even though they agree to live with it, they criticize each other and try to increase their power position for the next negotiations.

Identifying a Common Enemy. When two groups face a common enemy, they often develop a degree of cohesiveness between them as a means of protection. Differences of opinion and intergroup rivalry may be temporarily suspended while the two groups unite to defeat a common opponent. In the Robber's Cave experiment, the conflict between the two rival boys' groups was temporarily suspended by the challenge from another camp to an all-star baseball game. The best players from both sides were selected to form the all-star team, and the members of both groups directed their attention toward defeating the rival camp. In this experiment, however, it was noted that identifying a common enemy did not reduce the overall level of conflict. A high level of conflict still existed, but now it was directed at another source. When the common enemy was no longer present, the conflict between the two groups once again emerged. The conflict had not been resolved; it had only been suspended. Labor and management, for example, frequently face external threats in the form of foreign competition, government regulation, and declining sales. Although they may work together cooperatively in the face of these outside threats, the basic sources of the conflict have not been resolved, and conflict will soon reappear.

Resolution Strategies

The most effective method of resolving conflict is some form of **resolution strategy** that identifies the source of the conflict and resolves it. Research seems to indicate that resolution strategies are the most effective. One study investigated the conflict resolution styles of seventy-four managers. The least effective managers tended to ignore the conflict, while the most effective managers confronted the conflict directly by bringing the conflicting parties together to decide how to best meet the overall organizational goals.[37] Four types of resolution strategies include intergroup interaction, superordinate goals, problem solving, and structural change.

Intergroup Interaction. Since one of the consequences of intergroup conflict is a reduction in communication and interaction between groups, it would seem that bringing the groups together and increasing the contact between them would help to reduce the conflict. Unfortunately, when combative groups are brought together, the members of both groups are likely to use the occasion to demonstrate their loyalty for their own group and their dislike for the other. In the Robber's Cave experiment, for example, when the boys were required to eat together, rather than developing new friendships they used the occasion to express their hostility by throwing food.

Sometimes it is not good to bring warring groups together. A better strategy is to bring the leaders of both groups together to listen to the other group's position. When these discussions occur in private and the leaders are able to express their own opinions freely, the discussions are usually quite fruitful and represent an important first step in resolving the level of conflict. When the discussions are held in public, however, the leaders are expected to represent their own group. Consequently, the leaders are often more interested in looking good and impressing their constituents by being tough and combative rather than trying to resolve differences of opinion.

Another strategy is to exchange members for a period of time. Three members of the sales force, for example, could trade roles with three members of the credit department for a few weeks to help each group get a better understanding of the problems the other group faces. Another means of developing greater understanding is to share propaganda rather than members. For example, the members of each group could be asked to describe on paper their feelings toward the other group, along with a list of criticisms and suggestions. The groups could then exchange lists and respond to any questions or comments. This process of sharing information could continue until the emotional feelings are sufficiently diffused to allow the groups to work together in face-to-face problem solving.

Superordinate Goals. A superordinate goal is a goal that is more important to both parties than the relatively minor issues causing the conflict. In labor–management negotiations, for example, both sides may strongly disagree about the work rules and the number of paid vacation days but strongly agree about the survival of the company. If the company is unprofitable and cannot survive, work rules and paid vacations become meaningless issues. Using superordinate goals to resolve conflict involves three conditions. First, the groups must perceive their mutual dependency on each other; second, the superordinate goal must be highly desired by each group; and third, both groups must expect to be rewarded for accomplishing the goal.

Working to achieve a superordinate goal is a powerful motivation for the groups to resolve their basic differences and work together cooperatively. In the Robber's Cave experiment, for example, a series of superordinate goals were created. These goals were important to both groups and required joint cooperation such as fixing a break in the camp water supply, selecting a movie, pushing a stalled truck supplying camp food, and preparing a joint meal. By cooperating in these tasks, the level of tension and hostility between the two groups was reduced and feelings of cooperation and friendship were created.

Problem Solving. A joint problem-solving session is an effective resolution strategy if the two groups focus their attention on the problem rather than arguing about who is right or wrong or using the situation to get even. A problem-solving session usually involves a face-to-face meeting of the conflicting groups to identify the source of the problem and develop alternative solutions for solving it. This strategy is most effective when a thorough analysis of the problem can be made, when points of mutual interest are identified, and when alternatives are suggested and carefully explored. The disadvantage of this strategy is that it requires a great deal of time and commitment. Furthermore, if the conflict originates from value-laden issues and if people are emotionally involved, the tension may prevent them from progressing satisfactorily to an acceptable solution.[38]

Structural Change. Conflicts are frequently caused, or at least encouraged, by the way an organization is structured. Creating a marketing department, for example, means that a group of people will work together to solve marketing problems and plan a marketing strategy. As they become more specialized in their marketing functions, they will focus to a greater extent on marketing goals and disregard the goals of other departments. Other specialized groups in the organization develop an equally narrow focus. Some groups become so highly specialized, in fact, that they lose sight of the organization's goals and focus exclusively on their own group goals. Furthermore, the reward structures in organizations frequently recognize and reward group members for pursuing their group goals rather than organizational goals.

In these situations, an effective strategy for reducing conflict is to change the organizational structure. By emphasizing total organizational effectiveness rather than group effectiveness, cooperation rather than competition can be promoted.[39] Groups can be recognized and rewarded for their contribution to the effectiveness of other groups, and altruistic behavior across group lines can be encouraged. By reorganizing the departments and establishing clear, operational, and feasible goals for the organization, the source of conflict can be removed. For example, members of a marketing department could be assigned to specific projects so that they feel an allegiance not only to the marketing department but also to other departments and programs.

CREATING FUNCTIONAL CONFLICT

An earlier section suggested that there is an optimal level of conflict for each organization. While some organizations experience too much conflict, others would be more productive with more conflict. As conflict increases, individuals typically experience greater arousal and levels of motivation. Therefore, in a lethargic organization where ideas have become stale and behavior has become routine, greater conflict may be needed to generate creative ideas and motivate people to higher levels of performance. Four of the most popular methods for creating functional conflict in organizations include altering the communication flow, creating competition, altering the organizational structure, and recruiting outside experts.

Altering the Communication Flow. Information is a source of power in organizations, and conflict can be created by sharing or withholding information, especially if it is evaluative information. Managers rely on the information they receive to assess the performance of their group. This information may or may not be shared with other group members. Higher levels of conflict and concern for the performance of the group can be created by altering the communication flow so that group members know how well they have performed and what is expected of them.

Higher performance expectations can be created by showing groups how well they perform relative to other groups in the organization or by simply suggesting that they should do better. Some managers use the informal grapevine to create conflict by leaking confidential information and false rumors. Leaking false information, however, is not recommended because of its long-term consequence of destroying confidence.

Creating Competition. A competitive environment can be created by offering rewards to the individual or group with the best performance. If they are used properly, financial incentives and other extrinsic rewards can maintain a healthy atmosphere of competition that contributes to functional conflict. The rewards offered to the winners need to be sufficiently attractive and probable to motivate high performance, while those who lose should not feel that their defeat is a catastrophic loss.

Altering Organizational Structure. As noted earlier, an organization can be structured in a way that either stimulates or reduces conflict. As a general rule, higher levels of conflict occur when groups become smaller and more highly specialized, because the members tend to focus more exclusively on their group goals. Dividing a large group into smaller, specialized subgroups, for example, would create a situation more conducive to conflict, because each group would be competing for resources, materials, and clients.

Recruiting Outside Experts. Promotion-from-within policies have been criticized as inbreeding because new managers tend to follow old procedures that lead to stale thinking and a lack of creativity and imagination. To avoid the problem of inbreeding, organizations should recruit outside experts who will challenge established procedures and stimulate new thinking. Rather than promoting the best faculty member to be the new dean, for example, some business schools have recruited an executive from industry who can think about business education and the role of the business school much differently. An effective program that has been operating for several years allows faculty members and federal government employees to exchange places temporarily to stimulate new ideas both in government agencies and in academic institutions.

SUMMARY

1. The relationships between individuals and groups vary along a continuum representing different degrees of concern for others versus self-interest. Four points can be identified along this continuum: conflict, competition, cooperation, and altruism.

2. Competitive interactions are unusually prevalent in our Western civilization, even though competition has been highly criticized. Although competition reduces interpersonal attraction, it increases motivation and contributes to higher productivity on independent tasks. The effects of competition on satisfaction depend on the outcomes of the competition and whether the overall experience is rewarding or punishing.

3. Altruism is behavior that is intended to help others without compensation to the helper. People are more inclined to behave altruistically

when they feel a personal sense of responsibility for providing assistance, when they see others model helping behavior, when they have a clear perception of the need to render assistance, and when the person they are helping is similar to themselves.

4. Coalitions are a form of cooperation in which two or more parties agree to cooperate to achieve a majority. Two theories attempt to predict which parties will form a coalition: the minimum resource theory and the bargaining theory of coalitions. Both theories assume that coalitions are formed to increase the rewards to the winners. The first theory focuses on the potential resources each individual can contribute, and the latter theory focuses on the way the rewards are allocated.

5. A cohesive group consists of people who are highly attracted to the group and value their group membership. Group cohesiveness increases when people feel a strong interpersonal attraction for one another, when they interact more frequently, when their initiation into the group is more rigorous, when they agree on the group's goals, when the group is successful, and when there are outside threats forcing them to work together as a group.

6. Highly cohesive groups elicit greater participation from their members, demand greater conformity to group norms, and are generally more successful. Although highly cohesive groups are often more productive, they may also be rather unproductive if the group goals do not coincide with the organization's goals.

7. Although conflict is normally considered undesirable, some forms of conflict contribute to organizational effectiveness by raising levels of motivation and forcing decisions to be considered more carefully. Although we typically think conflict is dysfunctional to the organization, some forms of organizational conflict are functional.

8. Three of the most popular methods of studying conflict include the prisoner's dilemma game, the trucking company game, and observing interacting groups. These studies indicate that the most common causes of intergroup conflict include task interdependence, goal incompatibility, the use of threats, intergroup interaction, and the formation of win–lose attitudes in either group.

9. When two groups are engaged in intergroup conflict, predictable changes occur both within the group and between the groups. The changes that occur within each group include increased cohesiveness, increased loyalty, a rise in autocratic leadership, and inflated evaluations of the group's activities. The changes that occur between groups include a decrease in intergroup communication, distorted perceptions of the other group, and negative stereotypes of the opponent.

10. The major strategies for dealing with conflict can be classified into four categories: avoidance strategies, power intervention strategies, diffusion strategies, and resolution strategies. Avoidance strategies include ignoring the conflict or physically separating the two groups. Power intervention strategies include having upper management attempt to regulate the interaction, and political maneuvering among the two groups to resolve the conflict by a vote. Diffusion strategies include smoothing over the conflict, developing a compromise solution, and identifying a common enemy to distract the combative groups. Resolution strategies include having the two groups interact more frequently, developing a superordinate goal, changing the structure of the organization, and engaging in a joint problem-solving session to identify and eliminate the causes of the conflict.

11. Four of the most popular methods for stimulating conflict include altering the communication flow to raise expectations, creating competition within the organization, altering the organizational structure to create more highly specialized groups, and recruiting outside experts to bring fresh ideas.

DISCUSSION QUESTIONS

1. Compared to some Asian cultures, Western civilization is extremely competitive. Do you agree with those who say that competition is unhealthy and should be eliminated? Why or why not?

2. What are the different forms of competition that you have observed in schools, businesses, neighborhoods, and families? Which competitive situations should be changed to cooperative situations?

3. Should managers expect employees to behave altruistically in organizations? What can be done to obtain greater altruism in an organization?

4. How important is cohesiveness to athletic teams? Is cohesiveness important for the effectiveness of work groups? Identify a group to which you belong, and describe your recommendations for making that group more cohesive.

5. Explain the differences between functional and dysfunctional conflict. Describe two situations illustrating when conflict is functional and when it is dysfunctional.

6. The Robber's Cave experiment found that simply separating individuals into two different groups was sufficient to create intergroup conflict. What are the group dynamics that contribute to intergroup conflict? Is conflict between two interacting groups (fraternities, work groups, student groups) inevitable?

7. Suppose you were a member of a group and discovered that the group was unnecessarily creating a win–lose attitude toward an opposing group. What would you try to do to change your group orientation from a win–lose conflict to a win–win situation?

8. Describe a situation you have observed that demonstrates the spiraling escalation of conflict. The conflict situation could be between two nations, two student groups, or two individuals. How did the conflict start and why is it being perpetuated?

9. Which conflict resolution strategies would you recommend for the following situations: (a) two adjacent fraternities disagree about the use of the parking lot between them; (b) union and management representatives discontinued negotiations and the union has been on strike for two weeks; (c) two countries, such as Ecuador and Peru or Israel and Syria, have a border dispute between them; (d) a disagreement between roommates regarding dirty dishes being left in the kitchen.

10. What conditions indicate a need for greater conflict? Describe a situation where increased conflict would be functional and suggest a strategy for stimulating greater conflict.

GLOSSARY

altruism Behavior intended to help someone else with no expectation of an immediate extrinsic reward for helping.

avoidance strategies A method of responding to conflict situations by either ignoring the conflict or separating the conflicting parties.

bargaining theory of coalitions A theory explaining coalition formation that is based on the outcomes of negotiations between the parties as they attempt to maximize their rewards.

coalition Cooperation between two or more parties to achieve a majority vote.

cohesiveness The degree of interpersonal attraction of group members for each other and for membership in the group.

competition An interaction between two or more parties in which the parties cannot meet their goals simultaneously. The success of one individual or group prevents other groups or individuals from being successful.

conflict Interaction between individuals and groups in which each one attempts to defeat, destroy, or inflict damage on the other because of mutually exclusive goals or values.

cooperation The relationship that exists between two or more individuals who both benefit from working together and share the benefits of their joint efforts.

diffusion strategies A conflict resolution method that tries to reduce the emotional anger by either smoothing over the disagreement, developing a compromise, or creating a common enemy to distract attention.

dysfunctional conflict Any interaction between two parties that hinders or destroys the achievement of organizational or group goals.

functional conflict Conflict that contributes to the effectiveness of the organization by increasing motivation or improving the quality of decision making.

minimum-resource theory An explanation for the formation of coalitions that focuses on the relative resources contributed by each party.

mixed-motive conflict A situation in which an individual can either compete to maximize his or her personal gains or cooperate to maximize the joint gains.

organizational citizenship behavior (OCB) When an employee voluntarily helps other employees with no promise of reward. Behaviors directed toward helping individuals are also called *altruism* while behaviors directed toward helping the organization are called *compliance.*

pooled interdependence An additive group task that does not require group members to coordinate their efforts; instead, their individual efforts are simply summed or pooled to form the group product.

power intervention strategies A method of responding to conflict by having higher-level management impose a solution or political maneuvering among the conflicting members to obtain a majority vote.

prisoner's dilemma game A method of studying conflict by asking subjects to make either a competitive or a cooperative choice in a mixed-motive game.

reciprocal interdependence A conjunctive group task in which each member of the group is mutually dependent upon each of the other members of the group and successful task completion can be obtained only if each member does his or her part.

resolution strategies A method of trying to resolve conflict by identifying the cause of the problem through problem solving, removing the cause of the conflict by a structural change, or by creating a higher-level goal that requires cooperation.

sequential interdependence Situation in which the task structure is similar to an assembly line in which the performance of later groups depends upon the performance of earlier groups.

zero-sum conflict A type of conflict where the gains to one party represent losses to the other. For one party to win, the other must lose.

NOTES

1. Karen Horney, *New Ways in Psychoanalysis* (New York: Norton, 1939), p. 173.

2. Motion A. Deutsch, "Experimental Study on the Effects of Cooperation and Competition upon Group Processes," *Human Relations,* vol. 2 (1949), pp. 199–231.

3. L. K. Miller and R. L. Hamblin, "Interdependence, Differential Rewarding and Productivity," *American Sociological Review,* vol. 28 (1963), pp. 768–777.

4. David J. Cherrington, "Satisfaction in Competitive Conditions," *Organizational Behavior and Human Performance,* vol. 10 (1973), pp. 47–71.

5. Stephen Worchel and Joel Cooper, *Understanding Social Psychology,* 3rd ed. (Homewood, Ill.: Dorsey Press, 1983), chap. 8.

6. Larry J. Williams and Stella E. Anderson, "Job Satisfaction and Organizational Commitment as Predictors of Organizational Citizenship and In-Role Behavior," *Journal of Management,* vol. 17 (September 1991), pp. 601–617.

7. Jennifer M. George, "State or Trait: Affects of Positive Mode on Pro-Social Behaviors at Work," *Journal of Applied Psychology,* vol. 76 (1991), pp. 299–308.

8. Jiing-Lih Farh, Philip M. Podsakoff, and Dennis W. Organ, "Accounting for Organizational Citizenship Behavior: Leader Fairness and Task Scope Vs. Satisfaction," *Journal of Management,* vol. 16 (1990), pp. 705–721; Dennis W. Organ and Mary Konovsky, "Cognitive Vs. Affective Determinants of Organizational Citizenship Behavior," *Journal of Applied Psychology,* vol. 74 (1989), pp. 157–164.

9. Jon L. Pearce and Hal B. Gregersen, "Task Interdependence and Extrarole Behavior: a Test of the Mediating Affects of Felt Responsibility," *Journal of Applied Psychology,* vol. 76 (1991), pp. 838–844.

10. B. Latané and J. M. Darley, "Bystander Intervention in Emergencies," in J. R. Macaulay and L. Berkowitz (eds.), *Altruism and Helping Behavior* (New York: Academic Press, 1970), pp. 13–27.

11. P. Moriarty, "Crime, Commitment, and the Responsive Bystander: Two Field Experiments," *Journal of Personality and Social Psychology*, vol. 31 (1975), pp. 370–376.

12. Charlotte O. Phelps, "Caring and Family Income," *Journal of Economic Behavior and Organization*, vol. 10 (July 1988), pp. 63–96.

13. Lynette S. Unger, "Altruism as a Motivation to Volunteer," *Journal of Economic Psychology*, vol. 12 (March 1991), pp. 71–100.

14. J. H. Bryan and M. A. Test, "Models and Helping: Naturalistic Studies in Aiding Behavior," *Journal of Personality and Social Psychology*, vol. 6 (1967), pp. 400–407.

15. J. R. Macaulay, "A Shill for Charity," in J. R. Macaulay and L. Berkowitz, *Altruism and Helping Behavior* (New York: Academic Press, 1970), pp. 43–59.

16. J. M. Darley and C. D. Batson, "'From Jerusalem to Jericho': A Study of Situational and Dispositional Variables in Helping Behavior," *Journal of Personality and Social Psychology*, vol. 27 (1973), pp. 100–108.

17. D. L. Krebs, "Altruism—An Examination of the Concept and a Review of the Literature," *Psychological Bulletin*, vol. 73 (1970), pp. 258–302.

18. Jennifer M. George and Kenneth Bettenhausen, "Understanding Pro-Social Behavior, Sales Performance, and Turnover: A Group-Level Analysis in a Service Context," *Journal of Applied Psychology*, vol. 75 (1990), pp. 698–709.

19. W. A. A. Gamson, "A Theory of Coalition Formation," *American Sociological Review*, vol. 26 (1961), pp. 373–382.

20. W. A. A. Gamson, "Experimental Studies of Coalition Formation," in L. Berkowitz (ed.), *Advances in Experimental Social Psychology*, vol. 1 (New York: Academic Press, 1964).

21. J. M. Chertkoff and J. K. Esser, "A Test of Three Theories of Coalition Formation When Agreements Can Be Short-term or Long-term," *Journal of Experimental Social Psychology*, vol. 35 (1977), pp. 237–249; S. S. Komorita and J. M. Chertkoff, "A Bargaining Theory of Coalition Formation," *Psychological Review*, vol. 80 (1973), pp. 149–162; Michael H. Morris, Gordon W. Paul, and Don Rahtz, "Organizational Rewards and Coalition in the Industrial Buying Center," *International of Research and Marketing*, vol. 4 (1987), pp. 131–146.

22. E. Van de Vilert, "Siding and Other Reactions to a Conflict: A Theory of Escalation Toward Outsiders," *Journal of Conflict Resolution*, vol. 25 (1981), pp. 495–520; Anthony J. Venables, "Customs Union and Tariff Reform and Imperfect Competition," *European Economic Review*, vol. 31 (February–March 1987), pp. 103–110.

23. A. J. Lott and B. E. Lott, "Group Cohesiveness as Interpersonal Attraction: A Review of Relationships with Antecedent and Consequent Variables," *Psychological Bulletin*, vol. 64 (1965), pp. 259–309.

24. Jean M. Williams and Colleen Hacker, "Casual Relationships Among Cohesion, Satisfaction, and Performance in Women's Intercollegiate Field Hockey Teams," *Journal of Sports Psychology*, vol. 4 (1982), pp. 324–337.

25. Ralph M. Stogdill, "Group Productivity, Drive, and Cohesiveness," *Organizational Behavior and Human Performance*, vol. 8 (1972), pp. 26–43.

26. J. Hall and M. S. Williams, "A Comparison of Decision Making Performance in Established and Ad Hoc Groups," *Journal of Personality and Social Psychology*, vol. 3 (February 1966), pp. 217–222; L. R. Hoffman and N. R. F. Maier, "Quality and Acceptance of Problem Solutions by Members of Homogeneous and Heterogeneous Groups," *Journal of Abnormal and Social Psychology*, vol. 62 (April 1961), pp. 401–407.

27. Jeffrey Pfeffer, *Power in Organizations* (Marshfield, Mass.: Pitman, 1981), especially chap. 5.

28. William E. Scott, Jr., "Activation Theory and Task Design," *Organizational Behavior and Human Performance*, vol. 1 (1966), pp. 3–30.

29. L. D. Luce and H. Raiffa, *Games and Decisions: Introduction and Critical Survey* (New York: Wiley, 1957).

30. Morton Deutsch and Robert Krauss, "The Effect of Threat Upon Interpersonal Bargaining," *Journal of Abnormal and Social Psychology*, vol. 61 (1960), pp. 181–189.

31. Muzafer Sherif, O. J. Harvey, B. J. White, W. R. Hood, and Carolyn W. Sherif, *Intergroup Conflict and Cooperation: The Robber's Cave Experiment* (Norman, Okla.: Institute of Group Relations, University of Oklahoma, 1961).

32. See additional studies by Morton Deutsch, D. Canavan, and J. Rubin, "The Effects of Size of Conflict and Sex of Experimenter upon Interpersonal Bargaining," *Journal of Experimental Psychology*, vol. 7 (1971), pp. 258–267; S. C. Freedman, "Threats, Promises, and Coalitions: A Study of Compliance and Retaliation in a Simulated Organizational Setting," *Journal of Applied Social Psychology*, vol. 11 (1981), pp. 114–136.

33. G. H. Shure, R. J. Meeker, and E. A. Hansford, "The Effectiveness of Pacifist Strategies in Bargaining Games," *Journal of Conflict Resolution*, vol. 9 (1965), pp. 106–117; L. Solomon, "The Influence of Some Types of Power Relationships and Game Strategy upon the Development of Interpersonal Trust," *Journal of Abnormal and Social Psychology*, vol. 61 (1960), pp. 223–230; Friedel Bolle and Peter Ockenfels, "Prisoners' Dilemma as a Game with Incomplete Information," *Journal of Economic Psychology*, vol. 11 (March 1990), pp. 69–84.

34. C. P. Swingle (ed.), *The Structure of Conflict* (New York: Academic Press, 1970).

35. James E. Driskell and Eduardo Salas, "Group Decision-Making Under Stress," *Journal of Applied Psychology*, vol. 76 (1991), pp. 473–478.

36. Walter F. Daves and C. L. Holland, "The Structure of Conflict Behavior of Managers Assessed with Self- and Subordinate Ratings," *Human Relations,* vol. 42 (1989), pp. 741–756; Ronald C. Phillips, "Manage Differences: Before They Destroy Your Business," *Training and Development Journal,* vol. 42 (September 1988), pp. 66–71; Charles R. Schwenk, "Effects of Devil's Advocacy and Dialectical Inquiry on Decision-Making: A Meta-Analysis," *Organizational Behavior and Human Decision Processes,* vol. 47 (October 1990), pp. 161–176; Arthur Sondak, "What's Your Conflict Barometer?" *Supervisory Management,* vol. 35 (May 1990), pp. 1–2.

37. Ronald J. Burke, "Methods of Resolving Superior–Subordinate Conflict: The Constructive Use of Subordinate Differences," *Organizational Behavior and Human Performance,* vol. 5 (1970), pp. 393–411.

38. Marshall Scott Poole, Michael Holmes, and Gerardine DeSanctis, "Conflict Management in a Computer-Supported Meeting Environment," *Management Science,* vol. 37 (August 1991), pp. 926–953; Daniel Robey, Dana L. Farrow, and Charles R. Franz, "Group Process and Conflict in System Development," *Management Science,* vol. 35 (October 1989), pp. 1172–1191.

39. Richard A. Cosier and Dan R. Dalton, "Competition and Cooperation: Effects of Value Dissensus and Predisposition to Help," *Human Relations,* vol. 41 (1988), pp. 823–839.

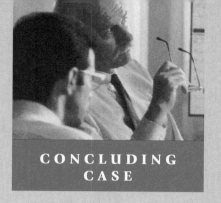

TOMAHAWK INDUSTRIES

Tomahawk Industries manufactures motor boats primarily used for water skiing. During the summer months, a third production line is normally created to help meet the heavy summer demand. This third line is usually created by assigning the experienced workers to all three lines and hiring college students who are home for summer vacation to complete the crews. In the past, however, experienced workers resented having to break up their teams to form a third line. They also resented having to work with a bunch of college kids and complained that they were slow, stubborn know-it-alls.

The foreman, Dan Jensen, decided to try a different strategy this summer and have all the college students work on the new line. He asked Mark Allen to supervise the new crew because Mark claimed that he knew everything about boats and could perform every job "with my eyes closed." Mark was happy to accept the new job and participated in selecting his own crew. Mark's crew was called "the Greek Team" because all the college students were members of a fraternity or sorority.

Mark spent many hours in training to get his group running at full production. The college students learned quickly, and by the end of June their production rate was up to standard, with an error rate that was only slightly above normal. To simplify the learning process, Dan Jensen had assigned the Greek Team long production runs to work on. These runs generally consisted of thirty to forty units that were exactly the same, and thus the train-ing period was minimized and errors were reduced. Shorter production runs were assigned to the experienced teams.

By the middle of July, a substantial rivalry had been created between the Greek Team and the older workers. At first the rivalry was good-natured, but after a few weeks, the older workers became resentful of the remarks made by the college students. The Greek Team often met its production schedules with time to spare at the end of the day for goofing around. It wasn't uncommon for someone from the Greek Team to go to another line pretending to look for materials and give the other workers a hard time. The experienced workers resented having to perform all the shorter production runs and began to retaliate with sabotage. They would sneak over during breaks and hide tools, dent materials, install something crooked, and in other small ways do something that would slow production for the Greek Team.

Dan Jensen was pleased with his decision to form a separate crew from the college students, but as he began to hear the reports of sabotage and rivalry, he became very concerned. Because of complaints from the experienced workers, Dan Jensen equalized the production requirements so that the types of production runs were equally distributed among all the crews. The rivalry, however, did not stop. Even after the distribution of production runs was equalized, the Greek Team continued to finish early and flaunt their performance in front of the other crews.

One day the Greek Team suspected that one of their assemblies was going to be sabotaged during the lunch break by one of the experienced crews. By skillful deception, they were able to substitute an assembly from the other experienced line for theirs. By the end of the lunch period, the Greek Team was laughing wildly because of their deception, while one experienced crew was very angry with the other one.

Dan Jensen decided that the situation had to be changed and announced that the job assignments between the different crews would be shuffled. The employees were told that when they appeared for work the next morning, the names of the workers assigned to each crew would be posted on the bulletin board. The announcement was not greeted with much enthusiasm, and Mark Allen decided to stay late to try to talk Dan out of his idea. Mark didn't believe the rivalry was serious enough for this type of action, and he suspected that many of the college students would quit if their team was broken up.

Questions

1. Is the relationship between the teams healthy competition or unhealthy conflict?

2. What are the reasons for the conflict, and how could the conditions be changed to reduce the conflict?

3. Is reassigning members to the different teams a useful way to resolve the conflict? What types of consequences will this likely create?

CONFLICT AND COLLABORATION—INTERGROUP EXERCISE

In many situations, two opposing sides will perpetuate a conflict, even though both sides know that neither side will win and that continued conflict can only increase the costs to both sides. Usually the conflict is perpetuated by a lack of trust in the other side. The purpose of this exercise is to illustrate the difficulty of developing a cooperative relationship between two teams, and to show how difficult it is to establish a spirit of trust once the relationship has been violated. In this exercise, two teams of students have to decide whether the relationship between them will be cooperative or competitive.

Directions. Divide the class into an even number of teams of three or four individuals each; each team should be paired with another team. A referee-timekeeper should be assigned to each pair of teams. Each team sets up its treasury and appoints a treasurer who collects and keeps track of team funds. The referee-timekeeper will collect funds from each team treasurer and establish the bank.

Each team takes fifteen minutes to (1) read these directions and ask questions; (2) appoint two negotiators who can be changed at any time by a majority vote; and (3) plan team strategy.

Each team member provides seventy-five cents; twenty-five cents is used for the bank and fifty cents is used to help establish the team's own treasury. Your treasury's money will be divided among your team's members at the end of the game. Bank money will *not* be returned at the end of the game.

1. This exercise involves two teams, each trying to win as much money from each other and/or the bank as possible.

2. Each team has ten weapons represented by ten cards. A card with its "X" side up is an active weapon. A card with its "X" side down is an inactive weapon. Each team begins the game with all ten cards in an active state. Cards should not be visible to the opposing team.

3. A total game consists of five moves. During each move a team may change two, one, or no weapons from an active position to an inactive position, or *vice versa*. Two total games are planned for the exercise.

4. A team has two minutes to make each move. If the team fails to decide on a move within that time, no cards will be turned. Referees will signal when moves are to begin and end.

5. At the end of each move, a team may (but does not have to) "attack" the other team. When an "attack" is called, the game ends. The team with fewer active weapons will pay to its opponents five cents per person for each active weapon it has less than the active weapons held by the other team.

6. If neither team is attacked by the end of the fifth move, the game is over.

7. At the end of the game, each team receives two cents per person from the bank for each inactive weapon. Conversely, each team pays the bank two cents per person for each active weapon.

8. Each team should appoint two negotiators who must meet with negotiators from the other team after the first and fourth moves. A team may also request negotiations at the end of any other move. The request may be either accepted or rejected by the other team. Negotiations take place on neutral territory and can last no longer than three minutes. Negotiators may or may not bargain in good faith. Teams are not bound by agreements made by their negotiators.

■ Organizational Theory
■ Organizational Structure and Design

ORGANIZATIONS

P revious sections have examined organizational behavior at the individual and group levels of analysis. This section moves to the next level of analysis and examines organizational behavior at the organizational level. It answers such questions as "What is an organization?" "What makes an organization effective?" "What is organizational structure?" and "What is the best way to structure an organization?"

The concept of an organization is usually the most difficult concept for students in an introductory organizational behavior class to understand for two reasons. First, we are not accustomed to thinking at an organizational level of abstraction. We are aware of individual differences and we have observed group dynamics, but organizational processes and structure are more abstract and more unfamiliar. Second, organizations are not physical objects that we can touch or feel. They are systems of activities, with subsystems that perform essential functions enabling the organization to survive and grow. If an organization were composed of something physical like buildings, organization charts, machines, or people, it would be easy to observe. But because it consists of nonphysical structures such as patterned activities and reporting relationships, it is more difficult to understand.

Chapter 11 uses open-systems theory to answer the question "What is an organization?" Open-systems theory explains the common characteristics of all social organizations, including manufacturing companies, service organizations, government agencies, religions, and voluntary associations. Chapter 11 also describes organizational culture and explains how culture influences attitudes and behavior.   ·

Chapter 12 describes organizational structure and design. When managers design an organization, they must decide how to arrange the jobs into meaningful departments and how the efforts of these departments will be coordinated. These structural decisions have a profound impact on organizational effectiveness and often make the difference between surviving and dying. Unfortunately, there are no universal principles to follow in designing an organization. The best organizational structure depends on the situation. Chapter 12 identifies some of the most important situational variables and explains their influence on design decisions.

Organizational Theory

LEARNING OBJECTIVES

After studying this chapter, you should be able to

1. Define open-systems theory, and identify the common characteristics of all social systems.

2. Describe the five subsystems of an organization, and provide an illustration of each.

3. Describe the institutional function of an organization, and identify the environmental sectors with which the organization must interact.

4. Describe the effects of environmental uncertainty on organizations, and explain how organizations reduce some of the uncertainty.

5. Identify the major criteria used to assess organizational effectiveness.

6. Describe the difference between official goals and operational goals, and explain why goals are important to an organization.

7. Define organizational culture and organizational climate, and explain the differences between them.

8. Describe the differences between type A and type Z cultures.

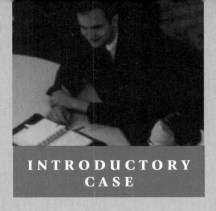

RETIREES: A NEW STAKEHOLDER

As part of an early retirement incentive, General Motors promised employees 55 years of age and older that they would receive low-cost medical coverage for life. When medical costs increased, General Motors decided it would be necessary to require the retirees to pay part of the benefits costs. To prevent this change, 84,000 retirees sued GM. Primerica Holding Incorporated was also sued by its 2,500 retirees when it attempted to raise the monthly cost of their health plan insurance from $5 to $50.

These lawsuits raise the question of where an organization's responsibilities end. Are retirees stakeholders, and do they have a legitimate ongoing interest in the company? Stakeholders are the groups of people who have a vital interest in the well-being of an organization and how it operates, because its operations somehow have a noticeable effect on their lives.

The latest stakeholders to attract attention are retirees. These people formerly worked for the organization and then left. But even though they are retired, they still expect to receive benefits and services from the organization and federal legislation has endorsed their expectations. Companies are not required to provide medical benefits; but if they do federal law requires companies to offer retirees the option of continuing their benefit coverage for at least 30 months, and some companies have promised coverage for life.

These promises have become a major financial strain to some companies. In these companies, retirees represent an enormous liability from a very large group that is getting larger. General Motors spends about $1 billion annually to pay for its retirees' health care costs. The bill is funded by General Motor's labor force of about 400,000, which is about the same size as its retiree population. Funding this bill in the future looks grim. Labor force reductions, early retirement incentives, and growing medical costs will make it very difficult for General Motors to meet its retirees' expectations in the future.

Growing militancy among retirees has forced companies to be much more careful in the promises they make to their employees and the kinds of incentives they offer for early retirement. Retirees are a not-to-be-ignored stakeholder group who represent a large unfunded liability for some companies threatening their financial health and future profitability.

Questions

1. Should retirees still be considered members of an organization? What obligations should an organization have to its former employees?

2. Is it possible or meaningful to define who is "in" versus "not in" an organization? Do organizations have boundaries?

Source: Susan B. Garland, "The Retiring Kind Are Getting Militant About Benefits," *Business Week* (May 28, 1990), p. 29.

Previous chapters have examined organizational behavior at the individual and group levels of analysis. This chapter moves to the next level of analysis and examines organizational behavior at the organizational level. It answers such questions as "What is an organization?" "What makes an organization effective?" "What is organizational structure?" and "What is the best way to structure an organization?"

For two reasons, the concept of an organization is usually the most difficult concept for students in an introductory organizational class to understand. First, we are not accustomed to thinking at an organizational level of abstraction. We are aware of individual differences and we have observed group dynamics, but organizational processes and structure are more abstract and more unfamiliar. Second, organizations are not physical objects that we can touch or feel. They are systems of activities, with subsystems that perform essential functions enabling the organization to survive and grow. If an organization were composed of something physical like buildings, organization charts, machines, or people, it would be easy to observe. But because it consists of nonphysical structures such as patterned activities and reporting relationships, it is more difficult to understand.

This chapter uses open-systems theory to answer the question, "What is an organization?" Open-systems theory explains the common characteristics of all social organizations, including manufacturing companies, service organizations, government agencies, religions, and voluntary associations.

OPEN-SYSTEMS THEORY

Organizations are hard to see even though we are surrounded by them and interact with them in almost everything we do. We are largely unaware of the complex organizations that provide the basic goods and services we have come to expect in our society. The food we buy at the supermarket is not provided by just one chain of food stores but by a complex combination of corporate farms, food-processing companies, transportation companies, and government agencies. Likewise, the gas that we buy at the corner station depends upon a complex web of national and international organizations that manufacture oil-drilling equipment, drill for oil, transport it, refine it, and market the products. Even simple activities like registering a car or renewing a driver's license require the coordinated efforts of large public organizations.

How well these organizations function has a significant influence on the quality of our lives. Inefficient organizations can create an enormous amount of inconvenience and unhappiness. We tend to attribute many of the problems caused by an inefficient organizational structure to a lack of motivation or leadership on the part of individuals. For example, consider the problem of the secretary who wanted to purchase a metal bookshelf for her office similar to the one she had bought for herself on sale for $39. Since the cost exceeded $25, she could not simply take the money out of petty cash and buy it herself. Following the correct procedures was almost impossible. Because the bookshelf was capital equipment and it had not been budgeted, the purchasing department could not accept her purchase order until another form with three signatures was obtained, authorizing the exception through the accounting department. Finally, in frustration the secretary took $25 from petty cash and paid the remainder herself to get the bookshelf before the sale ended. The hassle of buying a new bookshelf was so unpleasant that the secretary believed the accounting and purchasing staffs were consciously refusing to cooperate. In reality, however, both staffs were only trying to follow the proper procedures. The problem wasn't a lack of cooperation or motivation; the problem was the organizational structure.

Defining an Organization

When asked to define an organization, most students provide a definition that is largely useless and misleading. For example, an organization is often defined as "a group of people with a common goal who are all working together." This definition contains three elements: a group, a common goal, and working together. As we will see later, these three elements are misleading. Members have their own motives, and they are not equivalent to a "common goal." And to say that they are all working together would contradict the idea of a division of labor and would be true only in a limited way. Trying to distinguish between those who are "in" and those who are "not in" the organization overlooks the open nature of organizations, an important characteristic related to the fact that people are continually joining and leaving organizations. Furthermore, some people who would probably not be included in the organization make valuable contributions, such as recruiters, talent scouts, lobbyists, alumni, and members of the board of directors.

Some people believe an organization is defined by an organization chart showing the departments and their reporting relationships. Others think an organization is best described by a mission statement explaining the purpose of the organization. Although organization charts and mission statements are useful management tools, neither they nor other physical objects, such as buildings, campuses, machines, or refineries, properly focus our attention on the essential characteristics defining an organization.

An organization is best described as an open social system that consists of the patterned activities of a group of people that tend to be goal directed.[1] This definition contains three key elements: an open social system, patterned activities, and goal-directed behavior. Viewing an organization as a system of structured activities is especially useful when diagnosing organizational problems or analyzing the competitive advantages of a firm. Effective organizations consist of smoothly functioning patterned activities that occur at predictable times with a minimum of ongoing guidance or direction. People who think of an organization as a system of patterned activities are best prepared to identify organizational problems and opportunities.

What Is a System? To understand an organization, it must be viewed as a system. A *system* is a set of interrelated elements that acquires inputs from the environment, transforms them into some form of useful output, and discharges the outputs to the external environment. The idea of a system is generally a difficult concept for students to grasp. It is easier to understand how an organization is a system by examining other types of systems.

Kenneth Boulding describes different types of systems and arranges them in order from simple to complex.[2] Four levels of systems are illustrated in Exhibit 11.1. The simplest system is a *framework system,* such as an atom, a bridge, or a building. Simple framework systems may include some form of movement among the

EXHIBIT 11.1   Hierarchy of Systems

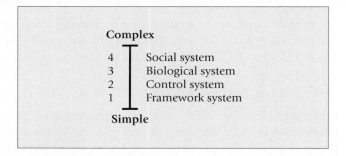

elements, but this movement is predictable like the motions of a clock. The second level of complexity is a self-regulating *control system.* Thermostats and other types of machine systems that can be regulated, such as assembly lines or oil refineries, are illustrations of control systems.

The third level of complexity is a *biological system,* which is a living, self-maintaining system. Plants and animal systems are far more complex than either framework or control systems. Plants and animals exchange resources with the environment and can adapt on their own to changes in the environment. These biological systems also contain subsystems that form the biological system. In fact, the human body is a useful analogy to help students understand the systems concepts. The human body consists of a series of subsystems that support the body and allow it to function, such as the respiratory, digestive, excretory, muscular, and skeletal systems. These subsystems interact in a predictable way to allow the organism to survive. The circulatory system, for example, obtains oxygen from the respiratory system and delivers it throughout the body for the muscular system to use. A breakdown in any system could result in serious illness or even death.

The most complex system is a *social system.* Social systems incorporate forms of complexity beyond machines and biological systems. This complexity explains why organizations cannot be designed to be like machines that are simply turned on and allowed to run without further direction. Social systems exist within a changing social environment that requires them to adapt to new demands.

Open Versus Closed Systems. All social systems are open systems. However, this statement is not very meaningful unless we contrast open systems with closed systems. A closed system does not depend on its environment; it is autonomous and isolated from the outside world. It has all the energy it needs and can function without consuming external resources. Many studies of organizational behavior have examined the internal functioning of organizations as if they were isolated from their environments. Scientific management has often been criticized for focusing exclusively on internal efficiency in its attempt to improve productivity, without recognizing the influence of the external environment. Many industrial engineering studies have assumed a closed-system logic assuming that the environment was constant and that organizational effectiveness depended only on improving internal efficiency. This logic assumed that the organization had a ready and constant supply of incoming resources and that the products were automatically consumed by a receptive public. Unfortunately, this closed-system logic is seriously flawed, since there are no closed social systems. Even organizations that try to minimize contact with society, such as prisons and some religious communities, still exist within an external environment that influences the availability of resources and the acceptability of outputs.

An **open system** must interact with the environment to survive. It must obtain resources from the environment and export products back to the environment. It cannot isolate itself nor seal itself off from the environment; nor can it ignore change within the environment. It must continuously adapt to the demands of a changing environment. Organizations must continue to obtain the necessary inputs and produce acceptable products in spite of an uncertain environment and fluctuations in the availability of resources or demand for the product. The human body is an open system, and so are churches, the military, businesses, cities, and the federal government.

Patterned Activities. The best way to think about an organization is to view it as a series of **patterned activities**—relatively stable and predictable events that continue to occur with regularity. All social systems, including organizations, consist of the patterned activities of individuals. These patterned activities are complementary and interdependent with respect to a common goal; that is, they are organized and coordinated to achieve a conscious purpose or objective. To analyze an organization we would want to first analyze these repeated, relatively enduring patterned activities. If an activity pattern occurs only once or at unpredictable intervals, we could not speak of an organization. A mob or a protest group, for example, would not be considered an organization until some type of structure emerged to provide stability and a recurrence of the activities. The patterned activities in a hospital include such activities as admitting patients, conducting diagnostic tests, performing operations, and providing health care. A significant patterned activity for a university consists of the hundreds of classes where students and teachers meet to share ideas. The patterned activities of a religion consist of worship services and other social events.

Describing an organization as a sequence of patterned activities explains why organizations are difficult to understand. Patterned activities are not objects that we can touch or feel; they are events that can only be viewed one at a time as they occur.

Common Characteristics of Organizations

Perhaps the best description of open-systems theory comes from the writing of Daniel Katz and Robert Kahn. They examined the patterned activities of organizations in terms of the energic input into the system, the transformation of energies within the system, and the resulting product or energic output. The two methods they used for identifying and determining the functioning of an organization were (1) tracing the pattern of energy exchange or activity of people as it results in an output; and (2) ascertaining how the output was then translated into energy within the environment to reactivate the pattern. The input, transformation, output, and recycling processes are illustrated in Exhibit 11.2. Katz and Kahn identified ten common characteristics of open systems that help us understand organizations.[3]

1. *Importation of energy.* All open systems import some form of energy from the external environment. This energy can appear in many forms, including human resources, raw materials, financial resources, status, recognition, satisfaction, or

EXHIBIT 11.2   Open-System Model of Organizations

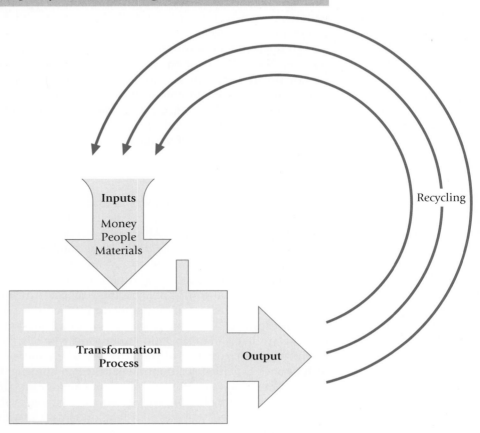

future expectations. New employees and venture capital may be the most important resources for a new enterprise. Satisfaction and future expectations, however, may be the most important resources for a religion or a sorority.

2. *The through-put or transformation process.* Open systems transform the energy into a product. Auto assembly plants transform inputs into cars, and universities conduct classes and seminars to educate students.

3. *The output.* Open systems produce a product and export it into the environment. The product might be an automobile, a consumer product, an educated mind, or restored health.

4. *Systems as cycles of events.* The product produced by an open system is recycled within the environment and transformed into more raw materials and labor to perpetuate the cycle of activities. Consumer goods are sold, and the money is used to purchase additional raw materials and to compensate employees. In a voluntary organization, the satisfaction from participating is the output, and it must be great enough to create the expectation that future participation will continue to be satisfying.

5. *Negative entropy.* The entropic process is a universal law of nature in which all forms of organization move toward disorganization or death. The open system,

however, by importing more energy from its environment than it expends in producing its products, can store energy and can achieve negative entropy. Business organizations hope to sell their products for more than it costs to produce them. These retained earnings and profit represent a form of negative entropy because they allow the organization to grow.

An illustration of entropy is when a research institute uses a research grant (energy) to study a problem and fails to produce any results. When all the money has been spent on salaries, supplies, and other research costs and the energy is exhausted, entropy has occurred and the institute dies. But the institute can achieve negative entropy if it produces reports or discoveries that it can sell for more than the initial grant. Negative entropy allows it to survive and even grow.

6. *Information input, feedback, and the coding process.* In addition to other forms of energic input, open systems must receive information or feedback on their performance. This information helps the systems of the organization know if they are on target or if change is needed. This information is necessary to help the organization adapt to a changing environment. If there are no feedback mechanisms to help the organization stay on course, it will lose its ability to survive and continue as a system. Customer satisfaction, new product information, and employee opinions are generally the most essential forms of feedback.

7. *The steady state and dynamic homeostasis.* The organization and its subsystems must be able to maintain a state of balance. However, this state of balance is a dynamic state that changes over time. For example, a marketing department and production department can both grow, but they need to maintain a balance as they grow together. A dramatic increase in the size of a marketing department could cause trouble if the production department could not produce what the marketing department sold. The same is true of the human body and the dynamic balance between its subsystems. The skeletal system must maintain a state of balance with the muscular system that moves it. Over time, however, both systems can grow, but they must maintain a dynamic state of balance as they grow together.

8. *Differentiation.* Differentiation is the development of specialized functions or a division of labor. Open systems move in the direction of greater differentiation and elaboration. Not every individual performs every function. Instead, specialized activities are identified and assigned to individuals and departments. In an emergency center at a hospital, for example, different people are responsible for admitting patients, cleaning wounds, taking blood samples, inserting IVs, setting bones, taking X rays, and transporting patients.

9. *Integration and coordination.* As organizations grow, they become more differentiated, with specialized activities and functions being performed by the various departments. This differentiation requires some sort of coordinating process to integrate the various activities and bring the system together for unified functioning. As organizations become more highly differentiated, the need for integrating activities increases. In living organisms, integration is achieved by the hormonal and nervous subsystems. In organizations, coordination is achieved by setting priorities, establishing routines, synchronizing functions, and scheduling events. In a university, for example, two major instruments of coordination are the university catalogue describing the degree requirements, courses, and faculty, and the class schedule announcing when and where each course will be taught.

10. *Equifinality.* The concept of equifinality is the idea that organizations can reach the same final state from a variety of paths. The process of development for an organization is not a fixed path, and it does not have the predictability of biological systems, as seen, for example, in the developmental stages of humans. Instead, an organization can grow to a specific size by following a variety of different paths.

Social organizations are essentially contrived systems. Since they are made by people, they are imperfect systems. They can come apart at the seams overnight, but they can also outlast by centuries the people who originally created them. Some organizations, such as Freemasonry and the Catholic Church, have survived for centuries in spite of dramatic social and cultural changes. Other organizations essentially disappear overnight, such as the political organization of an unsuccessful candidate. The campaign organization is a rapidly growing and thriving organization until election night. By the next morning, however, the organization is essentially dead, since all the speeches, campaigning, and rallies that represented its patterned activities have come to an end.

The cement holding organizations together is essentially psychological rather than biological. Social organizations are anchored in the attitudes, beliefs, motivations, and expectations of human beings. Some organizations can continue to survive and even to grow and flourish in spite of very limited involvement on the part of individuals. Such is the case with many political and volunteer associations, such as the parent-teacher associations (PTAs), which usually involve only a few minutes per year from most of their members. An organization can have a very high rate of turnover of personnel and still persist. The relationships of people, rather than the people themselves, provide the constancy of an organization.

Organizational Subsystems

As an open system, an organization is composed of several subsystems. Each of these subsystems can also be viewed as a system in its own right because it receives inputs from other subsystems and transforms them into outputs for use within the organization. Five subsystems that are necessary for any organization to survive and grow are the production, maintenance, supportive, adaptive, and managerial subsystems.[4] Although these subsystems are largely associated with particular departments, it is important to view them not as part of a particular department but as examples of the patterned activities that contribute to the functioning of the organization.

Production Subsystem. The **production subsystem** produces the products and services of the organization and represents the primary transformation activities. In a manufacturing firm, this subsystem consists largely of the activities of the production department; in a university, it consists of seminars and classes; and in a driver's license bureau, it consists of administering tests and issuing licenses. In most organizations, the production subsystem serves as the foundation around which other subsystems are organized.

Maintenance Subsystem. The **maintenance subsystem** is concerned with maintaining the social involvement of employees. Therefore, maintenance activities include compensating employees fairly, providing attractive benefits, creating favorable working conditions, rewarding outstanding performance, and providing other forms of recognition to satisfy human needs.

Adaptive Subsystem. The **adaptive subsystem** is responsible for helping the organization respond to a changing environment. Adaptive subsystem activities include gathering information about problems and opportunities in the environment and developing creative innovations to help the organization adapt and change. Most of the activities of a research and development department would be considered part of the adaptive subsystem.

Supportive Subsystem. The **supportive subsystem** includes two major functions: procurement and disposal. Procurement activities involve securing resources and energy from the environment and attempting to guarantee a stable source of future inputs. These activities are typically performed by the purchasing department in most organizations. The disposal functions include marketing and sales efforts to dispose of the product in the environment. Most manufacturing organizations have sales departments that specialize in performing the disposal function. In universities this function is performed by placement offices and alumni associations.

Supportive subsystem activities are sometimes called *boundary-spanning activities,* since they involve transactions at the organization's boundaries. Boundary-spanning activities regulate interactions between organizations and coordinate organizational demands with the environment.

Supportive subsystem activities also include lobbying efforts to create a favorable climate for the organization. This activity is also called the **institutional function,** since its goal is to protect the institution and create a friendly environment that supports the organization.[5] Most public relations activities, such as lobbying efforts and political action committee activities, would be considered part of the institutional function, because these activities are attempts to obtain favorable legislation to guarantee the survival and protect the special interests of the organization.

Managerial Subsystem. The **managerial subsystem** has the responsibility of directing the other subsystems of the organization. Management determines the strategy, goals, and policies that direct the entire organization. It also allocates resources and adjudicates disputes between people and departments. The managerial subsystem is also responsible for developing the organizational structure and directing the tasks within each subsystem.

Subsystems and the Value Chain

Every organization is a collection of patterned activities that are performed to design, produce, market, and deliver its products and services; and every organization contains the five subsystem activities just listed. An understanding of these subsystem activities is especially valuable for anyone doing strategic planning and analyzing the competitive advantages of a firm.

In his books *Competitive Strategy* and *Competitive Advantage,* Michael Porter explains how the competitive position of each firm depends on its ability to create value for buyers through what he calls a **value chain.**[6] Each firm represents a link in a chain of value: it receives inputs from suppliers, adds value to them, and passes them on to buyers. Within each firm, this value chain consists of nine strategically relevant activities that accomplish the firm's essential subsystem activities. Porter uses the value chain and its nine activities (1) to describe the firm's potential to provide a differentiated product and (2) to diagnose the relative costs and value added at each stage of the chain.

Every firm's value chain is composed of nine generic activities that are linked together in characteristic ways. How they are linked together within the firm plus how they are linked with outside firms determines whether a firm will have a competitive advantage that it can sustain. These nine activities consist of five primary and four support activities. Primary activities are involved in the physical creation of the product and its sale and transfer to the buyer. Support activities assist each of the primary activities by providing inputs, technology, human resources, and administration.

Primary activities include these five activities:

1. *Inbound logistics:* receiving, storing, materials handling, and controlling inventory
2. *Operations:* transforming inputs into the final product
3. *Outbound logistics:* collecting, scheduling, order processing, and distributing the product to the buyer
4. *Marketing and sales:* advertising, promoting, quoting, selecting distribution channels, and pricing
5. *Service:* installing, repairing, training, and supplying parts

Support activities include these four activities:

6. *Firm infrastructure:* administration, planning, financing, accounting, legal, and quality management
7. *Human resource management:* recruiting, hiring, training, compensating, and rewarding the various personnel
8. *Technology development:* improving the firm's products or its processes, such as improving the ordering process, the product design, the inventory system, consumer feedback or customer training
9. *Procurement:* obtaining inputs such as raw materials, office supplies, laboratory supplies, or travel and lodging for salespeople.

The four support activities support each other as well as the primary activities. Procurement activities, for example, are dispersed throughout an organization, because inputs are needed to support all the other activities. Likewise, human resource management activities support all other activities, because they require people who are trained and motivated to perform them.

ORGANIZATION–ENVIRONMENT INTERFACE

All organizations are required to interact with their environment. The interface between an organization and its environment has a great influence on the survival and effectiveness of the organization. This interface must be managed carefully to protect the future of the organization.

Organizations depend on the environment to provide necessary financial, human, and material resources and to consume the output produced by the organization. The products must be acceptable to society, and the organization needs to obtain a favorable exchange so that it can recycle the products and convert them into new resources. In addition, society must accept the mission of the organization and approve of how it operates. The existence of an organization can be threatened by public disapproval. Organizations can be terminated or drastically changed if society disapproves of the organization's products, of the way in which the products are produced, or of the organization's failure to comply with social expectations, such as safety requirements, environmental pollution standards, tariff agreements, and other legal requirements. The environment of tobacco companies, for example, has become increasingly hostile because of adverse scientific research, changing social customs, and antismoking laws.

Environmental Sectors

In a broad sense, the organizational environment is infinite; it includes everything outside the organization. It is more useful, however, to focus on specific aspects of the environment that influence the survival or functioning of an organization. These elements, which comprise the environmental field of action, are the organization's **domain**.[7]

The organization's domain can be divided into subenvironments or **sectors** that contain similar elements. Each sector represents an important segment of the environment that has the potential for influencing the survival and effectiveness of the organization. Eight of the most important sectors are shown in Exhibit 11.3: human resources, raw materials, financial resources, consumer markets, technology, industry, economic conditions, and government.[8] In strategic planning, a firm would want to examine each of these sectors to discover any competitive advantages it could adopt or weaknesses it should avoid.

1. *Human resources sector.* The human resources sector includes the labor market and all the sources from which potential employees may be obtained, including employment agencies, universities, technical schools, and other educational institutions. Employees can also be pirated from other organizations.

2. *Raw materials sector.* Raw materials must be obtained from the external environment. These materials include everything from paper and pencils to students for a university, patients for a hospital, iron ore for a steel mill, and insecticide for a farm. The raw materials sector for the auto industry includes a large number of suppliers and parts manufacturers.

3. *Financial resources sector.* Money is an essential input for most organizations and an especially crucial input for a new company. The financial resources sector includes places where needed money can be obtained, such as banks, savings and loan institutions, stock markets, and venture capitalists.

4. *Consumer markets.* The outputs produced by the organization must be consumed by customers who purchase the goods and services. The market sector includes the customers, clients, and potential users of the organization's products and services. For example, hospitals serve patients, schools serve students, supermarkets supply homemakers, airlines move travelers, and government agencies serve the public.

5. *Technology sector.* Technology is the use of available knowledge and techniques to produce goods and services. The technology sector includes scientific research

EXHIBIT 11.3   The Environmental Sectors of an Organization

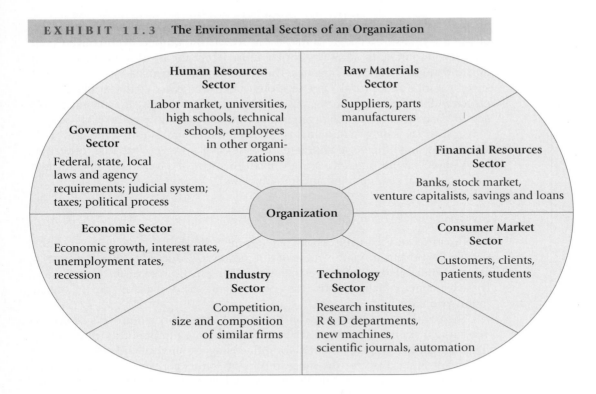

centers, universities, and the research and development efforts of other organizations that contribute to new production techniques and the creation of new knowledge.

6. *Industry sector.* An industry encompasses all the organizations in the same type of business, most of whom act as competitors to an organization. The size of the industry and the number of other competing firms create a unique industry sector for each organization. An industry dominated by one or two major corporations, such as heavy-equipment-manufacturing, is much different from an industry characterized by hundreds of small companies, such as the fast-food industry.

7. *Economics sector.* Organizations are not isolated from economic conditions. The success and effectiveness of an organization is influenced by the health of the overall economy and by such factors as whether the economy is expanding or contracting. Some of the most important aspects of this sector include economic growth, unemployment rates, recessions, inflation rates, and the rate of investment.

8. *Government sector.* Organizations are required to operate within the constraints imposed by federal, state, and local laws. These laws determine the political system in which organizations operate, such as capitalism versus socialism, and how much freedom organizations have to pursue their own ends. The government sector includes all the federal, state, and local laws plus the regulatory agencies that administer these laws, and the judicial system that resolves disputes. This sector also includes the political system and political action committees and lobbyists who try to change the laws and obtain favorable legislative treatment.

Boundary-Spanning Roles

Open-systems theory helps us realize that every organization depends on the environment and must interact with it to achieve a comfortable balance. Because of uncertainty about the environment, organizations create a series of buffering departments to help them absorb the impact of the environment. An organization can be viewed as a technical core surrounded by departments that buffer the organization.[9] The purpose of these buffering departments is to protect the organization and help it adapt to an uncertain environment. The goal of buffer departments is to make the technical core as stable as possible so it can function efficiently. Examples of buffering departments are shown in Exhibit 11.4.

The activities that occur in buffering departments are often referred to as **boundary-spanning roles.** Boundary-spanning roles link and coordinate the organization with key elements in the external environment. They serve two major purposes: (1) to gather and process information about environmental changes; and (2) to represent the organization to the environment. By communicating information between the environment and the organization, plans and activities can be coordinated and uncertainty can be reduced. This information helps the organization adapt to the environment or prepare to change the environment if needed.

Environmental Uncertainty

Organizations exist in an uncertain environment. However, the uncertainty is considerably greater for some organizations than others. The methods used for reducing uncertainty and the organization's success in doing so have important implications for survival.

EXHIBIT 11.4   Boundary-Spanning Roles That Buffer an Organization

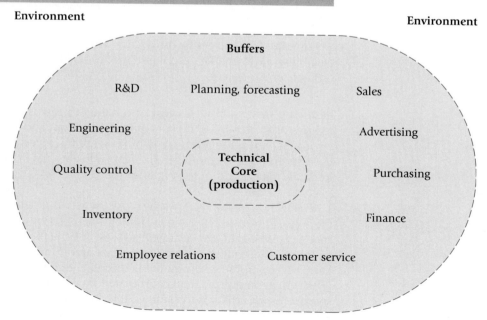

Complexity and Stability. Environmental uncertainty means that managers do not have sufficient information about environmental factors to make effective decisions. Therefore, they have a difficult time predicting external changes and predicting whether their decisions will be effective. The quality of organizational decisions and the ability to produce valuable products depends on having good information about such aspects of the environment as the availability of resources and consumer interests. Uncertainty increases the risk of failure for organizational actions and makes it difficult to compute the costs and probabilities associated with different decisions.

Organizational uncertainty is determined by two dimensions: (1) the extent to which the external environment is simple or complex, and (2) the extent to which the events are stable or unstable.[10] The combination of these two dimensions is shown in Exhibit 11.5. **Environmental complexity** concerns the number of external elements that are relevant to an organization. In a simple environment, the organization interacts with only a small number of external elements. For example, a family-operated chicken farm that sells most of its eggs to one food chain has a very simple environment. In a complex environment, however, the organization must interact with a large number of diverse external elements. Automobile companies, for example, interact with hundreds of parts suppliers located in many different countries plus hundreds of dealerships scattered throughout the world. Furthermore, they interact with hundreds of elements of the human resources sector in acquiring new employees plus dozens of agencies from the government sector.

The phrase **environmental stability** refers to whether the elements of the environment are dynamic and constantly changing, or whether they are stable. An environmental domain is stable if it remains the same over a period of several months or years. Some organizations enjoy a very stable environment, such as a company manufacturing lead pipe. Many of its products, such as the pipe and connecting joints, have remained virtually unchanged for many years. New production processes and technological improvements have been minimal. Other organizations are located in a very unstable environment. In the electronics industry, for example, new products may become obsolete overnight because of technological advances and new scientific discoveries. The actions of competitors and the unpredictability of the market also contribute to making the electronics industry a very unstable environment.

Reducing Uncertainty. Because uncertainty threatens organizational survival and reduces its effectiveness, most organizations adopt a variety of strategies to reduce environmental uncertainty. Most of these efforts focus on gaining greater control over environmental resources. The first two strategies listed here, however, involve internal changes within the organization.

1. *Changing organizational structures.* As the environment becomes more complex, the organization needs a larger number of buffering departments and boundary spanners. When the environment is stable, the internal structure and processes can be formal and centralized and can operate according to fixed rules and procedures. However, when the environment is unstable, the organization's structure must be informal, decentralized, and coordinated by the efforts of many individuals whose specific responsibility is to facilitate this control. This relationship between organizational structure and environmental uncertainty is one of the concepts that will be discussed in Chapter 12.

EXHIBIT 11.5 Framework for Evaluating Environmental Uncertainty

ENVIRONMENTAL COMPLEXITY

Simple | Complex

ENVIRONMENTAL CHANGE

Stable

Simple + Stable =
Low Uncertainty

1. Small number of external elements
2. Elements remain the same or change slowly

Examples: Soft drink bottlers, beer distributors, container manufacturers, local utilities

Complex + Stable =
Low Moderate Uncertainty

1. Large number of external elements
2. Elements remain the same or change slowly

Examples: Universities, hospitals, insurance companies

Uncertainty

Unstable

Simple + Unstable =
High Moderate Uncertainty

1. Small number of external elements
2. Elements change frequently, unpredictably, and reactively

Examples: Personal computers, fashion clothing, music industry, Atari, toy manufacturers

Complex + Unstable =
High Uncertainty

1. Large number of external elements
2. Elements change frequently, unpredictably, and reactively

Examples: American airlines, oil companies, electronic firms, aerospace firms, local utilities

Source: Reprinted from "Characteristics of Organizational Environments and Perceived Environmental Uncertainty," by Robert Duncan. Published in *Administrative Science Quarterly*, vol. 17 (September 1972), p. 320, Table 2. Reprinted by permission of *Administrative Science Quarterly*. Copyright *Administrative Science Quarterly*.

2. *Planning and forecasting.* Organizations can increase their capacity to respond to an unstable environment by forecasting environmental changes and creating contingency plans. Planning can soften the adverse impact of external shifts. Organizations that have unstable environments frequently create a separate planning department to help the organization adapt. Although planning does not reduce the amount of external change, it can help the organization adapt successfully to it. For example, economic forecasting may not change the economy any more than weather forecasting can change the weather. However, a good economic forecast maybe as helpful to organizational planning as a weather forecast is for scheduling a company picnic. An interesting paradox regarding economic forecasts is that their accuracy increases as the environment becomes more stable, but their usefulness increases as the environment becomes more unstable. Although forecasts

APPLYING ORGANIZATIONAL BEHAVIOR
RESEARCH

When Vertical Integration Fails to Reduce Uncertainty

 Vertical integration has been used extensively to reduce environmental uncertainty in such diverse industries as oil, steel, aluminum, rubber, food products, automobiles, and computers. Vertical integration is a form of diversification that allows a company to use the outputs from one line of business as inputs for another. The products in a vertically integrated firm move through successive stages of production in a value-added chain that involves internal transfers rather than transactions in the open market.

Vertical integration has been advocated as a method of reducing environmental uncertainty because the transactions are coordinated within the organizational hierarchy and the costs of exchange are eliminated. But these advantages have been questioned because some vertically integrated firms are so large and complex that they are inflexible and cannot adapt to competitive challenges and business cycles.

Although earlier studies of the oil industry during the 1970s endorsed vertical integration, a study of the forest products industry in the 1980s did not. This study examined a cross section of twenty-five firms having at least 50 percent of their sales in one or more segments of the industry: forestry and logging, lumber, plywood, paper mills, paperboard, wood boxes, milled-wood building materials, paper products, or cardboard boxes. This study examined how the degree of integration was related to financial factors, such as bankruptcy and the risk to stockholders.

The results revealed that the fully integrated firms were more prone to bankruptcy and high risk to stockholders when their environments were turbulent. In a volatile environment, the complexity of a firm's vertical integration is associated with high risk because the firm cannot adapt to dynamic environmental changes.

Many factors might explain why vertical integration is less effective in a highly volatile environment. For example, the inflexibility might occur because vertical integration prevents a firm from outsourcing (buying materials from another supplier) to obtain superior products, switching suppliers when new technologies appear, avoiding idle capacity and inventory swings during cyclical downturns, and substituting a competitor's components for inferior ones produced in-house. The advantages of vertical integration appear to depend on a more stable environment.

Source: Richard A. D'Aveni and Anne Y. Ilinitch, "Complex Patterns of Vertical Integration in the Forest Products Industry: Systematic and Bankruptcy Risks," *Academy of Management Journal,* vol. 35 (1992), pp. 596–625.

in an extremely unstable environment may not be as accurate, they are nevertheless more useful because of their contribution to organizational planning. Incorrect forecasts of future events can still be very useful because they identify the important variables and the relationships between them and because they can be updated periodically.

3. *Mergers and acquisitions.* An effective method of controlling environmental resources is to buy a controlling interest in a company that serves as a supplier or consumer of the company. If there is uncertainty about the source of a crucial raw material, this uncertainty can be removed by buying the supplier. For example, steel companies have acquired iron and coal mines, and soft drink manufacturers have acquired bottle makers. A similar method of controlling environmental resources is through joint ventures and contracts that create a legal and binding relationship between two or more firms. In a joint venture, organizations share the risks and costs associated with large projects. Contracts are designed to provide long-term

security for both the supplier and the consumer of raw materials by tying the consumer and the supplier to specific amounts and prices. For example, McDonald's Corporation will sometimes acquire an entire crop of potatoes to be certain of its supply of french fries.

4. *Cooptation.* **Cooptation** is any strategy of bringing outside people into the organization and making them feel obligated to contribute because of their organizational involvement. Cooptation occurs when leaders of important environmental sectors are brought into the organization by having them serve on an advisory committee or a board of directors. Cooptation explains why organizations in more uncertain environments tend to have larger boards of directors—a larger board can reduce uncertainty to a greater degree.[11] Some organizations reduce their resource uncertainty by creating a formal linkage called an *interlocking directorate* in which the members of the board of directors of one company sit on the board of directors of another company. These individuals influence the policies and decisions of each organization in a way that guarantees their cooperative association. Another form of cooptation is to recruit executives from another interdependent organization. For example, companies in the aerospace industry hire retired generals and executives from the Department of Defense to help them obtain better information about technical specifications and to improve their chances of obtaining defense contracts.

5. *Public relations and advertising.* Organizations spend enormous amounts of money to influence consumer tastes and public opinion. Advertising and public relations activities are designed to reduce uncertainty by providing a stable demand for the company's outputs or a constant level of inputs. Press reports and other news media shape the company's image in the minds of suppliers, customers, and government officials. Hospitals, for example, have begun to advertise their services to attract more patients.

6. *Political activity.* Since government legislation and agency enforcement can exert such a powerful influence on organizations, many of them spend a considerable amount of money on lobbyists and political action committees. These individuals strive to protect the interests of the organization by making members of governing bodies aware of the interests of the organization and the consequences of a proposed bill. Many organizations have formed trade associations for similar purposes, such as the National Association of Manufacturers. By pooling their resources, organizations expect the associations to have a larger voice in lobbying legislators, influencing new regulations, developing public relations campaigns, and blocking unfair competition.

7. *Illegal activities.* Although it is wrong, many organizations resort to illegal activities to control environmental uncertainty. Scarce environmental resources and pressures to succeed, especially from top managers, often lead managers to behave in illegal ways. Some examples of illegal behaviors include payoffs to foreign governments, illegal political contributions, promotional gifts, illegal kickbacks, price fixing, illegal mergers, franchise violations, refusals to bargain in good faith with a union, and espionage in market development and innovations.

Although organizations usually try to adapt to the environment, some try to change and control the environment. This is especially true of large organizations that command large resources. The environment is not fixed. Organizations can adapt when necessary, but they can also neutralize or alter a problematic sector in the environment. Although the potential of significantly influencing the environment is small when organizations act alone, a group of organizations can make a noticeable change within the environment when they act in concert.

ORGANIZATIONAL EFFECTIVENESS

When we study organizations, we need a method for measuring organizational performance. Performance measures are as important to managers as counting the number of strokes is to golfers. Without some method of measuring performance, we have no way to assess how well the organization is functioning or whether managerial decisions are good or bad.

The term *organizational effectiveness* refers to the concept of organizational success, or organizational performance. Basically, it is an indication of how well the organization is doing. Is it doing what it ought to do, or is it doing the best that it can? Athletic teams measure their performance by their win-loss record. The goal in each athletic contest is to outscore the opponent. Similarly, every organization defines success as a function of goal accomplishment. Individuals and groups are successful to the extent that they achieve their goals. Likewise, organizational effectiveness is a function of how well the organization achieves its goals.

The problem with defining organizational effectiveness in terms of goal accomplishment is that organizations don't have clear and concise goals. On the one hand, it can be argued that organizations don't have any goals; only people have goals. On the other hand, it can be argued that organizations have multiple goals. Indeed, organizations have multiple constituencies, including employees, managers, owners, and customers, and each constituency has multiple goals. Before we can understand organizational effectiveness, we need to analyze the concept of organizational goals.

Organizational Goals

Organizations exist for a purpose and are therefore considered goal-directed social entities. Yet it has also been argued that organizations *per se* do not have goals—only people have goals. Technically this criticism is correct. Organizations and other social entities do not have goals or other human properties, such as a soul, a mind, or feelings. However, as was noted in Chapter 1, most organizations have a goal that is commonly shared by most individuals, and there is sufficient agreement among people about the organization's goals to unite them in a common purpose. Therefore, it is appropriate to conclude that an organization and its members are trying to achieve a particular goal. Participants may have goals different from the organization's, and the organization may have several goals, but organizations exist for one or more purposes without which they would cease to exist. Therefore, it is meaningful to talk about organizational goals because of the consensual validation supporting them. The term *consensual validation* refers to a common belief or consensus that is so widely shared among a group of people

APPLYING ORGANIZATIONAL BEHAVIOR
IN THE NEWS

The Role of the Board of Directors

CNN Boards of directors are primarily responsible for two important functions: monitoring management's performance and monitoring the corporation's interaction with its external public. They are responsible for what happens in the corporation, and they represent the corporation to the outside world. In the past, neither function has been performed very well by most boards.

Board members are usually a combination of outside directors and internal managers. Only a very few companies invite employee or union representatives to participate on their boards. Board members are usually selected because they were recommended by other board members. Although board members must be approved by the stockholders, the approval process is usually a mere formality.

Although the board members are usually paid substantial fees for their service, it is generally believed that most outside directors have only a superficial knowledge about the internal functioning of the company. Outside board members do not spend enough time or take sufficient opportunity to become intimately familiar with all the cru-

cial corporate issues. Golf scores or the evening's entertainment are often discussed with greater enlightenment than the corporation's financial performance.

Inside board members who are members of management face a difficult compromising situation because they are expected to evaluate themselves. This conflict is especially troublesome when the chairperson of the board also is the president of the company. The chair can filter and bias all information reported to other board members. The major reason why some executives receive exorbitant salaries and enormous retirement packages is that board members feel compelled to reward their own members and it is difficult to make impartial decisions regarding another group member.

In recent years, however, many boards of directors have become increasingly active in replacing top management and telling them how to run the company. This activism is attributed to substantial losses and stockholder lawsuits. Board members are being forced by threat of lawsuit to examine their responsibilities more closely and fulfill their roles.

Source: CNN *Inside Business* news programing.

---

that most of the people accept it as true, even though it may not match their own personal feelings.

Organizational goals not only represent the reason for an organization's existence, they also increase the organization's effectiveness. Organizations have **official goals,** which define the general mission of the organization, and **operative goals,** which are more specific and describe what the organization is actually trying to accomplish. The management process of identifying goals and working to achieve them provides several benefits for the organization.

1. *Legitimacy.* The official goals of an organization provide a symbol of legitimacy both to the employee and to external constituencies. Goals describe the purpose of the organization, so people know what it stands for and accept its existence.

2. *Employee direction and motivation.* Operative goals provide a sense of direction and motivation for employees. Research on goal setting has shown that the performance of employees can be significantly increased by realistic goals.

3. *Decision guidelines.* Goals provide a standard for evaluating performance. Organizational goals can act as a set of constraints on individual behavior and decisions. The goals can serve as the criteria against which management decisions are made.

4. *Reduce uncertainty.* The process of goal setting tends to reduce uncertainty for members of the organization, especially top management. The process of arriving at a set of mutually acceptable goals helps to focus the energies and efforts of the entire organization.

Evaluating Organizational Effectiveness

How we evaluate organizational effectiveness depends on the time frame we use for measuring it. The most popular criteria for evaluating an organization are job satisfaction and productivity. Productive companies that provide pleasant jobs are considered highly effective. These short-run measures of productivity and satisfaction, however, are both theoretically and empirically different from long-term effectiveness measures. In the long run the survival of the organization is the ultimate measure of organizational effectiveness. If an organization survives for several centuries, we say it is effective because it has acquired resources from the environment, transformed them into usable products, and adapted to changing environmental demands. Although survival is the ultimate measure of organizational effectiveness, however, we need more immediate measures on a monthly or yearly basis to evaluate managerial decisions.

Efficiency Versus Effectiveness. The criteria for assessing organizational effectiveness must include an evaluation of how well the outputs are produced, plus how well the outputs are consumed by the environment and translated into additional inputs. The importance of considering the interaction between the organization and the environment illustrates the important distinction between efficiency and effectiveness.

The term *efficiency* refers to how well the organization converts inputs into outputs. Therefore, **efficiency** measures the quality of the transformation process. In contrast, **effectiveness** concerns both the efficiency of the transformation process plus how well the product is exported into the environment and recycled back into usable inputs for the organization. Organizational efficiency is typically assessed using cost–benefit ratios that compare the number of inputs required per level of output. The process of measuring organizational effectiveness, however, is much more difficult.

Organizational efficiency usually contributes to organizational effectiveness but not always. It is possible for an organization to be extremely efficient in transforming inputs into outputs, and yet this organization could be ineffective because its products are not accepted by the environment. However, an organization may be extremely effective because of a new innovation or a unique market strategy, even though it is not particularly efficient.

Organizations use a variety of efficiency measures, such as labor costs, productivity per employee hour, costs per unit, and tons per employee hours. These numbers are interpreted by examining historical trends or by making industry comparisons, and managers use this information to improve their organizational efficiency. In some industries the performance of different companies demonstrates wide variations in efficiency ratios. For example, in the auto industry the "efficiency ratio" of General Motors is only about 13 to 1. This efficiency ratio measures the number of cars produced per year per employee. The efficiency ratio of Ford, as shown in Exhibit 11.6, is about 18 to 1, while the efficiency ratio of Toyota is 59 to 1.[12] The relative efficiency ratios among different geographical locations or cultures have caused many business enterprises to move their factories from one state to another or to foreign countries.

Open-systems theory provides a useful model for evaluating organizational effectiveness. Effectiveness must be assessed in terms of the processes of input, transformation, output, and recycling. These processes can be used to categorize the most frequently used criteria of effectiveness, as illustrated in Exhibit 11.7.

Resource Acquisition Approach. One approach to measuring organizational effectiveness is to measure the organization's ability to exploit its environment by acquiring scarce and valued resources. According to this criterion, the most effective organizations are the ones that are the most successful in acquiring valued resources. This approach is used primarily by organizations in the early stage of development. New businesses often measure their success by their ability to acquire venture capital. Other organizations use resource acquisition to measure effectiveness because other effectiveness measures are difficult to obtain. For example, voluntary organizations such as the March of Dimes or the Muscular Dystrophy Association frequently report their success in terms of the contributions they receive from society. The number of new converts and new members is an important

EXHIBIT 11.6 Motor Vehicle Production, Number of Employees, and Efficiency Ratios for Selected Automobile Companies (1992)

Company	Vehicles	Employees	Vehicles per Employee
Chrysler			
United States	1,370,805	77,878	17.60
Worldwide	2,175,447	112,996	19.25
Ford			
United States	3,361,297	158,377	21.22
Worldwide	5,764,374	325,333	17.72
General Motors			
North American	4,975,000	396,000	12.56
Worldwide	7,452,000	571,000	13.05
Toyota[a]	4,022,550	67,814	59.31

[a]1989 data.

Source: Data taken from the published annual reports of each company for 1992.

EXHIBIT 11.7   Approaches to Measuring Organizational Effectiveness

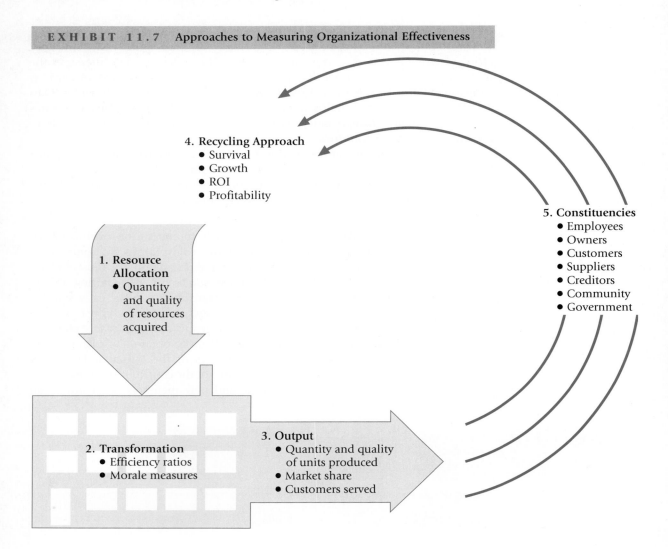

4. **Recycling Approach**
- Survival
- Growth
- ROI
- Profitability

5. **Constituencies**
- Employees
- Owners
- Customers
- Suppliers
- Creditors
- Community
- Government

1. **Resource Allocation**
- Quantity and quality of resources acquired

2. **Transformation**
- Efficiency ratios
- Morale measures

3. **Output**
- Quantity and quality of units produced
- Market share
- Customers served

measure of effectiveness for religious and social organizations. Some government agencies measure their effectiveness by the size of their budget or the amount of office space allocated to them. Along with their ability to attract new faculty or students, universities frequently use allocations from the state legislature as a measure of effectiveness. In their advertising commercials, car dealerships often emphasize the number of cars sent to them and consider this number an indication of their effectiveness.

The value of the **resource acquisition approach** is threefold: it takes the entire organization as a frame of reference, it considers the relationship of the organization to the external environment, and it can be used to compare organizations that have different goals. However, the resource acquisition approach also has its limitations. An organization that fails to use its resources effectively should not be considered effective. An athletic team that acquired many star players would not be considered effective if the team lost its games. A research institute that failed to create scientific discoveries with the money it received would not be considered effective.

Transformation Approach. Several measures of organizational effectiveness focus on internal organizational health and efficiency—whether the employees are happy and satisfied, whether departmental activities are coordinated to ensure high productivity, and whether the inputs are effectively translated into outputs. The **transformation approach** incorporates both human resource measures and economic efficiency measures. A wide variety of questionnaires have been developed to measure the attitudes of employees concerning internal organizational health. These questionnaires measure the amount of confidence, trust, and communication between workers and management; they measure how effectively decisions are made; they determine whether there is a feeling of teamwork, loyalty, and commitment; they determine whether the reward system is fair and adequate; and they determine whether the organization is organized efficiently and coordinated properly. These evaluations of internal health and functioning are often subjective, and they fail to consider adequately the interaction between the organization and its environment. However, the advantage of these perceptual measures is that they can be used to compare organizations whose outputs are not the same or not identifiable. Organizations producing different products can be compared on a similar basis.

To overcome the problem of subjectivity, many organizations have developed a variety of economic efficiency measures. Measures of efficiency inevitably are expressed in ratio terms comparing inputs with outputs. Some examples of efficiency measures include rate of return on capital or assets, unit cost, scrappage and waste, down time, cost per patient or per student or per client, and occupancy rates.

Output Approach. The **output approach** is generally viewed as the most relevant criterion of organizational effectiveness, since it appears to measure goal accomplishment. This approach seems logical because organizations try to maximize their profits and customer satisfaction. We must remember, however, that measures of output assess only one component of the open system model, and they are an incomplete index of organizational effectiveness. An organization may be very successful in producing a large volume of products or services, but unless the output is consumed by the public, the organization will not survive. Some of the most popular measures of output include profit, sales, market share, patients released, documents processed, clients served, students graduated, and the number of arrests or citations issued. In using the output approach to measure effectiveness, it is important to remember that organizations have multiple goals and multiple outcomes. High achievement on any one goal may mean low achievement on another. Therefore, effectiveness should not be assessed in only one dimension because this would oversimplify the objectives of the organization and produce a misleading conclusion.

Recycling Approach. The **recycling approach** concerns how well the products produced by the organization are consumed by society and translated into essential inputs. Unlike the earlier approaches, the recycling approach involves a long-term perspective and is more abstract. Three dimensions of the recycling approach include adaptability, development, and survival.

The term *adaptability* refers to how well the organization responds to internal and external changes. Management must be able to detect changes in the environment that require corresponding changes in the organization. To the extent that the organization cannot or does not adapt to its environment, its survival is in jeopardy. Changes in consumer taste and foreign competition are two environmental forces that have had a profound influence recently on many organizations. Some organizations measure their adaptability by examining their growth over time or the number of new products they have developed and brought to market.

To improve their adaptability and increase their chances for survival, many organizations invest in themselves through organizational development and training programs. By helping their employees develop new skills, organizations hope to adapt to a changing environment with less resistance and difficulty. The benefits of training and development activities are difficult to assess immediately.

Since organizational effectiveness is the organization's ability to take resources from the environment, transform them into products, and export them to the environment in a way that creates new inputs, this process involves a long-term assessment. Accordingly, the final test of organizational effectiveness is whether it is able to sustain itself in the environment. Therefore, survival of the organization is the ultimate measure of organizational effectiveness. Organizations that fail to respond to a changing environment or that lose their ability to produce products and transform them into new inputs do not survive and, by definition, they are not effective. Organizations that over time become larger and more powerful appear to do more than merely survive. However, the regulated breakup of AT&T reminds us that large and powerful organizations today may not survive tomorrow. Therefore, the only measure of organizational effectiveness in the long run is simply survival. However, this criterion is not very useful for managers who want more immediate feedback on the effectiveness of their organizations.

Constituency (Stakeholder) Approach. A contemporary method of assessing organizational effectiveness that uses a combination of other approaches is the **constituency** or *stakeholder* **approach.** A constituency is a group either inside or outside the organization that has a stake in the organization's performance. These groups are called stakeholders. Employees, customers, and stockholders are all constituencies whose assessment of the organization can serve as a measure of the organization's performance. Each constituency has a different criterion of success because it has a different interest in the organization. The effectiveness of the organization can be evaluated by surveying the attitudes of each constituency. Seven of the most important constituencies and the effectiveness criteria used by each are listed here.

Constituency	Effectiveness Criterion
1. Employees	Satisfaction with pay, supervision, and the work itself
2. Owners	Financial return on investment
3. Customers	Quality of goods and services
4. Suppliers	Satisfactory transactions
5. Creditors	Creditworthiness
6. Community	Social responsibility
7. Government	Compliance with laws and regulations

The strength of the constituency approach is that it uses a broad view of effectiveness and examines factors in the environment as well as within the organization. The concepts of social responsibility and community involvement, absent in the other approaches, are also included here. The constituency approach also tends to integrate several criteria regarding inputs, transformations, and outputs that overcome a serious flaw of many other measures. The constituency approach recognizes that there is no single measure of effectiveness and that the achievement of one criterion may be just as important as another. The well-being of employees, for example, is just as important as achieving the goals of the owners.[13]

The recognition of multiple constituencies and their multiple goals significantly influences major organizational decisions, such as whether to close a factory and where to build a new community hospital. The constituency approach also calls attention to the fact that effectiveness criteria reflect the values of different people. The organization must decide which values it wishes to pursue, which often means that some values will be excluded. Organizations cannot meet all criteria to the same extent at the same time. The leaders of an organization, the owners and/or managers, typically have the greatest influence over the direction of the organization. The dominant values expressed by this group usually have the greatest influence on the goals of the organization and the criteria that will be used to assess effectiveness.

ORGANIZATIONAL CLIMATE AND ORGANIZATIONAL CULTURE

Each organization has its own unique constellation of characteristics and properties. *Organizational climate* and *organizational culture* are two terms that have been used to describe these characteristics of organizations and their subunits. Although there is some inconsistency in the way these terms are defined, *culture* generally refers to organizational characteristics that are relatively enduring and resistant to change. *Climate*, in contrast, is used to describe characteristics that are temporary and capable of being changed. The weather has been used as a popular analogy to explain the differences between culture and climate. Like daily weather patterns, organizational climate can fluctuate from time to time because of organizational changes. Culture, in contrast, is like the seasons of the year, which change slowly over time. The seasons are associated with stable and enduring weather characteristics that transcend daily variations.

Organizational Climate

During the mid 1960s, organizational research identified climate as a significant independent and moderating variable influencing job attitudes and behavior. Although organizational climate is an ambiguous concept, studies have produced a generally accepted definition of climate and have identified some of its determinants.[14]

Defining Organizational Climate. The term *climate* refers to the set of characteristics or attributes that distinguish one organization from other organizations.[15] This definition is similar to the concept of personality, and, indeed,

organizational climate is often referred to as the personality of the organization. Just as *personality* refers to the stable characteristics of individuals, climate refers to the stable characteristics and properties of organizations.

Organizational climate influences behavior. Employees are more satisfied and perform better in some organizational climates than in others. A study of disadvantaged workers who entered a job training program after a lengthy period of unemployment found that the success of these trainees was influenced by the supportiveness of the climate. Employees who rated their climate as supportive were rated by the trainers as more competent and productive than those who perceived the climate as less supportive.[16] Another climate study found that the productivity of middle managers was greater in an innovative climate, provided that the climate of innovation was consistent with the amount of autonomy and the relative number of rules.[17] The value of harmony and consistency in the climate has also been confirmed in a study of executives. The satisfaction and productivity of a group of executives was highest for those executives who perceived their organizational climate as similar to their own personalities. However, the satisfaction and performance levels were lower among executives who described their personalities as different from the organizational climate.[18] It appears that the relationship between climate and behavior is a reciprocal interaction. Many individual and organizational factors influence climate, but climate also influences these factors. For example, creative people have an impact on an organization's climate, and climate can foster or discourage creativity.

Determinants of Organizational Climate. The variables influencing organizational climate include a variety of internal and external factors. Although a comprehensive list cannot be constructed, the following variables seem to have a significant impact on an organization's climate.

1. *Managerial values.* The values of managers have a strong influence on climate because values lead to actions that influence decisions. These values, or employees' perceptions of these values, have a significant influence on whether the organization is formal or informal, autocratic or participative, and impersonal or friendly. Research has shown that the values of managers can create a climate of honesty within, for example, retail organizations that reduces employee theft.[19]

2. *Leadership style.* Leaders who have confidence in their subordinates and want them to be involved in organizational decisions create a much different climate from that produced by managers who insist on making all important decisions and maintaining tight control.

3. *Economic conditions.* When the economy is growing and the organization is prosperous, managers tend to be more adventuresome and willing to take greater risks. In periods of economic decline, however, budgets are very tight and managers are forced to make more conservative decisions. New programs are not proposed and creative ideas are overlooked during economic decline.

4. *Organizational structure.* Several characteristics of the organizational structure tend to have a pervasive influence on the organizational climate. For

example, an organization with fixed reporting relationships and rigid rules and procedures tends to create a bureaucratic organizational climate that is perceived as cold and impersonal, but possibly very efficient.

5. *Characteristics of the members.* The personalities of organizational members contribute to the climate of the organization. Organizations with a high proportion of older or poorly educated employees will have a climate quite different from an organization with mostly young, highly educated, and ambitious employees. The climate is much more friendly in organizations whose members participate in social activities off the job.

6. *Unionization.* The presence or absence of a labor union has a pervasive influence on the organization. The relationships between management and labor tend to be more formal and antagonistic when the employees have voted to form a union and negotiated a labor agreement.

7. *Organizational size.* Large organizations tend to be more rigid, bureaucratic, and structured than smaller organizations. It is much easier to establish a climate of creativity, innovation, and cohesiveness in a small company than in a large organization. Most innovations and creative discoveries have emerged from small organizations.

8. *Nature of the work.* The kinds of jobs and the type of industry contribute to creating a unique organizational climate. Farming and food processing in rural communities is performed in a climate dramatically different from banking and financial investment companies in metropolitan areas. Time pressures and deadlines contribute to making the climate in a daily newspaper company much different from the climate of a textbook publisher.

Measuring Organizational Climate. Research studies measure organizational climate by asking employees to complete a questionnaire. An illustration of a portion of an organizational climate survey called the Organizational Analysis Questionnaire is shown in Exhibit 11.8. The dimensions of climate measured by this particular instrument include communication, leadership, decision making, problem solving, evaluating and rewarding performance, organizational structure, and organizational control.[20] When new questionnaires are developed, the items are typically taken from comments made by employees during interviews, and similar items are grouped together to measure a dimension of the climate.

A large number of organizational climate surveys have been developed and are used extensively by organizations. Unfortunately, there does not appear to be a consistent set of dimensions comprising organizational climate. Each instrument measures a different set of dimensions, with only a small amount of overlap with other instruments. Perhaps the most extensively developed questionnaire for measuring organizational climate is the Survey of Organizations (SOO) developed by the Survey Research Institute at the University of Michigan.[21] This questionnaire is patterned largely after the research of Rensis Likert described in Chapter 12. The dimensions of organizational climate measured by the SOO are shown in Exhibit 11.9. Research using the SOO has shown that a favorable organizational climate generally increases productivity and improves the quality of life for employees. One study, for example, found that alcoholism and drug abuse were significantly lower among companies with the highest scores on the SOO dimensions.[22]

EXHIBIT 11.8   Questionnaire for Measuring Organizational Climate

	How often is each statement an accurate description of the situation in your organization?					How important is it that this area be improved?			
	(Circle one)					(Circle one)			
Organizational Climate	Almost Always	More Often Than Not	About Half the Time	Less Often Than Not	Almost Never	Critical	High Priority	Low Priority	No Change Needed
Organizational Strategy and Understanding									
1. Your management does a good job of assessing the needs of those you serve and laying out a strategy that keeps ahead of the field.	1	2	3	4	5	1	2	3	4
2. Your management does a poor job of communicating their strategy to those who must implement it.	1	2	3	4	5	1	2	3	4
3. Adequate time is spent to make sure everyone understands the overall functioning of the organization and his or her place in it.	1	2	3	4	5	1	2	3	4
4. People don't really understand or appreciate the contribution their job makes to the success of the total organization.	1	2	3	4	5	1	2	3	4
5. People at all levels have a sense of dedication to the mission or goals of the organization.	1	2	3	4	5	1	2	3	4
6. What, if anything, should be done to make sure people understand the goals of the organization and feel a commitment to achieve them?									

Source: Organizational Analysis Survey, Novations Inc., Provo, Utah. Used by permission.

Organizational Culture

The people who study culture have sought to make a clear distinction between culture and climate. As noted earlier, *culture* refers to something that is more stable and enduring than climate, and it is more difficult to define and evaluate. While climate can be measured quantitatively by asking employees to complete a climate survey, culture is usually measured qualitatively using the ethnographic research methods of anthropology. Although some quantitative culture surveys have been used in organizational research to measure culture change, these surveys are deemed inadequate measures of the depth of an organization's culture.[23]

Defining Organizational Culture. Culture is the unwritten feeling part of the organization, and some researchers believe that it is so intangible and pervasive that

EXHIBIT 11.9   Organizational Indices Measured by the Survey of Organizations—SOO

Organizational Climate

1. Technological readiness
2. Human resource primacy
3. Communication flow
4. Motivational conditions
5. Decision-making practices
6. Lower-level influence

Supervisory Leadership

7. Support
8. Goal emphasis
9. Work facilitation
10. Team building

even the members of the organization cannot be relied on to describe it accurately. Culture is the set of key values, beliefs, and understandings that are shared by members of an organization. Culture defines the basic organizational values and communicates to new members the correct ways to think and act and the ways things ought to be done. Culture enhances the stability of the organization and helps members interpret organizational activities and events. The focus of culture is to provide members with a sense of identity and to generate within them a commitment to the beliefs and values of the organization.

An understanding of **organizational culture** helps organizations respond to external problems of adaptation and survival as well as internal problems of integration.[24] For example, an organization's culture creates a shared vision among members about the mission of the organization and the strategies and goals it should use to achieve success. This vision helps the organization adapt to a changing environment, especially during times of upheaval, because each member can decide what his or her responsibility is without waiting to be told. Internally, organizational culture helps to define the criteria for the allocation of power and status. Every organization establishes a pecking order and rules for how members acquire, maintain, and lose power. These rules help members manage their expectations and feelings of aggression. The criteria for allocating rewards and punishments are also defined by the organizational culture. The legends and myths let members know which behaviors are heroic or sinful—what gets rewarded with status and power and what gets punished through withdrawal of rewards or excommunication.

An excellent illustration of the effects of organizational culture is the "H-P way" at Hewlett-Packard Corporation. The H-P way consists of a constellation of attitudes and values, among which is an insistence on product quality, the recognition of achievement, and respect for individual employees. New employees are viewed with suspicion until they have demonstrated that they understand and follow the H-P way. Questions about sloppy work or careless performance are resolved immediately because sloppy work is inconsistent with the H-P way. The H-P way defines the internal culture of Hewlett-Packard.

The Creation of Organizational Culture. Since the term organizational culture refers to the underlying beliefs and values that are shared by organization members, culture cannot be dictated by top management. Indeed, many researchers argue that the pronouncements and speeches of top management do very little to create or change organizational culture. Instead, organizational culture is tied to more fundamental beliefs and values that are both created by and reflected in the ceremonies, stories, symbols, and slogans within the organization.[25]

Ceremonies Ceremonies are planned events that have special significance for the members and are conducted for their benefit. Ceremonies serve the same purpose for organizations that ordinations and initiations do for religious groups and social clubs. Ceremonies are special occasions when managers can reinforce specific values and create a bond among the members for sharing important values and beliefs. These occasions provide an opportunity to recognize heroes and induct them into the organizational hall of fame. For example, McDonald's Corporation conducts a nationwide contest to determine the best hamburger-cooking team in the country. Competition occurs among local teams and gradually progresses until the best teams from the company compete at the national level. The teams are judged on minute details that determine whether the hamburger is cooked to perfection. This ceremony communicates to all McDonald's employees the value of hamburger quality. It also requires store managers to become very familiar with the 700-page policy and procedures book.

Stories The stories that are told within an organization can have a profound impact on organizational culture regardless of whether the stories are true or false. Most stories are narratives based on true events that are shared among employees and told to new members to inform them about the organization. Some stories are considered legends because the events are historic, but may have been embellished with fictional details. Other stories may be myths, not supported by facts, but directionally consistent with the values and beliefs of the organization. Stories are important because they preserve the primary values of the organization and provide a shared understanding among all employees.

A classic story that serves to symbolize and preserve the H-P way at Hewlett-Packard involves one of the founders, David Packard. One evening as Packard was wandering around the Palo Alto lab after work hours he discovered a prototype constructed of inferior materials. Packard destroyed the model and left a note saying, "That's not the H-P way. Dave."

Symbols A symbol is something that represents something else. In one sense, ceremonies, rites, and stories are symbols because they represent the deeper values of the organization. Physical symbols in organizations are often used to represent and support organizational culture because they focus attention on a specific item and because they are so powerful. The value of physical symbols is that they communicate important cultural values. If the physical symbols are consistent with the ceremonies and stories, they are a powerful facilitator of culture.

Many organizations give ten- and twenty-year service pins as a form of recognition to employees who stay with the organization. Although these service pins are attractive pieces of jewelry, their significance to the employees far exceeds their economic value. Part of their value comes from the elaborate awards banquets at which they are presented. Such elaborate ceremonies and rites often contribute to the significance of physical symbols.

Language Almost every organization develops its own jargon and abbreviations, and these communication devices contribute to a unique organizational culture. Some companies use a specific slogan, metaphor, or saying to convey special meaning to employees. Metaphors are often rich with meaning and convey an entire sermon in only a short sentence. Slogans can be readily picked up and repeated by employees as well as customers of the company. "IBM means service" and "Everybody at Northrop is in marketing" are two slogans that are used by organizations. These slogans symbolize what the company stands for to both employees and the external public.

Theory Z Culture

A distinctive type of culture that has become well known in America is called the "theory Z" organizational culture. "Theory Z" refers to an American adaptation of the Japanese style of management and is sometimes referred to as a "hierarchical clan" type of culture.[26]

Comparisons between American and Japanese organizational cultures were particularly popular during the early 1980s. At this time, productivity comparisons between American and Japanese industry suggested that the Japanese style of management was far superior to the styles that were used in America.

The economic success of Japanese firms encouraged U.S. managers to adopt selected Japanese management practices. Some of the major American organizations that have attempted to duplicate theory Z characteristics include Kodak, Procter & Gamble, Hewlett-Packard, IBM, and Rockwell International.

The overriding feature of a type Z organization is a feeling of collaboration between managers and employees. When firms successfully implement a **theory Z management** structure, the employees experience a sense of equality and involvement, as if they were full partners in the enterprise. Since employees have a greater understanding of one another's point of view, shared norms and values begin to emerge. These shared values help the organization achieve more reliable performance from its employees and less resistance to change. In a type Z organization, seventy or eighty people may be involved in discussing a problem and generating creative ideas. Although a group discussion with so many people takes considerable time, the implementation is almost immediate. Furthermore, the sense of collective responsibility increases productivity.

A comparison of the basic properties distinguishing type A, the typical American corporation, from type Z, an organization patterned after the Japanese hierarchical clan organization, is illustrated in Exhibit 11.10. Perhaps the most significant difference between a type A and type Z organization is the long-term employ-

EXHIBIT 11.10 Comparison of Three Organizational Cultures

Type A (American)	Type J (Japanese)	Type Z (Modified American)
Short-term employment	Lifetime employment	Long-term employment
Individual decision making	Consensual decision making	Consensual decision making
Individual responsibility	Collective responsibility	Individual responsibility
Rapid evaluation and promotion	Slow evaluation and promotion	Slow evaluation and promotion
Explicit, formalized control	Implicit, informal control	Implicit, informal control with explicit, formalized measures
Specialized career path	Nonspecialized career path	Moderately specialized career path
Segmented concern	Holistic concern	Holistic concern, including family

Source: William G. Ouchi and Alfred M. Jaeger, "Type Z Organization: Stability in the Midst of Mobility," *Academy of Management Review,* vol. 3, no. 2 (April 1987), pp. 308, 311. Used by permission.

ment relationship between the employee and the organization. While American employees tend to move freely from one organization to another, the dominant career pattern in Japanese companies is lifetime employment within the same organization. The short-term employment of American employees contributes to the trend of rapid evaluation and promotion and highly specialized careers. With the long-term employment orientation of Japanese employees, however, there are fewer pressures for promotion and evaluation, and the employees pursue a broader and less specialized career.[27]

The group orientation of Japanese employees is much different from the individual orientation of Americans. While Americans focus on individual decision making and individual responsibility, Japanese employees are more concerned about consensual decision making and collective responsibility for the decisions they make.

The combination of collective decision making with a commonly shared culture reduces the need for close supervision, coordination, and evaluation among the Japanese. Since employees have a long-term relationship with the firm, superiors develop a holistic concern regarding the total quality of life of their subordinates. However, the lives of American employees tend to be more segmented, and managers are concerned about an employee's life away from work only if it influences job performance. Explicit rules and formal guidelines are used by American managers to control the behavior of their subordinates.

Japanese companies have a longer time horizon in the employment, evaluation, and promotion of their employees, and also a longer time horizon for evaluating organizational effectiveness. Japanese executives do not experience as many pressures as American executives to show short-term results. Part of the reason for this cultural difference comes from the shared ownership of Japanese companies by customers, suppliers, producers, and even the banks. Japanese electronics companies, for example, tend to have much higher debt-to-equity ratios than do American firms.

In summary, the ideal theory Z organization combines a basic cultural commitment to individual values with a highly collective group pattern of interaction. Employment is effectively a lifetime commitment; consequently, turnover is low

APPLYING ORGANIZATIONAL BEHAVIOR
ACROSS CULTURES

Does Japanese Management Work Outside Japan?

 The economic success of Japanese companies has led to a preoccupation on the part of scholars and executives with Japanese management styles. To boost productivity, some American firms have experimented with various Japanese management techniques, especially quality circles, with disappointing results. Their failure contributed to the conclusion that Japanese management only works in Japan with a Japanese culture.

The need for a full-scale cultural change, however, has been challenged by the successes of Japanese-owned companies in America with Japanese managers and American workers. Most of these companies have been remarkably successful without forcing their employees to adopt Japanese cultural values either in their personal lives or at work. Only in the movies are employees required to sing the company song, perform calesthenics, adopt an Asian religion, and learn a new language.

A good illustration of a successful Japanese-owned company in America is the TPC Company, located in the northeastern United States. The original company was founded in 1916 and grew to become the city's second largest employer in the 1970s. By 1983, however, after a period of declining profitability, tight budgets, frequent layoffs, a lack of renovation, high grievances, and a six-week strike, the company was sold to a holding company. In 1986, the TPC Company, headquartered in Tokyo, bought the company and began managing it. Although the hourly workers and middle managers were former employees, the top managers were Japanese.

To overcome prejudices and misperceptions, the new owners made it clear that TPC would be run as an "American" factory. Only three of the nine Japanese employees at this plant were members of top management. All the top American executives were sent to Japan for three weeks to learn the culture of the parent company.

The new management installed a new inventory control system (called Kanban) and a statistical process control system (SPC) to improve quality. These programs, which are characteristic of Japanese firms, required extensive training. They also renovated the existing machinery and made major capital expenditures to expand and improve the plant. The antagonistic relationship with the union was eliminated by attending union committee meetings to listen and answer questions. A new work schedule provided abundant opportunities for overtime work, which made employees much more content with their pay.

Two and a half years after the takeover, layoffs had ceased, the plant operated seven days a week, and it was highly profitable. To instill a group orientation (rather than individualistic) toward work, the new management reinstated the tradition of company parties and picnics, safety programs, suggestion boxes, and quality control groups.

The success of the TPC Company and other Japanese-owned companies in America suggests that their success is achieved by good Japanese managers who make good management decisions, rather than by unique Japanese management practices and the imposition of Japanese cultural values.

Source: Mary Yoko Brannen, "Culture as the Critical Factor in Implementing Innovation," *Business Horizons* (November–December 1991), pp. 59–67.

and individuals progress through a clearly defined sequence of career positions. Older employees who have limited physical stamina are placed in jobs that are more conducive to their levels of physical energy, something that would be considered a demotion by most Americans. Decision making is done by consensus, and there is a shared sense of collective responsibility for the success of a decision.

SUMMARY

1. All organizations are open social systems that consist of the patterned activities of a group of people; these activities tend to be goal directed. An open system is "open" in the sense that it relies on the external environment to obtain inputs of energy and other resources and to dispose of the product into society.

2. Social organizations are more complex than other types of systems, such as framework systems, control systems, and biological systems. However, biological systems, especially the human body, represent a useful analogy to help us understand the systems concept. Just as the human body is a system, with subsystems performing essential functions, so too is an organization a system with its central functions performed by its subsystems.

3. All open social systems have common characteristics defining them. Ten of these common characteristics are: the importation of energy, the transformation process, the output, systems as cycles of events, negative entropy, information input, dynamic homeostasis, differentiation, integration, and equifinality.

4. As an open social system, organizations are composed of several subsystems that are essential to the functioning of the organization. Five subsystems that are necessary for any organization to survive and grow are the production, maintenance, supportive, adaptive, and managerial subsystems.

5. Organizations depend on the environment for support and acceptance. Within the organization's domain, the environment can be divided into subenvironments, called "sectors," that contain similar elements. Eight of the most important sectors for each organization are human resources, raw materials, financial resources, consumer markets, technology, industry, economic conditions, and government. Within each organization, certain departments or positions are assigned to interact with these environmental sectors. These positions are called boundary-spanning roles.

6. Some organizations enjoy a reasonably safe and secure environment, while others face an extremely uncertain environment. The degree of environmental uncertainty is determined by two environmental variables: complexity and stability. Environmental complexity concerns the number of external sectors or forces that can be expected to influence the organization. Environmental stability concerns whether the environment is dynamic and constantly changing, or whether it is reasonably stable. Organizations typically use a variety of strategies to reduce the uncertainty of their environment, such as changing organizational structures, planning and forecasting, mergers and acquisitions, cooptation, public relations and advertising, political activity, or illegal activities.

7. Organizations have official goals that define the mission of the organization and operative goals that describe what the organization is actually trying to accomplish. Organizational goals serve a variety of purposes: to legitimate the organization, to direct and motivate employees, to guide decisions, to reduce uncertainty, and to serve as a criterion for measuring effectiveness.

8. Organizational effectiveness is the success or goal accomplishment of the organization and should be measured in terms of the entire input, transformation process, output, and recycling processes. The major approaches to measuring organizational effectiveness include the resource acquisition approach, the transformation approach, the output approach, and the recycling approach. The constituency approach involves surveying the opinions of the organization's constituencies, such as customers, stockholders, owners, and employees, to assess how well they think the organization is doing.

9. *Organizational climate* and *organizational culture* are terms that have been used to describe the characteristics of organizations. *Climate* typically refers to characteristics that describe the differences between organizations and includes such variables as managerial values, leadership style, economic conditions, unionization, organizational size, and nature of the work. Organizational surveys are often used as a means of measuring organizational climate.

10. Organizational culture encompasses the values, beliefs, and attitudes of members within an organization. These characteristics define the organization and are typically very stable, enduring, and difficult either to define or to evaluate. Organizational culture is reflected in the ceremonies, stories, symbols, and language of the employees.

11. Theory Z culture is a distinctive type of culture that has become particularly prominent in America. It is an American adaptation of the Japanese style of management and is characterized by a long-term employment relationship, intense company loyalty, a group orientation with collective decision making, and a holistic orientation toward life that combines life at work with life off the job.

DISCUSSION QUESTIONS

1. What is meant by the statement "Organizations are not physical objects"? If they are not physical, what are they?

2. Would a student protest group be considered an organization? What would need to happen before this group could be considered an organization?

3. Is it true that all social organizations are open systems? Why can't a religious group or a social commune withdraw from society and live as a closed system?

4. How does an organization achieve negative entropy? According to the second law of thermodynamics, entropy is a natural law of all physical sciences.

5. A group of friends who all play string instruments get together every Thursday night just to practice and play together. Would this group be considered an organization? What are its patterned activities, inputs, transformation process, and outputs? How are its outputs recycled to provide additional inputs?

6. What are the adaptive and supportive subsystem activities of a university?

7. How does open-system theory provide a useful framework for analyzing the competitive advantages of a firm?

8. Several critics have argued that recruiters from the military and industry should not be allowed on college campuses—that universities are in the business of educating students, not supporting the military-industrial complex. What type of subsystem activities are represented by recruiting and college placement offices, and how essential are these activities to the organization?

9. Why do organizations need to reduce environmental uncertainty? Why is that so essential for organizational survival?

10. What are the differences between organizational efficiency and effectiveness? What are the potential consequences of confusing these two terms?

11. If the constituency approach is used to measure organizational effectiveness, how much conflict should we anticipate? Can an organization expect to satisfy each of the different constituencies simultaneously?

12. What are the advantages and disadvantages of a theory Z organizational culture? How strongly would you recommend it to organizational leaders?

GLOSSARY

adaptive subsystem The patterned activities within an organization that help it adapt to a changing environment. Research and development are some of the most important adaptive subsystem activities.

boundary-spanning roles Positions within an organization that interact with environmental sectors.

constituency approach A method of measuring organizational effectiveness by surveying the attitudes of constituencies such as owners, customers, and employees.

cooptation A strategy of reducing uncertainty by bringing external individuals into the decision-making process of an organization, such as putting external people on the board of directors.

domain The elements within the environment that have a potential influence on an organization.

effectiveness A measure of the organization's success in bringing inputs into the organization, transforming them into usable outputs, and recycling them within the environment.

efficiency A ratio of inputs to outputs that measures the success of the transformation process according to how many outputs it achieves with a given level of inputs.

environmental complexity The number of external elements within the environment that can be expected to have an influence on an organization.

environmental stability A measure of how much change occurs within the environment and whether the environmental sectors are relatively stable or highly dynamic and constantly changing.

institutional function Part of the supportive subsystem activities that involve helping the organization to be accepted within the external environment and building support from other organizations.

maintenance subsystem Patterned activities within the organization that serve to maintain the willingness of individuals to continue their organizational membership. These include rewarding, recognizing, and encouraging individual members.

managerial subsystem Those patterned activities within an organization that are involved with administrative actions such as allocating resources, creating structure, and settling disputes.

official goals The formal goals stated by the organization that define its mission and purpose.

open system An organization that is influenced by its environment in procuring external resources such as energy and materials and disposing of its product into the environment. Ten common characteristics of open systems are importation of energy, the transformation process, the output, the recycling process, negative entropy, information input, dynamic homeostasis, differentiation, integration, and equifinality.

operative goals Organizational goals that tend to be relatively specific and reflect what the organization actually attempts to accomplish.

organizational climate The characteristics that describe an organization and distinguish it from other organizations. Although they are relatively stable, these characteristics are not permanent and include such variables as managerial values, leadership style, organizational structure, and the nature of the work.

organizational culture The relatively enduring and permanent characteristics of an organization that consist of the key values, beliefs, and understandings shared by members of the organization and that explain how new members should think and act within the organization.

output approach A method of measuring organizational effectiveness by measuring the output or products of the organization.

patterned activities The basic building blocks of an organization that consist of repeated activities that continue to occur with regularity and predictability.

production subsystem The patterned activities within an organization that transform the inputs into outputs and that are often represented by the production department.

recycling approach A method of measuring organizational effectiveness that focuses on how well the outputs are transformed into usable inputs for the organization.

resource acquisition approach A method of measuring organizational effectiveness that focuses on how successfully the organization can acquire valued resources from the environment.

sector An important segment of the environment that has the potential for influencing the organization. Eight of the most important sectors are human resources, raw materials, financial resources, consumer markets, technology, industry, economic conditions, and government.

supportive subsystem Patterned activities within the organization that focus on supporting the organization by procuring inputs from the environment, such as money and raw resources, and disposing of the product within the environment.

theory Z management An American adaptation of the Japanese management style, which is characterized by organizational loyalty, a long-term employment commitment, and a strong group orientation in making decisions.

transformation approach A method of measuring organizational effectiveness that focuses on how well inputs are transformed into usable outputs.

value chain The combination of interacting activities that brings resources into a firm, adds value to them, and sends them to the next link in the chain. These activities include five primary activities (inbound logistics, operations, outbound logistics, marketing, and service) and four support activities (firm infrastructure, human resource management, technology development, and procurement).

NOTES

1. Daniel Katz and Robert L. Kahn, *The Social Psychology of Organizations*, 2nd ed. (New York: Wiley, 1978).

2. Kenneth E. Boulding, "General Systems Theory: The Skeleton of Science," *General Systems, Yearbook of the Society for the Advancement of General System Theory*, vol. 1 (1956), pp. 11–17.

3. Katz and Kahn, op. cit., chap. 2.

4. Ibid., chap. 3.

5. Ibid., p. 52.

6. Michael E. Porter, *Competitive Strategy: Techniques for Analyzing Industries and Competitors* (New York: Free Press, 1980); Michael E. Porter, *Competitive Advantage: Creating and Sustaining Superior Performance* (New York: Free Press, 1985).

7. Richard L. Daft, *Organization Theory and Design*, 2nd ed. (Saint Paul, Minn.: West, 1986), chap. 2.

8. Ibid., pp. 49–55.

9. Ibid., pp. 59–66.

10. Ibid., p. 67.

11. Jeffrey Pfeffer, "Size and Composition of Corporate Boards of Directors: The Organization and Its Environment," *Administrative Science Quarterly*, vol. 17 (1972), pp. 218–228.

12. Don Hellriegel and John W. Slocum, Jr., "Organizational Climate: Measures, Research and Contingencies," *Academy of Management Journal*, vol. 17, no. 2 (June 1974), pp. 255–280.

13. Alfred A. Marcus and Robert S. Goodman, "Victims and Shareholders: The Dilemmas of Presenting Corporate Policy During a Crisis," *Academy of Management Journal*, vol. 34 (1991), pp. 281–305; Anne S. Tsui, "A Multiple-Constituency Model of Effectiveness: An Empirical Examination of the Human Resource Sub-Unit Level," *Administrative Science Quarterly*, vol. 35 (September 1990), pp. 458–483.

14. Hellriegel and Slocum, Jr., op. cit.

15. G. Forehand and B. Gilmer, "Environmental Variation in Studies of Organizational Behavior," *The Psychological Bulletin*, vol. 22 (1964), pp. 361–382; William H. Glick, "Conceptualizing and Measuring Organizational and Psychological Climate: Pitfalls in Multi-Level Research," *Academy of Management Review*, vol. 10, no. 3 (1985), pp. 601–616.

16. F. Friedlander and S. Greenberg, "Effect of Job Attitudes, Training, and Organizational Climates on Performance of the Hard-Core Unemployed," *Journal of Applied Psychology*, vol. 55 (1971), pp. 287–295.

17. N. Frederickson, "Some Effects of Organizational Climates on Administrative Performance," Research Memorandum RM-66-21 (Princeton, N.J.: Educational Testing Service, 1966). (Cited by Hellriegel and Slocum, op. cit.)

18. H. Kirk Downey, Don Hellriegel, and John W. Slocum, Jr., "Congruence Between Individual Needs, Organizational Climate, Job Satisfaction and Performance," *Academy of Management Journal*, vol. 18 (1975), pp. 149–155.

19. David J. Cherrington and J. Owen Cherrington, "The Climate of Honesty in Retail Stores," in William Terris (ed.), *Employee Theft: Research Theory and Applications* (Chicago: London House Publishing, 1985), chap. 1.

20. Developed by William G. Dyer, Gene W. Dalton, and Philip B. Daniels, and distributed by Novations, Inc., Provo, Utah.

21. James C. Taylor and David G. Bowers, *Survey of Organizations: A Machine-Scored Standardized Questionnaire Instrument* (Ann Arbor: University of Michigan Center for Research on Utilization of Scientific Knowledge, 1972).

22. Paul D. Steele and Robert L. Hubbard, "Management Styles, Perceptions of Substance Abuse, and Employee Assistance Programs in Organizations," *Journal of Applied Behavioral Science*, vol. 21, no. 3 (1985), pp. 271–286.

23. Robert A. Cooke and Denise M. Rousseau, "Behavioral Norms and Expectations: A Quantitative Approach to the Assessment of Organizational Culture," *Group and Organization Studies*, vol. 13 (September 1988), pp. 245–273; W. Gibb Dyer, Jr., and Alan L. Wilkins, "Better Stories, Not Better Constructs, to Generate Better Theory: A Rejoinder to Eisenhardt," *Academy of Management Review*, vol. 16 (1991), pp. 613–619; Kathleen M. Eisenhardt, "Better Stories and Better Constructs: The Case for Rigor and Comparative Logic," *Academy of Management Review*, vol. 16 (1991), pp. 620–627.

24. Edgar H. Schein, "Coming to a New Awareness of Organizational Culture," *Sloan Management Review*, vol. 25 (Winter 1984), pp. 3–16.

25. Terrence E. Deal and Allan A. Kennedy, *Corporate Cultures* (Reading, Mass.: Addison Wesley, 1982); Harrison M. Trice and Janice M. Beyer, "Studying Organizational Cultures Through Rites and Ceremonials," *Academy of Management Review*, vol. 9 (1984), pp. 653–669.

26. William G. Ouchi, *Theory Z* (Reading, Mass.: Addison-Wesley, 1981); Richard Pascale and Anthony Athos, *The Art of Japanese Management* (New York: Warner Books, 1981).

27. William G. Ouchi and Alfred M. Jaeger, "Type Z Organization: Stability in the Midst of Mobility," *Academy of Management Review*, vol. 3 (April 1978), pp. 305–314.

EVALUATING LAW SCHOOLS

We live in a world where everything is evaluated. Business organizations are ranked within their own industry and across all industries by both *Fortune* and *Forbes* according to size, profitability, and other economic measures. Musical artists live and die by the Top 40 rankings because they know that their economic fortunes rise and fall with their ratings. College football and basketball teams watch the Associated Press and United Press International Top 20 rankings very closely because they know their rankings will have a major impact on recruiting, alumni contributions, and attendance at games. These rankings influence the financial fortunes of the schools as much as their social prestige.

With all of the excitement about evaluating programs and organizations, it is interesting to observe the antievaluation policy of the American Bar Association regarding law schools. The ABA claims that rankings of law school programs are unreliable, misleading, and a disservice to the schools themselves. In 1976, the American Bar Association adopted the following statement:

> No rating of law schools beyond the simple statement of their accreditation status is attempted or advocated by the official organizations in legal education. Qualities that make one kind of school

good for one student may not be as important to another. The American Bar Association and its section of Legal Education and Admissions to the Bar have issued disclaimers of any law school rating systems. Prospective law students should consider a variety of factors in making their choice among schools.

The Education Council of the American Bar Association reissues this statement each year. In discrediting ratings that often appear, the council has stated in a bulletin to Deans of the ABA Approved Law Schools. "We have no knowledge of what scientific methodology, if any, is used in producing the published ratings. We have no knowledge of the accuracy of the ratings." The council is very concerned that published ratings will be used, and indeed cited, by individuals as a true assessment of a particular law school. "We would urge the Deans of ABA Approved Law Schools to carry the message that published law school ratings are of little value, and indeed may mislead the public. In an era of greater consumer protection, we must assist in preventing law schools' constituencies from being misled" (Memorandum D8586-50, from James P. White, Consultant on Legal Education to the American Bar Association to Deans of ABA Approved Law Schools, April 23, 1986).

Questions

1. Do you agree with the American Bar Association that the rating of law schools is a serious disservice to the schools and their programs? Are industrial rankings by *Forbes* and *Fortune* equally dysfunctional?

2. Although the American Bar Association discourages it, several rankings of law schools are published using the criteria of law school admission test (LSAT) scores, grade-point averages of entering students, faculty salaries, financial funding per student, publications by faculty members, and number of volumes in the law school library. Are these criteria reliable and objective? Would rankings based on these criteria be of interest to you and others?

3. People don't seem to mind using simple opinion polls to rank songs and football teams. What are the advantages and disadvantages of using a simple opinion poll to rank law schools?

ORGANIZATIONAL SYMBOLS

PART I ORGANIZATIONAL ART

Purpose. The purpose of this exercise is to learn more about organizations by visualizing them in ways that others can examine. Organizations represent a complex interaction of many interpersonal associations, and we often have difficulty sharing our interpretations of these complex interactions with others. Organizational art in the form of cartoons or metaphors is a useful method for illustrating an organization. This exercise asks you to develop a visual picture showing how you see an organization.

Activity. On a blank sheet of paper, draw a picture of an organization. Select an organization that you know well from your own personal experience, and create an illustration of it either by drawing a picture, creating a cartoon, or writing a metaphor. Here are some illustrations to help you get started.

A woman who worked in a large bureaucratic organization with rigid rules and procedures caricaturized her organization as a large dinosaur sinking in a pool of quicksand, which represented the rules. One of her colleagues illustrated the same idea by drawing a picture of an overweight cat entangled in a ball of twine, which represented the rules. A person who worked in the typesetting department of an advertising agency wrote a story about a hapless fool who was caught on a treadmill with fire-breathing dragons closing in behind. A union steward drew a picture of a battle scene between management and union. The company logo or union symbol on the warriors' swords and shields depicted the union's assault against the corporate castle.

Describe the picture you drew to your classmates, and share your feelings about it. As you explain your picture to them and listen to them describe their pictures, do you get a clearer view of how people view organizations?

PART II ORGANIZATIONAL METAPHORS

Purpose. The purpose of this exercise is to learn more about organizations through organizational metaphor. A metaphor is a figure of speech containing an implied comparison in which a word or phrase ordinarily used to describe one thing is applied to another. An organizational metaphor applies the characteristics and relationships found in one organization to another. Here are three organizational metaphors.

1. *A defensive football unit.* Working in the white-collar crime division was a lot like playing football. We were the defensive team trying to stop offensive teams who came at us with some really sophisticated schemes for committing fraud. Every morning we met in a huddle, and our captain called the play for the day. We each had our own assignments but we had to work as a team. If another team member was in trouble, we all helped out. It was always nice when our plays worked like they were planned, but it was more exciting when a broken play forced us to scramble and cover for each other. One time when we were closing in on a bust, one officer moved too soon. That off-sides penalty cost us more than just five yards; one officer was shot and two people we really wanted to catch got away.

2. *Roller derby.* Working for the daily newspaper is like a game of Roller Derby that never ends. Day after day we keep going around in the same circles, knocking each other down, trying to put on a good show for the public. We fight with the people in our department to see who gets the lead story and we fight with other departments to see who gets prime space. There doesn't need to be this much conflict, but there is anyway, and you always have to be looking over your shoulder to see who's closing in on you. If you're not

prepared to knock them down, they'll knock you down and run over you.

3. *The Symphony Conductor.* I supervise the clerical staff in the college of business, and in many ways I'm just like a symphony conductor directing an orchestra. All the players in my orchestra are assigned their own special jobs, and if we all do our jobs right, our efficiency is just as beautiful as a symphony. Our policies are standardized, so we all play in the same key, and our written procedures are just like a musical score. During the summer things are slow and our music is soft. But it reaches a crescendo at the beginning and end of each semester. If one typing center is too busy, we can move some of the work to another center, just like asking some first violins to play the second violin part. But we don't ask the student advisement center to help with the typing, any more than you would have a bassoon play the violin's part. Occasionally some of our people have nothing to do but wait for the phones to ring or for students to ask for help. But it is just as important for them to be there waiting as for a musician to sit and count measures of rest.

Activities

1. Develop one or two organizational metaphors that describe your experiences in organizations.

2. Use the following metaphors to illustrate some aspect of life in organizations: a cowboy, a family, an ocean beach, and an automobile.

Organizational Structure and Design

LEARNING OBJECTIVES

After studying this chapter, you should be able to

1. List the major bases of departmentalization, and describe the advantages and disadvantages of each.

2. Identify the variables that are conducive to wide versus narrow spans of control.

3. Explain the relative advantages of centralized versus decentralized decision making and authority.

4. Describe matrix structures, and explain when they are useful.

5. Identify the differences between mechanistic and organic organizational structures, and describe the advantages and disadvantages of each.

6. Compare the characteristics of bureaucracy and System Four organizational structures, and explain the advantages and disadvantages of each.

7. Explain the effects of technology on organizational structure, and explain the kinds of technologies and environments that are appropriate for mechanistic and organic structures.

8. Identify and describe the stages of an organization's life cycle.

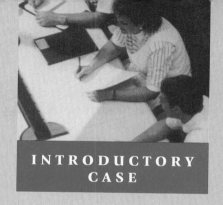

BUREAUCRATIC BATTLES AND UNORGANIZED EFFICIENCY

During his undergraduate years, Jim Tolman worked three summers for Land Managers, a real estate service company that provided accounting, legal, financial, and computer assistance to real estate investors. When he was hired, Jim was simply told to help some of the other employees or find his own clients to service. He was not assigned to a department, he was not given a job description, and he was not told when to start work. He was given a desk and a list of the five company officers and told to report to one of them at least monthly to justify what he was doing. The company had almost no formal policies or rules and no standard operating procedures, yet it seemed to function very efficiently.

Because Land Managers functioned so well with a loose structure, Jim could not understand why the university he was attending had so many formal rules and procedures. The formality of the rules was especially troublesome when Jim tried to get a tuition refund for a seminar that was canceled due to insufficient enrollment. When he asked for a refund from the registration office where he originally paid the tuition, he was told they didn't give refunds, only the finance office gives refunds. When he went to the finance office, however, he was told that before they could give him his full refund they would need verification that the course had been canceled and this verification would need to come from the department that offered the course.

When Jim asked the department chairman to send a memo to the finance office explaining that the course had been canceled, the chairman refused. He said that the cancelation decision was not made by the department but by an "archaic rule" within the college to which he objected. He instructed Jim to go to the dean's office to complain about the canceled course and to get a memo from someone there.

When he got to the dean's office, he learned that the dean was out of town for two weeks and no one else would help him. Both the dean's secretary and the associate dean said course listings were under the direction of the departments and the memo would have to come from the department.

When he returned to make an appointment with the department chairman, Jim was frustrated and angry. He felt trapped in the middle of a bureaucratic battle that was beyond his control, and he expressed his irritation to the departmental secretary. After learning of his plight, she told Jim that she knew someone who worked in the finance office and offered to call her and say that the course was canceled. Jim waited for her to make the call and then returned to the finance office for his refund.

Questions

1. Should the university be as loosely structured as the real estate company?

2. Are the elaborate rules and procedures in universities either necessary or desirable? Could a university operate with a more loosely organized structure, like that of the real estate company?

3. What are the benefits of rules and formal procedures? When do they make organizations more effective?

In the previous chapter, an organization was described as an open social system consisting of the patterned activities of a group of individuals. This chapter describes how these patterned activities are structured. The purpose of organizational structure is first to create and then to regulate and perpetuate the patterned activities. Organizational structure serves to reduce variability in human performance, or, in other words, it serves to control behavior by making it coordinated and predictable.

Although some people object to the idea of controlling human behavior because it appears to destroy individuality and autonomy, control is nevertheless essential. An organization cannot survive if its members behave in a random, unpredictable manner. Such a situation would produce chaos and disorganization. The difference between a well-organized and poorly organized group is as dramatic as the difference between the beauty of an orchestra playing a symphony versus the noise the musicians produce when they are warming up and tuning their instruments. To obtain the necessary patterned activities and thereby create an organization, the variability in human behavior must be reduced so that people behave in regular, predictable patterns. Although organizations vary in the amount of control they require from their members, at least some control is inherent in every organization.

The term *organizational structure* refers to the relatively fixed relationships among the jobs in the organization. The process of creating this structure and making decisions about the relative benefits of alternative structures is called **organizational design.**

CONCEPTS OF ORGANIZATIONAL DESIGN

The creation of an organizational structure requires an organization to respond to two basic issues: (1) differentiation, or division of labor among its members, and (2) integration, or coordination of what has been divided. Therefore, the field of organizational structure examines the manner in which an organization divides labor into specific tasks and achieves coordination among these tasks. Five design decisions are necessary for creating an organizational structure. These design decisions involve division of labor, departmentalization, span of control, delegation of authority, and coordinating mechanisms.

Division of Labor

The term **"division of labor"** refers to the process of dividing the total task of a unit into successively smaller jobs. Another term related to the division of labor is "job specialization." All jobs are specialized to some degree, since everyone can't do everything, but some jobs are considerably more specialized than others. One of the major benefits of organized activities is that a group of people working together through a division of labor are able to produce more than they could if they were working alone.

The key issue associated with division of labor concerns the extent to which jobs should be specialized. Specialization is low when employees perform a variety of different tasks and high when each person performs only a single task. In a word processing center, for example, the degree of specialization is low if three typists are allowed to edit, type, and proofread the manuscripts they type. However, if each of these functions is assigned to a different individual, the degree of specialization would be high. The degree of specialization can be represented along a continuum.

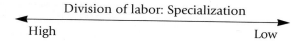

Deciding on the appropriate level of specialization is an important design decision because it has a great impact on organizational productivity. It is possible to create jobs that are so highly specialized that the organization suffers from a lack of coordination and there are times when there isn't enough work to keep everyone busy. Highly specialized jobs can also be extremely boring. Yet there are definite advantages to highly specialized jobs, and the chief advantage is that such jobs contribute to higher levels of productivity. Several reasons explain why specialization is more productive:

1. It creates greater proficiency by allowing employees to perform the same repetitive activity.
2. It requires less training to master the job.
3. Less time is lost going from one activity to another.
4. Special tools can be developed that can lead to complete automation of a task.
5. There is better quality control of the output.

In analyzing the results of a division of labor, a distinction is often made between line and staff activities. **Line activities** are functional activities directly related to the principal work flow of an organization. In a manufacturing firm, for example, all production-related activities, such as engineering, stamping, assembling, painting, inspection, and shipping, would be considered line activities. **Staff activities** are supportive activities that provide service and advice to line personnel. These activities might include the personnel, legal, and accounting departments of an organization.

Departmentalization[1]

Division of labor is the process of dividing a job into specialized tasks; **departmentalization** is the process of combining jobs into groups or departments. Managers must make a crucial decision regarding the most appropriate basis for forming departments, and central to this issue is the degree of similarity among the jobs within the department. Will it be a homogeneous department with all jobs involving similar activities or a heterogeneous department with jobs involving unrelated activities? Jobs can be grouped according to several criteria, and the most popular criteria include function, product, territory, and clientele, as illustrated in Exhibit 12.1.

Departmentalization: Job similarity

Homogeneous ←————————————————————————→ Heterogeneous

EXHIBIT 12.1   Bases of Departmentalization

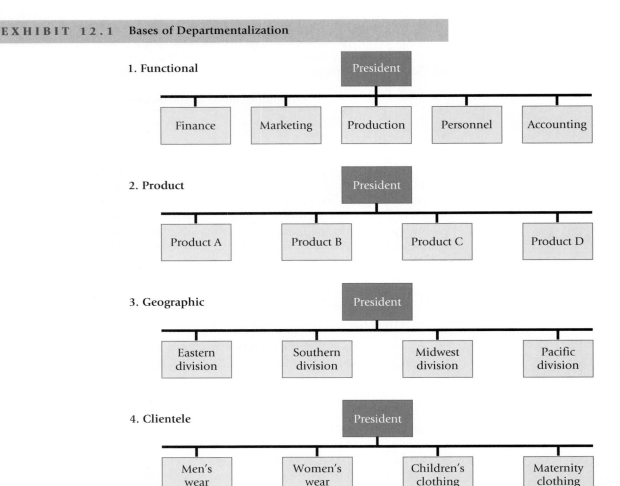

Functional Departmentalization. All the jobs associated with performing a particular function can be grouped together into the same department. For example, all the jobs associated with accounting, such as general ledger accountant, accounts payable clerk, accounts receivable clerk, and cost accountant, could all be combined into an accounting department. All these jobs involve similar activities, and they are related to a similar function that requires training in accounting. Organizing the departments by function would be a homogeneous form of departmentalization, since everyone in the department would share the same specialized skills. Other forms of departmentalization tend to be market-based and are more heterogeneous.

Functional departmentalization is probably the most widely used scheme in most organizations because in most situations it is the most effective method. This explains why a manufacturing company is typically departmentalized into production, marketing, finance, accounting, research and development, and personnel departments. Most hospitals are departmentalized in terms of such functions as surgery, nursing, psychiatry, pharmacy, personnel, and housekeeping.

Functional departmentalization has both advantages and disadvantages. Perhaps the most significant advantage is that it promotes skill specialization by having people who face similar problems and opportunities work together. The functional form also permits the maximum use of resources and encourages the use of specialists and specialized equipment, thereby eliminating duplication of equipment and effort. Communication and performance are usually improved because superiors share expertise with their subordinates.

The disadvantages of functional departmentalization are that it reduces communication and cooperation between departments and fosters a parochial perspective. This narrow orientation limits managers' capacities for coordination and encourages a short time horizon. Functional departmentalization has often led to a problem referred to as **suboptimizing.** Suboptimizing is said to occur when one department is pursuing its own goals and trying to look good at the expense of other departments or the organization as a whole. Suboptimizing is particularly problematic when departments are rewarded for achieving their own goals. Although departments should be rewarded for helping other departments, many departmental goals can best be achieved when each department pursues its own selfish interests. Custodial departments, for example, could keep the buildings cleaner if no one used the buildings. Likewise, the accounting and personnel departments could generate better reports if managers from whom the information was obtained spent all their time completing lengthy forms. Coordination and support across functional departments often become difficult because departments are separated both geographically and psychologically, and members come to view problems only from their limited functional perspectives.

Product Departmentalization. Product departmentalization consists of combining into a department jobs that involve producing similar products. This type of departmentalization typically occurs in large firms when it becomes difficult to coordinate the various functional departments. The members of a product-oriented department can develop greater expertise in researching, manufacturing, and distributing a specific product line. Managers have better control over the success or failure of each product if the authority, responsibility, and accountability are assigned according to products. This type of departmentalization is illustrated by the "brand" management structure that Procter & Gamble uses with its major products.

The product form of departmentalization also has both advantages and disadvantages and is often contrasted with the functional form of departmentalization. The major advantage of product departmentalization is that it creates greater interdepartmental coordination and focuses the efforts of each department on producing an effective and useful product. Companies organized by product are generally more customer oriented, and their employees tend to be more cohesive and involved in their work.

The major disadvantage of organizing by product is that the resources and skills of the organization are not fully employed unless the organization is extremely large. For example, a computer-driven lathe machine that is used for only one product and sits idle much of the time represents an inefficient use of capital resources. Another disadvantage is that product-oriented departments usually lead to increased costs because of duplication of activities, especially staff functions.

Geographic Departmentalization. Organizations use a geographic form of departmentalization when they assign all the activities in a geographic area to the same unit. This type of departmentalization typically occurs when organizations are dispersed over a large geographical area. The logic underlying this method is that all activities in a given area or region can be assigned to the same manager to oversee. The manager in each area can supervise both the functions that are performed and the products that are produced and sold within that area. This form of departmentalization is popular among retail companies that have stores located in many different cities. Each store manager is ultimately responsible for recruiting, hiring, training, advertising, sales promotions, security, and other diverse functions.

The major advantage of geographic departmentalization comes from minimizing problems created by distance, such as difficulties in communicating, observing, and making timely decisions. The disadvantage is that organizations are required to forgo the important advantages associated with the functional and product forms of departmentalization, which would have been far superior if distance hadn't precluded them.

Customer Departmentalization. Occasionally the most effective way of combining jobs is to organize them according to the customers who are served. These advantages typically occur when the clientele fall into distinct categories and the needs of each group are significantly different. Many universities, for example, have a separate evening class program or an executive MBA program because the interests and needs of the students in these two groups are significantly different from those of the regular day-time students. Many department stores have separate departments for men's clothing, women's clothing, maternity clothing, and children's clothing, because the customers served by each department have unique and separate interests.

Each form of departmentalization has both advantages and disadvantages. Therefore, managers are required to balance the various strengths and weaknesses of each form of departmentalization and identify the form that produces the highest efficiency. In most situations, managers use a mixed strategy that combines two or more forms of departmentalization.

For example, department stores combine the advantages of customer departmentalization with a functional form of organization among the staff units. The accounting, finance, personnel, and purchasing departments represent a functional departmentalization, while the men's clothing, women's clothing, boys' clothing, and maternity departments represent a customer form of departmentalization.

Span of Control

In selecting the **span of control,** managers decide how many people should be placed in a group under one supervisor: what is the appropriate size of a work group? The number of subordinates assigned to each supervisor could vary along a continuum from few to many.

Span of control: Number

Few   Many

The span-of-control decision has a major influence on the organization's shape and structure. Organizations that use a broad span of control have relatively few hierarchical levels, because many people work under the authority of a single supervisor. Where the span of control is narrow, however, each manager supervises only a few subordinates. As a result, a tall organizational structure is created. Tall and flat organizational structures are illustrated in Exhibit 12.2. Both hypothetical structures involve thirty-one positions. A narrow span of control, with only two subordinates per supervisor, produces a tall organizational structure with five hierarchical levels. However, a span of control of five produces a flat organizational structure with only three hierarchical levels.

A tall organizational structure with a narrow span of control allows for closer control over subordinates and greater personal contact between manager and subordinate. The risk, however, is that a manager with a narrow span of control comes to know only two or three subordinates very well and fails to become acquainted with others in the hierarchy. Consequently, tall organizations often inhibit interpersonal communication within the organization.

During the 1940s and 1950s, several management scholars were interested in prescribing the ideal span of control. One scholar calculated the geometric increase in the number of relationships a manager must supervise as the span of control increased and concluded that the maximum span of control should never exceed three or four subordinates.[2] In actual practice, however, several organizations had spans of control that exceeded twenty subordinates and the managers seemed to supervise their subordinates effectively. Consequently, it was concluded that the appropriate span of control should vary with the nature of the tasks being performed. Although a range of four to six subordinates is often recommended, a much larger span of control may be appropriate, depending on four situational variables:

1. *Contact required.* Jobs that require frequent contact and a high degree of coordination between superior and subordinates should use narrower spans of control. For example, jobs in medical technology and research and

EXHIBIT 12.2 Span of Control: Tall Versus Flat Organizational Structures

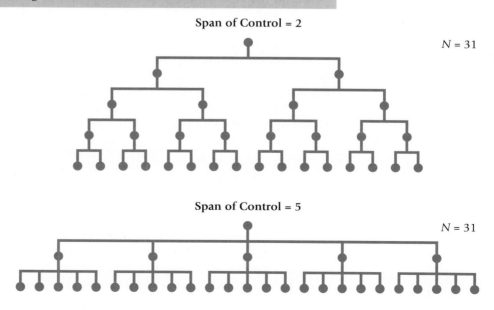

Span of Control = 2

$N = 31$

Span of Control = 5

$N = 31$

development often require frequent consultation of team members with a supervisor; therefore, a large span of control would preclude the necessary sharing of ideas and information that typically must occur on an informal basis.

2. *Level of subordinates' education and training.*   The skills and competence of subordinates influence how much supervision they need and whether the span of control should be broad or narrow. Highly skilled employees and professionals who are well trained generally require less supervision because they know their jobs well and they largely supervise themselves.

3. *Ability to communicate.*   Instructions, guidelines, and policies can be communicated to employees by a variety of methods. If all the necessary instructions can be written and then disseminated, it would be possible for one manager to supervise a large group. However, as communication becomes more difficult and job-related discussions become more important, a narrower span of control is appropriate to avoid overloading a supervisor.

4. *Nature of the task.*   Jobs that are repetitive and stable require less supervision and are more amenable to wide spans of control. For this reason, some field supervisors are able to supervise as many as sixty to seventy-five field hands in harvesting agricultural crops. However, when tasks are changed frequently, a narrower span of control is appropriate.

There seems to be a natural tendency for managers to adopt narrow spans of control, which increases the number of hierarchical levels. To improve organizational productivity, therefore, they are often encouraged to eliminate hierarchical levels by increasing spans of control. Productivity often increases after organizations have eliminated one or more hierarchical levels of administration.[3]

Delegation of Authority

The fourth issue in designing an organizational structure concerns delegation of authority and the extent to which authority is decentralized through the organizational hierarchy. Decentralization is the distribution of various types of power and authority to supervisors and production employees at lower hierarchical levels of the organizational structure. The more decentralized an organization, the greater the extent to which the rank-and-file employees can participate in and accept responsibility for decisions concerning their jobs and the activities of the organization. The amount of decision-making authority delegated to subordinates can vary along a continuum from highly **centralized** to highly **decentralized.**

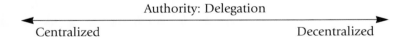

Authority: Delegation
Centralized   Decentralized

Centralization versus decentralization has been an important management issue since it was discussed by Alfred P. Sloan, Jr., president of General Motors from 1923 to 1937, who introduced the concept of the "central office." According to Sloan, authority for operating decisions should be delegated to the lowest levels possible in the various operating divisions, so that decisions could be made as close as possible to the information sources. However, the authority to make company-wide policy decisions should remain in the hands of corporate executives in the central office. Sloan argued that policies determined by the central office improve coordination and make their application more standardized and more fair. Yet, decentralized operating decisions lead to greater flexibility and increased autonomy among divisions.[4]

Most of the literature discussing the delegation of authority emphasizes the advantages of a decentralized structure. Increased decentralization often leads to greater organizational effectiveness, since it allows for greater autonomy and responsibility among employees at lower levels in the hierarchy, thereby more effectively using an organization's human resources. Supervisors in decentralized organizations typically report higher levels of job satisfaction and involvement, and they tend to be more productive because of increased autonomy and responsibility. A company that is struggling with declining sales may decide to decentralize its management structure to make it more responsive to customers and more conducive to new product development.[5]

A good example of a decentralized organization is the Minnesota Mining and Manufacturing Corporation (3M) of Minneapolis. 3M has a policy of maintaining small organizational units that have the responsibility and authority to manage themselves. 3M has over 640 business units in 52 countries, a high percentage of which employ less than 150 employees. 3M believes its strategy of decentralization contributes to significantly higher earnings and the development of new products. Like other companies, 3M has found that decentralized decision making encourages managers to improve their professional competence and makes the organization more responsive to customer needs.[6]

In spite of its benefits, however, decentralization is not universally superior and does not always contribute to greater organizational effectiveness. For example, one classic study discovered that decentralized control led to improved performance in research laboratories but caused poorer performance in production departments.[7] Even 3M has found that decentralization can be inefficient, especially in selling. When 3M was selling medical supplies to individual doctors, a decentralized sales force made sense. But when purchase decisions began to be made by large hospital groups rather than individual doctors, a small decentralized sales force was inefficient. Consequently, 3M merged two divisions and centralized its sales function.[8] Several weaknesses of decentralization have been noted, suggesting that centralized decision making is sometimes superior.

1. Decentralization makes it more difficult for certain shared functions, especially staff functions, to be executed.

2. Decentralization can create jurisdictional disputes and conflicts over priorities, since each unit essentially becomes an independent area.

3. Decentralization requires greater competence and expertise and greater commitment and involvement on the part of decision makers.

4. Decentralized decisions made by many lower-level managers create difficult problems of coordination and integration. An organization may become completely ineffective because of a lack of high-level coordination and integration.

To avoid the disadvantages of decentralization, organizations can either impose centralized standard operating procedures or rely on organizational culture to maintain control. A strong organizational culture creates a homogeneous set of

APPLYING ORGANIZATIONAL BEHAVIOR
ACROSS CULTURES

Centralization Versus Decentralization in Korea

 The top five conglomerates in South Korea are still largely run by their founding families and account for over 60 percent of the country's gross domestic product. These businesses, called *chaebols*, have traditionally been organized in highly centralized, mostly family-owned organizations that are managed under the tight control of the chairman. Decentralization is the latest trend in Korea, but it involves a significant cultural shift and it is not universally accepted.

The third- and fourth-largest corporations in South Korea are using opposite strategies to help them recover. Lucky-Goldstar, the number three conglomerate, is moving toward more decentralized decision making while the number four, Daewoo, is moving to greater centralization. Both corporations have made spectacular inroads into world markets, but they have stumbled recently because of high labor costs, a strong Korean currency, and intense Japanese competition. Consequently, both companies have been forced to make revolutionary structural changes, but they are pursuing different strategies to recover.

The Lucky-Goldstar group is extremely diversified in electronics, chemicals, trade, and financial services. Ever since it started in 1947, the strategic planning and operational decision making have been dominated by the founding Koo family. These decisions were primarily made during breakfast meetings hosted by a handful of family executives. As the company grew, however, this centralized process became too unwieldy and cumbersome. The chairman, Koo Cha-Kyung, eventually recognized that his hierarchical decision-making style did not fit the dynamic needs of the company and excessive decision-making delays were partially responsible for its problems. Employee dissatisfaction and alienation led to union unrest, defective parts went undetected, creating quality problems, and price increases reduced the company's market share. As a first step in correcting these problems, Koo delegated more decision-making authority to his front-line managers and created three special executive committees to determine strategic direction, budgeting, and personnel policies.

Going in the opposite direction, the chairman of Daewoo, Kim Woo-Choong, has centralized power and decision making by "retiring" scores of senior executives, by terminating a third of its middle management, and by making more decisions himself. The Daewoo Group is also extremely diversified in trade, auto machinery, consumer electronics, construction, shipping, computers and financial services. Many of these divisions were formerly operated as individual companies by presidents who were classmates of Kim in Seoul's elite Yonsei University. Kim delegated control to them while he spent his time traveling the world in pursuit of new markets. But Kim decided too much autonomy has been delegated to these division heads and more centralized planning and control are needed. Substantial losses in two successive years forced management to accept structural changes that eliminated many managerial positions and consolidated management functions and decision making. Two unprofitable joint ventures were dropped, as were other costly excesses, such as free haircuts for employees in the shipbuilding company.

Sources: Jie-Ae Sohn, "Lightening the Load at the Top," *Business Korea*, Vol. 8 (April 1991), pp. 26–28; Louis Kraar, "Korea's Tigers Keep Roaring," *Fortune*, vol. 125 (May 4, 1992), pp. 108–110; Laxmi Nakarmi, "At Lucky-Goldstar, the Koos Loosen the Reins," *Business Week* (February 18, 1991), pp. 72–73; Laxmi Nakarmi, "At Daewoo, a 'Revolution' at the Top," *Business Week* (February 18, 1991), pp. 68–69.

assumptions and decision premises that preserve coordination and centralization while still providing sufficient latitude for local interpretation and improvisation among decentralized units. It has been suggested that to function effectively, decentralized authority requires a strong organizational culture whose members have been socialized to use similar decision premises and assumptions. When centralization occurs via decision premises and assumptions provided by the culture, compliance occurs without surveillance. This is in sharp contrast to centralization by rules, regulations, and hierarchy, which require high surveillance.[9]

To design an effective organizational structure, managers must select the optimal amount of centralization and decentralization of authority. Power and authority should be decentralized to an extent that organizations use the knowledge and expertise of lower-level participants while simultaneously maintaining sufficient centralization to ensure adequate coordination and control. Like the other concepts of organizational design, the ideal policy depends on the situation.

Coordinating Mechanisms

Organizations need to process information and coordinate the efforts of their members. Employees at lower levels need to perform activities consistent with top-level goals, and the managers at the top need to know about the activities and accomplishments of people at lower levels.

Organizations use a variety of integrating mechanisms to achieve coordination. Five different methods of achieving coordination have been identified. They vary along a continuum of how much discretion is allowed for the worker.

Coordinating mechanisms: Personal discretion

←——→

Direct supervision and rules   Mutual adjustment

1. *Direct supervision.* Work is coordinated by designated supervisors who tell subordinates what to do.

2. *Standardization of work processes.* Jobs that are highly routine, such as assembly-line jobs, can be coordinated through standard operating procedures or the technology itself.

3. *Standardization of outputs.* When products must be produced according to technical specifications, these specifications may serve as an adequate basis for coordinating the activities. Individual workers are allowed some discretion in performing the work as long as the output meets the required specifications.

4. *Standardization of skills.* Highly skilled and trained employees can typically coordinate their own activities by performing activities consistent with their technical training. A surgical team or an ambulance crew is often coordinated by having people perform their jobs according to the way they were trained.

5. *Mutual adjustment.* **Mutual adjustment** consists of a constant interchange of informal communication; individuals coordinate their work through informal processes such as meetings, task forces, and liaison positions, mutually adjusting to one another's needs. Employees communicate with whomever they need to communicate with, without regard for formal lines of communication.

A crucial issue in choosing a coordinating mechanism concerns the need for information and the ways in which this information is collected, processed, and disseminated. The type of information collected by a driver's license bureau, for example, is mostly routine information that can be coordinated by rules and procedures. Companies that manufacture and sell fashion merchandise, however, require extensive market information that may be obtained from a variety of irregular sources and disseminated informally to anyone who needs to know. The demands that information processing make on the selection of an appropriate coordinating mechanism will be explained more completely later.

Coordinating mechanisms influence the degree of formalization in an organization. The term *formalization* refers to the degree to which rules and procedures guide the actions of employees. These rules and procedures can be either explicit or implicit. Explicit rules are written in job descriptions, policies and procedures manuals, or office memos. Implicit rules are often unwritten and develop as employees establish their own ways of doing things over time. Although they are unwritten, implicit rules often become standard operating procedures with the same effect on employee behavior as explicit rules.[10]

In a highly formal organization, employees are required to follow strict rules and procedures that tell them exactly how to perform their work. Informal organizations have very few rules and procedures; the employees are largely free to structure their own jobs. Formal organizations tend to rely on direct supervision and standardization of work processes, while informal organizations tend to use mutual adjustment and standardization of skills. An example of a formal structure in a university would be an administrative agency, such as the student loans office, while an example of an informal structure would be an academic department, such as the sociology department.

Matrix Organizational Structure

Many organizations have found that a combination of functional and product departmentalization provides the best reporting relationships and horizontal linkages, enabling them to achieve their organizational goals. This dual structure simultaneously organizes part of the organization along product lines and part of the organization along functional lines to gain the advantages of both. The simultaneous overlapping of these two functions is a **matrix organizational structure.** Although other types of departmentalization could be used to form a matrix organization, the most typical type of matrix structure is a combination of function and product, as illustrated in Exhibit 12.3.

In a matrix organization, each department reports simultaneously to both product managers and functional managers. The product managers and functional managers have equal authority within the organization, and employees report to both of them. For example, a member of the legal department may be assigned to assist with the development of a specific product and assume the responsibility for all the legal activities associated with the development, production, and distribution of the product. This individual would report to both the product manager and the supervisor of the legal department.

Although a dual hierarchy may seem awkward and unusual, it represents an effective structure in some situations. A matrix organization can quickly create new products or new responses to improved technical quality while retaining the benefits of its product and functional basis of organization. Consequently, a matrix structure is particularly effective when environmental pressures create a demand for both technical quality (functional) and frequent new products (product). These dual pressures require a dual authority structure to deal with them. A matrix struc-

EXHIBIT 12.3 Matrix Organizational Structure

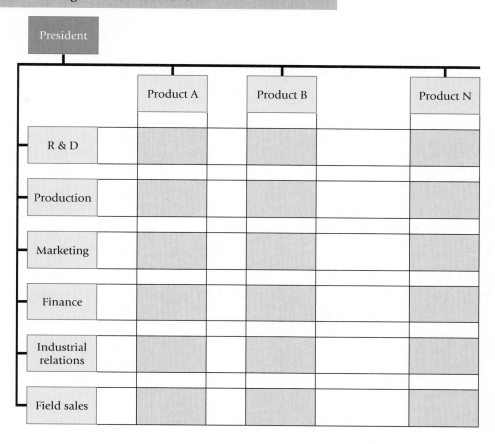

ture is particularly useful in an uncertain environment. Frequent external changes and high interdependence between departments require effective linkages between departments within an organization.

The disadvantage of a matrix structure is that it increases role ambiguity, stress, and anxiety because people are assigned to more than one department. Matrix structures violate the principle of unity of command. The employees who work in a matrix structure often feel that inconsistent demands are made on them, causing unproductive conflicts that call for short-term crisis management. Occasionally, employees abuse the dual-authority structure by playing one manager against another, thereby generating excuses for their incompetence or inactivity.

After a seven-year test, General Motors abandoned the matrix structure in favor of a product-oriented structure. Under the matrix structure, managers in charge of developing new cars for the Chevrolet-Pontiac-Canada division had to borrow workers from central staff operations and did not have ultimate control over their pay, promotions, or transfers. GM found that the decentralized structure of the Buick-Olds-Cadillac division, in which engineers, factory workers, and finance operatives reported to the same manager, was superior. This product-oriented structure proved to be more successful at developing higher-quality new models on a shorter schedule.[11]

APPLYING ORGANIZATIONAL BEHAVIOR
RESEARCH

Why Firms Adopt or Abandon Matrix Structures

The traditional explanation for why companies adopt a matrix organizational structure is that it makes them more innovative and responsive to customer needs by processing crucial information more efficiently. In short, dual reporting relationships are supposed to help companies adapt to complex and diverse environments.

Whether organizations actually adopt matrix structures for technical reasons was examined in a study of the hospital industry. During the 1960s, many hospitals began using a new organizational structure called *unit management*. Unit management is a type of matrix structure used in a hospital's clinical areas to promote the coordination of patient services and the integration of functional employees, such as nurses, housekeepers, dietary aides, and social workers.

Unit management was described in a flurry of articles that appeared in hospital administration journals, and its adoption by some of the major teaching hospitals gave it the appearance of being the latest fad. Between 1961 and 1978, about one-fourth of all large teaching hospitals implemented unit management. The study examined whether hospitals adopted unit management for technical reasons, such as the need to respond to organizational diversity, or whether it was just the latest fad.

Data were obtained from 1,375 hospitals in 1961, 1966, 1972, and 1978. The results indicated that 346 hospitals, or 27 percent, had adopted unit management between 1961 and 1978. Of these, 96 hospitals had subsequently abandoned it during the same period.

A comparison of the 346 hospitals that adopted unit management with the 901 hospitals that did not revealed that hospitals with high diversity were more likely to adopt matrix management. Diversity was measured by such factors as the hospital's mix of inpatient, outpatient, and emergency care services and whether it was affiliated with a medical school.

Diversity, however, was not the only explanation for adopting matrix structures. The decision to adopt was also significantly related to what was written in the professional media and whether other high-prestige hospitals in the area had adopted it. The pattern of adoptions suggested that once a high-prestige hospital adopted it, other hospitals in the region followed. In short, the decision to adopt unit management was often based more on glamour and appeal than on technical considerations.

The reasons for abandoning unit management were largely a lack of diversity and size. Smaller and less diverse hospitals had trouble implementing the program, or they adopted it for inappropriate reasons and then later dropped it. Comments from the hospitals that terminated their programs suggested that such issues as financing problems, turnover and staffing problems, and conflict between physicians and nurses caused abandonment. Thus, the reasons for abandonment seemed to be based more on issues of good design than were the decisions for adoption.

Source: Lawton R. Burns and Douglas R. Wholey, "Adoption and Abandonment of Matrix Management Programs: Effects of Organizational Characteristics and Interorganizational Networks," *Academy of Management Journal,* vol. 36 (1993), pp. 106–138.

UNIVERSAL THEORIES OF ORGANIZATIONAL DESIGN

The structure of an organization is determined by the five design decisions described in the previous section: division of labor, departmentalization, span of control, delegation of authority, and coordinating mechanisms. Different combinations of these factors can produce many different organizational structures. Which structure is the optimal design? Which structure is the most effective?

This section focuses specifically on universal theories of organizational design that were meant to be universally applicable—theories that proposed an ideal structure. Unfortunately, a universally superior organizational structure does not exist; the best structure depends on the situation, as explained in the next section.

Fayol's Principles of Management

One of the first authors to propose a universal design for organizations was Henri Fayol, a distinguished Frenchman who started as an engineer in a mining pit and twenty-eight years later became the director of the mining firm, a position he occupied for thirty years. Drawing on his successful experience, Fayol was the first to classify the essential functions of management: planning, organizing, commanding, coordinating, and controlling. In addition, he described fourteen principles of organizing that he considered essential for successful managers.[12]

Fayol's fourteen principles, shown in Exhibit 12.4, have been highly influential in the development of management and organizational theory. Fayol's unity of command means that employees should receive directions from only one person, and unity of direction means that tasks with the same objective should have a common supervisor. Combining these two principles with authority and responsibility and division of labor results in a system of tasks and reporting relationships that form the essence of organizing. Fayol's principles thus provide the framework for structuring and coordinating work. Even though his principles were supported by no evidence other than his own experience, they were widely accepted and followed by others.

EXHIBIT 12.4 Henri Fayol's Fourteen Principles of Management

1. *Division of work:* specialization belongs to the natural order.
2. *Authority and responsibility:* responsibility is a correlary with authority.
3. *Discipline:* discipline is what leaders make it.
4. *Unity of command:* people cannot bear dual command.
5. *Unity of direction:* one head and one plan for a group of activities having the same objectives.
6. *Subordination of individual interest to the general interest.*
7. *Renumeration:* fair, rewarding of effort, reasonable.
8. *Centralization:* Centralization belongs to the natural order.
9. *Scalar chain:* line of authority, gang-plank principle.
10. *Order:* A place for everyone and everyone in his or her place.
11. *Equity:* results from combination of kindness and justice.
12. *Stability and tenure of personnel:* prosperous firms are stable.
13. *Initiative:* great source of strength for business.
14. *Esprit de corps:* union is strength.

Source: Henri Fayol, *General and Industrial Management* (London: Pitman, 1949), pp. 19–20. Reprinted by permission of David S. Lake Publishers.

Mechanistic Versus Organic Organizational Structure

Two contrasting types of organizational structure have been recommended as universally appropriate for every organization. These two types differ greatly in the amount of formal structure and control they advocate. Several labels have been used to describe these two types. The labels used in this book are "mechanistic" versus "organic" organizational structures.

Mechanistic and organic organizational structures were first described in a classic study by Burns and Stalker.[13] They observed twenty industrial firms in England and discovered that the external environment was related to the internal organizational structure. When the external environment was stable, the internal organization was managed by rules, procedures, and a clear hierarchy of authority. Most managerial decisions were made at the top, and there was strong centralized authority. Burns and Stalker called this a **mechanistic organization structure.**

Some organizations, those in rapidly changing environments, had a much different organizational structure. The internal organization was much more adaptive, free-flowing, and spontaneous. Rules and regulations were generally not written, and those that were written were often ignored. People had to find their own way within the system and learn what to do. The hierarchy of authority was not clear, and decision-making authority was broadly decentralized. Burns and Stalker called this an **organic organizational structure.**

The differences between an organic and mechanistic organizational structure are illustrated in Exhibit 12.5. In a mechanistic structure, the work is divided into highly specialized tasks that are rigidly defined with a formal job description. In an organic structure, however, most tasks are not so highly specialized; employees are often expected to learn how to perform a variety of tasks and to frequently adjust and redefine their jobs as the situation changes. In a mechanistic structure, communication patterns follow the formal chain of command between superiors and

EXHIBIT 12.5   Mechanistic vs. Organic Organizational Structures

Mechanistic	Organic
1. Tasks are divided into separate, specialized jobs.	1. Tasks may not be highly specialized, and employees may perform a variety of tasks to accomplish the group's task.
2. Tasks are clearly and rigidly defined.	2. Tasks are not elaborately specified: they may be adjusted and redefined through employee interactions.
3. Strict hierarchy of authority and control with many rules.	3. Informal hierarchy of authority and control with few rules.
4. Knowledge and control of tasks are centralized, and tasks are directed from the top of the organization.	4. Knowledge and control of tasks are located anywhere in the organization.
5. Communication is vertical through the formal hierarchy.	5. Communication is horizontal; employees talk to whomever they need to communicate with.

EXHIBIT 12.6   **Structural Differences Between Mechanistic and Organic Organizations**

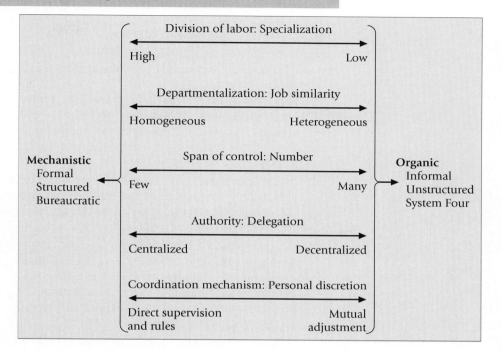

subordinates. In an organic structure, however, communication is horizontal, and employees talk with whomever they need to in order to do their work.[14]

Mechanistic and organic structures differ in each of the five dimensions of organizational structure, as illustrated in Exhibit 12.6. In addition to having highly specialized jobs, mechanistic structures are characterized by homogeneous departmentalization, a narrow span of control, highly centralized delegation of authority, and coordination through direct supervision and rules. Organic structures are just the opposite. The labor is divided in such a way that the level of specialization is reduced, the jobs are organized into heterogeneous departments, there is a broad span of control, decision-making authority is widely decentralized, and work is coordinated by mutual adjustment.

Bureaucratic Organizational Structure

Perhaps the best description of a mechanistic organizational structure is Max Weber's description of **bureaucracy**.[15] Highly bureaucratic organizations have a very mechanistic organizational structure. Unfortunately, the word *bureaucracy* is associated with a variety of negative feelings. Many people associate bureaucracy with excessive red tape, procedural delays, and organizational inefficiency. These connotations are not consistent with Max Weber's description of bureaucracy. According to Max Weber, bureaucracy was a sociological concept that referred to the rational collection of clearly organized activities. The word *bureaucracy* comes from the French word *bureau*, which means "office." In short, a bureaucracy is a collection of carefully organized offices performing specialized functions according to clearly defined rules and procedures. Weber's description of bureaucracy was intended as a description of the ideal form of a large organizational structure. The major attributes of this ideal form were rationality and efficiency. A bureaucratic structure was a well-organized collection of offices that combined the efforts of large numbers of people through a system of rules and procedures. Weber's description of a bureaucracy included the following identifying characteristics.

1. *A division of labor based on functional specialization.* All tasks necessary for accomplishing the goals of the organization are divided into highly specialized jobs. Such job specialization allows jobholders to become expert in their jobs and to be held responsible for the effective performance of their duties.

2. *A well-defined hierarchy of authority.* Each officeholder in the organization is accountable to a superior. The authority of superiors is based on expert knowledge and is legitimized by the fact that it is delegated from the top of the hierarchy. In this way a clearly defined chain of command is created.

3. *A system of rules covering the rights and duties of employees.* Each task is performed according to a consistent system of abstract rules to assure uniformity and coordination of different tasks. Through a system of clearly defined rules, officeholders can eliminate any uncertainty in performing their tasks that is caused by individual differences.

4. *Impersonal relationships* Each officeholder maintains a social distance from subordinates and clients and conducts the business of the office in a formal, impersonal manner. Strict adherence to the rules and impersonal relationships assure that personalities do not interfere with the efficient accomplishment of the office's objectives. There should be no favoritism resulting from personal friendships or ingratiating behaviors.

5. *Promotion and selection based on technical competence.* Employment in a bureaucratic organization is based on technical qualifications, and employees are protected against arbitrary dismissal. Similarly, promotions are based on seniority and achievement. Employment in the bureaucracy is viewed as a lifelong career that is designed to create loyalty and commitment.

6. *Written communications and records.* All administrative acts, decisions, and rules are recorded in writing. Since verbal conversations and discussions cannot be filed, all decisions, complaints, and administrative acts are to be written and filed. Recordkeeping provides an organizational memory, and written documents provide continuity over time.

Many of the characteristics that Weber recommended for an ideal bureaucracy seem quite obvious to us today because we are surrounded by organizations that have rules, a division of labor, written documents, and a hierarchy of authority. These characteristics provide an impersonal means of controlling organizations by guaranteeing that dependable work will be performed by qualified employees under the impartial direction of rational supervisors. These rational characteristics, however, were not so obvious a century ago when there were very few large organizations. Most organizations were family operated and characterized by nepotism and unfair treatment. Weber's recommendation of a rational, bureaucratic ideal was intended to both eliminate favoritism and increase organizational efficiency.

Advantages of a Bureaucracy. Bureaucracy has survived and even thrived because its advantages outweigh its disadvantages. The advantages of a bureaucracy stem logically from its ideal characteristics. At its best, a bureaucracy is a smooth-running organization where decisions and activities are processed efficiently and all members are treated equitably. Seven major benefits have been attributed to bureaucracy, as summarized in Exhibit 12.7.

1. *Technical efficiency.* The chief benefit of a bureaucracy is that the activities and functions have been carefully analyzed and rationally organized in a way that creates maximum efficiency. The process of dividing the labor into highly specialized jobs, assigning them to different offices, and coordinating them through a carefully designed system of rules and procedures produces what has sometimes been called *machine-like efficiency.*

2. *Elimination of favoritism.* By following the correct procedures and administering the rules impartially, clients and officeholders are treated equitably and fairly. No one is treated with special favors because of personal friendships or ingratiating behaviors. The rules and procedures are administered without regard to family, wealth, or status. This impartial treatment is consistent with bureaucratic ideals that condemn nepotism, partiality, and capricious judgment.

3. *Predictability in performance.* Strict adherence to clearly defined rules and procedures leads to greater predictability of performance. Both customers and employees know in advance the outcome of a decision. For example, if the vacation policy allows 3 weeks' paid vacation after five years of service, all employees with at least five years of service can expect to receive a 3-week paid vacation.

4. *Job security.* By following the rules and doing what the handbook or procedures manual says they are supposed to do, officeholders are assured that they will not be fired. Such a tenure policy maximizes vocational security. Officeholders tend to view their employment in the organization as a life-long career. Such an outlook minimizes turnover and engenders a high degree of loyalty and commitment.

EXHIBIT 12.7   Advantages and Disadvantages of Bureaucracies

Advantages	Disadvantages
1. Technical efficiency	1. Rigidity of behavior
2. Elimination of favoritism	2. Bureaucratic personality
3. Predictability of performance	3. Inversion of means and ends
4. Job security	4. Resistance to change
5. Technical competence	5. Peter Principle
6. Minimum direction needed	
7. Avoids impulsive action	

5. *Technical competence.* Since officeholders are hired on the basis of their ability rather than on the basis of whom they know, they are highly trained and competent officials.

6. *Minimum direction needed.* Since a bureaucracy has been rationally designed, and the officeholders are trained experts who are expected to follow standard rules and operating procedures, very little day-to-day direction is needed to keep the bureaucracy functioning. Like a carefully designed machine that operates smoothly after it is turned on, a bureaucracy is expected to operate smoothly with little direction or added input.

7. *Avoids impulsive decisions.* Since a bureaucracy operates according to standard operating procedures, it is not possible for an impulsive idea on the part of one officeholder immediately to disrupt the entire bureaucracy. Since they must be coordinated with other officeholders, new ideas and changes cannot be implemented quickly. Although reducing the possibility of impulsive action is sometimes an advantage, it can also be a disadvantage when change is required, which explains why bureaucracies are often associated with red tape and resistance to change.

Disadvantages of Bureaucracy. Although Weber described bureaucracies as an ideal organizational structure, they are not without their problems. Over the years, several dysfunctional consequences associated with bureaucracies have been identified. Some of these dysfunctional consequences are not created because the bureaucracy fails to operate properly. Instead, they are created because the bureaucracy is functioning exactly as it should, and the problems are inherent to the bureaucratic structure itself. In other words, these problems cannot be solved by having the bureaucracy operate more effectively; instead, a stricter application of bureaucratic principles would exacerbate the problems.

1. *Rigidity of behavior.* In a bureaucracy, officeholders are expected to know the rules and procedures and to follow them precisely. The bureaucracy can achieve greater control over individual behavior by demanding strict rule compliance. However, as they follow the rules more precisely, employees become more rigid in their behavior and more insensitive to individual problems. This rigidity of behavior inevitably leads to conflict with clients and customers. Many times individuals feel that their personal situation represents an exception to the rule, and occasionally they are right. For example, a rule that says second-year law students register on Wednesday and first-year law students register on Thursday does not contain a special provision for a student who did not finish the second semester because of illness. Wise bureaucrats know when to deviate from the rules and accept responsibility for their decisions. But bureaucrats who have been intimidated or threatened seek to protect themselves by following the rules. Despite the pleas of frustrated and perplexed clients for individual consideration, a devoted bureaucrat adheres to the regulations, and this behavior understandably produces difficulty with clients. As the level of conflict rises, the dysfunctional consequences of a bureaucratic structure become more obvious. Instead of responding to the complaints of clients and their demands for individual treatment, bureaucrats respond by following the rules more strictly. By strict adherence to the rules in their handbooks and policy manuals, they are able to defend their actions in the face of conflict. This dysfunctional conflict was described by sociologist Robert Merton and is illustrated in Exhibit 12.8.[16]

EXHIBIT 12.8   Merton's Model of the Dysfunctional
Consequences of Bureaucratic Control

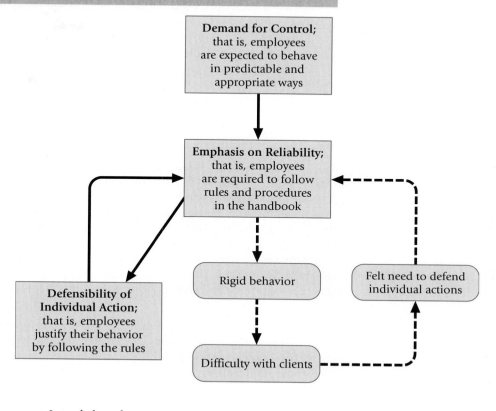

———— Intended results
━ ━ ━ Unintended results

Source: Adapted from Daniel Katz and Robert Kahn, *The Social Psychology of Organizations*, 2nd ed.
(New York: Wiley, 1978), p. 266. Used with permission.

Although bureaucracies do lead to rigid behavior, the dire consequences of bureaucracies seldom occur, because people recognize problems and make rational adjustments as needed. When bureaucratic controls are excessive and prevent people from doing their work, two individuals often form an informal relationship called a *dyadic alliance,* to get things done. These dyadic alliances are not under the control of the organization, and they are usually limited to the specific problem they were intended to circumvent. Although they tend to decrease the formal control of the organization, they help to solve problems and improve performance. These alliances are an important supplement to the structure of a bureaucracy.[17]

2. *Bureaucratic personality.* Employees who work in bureaucratic organizations tend to develop distinct personality patterns, and some of these characteristics are not considered particularly healthy. For example, some have suggested that extensive exposure to a bureaucratic structure tends to strip people of their personal conscience. Instead of allowing officeholders to adhere to their longstanding values and beliefs when deciding right and wrong, the bureaucracy imposes a new set of values

and beliefs. Officeholders come to believe that moral standards of right or wrong are defined by higher-level officers and by the rules they are expected to follow. Following the rules becomes more important than the possibly inhumane treatment required by strict rule compliance. For example, a pregnant student may be required to walk back to her apartment in a storm because she forgot to bring her computer lab pass to show that she is registered in a computer class.

Extended exposure to bureaucratic structures tends to cause individuals to respond to problems by creating more rules. This problem is particularly pronounced among managers who supervise specialists whose work they do not fully understand. Because of their bureaucratic orientation, they respond to this insecurity by issuing more rules and procedures. These regulations do not improve the functioning of the organization, but they help the manager feel more in control.

3. *Inversion of means and ends.* Rigid adherence to rules and regulations often results in a situation in which adherence becomes more important than achieving organizational goals—**means–ends inversion.** Thus, the means become more important than the end. Although the rules were originally designed to further organizational success, each officeholder comes to see the rules and regulations of that office as the ultimate goal. For example, advertising campaigns, sales incentives, and other programs are designed to increase sales. But each of these programs can come to be viewed as an end in itself, so that an elaborate awards banquet becomes so important that it dominates everyone's time and attention and replaces efforts to achieve high sales.

4. *Resistance to change.* As noted earlier, bureaucracies are intentionally designed to resist rapid change. This resistance is created by several aspects of a bureaucracy. First, officeholders tend to avoid responsibility when they are faced with decisions they prefer not to make. By redefining the problem, most officeholders are able to say, "That's not my job." Second, bureaucrats tend to be isolated from external feedback and outside evaluation. Bureaucracies tend to focus on their own internal functioning to the exclusion of external feedback. Their failure to respond to external evaluation prevents them from making corrective adjustments. Third, bureaucracies are not designed to foster goal setting or goal accomplishment. Rules and procedures focus the efforts of officeholders on activities rather than outcomes. Opportunities to produce innovative products or services tend to be overlooked because of a preoccupation with bureaucratic procedures. Fourth, bureaucracies move at a painfully slow pace in making complex decisions. The delay occurs because of the number of people who must concur before a decision is made about issues of importance. After the decision is finally made, there is an additional delay while new rules and procedures for each officeholder are created.

5. *The Peter Principle.* The **Peter Principle** was proposed as a satirical and humorous description of the incompetence that often occurs in bureaucratic organizations.[18] This principle states that in a hierarchy, every employee tends to rise to his or her level of incompetence. In a bureaucracy, promotions are supposed to be based on demonstrated ability. Therefore, the most competent individual at one level is promoted to the next level. The Peter Principle explains, however, that competence at one level does not guarantee competence at the next level. The skills and abilities required for a subordinate position are frequently different from the skills and abilities required for success at the next level. Therefore, the most competent individuals at one level are promoted from level to level within the organization until they reach their level of incompetence, at which time they are no longer considered for promotion. An example of the Peter Principle is the promotion of com-

petent technical or sales personnel into administrative positions for which they are ill suited by temperament. Outstanding grade school teachers, for example, do not necessarily make outstanding grade school principals. According to the Peter Principle, the only effective work that occurs in bureaucracies is performed by individuals who have not yet achieved their level of incompetence.

System Four Organizational Structure

A theory of organizational design that is significantly different from bureaucracy has been proposed by Rensis Likert.[19] Likert's theory has come to be known a **System Four organizational design.** Likert recommends his System Four as a universal "one best way" to design an organization. There is no question that Likert's views are widely shared by researchers and practitioners; indeed, extensive research by Likert and others has supported his theory.

System One Versus System Four. The central premise of Likert's theory is that organizational leaders develop different management systems that can be described as lying along a continuum from exploitive and authoritative at one end to participative and group oriented at the other end. Likert analyzed eight operating characteristics of organizations and placed each one along the exploitive–participative continuum. In his early work, Likert identified four management systems along this continuum.

The first style, called *exploitive-authoritative,* is characterized by the threat of punishment, hostile attitudes, downward communication, and distrust, with all decision making and goal setting performed by top management.

The second style, *benevolent-authoritative,* is slightly less hostile and threatening, since top management behaves more benevolently, but all decisions, goal setting, and communication are directly under the control of top management.

The third level, *consultative,* involves greater coordination between upper and lower levels of management. The ideas and interests of lower-level employees are considered, and lower-level employees have an opportunity to contribute to the decision making and goal setting in a limited way.

The fourth style, *participative-group oriented,* representing the other end of the continuum, is universally recommended as the ideal type of organizational structure. A participative-group-oriented system involves open communication channels, considerable responsibility and initiative on the part of individual members, decision making occurring at all levels through group processes, a decentralized authority structure, broad participation in the goal-setting processes whereby realistic objectives are set, and leadership processes that demonstrate a high level of confidence and trust between superiors and subordinates.

In his later writings, Likert simply described these four systems as System One through System Four. Likert also developed a comprehensive questionnaire for evaluating organizations in each of these dimensions. An abbreviated form of this questionnaire is illustrated in the experiential exercise at the end of the chapter.

System Four: An Ideal Design. Likert argued that System Four was an ideal organizational design; nevertheless, he recognized the reality of situational determinants and limited his recommendations to specific management characteristics. For example, Likert did not advocate a specific span of control or form of departmentalization. Likert recognized that these design decisions depended on the situation, but argued that there were higher-level principles that should guide management decisions in the design of an organization. Likert identified three principles that should be followed in organizational design: (1) the principle of supportive relationships, (2) the use of group decision making and group methods of supervision, and (3) the creation of high performance goals for the organization.

Principle of Supportive Relationships. The **principle of supportive relationships** is probably the most significant aspect of Likert's theory. In essence, this principle stated, "The leadership and other processes of the organization must be such as to ensure a maximum probability that in all interactions . . . each member . . . will view the experience as supportive and one which builds and maintains [a] sense of personal worth and importance."[20] This principle implies that the relationship between a superior and a subordinate is crucial to the structure and functioning of the organization. Both the behavior of the superior and the employee's perceptions of the situation must be such that the subordinate sees the experience as one that contributes to a sense of personal worth and importance and one that increases and maintains a sense of significance and human dignity.

Likert recommended the following kinds of questions to assess the degree to which relationships are supportive.

1. How much confidence and trust do you feel your superior has in you? How much do you have in him or her?

2. To what extent does your boss convey to you a feeling of confidence that you can do your job successfully?

3. To what extent is your boss interested in helping you to achieve and maintain a good income?

4. To what extent does your superior try to understand your problems and do something about them?

Group Decision Making and Supervision. Likert believed that decision making by the group and leadership by the group were universally superior to the traditional hierarchical organizational control. The traditional organizational structure consists of person-to-person interaction only between superiors and subordinates. In contrast, System Four management involves management by groups and recognizes overlapping group membership; each supervisor of a group also serves as a subordinate in another group at the next level above. Those who hold overlapping memberships are called "linking pins." At each hierarchical level, all members of a work group who are affected by the outcome of a decision should be involved in it. This does not mean, however, that supervisors abdicate their responsibility. Likert emphasized that the superior was still accountable for all decisions made by the group, for their execution, and for their results. It was the leader's responsibility to build an effective team. This principle has important implications for design decisions, since it encourages greater delegation of authority and coordination through the mutual adjustment that is brought about by self-management in each group. Again, however, Likert avoided specifying a span of control, but recommended that authority be decentralized to allow groups to make all decisions relevant to their performance.

High Performance Aspirations. Employees want stable employment, job security, and fulfilling work. Since these conditions can be provided only by successful firms, the goals of the organization need to be integrated with the goals of individuals. To achieve high levels of organizational performance, Likert argued that both managers and subordinates must have high performance aspirations. However, these high performance goals should not be imposed on employees. Therefore, the organization needs a mechanism through which employees can help to set high-level goals that satisfy their own needs as well. Likert believed that System Four provided such a mechanism through group decision making and overlapping group memberships. Such a design is consistent with the interests and objectives of the organization's multiple constituencies: employees, owners, shareholders, customers, and suppliers.

CONTINGENCY THEORIES OF ORGANIZATIONAL DESIGN

For many years, management scholars described various principles of management and recommended them as universally applicable guidelines for all organizations. Many other writers, in addition to Fayol, Weber, and Likert, contributed to what today represents an extensive literature on management theory, literature that describes rational approaches to organizational design.[21]

During the 1960s, however, the universal applicability of management principles was challenged, and recent management theory claims that organizational structure needs to adapt to the demands of the environment. This approach, called *contingency design theory,* has focused on identifying the most important environmental variables that should be taken into account when designing an organization for maximum effectiveness.

Most of the research on contingency design theories has focused on two situational factors: technology and environmental uncertainty. One line of research has shown that differences in technology determine the most effective organizational design, while the second suggests that differences in environmental uncertainty and the demands for processing information are the crucial factors. These two approaches are compatible and can be combined into a general model of organization design.

Technology

The term *technology* is difficult to define because it is used in so many ways. In general, **technology** is the actions that a person performs upon an object with or without the aid of tools or mechanical devices. It is the knowledge, tools, techniques, and actions used to transform organizational inputs into outputs. In this section, perhaps it is best to think of technology as the organization's transformation process; it includes machinery, employee education and skill, and work procedures that are used in the transformation process. Every organization has a unique type of technology. Knowledge is applied to work wherever work is done, whether in hospitals, universities, or government agencies. The first and most influential study of the relationship between technology and organizational structure was conducted by Joan Woodward, a British industrial sociologist.[22] Her research began as a field study of management principles in South Essex. At the time she designed her study, the so-called universal principles of management still taught that there was one best way for organizing every organization. For example, at that time it was recommended that every manager should have a span of control of six subordinates.

To test these "universal principles," Woodward surveyed 100 manufacturing firms firsthand to learn how they were organized. Through personal interviews, observations, and an examination of company records, Woodward and her research team obtained data on a wide range of structural characteristics, such as span of control, levels of management, ratios of management to clerical workers, and management style. Her data also included measures of performance regarding economic success.

At first, the analysis of the data did not make any sense. Firms varied widely in such things as span of control, number of hierarchical levels, administrative ratios, and the amount of verbal communication. For example, the spans of control of first-line supervisors varied from 10 to 90, with a median of 38, while the number of managerial levels varied from 2 to 12, with a median of 4. At first the research team was perplexed by their failure to find any meaningful relationships. The size of the firm did not account for differences in organizational structure, and the structural variables were not related to commercial success. They found no support for any of the "universal principles" of management.

The researchers tried to determine whether structural differences were related to effectiveness as measured by market share, profitability, capital expansion, and subjective factors such as reputation of the firm and employee attitudes. The firms were classified into three categories of effectiveness: average, above average, and below average. When the organizational structures were compared, however, no consistent patterns were found. Thus, there was no relationship between effectiveness and organizational structure.

Finally, the research team began to look at the variable of technology and discovered that technology influenced the appropriate organizational structure. Woodward developed a scale of technical complexity that represented the extent of mechanization and predictability of the manufacturing process. High technical complexity meant that most of the work was performed by machines and was very predictable. Low technical complexity meant that workers played a larger role in the production process. At first Woodward identified ten categories of technical complexity, and later consolidated them into three basic technology groups.

1. *Small-batch and unit production.* These firms are job shop operations that manufacture or assemble small orders to meet specific customer needs. This technology relies heavily on human operators and thus is not highly mechanized, such as printing shops and custom clothing stores.

2. *Large-batch and mass production.* This manufacturing process is characterized by long production runs of standardized parts. Output is placed in inventory from which orders are filled. Most assembly lines use a mass production technology.

3. *Continuous process production.* In this technology, the entire process is mechanized, and there is usually an ongoing flow of material without a starting or stopping point. This represents a high level of mechanization and standardization beyond an assembly line, such as that found in chemical plants, oil refineries, and nuclear power plants.

Using this classification of technology, Woodward discovered significant relationships between technology and structure and technology and performance. For example, as the technical complexity increased, Woodward found that there was an increase in the number of management levels, suggesting that greater management intensity is needed to manage complex technologies. As technical complexity increased, there was also a decrease in the ratio of direct to indirect labor because more indirect workers, such as clerical and administrative staff, are required to support and maintain complex machinery. Other characteristics, such as span of control, formalized procedures and centralization, were high for mass production technologies, but lower for the others because mass production work is standardized. With mass production, the jobs are standardized, with few exceptions; therefore, little communication is needed to direct them, even though the employees are less skilled. The other two technologies, however, require highly skilled workers to run the machines and verbal communication to adapt to changing conditions. The relationship between technical complexity and these structural characteristics are illustrated in Exhibit 12.9.

When Woodward examined the relationship between technology and performance, she discovered that successful firms had structures that fit their technology. In each of the three technology groupings, the successful firms had ratios and numbers that were close to the median, while the unsuccessful firms had ratios and numbers that were much higher or lower than the median. Another important conclusion was that successful small-batch and continuous process organizations tended to have organic structures, while successful mass production organizations tended to have mechanistic structures.

Woodward's research was a valuable step in the development of organization theories. Her findings signaled an end to the search for universal principles of management and introduced the search for situational variables. The important conclusion drawn from her research is that production technology has a systematic relationship with structure and management characteristics.

EXHIBIT 12.9   **Relationship Between Technological Complexity and Structural Characteristics**

Structural Characteristic	Technology		
	Unit Production	Mass Production	Continuous Process
Number of management levels	3	4	6
Supervisor span of control	23	48	15
Direct labor/indirect labor ratio	9:1	4:1	1:1
Manager/total personnel ratio	Low	Medium	High
Number "skilled" workers	High	Low	High
Formalized procedures	Low	High	Low
Centralization	Low	High	Low
Amount of verbal communication	High	Low	High
Amount of written communication	Low	High	Low
Overall structure	Organic	Mechanistic	Organic

Source: Joan Woodward, *Industrial Organization: Theory and Practice* (London: Oxford University Press, 1965). Used with permission.

After Woodward's pioneering research, many additional studies investigated the effects of technology on organizational structure. Technology has been most frequently analyzed in terms of the degree of routineness: what is the degree of continuity, automation, and rigidity in the production process? The technology is extremely routine when the production process is totally automated and highly mechanized and produces a consistent throughput. The structural variables most frequently analyzed in technology studies are centralization, formalization, and specialization, and all three of these variables are positively related to routineness. Although the relationships are influenced by the size of the organization and the kind of product it produces, the research generally concludes that when the technology is highly routine (1) decision making should be centralized, (2) the rules and procedures should be formalized, and (3) the process should be decomposed and performed by specialized people and equipment.[23]

Environmental Uncertainty

The degree of instability and uncertainty in the environment is another important situational variable that influences the appropriate type of organizational structure. Different organizational structures are required in order to cope with environmental uncertainty. Research is fairly consistent in indicating that organic structures tend to be most effective in uncertain environments while mechanistic structures are more effective in more stable environments. The classic study examining the effects of environmental uncertainty on organizational structure was conducted by Paul Lawrence and Jay Lorsch of Harvard University.[24]

Lawrence and Lorsch examined organizations in three industries: plastics, packaged food products, and paper containers. These three industries were selected because significant differences were found in the degree of environmental uncertainty. The environment of the plastics firms was extremely uncertain because of rapidly changing technology and customer demand. Decisions were required about new products even though feedback about the accuracy of the decisions often involved considerable delay. In contrast, the paper container firms faced a highly certain environment. Only minor changes in technology had occurred in the previous twenty years, and these firms focused on producing high-quality, standardized containers and delivering them to the customer quickly. The consequences of decisions could be ascertained in a short period. Between these two extremes, the producers of packaged foods faced a moderately uncertain environment.

Differentiation and Integration. In analyzing how these firms interacted with their environments, Lawrence and Lorsch identified two key concepts: differentiation and integration. **Differentiation** is the degree of segmentation of the organizational system into subsystems, which is similar to the concepts of specialization of labor and departmentalization. However, differentiation also includes the behavioral attributes of employees in highly specialized departments. As noted earlier, members of highly specialized functional departments tend to adopt a rather narrow-minded, department-oriented focus that emphasizes the achievement of departmental goals rather than organizational goals.

The consequence of high differentiation is that greater coordination between departments is required. More time and resources must be devoted to achieving coordination, since the attitudes, goals, and work orientations among highly specialized departments differ so widely. Lawrence and Lorsch developed the concept of **integration** to refer to this coordinating activity. Integration was defined as the coordinating process of achieving unity of effort among the various subsystems to accomplish the organization's goals.

Responding to Uncertainty. Lawrence and Lorsch discovered significant relationships between the degree of environmental uncertainty and the amount of differentiation and integration used within each of the three industries. For example, the firms in the container industry faced a fairly certain environment, and they were fairly undifferentiated. Therefore, they tended to adopt a mechanistic structure. The most successful container companies were organized along functional lines with a highly centralized authority structure. Coordination was achieved through direct supervision with formal written schedules. A bureaucratic organization structure was consistent with the degree of environmental certainty of the container industry.

In the plastics industry, however, facing an extremely uncertain environment, the most successful plastics companies adopted organic structures. A highly unstable environment required these companies to have a highly differentiated structure with highly specialized internal departments of marketing, production, and research and development, to deal with the uncertainty in the external environment. Coordination was achieved through mutual adjustment, ad hoc teams that cut across departments, and special coordinators who served as liaisons between departments. The most successful plastics firms achieved high levels of differentiation plus high levels of integration to coordinate them.

The study of Lawrence and Lorsch contributes to our understanding of organizational design by showing the effects of environmental uncertainty on organizational structure. When the environment is highly uncertain, frequent changes require more information processing to achieve coordination, so special integrators and coordinating mechanisms become a necessary addition to the organization's structure. Sometimes these integrators are called *liaison personnel, brand managers,* or *product coordinators.* Organizations that face a highly uncertain environment and a highly differentiated structure may have a fourth of their management personnel assigned to integration activities, such as serving on committees, task forces, or in liaison roles. Organizations that face a very simple and stable environment, however, may not have anyone assigned to a full-time integration role.

The analysis of Lawrence and Lorsch can be extended from the organization to the departmental level within an organization. A large firm may find it necessary to organize its production department quite differently from its research department. One department may tend toward a mechanistic design and the other toward an organic design. The differences between these two departments are due to the differences in environments to which the two departments must adapt. For example, if a marketing department of a large firm faced an extremely unstable environment because of transportation problems across international boundaries, the marketing department would need to adopt an organic organizational structure to respond to rapid developments. In contrast, the production department may face a very stable environment that allows for long production runs of standardized products. A mechanistic organizational structure with formal bureaucratic procedures would be most appropriate for the production department.

Information Processing

It has been proposed that the key integrating concept explaining the relationship between environmental uncertainty, technology, and organizational structure is the way the organization processes information.[25] Information flows into the organization from various environmental sectors, and the organization must respond and adapt to this information. The more rapid the changes in the external environment, the greater the necessity for incoming information. The consequence of environmental uncertainty on managers is an increase in the flow of information that leads to a communication overload. In essence, the organization becomes inundated with exceptional cases requiring individual attention. As a greater number of nonroutine demands are made on the organization from the environment, managers more and more are required to be involved in the day-to-day operations. Problems develop as plans become obsolete and the various coordinating functions break down. An effective organization requires a structure that allows it to adapt to such a situation.

Organic structures are able to deal with greater amounts of uncertainty than mechanistic structures. Organic structures have more highly connected communication networks that permit the efficient use of individuals as problem solvers and increase the opportunity for feedback. Because highly connected networks do not depend on any one individual, they are less sensitive to information overload or saturation. But while organic structures are able to deal effectively with greater amounts of uncertainty than mechanistic structures, there are costs associated with being able to process more information. Organic structures consume more time, effort, and energy and are less subject to managerial control. Thus, the benefits of increased efficiency and capacity to process information must be weighed against the costs of less control and greater effort and time.

Organizations in a dynamic and complex environment are unable to rely on traditional information processing and control techniques where all information is communicated through a chain of command. Changes in market demand, uncertain resources, and new technology disrupt the organization's plans and require adjustments while the task is being performed. Immediate adjustments to production schedules and task performance disrupt the organization. Coordination is made more difficult because it is impossible to forecast operations or revise standard operating rules or procedures. Organizations must obtain information that reflects the environmental changes.

ORGANIZATIONAL LIFE CYCLE

An important variable influencing organizational design is the age or maturity of the organization. However, it is not the chronological age that influences structure as much as the stage in the organization's **life cycle.** Organizations are born, grow larger, and get older, and they can die at any point in this life cycle.

Stages of Life Cycle

Organizational structure, leadership style, and administrative systems follow a predictable pattern of development and change as the organization progresses through its life cycle. The stages are sequential in nature and follow a natural progression. Four major stages have been proposed to describe an organization's life cycle.[26] Each stage is associated with a typical structure and a unique need that must be satisfied before the organization can move to the next stage. These stages are illustrated in Exhibit 12.10.

EXHIBIT 12.10 Organizational Life Cycles

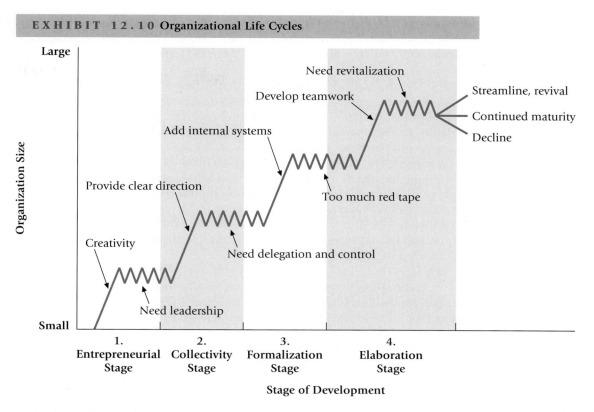

Source: Adapted from Robert E. Quinn and Kim Cameron, "Organizational Life Cycles and Some Shifting Criteria of Effectiveness: Some Preliminary Evidence," *Management Science*, vol. 29 (1983), pp. 33–51.

Stage 1: Entrepreneurial Stage. When an organization is first created, it starts with the entrepreneurial stage, and the emphasis is on creating a product that will survive in the marketplace. The entrepreneurs who start the organization typically devote their full energies to the technical activities of producing and marketing the product. While the organization is a small, one-person show, it adopts an organic structure. All structure and control are provided by the owner, whose energies are directed toward survival and the production of a single product or service. An organization needs dynamic leadership to move it from stage 1 to stage 2. Also, a strong manager is required who can introduce management techniques.

Stage 2: Collectivity Stage. If the leadership crisis is resolved and the organization receives managerial direction and control, a formal organizational structure begins to emerge. Departments are established based on a division of labor along with a hierarchy of authority. The structure, however, is a highly organic structure where members interact freely. Long hours of work are contributed by employees who are motivated by a sense of commitment and involvement. The goals and direction for the organization are provided by a strong, charismatic leader. To move an organization from stage 2 to stage 3, the organization has a need for delegation with control. Some organizations experience an autonomy crisis when top managers who were successful because of their strong leadership and vision do not want to relinquish any of their responsibility. Consequently, the organization must find mechanisms to coordinate and control departments that are allowed increasing levels of authority without direct supervision from the top.

Stage 3: Formalization Stage. As the organization enters the formalization period, during the middle of its life, bureaucratic characteristics emerge. Staff support groups are added to the organization along with formal procedures and a clear division of labor. Top managers must now focus their attention primarily on issues of strategy and planning and leave the day-to-day operation of the firm to lower-level managers. Incentive systems, such as executive bonuses and profit sharing, may be implemented to motivate managers to work toward the overall good of the company. If the organization can successfully implement coordination and control systems, it will continue to grow and operate effectively. For the organization to advance from stage 3 to stage 4, it must resolve the problem of excessive formality and bureaucratic red tape. Organizations tend to proliferate systems and programs that can overwhelm the organization.

Stage 4: Elaboration Stage. If the organization can eliminate unnecessary bureaucratic procedures, it can continue to grow and enter the elaboration stage. Here the organization is large and bureaucratic with extensive control systems, rules, and procedures. Managers learn to work within the bureaucracy without adding to it. The pervasiveness of bureaucratic procedures may reduce the effectiveness of the organization and force it to decline. The energies of individuals throughout the organization often focus more on maintaining the organization than on innovative and creative ideas. Innovation is formally institutionalized and assigned to the research and development department. Creative ideas that come from elsewhere in the organization are often ignored. For the organization to stay at this stage and not decline or die, it needs to be periodically revitalized. The renewal process tends to occur every few years when the organization slips out of alignment with the environment, and the problems are so severe that members feel a strong need for change. During these periods of change, top managers are often replaced by new managers with fresh ideas.

Organizational Decline[27]

Organizations are designed to grow, and there are inherent forces within the organization that naturally push for the organization to grow and expand. However, there are also environmental forces that threaten the survival of the organization. Indeed, some environmental forces require organizations to decline. Changing population patterns have reduced the number of students in schools and patients in urban hospitals. Foreign competition has closed steel mills and copper mines. Certain industries, especially automotive companies, have laid off record numbers of employees in response to a recessionary economy and decreased demand. **Organizational decline,** sometimes called "down-sizing," is a cutback in the size of the organization's workforce, profits, budget, or clients.

Managing an organization during a period of decline is much more difficult and usually much more unpleasant than managing a growing organization. In periods of growth, budgets are loose, new people are added, resources are plentiful, and bad decisions do not seem so serious. During periods of decline, resources are

APPLYING ORGANIZATIONAL BEHAVIOR
IN THE NEWS

The Death and Rebirth of Continental Can

CNN The term *equifinality* refers to the idea that organizations can grow by following many different pathways—they are not required to follow predictable growth patterns, as biological systems do. Today's Continental Can Company has certainly followed a unique pathway in its development. It died and was reborn by Donald Bainton, its former president.

Donald Bainton became the president of Continental Can Company, U.S. industrial giant at age 48. During his twenty-nine years at Continental Can, Bainton advanced from management trainee to the presidency. But at 52, he objected to the board's plans to sell the Canadian and Australian divisions, and his boldness cost him his job.

Although he was eligible for retirement, Bainton saw his termination from Continental Can as an opportunity to do something fun, and fun meant building another corporation. So, with his brother John he bought Viatech, a small engineering firm, for $6 million in 1983. While Continental Can was being divided and sold in pieces, Bainton and his brother were buying struggling companies and turning them around.

Bainton always maintained a sentimental attachment to Continental Can Company. Finally, he acquired the rights to the name Continental Can Company and to its distinctive red CCC logo. In 1992 he changed the name Viatech to Continental Can.

Although the newly named company bears little resemblance to its namesake, Bainton still identifies himself as being in the packaging industry and has been able to offer employment to some of the former employees. The new Continental Can does not produce cans, but it does produce plastic containers.

When asked what he wants to leave behind, Bainton says he wants to leave a financially successful company that cares for the people who work there and where people can be proud to work.

Source: CNN *Pinnacle* news programming.

scarce, faithful long-term employees may need to be terminated, the employees who remain are unhappy, and bad decisions are sometimes catastrophic.

During periods of decline, organizations are often required to make two types of adjustments: recentralization and reallocation.[28]

1. *Recentralization.* Decentralized authority often must be withdrawn during periods of decline. Decisions about the future of the organization and the types of adjustments that must be made to enable it to survive must be made by top management. Some departments may have to be eliminated, employees may have to be laid off, pay may be cut, and resources may be redirected. These decisions usually create such serious disagreement and debate that it is best for them to be made by top managers exercising centralized authority.

2. *Reallocation.* Organizations in decline are often required to eliminate some of their products or services. Low-priority management programs may also need to be eliminated. Making these decisions means reallocating resources among those who remain. The way the resources are allocated will reflect the survival strategy of top management.

Although organizational decline is an unpleasant time of stress and conflict, managers can take several actions to reduce the problems. The most effective managerial strategy is to recognize the change early and decide whether the decline is inevitable or whether a revitalization strategy is possible. If the decline is inevitable, it ought to be recognized and accepted, and members of the organization should be informed as early as possible. If people understand the need for decline and are notified in advance, they are more likely to accept the change and prepare for the future, so that being laid off will not be such a serious blow.

SUMMARY

1. Organizational design is the process of deciding what type of structure an organization should have. The major design decisions involve the division of labor, departmentalization, span of control, the delegation of authority, and coordinating mechanisms.

2. The key issue associated with the division of labor concerns the degree of specialization—whether jobs should be highly specialized and consist of separate specific tasks or should be left as enriched jobs with greater variety. Job specialization usually leads to high levels of productivity.

3. Departmentalization is the process of combining jobs into groups or departments. The key issue in departmentalization concerns whether jobs are grouped into homogeneous specialties or into heterogeneous units. The most popular method for forming departments is grouping jobs that are based on similar functions. Occasionally, however, departmentalization is based on product, geographic area, or clientele, and these criteria for departmentalization tend to be more market based.

4. The span of control decision concerns how many individuals should be placed in a group under one supervisor. A wide span of control creates a very flat organizational structure, while a narrow span of control creates a very tall organizational structure. The appropriate span of control depends on the amount of contact required with the supervisor, the amount of training and education of subordinates, the opportunity to communicate, and the nature of the task.

5. The decision-making authority within organizations can be centralized under the control of top management or decentralized to allow lower-level supervisors greater authority. Decentralized authority typically creates greater productivity and satisfaction; however, there are times when centralized authority is more effective, such as when there are shared functions between departments or crucial information controlled by top management.

6. Organizations can use a variety of mechanisms to coordinate their activities and subsystems. These coordinating mechanisms vary along a continuum of how much personal discretion employees are allowed to use. The least discretion occurs when direct supervision and rules are used to coordinate activities. The greatest degree of discretion occurs when organizations use mutual adjustment, such as committees, task forces, and liaison positions. Intermediate mechanisms involve coordinating activities through standardized outputs or standardized skills.

7. A matrix organizational structure combines two types of departmentalization, typically functional and product forms of departmentalization. A matrix structure is particularly effective when environmental pressures demand both technical quality (which is best produced by functional departmentalization) and frequent new products (which are best achieved through product departmentalization).

8. The five design concepts can be combined to produce either a mechanistic or an organic organizational structure. A mechanistic organizational structure is characterized by high job specialization, homogeneous departmentalization, narrow spans of control, centralized authority, and direct supervision. An organic structure, in contrast, is characterized by a low division of labor, heterogeneous departmentalization, broad spans of control, decentralized authority, and mutual adjustment.

9. The most widely known description of a mechanistic organizational structure is Max Weber's description of a bureaucracy, which was intended as a description of an ideal form for any large organization. The chief characteristics of a bureaucratic structure include an elaborate division of labor based on functional specialization, a well-defined hierarchy of authority, a system of rules covering the rights and duties of employees, impersonal relationships based on these rules, selection and promotion based on technical competence, and written communications and records.

10. Although most people respond negatively to bureaucracy, there are several advantages and disadvantages associated with it. The chief benefits of a bureaucracy include its technical efficiency, elimination of favoritism, predictability in performance, job security, technical competence of its office holders, minimum administration required to keep it operating, and protection from impulsive actions. However, bureaucracies also tend to create such problems as rigid behavior, bureaucratic personalities, an inversion of means and ends, and resistance to change.

11. Rensis Likert described four management systems along a continuum that ranged from System One to System Four. System One was called an exploitive-authoritative structure and was characterized by the threat of punishment, hostile attitudes, downward communication, and distrust. System Four, however, was called a participative-group-oriented structure and was characterized by considerable responsibility and initiative, decision making, decentralized authority, and goal setting. Likert believed that System Four was a universally ideal organizational structure. System Four structures are created by the principles of supportive relationships, group decision making and supervision, and high performance aspirations among employees.

12. Contingency theories claim that there are no universally appropriate design decisions for all organizations. Instead, the design decision should be based on the situation. One of the earliest studies supporting the contingency design theory was reported by Joan Woodward. Her study demonstrated a need for coordinating the technology of the organization with its structure. Woodward discovered that organizations using a mass production technology were most effective if they adopted a mechanistic organizational structure. However, companies using (a) a process manufacturing technology with a high level of technical complexity or (b) job order companies that manufacture small orders to meet specific demands were more effective if they used an organic organizational structure.

13. A study by Lawrence and Lorsch also supported the concept of contingency design theories by showing that the appropriate organizational structure depended on the amount of environmental uncertainty and the organization's need to respond to it. Organizations in an extremely unstable environment, such as electronics or plastics companies, need to adopt an organic structure, while organizations in an extremely stable environment, such as the container industry and the cast-iron industry, are more effective if they create a mechanistic structure with extensive rules.

14. The process that has the greatest impact on the appropriateness of an organizational structure is the organization's information-processing capacity. Stable environments place minimal information-processing demands on an organization, and organizations in stable environments are best suited for a mechanistic structure. However, organic structures are required in a dynamic environment that produces numerous exceptional cases and creates an information overload or saturation.

15. The appropriate organizational structure also depends on the life cycle of the organization. New organizations in the entrepreneurial stage contain very few rules and are highly organic. During the second stage of collectivity and the third stage of formalization, however, organizations begin to adopt bureaucratic characteristics that control behavior and structure organizational activities. In stage 4, the elaboration stage, organizations have acquired so many bureaucratic procedures that unless the procedures are contained, the organization will disintegrate.

DISCUSSION QUESTIONS

1. Select a typical everyday task, such as washing dishes or cleaning the house, and describe how this job could be divided into highly specialized tasks. Why does job specialization increase productivity?

2. The functional form of departmentalization is the most popular because it is supposed to be the most efficient. Can you explain why it is the most efficient? Also, can you explain why product departmentalization tends to be more customer oriented?

3. Jan Carlzon, former president of Scandinavian Airlines, recommends that companies turn their organization charts upside down and put power in the hands of the front-line employees who deal directly with customers. What does it mean to turn an organization's chart upside down? Is this change just "window dressing" in the form of customer service, or does it represent a significant change in decision making and responsibility?

4. The kind of control found in an organization is usually viewed as a function of management style. What happens when the style of control preferred by a manager differs greatly from the control mechanism called for by the situation?

5. Matrix structures violate Fayol's unity-of-command principle. Is Fayol's principle not really important, or is this a problem for matrix structures?

6. In recent years, some organizations have thrown away their organization charts and disregarded formal lines of authority. These organizations are typically small, innovative companies that appear to be highly successful. Their success has caused some to suggest that all organizations need to get rid of their organization charts and formal structure. Do you agree? How important is organizational structure?

7. What are the major advantages of a bureaucracy? Does a bureaucracy deserve the negative reaction it provokes in most people?

8. Describe a time in your life when you have experienced one of the dysfunctional consequences of a bureaucracy, such as rigid behavior by an officeholder, resistance to change, or an inversion of the means and the ends.

9. Is the Peter Principle really valid? Isn't everyone somewhat incompetent when beginning a new job?

10. Even though he was familiar with the contingency design research, Likert argued that System Four was a universally superior theory of organizational design. In what ways do you agree or disagree with him?

11. Explain why an unstable environment and extensive demands for information processing are more conducive to an organic structure.

12. Why do you suppose it is so much more difficult to manage an organization that is declining in size than one that is expanding?

GLOSSARY

bureaucracy An organizational structure that is characterized by an elaborate division of labor based on functional specialization, a hierarchy of authority assigned to different offices, a system of rules explaining how everyone is to perform, and impersonal relationships.

centralized authority A characteristic of organizations in which the authority to make organizational decisions is retained by top managers within the central office.

decentralized authority A characteristic of organizations in which authority to make organizational decisions is delegated to lower-level managers and supervisors.

departmentalization The process of assigning jobs to units or departments based on some criteria. Four of the most frequently used criteria include function, product, geographical area, or clientele.

differentiation The degree of segmentation or division of labor into specialized jobs. It includes the behavioral attributes brought about by creating a narrow, department-oriented focus in the minds of individuals.

division of labor The process of dividing work into specialized jobs that are performed by separate individuals.

integration The coordinating activity that is used to achieve a unity of effort among various subsystems within an organization. The five major methods of integration include direct supervision, standardization of work processes, standardization of outputs, standardization of skills, or mutual adjustment.

life cycle Organizational life cycles are the developmental stages that an organization experiences after it is first created. The four life cycle stages include the entrepreneurial stage, the collectivity stage, the formalization stage, and the elaboration stage.

line activity The activity of people who are directly involved in the central production of the organization.

matrix organizational structure A combination of two different forms of departmentalization, usually functional and product departmentalization.

means-end inversion A dysfunctional consequence of bureaucracy in which the means or processes that have been created to achieve an organizational purpose become an end in themselves, and are often viewed as more important than the objective for which they were designed.

mechanistic organizational structure A formal organizational structure characterized by highly specialized tasks that are carefully and rigidly defined, with a strict hierarchy of authority to control them. Bureaucracy is a type of mechanistic structure.

mutual adjustment A means of achieving organizational coordination by allowing people to coordinate their work through informal processes, mutually adjusting to each others' needs.

organic organizational structure A type of organizational structure characterized by people who work together in an informal arrangement, sharing ideas and information, and performing a variety of tasks based on whatever is needed to accomplish the group's task.

organizational decline The process of reducing the size of the organization by cutting back on its budget, clients, profits, and/or workforce.

organizational design The process of deciding on the type of structure appropriate for an organization, particularly regarding its division of labor, departmentalization, span of control, and delegation of authority.

Peter Principle A satirical explanation for incompetence in bureaucracies, suggesting that people rise to their level of incompetence.

principle of supportive relationships A universal principle, recommended by Rensis Likert as part of a System Four organizational structure, which suggests that every interaction between superiors and subordinates should be transacted in a way that builds and encourages each in the performance of their respective duties.

span of control The number of subordinates assigned to a supervisor.

staff activity The activity of employees who are not in a line position but whose responsibility is to provide advice or service to line managers.

suboptimizing Having individual units or subunits pursue their own goals at the expense of the overall unit objectives.

System Four A type of organizational structure that is at the opposite end of the continuum from a System One. A System Four style is called a "participative group" style, characterized by responsibility and initiative on the part of members, widely shared decision-making authority, decentralized decision making, and goal setting by employees.

technology The knowledge, tools, techniques, and actions that are used to transform organizational inputs into outputs. Essentially, technology is the organization's transformation process.

universal theories of organizational design Theories of organizational design that purport to be universally appropriate for every organization. Two widely contrasting universal design theories are bureaucracy and System Four.

NOTES

1. An early discussion of departmentalization is found in Luther Gulick and Lyndall Urwick (eds.), *Papers on the Science of Administration* (New York: Institute of Public Administration, 1937).

2. V. A. Graicunas, "Relationship in Organization," *Bulletin of the International Management Institute*, vol. 7 (March 1933), pp. 39–42; reprinted in Luther H. Gulick and Lyndall F. Urwick (eds.), *Papers on the Science of Administration* (New York: Institute of Public Administration, Columbia University, 1937), pp. 182–187; Arthur G. Bedeian, "Vytautas Andrius Graicunas: A Biographical Note," *Academy of Management Journal*, vol. 17 (1974), pp. 347–349; Lyndall F. Urwick, "V. A. Graicunas and the Span of Control," *Academy of Management Journal*, vol. 17 (1974), pp. 349–354.

3. Phoebe M. Carillo and Richard E. Kopelman, "Organization Structure and Productivity: Effects of Subunit Size, Vertical Complexity, and Administrative Intensity

on Operating Efficiency," *Group and Organization Studies,* vol. 91 (March 1991), pp. 44–59.

4. Alfred P. Sloan, *My Years With General Motors,* ed. J. McDonald with C. Stevens (Garden City, N.Y.: Doubleday, 1964); Nancy K. Austin, "The Death of Hierarchy," *Working Woman,* vol. 15 (July 1990), pp. 22–25.

5. Larry Reibstein, "IBM's Plan to Decentralize May Set a Trend—But Imitation Has Its Price," *Wall Street Journal* (February 19, 1988), p. 17.

6. Alan Radding and Tony Baer, "IS Helps 3M Stick Together," *Computer World,* vol. 25 (September 30, 1991), pp. S50–52; L. W. Lehr, "How 3M Develops Entrepreneurial Spirit Throughout the Organization," *Management Review,* vol. 69, no. 10 (1980), p. 31.

7. Paul R. Lawrence and Jay W. Lorsch, *Organization and Environment* (Boston: Harvard Business School, Division of Research, 1967).

8. Reibstein, op. cit.

9. Karl E. Weick, "Organizational Culture as a Source of High Reliability," *California Management Review,* vol. 29, no. 2 (1987), pp. 112–127.

10. Rachid M. Zeffane, "Centralization or Formalization? Indifference Curves for Strategies of Control," *Organization Studies,* vol. 10 (Summer 1989), pp. 326–352.

11. Joseph B. White, "GM Will Run Big Car Group Like Japanese," *Wall Street Journal* (June 10, 1991), p. A3.

12. Henri Fayol, *General and Industrial Management* (London: Pitman, 1949).

13. T. Burns and G. M. Stalker, *The Management of Innovation* (London: Tavistock Institute, 1961).

14. Christopher Gresov, "Effects of Dependence and Tasks on Unit Design and Efficiency," *Organization Studies,* vol. 11 (Fall 1990), pp. 503–529.

15. Max Weber, *The Theory of Social and Economic Organization,* trans. A. M. Henderson and T. Parsons (New York: Free Press, 1947).

16. Robert K. Merton, "Bureaucratic Structure and Personality," *Social Forces,* vol. 18 (1940), pp. 560–568.

17. James A. Gazell and Darrell L. Pugh, "Administrative Theory at Large Organizations in the Future: Whither Bureaucracy?" *International Journal of Public Administration,* vol. 13 (1990), pp. 827–858; Nancy C. Morey and Fred Luthans, "The Use of Dyadic Alliances in Informal Organization: An Ethnographic Study," *Human Relations,* vol. 44 (June 1991), pp. 597–618.

18. Lawrence F. Peter and Raymond Hull, *The Peter Principle* (New York: Morrow, 1969); Donald E. Walker, "The Peter Principle: A Simple Put-On About Complex Issues," *Change,* vol. 17 (July–August 1985), p. 11.

19. Rensis Likert, *New Patterns of Management* (New York: McGraw-Hill, 1961); Rensis Likert, *The Human Organization* (New York: McGraw-Hill, 1967).

20. Likert, *New Patterns of Management,* p. 103.

21. Reviewed by James G. March and Herbert A. Simon, *Organizations* (New York: Wiley, 1958); James D. Thompson, *Organizations in Action* (New York: McGraw-Hill, 1967).

22. Joan Woodward, *Industrial Organization: Theory and Practice* (London: Oxford University Press, 1965).

23. C. Chet Miller, William H. Glick, Yau-De Wang, and George P. Huber, "Understanding Technology-Structure Relationships: Theory Development and Meta-Analytic Theory Testing," *Academy of Management Journal,* vol. 34 (1991), pp. 370–399; Stephen R. Barley, "The Alignment of Technology and Structure Through Roles and Networks," *Administrative Science Quarterly,* vol. 35 (March 1990), pp. 61–103.

24. Paul R. Lawrence and J. W. Lorsch, *Organization and Environment* (Boston: Harvard Business School, 1967); Paul R. Lawrence and J. W. Lorsch, "Differentiation and Integration in Complex Organizations," *Administrative Science Quarterly,* vol. 12 (1967), pp. 1–47.

25. Michael L. Tushman and David A. Nadler, "Information Processing as an Integrating Concept in Organizational Design," *Academy of Management Review,* vol. 3 (1978), pp. 613–624.

26. Robert E. Quinn and Kim Cameron, "Organizational Life Cycles and Some Shifting Criteria of Effectiveness: Some Preliminary Evidence," *Management Science,* vol. 29 (1983), pp. 33–51; Larry E. Greiner, "Evolution and Revolution as Organizations Grow," *Harvard Business Review,* vol. 50 (July–August 1972), pp. 37–46; Henry Mintzberg, "Power and Organization Life Cycles," *Academy of Management Review,* vol. 9 (1984), pp. 207–224.

27. Kim S. Cameron, David A. Whetten, and Myung U. Kim, "Organizational Dysfunctions of Decline," *Academy of Management Journal,* vol. 30 (1987), pp. 126–138; William Weitzel and Ellen Jonsson, "Decline in Organizations: A Literature Integration and Extension," *Administrative Science Quarterly,* vol. 34 (March 1989), pp. 91–109.

28. Charles H. Levine, Irene S. Rubin and George G. Wolohojian, "Managing Organizational Retrenchment," *Administration and Society,* vol. 14 (1982), pp. 101–136.

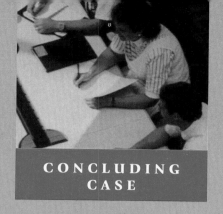

CONCLUDING CASE

GROWING FROM STAGE I TO STAGE II

PART I

CMP Publications Inc., a publisher of business newspapers and magazines was started in 1971 by Gerry Leeds and Lila, his wife and cofounder. As news entrepreneurs, the Leeds did just about everything they were supposed to do to build a successful family firm. By 1986 the company's ten publications were considered tops in their respective markets, and the firm was growing about 30 percent annually.

In every family firm, however, there comes a time when the entrepreneurial structure that worked so well at first was no longer adequate. The symptoms calling for a reorganization at CMP began to appear in annoying little ways. Employees would gather outside Gerry's and Lila's offices early in the morning hoping to share information. Requests and approvals were delayed unnecessarily in support departments, because the answers to operating decisions were difficult to obtain.

Questions

1. If the structure they used in the past was successful, why is it ineffective now? Can't the Leeds simply tell the division heads to act more independently?

2. Do they really need a major reorganization or just another executive to share the load?

PART II

The Leeds considered including their son Michael, who would some day inherit the firm, in the executive circle. But adding another executive, especially an inexperienced one, was not the solution. What they needed was to move to the next stage of organizational development by restructuring the company.

The Leeds divided the company into manageable divisions by creating companies within the company. A manager was placed in charge of each company with the authority to operate the company and make it grow. These managers were called *group publishers,* and they formed a board called the *publications committee.* As members of this committee, they assumed the titles and responsibilities of vice presidents.

This reorganization formed a new level of management and relieved the Leeds from some of their burden of leadership. These managers had authority to act on their own initiative consistent with the corporate strategic objectives they themselves helped formulate as members of the publications committee.

With the reorganization, CMP Publications has continued to grow and from the outside it looks like the same effective, growing company. But on the inside, the lines of communication and reporting relationships are very different and will allow the company to continue growing.

Questions

1. What are the advantages and potential disadvantages of creating companies within the company?

2. What are the major differences between companies in stage 1 versus stage 2 of organization development?

Source: Tom Richman, "Reorganizing for Growth," *Inc.,* vol. 13 (January 1991), pp. 110–111.

PROFILING ORGANIZATIONAL CHARACTERISTICS

Purpose. The purpose of this exercise is to improve your skill at diagnosing the effectiveness of an organization. This exercise is based on Rensis Likert's research, which identifies four significantly different management systems and the variables that characterize each system.

Activity. This exercise works best if all class members describe the same organization. However, if some have not experienced the same organization, they should select another organization that they know well enough to describe. Use the scales in Exhibit 12.11 to describe this organization. As you describe it, try to think of specific incidents you have personally experienced or illustrations you have heard of.

Discussion. Compare your evaluations with the evaluations of others who described the same organization. To what extent did you agree? If your evaluations were significantly different, talk about the differences and try to identify the specific experiences that led to your disagreements. Likert argued that every organization would be more effective if it moved closer to a System Four organization. How close is your organization to a System Four, and do you think it would be more effective if it were closer? Is it realistic or possible for your organization to become a System Four organization?

EXHIBIT 12.11 Profile of Organizational Characteristics

	Organizational Variables	System 1	System 2	System 3	System 4
Leadership	How much confidence is shown in subordinates?	None	Condescending	Substantial	Complete
	How free do they feel to talk to superiors about their job?	Not at all	Not very	Rather free	Fully free
	Are subordinates' ideas sought and used, if worthy?	Seldom	Sometimes	Usually	Always
Motivation	Is predominant use made of 1 fear, 2 threats, 3 punishment, 4 rewards, 5 involvement?	1, 2, 3, occasionally 4	4, some 3	4, some 3 and 5	5, 4 based on group
	Where is responsibility felt for achieving organizational goals?	Mostly at top	Top and middle	Fairly general	At all levels
	How much cooperative teamwork exists?	None	Little	Some	Great deal
Communication	What is the direction of information flow?	Downward	Mostly downward	Down and up	Down, up, and sideways
	How is downward communication accepted?	With suspicion	Possibly with suspicion	With caution	With a receptive mind
	How accurate is upward communication?	Often wrong	Censored for the boss	Limited accuracy	Accurate
	How well do superiors know problems faced by subordinates?	Know little	Some knowledge	Quite well	Very well
Decisions	At what level are decisions made?	Mostly at top	Policy at top, some delegation	Broad policy at top, more delegation	Throughout, but well integrated
	Are subordinates involved in decisions related to their work?	Not at all	Occasionally consulted	Generally consulted	Fully involved
	What does decision-making process contribute to motivation?	Nothing, often weakens it	Relatively little	Some contribution	Substantial contribution
Goals	How are organizational goals established?	Orders issued	Orders, some comments invited	After discussion, by orders	By group action (except in crisis)
	How much covert resistance to goals is present?	Strong resistance	Moderate resistance	Some resistance at times	Little or none
Control	How concentrated are review and control functions?	Highly at top	Relatively highly at top	Moderate delegation to lower levels	Quite widely shared
	Is there an informal organization resisting the formal one?	Yes	Usually	Sometimes	No—same goals as formal
	What are cost, productivity, and other control data used for?	Policing, punishment	Reward and punishment	Reward, some self-guidance	Self-guidance, problem solving

Source: Rensis Likert, *The Human Organization* (New York: McGraw-Hill, 1967). Reprinted by permission.

■ Communication

■ Decision Making

■ Leadership

■ Power and Politics in Organizations

■ Organization Change and Development

ORGANIZATIONAL PROCESSES

T he preceding sections have examined organizational behavior from three different levels of analysis: the individual, the group, and the organization. This section examines organizational processes.

Organizational processes are the activities and relationships that occur in organizations—they are the interactions between organizational members. The major organizational processes are communication, decision making, leadership, politics, and change.

These organizational processes occur throughout the organization and can be studied at each level of analysis. For example, communication can be examined at the individual level by studying the ways individuals transmit and receive information. At the group level, different communication networks influence the effectiveness of the group's performance. At the organization level, different structural arrangements influence the way information is collected and transmitted through both the formal and informal (or grapevine) communication systems. Communication problems can result from errors at any level.

The decision-making process is described in Chapter 14, while Chapter 15 examines different leadership styles and the conditions appropriate for each style. Some individuals and groups can significantly influence others because they know how to use power. Chapter 16 describes the sources of power and explains the difference between authority and power. Although we would like to think organizational decisions are rational decisions based on sound logic, this is generally not true. Most decisions are political decisions determined by the power positions of influential individuals or groups.

Chapter 17 examines the processes of organizational change and development. Organizations live in a changing environment, and their long-term survival depends on their ability to adapt to the demands of a changing environment. Organizations face an interesting paradox between structure and adaptability. An elaborate structure makes them more efficient; but the more highly structured they are, the more they tend to resist change. Although an elaborate organizational structure may contribute to effectiveness at one point in time, it also contributes to rigidity and a lack of adaptability that will threaten the organization's long-term survival after the environment changes.

CHAPTER 13

Communication

LEARNING OBJECTIVES

After studying this chapter, you should be able to

1. Describe the basic elements of the interpersonal communication process.

2. Explain the characteristics of persuasive communication.

3. Explain the characteristics of supportive communication.

4. Describe the skills required for effective listening.

5. Describe some of the major forms of nonverbal communication.

6. Explain the effects of different communication networks on the performance of groups.

7. Describe the directions of communication flow in organizations and the problems associated with each direction.

8. Explain the functions of formal and informal communication, and explain when grapevine information can be useful.

9. Identify the major barriers inhibiting effective communication in organizations.

10. List the major reactions to information overload, and indicate whether they are adaptive or dysfunctional responses.

11. Explain some of the strategies used to improve organizational communication.

AMTRAK'S COMMUNICATION SYSTEMS

Amtrak would like to improve the efficiency of its customer communications. When travelers need information, they call one of Amtrak's four regional reservations bureaus. The bureaus receive an average of 100,000 calls a day, with an average transaction time of 2.5 minutes per call. A reduction of just five seconds per call would mean a savings of over $1.2 million. But the increasing complexity in Amtrak's pricing tends to make the calls longer, not shorter.

During the past twenty years, Amtrak has recovered from being a national embarrassment. Although Amtrak still depends partially on federal subsidies, it plans to be completely self-sustaining by the year 2000. No other national passenger railroad has ever been financially self-sustaining. Amtrak is counting on two computerized information systems to help it reach its goals. A more efficient way to communicate with customers could also improve its profit picture.

Reservations and ticket sales for Amtrak are monitored by a computerized reservations system (CRS) called Arrow. This system supports 20,000 travel agents and can also be accessed by airline reservation agents who need to coordinate train and plane reservations. Arrow CRS is more complex than airline reservation systems, because there are 550 passenger train stations and the average number of stops on a train ride is about fifteen rather than two or three for a plane ride. The complexity is further compounded by a greater variety of accommodations, such as deluxe, standard, and economy bedrooms, as well as roomettes with facilities for the handicapped, all priced at different fares.

Arrow's statistical information helps Amtrak managers predict where the most money is to be made, when to raise prices, and when to offer promotions if demand is low. There used to be just two fares for a trip from Chicago to Washington—now there may be five or six, depending on demand. Although this complexity increases revenues, it also increases the average length of phone calls with customers. Amtrak would like to improve its customer communications, using new technology, the same way it improved its scheduling of trains.

The assignment of cars to trains and trains to tracks is handled by a centralized electrification and traffic control system (CETC) located in Philadelphia. Dispatchers sit before a 78-foot-long color projection TV screen and monitor the movement of trains and switches and overhead power wires. Instead of individual dispatchers in towers throwing switches manually, the big board provides instantaneous information on the location and status of every train. A dispatcher can reroute a train by simply touching a computer screen. This screen has improved service and safety by making better use of tracks and routes that are used by slower freight trains.

Questions

1. Does Amtrak really need to communicate directly with its customers? Could Amtrak rely on a form of communication other than phone calls to communicate with its customers?

2. If customers insist on calling for information, could Amtrak use an interactive recorded message system and avoid the wage expenses of reservation agents? How well might this work?

3. How important are these computerized systems to Amtrak's profitability? Would other companies benefit from similarly complex communication systems?

Source: Jason Forsythe, "The Big Train That Could," *Information Week* (May 21, 1990), pp. 29–33.

Communication is the exchange of information between a sender and a receiver. We typically think of communication as an exchange of verbal or written messages between two people. To understand organizational communication, however, this definition needs to be broadened. Writing and speaking are not the only channels for communicating, and the senders and receivers are not always people. For example, an airplane instrument panel (sender) sends messages to the pilot (receiver) and a smoke detector (sender) notifies the fire department (receiver) of a fire. In today's organizations, many messages are sent by complex management information systems, where data are input from numerous sources and analyzed by computer, and then electronically transmitted to receivers.

The importance of communication is indicated by the amount of time people spend communicating at work. One study found that production workers participated in communication episodes between 16 and 46 times per hour. This means that they communicated with someone every two to four minutes. This same study found that leadership responsibilities required supervisors to communicate even more frequently. First-level supervisors spent approximately 20 to 50 percent of their time in verbal communication. When written communication was included, the amount of time increased to as much as 29 to 64 percent. Some middle and upper-level managers spent as much as 89 percent of their time in verbal communication, either face-to-face or on a telephone.[1] Other surveys have reported that managers in many industries and across several management levels typically spend at least 70 to 80 percent of their time in interpersonal communication, and most of this communication occurs as oral, face-to-face interaction.[2]

Communication is the lifeblood of an organization; it is the thread that holds the various interdependent parts of an organization together. As noted in Chapter 11, an organization is a stable system of patterned activities where people work together to achieve common goals through a hierarchy of assigned roles and a division of labor. These patterned activities depend on communication for coordination and integration. If the communication flows could somehow be removed from an organization, the organization would cease to exist. The patterned activities that comprise the organization depend on the exchange of information.

The communication process can be analyzed from three different levels—interpersonal communication, communication in groups, and organizational communication—and managers need to understand all three levels. Each level gives rise to different communication problems and involves different levels of abstraction. The organizational communication process cannot be understood simply by extending the processes of interpersonal communication; organizational communication is not just the sum of many interpersonal conversations.

INTERPERSONAL COMMUNICATION

Interpersonal communication involves the exchange of information between two people. In this section we identify the basic elements of the communication process and the major characteristics of effective communication.

The Communication Process

The word *communication* is derived from the Latin word *communis,* which means "common." The communicator tries to establish a common understanding with a receiver. This shared understanding is achieved through the use of common symbols.

Symbolic Interaction. The communication process is a **symbolic interaction** between two people. For example, when a customer orders a turkey club sandwich and a strawberry milkshake at a fast-food restaurant, the customer is using words as symbols to indicate what he wants to eat. A symbol is something that stands for or represents something else. The words "turkey sandwich" are made from letters of the alphabet, but they are used to represent something made from slices of turkey and bread. The customer selected a turkey club sandwich after looking at a non-verbal representation showing a picture of the sandwich. The person behind the counter used even different symbols to inform the kitchen what to prepare—"One turkey deluxe, one strawberry."

Some symbols refer to physical objects, such as a table, a book, or a tree. Other symbols refer to activities, such as running, sleeping, and organizing. The most difficult symbols to understand, however, are hypothetical constructs, such as intelligence, loyalty, and diligence. These symbols refer to concepts that cannot be easily observed, and they often have slightly different meanings to different people.

Our ability to use symbols allows us to learn from the experience of others. People who lived many centuries ago can communicate their experiences to us symbolically through writing and art. Although receivers who have not experienced the same events as the senders may have difficulty comprehending the exact messages, highly complex messages can often be effectively communicated because of our ability to use symbols. For example, someone who has never experienced a tropical storm may not know exactly what such an event might be like, but a skilled communicator who has experienced such an event should be able to describe it vividly enough for the receiver to appreciate how powerful and frightening a tropical storm can be. A symbolic presentation using words, however, is almost always only a rough approximation of what actually occurred. Even when we are communicating information about physical objects, the meaning may be ambiguous and incomplete because of our inability to find a common ground in communication. Exhibit 13.1 illustrates the difficulty of describing a specific object.

Elements of Communication. The basic elements of the communication process are diagrammed in Exhibit 13.2. This model has been used extensively in the field of communication to analyze the communication process.[3]

The process begins with a *source* or a sender who has an intended message to communicate. The source is the originator of the message and may be one person or several people working together, such as a musical group or a television news team.

The *message* is the stimulus the source transmits to the receiver; it is composed of symbols designed to convey the intended meaning. Most messages contain words that are either written or spoken; however, a variety of nonverbal behaviors can also be used to communicate a message, such as body language, Morse code, sign language, winks, gestures, and electronic impulses.

EXHIBIT 13.1   Communication: A Symbolic Interaction

"I love my pet! It's really fun being with him."

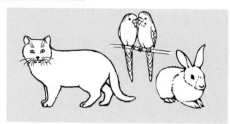

"He must be a really nice pet."

"Yeah, I play with him every day. Best dog in the world."

"Oh, it's a dog?"

"Uh-huh, he's a St. Bernard. We bought him as a pup."

"Now I see. He's a St. Bernard dog."

"He's real big. We've had him now for twelve years. He's mostly white with black spots."

"Oh, now I really understand. Your pet is a big St. Bernard that is white with black spots."

The process of transforming the intended message into the symbols used to transmit it is called the **encoding** process. Encoding can be fairly simple, such as seeing a picture of what you want and then ordering a sandwich and milkshake. On other occasions, encoding can be extremely difficult, such as finding the right words to explain why an employee's performance is inadequate.

EXHIBIT 13.2 The Communication Process

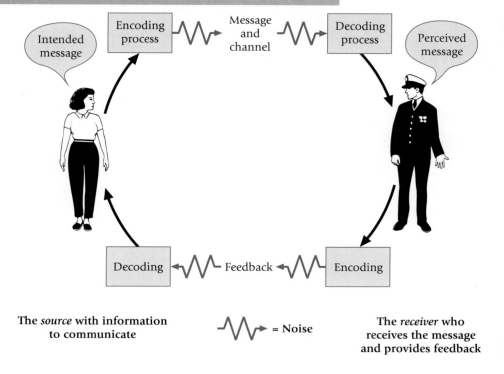

The *source* with information to communicate

—\/\/— = Noise

The *receiver* who receives the message and provides feedback

The *channel* is the means by which a message travels from a source to a receiver. It is the path through which the message is physically transmitted. The primary channel for interpersonal communication involves a face-to-face exchange between two people. Some of the major mass media channels include radio, television, films, newspapers, and magazines. Some of the newer electronic channels include facsimile machines, voice mail, videotape, teleconferencing, and electronic mail. Written messages are typically written on paper, but virtually anything can be used to convey written messages, including snow, slate, stone, twigs, and golden plates. Several organizations are moving toward a paperless office where all messages are sent by electronic mail, through networked computer systems, rather than by written memos. In the future, video display terminals will probably provide one of the major channels for written messages.

The *receiver* is the person who receives the message and has the responsibility for decoding it. **Decoding** is the process by which the symbols are interpreted by the receiver. Although some complex messages (such as those in a foreign language or in Morse code) require an actual translation, in most cases decoding is simply the interpretation of the message by the receiver.

Feedback from the receiver back to the sender is actually another message indicating the effectiveness of the communication. Feedback is desirable, because the source may discover that the initial message was not accurately communicated and needs to be repeated. Feedback may also indicate that subsequent messages need to be modified. One-way communication does not provide an opportunity for feedback.

In both transmitting the message and receiving feedback, the message may be disrupted by **noise,** which includes everything from ambiguous wording of a message to a poor telephone connection or static from a poor TV antenna. Any factor that disrupts, distorts, or interferes with the receiver's ability to receive the message is called *noise.*

Factors Influencing Accuracy. The accuracy of communication depends on the successful completion of each step in the communication process. It is not enough to carefully prepare and transmit a message and then simply assume that effective communication has occurred. The encoding, transmitting, decoding, and feedback processes are all essential for effective communication.

Most communication problems involve discrepancies between encoding and decoding. Accurate communication requires that the sender and the receiver share a common frame of reference. If their past experiences and perceptions of reality differ dramatically, communication errors are almost certain to occur. A discrepancy between the encoded and decoded messages can occur because of special jargon used by one of the parties, because of value judgments that distort the meaning, and because of semantic problems in which the symbols do not share a common meaning.

Communication failures can also be created by a variety of other problems. The encoding process often omits significant information that was necessary to convey the complete meaning of the message. To protect against omission, communicators frequently use redundancy and duplication, which means they express the same ideas in different words and repeat the message. Redundancy and duplication, however, contribute to information overload, leaving the receiver buried in information.

During the transmission of a message, the meaning often becomes distorted because of noise in the communication channel. Furthermore, when information is passed from person to person, significant parts of the message are often deleted through a process called *filtering.*

These problems represent barriers to effective communication and help to explain why communication is more complex than we typically appreciate. Each of these barriers is discussed more completely in a later section, along with recommended ways for overcoming them.

Interpersonal Communication Model. A useful model has been developed from empirical research describing the interpersonal communication process in organizations.[4] People were asked to describe the characteristics of effective and ineffective communicators, and from these interviews a communication audit in the form of a questionnaire was developed. An analysis of the questionnaire data from three organizations identified the central variables influencing interpersonal communication.

The interpersonal communication model shown in Exhibit 13.3 explains how the communication style of the focal person influences the behavior of that person's colleagues. Five characteristics were found to have a significant influence on a focal person's communication style: (1) being a careful transmitter; (2) being open and two-way; (3) being frank; (4) being a careful listener; and (5) being informal. These characteristics determine the credibility of the focal person, and specifically whether that person is perceived by colleagues as trustworthy, informative, and dynamic. Four important outcomes of the colleagues depend on the commu-

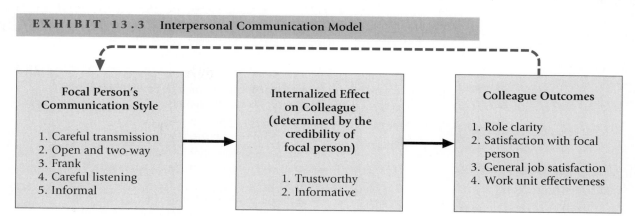

EXHIBIT 13.3 Interpersonal Communication Model

Focal Person's Communication Style

1. Careful transmission
2. Open and two-way
3. Frank
4. Careful listening
5. Informal

Internalized Effect on Colleague (determined by the credibility of focal person)

1. Trustworthy
2. Informative

Colleague Outcomes

1. Role clarity
2. Satisfaction with focal person
3. General job satisfaction
4. Work unit effectiveness

Source: Rudi Klauss and Bernard M. Bass, *Interpersonal Communication in Organizations* (New York: Academic Press, 1982), p. 69. Used by permission.

nication style and credibility of the focal person: (1) colleague role clarity; that is, how well colleagues understand their roles; (2) colleague satisfaction with the focal person; (3) overall job satisfaction of colleagues; and (4) the work unit effectiveness of the colleagues. Some of the questionnaire items measuring the various characteristics of communication style, communicator credibility, and colleague outcomes are shown in Exhibit 13.4. The relationships specified by the model have generally been confirmed by the communication audits in organizations.[5]

Persuasive Communication

Changing attitudes and swaying public opinion is an important issue for many organizations, such as political parties, religious organizations, business groups, and neighborhood committees. Consequently, persuasive communication has been investigated by scholars for many years; Aristotle was one of the first to construct a basic outline of the elements of persuasive communication. In his classic book, *Rhetoric*, Aristotle identified the three important dimensions for analyzing persuasive communication: the source, the message, and the audience.[6] Some of the characteristics associated with these three dimensions are summarized in Exhibit 13.5.

Characteristics of the Source. Extensive research has shown that the effectiveness of a message is largely influenced by the receiver's perception of the source's **credibility.** When changing attitudes, a highly credible communicator is more effective than one with low credibility.[7] Countless TV commercials attempt to get viewers to buy products because of recommendations by doctors or the American Dental Association or a panel of leading experts. Presumably, these authorities know the facts and should be listened to.

Communicators acquire credibility largely by possessing two characteristics: expertise and trustworthiness. Research scientists, for example, are more believable because they are considered experts who know the facts and are well informed about the issues. The fact that a doctor endorses a particular medication on

EXHIBIT 13.4   Sample Items from a Communication Audit

Dimensions of Communications Style

Factor	Sample Items
1. Careful transmitter	He speaks deliberately when he communicates. He chooses his words carefully.
2. Open and two-way	He is receptive to points of view that differ from his. He follows up conversations with feedback.
3. Frank	He is frank in saying what he really thinks. He levels with others when he disagrees with their viewpoints.
4. Careful listener	He keeps his mind on what the speaker is saying. He lets me finish my point before he comments.
5. Informal	He is very informal and relaxed when he communicates. He is very natural in the way he relates to others.

Credibility Dimensions

Factor	Sample Items
Trustworthy	He is very just in his dealings on the job. He is very kind to me.
Informative	He is very authoritative concerning issues that arise at work. He is very well informed on issues concerning his areas of responsibility.
Dynamic	He is very forceful at work. He is very energetic in his job.

Outcome Dimensions

Factor	Sample Items
Satisfaction with focal person	All in all, how satisfied are you with your focal person? In general, how satisfied are you that the way the focal person interacts with you is the right way for getting your job done?
Job satisfaction	All in all, how satisfied are you with your job? How satisfied are you that your own interests and abilities are being effectively used by the job you have?
Role clarity	I know what my own job responsibilities are. I know exactly what is expected of me in my job.
Effectiveness	Compared to other units you have known, how do you rate the effectiveness of the unit supervised by the focal person? How effective is the unit supervised by the focal person?

Source: Rudi Klauss and Bernard M. Bass, *Interpersonal Communication in Organizations* (New York: Academic Press, 1982), pp. 47, 50, 51. Used by permission.

EXHIBIT 13.5   Characteristics of Persuasive Communication

Characteristics of the Source

Credibility: expertise and trustworthiness
Similarity or dissimilarity from the receiver

Characteristics of the Message

Logical and reasonable
Pleasant versus fear appeal
One-sided versus two-sided arguments
Primacy versus recency
Overheard messages

Characteristics of the Audience

Level of intelligence
Initial position

---

television is effective both because doctors supposedly know what they are talking about and because they are perceived to have nothing to gain by recommending the particular product. The credibility of a communicator is destroyed, however, if the communicator has an ulterior motive or if the recommendation appears to be self-serving.

Several studies have shown that the effectiveness of a highly credible source lasts for only a short time. When measures of attitude are obtained immediately after the persuasion attempt, the studies show that highly credible sources produce significantly more attitude change than low-credibility sources. If the measures are obtained four to six weeks later, however, the credibility of the source appears to have no impact, and both groups show essentially equal amounts of attitude change.[8]

Another variable associated with the source is the similarity or dissimilarity of the communicator with the audience. People are more persuaded by communicators who share similar backgrounds and personality characteristics. Therefore, if you want to sell a computer to a word processing center, it may be better to get the endorsement of other users rather than a computer expert. Whether a communicator is more persuasive because of similarity or expertise depends largely on whether the issue in question is one of values or one of facts. If the persuasive message is a value issue, such as accepting new technology, learning new skills, or increasing productivity, the most effective communicator is one who shares similar characteristics with the audience. However, if the persuasive message concerns facts, such as which printer is the fastest and most reliable, the most effective communicator is one who possesses high credibility as a trustworthy expert.[9]

Characteristics of the Message. In general, the most persuasive communications consist of logical, well-reasoned presentations delivered in an eloquent and organized fashion. To persuade others, messages need to be reasonable and logical.

However, many other factors influence the persuasiveness of a particular message. For example, some attitudes are not changed very easily by logic or reason because they are based on emotion and feeling.[10]

In preparing a persuasive communication, the communicator needs to consider several issues: should only one side of the issue be presented, or both sides? And if both sides are presented, which one should be presented first? Should the communication reach a conclusion, or should it leave the receivers to draw their own conclusion?

Messages that make the receivers feel good tend to be more persuasive. Messages that evoke happy feelings and pleasant associations seem to attract attention and evoke a favorable response from the receiver. Favorable surroundings can also contribute to the persuasiveness of communications, such as pleasant music, good food, and beautiful scenery. The persuasive effect of pleasant surroundings explains why most TV commercials use beautiful scenery and pleasant music, with people who look as though they are having fun.

However, studies have also shown that communications tend to be more persuasive when they arouse the listener's level of fear. For example, advertisements about the effects of cigarette smoking on health tend to be more effective when they specifically describe the harmful effects of cancer and emphysema. Similarly, messages about taking injections for tetanus, adhering to safe driving standards, and improving dental hygiene practices tend to be more effective when the listeners are told specifically the serious consequences of failure to respond.[11] However, the level of arousal generated by a fear appeal can be too intense if the listeners are shown vivid portrayals of accidents, disease, and other revulsive scenes. The relationship between the degree of fear and the amount of attitude change appears to be an inverted-U relationship. As the level of fear increases, there is initially an increase in attitude change. As the level of fear becomes too intense, however, people cannot cope with the problem and respond by avoiding or denying the information.[12]

If a union leader tried to convince other workers to vote in favor of a union, would it be better to present a one-sided argument showing only the benefits of unionization, or would a two-sided argument that acknowledged some of the disadvantages of a union be more effective? Several studies have examined the relative effectiveness of one-sided versus two-sided presentations. Most of the evidence seems to indicate that they are almost equally effective. One-sided presentations may be superior when the listeners are not aware that a reasonable case could be made for the other issue. Yet two-sided communications were found to be far more effective in producing change that could withstand a counterattack on a subsequent occasion.[13]

If a communicator is going to present both sides of an argument, which side should be presented first—pro or con? Studies on the order of presenting arguments have generally produced rather mixed results. Some studies have shown a primacy effect, where the first argument presented was more persuasive than the second. Other studies, however, found a recency effect, in which the most recent argument had the greatest impact. Apparently the order of presentation does not make much difference as long as both messages are presented about the same time and attitudes are measured later. If there is a long time span between the two messages, however, and the attitudes are measured immediately following the second presentation, a recency effect typically occurs, in which the most recent message is accepted.[14]

Another variable influencing the credibility of a message is whether the listeners believe it was intended for them. Overheard messages tend to be very persuasive because the listeners are not worried about being intentionally manipulated and, therefore, the source is more credible. People are also influenced by messages that appear to be censored and kept from them. The effect of censorship, whether it be movies, books, or magazine articles, generally stimulates greater interest in obtaining the censored material, which then has a more persuasive impact than would have been anticipated if it had not been censored.

In interpersonal communication, both verbal and nonverbal messages may be communicated simultaneously. The total message is more persuasive when both the verbal and nonverbal messages are consistent. When they are inconsistent, however, the effectiveness of the verbal message is diminished. In fact, when the verbal and nonverbal communications are inconsistent, the listeners are usually influenced more by the nonverbal behavior, such as facial expressions, physical posture, and body language, rather than by the words. Furthermore, nonverbal cues portraying emotion are recognized more easily and remembered longer than inconsistent verbal messages.[15]

Videotaped messages such as television are generally considered the most persuasive form of mass communication because they combine the visual picture of the communicator with the verbal message. Audio messages, such as tape or radio, have generally been considered second in effectiveness, and the printed word, such as newspapers and magazines, has been considered third. Studies indicate, however, that the relative effectiveness of videotaped, audio, and written messages depends on the complexity of the message. Highly complex messages are more effective in a written form, which allows the receiver to reread and analyze the content of the message. Simple messages, however, are more effectively and persuasively communicated through videotape, where they are presented in living color.[16]

Characteristics of the Receiver. The effectiveness of a persuasive communication is limited by the receiver's ability to understand the message. A highly educated audience would be expected to respond to different types of arguments than those that appeal to a less intelligent audience. The relationship between intelligence and persuasiveness, however, appears to be mixed. Although highly intelligent people are more receptive to communications than less intelligent people, they are more resistant to influence. Therefore, if the full range of human intelligence is considered, people with moderate intelligence are generally the most easily influenced by the average communication. Those with very low intelligence do not understand the influence attempt, while those at very high levels of intelligence tend to resist the influence.[17]

The initial attitudes of the receivers influence the effectiveness of persuasive communication. People tend to have a **latitude of acceptance** that includes a range of attitudes slightly more or less favorable than their own. Their latitude of rejection consists of attitudes that differ significantly from their personal position. Persuasive communications are more successful when they advocate a position that falls within the listener's latitude of acceptance. When the message falls outside the latitude of acceptance, the listeners typically respond by changing their attitudes in the *opposite* direction. The results are quite different, however, if the source is a highly credible expert. Persuasive communication has a greater impact when the expert's position is significantly different from the listener's initial position. The wider the discrepancy, the greater the distress listeners have about the differences between their opinions and the expert's. If the communicator is not an expert, the listeners are inclined to disregard such a discrepant communication, thinking that only a fool could have such a far-out position. But, if the source is an expert, the wide discrepancy cannot be so easily dismissed, and the listeners are more prone to change their opinions.[18]

Supportive Communication

While the goal of persuasive communication is to change attitudes and sway public opinion, another form of communication is designed to build understanding and create a compatible interpersonal relationship. This form of communication, called **supportive communication,** is designed to avoid defensiveness.

Defensiveness on the part of either the sender or the receiver destroys the effectiveness of communication. When defensiveness occurs, people feel anger and hostility toward the other person, and communication breaks down. Defensiveness on the part of the sender results in incongruent messages, in which there is a mismatch between what the sender thinks and what is communicated. People are congruent when their feelings are consistent with their behavior.[19] Defensive communicators feel irritated and angry but refuse to express their feelings and attempt to deny them. Rather than dealing with their upset feelings openly, they allow their hostility to be expressed covertly through sarcasm and insincerity. When defensiveness occurs on the part of the listener, the message is typically not received. Defensive listeners do not listen effectively, and important elements of the message are either ignored or distorted. To the extent that a defensive communication is received, it usually results in a defensive response that further aggravates the problem of ineffective communication.[20]

Defensiveness is avoided, or at least reduced, by supportive communication. This type of communication is descriptive, problem-oriented, flexible, and owned rather than disowned, as summarized in Exhibit 13.6.

Descriptive. Supportive communication is descriptive and specific rather than evaluative or general. When people are told that their ideas or behaviors are good or bad, the evaluation process causes them to feel defensive. Evaluative statements create defensiveness and often result in arguments. For example, telling a cashier, "You did a terrible job handling that customer's complaint," would be an evaluative comment that creates defensiveness and antagonism. A descriptive comment would have been less threatening and more supportive, such as "The customer became upset because you interrupted him several times and raised your voice at him."

Using descriptive communication allows the situation to be discussed without arousing the need to defend or argue. Descriptive communication consists of three elements: (1) describing the event as objectively as possible; (2) describing your feelings about the event or consequences of the event; and (3) suggesting an alternative that would be more acceptable to you.

As a general rule, communication becomes more useful and arouses less defensiveness as it becomes more specific. For example, the statement "You are a poor cashier" is not a helpful comment because it does not indicate what behaviors need to be changed. In contrast, the statement "You interrupted the customer three times and spoke louder each time" is a specific statement telling a cashier what was wrong.

EXHIBIT 13.6   Characteristics of Supportive Communication

> 1. Descriptive and specific rather than general or evaluative
> 2. Problem-oriented rather than personality-oriented
> 3. Flexible rather than rigid
> 4. Owned rather than disowned

Problem-oriented. Supportive communication focuses on the specific problem rather than the personalities or status of the members. For example, the statement "You are too hotheaded when customers have a complaint" is a criticism of the cashier's personality. Problem-oriented communication focuses on the problem and its solution rather than discussing personal traits or ascribing blame. Focusing on the problem rather than personalities is particularly appropriate during performance appraisals since employees need to understand how to improve their performance, not how to change their personality. "You are unreliable, and we can't trust you to do your job" is a person-oriented statement that will generate defensiveness and hostility; whereas the statement "Your weekly reports have been late, and some of the information is so inaccurate we can't use it" is a problem-oriented statement that helps the individual know exactly what is wrong.

Problem-oriented communications also help to avoid making the listener feel inferior. The solution to a problem should be generated by a careful analysis of the problem, not by the invocation of status or power. Defensiveness is created when one person attempts to create an impression that says, "I know and you don't know" or "I am right and you are wrong" or "I have more power so we'll do it my way." These statements are examples of win–lose conflict, where one individual attempts to win at the expense of another or to look good by making others look inferior.

Flexible. Supportive communication is flexible, not rigid. When people adopt a know-it-all attitude and behave in a dogmatic manner, the other person becomes defensive, and effective communication is inhibited. "That sales projection has got to be wrong; I know it can't be that high" is a very rigid statement. A much more flexible statement is "It seems to me the sales projection is wrong; I don't see how it can be that high." People who are dogmatic in their conversation generally prefer to win an argument than to solve a problem, and being seen as the winner is more important to them than building a relationship. The consequence of such rigid communication is reciprocal rigidity, defensiveness, and interpersonal conflict.

Flexible communication means that the communicator is willing to accept additional information and acknowledges that other alternatives may exist. Being flexible is not synonymous with being insecure or easily influenced, but indicates a willingness to learn and grow by considering the contributions of others. Attitudes and opinions are stated provisionally rather than presented as firm facts. One consequence of flexible communication is that it affirms and acknowledges the potential contribution of other people. Other individuals are encouraged to share their attitudes and opinions because they are led to feel they can make a significant contribution to the conversation.

Owned. Supportive communication is owned, which means that the communicator takes responsibility for what is said. An example would be "After reviewing your qualifications, I have concluded that you have not satisfied the entrance requirements." Disowning communication, in contrast, is indicated by speaking in the third person or using plural pronouns, such as "We think that" or "They said" or "We've heard that." By attributing the source of a communication to some unknown party or external source, the communicator avoids having to take responsibility for the message and thereby avoids becoming invested in the communication. "The feeling of the committee is that you have not satisfied all the requirements and should not be admitted." One result of disowning communication is that the listener does not know whose point of view the message represents and often feels frustrated by not being able to pursue the problem further. Furthermore, disowned communications contain an implicit message that a certain psychological distance should be maintained rather than offering a close, interpersonal relationship.

Listening

Although listening is essential for effective communication, it is probably the most overlooked process in interpersonal communications. Reading, writing, and public speaking are taught in our educational system, and students spend many hours developing these skills, but students are usually left to falter along on their own when it comes to listening. Listening skills are developed to some extent by teaching students how to read and how to speak. But listening skills are different from reading and speaking skills, and students who are good at reading and speaking may still be very poor listeners.

Studies on listening indicate that most people are at best only mediocre listeners. One study found that most people remember less than half of what they hear immediately after hearing it, no matter how carefully they thought they listened. Two months after listening to a person talk, the average listener will remember less than one-fourth of what was said. Listening tests likewise indicate that people usually recall only about 25 percent of a conversation. Furthermore, when asked to rate the extent to which they are skilled listeners, 85 percent rate themselves as average or worse.[21] Clearly, listening is an important skill that needs to be more carefully developed. Effective listening comes from developing empathy and using effective listening skills.

Empathy. Effective listeners have been called *active listeners, reflective listeners,* and *empathic listeners.* Each of these labels implies that the listener must have the ability to listen to another's message empathically. Empathy is the capacity to participate in another's feelings or ideas; it involves understanding and relating to another's feelings. Empathic listeners imaginatively project themselves into the speaker's frame of reference and comprehend the full impact of the message. **Empathic listening** involves not only accurately perceiving the content of the messages but also understanding the emotional components and unexpressed meanings contained in the message.[22]

Empathic listening involves more than simply saying to the communicator, "I understand." It involves being able to reflect or restate the communicator's message on two different levels. The first level is called the **expressed level of empathy,** in which the listener simply paraphrases, restates, or summarizes the content of the communication. The second level, called the **implied level,** is more advanced and involves attending not only to what the communicator expresses but also to what was implied or left unstated.

The differences between the expressed and the implied levels can be illustrated by comparing alternative responses to a student who complains about not performing very well on a test. "I read and outlined every chapter in the text and spent twenty hours reviewing my notes and still scored ten points lower than my roommate, who didn't even read all the chapters." At the expressed level of empathy, the listener responds to the content and emotion of what was expressed: "You feel frustrated because you tried so hard to learn and still didn't do as well as your roommate." At the implied level of empathy, however, the listener responds not only to what was said but also to the implied or unstated component: "You sound discouraged about trying so hard and not doing as well as your roommate. It can be very frustrating when you try so hard and don't do as well as you think you should. When that happens, it's easy to get depressed and feel sorry for yourself."

Good empathizers need to know when to display each level of empathy. At the beginning of an interaction, listeners need to use the expressed level. After a feeling of trust and acceptance has been created, however, the implied level is appropriate. If the listener attempts to use the implied level of empathy too early in the interaction before a feeling of trust and acceptance has been developed, the communicator will probably feel threatened and feel as though he or she were being psychoanalyzed. If a listener continues to use the expressed level as the relationship becomes more intense, the expressed level may appear somewhat superficial and insincere.

Effective Listening Skills. Many listeners believe that listening is just a matter of sitting back and absorbing information like a sponge. Effective listening does not just happen, however; it requires much effort and hard work.

Different situations call for different kinds of listening. In a classroom, for example, students listen to obtain information and comprehend the most important concepts. In a political debate, the public often listens to confirm previously held biases supporting their points of view. In a courtroom, the opposing lawyer listens for faults, weaknesses, and contradictions in the testimony. In building a relationship, an empathic listener tries to understand the content and feeling of the message to enhance personal growth for both the communicator and the listener.

Several lists of guidelines have been proposed to explain the principles of good listening. Ten principles of effective listening are summarized in Exhibit 13.7. These ten principles identify the major differences between good and bad listeners. Good listeners look for areas of interest; overlook errors of delivery and objectionable personal mannerisms; postpone judgment until they understand the central point; listen for ideas and identify the main points; take careful notes to help them remember; are actively responsive in trying to listen; resist distractions; challenge their minds by trying to learn difficult material; capitalize on mind speed; and assist and encourage the speaker by asking for clarifying information and paraphrasing the ideas.[23]

Making Appropriate Responses. An important element in effective listening is responding to the communicator by making appropriate responses. Some listener responses stimulate the communicator to discuss the issue more extensively and

EXHIBIT 13.7   Principles of Effective Listening

Principle	The Good Listener	The Bad Listener
1. Look for areas of interest.	Seeks personal enlightenment and/or information; entertains new topics as potentially interesting	Tunes out dry subjects; narrowly defines what is interesting
2. Overlook errors of delivery.	Attends to meaning and content; ignores delivery errors while being sensitive to any messages in them	Ignores if delivery is poor; misses messages because of personal attributes of the communicator
3. Postpone judgment.	Avoids quick judgments; waits until comprehension of the core message is complete	Quickly evaluates and passes judgment; inflexible regarding contrary messages
4. Listen for ideas.	Listens for ideas and themes; identifies the main points	Listens for facts and details
5. Take notes.	Takes careful notes and uses a variety of note-taking or recording schemes depending on the speaker	Takes incomplete notes using one system
6. Be actively responsive.	Responds frequently with nods, "uh-huhs," etc.; shows active body state; works at listening	Passive demeanor; few or no responses; little energy output
7. Resist distractions.	Resists being distracted; longer concentration span; puts loaded words in perspective	Easily distracted; focuses on loaded or emotional words; short concentration span
8. Challenge your mind.	Uses difficult material to stimulate the mind; seeks to enlarge understanding	Avoids difficult material; does not seek to broaden knowledge base
9. Capitalize on mind speed.	Uses listening time to summarize and anticipate the message; attends to implicit messages as well as explicit messages	Daydreams with slow speakers; becomes preoccupied with other thoughts
10. Help and encourage the speaker.	Asks for clarifying information or examples; uses reflecting phrases; helps to rephrase the idea	Interrupts; asks trivial questions; makes distracting comments

Source: Developed by Kim Cameron and used with permission.

expand to related areas of interest. Other responses tend to restrict the topic of communication and terminate the conversation.

The appropriateness of the response largely depends on the purpose of the communication and the goal of the interaction. If the purpose of the conversation is to evaluate performance, an evaluative or reinterpretive response is generally best. However, if the purpose of the interaction is to help another individual solve a problem or make a decision, a reflective or probing response is generally most appropriate. Seven different response types have been identified that range from very directive responses, which close communication, to very nondirective responses, which tend to open additional topics for consideration, as shown in Exhibit 13.8. Each of these seven responses is appropriate for different purposes.[24]

EXHIBIT 13.8   Seven Alternative Types of Responses

These seven responses illustrate different ways of responding to an irate customer who states, "I ordered that part last month, and you said it would be here in a week. I think you're trying to take advantage of me."

1. *Evaluative responses:* Pass judgment, express agreement or disagreement, or offer advice; for example, "We are not trying to take advantage of you. You need to be patient longer." Evaluative responses are useful after a topic has been explored in depth, and it is appropriate for the responder to express an opinion.

2. *Confrontive responses:* Challenge the other person to clarify the message and identify points of inconsistency or contradictions; for example, "Just because we haven't been able to deliver the part yet doesn't mean we're taking advantage of you. No one else feels that way." Confrontation is useful for helping people clarify their thoughts and feelings or to think more broadly about the issue.

3. *Diverting responses:* Change the focus of the communicator's problem to a problem selected by the responder; for example, "Your comment reminds me of a problem I had last summer. I remember when . . ." Diverting responses often involve changing the subject and are helpful when a point of comparison is needed and the communicator needs to know that someone else has experienced a similar event.

4. *Probing responses:* Ask the communicator to clarify what was said or to provide additional information or an illustration; for example, "Yes, our deliveries are late, but could you tell me specifically why you think we're trying to take advantage of you?" Probing responses are useful when the respondent needs specific information to understand the message or when the communicator needs to respond to another topic in order to make the communication clearer.

5. *Reinterpretive responses:* Restate the message to examine an underlying cause, meaning, or interpretation of the message; for example, "Apparently you're upset because you think we promised you an unrealistic delivery date just so you wouldn't go to one of our competitors." Reinterpretive responses help clarify the message for both parties and encourage the communicator to pursue the topic in greater depth.

6. *Pacifying responses:* Reduce the intensity of emotions associated with the message and help to calm the communicator; for example, "There's no need to think that we're trying to take advantage of you, the delay is simply out of our control." Pacifying responses are useful when the communicator needs to be reassured that discussing the message is acceptable or when the intensity of feelings being experienced is inhibiting good communication.

7. *Reflective responses:* Reflect back to the communicator what was heard, but in different words; for example, "You're saying that we intentionally misrepresented our delivery date and are treating you unfairly." Reflective responses help communicators know they have been both heard and understood. Reflective responses should not simply mimic the communicator or be a direct restatement of what was said. Instead, they should contribute understanding, meaning, and acceptance to the conversation.

Nonverbal Communication

Face-to-face communication involves more than just the words we use. The verbal portion actually constitutes only a small part of the total message. The way in which the words are arranged and presented, including the tone, the rate of speech, inflection, pauses, and facial expressions, actually provide most of the message's content for the receiver. The words themselves do not stand alone but depend on nonverbal components for their true meaning. To illustrate, the expression "Isn't this just great!" could be used as an honest expression of happiness and joy. But if it is used with the appropriate facial expression and intonation, it becomes a sarcastic comment conveying disgust and contempt. The study of nonverbal communication has identified five major variables that influence the meaning of messages. These five variables include physical distance, posture, facial cues, vocal cues, and appearance.

Physical Distance. The study of the ways in which people structure their space and the distances between people in daily interactions is called *proxemics*.[25] The physical distance between the source and the receiver communicates a message itself, in addition to influencing the interpretation of what is said. We tend to stand closer when talking with people we know and like and further away from people we do not know or do not like. Shaking hands and touching is another way to communicate to people that you like them and have an interest in them. Physical distance is also an indication of status, and subordinates tend to maintain greater distance between themselves and people of higher status. Elevation can also be used as an indication of status, particularly in some cultures (such as Tonga). People of higher status are seated on higher-level platforms than people of lower status.

Posture. The study of posture and other body movements, including facial expressions and gestures, is called *kinesics*.[26] Posture, or body language, can be used to indicate numerous things, including liking or status. We tend to relax by leaning backward, maintaining an open-arm posture, and directly facing those we like. However, we tend to become rigid and tense around those of greater status or those whom we perceive as threatening. Higher-status individuals are generally more relaxed in posture than those of lower status. Standing, pacing, and putting your hands on your hips are all nonverbal cues of high status. When talking to another individual, we can communicate an element of responsiveness and interest in what they have to say by making spontaneous gestures, shifting our posture from side to side, and by moving closer to the individual.

Facial Cues. Although some people tend to be rather expressionless, others are very expressive and communicate many messages just using facial cues. In a job interview, for example, eye contact is an important indicator of an applicant's competence and strength of character. A pleasant facial expression also communicates a feeling of liking for another individual. We tend to maintain eye contact with people we like and avoid contact with those we dislike. High-status people tend to display less eye contact than do those of lower status. Smiling, furrowing one's eyebrows, and other facial expressions also indicate a degree of responsiveness to the communicator.[27]

Vocal Cues. The study of the human voice, including range, pitch, rhythm, resonance, and tempo, is called *paralinguistics*.[28] Interpersonal attraction and concern for another individual can be expressed through vocal cues. Speaking in a pleasant

APPLYING ORGANIZATIONAL BEHAVIOR
RESEARCH

Communicating with Clothes

What do the clothes you wear tell about you, and what do they say about your organization? Although we want people to judge us by what we do and say, our clothing communicates a first impression that influences how others interpret our behavior.

The messages clothing communicates about a person were examined in a study of how a salesman was perceived by purchasing agents in two industries: health care and retail sales. One sample consisted of 205 hospital purchasing agents, and the other sample consisted of 176 convenience store purchasing agents. Each purchasing agent was shown a photograph of a salesman and asked to evaluate him and the company he represented.

All the photographs showed the same person in an identical pose; but each purchasing agent saw him wearing one of seven different outfits. The seven outfits, ordered from most to least formal, were (1) a dark three-piece suit with white shirt; (2) a dark navy two-piece suit with white shirt; (3) a medium gray two-piece suit with white shirt; (4) a sport coat and slacks with white shirt; (5) a gray tweed jacket with casual knit open-neck shirt, black slacks, and a gold necklace; (6) a casual sweater with open-neck white shirt and khaki slacks; and

(7) a tourist-looking beige-colored jacket and peach-colored slacks with white shirt.

The results indicated that when the salesman was wearing one of the four more traditional outfits both he and the company he represented was perceived more favorably. He was not only perceived as better dressed, he was also perceived as being a better salesman, better educated, more ambitious, more conservative, and having greater product knowledge than when wearing less traditional clothing.

Similarly, when wearing one of the four traditional outfits, he was seen as representing a larger, more ethical company with more products, better credit, higher-quality products, and better service. The results were similar for both samples of purchasing agents. This study suggests that an organization's employees are indeed a symbol of the company.

Clothing communicates a symbolic message. Although our first impressions may later be replaced by other messages, it is clear that during initial contacts clothing has a sizable impact on many evaluations.

Source: Elnora W. Stuart and Barbara K. Fuller, "Clothing as Communication in Two Business-to-Business Sales Settings," *Journal of Business Research*, vol. 23 (1991), pp. 269–290.

---

tone of voice at a moderate rate of speed indicates a desire to communicate with the other individual. Anger is usually expressed in a loud, high-pitched tone of voice, while boredom is expressed through a deep, lethargic tone of voice. Lower-status people tend to have a lower voice volume than do those of higher status. Speaking loudly, rapidly, and in a moderate tone of voice generally conveys a sense of intensity and enthusiasm.

Appearance. Physical appearance, especially clothing, sends surprisingly strong nonverbal messages. High-status people often display appropriate ornaments, such as the badges and bars used in the military or police units. "Dress for success" seminars emphasize the importance of appearance in manipulating one's personal power and status in a group. For example, it is suggested that men wear long-sleeved rather than short-sleeved shirts if they want to increase their personal power and have greater influence on the outcome of a committee meeting.[29]

Although listeners may be unaware of it, they often look for nonverbal indicators as they listen to the message. The evidence suggests that women are rated more effective than men at both encoding and decoding nonverbal messages.[30] If the nonverbal component of the message supports the verbal message, it can reinforce the intended meaning of the message and assist the receiver in properly decoding the message. However, if communicators say one thing but nonverbally transmit a different message, the receiver tends to give more credence to the nonverbal components. For example, if supervisors use an apathetic, monotonic voice to say, "Thanks, I really appreciate what you've done," their vocal cues destroy their intended message.[31]

In a courtroom, jurors may ignore the testimony of witnesses when their verbal testimony is inconsistent with their nonverbal behaviors. Posttrial interviews with jurors have revealed that the testimony of a key witness may be discounted because the paralinguistic behaviors of the witness overwhelm the content of the testimony.[32]

COMMUNICATION IN GROUPS

The previous section examined interpersonal communication, in which a sender transmits a message to a receiver. This section examines the communication process in groups. Although there are still senders and receivers, each person is both a sender and a receiver, and the communication process is influenced by the presence of others and the way in which the group is structured.

Factors Influencing Communication

Several group variables influence the frequency and accuracy of communication, and the group can be structured in ways that alter the communication patterns. For example, the manager of a research unit may want to move offices and desks closer together to encourage more frequent communications among engineers, while elementary school teachers try to separate the desks in the classroom to discourage communication. Three variables influencing the frequency and direction of communication in groups are the opportunity to interact, status, and group cohesiveness.

Opportunity to Interact. Communication is influenced by the opportunity to interact. For example, if a manager wanted to increase the communication within a work group, desks could be moved closer together, walls could be removed, environmental noise could be eliminated, electronic mail and phone mail systems could be installed, and frequent opportunities to interact could be scheduled, such as lunch periods and rest breaks. In contrast, communication becomes more difficult and less frequent as people are separated by physical distance, walls, closed doors, and different work schedules, or by the removal of telephones and the creation of indirect lines of communication.[33] These kinds of changes have an enormous impact on the frequency and accuracy of communication and are far more powerful than simply telling people that they should or should not communicate.

Status. Communication patterns are influenced by status relationships regardless of whether superiors are communicating with subordinates or whether peers are communicating in the presence of a superior. In a group discussion, for example, members direct most of their communications to a higher-status person, even though that person may not be leading the discussion. Conversation among a group of peers is different when a higher-status person is present. Although the comments may still be directed toward one's peers, they are self-censored by the sender to reflect what they think the superior wants to hear.

People prefer to communicate with people who are either similar or at higher-status levels. One reason why people prefer communicating with high-status people is because they believe it will increase their standing in the eyes of others. Speaking with the president of the company, a famous movie star, or a political leader tends to increase one's feeling of importance within the group. High-status people also have the capacity of conferring rewards through praise, recognition, and other forms of reinforcement.

Cohesiveness. As groups become more cohesive, the members develop a stronger interpersonal attraction and they find communicating more satisfying, rewarding, and convenient. Furthermore, as they communicate more freely, their interpersonal attraction increases and they become even more cohesive. Thus, the relationship between cohesiveness and communication appears to be a two-way effect—cohesiveness increases communication, and communication leads to increased cohesiveness.

Communication Networks

Research has examined the effects of different communication networks. A communication network is the pattern of communication channels between group members or among positions in an organizational structure. Organizations may create official communication networks by requiring members to follow prescribed communication channels. This is done by creating physical barriers and by altering the accessibility of transmission and receiving devices, such as computers, telephones, and company reports.

Informal communication networks may also arise. Stable patterns of interaction may be created because of personal friendships, physical barriers, or other factors limiting the opportunity to communicate. These communication networks influence the functioning of a group, and different types of networks have been studied to examine their effects on such things as the speed of problem solving, accuracy in transmitting information, and the satisfaction of the group members.

Communication Network Studies. Studies of communication networks emerged from the research on small groups that began in the mid 1940s.[34] The major independent variables in these laboratory experiments were the size of the group, the structure of the network, and the complexity or simplicity of the task. The effects of group size on communication were fairly straightforward—larger groups reduced the speed and accuracy of communication and made communicating more difficult. The effects of network structure and task complexity, however, were more complex and more interesting.

Studies on the effectiveness of different network structures typically used five subjects who were seated at a table but separated from each other by partitions.

Slots in the partitions allowed members to communicate by passing written messages through the open slots. The experimenter created different network structures by allowing only certain slots to be opened.[35]

In most of these studies, the group task required group members to share information to solve a problem. In a typical study, each of the subjects was given a card containing six symbols, and the group was required to identify the one common symbol. Information was exchanged until all five group members knew the correct answer. Each group of five subjects was given a series of trials and allowed to transmit and receive messages according to the structure predetermined by the experimenter.

Five of the most frequently studied communication networks were the circle, the wheel, the chain, the Y, and the all-channel network, as illustrated in Exhibit 13.9. These five communication networks differ significantly in the degree of centralization or decentralization of their structure. The circle network, for example, is highly decentralized because each position can communicate directly with two other positions in the network, and no one can communicate directly with everyone. The wheel is the most centralized communication network, since all communications must pass through the center position.

The results of the early studies revealed that the centralized networks were clearly superior in the speed and accuracy of solving problems. Centralization increased the efficiency of the groups; they required fewer messages to solve the problem and inform all group members of the solution. The centralized wheel networks were the fastest to organize, because the person occupying the center position became the leader who collected information from the other members, solved the problem, and informed them of the solution. Decentralized groups, in contrast, were inefficient. The circle network, for example, was the slowest to organize, sent the most messages, made the most errors, and tended to be slower in solving problems than other networks.

Although the centralized networks were more efficient, they did not create the greatest satisfaction. Member satisfaction was related to the **centrality** of each position within the network. The centrality of each position was measured by counting the number of communication links that position required to communicate with every other position. In the wheel, for example, the centrality of position number five in the center is 4, since that position can communicate directly with each of the other four members. The centrality of the other four positions, however, is 7, because two communication links are required to communicate with each of the other three people plus one to communicate with the leader. The individual who occupied the most central position was most actively involved in the group discussion, reported higher satisfaction, and tended to be identified as the leader of the group.

Effects of Task Complexity. Although the early network studies found centralized networks to be more accurate and efficient, later studies, using more complex tasks, did not find the same results. With complex tasks, such as mathematics problems, group discussion issues, and sentence construction, the superiority of centralized networks seemed to disappear, and decentralized networks were frequently superior. Complex tasks required considerable communication to share and evaluate information. If all the information had to be channeled through one position, the person in that position became overloaded and acted as a bottleneck in performing the task.[36]

EXHIBIT 13.9   Communication Networks

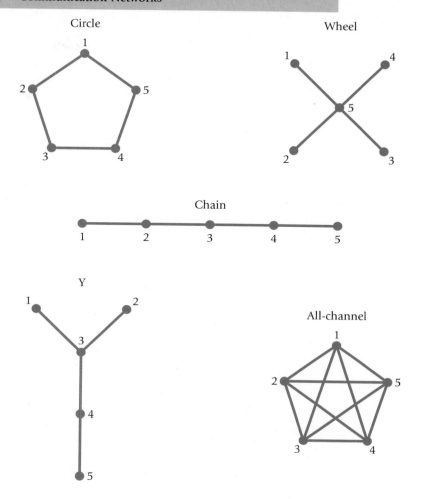

In summary, centralized networks are more efficient for solving simple tasks, while decentralized networks are more efficient for solving complex tasks. But regardless of the complexity of the task, centralized networks require fewer messages to perform the task, while decentralized networks create higher levels of satisfaction. These studies help us understand why complex organizational structures require a decentralized authority structure to help them process information, as explained in Chapter 12.

The results of these communication network studies also help us understand some of the concepts described in Chapters 15 and 16 by explaining why a person's position within a network has a great influence on that person's potential leadership and power. People in centralized organizations who can control the flow of information are able to exert leadership and influence regardless of their formal leadership position. These results explain why secretaries, administrative aides, and company clerks (like "Radar" O'Reilly in the TV program *M*A*S*H*) wield far more influence and power than their formal position would suggest.

Communication Roles

Communication network studies have been criticized because their laboratory conditions do not reflect real-life situations in large organizations. More recent network studies have attempted to correct these problems by studying communication networks in real organizations. Although the methodology of recent studies is limited by their inability to manipulate the independent variables such as size, task complexity, and network structure, they are at least successful in studying real organizational processes.

The methodology used in network analysis studies involves creating a matrix to show who speaks to whom. The members of the organization are listed down the side of a matrix and across the top, and the communication patterns of who speaks to whom are recorded. As the interpersonal communication patterns begin to emerge, the names of people are rearranged so that those who interact more frequently are placed closer together on the matrix. By analyzing the communication patterns over a period of time, the subgroupings, or cliques, gradually emerge within the matrix. An analysis of the interactions within the communication matrix reveals four different kinds of communication roles that occur in group communication networks.[37] The functions of these four group roles are illustrated in Exhibit 13.10.

Gatekeepers. A **gatekeeper** is someone who controls the flow of messages between two people or two groups in an organization structure. A gatekeeper in a communication network acts like a valve in a water pipe. One function of the gatekeeper is to decrease information overload by filtering the flow of messages from one group to another. An example is a quality control clerk who collects daily reports, summarizes them, and presents them to the plant manager.

Liaisons. A **liaison** is someone who connects two or more cliques within a system without belonging to either clique. Liaisons are the cement or the linking pin that holds the groups of an organization together. Liaisons are somewhat similar to gatekeepers, but while gatekeepers are typically in positions within an organizational structure where they govern the flow of upward communication, liaisons are typically positioned between two groups that are not arranged hierarchically one above the other. An example of a liaison between a football team and the faculty is a sports writer who tells the faculty about the team and when they will be gone and tells players how they are doing in class.

Opinion Leaders. **Opinion leaders** have the ability to influence informally the attitudes and behaviors of other members. Opinion leaders fill an important role in what is called the two-step flow model of attitude change. Persuasive messages flow from the mass media to opinion leaders, who interpret the information and pass it on to the public audience.[38] Within a group, opinion leaders are able to influence the attitudes of group members by helping them interpret new information and define the situation.

Boundary Spanners. **Boundary spanners** are people who communicate with the organization's environment. These people are typically top executives who travel widely and enjoy many types of contact with other organizations. They help the organization obtain acceptance within the environment and sense changes in the environment that will influence the organization. In one sense, boundary spanners

EXHIBIT 13.10 Communication Roles

Gatekeepers
Individuals who control the flow
of communication through a
communication channel

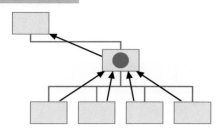

Liaisons
Individuals who connect
two or more groups within
an organization without
belonging to either group

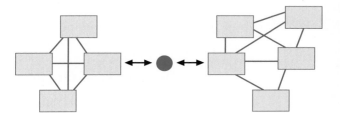

Opinion Leaders
Individuals who informally
influence the attitudes and
behaviors of other group members

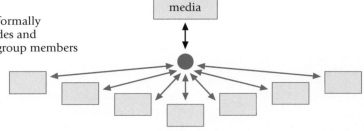

Boundary Spanners
Individuals who communicate with
the organization's environment

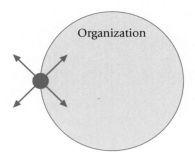

are a special type of gatekeeper, as they control the communication flows by which new ideas enter the organization. Boundary spanners help the organization cope with its environment and predict future changes.

ORGANIZATIONAL COMMUNICATION

This section looks at communication from an organizational perspective. Communication serves the crucial function of integrating and coordinating the various components of an organization and pervades all the activities within the organization. If communication were eliminated, the organization would cease to exist.[39] This section examines the functions of communication in an organization and the ways in which organizational structure restricts communication flows.

The Effects of Organizational Structure

There is a common misperception about communication problems in organizations. It is generally believed that most communication problems result from restricted or inadequate communication. This idea has been referred to as the "myth of free communication." The presence of problems seems to create a widely held idea that for organizations to function effectively, information must flow freely and unrestricted throughout the organization. In fact, just the opposite is true. One of the most important functions of organizational structure is to *restrict* communication flows and thus *decrease* problems of information overload. Some organizational problems are solved not by increasing but by restricting the flow of communication and clearly specifying how information is to be gathered, processed, and analyzed.

Consider the situation of sixty people who gather informally in an auditorium. As long as they interact with whomever they choose, they will remain a disorganized collection of people, regardless of their purpose for meeting. Unless the communication channels become organized and constraints are placed on the flow of information, this group will find it virtually impossible to accomplish anything, whether they are a state legislature, a college fraternity, or a group of concerned citizens. With an unorganized group of sixty people milling around at random, the number of potential communication links between two people is $N(N-1)/2$, or 1,770. However, if they are organized into six groups of 10 with a formally appointed leader, the number of communication channels is reduced to just nine in each group.

The situation is similar to an orchestra. If sixty musicians play whatever they want, such as they do when they are warming up, the result is unpleasant noise rather than beautiful music. To make beautiful music, the members must play exactly what they are supposed to play at exactly the right time. The same is true of communication patterns in organizations. To move from an unorganized state to an organized state requires that restrictions be placed on the flow of communication. People must use the appropriate communication channels, and only job-relevant information should be transmitted. Unrestricted communication produces noise and confusion in the organization. Without precision and timing, there may be sound but no music. Likewise, without structure and regulations there may be conversations but no meaning.

Direction of Communication Flow

One way to analyze organizational communication is to study the direction of information flow, that is, who communicates with whom. The three most important directions of formal communication flow are downward, upward, and horizontal. Informal communication is circulated through the grapevine system.

Downward Communication. Downward communication follows the organizational hierarchy and flows from people in higher levels to those in lower levels. The most common forms of downward communication include organizational procedures and practices, instructions about how to do the job, the rationale explaining why the job is important, feedback to subordinates about their performance, and an explanation of the goals and objectives of the organization.

This information teaches subordinates how to perform their jobs properly and makes them feel part of the organization. However, organizational members frequently complain that the information they receive is both inadequate and inaccurate. A typical complaint is "We have absolutely no idea what's happening." Although managers usually communicate job instructions adequately, they fail to provide an adequate rationale for the job or sufficient feedback to subordinates.

A problem in downward communication is inaccuracy as the information is passed from level to level. Orders are typically expressed in a language appropriate for the next level down rather than the lowest level, where the message is aimed. Therefore, as the information travels down the organizational structure, it needs to be adapted to the members at each successive level. A classic study of downward communications in 100 organizations estimated that 80 percent of the information was lost after passing through five levels of the organization.[40]

Serious distortions can occur as people interpret and redefine messages. During the Vietnam War, for example, newspaper reporters occasionally observed that army orders tended to be interpreted quite broadly and frequently with distortion as they passed to various levels in the chain of command. One war correspondent, for example, was present when the Army's First Air Cavalry division burned a hamlet. An inquiry revealed how the order had been changed as it was issued at four different levels. The order from division headquarters was "On no occasion must hamlets be burned down." The brigade radioed the battalion, "Do not burn down any hamlets unless you are absolutely convinced that the Viet Cong are in them." The battalion radioed the infantry company at the scene, "If you think there are any Viet Cong in the hamlet, burn it down." The company commander ordered his troops, "Burn down that hamlet."[41]

Upward Communication. Upward communication is designed to provide feedback on how well the organization is functioning. Lower-level employees are expected to provide upward communication about their performance and the organization's practices and policies. The most common forms of upward communication include memos, written reports, suggestion boxes, group meetings, and grievances.

One of the most serious problems of upward communication is that the information is biased and filtered. Upward communication is typically used to monitor the organization's performance and take corrective action. Subordinates are not inclined to give information to a supervisor if it will influence them adversely. Consequently, upward communication can best be described as what subordinates want the supervisors to hear rather than what the supervisors need to know. The small amount of information that gets filtered upward is typically biased to make people look good.

Another problem with upward communication is that organizations typically rely on lower-level members to initiate it. Instead of actively soliciting information and providing channels for receiving it, managers frequently adopt an open-door policy and assume that people who have something to say will voluntarily express it.

Horizontal Communication. Horizontal communication is lateral communication between peers; it does not follow the formal organizational hierarchy. Formal bureaucratic structures do not provide for horizontal communication, and one of the most difficult problems in creating an effective organization is providing for acceptable channels of horizontal communication. Expecting all of the communication between two departments to be passed up the organization until it reaches a common executive and then back down to the relevant group is unrealistic and inefficient. Adhering strictly to a formal chain of command is not only inefficient; it also creates a serious communication overload for upper-level executives. However, it is also true that unrestricted horizontal communication detracts from maximum efficiency. Therefore, organizations must provide for horizontal communication channels where they are necessary while restricting unnecessary channels.

In addition to helping people coordinate their work, horizontal communication among peers furnishes emotional and social support to people. Horizontal communication contributes to the development of friendships and informal work groups.

Informal Communication. Informal communication is called *grapevine communication,* and it exists in every organization. The **grapevine** is created by informal associations and cuts across formal lines of communication. Some of the major characteristics of grapevine information are as follows:

1. Grapevines are found in every organization, and they are virtually impossible to eliminate. It is only natural for employees to discuss matters of mutual concern, and even the closest monitoring of their conversations will not prevent them from occurring.
2. Information usually travels more rapidly through the grapevine than through official communication channels.
3. The grapevine is a more spontaneous form of expression and hence more intrinsically gratifying and credible than formal communication.
4. In situations where official censorship and filtering occur, grapevine information is more informative.
5. On noncontroversial topics related to the organization, most of the information communicated through the grapevine (estimated to be at least 75 percent) is correct. Emotionally charged information, however, is more likely to be distorted.
6. The number of people who serve as actual links in the grapevine is generally relatively small (estimated to be less than 10 percent of the group).[42]

APPLYING ORGANIZATIONAL BEHAVIOR
IN THE NEWS

Communicating from the Top

Richard Clarke, chairman of Pacific Gas and Electric, was driving his car to see the World Series game between the San Francisco Giants and the Oakland Athletics when he first felt the earthquake that registered 7.1 on the Richter scale. He thought he had a flat tire; but when he saw the pavement crumbling beneath him, he knew what it was. He also knew immediately that the Bay Area was probably experiencing devastating destruction from broken gas pipes. As chairman of PG&E, it was his responsibility to initiate actions to contain the damage and mobilize the repair crews. How do you communicate in a company that has 26,000 employees?

The communication problems in this crisis were not trivial. But the coordination was facilitated by the fact that the employees did what they had been trained to do. PG&E has a tradition that when a major event affects the company, such as a fire or an earthquake, the employees report to work. Within the next three weeks, the repair crews rebuilt a whole new gas system in the Marina district of San Francisco that involved over twenty miles of new gas mains.

Clarke must work hard to stay in touch with what is happening in PG&E. Although he has an open-door policy, he finds that his "brown-bag lunch" meetings are more helpful in sharing information. Clarke meets regularly with employees throughout the company in these informal lunches where employees are free to ask questions.

As the chairman of a nuclear utility company, Clarke also finds it necessary to communicate with outside groups, especially environmental groups. Clarke believes that the nuclear plant at Diablo Canyon is the safest place to be during an earthquake. But to satisfy environmentalists' concerns, he has had to provide extensive information about the facility and involve them in discussions about the problems of obtaining environmentally clean energy.

Source: CNN *Pinnacle* news programming.

Occasionally grapevines benefit the organization, and managers use them as a regular substitute for formal communication. For example, the grapevine can be used to test reactions to a proposed change without actually making a formal commitment. Managers have been known to leak ideas to the grapevine just to test their acceptability before implementing them.[43]

Grapevines tend to cause trouble in organizations characterized by a lack of trust and confidence among managers and workers. The unfortunate irony is that organizations most in need of an effective grapevine are usually plagued by a grapevine prone to disseminating vicious lies and distorted information. Grapevines provide a disservice when they become a constant source of false rumors. Rumors seem to spread fastest and farthest when the information is ambiguous, when the content of the rumor is important to those involved, and when the people are emotionally aroused.

Although rumors can be destructive to an organization, it has been shown that some stories and myths perpetuated in organizations contribute greatly to the organization's effectiveness by preserving valuable aspects of the organization's culture. At Hewlett-Packard Corporation, for example, feelings of job security among employees are perpetuated by a story describing how the workers at one point years ago went on a reduced workweek to avoid layoffs and preserve jobs.[44]

Improving Communication Effectiveness

Effective communication depends on the quality of the communication processes at both the interpersonal and organizational levels. Improving communication in organizations involves more accurate encoding, transmitting, decoding, and feedback at the interpersonal level and, at the organizational level, creating and monitoring appropriate communication channels. Several strategies can be used to help managers communicate more effectively.

Increasing Feedback. Misunderstandings are reduced when adequate feedback processes are used. If communicators know how well their messages have been received, they can correct errors and wrong impressions. If the message was ambiguous or didn't make sense, a communicator can start all over again, sending either the same message or a simplified version. Confusing messages can be explained more clearly.

Feedback mechanisms in organizations are just as important as they are in interpersonal communication. Top managers should not issue orders or policy statements and merely assume they have been understood. Feedback mechanisms need to be established so managers know whether their messages have been understood, accepted, and followed. Elaborate management information systems with reports and computer printouts are often used to monitor the operations of a company. Managers need to obtain similar feedback on subjective factors such as employee morale, leadership style, reward processes, and reactions to company policies.

Regulating Information Flow. The seriousness of communication overload requires managers to regulate the flow of information by establishing clear channels of communication. Although managers like to keep everyone informed so that everyone sees the "big picture," this practice typically requires lower-level managers to sift through an enormous volume of irrelevant material. Rather than trying to keep everyone involved, top-level managers need to follow the *"need-to-know" principle* in transmitting downward communication. The need-to-know principle suggests that managers ask whether lower-level personnel need this information to perform their tasks effectively. If the answer is no, the message should not be transmitted. Another useful principle in regulating the flow of information is the *exception principle*. This principle states that only significant deviations from standard policies and procedures should be brought to the attention of superiors. This principle involves developing standard operating procedures and identifying the range of acceptable performance. As long as performance falls within the acceptable range, the regular procedures are followed. When performance deviates from the accepted range, however, these exceptions are communicated.

Repetition. An effective strategy for increasing the effectiveness of communication is to repeat the message. Repetition helps the listener interpret messages that are ambiguous, unclear, or too difficult to understand the first time they are heard. Repetition also helps to avoid the problem of forgetting. In fact, forgetting is such a serious problem that many managers adopt the policy of having very important messages repeated at least three or four times. Effective communicators build repetition into their presentations by expressing the same idea in different ways. A popular strategy in both writing and speech communication to help the audience remember the main point is to use the strategy "Tell them what you're going to tell them, then tell them, then tell them what you've told them."

Simplifying Language. Complex language, technical terms, and jargon make communications difficult to understand and frustrating to the listener. It is not true that complex ideas require complex terms to explain them. Almost every idea can be explained in relatively simple language so that most people can understand it. When it is important for the listeners to understand the message, the communicators should make certain that the language they use is clear and easily understood.

There are times, however, when complex language using jargon and technical terms is appropriate. When a message is communicated to an audience that understands them, technical terms and jargon are useful. Scientific research reports, for example, are written for an audience of scientists who understand the technical terms that are used. Likewise, government reports are usually written for government agencies and administrators who understand the acronyms, abbreviations, and jargon contained in them. One advantage of using technical terms is that they have a precise meaning that conveys precise information without using many words. Although simple language tends to increase comprehension, complex language tends to save time and make communication more efficient for those who comprehend it.

One of the best ways to simplify an explanation is to provide an example or illustration. Complex ideas are not only difficult to understand but also difficult to remember. A simple illustration helps the listener comprehend the idea and remember it. Sometimes when listeners feel baffled and confused, the most effective thing they can do is to simply ask, "Can you give me an example to help me understand that?"

Effective Timing. A typical problem in interpersonal communication is that the speaker begins to speak before the listeners are ready to listen. Many managers find that messages come to them in a disorganized fashion, and they cannot switch effectively from one topic to another as rapidly as they need. Therefore, an effective strategy for both interpersonal and organizational communication is to manage the timing of the communication so that the messages are received in an orderly fashion, to the extent it is possible to do so. This principle is similar to the procedure many executives use in responding to their in-basket. Incoming mail is sorted into piles of related topics. A similar procedure can be used, to some extent, with verbal communication where specific time periods are scheduled for discussing a specific topic. Organizations can schedule conferences, meetings, and retreats to focus on identified problems without the influence of other distractions.

Barriers to Effective Communication

Because of the complexity of the communication process, problems can arise from difficulties at the individual, group, or organizational levels. Some of the major barriers to effective communication include omission, filtering, time pressures, differing frames of reference, selective listening, semantic problems, the use of jargon, premature value judgments, and information overload.

Omission. Regardless of the time available or the method of communication, messages are almost never 100 percent complete. The transmitted message is almost always an abbreviated representation of the intended meaning. Senders only transmit the most salient points of an intended message, and the amount of additional information is almost limitless. To illustrate, consider the situation of a verbal dispute that ends when an employee slugs the supervisor. The basic elements of this episode could be summarized in a few words. However, a skilled novelist could use the same episode as the basic plot for an entire chapter. Listeners may hear a message and feel secure, thinking they understood the communication, but what they may not realize is that what they heard was neither complete nor what the sender really intended to say.

Filtering. Filtering is the manipulation of information so that selected data, especially negative information, are either removed or altered before they are transmitted to the next individual. Filtering is a common occurrence in upward communication where only positive information is passed to higher levels in the organization.

Time Pressures. Limited time is a reality in every aspect of life, and time pressures create difficult problems in the communication process. Managers do not have unlimited time to talk with every subordinate, and because they are so rushed, important information is often deleted. Occasionally, people who should be included in the formal communication channel are overlooked, creating a situation called *short-circuiting*. Time pressures cause people to develop abbreviated phrases to communicate rapidly, and managers may insist that only abbreviated executive summaries of reports be submitted rather than full reports with supporting detail.

Jargon. Almost every group develops its own repertoire of unique words and phrases to help it communicate more rapidly and effectively. Most jargon consists of abbreviated words or simplified phrases summarizing more complex concepts, and it conveys a unique meaning to other group members. Consequently, jargon tends to increase the speed and accuracy of communication within the group and to build a more cohesive unit. But it creates a difficult barrier for members outside the group. New group members typically feel confused and alienated from the group until they master the jargon.

Value Judgments. The communication model presented earlier assumes that while the source is speaking, the receiver is listening. Rather than listening to the message, however, most receivers assign an overall worth to the message based on small samples of it and then become engaged in developing a rebuttal. Thus, before it is presented, management may reject a union proposal because "they're always trying to take advantage of the company." A personnel director may refuse to consider an employee's request to change work schedules because "He's always trying to get out of something." Effective listening requires the listener to suspend judgment until the entire message has been received and then evaluate the worth or accuracy of the message.

Information Overload. When receivers are sent more messages than they can possibly handle, they experience communication overload. A common complaint among managers is that they are drowned in communications. In fact, most chief executives can only respond to a small fraction of the information sent to them. Modern advances in communications have greatly exacerbated the problem of communication overload. In every organization, people at all levels can be flooded with memos, reports, personal letters, company newsletters, and other information that

APPLYING ORGANIZATIONAL BEHAVIOR
ACROSS CULTURES

Lost in Translation

When Japanese executives of N.E. Chemcat, Tokyo, were asked by their U.S. partners of Englehard Corporation, New Jersey, to go after a bid from a tough customer, they replied "It's difficult; we will try our best." But what the Japanese thought they had said and what the Americans thought they had heard were not the same.

What the interpreter had translated as "It's difficult" really means, in polite Japanese, "It's impossible." The Americans interpreted the Japanese executives' "we will try our best" as a commitment. But the Japanese were being *non*committal. The Japanese couldn't understand why the Americans were intent on pursuing something they had been told was impossible, and the Americans were upset that the Japanese were not coming through with their promises.

Effective communication is a challenge even when both parties speak the same language. Language barriers make communication even more difficult. International businesspeople have adopted a variety of methods for overcoming communication problems, such as using interpreters and studying foreign languages. But these methods are not foolproof.

When international executives learn a foreign language, they can communicate much more effectively with members of a different culture. For example, many U.S. managers in Mexico learn to speak Spanish so they can communicate directly with their employees without an interpreter. Nevertheless, although speaking the same language helps to communicate the words, cultural factors can still distort the meaning.

One word that has caused many problems for U.S. managers in Mexico is the Spanish word *ahorita*. Literally translated, *ahorita* means "right now." But if U.S. managers don't understand the varied meanings of the word as it is used in the Hispanic culture, they will be continually confused and frustrated.

"When can I expect your production report?" asks the manager.

"*Ahorita*," answers the employee, who knows that the report could not possibly be ready for several hours.

"When will your boss be back?" asks a potential customer.

"*Ahorita*," responds the secretary who knows that the boss is gone to lunch and won't be back for over an hour.

"When will you have that equipment fixed?" asks the shop floor manager.

"*Ahorita*," replies the engineer, who knows that the necessary parts are not in stock and must be ordered.

To an American, *ahorita* means right now, but to a Mexican it could mean a few seconds, a few minutes, or even a few hours. One U.S. manager says he won't allow his staff members to use *ahorita* as an answer to his time-related questions.

Sources: Jim Impoco, Betsy Streisand, and Susan Dentzer, "The Great Divide," *U.S. News and World Report* (July 6, 1992), pp. 52–54; Marjorie Miller, "A Clash of Corporate Cultures," *Los Angeles Times* (August 15, 1992), p. A1.

could literally bury them in a mountain of paper. Because communication overloads are so serious, the following section examines some of the major reactions to communication overload.

The wide variety of new and innovative communication channels that are now available, such as facsimile, voice mail, video technology, teleconferencing, and electronic mail, are making information transmittal in organizations easier, faster, and more convenient. But one disadvantage of having these electronic channels in the workplace is that they tend to be overused, thus increasing the volume of communication without necessarily adding to its effectiveness. Organizations are being forced to create usage guidelines for the efficient and effective use of communication channels.[45]

Differing Frames of Reference. Accurate communication requires that the encoding and decoding processes be based on a common field of experience. For example, two people would have difficulty talking about living in the mountains of Idaho if snowy winters mean skiing, snowmobiling, and ice skating to one while the other thinks about wet feet, cold hands, icy roads, and cars that won't start. A new sales campaign would be viewed differently by the marketing manager and by the credit manager. One sees the potential for increased sales; the other sees the possibility of uncollectible bills.

Selective Listening. The problem of selective listening is part of the larger problem of selective perception, in which people tend to listen to only part of a message and ignore other information for a variety of reasons. We hear only what we want to hear and tend to disregard information that creates cognitive dissonance or is threatening to our self-esteem. We try to ignore information that conflicts with established beliefs or values.

Semantic Problems. Communication is a symbolic process that relies largely on words to transmit the intended meaning. When people do not speak the same language, it is easy to understand why they have difficulty communicating. Occasionally people think they speak the same language, but the symbols they use do not have a common meaning. "You handled it as well as a scoutmaster" could be either a compliment or a criticism, depending on how you feel about scoutmasters. Semantic problems are particularly troublesome in communicating abstract concepts or technical terms. Words such as "discounted present value," "trusts," and "stock options" have special meanings to a finance executive that they do not have to someone in production.

Reactions to Communication Overload

The problem of information overload is both an individual and an organizational problem. People are obviously the ones who have to respond to the various communications. However, organizational processes are frequently responsible for generating the level of communication. Too much communication can be just as troublesome as inadequate communication. An example in the military illustrates this problem. A commander issued an unpopular order and found that for the next few weeks the reports he received were severely misleading and incomplete. Vital information necessary for making decisions was not being submitted. He responded by threatening disciplinary action if he did not receive more complete information. His company responded by burying him in memos and reports containing both essential and trivial information. The commander was no better off than he was before, since he could not isolate the relevant information. A similar situation occurred in a New York City school system when the superintendent of schools complained that the number of unnecessary and often unread reports was beyond belief and ordered a moratorium on all written reports.[46]

Individuals and organizations have developed a variety of reactions to communication overload. Each reaction can be analyzed according to whether it is an adaptive or maladaptive response. Adaptive, or coping, responses focus on solving the problem, whereas maladaptive or dysfunctional responses fail to solve the problem, although they may delay the collapse of the system momentarily.

Disregard. A common method of responding to too much information is to disregard and ignore what cannot be easily absorbed. Ignoring and disregarding are dysfunctional responses, since they deny information to the organization on an irrational basis. The information that is typically ignored is usually the information that seems the most difficult to comprehend or the least pleasant to attend to. In a large railroad company, a grievance case was not processed because it appeared too ambiguous and technical to receive serious consideration. When it finally went to court, the company was required to attend to it, but the failure to respond earlier cost the company the case, and a precedent was established that permitted thousands of workers to file suit. Failing to process this difficult case early cost the railroad company millions of dollars.

Queuing. Queuing consists of collecting the information in a pile, with the expectation of processing it at a later time. Queuing is only appropriate for recorded information such as letters, reports, and memos. Telephone calls and other verbal messages cannot be conveniently placed in a queue. Queuing, or delaying the processing of information, can be either an adaptive or dysfunctional response depending on the amount of overload. If messages continue to arrive faster than they can be processed, the pile becomes infinitely long. However, if there is adequate time between the surges of incoming messages to process them, queuing may be an effective way to respond.

Filtering. The process of filtering can also be either adaptive or dysfunctional. When appropriate guidelines have been established to help supervisors know which information should be deleted, filtering can be an adaptive response. But if the guidelines and priorities have not been assigned by the organization, supervisors will be inclined to delete information that they do not readily understand and that does not make them look good.

Approximating. Approximating consists of processing a sample of the information and using the sample to make inferences regarding the rest of the information. Approximation is typically an adaptive response, because most information is highly redundant, and processing only a small part of the information usually provides a fairly accurate understanding of the total message.

Multiple Channels. Multiple channels can be created for transmitting and receiving the information. Chief executive officers frequently use multiple channels by assigning different people or departments to be responsible for collecting and analyzing portions of the information. Using multiple channels is a form of decentralized information processing and is a highly adaptive response in terms of organizational effectiveness. An example of multiple channels is to have employee complaints sent to the employee relations department; questions about stock options referred to the finance department; and issues regarding product quality submitted to the quality control department.

SUMMARY

1. Communication is a symbolic process in which ideas are communicated from a sender to a receiver through the use of symbols. The most common communication symbols are words that are either written or spoken.

2. The basic elements of the communication process include the source, the message, the encoding process, the channel, the decoding process, the receiver, and feedback.

3. Persuasive communication attempts to change attitudes or opinions and is influenced by the characteristics of the source, the message, and the audience. The most important characteristic of the source is the source's credibility. Persuasive messages generally need to be logical and reasonable, but whether they should be one-sided or two-sided, pleasant or frightening, depends on the topic and the receiver's level of acceptance.

4. Supportive communication is designed to avoid defensiveness and create open, congruent communication. Supportive communication consists of comments that are descriptive, problem-oriented, flexible, and owned.

5. Effective listening is an essential communication skill that comes from developing empathy and using effective listening skills. Empathy, which is the capacity to anticipate someone's feelings or ideas, occurs at two levels: the expressed level and the implied level.

6. Communicators use a variety of responses to either stimulate greater communication or terminate a conversation. Evaluative, confrontive, and diverting responses tend to terminate a conversation, while probing, reinterpretive, pacify-

ing, and reflective responses tend to stimulate and expand the conversation.

7. Nonverbal messages are an important part of communication and are communicated by physical distance, posture, facial cues, vocal cues, and appearance.

8. Communication network studies found that centralized networks, such as the wheel, were more efficient on simple tasks, while decentralized networks were more efficient in solving complex tasks. Satisfaction was found to be related to the centrality of the member's position within the network.

9. An analysis of the communication patterns in ongoing groups reveals four different communication roles: gatekeepers, liaisons, opinion leaders, and boundary spanners.

10. Although communication is essential for an organization to exist, it must be restricted and properly channeled for the organization to function effectively. Increased communication does not always solve communication problems, especially when the problems are due to a communication overload.

11. Organizational communication typically flows in three directions: downward, upward, and horizontally. Organizations need to establish formal channels for messages going in all three directions.

12. Information is distributed through the grapevine system found in every organization. Grapevine information typically travels faster and is more spontaneous and credible than information traveling in formal channels.

13. Some of the major strategies for improving organizational communication involve increasing the amount of feedback, regulating the flow of information, providing for repetition in communication, simplifying the language, and scheduling the communication so that it occurs at more convenient times.

14. Although communication problems can result from many difficulties, the most serious barriers to effective communication include omission, filtering, time pressures, differing frames of reference, selective listening, semantic problems, the use of jargon, making premature value judgments, and information overload.

15. People use a variety of methods of responding to information overload, and these methods may be either adaptive or dysfunctional. Disregarding and ignoring information is almost always dysfunctional, while queuing, filtering, and approximating may be either dysfunctional or adaptive depending on the situation. Using multiple channels for receiving and processing information is almost always an adaptive response to overload.

DISCUSSION QUESTIONS

1. How would you respond to a supervisor who made the following comment during a communication seminar: "Why do you make such a big deal out of communication with all of this encoding and decoding stuff? I don't think it's such a big problem. When I have something to say to my crew, I just tell them."

2. In what way is communication a symbolic interaction? Provide some illustrations of communication in which symbols other than words are used.

3. If you were asked by one of the social clubs on campus to present a 15-minute persuasive message on why students should not plagiarize or pay others to write their research reports, what sort of message would you prepare, a one-sided or a two-sided message? A strong or moderate fear appeal? What message would have the greatest impact in changing behavior?

4. How is supportive communication different from persuasive communication? Should you use the principles of supportive communication to protest an improper parking ticket? And if so, how?

5. What are the nonverbal messages that indicate liking and attraction? Make a list of the cues you use to indicate an interpersonal attraction for someone else. Does it matter whether the individual is of the same or the opposite sex?

6. In *M*A*S*H*, Radar O'Reilly, the company clerk, exerts far more influence than his position as a clerk entitles him to. To what extent can Radar's power and influence be attributed to Hollywood screenwriters, and to what extent can it be explained by his position in the communication network?

7. Why must communication be restricted in an organization? Can you provide any examples, fictitious or real, illustrating how the free flow of communication can disrupt an organization?

8. If grapevine systems cannot be eliminated in organizations, is there any way managers can influence grapevines to help them perform beneficial functions?

9. Because the communication process is so complex and there are so many potential barriers to effective communication, what can you do to make certain that you have understood the true meaning of a complex message someone has attempted to send? Can you ever be really certain that you understand a complex message?

10. What are the advantages and disadvantages of using jargon? Would you recommend that organizations try to do more to develop a unique vocabulary, or would you discourage them from using any acronyms, abbreviations, or jargon?

GLOSSARY

boundary spanners Individuals who perform the role of communicating with the organization's environment by sensing environmental changes and selling the organization to the environment.

centrality An index in network studies indicating how many communication links each position requires to communicate with every other position.

credibility A characteristic of a communication source determined by the source's expertise and trustworthiness.

decoding The process of translating the symbols contained in a message into meaning and interpreting the message.

empathic listening Active listening that requires you to project yourself into the speaker's frame of reference to comprehend the full impact of the message.

encoding The process of translating the intended message into symbols that can be used to transmit the message.

expressed level of empathy The level of understanding at which the listener paraphrases, restates, or summarizes the content of the communication as it was stated.

gatekeeper A communication role in an organizational structure that controls the flow of information, especially between lower and upper levels in the organization.

grapevine The informal communication system through which messages are passed in an organization, especially rumors and myths.

implied level of empathy A more advanced level of listening in which the listener attends not only to what the communicator expresses, but also to what was implied or left unstated.

latitude of acceptance The range of attitudes or opinions that are sufficiently close to the receiver's opinion that the receiver is willing to attend to the message.

liaison A communication role within an organizational structure in which an individual serves as a communication link between two groups.

noise Any type of interference in the transmission of a message, either actual noise or interference within the channel.

opinion leader A communication role in an organizational structure in which noted personalities become the opinion leaders who receive information from the mass media and interpret it for other organizational members.

supportive communication Communication designed to help both parties maintain open and congruent communication by avoiding defensiveness.

symbolic interaction A description of the communication process that emphasizes the fact that communication consists of the transmission of messages through symbols that must be properly encoded and decoded to convey the intended meaning.

NOTES

1. M. Meissner, "The Language of Work," in Robert Duban (ed.), *Handbook of Work, Organization, and Society* (Chicago: Rand McNally, 1976).

2. Reviewed by Rudi Klauss and Bernard M. Bass, *Interpersonal Communication in Organizations* (New York: Academic Press, 1982), p. 3.

3. C. Shannon and W. Weaver, *The Mathematical Theory of Communication* (Urbana, Ill.: University of Illinois Press, 1949).

4. Klauss and Bass, op. cit.

5. Ibid, chap. 4.

6. Aristotle, *Rhetoric*. See also Annette N. Shelby, "The Theoretical Bases of Persuasion: A Critical Introduction," *Journal of Business Communication*, vol. 23 (Winter 1986), pp. 5–29.

7. Carl I. Hovland and W. Weiss, "The influence of Source Credibility on Communication Effectiveness," *Public Opinion Quarterly*, vol. 15 (1952), pp. 635–650.

8. H. C. Kelman and C. I. Hovland, " 'Restatement' of the Communicator in Delayed Measurement of Opinion Change," *Journal of Abnormal and Social Psychology*, vol. 48 (1953), pp. 326–335.

9. Roobina Ohanian, "Construction and Validation of a Scale to Measure Celebrity Endorsers' Perceived Expertise, Trustworthiness, and Attractiveness," *Journal of Advertising*, vol. 19, no. 3 (1990), pp. 39–52; Roobina Ohanian, "The Impact of Celebrity Spokespersons' Perceived Image on Consumers' Intention to Purchase," *Journal of Advertising Research*, vol. 31 (February–March 1991), pp. 46–54.

10. David Kipnis and Stuart Schmidt, "The Language of Persuasion; Hard, Soft, or Rational: Our Choice Depends on Power, Expectations, and What We Hope to Accomplish," *Psychology Today,* vol. 19 (April 1985), pp. 40–45.

11. H. Leventhal and P. Niles, "Persistence of Influence for Varying Duration of Exposure to Threat Stimuli," *Psychological Reports,* vol. 16 (1965), pp. 223–233; H. Leventhal and R. Singer, "Affect Arousal and Positioning of Recommendation in Persuasive Communications," *Journal of Personality and Social Psychology,* vol. 4 (1966), pp. 137–146; H. Leventhal, R. Singer, and S. Jones, "The Effects of Fear and Specificity of Recommendation upon Attitudes and Behavior," *Journal of Personality and Social Psychology,* vol. 2 (1965), pp. 20–29.

12. Irving L. Janis and Semour Feshbach, "Effects of Fear-Arousing Communications," *Journal of Abnormal and Social Psychology,* vol. 48 (1953), pp. 78–92.

13. R. A. Jones and J. W. Brehm, "Persuasiveness of One- and Two-Sided Communications as a Function of Awareness: There Are Two Sides," *Journal of Experimental Social Psychology,* vol. 6 (1970), pp. 47–56.

14. N. Miller and D. Campbell, "Recency and Primacy in Persuasion as a Function of the Timing of Speeches and Measurements," *Journal of Abnormal and Social Psychology,* vol. 59 (1959), pp. 1–9.

15. Paula T. Hertel and Alice Narvaez, "Confusing Memories for Verbal and Nonverbal Communication," *Journal of Personality and Social Psychology,* vol. 50, no. 3 (1986), pp. 474–481.

16. S. Chaiken and A. H. Eagly, "Communication Modality as a Determinant of Message Persuasiveness and Message Comprehensibility," *Journal of Personality and Social Psychology,* vol. 34 (1976), pp. 605–614.

17. Reviewed by Everett Rogers and Rekha Agarwala-Rogers, *Communication in Organizations* (New York: Free Press, 1976).

18. E. Aronson, J. Turner, and J. M. Carlsmith, "Communicator Credibility and Communicator Discrepancy as Determinants of Opinion Change," *Journal of Abnormal and Social Psychology,* vol. 67 (1963), pp. 31–36; Marvin E. Goldberg and Jon Hartwick, "The Effects of Advertiser Reputation and Extremity of Advertising Claim on Advertising Effectiveness," *Journal of Consumer Research,* vol. 17 (September 1990), pp. 172–179.

19. William G. Dyer, "Congruence," in *The Sensitive Manipulator* (Provo, Utah: Brigham Young University Press, 1972), pp. 9–22.

20. Jack R. Gibb, "Defensive Communication," *Journal of Communication,* vol. 2 (1961), pp. 141–148.

21. Ralph Nichols, "You Don't Know How to Listen," *Colliers Magazine* (July 1953), pp. 16–17; Lyman K. Steil, "Your Listening Profile" (Sperry Corporation, 1980).

22. Beatrice Hamilton, "Hearing, Analyzing, Empathizing, and Succeeding in Management," *Training and Development Journal,* vol. 44 (August 1990), p. 16; Thomas A. Herbek and Francis Y. Yammarino, "Empathy Training for Hospital Staff Nurses," *Group and Organization Studies,* vol. 15 (September 1990), pp. 279–295; Mark V. Redmond, "The Functions of Empathy," *Human Relations,* vol. 42 (July 1989), pp. 593–605.

23. Steven Golen, "A Factor Analysis of Barriers to Effective Listening," *Journal of Business Communication,* vol. 27 (Winter 1990), pp. 25–36.

24. David Whetten and Kim Cameron, *Developing Management Skills* (Glenview, Ill.: Scott, Foresman, 1984), chap. 5.

25. Philip V. Lewis, *Organizational Communication,* 3rd ed. (New York: Wiley, 1987), chap. 5.

26. R. H. Birdwhistell, *Kinesics and Context* (Philadelphia: University of Pennsylvania Press, 1970).

27. A. Mehrabian, "Communication Without Words," *Psychology Today* (1968), pp. 52–55; Neil R. Anderson, "Decision Making in the Graduate Selection Interview: An Experimental Investigation," *Human Relations,* vol. 44 (April 1991), pp. 403–417.

28. Lewis, op. cit.

29. John T. Malloy, *Dress for Success* (New York: Warner Books, 1975).

30. Gerald H. Graham, Jeanne Unruh, and Paul Jennings, "The Impact of Nonverbal Communication in Organizations: A Survey of Perceptions," *Journal of Business Communication,* vol. 28 (Winter 1991), pp. 45–62.

31. Patricia Buhler, "Managing in the 90s: Are You Really Saying What You Mean?" *Supervision,* vol. 52 (September 1991), pp. 18–20; Valerie McClelland, "Communication: Mixed Signals Breed Mistrust," *Personnel Journal,* vol. 66 (March 1987), pp. 24–29.

32. Aaron Abbott and Adam Davis, "Pre-Trial Assessments Make Witness Testimony Pay Off," *Risk Management,* vol. 36 (June 1989), pp. 22–29.

33. Everett M. Rogers and D. Lawrence Kincaid, *Communication Networks: Toward a New Paradigm for Research* (New York: Free Press, 1981), chap. 7.

34. Marvin Shaw, "Communication Networks," in L. Berkowitz (ed.), *Advances in Experimental Social Psychology,* Vol. 1 (New York: Academic Press, 1964).

35. Harold J. Leavitt, "Some Effects of Certain Communication Patterns on Group Performance," *Journal of Abnormal and Social Psychology,* vol. 46 (1951), pp. 38–50; Marvin E. Shaw, "Some Effects of Unequal Distribution of Information upon Group Performance in Various Communication Nets," *Journal of Abnormal and Social Psychology,* vol. 49 (1954), pp. 547–553.

36. Marvin E. Shaw, "Communication Networks," pp. 111–147; R. Burgess, "Communication Networks and Behavioral Consequences," *Human Relations,* vol. 22, no. 2 (1969), pp. 137–159; A. M. Sandowsky, "Communication Network Research: An Examination of Controversies," *Human Relations,* vol. 25, no. 4 (1972), pp. 283–306.

37. Everett M. Rogers and Rekha Agarwala-Rogers, *Communication in Organizations* (New York: Free Press, 1976), chap. 5; M. L. Tushman, "Special Boundary Roles in the Innovation Process," *Administrative Science Quarterly*, vol. 22 (1977), pp. 587–605.

38. V. O. Key, Jr., *Public Opinion and American Democracy* (New York: Knopf, 1961).

39. Daniel Katz and Robert L. Kahn, *The Social Psychology of Organizations* (New York: Wiley, 1978), chap. 14.

40. Reported in Rogers and Agarwala-Rogers, op. cit., p. 93.

41. Ibid.

42. Harold Sutton and Lyman W. Porter, "A Study of the Grapevine in a Governmental Organization," *Personnel Psychology*, vol. 21 (1968), pp. 223–230.

43. Robert Brody, "I Heard It Through the Grapevine," *Executive Female*, vol. 9 (September–October 1986), p. 22–23; Arthur R. Pell, "Rumors," *Managers Magazine*, vol. 66 (May 1991), p. 31; Mark Ward, "Swing on the Company Grapevine: More Than Just Gossip, It Can Be a Strategic Tool," *EDN*, vol. 36 (April 18, 1991), pp. 1–2.

44. Alan Wilkins, "The Culture Audit: A Tool for Understanding Organizations," *Organizational Dynamics*, vol. 12, no. 2 (Autumn 1983), pp. 24–38.

45. Susan K. Becker, "New Communication Technology: Helping or Hindering the Message?" *Employment Relations Today*, vol. 18 (Autumn 1991), pp. 303–312.

46. Reported by Rogers and Agarwala-Rogers, op. cit., p. 91.

OPEN COMMUNICATION IN TROUBLED TIMES

Because of an economic recession, Hugh Aaron, the CEO of a small closely held plastics manufacturer, told his employees that the company must eliminate overtime, wage increases, quarterly bonuses, and the purchase of new equipment; even his wages were being cut. The announcement was spurned with suspicion and resentment. To counter the snickers of doubt and innuendo, management decided to share the company's entire financial records with its employees.

The decision to open the company's records was difficult, because such information is usually kept from employees. But the biggest problem was helping employees understand how to interpret a profit-and-loss statement. A manager who enjoyed teaching held daily sessions with small groups of employees to explain basic accounting and finance.

Some employees were still skeptical and accused the company of keeping two sets of books for ulterior motives. In response, the company's outside accountant and auditor attended the next session to validate the figures and to explain their fiduciary responsibilities.

Gradually the employees' skepticism changed from questioning the profits to questioning the costs. They wanted to know, for example, why the company spent $4,000 each quarter on laundry expenses. When they were told it was for the uniforms they carelessly tossed into a laundry heap each night, they suggested buying washers and dryers and laundering their own uniforms. They also questioned why the company spent several thousand dollars on a Christmas party and suggested that it be eliminated. Each employee was given direct responsibility for making policy decisions that affected him or her, including the janitor, who chose the most efficient and economical broom to buy.

Although some employees could not see beyond their own narrow interests, open communication helped most of them see and accept the company's financial crisis. Open communication helped the company survive in difficult times.

Source: Hugh Aaron, "In Troubled Times, Run An Open Company," *Wall Street Journal* (December 10, 1990), p. A10.

Questions

1. Why are a company's financial records not usually open to all employees?

2. If sharing financial information with all employees made this company more efficient, is this something other companies should also consider? Why, or when?

3. The myth of universal information suggests that every group functions better when everyone knows everything. What are the problems with this idea, and do they arise here?

COMMUNICATION

PART 1: ONE-WAY VERSUS TWO-WAY COMMUNICATION

For this exercise, the class is divided into groups of six to eight members. One member of each group is selected as the demonstrator, and a sheet of paper containing figures is given to this individual. No one else in the group should see these figures until the end of the exercise.

Purpose. The purpose of this exercise is to help you improve your skill in organizing factual information and communicating your ideas to others. It is also designed to demonstrate the value of feedback in communication.

Instructions. The demonstrator will receive a sheet of paper containing four figures. Two of these figures will be described using one-way communication, and the other two will be described using two-way communication. The order of communication (one-way versus two-way) should be mixed among the different groups to control for the effects of learning. The goal for each group is to have each group member reproduce all four figures as rapidly as possible. During one-way communication, the demonstrator should assume that he or she is dictating instructions into a tape recorder and should not receive any form of feedback from members, such as groans, laughter, or facial expressions. During two-way communication, the demonstrator should assume that he or she is talking to the group in a committee meeting where they can ask questions, but the demonstrator cannot show them the piece of paper or use any type of physical gestures, such as hand motions. For both one-way and two-way communication, only verbal communication is allowed. Members should not be able to see the figures being drawn by other group members.

Scoring. Each group should time how long it takes to complete each figure, and the figures should also be scored for accuracy. An accuracy score is calculated for each member of the group by comparing the member's drawings with the figures on the demonstrator's page. Each individual receives one point for each rectangle in the correct position (horizontal, vertical or diagonal) and one point for each pair of rectangles connecting at the proper points. Since there are eight rectangles and seven connecting points, there is a maximum score of 8 plus 7, or 15 for each figure.

PART II: INFORMATION DISSEMINATION

Purpose. The purpose of this exercise is to determine how accurately information is passed from one individual to another. It is also designed to examine the kinds of distortion that occur and why.

Instructions. Five individuals should be selected from the class for this exercise, and four of them should be asked to leave the room. While they are out, the remaining person (person 1) receives a message by looking at a picture or listening to the description of an incident. Person 2 is then invited back into the room, and person 1 describes the message to person 2 in front of the class. Person 3 is invited back into the room, and person 2 then describes the message to person 3, who describes it to person 4, who describes it to person 5. While this information is being passed from person 1 to person 5, other class members identify the information that was added, deleted, or changed.

PART III: NONVERBAL COMMUNICATION

Purpose. The purpose of this exercise is to help you see how information is communicated through body language and to help you be more sensitive to nonverbal messages.

Instructions. For this exercise, the class should be divided into groups of six to ten members. Two individuals in each group should be identified as actors, preferably one male and one female. The actors will rearrange the order of the ten emotions in the following list in a random fashion and then try to portray these emotions to the group without saying anything. Each actor will have 2½ minutes to portray all ten emotions, 15 seconds per emotion.

The members of the group should try to identify the emotions and write them down without any group interaction.

Anger	Jealousy
Fear	Sympathy
Boredom	Passion
Happiness	Resentment
Enthusiasm	Despair

Decision Making

LEARNING OBJECTIVES

After studying this chapter, you should be able to

1. List and describe the steps of the decision-making process.

2. Explain why decision makers are not totally rational.

3. Describe the psychological forces that influence thought processes.

4. Describe some of the major personality variables influencing the way people make decisions.

5. Explain when individuals are superior to a group in making decisions and when groups are superior to individuals.

6. Describe how group dynamics influence individual decision-making and create such problems as groupthink and the risky-shift phenomenon.

7. Describe the differences between three popular decision-making techniques—brainstorming, the Delphi technique, and the nominal group technique—and explain the advantages of each.

8. Describe the creative thinking process, and identify some of the factors that inhibit or facilitate creativity.

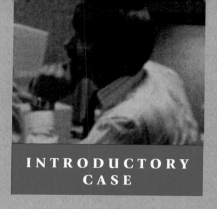

PROGRAMED DECISION MAKING AT K-MART

Ordering the right quantities of products has always been crucial to the success of retail firms. When inadequate supplies are ordered, customer service and sales are adversely affected. When too much of a product is ordered, profitability is harmed by unsold goods and high inventory investment. Increasingly, retail stores are centralizing their ordering decisions.

Decentralized decision making involves pushing decisions to lower levels of the organization and having fewer decisions made by top-level managers. Decentralization has been revered as an essential step in empowering employees. But some management decisions, such as ordering merchandise in retail firms, are becoming increasingly centralized and delegated to a computer rather than a manager.

To improve its ordering, K-Mart has developed a new system called CLAS (Classification and Assignment System), that has completely changed the way it orders and distributes merchandise to the stores. Rather than relying on store managers or manual methods to estimate product demand, CLAS assigns products to stores based on actual sales of the same or similar items. This computerized system maintains historical information about seasonal demands, price levels, and community characteristics, and uses this information to make programed decisions.

An illustration of how CLAS facilitates ordering decisions was a recent sale of microwave ovens.

When K-Mart featured a $119 microwave oven special in May, the demand for this new product was based on the sales of other microwave models. The data for these models were examined during the months of April, May, and June for the three previous years. Using CLAS, stores were then ranked according to their previous units sold and separated into fifteen groups. The computer decisions were briefly reviewed before CLAS was instructed to automatically process the orders.

Resistance to having ordering decisions made by a computer has been overcome because managers have seen its superiority. K-Mart reports that CLAS works very well and has been especially valuable in preparing for holidays such as Christmas and Valentine's Day. K-Mart achieved a significant reduction in inventory without experiencing any material shortages in merchandise.

Source: Bruce Fox, "K-Mart Tackles Distribution with CLAS," *Chain Store Age Executive* (January 1991), pp. 60–68.

Questions

1. What does centralized ordering imply regarding trends toward greater decentralized decision making and employee empowerment?

2. K-Mart's experience indicates that ordering decisions should be centralized. What other decisions should be centralized, and which ones should be decentralized?

Decision making involves making choices among alternative courses of action. Like communication, decision making is essential for organizations to survive. Management has sometimes been equated with decision making: What do managers do?—they make decisions. Most of the curricula in business schools contain courses designed to teach prospective managers how to make effective decisions in marketing, accounting, finance, and other business functions.

The systematic analysis of decision making has become known as **decision theory.** This field of study began during World War II and has become considerably more sophisticated in recent years. At first, decision theory proposed simple mathematical and statistical equations to help decision makers make good decisions. In recent years, decision theory has become far more complex; decision makers use computer simulations, expert systems, and operations research techniques to analyze complex situations and evaluate numerous alternatives.

Decision making occurs at all levels in the organization, and in this chapter it will be analyzed at the individual, group, and organizational levels. Decision making is also involved in creativity and innovation. Therefore, the concluding section of this chapter examines the creative process and methods of stimulating creativity. First, however, the decision-making process and some of the important factors influencing it need to be described.

THE DECISION-MAKING PROCESS

The basic elements of the decision-making process are illustrated in Exhibit 14.1. The process involves establishing goals and objectives, identifying a problem, developing and evaluating alternatives, choosing an alternative and implementing it, and evaluating its results. This model is somewhat misleading, since it implies that decision making follows a fixed series of logical steps. Actual decision making is not so organized or systematic. Nevertheless, this diagram lets us examine the elements in the normal decision-making process and identify some of the obstacles inhibiting effective decision-making.

Establishing Goals and Objectives

Decision makers must have goals and objectives to guide their decision making, whether they are specific, measurable objectives or only loosely defined goals. Without some form of goals or objectives, decision makers have no criteria for evaluating alternatives or selecting a course of action. In short, if there are no goals or objectives, it doesn't matter which decision is made. This point is illustrated by a classic exchange from Lewis Carroll's *Alice in Wonderland.* When Alice asks the cat which way she should go, the cat asks where she wants to go. Alice answers that she doesn't know, and the cat responds, "Then it doesn't much matter which way you go."

At the individual level of decision making, goals and objectives are created by each person according to that person's value system. At the group and organizational level, the goals and objectives are determined by power centers through group discussion, organizational infighting, mutual concessions, coalition forma-

EXHIBIT 14.1 The Decision-Making Process

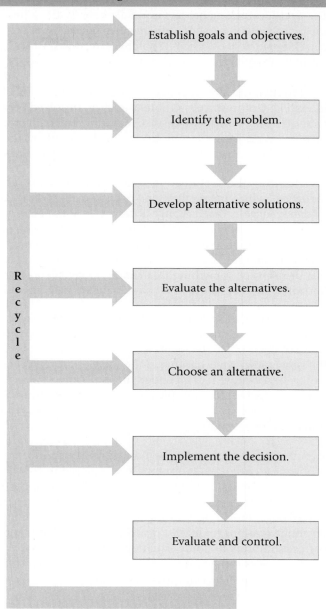

tion, or other social influence processes. It is important to remember, however, that groups and organizations do not have goals in the same way that individuals have goals. We should not make the mistake of thinking about the organization as though it were a "superperson" with a defined set of goals. When we make the mistake of thinking organizations have goals, we typically find inconsistencies and discontinuities in what we think are the organization's goals because of power shifts within the organization and turnover among key leaders.

Identifying the Problem

The decision-making process normally begins after a problem has been identified. Most problems consist of a discrepancy between the conditions that exist and the conditions that are desired. Problems can consist of such things as low productivity, high absenteeism, a malfunction in a major piece of equipment, or a conflict between two groups who want to use the conference room at the same time.

Effective decision making requires that the cause of the problem be clearly identified. Unfortunately, problems may go unsolved because of a faulty diagnosis. Four of the most frequent mistakes contributing to incorrectly identifying problems involve overlooking the seriousness of the problem, focusing on the symptoms, defining the problem by the solution, and engaging perceptual defenses.

Overlooking the Seriousness. Decision makers frequently display a "status quo tendency," which means they tend to pursue the existing course of action even when evidence suggests that a change is desirable. Sometimes it is difficult to know when a situation is bad enough to be considered a real problem. Two people can look at the same situation and disagree about whether it is serious enough to warrant attention. For example, is a 40 percent annual turnover among hourly employees a serious problem or something that can be tolerated? Recognizing real problems and knowing when to take action is a valuable managerial skill.

Focusing on the Symptoms. The symptoms of a problem are the visible indications that something is going wrong. Effective decision making requires that the cause of the problem be identified so that efforts will be directed toward striking at the roots rather than hacking at the leaves. For example, 40 percent turnover may simply be a symptom of an underlying problem, such as inadequate compensation, punitive supervision, or unpleasant working conditions. The problem can be more easily corrected by improving the compensation, supervision, or working conditions than by rewarding attendance.

Defining the Problem by the Solution. The following statements illustrate how problems are sometimes improperly diagnosed in terms of the solution: "Our performance appraisal isn't working very well because our supervisors haven't been trained"; "Our sales volume is down because we haven't spent enough money on advertising." Providing additional training and spending more money are popular recommendations for many organizational problems, and these actions may be the correct solutions in some situations. But performance evaluation problems and declining sales can be caused by many factors, which should be carefully analyzed before decision makers jump to the solution.

Perceptual Defense. Information that is threatening to our self-esteem is frequently overlooked or distorted. We try to protect ourselves from threatening and damaging information. Therefore, if the 40 percent turnover was actually caused by punitive supervision or a repressive work environment, we may be unwilling or even unable to admit that we are the real source of the problem.

Developing Alternatives

The identification of a problem typically results in a search for information to clarify the nature of the problem and identify alternative solutions. As a rule of thumb, the search for a solution begins by considering what was done in the past or what seems to be the most appropriate in the present. If a satisfactory solution is found, the search typically goes no further. Novel solutions are usually overlooked, regardless of how creative or insightful they may be. Old policies and procedures are usually redefined and revised before they are discarded and rewritten.

Another rule of thumb in searching for alternatives is to see what other organizations have done. If another organization has faced a similar problem and successfully solved it, managers are inclined to explore the same solution rather than "reinvent the wheel."

The rational decision-making process assumes that decision makers will investigate all the potential alternatives. In reality, however, the search process for most decisions is extremely limited, as the following section explains. Decision makers often look only long enough to find one acceptable solution, which they immediately select.

Evaluating and Choosing an Alternative

After the alternatives have been identified, they must be evaluated and the best alternative selected. Here, "best" is defined in terms of the original goals and objectives. Mathematical formulas are sometimes used to combine information and show the consequences of each course of action. The fields of statistics and operations research have contributed valuable insights and helpful models for evaluating alternatives. The appropriate decision-making tool depends on the amount of knowledge available and the cause–effect relationships. Three different decision-making conditions have been identified: certainty, uncertainty, and risk.

Certainty. In conditions of **certainty,** the decision maker has accurate knowledge about the outcomes of each alternative because the conditions that will exist are known. Investing money in a savings account at a bank is an example of making a decision under conditions of certainty. Because the interest rate is fixed and the bank is insured, the decision maker can use a simple mathematical formula to evaluate the value of this investment and feel reasonably certain of the outcome.

Risk. When making decisions under conditions of **risk,** the decision maker is willing to place a probability estimate on the outcome of each alternative. For example, the manager of the football concessions stand may not know whether to supply hot drinks or cold drinks to sell during the football game. If the weather is hot, the fans will want cold drinks, but if the weather is cold they will want hot drinks. The supplies have to be ordered three days in advance, and unsold drinks are perishable. If the manager is willing to place a probability estimate on the weather conditions and estimate how many drinks would be sold under those conditions, the decision of how much to stock can be made. This situation illustrates a decision made under conditions of risk, and various mathematical formulas, such as the expected value model shown in Exhibit 14.2, are available to help the decision maker reach a decision.

Uncertainty. Decisions are made under conditions of **uncertainty** when the decision maker does not know and is not willing to estimate the probability that certain conditions will exist. For example, if the manager of the concessions stand was not willing to assign a probability to the weather conditions, this decision would have to be made in conditions of uncertainty. In conditions of uncertainty, decision makers must use their own intuition, inspiration, or rough estimates in selecting an alternative.

EXHIBIT 14.2   Using Expected Value Formulas to Make a Decision

The expected value of an alternative is calculated by multiplying the probability of an event by the value of that event and then summing these products over all events. The formula is $EV = \sum p_i V_i$.

The concessions manager has identified four events (or weather conditions) and estimated the probability of that event and the likely demand for cold drinks associated with each event. For example, the probability that the temperature will be above 80 degrees is only .1 (or one in ten), but at that temperature, the demand will be for 10,000 drinks.

Each drink sells for $1, and the nonrecoverable cost for each drink is 15 cents. The concessions manager is considering three alternative amounts of cold drinks to stock: A = 10,000, B = 8,000, or C = 6,000. The profit for each alternative will depend on the weather and how many drinks are sold.

Event (weather temperatures, °F)	Probability	Demand for Cold Drinks	Profit		
			A = 10,000	B = 8,000	C = 6,000
80s	.1	10,000	$8,500	$6,800	$5,100
70s	.3	7,000	5,500	5,800	5,100
60s	.4	3,000	1,500	1,800	2,100
50s	.2	1,000	− 500	− 200	100

The expected value of stocking 10,000 drinks is

$$(.1)(8,500) + (.3)(5,500) + (.4)(1,500) + (.2)(-500) = \$3,000$$

The expected value of stocking 8,000 drinks is

$$(.1)(6,800) + (.3)(5,800) + (.4)(1,800) + (.2)(-200) = \$3,100$$

The expected value of stocking 6,000 drinks is

$$(.1)(5,100) + (.3)(5,100) + (.4)(2,100) + (.2)(100) = \$2,900$$

Although various mathematical models and statistical tools are available to help decision makers in conditions of certainty and risk, these tools are not useful in conditions of uncertainty. Here managers are left to follow what has been called the "science of **muddling through**."[1] This strategy involves developing broad statements of policy and objectives, and then proceeding to make intuitive decisions that seem the most expedient at the time. Hopefully, the consequences of earlier decisions can be assessed and used to revise later decisions. Like wading through a muddy river, the decision maker may be unsure of each step. But by stumbling along, the distant shore is finally reached.

Optimizing Versus Suboptimizing. Most decision-making situations involve multiple goals and objectives. For example, the decision to purchase a new machine can be examined in terms of its impact on the financial health of the organization, its impact on employee morale, and its effects on society by producing better products or polluting the environment. In such a situation, all the objectives cannot be optimized simultaneously; some objectives are optimized while the others are **suboptimized.** For example, the profitability of the company could increase because of the new machine, but at the expense of morale among the work group. If the new machine polluted the environment, the profitability of the company might be optimized while the quality of the environment would be suboptimized. Within organizations, different work groups frequently adopt practices that optimize the rewards to the group but suboptimize the organization's objectives, such as restrictive work rules and the careless use of company resources.

Escalation of Commitment. Once people have made a decision, they tend to feel emotionally committed to their decision and they want it to succeed. Most decision makers become ego invested in the projects they endorse, and they are willing to invest additional effort and resources if necessary to assure their success. This process, which has been referred to as "throwing good money after bad," is also known as "the escalation of commitment."

An example of commitment escalation is when a drug company invests money in developing a new medication. If the first allocation is spent without successfully developing a new product, there is a tendency to allocate more money. Studies suggest that in these situations the more people have already invested, and the closer they believe they are to a new discovery, the more they are willing to invest in further research. The danger is that decision makers can become so ego invested in their decisions that they are blind to contrary information and incapable of objectively evaluating the possibility of failure.[2]

The escalation of commitment does not appear to occur quite as much in group decision making when the group is asked to make a consensus decision. Apparently consensus decision making tends to diffuse the responsibility for the decision onto other group members, thereby reducing the feelings of personal responsibility and the need for self-justification.[3]

Implementing the Decision

Once the best alternative has been selected, it must be implemented. The most serious difficulties in implementing decisions are communicating them to others and overcoming resistance to change. A chief benefit of involving group members in making decisions is that it reduces problems of implementation, as will be discussed later.

Managers who make the decisions are usually not the ones responsible for implementing them. How well a solution can be implemented should be considered at the time it is being evaluated. Theoretically good solutions are not all that good if they cannot be implemented without undo resistance or difficulty. The policymakers in some organizations are so far removed from the everyday operations that they make decisions in terms of ideal goals with little regard for how they will be implemented in the practical operations. For example, managers may adopt a new safety plan for reducing accidents without considering how the workers will feel about the cumbersome equipment they are required to wear and the troublesome routines they are required to follow. In spite of how good the safety plan looked on paper, it may result in greater costs with no reduction in accidents.

APPLYING ORGANIZATIONAL BEHAVIOR
ACROSS CULTURES

Japanese Decision Making

 In 1990, Matsushita Electric, a $49.6 billion Japanese electronics firm, purchased MCA Inc., the parent company of Universal Pictures, Universal Studios' theme parks, and MCA music, for $6.1 billion. But the marriage of the two firms was hardly a match made in heaven. MCA executives struggled with cultural differences and language barriers, but the most frustrating aspect of the Japanese acquisition for MCA was the very different way in which Matsushita conducted business.

MCA spent months preparing a bid to purchase British-based Virgin Records. MCA saw the acquisition as an excellent opportunity to improve its international competitive position. Matsushita, however, refused without explanation to provide the necessary funds for the acquisition, and Virgin Records went to a competitor.

Although MCA is considered the most "rock solid and corporate of the Hollywood studios," to the Japanese firm it seemed reckless and impetuous. Matsushita, like many other Japanese companies, adheres to the Japanese business principles of *kaizen*, which prescribes slow, incremental growth and exacting analysis. The Japanese simply take longer to make decisions than the Americans.

Decision making in Japan is based on a collaborative decision-making process called *ringi*. The word *ringi* can be broken into two parts: *rin*, which means "submitting to the superior's will and receiving his or her approval," and *gi*, which means "decisions and deliberations."

This traditional decision-making process begins when someone in the organization has an idea. This person asks subordinates for their input and uses the information to prepare a formal statement called a *ringisho*. The *ringisho* is given to the individual's superior for approval and is passed upward through higher levels of superiors until it reaches the top of the organization. After the *ringisho* receives approval from the top level, it is passed back down to its originator as an order that can be carried out.

Sources: Abbass F. Alkhafaji, "Comparative Management in Developed and Developing Countries," *Management Challenges: A Worldwide Perspective*, vol. 29 (November 1991), pp. 36–40; Jim Impoco, Betsy Streisand, and Susan Dentzer, "The Great Divide," *U.S. News & World Report* (July 6, 1992), pp. 52–54.

Evaluation and Control

After a decision has been implemented, decision makers cannot simply assume that the problem is solved. Control and evaluation are necessary to make certain the actual results are consistent with the results expected when the decision was made. The value of clearly defined goals and objectives can be seen again at this point in the decision-making process. Specific objectives that are stated in measurable terms allow decision makers to determine quickly whether the decision achieved the desired results. If there is a discrepancy, a problem still exists, and the decision makers need to go through the decision-making process again. Each step needs to be carefully considered, including the original statement of goals and objectives. The discrepancy may exist because the original goals and objectives were unrealistic. Before initiating an exhaustive search for better solutions, the decision makers may want to question whether any solution is capable of producing the desired goal or if more modest goals and objectives should be sought.

INDIVIDUAL FACTORS IN DECISION MAKING

The previous section described the decision-making process as though individuals actually followed it in making decisions. In reality, individual decision making is far less orderly and systematic than this process suggests. This section examines the ways people make decisions and explains why we typically do not make completely rational and well-informed decisions.

Cognitive Limits of Rationality

To appreciate why we are not totally rational in making decisions, it is useful to look at the assumptions underlying the model of the perfectly rational decision maker. Human beings are not necessarily irrational, but there are at least limits to their rationality.

The Rational Decision Maker. The early decision-making models were derived from classical decision theory and assumed that people were perfectly rational in making optimal decisions. This model of human behavior contained the following assumptions:

1. The decision maker had ready access to perfect information concerning all aspects of the decision situation.
2. The decision maker could process and remember all relevant information in identifying and diagnosing problems.
3. The decision maker was able to identify all feasible solutions to a problem and evaluate the outcomes of each alternative.
4. Multiple goals could be combined mathematically into a single, simplifying equation.
5. As a rational person, the decision maker always selects the alternative that produces the maximum benefit.
6. All decision makers process information in the same manner and make similar decisions.

Although no one really argued in favor of this rational model, most of the economic theories of human behavior during the first half of this century were based on these assumptions. These theories assumed that people had a complete system of personal preferences that allowed them to choose among the alternatives open to them; they were always completely aware of the feasible alternatives; and there were no limits on their ability to make complex computations to determine which alternatives were best.

Bounded Rationality. The model of the perfectly rational decision maker was challenged by Herbert Simon, a Nobel Prize winner, who suggested that administrators exhibit **bounded rationality** rather than perfect rationality.[4] The concept of bounded rationality implies that people are forced to make decisions under a

APPLYING ORGANIZATIONAL BEHAVIOR
IN THE NEWS

Should the United States Close Its Doors to Immigration?

A crucial decision Americans need to make is whether they should close their doors to immigration. During the 1980s, 10 million immigrants came to the United States. That was more than during the first decade of the 1900s, when Congress decided it was too many and passed federal legislation limiting immigration. Some people feel the time has come to further restrict immigration, but the feelings are not universal.

Should immigration be further reduced? The decision-making process should provide a way for rational people to discuss the immigration issue and reach a consensus—identify the problem, develop alternative solutions, evaluate them, choose the best one and implement it, and then evaluate it. Unfortunately, this issue is surrounded with disagreement from start to finish. Is immigration really a problem? What are some realistic solutions to this problem, and how good are they? What is the best alternative, and how should it be implemented?

What criteria should be applied to the decision—helping the oppressed, adding skilled workers to the labor force, increasing the tax base, or providing a cheap source of labor?

What are the consequences of immigration—additional welfare costs, a cheap source of labor, a loss of jobs?

The alternatives that could be considered are almost endless, but evaluating them is hopeless without acceptable criteria. Deciding whether to further limit immigration is not an easy decision.

Source: CNN *Inside Business* news programming.

number of external and psychological constraints. People do not have perfect information regarding the problem, nor are they aware of all feasible solutions. And even if this information were available, they would probably not have the cognitive capacity to understand and remember it all, nor would they want to even if they could. The decision maker's ability to analyze only a few things at a time is referred to as *cognitive limits of rationality*. Contrary to the rational decision maker model, most people explore very few alternatives and make decisions after considering only a small amount of information.

Maximizing Versus Satisficing. A major implication of bounded rationality is that decision makers are *satisficers* rather than *maximizers*. "Satisficing" means establishing a minimum level of acceptability for a solution and then evaluating the alternatives until one reaching the minimum level is found. The first alternative that meets the minimum level is accepted, and the search for additional alternatives is terminated. The rational decision maker model implied that decision makers were **maximizers** who evaluated all possible solutions against a unitary goal and selected the alternative producing the maximum benefit.

One implication of bounded rationality is that people limit their search for information to the most convenient and least expensive data. Obtaining information is a double problem: obtaining additional information requires time, effort, and money, and once it is obtained decision makers are required to process it and they may be inundated with information.

Another crucial implication of bounded rationality is that the search for alternative solutions and the process of evaluating them is influenced by the decision maker's attitudes, values, and thought processes. Some of the most important personality variables and psychological forces influencing the ways people think are described in the following sections.

Psychological Aspects of the Thought Process

Two decision makers facing the same problem with identical information and similar alternatives will not necessarily select identical solutions. Our thought processes are influenced by at least seven cognitive variables.[5]

Social Position. Our thought processes are influenced by our social position not only in the organization, but also in the family, the community, and society. Our social position influences the information we allow ourselves to be exposed to and how we evaluate it. Upper-level managers are conditioned to focus on different problems and to analyze them according to different criteria from those used by lower-level managers.

The effects of social position on how decisions are made is particularly obvious to the children of military officers who compare their family environment with the environment of their friends. Military officers tend to use the same military mind-set at home that they use on the base, which tends to be heavily oriented toward discipline, obedience, orderliness, and accepting as right what higher-level officers say is right. Authority, discipline, and order are much less obvious in nonmilitary homes. Similarly, if a supervisor and a union steward were analyzing a declining sales problem, their social positions would cause them to consider different issues. While the supervisor would be more inclined to attribute the problem to poor-quality work, the union steward would attribute it to management's failure to improve the product design.

Reference Groups. A reference group can be either an imaginary or an actual group that individuals use as a basis for evaluating their ideas. People tend to identify with outside reference groups by developing emotional ties and affective feelings for them. These ties tend to influence the decisions we make. Studies have indicated, for example, that an individual's family unit is a very powerful reference group that influences the quality of work an individual displays on the job. People who have a strong work ethic and take pride in their work generally report that their families at home expect them to perform well on the job.[6] Another example of the influence of an outside reference group is an accountant serving on a product development committee who adamantly insists that the product development costs be properly allocated, even though doing so would be time consuming and seemingly irrational, because the accountant knows that other members of the accounting staff would be disappointed if an incorrect procedure were followed.

Projection of Attitudes and Values. We tend to project our own attitudes and values onto others and assume that their attitudes and values are similar to ours. Projecting our attitudes and values onto others can cause us to make errors when we falsely assume that others have the same interests and desires we do. For example, managers frequently project their own attitudes and values regarding such things as promotions, opportunities for overtime, and loyalty to the company, and they are surprised when new employees refuse promotions, resist working overtime, and show no sense of loyalty to the company.

Global or Undifferentiated Thinking. Undifferentiated thinking is thinking about a concept or an object as one homogeneous idea without appreciating that the concept may actually consist of numerous subconcepts that should be considered separately. Russia, for example, is not simply one large, homogeneous country but a very diverse nation with many ethnic groups possessing a vast array of political, economic, and religious views. Another concept often treated as an undifferentiated concept is job satisfaction. Although we talk about the effects of different organizational variables on satisfaction, we usually fail to appreciate that job satisfaction consists of many components, and a particular change seldom influences all components equally.

Dichotomized Thinking. Another common error stems from our tendency to view the world in terms of opposites—good or bad, right or wrong, high or low. For example, students in organizational behavior frequently want to know if a particular theory is true. The assumption is that if it is not true, then it must be false. Many students have difficulty learning that the appropriate question is not whether a theory is true or false, but when is it useful. Similarly, most people have firmly entrenched attitudes that labor unions are either good or bad, without realizing that in some situations and for specific problems unions can be either good or bad.

Cognitive Nearsightedness. Most people have a tendency to respond to that which is urgent, immediate, and visible and to neglect problems that may be more significant but removed in time and place. The problems in front of us tend to be perceived as urgent and take precedence over issues that may be far more important but do not have the same degree of urgency. For example, many college seniors spend their time on urgent matters, such as writing papers, preparing for exams, and doing daily homework. These urgent daily activities may not be as important as preparing a résumé, registering with the placement office, and initiating an aggressive job search.

Oversimplified Explanations of Causation. In analyzing organizational problems, decision makers frequently try to restrict the diagnosis to a limited number of variables. A large number of variables is awkward to consider and not as easy to explain or use as a simple cause–effect model with two or three variables. Furthermore, we occasionally make the mistake of labeling the problem and assume that once it is labeled, it is then explained. For example, labeling the problems of performance appraisals, such as halo effect, central-tendency effect, and leniency–strictness effect, seems to create the impression that now that they have been identified, nothing further needs to be done to solve them. Simple cause–effect models may simplify the decision-making process but be very misleading. For example, turnover is not simply caused by job dissatisfaction. Many individual, organizational, and economic variables influence a company's turnover rate. Likewise, inflation is caused not only by the supply of money but by a host of other economic variables. Simple linear thinking, such as A causes B, can create serious decision-making problems when A, B, C, and D all influence each other.

Personality Determinants

In addition to the general limitations of our thought processes, our decisions are influenced by fairly stable and enduring personality orientations. These basic personality characteristics influence the decisions we make in a wide variety of situations. Four personality variables that influence decision making include ideology versus power orientation, emotionality versus objectivity, creativity versus common sense, and action orientation versus contemplation.[7]

Ideology Versus Power. Some decision makers possess an ideology orientation, which means that their decisions are based on a coherent philosophy or set of principles. Other decision makers base their decisions on what appears to be politically expedient and serves to increase their own personal power. Most politicians adopt a power orientation designed to keep them in office by catering to the voting public. Some political leaders, however, are more inclined to base their decisions on what they think is right in spite of its lack of popularity, such as President Ronald Reagan's decision to support the contra rebels fighting the Sandinistas in Nicaragua. Social reform movements typically have leaders who have a very strong ideology orientation, so that their decisions are based on considerations of what is right rather than what is expedient. It has been suggested that organizations dominated by power-oriented leaders tend to move in the direction of aggrandizement of the leaders rather than organizational improvement. Significant organizational contributions are typically made by leaders with a strong ideology orientation.

Emotionality Versus Objectivity. Some decision makers allow their emotions to have a great influence on the decisions they make. These emotions may be either conscious personal preferences or subconscious emotions stemming from deeper defensive needs. Emotions can influence the ways problems are analyzed and the kinds of information and alternatives considered in making a decision. Objective information may be ignored, and the decision may be based strictly on personal feelings.

Other decision makers are more objective; they prevent their emotions from distorting their perception of the problem or the facts surrounding it. For example, if one of the applicants applying for a job was a friend of the person making the decision, an emotional decision maker would hire the friend even though objective performance indicators suggested that other applicants had a higher probability of success. The objective decision maker would be less inclined to allow feelings of friendship to influence the evaluation process and, instead of offering the job to the friend, would offer it to the most qualified candidate.

When decisions are based on conscious emotions and feelings, they tend to show a greater humanitarian concern for people and their welfare. However, when emotional decisions are based on deeper, defensive needs, they are usually dysfunctional for both the organization and individuals. Defensive needs indicate a psychological weakness that causes people to interpret situations as a threat to their self-esteem. To the extent that decisions are designed to protect one's self-esteem rather than benefit the organization, the organization suffers. Defensive decision makers tend to surround themselves with individuals who filter incoming information and act to protect an unstable leader rather than help the organization respond to its environment.

Creativity Versus Common Sense. When facing a new problem, some decision makers try to redefine the problem and discover new relationships that represent a creative solution to the problem. Other decision makers tend to focus more on what has worked in the past and what seems to make good sense. In general, top managers tend to be people who use common sense and good judgment in making decisions, while those who focus on creative solutions typically serve in supporting staff positions. Both these orientations, creativity and common sense, make an important contribution to organizational effectiveness, but the same individual rarely possesses both.

Action Orientation Versus Contemplation. People differ in terms of their propensity for taking action. Decision makers who are prone to contemplation tend to become fixated on identifying and evaluating problems; they seem to find satisfaction in debating the issues and exploring the possible implications. Decision makers with an action orientation focus on making a decision and implementing the solution as rapidly as possible. These people want to translate decisions into action without spending any more time than is necessary in considering the alternatives. As a general rule, supervisory positions tend to attract people who have a greater capacity for action, while college faculty positions tend to attract people who like to explore issues and think about them. Successful work groups need both kinds of personalities. For example, a successful research and development team requires people who can generate creative ideas and others who can translate them into action.

GROUP DECISION MAKING

A common method for making organizational decisions is to delegate the task to a group and ask the members to reach a group decision. In fact, group decision making is one of the most popular techniques for making important organizational decisions. As a general rule, the most complex problems are assigned to committees, task forces, and other decision-making groups for a solution. Since so many decisions are made by groups, it is important to understand the effects of groups on the decision-making process and to know when groups produce superior decisions and when their decisions are inferior.

Individual Versus Group Decision Making

Suppose a manufacturing company decided to build an additional production facility and needed to know where it should be located. This problem could be assigned to an individual to identify alternative locations, evaluate them, and select the best one. Individual decision making has become increasingly rare, however, as most decisions of this magnitude are almost always delegated to a committee.

The growing use of group decision making comes from the assumptions we tend to make about the benefits of group decision making. Most people expect groups to make decisions that are more accurate than individual judgments. A group of several individuals supposedly has a larger reservoir of insight and knowledge than a single individual; therefore, shouldn't it produce more accurate decisions that are also more creative and insightful? Group decisions are also expected to produce greater commitment and acceptance among group members, who should be more likely to implement the decision properly and without resistance.

Finally, allowing people to participate in making group decisions is consistent with the democratic values espoused by our society. Individuals expect to have a voice in deciding what should happen. Through the democratic participation of many individuals, favoritism and bias should be eliminated, thereby producing decisions that are more fair.

Although there is a general feeling that group decisions are superior to individual decisions, committee decisions do not have a very favorable reputation. Committee meetings have been criticized as a waste of time for highly paid administrators, who are said to squander the majority of their valuable time there. Committee decisions are notoriously slow. Indeed, some executives delegate unpopular issues to a committee knowing that the issue will die before the committee ever reaches a decision. If the committee ever succeeds in reaching a decision, its recommendations are frequently criticized as being biased by one or two dominant people who manipulated the group. Just because several people participated in making the decision does not mean that the decision is more effective or brilliant than any member could have produced alone. The decision may be an irrational compromise for which no one is willing to accept responsibility.

Some of the assets and liabilities of groups are listed in Exhibit 14.3. The size of the group is relevant, since a larger group will enhance the value of the assets and exacerbate the liabilities. Although groups generally are superior to individuals in making decisions, their superiority is not universal. A comparison of individual versus group decision making must consider these criteria: accuracy and judgment, creativity, commitment and acceptance, and time and cost.

EXHIBIT 14.3 Assets and Liabilities of Groups in Making Decisions

Assets of Groups

1. Greater knowledge and information
2. Greater variety of approaches to a problem
3. Increased acceptance of the decision
4. Reduced communication problems

Liabilities of Groups

1. Social pressures to conform
2. Loss of valuable time of group members
3. Hasty convergence on a solution
4. Possibility of control by a dominant individual
5. Distraction by hidden agenda and secondary goals
6. Insufficient time to reach a decision
7. Problems with disagreement and interpersonal conflicts
8. Possibility of final decision being an irrational compromise

Accuracy and Judgment. As a general rule, group decisions tend to be more accurate than individual decisions, but for only certain kinds of problems. Group decisions tend to be superior when (1) the problems have multiple parts, allowing for a division of labor among the group members, (2) group members have complementary skills and information, (3) the problem involves estimation rather than creativity, or (4) the problem involves remembering information.[8] In contrast, individual decision making tends to be superior when (1) the situation requires a sequence of multiple stages, (2) the problem is not easily divided into separate parts, and (3) the correctness of the solution cannot be easily demonstrated.[9]

A group decision would normally be superior to an individual decision in developing a new product. This decision requires information from several different functional departments within the organization, including accounting, finance, marketing, production, and legal. It is virtually impossible for any single individual to comprehend adequately all these areas of knowledge, and experts from each area would need to be consulted even if individuals tried to make the decision alone. A committee composed of experts from each area has the potential to make a more accurate decision.

The mere presence of complementary information, however, does not guarantee a superior decision. Various group dynamics may inhibit the group from effectively sharing information or using it effectively to make a good decision. The status and expertise of group members can interfere with the deliberations of the group. For example, the presence of a perceived expert or a higher-level manager tends to create an autocratic rather than a democratic group atmosphere. Their presence inhibits the open exchange of ideas, and their comments are usually not challenged or reviewed as critically as the comments of others.[10]

In the decision-making process, group members need to challenge the information and assumptions of other members and strive to reach a consensus decision. Guidelines for effective group decision making are presented in Exhibit 14.4.

Group decisions are generally more accurate than individual decisions on estimation problems. Estimating the size of an audience, forecasting the demand for next year's sales, and guessing how many items of inventory are in a large container are examples of problems that generally produce superior decisions by groups. The group decision is generally more accurate than the average of the individual decisions.[11]

An example of a problem that is more conducive to individual decision making than group decision making is a problem that involves complex computations, such as developing an inventory-control model or a cost–benefit analysis. Such problems cannot be easily subdivided and delegated to group members, and they involve a sequence of multiple stages requiring the concentration of one individual rather than many.

Through experience and training, group members can learn how to improve the effectiveness of their group decisions. Groups that have learned to work well together make consensus decisions that are typically superior to the average level of the group or the level of the most knowledgeable group member. Groups that have learned how to make consensus decisions are more effective than groups that rely on other techniques, such as majority votes, coin tosses, or autocratic pronouncements. A longitudinal study of student groups who worked together for a semester on class projects and exams found that the group outperformed the most proficient group member 97 percent of the time. The average improvement of the group's

EXHIBIT 14.4   Guidelines for Achieving Consensus in Group Decisions

1. Avoid arguing for your own position. Present your position as lucidly and logically as possible, but listen to the other members' reactions and consider them carefully before you press your point.

2. Do not assume that someone must win and someone must lose when the discussion reaches a stalemate. Instead, look for the next-most-acceptable alternative for all parties.

3. Do not change your mind simply to avoid conflict and to reach agreement and harmony. When agreement seems to come too quickly and easily, be suspicious. Explore the reasons, and be sure everyone accepts the solution for basically similar or complementary reasons. Yield only to positions that have objective and logically sound foundations.

4. Avoid conflict-reducing techniques such as majority vote, averages, coin flips, and bargaining. When a dissenting member finally agrees, don't feel that he or she must be rewarded by having his or her own way on some later point.

5. Differences of opinion are natural and expected. Look for them and try to involve everyone in the decision process. Disagreements can help the group's decision because a wide range of information and opinions increases the chance that the group will find a more adequate solution.

score over the most knowledgeable member's score was 8.8 percent. Therefore, on tasks that require analyzing, synthesizing, and remembering information the optimal decision-making strategy appears to be consensus group decision making.[12]

Creativity. As a general rule, individual decision making generates higher levels of creativity than group decision making. Research studies show that group decision making tends to inhibit creativity, and individuals working alone produce ideas of higher quantity and quality than individuals working in a group.[13] These conclusions, however, are not consistent with common beliefs: most people believe that groups are more creative than individuals.

The myth about the superiority of group creativity originated with a technique developed by Alex Osborn in 1939 called **brainstorming**.[14] The purpose of this technique was to enhance creativity through group discussion. It was particularly recommended to help advertising executives develop new promotional ideas. In a group brainstorming session, individuals are instructed to concentrate on a topic and express every idea that comes to mind regardless of how outlandish or absurd the thought may be. Criticizing another's ideas is not allowed; in fact, members are encouraged to think about absurd ideas with the hope that they will eventually stimulate a totally novel and creative solution.

Although brainstorming continues to be used quite frequently, some of the enthusiasm for it declined when studies failed to support its claims. One study compared the creativity of four individuals working together as a group versus four individuals working alone.[15] Four problems were used in this study: one concerning the problems of handling increased school enrollments in subsequent decades, one seeking ways to increase tourism in America, one assessing the advantages and disadvantages of being born with an extra thumb on each hand, and one assessing the consequences to society if the average adult height increased by 10 inches. Each group of 4 individuals worked together on two of these problems and alone on the other two. Since the brainstorming technique had been recommended for advertising executives, the study used a sample of advertising people along with a sample of employees in research and development.

The results for both groups, as illustrated in Exhibit 14.5, indicated that individuals consistently generated a greater number of nonredundant ideas when working alone than when working in a group. A panel of judges evaluated the quality of each idea, and the results indicated that individuals working alone not only produced more ideas, but their ideas were qualitatively superior than when they were working in a group. These results are consistent with the results of other studies indicating that group processes inhibit creativity. Even though people in a brainstorming group are instructed to ignore the influence of the group, they cannot entirely ignore the presence of others. Idea generation is apparently an individual process requiring concentration and insight, and it seems to be inhibited by the presence of others.

One reason why brainstorming continues to be used is because when individuals are in the group, they are at least forced to think about the problem. If they were by themselves concentrating on the problem, individuals would be more creative, but only if they were motivated to concentrate. In some situations, apparently the motivation produced by the presence of others pushes people into thinking about the problem and may offset some of the loss of concentration. A second reason why brainstorming might be helpful is because it teaches members how to engage in divergent thinking. A brief experience in a brainstorming group might help a newcomer grasp the freewheeling nature of divergent thinking.

One technique designed to minimize the distraction of the group in brainstorming sessions is to require people to speak in sequence or to pass if they have no ideas to contribute. This technique prevents one individual from dominating the discussion and helps timid members participate more openly. One report indicated that this technique resulted in an 80 percent increase in the number of ideas generated over the normal brainstorming technique.[16]

Commitment and Acceptance.   One of the most significant reasons for delegating a problem to a group stems from the positive benefits of participation. People want to be involved in the decisions that affect them. When people participate in making a decision, they feel greater commitment and loyalty to the decision and are willing to commit more of their own time and energy to implement it successfully. Furthermore, there is a greater chance that the solution will be implemented properly, since people will have a better understanding of the situation.

The powerful influence of participative decision making was revealed in an early series of studies on the food selections of homemakers. During World War II several food items were in short supply because the country was committed to providing one pound of meat per day for every American soldier. In spite of the shortage of desirable cuts of meat, there was a surplus of undesirable items, especially brains, kidneys, and tripe, which are an excellent source of protein and minerals. Although these undesirable animal parts are nutritious and Europeans considered them edible and even delicacies, American consumers refused to eat them.

Government food experts asked Kurt Lewin to study the conditions necessary for changing eating habits. Kurt Lewin, a leader in the field of group dynamics, believed that participating in a group discussion would influence the level of commitment and acceptance of the group members. Using groups of homemakers and Red Cross volunteers, Lewin had some women participate in a group decision while

EXHIBIT 14.5	Number of Different Ideas and/or Solutions to Problems Generated Under Conditions of Individual and Group Brainstorming

	Research	Personnel	Advertising	Personnel
Thumbs and People	78.3	60.9	82.9	59.8
Education and Tourists	62.2	49.3	58.5	37.3
Total	140.5	110.2	141.4	97.1

Source: Marvin D. Dunnette, John P. Campbell, and Kay Jaastad, "The Effect of Group Participation on Brainstorming Effectiveness for Two Industrial Samples," *Journal of Applied Psychology,* vol. 47 (1963), pp. 30–37. Copyright 1963 by the American Psychological Association. Reprinted by permission.

others listened to a persuasive communication.[17] In the persuasive sessions, the women listened to panels of experts describe the value of the undesirable products and exhort them to support the government's efforts. In the group decisions, experts were available to answer questions, but the women were expected to discuss the pros and cons of eating the undesirable animal parts and reach a consensus.

The effects of these conditions were assessed by observing what the women actually purchased and consumed two and four weeks after the session. The results indicated that the group discussions had a much greater influence than the lectures. After four weeks, the consumption of kidneys, brains, and hearts increased 32 percent among those who participated in the group decisions but only 3.7 percent among those who attended the lectures. The group discussions were also found to have a much greater impact than the lectures on the consumption of other products such as evaporated milk and cod liver oil. Subsequent research has produced similar results and helped to identify the factors in group decision making that contribute to commitment and behavior change. Group decisions reached by consensus create intense social pressures for individuals to accept the group decision and follow it. Unlike the individuals who attend a lecture, group members are forced to reach a decision and publicly declare their intention. Furthermore, their decision to change is reinforced by observing the change in others.[18]

Time and Cost. Although group decision making has the advantage of creating greater acceptance and commitment, these benefits are not free: group decisions are typically very time consuming. If the decision is accompanied by conflict, some groups never reach a decision. A management strategy for delaying an issue or avoiding it altogether is to delegate it to a committee without appointing a leader. If the committee is large enough, there is a good chance it will never succeed in recommending a solution.

The enormous cost associated with committee assignments can be estimated by counting the number of employee hours executives spend in committees and calculating the total cost of a meeting based on the hourly rate of the members in attendance. As the size of the committee increases, both the length of time needed to reach a decision and the cost of the meeting increase dramatically. When speed in reaching a decision is a major factor, group decision making with large groups should be avoided.

Group Influences on Decisions

The presence of others has a significant influence on the way people make decisions. Although the combined efforts of several people should increase the acquisition, retention, and recall of relevant information, studies of group remembering and decision making have found that the dynamics of the group often prevent it from making a good decision. Decision-making groups have often been observed to fumble in search of relevant information until one member claims to recall it. If the information, right or wrong, is asserted with enough conviction, it may be accepted by the group, who then confer expert status on the individual who provided the information. Groups also have a tendency to selectively recall information supporting only one side of an issue and selectively suppress or ignore information consistent with an opposing position.[19] The influence of the group can be analyzed by examining changes in risk taking and a phenomenon called "groupthink."

Risk Taking. Decision making typically involves some degree of risk and uncertainty, and an important question is whether group decisions tend to be more risky or more conservative than the decisions of individuals. For example, a traditional principle of military leadership is that individuals, not groups, should make decisions because groups are not capable of the boldness and courage needed for a successful military strategy. This principle assumes that group decisions tend to be conservative.

Early research studies found just the opposite, however: group decisions tended to be more risky than individual decisions. Individuals were asked to review hypothetical cases involving career choices, investment decisions, and medical operations. In each case they were faced with a dilemma requiring them to choose between a relatively safe alternative with a moderate payoff and a riskier alternative with a higher potential payoff, such as a secure job with a big corporation or an uncertain job with a new but potentially more rewarding and exciting company and a larger salary. Individuals were asked to determine the highest level of risk they would tolerate before rejecting the uncertain alternative. After reaching their individual decisions, they were formed into groups where they discussed each case and reached a consensus decision. The early results indicated that groups were willing to make more risky decisions, and this effect was called the **risky-shift phenomenon.**[20]

Early attempts to explain why groups made more risky decisions focused on the "diffusion of responsibility." According to this explanation, individual decision makers are more conservative because they are totally responsible for their decisions. If the consequences are bad, the individual must bear the full responsibility for failure. However, groups need not be so conservative, since the criticism for a bad decision can be shared by the entire group.

Although diffusion of responsibility was a reasonable explanation, additional studies found that some groups produced conservative shifts in which the group decisions were less risky than the individual decisions. It is now clear that group discussion can produce both risky and conservative shifts in a wide variety of settings, such as investment, purchasing, and termination decisions. In addition to the diffusion of responsibility, two additional explanations have been proposed to explain the effects of groups on risk taking: the polarization explanation and the cultural values explanation. The polarization explanation suggests that the group discussion seems to polarize or exaggerate the initial positions of group members. While the initial positions of individuals tend to be only slightly conservative or risky, they tend to move toward the nearest end of the continuum as a result of the group discussion. Thus, individuals who are only slightly risky before the group discussion adopt a much more risky position afterward, while people who are only a little conservative become much more conservative after the discussion. If the majority of the group members are slightly risky, the discussion will produce a risky shift, while a conservative shift will occur if the majority of the group members are slightly conservative.

The cultural values explanation for changes in risk taking suggests that the group discussion tends to reinforce the significance of dominant cultural values. If the dominant social value tends to be conservative, such as saving the life of the mother in abortion decisions, then the group discussion tends to produce a conservative shift. However, if the dominant social value tends to be risky, such as investing in a new product, the group decision tends to produce a risky shift.[21]

Groupthink. Although group decision making provides several potential advantages, one of the most serious disadvantages is the phenomenon identified by Irving Janis called "**groupthink**." Groupthink occurs in highly cohesive groups when group pressures lead to reduced mental effort, poor testing of reality, and careless moral judgments. Janis has used the phenomenon of groupthink to study several of the major fiascoes involving high-level decisions such as the Bay of Pigs incident of the Kennedy administration, the decision to escalate war in Vietnam during the Johnson administration, and the failure to adequately protect Pearl Harbor against Japanese attack during World War 11.[22] The destruction of the *Challenger* spacecraft disaster appears to be a more recent illustration of groupthink. Public testimony has suggested that NASA officials failed to heed relevant warnings in their decision to launch another space shuttle mission.[23] Although groupthink does not necessarily occur with all cohesive groups, Janis identified eight of the main symptoms of groupthink.

1. *Illusion of invulnerability.* Group members develop an illusion of invulnerability that leads them to ignore obvious dangers. As a consequence, they become overconfident and willing to assume greater risks.

2. *Rationalization.* Problems and counterarguments that should not be ignored are rationalized away. Group members collectively construct rationalizations to discount warnings or other sources of information challenging their thinking. Therefore, negative information is discredited in the group discussion.

3. *Illusion of morality.* Group members believe unquestioningly in the inherent morality of their position and ignore the ethical or moral consequences of their decisions. The decisions adopted by the group are not only perceived as sensible, they are also perceived as morally correct.

4. *Shared stereotypes.* Members develop stereotyped views about leaders of outside groups. Opposing leaders, for example, are viewed as evil, stupid, or too weak to deal effectively with whatever the group decides. Such stereotypes effectively block any reasonable negotiations between differing groups.

5. *Pressure for conformity.* Members pressure each other to conform with the group views and accept the group consensus. Dissenting views among the members are not acceptable.

6. *Self-censorship.* Group members convince themselves that they should avoid expressing opinions contrary to the group. Personal reservations and doubts are self-censored by members who do not want to "rock the boat."

7. *Illusion of unanimity.* Because no one expresses doubt or disagreement, members perceive unanimous support for the group decision. The group falsely assumes that because no one says otherwise, everyone in the group is in full agreement.

8. *Mind guards.* Just like bodyguards who protect people from physical harm, mind guarding occurs when individual members adopt the role of protecting the group from information that contradicts its decision.

The Bay of Pigs fiasco was a serious embarrassment to President John F. Kennedy and his new administration. On April 17, 1961, a brigade of about 1,400 Cuban exiles aided by the U.S. military invaded the coast of Cuba at the Bay of Pigs. The planning for this event had been seriously flawed and inadequate. On the first day none of the four ships containing reserve ammunition and supplies arrived. By the second day the brigade was completely surrounded by 20,000 Cuban troops, and by the third day those who had not been killed were captured and led to prison camps. This embarrassing event forced Kennedy and other top administration officials to carefully review the poor method by which their group decisions had been made.

A careful review of their failure enabled them to respond much more effectively eighteen months later to the Cuban missile crisis, when Soviet missile sites were being constructed in Cuba. This time Kennedy took several precautions to avoid the problem of groupthink. He assigned each cabinet member the role of critical evaluator responsible for voicing objections and doubts; he did not state his personal preferences and expectations at the beginning; he invited outside experts to share information and challenge the views of the group; and he divided the group into subgroups to consider issues separately. By avoiding the problems of groupthink, the Kennedy administration was able to handle the Cuban missile crisis much more successfully than it did the Bay of Pigs invasion.[24]

Very similar to the groupthink phenomenon is the Abilene Paradox. The Abilene Paradox occurs when members of an organization take an action contrary to what they really want to do and, as a result, defeat the very purposes they are trying to achieve. This label comes from the story of a father, mother, daughter, and son-in-law who endured a miserable trip to Abilene and ate a terrible Sunday dinner, only to discover when they returned that none of them wanted to go even though they all expressed interest when the idea was first proposed. The Abilene Paradox occurs in organizations when members fail to communicate their true ideas and desires because they think it is better to be agreeable.[25]

To prevent groupthink and the Abilene Paradox, groups should create a climate that tolerates disagreement and accepts debates. Leaders can reduce groupthink if they refrain from expressing their desires, encourage criticism, assign members to express dissenting views, and recruit outside experts to review and assist in decision making.[26]

Programed Conflict. The Abilene Paradox and the groupthink phenomenon occur when group members feel a need to be agreeable and they want to maintain harmony in their deliberations. Conflict threatens the unity of the group, and members often want to avoid any appearance of disrupting the group. But conflict can also be functional.

Knowing that contrasting viewpoints can improve the quality of a group decision, some groups use a form of programed conflict where opposing arguments are presented in a structured format. The two most prominent forms of programed conflict are the devil's advocacy and dialectical inquiry.

The *devil's advocacy* technique gets its name from the traditional practice used by the Catholic Church when the College of Cardinals considers someone for sainthood. One person is assigned the role of devil's advocate and expected to expose and examine all possible objections to the person's canonization. When this technique is used in organizations, one member of the group is assigned the role of critic and expected to criticize every proposal and decision. A good devil's advocate challenges and exposes bad ideas, thereby reducing the likelihood of groupthink.

The method of *dialectical inquiry* traces its beginnings to the dialectic school of philosophy in ancient Greece. Plato and his followers developed the art of logically examining issues by discussing a principle (thesis) and then considering its opposite (antithesis). When this approach is used in organizations, the assumptions underlying a proposal are identified, and then a conflicting counterproposal is presented, using different assumptions. Different teams are usually asked to represent each side. Advocates of each position present the merits of their arguments to help a decision maker make an informed decision. This method is used extensively in the legal systems of most countries.

Although the devil's advocacy and dialectical inquiry techniques are slightly different, research indicates that they have about the same effects.[27] Both methods help groups produce higher-quality decisions than the average produced by individual members. It is usually a good idea to rotate the role of critic so no one person or group develops a reputation of being negative and uncooperative. Furthermore, learning to challenge assumptions is good training for developing better analytical skills.

DECISION MAKING IN ORGANIZATIONS

The structure of an organization largely determines who is involved in the decision-making process and what kinds of decisions they will make. Whether an organization has a centralized or decentralized organizational structure depends on whether the decision making rests primarily with top-level managers or whether important decisions have been delegated to lower levels in the organization.

In analyzing organizational decision making, we need to understand what kinds of decisions need to be made, who should make them, and what organizational procedures are needed to gather information, evaluate alternatives, and implement a decision.

Types of Decisions

Many different kinds of decisions are made in organizations, concerning marketing, finance, human resources, and production. Policy decisions made by top administrators influence the entire organization. Other decisions are made lower in the organization and involve very few people, such as scheduling a committee meeting.

In analyzing the kinds of decisions made in organizations and the individuals who make them, a useful classification was suggested by Herbert Simon, who distinguished between programed and nonprogramed decisions.[28]

Programed Decisions. **Programed decisions** are repetitive and routine decisions for which a procedure can be developed. Programed decisions are possible when the problems are well structured and when people know how to achieve the desired consequences. These problems are generally rather simple, and their solutions are noncontroversial. College students observe dozens of programed decisions as they interact with the university staff. These decisions are made by lower-level staff members as students register for classes, buy a parking permit, purchase an activity card, request a copy of their grade transcript, apply for graduate school, and try to appeal a parking ticket.

Many complex business decisions have been reduced to programed decisions by the use of mathematical formulas, statistics, and operations research. These methods have helped decision makers identify the relevant information and process it in a way that produces a straightforward decision. In some situations, very complex conditions involving a large volume of information can be effectively reduced to a simple decision.

Nonprogramed Decisions. **Nonprogramed decisions** are novel and unstructured decisions. Established procedures cannot be created for handling certain problems, either because they have not occurred in exactly the same manner or because they are extremely complex and important. Nonprogramed decisions are not well structured, either because the current conditions are unclear, the methods of obtaining the desired results are unknown, or there is disagreement about what constitutes a desired result. An example of an unstructured problem that many students experience as they near graduation is deciding whether to attend graduate school and, if so, where. Deciding whether to go to graduate school is not a decision students make every day, and they cannot refer to rules of thumb or standard operating procedures to make this decision. In fact, most students don't even have a clear criterion to help them make the decision; is their goal to maximize their future earnings, acquire knowledge, secure a better job, achieve higher social status, or something else?

Nonprogramed decisions have typically been handled by general problem-solving processes involving intuition, judgment, and creativity. The group decision-making techniques were primarily developed to help make nonprogramed decisions. Because nonprogramed decisions are typically unique, complex, and without a clear criterion, they are usually surrounded by controversy and political maneuvering. An interesting irony is that while modern decision theory has created many decision rules to help with programed decisions, very little exists to help with nonprogramed decisions, and yet nonprogramed decisions have the greatest impact on the survival and effectiveness of an organization.

Ideally, top management should be primarily concerned with nonprogramed decisions, while first-level managers should be more concerned with programed decisions, as illustrated in Exhibit 14.6. Unfortunately, many top-level managers spend inordinate amounts of time on programed decisions that should be made much more rapidly and efficiently, leaving time for them to contemplate more significant nonprogramed decisions. Herbert Simon referred to an important principle of organizational decision making called Gresham's law of plan-

EXHIBIT 14.6 Types of Decisions Made at Different Levels of Management

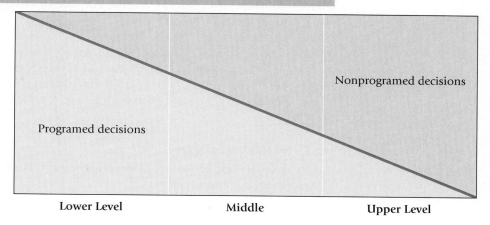

ning. This law suggests that programed activity tends to replace nonprogramed activity. If a leader's job involves both programed and nonprogramed decisions, programed decisions tend to be emphasized at the expense of nonprogramed decisions. Therefore, managers need to identify which decisions should be treated as programed decisions and develop a procedure for handling them quickly and efficiently.[29]

The variables that should determine whether a decision is programed or nonprogramed are the nature of the problem, the frequency with which it occurs, and the degree of certainty involved. To the extent that problems are routine, easily categorized, frequently observed, and exist within fairly stable conditions, they should be treated as programed decisions for which standard operating procedures or policies have been created. For example, deciding whether to contribute to the purchase of new band uniforms for the local high school or allowing an employee to have two weeks off with pay for military duty may be treated as nonprogramed decisions the first time they occur. But if organizations receive numerous requests for charitable contributions or personal leave time, policies should be created allowing members of the finance and personnel departments to make these decisions without referring them to upper-level managers. Organizational effectiveness suffers when top managers spend considerable time and effort on programed decisions. The unfortunate consequence of this practice is the neglect of long-range planning. Top managers cannot attend to the long-range issues of survival and change if they are overly preoccupied with day-to-day programed decisions.

Decision-Making Techniques

One of the major purposes of organizational communication systems is to provide relevant information for those making decisions. Reporting procedures are designed to help managers identify problems, evaluate the alternatives, and make effective decisions. Collecting and disseminating information, however, is not a free service. Making information available to managers requires time and effort, but the cost is justified if it helps them make more effective and timely decisions.

Three decision-making techniques that could be classified as either group or organizational techniques have been recommended to help organizations make effective decisions. These three techniques include brainstorming, the Delphi technique, and the nominal group technique.[30]

Brainstorming. As noted earlier, brainstorming was originally proposed as an ideal method for generating creative ideas in advertising. The purpose of the technique was to enhance creativity in group discussions by creating an environment that stimulated the generation of new ideas. The four basic rules of brainstorming include[31]

1. No ideas are criticized.
2. Freewheeling, or the free association of ideas, is encouraged. The more far-fetched an idea the better.
3. The quantity of ideas produced is stressed. The larger the number of ideas, the greater the probability of getting a winner.
4. "Hitchhiking" is encouraged; that is, participants are urged to improve on the ideas of others and combine ideas to form new and more complex solutions.

Although brainstorming looks like an effective method for generating creative ideas, empirical results have forced the proponents of brainstorming to be a bit more cautious in their enthusiasm. Studies on the effectiveness of brainstorming indicate that rather than aiding creative thinking, it actually inhibits it. Consequently, although brainstorming continues to be a rather popular method for generating new ideas, research suggests that other methods are superior.

The Delphi Technique. The **Delphi technique** was developed by employees at the Rand Corporation as a method of combining the information and insights of a group of people without suffering the adverse effects of face-to-face interaction.[32] The Delphi technique consists of the following steps:

1. After the problem has been clearly identified, several experts are identified and asked to participate in the project.
2. The basic problem is presented to each expert, but the experts are not brought together.
3. Each expert, independently and anonymously, answers the problem and provides comments, suggestions, and justifications for the proposed solution.
4. The experts' comments are compiled at a central location, summarized, and reproduced.
5. Each expert receives a summary of the group's answers along with comments and explanations.
6. Each expert evaluates and comments on the justifications provided by the other experts and revises his or her decision if necessary as a result of the comments of others.

7. The explanations and revised estimates of the experts are once again compiled at a centralized location, summarized, and redistributed. Several iterations of compiling and disseminating information may be used until a consensus is reached.

The Delphi technique has two major advantages over typical group decision making. First, since the individuals do not engage in face-to-face interaction, the group decision is not swayed by a dominant individual and is reasonably free of the biases created by individual personalities. By avoiding face-to-face interaction, they also avoid the problems of groupthink found in cohesive groups. The second major advantage of the Delphi technique is its ability to combine the expertise, experience, and wisdom of several people without incurring the cost in time and money by meeting at a common location. Rand Corporation, for example, has been able to have renowned scientists from around the world work on some of its problems using the Delphi technique, while a traditional group discussion would have been impossible because of prohibitive transportation costs and scheduling problems.

The disadvantages of the Delphi technique include time and motivation. Going through successive iterations of collecting information, submitting it to experts, and compiling their revised estimates requires a great deal of time. Without the pressures of face-to-face interaction, some experts tend to procrastinate in responding, and the long gaps of time between each iteration tend to dilute the experts' enthusiasm for participating.

Nominal Group Technique. The **nominal group technique** incorporates some of the features of brainstorming and the Delphi technique. As in brainstorming, individuals work together as a group on a problem, but, as with the Delphi technique, the process for generating alternatives and evaluating them is intended to protect individuals from unfettered group biases.[33] The procedure for conducting a nominal group technique consists of the following steps:

1. After the problem has been clearly identified, individual members are asked to develop their own solutions to the problem or task. This step is accomplished silently and independently and may even occur before the individuals are brought together in a group.

2. A recorded round-robin procedure is followed in which group members, one at a time, present one of their ideas to the group without discussion. The ideas are summarized and recorded on a blackboard or sheet of paper.

3. After all the initial ideas have been presented, the group discusses the ideas, clarifying and evaluating them.

4. The meeting concludes with a silent, independent vote in which each member ranks the solutions. The idea with the highest aggregate ranking is the group decision.

Since the nominal group technique provides a more structured form of eliciting ideas and evaluating them, larger groups can be used effectively with this technique. Although five or six individuals tends to be the maximum size for typical discussion groups, nominal groups of ten members have been found to be optimal when both productivity and satisfaction are considered.

A high-tech adaptation of the nominal group technique involves electronically compiling information. Group members are placed in front of a computer or key-pad connected to a computer. During the group discussion, the facilitator can ask group members to type their ideas into their computers, and the ideas can be anonymously shown on a screen. Each idea can be examined by asking the participants to evaluate it anonymously by responding to a series of multiple-choice questions on a keypad. Computer software programs can compile the group decisions instantaneously so all members know the feelings of the group without the biasing effect of strong personalities and powerful individuals.[34]

Studies have examined the effectiveness of the Delphi technique, nominal group technique, and traditional interaction groups. These studies have generally revealed that the nominal and Delphi groups generate significantly more unique ideas than traditional groups, and satisfaction tends to be highest using the nominal group technique than either of the other two.[35]

CREATIVITY AND INNOVATION

Every organization demands creativity and innovation to avoid becoming stagnant and obsolete. Change is a way of life, and organizations must respond to the demands of an ever-changing environment. Organizations that resist innovation and change are doomed to failure, regardless of how successful they are in the beginning. Every organization competes with every other organization for time, resources, talent, and markets. As the environment changes, organizations require new ideas and creative insights to adapt.

The following section describes the creative process and attempts to answer some important questions. What is creativity? What factors influence creative behavior? What can an organization do to facilitate creativity?

The Creative Process

Sometimes we make the mistake of thinking that creativity results from a sudden flash of insight that comes to a few highly intelligent people. This idea is wrong. Creative insights do not come just to highly intelligent people. The relationship between creativity and intelligence is at best very weak. A minimum threshold level of intelligence may be necessary for significant creative behavior; however, not all highly intelligent people are necessarily creative, nor are highly creative people always intelligent. Most studies have found a very small overlap between creativity and intelligence, which appears to be no greater than 10 percent.[36]

Another false assumption is that creativity belongs exclusively to only a few gifted individuals. Tests have been developed to measure individual creativity, and the results indicate that creativity is widely distributed throughout the general population. Although some individuals have more creative talent than others, apparently everyone has some degree of creativity regardless of age, race, or education.[37]

APPLYING ORGANIZATIONAL BEHAVIOR
RESEARCH

Organizational Size and Innovation

 A common idea suggests that small organizations are more innovative because they have more flexibility, it is easier for them to adapt and improve, and they have less difficulty accepting and implementing change. Although it sounds good, the research evidence fails to support this popular myth.

The results of a meta-analysis confirms that organizational size facilitates innovation. This meta-analysis examined the results of twenty empirical studies that reported data on the relationship between organizational size and innovation.

A meta-analysis is a statistical analysis of many research studies all focused on the same issue. It summarizes the results of numerous studies and also has the advantage of being able to identify moderating factors that help to explain why the relationships are stronger in some situations than others.

Some of the moderators examined in this study included the type of organization (manufacturing versus service, and profit versus nonprofit), how size was measured (number of employees versus other measures such as number of assets or financial resources), scope of innovation (whether there were just a few innovations or a large number of them), and stage of adoption (whether the innovations were only initiated or if they also had to be implemented). In this study, an innovation was defined as the adoption of any new idea or behavior by a company, including new products, services, policies, programs, processes, or systems.

Since some of the empirical studies reported multiple experiments, there were thirty-six correlations between organizational size and innovation. The average correlation was .32, indicating that larger companies are more innovative.

The moderator analysis found that size is more positively related to innovation

- In manufacturing than service companies
- In profit than nonprofit organizations
- When size is measured by something other than number of employees
- When the innovation involves a broad scope of innovations rather than just one or two changes
- When innovation consists of implementation and not just initiation

Many suggestions were offered to explain why larger organizations are more innovative. Larger organizations have greater knowledge resources, more differentiated structures, and higher professionalism. A survey of 4,000 innovations and innovative firms in Great Britain over four decades has shown that the average size of innovative firms is increasing, but the average size of divisions within those firms is decreasing. Therefore, it appears that larger organizations are creating the flexibility to be innovative by forming smaller specialized units that focus on innovation, but that have access to the knowledge and resources of a larger organization.

Sources: K. Pavitt, M. Robson, and J. Townsend, "Technological Accumulation, Diversification, and Organization in U.K. Companies," *Management Science*, vol. 35 (1989), 81–99; Fariborz Damanpour, "Organizational Size and Innovation," *Organization Studies*, vol. 13 (1992), pp. 375–402.

The most creative individuals appear to be people who are open to experience and personally motivated to engage in divergent thinking. People who are closed to new experiences or preoccupied with personal problems, however, do not engage in divergent thinking and are not creative.[38]

Sudden flashes of insight do not magically appear without any preparation or contemplation. The creative process involves the cognitive manipulation of elements already known to the individual. This cognitive manipulation involves the nonverbal association of symbols in ways that produce unique combinations.

Although the creative process appears somewhat mystical and mysterious, it can be divided into four phases. These four phases are preparation, incubation, insight, and verification.[39]

Preparation. Creative insights do not simply flash unexpectedly like bolts of lightning. Instead, creativity is usually preceded by much hard work in collecting information and studying the situation. Many creative insights are a combination of two or more large bodies of information that become associated in new and unique ways. Unless individuals have mastered these bodies of knowledge thoroughly, they are not prepared to combine them in new and insightful ways. Creativity requires a high degree of motivation because the creative insight follows the preparation, and the preparation involves an enormous amount of effort and dedication.

Incubation. The period of incubation is described as a period of relaxation or withdrawal from the intense preparation period. This period has sometimes been considered a period of unconscious thinking, where the individual is actually thinking without being aware of it. Unfortunately, if it is unconscious, we cannot know for sure what is happening, and for all we know, no thinking whatsoever may be occurring. The best explanation of what happens during the incubation period is that the individual takes time to step back from the trees to examine the forest in order to gain a clearer perspective. After being so intensely immersed in technical details during the preparation period, the individual now stands back and asks what it all means, how it can be useful, and if it can be reorganized.

Insight. Insight occurs when individuals begin to discover new associations and patterns that provide a useful solution to a problem. This phase has also been called the *hypothesis formation phase*. Occasionally insight comes as a sudden flash of inspiration in which the solution to the problem is obvious. More frequently, however, the creative insight comes from a gradual awareness that stems from a solution that solves part of the problem, and this partial solution motivates the individual to pursue the problem until it is completely solved. This process may start as a small idea, stimulated by a new association or symbolic representation, that is followed by a gradual unfolding of deeper meanings and applications.

Verification. Verification involves testing, refining, demonstrating, and communicating the creative ideas following the insight period. Additional insight frequently occurs during verification as the initial insight is tested for accuracy and usefulness and is translated into a form that allows it to be shared with others. Verification ought to occur immediately after the insight has been obtained, because valuable ideas are often lost by even a short time delay.

Although these four phases are described as a sequential process of creative behavior, the interaction between the phases should not be forgotten. Partial insights frequently occur during the preparation phase as new ideas are stimulated and possible associations are conceived. Insights are further refined during the verification or testing as the individual realizes that alterations and revisions are necessary. Verification and testing may also occur during the preparation period as new associations and combinations are considered.

Stimulating Creativity

Organizations need people who can generate creative ideas and make innovative contributions. Efforts to increase creativity in organizations tend to focus on three methods: selection, training, and organizational redesign. As a selection problem, organizations try to select individuals who have high creative potential. Several tests of creativity have been developed, and these tests can be used as a selection instrument to identify individuals possessing high creativity.[40] Organizations can provide people with creativity training to help them learn how to make more creative contributions to the organization. Studies have shown that creativity training increases the number of creative suggestions offered by employees.[41] The organization itself can be redesigned to facilitate the creative process. Like any other desired behavior, creativity must be identified, actively encouraged, recognized, rewarded, and used.[42] If the organization ignores, belittles, or punishes creative expression, then creative ability will not be used. The organization can either inhibit or facilitate creativity. The characteristics of a creative organization are listed in Exhibit 14.7.

Factors Inhibiting Creativity. Creativity is inhibited by defensiveness, fear, and anxiety. Therefore, organizations that have an oppressive climate, punitive supervision, and excessive criticism of mistakes tend to inhibit creativity.

EXHIBIT 14.7   Characteristics of a Creative Organization

Communication channels are open, and people feel free to discuss ideas.

Outside contacts are encouraged.

Staffing includes heterogeneous, unusual types of people.

Nonspecialists are included in task forces.

Eccentricity is allowed.

Ideas are evaluated on merit, not on the status of the originator.

Promotion and selection are based on merit.

The organization invests in basic research with flexible long-range planning.

Experiments with new ideas rather than prejudging on "rational" grounds; everything gets a chance.

Organizational structure is decentralized and diversified.

There is some administrative slack with sufficient time and resources to absorb errors.

There is a norm of risk taking that tolerates and expects people to take chances.

People are free to pursue problems and choose what to do.

The organization is pursuing its distinctive competence and striving to be original and unique.

Source: Adapted from Morris L. Stein, "Creativity, Groups, and Management," in Richard A. Guzzo (ed.), *Improving Group Decision Making in Organizations* (New York: Academic Press, 1982), p. 143; and G. Steiner (ed.), *The Creative Organization* (Chicago: University of Chicago Press, 1965), pp. 16–17.

Creativity can also be inhibited by an extremely unstable or rigid organizational climate. In extremely unstable organizations, employees may be so confused by frequent job changes and ambiguity that they do not have adequate time for preparation and incubation of insightful ideas. Likewise, if the organization is extremely rigid because of highly formalized rules, policies, and procedures, employees may be discouraged or even prevented from studying the problems or generating new alternatives. The formal rules may prohibit people from experimenting with new ideas, discussing new alternatives, or thinking about new methods. One problem of a highly centralized organization is its effect on inhibiting creativity, since lower-level members do not have access to the needed information to generate creative insights.

Another factor contributing to a decline in creativity is inadequate time. Preparation and incubation periods take time; consequently, insights will not occur if short-term emergencies continually destroy opportunities for thinking and planning.

Factors Facilitating Creativity. Organizations desiring to stimulate creative ideas can do so by following an appropriate strategy. However, the results of research into the effects of money and other extrinsic rewards on creativity are not entirely consistent. Several laboratory studies of grade school and college students have found that those who were offered money or prizes produced less creative paintings and invented fewer stories than students who were motivated by the intrinsic satisfaction of being creative. The results suggested that extrinsic rewards diverted the students' concentration away from creative activities and centered their thinking on the rewards.[43]

The negative effects of extrinsic rewards on creativity, however, are not observed in organizations. Creative behavior appears to be positively influenced by both the intrinsic and extrinsic rewards available for it. Significant monetary rewards, for example, serve to increase the number of creative suggestions made by employees in suggestion boxes. Greater creativity can be elicited even by simple acts of recognition such as inviting the employee to lunch with the president, bestowing an employee-of-the-month award, or having the employee's picture placed in the company newsletter. On the other hand, if creativity is ignored by managers who show no interest in it or if it is punished by co-workers who make belittling comments, creativity tends to diminish.

Another organizational strategy for increasing creativity is to set appropriate goals and deadlines. A study that examined the effects of creativity goals found that the highest levels of creativity occurred when students were assigned difficult goals rather than no goals.[44] Time constraints and deadlines sometimes produce a flurry of creative ideas. When people do not have deadlines, they tend to postpone action and delay serious consideration until the deadline approaches. As long as people do not feel pressed to solve a problem, they tend to either ignore it or fill their time with additional preparation. Time constraints help people move from the preparation phase to the insight phase.

Occasionally, tight deadlines force people to make rash decisions because they were not given enough time. Managers may get better ideas by discarding the first solution and asking for a second solution with an extended deadline. Evidence suggests that the second solution will be superior to the first solution.

While an oppressive organizational climate inhibits creative ideas, a stimulating and supportive organizational climate can facilitate creativity by providing the flexibility and autonomy needed to explore ideas and test them. Knowing that new ideas are valued and will be tried is a great stimulus to employees to express their ideas. Creativity can also be stimulated by forming heterogeneous work teams. Work groups should be composed of people from diverse backgrounds and specialties, since this diversity allows people to identify new combinations and associations of ideas that emerge from the group interaction. The organization also needs to provide opportunities for the members to meet and share ideas. Conferences, luncheons, and informal gatherings allow members to interact, explore new discoveries, and share information.

SUMMARY

1. The decision-making process consists of establishing goals and objectives, identifying the problem, developing and evaluating alternatives, choosing an alternative, implementing the solution, and evaluating its results. Each of these steps is involved in the decision-making process, although the actual process is generally more abbreviated and less systematic.

2. In evaluating and choosing alternatives, decisions are made under conditions of certainty, uncertainty, or risk. In conditions of certainty and risk, where the outcomes are either known or can be estimated, decision makers can use a variety of mathematical and statistical tools to help make decisions. In conditions of uncertainty, however, decision makers must make decisions based on intuition or inspiration.

3. Although economic models of decision making assume that people are thoroughly informed and rational, these assumptions are not correct. Individuals are subject to bounded rationality because they do not have perfect information about the problem and they are aware of only a limited number of alternatives.

4. Rather than trying to maximize their outcomes by investigating all alternatives and selecting the optimal one, most decision makers are content to "satisfice"; that is, to choose the first solution that seems minimally acceptable.

5. Our ability to think rationally is limited by several psychological aspects that influence our thought processes. Some of the major variables

influencing our ability to think include our position in society; outside reference groups; our tendency to project our own attitudes and values onto others; the tendency to use global or undifferentiated thinking; the tendency to use dichotomized thinking; cognitive nearsightedness, which emphasizes short-term urgent problems; and oversimplified explanations of causation.

6. Decision making is influenced by several personality variables. Four of the most important personality characteristics influencing the way decisions are made are ideology versus power orientation, emotionality versus objectivity, creativity versus common sense, and action orientation versus contemplation.

7. Although some of the most important organizational decisions are made by groups, groups are not necessarily superior to individuals in making decisions. Group decisions tend to be superior to individual decisions when the problems have multiple parts, allowing for a division of labor among the group members; when group members have complementary skills and information; or when the problem involves estimation or forecasting.

8. Individual decision making tends to be superior to group decision making when the problem requires a sequence of stages, when the problem is not easily divided into separate parts, or when the problem involves the development of creative ideas.

9. Although creativity in brainstorming sessions seems to be inhibited by the presence of other group members, group decisions are an effective way to obtain greater levels of commitment and acceptance.

10. Group decision making frequently produces a risky-shift phenomenon in which the group decision is riskier than the individual decisions of each member. In some situations, however, groups may produce conservative shifts, depending on the diffusion of responsibility, the polarization of individual attitudes, and the emergence of dominant social values.

11. Cohesive decision-making groups are often the victims of groupthink, so that their group decisions are flawed and distorted because of pressures within the group.

12. Programed decisions are routine decisions for which procedures should be developed, while nonprogramed decisions are made in response to unstructured problems requiring considerable insight and thoughtfulness. Programed decisions should be made at lower levels in the organization based on approved policies or decision-making routines, leaving top managers free to spend their time making nonprogramed decisions.

13. Three methods used by organizations for making decisions include brainstorming, the Delphi technique, and the nominal group technique. Although brainstorming is not a particularly effective method of generating creative ideas, evidence demonstrates that the Delphi technique and the nominal group technique are effective methods for collecting information from many individuals and analyzing it objectively.

14. Creativity is an ability that is widely dispersed throughout society and is not directly related to intelligence. Four stages are involved in the creative process: preparation, incubation, insight, and verification.

15. Various organizational conditions tend to either inhibit or facilitate creativity. Punitive supervision, defensiveness, fear, and excessive criticism tend to inhibit creativity. In contrast, rewards, a stimulating and supportive organizational climate, heterogeneous work groups, and opportunities for employees to interact tend to facilitate creativity.

DISCUSSION QUESTIONS

1. How well does the decision-making process outlined in the chapter correspond with the actual way you make decisions? Identify a major decision you have made in the past few months, and look for each of the decision-making steps in your behavior.

2. In decision making, the difference between conditions of uncertainty and conditions of risk is the willingness of the decision maker to assign a probability to the outcomes. It could be argued that all decision making involves an element of risk and, therefore, every decision maker ought to be willing to assign a probability estimate. Do you agree that decision makers should be forced to assign probability estimates and thereby change conditions of uncertainty into conditions of risk?

3. What is bounded rationality? Provide two or three illustrations from your own experience to demonstrate the concept of bounded rationality.

4. Since decision makers do not really maximize their outcomes, it could be argued that business schools should teach students to satisfice rather than maximize. Do you agree with this position?

5. Why is group decision making becoming such a popular method of making decisions? When are group decisions expected to be superior to individual decisions, and when are they expected to be inferior?

6. Explain whether you would expect a conservative or a risky shift, and why, in the following groups: (a) a parole board deciding whether or not to release a convict, (b) a jury deciding whether or not to impose the death penalty on a convicted murderer, (c) a hospital review board discussing the approval of an artificial heart, and (d) an army unit deciding whether to continue negotiating with a terrorist group or to storm their positions.

7. Suppose you were chairing a strategic planning committee for an organization and wanted to avoid the pitfalls of groupthink. What precautions would you take?

8. Explain the differences between programed and nonprogramed decisions, and provide some illustrations of both from your own life. When should nonprogramed decisions become programed decisions?

9. Explain the similarities and differences between the Delphi technique and the nominal group technique. What are the advantages and disadvantages of each, and when would you use them?

10. We may say that necessity is the mother of invention, and yet we usually think creativity comes by sudden flashes of insight. Why do problems contribute to creativity? Why is creativity enhanced by problems, deadlines, and rewards? What do these factors have to do with our ability to think?

11. An example of global, dichotomous thinking is the popular myth that all bureaucracies are large, impersonal, inefficient, bungling organizations. Describe a more differentiated and carefully analyzed view of a bureaucracy.

12. What kinds of organizational problems are caused by leaders who continually look for creative solutions to problems? What problems are caused by those who rely on commonsense solutions?

GLOSSARY

bounded rationality The idea that there are limits to our capacity to think rationally because of our inability to gather infinite information and process it accurately. Therefore, there are cognitive limits to our rationality based on limits in our ability to think, reason, and process information.

brainstorming A group technique for generating creative ideas in a freewheeling session in which ideas are proposed without being evaluated or criticized.

certainty Decision making occurs under conditions of certainty when the decision maker knows the outcomes of each decision.

decision theory A field of knowledge that encompasses the systematic analysis of the decision-making process.

Delphi technique A method of group decision making in which information is individually gathered from the group members, summarized, and then redistributed to the group members to see if any of them would like to change their evaluations. Group members are not brought together in a face-to-face interaction.

groupthink The tendency for a highly cohesive group to agree with what appears to be a unanimous group consensus without challenging the consensus or realizing that it may not represent the group.

maximizing The unrealistic notion that decision makers carefully consider all possible alternatives and select the one that maximizes their rewards.

muddling through An uncertain decision-making procedure in which individuals try to make decisions that move them gradually toward a general goal rather than following a clearly defined decision-making process.

nominal group technique A group decision-making method that structures the way group members propose solutions, discuss them, and select an alternative.

nonprogramed decisions Unstructured decisions in response to new or unique problems requiring decision makers to go carefully through the decision-making process in order to reach a solution.

programed decisions Highly structured decisions that can be made by following established rules of thumb or procedures created for handling them.

risk Decision making under conditions of risk occurs when the decision maker is willing to assign a probability estimate to the likely outcome of each alternative.

risky-shift phenomenon A phenomenon that occurs when a group discussion causes a group to choose a more risky alterative than the group members would have been willing to accept on their own.

satisficing Rather than evaluating every alternative and selecting the optimal one, decision makers look until they find the first satisfactory alternative that achieves a minimum level of outcome.

suboptimizing Making decisions that do not provide an optimal solution for everyone simultaneously. While a decision may be optimal according to one criterion, it is suboptimal or inferior according to other criteria.

uncertainty Decision making occurs in conditions of uncertainty when the decision maker does not know the outcomes of a decision and is not willing to assign a probability estimate.

NOTES

1. C. E. Lindblom, "The Science of 'Muddling Through,' " *Public Administration Review*, vol. 19 (1959), pp. 78–88.

2. Howard Garland, "Throwing Good Money After Bad: The Effect of Sunk Costs on the Decision to Escalate Commitment to an On-Going Project," *Journal of Applied Psychology*, vol. 75 (1990), pp. 728–731.

3. Glen Whyte, "Diffusion of Responsibility: Effects on the Escalation Tendency," *Journal of Applied Psychology*, vol. 76 (1991), pp. 408–415.

4. James G. March and Herbert A. Simon, *Organizations* (New York: Wiley, 1959); Herbert A. Simon, *Behavioral Economics and Business Organization*, vol. 2 (Cambridge, Mass.: MIT Press, 1982).

5. This section is based largely on Daniel Katz and Robert L. Kahn, *The Social Psychology of Organizations*, 2nd ed. (New York: Wiley, 1978), chap. 15.

6. David J. Cherrington, *The Work Ethic: Working Values and Values That Work* (New York: AMACOM Publishing, 1980), chap. 7.

7. Based on Katz and Kahn, op. cit.

8. Jon Hartwick, Blair H. Sheppard, and James H. Davis, "Group Remembering: Research and Implications," in Richard A. Guzzo (ed.), *Improving Group Decision Making in Organizations* (New York: Academic Press, 1982), pp. 40–72; Janet A. Sniezek and Rebecca A. Henry, "Accuracy and Confidence in Group Judgment," *Organizational Behavior and Human Decision Processes*, vol. 43 (February 1989), pp. 1–28.

9. Harold H. Kelley and John W. Thibaut, "Group Problem Solving," in Gardner Lindsey and Eliot Aronson (ed.), *Handbook of Social Psychology*, 2nd ed. (Reading, Mass.: Addison-Wesley, 1969), chap. 29.

10. Joseph S. Fiorelli, "Power in Work Groups: Team Members' Perspectives," *Human Relations*, vol. 41 (January 1988), pp. 1–12.

11. Kelley and Thibaut, op. cit.

12. Larry K. Michaelson, Warren E. Watson, and Robert H. Black, "A Realistic Test of Individual Versus Group Consensus Decision Making," *Journal of Applied Psychology*, vol. 74 (1989), pp. 834–839; Warren Watson, Larry K. Michaelson, and Walt Sharp, "Member Competence, Group Interaction, and Group Decision Making: A Longitudinal Study," *Journal of Applied Psychology*, vol. 76 (1991), pp. 803–809.

13. Donald W. Taylor, Paul C. Berry, and Clifford H. Block, "Does Group Participation When Using Brainstorming Facilitate or Inhibit Creative Thinking?" *Administrative Science Quarterly*, vol. 3 (1958), pp. 23–47; Terry Connolly, Leonard M. Jessup, and Joseph S. Valacich, "Effects of Anonymity and Evaluative Tone on Idea Generation in Computer-Mediated Groups," *Management Science*, vol. 36 (June 1990), pp. 689–703.

14. Alex F. Osborn, *Applied Imagination* (New York: Scribners, 1957).

15. John P. Campbell, Marvin D. Dunnette, and Kay Jaastad, "The Effect of Group Participation on Brainstorming Effectiveness for Two Industrial Samples," *Journal of Applied Psychology*, vol. 47 (1963), pp. 30–37.

16. T. J. Bouchard. "Whatever Happened to Brainstorming?" *Journal of Creative Behavior*, vol. 5, no. 3 (1971), pp. 182–189.

17. Kurt Lewin, "Group Decision and Social Change," in E. E. Maccoby, T. M. Newcomb, and E. C. Hartley (eds.), *Readings in Social Psychology*, 3rd ed. (New York: Holt, Rinehart and Winston, 1958).

18. Betty W. Bond, "The Group-Discussion-Decision Approach: An Appraisal of Its Use in Health Education," *Dissertation Abstracts*, vol. 16 (1956), pp. 903–904.

19. Hartwick, Sheppard, and Davis, op. cit.

20. J. A. F. Stoner, "A Comparison of Individual and Group Decisions Involving Risk" (Master's thesis, MIT, Sloan School of Industrial Management, 1961); J. A. F. Stoner, "Risky and Cautious Shifts in Group Decisions: The Influence of Widely Held Values," *Journal of Experimental Social Psychology*, vol. 4 (1968), pp. 442–459.

21. D. G. Marquis and H. Joseph Reitz, "Effects of Uncertainty on Risk Taking in Individual and Group Decisions," *Behavioral Science*, vol. 4 (1969), pp. 181–188.

22. Irving L. Janis, *Victims of Groupthink* (Boston: Houghton Mifflin, 1972).

23. Gregory Moorhead, Richard Ference, and Chris P. Neck, "Group Decision Fiascoes Continue: Space Shuttle Challenger and a Revised Groupthink Framework," *Human Relations*, vol. 44 (1991), pp. 539–550; Glen Whyte, "Groupthink Reconsidered," *Academy of Management Journal*, vol. 14 (January 1989), pp. 41–56.

24. Ibid., Irving L. Janis, "Sources of Error in Strategic Decision Making," in Johannes M. Pennings and Associates, *Organizational Strategy and Change* (San Francisco: Jossey-Bass, 1985), pp. 157–197.

25. Jerry B. Harvey, Rosabeth Moss Kanter, and Arthur Elliott Carlisle, "The Abilene Paradox: The Management of Agreement," *Organizational Dynamics*, vol. 17 (Summer 1988), pp. 16–43; Daphne Gottlieb Taras, "Breaking the Silence: Differentiating Crisis of Agreement," *Public Administration Quarterly*, vol. 14 (Winter 1991), pp. 401–418.

26. Michael Kettelhut, "Avoiding Group-Induced Errors in Systems Development," *Journal of Systems Management*, vol. 42 (March 1991), pp. 13–70; Sami M. Abbasi and Kenneth W. Hollman, "Dissent: An Important but Neglected Factor in Decision Making," *Management Decision*, vol. 29, no. 8 (1991), pp. 7–11.

27. David M. Schweiger and William R. Sandberg, "The Utilization of Individual Capabilities in Group Approaches to Strategic Decision Making," *Strategic Management Journal*, vol. 10 (January–February 1989), pp. 31–43; Charles Schwenk, "A Meta-Analysis on the Comparative Effectiveness of Devil's Advocacy and Dialectical Inquiry," *Strategic Management Journal*, vol. 10 (May–June 1989), pp. 303–306.

28. Herbert A. Simon, *The New Science of Management Decision* (New York: Harper & Row, 1960), p. 5.

29. David J. Hickson, "Decision-making at the Top of Organizations," *Annual Review of Sociology*, vol. 13 (1987), pp. 165–192.

30. Douglas R. Anderson, "Increased Productivity Via Group Decision Making," *Supervision*, vol. 51 (September 1990), pp. 6–10.

31. Osborn, op. cit.

32. Andre L. Delbecq, Andrew H. Van de Ven, and David H. Gustafson, *Group Techniques for Program Planning: A Guide to Nominal Group and Delphi Processes* (Glenview, Ill.: Scott, Foresman, 1975).

33. Ibid.

34. Michael Finley, "Welcome to the Electronic Meeting," *Training*, vol. 28 (July 1991), pp. 28–32.

35. N. C. Dalkey and Olaf Helmer, "An Experimental Application of the Delphi Method to the Use of Experts," *Management Science*, vol. 9 (1963), pp. 458–467; A. H. Van de Ven and Andre L. Delbecq, "The Effectiveness of Nominal, Delphi, and Interacting Group Decision Making Processes," *Academy of Management Journal*, vol. 17 (1974), pp. 605–632.

36. R. J. Sternberg, "Implicit Theories of Intelligence, Creativity, and Wisdom," *Journal of Personality and Social Psychology*, vol. 49 (1985), pp. 607–627; W. C. Ward, Nathan Kogan, and Ethel Pankove, "Incentive Effects in Children's Creativity," *Child Development*, vol. 43 (June 1972), pp. 669–676.

37. Anne Anastasi and C. E. Schaefer, "Note on the Concepts of Creativity and Intelligence," *Journal of Creative Behavior*, vol. 5 (2nd quarter 1971), pp. 113–116.

38. Robert R. McCrae, "Creativity, Divergent Thinking, and Openness to Experience," *Journal of Personality and Social Psychology*, vol. 52 (1987), pp. 1258–1265.

39. See H. Joseph Reitz, *Behavior in Organizations*, rev. ed. (Homewood, Ill.: Irwin, 1981), chap. 7; Morris I. Stein, "Creativity, Groups, and Management," in Richard A. Guzzo (ed.), *Improving Group Decision Making in Organizations* (New York: Academic Press, 1982), pp. 127–157, especially p. 131.

40. See T. M. Amabile, "Social Psychology of Creativity: A Consensual Assessment Technique," *Journal of Personality and Social Psychology*, vol. 43 (1982), pp. 997–1013; F. Barron, *Creative Person and Creative Process* (New York: Holt, Rinehart and Winston, 1969).

41. D. M. Harrington, "Effects of Explicit Instructions to 'Be Creative' on the Psychological Meaning of Divergent Thinking Test Scores," *Journal of Personality*, vol. 43 (1975), pp. 434–453; A. N. Katz and J. R. Poag, "Sex Differences in Instructions to 'Be Creative' on Divergent and Nondivergent Test Scores," *Journal of Personality*, vol. 47 (1979), pp. 518–530; Marc Hequet, "Creativity Training Gets Creative," *Training*, vol. 29 (February 1992), pp. 41–46; Paul C. Michell, "Creativity Training: Developing the Agency–Client Creative Interface," *European Journal of Marketing*, vol. 21, no. 7 (1987), pp. 44–56.

42. G. Steiner (ed.), *The Creative Organization* (Chicago: University of Chicago Press, 1965); John W. Lewis, III, "Breaking the Quality Circle," *Personnel Administrator*, vol. 34 (October 1988), pp. 72–79; James Braham, "Creativity: Eureka!" *Machine Design*, vol. 64 (February 6, 1992), pp. 32–36.

43. Teresa M. Amabile, "Motivation and Creativity: Effects of Motivational Orientation on Creative Writers," *Journal of Personality and Social Psychology*, vol. 48 (1985), pp. 393–399; Alfie Kohn, "Art for Art's Sake," *Psychology Today*, 21 (September 1987), pp. 52–57.

44. Christina E. Shalley, "Effects of Productivity Goals, Creativity Goals, and Personal Discretion on Individual Creativity," *Journal of Applied Psychology*, vol. 76 (1991), pp. 179–185.

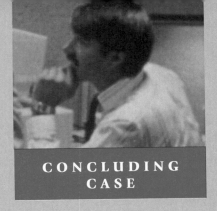

CONCLUDING CASE

HOVEY AND BEARD COMPANY

Note: This is a segmented case. Your instructor may wish to have you discuss each part of the case before reading subsequent parts.

PART I

The Hovey and Beard Company manufactured wooden toys of various kinds: wooden animals, pull toys, and the like. One part of the manufacturing process involved spraying paint on the partially assembled toys. The operation was staffed entirely by women.

The toys were cut, sanded, and partially assembled in the wood room. They were dipped into shellac and then painted. The toys were predominantly two-colored; a few were made in more than two colors. Each color required an additional trip through the paint room.

For a number of years, production of these toys had been entirely handwork. However, to meet tremendously increased demand, the painting operation had recently been re-engineered so that the eight women who did the painting sat in a line by an endless chain of hooks. These hooks were in continuous motion, going past the line of women and into a long horizontal oven. Each woman sat at her own painting booth, designed to carry away fumes and to backstop excess paint. The woman would take a toy from the tray beside her, position it in a jig inside the painting cubicle, spray on the color according to a pattern, then release the toy and hang it on the hook passing by. The rate at which the hooks moved had been calculated by the engineers so that each woman, when fully trained, would be able to hang a painted toy on each hook before it passed beyond her reach.

The women working in the paint room were on a group bonus plan. Since the operation was new to them, they were receiving a learning bonus that decreased by regular amounts each month. The learning bonus was scheduled to vanish in six months, by which time it was expected that they would be on their own—that is, able to meet the standard and to earn a group bonus when they exceeded it.

Question

Are there any obvious problems here? Do the work flow and job design seem to be reasonable?

PART II

By the second month of the training period, trouble had developed. The women learned more slowly than had been anticipated, and it began to look as though their production would stabilize far below what was planned. Many of the hooks were going by empty. The women complained that they were going by too fast and that the time study expert had set the rates wrong. A few women quit and had to be replaced, which further aggravated the learning problem. The team spirit that the management had expected to develop automatically through the group bonus was not in evidence except as an expression of what the engineers called "resistance." One woman whom the group regarded as its leader (and the management regarded as the ringleader) was outspoken in making the various complaints of the group to the foreman: the job was a messy one, the hooks moved too fast, the incentive pay was not being correctly calculated, and it was too hot working so close to the drying oven.

Question

What are the specific issues the company had overlooked? What approach should the company use to examine this problem? What alternatives should be considered, and how good are they?

PART III

A consultant who was brought into the picture worked entirely with and through the foreman. After many conversations with him, the foreman felt that the first step should be to get the women together for a general discussion of the working conditions. He took this step with some hesitation, but he took it on his own volition.

The first meeting, held immediately after the shift was over at 4 in the afternoon, was attended by all eight women. They voiced the same complaints again: the hooks went by too fast, the job was too dirty, the room was hot and poorly ventilated. For some reason, it was this last item that they complained of most. The foreman promised to discuss the problem of ventilation and temperature with the engineers, and he scheduled a second meeting to report back to the women. In the next few days the foreman had several talks with the engineers. They and the superintendent felt that this was in reality a trumped-up complaint and that the expense of any effective corrective measure would be prohibitively high.

The foreman came to the second meeting with some apprehension. The women, however, did not mind because they had a proposal of their own to make. They felt that if several large fans could circulate the air around their feet they would be much more comfortable. After some discussion, the foreman agreed that the idea might be tried out. The foreman and the consultant discussed the question of the fans with the superintendent, and three large propeller-type fans were purchased.

Question

How good is this solution? Does it really address the actual problem?

PART IV

The fans were brought in. The women were jubilant. For several days, the fans were moved about in various positions until they were placed to the satisfaction of the group. The women seemed completely satisfied with the results, and relations between them and the foreman improved visibly.

The foreman, after this encouraging episode, decided that further meetings might also be profitable. He asked the women if they would like to meet and discuss other aspects of the work situation. The women were eager to do this. The meeting was held, and the discussion quickly centered on the speed of the hooks. The women maintained that the time-study expert had set them at an unreasonably fast speed and that they would never be able to fill enough of them to earn a bonus.

The turning point of the discussion came when the group's leader frankly explained that the point wasn't that they couldn't work fast enough to keep up with the hooks, but that they couldn't work at that pace all day long. The foreman explored the point. The women were unanimous in their opinion that they could keep up with the belt for short periods if they wanted to, but they didn't want to because if they showed they could do this for short periods, they would be expected to do it all day long. The meeting ended with an unprecedented request: "Let us adjust the speed of the belt and make it go faster or slower depending on how we feel." The foreman agreed to discuss this with the superintendent and the engineers.

The reaction of the engineers to the suggestion was negative. However, after several meetings, it was granted that there was some latitude within which variations in the speed of the hooks would not affect the finished product. After considerable argument with the engineers, it was agreed to try out the women's idea.

With misgivings, the foreman had a control with a dial marked "low, medium, fast" installed at the booth of the group leader; she could now adjust the speed of the belt anywhere between the lower and upper limits that the engineers had set.

Question

How good is this solution? Does it address the real problem? What outcome would you predict?

PART V

The women were delighted, and they spent many lunch hours deciding how the speed of the belt should be varied from hour to hour throughout the day. Within a week the pattern had settled down to one in which the first half hour of the shift was run on what the group called medium speed (a dial setting slightly above the point marked "medium"). The next two and one-half hours were run at high speed; the half hour before lunch and the half hour after lunch were run at low speed. The rest of the afternoon was run at high speed with the exception of the last 45 minutes of the shift, which was run at medium.

Considering the women's reports of satisfaction and ease in their work, it is interesting to note that the constant speed at which the engineers had originally set the belt was slightly below medium on the control dial. The average speed at which the women were running the belt was on the high side of the dial. Few, if any, empty hooks entered the oven, and inspection showed no increase of rejects from the paint room.

Production increased, and within three weeks (some two months before the scheduled ending of the learning bonus) the women were operating at 30 to 50 percent above the level that had been expected under the original arrangement. They were collecting their base pay, a considerable piece-rate bonus, and the learning bonus—which, it will be remembered, had been set to decrease with time and not as a function of current productivity. The women were earning more now than many skilled workers in other parts of the plant.

Question

Is the problem solved, and is this incident resolved?

PART VI

Skilled workers were envious of the women's high incentive pay. Management was besieged by demands that this inequity be resolved. With growing irritation between superintendent and foreman, engineers and foreman, superintendent and engineers, the situation came to a head when the superintendent revoked the learning bonus and returned the painting operation to its original status. The hooks moved again at their constant, time study-designated speed; production dropped again; and within a month, all but two of the eight women had quit. The foreman himself stayed on several months but, feeling aggrieved, then left for another job.

Question

What went wrong? What variables and relationships were overlooked?

Source: Abridgement of "Group Dynamics and Intergroup Relations" by George Strauss and Alex Bauelas from *Money and Motivation* by William Foote Whyte. Copyright 1955 by Harper & Row Publishers Inc. Copyright © renewed 1983 by William Foote Whyte. Reprinted by permission of HarperCollins Publishers Inc.

INDIVIDUAL VERSUS GROUP DECISION MAKING

Purpose. The purpose of this exercise is to identify the times when individuals are superior at making decisions and when groups are superior.

Activity. For this exercise the class should be divided into groups of three to five individuals. On some of the problems, the groups should work as *interacting* groups sharing ideas and feedback. On other problems, however, the group should be a *nominal* group; that is, a group in name only, and the members should work individually without any interaction. The decision regarding which groups will be nominal groups and which groups will be interacting groups for the various problems should be decided by the instructor for the class as a whole.

PROBLEM 1   *Collecting and Synthesizing Factual Information*

On a blank sheet of paper, draw a map of the United States, showing each of the forty-eight contiguous states. Label each state and identify its capital city.

PROBLEM 2   *Generating Creative Ideas*

Suppose you were Robinson Crusoe and one day you saw a Coke bottle float ashore. In twenty minutes, list the possible uses that could be made of the Coke bottle, regardless of how outlandish they are.

PROBLEM 3   *Solving Problems.*

Solve the following problems:

1. Suppose you were given nine coins, identical in every respect, except that one is counterfeit and slightly heavier than the genuine coins. Using only a sensitive balance scale, one with two pans and no weights, how would you identify the counterfeit coin by making only two weighings?

2. The Big Chew Bubble Gum Company has ten bubble gum machines that normally produce gum balls weighing 1 ounce each. However, one of the ten machines is defective and makes hollow gum balls weighing only 1/2 ounce. Using a scale, how could you find the defective machine in only one weighing? An unlimited number of gum balls is available from each machine.

3. Two friends had an eight-quart jug of cider that they wanted to share equally. They had two empty jars, a five-quart jar and a three-quart jar. They were able to divide the cider equally without spilling a drop. How were they able to do this?

4. Sam and Jim, who live two and a half miles apart, decide to meet for a visit. Jim walks two miles per hour, Sam walks three miles per hour, and Sam has a pet swallow that flies twenty-six miles per hour. When the two men begin walking toward each other, Sam's swallow flies to meet Jim and then returns immediately to Sam and continues to fly back and forth between the two men until they meet. Assuming the swallow does not lose any time in reversing directions, how far does the swallow fly?

Leadership

CHAPTER OUTLINE

LEARNING OBJECTIVES

After studying this chapter, you should be able to

1. Explain the differences between management and leadership, and identify some major personal traits associated with leadership.

2. Explain the limitations of using personal traits to understand leadership.

3. Identify and describe the two major leadership behaviors that occur within a group.

4. Identify some of the major situational factors influencing leadership, and explain how they influence group performance.

5. List and describe the major variables that determine the appropriate leadership style.

6. Explain some of the strategies for improving leadership effectiveness.

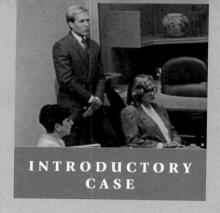

JOHN F. WELCH, JR.

In 1981, at age 45, John Francis Welch, Jr., became the youngest executive to take the reins of General Electric Company, a U.S. institution founded by Thomas Edison in 1878. Although the company was profitable under his predecessor, Welch believed the company was not poised to compete aggressively in an increasingly competitive international economy, and he began a drastic restructuring program.

During his first six years, Welch closed at least thirty factories and eliminated over 100,000 jobs, reducing GE's workforce by a fourth. His critics described him as one of the world's most ruthless managers and nicknamed him "Neutron Jack" (he "leaves the factories standing, but wipes out the people in them"). An angered union official said the company was suffering from a disease called Welchitis—caused by corporate greed, arrogance, and contempt for its employees. Some of his cuts included the production of GE's televisions and other appliances that for years were considered the heart of General Electric.

More recently his actions have been praised and he has been regarded as a model CEO. In 1991, *Industry Week* listed Jack Welch as one of the twelve best CEOs in the United States, and the National Management Association honored him as "American Manager of the Year." Rather than condemning him for being ruthless and unfeeling, *Working Woman* praised his management style and the decentralized environment he has created because it allows more women to participate in management decisions.

Welch stands 5 feet, 8 inches, and maintains his physical conditioning by 6:30 A.M. workouts at the GE gym. He is described as smart, unpretentious, and eager to laugh. His competitive spirit was honed in his earlier life by participating in school sports. He refers to his subordinates as *leaders,* instead of *managers:*

> Call people *managers* and they are going to start managing things, getting in the way. The job of a leader is to take the available resources—human and financial—and allocate them rigorously. Not to spread them out evenly, like butter on bread. That's what bureaucrats do. It takes courage and tough-mindedness to pick the bets, put the resources behind them, articulate the vision to the employees, and explain why you said yes to this one and no to that one.

Whether Jack Welch changed his fundamental leadership style after the first six years is not clear. One person described him as a tough guy who has found a new religion; others suggest that his actions have always reflected a strategic direction that values strengthening the enterprise to make it more secure for the remaining employees.

Questions

1. How would you describe John Welch's leadership style? Do you think he has changed his basic leadership style since the time he became GE's CEO?

2. How important are trust and loyalty for a leader? How could a leader create feelings of trust and loyalty after making drastic cuts in employment?

Source: Stratford P. Sherman and Cynthia Hutton, "Inside the Mind of Jack Welch," *Fortune* (March 27, 1989), pp. 39ff.

LEADERSHIP

Leadership is an extremely popular topic in organizational behavior because of the role we assume it plays in group and organizational effectiveness. We assume that the success of a group depends primarily on the quality of leadership. To have a winning season requires a good coach; to achieve a military victory requires a great commander; and to have a productive work group requires a competent supervisor. Whether they deserve it or not, leaders are usually credited for the group's success and blamed for the group's failure. When a team has a losing season, instead of firing the team, the coach is fired.

Defining Leadership

Defining leadership seems unnecessary because it is such a common topic. Intuitively, everyone understands that leadership involves leading people and influencing what they do. But the lack of a precise definition of leadership has contributed to extensive conflict and inconsistency in a century of leadership research. In 1974, Ralph Stogdill reviewed more than three thousand leadership studies and concluded that several decades of research have failed to produce an integrated understanding of leadership.[1]

One controversy is whether leadership is an individual or a group phenomenon. Some theorists define leadership in terms of the actions of formally appointed leaders, which tends to focus their analysis on the personalities and behaviors of these people. Other theorists say leadership includes all efforts to influence the behavior of others, which means leadership is a group function that can be widely shared among all members of a group.

Another controversy concerns the definition of leadership. To emphasize a particular kind of leadership, some theorists limit the definition of leadership to successful influence attempts that result in enthusiastic commitment by followers. Proponents of this view argue that leadership should have a profound effect on followers; those who simply use formal authority or who rely on rewards and punishments to manipulate or coerce followers are not really "leading" them. Those who disagree with this definition insist that leadership also includes routine direction that maintains the status quo—a manager's influence need not be successful to be leadership. These disagreements help to explain why the leadership research has been so inconsistent and why it is important to understand the different definitions.

Incremental Influence. The most useful definition of leadership, and the one we will use in this chapter, considers it a form of behavior in which one person influences others. In other words, **leadership** is the *incremental influence* one individual exerts over another above and beyond mechanical compliance with routine directives. Leadership occurs when one individual influences others to do something voluntarily rather than because they were required to do it or because they feared the consequences of noncompliance. It is this voluntary aspect of leadership that distinguishes it from other influence processes such as power and authority.[2]

Although leaders may use force or coercion to influence the behavior of followers, leaders by our definition use their ability to induce voluntary compliance.

By this definition, anyone in the organization can be a leader whether or not that individual is formally identified as such. Indeed, informal leaders are extremely important to the effectiveness of most organizations.

Charismatic Leadership. **Charismatic leadership** is a special kind of influence that has been attributed to outstanding and gifted individuals. Followers not only trust and respect charismatic leaders, they also idolize and worship them as super-human heroes or spiritual figures. Charismatic leadership is evidenced by the amount of trust followers hold in the correctness of the leader's beliefs, their unquestioning acceptance of the leader, their willing obedience, and their affection for the leader.

Many writers have tried to explain what makes a charismatic leader. Charis-matic leaders generally have a strong need for power, high self-confidence, and strong convictions about the morality of their cause.[3] Charismatic leaders establish their influence most importantly by the example they model in their own behavior for followers. Other behaviors that help them maintain their status include man-aging their charismatic perception (impression management) to preserve the fol-lower's confidence, articulating an appealing vision of the group's goals in ideological terms, communicating high expectations for followers, and expressing confidence in followers' abilities to build their self-confidence.[4] Studies of the self-fulfilling prophecy, described in Chapter 2, show that followers perform better when leaders express confidence in them.

Managers Versus Leaders

Although leadership is similar to management, some theorists make a clear differ-ence between these topics as a way to highlight the distinctive nature of leadership.

Managing Things Versus Leading People. One contrast between management and leadership focuses on what is influenced: managers manage things, while lead-ers lead people.[5] Managers focus their efforts on inanimate objects, such as budgets, financial statements, organization charts, sales projections, and productivity re-ports. Leaders focus their efforts on people as they encourage, inspire, train, empathize, evaluate, and reward. Leaders are the ones who build organizations, cre-ate organizational cultures, and shape society. Managers maintain bureaucratic pro-cedures and keep organizations running smoothly by solving problems.[6] Although they perform a crucial role, managers are sometimes disparagingly referred to as "bean counters."

Warren Bennis and Burt Nanus highlight the differences between managers and leaders by saying that "managers are people who do things right, and leaders are people who do the right thing."[7] This statement suggests a difference in focus and purpose. To manage means to direct, to bring about, to accomplish, and to have responsibility for. The functions of management, as described in Chapter 1, are planning, organizing, directing, and controlling. The successful manager is viewed as someone who achieves results by following the prescribed activities and by main-taining behaviors and products within prescribed limits.

To lead, however, is to inspire, to influence, and to motivate. Effective leaders inspire others to pursue excellence, to extend themselves, and to go beyond their perfunctory job requirements by generating creative ideas. This distinction is some-what overstated, because effective leaders do a lot of managing, and effective managers need to lead. But it serves to emphasize an important organizational outcome: the creation of an energetic and highly committed work force that is successfully adapting to the demands of a changing environment and competently producing viable products and services.

Controlling Complexity Versus Producing Change. John Kotter has proposed another way to examine the differences between managers and leaders by studying the specific focus of each. Management focuses on *controlling complexity*—creating order in the organization, solving problems, and ensuring consistency. Leadership focuses on *creating change*—recognizing the demands of a changing environment, sensing opportunities for growth, and communicating a vision that inspires others. Here, leadership is not necessarily better than management, nor is it a replacement for it. Both functions are needed in organizations, but they may need to be performed by different individuals. Although some have suggested that management and leadership are skills anyone can learn, Kotter argues that good leaders and good managers focus on such different outcomes that they require very different personalities.[8]

Management and leadership are both involved in influencing others, and they share four common roles: (1) planning—deciding what needs to be done, (2) organizing—creating a structure of networks and relationships to get work done, (3) directing the work, and (4) controlling—ensuring performance. As they perform each of these roles, managers and leaders behave very differently because they focus on different outcomes, as summarized in Exhibit 15.1.

1. *Planning—deciding what needs to be done.* Managers decide what to do by planning and budgeting—setting targets and goals for the future, establishing detailed steps for achieving them, and allocating resources to accomplish those plans. Planning and budgeting are the processes managers use to control complexity and produce orderly results. But they are not used to create change.

Leadership involves helping an organization achieve constructive change, which requires setting a direction—developing a vision of the future and strategies for producing the changes needed to accomplish the vision.

2. *Organizing—creating networks and relationships to get work done.* Managers perform a variety of organizing and staffing activities to create a structure for getting work done. These activities include dividing the work into distinct jobs, staffing the jobs with qualified workers, structuring jobs in defined units, establishing reporting relationships, and delegating authority for following the assigned procedures. Through organizing and staffing, managers control a complex environment and create a stable structure for getting work done.

The corresponding leadership activity is aligning people behind a shared vision of how the organization needs to change. Aligning people involves communicating a new direction to the relevant people who can work unitedly and form coalitions with a common vision and sense of direction. Change is not an orderly process, and it will be staggered and chaotic unless many people coalesce and move together in the same direction.

3. *Directing productive work.* Managers are problem solvers. They tend to view work as an enabling process, involving people with multiple talents and interests that may not coincide with each other or with the interests of the organization. They strive to create an acceptable employment exchange by negotiating agreements that satisfy the expectations of workers and the demands of the organization. Bargain-

EXHIBIT 15.1 Comparison Between Leadership and Management

	Leadership	Management
Focus	**Producing useful change**	**Controlling complexity**
Role 1. Deciding what needs to be done	Setting direction Creating a vision and strategy	Planning and budgeting
Role 2. Creating a structure of networks and relationships to get work done	Aligning people with a shared vision Communicating with all relevant people	Organizing and staffing Structuring jobs Establishing reporting relationships Providing training Delegating authority
Role 3. Directing productive work	Empowering people	Solving problems Negotiating compromises
Role 4. Ensuring performance	Motivating and inspiring people	Implementing control systems

ing and compromise are used to establish an agreement, and rewards and punishment are used to maintain it.

Leaders, in contrast, rely on empowering people and letting them work autonomously according to their shared vision. Free to exercise individual initiative and motivated by a sense of ownership, people throughout the organization respond quickly and effectively to new opportunities and problems. Lower-level employees feel free to initiate actions without feeling vulnerable.

4. *Controlling—ensuring performance.* Managers ensure performance by implementing control systems—establishing measurable standards, collecting performance data, identifying deviations, and taking corrective actions. Leaders, in contrast, ensure performance by motivating and inspiring people to go above and beyond the formal job expectations. Motivation and inspiration energize people, not by monitoring their behavior as control mechanisms do, but by satisfying basic human needs for fulfillment, a sense of accomplishment, recognition, self-esteem, a feeling of control over one's life, and the ability to achieve one's ideals. These feelings touch people deeply and elicit a powerful response.

For many of the same reasons that control is so central to management, highly motivated and inspired behavior is inappropriate. Control systems are supposed to ensure that normal people perform their work in normal ways, day after day. Managing routine performance is not glamorous, but it is necessary. Leadership that inspires excellence and helps organizations thrive in an uncertain world is glamorous, but it may not be any more necessary than management.

Transformational Leadership

Another contrast used to highlight a particular kind of leadership is transformational versus transactional leadership. **Transactional leaders** manage the transactions between the organization and its members; they get things done by giving contingent rewards, such as recognition, pay increases, and advancement for employees who perform well. Employees who do not perform well are penalized. Transactional leaders frequently use the management-by-exception principle to monitor the performance of employees and take corrective actions when performance deviates from standard.

Transformational leadership focuses on changing the attitudes and assumptions of employees and building commitment for the organization's mission, objectives, and strategies. This form of leadership occurs when leaders broaden and elevate the interests of their employees, when they generate awareness and acceptance of the purposes and mission of the group, and when they stir their employees to look beyond their own self-interest for the good of the group.[9]

A result that is attributed to transformational leadership is the empowerment of followers, who are capable of taking charge and acting on their own initiative. **Empowerment** involves providing the conditions that stimulate followers to act in a committed, concerned, and involved way in doing their work. The kinds of conditions that contribute to empowerment include providing relevant factual information; providing resources such as time, space, and money; and providing support such as backing, endorsement, and legitimacy. Empowered followers make things happen and get things done without waiting for detailed instructions or administrative approvals.[10]

The differences between transformational and transactional leadership were first described by James MacGregor Burns in 1978.[11] According to Burns, transformational leaders seek to raise the consciousness of followers by appealing to higher ideals and values such as liberty, justice, equality, peace, and humanitarianism, rather than baser emotions such as fear, greed, jealousy, or hatred. Burns used this distinction to describe a kind of leadership he thought was sorely needed to rejuvenate society and reform institutions. Other writers agree with Burns that society needs more transformational leaders. They claim that many social and economic problems, including unemployment and the decline in international competitiveness, stem from insufficient transformational leaders who dream inspired visions and motivate followers to pursue them.[12]

Empirical support for the importance of transformational leadership comes from the research of Bernard Bass, who developed an instrument called the Multifactor Leadership Questionnaire (MLQ) to measure transformational and transactional leadership behaviors.[13] According to Bass, transformational leadership is largely a function of three processes: (1) being charismatic, (2) showing individual consideration, and (3) being intellectually stimulating, as shown in Exhibit 15.2. Being charismatic involves providing followers with a vision and sense of mission, instilling pride in the group regarding its performance, and gaining the respect and trust of followers. Showing individual consideration involves giving followers personal attention by treating people individually, helping them improve their personal skills, and advising them about their careers. Being intellectually stimulating involves promoting rationality and careful problem solving, and sharing new insights and personal learning.

Bass claims that transformational leadership is superior to transactional leadership and presents data to support his claim. In one study, for example, data were collected from 228 employees of 58 managers in an engineering firm who evaluated their leaders and also rated themselves on how often they exerted extra effort.[14] Leaders who were rated high on transformational leadership factors had a much larger percentage of employees who said they exerted extra effort, than did leaders

EXHIBIT 15.2   Characteristics of Transactional and
                Transformational Leadership

Transactional Leadership

- Establishes goals and objectives
- Designs work flow and delegates task assignments
- Negotiates exchange of rewards for effort
- Rewards performance and recognizes accomplishments
- Searches for deviations from standards and takes corrective actions

Transformational Leadership

- *Charismatic:* Provides vision and a sense of mission, gains respect and trust, instills pride
- *Individualized consideration:* Gives personal attention, and treats each person individually, coaches
- *Intellectually stimulating:* Promotes learning, encourages rationality, uses careful problem solving
- *Inspirational:* Communicates high performance expectations, uses symbols to focus efforts, distills essential purposes

---

rated low. Transactional leadership factors, however, did not have as great an impact on eliciting extra efforts from employees. A study of 186 Navy officers on active duty also found that transactional leadership was related more strongly to their subordinates' extra efforts and satisfaction than did transactional or laissez-faire leadership.[15] Other research studies have likewise found that transformational leadership is associated with greater leader effectiveness and employee satisfaction.[16]

Bass claims that transformational leadership can be learned, and is greatly influenced by the kind of leadership behaviors modeled by the top leaders in an organization. His research shows that leaders at all levels can be trained to be more charismatic, to be more intellectually stimulating, and to show more individual consideration. Successful training programs have been conducted for a variety of groups, such as first-level supervisors in high-tech computer firms, as well as senior executives of insurance firms, and officers in the Israeli military.[17]

Patterns of Organizational Leadership

The type of influence required for effective leadership is not the same for all leaders. Depending on their level in the organization, different cognitive and affective skills are required of leaders. Three basic leadership roles have been identified: origination, interpolation, and administration.[18]

1. *Origination.* Origination refers to strategic decision making regarding policy formulation or structural change. These crucial decisions determine the culture and mission of the organization.

APPLYING ORGANIZATIONAL BEHAVIOR
IN THE NEWS

Leading from in Front

CNN A. B. "Buzzy" Krongard is the president of Alex Brown and Company, a Baltimore-based investment bank. The company has 1,700 employees and is the oldest investment bank in the United States. Because investment banking is so competitive, the company demands flawless leadership.

Buzzy Krongard is regarded as an excellent leader because of his intelligence, his clarity of thought, and his fairness. He does not claim any special leadership gifts; he says he was selected simply because he happened to be in the right place and was willing to serve. Nevertheless, he is a dynamic leader who inspires excellence in his associates.

Krongard credits his leadership style to his experience in the Marine Corps, where he learned both to lead and to follow. The military taught him that effective leaders must "lead from in front"—you don't ask your people to do anything you wouldn't be willing to do yourself. Competitive athletics also contributed to his leadership skills by teaching him the value of teamwork.

Krongard describes his management style as management by confrontation. He expects his managers to challenge him and each other until they reach a decision. But then he expects total cooperation, especially from those whose ideas were not accepted. Consistent with surveys of other leaders, Krongard agrees that in his leadership he tries to portray a clear sense of values, he has a high tolerance for frustration, and he has a strong dedication to the work ethic.

Source: CNN *Pinnacle* news programming.

2. *Interpolation.* Interpolation means interpreting strategic decisions and designing a method for implementing them within the organization. Interpolation includes adapting or supplementing the present structure to new policy directives.

3. *Administration.* Administration consists of implementing the policies and procedures that have been provided to keep the organization operating efficiently.

These three types of leadership are typically performed at different levels in the organization and require different abilities and skills, as shown in Exhibit 15.3. The origination of new programs and policies, which may involve a change in the organization's structure or a reinterpretation of the organization's mission, occurs at the top level of the organization. People at this level must have an understanding of the entire organization and of the ways it interacts with the external environment. Top-level managers symbolize the organization and what it stands for and need to display transformational leadership.

Interpolation—interpreting policy decisions and applying them to the existing organization—is typically done by intermediate-level managers. Middle-level managers must maintain a two-way orientation by taking directives from those above and accommodating them for people below.

Lower-level supervisors administer the policies and procedures of the organization. Successful supervisors are transactional leaders who need to possess both technical knowledge and a clear understanding of the organization's rules. Lower-level supervisors must be concerned with equity and with the administration of rewards and punishments, because they continually deal with these issues in leading others.

EXHIBIT 15.3 Three Leadership Patterns, Their Location in the Organization, and Their Skill Requirements

Type of Leadership Process	Typical Organizational Level	Abilities and Skills	
		Cognitive (knowledge)	Affective (emotion)
Origination: change, creation, and elimination of structure	Top echelons	System perspective	Charisma
Interpolation: supplementing and piecing out of structure	Intermediate levels: pivotal roles	Subsystem perspective: two-way orientation	Integration of primary and secondary relations: human relations skills
Administration: use of existing structure	Lower levels	Technical knowledge and understanding of system of rules	Concern with equity in use of rewards and sanctions

Source: Adapted from Daniel Katz and Robert Kahn, *The Social Psychology of Organizations* (New York: Wiley, 1979), p. 539.

LEADERSHIP TRAITS

Leadership plays an essential role in organizational dynamics and often separates effective and ineffective organizations. As defined earlier, leadership occurs when one person influences others to do something of their own volition they would not ordinarily do. Leadership is an essential organizational process, and like other processes it can be studied on three different levels—the individual, the group, and the organization.

At the individual level of analysis, leadership studies focus on the traits of successful leaders. At the group level, leadership studies focus on leadership behaviors of both formal and informal leaders. The organizational level of analysis examines how organizational effectiveness is determined by the interaction between the leader, the follower, and the situation. These studies have given rise to *situational leadership theories* or *contingency theories of leadership*.

These three levels of analysis also correspond roughly with the chronology of leadership research, because the earliest studies examined individual traits, followed by studies of leader behaviors in a group, and then contingency leadership theories in organizations. Each level is analyzed separately, beginning with leadership traits.

In Search of Leadership

Although early writers attempted to describe the characteristics of effective leaders, systematic investigations of leadership traits first began after the turn of the century. World War I highlighted the need for selecting and training effective leaders, and for the quarter century between World War I and World War II, numerous studies investigated the personal traits of good leaders. These studies are generally referred to as *trait studies,* because their primary goal was to identify the traits and personal characteristics of effective leaders.

A variety of methods was used to study leadership traits, and this variety is probably one reason why the results were so inconsistent. Most studies compared effective leaders with ineffective leaders or leaders with nonleaders. The studies were inconsistent in the methods used to identify leaders. Some were identified by outside observers, some were selected by the group via nominations or voting, others were named by qualified observers such as teachers, and some were selected because they occupied a position of leadership such as student body president or team captain. The studies were also inconsistent in the way they measured traits. In some studies the traits were measured by psychological tests; other studies relied on observers to identify the traits they saw; and some studies relied on the individuals to report their own character traits.

In general, the trait studies were quite disappointing, especially to researcherswho had hoped to develop a measure of leadership that predicted leader effectiveness as accurately as intelligence tests predicted problem-solving ability. Because of weak results, the focus of leadership research shifted from trait studies to contingency studies, which examined more than just the traits of the leader.

Research on leadership traits should not be dismissed too quickly, however. Although the traits studies were disappointing, they were not worthless. Several traits produced a significant difference in leadership effectiveness, but they did not act alone. Instead, they interacted with other situational variables to influence leader effectiveness. Four major reviews have surveyed the trait studies, and the results can be summarized according to physical traits, intelligence, and personality traits.[19]

Physical Traits

Trait studies examined such physical factors as height, weight, physique, energy, health, and appearance. To the extent that anything can be concluded regarding the relationship between these factors and leadership, it appears that leaders tend to be slightly taller and heavier, have better health, a superior physique, a higher rate of energy output, and a more attractive appearance.

To illustrate, one early study on the effects of height found that executives in insurance companies were taller than policyholders, that bishops were taller than clergymen, that university presidents were taller than college presidents, that sales managers were taller than sales representatives, and that railway presidents were taller than station agents.[20] Results of this sort, however, have not always been consistent. While one literature review found nine studies showing that leaders tend to be taller, it reported two studies showing that leaders tended to be shorter. Attractiveness and a pleasant appearance were found to be highly correlated with leaders among Boy Scouts; but among groups of delinquent youth, leaders were rated as more slovenly and unkempt.[21]

In summary, studies of personal characteristics are not particularly interesting or useful. The results are generally too weak and inconsistent to be useful in selecting leaders, nor are they useful for training purposes, because very little can be done to change most of these physical traits. The results seem to say more about cultural stereotypes than about leadership.

Intelligence

Many studies have investigated the relationship between leadership and general intelligence, and they generally agree that leaders are more intelligent than nonleaders. The relationship between intelligence and leadership probably stems from the fact that so many leadership functions depend on careful problem solving. All three leadership roles—origination, interpolation, and administration—require significant mental ability.

One review of leadership studies reported twenty-three experiments showing that leaders were brighter and had greater levels of intelligence.[22] Only five studies reported that intelligence made no difference. In general, it appears safe to conclude that leaders are more intelligent than nonleaders, but again the correlations are small. Obviously, many other variables beside intelligence influence leadership effectiveness.

An interesting conclusion from these studies is the suggestion that leaders should be more intelligent than the group, but not by too wide a margin. Members who are significantly brighter than other group members are seldom selected as leaders. Because of their superior intellect, other group members tend to reject them; they are too different from and out of touch with the rest of the group. People with high IQs tend to have different vocabularies, interests, and goals, which create communication and interpersonal relations problems.

Leadership effectiveness also appears to be related to two other variables closely associated with intelligence: scholarship and knowledge. Leaders generally excel scholastically and receive better-than-average grades. General information, practical knowledge, and simply knowing how to get things done appears to be important for effective leadership, and several studies have shown a positive relationship between general knowledge and leadership ability.

Personality Traits

Studies of the relationship between leadership and personality traits have examined a lengthy list of factors. Unfortunately, most of the results have been inconsistent and even contradictory. Several personality traits appear to be related to leadership, although most of these relationships are not especially strong.

A list of the personality traits most frequently associated with leadership is shown in Exhibit 15.4. This list is based on the 1948 review by Ralph Stogdill of 124 studies of leadership traits.[23] This list suggests that the average leader is more social, displays greater initiative, is more persistent, knows how to get things done, is more self-confident, displays greater cooperativeness and adaptability, and possesses greater verbal skills to facilitate communication. Studies examining personality integration or emotional adjustment consistently found that leaders were more emotionally mature than nonleaders. Rather consistent support was also found for the relationship between leadership and self-confidence or self-esteem. Indeed, the relationship between self-confidence and leadership generally produced some of the highest correlations of any of the personality traits tested.

EXHIBIT 15.4   Personality Factors Most Frequently
Associated with Effective Leadership

Capacity	Achievement	Responsibility	Participation	Status
Intelligence	Scholarship	Honesty	Activity	Socioeconomic position
Alertness	Knowledge	Dependability	Sociability	Popularity
Verbal facility	Athletic accomplishment	Initiative	Cooperation	
Originality	Personality adjustment	Persistence	Adaptability	
Judgment		Aggressiveness	Humor	
		Self-confidence		
		Desire to excel		

Honesty or integrity is another characteristic attributed to good leaders. Several reviews of the characteristics people admire most in leaders report that honesty is the most important trait.[24]

Consequently, it is not correct to conclude that personal characteristics are unrelated to leadership; there are indeed some relationships, but they are more complex than they first appear to be.

After four major reviews of the trait studies, researchers concluded that effective leadership does not depend solely on a combination of personality traits. Situational variables were also important; the situation frequently determined whether a personality characteristic was positively or negatively associated with effective leadership. Each review concluded that leadership must be examined as an interaction of three variables: characteristics of the leader, characteristics of the subordinate, and the nature of the task.

LEADER BEHAVIORS

While the trait studies focused on individual leaders, another line of research examined leader behaviors within the context of a group and attempted to describe what leaders actually do. These studies essentially asked whether certain ways of behaving were more effective than others: How do effective leaders behave differently from other group members? Most of these studies occurred during the 1940s and 50s.

Various styles of leadership were defined as a result of these studies of leader behaviors. One of the earlier studies compared three leadership styles: authoritarian, democratic, and laissez-faire. Perhaps the best research on styles of leadership, however, occurred simultaneously at The Ohio State University and the University of Michigan. At each university, researchers identified two leader behaviors that were essentially similar, even though both investigations were conducted independently. These two dimensions of leadership have been used to form an instrument, called the **Leadership Grid®,** that has been used for research and training.

Authoritarian, Democratic, and Laissez-faire Leadership

The contrasting political systems in the United States and Germany preceding World War II inspired one of the early classic studies of leadership that compared the effects of three leadership styles: authoritarian, democratic, and laissez-faire.[25] This study involved groups of 10-year-old boys who were organized in groups of five. Each group met regularly after school to engage in hobbies and other activities under the direction of a leader who adopted one of the three styles of leadership. Every six weeks the leaders were rotated among the groups so that each group experienced each type of leadership. The leaders of these groups, who were graduate students in social psychology, were trained to lead the boys using one of three leadership styles. Under the democratic style of leadership, group decisions were made by majority vote in which equal participation was encouraged and criticism and punishment were minimal. Under the autocratic leader, all decisions were made by the leader and the boys were required to follow prescribed procedures under strict discipline. Under the laissez-faire leader, the actual leadership was minimized and the boys were allowed to work and play essentially without supervision.

During the 18 weeks of this study, the performance of the boys was observed in order to assess the effects of the three leadership styles. Under democratic leadership, the groups were more satisfied and functioned in the most orderly and positive manner. Aggressive acts were observed most frequently under the autocratic leadership. The effects of the leadership styles on productivity were somewhat mixed, although actual objective measures of productivity were not obtained. Under autocratic leadership, the groups spent more time in productive work activity and had more work-related conversations. However, the autocratic groups appeared to be more productive only when the leader was present. When the leader left the room, the amount of work-related activity dropped drastically.

The results of this study were somewhat surprising to the researchers, who had expected the highest satisfaction and productivity under democratic leadership. This study was conducted under the direction of Kurt Lewin, a behavioral scientist who came to America from Germany just prior to World War II. Lewin believed that the repressive, autocratic political climate he had left in Germany was not as satisfying, productive, or desirable as a democratic society. He expected the results of the experiment to confirm his hypothesis. Although the boys preferred a democratic leader, they appeared to be more productive under autocratic leadership.

Other studies have also shown that democratic leadership styles are not always the most productive. In fact, some studies have found that both the satisfaction and the productivity of group members is higher under directive leaders than democratic leaders. For example, a study of 488 managers in a consumer loan company found that employees who had high authoritarianism scores (high acceptance of strong authority relationships) were more satisfied and productive when they worked for supervisors who had little tolerance for freedom.[26] Greater satisfaction with an authoritarian leader was also found in another study of over 1,000 workers.[27] This study found that employees who worked independently but were required to have frequent interaction with their superior preferred and were more satisfied with an autocratic leader. Some examples of such employees are fire fighters, police officers, and administrative aides.

Initiating Structure and Consideration

Following World War II, a major research effort studying **leader behaviors** was conducted at The Ohio State University. This project involved a series of studies that ultimately produced a two-factor theory of leader behavior. The two leadership factors were referred to as **initiating structure** and **consideration**.[28] Initiating structure consisted of leadership behaviors associated with organizing and defining the work, the work relationships, and the goals. A leader who initiated structure was described as one who assigned people to particular tasks, expected workers to follow standard routines, and emphasized meeting deadlines. The factor of consideration involved leader behaviors that showed friendship, mutual trust, warmth, and concern for subordinates.

These two factors were identified by administering questionnaires containing numerous descriptions of leader behaviors and combining the items that seemed to measure the same dimension, through a statistical technique called *factor analysis*. Some of the statements that were used to describe leader behavior are illustrated in the experiential exercise at the end of the chapter. After the data from many employees had been collected and analyzed, the researchers concluded that the responses were measuring just two factors: initiating structure and consideration. These two leader behaviors accounted for about 80 percent of the variance in the responses.

The research indicates that initiating structure and consideration are separate and independent dimensions of leadership behavior. Therefore, a leader could be high on both dimensions, low on both dimensions, or high on one and low on the other. Since both factors were considered important dimensions of leadership, the early studies assumed that the most effective leaders were high on both dimensions.

Subsequent research failed to support the initial expectations. In a study of the behavior of supervisors at International Harvester, for example, it was found that supervisors scoring high on initiating structure had high proficiency ratings but many employee grievances. Those who had high consideration scores had low proficiency ratings and also low absences.[29]

After extensive research, it can now be concluded that the most effective leaders are not always high on both initiating structure and consideration. Although most studies show that leadership effectiveness is associated with high scores on both dimensions, occasionally other combinations have produced the highest levels of satisfaction and performance, such as being high on one scale and low on the other or being at moderate levels on both dimensions.[30]

Production-centered and Employee-centered Leader Behaviors

About the same time as the Ohio State University researchers were discovering the dimensions of initiating structure and consideration, a similar research program at the University of Michigan identified two similar dimensions of leadership behavior, which they labeled production-centered and employee-centered behaviors.[31] *Production-centered* behaviors were similar to initiating structure, in which leaders established goals, gave instructions, checked on performance, and structured the work of the group. *Employee-centered* behaviors were similar to the dimension of consideration, in which the leader developed a supportive personal relationship with subordinates, avoided punitive behavior, and encouraged two-way communication with subordinates.

Studies on the relationship between production-centered and employee-centered behaviors also found them to be independent dimensions of leadership. A review of twenty-four studies dispelled a popular myth suggesting that supervisors focused on either production or employees, and to the extent they focused on one, they were necessarily disinterested in the other. These studies indicated instead that supervisors can be interested in both production and employees.[32] Therefore, a leader who has a strong production orientation is not necessarily disinterested in the employees. Knowing an individual's orientation on one leader dimension says nothing about that person's orientation on the other.

The Leadership Grid®

A conceptual framework combining a concern for task accomplishment and a concern for people was created by Robert Blake and Jane Mouton called the Leadership Grid, formerly called the Managerial Grid.[33] An illustration of the Leadership Grid is shown in Exhibit 15.5. The concern for production dimension is measured on a nine-point scale and represented along the horizontal dimension, while the vertical dimension measures an individual's concern for people, again using a nine-point scale. Blake and Mouton assume that the most effective leadership style is a 9,9 style, demonstrating both concern for production and concern for people.

By responding to a questionnaire developed by Blake and Mouton, individuals can place themselves in one of the eighty-one cells on the Leadership Grid. Five different grid positions are typically used to illustrate different leadership styles. A 9,1 leader is primarily concerned with production and task accomplishment and unconcerned about people. This person wants to get the job done and wants a schedule followed at all costs. The 1,9 leadership style reflects a maximum concern for people with minimum concern for production. This individual is not concerned whether the group actually produces anything, but is highly concerned about the members' personal needs, interests, and interpersonal relationships. The 1,1 leadership style reflects minimal concern for both production and people and is characteristic of a person who essentially abdicates the leadership role. The 5,5 leadership style reflects a moderate concern for both people and production, while the 9,9 leadership style reflects a maximum concern for both production and people. A 9,9 leader wants to meet schedules and get the job done, but at the same time is highly concerned about the feelings and interests of the group members.

The Leadership Grid is popular among managers, and they have used it rather extensively to assess their leadership style as part of a training program designed to move them to the 9,9 style. In spite of its popularity, however, the usefulness of the Leadership Grid has not been consistently supported by research. Most of the available research consists of case analyses that have been loosely interpreted to support it. However, empirical research has failed to show that a 9,9 leadership style is universally superior. The demands of the situation, the expectations of other group members, and the nature of the work being performed interact in complex ways that call for a variety of leadership styles. Consequently, the 9,9 leadership style is not always the most effective.[34]

Although the research has not shown that one leadership style is universally superior, this research helps to identify the important leadership roles that occur within a group. Rather than thinking of leadership strictly in terms of the behavior of the formal leader, it is helpful to think of leadership as leadership roles performed within a group. Thinking of leadership this way implies that leadership

EXHIBIT 15.5   The Leadership Grid®

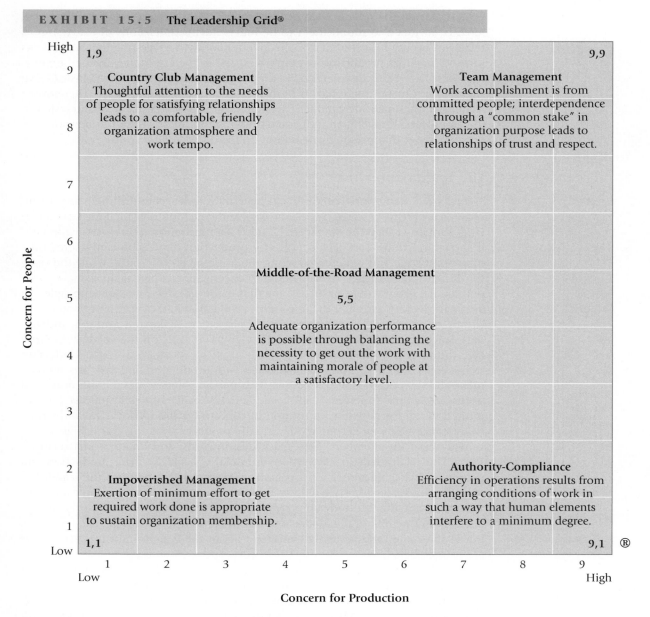

Source: R. R. Blake and Anne Adams McCanse, *Leadership Dilemmas—Grid Solutions* (Houston: Gulf Publishing, 1991), p. 129. Reproduced by permission.

consists of leader behaviors performed by any group members, whether they are formally appointed as leaders or not.

The two major leadership roles, initiating structure and consideration, are similar to the work roles and maintenance roles described in Chapter 9.[35] These two roles are necessary for a group to be effective and can be performed either by the formally appointed leader or by other group members. If a task is already highly structured, or if other group members are adequately structuring the task, then efforts by

APPLYING ORGANIZATIONAL BEHAVIOR
ACROSS CULTURES

Cultural Preferences for Participative Leadership

 Cultural differences in leadership styles have largely been overlooked because most leadership theories have been developed and tested in the United States. Extensive research has also been limited because contingency leadership theory, the idea that the appropriate leadership style depends on the situation, seems to be widely accepted in every culture. Indeed, one of the first cross-cultural comparisons suggested that there are more similarities than differences in leadership. Nevertheless, significant cultural differences have been observed in the acceptance of participative leadership.

Cultural differences in the willingness to accept participative management were observed in a study of managers from various countries. These managers were asked whether they thought it was essential for them to have answers to all their subordinates' questions. The percentage of managers from various countries agreeing with this statement varied significantly.

"It is important for managers to have on hand precise answers to most of the questions that his or her subordinates may raise about their work."

	Percent Agreement
Sweden	10%
The Netherlands	17%
United States	18%
Denmark	23%
Great Britain	27%
Switzerland	38%

	Percent Agreement
Belgium	44%
Germany	46%
France	53%
Italy	66%
Brazil	72%

Participative leadership assumes employees want to contribute to management decision making; but this assumption is not universally true. In cultures that emphasize management expertise and power relationships, employees want their managers to act decisively and they are willing to accept authoritarian leadership. Managers are expected to be experts, and inviting employees to help make decisions is viewed as a sign of weakness. In cultures where people expect managers to lead, employees are uncomfortable with the delegation of discretionary decisions.

Participative leadership styles are highly recommended by the earlier leadership theories, such as McGregor's Theory X and Theory Y, Likert's System Four theory, Blake and Mouton's Leadership Grid®, and also by more recent writing about employee empowerment. But involving subordinates in decisions is not equally recommended in every culture.

Source: Gilles Amado and Haroldo Vinagre Brasil, "Organizational Behaviors and Cultural Context: The Brazilian 'Jeitinho,' " *International Studies of Management and Organization,* vol. 21, no. 3 (1991), pp. 38–61; A. Laurent, "The Cultural Diversity of Western Conceptions of Management," *International Studies of Management and Organization,* vol. 13 (1983), pp. 75–96.

the leader to add additional structure are unnecessary and ineffective. Likewise, the maintenance role of showing consideration and concern for group members may be performed by other group members, thereby eliminating the need for the formal leader to perform this role. In summarizing research on consideration and initiating structure, one review concluded that when the formally appointed leaders fail to perform either of these leader behaviors, an informal leader will emerge and perform them if it is necessary for success and if the group desires success.[36]

SITUATIONAL LEADERSHIP

In analyzing leadership at the organizational level of analysis, the effectiveness of the different leadership styles must be combined with different organizational factors to assess their effectiveness. At this level of analysis, the study of leadership has given rise to contingency theories of leadership or situational leadership theories. Four situational leadership theories have received the primary attention: Paul Hersey's and Ken Blanchard's situational leadership model, Fred Fiedler's contingency theory of leadership, Robert House's path–goal theory of leadership, and Victor Vroom and Philip Yetton's normative decision-making model of leadership.

The Situational Leadership Model: Life Cycle Theory

Paul Hersey and Ken Blanchard developed a situational leadership model that combined three variables: (1) the amount of guidance and direction (task behavior) a leader gives; (2) the amount of emotional support (relationship behavior) a leader provides; and (3) the readiness level (maturity) that followers exhibit in performing a specific task or function.[37] The focus of this model is on the relationship between the leaders and followers, and the maturity of the followers is viewed as the most important situational variable influencing leader behaviors. Therefore, this theory is also called the **"life cycle theory of leadership."**

Maturity is defined as the ability and willingness of people to take responsibility for directing their own behavior as it relates to the specific task being performed. An individual or group may demonstrate maturity on some tasks and immaturity on others. Effective leadership requires that the leader's task behaviors and relationship behaviors must change to match the maturity of the group.

The maturity of followers varies along a continuum and is determined by two components: job maturity (ability) and psychological maturity (willingness). Job maturity is the ability to do something and is a function of the follower's knowledge and skills. Psychological maturity is the willingness or motivation to do something and is a function of the follower's commitment and confidence. The appropriate combination of task and relationship behaviors for four different levels of follower maturity are shown in Exhibit 15.6. The bell-shaped curve is called a "prescriptive" curve because it shows the appropriate leadership style directly above the corresponding level of maturity. Four potential leadership styles are created by combining different amounts of task and relationship behaviors.

S1. *Telling.* Provide specific instructions and closely supervise performance. This style is suited for followers of low maturity who are unable and unwilling.

S2. *Selling.* Explain your decisions, and provide opportunity for clarification. This style is appropriate for followers who are willing but unable.

S3. *Participating.* Share ideas and facilitate in making decisions. This style is suited for followers who are able but unwilling.

S4. *Delegating.* Turn over responsibility for decisions and implementation. This style is appropriate for followers who are able and willing.

EXHIBIT 15.6   Hersey and Blanchard's Situational Leadership Model: Defining Maturity and Four Leadership Styles

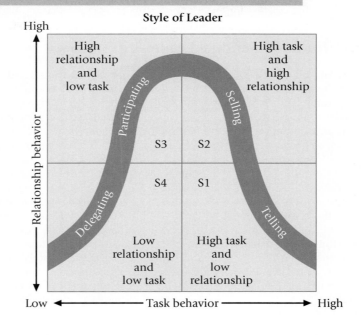

Style of Leader

Maturity of Follower(s)

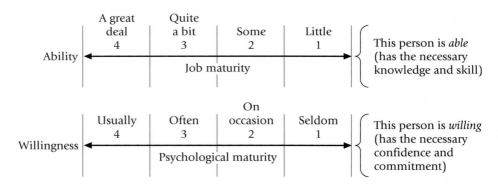

Source: Paul Hersey and Ken Blanchard, *Management of Organizational Behavior: Utilizing Human Resources,* 4th ed., © 1982, p. 152. Adapted by permission of Prentice-Hall, Inc., Englewood Cliffs, New Jersey.

APPLYING ORGANIZATIONAL BEHAVIOR
RESEARCH

An Empirical Test of Situational Leadership Theory

 Hersey and Blanchard's situational leadership theory (SLT) is one of the most widely used models in leadership and supervisory training. The theory seems plausible and it has a natural intuitive appeal; however, prior research has not consistently supported it.

An example of the mixed empirical support for SLT is a study of 105 full-time nurses at a private hospital. These nurses were asked to evaluate their satisfaction with their supervisor, the quality of their leader–member relationship, and how much their supervisor displayed consideration and initiating (task) structure. Their job maturity and psychological maturity were evaluated by the head nurses, who also rated each nurse on a four-point performance scale.

According to SLT, low-maturity followers require a high level of task-oriented but a low level of relationship-oriented supervision, whereas high-maturity followers require a low level of both task- and relationship-oriented supervision. Followers with intermediate-maturity require a style of supervision that is intermediate on the task dimension but comparatively high on the relationship dimension.

Previous studies have found that the number of matches between the maturity of the followers and the appropriate leadership situation have been greatly outnumbered by the number of mismatches. This study was no exception. Only 12 nurses were judged as properly matched, while 74 were classified as mismatched.

The results indicated that the matched nurses had higher performance ratings than the mismatched nurses (2.58 versus 2.44). The matched nurses also reported slightly higher satisfaction with the leader–member relationship (11.41 versus 10.70) and satisfaction with supervision (44.83 versus 42.32). However, none of these differences were statistically significant even though they were in the predicted direction.

This study adds to the mixed results for SLT. It also illustrates some of the difficulties involved in testing this and other leadership theories. The small number of matches suggests that a much larger sample size is needed to test the theory, but larger sample sizes are inconvenient and they introduce other confounding factors. Some studies should be longitudinal to examine the effects of leadership over time; but longitudinal studies pose the same difficulties. More precise instruments also need to be developed to measure the variables, especially for ambiguous constructs such as maturity.

Source: William R. Norris and Robert P. Vecchio, "Situational Leadership Theory: A Replication," *Group and Organization Management,* vol. 17 (1992), pp. 331–342.

Hersey and Blanchard have developed instruments for measuring maturity to determine the appropriate leadership style, and they have applied their model to a variety of settings, including manager–follower relationships, teacher–student relationships, and parent–child relationships. Support for their theory is provided by the experiences of managers who have used it to help them learn how to adapt their leadership style to different situations.

Their theory has also been favorably received in training seminars, where it is used to interpret and understand the inconsistent findings of other leadership studies. Empirical support, however, has been mixed. Several studies have failed to find that the maturity of the followers moderates the relationship between leader behavior and group effectiveness. These negative findings suggest that the maturity of the followers may not have as much impact as the theory claims when leaders are trying to decide on the optimal levels of initiating structure and consideration.[38]

The Contingency Theory of Leadership

The most popular and extensively researched situational theory of leadership was first proposed by Fred Fiedler during the 1960s. Fiedler's model claims that group performance depends on the interaction of the leader style and the favorableness of the situation. Fiedler's major contributions consist of (1) identifying a unique leadership orientation of the leader and developing a way to measure it, and (2) identifying three situational factors influencing leadership and developing a method of measuring them.[39]

Leader Orientation. Fiedler's definition of the leader's orientation emerged largely from earlier studies in which leaders were classified as either relationship oriented or task oriented. **Relationship-oriented leaders** look at others as co-workers and see close interpersonal relations as a requirement for accomplishing the task. **Task-oriented leaders** show a strong emotional reaction against people with whom they have difficulty working. If they are forced to make a choice between getting the job done or worrying about interpersonal relations, they choose the task first and worry about interpersonal relations later. Following earlier research, Fiedler suggested that people could be placed along one continuum characterized by two basic leader orientations: relationship oriented versus task oriented.

LPC Scale. Leadership orientation is measured by the least-preferred-co-worker or **LPC scale,** as illustrated in Exhibit 15.7. People are asked to think of a person with whom they have worked who they least preferred as a co-worker, and they are asked to describe this person using sixteen scales. When the responses are summed, someone with a favorable description of their least preferred co-worker would have a high LPC score, suggesting a relationship-oriented leader. An unfavorable description of the least preferred co-worker would result in a low score, suggesting a task-oriented leader.

Difficulty in interpreting the LPC scores has been a problem for Fiedler's contingency theory. The LPC scale is not related to any of the well-known personality measures. In spite of uncertainty about what exactly it measures, however, the evidence indicates that it is a reliable measure of something, and Fiedler concludes that "there can be little doubt that we are dealing with a very important aspect of personality."[40] A review of twenty-five years of research using the LPC scale concluded that high LPC leaders are primarily relationship oriented, while low LPC leaders are primarily task oriented, consistent with Fiedler's claims.[41] In general, a low LPC leader is more directive, more structuring, more goal oriented, and more concerned with efficiency. A high LPC leader is more considerate, more human relations oriented, more participative, and more sensitive to the feelings of others.

Situational Favorableness. Fiedler's model claims that whether a high LPC leader or low LPC leader will be more effective depends on the favorableness of the situation. In some situations, a high LPC leader is most effective, while a low LPC leader is more effective in other situations. Fiedler claimed that the favorableness of the situation is determined by three variables: (1) whether the relationships between the leader and the members are good or poor, (2) whether the task is relatively structured or unstructured, and (3) whether the power position of the leader is relatively strong or weak.

EXHIBIT 15.7   LPC Scale

Think of the person with whom you can work least well. It may be someone you work with now, or it may be someone you knew in the past. It does not have to be the person you like least well, but should be the person with whom you had the most difficulty in getting a job done. Describe this person as he or she appears to you.

	8	7	6	5	4	3	2	1	
Pleasant									Unpleasant
Friendly	8	7	6	5	4	3	2	1	Unfriendly
Rejecting	1	2	3	4	5	6	7	8	Accepting
Helpful	8	7	6	5	4	3	2	1	Frustrating
Unenthusiastic	1	2	3	4	5	6	7	8	Enthusiastic
Tense	1	2	3	4	5	6	7	8	Relaxed
Distant	1	2	3	4	5	6	7	8	Close
Cold	1	2	3	4	5	6	7	8	Warm
Cooperative	8	7	6	5	4	3	2	1	Uncooperative
Supportive	8	7	6	5	4	3	2	1	Hostile
Boring	1	2	3	4	5	6	7	8	Interesting
Quarrelsome	1	2	3	4	5	6	7	8	Harmonious
Self-assured	8	7	6	5	4	3	2	1	Hesitant
Efficient	8	7	6	5	4	3	2	1	Inefficient
Gloomy	1	2	3	4	5	6	7	8	Cheerful
Open	8	7	6	5	4	3	2	1	Guarded

Source: Fred Fiedler, *A Theory of Leadership Effectiveness* (New York: McGraw-Hill, 1967), p. 41.

In studies testing the model, Fiedler and his colleagues developed instruments to measure each of these three situational variables.[42] Of the three situational variables, the leader–member relations variable was considered to be the most important for determining the favorableness of the situation. Leader–member relations were measured using a simple questionnaire with ten scales on which the leader was asked to describe the group. This instrument was called a "group atmosphere scale," and two sample items are shown here.

Pleasant	8 7 6 5 4 3 2 1	Unpleasant
Unfriendly	1 2 3 4 5 6 7 8	Friendly

The second most important situational variable was the task structure, which was evaluated by judges who examined four aspects of the task structure:

1. *Goal clarity:* the degree to which the requirements of the job are clearly stated and known by the people performing them
2. *Path–goal multiplicity:* the degree to which the problems encountered in the job can be solved by a variety of procedures
3. *Decision verifiability:* the degree to which the correctness of the solutions or decisions can be demonstrated and ascertained
4. *Decision specificity:* the degree to which there is generally more than one correct solution involved in performing the task

In a highly structured task, goals are very clear, there is only one correct procedure for performing the task, the correctness of the decisions can be immediately verified, and there is only one correct solution. Obviously, a highly structured task does not require leaders to provide additional structure.

The third situational variable was the power position of the leader. This factor was measured by a series of questions asking whether the leaders could recommend rewards or promotions, whether they could assign tasks and evaluate performance, and whether they had been given official titles by the organization to differentiate them from subordinates.

By determining whether a group is high or low on each of the three situational factors, Fiedler classified each group into one of eight categories, which ranged along a scale from extremely favorable situations to extremely unfavorable situations for the leader. A highly favorable situation consisted of good leader–member relations, a highly structured task, and a strong power position, as illustrated in Exhibit 15.8. An extremely unfavorable situation existed when the leader–member relations were poor, the task was unstructured, and the leader possessed a weak power position.

Group Effectiveness. Fiedler examined the relationship between the leaders' LPC score and the effectiveness of the group in a variety of situations. The results indicated that a high LPC leader was most effective when the situation was moderately favorable. If the situation was extremely favorable or unfavorable, however, low LPC leaders tended to have the most effective groups. These relationships are illustrated in Exhibit 15.9.

Although these results may look rather complex and difficult to understand, they seem plausible after a brief consideration. Relationship-oriented leaders (high LPC) tend to excel in situations of intermediate favorableness where concern for the group members is apparently a necessary prerequisite for motivating them to perform well. In these situations, people want to have leaders who care about them. Task-oriented leaders (low LPC), however, are more effective when the situation is either very favorable or very unfavorable. In a highly favorable situation, the personal needs of members are apparently already satisfied and what is needed is a task-oriented leader to get the job done. In an extremely unfavorable situation, however, satisfying individual needs is probably impossible. A task-oriented leader who simply focuses on getting the work done is more effective than a relationship-oriented leader who spends time fruitlessly trying to build good relationships in an impossible situation.

EXHIBIT 15.8   The Situation Favorableness Dimension:
Measured by Three Situational Variables

	Very Favorable							Very Unfavorable
	I	II	III	IV	V	VI	VII	VIII
Leader–Member Relations	Good	Good	Good	Good	Poor	Poor	Poor	Poor
Task Structure	High	High	Low	Low	High	High	Low	Low
Power Position	Strong	Weak	Strong	Weak	Strong	Weak	Strong	Weak

Source: Adapted from Fred E. Fiedler and Martin M. Chemers, *Leadership and Effective Management* (Glenview, Ill.: Scott Foresman, 1974), p. 70. Used by permission.

Fiedler's theory has some interesting implications for the selection and training of leaders in organizations. Candidates for leadership positions should be evaluated to assess their basic orientations, and they should be placed in jobs consistent with their leadership orientation. The favorableness of a situation should be assessed before assigning a leader to that position. Leaders who are struggling may need to be placed in a different situation, or their current situation may need to be changed.

When leaders are not successful, it is tempting to suggest that they need to change their leadership orientation. Fiedler does not recommend this approach, however, and argues that the basic leadership orientation of an individual is a relatively stable personality characteristic that cannot be easily changed. Rather than changing the leader to fit the situation, Fiedler recommends changing the situation to fit the leader through what he calls job engineering.[43] *Job engineering* consists of changing one of the situational factors to increase or decrease the favorability of the situation. For example, the task structure and power position can be effectively changed through job redesign programs or changes in personnel policies.

The validity of Fiedler's contingency theory has been examined in numerous studies. Although most of the studies have been supportive, there have been enough contradictory findings for the model to remain somewhat controversial among leadership scholars. The most serious controversy about Fiedler's model concerns the LPC scale. Although the theory seems to predict leader effectiveness, the ambiguity over what the LPC score is actually measuring is disturbing.

The Path–Goal Model

Another situational leadership theory is the **path–goal model** developed primarily by Robert House.[44] This model is fairly well known because it is based upon a popular theory of motivation—expectancy theory. The path–goal model explains how

EXHIBIT 15.9	Fiedler's Contingency Model: Leader–Situation Match

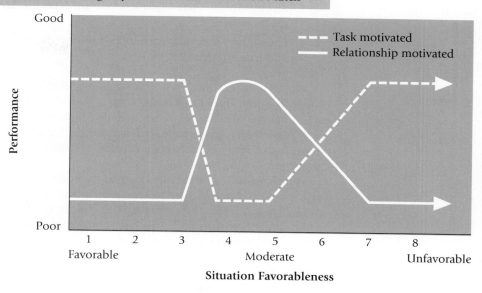

leaders can facilitate task performance by showing subordinates how their performance can be instrumental in achieving desired rewards. Expectancy theory explains how an individual's attitudes and behavior are influenced by the relationships between effort and performance (goal paths) and the valence of the rewards (goal attractiveness). Therefore, people are satisfied and productive when they see a strong relationship between their effort and performance and when their performance results in highly valued rewards. The path–goal model claims that the most effective leaders are those who help subordinates follow the path to receiving valued rewards.

Essentially, the model explains what leaders should do (a) to influence the perceptions of subordinates about their work, (b) to identify important personal goals for subordinates, and (c) to clarify the various paths to goal attainment. The model claims that leader behavior is motivating and satisfying to the extent that it clarifies the paths to the goals and increases goal attainment.

Leader Behaviors. The path–goal model suggests that leadership consists of two basic functions. The first function is path clarification: the leader helps subordinates understand which behaviors are necessary to accomplish the tasks. The second function is to increase the number of rewards available to subordinates by being supportive and paying attention to their personal needs. To perform these functions, leaders may adopt a variety of leadership styles. Four distinct leadership styles are explained in the model:

1. *Directive leadership:* tells subordinates what is expected of them and provides specific guidance, standards, and schedules of work
2. *Supportive leadership:* treats subordinates as equals and shows concern for their well-being, status, and personal needs; seeks to develop pleasant interpersonal relationships among group members.

3. *Achievement-oriented leadership:* sets challenging goals, expects subordinates to perform at their highest level, and continually seeks improvement in performance

4. *Participative leadership:* consults with subordinates and uses their suggestions and ideas in decision making

Unlike Fiedler's model, which suggested that leadership style was resistant to change, the path–goal model suggests that these four styles can be performed by the same manager at different times and in different situations. In other words, the path–goal theory suggests that if a directive leader discovers the situation has changed and now requires a participative leader, it is possible for the leader to change.

A fifth leadership style that ought to be added to the model is punitive leadership. The path–goal model focuses almost exclusively on the leader's ability to administer positive reinforcement and ignores the powerful impact of carefully administered punishment. While both contingent and noncontingent rewards typically create positive feelings toward the leader, significant task improvement is sometimes best accomplished by contingent punishment. For punishment to be effective, however, it should be administered fairly and timely, the punishment should not be severe, clear expectations and explanations should be communicated, and there should be an atmosphere of genuine concern and caring for those being punished.[45]

The appropriate leadership style depends on the situation. Although the path–goal model does not explain how to identify the appropriate leadership style, the model does present a list of situational factors that need to be considered.

Situational Factors. Two types of situational factors are proposed—the characteristics of the follower and environmental factors. Three characteristics of the followers have been identified as significant variables determining the appropriate leadership style:

1. *Locus of control.* As explained in Chapter 2, locus of control concerns the individual's belief concerning the determinants of reward. Individuals with an internal locus of control believe their rewards are based on their own efforts, while those with an external locus of control believe their rewards are controlled by external forces. Internals prefer a participative leadership style, while externals are generally more satisfied with a directive leadership style.

2. *Authoritarianism.* Authoritarianism is an individual's willingness to accept the influence of others. Highly authoritarian followers tend to be less receptive to a participative leadership style and more responsive to directive leadership.

3. *Abilities.* The ability and experience of the followers will influence whether they are able to work more successfully with an achievement-oriented leader who sets challenging goals and expects high performance, or a supportive leader who is willing to patiently encourage and instruct them.

The path–goal model identifies three environmental factors moderating the effects of leadership styles: (1) the nature of the task, (2) the formal authority system within the organization, and (3) the group norms and dynamics. These environmental factors can influence the effectiveness of different leadership styles in a variety of ways. A highly structured task, for example, may reduce the need for a directive leader and even make a directive leader's attempt to provide additional structure seem unwarranted and unwanted. However, a directive leader would be more likely to succeed than a participative leader if the organization had a highly formal authority structure that followed a strict chain of command. Likewise, a concern for the personal needs of subordinates by a supportive leader may seem superficial and unnecessary in a highly cohesive work group.

The basic elements of the path–goal model of leadership are illustrated in Exhibit 15.10. This model shows how leadership styles interact with follower characteristics and environmental factors to influence the personal perceptions and motivation of the followers. The perceptions of the followers concerning the situation and the followers' level of motivation determine their job satisfaction, performance, and acceptance of the leader.

Some simplified applications of the path–goal model are shown in Exhibit 15.11. In the first two situations, subordinates have an ambiguous job or they feel insufficiently rewarded. Both situations call for a directive leader who explains the job and helps subordinates know how to get rewarded for performing it. The next two situations, boring work and a lack of self-confidence, call for a supportive leader. Repetitive jobs are not as boring if a supportive leader helps subordinates see that their work is meaningful and significant. Likewise, a supportive leader can help subordinates feel greater self-confidence by coaching them and praising their accomplishments. In situation 5, subordinates are not challenged by the task. An achievement-oriented leader will set high goals and emphasize the intrinsic and extrinsic rewards from more effort. Finally, situation 6 involves a task that is

EXHIBIT 15.10 Path–Goal Model of Leadership

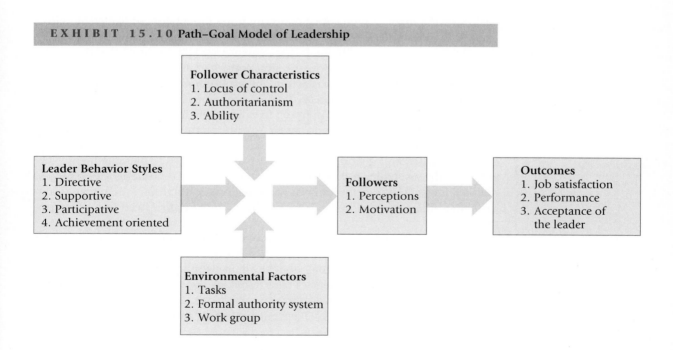

EXHIBIT 15.11 Applications of the Path–Goal Model to Six Situations

Situation		Leader Behavior		Impact on Subordinate		Outcome
1. Ambiguous job	$\longrightarrow$	Directive leader	$\longrightarrow$	Provides guidance and clarity of direction	$\longrightarrow$	More effort
2. Insufficient reward	$\longrightarrow$	Directive leader	$\longrightarrow$	Clarifies path to reward and/or increases reward	$\longrightarrow$	More effort
3. Boring job	$\longrightarrow$	Supportive leader	$\longrightarrow$	Increases interest in work	$\longrightarrow$	More effort
4. Lack of self-confidence	$\longrightarrow$	Supportive leader	$\longrightarrow$	Increases role competence and reward expectation	$\longrightarrow$	More effort
5. Lack of challenge	$\longrightarrow$	Achievement-oriented leader	$\longrightarrow$	Sets high goals	$\longrightarrow$	More effort
6. Undefined task	$\longrightarrow$	Participative leader	$\longrightarrow$	Clarifies objectives and task specifications	$\longrightarrow$	More effort

Source: Adapted from Gary A. Yukl, *Leadership in Organizations* (Englewood Cliffs, N.J.: Prentice-Hall, 1981).

unstructured and poorly defined, calling for participative leadership. By participating in the decision making, subordinates help to create an effective solution to the problem and, as a result of their involvement, feel committed to making it work.

Research on the Path–Goal Model. The relationships specified by the path–goal model have been examined in a modest number of empirical studies. This research has tested the theory's predictions concerning the moderators of leadership effectiveness to determine whether the situational variables interacted with the leadership styles in the predicted manner. The evidence seems to indicate that the model does quite well in predicting how the situational variables and leader styles combine to influence individual satisfaction and group morale.[46] However, the model has not been shown to be a good predictor of individual or group performance. Perhaps the greatest disadvantage in trying to validate the model empirically is that it contains too many variables and tries to explain too much. An experiment testing the full path–goal model is difficult because too many variables have not been clearly identified and instruments have not been developed to measure them. Nevertheless, the available studies tend to support the model, although they suggest that it understates the complexity of the situation. Furthermore, the research suggests that other variables, such as conflict and structure, also need to be incorporated into it.

Perhaps the major contribution of the path–goal model is that it provides a method for viewing leadership in terms of the rewards and punishments administered by the leader. The path–goal model explains why a particular style works best because of the reward contingencies determined by the environment and the leader's capacity to administer rewards and punishments. As more research accumulates, this type of explanation will have practical applications for those interested in the leadership process.[47]

The Normative Decision-making Model of Leadership

Another situational leadership theory is the **normative decision-making model** formulated by Victor Vroom and Philip Yetton.[48] It is considered both a decision-making model and a theory of leadership, because it explains how leaders should make decisions. This model tends to equate leadership with decision making, suggesting that making decisions is one of the most important functions a leader performs.

The normative decision-making model is a contingency theory of leadership since it assumes that no single leadership style is appropriate for all situations. Instead, leaders must develop a repertoire of leadership styles and adopt the style that is most appropriate to the situation. This model also disagrees with Fiedler by suggesting that leaders can use a variety of decision-making strategies.

Knowing whether to involve others in the decision-making process or whether to make the decision alone is an important leadership issue that depends on several considerations. Leaders need to know when to consult others and when consultation is a waste of time. Briefly stated, Vroom and Yetton's classic model identifies five decision-making styles, along with a series of diagnostic questions to determine which style is most appropriate. These diagnostic questions are arranged sequentially in the form of a decision tree to help managers select the appropriate leadership style.

Decision-making (Leadership) Styles of Leaders. The Vroom-Yetton model identifies five decision-making styles: two types of autocratic decision making (AI and AII), two types of consultative decision making (CI and CII), and a group decision making style (GII). These five styles are defined as follows:

AI   The leader decides alone without soliciting any input from members.

AII The leader decides alone after obtaining the necessary information from members.

CI   The leader makes the decision after consulting with group members individually. The leader shares the problem with them and obtains information, ideas, suggested alternatives, and evaluation.

CII The leader makes the decision after meeting with the members *as a group* to collect their information, ideas, suggested alternatives, and evaluation.

GII The leader and members arrive at a group decision through consensus decision making. The leader may chair the group, but is simply one of the group and does not try to influence the group to adopt a particular solution.

Criteria for Selecting a Leadership Style. Two criteria are used for assessing the effectiveness of a leadership style: quality and acceptance. The quality of the decision concerns its accuracy and the extent to which it will achieve some objective, such as increase profitability, raise productivity, lower costs, reduce turnover, or increase sales. Decision quality depends on gathering accurate and relevant information, identifying good alternatives, and evaluating them carefully to select the best solution. Consulting other group members often provides additional information, but when there are severe time constraints or vested interests on the part of the members, participative decision making would be inappropriate. For example, participative decision making is quite inappropriate during a commando raid, in the middle of a police rescue action, or during the twenty-second huddle of a football team.

Decision acceptance concerns the degree to which the subordinates or group members are willing to implement the decision. There are two questions that leaders should consider in order to determine whether acceptance is an issue: (1) do subordinates feel strongly about the decision? and (2) is individual initiative and judgment on the part of members required to implement the decision? If the answer to either of these questions is yes, then the acceptability of the decision is important. Regardless of the technical quality of the solution, the decision may be a failure if the members are not willing to accept it.

Diagnostic Decision Rules. Vroom and Yetton suggest that leaders select an appropriate decision-making style by diagnosing the situation using a sequence of decision rules. These decision rules are designed to help the leader know how to involve subordinates in decisions in a way that enhances the quality and acceptability of the decision. The first three rules focus on the quality of the decision.

The decision rules are contained in eight questions that a leader answers either yes or no.[49]

1. As long as it is accepted, does it make any difference which decision is selected? Are some decisions qualitatively superior to others?
2. Do I have enough information to make a high-quality decision?
3. Do subordinates have sufficient additional information that must be considered to result in a high-quality decision?
4. Do I know exactly what information is needed, who has it, and how to collect it?
5. Is acceptance of the decision by subordinates crucial to effective implementation?
6. If I were to make the decision by myself, is it certain to be accepted by my subordinates?
7. Can subordinates be trusted to base their solutions on considerations consistent with the organization's goals?
8. Is conflict among the subordinates likely, given the preferred solutions?

These diagnostic questions are used to determine the appropriate decision-making style. The application of these diagnostic questions is contained in the decision tree chart shown in Exhibit 15.12. The chart reads from left to right, and the letters A through H represent the questions shown below the decision tree. The circles in the decision tree below each number represent the point where that question is asked. The lines connecting the circles indicate the decision making path the manager follows, depending on whether the answers to the questions are yes or no. The symbols in the center illustrate which decision style is appropriate for the various paths through the decision tree.

At the end-points of some of the decision sequences, several alternative styles are feasible. For example, at the starting point all five decision styles are appropriate, and the model suggests that each style is likely to lead to a high-quality decision acceptable to subordinates. When more than one decision style is acceptable,

EXHIBIT 15.12 Vroom-Yetton Decision Process Flow Chart

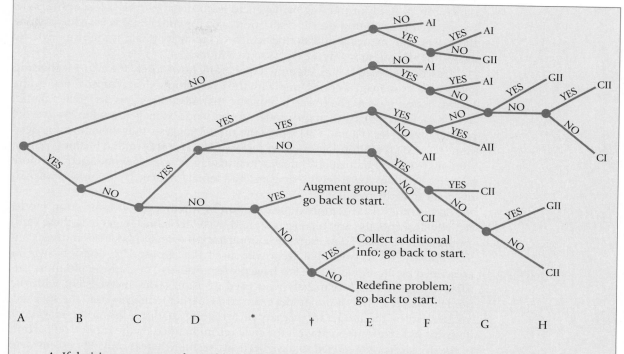

A. If decision was accepted, would it make a difference which course of action was adopted?
B. Do I have sufficient information to make a high-quality decision?
C. Do subordinates have sufficient additional information to result in high-quality decision?
D. Do I know exactly what information is needed, who possesses it, and how to collect it?
* Is necessary additional information to be found within my entire set of subordinates?
† Is it feasible to collect additional information outside group prior to making decisions?
E. Is acceptance of decision by subordinates critical to effective implementation?
F. If I were to make the decision by myself, is it certain that it would be accepted by my subordinates?
G. Can subordinates be trusted to base solutions on organization considerations?
H. Is conflict among subordinates likely in preferred solutions?

Source: Reprinted from Victor H. Vroom and Philip W. Yetton, *Leadership and Decision Making,* by permission of the University of Pittsburgh Press, 1973.

the model recommends that managers choose the most autocratic style to save time and minimize costs. If saving time and minimizing costs are not the most important objectives, one of the other styles might be recommended when more than one style is acceptable. For example, if the goal is to further the personal development of subordinates, the participative styles, GII and CII, are preferred more frequently.

In half the situations the model recommends either AI, AII, or CI strategies, in which the manager decides alone. In four situations the model recommends the CII strategy, where the manager makes the decision alone after consulting with the subordinates as an advisory group. In only three situations does the model indicate that the group decision-making strategy, GII, is the only acceptable method.

Applying the Vroom-Yetton Model. Vroom and Yetton have developed a series of decision-making scenarios that portray how the model can be applied. These scenarios can be used for training managers to learn the appropriate leadership style. Each scenario presents a decision situation, and the individual is asked to assume the role of the manager and decide which is the appropriate leadership style by answering the questions in the decision tree model.

Descriptive research has attempted to identify how closely the actual leadership styles used by managers correspond with the leadership styles recommended by the Vroom-Yetton model. The research indicates that most managers use greater participative decision making than the model recommends. Managers tend to overuse the consultative styles (CI and CII) where the model suggests that the autocratic decision style (AI) is appropriate.[50] Other research has also shown that business school students are more participative than actual managers; top-level managers are more participative than lower-level managers; and female managers are more participative than male managers.[51]

Two studies have examined the question of whether the Vroom-Yetton model actually describes the way managers should make decisions. In general, these studies support the model. For example, among forty-five retail franchises in the cleaning industry, those store managers who used the appropriate decision style as prescribed by the model tended to have more productive operations and more satisfied employees than managers who used decision styles inconsistent with the model.[52] Another test of the model examined whether managers used the style recommended by the model in a variety of decision situations. When the manager's decision style corresponded with the style recommended by the model, 68 percent of the decisions were judged to have been successful, whereas only 22 percent were successful when the actual style failed to correspond with the style recommended by the model.[53] These data suggest that managers would do well to consider the diagnostic questions in deciding whom to involve in decision making.

Comparing the Leadership Models. All four situational leadership models contribute to our understanding of leadership by emphasizing the influence of external factors on the effectiveness of a particular leadership style. Fiedler's contingency model has been subjected to the most extensive empirical research and has been more carefully defined than the other models. A common characteristic of all four models is that each model identifies different leadership styles and suggests that the effectiveness of the style is determined by various situational factors. However, the models focus on different styles, different situational factors, and different criteria for selecting the best style.

The models developed by Hersey and Blanchard and by Fiedler both identify two leadership styles: task oriented versus relationship oriented. But while Hersey and Blanchard view them in a two-dimensional matrix as two independent leader behaviors, Fiedler views them as ends of a single continuum. The path–goal model identifies four leadership styles: directive, supportive, participative, and achievement oriented. The normative decision-making model identifies three leadership styles: autocratic, consultative, and participative.

The situational factors influencing the effectiveness of leadership are quite different in each model. An important reason for some of this difference is that the normative decision-making model equates leadership with making decisions and looks at only this function of leadership. In addition, the models use rather different criteria for evaluating the effectiveness of leadership. Both the Hersey-Blanchard and the Fiedler models evaluate the effectiveness of different leadership styles according to group performance. The path–goal model evaluates leadership according to job satisfaction, performance, and acceptance of the leader. The normative decision-making model focuses on decision quality, decision acceptance, and time required to reach a decision.

The Leader–Member Exchange Theory

Most leadership theories assume that leaders treat all their followers the same and overlook the fact that some followers usually receive considerably more courtesy, autonomy, and trust than others. Some leaders show favoritism to certain followers and give them more resources and greater latitude in deciding what to do.

The **leader–member exchange (LMX) theory** is a situational leadership theory that recognizes the special relationships that leaders develop with certain group members. Members who receive special attention form the in-group while the others form the out-group. Members of the in-group receive a disproportionate amount of the leader's attention and have greater latitude in negotiating special deals with the leader. Members in the out-group receive fewer special favors, and their interactions with the leader are generally based on formal authority interactions.[54]

The LMX theory proposes that the special status of in-group members is determined early in the formation of a group as the leader implicitly categorizes them. It is unclear what criteria leaders use to decide which members will receive special treatment. Some evidence suggests that the leader's perceptions of the members' skills and abilities weighs heavily in this decision. There is also good reason to think that this decision is highly individual and based on personal characteristics such as age, personality, cultural interests, hobbies, and athletic skills.[55]

Differential treatment is more pronounced in some groups than others. In some groups, leaders make a special effort to treat all members similarly, while other groups have highly differentiated in-groups and out-groups.

Research testing LMX theory generally finds that leaders do indeed treat some members better than others, and those who are favored usually report higher levels of satisfaction and productivity. However, highly differentiated groups with sizable status differences between in-groups and out-groups have lower group performance and overall satisfaction than groups whose members are treated more equally.[56] These results suggest that leaders will be more successful if they take the time to build a personal relationship with each follower and make each feel special.

DETERMINANTS OF LEADERSHIP EFFECTIVENESS

Although deciding what makes an effective leader seems as if it should be a simple decision, the theories and research reviewed earlier illustrate the complexity of the issue. In spite of the complexity, however, people who are in positions of leadership are still faced with the practical question of deciding which leadership pattern to adopt.

Choosing a Leadership Style

One of the most popular models for selecting an appropriate leadership style is one proposed by Robert Tannenbaum and Warren Schmidt.[57] This model describes a variety of leadership styles along a continuum from highly autocratic at one end to highly participative at the other, as illustrated in Exhibit 15.13. Seven different leadership styles along this continuum are identified in the exhibit. At one extreme the manager uses his or her authority to simply make the decision and announce it. At the other extreme, the manager provides an area of freedom for subordinates and permits them to function within these limits to make decisions and direct their own activities. According to Tannenbaum and Schmidt, the appropriate leadership style is determined by (1) forces in the manager, (2) forces in the subordinates, and (3) forces in the situation.

Some of the important forces in the manager include the manager's value system and the value the manager places on participation and involvement by subordinates. The amount of confidence managers have in their subordinates and the manager's ability to handle uncertainty are also relevant.

The forces in a subordinate include such things as whether subordinates have high needs for independence, whether they are ready to assume responsibility for decision making, whether they are interested in the problems, and whether they have enough experience to deal with them. As subordinates gain greater skill and competence in managing themselves, leaders ought to provide more autonomy for them.

The forces in the situation include the culture of the organization and its history of allowing subordinates to exercise autonomy, cohesiveness in the group and the degree to which the members work together as a unit, the nature of the problem itself and the question of whether subordinates have the knowledge and experience needed to solve it, and the pressures of time, since group decision making is time consuming and ineffective in a crisis situation.

The framework provided by Tannenbaum and Schmidt provides a useful way to analyze a leadership situation and choose a successful leadership pattern. The successful leader is one who is aware of the situational forces and responds appropriately to them. Effective leaders need to understand themselves, the members of the group, the company, and the broader social environment in which they operate. As a long-term strategy, Tannenbaum and Schmidt encourage leaders to change their subordinates and the situation in a way that allows them to gradually provide greater opportunities for subordinate involvement.

Strategies for Improving Leadership

Since the quality of leadership contributes so greatly to the effectiveness of an organization, knowing how to increase leader effectiveness is a serious issue. Improved leader behavior is not a panacea for all organizational problems; nevertheless, quality leadership is so important that improving the quality of leadership should be an ongoing effort in every organization. Four of the most popular methods for increasing leadership effectiveness include leadership training, managerial selection and placement, organizational redesign, and rewarding leader behavior.

Leadership Training. Although there is some uncertainty about whether basic leader orientations can be effectively changed through training, millions of dollars are spent annually to train leaders. This training includes both training in basic

EXHIBIT 15.13   Continuum of Leader Behavior

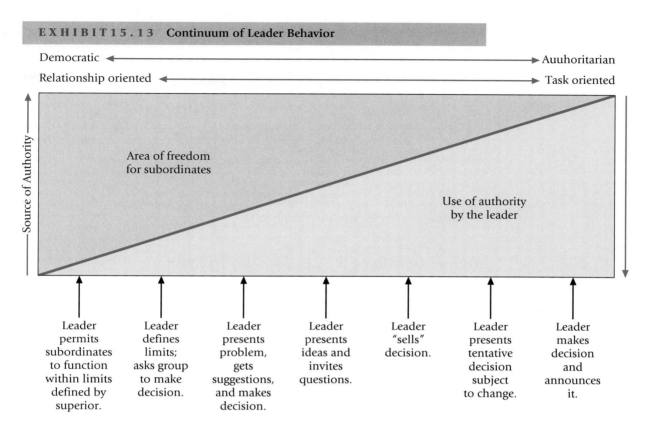

Democratic ⟵⟶ Auuhoritarian

Relationship oriented ⟵⟶ Task oriented

Source of Authority

Area of freedom for subordinates

Use of authority by the leader

| Leader permits subordinates to function within limits defined by superior. | Leader defines limits; asks group to make decision. | Leader presents problem, gets suggestions, and makes decision. | Leader presents ideas and invites questions. | Leader "sells" decision. | Leader presents tentative decision subject to change. | Leader makes decision and announces it. |

Source: Reprinted by permission of the *Harvard Business Review*. An exhibit from "How to Choose a Leadership Pattern," by Robert Tannenbaum and Warren Schmidt (May–June 1973). Copyright 1973 by the President and Fellows of Harvard College; all rights reserved.

skills, such as managing time and evaluating performance, and training in interpersonal relations designed to change the leader's basic personality. Although training appears to help leaders acquire better leadership skills, it is doubtful that such training will change a leader's basic leadership orientation or personality structure.[58]

Managerial Selection and Placement. Since basic leadership orientations are not easily changed, an individual's leadership style should be matched to the situation. This idea is consistent with Fiedler's recommendation to measure both the LPC score of the leader and the favorableness of the situation and place the leader in an appropriate situation. When companies are recruiting top-level leaders, they often spend considerable time and money trying to make a careful selection. Some companies pay sizable consulting fees to executive search firms to help them identify outstanding leadership talent. Biographical information examining a person's previous leadership experiences can help to predict leadership effectiveness.[59]

Organizational Engineering. When people are placed in situations inconsistent with their leadership style, they will probably be unsuccessful and experience frustration and discouragement until they are placed in a new situation or their situation is changed. Fiedler recommends that organizations engineer the job to fit the manager. This approach is particularly useful when a specific individual is necessary to the organization, yet that person does not possess a compatible leadership style. The job can be changed most easily by changing the degree of task structure or the power position of the leader.

Rewarding Leader Behavior. Leaders can acquire new leadership skills and learn different leader behaviors if they are sufficiently motivated to experiment and learn. A variety of incentives can be provided to reward leaders for learning and developing. Pay increases and promotions are popular incentives encouraging most leaders to improve. However, the most powerful incentive is probably the intrinsic satisfaction that comes from greater self-confidence and improved interpersonal relationships between leaders and members.

Reciprocal Influence of Leader and Follower

With thousands of books and articles written about leadership, it is surprising that so little has been written about "followership." We seem to assume that leadership is a one-way process in which leaders influence followers, and we overlook the potential influence in the opposite direction. Only meager efforts have attempted to describe the influence of the group on the leader.

The discussion to this point has assumed that leaders influence followers—the satisfaction and performance of the followers is caused by the leader's behavior. There are good reasons to reverse this statement, however, and argue that the behavior of the leader is caused by the performance and satisfaction of the followers. When we acknowledge the leader's capacity to reward the behavior of followers, we should not overlook the capacity of the followers to reward the leader by the ways they perform. For example, organizations reward managers according to the performance of their group. Consequently, the managers of high-performing groups are highly rewarded by the organization.

One study has demonstrated the reciprocal nature of influence between leaders and subordinates. In this study, data were collected from first-line managers and two of the supervisors who reported to them. Leaders who were more considerate created greater satisfaction among their subordinates; but, at the same time, the performance of the subordinates caused changes in the behavior of the leaders.[60] Employees who performed well caused their supervisors to reward them and treat them with greater consideration. Although research on the reciprocal influence between leaders and followers is still rather limited, it is important to remember that leadership may be significantly constrained by the followers.

Some observers contend that the leadership crisis in society is not really caused by bad leaders, but by incompetent or uncooperative followers who fail to complete their work in an active, intelligent, and ethical way.[61] Effective followers are characterized as having (1) personal integrity that demands loyalty to the organization and a willingness to follow their own beliefs, (2) an understanding of the organization and their assigned role, (3) versatility, and (4) personal responsibility.[62]

Constraints on Leader Behavior. Leaders do not have unlimited opportunities to influence others. Leadership effectiveness is constrained by a variety of factors, such as the extent to which managerial decisions are preprogramed due to precedent, structure, technological specifications, laws, and the absence of available alternatives. Leadership can also be constrained by a variety of organizational factors limiting the leader's ability to either communicate with or to reinforce the behavior of subordinates.[63] The constraints imposed on leaders include external factors, organizational policies, group factors, and individual skills and abilities.

1. *External factors.* Leaders are constrained in what they can do because of various economic realities and a host of state and federal laws. For example, leaders are required to pay at least the minimum wage and they are required to enforce safety standards. Leaders who have unskilled followers will have difficulty leading regardless of their leadership style, and the availability of skilled followers is influenced by the external labor market. Some geographical areas have a much better supply of skilled employees than others.

2. *Organizational policies.* The organization may constrain a leader's effectiveness by limiting the amount of interaction between leaders and followers and by restricting the leader's ability to reward or punish followers.

3. *Group factors.* Group norms are created by the dynamics of the group. If the group is highly cohesive and very determined, it can limit the leader's ability to influence the group.

4. *Individual skills and abilities.* The leader's own skills and abilities may act as constraints since leaders can only possess so much expertise, energy, and power. Some situations may simply require greater skills and abilities than the leader may possibly hope to possess.

Substitutes for Leadership. While some situations constrain leaders, other situations make leadership unnecessary. These variables are referred to as *substitute variables* because they **substitute for leadership** either by making the leader's behavior unnecessary or by neutralizing the leader's ability to influence subordinates. Some of the variables that tend to substitute for, or **neutralize leadership** are illustrated in Exhibit 15.14. For example, subordinates who have extensive experience, ability, and training tend to eliminate the need for instrumental leadership. The task-oriented instructions from an instrumental leader are simply unnecessary when subordinates already know what to do. If the subordinates are indifferent toward rewards offered by the organization, the influence of both supportive leaders and instrumental leaders is neutralized.

Although the concepts of substitutes and neutralizers for leadership are relatively new, early studies seem to support them. For example, studies have shown that a highly structured situation neutralizes a leader's efforts to structure the group's behavior.[64]

Realizing that there are constraints on a leader's behavior and that other factors may serve to neutralize or substitute for the influence of a leader helps explain why the research on leadership has produced such inconsistent results. The fact that the results are inconsistent and generally weak does not necessarily mean that leadership is unimportant or that leaders don't really account for much. Instead, it illustrates the complexity of the world in which leaders are required to function. Leadership is an extremely important function that has an enormous influence on the effectiveness of groups and organizations. The complexity of the situation, however, may prevent us from knowing in advance which leadership behaviors will be the most effective.

EXHIBIT 15.14 Substitutes and Neutralizers for Leadership

	Leader Behavior Influenced	
Substitute or Neutralizer	Supportive Leadership	Instrumental Leadership
A. *Subordinate Characteristics:*		
1. Experience, ability, training		Substitute
2. "Professional" orientation	Substitute	Substitute
3. Indifference toward rewards offered by organization	Neutralizer	Neutralizer
B. *Task Characteristics:*		
1. Structured, routine, unambiguous task		Substitute
2. Feedback provided by task		Substitute
3. Intrinsically satisfying work	Substitute	
C. *Organization Characteristics:*		
1. Cohesive work group	Substitute	Substitute
2. Low position power (leader lacks control over organizational rewards)	Neutralizer	Neutralizer
3. Formalization (explicit plans, goals, areas of responsibility)		Substitute
4. Inflexibility (rigid, unyielding rules and procedures)		Neutralizer
5. Leader located apart from subordinates with only limited communication possible	Neutralizer	Neutralizer

Source: Adapted from Stephen Kerr and J. Jermier, "Substitutes for Leadership: Their Meaning and Measurement," *Organizational Behavior and Human Performance,* vol. 22 (1978), pp. 375–403.

SUMMARY

1. Leadership is incremental influence and is said to occur when one individual influences others to do something voluntarily that they otherwise would not do. A need for leadership within organizations stems from the incompleteness of the organization design and the dynamic nature of the internal and external environments. Three basic leadership roles include origination of policy and structure, interpolation, and administration.

2. Leadership has been distinguished from management. One distinction focuses on what they do: managers manage things and leaders lead people. Another distinction focuses on how each responds to change: managers control complexity and stabilize organizational activities while leaders produce useful change. A distinction is also made between transactional leadership, which motivates people with contingent rewards and pay increases, and transformational leadership, which motivates people using an inspired vision that empowers people and builds commitment.

3. The earliest studies of leadership were primarily trait studies that attempted to identify the characteristics of effective leaders. These studies

focused primarily on physical traits, intelligence, and personality. Although some personal characteristics were frequently related to leadership, the results were generally weak and often inconsistent. Many studies concluded that the characteristics of the subordinate and the nature of the task were as important as the characteristics of the leader in determining success.

4. A second approach to studying leadership focused on leader behaviors—how leaders actually behave. One of the earliest studies compared three leadership styles: authoritarian, democratic, and laissez-faire. Although democratic leadership created the greatest satisfaction, autocratic leadership created the highest levels of productivity.

5. Research conducted simultaneously at two universities identified two similar leadership behaviors. At The Ohio State University, the researchers labeled these two leader behaviors *initiating structure* and *consideration*. At the University of Michigan, the same two factors were labeled *production-centered* and *employee-centered leader behaviors*. These two leader behaviors appear to identify leadership functions essential to the effectiveness of a group. The two factors have been used to form a matrix called the Leadership Grid®, which places a concern for production on one side of the grid and concern for people on the other. Each dimension is measured on a nine-point scale, and the ideal leadership style is considered to be 9,9, indicating a leader who is high in both dimensions. The research evidence, however, does not consistently support this conclusion.

6. The failure of leadership research to identify leadership traits or universally superior leader behaviors resulted in the development of four situational theories of leadership. These theories suggest that the most effective leadership style depends on situational variables, especially the characteristics of the group and the nature of the task.

7. Hersey and Blanchard developed a situational leadership model that matched different combinations of task behavior and relationship behavior with the maturity of the followers. As the maturity of the followers increases, the appropriate leadership style is first telling, then selling, then participating, and finally, for highly mature followers, delegating.

8. The most extensively researched situational leadership theory is Fred Fiedler's contingency theory of leadership. Fiedler used the LPC scale to measure the leader's orientation toward either the task or the person. The most appropriate leadership style was then determined by assessing three situational variables: whether the relationships between the leader and the members were good or poor, whether the task was structured or unstructured, and whether the power position of the leader was strong or weak. When these three situational variables created an extremely favorable or extremely unfavorable situation, the most effective leadership style was a task-oriented (low LPC) leader. However, a leader with a high concern for interpersonal relationships (high LPC) was more effective in situations where there were intermediate levels of favorableness.

9. The path–goal model is another situational leadership theory. This theory is derived from expectancy theory and suggests that effective leaders must clarify the goal paths and increase the goal attractiveness for followers. Four distinct leadership styles are proposed in the model: directive, supportive, achievement oriented, and participative leadership styles. The most appropriate style depends on two types of situational factors: the characteristics of the follower and characteristics of the environment. Three of the most important follower characteristics include the locus of control, authoritarianism, and personal abilities. The three environmental factors include the nature of the task, the formal authority system within the organization, and the group norms and dynamics.

10. Vroom and Yetton's normative decision-making model is also a situational leadership theory, because it identifies the appropriate styles leaders should use in making decisions. The three leadership styles include autocratic decision making, consultative decision making, and group decision making. The decision rules determining which style is most appropriate

include such questions as whether the leader has adequate information to make the decision alone, whether the subordinates will accept the goals of the organization, whether subordinates will accept the decision if they do not participate in making it, and whether the decision will produce a controversial solution.

11. Although most of the literature on leadership emphasizes the influence of the leader on the group, the influence of the group on the leader should not be overlooked. The relationship between the leader and the group implies a reciprocal influence. Groups have the capacity to influence the behavior of their leaders by responding selectively to specific leader behaviors. The influence of a leader can also be constrained by several external factors, such as organizational policies, group norms, and individual skills and abilities. Other variables have been found to neutralize or substitute for the influence of a leader, such as the skills and abilities of followers and the nature of the task itself.

DISCUSSION QUESTIONS

1. Can a person be a good manager and a poor leader? Can a person be a good leader and a poor manager?

2. Identify someone you have associated with who was a transformational leader and someone who was a transactional leader. How were they different, and what were the effects of these differences?

3. Studies of the relationship between physical traits and leadership suggest that leaders tend to be tall, dark, and handsome. How do you account for these results?

4. Why is honesty such an important leadership trait?

5. What is the relationship between the two leader behaviors, initiating structure and consideration, and the two group roles discussed in Chapter 9: work roles and maintenance roles? What does this association suggest in terms of essential activities for group functioning?

6. What is your leadership style on the managerial grid? The experiential exercise at the end of the chapter might help you decide. Is your leadership style the same for all situations?

7. Is it realistic to expect a leader to be proficient in all four life cycle leadership styles: telling, selling, participating, and delegating?

8. Apply Fiedler's contingency theory of leadership by identifying two extremely different situations, one extremely favorable and the other extremely unfavorable, and explain why a task-oriented (low LPC) leader is most effective in each situation.

9. What is the relationship between expectancy theory and the path–goal model of leadership?

10. In Vroom and Yetton's normative decision-making model of leadership, the conflict rule (number 8) advocates group decision making when acceptance of the decision is crucial but conflict among subordinates is anticipated. How valid is this rule? How can you expect group decision making to produce an acceptable decision when there is conflict?

11. What are the social, moral, and legal ramifications of having a clearly defined in-group?

12. An important difference in the implications of situational leadership theories is whether leadership styles can be learned or changed. What is your opinion about the possibility of significantly changing an individual's basic leadership style?

13. The relationship between the leader and the group involves a reciprocal influence relationship. Who do you think exerts the greatest influence, the leader or the group? Using the principles of operant conditioning, describe how a group would need to behave in order to create a punitive, authoritarian supervisor or a rewarding, participative supervisor.

GLOSSARY

charismatic leadership A type of leadership attributed to outstanding and highly esteemed leaders who gain the confidence and trust of followers.

consideration Leader behavior that focuses on the comfort, well-being, satisfaction, and need fulfillment of subordinates.

contingency theories of leadership Leadership theories that recognize the influence of situational variables in determining the ideal styles of leadership. Four contingency leadership theories include Hersey and Blanchard's situational leadership model, Fiedler's contingency theory, House's path–goal theory, and Vroom and Yetton's normative decision-making model.

empowerment A condition created by leaders that stimulates followers to act on their initiative and perform in a highly committed, intelligent, and ethical way.

initiating structure Leader behavior that focuses on clarifying and defining the roles and task responsibilities for subordinates.

LPC scale A questionnaire with sixteen semantic differential scales that are used to measure the least preferred co-worker. This scale measures a person's leadership orientation.

leader behaviors The kinds of behaviors that leaders actually perform in a group. The two leader behaviors that have been consistently observed include task-related activities, called *initiating structure* or *production-centered activities,* and interpersonal relations activities, sometimes called *consideration* or *employee-centered activities.*

leader–member exchange (LMX) theory A situational leadership theory that explains how leaders form special relationships with selected group members who form an in-group and are more trusted and favored.

leadership The incremental influence that one individual exerts on another and that causes the second person to change his or her behavior voluntarily. Three leadership roles include origination of structure by top-level managers, interpolation or adapting the structure by middle-level managers, and administra-

tion or implementation of the policies and procedures by lower-level supervisors.

Leadership Grid® (formerly Managerial Grid®) A matrix that combines two factors: concern for people and concern for production. Each factor is measured with a nine-point scale.

life cycle theory of leadership The situational leadership theory developed by Hersey and Blanchard, which suggests that leaders should use either a telling, selling, participating, or delegating style of leadership depending on the maturity of the followers.

neutralizers of leadership Forces that tend to destroy the influence of a leader or make it ineffective.

normative decision-making model A decision-making model that is also a theory of leadership that suggests the most appropriate decision-making style for a leader depends on situational factors, such as the information possessed by leader and followers and whether group members will accept the decision.

path–goal model A contingency theory of leadership based on expectancy theory that suggests the characteristics of the follower and environmental factors should determine which of four leadership styles is most appropriate.

relationship-oriented leader (high LPC) According to Fiedler, a leader who sees desirable characteristics even in his or her least preferred co-worker.

substitutes for leadership Subordinate, task, or organizational factors that decrease the importance of a leader's influence; forces within the environment that supplant or replace the influence of the leader.

task-oriented leader (low LPC) According to Fiedler, a leader who shows a strong emotional dislike for his or her least preferred co-worker.

transactional leadership A style of leadership that focuses on accomplishing work by relying on contingent rewards, task instructions, and corrective actions.

transformational leadership A style of leadership that focuses on communicating an organizational vision, building commitment, stimulating acceptance, and empowering followers.

NOTES

1. Ralph M. Stogdill, *Handbook of Leadership: A Survey of the Literature* (New York: Free Press, 1974).

2. Daniel Katz and Robert L. Kahn, *The Social Psychology of Organizations*, 2nd ed. (New York: Wiley, 1978), pp. 530–535.

3. Robert J. House, "A 1976 Theory of Charismatic Leadership," in J. G. Hunt and L. L. Larson (eds.), *Leadership: The Cutting Edge* (Carbondale: Southern Illinois University Press), pp. 189–207; Leanne Atwater, Robert Penn, and Linda Rucker, "Personal Qualities of Charismatic Leaders," *Leadership and Organization Development Journal*, vol. 12, no. 2 (1991), pp. 7–10.

4. J. A. Conger and R. N. Kanungo, "Behavioral Dimensions of Charismatic Leadership," in J. A. Conger and R. N. Kanungo (eds.), *Charismatic Leadership: The Elusive Factor in Organizational Effectiveness* (San Francisco: Jossey-Bass, 1988), pp. 78–97.

5. Warren Bennis, *On Becoming a Leader* (Reading, Mass.: Addison-Wesley, 1989); Warren Bennis, "Why Leaders Can't Lead," *Training and Development Journal*, vol. 43 (April 1989), pp. 35–39.

6. Abraham Zaleznik, "Managers and Leaders: Are They Different?" *Harvard Business Review*, vol. 70 (March–April 1992), pp. 126–135.

7. Warren Bennis and Burt Nanus, *Leaders: The Strategies for Taking Charge* (New York: Harper & Row, 1985), p. 21.

8. John P. Kotter, "What Leaders Really Do," *Harvard Business Review*, vol. 68 (May–June 1990), pp. 103–111.

9. Bruce J. Avolio, David A. Waldman, and Francis J. Yammarino, "Leading in the 1990s: The Four I's of Transformational Leadership," *Journal of European Industrial Training*, vol. 15, no. 4 (1991), pp. 9–16; Philip Atkinson, "Leadership: Total Quality and Cultural Change," *Management Services*, vol. 35 (June 1991), pp. 16–19; Jane M. Howell and Christopher A. Higgins, "Champions of Technological Innovation," *Administrative Science Quarterly*, vol. 35 (June 1990), pp. 317–341; Arthur K. Smith, "Good Leaders," *Business and Economic Review*, vol. 37 (October–December 1990), pp. 10–12.

10. Ron Zemke, "Empowerment: Helping People Take Charge," *Training: The Magazine of Human Resource Development*, vol. 25 (January 1988), pp. 63–64.

11. James M. Burns, *Leadership* (New York: Harper & Row, 1978).

12. Bennis, *On Becoming a Leader.*

13. Bernard M. Bass, *Leadership and Performance Beyond Expectations* (New York: Free Press, 1985); John J. Hater and Bernard M. Bass, "Superiors' Evaluations and Subordinates' Perceptions of Transformational and Transactional Leadership," *Journal of Applied Psychology*, vol. 73 (November 1988), pp. 695–702.

14. Bernard M. Bass, "From Transactional to Transformational Leadership: Learning to Share the Vision," *Organizational Dynamics*, vol. 18 (Winter 1990), pp. 19–31.

15. Francis J. Yammarino and Bernard M. Bass, "Transformational Leadership and Multiple Levels of Analysis," *Human Relations*, vol. 43 (October 1990), pp. 975–995.

16. Ronald J. Deluga, "Relationship of Transformational and Transactional Leadership with Employee Influencing Strategies," *Group and Organization Studies*, vol. 13 (December 1988), pp. 456–467; Joseph Seltzer and Bernard M. Bass, "Transformational Leadership: Beyond Initiation and Consideration," *Journal of Management*, vol. 16 (December 1990), pp. 693–703; William D. Spangler and Lewis R. Braiotta, "Leadership and Corporate Audit Committee Effectiveness," *Group and Organization Studies*, vol. 15 (June 1990), pp. 134–157; David A. Waldman, Bernard M. Bass, and Francis J. Yammarino, "Adding to Contingent-Reward Behavior: The Augmenting Effect of Charismatic Leadership," *Group and Organization Studies*, vol. 15 (December 1990), pp. 381–394; Francis J. Yammarino and Bernard M. Bass, "Transformational Leadership and Multiple Levels of Analysis," *Human Relations*, vol. 43 (October 1990), pp. 975–995.

17. Bernard M. Bass and Bruce J. Avolio, "Developing Transformational Leadership: 1992 and Beyond," *Journal of European Industrial Training*, vol. 14, no. 5 (1990), pp. 21–27; Brian P. Niehoff, Cathy A. Enz, and Richard A. Grover, "The Impact of Top Management Actions on Employee Attitudes and Perceptions," *Group and Organization Studies*, vol. 15 (September 1990), pp. 337–352; Micha Popper, Ori Landau, and Ury M. Gluskines, "The Israeli Defence Forces: An Example of Transformational Leadership," *Leadership and Organization Development Journal*, vol. 13, no. 1 (1992), pp. 3–8.

18. Katz and Kahn, op. cit., chap. 16.

19. Bernard M. Bass, *Leadership, Psychology, and Organizational Behavior* (New York: Harper & Row, 1960); Cecil A. Gibb, "Leadership," in G. Lindzey and E. Aronson (eds.), *The Handbook of Social Psychology*, 2nd ed., Vol. 4 (Reading, Mass.: Addison-Wesley, 1969); R. D. Mann, "A Review of the Relationships Between Personality and Performance in Small Groups," *Psychological Bulletin*, vol. 56 (1959), pp. 241–270; Ralph M. Stogdill, "Personal Factors Associated with Leadership: A Survey of the Literature," *Journal of Psychology*, vol. 25 (1948), pp. 35–71.

20. E. B. Gowin, *The Executive and His Control of Men* (New York: Macmillan, 1915).

21. E. C. Hunter and A. M. Jordan, "An Analysis of Qualities Associated with Leadership Among College Students," *Journal of Educational Psychology*, vol. 30 (1939), pp. 497–509.

22. Stogdill, op. cit.

23. Ibid.

24. Shelley A. Kirkpatrick and Edwin A. Locke, "Leadership: Do Traits Matter?" *Academy of Management Executive*, vol. 5 (May 1991), pp. 49–60; James M. Kouzes and Barry Z. Posner, "The Credibility Factor: What Followers Expect from Their Leaders," *Business Credit*, vol. 92 (July–August 1990), pp. 24–28.

25. Kurt Lewin, R. Lippitt, and R. K. White, "Patterns of Aggressive Behavior in Experimentally-Created Social Climates," *Journal of Social Psychology*, vol. 10 (1939), pp. 271–301.

26. Henry Tosi, "Effect of the Interaction of Leader Behavior and Subordinate Authoritarianism," *Proceedings of the Annual Convention of the American Psychological Association*, vol. 6, part 1 (1971), pp. 473–474.

27. Victor H. Vroom and Floyd C. Mann, "Leader Authoritarianism and Employee Attitudes," *Personnel Psychology*, vol. 13 (1960), pp. 125–140.

28. John K. Hemphill, *Leader Behavior Description* (Ohio State Leadership Studies Staff Report, 1950); Ralph M. Stogdill, *Handbook of Leadership* (New York: The Free Press, 1974), chaps. 11 and 12.

29. E. A. Fleishman, "Twenty Years of Consideration and Structure," in E. A. Fleishman and J. G. Hunt (eds.), *Current Developments in the Study of Leadership* (Carbondale: Southern Illinois University Press, 1973), pp. 1–40; E. A. Fleishman and E. F. Harris, "Patterns of Leadership Behavior Related to Employee Grievances and Turnover," *Personnel Psychology*, vol. 15 (1962), pp. 43–56.

30. Fleishman, op cit.; Jane N. Howell and Peter J. Frost, "A Laboratory Study of Charismatic Leadership," *Organizational Behavior and Human Decision Processes*, vol. 43 (April 1989), pp. 243–269.

31. Daniel Katz, N. Maccoby, and N. C. Morse, *Productivity, Supervision, and Morale in an Office Situation* (Ann Arbor: University of Michigan Survey Research Center, 1950).

32. Peter Weissenberg and M. H. Kavanagh, "The Independence of Initiating Structure and Consideration: A Review of the Evidence," *Personnel Psychology*, vol. 25 (Spring 1972), pp. 119–130.

33. Robert R. Blake and Anne Adams McCanse, *Leadership Dilemmas—Grid Solutions* (Houston: Gulf Publishing, 1991).

34. See the review by Paul Hersey and Ken Blanchard, *Management of Organizational Behavior*, 4th ed. (Englewood Cliffs, N.J.: Prentice-Hall, 1982), chap. 4.

35. Kenneth D. Benne and Paul Sheats, "Functional Roles and Group Members," *Journal of Social Issues*, vol. 4 (Spring 1948), pp. 42–47.

36. Robert J. House and M. L. Baetz, "Leadership: Some Generalizations and New Research Directions," in Barry M. Staw (ed.), *Research in Organizational Behavior* (Greenwich, Conn.: J.A.I. Press, 1979).

37. Hersey and Blanchard, op. cit., chap. 7.

38. Reviewed by Hersey and Blanchard, op. cit., pp. 171–172. See also Warren Blank, John R. Weitzel, and Stephen G. Green, "A Test of the Situational Leadership Theory," *Personnel Psychology*, vol. 43 (Autumn 1990), pp. 579–597; Jane R. Goodson, Gail W. McGee, and James F. Cashman, "Situational Leadership Theory: A Test of Leadership Prescriptions," *Group and Organization Studies*, vol. 14 (December 1989), pp. 446–481.

39. Fred E. Fiedler and Martin M. Chemers, *Leadership and Effective Management* (Glenview, Ill.: Scott, Foresman, 1974).

40. Ibid., p. 99.

41. Robert W. Rice, "Construct Validity of the Least Preferred Coworker Score," *Psychological Bulletin*, vol. 85 (1978), pp. 1199–1237.

42. Fred E. Fiedler, L. Mahar, and Martin M. Chemers, "Leadermatch IV: Programmed Instructor and Leadership for the U.S. Army" (Seattle: University of Washington Department of Psychology, 1977); Associates in the Department of Behavioral Sciences and Leadership, *Leadership in Organizations* (New York: United States Military Academy at West Point, 1981), chap. 13.

43. Fred E. Fiedler, "Change the Job to Fit the Manager," *Harvard Business Review*, vol. 43 (1965), pp. 115–122.

44. Robert J. House and G. Dessler, "The Path–Goal Theory of Leadership: Some *Post Hoc* and *A Priori* Tests," in James G. Hunt and Lars L. Larson (eds.), *Contingency Approaches to Leadership* (Carbondale, Ill.: Southern Illinois University Press, 1974); Robert J. House and Terrence R. Mitchell, "Path–Goal Theory of Leadership," *Journal of Contemporary Business* (Autumn 1974), pp. 81–98.

45. Appa Rao Korukonda and James G. Hunt, "Pat On the Back Versus Kick in the Pants: An Application of Cognitive Inference to the Study of Leader Reward and Punishment Behaviors," *Group and Organization Studies*, vol. 14 (September 1989), pp. 299–324.

46. Charles N. Greene, "The Reciprocal Nature of Influence Between Leader and Subordinate," *Journal of Applied Psychology*, vol. 60 (1975), pp. 187–193; Randall S. Schuler, "Participation with Supervisor and Subordinate Authoritarianism: A Path–Goal Theory Reconciliation," *Administrative Science Quarterly*, vol. 21 (1976), pp. 320–325; J. E. Sheridan, H. K. Downey, and J. W. Slocum, Jr., "Testing Causal Relationships of House's Path–Goal Theory of Leadership Effectiveness," in J. G. Hunt and L. L. Larson (eds.), *Leadership Frontiers* (Kent, Ohio: Kent State University Press, 1975); Robert T. Keller, "A Test of the Path–Goal Theory of Leadership with Need for Clarity as a Moderator in Research and Development Organizations," *Journal of Applied Psychology*, vol. 74 (April 1989), pp. 208–212.

47. Timothy R. Barnett and Danny R. Arnold, "Justification and Application of Path–Goal Contingency

Leadership Theory to Marketing Channel Leadership," *Journal of Business Research,* vol. 19 (December 1989), pp. 283–292; Linda L. Neider and Chester A. Schriesheim, "Making Leadership Effective: A Three-Stage Model," *Journal of Management Development,* vol. 7, no. 5 (1988), pp. 10–20.

48. Victor H. Vroom and Philip W. Yetton, *Leadership and Decision-Making* (Pittsburgh: University of Pittsburgh Press, 1973).

49. Ibid., chap. 3.

50. Victor H. Vroom and Arthur G. Jago, "On the Validity of the Vroom-Yetton Model," *Journal of Applied Psychology* (April 1978), pp. 151–162.

51. Arthur Jago and Victor H. Vroom, "Predicting Leader Behavior from a Measure of Behavioral Intent," *Academy of Management Journal,* vol. 21 (1978), pp. 715–721; Richard Steers, "Individual Differences in Participative Decision-Making," *Human Relations* (September 1977), pp. 837–847; Richard H. G. Field and Robert J. House, "A Test of the Vroom-Yetton Model Using Manager and Subordinate Reports," *Journal of Applied Psychology,* vol. 75 (June 1990), pp. 362–366; Robert J. Paul and Yar M. Ebadi, "Leadership Decision Making in a Service Organization: A Field Test of the Vroom-Yetton Model," *Journal of Occupational Psychology,* vol. 62 (September 1989), pp. 201–211.

52. C. Margerison and R. Glube, "Leadership Decision-Making: An Empirical Test of the Vroom and Yetton Model" (manuscript, 1978); Jennifer T. Ettling and Arthur G. Jago, "Participation Under Conditions of Conflict: More on the Validity of the Vroom-Yetton Model," *Journal of Management Studies,* vol. 25 (January 1986), pp. 73–83.

53. Vroom and Jago, "On the Validity of the Vroom-Yetton Model."

54. Fred Dansereau, Jr., George Graen, and W. J. Haga, "A Vertical Dyad Linkage Approach to Leadership Within Formal Organizations: A Longitudinal Investigation of the Role Making Process," *Organizational Behavior and Human Performance,* vol. 13 (1975), pp. 46–78; George Graen, M. Novak, and P. Sommerkamp, "The Effects of Leader–Member Exchange and Job Design on Productivity and Satisfaction: Testing a Dual Attachment Model," *Organizational Behavior and Human Performance,* vol. 30 (1982), pp. 109–131.

55. Terry M. Dockery and Dirk D. Steiner, "The Role of the Initial Interaction in Leader–Member Exchange,"

Group and Organization Studies, vol. 15 (December 1990), pp. 395–413.

56. William E. McClane, "Implications of Member Role Differentiation: Analysis of a Key Concept in the LMX Model of Leadership," *Group and Organization Studies,* vol. 16 (March 1991), pp. 102–113.

57. Robert Tannebaum and Warren H. Schmidt, "How to Choose a Leadership Pattern," *Harvard Business Review,* vol. 51 (May–June, 1973).

58. Chris Lee, "Can Leadership Be Taught?" *Training,* vol. 26 (July 1989), pp. 19–26.

59. Karl W. Kuhnert and Craig J. Russell, "Using Constructive Developmental Theory and Biodata to Bridge the Gap Between Personnel Selection and Leadership," *Journal of Management,* vol. 16 (September 1990), pp. 595–607.

60. Charles N. Greene, "The Reciprocal Nature of Influence Between Leader and Subordinate," *Journal of Applied Psychology,* vol. 59 (April 1975), pp. 187–193; Ifechukude B. Mmobuosi, "Followership Behavior: A Neglected Aspect of Leadership Studies," *Leadership and Organizational Development Journal,* vol. 12, no. 7 (1991), pp. 11–16.

61. Joe Flower, "The Art and Craft of Followership: A Conversation with Robert E. Kelley," *Health Care Forum,* vol. 34 (January–February 1991), pp. 56–60; Stephen C. Lundin and Lynne C. Lancaster, "Beyond Leadership . . . the Importance of Followership," *Futurist,* vol. 24 (May–June 1990), pp. 18–22; Deborah Murphy, "Followers for a New Era, *Nursing Management,* vol. 21 (July 1990), pp. 68–69.

62. Chris Lee, "Followership: The Essence of Leadership," *Training,* vol. 28 (January 1991), pp. 27–35.

63. Stephen Kerr and J. Jermier, "Substitutes for Leadership: Their Meaning and Measurement," *Organizational Behavior and Human Performance,* vol. 22 (1978), pp. 375–403.

64. J. P. Howell and P. W. Dorfman, "Substitutes for Leadership: Test of a Construct," *Academy of Management Journal,* vol. 24 (1981), pp. 714–728; Jon P. Howell, David E. Bowen, Peter W. Dorfman, Stephen Kerr, and Philip M. Podsakoff, "Substitutes for Leadership: Effective Alternatives to Ineffective Leadership," *Organizational Dynamics,* vol. 19 (Summer 1990), pp. 20–38.

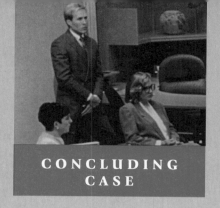

DECISION TREE FOR PARTICIPATIVE LEADERSHIP

Use the questions and decision tree by Victor H. Vroom and Philip W. Yetton illustrated in Exhibit 15.12 to analyze these three cases.

CASE 1: SCHEDULING HOLIDAY WORK

You are the manager of a hotel, and it is your responsibility to develop a work schedule for the Christmas holiday. The occupancy rate is very low since most people prefer to be home for the holidays. Unfortunately, all the employees also want to be home for the holidays, but it is necessary that a reduced staff of dependable employees cover key jobs around the clock. The holiday schedule last year created intense dissatisfaction, and some employees quit because the schedule was changed several times and many employees felt unfairly treated. Although some employees are more proficient than others, virtually everyone has adequate knowledge to perform the work at both the reservation's desk and cashier's desk. How should you decide which employees to assign to work on Christmas?

CASE 2: PERSONNEL BUDGET

You are the personnel manager of a corporation with 4,600 employees. As the vice president of personnel, you have five department managers who report to you. These department managers are responsible for employment, wage and salary administration, labor relations, training and devel-

opment, and safety. Each year you are required to develop an itemized budget divided into quarters. You have attempted to delegate to each manager full responsibility for the activities under his or her direction. Your company encourages management by objectives. You have learned from past experience that your managers all seem to excel and adhere more closely to the budget targets when they feel a sense of ownership in their goals. How should you proceed to develop the budget for the personnel department?

CASE 3: NEW TRUCK ASSIGNMENT

You are the supervisor of a crew of repair technicians. Every so often your department receives a new truck in exchange for an old one, and you have the problem of deciding which technician should receive the new truck. When these decisions have been made in the past, there have been seriously hurt feelings because each technician seems to think he or she is entitled to the new truck. You have a difficult time being fair. In fact, in the past it seems that no matter what you decide, your decision is considered wrong by the majority. Although you consider all six of your technicians highly competent and skilled, you are also convinced that they are a bunch of uncooperative prima donnas. How should you make the decision about who gets the new truck?

LEADERSHIP ORIENTATION

LEADERSHIP ORIENTATION QUESTIONNAIRE

Directions: The following statements describe aspects of leadership behavior. Think about the way you usually act when you are the leader of a group. Respond to each item according to the way you would most likely act if you were the leader of a work group. Circle whether you would most likely behave in the described way: *always* (A), *frequently* (F), *occasionally* (0), *seldom* (S), or *never* (N).

A F O S N 1. I would consult the group before making any changes.

A F O S N 2. I would encourage the group to set specific performance standards.

A F O S N 3. I would trust the group to exercise its own good judgment.

A F O S N 4. I would urge the group to beat its previous record.

A F O S N 5. I would try to make certain all group members were comfortable and happy.

A F O S N 6. I would assign group members to specific tasks.

A F O S N 7. I would represent the group and defend them at outside meetings.

A F O S N 8. I would be the one to decide what should be done and how it should be done.

A F O S N 9. I would permit group members to use their own judgment in solving problems.

A F O S N 10. I would try to keep the work moving at a rapid pace.

A F O S N 11. I would invite group members to share their personal concerns with me.

A F O S N 12. I would carefully plan how to do the work most efficiently.

A F O S N 13. I would eliminate conflicts and make certain there were friendly feelings in the group.

A F O S N 14. I would encourage overtime work.

A F O S N 15. I would allow members complete freedom in their work.

A F O S N 16. I would encourage members to follow the standard procedures.

A F O S N 17. I would encourage members to get to know each other.

A F O S N 18. I would establish a schedule for getting the work done.

A F O S N 19. I would encourage members to share their ideas with me.

A F O S N 20. I would emphasize quality and insist that all mistakes be corrected.

Scoring: These 20 items measure two leadership orientations: the odd-numbered items measure concern for people and the even-numbered items measure concern for the task.

The responses to each item are scored as follows: A = four points, F = three points, O = two points, S = one point, and N = zero points. Calculate your score for both leadership orientations by adding the points for the odd items and then adding your points for the even items. Your score for each variable will be a number between 0 and 40.

Sum of the odd items: _____ Concern for People score

Sum of the even items: _____ Concern for the Task score

Evaluating Your Leadership Style: To help you evaluate your style of leadership, mark your Concern for People score on the left arrow of the diagram below and your Concern for the Task score on the right arrow. Draw a straight line between the two points on the two arrows. The point at which that line crosses the team leadership arrow in the middle indicates your score on that dimension. Shared leadership comes from a balanced concern for the task and a concern for people.

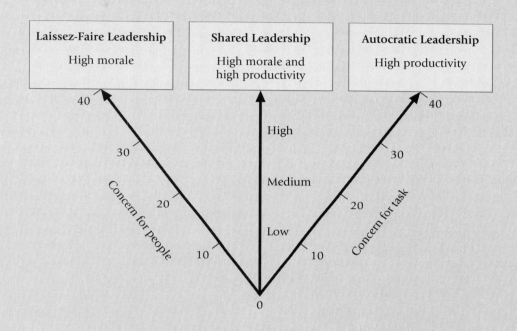

Power and Politics in Organizations

LEARNING OBJECTIVES

After studying this chapter, you should be able to

1. Identify and describe the different forms of interpersonal influence: power, authority, control, and leadership.

2. Identify three types of authority.

3. Describe the five bases of power, and explain when each type of power is most appropriate.

4. Describe the conditions that contribute to the acquisition of individual and subunit power.

5. Explain why political activities occur in organizations, and describe some of the major political strategies that are used.

6. Explain how positions of power can be maintained within an organization.

7. Describe the principles involved in influencing subordinates, superiors, and peers.

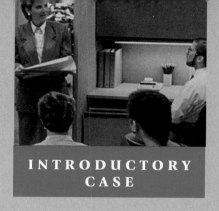

THE GOLDEN RULE LAYS A GOLDEN EGG

In 1990, the top management at General Motors announced a simple change in their pension plan. Rather than calculating pensions as a percentage of *straight* salary, it would be a percentage of *total* compensation, which includes salary *and* bonuses. For most of GM's 3,350 managers, this change was a small addition to their previous pension. But for a few top executives, and most importantly those who made this decision, this change was an enormous increase. For example, the annual pension of chairman Roger B. Smith, who retired just three months later, was increased from $700,000 to $1,250,000.

As part of the strategy for assuring the acceptability of this change, GM commissioned a study of pension plans and announced that any changes would be submitted for stockholder ratification at the annual meeting. The commission collected pension and salary data from other U.S. industries and reported that when pensions were calculated as a percentage of prior earnings, GM's percentage was only at the twenty-first percentile, well below the national norm. GM executives used these data to justify improving the pension plan even though the data could have been interpreted just as easily to argue that their earnings were too high rather than that their pensions were too low.

GM executives regretted offering to submit their proposal for stockholder ratification. Their decision was criticized as a bad decision that was made at the wrong time for the wrong reasons. Extravagant pensions for top executives were inconsistent with GM's economic performance. During the previous decade, GM's share of the U.S. passenger car market slid from 46 to 35 percent, and domestic car profits declined as productivity trailed the industry as a whole.

The pension announcement was also inconsistent with the changes GM was trying to negotiate with the United Auto Workers union. GM was pushing for a new labor agreement that contained labor force reductions, cost-cutting programs, and sharing of medical benefits expenses.

Stung by criticism of its new pension plan, GM announced that in the future it would not seek stockholder ratification of board decisions. This move will serve to further centralize the power of the board even though stockholder ratification typically amounts to a "rubber stamp" process. Unless the current policy is changed, GM executives will continue to receive sizable pensions in addition to enormous salaries and bonuses.

Questions

1. How does the change in pension calculations illustrate the use of power?

2. Since the decision was ratified by the stockholders, why wouldn't this be an illustration of rational decision making rather than an illustration of power?

Source: James D. Treece, "GM: Wrong Move. Wrong Time. Wrong Reason," *Business Week* (May 28, 1990), p. 32.

POLITICAL VERSUS RATIONAL DECISION MAKING

The topics of power and politics provide an alternative way to think about organizations. Seeing organizational activities from the perspective of power and politics is quite different from seeing the same activities from the perspective of effectiveness and rationality that has been the case in earlier chapters. This chapter focuses not on effectiveness, but on power and influence.

Power and organizational politics are topics that make people feel uncomfortable. "Power" is a word that has an emotional tinge. When people use politics to accomplish something they want, we are quick to condemn their behavior as immoral and unethical. Nevertheless, power, influence, and political activity exist in organizations, and some have argued persuasively that the use of power is not only inevitable but often beneficial to both organizations and individuals. An important objective of this chapter is to show that power and politics are inevitable and important parts of administrative activity. It is important for us to recognize when power is being used by ourselves or others and to know how to use it more effectively.

Power Orientation: A Way to View Organizations

The effects of power can be seen in almost every aspect of organizational life, such as (1) when budgets are allocated to organizational subunits, (2) when promotion and hiring decisions are made, and (3) when organizational structures are redesigned. We typically dislike admitting that politics plays an important role in making organizational decisions, because we think our behavior should be based on socially accepted values of rationality and effectiveness. It is socially more acceptable to believe that budget allocations are based upon a rational assessment of departmental needs rather than the political power of the department managers.

Exorbitant executive salaries illustrate the use of power. The golden rule of power says that those who have the gold get to rule; in other words, those who have power can successfully manipulate the situation to retain power and increase their share of the rewards. The major reason why executive pay is so enormous is because executives have the power to play a central role in deciding their own pay. Technically, executive pay is determined by the board of directors, and someone who didn't know better might think executive pay was based on an impartial evaluation of their performance. It sounds good, but it's not true. This naive belief fails to recognize (1) how top managers manipulate and control the information presented to the board and (2) the fact that in many corporations the top executives are members of the board. Although executives may not comprise a majority of the board, they control the kinds of information seen by the board and many of the comparisons the board uses to make salary and bonus decisions.

Chapter 14 explains how rational decision makers define the organization's objectives, identify the problem and potential solutions, evaluate each alternative, select the best alternative, and implement it. This process assumes that everyone can agree on the objectives of the organization and, after a careful review, everyone will also agree on the ideal alternative. Two leading researchers on power, Jeffrey Pfeffer and John Kotter, both argue that in reality the rational decision-making model is seldom used.[1] Pfeffer argues that rational decision-making models fail to account for the diversity of interests and goals within organizations, and he concludes that the decision-making processes in organizations must be understood from the perspective of power and organizational politics. This does not necessarily mean that most decisions are contrary to the best interests of the organization. Indeed, Pfeffer argues that political decision making is often beneficial if not necessary for organizational effectiveness, because it provides a mission and direction for the organization. Trying to achieve a consensus decision regarding the objectives of the organization and the alternatives that best serve the interests of the organization, he argues, would be extremely time consuming and ineffective, particularly in today's large and complex organizations with their diverse cultures and interests.

Although power may be necessary for organizational decision making, the prevalence of politics among top management teams has been found to be associated with poor firm performance. Political decision making is not necessarily the most effective.[2]

Kotter agrees that most organizational decisions are heavily laced with power and political influence, but he emphasizes the importance of maintaining a position between naïveté and cynicism regarding the use of power. Individuals who are politically naive fail to see the diversity in organizational cultures and are shocked when they see political maneuvering that provides a larger share of the resources for those with the greatest power. However, those who are cynical about organizational politics make the mistake of assuming that every organizational interaction involves built-in conflicts that lead to destructive power struggles, bureaucratic infighting, and parochial politics. Conflict becomes a self-fulfilling prophecy for these cynics, and they are unprepared to contribute to the success of the organization by compromise and joint problem solving.

Organizational politics and power provide us with a very different way of conceptualizing organizational behavior from the open-systems model that has been used throughout most of this text. Open-systems theory describes organizations as a set of patterned activities that are structured in a variety of effective and ineffective ways. Political models view organizations as pluralistic collections of people and subcultures competing for scarce resources and the right to determine the organization's strategy and objectives. Conflict is viewed as normal or at least a customary part of the organization. The activities of individuals and groups are not viewed as goal-directed behaviors but as games among players who are pursuing their own individual or subunit objectives. Political models of organizations assume that when the interests of people conflict, decisions will be determined by the relative power of the individuals or subunits involved. Those who possess the greatest power will receive the greatest rewards as a result of the interplay of organizational politics. Power is used to overcome the resistance of others and to get one's way in the organization.

Types of Influence: Power, Authority, Control, and Politics

In organizations, some people exert more influence than others. The hierarchical structure in organizations calls for top-level officers to influence lower-level workers. Sometimes the actual influence patterns correspond with the way influence is prescribed by the organizational structure, but not always. Some individuals or groups typically exert far more influence than their position in the organization would suggest. This raises two questions: how do individuals acquire power, and why do others voluntarily submit to it?

The need for leadership and influence (introduced in Chapter 11) stems from the need to reduce the variability of human behavior. In every organization, people must behave in prescribed ways; employees are not free to behave as they please. Although we enjoy considerable freedom in organizations, we are still required to behave in specified ways and follow prescribed behaviors. Doing the right thing at the right time is particularly important for such groups as athletic teams, orchestras, and assembly-line workers. In these groups the need to reduce the variability of human behavior is quite evident. Getting people to reliably perform their assigned roles involves influencing human behavior. This influence appears in several forms, as summarized in Exhibit 16.1, and is typically described in terms of power, authority, control, and leadership.

Power. Most definitions of **power** agree with the early definition provided by the great German sociologist Max Weber: power is "the probability that one actor within a social relationship would be in a position to carry out his own will despite resistance."[3] Essentially, power is the ability of one person or a group of persons to influence the behavior of others. This definition implies that power is a force producing a change in behavior that would not have occurred if the force had not been present. This definition highlights three important characteristics of power:

1. Power is the ability to influence others, and individuals may have power whether or not they use it. This is called *potential power.*
2. Power is in the eye of the beholder. People have power only to the extent that others perceive them to possess it.
3. Power in organizations is acquired, and people have the potential to increase or decrease their power base.

Power has been referred to as "America's last dirty word." The implication here is that we are uncomfortable with the concept of power because power seems to imply some form of illegitimate influence on others. Although power can be used in a repressive manner, it need not be. Power exists in every organization, and it can create either desirable or undesirable outcomes. The concept of power is closely related to the concepts of leadership and authority, and it is important to understand when one type of influence ends and another begins. When, for example, does a manager stop using legitimate authority in a work situation and start using unauthorized power?

Authority. Although *power* and *authority* are often used in the same context, there is an important difference between them. Power is the capacity of one person or group to secure compliance from another person or group. There is nothing in this definition about the right to secure compliance—only the ability. Authority is the right to seek compliance by others. **Authority** is legitimate power and is conferred on an individual by the organization or by social custom.[4]

Within an organization, an authority structure is specified by the organizational hierarchy. The structure is clearly visible on the organization chart. At each level, supervisors are expected to influence the behavior of their subordinates as part of their supervisory responsibility. But at the same time, they are expected to

EXHIBIT 16.1 Types of Influence

Influence	Definition
Power	The capacity to influence the behavior of others; the ability of one party to overcome resistance in others to achieve a desired objective
Authority	The legitimate exercise of power, where "legitimate" means role relevant
Control	The capacity to determine acceptable behavior and prevent someone from behaving unacceptably
Leadership	Incremental influence; the ability to induce voluntary compliance by inspiring and motivating others
Politics	The use of power in organizations to obtain one's preferred outcomes

respond to the influence of those above them. The flow of influence between the different hierarchical levels constitutes an **authority structure** that provides for a highly specialized set of influence transactions.

Influence can also be exerted without formal authority by creating alliances and informal work relationships based on mutual exchange. These relationships are maintained by shared expectations of a reciprocal exchange, which is called the *norm of reciprocity.*[5] It is reasonable for person A to accept the influence of person B if person A expects to receive something in return from person B either now or in the future. It is important for these exchanges to be perceived as roughly equivalent over time, or feelings of inequity and resistance will result.

Control. **Control** is the ultimate form of influence wherein acceptable behavior is specified and people or groups are prevented from behaving otherwise. For example, internal accounting procedures are designed to control financial transactions and prevent employee theft. Locked gates, hidden cameras, and other physical security devices are designed to control the flow of merchandise and prevent shoplifting. Safety devices are designed to prevent unsafe actions that could cause serious injury. Traffic lights, speed limits, and barricades are designed to control the driving of motorists and provide greater safety.

Politics. **Politics** is the exercise of power in organizations. When people acquire, develop, and use power in a conscious attempt to obtain their preferred outcomes, these activities are called *political activities*. Political activity is used to overcome opposition or resistance. If there were no opposition, there would be no need for political activity.[6]

People typically engage in political activity for their own benefit or the benefit of their subunit; but political activity is not necessarily dysfunctional to the subunit or suboptimal for the organization. In fact, many managers engage in political activities that they sincerely believe will benefit the organization. Politics, like power, is not inherently bad. Indeed, the survival of some organizations occasionally depends on the successful political maneuvering of people or dominant coalitions who succeed in changing the mission of the organization and in helping it adapt to a changing environment. Some excellent examples of political struggles that greatly benefited the auto industry are vividly described in Lee Iacocca's autobiography, in which he describes the development of the Mustang at Ford and the K-car at Chrysler.[7] The political battles in both organizations eventually produced superior products and caused their internal structures to be more customer oriented.

Conditions Necessary for the Use of Power

Because of their nature, some situations are not susceptible to organizational politics and power. For example, in a physical exercise program there is no reason for one jogger to exert power over other joggers, since all the joggers are independent—they can run whenever they want, wherever they want, as far as they want. Among a group of engineers, the power of one engineer who has access to a personal computer would disappear if computers were provided for all the engineers. Also, the positions on a basketball team would probably be assigned rationally by the height of the players rather than by political considerations. These illustrations suggest that some conditions are not as conducive to the use of power as others. In other situations, however, it has been argued, especially by Jeffrey Pfeffer, that the introduction of power is both a necessary and a sufficient condition for making a choice. Three conditions are necessary for the use of power: interdependence, scarcity, and heterogeneous goals.[8]

Interdependence. A state of interdependence provides an opportunity for conflict and a corresponding need for some way to resolve the conflict. Interdependence arises from joint activity in which the work of one individual or group affects the work of others. Interdependence ties the activities of organizational members together, and each member becomes concerned with what others do and what they obtain. In the absence of interdependence, there would be no basis for conflict and no reason for one individual to exert influence over others.

Scarcity. When there are ample resources and people can have everything they want, conflict tends to be eliminated and there is little reason for people or groups to exert influence over others. When resources are scarce, however, choices must be made concerning their allocation. The greater the **scarcity** relative to the demand, the greater the opportunity for power and influence to be used in resolving the conflict.

Heterogeneous Goals. When everyone agrees on the goals of the organization and the ways to achieve them, the amount of conflict and opportunity for political activity is less than when there is disagreement. Most organizations experience considerable disagreement because they have *heterogeneous goals*. In complex organizations, there is usually a wide variety of inconsistent goals and incompatible beliefs about how these goals should be achieved. Managers may strongly disagree about which products should be promoted or which innovations will be the most profitable. They may also disagree about the long-term effects of organizational policies and personnel practices. For example, it may be difficult to assess whether a job

Surplus Labor in Germany Erodes Union Power

The conditions necessary for the use of power are scarcity, interdependence, and heterogeneous goals. For many years, labor unions in West Germany had all three of these conditions and they used them to obtain some of the highest factory wage rates in the world. With the German unification in 1990, however, labor was no longer as scarce as before and negotiations between labor unions and management changed significantly.

In 1990, I. G. Metall, West Germany's most powerful trade union, demanded pay increases of 8.5 percent and a 35-hour workweek. On May 3, the 2.6 million members of the union closed the machine tool industry with a one-day warning strike to underscore their demands. Within 24 hours, however, the union suddenly accepted a new five-year agreement that provided for an increase of only 6 percent in wages, with no reduction in the length of the workweek.

The union quickly dropped its demands and settled because of the availability of 9 million East Germans whose average wage is only a quarter of what the West Germans make. The average factory wage in West Germany was $21 per hour, with a 38-hour workweek and 30 holidays per year while the East Germans had an average wage of only $5.40 with a 44-hour workweek and 21 holidays per year.

The printers union, I. G. Medien, also accepted a reduced pay increase of only 6.8 percent and agreed to stay with a 38 1/2-hour workweek because of the availability of former East German laborers. The wage disparities in a unified Germany will ensure an ample supply of workers willing to accept high-paying jobs and limit the bargaining power of unions until greater parity in wages is achieved. To improve their bargaining position, Germany's powerful unions are pushing to ensure that eastern German labor costs reach those of the western region by 1995 despite lagging increases in productivity.

Source: Igor Reichlin and Gail E. Schares, "What's Haunting West German Unions: East Germans," *Business Week,* May 21, 1990), p. 60; Amity Shales, "Anywhere But Germany," *Wall Street Journal* (January 22, 1993), p. A10.

enrichment program or improved employee benefits will reduce employee turnover, or whether reduced turnover itself is even desirable.

When interdependence, scarcity, and heterogeneous goals are present, as illustrated in Exhibit 16.2, the likelihood that some form of power will be exerted is very high. Indeed, Pfeffer argues that under these conditions the use of power is virtually inevitable and essentially the only way to arrive at a decision. The use of power is inevitable because there is no rational way other than chance to determine whose preferences should prevail or whose beliefs about the goals or the methods of achieving them should guide the decision. Prolonged discussions using rational decision-making processes will generally serve to heighten awareness of the goal incompatibility. In these situations, social customs, traditions, and group norms may be called on to guide the decision, but in actuality they are only used by the most powerful to make the use of power appear less obtrusive and more legitimate.

In many situations, power can be used so effectively by those who are powerful that others are not even aware that it is happening and they feel no conflict or resistance. By manipulating the situation, redefining the objectives, and using other political tactics, high-power people can make low-power people believe they are engaged in a cooperative rather than a competitive situation.[9] Here the use of power is perceived as contributing to greater effectiveness.

EXHIBIT 16.2   Conditions Necessary for the Use of Power

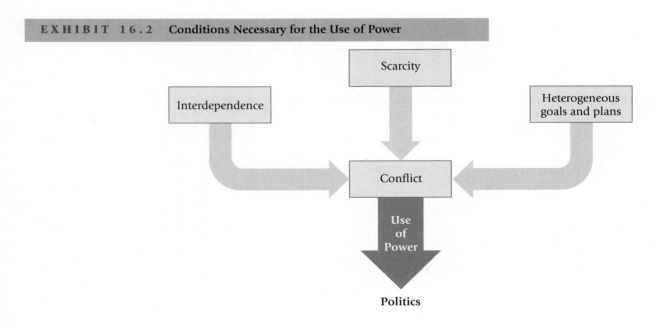

AUTHORITY

People usually do what they are told to do when they think the person issuing the commands has the proper authority. Executives are expected to exercise their authority by telling subordinates what to do. But there are also times when subordinates have the authority to command superiors, such as when a secretary requests financial information from executives or schedules their activities.

Authority Versus Power

It is important to distinguish between power and authority. As noted earlier, power represents the capacity of one person to secure compliance from another person, while authority represents the *right* of this person to seek compliance by others. Therefore, authority is defined as legitimate power and is conferred on an individual by the organization or social customs. Authority is backed by legitimacy.

Defining authority as legitimate power raises the question of what is legitimate. In their discussion of authority, Katz and Kahn define "legitimate" as "role relevant" or, in other words, "related to one's job or position within the organization."[10] Behaviors, attitudes, and even manners of dress and grooming, if they are related to successful job performance, are considered role relevant. However, behaviors and attitudes that have nothing to do with job performance are not role relevant; for example, food preferences, the choice of friends, or hairstyles.

If a manager asks an assistant to prepare a report, this request would be role relevant and the manager would be exercising authority. However, if the manager asks the assistant to perform personal errands during the lunch hour, this would not be a role-relevant request and would not constitute an exercise of authority. If the assistant performed the personal errands, it would not be because of legitimate power but because of some other form of power. Sometimes managers admit that some of their directives are not role relevant. Usually they say that their directives are requests or suggestions rather than orders or commands.

Types of Authority

Max Weber defined authority by using a historical perspective to contrast three types of authority: traditional, charismatic, and rational-legal.[11]

Traditional Authority. **Traditional authority** is the influence exerted by an individual who has rightfully inherited a position of status. This form of authority is characteristically found in cultures where kings or chiefs occupy a position of status that is widely accepted within the society. The authority possessed by the king or the chief is based on inheritance or a natural order that has always been followed and presumed always to have existed. In some family businesses, the children of the founder, because of the traditional authority conferred on them, exert considerable influence on others even though they do not occupy a formal position in the company.

Charismatic Authority. **Charismatic authority** stems from the alluring and mystical quality of a leader who is highly respected and revered. A true charismatic leader possesses a special quality of leadership that captures the popular imagination and inspires unwavering allegiance and devotion. Therefore, charismatic leaders are able to exert influence because of the respect and devotion others have for them. Their directives are seen as legitimate because the followers assume that a charismatic leader has the vision or inspiration to know what must be done.

Rational-Legal Authority. The authority that comes from a person's formal position within an organizational hierarchy is called **rational-legal authority.** Weber's description of rational-legal authority was derived from his definition of a bureaucracy in which officeholders had the authority to issue official directives and sanctions based on the rules and official procedures associated with their offices.

Obedience to Authority

An important question is why people respond to authority. Why do people join an organization and submit to the influence of others? Why do organizational members obey rules and comply with norms and expectations? One reason people obey is because obedience is necessary for continued membership. If they refuse to comply with the accepted rules and norms, they can be expelled from the organization. People who fail to comply with an organization's expectations are fired from business organizations, expelled from voluntary organizations, or excommunicated from religious organizations.

Most people also realize, however, that rule compliance is necessary for the organization to survive. Therefore, they do what they are told to do not simply to avoid punishment or termination but because they think it is necessary for the organization. A research study examined the reasons for compliance among industrial workers in five countries: Italy, Austria, the United States, Yugoslavia, and Israel. The workers and supervisors were asked directly, "When you do what your immediate supervisor requests you to do on the job, why do you do it?" The people were asked to evaluate six explanations for their compliance. The most important reasons given was "It is my duty." Other explanations, such as the supervisor has the ability to reward or punish, the supervisor is a nice guy, or they respect the supervisor's competence were considered less important in explaining why people complied.[12]

The willingness of people to comply with a legitimate authority is a highly developed tendency in our society. People have been taught to obey people in authority as part of the basic socialization process. Willingness to comply with authority has been illustrated in a series of surprising studies conducted by Stanley Milgram.[13] These studies demonstrated that experimental subjects willingly obeyed the instructions of the experimenter even when they thought they were inflicting intense pain on another person.

In Milgram's study, volunteers were paid to participate in a study that was ostensibly testing the effects of punishment on learning. Through a drawing that appeared to be random, the actual subject was assigned to teach the "learner" a series of word association pairs. For each incorrect response, the teacher was instructed to administer an electrical shock. The instrument panel facing the "teacher" contained 30 shock levers, which increased from 15 volts to 450 volts, with labels describing each shock, ranging from "slight shock" to "danger: severe shock."

The learner, who was actually a confederate, gave many wrong answers according to plan. The teacher was instructed to administer one shock for each error and to increase the voltage each time. Starting with 75 volts, the learner began to moan and complain. At 150 volts he demanded to be released from the experiment. At 180 volts he cried out that he could no longer stand the pain, and at 300 volts he vehemently protested and refused to provide any more answers. After 300 volts there were no further responses from the learner. The experiment ended when the teachers refused to administer the next level of shock or when they reached the last shock level. If the teacher at any time hesitated to administer the next shock level, the experimenter used a sequence of mild instructions to encourage the teacher to continue: (1) "Please go on," (2) "The experiment requires that you continue," (3) "It is absolutely essential that you continue," and (4) "You have no other alternative, you must go on."

Milgram varied the experimental methodology to test various levels of authority and tested 40 people in each condition. More than 1,000 people participated in these obedience experiments. Before the results were published, 40 psychiatrists were asked to predict how many people would administer the different levels of shock. The psychiatrists predicted that most teachers would not continue after the learner requested to be freed at 150 volts. They estimated that less than 1 in 1,000 would obediently administer the highest shock levels. The results, however, were quite different from the psychiatrists' predictions. In fact, 62 percent of the subjects (620 out of 1,000) obeyed the experimenter's authority and administered the maximum shocks of 450 volts to a moaning, protesting, and then ominously silent learner.

In most of the studies, the confederate learner was in an adjacent room and could not be seen by the subject. Milgram discovered that the subject's decision to disobey the experimenter was influenced by his ability to see and hear the learner. When the teachers could neither see nor hear the protests of the learner, virtually all teachers, once commanded, proceeded to administer the highest shock level in spite of the warning labels. The proportion of obedient teachers dropped to 62 percent when the moans and protests of the learner could be heard, dropped a little more when the teacher could also see the victim, and dropped to 30 percent when the teacher was compelled to touch the victim by forcing his hand onto a metal plate in order to administer the shock.

Milgram noted that although he was surprised with his subjects' obedience to authority, the obedience was not a blind obedience. The subjects were not acting without feeling. Instead they exhibited considerable anxiety, a conflict of conscience, and sympathy for the learner. They were critical of the research, the experimenter, and the research organization. Nevertheless, they continued to administer shocks.

Milgram's studies indicate just how influenceable people can be. The experimenter did not pretend to have any reward or coercive power over the subjects. His only powers were limited to legitimate or expert power. The studies on conformity discussed in Chapter 9 showed how people are influenced by the social pressures of group norms when they face a unanimous authority. Milgram's studies, however, found that an individual facing an authority of only one person can be induced to behave in ways that are socially inappropriate, immoral, unethical, disloyal, or even dangerous.

The Democratic Alternative

Most organizations are arranged hierarchically with power and authority concentrated in upper levels of the hierarchy. An alternative to the hierarchical authority structure has been suggested. This alternative, referred to as the **democratic alternative,** tries to separate two important administrative functions performed by top management.[14] These two functions are the legislative function and the executive function, similar to the legislative and executive branches in the federal government of the United States. In a democratic system, the legislative function is performed by everyone in the organization, including lower-level members who participate equally in deciding the organization's policies and rules. Labor unions are supposed to operate democratically—each union member should participate equally in expressing opinions and ratifying contracts.

The executive function, however, is performed by designated leaders who are either appointed or elected to their office. In performing their responsibilities, these leaders are expected to influence others. However, the legitimate power they exercise has been granted to them by the vote of the membership.

Although this democratic alternative is rather appealing, there is evidence suggesting that it is not the most effective way to structure the power relationships within an organization. In fact, studies on the structure and distribution of power within society have identified what is called the **"irony of democracy."**[15] Briefly stated, this irony is that the basic democratic values of our society are not preserved by the masses of population they are intended to protect. Instead, our basic democratic values are preserved by small numbers of people belonging to an elite; these people exercise tremendous power even though they are not formally elected as leaders. Important freedoms protecting political, social, and economic interests are preserved by the efforts of the small elite groups who are willing to be involved in social issues.

Although "power to the people" and "democracy for all" represent popular slogans endorsing the transfer of greater influence to lower-level organizational

**EXHIBIT 16.3   Control Graph Created by Asking Individuals
"How Much Influence Do People Have?"**

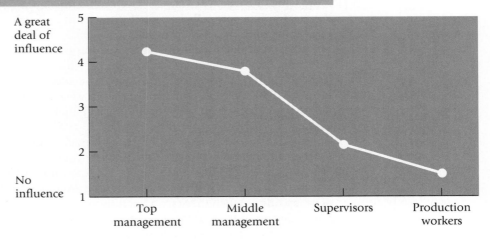

members, there appears to be an almost universal acceptance of the hierarchical power structure within organizations. A method of measuring the relative amount of influence desired by people at different levels in the organizational hierarchy has been developed by Arnold Tannenbaum. This method consists of asking people at different levels in the organization the following question: "In general, how much say or influence do you feel each of the following groups actually has in what they want in your plant?" The employees then rate the amount of influence people at different levels exert, using a five-point scale (1 = little or no influence and 5 = a very great deal of influence). When the responses from people at all levels in the organization are averaged, they form a graph similar to the one shown in Exhibit 16.3, called a **control graph.** The research conducted by Tannenbaum and his followers has provided the following conclusions:[16]

1. The data collected from a wide variety of organizations, including military organizations, voluntary associations, industrial organizations, labor unions, municipal organizations, and universities all produced a similar control graph in which members at the top of the organization exercise more control and influence than lower-level members.

2. The results from similar companies in five different areas, Italy, Yugoslavia, United States, Austria, and Israeli kibbutzim, produced substantially the same pattern of hierarchical control in spite of significantly different political and ideological values. Even the factories in the socialist kibbutzim show this familiar hierarchical pattern of greater control exerted by upper-level managers.

3. When people at lower levels in the organization are asked how much control and influence they would like to have, they typically indicated that they would prefer to have more control and influence. Nevertheless, their ideal control is still less than the amount of control they would choose to delegate to upper-level managers.

4. The amount of total control in an organization is not a fixed sum or a constant. Increasing the amount of influence at one level does not necessarily mean decreasing the influence of another level. Thus, delegating greater influence and control to lower levels in the organization does not necessarily detract from the amount of influence and control possessed by top management. The total amount of influence and control within the organization can increase.

POWER

One of the greatest concerns about power is its effects on those who use it. The more people use power, the more they tend to perceive situations in terms of power relationships, and the more they are inclined to use power for their own personal ends. This danger is expressed in the statement "Power tends to corrupt; and absolute power corrupts absolutely." The addictive effects of power have been recognized for many years. Plato was convinced that power would continue to corrupt unless philosophers became ruler and rulers were philosophers.17

Power: Good or Bad?

In studying the use of power, an important question is when is it appropriate or inappropriate. If you have sufficient power, you can influence other people and even compel them to behave against their will. Consequently, there are ethical and moral issues associated with acquiring and using power. People who adopt political strategies ought to be aware of the moral implications of their behavior.

Some ethical and moral questions regarding the use of power are very difficult to answer. Most people agree that inflicting physical or psychological damage on another individual is an abuse of power, but other issues regarding the use of power are not so clear. Should power be used to require employees to perform their jobs the way they agreed to do them when they first joined the organization? Are organizational policies an abuse of power because they reduce human variability and require members to follow prescribed procedures in performing their work? Who should decide whether a political strategy is moral or immoral?

Deciding whether the use of power is moral or immoral is necessarily a personal value decision. Moral issues and value judgments are always decided by people who use their personal standards of right and wrong to decide. Although they may attempt to follow a set of organizational guidelines or professional ethics in making value judgments, ultimately their decisions rest on their own value framework.

Political activities and the use of power are not necessarily good or bad. Although we typically think political activities are bad because they are defined as the self-serving use of power, the consequences may also be desirable for the organization and society. For many years there existed the common belief that what was good for business was good for society.18 Although this statement is not universally true, it is probably true more often than it is false. A basic principle of economic theory is that people will work for the betterment of society by pursuing their own self-interest.19 Unfortunately, the unrestricted pursuit of personal power does not always work for the good of society. And whether business transactions are good or bad needs to be determined not by the economic laws of supply and demand but by the personal values of individuals relying on their own standards of morality.

A survey of 428 managers provides some interesting insights into their perceptions of political behavior in organizations. Almost 90 percent of them agreed that successful executives must be good politicians, and 70 percent agreed that managers have to behave politically to get ahead in organizations. In spite of its perceived importance, however, 55 percent of the managers said that politics in organizations is detrimental to efficiency, and almost 50 percent agreed that top management should try to get rid of organizational politics.[20]

Sexual Harassment: An Abuse of Power

Some forms of sexual harassment, especially the more subtle forms, result from an abuse of interpersonal power. Although women are the most frequent victims of sexual harassment, it happens to both men and women. Sexual harassment includes unwelcome sexual advances, requests for sexual favors, and other verbal or physical conduct of a sexual nature that affect an individual at work. Advances that are welcomed are not harassment, which means that it is not the behavior itself, but how the behavior is interpreted that makes it harassment.

As stated earlier, power is the ability to influence others and some people use their positions in organizations to make unwelcome sexual advances. Physical size and strength can serve as a source of power to intimidate or coerce others. Even one's physical surroundings contribute to one's power position. For example, being outnumbered in a group, such as one woman in a group of men, can be intimidating and uncomfortable.

Earlier it was also noted that power is in the eye of the beholder. Some forms of sexual harassment are very blatant, such as requiring sexual favors as a condition of continued employment. Other forms, however, are very subtle and not universally perceived as objectionable, such as commenting about someone's clothing and appearance or watching one's movements. Most men consider it a compliment to be told they have a good-looking rear end; most women find it objectionable.[21]

The targets of abuse often face a very difficult situation when they try to rebuff the unwelcome advances of others. Resisting unwelcome advances is interpersonally uncomfortable, especially when the person is in a dependent position. Sometimes the victims feel too embarrassed to say anything and they try to ignore the problem. There is also a concern that complaining about an unpleasant situation will just make it worse. When asked why they didn't report sexual harassment earlier, women state several reasons: they were too embarrassed, they thought they were partially at fault, they thought nothing would be done about it, they feared losing their job, or at least they feared that the work environment would be so hostile after complaining that they would feel compelled to leave.

Sexual harassment violates the Civil Rights Act, and the Equal Employment Opportunity Commission (EEOC) is charged with enforcing the law. To prevent problems of sexual harassment, many companies have adopted policies that prohibit both implicit and explicit forms of harassment. Employees who are harassed are told who they should contact to register their complaint. Those guilty of harass-

> ## APPLYING ORGANIZATIONAL BEHAVIOR
> ### IN THE NEWS
>
> ### Sexual Harassment on the Job
>
> **CNN** The confirmation hearing of U.S. Supreme Court Justice Clarence Thomas in 1991 brought the subject of sexual harassment in the workplace to the attention of the American people. Sexual harassment claims filed with the Equal Employment Opportunity Commission, the agency charged with enforcing equal opportunity laws, rose from 5,300 in 1988 to 5,700 in 1990. According to Ellen Bravo of the Nine to Five National Association of Working Women, "The silence has been broken." However, others estimate that many victims of sexual harassment—both men and women—remain silent out of concern for their jobs or reputations.
>
> Major companies such as AT&T realized it was in their best interest to take sexual harassment charges seriously. AT&T has had policies regarding sexual harassment in place since the 1970s, and has sponsored employee training on that and related issues since the 1980s. AT&T's policy today is described as "proactive" by company spokesper-
>
> son JoAnn McPherson. Employees are informed of the company's policy banning sexual harassment in annual training sessions, and special EEOA (Equal Employment Opportunity Advisor) counselors are available to receive employee complaints. If someone is found to have violated the company's policy against harassment, the punishment can range from a verbal or written warning to dismissal, depending on the nature of the offense. Companywide, about 21 percent of those who violate the guidelines are fired, while the rest are either demoted or transferred to other branches.
>
> Ellen Bravo of Nine to Five recommends that all companies take proactive measures as AT&T has done, to prevent the problem at its inception through education and training. The intent, she says, is "to try to change attitudes, but also let it be known that behavior has to change too."
>
> *Source:* CNN *Inside Business* program, "Sexual Harassment."

ing others are warned that they could be terminated. Some companies also spend considerable time and money in training programs designed to make employees more sensitive to the problems of sexual harassment.

Power Indicators

Sometimes it is difficult to tell when power is being used. Those who use power usually do not want others to know about it. Indeed, power is most effective when it is not visible. People tend to resist the use of power when they see themselves being influenced in a way that is contrary to their own desires. However, if the influence attempt appears to be legitimate and rational, we are more willing to comply and subject ourselves to the wishes of others.

Frequently, people who are using power fail to recognize what they are doing. They honestly feel that they are exerting rational influence that can be justified for legitimate reasons other than their personal wishes. They sincerely think their influence is rational rather than political. There is often considerable disagreement about when power is actually being used.

A good illustration of the disagreement about whether decisions are made politically or rationally comes from the research on budget allocations in universities. Studies of university budgeting processes have indicated that most of the participants, department heads, deans, and administrators, believe that the budgets are determined by rational criteria based on the relative importance and needs of the different departments. Some participants have been extremely irritated and incensed by the suggestion that the budgets are determined more by political influence than by rational criteria. Nevertheless, research studies examining the variables most directly related to budget allocations have found that the best predictors of who gets the most money are political variables, especially the departmental representation on the budget committee and other important university committees.[22]

To diagnose whether decisions are being made by power rather than by logic and reason, Jeffrey Pfeffer has identified five criteria for assessing power. He suggests that the most reasonable way to diagnose power is to look for a convergence of power indicators from all five sources. As illustrated in Exhibit 16.4, these five indicators include the determinants of power, the consequences of power, power symbols, reputation, and representation on important boards or committees.

Determinants of Power.   One method of assessing power focuses on the potential to exert influence and consists of measuring how many determinants of power are available to each group member. French and Raven's classical analysis of power, for example, identified five bases of personal power; how many of these bases of power does each individual possess? One base of power is expertise; therefore, people who possess greater knowledge and expertise can exert greater influence in situations where their knowledge is important. In assessing the relative power of students who have formed a study group, we find that the student who seems to possess the greatest knowledge will have the greatest power.

Consequences of Power.   The distribution of power can also be assessed by examining the consequences of a decision-making process. Since power is used to influence decisions, those with the greatest power should be the ones who obtain the most favorable decision outcomes. For example, in allocating money to university departments, those who receive the largest allocations are generally perceived as the most powerful.[23] In labor negotiations, wage increases and employment guarantees reflect the relative power of the unions.[24]

This relationship between power and consequences needs to be interpreted carefully. The assessment of power requires knowing what would have happened in the absence of the power holder. For example, would a university department have received the same budget resources if the department chairperson had not been present? It is also important to distinguish between the ability to influence a situation and the ability to forecast what would have occurred in any event. Typically we assume that the most powerful people are the ones who can persuade others. Therefore, they would usually be on the winning side of a vote. Sometimes, however, the outcome of a decision is obvious long before it is made and to avoid being on the losing side, people will jump on the bandwagon to become part of the winning team. The fact that the ultimate decision turns out to be the same as what they were arguing for does not necessarily indicate anything about their relative power. Instead, it simply means that they had the foresight to know which alternative was the most likely one to win.

EXHIBIT 16.4   Indicators of Power

Indicator	Examples
1. Determinants of power	The capacity to use any of the bases of power: reward power, coercive power, referent power, legitimate power, or expert power.
2. Consequences of power	Budget allocations, win–loss record in debated issues, ability to authorize exceptions to policy, authority to hire and fire others.
3. Symbols	Size, location, and furnishings of one's office. Invitations to attend social events and seating at those events.
4. Reputation	Comments by others acknowledging one's power. Seeking one's advice. Asking for one's opinion.
5. Representation on committees	The number and status of committee memberships: boards of directors, advisory councils, presidential task forces, and executive committees.

Symbols. The power of different people can be assessed by examining how many symbols of power they possess. Symbols include such things as titles, office size and location, special parking privileges, special eating facilities, automobiles, airplanes, and office furnishings. Since the executive offices are typically on the top floor of a building, the location of offices on other floors often reflect the relative power of the officeholders. Jeffrey Pfeffer has shown that the layout of buildings at the University of California Berkeley campus reflects the relative power of the different departments. Departments that are relatively higher up the hillside, with a view of San Francisco and the Golden Gate Bridge, have tended to be more powerful within the university.[25]

Reputation. Another way of assessing power in organizations is to ask members of the organization who possesses the greatest power or exerts the greatest influence. This method measures the reputation of organizational members as perceived by others and assumes that people are knowledgeable about power relationships and willing to report what they know. These assumptions are often incorrect, especially when power is effective, because then it is not perceived as an exercise of power. Consequently, the political activities of the most powerful and influential people may be understated and overlooked by both themselves and others.

Representation on Committees. Finally, the last way of assessing power is to determine which people and groups are the most heavily represented on committees and other significant administrative posts. In universities, for example, as already noted, the departments with the greatest representation on the budget committees receive the largest budget allocations. Evidence of power can also be seen by representation on other committees such as the educational policy committee, the graduate council, and fellowship and scholarship committees. As a general rule, people who are invited to participate on significant administrative councils acquire greater power for their departments, such as when accountants participate in executive committee meetings or when engineers participate in quality circles.

INTERPERSONAL POWER

Where does power come from? Why can some people prevail over others in the allocation of resources or in the hiring and promotion of personal friends? In short, these questions ask how some people are able to acquire power and use it successfully to achieve their own goals.

Five Bases of Power

Power can be derived from a combination of sources. In a classic article, John R. P. French, Jr., and Bertram Raven identified and described five bases of social power: reward power, coercive power, legitimate power, referent power, and expert power.[26]

Reward Power. Person A has **reward power** over person B to the extent that A controls desired rewards that B wants. These rewards include a wide variety of incentives such as pay increases, promotions, desirable job assignments, an opportunity to work overtime, or time away from work. Person B must value the reward and think that A has the ability to either provide it or withhold it. Reward power loses its effectiveness when B does not value the reward or fails to perceive A's ability to provide it. For example, the manager of an engineering department who can reward engineers with cash bonuses, challenging job assignments, and additional funds for research can exert reward power.

Coercive Power. Person A has **coercive power** over person B to the extent that A can administer some form of punishment to B. The punishment can be in the form of pain, such as public humiliation or a physical beating, or it can be administered by removing reinforcers, such as by firing an employee, taking a player out of the game, or removing an employee from a training program. The punishment must be important to person B, who must also see A as having the ability to administer or withhold it. Coercive power is the opposite of reward power, and followers typically comply because of fear.

Legitimate Power. Person A has **legitimate power** over person B to the extent that person A is perceived as having the right to influence person B. Legitimate power is typically based on the formal organizational hierarchy and is similar to Weber's concept of rational-legal authority, by which superiors have the right to influence subordinates. Legitimate power may also exist outside the organizational hierarchy when the right to influence is prescribed by cultural values. For example, social values say it is legitimate for adults to influence children, and a voting district chairperson has the legitimate right to conduct a public mass meeting. Legitimate power can be acquired through assignment, election, or some other form of formal recognition. Subordinates play a major role in the exercise of legitimate power since their compliance is influenced by whether they perceive the use of power as legitimate.

Referent Power. Person A has **referent power** over person B to the extent that person B admires the personal qualities, characteristics, or reputation of person A. Referent power has also been called *charismatic power* because it is similar to Weber's concept of charismatic authority, where allegiance is based on the interpersonal attraction of one individual for another. People who are highly admired and respected are able to exert referent power because other people seek their approval and want to please them. A major source of referent power comes from a sense of identification by which person B wants to be like A or be part of person A's life. Imitation and conformity tend to increase the degree of referent power.

Expert Power. Person A possesses **expert power** over person B to the extent that person A has knowledge or expertise relevant to a particular problem or situation. To possess expert power a person must be perceived as credible and trustworthy. Person B must believe that person A actually possesses the crucial information and skills. If a group is traveling in a strange city, someone who knows the geography of the city would possess expert power. If the group has car trouble, however, the power shifts to someone who has mechanical knowledge. Expert power tends to be very limited in its range of influence relative to referent power. Referent power has the capacity to influence a wide range of behaviors in person B; expert power is generally limited to specific situations where the information is relevant and needed.

Techniques that help leaders acquire expert power include developing an image of expertise, maintaining credibility, acting in a confident and decisive manner, keeping informed, and recognizing opportunities to display the expertise.

Interactions Among the Bases of Power. The five sources of power are not independent of one another. How one base of power is used can affect the availability of the others.

The use of reward power tends to increase the availability of referent power, since people are attracted to those whom they admire and who reward them. In contrast, the use of coercive power tends to decrease referent power for the same reason. People tend to avoid and dislike those who administer punishment or withhold rewards. Therefore, by properly administering or withholding rewards for legitimate reasons, people can increase their referent power.

Referent power is also influenced by the appropriate use of legitimate power. Because organizational leaders are typically respected, they are endowed with a certain amount of referent power when they perform their jobs competently. Thus, their referent power tends to increase.

Referent power is also influenced by expert power, since people tend to be impressed by those who possess valuable knowledge and skills. Therefore, to the extent that people have greater knowledge and use it at appropriate times, they are well liked and admired and their referent power increases.

Guidelines have been proposed explaining how managers should use each of these five bases of power.[27] These guidelines are illustrated in Exhibit 16.5. How person B responds to the influence attempt of person A will be largely determined by the way person A behaves. Person B may respond with commitment, compliance, or resistance, depending on the influence attempt. Commitment means that person B accepts and is highly motivated to carry out the wishes of person A. Compliance

EXHIBIT 16.5   Guidelines for Using Power

Bases of Power	Guidelines for Use
Reward Power	Verify compliance.
	Make feasible and reasonable requests.
	Make only ethical and proper requests.
	Offer rewards desired by subordinates.
	Offer only credible rewards.
Coercive Power	Inform subordinates of rules and penalties.
	Warn before punishing.
	Try to administer punishment consistently.
	Try to administer punishment uniformly.
	Understand the situation before acting.
	Maintain credibility.
	Fit punishment to the infraction.
	Punish in private.
Referent Power	Treat subordinates fairly.
	Defend subordinates' interests.
	Be sensitive to subordinates' feelings.
	Select subordinates similar to oneself.
	Engage in role modeling.
Expert Power	Promote image of expertise.
	Maintain credibility.
	Act confident and decisive.
	Stay informed.
	Recognize employee concerns.
	Do not threaten subordinates' self-esteem.
Legitimate Power	Be cordial and polite.
	Be confident.
	Delegate clearly with timely follow-up.
	Make certain that requests are appropriate.
	Explain reasons for requests.
	Follow proper channels of communication.
	Exercise power discretely.
	Enforce compliance with reasonable force.
	Be sensitive to subordinates' concerns.

Source: Adapted from Gary A. Yukl, *Leadership in Organizations.* © 1981. Used with permission of Prentice-Hall, Inc., Englewood Cliffs, N.J., pp. 44–58.

means that person B is willing to fulfill person A's wishes but only as long as the extra effort and energy are adequately rewarded. Resistance, however, means that person B opposes person A's wishes and will try to deliberately neglect or sabotage the request. The guidelines proposed in Exhibit 16.5 explain how to obtain commitment from employees rather than resistance. However, these guidelines generally assume that the goals of employees are in harmony with the goals of the leader and the organization. When the individual's goals do not match the organization's goals, the subordinate may or may not comply, depending on whether the supervisor is perceived as genuine and concerned or as arrogant and insulting.

Other Sources of Power

The five bases of power defined by French and Raven represent the classical explanation for how one person influences others as well as the foundation for most research on power. Recently, however, other sources of power have been defined, explaining other sources of influence.

Information Power. Information is power. Person A can exert influence over Person B if A has information that B needs and is not otherwise available to B. Knowledge is a source of power because it allows those who are informed to control situations and influence the allocation of resources. A valuable kind of information is knowledge of the friendships and informal networks within a group. Those who have a better understanding of the friendships and advice networks in a group tend to be more powerful because they can use this information to advantageously disseminate information and influence how it is received.[28]

Persuasiveness. Person A has power over Person B to the extent that A can present logical arguments to convince B that A's recommendation or request is the best way to accomplish an objective or perform a task. The ability to develop logical arguments and reasonable explanations is an important source of power because people respond to rational and sensible ideas. People who can talk persuasively about an idea can generally obtain the cooperation and support of others.

Charisma. The ability to inspire others can be a source of personal power. Person A can influence Person B if A can appeal to B's values and inspire enthusiasm for a cause or a task. Charismatic power is similar to referent power; but while referent power depends on one person liking and wanting to please another, charismatic power depends on one's ability to inspire others and draw on their commitment to shared values. Leaders of voluntary organizations, religious groups, and organizations that have strong cultures typically use charismatic power when they appeal to the inherent nobility of their cause to generate enthusiasm and commitment.

Research examining the effects of these sources of power are limited, but at least one study has found that all three sources of power are positively associated with commitment and managerial effectiveness. As judged by both subordinates and peers, managers who use information power, persuasiveness, and charisma stimulate greater organizational commitment in others and they are perceived as more effective.[29]

Social Versus Personal Power. In his research on learned needs, David McClelland described the need for power and the characteristics of people who have a high need for power. McClelland's research indicated that successful business executives and entrepreneurs typically have rather high power needs, as described earlier in Chapter 4. However, McClelland distinguished between "two faces of power": personal power and social power.[30]

Personal power is expressed through a desire for authority and control over others. Winning by defeating others and by feeling powerful are important to those who value personal power. They enjoy the status and prestige associated with control; they derive personal gratification from their ability to coerce others and restrict their freedom.

APPLYING ORGANIZATIONAL BEHAVIOR
RESEARCH

A Better Measure of Power

 The five bases of power that French and Raven defined in their classic 1959 article are well known and widely accepted as a useful explanation for how one person influences another. But even though the classification is conceptually well accepted, research examining the effects of these power bases has not been as intuitively appealing. A quarter century of research has produced results that are often inconsistent and difficult to interpret. Occasionally negative correlations have been found when positive relationships were expected.

Finally, in 1985, Philip Podsakoff and Chester Schriesheim suggested that the previous research was flawed by a poor method of measuring the bases of power. The method typically used involved presenting five statements to respondents, each statement describing one of the bases of power, and asking the respondents to rank-order the statements according to the reasons why they complied with their supervisor's requests. Podsakoff and Schriesheim criticized this method because ranking forces some items to be rated low and others high regardless of how important they are, plus the rankings are not very reliable or consistent because they are single items subject to misinterpretation and greatly influenced by recent events.

A study by Schriesheim, Hinkin, and Podsakoff demonstrated that the ranking method was not reliable enough. Using a test–retest method to measure reliability, they asked forty-two secretaries to rank-order the five statements twice with a two-week interval between the test and retest. The correlations between the two measures for the five statements ranged from .22 to .39, which is much too low to be considered acceptable. A measuring instrument this unreliable cannot be effectively used to analyze the effects of the bases of power.

To avoid the problems of ranking, they used Likert scales to see if the test-retest reliabilities would be any better. The Likert scales were five-point scales ranging from "strongly disagree" to "strongly agree." When they used a Likert scale with the five single statements, the correlations between the test and retest ranged from .28 to .43, which was better but still not reliable enough. When they created additional statements so that five items were combined to measure each base of power, this twenty-five-item questionnaire was much more reliable: the test–retest reliabilities ranged from .72 to .81.

With a reliable instrument, Schriesheim, Hinkin, and Podsakoff examined the effects of power on two additional samples of people: fifty-three research scientists and sixty-three restaurant employees. The results indicated that reward, coercive, and legitimate power were essentially unrelated to any of the dependent measures. However, referent and expert power were significantly related to overall job satisfaction, satisfaction with the supervisor's technical ability, and satisfaction with the supervisor's human relations. Referent and expert power were also positively correlated with organizational commitment and negatively correlated with role conflict, but only among the research scientists.

These results suggest that power derived from one's organizational position has little, if any, impact on satisfaction or commitment. But expert and referent power that are derived from one's personal competence appear to have a significant impact on the reactions of subordinates. Employees are apparently more satisfied and committed to organizations that are led by leaders who use referent and expert power to influence them.

Source: Philip M. Podsakoff and Chester A. Schriesheim, "Field Studies of French and Raven's Bases of Power: Critique, Reanalysis, and Suggestions for Future Research," *Psychological Bulletin*, vol. 97 (1985), pp. 387–411; Chester A. Schriesheim, Timothy R. Hinkin, and Philip M. Podsakoff, "Can Ipsative and Single-Item Measures Produce Erroneous Results in Field Studies of French and Raven's (1959) Five Bases of Power? An Empirical Investigation," *Journal of Applied Psychology*, vol. 76 (1991), pp. 106–114.

Social power stems from the motive to exercise power for the benefit of others. People who have high needs for social power show a concern for those being influenced and for effective solutions to problems that benefit organizations and society. They are willing to help others feel powerful, and they empower others to act on their own.

The differences between personal and social power are significant. Research indicates that people who are high in social power are more profitable entrepreneurs, better liked as managers, and more effective as managers than those high in personal power. Entrepreneurs who are high in social power have a greater desire to build an organization for the benefit of society, and they are more willing to engage in succession planning. In contrast, entrepreneurs who are high in personal power are unwilling to relinquish their positions of power, and they resist succession planning. Consequently, entrepreneurs with high personal power needs tend to precipitate leadership crises because successors have not been groomed to replace them.[31]

Acquisition of Interpersonal Power

Most illustrations of power create the impression that power is something desirable to have. For example, the desirability of power is observed when top management or the news media consult an individual asking for his or her opinion on important matters. The advantages of interpersonal power are also visible when an individual has quick access to top decision makers to obtain early information about decisions and policy changes, when a manager can hire a talented replacement or reinstate a terminated employee, or when a manager can approve expenditures exceeding the budget or grant above-average salary increases for subordinates who are excellent performers. Some individuals clearly have greater power than others. They receive more than their share of the organization's resources and they exert greater influence on decisions and activities.

A relevant question is why large differences in power exist and how some people succeed in gaining more power. Two answers to this question have been provided by Rosabeth Moss Kanter, who claims that people acquire power by (1) doing the right things and (2) cultivating the right people.[32]

Doing the Right Things. Although most employees faithfully perform their assigned role, methodical and dependable role performance does not necessarily increase an individual's power. Kanter suggests that some activities are considerably better than others for increasing personal power. The power of people increases when their activities are extraordinary, highly visible, and especially relevant to organizational problems.

Extraordinary Activities Routine job performance does not contribute much to personal power even when the performance is excellent. To increase their power significantly, people need to perform unusual or nonroutine activities that commonly involve an element of risk. Examples of extraordinary activities include negotiating a new contract, developing a new program, or designing a new product.

Visible Activities Extraordinary activities will not generate much power if no one knows about them. Therefore, the extraordinary activities must be visible to others in the organization, preferably without the individual having to "play his own horn." Individuals who are required to advertise their own extraordinary activities do not gain as much power as those whose activities are announced by top management or influential people outside the organization.

Relevant Activities Besides being extraordinary and visible, the activities need to be seen as relevant to the mission of the organization or to the solution of important organizational problems. Trivial activities do not produce the same degree of personal power as activities that are central to the survival of the organization.

Cultivating the Right People. In addition to doing the right things, people can increase their personal power by developing informal relationships with the right people. Kanter suggests that if the interpersonal relationships are properly managed, virtually everyone can contribute to the development of the individual's personal power, including superiors, subordinates, and peers.

Superiors Higher-level managers can significantly increase an individual's personal power, as suggested by the phrase "It's not what you know but who you know that counts." Superiors who show a special interest and willingness to help a promising subordinate are referred to as *mentors* or *sponsors*. These people may be an immediate supervisor or any higher-level officer. They can be extremely helpful in increasing personal power by speaking favorably of subordinates, recommending them for new assignments, and providing introductions to other influential people.

Subordinates Although it may seem unusual for subordinates to have the capacity to increase their superiors' power, they may indeed play a very significant role by making their superior look good or by endorsing their superiors' views and recommendations. Professors who train brilliant doctoral students and managers who train outstanding new leaders are able to exert greater influence not only because of their reputation as outstanding trainers but also because of their continuing relationships with their former subordinates.

Peers An individual's personal power can be enhanced or destroyed by favorable or unfavorable relationships with peers. People cannot succeed alone. They depend on the support and cooperation of their peers. An antagonistic relationship with peers can destroy personal power and prevent people from being effective within the organization.

Perpetuation of Personal Power

People who have power usually become more powerful because they can manipulate the situation and engage in political strategies to perpetuate their own personal power. Once they have achieved a position of power, most people either intentionally or unintentionally structure the situation so that they increase their control over the outcomes for others.

Some strategies are so subtle that they go unrecognized. Powerful people can enhance their power position through such simple acts as creating new jargon or telling jokes. For example, a study of humor in the workplace revealed how certain group members are more frequently chosen as the target, or butt, of the jokes and how their jokes tend to be rejected.[33] The four stereotypical group members who are most likely to be the target of humor and who suffer a loss in their personal power are the arrogant executive, the benign bureaucrat, the solid citizen, and the novice. Humor can be used to "keep people in their place." Not only are their jokes rejected, their ideas and suggestions are also ignored.

Reward power, coercive power, and legitimate power are conferred by the organization. Consequently, maintaining organizationally based power depends largely on continued organizational support. If the organization withdraws support by terminating an individual or refusing to endorse this person's use of rewards and punishment, the person's power suddenly ends.

Individuals whose personal power is based on expert or charismatic power do not depend on the organization for their ability to influence others, and they can use a variety of strategies to help them maintain their power position.

Maintaining Expert Power. Three conditions are necessary to maintain expert power. First, since expert power is based on knowledge and skill, the experts must continue to be perceived as competent; those who become obsolete lose their expert power. The second requirement is to make certain that the organization continues to need the expert's knowledge and skill. The expert power of many accountants and lawyers is created by complex laws and tax regulations. If these laws were repealed, the expertise of accountants and lawyers would suddenly become unnecessary. Finally, experts must prevent other experts from replacing them. In short, expert power can be maintained only if there is a crucial need for the skills and knowledge of the expert that cannot be conveniently obtained elsewhere.

The way university faculty members maintain their expert power and thereby obtain enhanced salaries was described in a study of a large national sample of college faculty. Individual earnings were affected by the things faculty did to perpetuate their expert power. Specifically, having an outside job offer, having more extensive communications with faculty at other schools, obtaining outside research grants, and being influential in departmental decision making had a direct effect on both salaries and individual productivity.[34]

Maintaining Charismatic Power. Charismatic power typically develops when a group of people are feeling uncertainty or anxiety, particularly at a time of crisis, and a leader emerges who provides a sense of direction and inspiration. As long as the crisis continues and the leader can provide inspiration and a sense of mission, the charismatic influence of the leader will be maintained. Once the crisis has ended and operations have returned to normal, however, the power of a charismatic leader will depend on whether the power has become institutionalized. If so, the leader will remain in power and continue to lead the group. The story of Fidel Castro illustrates the ability of a charismatic leader to perpetuate his power. In the late 1950s Fidel Castro led a revolution in Cuba as a young charismatic rebel. Today he is still the head of the government and relies heavily on his charismatic power to maintain his position. Castro's success in institutionalizing his charismatic power is a result of his using these four ways for maintaining charismatic power.

1. *Perpetuate the charismatic image.* By emphasizing the symbols associated with the rise of the charismatic leader, the perception of charisma can be maintained. Pictures of Castro are displayed everywhere in Cuba, and his physical appearance is similar to what it was during the revolution—he keeps his beard and continues to dress in battle fatigues.

2. *Controlled interactions with others.* Charismatic leaders are able to set themselves apart from the rest of society and rise above the crowd by controlling their interactions with others and regulating their public contact. Castro is

typically seen in controlled settings such as speeches, rites, or ceremonies that allow him to look "presidential."

3. *Recall past atrocities.* Remembering how bad it used to be helps people think kindly of the charismatic leader. Positive feelings for a charismatic leader are particularly strong when specific negative images of atrocities and injustices are recalled.

4. *Provide a general vision of the future.* By speaking in general terms about the future, a charismatic leader can help people acquire a sense of meaning and direction. If the future is described in only general terms, people can interpret the description in terms of their own specific goals. Believing that the future will be better often helps people endure the frustrations and injustices of the present.

GROUP AND SUBUNIT POWER

In examining the issues of power within groups, we are largely concerned with the acquisition of subunit power and the ways in which this power becomes institutionalized or perpetuated. The term *subunit* applies to any organizational department, such as finance, nursing, intensive care unit, marketing, personnel, research and development, or word processing.

Acquisition of Subunit Power

How do subunits acquire power? Why are some subunits able to exert greater power than others? Although the strategies for acquiring interpersonal power and group power are largely interchangeable, five specific methods of acquiring group power are listed in Exhibit 16.6: controlling resources, controlling strategic contingencies, coping with uncertainty, being irreplaceable, and being central to the organization.[35]

Control of Resources. The most powerful subunits of an organization are those which control or have the capacity to provide crucial organizational resources. Resource control largely explains the "golden rule of power"—those who have the gold are able to rule. Because they control the resources, they can exert greater influence, and other groups will look to them for direction and respond to their directives. Crucial organizational resources include anything of value to the organization, such as money, time, materials, patents, expertise, or market survey information.

A study of the power relationships between the departments of a university found that the most important variable influencing the relative power was the department's ability to secure outside funds for the university in the form of contracts and research grants.[36] Contracts and research grants are valuable resources to a university, and the department that provided the most exerted the greatest influence.

Relative differences between the power of groups tend to become magnified when resources become scarce. When resources are plentiful, groups tend to spend

EXHIBIT 16.6 Acquiring and Institutionalizing Subunit Power

Acquiring Subunit Power

1. Controlling resources
2. Controlling strategic contingencies
3. Helping to control uncertainty
4. Being irreplaceable
5. Performing central functions

Institutionalizing Subunit Power

1. Controlling the organization's business strategy
2. Controlling the selection of new personnel
3. Controlling who gets promoted
4. Controlling training and socialization activities

less time maneuvering for an advantageous political position. During lean times, however, subgroups in a weak power position are either reduced or eliminated from the organization. Because of their weak power position, weak subunits are perceived as irrelevant and superfluous to the basic mission of the organization and gradually eliminated.

Control of Strategic Contingencies. Controlling **strategic contingencies** means having control of an activity or function that other subunits depend on. When one department cannot perform its function until another department has done its job, the first activity is contingent on the second. For example, the sales department in an engineering company has far more power than their limited expertise and training would suggest in a high-tech organization. In spite of their limited educational background, the sales force yields enormous power because others with more training and expertise cannot perform their function until the sales have been made. Thus, a contingency represents a source of uncertainty in the decision-making process, and a contingency becomes strategic when it has the potential to change the balance of power between subunits in such a way that one unit depends on another.[37]

An excellent example of power derived from controlling strategic contingencies comes from the classic study by Lawrence and Lorsch discussed in Chapter 12.[38] This study showed that significant influence patterns were created by the control of strategic relationships between the subunits of the three industries. The results indicated that in the most successful firms, power was distributed according to the strategic contingencies. That is, the units that possessed the greatest power were those units on which other units depended. For example, in the food processing firms, where the strategic contingencies focused on expertise in food sciences and marketing, the major power of the most successful firms rested in the sales and research units. However, in the container manufacturing companies, where the strategic contingencies were customer delivery and product quality, the major power resided in the sales and production staffs. In other words, the departments who held the power in the most successful firms were those units who performed vital functions for the organization in terms of its survival. The subunits that were the most important for organizational success were controlled by the most powerful decision makers. In the less successful firms, however, power was not distributed according to these strategic contingencies.

Ability to Cope with Uncertainty. Subunits are able to acquire power when they have the capacity to help other departments cope with uncertainty or minimize the consequences of uncertainty. For example, if department A is able to help reduce some of department B's uncertainties, then department A has power over department B. The uncertainty itself does not give power; the power comes from helping another department reduce the uncertainty or cope with it.

A study of the power relationships between departments within a manufacturing company illustrated how one department could successfully exert power over another because of its ability to help the second cope with uncertainty. This study was conducted in a large manufacturing company owned by the French government.[39] One group, the production workers, enjoyed tremendous job security because they were a special group, entitled to government employment under French law. The other group, the maintenance workers, were skilled technicians who were required to pass a difficult, competitive examination. The production workers were paid according to a piece-work incentive plan while the maintenance workers were salaried and controlled by strict seniority rules. Because of their job security, one would expect the production workers to exert considerable power over the maintenance people, who were expected to keep the machines in working order. The power relationships, however, were just the opposite of what one would expect. Since the production workers depended on the maintenance workers to keep their machines in working order, the maintenance workers exerted considerable power over the production workers. In the routine of the factory, machine stoppages were the only major events that could not be predicted or programed. Therefore, the production workers were clearly dependent on the salaried maintenance workers, who in their turn were not dependent on the production workers. Consequently, the maintenance workers not only controlled a strategic contingency within the factory, they also helped the production workers cope with the uncertainties of their jobs.

One subunit can reduce another subunit's uncertainty in a variety of ways. One method is by providing information so the other subunit can predict its future and prepare for change. A second method is to forestall the uncertainty by preventing unwanted events from occurring. Finally, a third method is to absorb the pressures by helping the subunit deal with its problems after they occur.

Irreplaceability. Individuals or departments who provide a crucial resource or perform a vital function for the organization and who cannot be readily replaced in that function are able to exert greater power. This basis of power is frequently discussed in terms of **substitutability,** which refers to the ability of other subunits to perform the activities of a particular subunit. If an organization can obtain alternative sources of skill, information, or resources to perform the job of another subunit, that subunit's power will be diminished. The training department loses its power if training can be provided by line managers, and the computer department loses its power over the accounting department if the accountants know enough computer programing to revise the management information systems.

Yet as subunits become more **irreplaceable**, they acquire greater power. When programers and systems analysts develop lengthy and complex computer programs, they acquire more power within the organization, especially when the output is used to make important decisions.[40] To increase their power even further, programers and systems analysts often fail to document their programs adequately so that others cannot understand them or revise them and it would be too time consuming and expensive to develop new programs from scratch. Using specialized language and symbols that makes one's expertise difficult to comprehend makes some positions appear more irreplaceable than they are in reality. The use of Greek letters in statistics and engineering create an aura of complexity and sophistication that makes these disciplines appear off limits to the untrained.

A political strategy that is often used to maintain a subunit's irreplaceability involves monitoring the organization's hiring policies to prevent the hiring of people with the same scarce skills. If an organizational subunit can maintain a monopoly on certain types of expertise and the capacity to cope with uncertainty, they become increasingly irreplaceable and powerful within the organization. For example, studies of the distribution of power in hospitals indicate that physicians gain their power because they are perceived to be irreplaceable. Nurses, however, are not irreplaceable, and their power comes from reducing uncertainty and from being central to the work of the hospital.[41]

Centrality. Subunits that are the most central to the workflow in an organization typically acquire the greatest power. Although all the subunits are interdependent, some subunits contribute more directly to the final output of the organization and therefore have greater **centrality**. The power that comes from centrality was discovered in some of the earliest communication network experiments. In the wheel structure, for example, the person in the center who communicated with each of the other members was the one who occupied the most central role and was usually perceived as the leader of the group and the most powerful figure. This individual's power stemmed largely from being able to control the flow of information throughout the group. Subsequent research on technological gatekeepers, those who control the flow of crucial technological information in an organization, has shown that these people have great power within the organization. Physical centrality can be just as important as work flow centrality in increasing a subunit's power.

In companies that have adopted a computerized information system, the centrality of each subunit is a crucial determinant of that unit's power. Even when all subunits have equal access to all information, some subunits have more power because they can regulate what information goes into the system.[42]

Institutionalization of Subunit Power

The power structure in most organizations is fairly constant over time. The relative power doesn't change much because powerful subunits can do many things to maintain their supremacy over less powerful subunits even though the people change. Studies of power usually find that the best predictor of which subunit will emerge as the most powerful during times of change is the amount of power it had before the change.[43] Power relationships in organizations can be perpetuated by maintaining the subsystem relationships and the organizational culture that support the current power positions. Four of the best ways to institutionalize power, as listed in Exhibit 16.6, come from controlling (1) the organization's strategy, (2) the selection of personnel, (3) the promotion of people, and (4) the socialization process, especially training and development.

Influencing Strategy. Powerful subunits can use their power to keep the organization focused on strategic contingencies that they control. For example, if the marketing department is the most powerful subunit, it may decide to block the acquisition of a new company that would give greater power to the finance department or to oppose the development of a new product that would transfer power to the engineering department. The most powerful subunit can force the organization to pursue a strategy that will allow it to maintain control over strategic contingencies and retain its centrality and nonsubstitutability. As noted earlier, these are the strategies that lead to the acquisition of power and by pursuing them, powerful subunits can increase their power and maintain their influence.

Personnel Selection. By defining the selection criteria and controlling the hiring of new applicants, powerful subunits can increase their relative power within organizations.[44] If one department succeeds in acquiring the best and brightest new employees, the status and power of that department increases. By influencing the selection process, some academic departments in universities have succeeded in strengthening their power positions. For example, if those faculty members who have a quantitative orientation have more power than others, they can change the curriculum to require students to take additional quantitative classes. This change increases the enrollment in quantitative classes and requires the university to hire more quantitatively trained faculty to teach them. The addition of new faculty with quantitative training strengthens the power position of those who are already there.

Personnel Promotion. Unless the organizational culture changes, it is difficult for power to shift to other subunits, and the culture is not likely to change if the values and perspectives of people at the top stay the same. Securing employees who have the right perspective can be controlled by influencing the advancement and promotion policies. Even if an error is made by selecting the wrong person, it can be corrected by passing over for promotion the person who failed to meet expectations. If those who are in powerful positions can succeed in defining both the required competence and the right perspective, they can protect their power position and reinforce the present power structure. Individuals who rock the boat by challenging those in power can be kept in lower-level positions or transferred to a weak subunit.

Training and Socialization. Training activities in an organization are important in instilling important values and expectations in employees. New employee orientation programs are particularly crucial in the socialization process, when new employees learn which behaviors and attitudes are acceptable to the organization. Because of their position, powerful subunits are better able to control the content of training and present their interpretation of the topics. Consequently, the norms and values transmitted through organizational training programs tend to reflect those of the key power groups. For example, in a manufacturing company whose safety department was the most powerful subunit, a major part of the new employee orientation and other training programs emphasized the importance of safe operating procedures.

ORGANIZATIONAL POLITICS

Power can be exercised within organizations in many different ways. Suppose, for example, that the president of the company asked the marketing vice president to recommend which one of five new products the firm should develop. The vice president could use a rational, nonpolitical decision-making process that rigorously assessed the costs and benefits of each product. However, if the vice president has a clear preference for one product over the others, a variety of political strategies are available to this vice president to make certain that the preferred product is the one selected.

Political Strategies

As defined earlier, organizational politics refers to activities within organizations designed to acquire, develop, or use power in a conscious way to obtain one's preferred outcomes or to manipulate a situation for one's own purposes. Using power for one's personal interest may sound a bit self-serving and appear to be an abuse of power; however, organizational politics occur in every organization for a variety of reasons, both good and bad. Individuals and subunits who want to exert political influence can select from a fairly long list of political strategies. Exhibit 16.7 identifies some of the most popular political strategies. Which strategy is the most effective depends on the situation.

Control the Agenda. The decisions made in most committee meetings depend not only on the opinions of the committee members but also on whether the committee has time to make a decision. Decisions can be stalled by removing items from the agenda, or they can be manipulated by placing them in particular places on the agenda. The items at the beginning of an agenda are typically discussed in greater detail, allowing greater tolerance for ambiguity and broader consideration of empirical information than items placed at the end of an agenda. Many items at the end of the agenda are either superficially decided or completely overlooked.

EXHIBIT 16.7   Political Strategies

1. Control the agenda.
2. Select the criteria for making decisions.
3. Control access to information.
4. Use outside experts.
5. Control access to influential people.
6. Form a coalition.
7. Co-opt the opposition.
8. Manipulate symbols by redefining them.
9. Manipulate people through persuasion or ingratiation.

Select the Decision Criteria. As explained in the chapter on decision making, people try to make decisions according some type of objective criteria. Therefore, people who can change the criteria for making the decision can control the decision as well. For example, if a member of a university admissions committee wanted to accept a minority female who had low test scores and a low GPA into a graduate program, the committee member should try to change the criteria for deciding this case and emphasize the committee's social responsibility rather than objective test scores and grades. Decision making can be easily manipulated by changing the criteria. In any decision-making situation, multiple measures are available for assessing alternatives. Rather than arguing for one's preferred alternative, a much more effective political strategy is to simply suggest that the decision should be based on the criteria favoring the preferred alternative.

Control Access to Information. Information is a powerful weapon in a fight for power, and those who have access to information or who have the capacity to filter or manipulate information can often succeed in controlling decisions. Sales projections, salary information, quality reports, and many other items of information are frequently treated as confidential information in order to increase the political power of those possessing the information. Labor–management negotiations are also filled with distrust because each side attempts to manipulate the information to increase its power. Although information is frequently manipulated intentionally as a political power strategy, this process occurs most frequently in an innocent way. The process of selective perception described earlier in Chapter 2 explains how people show differential attention to and retention of facts that favor their position on an issue. In an early study of a company's decision to purchase a computer, it was found that people selectively collected and used information in the decision-making process that provided support for the decision that they already favored.[45] The processes of selective perception and manipulation of information are illustrated by a remark attributed to Peter Drucker that anyone over age 21 should be able to find enough facts to support his or her position.

Use Outside Experts. Outside experts can usually be found to support any point of view, regardless of the issue. Therefore, people can influence the outcome of the decision by carefully selecting the right outside expert and providing a forum for that individual to express an opinion. The use of outside experts as a political strategy is particularly obvious in jury trials, where the names and reputations of the experts are more important than the substance of their testimony.

Control Access to Influential People. Many great ideas and quality suggestions are killed or ignored because they never reach the people who have the capacity to do anything with them. New ideas often rock the boat and threaten people's jobs. Middle managers often succeed in preventing lower-level members from submitting creative ideas or constructive criticisms by preventing lower-level members from communicating with top management. Being able to communicate regularly with members of top management increases one's ability to use power, whether the interaction comes from a scheduled meeting, a weekly game of golf, or commuting to work together.

Form a Coalition. When groups of people discover they lack the power to influence the decision process, they can increase their power by forming a coalition with other groups. As described in Chapter 10, coalitions are typically formed to maximize the rewards or outcomes to the group and its members. Therefore, most coalitions are comprised of the minimum number of members required to achieve a successful decision. Coalitions tend to be unstable and temporary unless there are philosophical or ideological commonalities that keep the parties together.

Co-opt the Opposition. The strategy of co-opting is similar to the strategy of forming a coalition. However, **co-optation** generally refers to an enduring relationship rather than a temporary alliance of a coalition. Co-opting occurs, for example, when a subunit asks a local critic to join their group and work with them in solving their problems. School systems, hospitals, and other civic organizations use a co-opting strategy of placing influential citizens on their board of directors as a conscious strategy of reducing their uncertainty and minimizing outside criticism.

Manipulate Symbols. Politics, either in organizations or in government, has a language of its own that is designed to rationalize and justify decisions by using the appropriate symbolic labels. Without this legitimization, the exercise of power would be unacceptable and would create resistance. Political actors need to use appropriate language and symbols to generate support when their decisions are made on the basis of power. Decisions that are largely based on power can often be made to appear as though they resulted from rational decision making.

Two federal laws provide excellent illustrations of the effects of political language: the "right to work" section of the Taft-Hartley Act (1947) and the windfall profits tax (1980). Section 14b of the Taft-Hartley Act allows states to pass a law guaranteeing workers the right to refuse to join a union even though the majority of the workers vote in favor of it. This section has been labeled the "right to work," and union leaders claim that personal rights and freedom are such widely accepted social values that this label contains a misleading bias. Union leaders complain that this law allows workers to refuse to join the union even though they benefit from the negotiations and sacrifices of their co-workers. It is doubtful that the "right to work" provision would enjoy the same degree of popularity if it carried a negative label, such as the "freeloader bill." Likewise, the Windfall Profits Tax was an excise tax based on the price of oil that actually had nothing to do with profits. Nevertheless, it was passed at a time when the oil companies appeared to be making large profits, and a tax on "windfall profits" was politically appealing. Support for this tax probably would have been considerably less if it had been called an "Excise Tax on Gasoline" or an "Oil Price Increase" tax.

Actions, ceremonies, and myths are also symbolic events that have a large influence in organizations. Administrators perform a variety of symbolic activities that influence the power relationships in organizations. Here is a list of four symbolic administrative actions and an explanation of why each action is effective:

1. *Spend time on activities that are important.*   The amount of time an administrator spends on an activity is one measure of the importance of that goal or function.

2. *Change or enhance the setting.*   A new setting conveys the feeling that something new is happening. An enhanced setting with more elaborate furnishings generally means that the activity is more consequential and important. Changing the meeting from the lunchroom to the boardroom communicates a message of significance to the attendees.

3. *Review and interpret history.*   Events have meaning only through our interpretations of them. The most important interpretations are those derived from a historical analysis demonstrating a consistent line of meaning and direction. If current events appear to be consistent with historic trends, it is easier to obtain a consensus on a chosen course of action. For example, wage cuts and extra hours are more acceptable if it can be shown that the employees have always responded with loyalty and sacrifice during hard times.

4. *Provide a dominant value expressed in a simple phrase.*   A simple phrase, one that reflects a dominant value and is easily remembered, can influence the behaviors of organizational members by creating a consensus about appropriate behavior. For example, a simple slogan such as "Pride in performance brings excellence in service" can mobilize support for greater organizational commitment and dedication to work.

Use Interpersonal Manipulation. Perhaps the most blatant political strategy is when people directly pursue their goals through persuasion, manipulation, or ingratiation. Persuasion is an overt attempt to influence others by asking for cooperation and by providing information that supports the request. There is no effort to conceal the intentions of the persuader, and for the most part the information is considered accurate.

There is an important difference between persuasion and manipulation. Both involve the presentation of information designed to obtain one's desired goal. In manipulation, however, the intent of the person is concealed from the other person and crucial information is either distorted or withheld to influence the decision.

Ingratiation is a form of interpersonal manipulation that is accomplished through flattery and a display of sincerity. Flattery is a form of positive reinforcement designed to alter the target person's perception of the flatterer. The most direct form of ingratiation is when person A goes to person B and makes flattering comments. However, the effectiveness of this strategy is limited, because person B may be skeptical of person A's motives. A more effective strategy is for person A to make flattering comments about B to someone else who could be expected to report the comments back to B. Flattering comments by person A do not create suspicion if they come through person C.[46]

Influence Strategies

Managers can exert power in three directions: on their subordinates, on their superiors, and on their peers. To effectively use power, managers need to know how to exert influence in all three directions.[47]

Influencing Subordinates. Because supervisors have the legitimate right to hire, fire, and discipline subordinates, we often overestimate the power of supervisory jobs. What we typically overlook is the power that subordinates *as a group* have over their bosses. Subordinate power comes in many forms and is based on (1) skills that are difficult to replace quickly or easily, (2) specialized information and knowledge that others do not have, (3) good personal relationships that prevent a supervisor from reprimanding or replacing a subordinate without alienating other employees, and (4) the centrality of the subordinate's job, which may be crucial to the performance of the supervisor's job.

The combination of these factors creates a situation in which the power of the subordinates is greater than the power of the supervisor despite the formal power that comes from the organization. Consequently, supervisors need to expand their power base beyond the legitimate power conferred by the organization. Effectively leading subordinates demands that supervisors bring additional sources of power to the job. The following suggestions have been made for supervisors to increase their clout during their early tenure as supervisors.

1. *Acquire the relevant interpersonal skills and abilities.* Being a good supervisor and successfully exerting power requires good interpersonal skills, persuasiveness, and the ability to identify and resolve conflicts quickly. Good verbal skills in listening and communicating are essential for influencing subordinates.

2. *Establish good working relationships.* Good working relationships are based on a combination of respect, admiration, obligation, and friendship. To be perceived as effective and a credible source of influence, supervisors need to maintain good relationships not only with subordinates but with superiors and others outside the chain of command.

3. *Acquire information.* Knowledge is power, but the most important knowledge in leadership jobs is detailed information about the social reality in which the job is embedded. Supervisors need to know who the relevant parties are, their different perspectives, and when these perspectives may be in conflict.

4. *Maintain a good track record.* Being perceived as a successful supervisor contributes to the supervisor's power position. A credible track record and the reputation it earns can help a supervisor obtain compliance in a fraction of the time that is required if credibility is lacking. Success breeds success, and the successful application of power in one situation increases the supervisor's potential power for the next occasion.

Influencing Superiors. Successful employees need an effective boss to provide them with the necessary job opportunities, resources, organizational protection, and job security. Unfortunately, many employees do not feel they receive the support and encouragement they need to perform their jobs adequately. Even more serious is the fact that many employees think their supervisor is unfair, incompetent, biased, and unqualified to lead. These problems highlight the importance of being able to exert influence upward in the organization. They also explain why one of the most popular new courses at some universities is a course on boss management.

Although we typically think of power being exerted downward in an organization, it is equally important for subordinates to effectively exert power upwards. To obtain sufficient resources, support, and encouragement, subordinates must develop and maintain good working relationships with their superiors. The following principles have been suggested for developing good relationships with superiors and exerting upward influence.

1. Creative, competent subordinates take some of the load off their boss's shoulders. Effective subordinates solve problems rather than create them, and whenever possible they bring good news of successful solutions to the boss rather than failures and problems.

2. Change your boss's bad behavior with rewards. Catching your boss doing something good and rewarding this behavior is far more effective than criticizing or complaining. If your boss has traits you would like to change, reward positive behavior with thanks or sincere praise.

3. Look beyond the boundaries of your job description to let others benefit from your ideas and efforts. Bosses enjoy being told by outsiders that they have an exemplary subordinate. Take advantage of opportunities outside work to make yourself visible and manage your own public relations without devoting too much time and effort to it.

4. Recognize your boss's weaknesses and let them be your strengths. If the boss hates to attend meetings, offer to go instead and give a briefing later. If the boss hates to write reports, be a ghost writer and prepare a first draft. If the boss relates badly with certain people, perform those functions yourself that entail meeting these people. By becoming a representative of your boss, you will be given the knowledge and stature to do so properly.

5. Maintain a good working relationship by keeping the boss informed, behaving dependably and honestly, and using the boss's time and resources very selectively. Subordinates who are undependable, dishonest, or who waste their boss's limited time and energy are certain to destroy their relationship with their boss.

Influencing Peers. Almost everyone in an organization depends on someone outside the formal chain of command. For example, supervisors depend on the personnel department to screen new employees, while the personnel department depends on the supervisors to submit their staffing requirements. The success of most employees is influenced by how well they manage relationships outside the chain of command. Being able to influence one's peers often means the difference between effective and ineffective performance. Four suggestions have been offered for managing peer relationships.

1. Identify all the relevant lateral relationships both inside and outside the organization. This list represents the group of people whose performance and interactions must be monitored.

2. Assess who among these people may resist cooperation, why, and how strongly. This assessment will identify the leadership challenges and power struggles likely to occur.

3. Develop wherever possible a good relationship with these people to facilitate the communication, education, and negotiation processes required to reduce or overcome resistance. A good working relationship requires dependability and reciprocity from both parties.

4. When a good working relationship cannot be developed, some additional type of power intervention that is more subtle and more forceful should be developed to deal with the resistance.

SUMMARY

1. Power and politics provide a very different model for analyzing organizational behavior from the model of effectiveness and efficiency that is assumed in other chapters. Political models of organizational behavior view organizations as collections of people and subgroups competing for scarce resources and for the right to determine the organization's strategies and objectives. Political models of decision making focus on allocating resources according to the relative power of people and subunits rather than an objective assessment of organizational effectiveness.

2. Power represents the capacity of one person or group to secure compliance from another person or group. Authority is legitimate power and represents the right of one party to seek compliance from another. Control is the epitome of influence, where behavior is constrained and individuals are prevented from behaving in ways not allowed by the organization. Politics is the exercise of power within an organization.

3. Three conditions are necessary for the use of power: interdependence, scarcity, and heterogeneous goals. When the activities of one individual or group depend on others, when there are not enough resources for everyone, and when the goals of the organization and the means of achieving these goals are uncertain, then the likelihood that some form of power or political activity will be exerted is very high. Furthermore, it has been argued that when these three conditions exist, the use of power is inevitable and virtually the only way to make a decision.

4. The most important difference between the use of power and authority is that authority is defined as legitimate power where *legitimate* refers to role-relevant influence. Three types of authority have been defined using a historical perspective: traditional authority based on inheritance or an accepted social order as found in certain cultures, charismatic authority derived from the mystical personal quality of a highly respected and revered leader, and rational-legal authority derived from a person's formal position in an organizational structure.

5. The authority structure found in most organizations is widely accepted in different cultures and nationalities. Research studies have shown that people are remarkably obedient to the commands of people in authority.

6. Although the use of power is associated with important ethical concerns, it is not necessarily good or bad. In some situations, the use of power is the best way, if not the only way, to make timely decisions.

7. Sometimes it is difficult to know when power is being used because the most successful applications of power occur when it is subtle and least recognized. Five objective indicators of power that can be used to assess the application of power involve measuring (a) the determinants of power, such as how many bases of power each person possesses; (b) the consequences of power, in terms of who receives the most resources or achieves the greatest agreement in decision-making episodes; (c) symbols of power in terms of titles, office size, and special privileges; (d) reputation as reported by others; and (e) representation on committees, especially important policymaking committees.

8. Five sources of social power have been identified to explain how person A exerts power over person B. Reward power is based on person A's ability to reward person B. Coercive power is based on person A's ability to punish person B. Legitimate power is based on person A's assigned position in an organizational structure that authorizes person A to exert influence over person B. Referent power exists when person A is highly admired and respected by person B. Expert power exists when person A possesses knowledge and skills that are valuable to person B.

9. Two activities have been recommended to increase an individual's personal power: doing the right things and cultivating the right people. Doing the right things includes performing extraordinary activities that are highly visible and relevant to the success of the organization. Cultivating the right people involves developing good working relationships with superiors, subordinates, and peers.

10. In most organizations, the power structure is fairly constant over time because people are able to perpetuate their own personal power, and subunit power is institutionalized by a stable organizational culture. Although organizationally based power depends on continued support from the organization, individually based power in the form of expert or charismatic power can be enhanced by the ways people behave.

11. Subunits within an organization are able to acquire power by (a) controlling valuable resources either by being able to secure them from outside the organization or allocate them to other subunits, (b) controlling strategic contingencies, (c) helping the organization or other subunits within the organization to cope with uncertainty, (d) being irreplaceable by performing crucial functions that cannot be performed by others, and (e) being central to the organization by performing the most important functions.

12. Powerful subunits within an organization can maintain their power by preserving the organizational culture and maintaining the current relationships among the subsystems.

Four methods by which powerful subunits institutionalize the power relationships in an organization come from controlling the organization's strategy, influencing the selection of personnel, controlling the promotion of organization members, and influencing the socialization process, especially the training of new employees.

13. After they acquire power, individuals and subunits can exert political influence through a variety of political strategies, including controlling the agenda of committee meetings; selecting the criteria by which decisions will be made; controlling access to information; using outside experts to influence a decision; controlling access to influential people; forming a coalition with other members; co-opting the opposition by asking them to join the group; manipulating the symbols of power; and using persuasion, manipulation, or ingratiation to exert direct interpersonal influence.

14. Power is exerted in many directions, and to perform their jobs effectively, employees are usually required to exert influence on their subordinates, superiors, and peers outside the formal chain of command. Learning how to manage one's boss is a popular idea that is particularly appealing to college students and involves such suggestions as taking the load off the boss's shoulders, changing the boss by rewarding good behavior, compensating for the boss's weaknesses by performing those functions yourself, and being honest and dependable.

DISCUSSION QUESTIONS

1. How do power and politics represent an alternative way of thinking about an organization?

2. Evaluate this statement: "A has power over B only to the extent that B allows A to exert such power."

3. Authority is defined as legitimate power, and legitimate is defined in terms of being role relevant. But what criteria do we use to decide what is role relevant? Is the banning of beards and long hair a role-

relevant prohibition among employees who do not interact with the public? Is a chemical company's ban on smoking either on or off the job a role-relevant demand?

4. The conditions necessary for the use of power are interdependence, scarcity, and heterogeneous goals. Are there heterogeneous goals in a university? Discuss the heterogeneous nature of both the

goals and the means of achieving them in a major university.

5. Is the use of power inevitable? One manager does not believe that power is necessary and argues instead that the use of power in one decision situation only increases the likelihood that it will be used in the future. Is it true that the use of power increases the use of power?

6. How do you explain the widespread acceptance of obedience to authority? Do you consider it unhealthy for people to comply so willingly to the directives of someone in authority?

7. Discuss this statement: "Control and influence are not fixed, they are expandable. Allowing production workers to have more influence does not necessarily reduce the influence of top management."

8. Explain what is meant by "Power tends to corrupt; and absolute power corrupts absolutely." Why does this happen?

9. If you were going to study the power relationships between student organizations such as fraternities, sororities, and service clubs, what objective indicators would you use to assess the use of power?

10. Since people dislike being punished, why would they stay in a situation where someone was using coercive power? How can coercive power be maintained in situations where people are free to leave?

11. Personal power comes from doing the right things. If you were the secretary of a preprofessional student organization such as the dental club, what are some things you would need to do to increase your personal power?

12. Explain how humor can be used as a tactic to exert power on others or to blunt the power of others. Describe situations that illustrate this process.

13. Subunits within an organization can increase their power by controlling strategic contingencies. Choose an organization and identify which strategic contingencies are being controlled by which subunits and with what effect.

14. What is the difference between coalition formation and co-optation? Which strategy is the most permanent, and when would each strategy be useful?

15. How is ingratiation different from positive reinforcement? How effective is ingratiation? Regardless of the insincerity, don't most people enjoy flattery?

16. How much actual influence do you think subordinates have over their boss? Is it realistic for employees to think they can change their boss's undesirable traits or behavior?

GLOSSARY

authority The legitimate use of power.

authority structure The hierarchical patterns of authority relationships illustrated by an organizational chart.

centrality A method of acquiring subunit power by occupying an important role in the work flow of an organization, particularly within the communication network.

charismatic authority The authority derived from the alluring or mystical personal qualities of a highly respected and revered leader.

coercive power One of the bases of social power that is derived from the ability to punish others or deprive them of rewards.

control The epitome of influence, in which people are constrained from behaving contrary to the way intended.

control graph A graph showing the relative influence of people at different levels in the organization as perceived by organizational members.

co-optation A strategy of bringing opposition members into the organization to obtain their support and cooperation.

democratic alternative An alternative political strategy for making decisions and exerting influence within organizations that allows everyone to participate equally in making decisions and approving policies.

expert power A basis of social power derived from the special knowledge and ability an individual possesses.

heterogeneous goals One of the conditions contributing to power that exists when people disagree about the organizations's goals and objectives and the means that should be used to achieve them.

irony of democracy Democratic values and freedoms in our society are not protected by the political activities of the entire population as much as they are by the political activities of a few members of an elite within society.

irreplaceability A method of acquiring power that comes from being the only one capable of performing a crucial function or providing a crucial resource.

legitimate power A basis of social power that is derived from one's position in the organizational hierarchy.

mentor A higher-level member, sometimes called a *sponsor*, who provides resources, ideas, information, introductions and personal contacts for someone lower in the organization.

politics The use of power in organizations to allocate resources or make decisions.

power The capacity to influence the behavior of others; the probability that one individual within a social relationship can carry out his or her own will despite resistance.

rational-legal authority A type of authority that is derived from the hierarchical structure of the organization, which grants officeholders the right to exert influence over others.

referent power A basis of social power derived from the interpersonal attraction that person A has for person B because of A's personal qualities, reputation, and charismatic leadership.

reward power A basis of social power that is derived from an individual's ability to reward others.

scarcity A condition, necessary for the use of power, that exists when insufficient resources are available for everyone.

strategic contingencies The crucial interactions and work flow interdependencies within organizations that make one subunit dependent on another. Subunits are able to increase their power by controlling the most crucial of these contingencies.

substitutability The capacity of not having to depend on a particular subunit for resources or the performance of crucial functions. To the extent that a subunit is not substitutable, it is irreplaceable and, therefore, more powerful.

traditional authority Authority derived from inheritance or social custom.

NOTES

1. Jeffrey Pfeffer, *Power in Organizations* (Marshfield, Mass.: Pitman, 1981); John P. Kotter, *Power and Influence* (New York: Free Press, 1985); Jeffrey Pfeffer, *Managing With Power* (Boston: Harvard Business School Press, 1992).

2. Kathleen M. Eisenhardt, "Politics of Strategic Decision Making in High-Velocity Environments: Toward a Midrange Theory," *Academy of Management Journal*, vol. 31 (1988), pp. 737–770.

3. Cited in A. M. Henderson and Talcott Parsons, *Max Weber: The Theory of Social and Economic Organization* (New York: Free Press, 1947); Stewart R. Clegg, "Radical Revisions: Power, Discipline, and Organizations," *Organizational Studies*, vol. 10, no. 1 (1989), pp. 97–115.

4. Daniel Katz and Robert Kahn, *The Social Psychology of Organizations*, 2nd ed. (New York: Wiley, 1978), chap. 10; Edgar H. Schein, "Reassessing the 'Divine Rights' of Managers," *Sloan Management Review*, vol. 30 (Winter 1989), pp. 63–68.

5. Allan R. Cohen and David L. Bradford, "Influence Without Authority: The Use of Alliances, Reciprocity, and Exchange to Accomplish Work," *Organizational Dynamics*, vol. 17 (Winter 1989), pp. 4–17.

6. Amos Drory and Tsilia Romm, "The Definition of Organizational Politics: A Review," *Human Relations*, vol. 43 (November 1990), pp. 1133–1154.

7. Lee Iacocca and William Novak, *Iacocca: An Autobiography* (New York: Bantam Books, 1984).

8. Pfeffer, op. cit., chap. 3.

9. Dean Tjosvold, Robert I. Andrews, and John T. Struthers, "Power and Interdependence in Work Groups—Views of Managers and Employees," *Group and Organization Studies*, vol. 16 (September 1991), pp. 285–299.

10. Katz and Kahn, op. cit., pp. 300–330, especially p. 324.

11. Henderson and Parsons, op. cit.

12. Arnold S. Tannenbaum, *Hierarchy in Organizations* (San Francisco: Jossey-Bass, 1974).

13. Stanley Milgram, *Obedience to Authority* (New York: Harper & Row, 1973); Stanley Milgram, "Behavioral Study of Obedience," *Journal of Abnormal and Social Psychology*, vol. 67 (1963), pp. 371–378.

14. Katz and Kahn, op. cit., chap. 10.

15. Thomas R. Dye and L. Harmon Zeigler, *The Irony of Democracy: An Uncommon Introduction to American Politics* (Belmont, Calif.: Wadsworth, 1970).

16. Arnold S. Tannenbaum, *Control in Organizations* (New York: McGraw-Hill, 1968); Arnold S. Tannenbaum and R. A. Cooke, "Organizational Control: A Review of Research Employing the Control Graph Method," in C. J. Lammers and D. J. Hickson (eds.), *Organizations Alike and Unlike* (London: Routledge & Kegan Paul, Ltd., 1978); Leslie H. Brown, "Locus of Control and Degree of Organizational Democracy," *Economic and Industrial Democracy*, vol. 10 (November 1989), pp. 467–498.

17. Quotation is by John Emrich Edward Dalberg, Lord Acton, in a Letter to Bishop Mandell Creighton, 1887. Cited in John Bartlett, *Familiar Quotations*, 12th ed., edited by Christopher Morley and Louella D. Everett (Boston: Little, Brown, 1949), p. 1041; Manfred F. R. Kets De Vries, "Whatever Happened to the Philosopher-King? The Leader's Addiction to Power," *Journal of Management Studies*, vol. 28 (July 1991), pp. 339–351.

18. This belief is typified by the famous quote by Charles Wilson when he was being confirmed for secretary of defense and was asked by Senator Hendrickson, "If a situation did arise where you had to make a decision which was extremely adverse to the interest of your stock and General Motors . . . in the interest of the United States Government, could you make that decision?" Mr. Wilson replied, "Yes, sir, I could. I cannot conceive of one because for years I've thought what was good for our country was good for General Motors and vice versa. The difference did not exist."

19. The desirability of having people pursue their own selfish interest is often attributed to the "invisible hand" guiding the marketplace as described by Adam Smith in *The Wealth of Nations* (1776).

20. Jeffrey Gandz and Victor Murray, "The Experience of Workplace Politics," *Academy of Management Journal*, vol. 23 (1980), pp. 237–251.

21. In sexual harassment seminars, when the audience has been asked this question, about 80 percent of the men report it would be a compliment while 80 percent of the women find it objectionable.

22. Jeffrey Pfeffer and Gerald R. Salancik, "Organizational Decision-making as a Political Process: The Case of a University Budget," *Administrative Science Quarterly*, vol. 19 (1974), pp. 135–151.

23. Pfeffer, op. cit., chap. 2.

24. Kevin M. O'Brien, "Compensation, Employment, and the Political Activity of Public Employee Unions," *Journal of Labor Research*, vol. 13 (Spring 1992), pp. 189–203; J. Lawrence French, "The Power and Pay of International Union Officials," *Journal of Labor Research*, vol. 13 (Spring 1992), pp. 157–172.

25. Pfeffer, op. cit., p. 51.

26. John R. P. French, Jr., and Bertram Raven, "The Bases of Social Power," in Dorwin Cartwright (ed.), *Studies of Social Power* (Ann Arbor: Institute for Social Research, University of Michigan, 1959), pp. 150–165.

27. Gary A. Yukl, *Leadership in Organizations* (Englewood Cliffs, N.J.: Prentice-Hall, 1981), pp. 44–58.

28. David Krackhardt, "Assessing the Political Landscape: Structure, Cognition, and Power in Organizations," *Administrative Science Quarterly*, vol. 35 (June 1990), pp. 342–369.

29. Gary Yukl and Cecilia M. Falve, "Importance of Different Power Sources in Downward and Lateral Relations," *Journal of Applied Psychology*, vol. 76 (June 1991), pp. 416–423.

30. David C. McClelland, "The Two Faces of Power," *Journal of International Affairs*, vol. 24 (1970), pp. 29–47; David C. McClelland, *Power: The Inner Experience* (New York: Irvington, 1975).

31. T. Roger Peay and W. Gibb Dyer, Jr., "Power Orientations of Entrepreneurs and Succession Planning," *Journal of Small Business Management*, vol. 27 (January 1989), pp. 47–52.

32. Rosabeth Moss Kanter, *Men and Women of the Corporation* (New York: Basic Books, 1977).

33. W. Jack Duncan and J. Philip Feisal, "No Laughing Matter: Patterns of Humor in the Workplace," *Organizational Dynamics*, vol. 17 (Spring 1989), pp. 18–30.

34. Jeffrey Pfeffer and Alison M. Konrad, "The Effects of Individual Power on Earnings," *Work and Occupations*, vol. 18 (November 1991), pp. 385–414.

35. Pfeffer, op. cit., chap. 4.

36. Pfeffer and Salancik, op. cit.

37. W. Graham Astley and Edward J. Zajac, "Beyond Dyadic Exchange: Functional Interdependence and Sub-Unit Power," *Organization Studies*, vol. 11 (1990), pp. 481–501; Carol Stoak Saunders, "The Strategic Contingency's Theory of Power: Multiple Perspectives," *Journal of Management Studies*, vol. 27 (January 1990), pp. 1–18.

38. Paul R. Lawrence and Jay W. Lorsch, *Organization and Environment* (Boston: Harvard University Graduate School of Business Administration, 1967).

39. M. Crozier, *The Bureaucratic Phenomenon* (Chicago: University of Chicago Press, 1964).

40. Sid L. Huff, "Power and the Information Systems Department," *Business Quarterly*, vol. 55 (Winter 1991), pp. 50–53.

41. Genevieve E. Chandler, "Creating an Environment to Empower Nurses," *Nursing Management*, vol. 22 (August 1991), pp. 20–23; Bruce J. Fried, "Power Acquisition in a Health Care Setting: An Application of Strategic Contingencies Theory," *Human Relations*, vol. 41 (December 1988), pp. 915–927; Jennifer E.

Jenkins, "Professional Governance: The Missing Link," *Nursing Management*, vol. 22 (August 1991), pp. 26–30.

42. Marlene E. Burkhardt and Daniel J. Brass, "Changing Patterns or Patterns of Change: The Effects of a Change in Technology on Social Network Structure and Power," *Administrative Science Quarterly*, vol. 35 (March 1990), pp. 104–127.

43. Ron Lachman, "Power from What?" A Reexamination of Its Relationships with Structural Conditions," *Administrative Science Quarterly*, vol. 34 (June 1989), pp. 231–251.

44. Gerald R. Ferris and Thomas R. King, "Politics in Human Resources Decisions: 'A Walk on the Dark Side'," *Organizational Dynamics*, vol. 20 (Autumn 1991), pp. 59–71.

45. Richard M. Cyert, Herbert A. Simon, and Donald B. Trow, "Observation of a Business Decision," *Journal of Business*, vol. 29 (1956), pp. 337–348.

46. Edward E. Jones, *Ingratiation: A Social Psychological Analysis* (New York: Appleton-Century-Crofts, 1964).

47. John P. Kotter, *Power and Influence* (New York: Free Press, 1985).

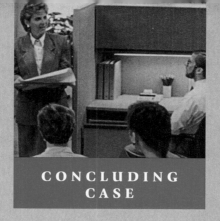

A POWER CAGE PROTEST

On Tuesday morning at 6:30 A.M., two young auto workers, disgruntled over failing to get their supervisor fired, scaled the 10-foot fence of a power control area, shut off the power and closed down a Transpower Corporation assembly line. They simply took matters into their own hands when the union's grievance procedure did not work fast enough to satisfy them. For thirteen hours thereafter, William Strong and Larry Kane carried on their protest in the 6-by-7 foot facility known as the *power cage*, as fellow workers shouted encouragement.

This dramatic protest ended in victory with the delivery to the power cage of a signed statement from the plant manager, officially reporting that the supervisor had been fired and that there would be no reprisal against the protesters. Strong and Kane were carried from the plant on the shoulders of their fellow workers. They were back in the plant working as spot welders the next day but the fired supervisor, Fred Winfare, was out of his job, although he hoped to get another job with the company.

Winfare, who has four children and who was fired for "personnel violations," claimed the action was unjust. In explaining the events that led to the power cage protest and his subsequent firing, Winfare said that production on the assembly line had been chronically below quota before he was named supervisor. At the time Winfare was made supervisor, the plant manager had plainly told him that his job was to improve the production rate, and pro-

duction had, in fact, improved markedly in the short time that he was supervisor.

Winfare said his firing would set a damaging precedent. "The company's action creates a situation where the operations of the plant are subject to the whims of any employee with a grudge," he said. This possibility was emphasized by the comment of a union steward who said there were other conditions in the plant that needed improving—such as the cafeteria food and relief from the more than 100°F heat in the metal shop. Moreover, the steward said, there was at least one other supervisor who should be fired. His manner implied that the successful power cage protest would facilitate attaining these ends, too. The union steward's final comment was that two men on an unauthorized wildcat strike had clearly accomplished the same thing as a full-blown strike.

Commenting to a news reporter about the power cage strike, the two auto workers reportedly said, "We knew we were going to win. When you cut the power, you've got the power. Every minute we were in there was costing the company money, and we weren't going to leave. It showed the power of the workers to control the company."

The protest at the Transpower plant cost the company the production of 900 to 950 automotive units valued at $8,000 each and one reliable supervisor, according to newspaper accounts.

As the plant manager began to prepare a report on the power cage protest for his superior, the division vice president, he reviewed the events of the day, the decisions he had made, and the implications for the future. He wondered if the situation might not have been dealt with more effectively.

Questions

1. Did William Strong and Larry Kane actually have as much power as they claimed to have?

2. What other alternatives did the company have? How good were these alternatives?

3. What will be the long-term consequences of the company's decision? What did the company gain or lose by this incident?

Source: Adapted from John M. Champion and John H. James, *Critical Incidents in Management* (Homewood, Ill.: Richard D. Irwin, Inc., 1975), p. 1.

SUPERVISING A STUDENT TEACHER

Purpose. The purpose of this exercise is to help you improve your negotiating skills and gain a better understanding of how conflicts can be resolved.

Activity. This exercise is a role-play activity among five individuals who have to decide which one of them has the privilege of supervising a student teacher. This exercise works best if there are five or more observers assigned to watch the five people playing the roles.

Situation. You are one of five English teachers at Valley View High School, and you have just learned that a student teacher from the local university has been assigned to your school. The student teacher, Kim Phillips, has had considerable teaching experience in the past and will require very little supervision. Therefore, all five of you very much want to supervise Kim. Your principal has decided to let the group decide who will have that privilege. However, if you fail to make a decision within the allotted time, the decision will be made by drawing names out of a hat. Listed here is the information regarding the five teachers. Only read the information relevant to your role assignment.

Role for Lynn Abbott. You have been teaching high school for twelve years and during the past four years you have worked hard to develop the AP (advanced placement) program for the high school. You have the major responsibility of working with the seniors in writing letters of recommendation to help them get into college and obtain scholarships. The literature books that you are using are the oldest ones in the school, and you feel that if anyone deserves the next "favor" it should be you.

Role for Pat Schow. You have been teaching English at the high school for eight years. Because you relate well with problem students, your teaching assignment includes teaching all the remedial English classes that contain students who are academically weak or who have behavior problems. Many weeks you spend as many as two and three hours per week talking with parents and students by phone trying to help them stay in school. A student teacher would make it much easier for you to help students with problems.

Role for Murray Linden. You have been teaching high school English for the past seven years. Because of your outstanding academic record in college, you were invited to teach the honors sections. Last year you received new literature books for your classes and a student teacher would allow you more time to develop classroom activities and homework assignments from these books. You are also responsible for the school yearbook, a major assignment for which you could use additional time.

Role for Chris Joelson. You have been teaching English at the school for the past three years. You have been teaching large sections of junior English and would like to have developmental time so that you can prepare to teach other classes. You are responsible for the junior prom assembly and dance, which is the largest social event in your school. Supervising these events is an enormous time requirement and a student teacher would make it considerably easier.

Role for Liang Chen. This is your first year of teaching English in the high school and having a student teacher to help you would be an enormous benefit. You have been assigned to teach sophomore English, which is largely a writing class. All your sections are extremely large, and it is simply impossible for you to adequately read all the writing assignments you expect your students to write.

CHAPTER 17

Organization Change
and Development

LEARNING OBJECTIVES

After studying this chapter, you should be able to

1. Identify some of the internal and external forces requiring organizations to change.

2. Explain why organizational change is often resisted by both individual and organizational forces.

3. List the potential targets of a change effort.

4. Contrast the effectiveness of different methods of change.

5. Describe the underlying assumptions and values of organizational development.

6. List some of the major organizational change interventions, and explain how they are conducted.

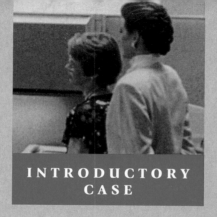

WORK-OUT AT GENERAL ELECTRIC

For more than a century, General Electric Company has been a pioneering U.S. company whose management practices have been copied by other companies. Consequently, in the 1980s many were surprised to watch GE shed more than thirty plants and terminate over 100,000 jobs, a quarter of its workforce. Although the company had been profitable before, the future looked uncertain because of increasing global competition and growing bureaucracy. Any unit that wasn't first or second in its industry was a likely candidate for the auction block.

After GE completed the restructuring of its "hardware," it began to build its "software." The goal was to make the organization less bureaucratic by moving away from centralized controls, multilevel approvals, and formal reports, toward an operation characterized by "speed, simplicity, and self-confidence." GE used three change interventions to revitalize the company: Work-Out sessions, Best Practices, and Process Mapping.

Work-Out started in 1989 when GE's chairman, John Welch, and his two vice chairmen, began holding a series of meetings with the heads of the fourteen main business units and their salaried employees. Work-Out was envisioned as a series of New England-style town meetings with people of every conceivable rank and function chipping away at the bureaucratic inefficiencies and nonsense that develop in large corporations as they age. Employees were empowered to express their feelings openly because Welch made it plain that any efforts to obstruct the progress of a Work-Out team would be a "career-limiting move." Furthermore, support for Work-Out was one of the criteria in their annual performance reviews.

The initial targets of Work-Out focused on eliminating wasteful paperwork, duplication of effort, and unnecessary approvals. During the first year, some of the most obvious inefficiencies were identified and changed. But the greatest accomplishment of the early sessions was the development of trust and openness that paved the way for more significant improvements in later years. Customers and suppliers were included in some Work-Out sessions to identify a broader array of problems and solutions.

Best Practices was another strategy GE used to improve efficiency. From an initial list of 200 well-run companies, a final list of about two dozen was compiled that had achieved faster productivity growth than GE and sustained it for at least ten years. About half of these companies agreed to let GE send some of its people to their firms to learn about their best management practices, and in return GE agreed to share what they learned. From this review, GE changed the way it managed and measured performance. GE continues to interact with some of these companies, which provides an ongoing source of new ideas.

Process mapping is an old technique that sounds simple, but it can be quite complex. A process map is a flow chart showing every step, no matter how small, that goes into making or doing something.

Elaborate process maps use diamonds, circles, and squares to distinguish work that adds value from work that doesn't, such as inspections and reports. Some Work-Out sessions are devoted to building process maps and revising them to improve efficiencies.

Work-Out sessions and process mapping were used to remove the horizontal barriers interrupting the flow of work in GE's huge appliance operation in Louisville. This program, called Quick Response, was an astonishing success. Every function in the business, including finance, distribution, customer service, marketing, and manufacturing, worked together to reduce average inventory by $200 million and to speed the order-to-delivery cycle time from eighteen weeks to five weeks.

In recent years, so many productivity improvements have occurred almost simultaneously that the effects of Work-Outs have been described as explosive. Due to the volume of Work-Outs at GE, outside facilitators who helped with the earlier sessions are having to train GE employees to take their place. A trained facilitator is considered essential because the sessions often get very heated. A skilled facilitator needs to know when to step in, when to keep out, and how to get help from engineers and other experts if the team needs it.

Questions

1. What group dynamics contribute to the success of a Work-Out session? How does GE's Work-Out program overcome resistance to change, and why do employees feel free to participate openly?

2. How is a Work-Out session any different from a quality control meeting? Why is GE's Work-Out program so successful when most companies have struggled with their quality control committees?

Sources: Thomas A. Stewart, "G. E. Keeps Those Ideas Coming," *Fortune* (August 12, 1991), pp. 41–49. Russell Mitchell and Judith H. Dobrzynski, "Jack Welch: How Good a Manager?" *Business Week* (December 14, 1987), p. 92; Joseph M. Winski, "Black Monday in Cicero: Why GE Plant Was Doomed," *Crain's Chicago Business* (October 5, 1987), p. 2; Tracy E. Benson, "America's Best CEOs," *Industry Week* (December 2, 1991), pp. 28–36; "The National Management Association Honors John F. Welch, Jr., as 1991 American Manager of the Year," *Manage*, vol. 43, no. 1 (1991), pp. 18–19; Jill Andresky Fraser, "Women, Power and the New GE," *Working Woman*, vol. 17 (December 1992), pp. 58–62; see also Michael Morris, "The New Breed of Leaders Taking Charge in a Different Way," *Working Woman*, vol. 15 (March 1990), pp. 73 ff.

ORGANIZATIONAL SURVIVAL AND ADAPTATION

Organizations live in an ever-changing environment and their survival depends on their ability to adapt to new demands and opportunities. Organizational development is a series of planned systematic changes introduced into an ongoing organization. These changes, typically referred to as **interventions,** are designed to improve the effectiveness of the organization and to help it respond to a changing environment. Organizational development (OD) includes a wide range of change-inducing activities that may be targeted for individuals, groups, or the entire organization. Regardless of the target, the purpose of OD is to facilitate organizational renewal—to help the organization avoid decay, obsolescence, and rigidity. Because organizations exist in a world of rapid change, they must be innovative and creative to maintain their vitality. Conditions must be established to encourage people to share their creative ideas, and the organization must have the flexibility to adjust to new environments.

In 1917, *Forbes* magazine published a list of the top 100 companies in terms of their total assets. Fifty years later, *Forbes* published a special fiftieth-anniversary issue, which again listed the top 100 companies. Of the top 100 companies in 1917, only 43 were still among the top 100 fifty years later. Of the 57 companies that had dropped out, 28 had disappeared entirely through either merger or liquidation. An analysis of the companies that died provides an interesting postmortem examination of the causes of business failures.[1]

According to the editors of *Forbes,* the most important reason for the failure of these organizations was poor management. In each situation, external factors could be identified that contributed to the companies' failure; however, the successful companies faced the same external factors and, instead of failing, they became stronger. Although some corporate failures were attributed to internal conflict or fraud, most of these companies failed primarily because they did not respond appropriately to a changing environment. Koppers Company, for example, failed to see the change in the extraction of chemicals from oil rather than coal. Baldwin Locomotive and American Locomotive failed to see that the steam locomotive would give way to the diesel. When the jet engine was introduced, the mighty Curtiss-Wright Corporation assumed it was a passing fad and that a souped-up version of their old-fashioned piston engine would compete effectively with jets. The meat-packing industry was first rocked by Upton Sinclair's book *The Jungle,* with its lurid descriptions of filthy packing houses, and then by the Packers Act of 1921 which brought federal inspections, regulations, and the elimination of price-fixing. Lehigh Coal Company was an effective and profitable company as long as the demand for anthracite coal continued. However, Lehigh Coal was first threatened by the advantages of bituminous coal, and ultimately destroyed when oil and gas became more convenient and less expensive.

In 1917 the top-100 list was led by U.S. Steel. In 1967 U.S. Steel had dropped to sixth place. Since 1967, U.S. Steel has had to fight for its very existence because of high labor costs, less expensive foreign imports, and obsolete equipment. To survive, U.S. Steel found it necessary to terminate thousands of jobs and idle several steel mills. In 1986, U.S. Steel changed its name to USX after acquiring Marathon Oil Company and Texas Oil and Gas, and since then steel is no longer its major product. Although some of these problems are unique to the steel industry, every organization faces an ever-changing environment that requires it to adapt and change.

Changes in the computer industry since 1970, as shown in Exhibit 17.1, illustrate how drastically and quickly change can occur. Before 1970, revenue in the computer industry was primarily derived from the sale of large mainframe computers. In 1971, 77 percent of the total industry revenue was derived from the sale of mainframe computers. About then the computer industry began moving away from large mainframes to smaller computers; first in the form of minicomputers and then to personal computers. The sale of minicomputers peaked in 1979 at 71 percent of the market, and personal computer sales peaked in 1984 at 51 percent. In recent years, computer sales are primarily in the form of distributed computing with networked computers. In 1992, distributed computing controlled 76 percent of the market.[2]

Although changes in the computer industry may seem rather mild, they were monumental for computer firms. International Business Machines (IBM) and Digital Equipment Company (DEC), two producers of large mainframe computers, enjoyed tremendous growth and stability before the sale of mainframes began to decline. In recent years, however, both companies have suffered economically and been forced to reduce their workforces. IBM was slow to recognize the growing popularity of PCs and, when it finally did recognize the shift, responded too slowly. Much of the PC market share was captured by smaller and more adaptable computer makers who cloned IBM's products.[3]

The market changes were even more severe for smaller computer companies. Data General, for example, was founded in 1968 by defectors from DEC who recognized the coming popularity of minicomputers. By specializing in producing minicomputers, Data General reached its peak in 1984 with over 17,000 employees and annual sales in excess of $1 billion. In its days of glory, Data General was

EXHIBIT 17.1   Growth of the Computer Networking Industry

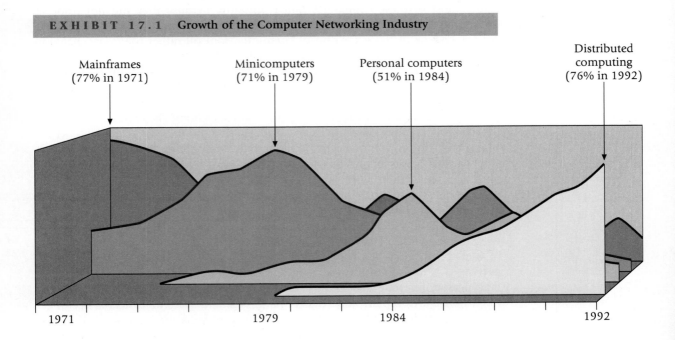

Mainframes (77% in 1971)   Minicomputers (71% in 1979)   Personal computers (51% in 1984)   Distributed computing (76% in 1992)

1971   1979   1984   1992

known for its aggressive sales tactics and for developing new computers that cost less and performed better than its rivals' machines. But Data General failed to catch the next technological wave of personal computers, and within five years it was posting substantial losses. The experience of Data General is typical of many successful firms who are blinded by their success and fail to see the changing environmental conditions.[4]

Forces of Change

Organizations are required to change because of a broad variety of different forces. These forces can be analyzed in terms of both internal forces within the organization and external forces in the environment, as shown in Exhibit 17.2.

Internal Forces of Change. Several forces within the organization may require it to change:

1. *Technology.* The rate of technological change seems to increase every year with new machines, new manufacturing processes, and scientific discoveries. New jobs are created and old jobs deleted because of technological change. Advances in computer technology and communication systems are probably the most significant technological changes in recent years. In future years, the use of computers will continue to increase, influencing every industry. Many universities now require students to have their own personal computers for class assignments. Communication will be facilitated by mobile phones that people carry with them at all times. Facsimile machines will be common in offices, homes, and vans that serve as mobile offices.

2. *Work values.* Organizations are forced to respond to the changing values of their members. Some of the most significant changes include a change in priorities that puts family responsibilities ahead of work, a decline in the moral obligation to have a job, a decline in the sense of organizational loyalty, greater indifference toward promotions and advancement, greater variety in lifestyle and work schedules, and greater career mobility. Many managers are asking, "Why should I be loyal to the company if the company is not loyal to me?" Years of dedicated service seem to be ignored as layers of managerial jobs are deleted from the organizational chart after a merger or acquisition.[5]

3. *Knowledge explosion.* The creation of new knowledge requires organizations to operate differently, and new knowledge is being created at a very rapid rate. The creation of new knowledge requires managers to find methods for assimilating and storing useful information and converting it into profitable products and services.

4. *Product obsolescence.* Technological advances and the explosion of knowledge combine to make many products obsolete in a very short time. In an average supermarket, for example, approximately 55 percent of the items sold today did not exist ten years ago. Of the products sold then, about 40 percent are no longer produced. When the first pocket calculator was sold in the early 1970s, it was priced at approximately $250. Ten years later, a pocket calculator that was both more complex and more compact could be

EXHIBIT 17.2   Forces of Change

Driving Forces for Change	Forces Resisting Change
Internal Forces	Individual Resistance
1. New technology	1. Fear of the unknown
2. Changing work values	2. New learning
3. Creation of new knowledge	3. Disruptions of stable friendships
4. Product obsolescence	4. Distrust of management
5. Desire for leisure and alternative work schedules	
Environmental Forces	Organizational Resistance
1. Competition	1. Threat to the power structure
2. Changes in consumer demands	2. Inertia of organizational structure
3. Resource availability	3. System relationships
4. Social and political change	4. Sunk costs and vested interests
5. International changes	

purchased for less than a tenth of its earlier price. In recent years, calculators have been built into wallets, watches, and even matchbooks and have been given away free as party favors at luncheons. Rapid product obsolescence requires organizations to shorten production lead times and develop the capacity to adjust rapidly.

5. *Alternative work schedules.* More attractive opportunities for leisure and hobbies have encouraged employees to place greater demands on the organization for alternative schedules of work, such as job sharing and flextime, plus time away from work. With the increasing use of electronic mail and facsimile (fax) machines, some people avoid commuting to work by working at home on a computer connected to their office.

Environmental Forces of Change. Organizations cannot control the environment; nevertheless, astute managers identify the external forces for change and respond appropriately to them.

1. *Competition.* Changes in the marketplace can destroy a company's profitability. Consequently, managers need to know when their competitors introduce new products, change their advertising, reduce their prices, or improve their customer service. Although competition creates uncertainty, it contributes to the development of better consumer products and services. These benefits are illustrated most dramatically by comparing the cost and quality of consumer goods in competitive economies with the limited consumer goods available in regulated socialist economies.

2. *Consumer demand.* Managers must be concerned about changes in consumer tastes and preferences because a firm's products may lose their appeal for very trivial and superficial reasons. Fashions change frequently, regardless of

whether the previous style was functional or comfortable. Rumors that a product causes cancer, high blood pressure, or some other health hazard can destroy consumer products even though the rumors may be false.

3. *Resource availability.* Organizations depend on the external environment for raw materials and other resources. Disruptions in the supply of crucial resources can force organizations to drastically alter their operations, as was illustrated by the oil embargo in the mid 1970s and the shortages during World War II. Uncertainty in obtaining resources has prompted many organizations to extend their boundaries in an attempt to reduce this uncertainty. For example, electric power companies have purchased their own coal mines, steel companies produce their own coke, and food industries have purchased their own trucking lines.

4. *Social and political change.* As social and political changes occur, organizations are required to adapt. The Civil Rights Act of 1964, for example, had a very powerful impact in reducing discrimination by requiring organizations to eliminate discriminatory employment practices. Federal regulations regarding environmental pollution, toxic wastes, and safety hazards require organizations to either comply or cease doing business.

5. *International forces.* International economic forces, such as wars, balance-of-payments problems, and lower labor rates in foreign countries exert an ever-increasing influence on organizations. Managers are learning that the flow of oil out of the Middle East, monetary transactions in Switzerland, the war in Central Europe, and low wages in Asian nations are having as large an impact on the success of their organization as are their competitors down the street.

The process of analyzing future trends is called "environmental scanning," and some organizations have a strategic planning committee responsible for identifying environmental changes and how they might impact the organization. This group examines economic forecasts, changes in the demographic composition of the labor force, international events, and pending government legislation.[6]

Organizational effectiveness depends in part upon the degree of predictability and stability in the organization. However, organizations can expect to improve their effectiveness by creating a highly structured organization with clearly defined rules and procedures. If the environment remains constant, a stable structure contributes to effectiveness. However, conditions do not remain the same, so organizations are constantly caught in the dilemma, between being highly structured and being adaptable. Highly structured organizations that are rigid and inflexible are doomed to inefficiency and will eventually disappear. Therefore, organizations face a constant dilemma, trying to balance between being sufficiently organized to operate efficiently, while at the same time being sufficiently adaptable to respond to new forces demanding change. [7]

Resistance to Change

Although change is inevitable, people tend to resist it. Some evidences of resistance to change are very overt, such as wildcat strikes, work stoppages, turnover, and protests about a proposed change. Resistance to change may also be very subtle and indirect, such as dissatisfaction, grievances, requests for transfers, absenteeism, excessive damage to machines, and conflict among members of a work crew. The reasons explaining resistance to change can be divided into individual and organizational forces of resistance, as shown in Exhibit 17.2.

Individual Resistance. People resist change for a variety of reasons, and before implementing change managers should try to understand why people are likely to object.

1. *Fear of the unknown.* Although change may improve life, the outcome is not certain, and fear of the unknown causes a powerful resistance to change. Significant change presents a realistic possibility that jobs will be terminated and employees laid off. These fears can be very frightening and persist in spite of management's attempt to assure employees that jobs will not be eliminated.

2. *New learning.* Learning a new task or procedure requires a conscious effort and is not as comfortable as doing it the "same old way." Some changes are small; others are far more significant, requiring people to learn a new language, develop a new technology, learn how to operate a computer, or adjust to a totally new culture. Although learning new ideas can be exciting, most people report that the excitement came after the learning occurred, not before.

3. *Disruption of stable friendships.* By working together, employees develop stable friendships. When these social interactions are disrupted, the resulting dissatisfaction is quite understandable. Almost any organizational change has the potential of destroying stable interactions and creating uncomfortable feelings of social isolation and loneliness.

4. *Distrust of management.* Employees often suspect the reason for change is to make them work faster for the same pay. Management usually has difficulty assuring employees of their motives because too many times in the history of labor relations, managers have exploited labor. Workers on piece-rate incentive plans, for example, have learned by sad experience that if they work rapidly to earn more money, their jobs are likely to be retimed, requiring them to work at the same speed for less money.

Organizational Resistance to Change. The organizational structure itself also resists change. Necessary changes may be resisted even when the survival of the organization depends on changing.

1. *Threats to the power structure.* Most changes have the capacity to disrupt the organization's power structure. Participative changes may be particularly threatening to managers because group decisions tend to restrict the manager's influence. Decentralized decision making may be a welcomed improvement for lower-level employees while higher-level employees are threatened by it.

2. *The inertia of organizational structure.* Control systems within organizations are overdetermined in the sense that they have several mechanisms designed to produce stability. Organizational structures are designed to maintain a stable pattern of interactions among people. Therefore, job assignments, the selection of new personnel, training of new employees, performance and reward systems, and many other aspects of the organizational structure are

designed to maintain stable interactions, thereby resisting change. To the extent that an organization is more highly structured, it tends to be more resistant to change.

3. *System relationships.* Since organizations are a complex collection of interacting subsystems, it is difficult to make a change in one subsystem without that change affecting other subsystems. A change in the accounting department may influence the methods of reporting and recordkeeping of every other department. A revised regulation in a labor contract may require supervisors throughout the organization to behave differently.

4. *Sunk costs and vested interests.* "Sunk costs" are investments in fixed assets, such as equipment, land, and buildings. "Vested interests" are the personal commitments of individuals to programs, policies, or other people. Vested interests may be as difficult for individuals to abandon as sunk costs are difficult for an organization to recoup. Sunk costs and vested interests make it difficult to assess objectively the benefits of doing things differently.

A principle that seems rather well accepted among change agents is that significant change only occurs when people are feeling pain. Unless their present conditions create enough discomfort, there is no motive for change. Change agents usually try to assess how much emotion people feel regarding the change issues before they try to initiate a change strategy.[8]

ORGANIZATIONAL CHANGE

A common mistake in initiating change is assuming that because an organization is a collection of people it can be changed by changing each individual. This assumption is wrong, because it overlooks the complexity of individual behavior and the influence of organizational processes. Organizational change is a complex process, and many different strategies have been proposed for creating change. In the field of psychology, most change strategies focus on changing the behavior of a single individual. In organizational behavior, efforts to change a single personality are rare because organizational problems are seldom problems of isolated people. Most problems are caused by the interactions of individuals within groups and between interacting groups. Consequently, successful change strategies require the active involvement of many people.

Kinds of Change

Organizations are constantly involved in change, but not all change is the same. Although some organizations make minor adjustments to take advantage of new opportunities, other organizations are devoured in corporate takeovers that move them into entirely different industries. Therefore, some changes have a larger impact on people and are more difficult to implement than others. Three kinds of change have been categorized according to their degree of complexity and their potential for resistance to change, as shown in Exhibit 17.3: developmental, transitional, and transformational.[9]

EXHIBIT 17.3   Kinds of Organizational Change

Developmental Change

Transitional Change

Transformational Change

- Degree of complexity, cost, uncertainty, and frustration

- Potential for resistance to change

Developmental Change. Developmental change is a gradual improvement in skills, methods, or processes to help an organization function more efficiently. This kind of change might be considered fine-tuning, because it is usually a small adjustment that helps to raise individual productivity, reduce conflict, improve communication, eliminate wasted motions, or otherwise contribute to organizational effectiveness. Developmental change results in an improvement in what is currently happening rather than the formation of an entirely new process. This kind of change should be incorporated into the company's training and development programs and reviewed as part of its performance evaluation process. Resistance to developmental change is usually not manifested in open opposition but as a subtle refusal of individuals to learn new skills or adopt new procedures.

Transitional Change. Transitional change is having an organization evolve slowly from an old state to a new state. The change occurs gradually over time, but it involves more than improving what is already there, as in developmental change. Transitional change involves new processes, new activities, new products, and sometimes a new organizational structure. This kind of change usually occurs in defined transition steps such as a series of delineated stages, pilot projects, phase-in operations, temporary arrangements, and reorganizations.

Transformational Change. The most dramatic kind of change is **transformational change,** which is characterized by a radical reconceptualization of the organization's mission, culture, products, leadership, or structure. This kind of change occurs in companies that have become stagnant and started to disintegrate. A typical scenario is a mature company whose sales plateaued several years earlier and has recently experienced chaos because of declining sales and a loss of market share due to foreign competition.

It is also possible for an entire industry to be threatened by technological improvements that make the old ways of doing business obsolete, such as the shift in the steel industry from large, integrated steel mills with their open-hearth furnaces to the small minimills with their electric furnaces. The minimills produce about four times as many tons of steel per employee hour and their process is superior in terms of safety, speed, and reduced environmental pollution.[10]

Transformational change often occurs because of a significant **paradigm change** within the industry. The word *paradigm* comes from the Greek word for "pattern," and the new paradigm is a new pattern of behavior or a new way of looking at the world. Paradigm changes often result from a new set of assumptions, a new way of structuring an issue, a new way of thinking about a problem, or a new technological innovation that makes the former technology obsolete.[11]

Paradigm changes within an industry affect every organization in that industry. For example, the efficiency of electric furnaces influences all steel mills worldwide, including both the minimills and the large integrated mills. Organizations that cannot or choose not to change usually die. The industrial graveyard is filled with organizations that dissolved because their success kept them from recognizing the paradigm shift and the need to change. Organizations that recognize a paradigm shift early enough can plan for gradual systematic transitional change. Organizations that fail to recognize the need for change until they are in the middle of chaos and turmoil are forced into transformational change that is usually associated with frustration, uncertainty, and crisis planning.

Another way to describe transformational change is called "punctuated equilibrium," which refers to an alternation between long periods when stable organizational structures permit only incremental adjustments separated by brief periods of revolutionary upheaval. During periods of calm, only developmental changes are happening. But every so often, massive restructuring or realignment occurs that fundamentally alters the structure and direction of the organization. Punctuated equilibrium has been observed not only in organizational change, but also in other domains, such as individual development, group dynamics, biological evolution, and the history of science.[12] Punctuated equilibrium is illustrated by the paradigm changes described earlier in the computer industry.

Targets of Change

Organizational change strategies are generally designed to create change at a specific level in an organization. The seven most common targets of change are as follows:

Individual Personality. Occasionally organizational difficulties stem from the personality of a specific individual. For example, a supervisor could be excessively punitive and dictatorial, or a worker might be constantly critical, negative, or otherwise offensive. Key individuals who work in administrative or executive positions are often criticized because of their supervisory style.

Dyad. The term **dyad** refers to the relationship between two people, such as two co-workers or a married couple. Occasionally the problems between two people are not specifically caused by either person; they are caused by the relationship between them. In an interdependent relationship, both members develop expectations regarding one another. When these expectations are violated, serious conflicts can occur. The cause of the problem may have nothing to do with inadequacy or immaturity on the part of either individual. Both may be healthy individuals, but they may have unrealistic or inconsistent expectations regarding their relationship. Here the problem is not people but the relationship between them.

Group. Work groups are probably the most popular target of OD interventions. These change strategies can focus on conflict within the group or on changing group norms. Each group develops its own goals and norms influencing member behavior. Occasionally the group norms are inconsistent with the goals of the organization or unacceptable to members of the group. Groups may also develop a hostile climate in which some group members are not accepted.

Family Groups. Family groups consist of a supervisor and the immediate subordinates who report to that supervisor. Specific problems can exist within family groups in addition to the typical problems that occur in peer groups. Issues regarding leadership style, authority, delegation of work assignments, and performance evaluations are sources of potential conflicts.

The Entire Organization and Its Divisions. Greater cohesiveness within groups usually inspires more conflicts between groups. Change strategies may need to focus on the relationships between groups and the ways in which the major divisions of a company coordinate their efforts. The contributions of all the separate departments should result in a carefully balanced and highly integrated organization.

Organizational Structure. Occasionally the structure of the organization must change to meet new demands or provide greater efficiency. Change strategies may focus on a variety of structural characteristics, such as the division of labor, pattern of departmentalization, the span of control, or the reporting relationships.

Organizational Strategy. Significant changes in technology or competition may require organizations to alter their strategic direction. Therefore, the target of some change efforts focuses on clarifying the mission of the organization and what it must do to survive. The outcome of this change could be something as simple as adding or deleting product lines or as drastic as moving into a different industry or merging with another company.

Theories of Change

One of the earliest theories of change was the force field analysis proposed by Kurt Lewin. Although this model was derived from the physical sciences, it continues to provide a valuable framework for thinking about change and diagnosing problems. Other change models have come from psychology, social psychology, and group dynamics.

Kurt Lewin's Force Field Analysis. Kurt Lewin's theory of change was derived from the laws of physics, which state that the position of an object and its direction are determined by the forces operating on it. Change occurs when the forces pushing in one direction are greater than the forces pushing in the opposite direction. A state of balance exists when the restraining forces acting to prevent change are equal to the driving forces attempting to produce change. The equilibrium point is determined by the resultant forces operating in different directions, as shown in Exhibit 17.4. According to Kurt Lewin, planned change occurs in three stages: unfreezing, change, and refreezing.[13]

EXHIBIT 17.4 **An Illustration of Kurt Lewin's Force Field Analysis**

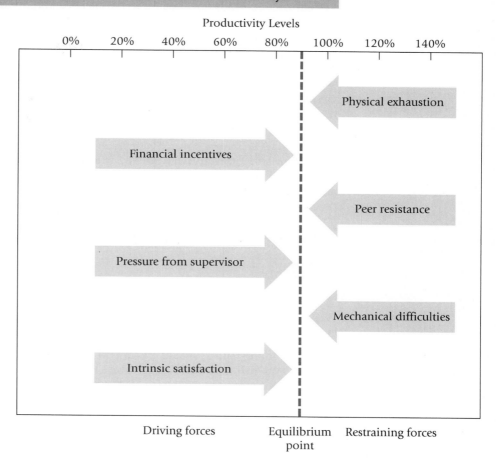

Productivity Levels

0%   20%   40%   60%   80%   100%   120%   140%

Physical exhaustion

Financial incentives

Peer resistance

Pressure from supervisor

Mechanical difficulties

Intrinsic satisfaction

Driving forces   Equilibrium   Restraining forces
                        point

1. *Unfreezing* occurs when people see a need for change. The status quo is disturbed by unsettling forces that challenge current values, attitudes, and behaviors.

2. *Change* is the action-oriented stage, in which the situation is diagnosed, improved patterns of behavior are selected, and a new equilibrium is created. As a result of change, people develop new values, attitudes, and/or behaviors.

3. *Refreezing* stabilizes the change and solidifies the new patterns of behavior. Refreezing requires continued management of the change process beyond the immediate implementation. Refreezing also requires that people experience positive consequences to strengthen their continuing commitment to the new change. The new state then becomes the status quo for future behavior.

According to Lewin's **force field analysis,** managers create planned change by altering the restraining and driving forces. A careful analysis is needed to determine how the restraining forces can be reduced and/or how the driving forces can be strengthened. Lewin's force field analysis has been a popular model for analyzing change programs and predicting the effects of future changes.

Three theoretical explanations, based on different underlying motives for behavior, have been proposed to explain why change occurs: education, reinforcement, and peer group influences. These strategies of change are also called *rational empirical, power coercive,* and *normative re-educative.*[14] These strategies can also be viewed as methods for dealing with resistance to change. Exhibit 17.5 summarizes the times when each method is most effective and the advantages and disadvantages of each method.

Education and Communication. Many change efforts are based on the assumption that new information creates change. People are expected to behave differently after they acquire new attitudes, insights, or self-awareness. This theory of change

---

EXHIBIT 17.5   Methods for Overcoming Resistance to Change

Method of Change	When It Should Be Used	Advantages	Disadvantages
1. *Education and Communication:* Explain the need for change, what will happen, and how it will affect each person. Help them see the logic and rationale for change.	When there is a lack of information or when the situation is novel or uncertain. It should normally accompany other change methods.	Highly effective in ambiguous situations. It provides cognitive support for other change methods. Once persuaded, people help to implement the change.	New information seldom motivates a change in behavior. Providing new knowledge or rational justifications can also be very time consuming.
2. *Reinforcement:* a. *Incentives:* Offer additional incentives for compliance and negotiate agreement.	When employees want what management has to offer; when the incentives are not too costly; and when it is important for the employees to perceive a fair exchange.	A fair exchange helps to preserve dignity and equity. It can be a relatively easy way to avoid resistance.	It can be very costly and the costs may escalate in future encounters.
b. *Coercion:* Force employees to accept change by using either implicit or explicit threats, such as pay cuts, job loss, or undesirable assignments	When speed is essential and management has sufficient power to enforce the threats.	It takes little time and allows the company to begin rebuilding faster.	If it makes people angry, they may retaliate or leave.
3. *Peer Group Influence:* Allow groups of people to participate in the change process by discussing issues, recommending creative ideas, and implementing the change.	When management needs the insight or cooperation of members. When group norms impede the group. When people are contemplating changes in their attitudes or values.	People who participate in change are more prepared to implement it and more committed to its success. Group influence is a powerful impetus for personal change.	Can be very time consuming, and it is possible the group may decide to oppose the change.

has been called a *rational empirical* change strategy, because it assumes that people are rational and will follow their self-interest once this is identified for them.[15]

Because we assume people are rational and motivated by self-interest, it is reasonable to assume they will adopt a proposed change if it can be rationally justified and if it can be shown they will gain by the change. For example, salesclerks would be expected to lock their lockers after they are told that their personal items may be stolen, and they would be expected to be less "pushy" after they discover that customers are offended by their behavior.

New information is not always effective in changing behavior, however. As was explained in Chapter 7, the relationship between attitudes and behaviors is usually extremely weak. Changing a person's attitudes will not necessarily change the person's behavior. The effectiveness of empirical evidence or new information in changing behavior depends largely on whether there was a lack of information to begin with. New information is a powerful force for change in ambiguous situations. For example, new employee orientations are particularly effective in changing the behavior of new employees, because they wouldn't have known how to behave otherwise. However, new information is not an effective impetus for change when people already know the correct way of behaving but fail to conform. For example, employees already know that absenteeism and sloppy work are wrong, and training programs discussing attendance and careful work will do little to create new knowledge. Likewise, many people continue to smoke in spite of frequent warnings and mounting evidence showing the health hazards of tobacco use. Information alone is often not adequate to change behavior.

Reinforcement. Another explanation for change is that people do what they are reinforced for doing. This method has been called a *power coercive* change strategy because it involves the application of power in which people with less power are forced to comply with the plans, directions, and leadership of those with greater power.[16] People tend to change quite quickly when there are sufficient incentives to reward change or punishments if they resist change. The reinforcement may be overt, such as bribes, payoffs, and bonuses, or subtle, such as social approval, self-esteem, and peer group pressure.

People can be forced to accept change under implicit or explicit threats, such as job loss, pay cuts, demotions, or undesirable transfers. Coercion can be effective when speed is essential and the change agents have considerable power. But it is not highly recommended, because it can be risky if it makes people angry and people tend to be uncooperative if they feel abused or ignored. A lack of cooperation may lead to periodic sabotage and prevent even good ideas from succeeding.

As explanations for change, new learning and reinforcement are similar to the concepts of information dependence and effect dependence described in Chapter 9. Change seems to occur when people are provided with new information justifying the change, or when there are specific reinforcers supporting the change.

Peer Group Influence. Another theory of change recognizes the influence of social norms, especially at the level of the group. This method of change has been called a *normative re-educative* change strategy, because it is based on the assumption that change occurs as people learn new normative orientations that result in new attitudes, values, and interpersonal relationships.[17]

Peer pressure is perhaps the most subtle and powerful impetus for change and partially explains why group discussions are one of the most frequently used change methods in organizational development. The effectiveness of peer group discussions in changing behavior was identified in some of the early group dynamics research.[18]

The advantages of peer group discussions on overcoming resistance to change was demonstrated in a classic study in a garment factory. When job changes had to be introduced, a control group received the conventional explanation, which simply told them their jobs had to be changed. A second group received an elaborate explanation of the need for change and then selected representatives from the group to help make the change. Two other experimental groups also received a careful explanation of the need for change and then participated as a total group in redesigning the new jobs. After the changes were implemented, the control group showed hardly any improvement over its earlier efficiency ratings, and the hostility of this group toward management resulted in a 17 percent turnover within the first forty days. The group that selected representatives demonstrated quick relearning and was able to reach standard performance within fourteen days, as well as continued improvement thereafter. The two groups that were allowed total participation showed the greatest performance improvement and the highest levels of morale. Only in the control group did any of the employees quit.[19]

Four reasons have been proposed to explain why group discussions are so effective in changing the attitudes and behavior of their members.

1. People who are contemplating a change in their attitudes or behavior are reinforced by seeing other group members make the same change.

2. The group discussion forces members to come to a decision point. Rather than just passively considering the issue, they are required to decide whether they accept or reject the change.

3. As they talk about the change and arrive at a group consensus, members are forced to make a public commitment to change their behavior. If they fail to follow through after the group discussion, there is a sense of dishonesty and loss of self-esteem.

4. Some aspect of the decision making process itself helps people accept the change, such as the risky-shift phenomenon described in Chapter 14, or the process of emotional catharsis described in Chapter 2.

Action Research Model

A useful model describing the basic approach of most organizational change activities is the **action research model**.[20] This model is consistent with the scientific method of inquiry and its reliance on data gathering and analysis to solve problems. This model has also been called the *action learning model* to emphasize the collective involvement of members to discover and adopt new behaviors.[21] Exhibit 17.6 illustrates the six basic steps in this model: data gathering, feedback of the data to the target group, data discussion and diagnosis, action planning, action, and recycling. Each of these six processes is important to successful change efforts.

Data Gathering. When evidence of a problem exists and is serious enough to merit attention, the first step is to gather information about the problem. Data may be collected about the causes of the problem and its seriousness from a variety of

EXHIBIT 17.6 An Action Research Model for Organizational Development

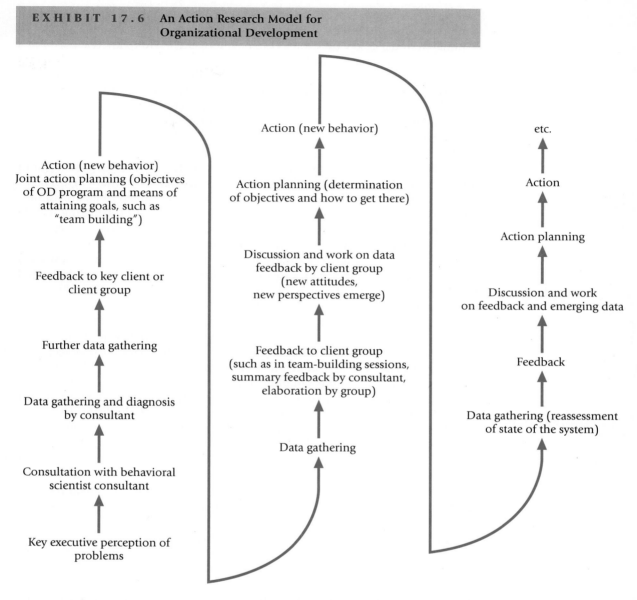

Action (new behavior)
Joint action planning (objectives of OD program and means of attaining goals, such as "team building")

↑

Feedback to key client or client group

↑

Further data gathering

↑

Data gathering and diagnosis by consultant

↑

Consultation with behavioral scientist consultant

↑

Key executive perception of problems

Action (new behavior)

↑

Action planning (determination of objectives and how to get there)

↑

Discussion and work on data feedback by client group (new attitudes, new perspectives emerge)

↑

Feedback to client group (such as in team-building sessions, summary feedback by consultant, elaboration by group)

↑

Data gathering

etc.

↑

Action

↑

Action planning

↑

Discussion and work on feedback and emerging data

↑

Feedback

↑

Data gathering (reassessment of state of the system)

Source: Wendell French, "Organization Development Objectives, Assumptions, and Strategies," *California Management Review*, vol. 12 (1969), p. 26. By permission of the Regents.

sources including interviews, observations, questionnaire surveys, and archival data. Each method contains advantages and disadvantages and successful change agents develop the ability to use all four methods rather than rely solely on one or two.

Interviews tend to produce the "richest" information, which means that they generate information about the specific problem plus valuable insights into related concerns. During an interview, a skilled interviewer can uncover a variety of problems by sensitive listening. However, interviews are very time consuming, and only a limited number of key individuals can be interviewed. Group interviews conserve time and allow more people to be included in the data-gathering process; however, they also require greater skill on the part of the interviewer to make group members feel free to share their feelings. Group interviews work best for homogeneous groups of no more than seven to ten individuals who share common attitudes. When individuals disagree with the remainder of the group, they often feel inhibited in expressing their opinions.

The least obtrusive data-gathering method is *observation* by a skilled observer, usually the change agent. Observations are particularly useful for diagnosing group processes, interpersonal interactions, and task efficiency. Industrial engineers, for example, rely on their ability to observe a task being performed to identify unnecessary motions and improve task efficiency. One advantage of gathering data by observation is that the data can be reliable measures of actual behaviors that can be counted, such as how many comments a committee member made or how many units a worker produced. The disadvantage of observations is that the causes of many problems involve feelings or expectations that cannot be easily observed. Knowing what happened may not be as meaningful as understanding why it happened or how others perceived the problem.

Questionnaires can be used to gather large volumes of information from many people in a short time. Everyone can be involved in the diagnosis stage, and the information can be summarized in a short time. Questionnaire surveys keep individuals who have specific complaints from creating the impression that everyone shares their opinion. Various sampling techniques allow researchers to survey only a small number of people and make remarkably accurate inferences about the attitudes of others, as is done with political surveys. The major disadvantage of questionnaires is that the information obtained from them is largely limited to confirming or disconfirming the expectations of those who designed the questionnaire. If the relevant issues are not covered in a questionnaire, the information will be inadequate or misleading. The best solution to this dilemma is (1) to interview a sample of workers to identify the relevant issues and use this information to construct the questionnaire or (2) to ask for open-ended comments at the end of the questionnaire.

Archival data are the kinds of data contained in the personnel files, such as turnover, absenteeism, productivity, accidents, grievances, wages, and medical expenses. The advantages of using archival data are that they already exist without having to be collected and may cover a fairly lengthy historical period, thereby providing a long-term perspective. Care must be used in interpreting these data, however, because they are influenced by many variables.

Feedback of Data to Target Group. After the data have been collected and summarized, they are presented to the **target of change.** The target group encompasses those involved in the problem, which could be an individual, a group, or the total organization. The data are not simply reported to top management and kept locked in confidential files. The data should be open to anyone for whom it is relevant. Information about group conflicts should be shared with the group; information about the total organization should be open to the entire organization, but not criticisms about a particular supervisor.

Data Discussion and Diagnosis. The data should be used to identify and diagnose organizational problems. A careful analysis is needed to identify the real problems rather than just surface symptoms. This analysis generally involves a group discussion by the target group. To reduce the likelihood of misinterpreting the data, the group should explore alternative causes of the problem.

The diagnosis may focus on either a specific problem or a general issue. Insufficient supplies, incorrect reports, and scheduling problems are examples of specific problems that need to be resolved. Declining sales, high turnover, and low morale are indications of a general problem that requires a more careful diagnosis.

Action Planning. After the cause of the problem has been identified, the target group should develop an action plan to solve the problem. The action plan may involve more than just the target group because corresponding changes in other parts of the organization may be necessary to avoid dysfunctional consequences. A variety of change strategies that are described later in the chapter are typically used in the action-planning process.

Action. After the change has been carefully planned, it is implemented. Some OD interventions are very narrow and shallow, others are broad and deep. The change may involve something as simple as having supervisors complete a new form or as complex as restructuring the entire organization or revising the compensation system.

Recycling. Organizational development is not a one-shot event; it is an iterative process. After the change has been implemented, the situation is reassessed to see if the original problem has been eliminated and if new problems have appeared. This iterative process involves recycling through the previous steps as shown in Exhibit 17.6. Each recycling is in essence an evaluation of the previous cycle.

Re-energizing the Mature Organization

Organizations evolve through a lifecycle, and each evolving stage is characterized by a dominant issue and a specific change challenge that must be faced before it advances to the next stage.

As explained in Chapter 12, organizations begin with the *entrepreneurial stage,* which focuses on identifying and developing new products. During this life cycle stage, the organization revolves around the creative efforts of an entrepreneur and the dominant issue consists of learning how to establish a market niche.[22]

The change challenge that moves the organization to stage 2, the *collectivity* or *growth* stage, is the need for leadership. Directing an organization through a growth period requires managerial direction and control. The dominant issue at stage 2 is how to delegate responsibilities and provide clear direction so that the collective efforts of many people will combine effectively to produce the desired product or services.

The change challenge that moves an organization to stage 3, the *formalization* or *maturity* stage, is the need for delegation and control. The establishment of formal procedures contributes to predictable, patterned activities. As responsibilities are delegated, internal control systems are required to integrate diverse activities and the dominant issue focuses on selecting the most appropriate control systems.

The change challenge that organizations face as they move to stage 4, the *elaboration* stage, is the need to control bureaucratic inefficiencies. As organizations enter the elaboration stage, they usually begin to decline as a result of excessive bureaucratic procedures: unnecessary reports, useless meetings, needless approvals, and meaningless activity measures. At this stage, organizations will continue to decline unless they can be revitalized.

It is very unlikely that a mature organization can maintain its size and market domination for an extended period without some form of revitalization. Even large and once-powerful organizations, such as GM, GE, and IBM, have found they cannot continue to produce the same products with the same technology and the same organizational structure year after year. The process of revitalizing mature organizations, as shown in Exhibit 17.7, occurs in five stages: restructuring, bureaucracy "bashing," employee empowerment, continuous improvement, and cultural change.[23]

EXHIBIT 17.7   A Process for Re-Energizing Mature Organizations

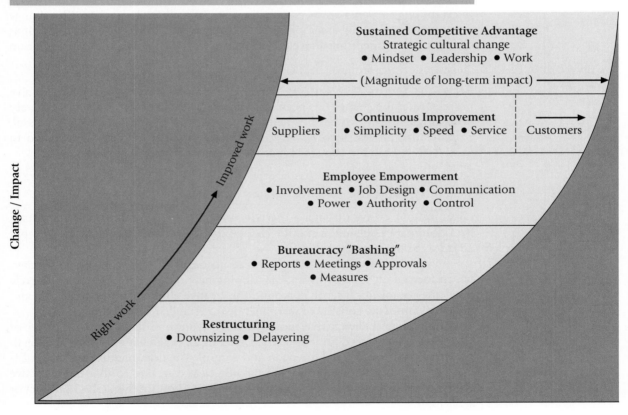

Source: Richard W. Beatty and David O. Ulrich, "Re-Energizing the Mature Organization," in Todd D. Jick, *Managing Change: Cases and Concepts* (Homewood, Ill.: Irwin, 1993), p. 68. Used with permission.

Restructuring. The first stage of renewal generally begins with a significant restructuring effort focused on downsizing or delayering the organization. Complacent organizations usually have more employees than they need. The leadership challenge at this stage is knowing which positions to eliminate and having the courage to make difficult but fair termination procedures.

Bureaucracy "Bashing." The next step is to remove bureaucratic inefficiencies, such as unnecessary reports, approvals, meetings, policies, and other activities that waste effort or impede productive work. Reducing bureaucratic inefficiencies involves getting rid of work that fails to add value to customers. Unless they are essential for coordinating work, activity reports and productivity measures result in wasted time preparing them and wasted time reading them.

Employee Empowerment. Employees should be free to identify better work procedures and implement them. Self-directed work teams, employee involvement activities, and job redesign help to remove barriers between people and give them the authority to act. In a bureaucracy, only the top managers are empowered. By reducing bureaucratic inefficiencies, all employees are empowered to suggest process improvements and new product ideas. Empowerment allows the organization to benefit from the creativity and ingenuity of employees.

Continuous Improvements. After the organization is restructured, bureaucratic inefficiencies are eliminated, and employees are empowered, renewal efforts should focus on achieving continuous improvements in the value chain. These improvements could involve better relationships with upstream suppliers or downstream customers in the value chain. Barriers between suppliers and customers should become more permeable, allowing for a smoother flow of products and information. Problems are identified, complexities are simplified, and delays are eliminated to improve the quality of the product or service.

Cultural Change. The final renewal stage, cultural change, is a consequence of the previous stages if they have been successful. Employees will not think of themselves as part of a mature organization, but they will feel an enthusiasm for trying new approaches and looking for better ways to serve customers. How they think about their work and the company will form a new mind-set that amounts to a fundamental cultural change. With an involved and committed workforce, the organization will achieve a sustained competitive advantage in its industry.

THE ORGANIZATIONAL DEVELOPMENT PROCESS

Organizational development is a process of preparing for and managing a planned change effort. However, not all change efforts are considered organizational development, because OD is typically differentiated from management training and other educational interventions. Organizational development involves a collaborative diagnosis and problem-solving approach for avoiding organizational decay and for creating organizational renewal.

Historical Stems

OD is a relatively recent application of applied behavioral science knowledge to organizational change. By the early 1970s, several successful OD interventions had occurred and many managers had learned about the benefits of OD. The foundations of OD, however, go back to earlier change strategies that started in the 1940s and 1950s: laboratory training, survey feedback, quality management, and sociotechnical systems.[24]

Laboratory Training. Laboratory training, called **T-group** training or **sensitivity training** today, was started by Kurt Lewin and others in the 1940s. Lewin found that informal discussions about individual and group behavior combined with feedback at the end of each day appeared to produce more insight and learning than lectures and seminars. Kurt Lewin died in 1947, but the basic design of sensitivity training was continued by other behavioral scientists.

For many years, three-week sensitivity training sessions were held at the National Training Laboratories in Bethel, Maine. During the first decade, however, the trainers were disturbed by the difficulty participants experienced in transferring what they learned during training to problems in their organizations after they returned. Gradually the training at Bethel moved away from "stranger" T-groups to the training of teams from the same organization. Some of the first major corporations to use T-groups were Esso-Standard Oil (now Exxon), Union Carbide, and General Mills.

For many years, organizational development specifically meant sensitivity training; when managers or consultants were talking about organizational development, they were referring specifically to sensitivity training. Today, however, organizational development has been defined much more broadly, and sensitivity training is only one of many OD interventions.

Survey Feedback. Survey research and feedback were started by the Survey Research Center founded in 1946 at the University of Michigan by Rensis Likert and others. This group pioneered the development and use of carefully constructed questionnaires, rigorous probability sampling, and information feedback to managers and supervisors. They found that the information helped to improve the organization if managers shared the results with their subordinates and discussed with them how to make improvements.

One early success of survey feedback took place at the Detroit Edison Company. The opinions of the employees had been assessed with a questionnaire, and the results of the survey were reported to managers. Likert and his associates discovered that when managers shared the results with subordinates and involved them in discussing the problems, substantial improvement occurred. However, little or no change occurred when managers failed to share the data with their subordinates. The results of this study led to the creation of survey feedback as an OD intervention.

Quality Management. During the reconstruction of Japan after World War II, W. Edwards Deming was invited to share his ideas about continuous quality improvement. He designed a four-day seminar for Japanese executives in 1950 and subsequently became a national hero to Japanese industry. To honor his contributions, Japanese industry created the Deming Prize in 1951. This annual prize, highly esteemed in Japan, recognizes the company that attains the highest level of quality that year.

Deming's ideas attracted little attention in America until a NBC documentary in 1980 featured the work of Deming, J. M. Juran, and other colleagues in Japan. Illustrations of dramatic quality improvements in Japanese manufacturing attracted considerable interest and drew attention to the problems of poor quality in the United States. Many U.S. manufacturers, such as Ford, Motorola, Federal Express, and Xerox, began to use Deming's ideas and consulting services. Deming taught that poor quality is 85 percent a management problem and 15 percent a worker problem. Management must plan for quality, and quality must be built into the product rather than inspected into it. In 1987, the United States started the Malcolm Baldridge National Quality Award to recognize U.S. companies that excel in quality achievement and management.

Sociotechnical Systems. Sociotechnical systems redesign originated in the early 1950s when researchers from England's Tavistock Institute proposed an alternative method of structuring the work of coal miners in Great Britain. Before the advent of machinery, the miners worked in groups of six and each miner performed all the work functions: extracting coal from the face of the wall, loading and transporting it from the mine, and advancing the roof supports and equipment. The new long-wall method, with conveyors and coal-cutting machinery, created specialized jobs that destroyed the stable work group culture and caused considerable resistance. But social support from the group was essential because they were performing difficult and hazardous jobs.

To combine the advantages of the new machine technology with the essential social support of work groups, Eric L. Trist and Kenneth W. Bamforth experimented with a "composite longwall" system where forty-one miners worked as a team performing all the necessary functions. Workers were trained to perform multiple tasks, and they were paid as a group. The group was responsible for selecting and training new members, making job assignments, scheduling work, and rotating the shifts. The performance of the composite longwall system was far superior to the traditional longwall system: voluntary absenteeism was only a tenth as much, output per person-shift was 5.3 tons versus 3.5 tons, operating potential was 95 percent versus 78 percent, and the company was saved the salary of a supervisor, since the group managed itself.[25]

Sociotechnical system design emphasizes the need to balance the technological factors associated with machines and work processes with the social needs of workers for interesting work and meaningful social interactions. Sociotech interventions usually involve forming work teams and allowing them to direct themselves. Since every work group has some form of technology and social interaction, some people consider every change effort as a sociotech intervention.

Assumptions of OD

OD interventions are based on a number of underlying assumptions and values concerning people, groups, and organizations.[26] These assumptions and values play a large role in understanding the processes that are used in OD. Most of these processes depend heavily on individual involvement and effective group functioning for success.

Assumptions About People. OD interventions are based on the assumption that most people want to make, and are capable of making, a greater contribution to the organization than they are normally permitted to make. Many people feel constrained in their present environment and unable to exert constructive energy toward the attainment of organizational goals. OD attempts to unleash the energy and enthusiasm of employees and provide a means for channeling this constructive energy into creative and insightful avenues.

Assumptions About Groups. OD interventions recognize the powerful influence of peer groups on individual behavior. Small groups are generally considered the basic organizational building blocks of excellent companies. To help the group function effectively, most interventions assume that a formal leader cannot perform all the leadership and maintenance functions necessary for group effectiveness, hence other group members must act to supplement and help with the leadership functions. Many interventions try to improve the effectiveness of groups because groups cannot function effectively when there is a lack of interpersonal trust, support, and cooperation among group members.

Assumptions About Organizations. Most OD interventions assume that organizational conflict does not have to be viewed as an us-against-them confrontation. Instead, conflict is reinterpreted from a win–lose situation to a win–win strategy by approaching it in terms of "how can we all win?" OD interventions reject the idea that the goals of individuals are inconsistent and incompatible with organizational goals. Instead, the goals of individuals and the goals of the organization are viewed as consistent, where individuals can pursue their own best interests while working simultaneously to help the organization become successful.

Another important assumption about organizations, derived from open-systems theory, is that a change in one subsystem of an organization will have an impact on other subsystems. Therefore, organizational development efforts need to be sustained by appropriate changes in every subsystem of the organization.

Values in OD. OD interventions also place a high value on two aspects of human behavior. A high value is placed on the dignity and worth of a human being. Individuals do not exist to serve the organization; organizations are created to serve people. Even though individual behavior must be controlled to some extent for the organization to exist, OD is based on the premise that excessive control and destructive influences should be changed or eliminated to preserve the dignity of the individual.

A high value is also placed on personal growth and development. The individual is viewed as a growing and developing person progressing toward self-actualization and self-improvement. Helping people to attain high levels of maturity and growth is an important aspect of OD interventions.

Vision and Mission Statements

Vision and mission statements facilitate organizational change by providing guidance and direction. Organizational change frequently requires people to do things differently—to change directions, to pursue other goals, or to perform different functions. To get people to march to the beat of a different drummer, it helps to have a clear signal coming from the new drummer. Vision and mission statements

APPLYING ORGANIZATIONAL BEHAVIOR
IN THE NEWS

Responding to Environmental Awareness

CNN Dramatic changes in consumer buying have been observed in the cosmetics industry. In 1976, Anita Roddick opened her first Body Shoppe cosmetics store in Brighton, England, with $6,000 and made $208 the first day. Eight years later, her company raised $10 million by selling shares to the public. By 1991, the company had 620 shops in thirty-nine countries.

Roddick attributes her company's growth to two major factors: providing "safe" health care products and being environmentally responsible. According to Roddick, the cosmetics industry sells unattainable dreams about product results that exploit women and make them unhappy. But satisfying these narcissistic needs is a very profitable industry; the Body Shoppe grew about 40 percent in 1991 and expects to open one new shop every three working days somewhere in the world.

The Body Shoppe recognized the potential profitability of being concerned about personal health and the environment. The major appeal of Body Shoppe products is that they are natural products made from vegetables and herbs. While Roddick lived with tribal groups in underdeveloped nations, she learned that such natural products as aloe vera, cocoa butter, and monsoon mud could be used for cleaning your body and washing your hair. The Body Shoppe advertisements capitalize on the "natural" contents of the products. To appeal to the buyer's conscience, product labels also state that the contents have not been tested on animals.

The Body Shoppe's success has prompted other cosmetics companies to adopt similar environmental and social concerns. Estée Lauder has developed a new division, Origins, that specializes in natural cosmetics. It advertises that the new Origins products are made from natural materials, they are not tested on animals, they do not use aerosol cans, and all their containers are recyclable.

Source: CNN *Inside Business* news programing.

provide a shared direction that helps align the efforts of many members behind a common idea that energizes and excites them.[27]

A vision statement is a document describing the way things could be. It is a declaration of the organization's most desirable future and serves as a foundation for building the organization's culture. The Declaration of Independence is cited as an example of a vision statement that has helped to frame the U.S. culture. Vision statements are most helpful for emerging companies that seem to be out of control because of rapid growth, or for retrenched companies whose employees feel demoralized and insecure because of downsizing or restructuring. The highest level of management is responsible for creating a vision statement, although they need input from others who might be key players in implementing the vision.

Mission statements are often very similar to vision statements; however, mission statements are generally more specific. A mission statement explains what the organization is striving to accomplish and is usually specific enough for members to determine whether they have achieved their objectives. Good mission statements are challenging and require members to exert sincere efforts to accomplish them. They should also have a time horizon that is within reach of most employees, such as five years. A popular illustration of a mission statement was President John Kennedy's charge to NASA in 1962 of achieving the goal, before the decade was out, of landing someone on the moon and returning him or her safely to earth.

Change Agents

OD interventions are typically supervised and guided by a person or group of people who serve as a catalyst facilitating the process. The catalysts, who are typically referred to as **change agents,** may be either internal or external to the organization.

External Change Agents. An external change agent is someone from outside the organization who is asked to intervene and help bring about change. Coming from the outside presents both advantages and disadvantages. One advantage is that this person is unbiased, sees problems more objectively, and can contribute valuable insights from other organizations. Another advantage is that after a feeling of trust has been established, employees are usually more willing to speak openly about sensitive problems and difficulties with an external change agent.

The disadvantage is that external change agents sometimes have difficulty establishing a feeling of trust, and their lack of experience with the organization prevents them from identifying the root causes of the problems. Coal miners, for example, typically feel that no one can truly understand their problems until they have spent time working underground. Another disadvantage of external change agents is that they are typically inclined to recommend more drastic changes, which may be overly disruptive to the organization.

Managers use external change agents for a variety of purposes to help them perform their work. Normally, external change agents are expected to provide technical assistance and information or to assist in diagnosing and resolving problems. But external change agents are sometimes employed by a company to make unpopular decisions, such as recommending that a branch office be closed, or to perform undesirable chores, such as terminating an employee. Consequently, external change agents are justifiably viewed with suspicion by employees until their motives are clear.[28]

Internal Change Agents. Internal change agents are typically staff employees who have been specifically trained in organizational development. However, managers and supervisors can also be trained to serve as change agents and conduct OD interventions to improve the functioning of their own units.[29] Internal change agents have the advantage of being familiar with the organization and its personnel and can develop the long-term relationship and feeling of trust sometimes needed for successful change. The disadvantage of internal change agents is that they are often viewed as agents of management who are only interested in the good of the company, not in the good of the workers.

Transfer and Diffusion of Change

Organizational development interventions must contend with two troublesome problems: the transfer-of-training problem and the intervention-diffusion problem.

Transfer of Training. Transfer concerns the extent to which changes brought about during a training situation are actually carried over into the work environment. Training programs, for example, may help employees acquire new skills, but if they fail to use these skills when they return to the job the training is ineffective. The transfer-of-training problem was a serious difficulty limiting the success of early sensitivity training programs. Evidence indicates that positive transfer is most likely to occur in the following situations:

1. When the environment of the training situation is similar to the environment of the actual work situation
2. When the new skills, attitudes, and behaviors are supported and reinforced by other individuals and by the reward system in the organization
3. When the change is implemented immediately and is perceived as being useful in the work environment

Diffusion. The **diffusion** of an OD intervention is the extent to which the initial change produces complementary changes in other individuals or programs and spreads throughout the organization. It may be possible, for example, for an OD intervention to have a limited impact in one unit of an organization without benefiting other units of the organization or making the organization more effective. An otherwise useful intervention may die if diffusion does not occur. The problem of limited diffusion may occur because of resistance within other parts of the organization or because the sequential process linking one change with subsequent changes was never clearly specified in the beginning. An excellent team-building meeting, for example, may help one work group produce more efficiently; but unless corresponding changes can be made in adjacent groups, there may be no increase in organizational effectiveness.

Several factors contribute to the problems of diffusing of OD interventions:

1. The intervention lacks the support and commitment of top management.
2. Other departments are content with the status quo and feel no pain or dissatisfaction motivating them to accept a change.
3. The reward system does not recognize or reinforce the change.
4. Structural and technological changes necessary to support the change are not made.
5. Other problems are perceived as more pressing and demand attention.

Evaluating OD

Most of the literature evaluating the effectiveness of OD interventions, especially the early reports, relied on anecdotal observations rather than sound empirical assessments. The literature largely consisted of case studies that were reported by the same people who served as the change agents. One study reviewed 574 case studies of OD and found that the vast majority of these were considered successful.[30] These studies included a wide variety of OD interventions, including team building, conflict resolution, survey feedback, and process consultation. In contrast, fewer than half of the senior executives in Fortune 500 companies reported in a survey that their change initiatives were successful. Not surprisingly, they said the major barrier to success was employee resistance to adopting new ways. They also said that the main impetus for achieving successful change was a change in management,[31] which was not something they were likely to recommend.

Over the years, the quality of the research evaluating OD has improved, and a growing number of change efforts have been evaluated with acceptable

APPLYING ORGANIZATIONAL BEHAVIOR
ACROSS CULTURES

Global Change

 The *Harvard Business Review* conducted a World Leadership Survey with the cooperation of twenty-five business magazines in 25 countries on six continents. The survey contained 91 items, printed in the language of the country, and 11,678 readers responded to the surveys. Two important conclusions were observed by the researchers.

First, change is universal. Significant restructuring, downsizing, merging, divesting, and international expansion were found in every country. Second, cultural differences persist. In spite of extensive international transactions, a common culture of management has not emerged. Business is transacted within the unique cultural context of each country.

Organizational change is a reality for companies in every country of the world. When the respondents were asked if their organization had experienced a major restructuring in the past two years, a sizable percentage said yes:

South Korea	71%
Mexico	63
Germany	60
United States	59
Japan	44
Hungary	36

The walls between countries are crumbling, but the results indicated that there were still significant cultural differences between countries. A degree of homogeneity has emerged, however, among some "cultural allies." Three groups of cultural allies and their commonalities were identified. Group 1 consists of English-speaking people in Australia, Canada, Great Britain, New Zealand, Singapore, and the United States, who expressed a preference for family over work and were the least cosmopolitan. Group 2 were people of Hispanic cultures in Argentina, Brazil, Italy, Mexico, Spain, and Venezuela, who prefer more privately held companies, fewer joint ventures, and a higher reliance on trade policies for economic protection. Group 3 were Europeans in Austria, Belgium, Finland, France, Germany, the Netherlands, and Sweden, who prefer close partnerships, are pessimistic about the future, and are the most cosmopolitan. (Being cosmopolitan involves being multilingual, having an international perspective, rejecting protectionism, and ignoring cultural boundaries.)

Four countries were identified as cultural islands with their own unique interests and orientations: Japan, with its interest in the work ethic; South Korea, with its willingness to put country ahead of company; India, with its strong interest in protectionism; and Hungary, with its unique organizational structures.

Source: Rosabeth Moss Kanter, "Transcending Business Boundaries: 12,000 World Managers View Change," *Harvard Business Review,* vol. 69 (May–June 1991), pp. 151–164.

experimental or quasi-experimental designs. One study examined the results of almost 100 research studies and concluded that the results were quite encouraging.[32] Eleven types of OD interventions were included in this review, and they all had generally positive effects on various performance measures, such as output, turnover, absenteeism, and grievances. This review concluded that the average improvement, expressed statistically, was an increase of almost one half of a standard deviation unit.

Although most evaluations suggest that OD improves both job performance and worker satisfaction, several studies have found that the perceived changes in the quality of work life are negative when the change focuses on work redesign and productivity improvements. One review of fifty-six studies that measured both productivity changes and changes in the self-perceived quality of work life found substantial positive effects on performance measures but almost uniformly negative changes in quality of work life.[33] These negative effects were attributed to the performance pressures placed on the workers as a result of the "action levers" and control mechanisms implemented as part of the change.[34]

A crucial question concerning the favorable conclusions regarding OD research is whether the change is caused by the OD intervention itself or by the self-fulfilling prophecy (described in Chapter 2). OD interventions are implemented with the expectation that they will improve organizational functioning; therefore, positive results should be obtained, due to the self-fulfilling prophecy, even if the intervention is worthless. At least one study has found that an OD intervention improved actual performance measures when those involved were led by the experimenter to expect it to, whereas the same intervention failed when organizational members were led not to expect strong positive results.[35] Very few studies have attempted to control for the effects of the self-fulfilling prophecy, and it seems safe to conclude that it has contributed importantly to the positive results of OD.

A study of the benefit of team building in the Israeli military controlled for the effects of the self-fulfilling prophecy by creating success expectations for both the experimental and control groups. The results indicated that the team-building intervention significantly improved the teamwork and conflict handling of the experimental groups more than the control groups.[36] Therefore, even though the self-fulfilling prophecy may contribute importantly to the success of OD interventions, it appears that the interventions also make an important contribution to organizational functioning.

OD INTERVENTIONS

An OD intervention is a set of structured activities designed to improve some aspect of organizational functioning. The set of activities does not have to be a rigid procedure; most OD interventions involve only a loosely defined sequence of activities that are adapted to the situation. A convenient way to classify OD interventions is according to the group for which they are intended. The major targets to be considered here are (1) interpersonal relationships, (2) group processes, (3) intergroup processes, and (4) the total organization. Some interventions are appropriate for more than one target, but most interventions are specifically designed to create change at one of these target areas. Only some of the most prominent interventions for each target are described here, but many additional interventions are described in the literature.

Interpersonal Interventions

Interpersonal interventions are directed primarily toward individual learning, insight, and skill building. They are designed to improve the effectiveness of individuals and to contribute to personal growth and adjustment.

Coaching and Counseling. An organization's formal performance appraisal system should provide feedback to employees regarding their performance. This information, however, is often inadequate because it does not tell a person what to do differently. A skilled observer is needed to identify problems and to suggest new behaviors. Usually the skilled observer is an external consultant who is able to take a fresh look at the situation. The consultant must be highly trained in observing human behavior and must know which behaviors are inappropriate. The role of the consultant is to respond to such questions as "What do you think I should do in this instance to improve my performance?" or "Now that I can see some areas for improvement, how can I change my behavior?" Management education programs could be viewed as OD interventions of **coaching and counseling.**

Sensitivity Training. Sensitivity training (or T-groups, with "T" standing for training) basically consists of unstructured group discussions by a small face-to-face group of not more than twelve to fifteen people. The focus of the discussions is on the "here and now" as opposed to what has happened in the past. The here and now consists mostly of the feelings and emotions experienced by the group members. Group members share their perceptions of each other and describe the attributes they admire in one another and the things that irritate them.

A trainer is usually present during sensitivity training, but not in a leadership role. The trainer usually refuses either to lead the group or to recognize other forms of leadership or status among group members, such as organizational position. Typically, no activities or topics of discussion are planned although short questionnaires are sometimes used at the beginning to spur participants to think about themselves and to reveal their feelings to others. When the participants are asked to respond to a questionnaire as a means of facilitating the session, these sessions are referred to as **"instrumented T-group"** sessions.

The lack of structure in a T-group often creates feelings of frustration, expressions of hostility, and attempts by some members to organize the group. Organizing attempts usually fail, however, and the group ultimately discusses why some members felt the need for structure. The ambiguity and frustration created in a T-group are not undesirable, since they force the participants to respond to new situations and help them to obtain greater self-insight. The primary objectives of sensitivity training are greater self-insight and self-awareness, greater sensitivity to the feelings and behaviors of others, and greater awareness of the processes that facilitate or inhibit group functioning.

Because of its popularity during the 1960s, T-group training stimulated much research and controversy. The research generally indicated that T-group training had a significant influence on changing interpersonal behavior, but the direction of the change was unclear.[37] Some participants said the change they experienced was not desirable. Empirical research found both positive and negative results. Most participants indicated that their T-group experience increased their interpersonal skills and made them more aware of others. However, some described it as a threatening experience that left them feeling inadequate and destroyed their self-confidence.

Sensitivity training continues to be used to help people improve their interpersonal competence, but it is generally not appropriate when the target of change is the organization or intergroup processes. Other interventions are more effective at creating change at those levels.[38] The transfer-of-training problem, a serious problem limiting the value of sensitivity training, has already been noted. To overcome this problem, "stranger T-groups" were replaced by "family T-groups" where the participants were members of an organizational family (a supervisor and his or her immediate subordinates).

Process Consultation. No organization operates perfectly, and managers often realize there are problems but don't know precisely what caused them or how to solve them. Consultants are frequently asked to help managers diagnose organizational problems and evaluate alternative solutions. "Process consultation" refers to activities on the part of a consultant that help the client perceive, understand, and alter the processes occurring in the organization.[39]

Like sensitivity training, process consultation assumes that organizational effectiveness can be improved by resolving interpersonal problems. However, process consultation is much more task oriented than sensitivity training. A process consultant observes the interactions between the client and other people and helps the client understand these interactions. They do not solve the organization's problems but serve as a guide or coach advising the client on the processes and interpersonal relationships needing improvement.

One major role of a successful process consultant is to teach the client how to diagnose group activities and interpersonal relationships. Therefore, process consultation is a joint effort in diagnosing and solving problems with the goal of helping managers acquire problem-solving skills that they can use after the consultant is gone. Process consultation often occurs as a one-on-one coaching process in which the consultant observes the interactions of a manager in meetings, interviews, and conversations, and tries to help the manager understand what occurred and how the interactions could be improved.

Group Interventions

The OD interventions that focus on group functioning receive the most attention. This attention primarily stems from the significant influence that the work group culture exerts on the behavior and attitudes of group members. The attention also stems from the realization that much of the work in today's organizations is accomplished directly or indirectly through groups. Therefore, both organizational effectiveness and the quality of work life are influenced greatly by how well a group functions.

Studies in group dynamics have identified some of the characteristics of an effective work group. In an effective group, there is a norm of cooperation and teamwork. The members communicate with each other openly and without defensiveness. Everyone participates in task-relevant discussions, and members listen well to one another. Decisions are usually based on consensus rather than on organizational position or a majority vote. The decisions and group goals are widely accepted. Conflict and disagreement are not necessarily eliminated, but they are focused on ideas and methods rather than on personalities and are used to stimulate creative problem solving.

Effective teams help their members satisfy their personal needs while cooperating to achieve the group's goal. Sometimes employees want to improve the group but do not know what to do. Individual efforts to create a more effective group are often resisted by other group members and only create more antagonism and conflict. Successful group interventions usually require the involvement of all group members. Four of the most popular group interventions include (1) the group diagnostic meeting, (2) the team-building meeting, (3) the role analysis technique (RAT), and (4) responsibility charting.

Group Diagnostic Meetings. **Group diagnostic meetings** are usually held by organizational "family" groups consisting of a supervisor and his or her immediate subordinates. The purpose of the diagnostic meeting is not to solve problems but simply to identify them and decide which are the most crucial. Solutions come later and may involve further interventions.

Group diagnostic meetings usually require an outside consultant to facilitate the discussion; however, supervisors can serve just as well if they possess adequate interpersonal skills and are not overly defensive. Being able to conduct a group diagnostic meeting is a valuable supervisory skill, but it is easy for a supervisor to feel defensive during the meeting since the discussion focuses on such questions as "What are we doing right?" "What are we doing wrong?" "Are we taking advantage of our opportunities?" "What problems do we need to address?" "How good are our relationships with each other?"

A group diagnostic meeting consists of an open discussion of the group's problems. If there are intense hostilities or if the group is too large for everyone to participate, the group may be divided into small subgroups. The subgrouping could be as small as peers who interview each other and then report to the total group. Typically, the problems are written on a chalkboard or on large pieces of paper taped to the walls. The group members discuss the problems, sharing their feelings about the cause of each problem and its seriousness.

The outcome of a group diagnostic meeting should be a careful analysis of the group's problems and a priority ranking showing which problems are the most crucial. Formal scaling procedures have been proposed to help the group evaluate the problems.[40] Later interventions may involve the group in generating and implementing solutions to the problems. But the goal of the diagnostic meetings is simply problem diagnosis. If the group members discuss the problems, sharing their feelings about the cause of each problem and its seriousness, many problems can be resolved without further interventions.

Team-Building Meetings. The goal of a **team-building meeting** is to build a better functioning team. This goal includes greater goal accomplishment and improved group processes, such as better communication, decision making, personal interactions, and problem solving. Group processes tend to improve as a by-product of learning to solve problems that prevent the group from achieving its goals.[41]

Most team-building meetings involve getting the work group together, away from the workplace, for an extended period of time, such as one to three days. The group identifies the important problems, usually with the help of a consultant or an outside facilitator. As these problems are discussed, alternative solutions are developed and evaluated. The outcome of the meeting should be a carefully planned procedure that identifies the action steps and specifies who will do what and when. This plan should be a realistic solution acceptable to all group members.

If the meeting is dominated by a leader, the action plan probably will not be accepted by the group, nor will the group function as a coordinated team. All team members should be involved in the discussions, and all the decisions should be reached by consensus rather than majority vote.

There are several ways to conduct a team-building meeting. One method used at an oil refinery started by asking each member to estimate how effective the refinery was relative to how effective it could be. When the estimates were discussed, they agreed that it was only 60 percent effective. The facilitator drew a football field on the chalkboard and said the ball was forty yards away from the goal. The group used Lewin's force field analysis to analyze forces pushing in both directions in an attempt to diagnose their problems. After the group had agreed on the problems and their causes, they divided into subgroups to study them. The next day they met to discuss the recommended solutions and to decide on an action plan. By working late into the night, they developed a tentative plan. The next morning the plan was modified until it was finally accepted. This form of concentrated involvement away from the day-to-day pressures of work is usually necessary to resolve group conflicts and to build an effective team.

Role Analysis Technique. An organizational role consists of the task assignments and responsibilities of a particular job. A role also involves relationships with other jobs, and these relationships have to be understood for the roles to be performed effectively. The role analysis technique (RAT) is designed to reduce the uncertainty surrounding an employee's task assignments and responsibilities. Although the **RAT intervention** is used most frequently for managerial jobs, it can also be used to clarify the responsibilities of any job. It is particularly applicable when new teams are created or when a new member is added to an established team.[42]

The RAT intervention defines the requirements of a *focal role*; that is, the role being examined. This intervention basically involves two steps. The first step consists of the person in the focal role defining his or her perception of the role—what it entails, why it exists, and what its place is in achieving the organization's goals. The specific duties are listed on a chalkboard and discussed by the entire group. Responsibilities are added and deleted until the role incumbent and the group are satisfied with the description. The second step consists of clarifying the expectations that the focal role person has of others. These expectations are likewise listed and discussed until the group and the role incumbent agree on them.

RAT interventions focus on one role at a time, and it is usually wise to repeat the process until all crucial roles in the group have been clarified. Role confusion can be a serious cause of conflict in a work group. This conflict is illustrated by the confusion that existed between a personnel director and a plant manager concerning the personnel director's job. As part of a training program, the managers were asked to prepare a written job description of their own jobs and their subordinates' jobs. When the personnel director's description of her job was compared with the plant manager's description of her job, it was obvious that they did not agree. The two descriptions were very different. Both individuals were surprised to learn what the other expected, and they concluded that the confusion had been a major cause of conflict between them. The personnel director had held the job for eight months but had never been clear about her role.

Responsibility Charting. The effectiveness of a work group depends on the quality of decisions that are made, how carefully they are implemented, and whether task assignments and other responsibilities are carefully delegated and clearly understood. Clarifying responsibilities is typically easier to accomplish on paper than through informal discussions. **Responsibility charting** is an intervention that helps to clarify who is responsible for what regarding various decisions and actions.[43]

The first step in responsibility charting is to construct a matrix. The types of decisions and classes of actions that need to be taken are placed along the left side of the matrix, and the group members are listed across the top of the matrix, as shown in Exhibit 17.8. The second step is to determine how each actor should be involved in each of the decisions. Group members may be assigned to make any one of four possible responses to each decision.

1. R: responsibility to initiate action.
2. A–V: right to approve or veto the decision.
3. S: providing support and resources.
4. I: being informed about the decision.

EXHIBIT 17.8   Responsibility Chart for an Employment Office

	R Responsibility (initiates) A-V Approval (right to veto) S Support (put resources against) I Inform (to be informed)					
Members → **Decisions ↓**	**Karen**	**Jill**	**Ken**	**Bob**	**Dick**	**Janet**
Advertise jobs.	R	I	—	S	—	A-V
Screen applicants.	I	R	I	I	—	A-V
Interview applicants.	I	I	R	—	S	S
Contact references.	—	I	R	—	S	S
Make job referrals.	I	I	—	I	S	R
Update data files.	—	R	—	—	—	A-V
Administer tests.	—	I	—	—	R	S

If a group member is totally removed from a particular decision, such noninvolvement is indicated by a simple dash in that cell of the matrix.

The responsibility for most decisions should be assigned to only one person in order to maintain personal accountability. The authority to approve or veto a decision should also be limited, because it is too time consuming to get approval from a large group. Furthermore, if one individual is involved in too many approval–veto roles, that person could become a bottleneck inhibiting the group's progress. One of the immediate insights that usually comes from responsibility charting is the realization that many decisions are not adequately supported by enough people. While people like having the authority to approve or veto decisions, providing the necessary support is not as popular.

Intergroup Interventions

Conflict and tension between two groups typically produce undesirable consequences for an organization. Each group pursues its own self-serving goals with little regard for the success of the other groups or the total organization. Communication between the two groups becomes distorted or is completely severed. Each group blames the other for problems and justifies its own actions. Gradually the other group is viewed as an enemy and perceived in terms of negative stereotypes. The groups may even resort to acts of sabotage or violence, and each group may become more interested in damaging the other group than in pursuing its own goals. These problems were described in detail in Chapter 10.

The typical conflict between union and management is an excellent example of intergroup conflict. Several strategies have been proposed for reducing intergroup conflict, and some of the most popular strategies include the following.[44]

Finding a Common Enemy. This strategy involves finding an outside object or group that both groups dislike. Fighting a common enemy requires the groups to coordinate their efforts in order to achieve success. An example of a common enemy in union–management conflict is government regulation that threatens to eliminate jobs or foreign competition that threatens to dominate the industry.

Joint Activities. In pursuing joint activities, the groups are required to interact and communicate with each other. Although the initial interaction may be a bit strained, increased interaction under favorable conditions tends to create more positive feelings and sentiments toward members of the other group. Pursuing joint activities is especially effective for reducing conflict when there is a goal that both groups desire to achieve that neither can obtain without the help of the other. Some examples of joint activities that have helped to resolve labor–management conflicts are the quality-of-work-life programs discussed in Chapter 6.

Rotating Membership. This strategy consists of moving members from one group to the other. The expectation is that the transferred members will be able to share their feelings with the new group and help the groups understand each other better. This strategy has helped to improve international relationships by having foreign student exchanges. In union–management relations, this strategy has been limited mostly to promoting union members into management. A small number of managers have also been demoted to union member status. The evidence indicates that employee attitudes are strongly influenced by their group membership. When they were union members, they held prounion attitudes; when they became managers, they adopted promanagement attitudes; and when they were demoted back to union status, they reverted again to prounion attitudes. Apparently, the forces that create intergroup conflict can be very powerful.[45]

Conflict Resolution Meetings. Another strategy for resolving intergroup conflict involves a series of steps that gradually bring the groups together to share feelings and to engage in joint problem solving.[46]

The first step usually involves bringing the leaders of both groups together to give them instructions and to gain their commitment to seek better cooperation. In the second step, the two groups meet alone to develop two lists. Each group describes its feelings about the other group in one list, and then indicates what it thinks the other group is saying about it in the other list. In the third step the groups come together and share lists. Discussion is limited to questions for clarification; justifications and explanations are not allowed. In the fourth step the groups move toward a joint problem-solving session if they are ready for it. The number of steps in this intervention should be influenced by the degree of conflict. The groups should not be brought together in open discussion until they are ready to focus on the issues without having to defend themselves or blame one another. They continue to share lists until the hostility is diffused.

Group conflict may be caused by substantive issues, emotional issues, or both. Substantive issues involve disagreement over policies and practices, competition for scarce resources, and differing expectations about role relationships. Emotional issues involve negative feelings caused by resentment, distrust, and anger. The conflict resolution meetings should focus on the relevant issues. If conflict exists over substantive issues, the meeting should include problem solving and negotiation. If conflict exists over emotional issues, the meeting should focus on restructuring attitudes and discussing negative feelings.

Organizational Interventions

The preceding interventions can be used throughout a company to change the total organization. Sensitivity training and team-building sessions, for example, could start with top management groups and cascade down to successively lower levels in the organizational hierarchy until every member has participated. In a family group, everyone would participate as both a subordinate and as a supervisor except for the lowest levels, which would participate only as subordinates. These sessions could focus on goal setting, task redesign, role clarifications, group processes, performance evaluation, or whatever the problems happen to be. If they were successfully held at each level of the organization, these sessions could greatly increase the effectiveness of the organization by identifying problems, resolving conflicts, creating shared goals, and clarifying accountabilities for individuals and groups.

Organizational interventions do not necessarily have to start at the top. An alternative is to start at the periphery and move toward the corporate core by putting employees in a new corporate context that imposes new roles and responsibilities on them. This approach to change focuses on task alignment and developing a shared vision.[47] A new corporate culture emerges over time as new policies and systems become institutionalized.

Although most interventions can be implemented throughout the entire organization, some interventions are generally considered companywide interventions. These interventions are called **comprehensive interventions** because they usually involve the entire organization and are implemented throughout a company. Five of the most widely known comprehensive interventions include (1) survey feedback, (2) structural interventions, (3) sociotechnical system design, (4) total quality management, and (5) cultural interventions.

Survey Feedback. Survey feedback interventions consist of two major activities. The first step is administering the attitude survey to assess the opinions of employees. The second step is reporting this data back to members of the organization, analyzing what they say and using them to design corrective actions.

Many companies have used opinion surveys to measure employee attitudes. There are important differences, however, between the typical opinion survey and a survey feedback intervention. The traditional opinion survey measures employee opinions and reports data to top management. The data are often buried in a lengthy report that is conveniently lost in a file drawer and improvements are seldom made. Employees are usually suspicious of traditional opinion surveys and do not always report their true feelings.

When survey feedback is used as an OD intervention, everyone participates in providing information and reviewing the data. Each group is the first to receive a report on its own group attitudes; the data are used to identify problems and diagnose the organization. During the feedback session, the groups engage in problem-solving activities to correct problems and to increase organizational effectiveness.

Survey feedback interventions have been used successfully by many organizations, but their success depends primarily on three factors.[48] The first factor involves the commitment of organizational members to each other and to the success of the organization. They must be willing to share their feelings and to participate openly in the feedback and problem solving sessions. Second, top management must support the intervention and create an open environment so that employees feel their efforts are worthwhile. Finally, the questionnaire must address the major issues and accurately assess employee feelings. The development of a good questionnaire is a creative endeavor that usually requires some preliminary interviewing to make certain it focuses on relevant employee concerns. Part of a questionnaire used in survey feedback is shown in Exhibit 17.9.

A questionnaire developed by Rensis Likert measuring System One versus **System Four** style is especially useful for survey feedback interventions because it focuses on vital organizational variables. Likert argued that an autocratic, exploitative, System One management style was not as effective as a participative, democratic and employee-centered System Four management style. Likert collected extensive data to support his argument that organizations become more effective as they move from a System One to a System Four style of management.[49] Members of the organization are asked to describe the current style of management using a questionnaire similar to the one in Exercise 12.1. This questionnaire focuses specifically on the dimensions of management style that Likert's research indicates are important determinants of organizational effectiveness.

Structural Change. Perhaps the easiest change to make in an organization is a change in the organizational structure. Structural changes include such changes as altering the span of control, changing the basis of departmentalization, revising the authority system by creating a different hierarchical reporting relationship, or revising the organization's policies. These changes often have an enormous and relatively permanent impact on individual behavior and organizational functioning. Structural changes are often suggested as part of the problem solving and action planning of other OD interventions. However, the structure also can be changed by a unilateral decision of top management. Some examples of structural changes include

- Moving a job from one department to another
- Reducing a supervisor's span of control
- Dividing a large department into two smaller departments
- Transferring an entire department to a different division (such as taking security out of the personnel department and assigning it to the operations division)
- Creating a new department to centralize a particular function (such as creating a word processing center rather than allowing managers to have personal secretaries)
- Reorganizing an entire organization along different lines (such as eliminating the management, finance, accounting, and economics departments within a college of business and assigning the faculty instead to undergraduate or graduate degree programs)

In recent years some companies have experimented with new structural arrangements to respond to a rapidly changing environment. Many companies have

EXHIBIT 17.9   **Questionnaire Used for Survey Feedback**

	Strongly Disagree		Neither		Strongly Agree		
1. Considering everything about the company, I'm very well satisfied with it.	1	2	3	4	5	6	7
2. People in top management respect my personal rights.	1	2	3	4	5	6	7
3. The company frequently expects me to do things that are not reasonable.	1	2	3	4	5	6	7
4. I have a lot of confidence in the business judgment of top management.	1	2	3	4	5	6	7
5. There's a friendly feeling between the employees and management.	1	2	3	4	5	6	7
6. Management usually keeps us informed about the things we want to know.	1	2	3	4	5	6	7
7. The company tries to unfairly take advantage of its employees.	1	2	3	4	5	6	7
8. This company is a good one for a person trying to get ahead.	1	2	3	4	5	6	7
9. The company offers good opportunities for self-improvement and training.	1	2	3	4	5	6	7
10. Management is not very interested in the feelings of the employees.	1	2	3	4	5	6	7
11. I know exactly what's expected of me in my job.	1	2	3	4	5	6	7
12. The employees frequently don't know what they're supposed to be doing.	1	2	3	4	5	6	7
13. This company is a better place to work than most companies around here.	1	2	3	4	5	6	7
14. The jobs in this company are well organized and coordinated.	1	2	3	4	5	6	7
15. There is a lot of time and effort wasted in this company due to poor planning.	1	2	3	4	5	6	7
16. Our job assignments all seem to be fouled up.	1	2	3	4	5	6	7
17. My company is just a place to work and is separate from my personal interests.	1	2	3	4	5	6	7
18. The needs of the company are more important than my own personal interests.	1	2	3	4	5	6	7

used a project structure in which employees are assigned to work on special projects under the direction of the project leader. However, the employees still retain their memberships in their original departments while they work on the project. During this time, they report to two supervisors.

Because an organization's structure has a strong influence on its effectiveness, structural changes can have a significant and immediate impact. Therefore the structure of an organization must be periodically evaluated. Frequent changes in the structure can create confusion, but an obsolete structure can place a serious constraint on organizational effectiveness.

Sociotechnical System Design. A sociotechnical system intervention could involve any change in either the social or technical systems of an organization; however, sociotech interventions typically involve organizing workers in teams and allowing them to structure their work in the optimal way. Sociotech redesign is especially popular in middle-sized manufacturing and service companies that must be highly responsive to changing customer demands.

Although sociotech interventions can be started in an existing workforce, they are best implemented in a **"greenfield,"** which is a startup operation with new plant and equipment and a new workforce.[50] The advantage of a greenfield is that the new work environment can be designed to maximize both productive efficiency and optimal social interaction. Machines, desks, partitions, and other physical design features can be arranged to facilitate the flow of work and the needs of employees.

Sociotech redesign typically involves the formation of autonomous or semiautonomous groups who supervise themselves. The responsibilities of these teams may include selecting and training their own team members, disciplining and terminating team members, administering salary and benefits, ensuring adequate multicultural diversity through affirmative action, budgeting, planning and distributing materials, shipping the end product, evaluating performance, engineering changes, monitoring product quality, maintaining equipment, providing safety and first aid, setting goals, solving problems, and scheduling work.

In most sociotech systems, a strong emphasis is placed on training and skill development. Team members are encouraged to learn how to perform all the jobs in the team so they can rotate freely to any job that needs to be performed. Multiskilling is rewarded by the compensation system, which is typically based on a philosophy of pay for knowledge rather than pay for performance. The base rate of pay for each employee is determined by how many skills and work functions the employee can demonstrate proficiency in performing.

Research evaluating the effectiveness of sociotechnical system designs has generally been positive.[51] A survey of seventeen studies found that sociotech interventions generally increase productivity and the increases are greater when they involve the formation of autonomous rather than semiautonomous groups, when they include increases in monetary incentives, and when they occur in countries other than the United States.[52] However, many sociotech interventions have also failed, and they have been criticized for lacking a clear conceptual focus and for not maintaining a consistent direction or application. There is no model to follow in designing a sociotech system, and sometimes a better balance in the social and technical systems of a company fails to improve productivity or satisfaction.[53]

Total Quality Management (TQM). **Total quality management** is characterized by three primary principles: doing things right the first time, striving for continuous improvement, and being responsive to the interests of customers. TQM interventions involve making quality a major responsibility of all employees. Continuous improvement usually includes working with suppliers to improve the quality of incoming parts and ensuring that manufacturing processes are capable of consistently high quality. Statistical process control (SPC) is a popular TQM technique that is used to improve quality. SPC involves carefully measuring the production process and using the data to identify problems and to monitor quality improvement.[54]

The steps that might be used in a TQM intervention include

1. Defining the major functions and services that must be performed
2. Determining the customers and suppliers of these services
3. Identifying the customer's requirements, and developing quantitative measures to assess customer satisfaction regarding these requirements
4. Identifying the requirements and measurement criteria that the suppliers to the process must meet
5. Mapping, or flow-charting, the processes that occur within each department and between departments
6. Continuously improving the process with respect to effectiveness, quality, cycle time, and cost.[55]

TQM interventions are often combined with other production management interventions, such as just-in-time inventory (JIT) and advanced manufacturing technology (AMT).[56] Just-in-time inventory control is a set of practices for reducing lead time and inventory. Its name derives from the practice of receiving or producing each subcomponent just in time for it to be used in the next step of production. JIT is usually associated with a "kanban" replenishment system. A kanban is a ticket in a container of parts that initiates the production of more parts so they will arrive just before the container is empty.[57]

Advanced manufacturing technology includes a variety of computerized technologies, such as computer-aided manufacturing (CAM) and computer-aided process planning (CAPP). These technologies have facilitated the use of robots in the assembly process and have greatly increased both productivity and quality.

TQM interventions have produced mixed results. Some companies have reported tremendous success and credited TQM for their competitive advantage, such as Motorola, Xerox, Federal Express, and Harley-Davidson. In other companies, however, TQM failed to produce the anticipated spectacular results. Florida Power & Light implemented what appeared to be a successful TQM project and won Japan's Deming Prize for quality management. However, worker complaints of excessive paperwork prompted Florida Power to slash its program. Likewise, the Wallace Company, a Houston oil supply company that won the Commerce Department's Malcolm Baldridge National Quality Award, found the honor did not protect it from economic hard times—it had to file for bankruptcy.[58]

Many authors have tried to explain why TQM succeeds or fails; but the advice is mostly anecdotal. The most popular suggestions call for employee training and the support of top management; but these suggestions did not guarantee success for Douglas Aircraft. After two years, Douglas Aircraft's TQM program was in shambles in spite of extensive preparation and training, which included two-week training seminars for its 8,000 employees.[59] These failures highlight the need for more information about how to involve employees in a successful quality program. The total quality movement is important to organizational success and better research is needed to identify when and how to implement TQM interventions.

APPLYING ORGANIZATIONAL BEHAVIOR
RESEARCH

Evaluating Total Quality Management in a Health Care Organization

The health care industry has traditionally assumed that efforts to control costs would reduce the quality of services. Total quality management programs in the health care industry have served to dispel this myth. TQM programs are designed to raise the standards of health care services and improve relationships with health care providers and customers.

A survey of health care employees in a large Midwestern academic medical center examined the effects of a TQM program on job satisfaction, organizational climate, and perceptions of the work environment. Responses were obtained from 5,174 employees, of which 52 percent had participated in a TQM training program that focused on value-added production processes, customer–supplier relationships, and the importance of customer satisfaction, quality measurement, quality planning, quality control, and continuous improvement strategies.

The results indicated that those who had participated in the TQM program reported only slightly higher intrinsic satisfaction scores than the nonparticipants; while the extrinsic satisfaction scores and general satisfaction scores were the same. TQM did not seem to make work more satisfying.

Other attitudes toward the TQM program, however, were more favorable for the participants than the nonparticipants. Those who participated in the TQM program were more likely to say they would recommend the hospital as a good place to work and a good place for patient care. They said they were more involved in job decisions, the organization had a stronger emphasis on teamwork, they were more aware of the organization's goals, and they felt the institution did a better job of using goals and performance standards for job evaluation. They also indicated they were more likely to continue working there the next year.

This study did not assess the effects of the TQM program on the delivery of health care services or actual costs. However, the perceptions of employees indicated that the TQM program was a valuable intervention for improving patient care.

Source: Michael A. Counte, Gerald L. Glandon, Denise M. Oleske, and James P. Hill, "Total Quality Management in a Health Care Organization: How Are Employees Affected?" *Hospital and Health Services Administration,* vol. 37 (Winter 1992), pp. 503–518.

Cultural Interventions. It has been suggested that significant changes in organizational structures or processes requires concomitant changes in the organization's culture; that formal change in the way the organization operates will endure only if consistent changes occur at the informal level of interpersonal relations and social expectations.[60] Unless there is a cultural change, formal changes will be resisted. Organizational stories and myths that serve to legitimize and rationalize a change strategy have been shown to contribute greatly to the acceptance of change because these stories (1) create a new organizational image and identity, (2) reward new behaviors, (3) facilitate organizational diagnosis, (4) establish new standards of behavior, and (5) serve as an effective source of social control.[61]

Cultural interventions are the most difficult interventions to implement, and some scholars question whether organizational culture can even be changed by a conscious change strategy.[62] The culture of an organization consists of the shared feelings, beliefs, and expectations of members within the organization. These variables are not physically observable and can only be inferred indirectly by observing members of the organization and talking with them.

Most cultural interventions are actually attempts to clarify the culture of the organization. These interventions are typically conducted with top-level managers in the organization in a series of group discussions. These administrators discuss such questions as "What is our unique mission?" "What do we want to be known for?" "What are the ten commandments of this organization?"[63]

Some cultural interventions seek to specifically change the culture of the organization. For example, one organization sought to create a culture that was centered around the concept of a commitment to excellence. This intervention involved a series of meetings attended by all employees in which the top administrators presented talks on the theme "What it means to me to have a commitment to excellence." People in the organization were asked to identify everyday common practices that did not reflect a commitment to excellence. Department supervisors and division heads were asked to analyze careless and sloppy practices that failed to conform to the commitment to excellence, and eliminate them.

Another illustration of a cultural intervention is the efforts of a retail company to create a climate of honesty. This company had been plagued for several years by high inventory shrinkage rates, and the evidence seemed to indicate that the majority of the losses could be attributed to employee theft rather than shoplifting. The intervention was introduced by an announcement from top management that the organization desired to create a code of ethics for all employees, and everyone was invited to participate in creating it. Employees at all organizational levels participated in a series of meetings that identified ethical issues and dishonest practices. Several drafts of a proposed code of ethics were circulated to all employees, and everyone was asked to help refine it and clarify unresolved issues. Several issues were difficult to resolve because of differences of opinion, such as what types of gifts employees in purchasing should be allowed to accept from suppliers. For this issue, it was ultimately decided that the only acceptable gifts were edible gifts that could be eaten on the spot. Like many of the other issues, the issue of acceptable gifts was debated extensively until a consensus of what was legitimate and acceptable began to emerge. After several months and many meetings, an acceptable code of ethics finally emerged. This code had been written and rewritten many times, and all the employees had reviewed many earlier drafts before the final product was accepted. Eventually a fifteen-page code of ethics identifying principles of right and wrong with accompanying illustrations was published by the company, and employees were asked to sign a statement that they were willing to abide by it. The process of creating the code was both difficult and time consuming, but top management believed the process was more important than the document itself in creating higher levels of personal integrity among the employees. Inventory shrinkage rates were significantly lower after this intervention, indicating that the time had been profitably spent.[64]

An important element in creating a new culture is creating cultural artifacts that support the new culture, such as the language, the metaphors, the stories, the labels, and other supporting systems. For example, British Rail conducted a three-year development project designed to change its bureaucratic culture and relied greatly on being able to eliminate dysfunctional modes of thinking by labeling them ("isms").[65] Similarly, General Mills used a label, Company of Champions, to describe the new culture it wanted to create and used three words to define a "company of champions": innovation, speed, and commitment. To implement and reinforce its new culture, General Mills made corresponding changes in its reward systems, its recognition program, and its education and training programs.[66] The words used by General Electric to support its new culture were *simplicity, self-confidence,* and *speed.*[67]

Metaphors can play an important role in cultural change. Acquiring new ways of thinking requires a departure from an "old world" view to a new set of ideas, values, and beliefs that are reflected in a new language. Metaphors can refocus familiar images in a new light and provide a shared vision that guides future actions and gives its members meaning and purpose. Metaphors from war, religion, and sports are common in business (and some of these metaphors have been criticized because they are associated with a predominantly male language that women feel uncomfortable using).[68] An important part of Jack Welch's success in changing the culture of General Electric to a leaner and more adaptable company was his frequent criticism of bureaucratic inefficiencies. Like fat on a bloated bureaucracy, these inefficiencies had to be eliminated in Work-Out sessions. This metaphor of a physical exercise program helped overcome resistance to removing layers of management and departmental boundaries. The metaphor also made employees think the company would ultimately be in "better shape," which ultimately provided an acceptable foundation for building trust and cooperation. Metaphors are an essential medium through which reality is constructed, and they help to encourage and control change.[69]

SUMMARY

1. Organizations are required to change because of a variety of internal and external forces of change. Internal forces include new technology, changing work values, knowledge explosion, product obsolescence, and alterative work schedules. External forces for change include competition, consumer demand, resource availability, social and political change, and international forces.

2. People have a tendency to resist change because they fear the unknown, they dislike having to learn new skills, change disrupts stable friendships, and they have a lack of trust in management. The organizational structure also tends to resist change because change is a threat to the power structure, the existing organizational systems are designed to maintain the status quo, other subsystems within the organization resist change, and previous commitments have been made in the form of sunk costs or vested interests.

3. Organizations are constantly involved in change, but some changes are much more complex than others and create greater resistance to change.

Three kinds of change are developmental change, transitional change and transformational change. While developmental change involves gradual improvements in existing processes, transitional change involves new or different processes. Transformational change is the most chaotic and usually results from a major upheaval in the organization. Paradigm changes often create transformational change and require every company in an industry to change or become obsolete.

4. Organizational change strategies are generally designed to create change in any of the following seven targets of change: individual personality, dyad, group, family group, the entire organization, the organizational structure, and organizational strategy.

5. The major theories of change include Kurt Lewin's force field analysis, education, reinforcement, and peer group influence. The action research model is useful in illustrating the organizational development process. This model consists of gathering data about a problem, feeding the data back to the target group, having the

target group discuss the data and diagnose the problem, action planning to solve the problem, implementing the actions, and recycling to assess whether the problem was solved by the action or if further changes are needed.

6. Organizations typically evolve through a life cycle of stages: the entrepreneurial stage, the growth stage, the maturity stage, and then the elaboration stage, when bureaucratic rigidities cause the organization to begin to decline. To revitalize the organization, it needs to go through five processes: restructuring to remove unnecessary employees, bureaucracy bashing to eliminate rigid procedures and policies, empowering employees so they are free to act, making continuous improvements in the value chain, and changing the culture to achieve a continuous competitive advantage.

7. Organizational development interventions have evolved from four historical sources: T-group training, survey feedback, quality management, and sociotechnical systems designs.

8. Organizational development interventions are based on a variety of assumptions about individuals, groups, and organizations. OD assumes that individuals can and want to be involved in improving organizations. OD also places a high value on the personal growth and development of individuals.

9. OD interventions generally focus on creating change in a specific target area. The major targets

of change include interpersonal relationships, group processes, intergroup processes, and the total organization.

10. The major interpersonal OD interventions include coaching and counseling, sensitivity training, and process consultation. These interventions are designed to help people function more effectively in their positions.

11. Many OD interventions focus on group functioning. Four of the most popular group interventions are group diagnostic meetings, team building, role analysis technique interventions, and responsibility charting. These interventions are designed to assist the group in functioning more effectively as a group and achieving group goals.

12. Four of the most common intergroup interventions for helping groups resolve intergroup conflict are finding a common enemy, having the groups participate in joint activities, rotating membership among the group members, and having the groups participate in a conflict resolution meeting.

13. Organizational interventions are also called *comprehensive interventions* because they involve the entire organization and are implemented throughout a company. Five of the most widely known comprehensive interventions include survey feedback, structural changes, sociotechnical systems design, total quality management, and cultural interventions.

DISCUSSION QUESTIONS

1. If organizations are collections of people, why can't you change an organization by simply changing each individual?

2. What are the major targets of organizational change, and why is it important to identify the right targets?

3. Describe the action research model, and illustrate how you would use it to resolve a problem in a student dormitory.

4. What happens in a sensitivity training session? Why could a T-group produce both good and bad results?

5. What is a team-building meeting? Is an external consultant needed to help conduct a team-building meeting or a group diagnostic meeting, or can a supervisor do it just as well?

6. What would be the best strategy for reducing conflicts between two fraternities with a long history of bad feelings and sabotage?

7. What are the advantages of using Likert's System Four questionnaire as part of a survey feedback intervention rather than just some satisfaction scales?

8. How do the organizational structure and formal organizational policies make an organization resistant to change? How can an organization know when it is too highly structured?

9. Organizational development assumes that individual goals and organizational goals are consistent with each other and with the goals of society.

How safe are these assumptions, and when are they not true?

10. Suppose the leadership of a sorority wanted to change the culture of the sorority from parties and games to academic excellence. Do you think it is possible to create such a cultural change within a sorority, and how would you try to do it?

GLOSSARY

action research model A strategy of organizational development that typically involves the processes of problem identification, data gathering, feedback of the data to the client group, data discussion and diagnosis, action planning, action, and reevaluation. These processes are recycled as needed to increase organizational effectiveness.

change agent A person or persons who serve as a catalyst facilitating an OD intervention.

coaching and counseling An interpersonal OD intervention that provides feedback and insights to a person to help in that individual's personal development.

comprehensive interventions OD interventions that influence the entire organization, such as survey feedback or a structural change.

cultural interventions An OD intervention that attempts to diagnose the current culture of the organization and either clarify it or change it.

developmental change Gradual improvement in the skills, methods, and current processes of an organization.

diffusion Extending a change in one part of the organization to additional areas and arranging for complementary changes in these areas to facilitate implementation of the change.

dyad Two people and the relationship between them.

family group A work group composed of a supervisor and his or her immediate subordinates.

focal role The central role being evaluated in a role analysis technique intervention.

force field analysis A method for analyzing a change situation by looking at the driving and restraining forces operating on a situation.

greenfield A startup company with a new plant and equipment and a new workforce.

group diagnostic meeting A group meeting that allows members of the group to identify problems confronting the group and rank them in priority.

instrumented T-group A sensitivity training group that uses some form of a questionnaire to facilitate the discussion.

intervention A series of structured activities designed to improve the functioning of an organization or subgroup.

paradigm change A change in the basic assumptions and ways of structuring an issue or thinking about a problem. Paradigm changes typically create significant change throughout an industry.

RAT intervention Role analysis technique; an OD intervention designed to clarify the roles and responsibilities of key employees.

responsibility charting An OD intervention that clarifies the responsibilities of group members for each decision in terms of initiating action, approving or vetoing, providing resources, or being informed.

sensitivity training An unstructured group discussion in which members of the group share their perceptions and feelings of each other and of what is happening in the organization. Such a discussion is designed to create greater self-awareness and sensitivity to other individuals and to group processes.

sociotechnical systems A type of work redesign that recognizes the importance of balancing the social needs of employees with the technical demands of the work process. Sociotech interventions usually involve autonomous work groups that structure and assign work to team members in the way they think is optimal.

System Four A style of management that is characterized by open communication, full participation in problem solving and decision making, commitment by all employees to the organization's goals and objectives, intrinsic motivation, and participative leadership. System Four is the opposite of the bureaucratic, restrictive, and repressive climate that characterizes System One.

T-group *T-group* ("T" for "training") is another name for sensitivity training group.

target of change The focus of an OD intervention that may be either an individual personality, a dyad, a group, a family group, the entire organization, or the organizational structure.

team building An OD intervention that attempts to build a more cohesive work group by having the group create better communication, better decision making, improved personal interactions, and greater goal accomplishment.

total quality management (TQM) A change strategy that emphasizes flawless quality performance, con-tinuous improvement, and being responsive to customers.

transformational change Change that is highly disruptive and chaotic and usually results in the adoption of significantly different products, processes, or relationships.

transitional change Changes that could involve adopting new methods, revising the organization's processes, or producing new products; but these changes occur in a series of defined stages.

NOTES

1. *Forbes,* vol. 100, no. 6 (September 15, 1967), pp. 51–200.

2. Data supplied by Berkeley Geddes, program manager for the Certified Network Engineer Professional Association, Novell Inc., 1993.

3. John W. Verity, "Deconstructing the Computer Industry," *Business Week* (November 23, 1992), pp. 90–100.

4. John R. Wilke, "Data General Board Ousts Co-Founder," *Wall Street Journal* (December 14, 1990), p. B1.

5. Bruce Nussbaum, "The End of Corporate Loyalty," *Business Week* (August 4, 1986), pp. 42–49.

6. Randall S. Schuler, "Scanning the Environment: Planning for Human Resource Management and Organizational Change," *Human Resource Planning,* vol. 12 (1989), pp. 257–276.

7. Heather A. Haveman, "Between a Rock and a Hard Place: Organizational Change and Performance Under Conditions of Fundamental Environmental Transformation," *Administrative Science Quarterly,* vol. 37 (March 1992), pp. 48–75.

8. Bert A. Spector, "From Bogged Down to Fired Up: Inspiring Organizational Change," *Sloan Management Review,* vol. 30 (Summer 1989), pp. 29–34.

9. Linda Ackerman, "Development, Transition or Transformation: The Question of Change in Organizations," *O.D. Practitioner* (December 1986), pp. 1–8; Dexter C. Dunphy and Doug A. Stace, "Transformational and Cohesive Strategies for Planned Organizational Change: Beyond the O.D. Model," *Organizational Studies,* vol. 9 (1988), pp. 317–334.

10. Dana Milbank, "Changing Industry: Big Steel Is Threatened by Low-cost Rivals, Even in Japan, Korea," *Wall Street Journal* (February 2, 1993), p. A1.

11. Joel Barker, "Discovering the Future: The Business of Paradigms" (videotape produced by Public Media Inc., 1989); Joel Barker, "Discovering the Future: The Power of Vision" (videotape produced by Public Media Inc., 1990).

12. Connie J. G. Gersick, "Revolutionary Change Theories: A Multilevel Exploration of the Punctuated Equilibrium Paradigm," *Academy of Management Review,* vol. 16 (1991), pp. 10–36.

13. Kurt Lewin, *Field Theory in Social Science* (New York: Harper & Row, 1951), pp. 228–229.

14. Robert Chin and Kenneth D. Benne, "General Strategies for Effecting Changes in Human Systems," in W. G. Bennis, K. D. Benne, R. Chin, and K. E. Corey (eds.), *The Planning of Change,* 3rd ed. (New York: Holt, Rinehart and Winston, 1976), pp. 22–45.

15. Ibid.

16. Ibid.

17. Ibid.

18. Kurt Lewin, "Group Decision and Social Change," in G. E. Swanson, T. M. Newcomb, and E. L. Hartley (eds.), *Readings in Social Psychology,* rev. ed. (New York: Holt, Rinehart and Winston), pp. 459–473.

19. Lester Coch and John R. P. French, "Overcoming Resistance to Change," *Human Relations,* vol. 1 (1948), pp. 512–533.

20. Wendell French, "Organization Development: Objectives, Assumptions, and Strategies," *California Management Review,* vol. 12 (Winter 1969), pp. 23–34; Chris Lee, "Action Research: Harnessing the Power of Participation," *Training: The Magazine of Human Resources Development,* vol. 27 (1990), pp. 85–87.

21. Rafael Ramirez, "Action Learning: A Strategic Approach for Organizations Facing Turbulent Conditions," *Human Relations,* vol. 36 (1983), pp. 725–742.

22. Robert E. Quinn and Kim Cameron, "Organizational Life Cycles and Some Shifting Criteria of Effectiveness: Some Preliminary Evidence," *Management Science,* vol. 29 (1983) pp. 33–51.

23. Richard W. Beatty and David O. Ulrich, "Re-energizing the Mature Organization," in Todd D. Jick, *Managing Change: Cases and Concepts* (Homewood, Ill.: Irwin, 1993), pp. 60–74.

24. Wendell L. French and Cecil H. Bell, Jr., "A Brief History of Organization Development," *Journal of Contemporary Business*, vol. 1 (Summer 1972), pp. 1–8.

25. Eric L. Trist and Kenneth W. Bamforth, "Some Social and Psychological Consequences of the Longwall Method of Coal-getting," *Human Relations*, vol. 4 (1951), pp. 3–38; Eric L. Trist, "The Assumptions of Ordinariness as a Denial Mechanism: Innovation and Conflict in a Coal Mine," *Human Resource Management*, vol. 28 (Summer 1989), pp. 253–264.

26. Wendell L. French and Cecil H. Bell, Jr., *Organization Development*, 3rd ed. (Englewood Cliffs, N. J.: Prentice-Hall, 1984), chap. 4.

27. Jerome H. Want, "Managing Change in a Turbulent Business Climate," *Management Review*, vol. 79 (November 1990), pp. 38–41.

28. Thomas L. Case, Robert J. Van den Berg, and Paul H. Meredith, "Internal and External Change Agents," *Leadership and Organization Development*, vol. 11 (1990), pp. 4–15.

29. W. Warner Burke, Janet L. Spencer, Lawrence P. Clark, and Celeste Coruzzi, "Managers Get a 'C' in Managing Change," *Training and Development*, vol. 45 (May 1991), pp. 87–90; John Lawrie, "The Differences Between Effective and Ineffective Change Managers," *Supervisory Management*, vol. 36 (June 1991), pp. 9–10.

30. R. T. Golembiewski, C. W. Proehl, and D. Sink, "Estimating the Success of OD Applications," *Training and Development Journal*, vol. 36 (April 1982).

31. William A. Schiemann, "Why Change Fails," *Across the Board*, vol. 29 (April 1992), pp. 53–54.

32. R. A. Guzzo, R. D. Jette, and R. A. Katzell, "The Effects of Psychologically Based Intervention Programs on Worker Productivity: A Meta-Analysis," *Personnel Psychology*, vol. 38 (1985), pp. 275–291.

33. B. A. Macy, H. Izumi, C. C. M. Hurts, and L. W. Norton, "Meta-Analysis of United States Empirical Organizational Change and Work Innovation Field Experiments," paper presented at the National Academy of Management Meetings, Chicago, 1986.

34. See Marshall Sashkin and W. Warner Burke, "Organization Development in the 1980's," *Journal of Management*, vol. 13 (1987), pp. 393–417.

35. A. S. King, "Expectation Effects of Organizational Change," *Administrative Science Quarterly*, vol. 19 (1974), pp. 221–230.

36. Dov Eden, "Team Development: Quasi-Experimental Confirmation Among Combat Companies," *Group and Organization Studies*, vol. 11, no. 3 (1986), pp. 133–146.

37. John P. Campbell and Marvin D. Dunnette, "Effectiveness of T-Group Experiences in Managerial Training and Development," *Psychological Bulletin*, vol. 70, no. 2 (August 1968), pp. 73–104.

38. Eric Berne, *Games People Play* (New York: Grove Press, 1964); Eric Berne, *Transactional Analysis and Psychotherapy* (New York: Grove Press, 1961).

39. Edgar H. Schein, *Process Consultation: Its Role in Organization Development* (Reading, Mass.: Addison-Wesley, 1969).

40. Richard N. Ottaway and Linda Terjeson, "A Proposed Change Evaluation Scaling Method," *Journal of Managerial Psychology*, vol. 1, no. 2 (1986), pp. i–ii.

41. William G. Dyer, *Team Building. Issues and Alternatives*, 2nd ed. (Reading, Mass.: Addison-Wesley, 1987).

42. French and Bell, *Organization Development*, pp. 146–148.

43. Ibid., pp. 149–151; Richard Beckhard and Reuben T. Harris, *Organizational Transactions: Managing Complex Change* (Reading, Mass.: Addison-Wesley, 1977), chap. 6.

44. Muzafer Sherif and Carolyn W. Sherif, *Social Psychology* (New York: Harper & Row, 1969), chaps. 6–12.

45. Seymour Liberman, "The Effects of Changes in Roles on the Attitudes of Role Occupants," *Human Relations*, vol. 9 (1956), pp. 385–402.

46. Wendell L. French and Cecil H. Bell, Jr., *Organization Development*, pp. 175–178.

47. Michael Beer, Russell A. Eisenstat, and Bert Spector, "Why Change Programs Don't Produce Change," *Harvard Business Review*, vol. 68 (November–December 1990), pp. 158–166.

48. William J. Rothwell and H. C. Kazanas, "The Attitude Survey as an Approach to Human Resource Strategic Planning," *Journal of Managerial Psychology*, vol. 1, no. 2 (1986), pp. 15–18; David Jacobs, "Management Audits as Instruments of Change," *International Management*, vol. 42, no. 3 (1987), p. 54.

49. Rensis Likert, *New Pattern of Management* (New York: McGraw-Hill, 1961); Rensis Likert, *The Human Organization* (New York: McGraw-Hill, 1967).

50. Gaye E. Gilbert, "Framework for Success: Socio-technical Systems at Lake Superior Paper Industries," *American Productivity & Quality Center* (July 1989), pp. 1–8; Barcy H. Proctor, "A Socio-technical Work-Design System at Digital Enfield: Utilizing Untapped Resources," *National Productivity Review* (Summer 1986), pp. 11–19.

51. Rupert F. Chisholm, "Introducing Advanced Information Technology into Public Organizations," *Public Productivity Review*, vol. 11 (Summer 1988), pp. 39–56.

52. Rafik I. Beekun, "Assessing the Effectiveness of Socio-technical Interventions: Antidote for Fad?" *Human Relations*, vol. 42 (1989), pp. 877–897.

53. Bob Maton, "Socio-technical Systems: Conceptual and Implementation Problems," *Industrial Relations*, vol. 43 (1988), pp. 869–887.

54. Bob Krone, "Total Quality Management: An American Odyssey," *Bureaucrat*, vol. 19 (Fall 1990), pp. 35–38; Drew R. Lathin, "A Marriage in the Making? High Commitment Systems and Total Quality," *Journal for Quality and Participation* (December 1990), pp. 44–46.

55. R. Henkoff, "What Motorola Learns from Japan," *Fortune* (April 24, 1989), pp. 157–168.

56. Scott A. Snell and James W. Dean, Jr., "Integrated Manufacturing and Human Resource Management: A Human Capital Perspective," *Academy of Management Journal*, vol. 35 (1992), pp. 467–504.

57. Janice A. Klein, "A Reexamination of Autonomy in Light of New Manufacturing Practices," *Human Relations*, vol. 44 (January 1991), pp. 21–38.

58. J. Matthews and Peter Katel, "The Cost of Quality: Faced with Hard Times, Business Sours on 'Total Quality Management,'" *Newsweek* (September 7, 1992), pp. 48–49.

59. Ibid.; Gilbert Fuchsberg, "'Total Quality' Is Termed only Partial Success," *Wall Street Journal* (October 1, 1992), p. B1.

60. Edgar H. Schein, *Organizational Culture and Leadership* (San Francisco: Jossey-Bass, 1985); Edgar H. Schein, "Coming to a New Awareness of Organizational Culture," *Sloan Management Review*, vol. 25 (Winter 1984), pp. 3–16.

61. Mark L. McConkie and Wayne R. Boss, "Organizational Stories: One Means of Moving the Informal Organization During Change Efforts," *Public Administration Quarterly*, vol. 10, no. 2 (1986), pp. 189–205.

62. Alan Wilkins and Kerry Patterson, "You Can't Get There From Here: What Will Make Culture Change Projects Fail," in R. H. Kilman and Associates, *Gaining Control of the Corporate Culture* (San Francisco, Calif.: Jossey-Bass, 1985).

63. David Bradford, "Cultural Interventions," paper presented at the 1984 Organizational Behavior Teaching Conference, Boise, Idaho, May 1984; Larry B. Meares, "A Model for Changing Organizational Culture," *Personnel*, vol. 63 (July 1986), pp. 38–42.

64. This intervention occurred in two organizations, J. C. Penney and Security Pacific Bank and parts of their codes of ethics are described in *Corporate Ethics Research Report No. 900* (New York: The Conference Board, 1988), pp. 21–27.

65. Paul Bate, "Using the Culture Concept in an Organization Development Setting," *Journal of Applied Behavioral Science*, vol. 26 (1990), pp. 83–106.

66. Stephanie Overman, "A Company of Champions," *HR Magazine*, vol. 35 (October 1990), pp. 58–60.

67. John F. Welch, Jr., "Working Out of a Tough Year," *Executive Excellence*, vol. 9 (April 1992), pp. 14–16.

68. Catherine Cleary, Thomas Packard, Achilles Armenakis, Arthur Bedeian, Laurie Larwood, and W. Warner Burke, "The Use of Metaphors in Organizational Assessment and Change: The Role of Metaphors in Organizational Change," *Group and Organization Management*, vol. 17 (September 1992), pp. 229–259; Fiona Wilson, "Language, Technology, Gender and Power," *Human Relations*, vol. 45 (September 1992), pp. 883–904.

69. Stratford P. Sherman and Cynthia Hutton, "Inside the Mind of Jack Welch," *Fortune* (March 27, 1989), pp. 39–49.

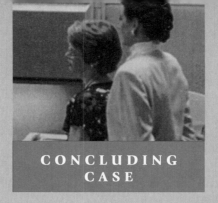

INADEQUATE INNOVATION AT SOUTHEAST BANK

Most banks get into trouble for being too risky, but Southeast Banking Corporation had been criticized for being too conservative. A *Wall Street Journal* article concluded that its troubles stem from "sticking to its stodgy ways."

The chief executive at Southeast Bank, Charles J. Zwick, has been praised by some for following a solid and proven path of solvency and success. But some have criticized him for resisting change. He refused to grow by merging with smaller banks because of his determination to maintain independence. And he overlooked opportunities to expand into the consumer retail market because he insisted that Southeast Bank's clients were corporations.

As Florida's population expanded, Zwick scoffed at other banks for spending so heavily on building a decentralized banking system. He chose instead to emphasize corporate and international loans and opened an office in London. Since a disproportionately larger share of corporate and international loans have soured, Southeast Bank has had more than its share of bad loan writeoffs.

While Southeast Bank was mired in its corporate lending strategy, Burnett Banks Incorporated built a successful network of branch banks across Florida to serve cash-rich retirees and small businesses. By emphasizing service, Burnett overtook Southeast in deposits in 1983 and soon doubled Southeast's assets. When Zwick finally recognized the profitability of the retail banking market and decided to enter it, he tried to catch up all at once. Rather than pursuing the business one customer at a time, Southeast Bank

bought packages of auto loans and acquired small thrift institutions. This strategy provided large chunks of the consumer market overnight, but it created serious losses because of the high number of bad loans included in the portfolios.

Although Southeast Bank is still profitable and operating independently, which is more than some banks can claim, it is not as healthy as it could have been. Other banks that responded to consumer needs and opportunities for growth were able to grow and acquire a strong competitive position. Southeast Bank's cautious conservativism has helped it avoid the disasters associated with jumping on each new industry fad. But its resistance to change has also caused it to forgo valuable opportunities.

Questions

1. Given that so many banks have failed because of risky and unsound financial decisions, how do you feel about the criticism of Southeast Bank's president for being too conservative?

2. Southeast Bank specialized in corporate banking and overlooked the growth in the consumer market. What are the individual and organizational forces that resist change in this situation? What are the forces supporting the change?

3. What are the problems that a bank or any other organization might face that fails to distinguish between real change versus fads?

Source: Martha Brannigan, "Costly Strategy: Southeast Banking Got in Trouble by Sticking to Its Stodgy Ways," *Wall Street Journal* (January 9, 1991), p. A1.

SENSITIVITY TRAINING

Sensitivity training consists of a series of unstructured group discussions. The discussions usually proceed without clearly defined goals, rules, procedures, agenda, or member roles. The focus of the discussion is on feelings and perceptions rather than intellectual conversations or personal histories.

Participants are expected to learn about themselves as individuals and how they customarily behave in groups. They should learn how others respond to them and how they in turn view others. Sensitivity training reveals to participants how others influence them, how groups function, and how to cooperate with others to be effective group members.

Directions. For this exercise, the class will be organized into groups of five to eight individuals. This exercise works best if the members of each group have worked together as a group through the semester. Each group will set a date when they can meet together for at least two hours of uninterrupted time. The meeting place should be free from distractions, preferably a location that creates a relaxed and comfortable atmosphere such as a living room. Each group should hold an unstructured discussion in which the members share their personal feelings, their perceptions of each other, their personal interests, their personal gripes, and other attitudes and opinions that might be relevant as feedback to each other. Sensitivity training groups typically do not have a leader, although they usually have a facilitator who helps to create the proper climate and interpret the group discussion. Since the groups will meet for only a limited time, the following questions may be useful in helping the discussion to get started.

1. What traits do you most admire in each group member?
2. What are the dominant traits of each group member?
3. Which group members are most highly accepted by the group?
4. Which group members are most rejected by the group?
5. Which group members tend to be sarcastic or critical in their remarks?
6. Which group members tend to protect and support members who feel threatened?
7. Which group members perform best without direction and support from the teacher?
8. Which group members try to keep themselves in the limelight as much as possible?
9. Which group members would you most like to vacation with?
10. Which group members would you most like to have as co-workers?
11. Which group members would you least like to have as co-workers?
12. Which group members do you think you can most easily influence to change their opinions?
13. Which group members do you think can most easily influence you to change your opinions?